New Perspectives

Microsoft® Office 365®
Excel® 2021

Comprehensive

※ Cengage

Australia • Brazil • Canada • Mexico • Singapore • United Kingdom • United States

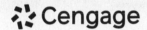

**New Perspectives Series®, Microsoft®
Office 365® & Excel® 2021 Comprehensive**
Patrick Carey

SVP, Product: Erin Joyner

VP, Product: Thais Alencar

Product Director: Mark Santee

Senior Product Manager: Amy Savino

Product Assistant: Ciara Horne

Learning Designer: Zenya Molnar

Content Manager: Christina Nyren

Digital Delivery Quality Partner: Jim Vaughey

Developmental Editors: Robin Romer

VP, Product Marketing: Jason Sakos

Director, Product Marketing: Danaë April

Executive Product Marketing Manager: Jill Staut

IP Analyst: Ann Hoffman

IP Project Manager: Anjali Kambli

Production Service: Lumina Datamatics, Inc.

Designer: Erin Griffin

Cover Image Source: Artur Debat/Getty Images

Mac Users: If you're working through this product using a Mac, some of
the steps may vary. Additional information for Mac users is included with
the Data files for this product.

Disclaimer: This text is intended for instructional purposes only; data is
fictional and does not belong to any real persons or companies.

Disclaimer: The material in this text was written using Microsoft
Windows 10 and Office 365 Professional Plus and was Quality Assurance
tested before the publication date. As Microsoft continually updates the
Windows 10 operating system and Office 365, your software experience
may vary slightly from what is presented in the printed text.

Windows, Access, Excel, and PowerPoint are registered trademarks of
Microsoft Corporation. Microsoft and the Office logo are either registered trademarks or trademarks of Microsoft Corporation in the United
States and/or other countries. This product is an independent publication and is neither affiliated with, nor authorized, sponsored, or
approved by, Microsoft Corporation.

Some of the product names and company names used in this book have
been used for identification purposes only and may be trademarks or
registered trademarks of Microsoft Corporation in the United States and/
or other countries.

For product information and technology assistance, contact us at
**Cengage Customer & Sales Support, 1-800-354-9706 or
support.cengage.com.**

For permission to use material from this text or product, submit all
requests online at **www.copyright.com.**

Library of Congress Control Number: 2022935121

Student Edition ISBN: 978-0-357-67222-8
Looseleaf ISBN: 978-0-357-67223-5*
*Looseleaf available as part of a digital bundle

Cengage
200 Pier 4 Boulevard
Boston, MA 02210
USA

Cengage is a leading provider of customized learning solutions with
employees residing in nearly 40 different countries and sales in more
than 125 countries around the world. Find your local representative at
www.cengage.com.

To learn more about Cengage platforms and services, register or access
your online learning solution, or purchase materials for your course, visit
www.cengage.com.

Notice to the Reader

Printed in the United States of America
Print Number: 01   Print Year: 2022

BRIEF CONTENTS

Getting to Know Microsoft Office Versions. OFF-1

Using SAM Projects and Textbook Projects SAM-1

EXCEL

Module 1 Getting Started with Excel. . . . . EX 1-1
Tracking Miscellaneous Expenses for a Conference

Module 2 Formatting Workbook Text and Data . . . . EX 2-1
Creating a Sales Report

Module 3 Performing Calculations with Formulas and Functions . . . . EX 3-1
Staffing a Call Center

Module 4 Analyzing and Charting Financial Data . . . . EX 4-1
Preparing an Investment Report

Module 5 Generating Reports from Multiple Worksheets and Workbooks . . . . EX 5-1
Summarizing Profit and Loss Statements

Module 6 Managing Data with Data Tools. . . . . EX 6-1
Analyzing Employment Data

Module 7 Summarizing Data with PivotTables. . . . . EX 7-1
Preparing a Social Media Marketing Report

Module 8 Performing What-If Analyses . . . . EX 8-1
Maximizing Profits with the Right Product Mix

Module 9 Exploring Financial Tools and Functions . . . . EX 9-1
Analyzing a Business Plan

Module 10 Analyzing Data with Business Intelligence Tools . . . . EX 10-1
Presenting Sales and Revenue Data

Module 11 Exploring PivotTable Design . . . . EX 11-1
Summarizing Sales and Revenue Data

Module 12 Developing an Excel Application. . . . . EX 12-1
Creating a Data Entry App

Index   **IDX 1**

TABLE OF CONTENTS

Getting to Know Microsoft Office Versions OFF-1

Using SAM Projects and Textbook Projects SAM-1

EXCEL MODULES

Module 1 Getting Started with Excel
Tracking Miscellaneous Expenses for a
Conference . . . . **EX 1-1**

Session 1.1 Visual Overview: . . . . EX 1-2

The Excel Workbook . . . . EX 1-3

Introducing Excel and Spreadsheets. . . . . EX 1-4

Getting Help. . . . . EX 1-6

Using Keyboard Shortcuts to Work Faster . . . . EX 1-6

Using Excel in Touch Mode. . . . . EX 1-6

Exploring a Workbook. EX 1-8

Changing the Active Sheet. . . . . EX 1-8

Navigating Within a Worksheet . . . . EX 1-9

Selecting a Cell Range . . . . EX 1-12

Closing a Workbook . . . . EX 1-13

Planning a Workbook . . . . EX 1-14

Starting a New Workbook. . . . . EX 1-15

Renaming and Inserting Worksheets . . . . EX 1-16

Moving Worksheets . . . . EX 1-17

Deleting Worksheets . . . . EX 1-17

Saving a Workbook. . . . . EX 1-18

Entering Text, Dates, and Numbers . . . . EX 1-18

Entering Text. . . . . EX 1-18

Undoing and Redoing an Action . . . . EX 1-20

Editing Cell Content . . . . EX 1-20

Understanding AutoComplete . . . . EX 1-21

Displaying Numbers as Text. . . . . EX 1-22

Entering Dates . . . . EX 1-23

Entering Numbers. . . . . EX 1-26

Resizing Columns and Rows . . . . EX 1-27

Setting a Column Width . . . . EX 1-27

Wrapping Text Within a Cell. . . . . EX 1-29

Changing Row Heights . . . . EX 1-30

Session 1.1 Quick Check . . . . EX 1-31

Session 1.2 Visual Overview: Excel Formulas
and Functions . . . . EX 1-32

Calculating with Formulas . . . . EX 1-34

Entering a Formula . . . . EX 1-34

Copying and Pasting Formulas. . . . . EX 1-37

Calculating with Functions . . . . EX 1-38

Understanding Function Syntax . . . . EX 1-38

Inserting Functions with AutoSum . . . . EX 1-39

Modifying a Worksheet. . . . . EX 1-41

Moving and Copying a Cell or Range. . . . . . . EX 1-41

Using the COUNT Function. . . . . EX 1-43

Modifying Rows and Columns. . . . . EX 1-44

Inserting Rows and Columns . . . . EX 1-45

Deleting Rows and Columns. . . . . EX 1-46

Inserting and Deleting a Range . . . . EX 1-47

Using Flash Fill. . . . . EX 1-49

Formatting a Worksheet . . . . EX 1-51

Adding Cell Borders . . . . EX 1-51

Changing the Font Size. . . . . EX 1-52

Printing a Workbook . . . . EX 1-53

Changing Worksheet Views . . . . EX 1-53

Changing the Page Orientation . . . . EX 1-55

Setting the Scaling Options . . . . EX 1-55

Setting the Print Options . . . . EX 1-56

Viewing Worksheet Formulas . . . . EX 1-57

Session 1.2 Quick Check . . . . EX 1-59

Review Assignments . . . . EX 1-60

Case Problem 1 . . . . EX 1-62

Module 2 Formatting Workbook Text and Data
Creating a Sales Report . . . . **EX 2-1**

Session 2.1 Visual Overview: . . . . EX 2-2

Formatting a Worksheet . . . . EX 2-3

Formatting Cell Text . . . . EX 2-4

   Applying Fonts and Font Styles . . . . EX 2-4

   Applying a Font Color . . . . EX 2-6

   Formatting Text Selections Within a Cell . . . . . EX 2-8

Working with Fill Colors and Backgrounds . . . . . . EX 2-9

   Changing a Fill Color . . . . EX 2-9

   Setting the Worksheet Tab Color . . . . EX 2-10

   Adding a Background Image . . . . EX 2-11

Using Functions and Formulas with Sales Data . EX 2-12

Formatting Numbers . . . . EX 2-16

   Applying Number Formats . . . . EX 2-16

   Displaying Percentages . . . . EX 2-19

   Formatting Dates and Times . . . . EX 2-19

Formatting Worksheet Cells . . . . EX 2-20

   Aligning Cell Content . . . . EX 2-20

   Indenting Cell Content . . . . EX 2-21

   Adding Borders to Cells . . . . EX 2-21

   Merging Cells . . . . EX 2-23

   Rotating Cell Contents . . . . EX 2-24

Exploring the Format Cells Dialog Box . . . . EX 2-25

Session 2.1 Quick Check . . . . EX 2-29

Session 2.2 Visual Overview: . . . . EX 2-30

Designing a Printout . . . . EX 2-31

Calculating Averages . . . . EX 2-32

Applying Cell Styles . . . . EX 2-35

   Creating a Custom Cell Style . . . . EX 2-37

   Merging Custom Cell Styles . . . . EX 2-38

Copying and Pasting Formats . . . . EX 2-38

   Copying Formats with the Format
   Painter . . . . EX 2-8

   Copying Formats with the Paste Options
   Button . . . . EX 2-40

   Copying Formats with Paste Special . . . . EX 2-40

   Transposing Data . . . . EX 2-41

Finding and Replacing Text and Formats . . . . . . EX 2-42

Working with Themes . . . . EX 2-44

   Applying a Theme . . . . EX 2-44

   Setting Theme Colors and Fonts . . . . EX 2-45

   Saving a Theme . . . . EX 2-46

Highlighting Data with Conditional
Formats . . . . EX 2-46

   Highlighting Cells Based on Their
   Values . . . . EX 2-46

   Highlighting Cells with a
   Top/Bottom Rule . . . . EX 2-48

   Editing a Conditional Formatting Rule . . . . . . EX 2-49

   Clearing Conditional Formatting Rules . . . . . EX 2-51

   Documenting Conditional Formats . . . . EX 2-51

Formatting a Worksheet for Printing . . . . EX 2-53

   Using Page Break Preview . . . . EX 2-53

   Defining the Print Area . . . . EX 2-54

   Inserting Page Breaks . . . . EX 2-55

   Adding Print Titles . . . . EX 2-56

   Designing Headers and Footers . . . . EX 2-58

   Setting the Page Margins . . . . EX 2-60

Session 2.2 Quick Check . . . . EX 2-63

Review Assignments . . . . EX 2-64

Case Problem 1 . . . . EX 2-66

Module 3 Performing Calculations with Formulas and Functions

Staffing a Call Center . . . . .EX 3-1

Designing a Workbook for Calculations . . . . .EX 3-4

    Documenting Calculations . . . . .EX 3-5

    Constants and Units . . . . .EX 3-5

Calculating with Dates and Times. . . . . .EX 3-6

AutoFilling Formulas and Data Patterns . . . . .EX 3-7

    AutoFilling a Formula .EX 3-8

    Exploring Auto Fill Options . . . . .EX 3-8

    Filling a Series . . . . .EX 3-10

Applying Excel Functions . . . . .EX 3-12

    Rounding Data Values. . . . . .EX 3-13

    Calculating Minimums and Maximums. . . . . . .EX 3-16

    Measures of Central Tendency . . . . .EX 3-18

    Nesting Functions. . . . . .EX 3-21

    The Role of Blanks and Zeroes . . . . .EX 3-23

    Date and Time Functions . . . . .EX 3-23

Interpreting Error Values . . . . .EX 3-25

Session 3.1 Quick Check . . . . .EX 3-27

Calculating Running Totals with the Quick Analysis Tool . . . . .EX 3-30

Exploring Cell References. . . . . .EX 3-32

    Relative Cell References . . . . .EX 3-32

    Absolute Cell References . . . . .EX 3-32

    Mixed Cell References . . . . .EX 3-33

    Entering an Absolute Cell Reference . . . . . . .EX 3-34

Working with the IF Logical Function . . . . .EX 3-35

Formatting Input, Calculated, and Output Values. . . . . .EX 3-39

Looking Up Data . . . . .EX 3-40

    Finding an Exact Match with the VLOOKUP Function . . . . .EX 3-41

Performing What-If Analyses with Formulas and Functions . . . . .EX 3-45

    Using Trial and Error .EX 3-45

    Using Goal Seek . . . . .EX 3-48

Session 3.2 Quick Check . . . . .EX 3-51

Review Assignments . . . . .EX 3-52

Case Problem 1 . . . . .EX 3-53

Module 4 Analyzing and Charting Financial Data

Preparing an Investment Report. . . . . **EX 4-1**

Getting Started with Excel Charts . . . . EX 4-4

Creating a Pie Chart . . . . EX 4-6

    Selecting the Data Source . . . . EX 4-6

    Charting with the Quick Analysis Tool . . . . . . .EX 4-7

    Moving and Resizing a Chart . . . . .EX 4-8

Working with Chart Elements . . . . .EX 4-10

    Formatting a Chart Element. . . . . .EX 4-11

    Choosing a Chart Style . . . . .EX 4-14

    Changing the Color Scheme. . . . . .EX 4-15

Performing What-If Analyses with Charts . . . . . .EX 4-16

Creating a Column Chart . . . . .EX 4-18

    Comparing Column Chart Subtypes . . . . . . .EX 4-18

    Creating a Clustered Column Chart. . . . . . . .EX 4-19

    Editing a Chart Title .EX 4-20

    Setting the Gap Width . . . . .EX 4-21

    Adding Gridlines to a Chart . . . . .EX 4-22

Creating a Line Chart . . . . .EX 4-23

    Editing the Category Axis. . . . . .EX 4-24

    Formatting Data Markers . . . . .EX 4-24

Creating a Combination Chart . . . . .EX 4-26

    Adding an Axis Title . . . . .EX 4-28

    Editing a Value Axis Scale. . . . . .EX 4-29

Session 4.1 Quick Check . . . . .EX 4-31

Creating a Scatter Chart . . . . .EX 4-34

Editing the Chart Data Source . . . . .EX 4-37

Adding Graphic Objects to a Workbook . . . . . .EX 4-39

Adding a Data Callout to a Chart. . . . . EX 4-40

Inserting a Graphic Shape . . . . .EX 4-41

Inserting Graphic Icons. . . . . .EX 4-42

Tools for Managing Graphic Objects . . . . . . EX 4-44

Exploring Other Chart Types . . . . .EX 4-45

Hierarchy Charts . . . . .EX 4-45

Pareto Charts . . . . EX 4-46

Histogram Charts . . . . EX 4-46

Waterfall Charts . . . . .EX 4-47

Creating Data Bars . . . . EX 4-48

Modifying a Data Bar Rule . . . . .EX 4-49

Creating Sparklines . . . . .EX 4-50

Formatting a Sparkline . . . . .EX 4-54

Sparkline Groups and Sparkline Axes. . . . . . .EX 4-55

Session 4.2 Quick Check . . . . .EX 4-57

Review Assignments . . . . .EX 4-58

Case Problem 1 . . . . .EX 4-59

**Module 5 Generating Reports from
Multiple Worksheets and Workbooks**
Summarizing Profit and Loss Statements . . . . . . **EX 5-1**

Session 5.1 Visual Overview: Worksheet
Groups and 3-D References . . . . EX 5-2

Working with Multiple Worksheets. . . . . EX 5-4

Copying a Worksheet . . . . EX 5-4

Viewing a Workbook in Multiple Windows . . . . EX 5-6

Arranging Multiple Workbook Windows . . . . EX 5-7

Using Synchronized Scrolling Between
Windows . . . . EX 5-9

Working with Worksheet Groups . . . . .EX 5-10

Editing a Worksheet Group . . . . .EX 5-11

Ungrouping a Worksheet Group . . . . .EX 5-13

Writing 3-D References. . . . . .EX 5-14

Referencing Cells in Other Worksheets . . . . .EX 5-14

Applying 3-D References to Formulas
and Functions . . . . .EX 5-14

Session 5.2 Visual Overview: External
References and Links. . . . . EX 5-20

Linking to External Workbooks. . . . . EX 5-22

Creating an External Reference . . . . EX 5-22

Updating Workbook Links . . . . EX 5-25

External References and Security Concerns. EX 5-26

Reviewing Links Within a Workbook. . . . . . . EX 5-27

Managing Workbook Links. . . . . EX 5-28

Creating Hyperlinks. . . . . EX 5-29

Linking to a Location Within a Workbook . . EX 5-29

Linking to an Email Address . . . . EX 5-31

Session 5.3 Visual Overview: Named
Ranges and Templates . . . . EX 5-34

Simplifying Formulas with Named Ranges . . . . EX 5-36

Defining a Named Range . . . . EX 5-36

Using Named Ranges in Formulas . . . . EX 5-39

Determining the Scope of Named
Ranges. . . . . EX 5-42

Using Defined Names in Existing
Formulas . . . . EX 5-44

Exploring Workbook Templates . . . . EX 5-47

Setting Up a Workbook Template . . . . EX 5-48

Creating a Workbook Based on a Template. . . .EX 5-50

Review Assignments . . . . EX 5-54

Case Problem 1 . . . . EX 5-55

Case Problem 2 . . . . EX 5-56

Module 6 Managing Data with Data Tools
Analyzing Employment Data. . . . . **EX 6-1**

Session 6.1 Visual Overview: Data Ranges,
Workbook Panes, and Subtotals . . . . EX 6-2

Handling Data in Excel . . . . EX 6-4

Using Panes to View Data . . . . EX 6-6

Dividing the Workbook Window into Panes . . . . EX 6-6

Freezing Panes . . . . EX 6-8

Locating Duplicate Records . . . . EX 6-10

Highlighting Duplicate Values . . . . EX 6-10

Removing Duplicate Records . . . . EX 6-12

Sorting Records in a Data Range . . . . EX 6-13

Sorting by a Single Field . . . . EX 6-13

Sorting by Multiple Fields . . . . EX 6-15

Sorting with a Custom List . . . . EX 6-17

Calculating Subtotals . . . . EX 6-19

Creating a Subtotal Row . . . . EX 6-19

Using the Subtotal Outline View . . . . EX 6-21

Session 6.2 Visual Overview: Filters and Excel Tables . . . . EX 6-24

Locating Cells Within a Worksheet . . . . EX 6-26

Finding and Selecting Multiple Cells . . . . . . EX 6-26

Finding Cells by Type . . . . EX 6-27

Filtering Data . . . . EX 6-27

Filtering Based on One Field . . . . EX 6-28

Filtering Based on Multiple Fields . . . . EX 6-29

Using Criteria Filters . . . . EX 6-30

Clearing Filters . . . . EX 6-33

Applying an Advanced Filter . . . . EX 6-33

Creating an Excel Table . . . . EX 6-37

Converting a Range to a Table . . . . EX 6-37

Using Table Styles . . . . EX 6-39

Adding a Total Row . . . . EX 6-41

Adding and Deleting Records . . . . EX 6-42

Creating a Calculated Field . . . . EX 6-43

Structural References and Excel Tables . . . . . EX 6-45

Session 6.3 Visual Overview: Slicers and Dashboards . . . . EX 6-48

Filtering Data with Slicers . . . . EX 6-50

Creating a Dashboard . . . . EX 6-52

Formatting a Slicer . . . . EX 6-54

Using the SUBTOTAL Function . . . . EX 6-55

Creating Dynamic Charts . . . . EX 6-58

Looking Up Data with Tables . . . . EX 6-62

Review Assignments . . . . EX 6-64

Case Problem 1 . . . . EX 6-66

Case Problem 2 . . . . EX 6-67

Module 7 Summarizing Data with PivotTables
Preparing a Social Media Marketing Report . . . . **EX 7-1**

Session 7.1 Visual Overview: Summary IF Functions and VLOOKUP . . . . EX 7-2

Using Lookup Functions . . . . EX 7-4

Creating Approximate Match Lookups . . . . . EX 7-6

Performing Two-Way Lookups with the XLOOKUP Function . . . . EX 7-12

Retrieving Data with Index Match Lookups . . . . EX 7-14

Exploring Logical Functions . . . . EX 7-16

Using the IFS Function . . . . EX 7-17

Combining Conditions with the OR and AND Functions . . . . EX 7-17

Applying Summary IF Functions . . . . EX 7-19

Conditional Counting with COUNTIF . . . . . EX 7-20

Calculating Conditional Sums with SUMIF . . EX 7-22

Calculating Conditional Averages with AVERAGEIF . . . . EX 7-24

Using Summary IFS Functions . . . . EX 7-25

Session 7.2 Visual Overview: PivotTables . . . . EX 7-28

Creating PivotTables . . . . EX 7-30

Inserting a PivotTable . . . . EX 7-31

Creating a PivotTable Layout . . . . EX 7-33

Modifying the PivotTable Layout . . . . EX 7-34

Adding Multiple Fields to a Row or Column . . . EX 7-35

Filtering a PivotTable. . . . . EX 7-37

Formatting a PivotTable. . . . . EX 7-39

Changing Labels and Number Formats . . . . EX 7-40

Choosing a PivotTable Summary Function . . EX 7-42

Reordering PivotTable Categories . . . . EX 7-45

Setting PivotTable Options . . . . EX 7-46

Setting the PivotTable Design. . . . . EX 7-47

Session 7.3 Visual Overview: PivotCharts
and Slicers . . . . EX 7-50

Introducing PivotCharts. . . . . EX 7-52

Creating a PivotChart . . . . EX 7-53

Moving a PivotChart to Another
Worksheet. . . . . EX 7-55

Creating a Pie PivotChart . . . . EX 7-56

Using Slicers and PivotTables . . . . EX 7-60

Applying a Slicer to Multiple PivotTables . . . EX 7-61

Creating a Timeline Slicer . . . . EX 7-63

Drilling Down a PivotTable. . . . . EX 7-65

Review Assignments . . . . EX 7-68

Case Problem 1 . . . . EX 7-70

Case Problem 2 . . . . EX 7-71

Module 8 Performing What-If Analyses
Maximizing Profits with the Right Product Mix 1

Session 8.1 Visual Overview: Data Tables
and What-If Analysis . . . . .EX 8-2

Understanding Cost-Volume Relationships. . . . . .EX 8-4

Comparing Expenses and Revenue . . . . .EX 8-4

Exploring the Break-Even Point . . . . .EX 8-6

Finding the Break-Even Point with
What-If Analysis. . . . . .EX 8-7

Working with Data Tables . . . . .EX 8-9

Creating a One-Variable Data Table. . . . . . . .EX 8-9

Charting a One-Variable Data Table. . . . . . . EX 8-12

Modifying a Data Table. . . . . EX 8-13

Creating a Two-Variable Data Table . . . . EX 8-14

Formatting the Result Cell . . . . EX 8-17

Charting a Two-Variable Data Table . . . . EX 8-18

Session 8.2 Visual Overview: What-If Scenarios. . . EX 8-22

Exploring Financial Scenarios with Scenario
Manager . . . . .EX 8-24

Defining a Scenario. . . . . .EX 8-25

Viewing Scenarios. .EX 8-28

Editing a Scenario .EX 8-29

Creating Scenario Summary Reports . . . . .EX 8-30

Session 8.3 Visual Overview: Optimal
Solutions with Solver .EX 8-36

Optimizing a Product Mix . . . . .EX 8-38

Finding the Optimal Solution with Solver . . . . . EX 8-40

Activating Solver. . . . . .EX 8-41

Setting the Objective Cell and
Variable Cells. . . . . .EX 8-42

Adding Constraints to Solver . . . . EX 8-44

Exploring the Iterative Process . . . . .EX 8-50

Creating a Solver Answer Report . . . . .EX 8-51

Saving and Loading Solver Models. . . . . .EX 8-53

Review Assignments .EX 8-58

Case Problem 1 . . . . .EX 8-59

Case Problem 2 . . . . .EX 8-61

**Module 9 Exploring Financial Tools
and Functions**
Analyzing a Business Plan. . . . . **EX 9-1**

Session 9.1 Visual Overview: Loan
and Investment Functions . . . . .EX 9-2

Introducing Financial Functions. . . . . .EX 9-4

Calculating Borrowing Costs. . . . . .EX 9-4

Calculating Payments with the
PMT Function . . . . .EX 9-5

Calculating a Future Value with the
FV Function. . . . . .EX 9-7

Calculating the Payment Period with the
NPER Function . . . . .EX 9-9

Calculating the Present Value with the
PV Function. . . . . EX 9-10

Creating an Amortization Schedule . . . . EX 9-12

Calculating Interest and Principal
Payments. . . . . EX 9-13

Calculating Cumulative Interest and
Principal Payments . . . . EX 9-16

Session 9.2 Visual Overview: Income
Statements and Depreciation . . . . EX 9-20

Projecting Future Income and Expenses . . . . . . EX 9-22

Exploring Linear and Growth Trends . . . . EX 9-22

Interpolating from a Starting Value to
an Ending Value . . . . EX 9-23

Calculating the Cost of Goods Sold. . . . . EX 9-26

Extrapolating from a Series of Values. . . . . . . EX 9-27

Calculating Depreciation of Assets. . . . . EX 9-29

Straight-Line Depreciation . . . . EX 9-30

Declining Balance Depreciation . . . . EX 9-30

Adding Depreciation to an Income
Statement . . . . EX 9-34

Adding Taxes and Interest Expenses to
an Income Statement . . . . EX 9-35

Session 9.3 Visual Overview: NPV and
IRR Functions and Auditing. . . . . EX 9-38

Calculating Interest Rates with the
RATE Function. . . . . EX 9-40

Viewing the Payback Period of an Investment . . . EX 9-41

Calculating Net Present Value. . . . . EX 9-43

The Time Value of Money. . . . . EX 9-43

Using the NPV Function . . . . EX 9-43

Choosing a Rate of Return . . . . EX 9-44

Calculating the Internal Rate of Return. . . . . . . EX 9-46

Using the IRR Function . . . . EX 9-47

Exploring the XNPV and XIRR Functions . . . .EX 9-49

Auditing a Workbook . . . . EX 9-51

Tracing an Error. . . . . EX 9-52

Evaluating a Formula. . . . . EX 9-55

Using the Watch Window . . . . EX 9-57

Review Assignments . . . . EX 9-60

Case Problem 1 . . . . EX 9-62

Case Problem 2 . . . . EX 9-63

**Module 10 Analyzing Data with Business
Intelligence Tools**
Presenting Sales and Revenue Data. . . . . **EX 10-1**

Session 10.1 Visual Overview: Queries
and Trendlines. . . . . EX 10-2

Introducing Business Intelligence . . . . EX 10-4

Writing a Data Query . . . . EX 10-4

Using Power Query. EX 10-4

Retrieving Data into an Excel Table . . . . EX 10-8

Editing a Query. . . . . EX 10-9

Refreshing Query Data . . . . EX 10-10

Transforming Data with Queries . . . . EX 10-11

Adding a New Column . . . . EX 10-12

Grouping Values in a Query . . . . EX 10-13

Charting Trends. . . . . EX 10-16

Creating a Forecast Sheet. . . . . EX 10-18

Session 10.2 Visual Overview: Power Pivot
and the Data Model . . . . EX 10-24

Introducing Databases . . . . EX 10-26

Relational Databases. . . . . EX 10-26

Querying an Access Database . . . . EX 10-27

Exploring the Data Model. . . . . EX 10-28

Transforming Data with Power Pivot.........EX 10-30

  Exploring the Data Model in
  Diagram View ....EX 10-32

  Managing Table Relationships ....EX 10-32

Creating a PivotTable from the Data Model ...EX 10-34

  Tabulating Across Fields from
  Multiple Tables ....EX 10-37

  Applying Slicers and Timelines from the
  Data Model ....EX 10-38

Session 10.3 Visual Overview: Hierarchies
and Maps.................................EX 10-42

Working with Outlines and Hierarchies.......EX 10-44

  Outlining a PivotTable by Nested Fields....EX 10-44

  Drilling Down a Field Hierarchy ....EX 10-46

  Viewing Data with the Quick Explore Tool ... EX 10-51

Viewing Data with Map Charts ....EX 10-53

  Creating a Value Map Chart ....EX 10-54

  Formatting a Map Chart................EX 10-58

  Visualizing Data with 3D Maps ....EX 10-60

  Choosing a Map Style.................EX 10-62

  Creating New Scenes ....EX 10-63

  Setting Scene Options ....EX 10-64

  Playing a Tour ....EX 10-66

Review Assignments ....EX 10-68

Case Problem 1 ....EX 10-69

Case Problem 2 ....EX 10-71

Module 11 Exploring PivotTable Design
*Summarizing Sales and Revenue Data ....***EX 11-1**

Session 11.1 Visual Overview: Layouts,
Sorting, Filtering, and Grouping...........EX 11-2

Laying Out a PivotTable...................EX 11-4

  Working with Grand Totals and
  Subtotals.........................EX 11-4

  Changing the PivotTable Layout..........EX 11-7

Sorting a PivotTable......................EX 11-9

  Manually Sorting a Field ....EX 11-9

  Sorting by Value ....EX 11-9

Filtering a PivotTable....................EX 11-12

Grouping PivotTable Fields ....EX 11-15

  Manual Grouping ....EX 11-16

  Grouping by Dates ....EX 11-18

  Grouping by Numeric Fields............EX 11-21

Session 11.2 Visual Overview: Conditional
Formats and Calculations ....EX 11-24

Calculations with PivotTables ....EX 11-26

  Calculating Ranks ....EX 11-28

  Calculating Percent Differences ....EX 11-29

Displaying PivotTables with Conditional
Formats ....EX 11-31

  Creating an Icon Set ....EX 11-32

  Working with Color Scales ....EX 11-34

Exploring the PivotTable Cache ....EX 11-35

  Sharing a Cache Between PivotTables .....EX 11-35

  Creating a New Cache ....EX 11-37

Working with Calculated Items and
Calculated Fields.........................EX 11-39

  Creating a Calculated Item..............EX 11-39

  Creating a Calculated Field ....EX 11-42

  Behind the Math of Calculated Items
  and Fields ....EX 11-46

Session 11.3 Visual Overview: PivotTable
Measures ....EX 11-48

Introducing PivotTable Design Under the
Data Model ....EX 11-50

Calculating Distinct Counts................EX 11-51

Creating a Measure......................EX 11-53

  Introducing DAX.....................EX 11-53

  Adding a Measure to a Table ....EX 11-54

Calculating Measures Across Tables and Rows ....EX 11-57

The RELATED Function.................EX 11-58

The SUMX Function ....EX 11-58

Retrieving PivotTable Data with GETPIVOTDATA.......................EX 11-61

Exploring Database Functions ....EX 11-65

Review Assignments ....EX 11-68

Case Problem 1 ....EX 11-69

Case Problem 2 ....EX 11-71

Module 12 Developing an Excel Application
Creating a Data Entry App ....**EX 12-1**

Session 12.1 Visual Overview: WordArt and Funnel Charts.......................EX 12-2

Planning an Excel Application...............EX 12-4

Creating a WordArt Graphic................EX 12-4

Displaying Data with a Funnel Chart.........EX 12-8

Hiding Error Values with the IFERROR Function..............................EX 12-11

Session 12.2 Visual Overview: Data Validation and Workbook Protection ....EX 12-14

Validating Data Entry.....................EX 12-16

Validating Dates ....EX 12-17

Creating a Validation Error Message ......EX 12-18

Creating an Input Message..............EX 12-20

Validating Against a List ....EX 12-21

Creating a Custom Validation Rule........EX 12-23

Validating Data Already in the Workbook............................EX 12-25

Hiding Workbook Content ....EX 12-25

Protecting Workbook Contents ....EX 12-27

Protecting a Worksheet ....EX 12-27

Protecting a Workbook..................EX 12-28

Unprotecting a Worksheet and a Workbook ....EX 12-29

Locking and Unlocking Cells.............EX 12-30

Session 12.3 Visual Overview: Macros and Visual Basic for Applications ....EX 12-34

Loading the Excel Developer Tab ....EX 12-36

Automating Tasks with Macros ....EX 12-37

Recording a Macro ....EX 12-37

Running a Macro......................EX 12-39

Saving and Opening a Macro-Enabled Workbook .... EX 12-40

Assigning Macros to Shapes and Buttons ....EX 12-41

Assigning a Macro to a Shape ....EX 12-41

Assigning a Macro to a Button.......... EX 12-43

Working with the VBA Editor ....EX 12-50

Opening the VBA Editor................EX 12-50

Understanding Sub Procedures ....EX 12-51

Editing a Macro with the VBA Editor ......EX 12-52

Protecting Against Macro Viruses..........EX 12-55

Macro Security Settings ....EX 12-55

Adding a Digital Signature to a Workbook ....EX 12-57

Review Assignments ....EX 12-58

Case Problem 1 ....EX 12-59

Case Problem 2 .... EX 12-60

Index ....**IDX 1**

Getting to Know Microsoft Office Versions

Cengage is proud to bring you the next edition of Microsoft Office. This edition was designed to provide a robust learning experience that is not dependent upon a specific version of Office.

Microsoft supports several versions of Office:

- **Office 365:** A cloud-based subscription service that delivers Microsoft's most up-to-date, feature-rich, modern productivity tools direct to your device. There are variations of Office 365 for business, educational, and personal use. Office 365 offers extra online storage and cloud-connected features, as well as updates with the latest features, fixes, and security updates.

- **Office 2021:** Microsoft's "on-premises" version of the Office apps, available for both PCs and Macs, offered as a static, one-time purchase and outside of the subscription model.

- **Office Online:** A free, simplified version of Office web applications (Word, Excel, PowerPoint, and OneNote) that facilitates creating and editing files collaboratively.

Office 365 (the subscription model) and Office 2021 (the one-time purchase model) had only slight differences between them at the time this content was developed. Over time, Office 365's cloud interface will continuously update, offering new application features and functions, while Office 2021 will remain static. Therefore, your onscreen experience may differ from what you see in this product. For example, the more advanced features and functionalities covered in this product may not be available in Office Online or may have updated from what you see in Office 2021.

For more information on the differences between Office 365, Office 2021, and Office Online, please visit the Microsoft Support site.

Cengage is committed to providing high-quality learning solutions for you to gain the knowledge and skills that will empower you throughout your educational and professional careers.

Thank you for using our product, and we look forward to exploring the future of Microsoft Office with you!

Using SAM Projects and Textbook Projects

SAM Projects allow you to actively apply the skills you learned live in Microsoft Word, Excel, PowerPoint, or Access. Become a more productive student and use these skills throughout your career.

To complete SAM Textbook Projects, please follow these steps:

SAM Textbook Projects allow you to complete a project as you follow along with the steps in the textbook. As you read the module, look for icons that indicate when you should download **sam**⬇ your SAM Start file(s) and when to upload **sam**⬆ the final project file to SAM for grading.

Everything you need to complete this project is provided within SAM. You can launch the eBook directly from SAM, which will allow you to take notes, highlight, and create a custom study guide, or you can use a print textbook or your mobile app. Download IOS or Download Android.

To get started, launch your SAM Project assignment from SAM, MindTap, or a link within your LMS.

Step 1: Download Files

- Click the "Download All" button or the individual links to download your **Start File** and **Support File(s)** (when available). You <u>must</u> use the SAM Start file.

- Click the Instructions link to launch the eBook (or use the print textbook or mobile app).

- Disregard any steps in the textbook that ask you to create a new file or to use a file from a location outside of SAM.

- Look for the SAM Download icon **sam**⬇ to begin working with your start file.

- Follow the module's step-by-step instructions until you reach the SAM Upload icon **sam**⬆.

- Save and close the file.

Step 2: Save Work to SAM

- Ensure you rename your project file to match the Expected File Name.

- Upload your in-progress or completed file to SAM. You can download the file to continue working or submit it for grading in the next step.

Step 3: Submit for Grading

- Upload the completed file to SAM for immediate feedback and to view the available Reports.

  - The **Graded Summary Report** provides a detailed list of project steps, your score, and feedback to aid you in revising and re-submitting the project.

  - The **Study Guide Report** provides your score for each project step and links to the associated training and textbook pages.

- If additional attempts are allowed, use your reports to assist with revising and resubmitting your project.

- To re-submit the project, download the file saved in step 2.

- Edit, save, and close the file, then re-upload and submit it again.

<u>For all other SAM Projects, please follow these steps:</u>

To get started, launch your SAM Project assignment from SAM, MindTap, or a link within your LMS.

Step 1: Download Files

- Click the "Download All" button or the individual links to download your **Instruction File**, **Start File**, and **Support File(s)** (when available). You <u>must</u> use the SAM Start file.

- Open the Instruction file and follow the step-by-step instructions. Ensure you rename your project file to match the Expected File Name (change _1 to _2 at the end of the file name).

Step 2: Save Work to SAM

- Upload your in-progress or completed file to SAM. You can download the file to continue working or submit it for grading in the next step.

Step 3: Submit for Grading

- Upload the completed file to SAM for immediate feedback and to view available Reports.

  - The **Graded Summary Report** provides a detailed list of project steps, your score, and feedback to aid you in revising and resubmitting the project.

  - The **Study Guide Report** provides your score for each project step and links to the associated training and textbook pages.

- If additional attempts are allowed, use your reports to assist with revising and resubmitting your project.

- To re-submit the project, download the file saved in step 2.

- Edit, save, and close the file, then re-upload and submit it again.

For additional tips to successfully complete your SAM Projects, please view our Common Student Errors Infographic.

Objectives

Session 1.1
- Open and close a workbook
- Navigate through a workbook and worksheet
- Select cells and ranges
- Plan and create a workbook
- Insert, rename, and move worksheets
- Enter text, dates, and numbers
- Undo and redo actions
- Resize columns and rows

Session 1.2
- Enter formulas and the SUM and COUNT functions
- Copy and paste formulas
- Move or copy cells and ranges
- Insert and delete rows, columns, and ranges
- Create patterned text with Flash Fill
- Add cell borders and change font size
- Change worksheet views
- Prepare a workbook for printing

Getting Started with Excel

Tracking Miscellaneous Expenses for a Conference

Case | MedIT

Carmen Estrada is an event coordinator for MedIT, a company that develops information technology for hospitals and clinics. Carmen is planning the upcoming regional conference for MedIT customers and vendors in Boston, Massachusetts. An important aspect of event planning is reviewing budget data and supplying additional expense information for the conference. Carmen wants you to review the conference planning documents and then create a document that she can use to detail miscellaneous expenses for the conference event.

EXCEL

Starting Data Files

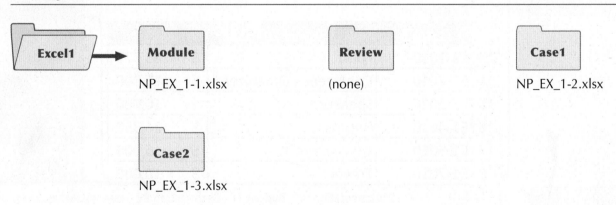

Excel1 → Module
NP_EX_1-1.xlsx

Review
(none)

Case1
NP_EX_1-2.xlsx

Case2
NP_EX_1-3.xlsx

Session 1.1 Visual Overview:

The ribbon is organized into tabs. Each **tab** has a group of related commands for particular activities or tasks.

Buttons for related commands are organized on a tab in **groups**.

Excel stores a collection of sheets within a single file called a **workbook**. The name of the current workbook appears in the title bar.

The **ribbon** contains grouped command buttons that you click to interact with Excel and execute commands.

The **Name box** displays the cell reference of the active cell. In this case, the active cell is cell K16.

The area above the worksheet grid is the **formula bar** where you can enter or edit data in the active cell.

A group of cells in a rectangular block is called a **cell range** (or **range**). If the blocks are not connected, as shown here, it is a **nonadjacent range**.

The **row headings** are numbers in boxes along the left side of the workbook window that identify the worksheet rows.

The **status bar** is a bar at the bottom of the Excel window that shows information about the current worksheet as well as view buttons and Zoom controls.

The sheet currently displayed in the workbook window is the **active sheet**. Its sheet tab is underlined, and the sheet name is green and bold.

Inactive sheets are not visible in the workbook window. Their sheet tabs are not underlined, and their sheet names are black.

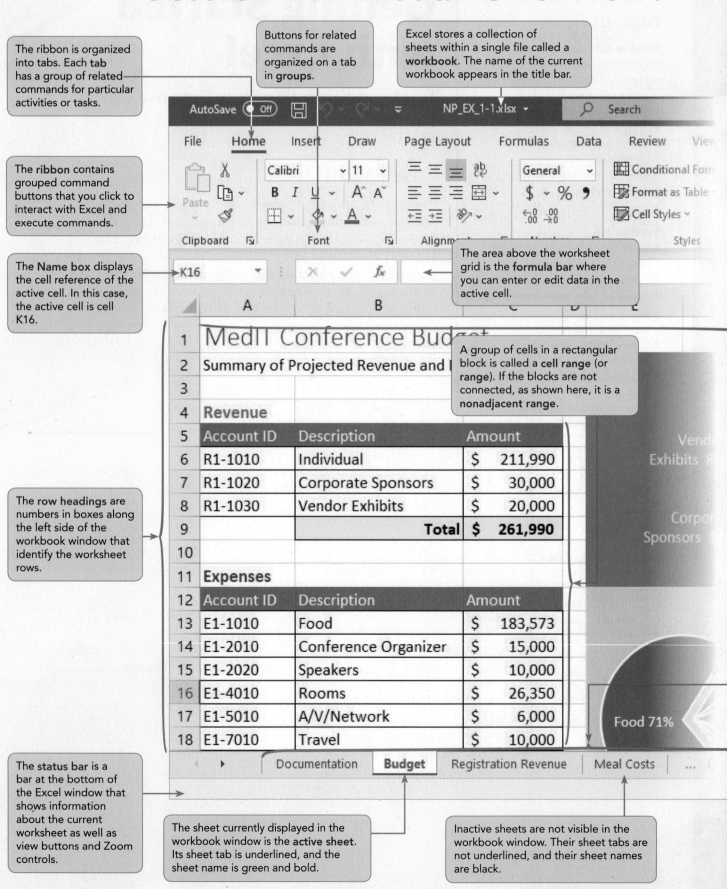

	A	B		C
1	MedII Conference Budget			
2	Summary of Projected Revenue and			
3				
4	Revenue			
5	Account ID	Description	Amount	
6	R1-1010	Individual	$	211,990
7	R1-1020	Corporate Sponsors	$	30,000
8	R1-1030	Vendor Exhibits	$	20,000
9		Total	$	261,990
10				
11	Expenses			
12	Account ID	Description	Amount	
13	E1-1010	Food	$	183,573
14	E1-2010	Conference Organizer	$	15,000
15	E1-2020	Speakers	$	10,000
16	E1-4010	Rooms	$	26,350
17	E1-5010	A/V/Network	$	6,000
18	E1-7010	Travel	$	10,000

Documentation | **Budget** | Registration Revenue | Meal Costs

K16

AutoSave Off | NP_EX_1-1.xlsx | Search

File | Home | Insert | Draw | Page Layout | Formulas | Data | Review | View

Food 71%

The Excel Workbook

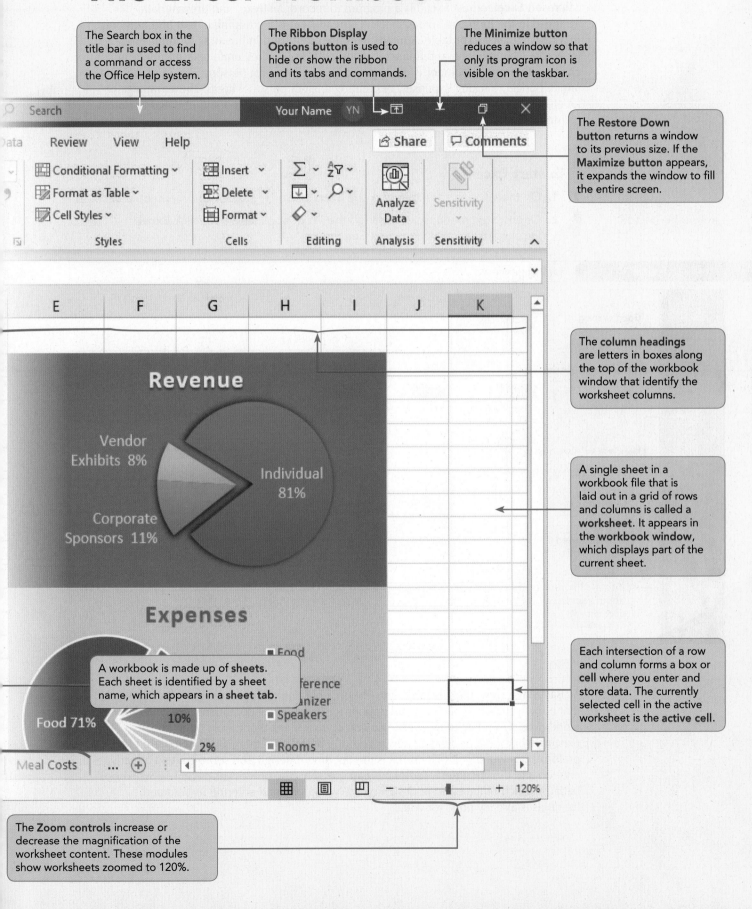

The Search box in the title bar is used to find a command or access the Office Help system.

The Ribbon Display Options button is used to hide or show the ribbon and its tabs and commands.

The Minimize button reduces a window so that only its program icon is visible on the taskbar.

The Restore Down button returns a window to its previous size. If the Maximize button appears, it expands the window to fill the entire screen.

The column headings are letters in boxes along the top of the workbook window that identify the worksheet columns.

A single sheet in a workbook file that is laid out in a grid of rows and columns is called a worksheet. It appears in the workbook window, which displays part of the current sheet.

A workbook is made up of sheets. Each sheet is identified by a sheet name, which appears in a sheet tab.

Each intersection of a row and column forms a box or cell where you enter and store data. The currently selected cell in the active worksheet is the active cell.

The Zoom controls increase or decrease the magnification of the worksheet content. These modules show worksheets zoomed to 120%.

Introducing Excel and Spreadsheets

Microsoft Excel (or just **Excel**) is a program to record, analyze, and present data arranged in the form of a spreadsheet. A **spreadsheet** is a grouping of text and numbers in a rectangular grid or table. Spreadsheets are often used in business for budgeting, inventory management, and financial reporting because they unite text, numbers, and charts within one document. They can also be employed for personal use in planning a family budget, tracking expenses, or creating a list of personal items. The advantage of an electronic spreadsheet is that the content can be easily edited and updated to reflect changing financial conditions.

To start Excel:

1. On the Windows taskbar, click the **Start** button ⊞. The Start menu opens.
2. On the Start menu, scroll through the list of apps, and then click **Excel**. Excel starts in Backstage view. See Figure 1-1.

Figure 1-1   Backstage view

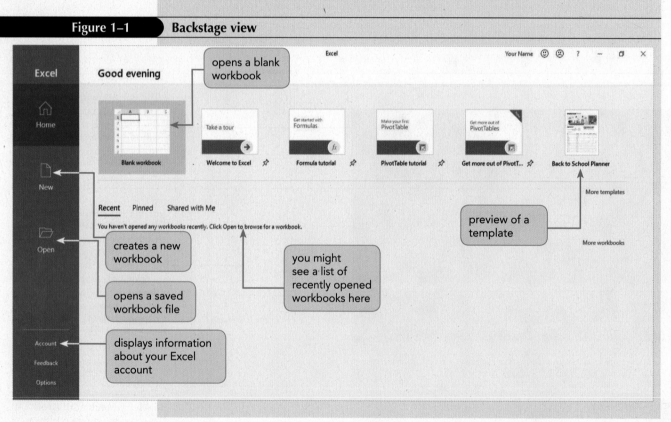

Backstage view, the File tab of the ribbon, contains various screens with commands that allow you to manage files and options for Excel. Excel documents are called workbooks. From Backstage view, you can open a blank workbook, open an existing workbook, or create a new workbook based on a template. A **template** is a preformatted workbook that contains the document design and some content already entered into the document. Templates can speed up the process of creating a workbook because much of the effort in designing the workbook and entering its data and formulas is already done for you.

Carmen created an Excel workbook containing information on the budget for the upcoming Boston conference. You'll open that workbook now.

To open the Conference workbook:

▶ **1.** In the navigation bar in Backstage view, click **Open**. The Open screen is displayed and provides access to different locations where you might store files.

▶ **2.** Click **Browse**. The Open dialog box appears.

▶ **3.** Navigate to the **Excel1 > Module** folder included with your Data Files.

   Trouble? If you don't have the starting Data Files, you need to get them before you can proceed. Your instructor will either give you the Data Files or ask you to obtain them from a specified location (such as a network drive). If you have any questions about the Data Files, see your instructor or technical support person for assistance.

▶ **4.** Click **NP_EX_1-1.xlsx** in the file list to select it.

   If your instructor wants you to submit your work as a SAM Project for automatic grading, you must download the Data File in Step 4 from the assignment launch page.

▶ **5.** Click the **Open** button. The workbook opens in Excel.

   Trouble? If you don't see the full ribbon as shown in the Session 1.1 Visual Overview, the ribbon may be partially or fully hidden. To pin the ribbon so that the tabs and groups are fully displayed and remain visible, click the Ribbon Display Options button ⊞, and then click Show Tabs and Commands.

▶ **6.** If the Excel window doesn't fill the screen, click the **Maximize** button ☐ in the upper-right corner of the title bar. See Figure 1–2.

Figure 1–2   **Conference workbook**

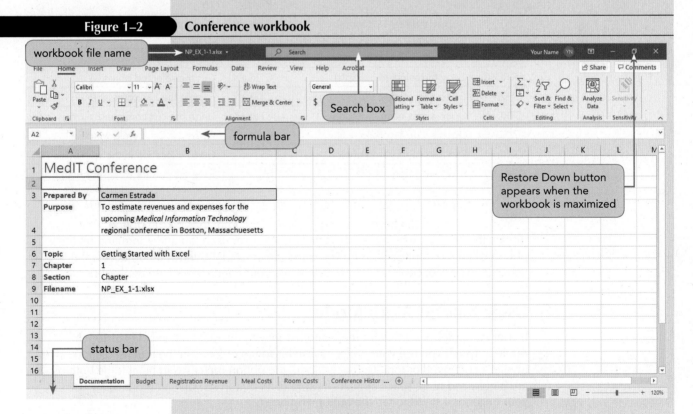

Before reviewing the contents of this workbook, you first should understand how to work with the Excel interface.

Getting Help

Excel is an extensive and powerful program supporting a wide variety of commands and tools. If you are unsure about the function of an Excel command or you want information about how to accomplish a task, you can use the Help system. To access Excel Help, you press F1. You can also enter a phrase or keyword into the Search box next to the file name in the title bar. From this box, you can get quick access to detailed information on all of the Excel features.

Using Keyboard Shortcuts to Work Faster

There are several ways of accessing an Excel command. Perhaps the most efficient method is entering the command through your device's keyboard through the use of keyboard shortcuts. A **keyboard shortcut** is a key or combination of keys that you press to access a feature or perform a command. Excel provides keyboard shortcuts for many commonly used commands. For example, CTRL+S is the keyboard shortcut for the Save command, which means you hold down CTRL while you press S to save the workbook. (Note that the plus sign is not pressed; it is used to indicate that an additional key is pressed.) When available, a keyboard shortcut is listed next to the command's name in a ScreenTip. A **ScreenTip** is a label that appears next to an object, providing information about that object or giving a link to associated help topics. Figure 1–3 lists some of the keyboard shortcuts commonly used in Excel.

| Figure 1–3 | Excel keyboard shortcuts |

Press	To	Press	To
ALT	Display the Key Tips for the commands and tools on the ribbon	CTRL+V	Paste content that was cut or copied
CTRL+A	Select all objects in a range	CTRL+W	Close the current workbook
CTRL+C	Copy the selected object(s)	CTRL+X	Cut the selected object(s)
CTRL+G	Go to a location in the workbook	CTRL+Y	Repeat the last command
CTRL+N	Open a new blank workbook	CTRL+Z	Undo the last command
CTRL+O	Open a saved workbook file	F1	Open the Excel Help window
CTRL+P	Print the current workbook	F5	Go to a location in the workbook
CTRL+S	Save the current workbook	F12	Save the current workbook with a new name or to a new location

You can also use the keyboard to quickly select commands on the ribbon. First, you display the **KeyTips**, which are labels that appear over each tab and command on the ribbon when ALT is pressed. Then you press the key or keys indicated to access the corresponding tab, command, or button while your hands remain on the keyboard.

Using Excel in Touch Mode

If your computer has a touchscreen, another way to interact with Excel is in **Touch Mode** in which you use your finger or a stylus to tap objects on the touchscreen to invoke a command or tool. In Touch Mode, the ribbon increases in height, the buttons are bigger, and more space appears around each button so you can more easily use your finger or a stylus to tap the button you need.

The figures in these modules show the screen in **Mouse Mode**, in which you use a computer mouse to interact with Excel and invoke commands and tools. If you plan on doing some of your work on a touch device, you'll need to switch between Touch Mode and Mouse Mode. You should turn Touch Mode on only if you are working on a touch device.

To switch between Touch Mode and Mouse Mode:

▶ **1.** On the Quick Access Toolbar, click the **Customize Quick Access Toolbar** button ▼ . A menu opens, listing buttons you can add to the Quick Access Toolbar as well as other options for customizing the toolbar.

Trouble? If the Touch/Mouse Mode command on the menu has a checkmark next to it, press ESC to close the menu, and then skip Step 2.

▶ **2.** From the Quick Access Toolbar menu, click **Touch/Mouse Mode**. The Quick Access Toolbar now contains the Touch/Mouse Mode button 👆▾ , which you can use to switch between Mouse Mode and Touch Mode.

▶ **3.** On the Quick Access Toolbar, click the **Touch/Mouse Mode** button 👆▾ . A menu opens listing Mouse and Touch, and the icon next to Mouse is shaded to indicate that it is selected.

Trouble? If the icon next to Touch is shaded, press ESC to close the menu and continue with Step 5.

▶ **4.** Click **Touch**. The display switches to Touch Mode with more space between the commands and buttons on the ribbon. See Figure 1–4.

Figure 1–4	Excel displayed in Touch Mode

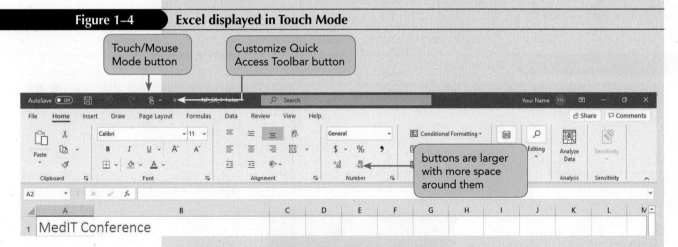

Next, you will switch back to Mouse Mode. If you are working with a touch-screen and want to use Touch Mode, skip Steps 5 and 6.

▶ **5.** On the Quick Access Toolbar, click the **Touch/Mouse Mode** button 👆▾ , and then click **Mouse**. The ribbon returns to Mouse Mode, as shown earlier in Figure 1–2.

▶ **6.** On the Quick Access Toolbar, click the **Customize Quick Access Toolbar** button ▼ , and then click **Touch/Mouse Mode** to deselect it. The Touch/Mouse Mode button is removed from the Quick Access Toolbar.

Now that you've seen how to interact with the Excel program, you ready to explore the workbook that Carmen has prepared.

Exploring a Workbook

The contents of a workbook are shown in the workbook window, which is below the ribbon. Workbooks are organized into separate pages called sheets. Excel supports two types of sheets: worksheets and chart sheets. A worksheet contains a grid of rows and columns into which you can enter text, numbers, dates, and formulas. Worksheets can also contain graphical elements such as charts, maps, and clip art. A **chart sheet** is a sheet that contains only a chart that is linked to data within the workbook. A chart sheet can also contain other graphical elements like clip art, but it doesn't contain a grid for entering data values.

Changing the Active Sheet

Worksheets and chart sheets are identified by the sheet tabs at the bottom of the workbook window. The workbook for the MedIT conference in Boston contains eight sheets labeled Documentation, Budget, Registration Revenue, Meal Costs, Room Costs, Conference History, Budget History, and Registration List. The sheet currently displayed in the workbook window is the active sheet, which in this case is the Documentation sheet. The sheet tab of the active sheet is highlighted, and the sheet tab name appears in bold.

If a workbook contains more sheet tabs than can be displayed in the workbook window, the list of tabs will end with an ellipsis (…), indicating the presence of additional sheets. You can use the sheet tab scrolling buttons, located to the left of the sheet tabs, to scroll through the tab list. Scrolling through the sheet tab list does not change the active sheet; it changes only which sheet tabs are visible within the workbook window.

You will view the contents of the Conference workbook by clicking the tabs for each sheet.

> **Tip**
>
> Some Excel documents have hidden sheets, which are still part of the workbook but do not appear within the workbook window.

To change the active sheet:

1. Click the **Budget** sheet tab. The Budget worksheet becomes the active sheet, and its name is in bold green. See Figure 1–5.

Figure 1–5 ▶ Budget worksheet

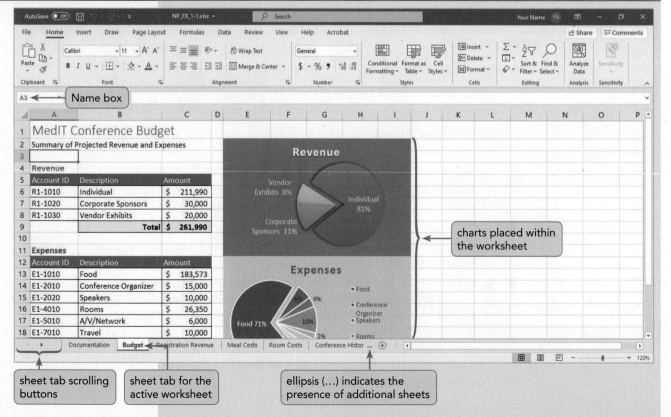

sheet tab scrolling buttons

sheet tab for the active worksheet

ellipsis (…) indicates the presence of additional sheets

The Budget sheet contains estimates of the conference's revenue and expenses. The sheet also contains charts of the revenue and expense categories. From the charts, it's easily apparent that the major source of revenue for the conference comes from individual registrations and the major expense comes from feeding all the attendees over the three conference days.

2. Click the **Registration Revenue** sheet tab to make it the active sheet. The Registration Revenue tab provides a more detailed breakdown of the revenue estimates for the conference.

3. Click the **Meal Costs**, **Room Costs**, and **Conference History** sheet tabs to view each worksheet. Figure 1–6 shows the contents of the Conference History chart sheet. Because this is a chart sheet, it contains only the Excel chart and not the rows and columns of text and numbers you saw in the worksheets.

Figure 1–6	Conference History chart sheet

chart sheet contains a chart but no grid of text and data

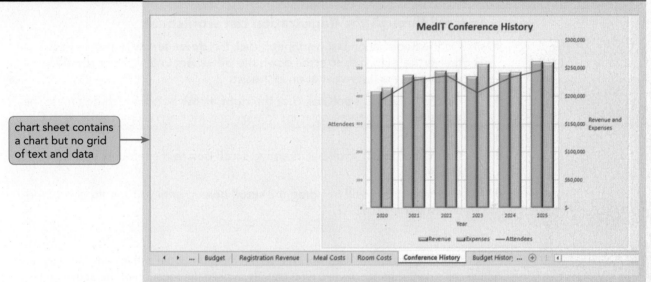

4. Click the **Budget History** and **Registration List** sheet tabs to view the remaining two worksheets in the workbook.

Trouble? If you can't see the sheet tabs for the last few sheets in the workbook, click the sheet tab scrolling buttons to scroll through the tab list.

Now you know how to switch between the eight sheets in the workbook. Next, you will move around the individual worksheets so you can review their contents.

Navigating Within a Worksheet

A worksheet is organized into a grid of cells, which are formed by the intersection of rows and columns. Rows are identified by numbers, and columns are identified by letters. Row numbers range from 1 to 1,048,576. Column labels start with the letters A to Z. After Z, the next column headings are labeled AA, AB, AC, and so forth. The last possible column label is XFD, which means there are 16,384 columns available in a worksheet. The total number of possible cells in a single Excel worksheet is more than 17 billion, providing an extremely large worksheet for reports.

Each cell is identified by a **cell reference**, which indicates the column and row in which the cell is located. For example, as shown in Figure 1–5, the total expected revenue from the conference, $261,990, is displayed in cell C9. Cell C9 is the intersection of column C and row 9. The column letter always appears before the row number in any cell reference.

The cell that is currently selected in the worksheet is the active cell and has a thick green border. The corresponding column and row headings for the active cell are also highlighted. The cell reference of the active cell appears in the Name box, located just below the left side of the ribbon. The active cell in Figure 1–5 is cell A3.

To move different parts of the worksheet into view, you can use the horizontal and vertical scroll bars located at the bottom and right edges of the workbook window, respectively. A scroll bar has arrow buttons that you can click to shift the worksheet one column or row in that direction, and a scroll box that you can drag to shift the worksheet larger amounts in the direction you choose.

You will scroll the active worksheet so you can review the rest of the Registration List worksheet.

To scroll through the Registration List worksheet:

▶ **1.** On the Registration List worksheet, click the **down arrow** button ▼ on the vertical scroll bar to scroll down the worksheet until you see row 496 containing the last registration in the list.

▶ **2.** On the horizontal scroll bar, click the **right arrow** button ▶ three times. The worksheet scrolls three columns to the right, moving columns A through C out of view.

▶ **3.** On the horizontal scroll bar, drag the **scroll box** to the left until you see column A.

▶ **4.** On the vertical scroll bar, drag the **scroll box** up until you see the top of the worksheet and cell A1.

Scrolling the worksheet does not change the location of the active cell. Although the active cell might shift out of view, you can always see the location of the active cell in the Name box. To make a different cell active, you can either click a new cell or use keyboard shortcuts to move between cells, as described in Figure 1–7.

Figure 1–7	Excel navigation keyboard shortcuts

Press	To move the active cell
↑ ↓ ← →	Up, down, left, or right one cell
HOME	To column A of the current row
CTRL+HOME	To cell A1
CTRL+END	To the last cell in the worksheet that contains data
ENTER	Down one row or to the start of the next row of data
SHIFT+ENTER	Up one row
TAB	One column to the right
SHIFT+TAB	One column to the left
PGUP, PGDN	Up or down one screen
CTRL+PGUP, CTRL+PGDN	To the previous or next sheet in the workbook

Keyboard shortcuts are especially useful in worksheets in which the data is spread across many rows or columns. For example, some financial worksheets can have tens of thousands of rows of data. You will use these shortcuts to move through the Registration List worksheet.

To change the active cell using keyboard shortcuts:

▶ **1.** On the Registration List worksheet, move the pointer over cell **C10** and then click the mouse button. The active cell moves from cell A2 to cell C10. A green border appears around cell C10 to indicate that it's now the active cell. The labels for row 10 and column C are highlighted, and the cell reference in the Name box is C10.

▶ **2.** Press **RIGHT ARROW**. The active cell moves one column to the right to cell D10.

▶ **3.** Press **PGDN**. The active cell moves down one full screen.

▶ **4.** Press **PGUP**. The active cell moves up one full screen, returning to cell D10.

▶ **5.** Press **CTRL+END**. The active cell is cell H496, the last cell containing data in the worksheet.

▶ **6.** Press **CTRL+HOME**. The active cell returns to the first cell in the worksheet, cell A1.

To change the active cell to a specific cell location, you can use the Go To dialog box or the Name box. These methods are especially helpful when you are working in worksheets with many rows or columns. You'll try both these methods now.

To change the active cell using the Go To dialog box and Name box:

▶ **1.** On the Home tab, in the Editing group, click the **Find & Select** button, and then click **Go To** on the menu that opens (or press **CTRL+G** or **F5**). The Go To dialog box opens.

▶ **2.** Type **A100** in the Reference box. See Figure 1–8.

Figure 1–8   Go To dialog box

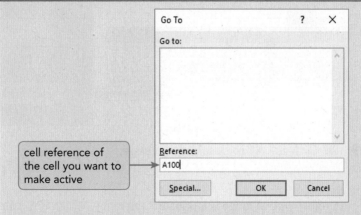

cell reference of the cell you want to make active

▶ **3.** Click **OK**. Cell A100 becomes the active cell showing the registration information for Anjali Cunha of New Bedford, Massachusetts.

▶ **4.** Click the Name box, type **A3**, and then press **ENTER**. Cell A3 becomes the active cell in the worksheet.

Selecting a Cell Range

Many tasks in Excel require you to work with a group of cells. A group of cells in a rectangular block is called a cell range (or simply a range). Each range is identified with a **range reference** that includes the cell reference of the upper-left cell of the rectangular block and the cell reference of the lower-right cell separated by a colon. For example, the range reference A1:G5 refers to all the cells in the rectangular block from cell A1 through cell G5.

As with individual cells, you can select cell ranges using your mouse, the keyboard, or commands. You will select a range in the Budget worksheet.

To select a cell range in the Budget worksheet:

1. Click the **Budget** sheet tab. The Budget worksheet becomes the active sheet.

2. Click cell **A5** to select it and, without releasing the mouse button, drag down and right to cell **C8**.

Tip

You can also select a cell range by typing its range reference in the Name box and pressing ENTER.

3. Release the mouse button. The range A5:C8 is selected. The selected cells are highlighted and surrounded by a green border. The first cell you selected in the range, cell A5, is the active cell in the worksheet. The Quick Analysis button appears next to the selected range, providing options for working with the range. See Figure 1–9.

| Figure 1–9 | Range A5:C8 selected |

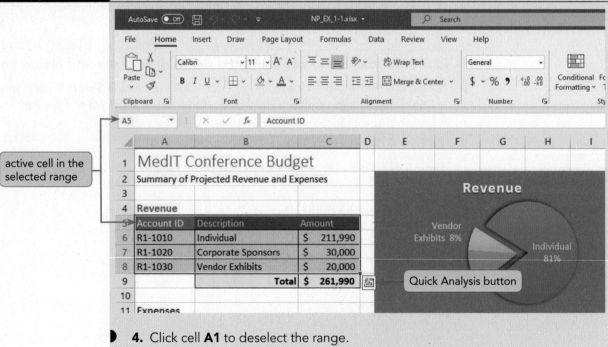

active cell in the selected range

4. Click cell **A1** to deselect the range.

Another type of range is a nonadjacent range, which is a collection of separate rectangular ranges. The range reference for a nonadjacent range includes the range reference to each range separated by a comma. For example, the range reference A1:G5,A10:G15 includes two ranges—the first range is the rectangular block of cells from cell A1 to cell G5, and the second range is the rectangular block of cells from cell A10 to cell G15.

You will select a nonadjacent range in the Budget worksheet.

To select a nonadjacent range in the Budget worksheet:

1. Click cell **A5**, hold down **SHIFT** as you click cell **C8**, and then release **SHIFT** to select the range A5:C8.

2. Scroll down the worksheet using the vertical scroll bar and then hold down **CTRL** as you drag to select the range **A12:C19** and then release **CTRL**. The two separate blocks of cells in the nonadjacent range A5:C8,A12:C19 are selected. See Figure 1–10.

Figure 1–10   **Range A5:C8,A12:C19 selected**

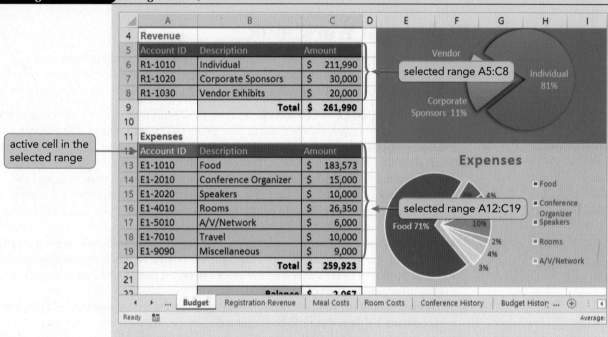

You can also use the Name box and Go To dialog box to select entire columns or rows. Just enter the column letters or row numbers as the reference separated by a colon. For example, the range reference E:E selects all cells in column E and the range reference 5:5 selects all cells in row 5.

Closing a Workbook

Once you are finished with a workbook, you can close it. When you close a workbook, a dialog box might appear, asking whether you want to save any changes you may have made to the workbook. If you have made changes that you want to keep, you should save the workbook. Because you have finished reviewing Carmen's workbook for MedIT, you will close the workbook without saving any changes you may have inadvertently made to its contents.

To close Carmen's workbook:

▶ **1.** On the ribbon, click the **File** tab to display Backstage view, and then click **Close** in the navigation bar (or press **CTRL+W**).

▶ **2.** If a dialog box opens, asking whether you want to save your changes to the workbook, click **Don't Save**. The workbook closes without saving any changes. Excel remains opens, ready for you to create or open another workbook.

Now that you've reviewed Carmen's workbook estimating the revenues and expenses for the upcoming conference in Boston, you are ready to create a new workbook. Carmen wants you to create a workbook in which you will estimate the miscellaneous expenses from the conference.

Planning a Workbook

A good practice is to plan your workbooks before you begin creating them. You can do this by using a planning analysis sheet, which includes the following questions that help you think about the workbook's purpose and how to achieve your desired results:

1. **What problems do I want to solve?** The answer identifies the goal or purpose of the workbook. In this case, Carmen wants you to come up with reasonable estimates for the conference's miscellaneous expenses.
2. **What data do I need?** The answer identifies the type of data that you need to collect for the workbook. Carmen needs a list of all the miscellaneous expenses and the estimated cost of each so that MedIT will not be surprised by unexpected expenses. Miscellaneous expenses include printing brochures and schedules, decorations for the conference banquet, and gifts for the conference attendees and keynote speakers.
3. **What calculations do I need?** The answer identifies the formulas you need to apply to your data. Carmen needs you to calculate the charge for each miscellaneous item, the total number of items ordered, the sales tax on all purchased items, and the total cost of all miscellaneous expenditures.
4. **What form should my solution take?** The answer impacts the appearance of the workbook content and how it should be presented to others. Carmen wants the estimates stored in a single worksheet that is easy to read and prints clearly.

You will create a workbook based on this plan. Carmen will then incorporate your projections for miscellaneous expenses into her full budget to ensure that the conference costs will not exceed the projected revenue.

Proskills

Written Communication: Creating Effective Workbooks

Workbooks convey information in written form. As with any type of writing, the final product creates an impression and provides an indicator of your interest, knowledge, and attention to detail. To create the best impression, all workbooks—especially those you intend to share with others such as coworkers and clients—should be well planned, well organized, and well written.

A well-designed workbook should clearly identify its overall goal and present information in an organized format. The data it includes—both the entered values and the calculated values—should be accurate. The process of developing an effective workbook includes the following steps:

1. Determine the workbook's purpose, content, and organization before you start.
2. Create a list of the sheets used in the workbook, noting each sheet's purpose.
3. Insert a documentation sheet that describes the workbook's purpose and organization. Include the name of the workbook's author, the date the workbook was created, and any additional information that will help others to track the workbook to its source.
4. Enter all the data in the workbook. Add labels to indicate what the values represent and, if possible, where they originated so others can view the source of your data.
5. Enter formulas for calculated items rather than entering the calculated values into the workbook. For more complicated calculations, provide documentation explaining them.
6. Test the workbook with a variety of values; edit the data and formulas to correct errors.
7. Save the workbook and create a backup copy when the project is completed. Print the workbook's contents if you need to provide a hard-copy version to others or for your files.
8. Maintain a history of your workbook as it goes through different versions, so that you and others can quickly see how the workbook has changed during revisions.

By including clearly written documentation, explanatory text, a logical organization, and accurate data and formulas, you will create effective workbooks that others can easily use.

Starting a New Workbook

You create new workbooks from the New screen in Backstage view. The New screen includes templates that you can use to preview different types of workbooks you can create with Excel. You will create a new workbook from the Blank workbook template, and then add all the content that Carmen wants for the miscellaneous expenses workbook.

To start a new, blank workbook for miscellaneous expenses:

1. **sam** ↓ On the ribbon, click the **File** tab to display Backstage view.

2. Click **New** in the navigation bar to display the New screen, which includes access to templates for a variety of workbooks.

Tip

You can also create a new blank workbook by pressing CTRL+N.

3. Click **Blank workbook**. A blank workbook opens.

   In these modules, the workbook window is zoomed to 120% for better readability. If you want to zoom your workbook window to match the figures, complete Step 4. If you prefer to work in the default zoom of 100% or at another zoom level, read but do not complete Step 4; you might see more or less of the worksheet on your screen, but this will not affect your work in the modules.

4. If you want your workbook window zoomed to 120% to match the figures, on the Zoom slider at the lower-right of the program window, click the **Zoom In** button ⊞ twice to increase the percentage to **120%**. The 120% magnification increases the size of each cell but reduces the number of worksheet cells visible in the workbook window. See Figure 1-11.

Figure 1-11	Blank workbook

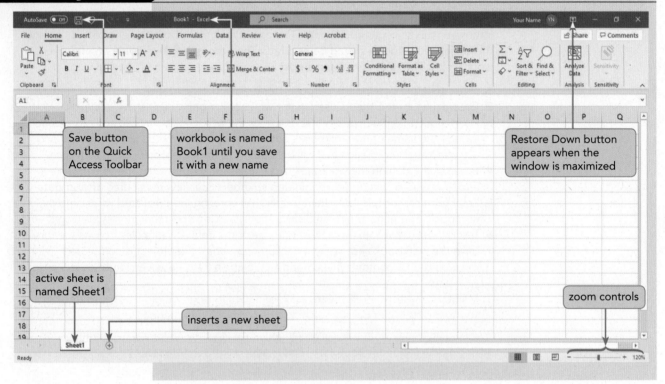

The name of the active workbook, Book1, appears in the title bar. If you open multiple blank workbooks, they are named Book1, Book2, Book3, and so forth until you save them with a more descriptive name.

Renaming and Inserting Worksheets

Blank workbooks open with a single blank worksheet named Sheet1. It's a good practice to give your sheets more descriptive names that indicate the purpose and content of the sheet. Sheet names cannot exceed 31 characters, but they can contain blank spaces and include uppercase and lowercase letters.

Because Sheet1 is not a very descriptive name, Carmen wants you to rename the worksheet as Miscellaneous Expenses.

To rename the Sheet1 worksheet:

1. Double-click the **Sheet1** tab to select the text of the sheet name.

2. Type **Miscellaneous Expenses** as the new name, and then press **ENTER**. The width of the sheet tab expands to fit the longer sheet name.

Many workbooks include multiple sheets so that data can be organized in logical groups. A common business practice is to include a documentation worksheet that contains a description of the workbook, the name of the person who prepared the workbook, and the date it was created.

Carmen wants you to create two new worksheets. You will rename one worksheet as Documentation and the other worksheet as Site Information. The Site Information worksheet will be used to store information about the convention center that is hosting the conference.

To insert and name the Documentation and Site Information worksheets:

1. To the right of the Miscellaneous Expenses sheet tab, click the **New sheet** button ⊕. A new sheet named Sheet2 is inserted to the right of the Miscellaneous Expenses sheet.
2. Double-click the **Sheet2** sheet tab, type **Documentation** as the new name, and then press **ENTER**. The worksheet is renamed.
3. To the right of the Documentation sheet, click the **New sheet** button ⊕ and then rename the inserted Sheet3 worksheet as **Site Information**.
4. If you want these worksheets zoomed to 120% to match the figures, go to each worksheet, and then on the Zoom slider, click the **Zoom In** button + twice to increase the percentage to **120%**.

Moving Worksheets

Another good practice is to place the most important sheets at the beginning of the workbook (the leftmost sheet tabs) and the least important sheets at the end (the rightmost sheet tabs). To change the placement of sheets in a workbook, you drag them by their sheet tabs to the new location.

Carmen wants you to move the Documentation worksheet to the front of the workbook, so that it appears before the Miscellaneous Expenses sheet.

To move the Documentation worksheet:

1. Point to the **Documentation** sheet tab. The sheet tab name changes to bold.
2. Press and hold the mouse button. The pointer changes to ⇱, and a small arrow appears in the upper-left corner of the tab.
3. Drag to the left until the small arrow appears in the upper-left corner of the Miscellaneous Expenses sheet tab, and then release the mouse button. The Documentation worksheet is now the first sheet in the workbook.

You can copy a worksheet by holding down CTRL as you drag and drop the sheet tab. Copying the worksheet duplicates all of the worksheet data and its structure.

Deleting Worksheets

In some workbooks, you will want to delete an existing sheet. The easiest way to delete a sheet is by using a **shortcut menu**, which is a list of commands related to an object that opens when you right-click the object. Carmen asks you to include site information on the Miscellaneous Expenses worksheet so all the information about the conference site and the miscellaneous expenses is on one sheet.

To delete a worksheet:

▶ **1.** Right-click the **Site Information** sheet tab. A shortcut menu opens.

▶ **2.** Click **Delete**. The Site Information worksheet is removed from the workbook.

When you delete a sheet, you also delete any text and data it contains. So be careful that you do not remove important and irretrievable information.

Saving a Workbook

Tip

To save a new workbook to OneDrive, click the Save button on the Quick Access Toolbar, enter a file name, and then select a OneDrive folder. The AutoSave button in the title bar can save the workbook as it is edited.

As you modify a workbook, you should save it regularly—every 10 minutes or so is a good practice. The first time you save a workbook, the Save As dialog box opens so you can name the file and choose where to save it. You can save the workbook on your computer or network or to your account on OneDrive.

You will save the miscellaneous expenses workbook that you just created.

To save the miscellaneous expenses workbook for the first time:

▶ **1.** On the Quick Access Toolbar, click the **Save** button 🖫 (or press **CTRL+S**). The Save this file dialog box opens.

▶ **2.** Click **More options**. The Save As screen in Backstage view opens.

▶ **3.** Click the **Browse** button. The Save As dialog box opens.

▶ **4.** Navigate to the location specified by your instructor.

▶ **5.** In the File name box, select **Book1** (the default name assigned to your workbook) if it is not already selected, and then type **NP_EX_1_Misc** as the new name.

▶ **6.** Verify that **Excel Workbook** appears in the Save as type box.

▶ **7.** Click **Save**. The workbook is saved, the dialog box closes, and the workbook window reappears with the new file name in the title bar.

As you modify the workbook, you will need to resave the file. Because you already saved the workbook with a file name, the next time you save, the Save command saves the changes you made to the workbook without opening the Save As dialog box.

Tip

You can save the workbook to your OneDrive account by clicking the file name in the title bar and then clicking Upload.

Sometimes you will want to save a current workbook under a new file name. This is useful when you want to modify a workbook without losing its content and structure or when you want to save a copy of the workbook to a new location. To save a workbook with a new name, click the File tab to return to Backstage view, click Save As on the navigation bar, specify the new file name and location, and then click Save.

Entering Text, Dates, and Numbers

Worksheet cells can contain text, numbers, dates, and times. **Text data** is any combination of letters, numbers, and symbols. A **text string** is a series of text data characters. **Numeric data** is any number that can be used in a mathematical operation. **Date data** and **time data** are values displayed in commonly recognized date and time formats. For example, Excel interprets the cell entry April 15, 2025, as a date and not as text. By default, text is left-aligned within worksheet cells, and numbers, dates, and times are right-aligned.

Entering Text

Text is often used in worksheets as labels for the numeric values and calculations displayed in the workbook. Carmen wants you to enter text content into the Documentation sheet.

To enter text in the Documentation sheet:

▶ **1.** Go to the **Documentation** sheet, and then press **CTRL+HOME** to make sure cell A1 is the active cell.

▶ **2.** Type **MedIT** in cell A1. As you type, the text appears in cell A1 and in the formula bar.

▶ **3.** Press **ENTER** twice. The text is entered into cell A1, and the active cell moves down two rows to cell A3.

▶ **4.** Type **Author** in cell A3, and then press **TAB**. The text is entered and the active cell moves one column to the right to cell B3.

▶ **5.** Type your name in cell B3, and then press **ENTER**. The text is entered and the active cell moves one cell down and to the left to cell A4.

▶ **6.** Type **Date** in cell A4, and then press **TAB**. The text is entered, and the active cell moves one column to the right to cell B4, where you would enter the date you created the worksheet. For now, you will leave the cell for the date blank.

▶ **7.** Press **ENTER** to make cell A5 the active cell, type **Purpose** in the cell, and then press **TAB**. The active cell moves one column to the right to cell B5.

▶ **8.** Type **To estimate expenses at the MedIT convention** in cell B5, and then press **ENTER**. Figure 1–12 shows the text entered in the Documentation sheet.

Figure 1–12	Text entered in the Documentation sheet

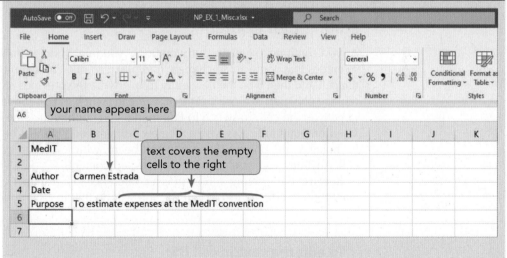

The text strings you entered in cells B3 and B5 are so long that they cover the adjacent cells. Any text that doesn't fit within a cell will cover the adjacent cells to the right if they are empty. If the adjacent cells contain data, only the text that fits into the cell is displayed and the rest of the text string is hidden. The complete text is still stored in the cell; it is just not displayed. (You will learn how to display all text in a cell in the next session.)

Undoing and Redoing an Action

As you enter data in a workbook, you might need to undo a previous action. Excel maintains a list of the actions you performed in the workbook during the current session, so you can undo most of your actions. You can use the Undo button on the Quick Access Toolbar or press CTRL+Z to reverse your most recent actions one at a time. If you want to undo more than one action, you can click the Undo arrow and then select the earliest action you want to undo—all actions after that initial action will also be undone.

You will undo the most recent change you made to the Documentation sheet—the text you entered into cell B5. Then you will enter a different description of the workbook's purpose in cell B5.

To undo the text entry in cell B5:

▶ **1.** On the Quick Access Toolbar, click the **Undo** button ⟲ (or press **CTRL+Z**). The last action is reversed, removing the text you entered in cell B5.

▶ **2.** Type **To estimate miscellaneous expenses at the MedIT convention in Boston** in cell B5, and then press **ENTER**. The new purpose statement is entered in cell B5.

If you want to restore actions you have undone, you can redo them. To redo one action at a time, you can click the Redo button ⟳ on the Quick Access Toolbar or press CTRL+Y. To redo multiple actions at once, you can click the Redo arrow ⟳▾ and then click the earliest action you want to redo. After you undo or redo an action, Excel continues the action list starting from any new changes you make to the workbook.

Editing Cell Content

As you continue to create your workbook, you might find mistakes you need to correct or entries that you want to change. To replace all of a cell's content, you simply select the cell and then type the new entry to overwrite the previous entry. If you want to replace only part of a cell's content, you can switch to **Edit mode** to make the changes directly in the cell. To switch to Edit mode, you double-click the cell. A blinking insertion point indicates where the new content you type will be inserted. In the cell or formula bar, the pointer changes to an I-beam, which you can use to select text in the cell. Anything you type replaces the selected content.

Because the meeting in Boston is a conference rather than a convention, Carmen wants you to edit the text in cell B5. You will do that in Edit mode.

To edit the text in cell B5:

▶ **1.** Double-click cell **B5** to select the cell and switch to Edit mode. A blinking insertion point appears within the text of cell B5. The status bar displays Edit instead of Ready to indicate that the cell is in Edit mode.

▶ **2.** Press **LEFT ARROW** or **RIGHT ARROW** as needed to move the insertion point directly to the right of the word "convention" in the cell text.

▶ **3.** Press **BACKSPACE** 10 times to delete the word "convention," and then type **conference** in the entry. See Figure 1–13.

Figure 1–13   **Edited text in the Documentation sheet**

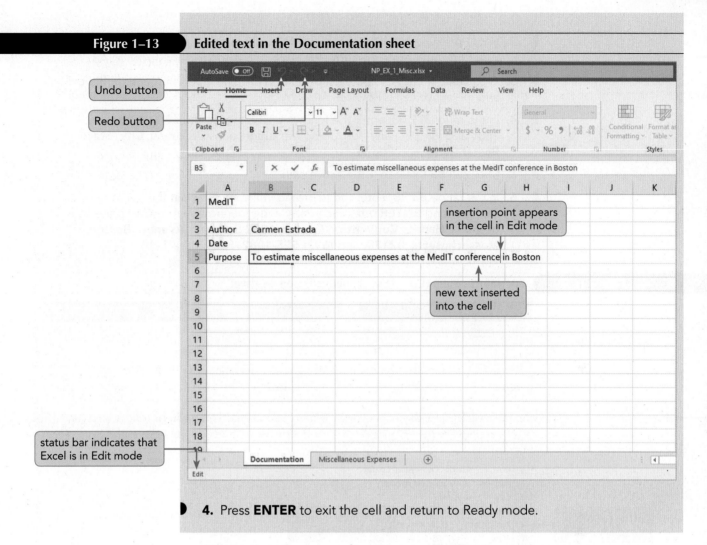

4. Press **ENTER** to exit the cell and return to Ready mode.

Now that you have returned to Ready mode, you can continue to insert and edit content from other cells and sheets in the workbook.

Understanding AutoComplete

As you type text in the active cell, Excel tries to anticipate the remaining characters by displaying text that begins with the same letters as a previous entry in the same column. This feature, known as **AutoComplete**, helps make entering repetitive text easier and reduces data entry errors. To accept the suggested text, press TAB or ENTER. To override the suggested text, continue to type the text you want to enter in the cell. AutoComplete does not work with dates or numbers or when a blank cell is positioned between the previous entry and the text you are typing.

You will see AutoComplete entries as you enter descriptive text about the Boston conference in the Miscellaneous Expenses worksheet.

To enter information about the conference site:

1. Click the **Miscellaneous Expenses** sheet tab to make Miscellaneous Expenses the active sheet.

2. In cell A1, type **MedIT Conference Miscellaneous Expenses** as the work-sheet title, and then press **ENTER** twice to change the active cell to A3.

3. Type **Host** in cell A3, and then press **ENTER**. The label is entered in the cell and the active cell is now cell A4.

4. In the range A4:A8, enter the following labels, pressing **ENTER** after each entry and ignoring any AutoComplete suggestions: **Address**, **City**, **State**, **Postal Code**, and **Phone**.

5. Click cell **B3** to make it the active cell.

6. In the range B3:B8, enter the following information about the conference site, pressing **ENTER** after each entry and ignoring any AutoComplete suggestions: **Harbor Convention Center**, **1082 Suncrest Avenue**, **Boston**, **Massachusetts**, **02128**, and **(617) 555-1082**. See Figure 1–14.

Figure 1–14	Site information in the Miscellaneous Expenses sheet

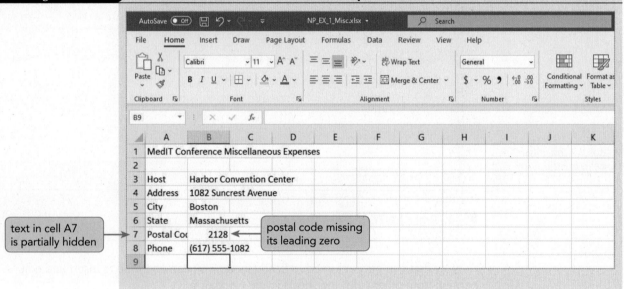

text in cell A7 is partially hidden

postal code missing its leading zero

The postal code value in cell B7 is missing its leading zero, you will fix that problem next.

Displaying Numbers as Text

When you enter a number in a cell, Excel removes leading zeroes from integer values. So a number like 02128 that you entered in cell B7 is changed to 2128. Because the number you entered in cell B7 is actually a postal code, it needs the leading zero. In these instances, you can instruct Excel to treat a number as text so that the leading zero is not dropped. You'll make this change the for the postal code in cell B7.

To display the postal code as text:

1. Click cell **B7** to select it. The number is right-aligned in the cell.

2. On the Home tab, in the Number group, click the **Number Format arrow**. A list of number display options appears.

Tip

You can also display a number as text by typing an apostrophe (') before the number.

3. Scroll down the list, and then click **Text**. Anything entered in the cell will now be considered text.

4. Type **02128** in cell B7, and then press **ENTER**. The leading zero remains in the entry, and the entry is left-aligned in the cell just like other text. See Figure 1–15.

Figure 1–15   Number displayed as text

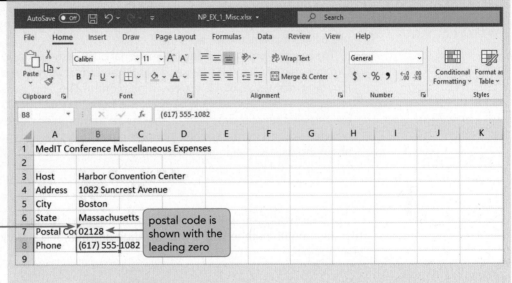

green triangle warns about a potential error

postal code is shown with the leading zero

Tip

To remove a green triangle, click the cell, click the icon that appears, and then click Ignore Error.

Notice that a green triangle appears in the upper-left corner of cell B7. Excel uses green triangles to flag potential errors in cells. In this case, it is simply a warning that you displayed a number as text. Because this is intentional, you do not have to edit the cell to fix the "error."

Entering Dates

Excel recognizes dates in any standard date formats. For example, in Excel, all the following entries represent the same date:

- 4/6/2025
- 4/6/25
- 4-6-2025
- April 6, 2025
- 6-Apr-25

Even though dates are entered as text, Excel stores the date as a number equal to the number of days between the specified date and January 0, 1900. Times are also entered as text and stored as fractions of a 24-hour day. For example, a date and time of April 15, 2025, 6:00 PM is stored as the number 45,762.75, which is 45,762 days after January 0, 1900, plus 3/4 of one day. Excel stores dates and times as numbers so they can be used for date and time calculations, such as determining the elapsed time between one date and another.

Based on how your computer displays dates, Excel might change the appearance of a date after you type it. For example, if you enter the date 4/15/25 into the active cell, Excel might display the date with the four-digit year value, 4/15/2025. If you enter the text April 15, 2025, Excel might change the date format to 15-Apr-25. Changing how the date or time is displayed does not affect the underlying date or time value.

Insight

International Date Formats

For international business transactions, you may need to adopt international standards for expressing dates, times, and currency values in your workbooks. For example, a worksheet cell might contain the date 06/05/25, which could be interpreted as either the 5th of June 2021, or the 6th of May 2021.

The interpretation depends on which country the workbook has been designed for. You can avoid this problem by entering the full date, as in June 5, 2025. However, this might not work with documents written in foreign languages, such as Japanese, that use different character symbols.

To solve this problem, many international businesses adopt ISO (International Organization for Standardization) dates in the format *yyyy-mm-dd*, where *yyyy* is the four-digit year value, *mm* is the two-digit month value, and *dd* is the two-digit day value. So, a date such as June 5, 2025, is entered as 2025/06/05. If you choose to use this international date format, make sure that everyone else using your workbook understands this format so they interpret dates correctly. You can include information about the date format in the Documentation sheet.

For your work, you will enter dates in the format *mm/dd/yyyy*, where *mm* is the two-digit month number, *dd* is the two-digit day number, and *yyyy* is the four-digit year number.

To enter a date into the Documentation sheet:

▶ **1.** Click the **Documentation** sheet tab to make the Documentation sheet the active worksheet.

▶ **2.** Click cell **B4** to make it the active cell, type the current date in the *mm/dd/yyyy* format, and then press **ENTER**. The date is entered in the cell.

   Trouble? Depending on your system configuration, Excel might change the date to the date format *dd-mmm-yy*. This difference will not affect your work.

▶ **3.** Click the **Miscellaneous Expenses** sheet tab to return to the Miscellaneous Expenses worksheet.

The next part of the Miscellaneous Expenses worksheet will list the miscellaneous expenses that will be tracked in the conference budget. As shown in Figure 1–16, the list includes each expense's category, subcategory, description, number of units, and the cost per unit.

Figure 1–16   Miscellaneous expenses

Expense Category	Subcategory	Description	Units	Cost per Unit
E2	9010	printing of brochures and conference materials	1600	$2.45
E2	9030	transportation shuttles	3	$335.75
E2	9020	decorations for banquet	1	$850.55
E2	9040	gift bags for conference attendees	525	$6.25
E2	9045	gifts for banquet speakers	6	$55.25

You will enter the first three columns of this table into the worksheet.

To enter the first part of the table of miscellaneous expenses:

1. In the Miscellaneous worksheet, click cell **A10** to make it the active cell, type **Expense Category** as the column label, and then press **TAB** to move to cell B10.

2. Type **Subcategory** in cell B10, press **TAB** to move to cell C10, type **Description** in cell C10, and then press **ENTER**.

3. In the range A11:C15, enter the Expense Category, Subcategory, and Description text for the five miscellaneous expenses listed in Figure 1–16, pressing **TAB** to move from one cell to the next, and pressing **ENTER** to move to a new row. Note that the text in some cells will be partially hidden; you will fix that problem shortly. See Figure 1–17.

Figure 1–17   Miscellaneous expense categories, subcategories, and descriptions

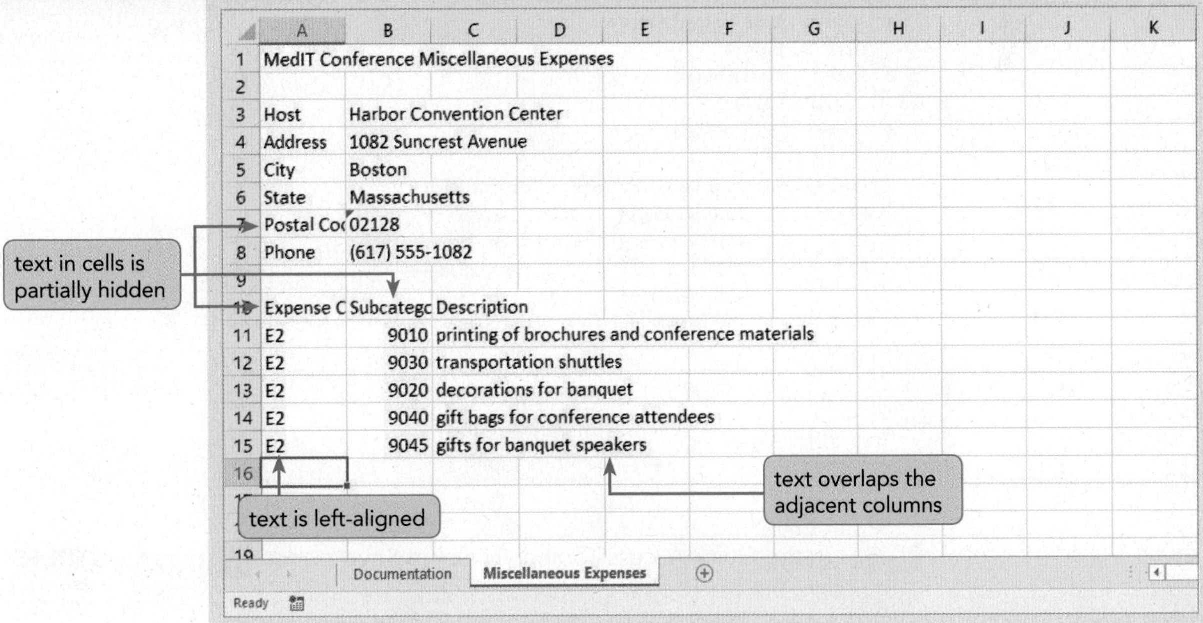

text in cells is partially hidden

text is left-aligned

text overlaps the adjacent columns

Next you will enter the miscellaneous expenses.

Entering Numbers

In Excel, numbers can be integers such as 378, decimals such as 1.95, or negative values such as –5.2. In the case of currency and percentages, you can include the currency symbol or the percent sign when you enter the value. Excel treats a currency value such as $87.25 as the number 87.25, and a percentage such as 95% as the decimal 0.95. Much like dates, currency and percentages are displayed with their symbols but stored as numbers.

You will complete the list of miscellaneous expenses by inserting their number of units and costs per unit.

To enter the miscellaneous expenses:

1. Click cell **D10**, type **Units** as the label, and then press **TAB**. Cell E10 becomes the active cell.

2. Type **Cost per Unit** in cell E10, and then press **ENTER**. Cell D11 becomes the active cell.

3. Type **1600** in cell D11, press **TAB** to make cell E11 the active cell, type **$2.45** in cell E11, and then press **ENTER**. Cell D12 becomes the active cell.

4. In the range D12:E15, enter the number of units and cost per unit for the remaining four expense categories shown in Figure 1–16. See Figure 1–18.

Figure 1–18	Miscellaneous expense units and costs per unit

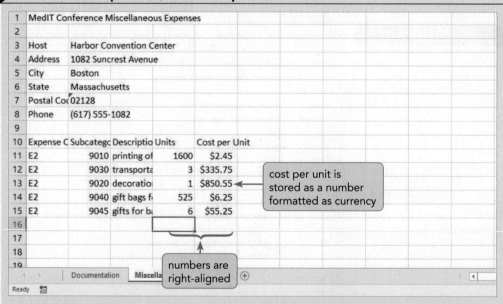

5. On the Quick Access Toolbar, click the **Save** button 🖫 (or press **CTRL+S**) to save the workbook.

Much of the information from the miscellaneous expenses table is difficult to read because of the hidden text. You can display all the cell contents by changing the size of the columns and rows in the worksheet.

Resizing Columns and Rows

There are several ways to resize columns and rows, including changing column widths, wrapping text within cells, and changing row heights. You can use a combination of these in a worksheet to create the best fit for your data.

Setting a Column Width

Column widths are expressed as the number of characters the column can contain. The default column width is 8.43 standard-sized characters. In general, this means that you can type eight characters in a cell. Any additional text is hidden or overlaps the adjacent cell. Column widths are also expressed in terms of pixels. A **pixel** is an individual point on a computer monitor or printout. A column width of 8.43 characters is equivalent to 64 pixels.

Insight

Setting Column Widths

On a computer monitor, pixel size is based on screen resolution. As a result, cell content that looks fine on one screen might appear differently when viewed on a screen with a different resolution. If you work on multiple computers or share your workbooks with others, you should set column widths based on the maximum number of characters you want displayed in the cells rather than pixel size. This ensures that everyone sees the cell contents the way you intended.

You will increase the width of column A so that all of the text labels within that column are completely displayed.

To increase the width of column A:

1. Point to the **right border** of the column A heading until the pointer changes to ↔.

2. Click and drag to the right until the width of the column heading reaches **18** characters, but do *not* release the mouse button. The ScreenTip that appears as you resize the column shows the new column width in characters and in pixels. See Figure 1–19.

Figure 1–19   Width of column A increased to 18 characters

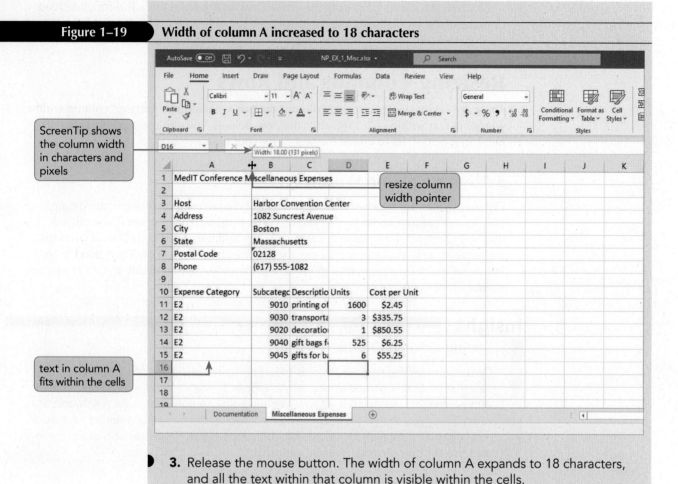

ScreenTip shows the column width in characters and pixels

resize column width pointer

text in column A fits within the cells

3. Release the mouse button. The width of column A expands to 18 characters, and all the text within that column is visible within the cells.

You can change the width of multiple columns at once. To select a range of columns, click the first column heading in the range, hold down SHIFT, and then click the heading of the last column or click and drag the pointer over the column headings. To select nonadjacent columns, hold down CTRL and click the heading of each column you want to select. When you change the width of one column, the widths of all the other columns that are selected also change.

Using the mouse to resize columns can be imprecise and a challenge to some users with special needs. The Format command on the Home tab gives you precise control over column width and row height settings. You will use the Format command to set the width of column B to exactly 12 characters so that the hidden text in cell B10 is completely visible.

To set the width of column B using the Format command:

1. Click the **column B** heading. The entire column is selected.

2. On the Home tab, in the Cells group, click the **Format** button, and then click **Column Width**. The Column Width dialog box opens.

3. Type **12** in the Column width box to specify the new column width.

4. Click **OK**. The width of column B is set to exactly 12 characters.

5. Click cell **A2** to deselect column B. See Figure 1–20.

Figure 1–20	Width of column B set to 12 characters

	A	B	C	D	E	F	G	H	I	J	K
1	MedIT Conference Miscellaneous Expenses										
2											
3	Host	Harbor Convention Center									
4	Address	1082 Suncrest Avenue									
5	City	Boston									
6	State	Massachusetts									
7	Postal Code	02128									
8	Phone	(617) 555-1082									
9											
10	Expense Category	Subcategory	Descriptio	Units	Cost per Unit						
11	E2		9010	printing of	1600	$2.45					
12	E2		9030	transporta	3	$335.75					
13	E2		9020	decoratio	1	$850.55					
14	E2		9040	gift bags f	525	$6.25					
15	E2		9045	gifts for ba	6	$55.25					
16											
17											
18											
19											

width of column B set to 12 characters

Documentation   **Miscellaneous Expenses**   ⊕

Ready

You can also use the **AutoFit** feature to automatically adjust a column width or row height to accommodate its widest or tallest entry. To AutoFit a column to the width of its contents, double-click the right border of the column heading. You'll use AutoFit to resize columns C and E so that all the content is fully displayed.

To use AutoFit to display all the contents of columns C and E:

1. Point to the **right border** of column C until the pointer changes to the resize column width pointer ↔.

2. Double-click the **right border** of the column C heading. The width of column C increases to about 43 characters so that the longest item description is completely visible.

3. Double-click the **right border** of the column E heading. The width of column E increases to about 12 characters.

Sometimes when you use AutoFit, the column becomes wider than you want. Another way to display long text entries is to wrap the text within each cell.

Wrapping Text Within a Cell

When you wrap text within a cell, any content that doesn't fit on the first line is displayed on a new line in the cell. Wrapping text increases the row height to display any additional new lines added in the cell. You can wrap only text within a cell; numbers, dates, or times do not wrap.

You'll reduce the width of column C to 30 characters, and then wrap the category descriptions so all of the text is visible.

To wrap text in column C:

1. Resize the width of column C to **30** characters.

2. Select the range **C11:C15**, which has the expense descriptions.

3. On the Home tab, in the Alignment group, click the **Wrap Text** button. The Wrap Text button is highlighted, indicating that it is applied to the selected range. Any text in the selected cells that exceeds the column width wraps to a new line in those cells.

4. Click cell **A2** to make it the active cell. See Figure 1–21.

Figure 1–21   **Text wrapped within a cell**

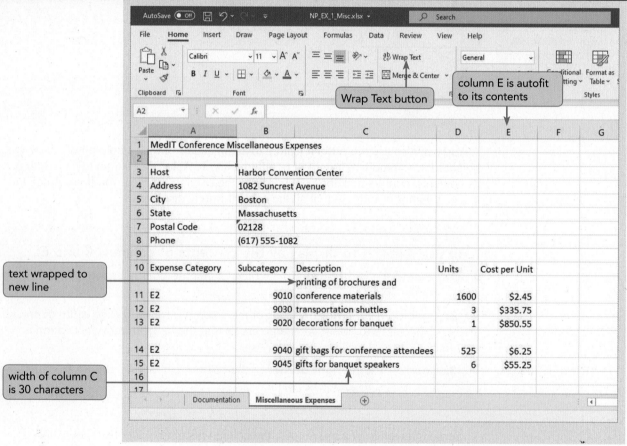

Another way to create a new line within a cell is to press ALT+ENTER where you want the new line to start. Subsequent characters will be on a new line.

Changing Row Heights

Row heights are measured in points or pixels. A **point** is approximately 1/72 of an inch. The default row height is 15 points or 20 pixels. There are several ways to set row heights. You can drag the bottom border of the row heading. You can click the Format button in the Cells group on the Home tab, and then click Row Height. Or, you can double-click the bottom border of the row heading to AutoFit a row to its tallest cell.

The height of row 14 is a too tall for its contents. Carmen asks you to reduce it.

> **To change the height of row 14:**
>
> ▶ **1.** Point to the **bottom border** of the row 14 heading until the pointer changes to the resize row height pointer ✛ .
>
> ▶ **2.** Drag the bottom border up until the height of the row is equal to **18** points (or **24** pixels), and then release the mouse button. The height of row 14 better matches its contents.
>
> ▶ **3.** Press **CTRL+S** to save the workbook.

You have entered the table of miscellaneous expenses for the Boston conference. In the next session, you will use formulas and functions to calculate the total cost of all of those expenses.

Review

Session 1.1 Quick Check

1. How are chart sheets different from worksheets?
2. What is the cell reference for the cell located in the third column and fourth row of a worksheet?
3. What is the range reference for the block of cells D3 through E10?
4. What is the range reference for cells A1 through C5 and cells A8 through C12?
5. How is text aligned within a worksheet cell by default?
6. How would the number 00514 appear in a cell?
7. Cell B2 contains the entry May 3, 2025. Why doesn't Excel consider this a text entry?
8. How do you autofit a column to match its longest cell entry?

1.) Chart sheets contain charts and graphs while worksheets contain grids in which text and formulas can be entered.

2.) C4

3. D3 : E10

4. A1 : C5, A8 : C12

5. left aligned

6. 514

7. Dates and times are stored as numbers

8. Autofit Column width

Session 1.2 Visual Overview:

The **font size** specifies the size of text characters measured in units called points.

The Page Layout tab is used to specify how the worksheet will be arranged and printed.

In Excel, every formula begins with an equal sign (=).

When the active cell contains a formula, the formula appears in the formula bar and the result of the formula appears in the cell.

The worksheet cells are surrounded by **gridlines**, which are horizontal and vertical lines in a worksheet or chart that make it easier to read.

A border is a line added along the edge of a cell, row, column, or table.

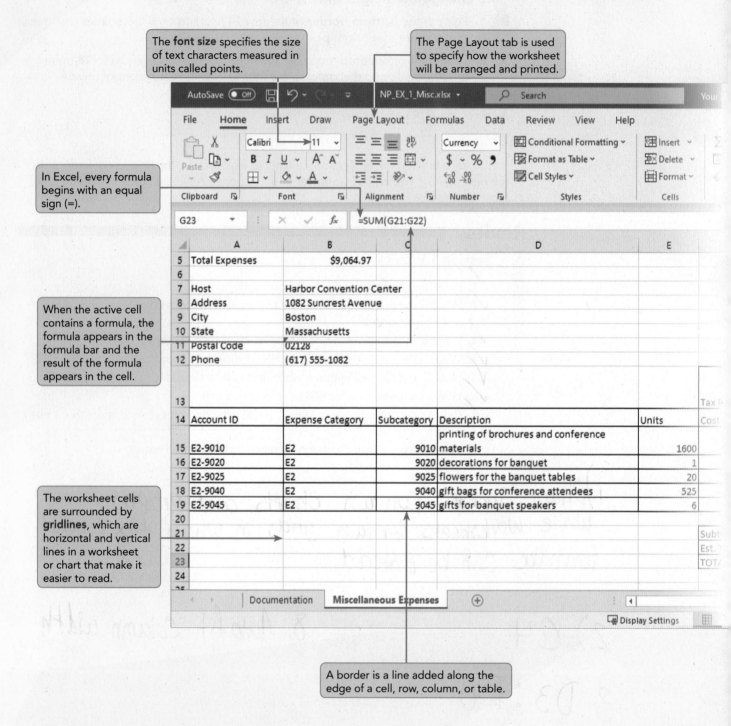

▲	A	B	C	D	E
5	Total Expenses	$9,064.97			
6					
7	Host	Harbor Convention Center			
8	Address	1082 Suncrest Avenue			
9	City	Boston			
10	State	Massachusetts			
11	Postal Code	02128			
12	Phone	(617) 555-1082			
13					Tax
14	Account ID	Expense Category	Subcategory	Description	Units	Cost
15	E2-9010	E2	9010	printing of brochures and conference materials	1600	
16	E2-9020	E2	9020	decorations for banquet	1	
17	E2-9025	E2	9025	flowers for the banquet tables	20	
18	E2-9040	E2	9040	gift bags for conference attendees	525	
19	E2-9045	E2	9045	gifts for banquet speakers	6	
20					
21					Subt
22					Est.
23					TOTA
24					

G23   =SUM(G21:G22)

Documentation | **Miscellaneous Expenses** | ⊕

Display Settings

Excel Formulas and Functions

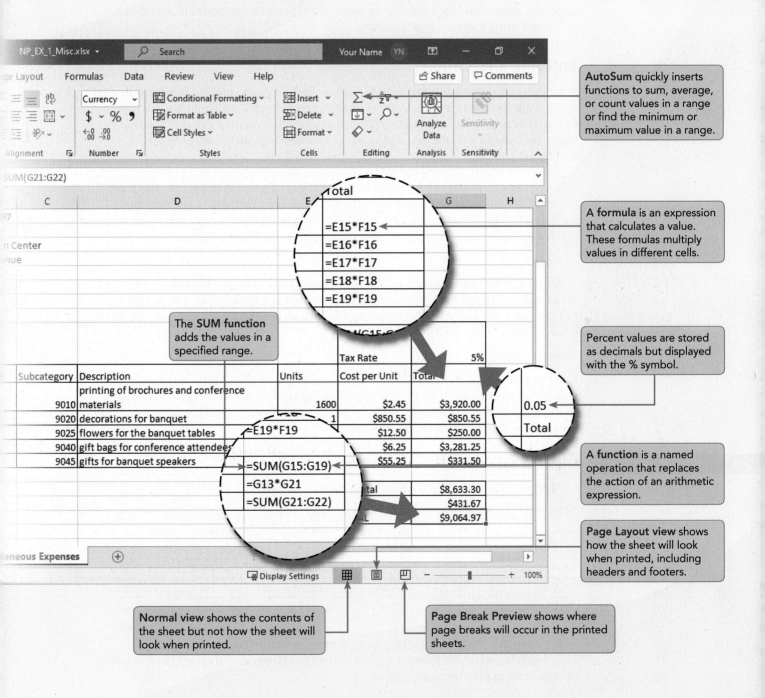

AutoSum quickly inserts functions to sum, average, or count values in a range or find the minimum or maximum value in a range.

A **formula** is an expression that calculates a value. These formulas multiply values in different cells.

The **SUM function** adds the values in a specified range.

Percent values are stored as decimals but displayed with the % symbol.

A **function** is a named operation that replaces the action of an arithmetic expression.

Page Layout view shows how the sheet will look when printed, including headers and footers.

Normal view shows the contents of the sheet but not how the sheet will look when printed.

Page Break Preview shows where page breaks will occur in the printed sheets.

Formulas shown in worksheet:
- =E15*F15
- =E16*F16
- =E17*F17
- =E18*F18
- =E19*F19
- =E19*F19
- =SUM(G15:G19)
- =G13*G21
- =SUM(G21:G22)

Subcategory	Description	Units	Cost per Unit	Total
9010	printing of brochures and conference materials	1600	$2.45	$3,920.00
9020	decorations for banquet	1	$850.55	$850.55
9025	flowers for the banquet tables		$12.50	$250.00
9040	gift bags for conference attendees		$6.25	$3,281.25
9045	gifts for banquet speakers		$55.25	$331.50

Tax Rate 5%   0.05

	$8,633.30
	$431.67
	$9,064.97

Calculating with Formulas

So far you have entered text, numbers, and dates in the worksheet. However, the main reason for using Excel is to perform calculations and analysis on data. For example, Carmen wants the workbook to calculate the number of items in the miscellaneous expense category and the total cost of those items. Such calculations are added to a worksheet using formulas and functions.

Entering a Formula

A formula is an expression that returns a value. In most cases, this is a number—though it could also be text or a date. In Excel, every formula begins with an equal sign (=) followed by an expression containing the operations that return a value. If you don't begin the formula with the equal sign, Excel assumes that you are entering text or numbers.

A formula is written using **operators**, or mathematical symbols, that combine different values, resulting in a single value that is then displayed in the cell. The most common operators are **arithmetic operators** that perform mathematical calculations such as addition (+), subtraction (–), multiplication (*), division (/), and exponentiation (^). For example, the following formula adds 3 and 8, returning a value of 11:

=3+8

Most Excel formulas contain references to cells rather than specific values. This allows you to change the values used in the calculation without having to modify the formula itself. For example, the following formula returns the result of adding the values stored in cells C3 and D10:

=C3+D10

If the value 3 is stored in cell C3 and the value 8 is stored in cell D10, this formula would also return a value of 11. If you later changed the value in cell C3 to 10, the formula would return a value of 18. Figure 1–22 describes the different arithmetic operators and provides examples of formulas.

Figure 1–22   Arithmetic operators

Operation	Arithmetic Operator	Example	Description
Addition	+	=B1+B2+B3	Adds the values in cells B1, B2, and B3
Subtraction	–	=C9-B2	Subtracts the value in cell B2 from the value in cell C9
Multiplication	*	=C9*B9	Multiplies the values in cells C9 and B9
Division	/	=C9/B9	Divides the value in cell C9 by the value in cell B9
Exponentiation	^	=B5^3	Raises the value of cell B5 to the third power

If a formula contains more than one arithmetic operator, Excel performs the calculation based on the following order of operations, which is the sequence in which operators are applied in a calculation:

1. Calculate any operations within parentheses
2. Calculate any exponentiations (^)
3. Calculate any multiplications (*) and divisions (/)
4. Calculate any additions (+) and subtractions (–)

For example, the following formula returns the value 23 because multiplying 4 by 5 is done before adding 3:

=3+4*5

If a formula contains two or more operators with the same level of priority, the operators are applied in order from left to right. In the following formula, Excel first multiplies 4 by 10 and then divides that result by 8 to return the value 5:

=4*10/8

When parentheses are used, the value inside them is calculated first. In the following formula, Excel calculates (3+4) first, and then multiplies that result by 5 to return the value 35:

=(3+4)*5

Figure 1–23 shows how changes in a formula affect the order of operations and the result of the formula.

Figure 1–23	Order of operations applied to formulas

Formula	Order of Operations	Result
=50+10*5	10*5 calculated first and then 50 is added	100
=(50+10)*5	(50+10) calculated first and then 60 is multiplied by 5	300
=50/10–5	50/10 calculated first and then 5 is subtracted	0
=50/(10–5)	(10–5) calculated first and then 50 is divided by that value	10
=50/10*5	Two operators at same precedence level, so the calculation is done left to right with 50/10 calculated first and that value is then multiplied by 5	25
=50/(10*5)	(10*5) is calculated first and then 50 is divided by that value	1

Carmen wants the miscellaneous expenses workbook to calculate the total cost of each item. The total cost is equal to the number of units ordered multiplied by the cost per unit. You already entered this information in columns D and E. Now you will enter a formula in cell F11 to calculate the total cost of printing for the conference.

To enter a formula that calculates the total cost of printing:

1. If you took a break after the previous session, make sure the NP_EX_1_Misc.xlsx workbook is open and the Miscellaneous Expenses worksheet is active.

2. Click cell **F10**, type **Total** as the label, and then press **ENTER**. The label is entered in cell F10 and cell F11 is the active cell.

3. Type **=D11*E11** (the number of units multiplied by the cost per unit). As you type the formula, a list of Excel function names appears in a ScreenTip, which provides a quick method for entering functions. The list will close when you complete the formula. You will learn more about Excel functions shortly. Also, Excel color codes each cell reference and its corresponding cell with the same color. See Figure 1–24.

| Figure 1–24 | Formula being entered in cell F11 |

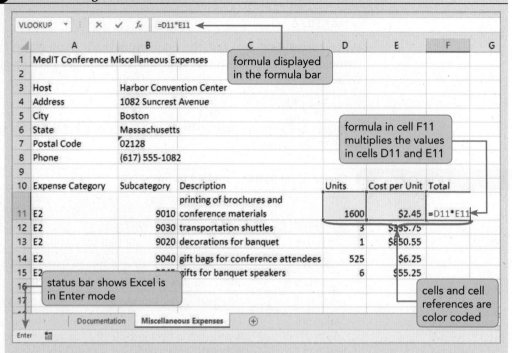

4. Press **ENTER**. The formula result $3,920.00 appears in cell F11. This value is the total cost of printing 1600 brochures and other conference materials. The result is displayed as currency because cell D11, which is referenced in the formula, contains a currency value.

5. Click cell **F11** again to make it the active cell. The cell displays the result of the formula, but the formula bar displays the formula you entered so that you can see at a glance both the formula and its value.

For the first item, you entered the formula by typing each cell reference in the expression. You can also insert a cell reference by clicking the cell as you type the formula. This technique reduces the possibility of error caused by typing an incorrect cell reference. You will use this method to enter the formula to calculate the charge for renting vans to shuttle conference attendees between the airport and the hotel.

To enter a formula to calculate the cost of shuttle using the mouse:

1. Click cell **F12** to make it the active cell.

Be sure to type = first; otherwise, Excel will not recognize the entry as a formula.

2. Type = to indicate that you are entering a formula. Any cell you click from now on inserts the cell reference of the selected cell into the formula until you complete the formula by pressing Enter or Tab.

3. Click cell **D12**. The cell reference is inserted into the formula in the formula bar. At this point, any cell you click changes the cell reference used in the formula. The cell reference isn't locked until you type an operator.

4. Type * to enter the multiplication operator. The cell reference for cell D12 is locked in the formula, and the next cell you click will be inserted after the operator.

5. Click cell **E12** to enter its cell reference in the formula. The formula, =D12*E12, is complete.

6. Press **ENTER**. Cell F12 displays the value $1,007.25, which is the cost of renting vans to transport attendees to and from the conference.

Next, you will enter formulas to complete the calculations of the remaining miscellaneous expenses.

Copying and Pasting Formulas

Many worksheets have the same formula repeated across several rows or columns. Rather than retyping the formula, you can copy a formula from one cell and paste it into another cell. When you copy a formula, Excel places the formula onto the **Clipboard**, which is a temporary storage area for selections you copy or cut. When you **paste**, Excel retrieves the formula from the Clipboard and places it into the selected cell or range.

The cell references in the copied formula change to reflect the formula's new location in the worksheet. For example, consider a formula from a cell in row 12 that adds other values in row 12. When that formula is copied to row 15, the formula changes to add the corresponding values in row 15. By automatically updating the formula based on its new location, Excel makes it easy to quickly enter the same general formula throughout a worksheet.

You will calculate the costs of the remaining expense categories by copying the formula you entered in cell F12 and pasting it to the range F13:F15.

To copy and paste the formula in cell F12:

1. Click cell **F12** to select the cell that contains the formula you want to copy.

2. On the Home tab, in the Clipboard group, click the **Copy** button (or press **CTRL+C**). Excel copies the formula to the Clipboard. A blinking green box surrounds the cell being copied.

3. Select the range **F13:F15**. You want to paste the formula into these cells.

4. In the Clipboard group, click the **Paste** button (or press **CTRL+V**). Excel pastes the formula into the selected cells, adjusting each formula so that the total cost of each item is based on the Units and Cost per Units values in that row. A button appears below the selected range, providing options for pasting formulas and values. See Figure 1–25.

| Figure 1–25 | **Copied and pasted formulas** |

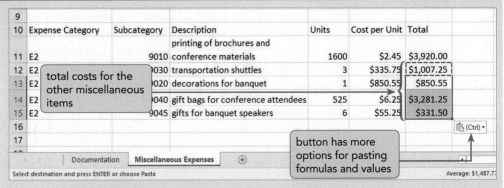

▶ **5.** If necessary, click cell **F13** to make it the active cell. The formula =D13*E13 appears in the formula bar. Notice that the cell references in the formula were updated to reflect its current position of the cell in the worksheet.

▶ **6.** Click cell **F14** to verify that the formula =D14*E14 appears in the formula bar, and then click cell **F15** to verify that the formula =D15*E15 appears in the formula bar.

Another way of performing calculations is to use functions.

Calculating with Functions

A function is a named operation that replaces the arithmetic expression in a formula. Functions are used to simplify long or complex formulas. For example, to add the values from cells A1 through A10, you could enter the following long formula:

    =A1+A2+A3+A4+A5+A6+A7+A8+A9+A10

Or, you could use the SUM function to calculate the sum of those cell values by entering the following formula:

    =SUM(A1:A10)

In both instances, Excel adds the values in cells A1 through A10, but the SUM function is faster and simpler to enter and less prone to a typing error. You should always use a function, if one is available, in place of a long, complex formula. Excel supports more than 300 functions from the fields of finance, business, science, and engineering, including functions that work with numbers, text, and dates.

Understanding Function Syntax

Every function follows a set of rules, or **syntax**, which specifies how the function should be written. The general syntax of all Excel functions is

    FUNCTION(arg1,arg2,[arg3],[arg4],…)

where *FUNCTION* is the function name, and **arg1**, **arg2**, and so forth are arguments. An **argument** is information that the function uses to calculate an answer. Arguments can be required or optional. Required arguments, shown in bold, are needed by the function to operate. Optional arguments, enclosed in square brackets, are not required but may be used by the function. Optional arguments are always placed at the end of the argument list. In this case, **arg1**, **arg2**, are required arguments and *arg3*, *arg4* are optional arguments.

The SUM function shown earlier has the syntax

    SUM(number1,[number2],[number3],…)

where **number1** is a required argument that indicates the range of values to sum and *number2*, *number3*, and so on are optional arguments used for nonadjacent ranges or lists of numbers. For example, the following SUM function calculates the sum of values from the ranges A1:10 and A21:A30:

    SUM(A1:A10,A21:A30)

Some functions do not require any arguments and have the syntax *FUNCTION( )*. Functions without arguments still must include the opening and closing parentheses after the function name. For example, the NOW function does not require any argument values to return the current date and time, as shown in the following formula:

    =NOW()

You can learn more about function syntax using Excel Help.

Inserting Functions with AutoSum

A fast and convenient way to enter commonly used functions is with AutoSum. The AutoSum button, located on the Home tab of the ribbon, includes options to insert the following functions into a selected cell or cell range:

- SUM—Sum of the values in the specified range
- AVERAGE—Average value in the specified range
- COUNT—Total count of numeric values in the specified range
- MAX—Maximum value in the specified range
- MIN—Minimum value in the specified range

After you select one of the AutoSum options, Excel determines the most appropriate range from the available data and enters it as the function's argument. You should always verify that the range included in the AutoSum function matches the range that you want to use.

You will use AutoSum to enter the SUM function to add the total cost from all miscellaneous expense categories.

To use AutoSum to sum the miscellaneous expense values:

1. Click cell **E16** to make it the active cell, type **Subtotal** as the label, and then press **TAB** to make cell F16 the active cell.

2. On the Home tab, in the Editing group, click the **AutoSum arrow**. The button's menu opens and displays five common functions: Sum, Average, Count Numbers, Max (for maximum), and Min (for minimum).

Tip

You can quickly insert the SUM function by clicking the worksheet cell where the sum should be calculated and pressing ALT+=.

3. Click **Sum** to enter the SUM function. The formula =SUM(F11:F15) is entered in cell F16. The cells being summed are selected and highlighted on the worksheet so you can quickly confirm that Excel selected the appropriate range from the available data. A ScreenTip appears below the formula describing the function's syntax. See Figure 1–26.

Figure 1–26   SUM function entered using the AutoSum button

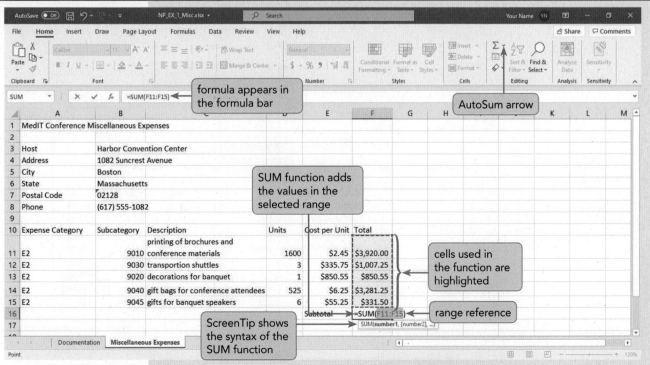

◗ **4.** Press **ENTER** to accept the formula. The sum of the miscellaneous expenses is $9,390.55.

Carmen wants you to include a 5% sales tax on the miscellaneous expenses. You will calculate the tax, and then add the subtotal value to the tax.

To calculate the sales tax and total expenses:

◗ **1.** Click cell **E9**, type **Tax Rate** as the label and then press **TAB** to make cell F9 the active cell.

◗ **2.** Type **5%** in cell F9, and then press **ENTER**. The 5% value is displayed in cell F9, but the stored value is 0.05. Percentages are displayed with the % symbol but stored as the decimal value.

◗ **3.** Click cell **E17** to make it the active cell, type **Est. Tax** as the label, and then press **TAB** to make F17 the active cell.

◗ **4.** Type the formula **=F9*F16** in cell F17 to calculate the sales tax on all of the miscellaneous expenditures, and then press **ENTER**. The formula multiplies the sales tax in cell F9 by the order subtotal in cell F16. The estimated taxes of $469.53, which is 5% of the subtotal value of $9,390.55, is displayed in cell F17.

◗ **5.** In cell E18, type **TOTAL** as the label, and then press **TAB** to make cell F18 the active cell.

◗ **6.** Type the formula **=SUM(F16:F17)** in cell F18 to calculate the total cost of the miscellaneous expenditures plus tax, and then press **ENTER**. The overall total is $9,860.08.

◗ **7.** Click cell **F18** to view the formula in the cell. See Figure 1–27.

Figure 1–27   **Total miscellaneous expenses**

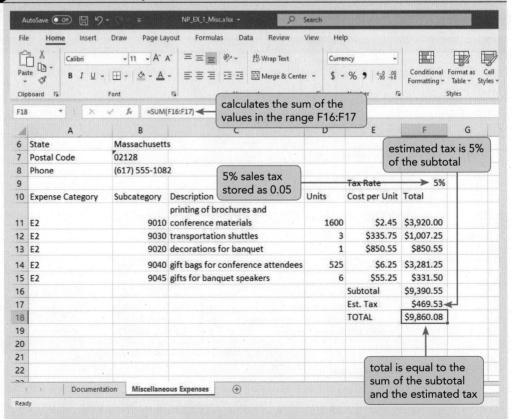

If you want to add all of the numbers in a column or row, you need to reference the entire column or row in the SUM function. For example, SUM(E:E) will return the sum of all numeric values in column E and SUM(5:5) will return the sum of all numeric values in row 5.

Proskills

Problem Solving: Writing Effective Formulas

You can use formulas to quickly perform calculations and solve problems. First, identify the problem you need to solve. Then, gather the data needed to solve the problem. Finally, create accurate and effective formulas that use the data to answer or resolve the problem. To write effective and useful formulas, consider these guidelines:

- **Keep your formulas simple.** Use functions in place of long, complex formulas whenever possible. For example, use the SUM function instead of entering a formula that adds individual cells, which makes it easier to confirm that the formula is making an accurate calculation as it provides answers needed to evaluate the problem.

- **Do not hide data values within formulas.** The worksheet displays formula results, not the actual formula. For example, to calculate a 5% interest rate on a currency value in cell A5, you could enter the formula =0.05*A5. However, this doesn't show how the value is calculated. A better approach places the 5% value in a cell accompanied by a descriptive label and uses the cell reference in the formula. Your worksheet will then display the interest rate as well as the resulting interest, making it clear to others what calculation is being performed.

- **Break up long formulas to show intermediate results.** Long formulas can be difficult to interpret and are prone to error. For example, the formula =SUM(A1:A10)/SUM(B1:B10) calculates the ratio of two sums but hides the two sum values. Instead of one long formula, consider calculating each sum in a separate cell, such as cells A11 and B11, and use the formula =A11/B11 to calculate the ratio. The worksheet will then show both the sums and the calculation of the ratio, making the workbook easier to interpret and manage.

- **Test complicated formulas with simple values.** Use values you can calculate in your head to confirm that your formula works as intended. For example, using 1s or 10s as the input values makes it easier to verify that your formula is working as intended.

Finding a solution to a problem requires accurate data and analysis. With workbooks, this means using formulas that are easy to understand, clearly showing the data being used in the calculations and demonstrating how the results are calculated. Only then can you be confident that you are choosing the best problem resolution.

Modifying a Worksheet

As you develop a worksheet, you will often need to modify its content and structure to create a cleaner and more readable document. You might need to move cells and ranges of cells or you may want to delete rows and columns from the worksheet. You can modify the worksheet's layout without affecting any data or calculations.

Moving and Copying a Cell or Range

One way to move a cell or range is to select it, position the pointer over the bottom border of the selection, drag the selection to a new location, and then release the mouse button. This technique is called **drag and drop** because you are dragging the range and dropping it in a new location. If the drop location is not visible, drag the selection to the edge of the workbook window to scroll the worksheet, and then drop the selection.

You can also use the drag-and-drop technique to copy cells by pressing CTRL as you drag the selected range to its new location. A copy of the original range is placed in the new location without removing the original range from the worksheet.

Reference

Moving or Copying a Cell Range

- Select the cell range to move or copy.
- Move the pointer over the border of the selection until the pointer changes shape.
- To move the range, click the border and drag the selection to a new location. To copy the range, hold down CTRL and drag the selection to a new location.

or

- Select the cell range to move or copy.
- On the Home tab, in the Clipboard group, click the Cut or Copy button; or right-click the selection, and then click Cut or Copy on the shortcut menu; or press CTRL+X or CTRL+C.
- Select the cell or the upper-left cell of the range where you want to paste the copied content.
- In the Clipboard group, click the Paste button; or right-click the selection and then click Paste on the shortcut menu; or press CTRL+V.

Carmen wants the labels and value in the range E16:F18 moved down one row to the range E17:F19 to set those calculations off from the list of miscellaneous expenses. You will use the drag-and-drop method to move the range.

To drag and drop the range E16:F18:

1. Select the range **E16:F18**. This is the range you want to move.

2. Point to the **bottom border** of the selected range so that the pointer changes to the move pointer 🕂.

3. Press and hold the mouse button to change the pointer to the arrow pointer ⬉, and then drag the selection down one row. Do not release the mouse button. A ScreenTip appears, indicating that the new range of the selected cells will be E17:F19. A dark green border also appears around the new range. See Figure 1–28.

Figure 1–28	Range being dragged

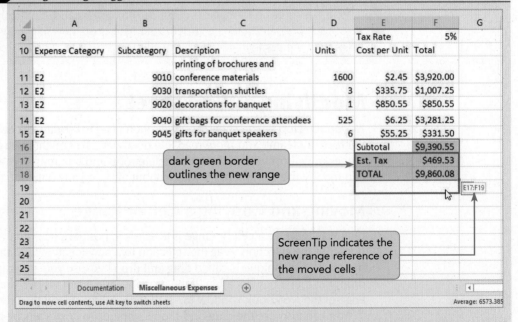

▶ **4.** Make sure the ScreenTip displays the range E17:F19, and then release the mouse button. The selected cells move to their new location.

Some people find dragging and dropping a range difficult and awkward, particularly if the selected range is large or needs to move a long distance in the worksheet. In those situations, it is often more efficient to cut or copy and paste the cell contents. Cutting moves the selected content. Copying duplicates the selected content in the new location.

Carmen wants the worksheet to include a summary of the miscellaneous expenses at the top of the worksheet. To free up space for this summary, you'll cut the contents of the range A3:F19 and paste them into the range A7:F23.

To cut and paste the range A3:F19:

▶ **1.** Click the Name box to the left of the formula bar, type **A3:F19** as the range to select, and then press **ENTER**. The range A3:F19 is selected.

▶ **2.** On the Home tab, in the Clipboard group, click the **Cut** button (or press **CTRL+X**). The range is surrounded by a moving border, indicating that it has been cut.

▶ **3.** Click cell **A7** to select it. This is the upper-left corner of the range where you want to paste the range that you cut.

▶ **4.** In the Clipboard group, click the **Paste** button (or press **CTRL+V**). The range A3:F19 is pasted into the range A7:F23. Note that the cell references in the formulas were automatically updated to reflect the new location of those cells in the worksheet.

Using the COUNT Function

Many financial workbooks need to report the number of entries, such as the number of products in an order or the number of items in an expense or revenue category. To calculate the total number of items, you can use the COUNT function. The COUNT function has the syntax

```
COUNT(value1,[value2],[value3],…)
```

where **value1** is the range of numeric values to count and *value2*, *value3*, and so forth specify other ranges.

The COUNT function counts only numeric values. Any cells containing text are not included in the tally. To include cells containing non-numeric data such as text strings, you need to use the COUNTA function. The COUNTA function has the syntax

```
COUNTA(value1,[value2],[value3],…)
```

where **value1** is the range containing numeric or non-numeric values and *value2*, *value3*, and so forth specify other ranges to be included in the tally.

Next, you will enter a summary of the miscellaneous expenses by displaying the number of miscellaneous expense categories and the total cost of all the expenses. Because you are interested only in numeric values, you will use the COUNT function to count the number of miscellaneous expense values in the worksheet.

To use the COUNT and SUM functions to create an expense summary:

▶ **1.** Scroll up the worksheet, click cell **A3** to make it the active cell, type **Summary** as the label, and then press **ENTER** to make cell A4 the active cell.

▶ **2.** In cell A4, type **Expense Categories** as the label, and then press **TAB** to make cell B4 the active cell.

▶ **3.** In cell B4, type **=COUNT(** to begin the COUNT function.

▶ **4.** Select the range **F15:F19**. The range reference F15:F19 is entered into the COUNT function.

▶ **5.** Type **)** to complete the function, and then press **ENTER** to make cell A5 the active cell. Cell B4 displays 5, indicating that the report includes five types of miscellaneous expenses.

▶ **6.** In cell A5, type **Total Expenses** as the label, and then press **TAB** to make cell B5 the active cell.

▶ **7.** In cell B5, type **=F23** as the formula, and then press **ENTER**. This formula displays contents of cell F23, which is the cell where you added the subtotal and taxes. See Figure 1–29.

> **Tip**
>
> To count all the values in a column, include only the column letter in the range reference; such as =COUNT(F:F) to count all values in column F.

Figure 1–29   Miscellaneous expenses summary

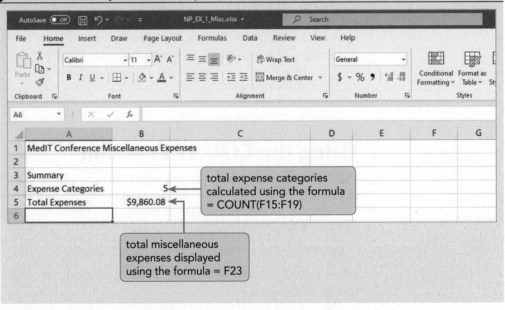

The formula in cell B5 that displays the sum of miscellaneous expenses calculated in cell F23 illustrates an important practice: Don't repeat the same calculation multiple times. Instead, use a formula that references the cell containing the formula results you wish to repeat. This way, if you must later change the formula, you need to edit only that one cell.

Modifying Rows and Columns

Another way to modify the structure of a workbook is by inserting or removing whole rows and columns from a worksheet.

Inserting Rows and Columns

When you insert a new column, the existing columns are shifted to the right, and the new column has the same width as the column directly to its left. When you insert a new row, the existing rows are shifted down, and the new row has the same height as the row above it. Because inserting a new row or column moves the location of the other cells in the worksheet, any cell references in a formula or function are updated to reflect the new layout.

Reference

Inserting and Deleting Rows or Columns

To insert rows and columns into a worksheet:
- Select the row or column headings where you want to insert new content.
- On the Home tab, in the Cells group, click the Insert button; or right-click the selected headings and click Insert on the shortcut menu; or press CTRL+SHIFT+=.

To delete rows or columns:
- Select the row or column headings for the content you want to delete.
- On the Home tab, in the Cells group, click the Delete button; or right-click the selecting headings, and then click Delete on the shortcut menu; or press CTRL+-.

MedIT is providing the flower arrangements for the tables at the closing banquet of the conference. Carmen asks you to add that expense category to the worksheet. You will insert a new row and enter that expense.

To insert the flower expense category:

1. Scroll down and click the **row 18** heading to select the entire row. You want to add the new expense category as row 18.

2. On the Home tab, in the Cells group, click the **Insert** button (or press **CTRL+SHIFT+=**). A new row 18 is inserted in the worksheet, and all the rows below the new row are shifted down.

3. Enter **E2** in cell A18, enter **9025** in cell B18, enter **flowers for the banquet tables** in cell C18, enter **20** in cell D18, and enter **$12.50** in cell E18.

4. Copy the formula from cell **F17** and paste it into cell **F18**. The formula =D18*E18 entered in cell F18, displaying $250.00 as the category expense total. The formula calculating the overall total of miscellaneous expenses in cell F22 is updated to include the new row. The subtotal, estimated taxes, and grand total are recalculated to include the new category. Cell F24 displays the grand total as ######## because the column is too narrow to display the entire value.

5. Increase the width of column F to **12** characters using whatever method you choose.

6. Click cell **F22**. See Figure 1–30.

Figure 1–30	New row inserted into the worksheet

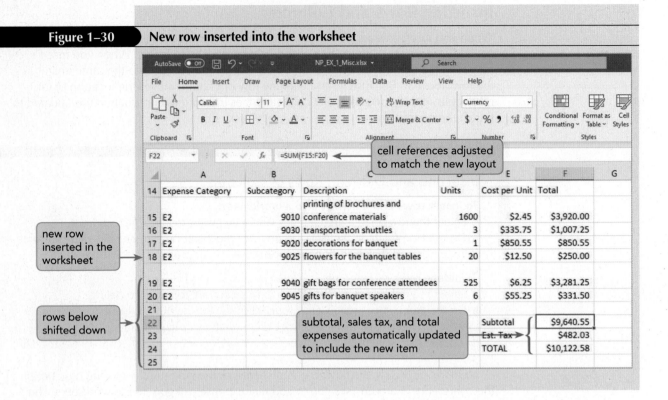

new row inserted in the worksheet

rows below shifted down

cell references adjusted to match the new layout

subtotal, sales tax, and total expenses automatically updated to include the new item

F22 =SUM(F15:F20)

	A	B	C	D	E	F	G
14	Expense Category	Subcategory	Description	Units	Cost per Unit	Total	
15	E2		9010	printing of brochures and conference materials	1600	$2.45	$3,920.00
16	E2		9030	transportation shuttles	3	$335.75	$1,007.25
17	E2		9020	decorations for banquet	1	$850.55	$850.55
18	E2		9025	flowers for the banquet tables	20	$12.50	$250.00
19	E2		9040	gift bags for conference attendees	525	$6.25	$3,281.25
20	E2		9045	gifts for banquet speakers	6	$55.25	$331.50
21							
22					Subtotal	$9,640.55	
23					Est. Tax	$482.03	
24					TOTAL	$10,122.58	
25							

Notice that the formula in cell F22 is now =SUM(F15:F20). The range reference was updated to reflect the inserted row. The tax amount increased to $482.03 based on the new subtotal value of $9,640.55, and the total charge increased to $10,122.58 because of the added item. Also, the result of the COUNT function in cell B4 increased to 6 to reflect the added expense.

Deleting Rows and Columns

There are two ways of removing content from a worksheet: deleting and clearing. **Deleting** removes both the data and the selected cells from the worksheet. The rows below the deleted row shift up to fill the vacated space. Likewise, the columns to the right of the deleted column shift left to fill the vacated space. Also, all cell references in worksheet formulas are adjusted to reflect the change that removing the row or column makes to the worksheet structure. You click the Delete button in the Cells group on the Home tab to delete selected rows or columns.

Clearing removes the data from the selected cells, leaving those cells blank but preserving the current worksheet structure. You clear data from the selected cells by pressing DELETE.

The Boston conference isn't intended to make money for MedIT, but the company doesn't want to lose money either. Carmen needs to watch expenses and keep the total miscellaneous costs under $9,000. Carmen negotiated with the hotel to provide the transportation shuttles for free and asks you to remove that expense from the worksheet.

To delete the transportation shuttles row from the worksheet:

1. Click the **row 16** heading to select the entire row.

2. On the Home tab, in the Cells group, click the **Delete** button (or press **CTRL+−**). Row 16 is deleted, and the rows below it shift up to fill the space.

All the cell references from the formulas in the worksheet are again updated automatically to reflect the impact of deleting row 16. The subtotal value in cell F21 is now $8,633.30, which is the sum of the range F15:F19. The estimated tax in F22 decreases to $431.67. The total miscellaneous expenses are now $9,064.97, which is closer to the budget that Carmen must meet. Also, the result of the COUNT function in cell B4 returns to 5, reflecting the deleted expense category. As you can see, one of the great advantages of using Excel is that it modifies cell references within the formulas to reflect the additions and deletions made in the worksheet.

Inserting and Deleting a Range

You can also insert or delete cell ranges within a worksheet. When you use the Insert button to insert a range of cells, the existing cells shift down when the selected range is wider than it is long, and they shift right when the selected range is longer than it is wide, as shown in Figure 1–31. When you use the Insert Cells command, you specify whether the existing cells shift right or down, or whether to insert an entire row or column into the new range.

Figure 1–31   **Cells inserted into a worksheet**

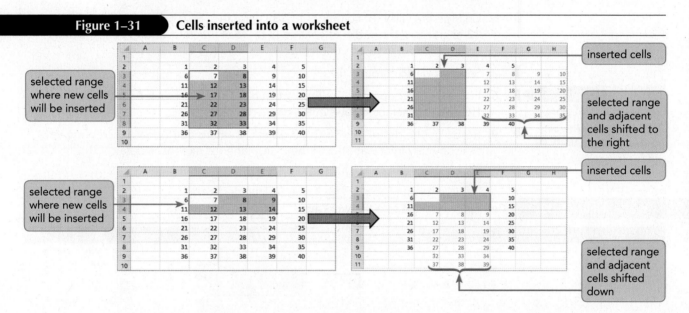

The process works in reverse when you delete a range. As with deleting a row or column, the cells adjacent to the deleted range either move up or left to fill in the space vacated by the deleted cells. The Delete Cells command lets you specify whether you want to shift the adjacent cells left or up or whether you want to delete the entire column or row.

When you insert or delete a range, cells that shift to a new location adopt the width of the columns they move into. As a result, you might need to resize columns and rows in the worksheet.

Reference

Inserting and Deleting a Range

- Select a range that matches the area you want to insert or delete.
- On the Home tab, in the Cells group, click the Insert button or the Delete button.

or

- Select the range that matches the range you want to insert or delete.
- On the Home tab, in the Cells group, click the Insert arrow and then click Insert Cells or click the Delete arrow and then click Delete Cells; or right-click the selected range, and then click Insert or Delete on the shortcut menu.
- Click the option button for the direction to shift the cells, columns, or rows.
- Click OK.

MedIT assigns an account ID for each type of revenue and expense item. Carmen asks you to insert this information into the worksheet. You will insert these new cells into the range A13:A23, shifting the adjacent cells to the right.

To insert a range to enter the account IDs:

1. Select the range **A13:A23** using any method you choose.

2. On the Home tab, in the Cells group, click the **Insert arrow**. A menu of insert options appears.

3. Click **Insert Cells**. The Insert dialog box opens.

4. Verify that the **Shift cells right** option button is selected.

5. Click **OK**. New cells are inserted into the selected range, and the adjacent cells move to the right. The shifted content does not fit well in the adjacent columns. You'll resize the columns and rows to fit their data.

6. Change the width of column B to **18** characters, the width of column C to **12** characters, the width of column D to **36** characters, and the widths of columns F and G to **14** characters.

7. Select rows **15** through **19**.

8. In the Cells group, click the **Format** button, and then click **AutoFit Row Height**. The selected rows autofit to their contents.

9. Resize the height of row 13 to **42** points, creating additional space between the summary information and the miscellaneous expenses data.

10. Click cell **A14**. See Figure 1–32.

> **Tip**
>
> You can also autofit rows by double-clicking the bottom border of the selected rows.

Figure 1–32 Cell range inserted into the worksheet

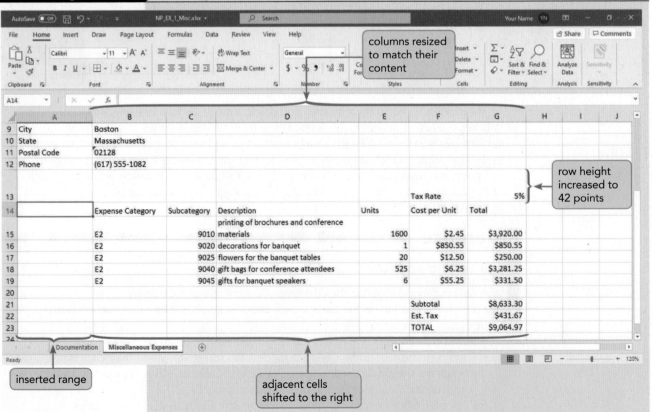

Notice that even though the account IDs will be entered in the range A14:A19, you inserted new cells into the A13:A23 range to retain the layout of the worksheet contents. Selecting the additional rows ensures that the tax rate and summary values still line up with the Cost per Unit and Total columns. Whenever you insert a new range, be sure to consider its impact on the layout of the entire worksheet.

Insight

Hiding and Unhiding Rows, Columns, and Worksheets

Workbooks can become long and complicated, filled with formulas and data that are important for performing calculations but are of little interest to readers. In those situations, you can simplify these workbooks by hiding rows, columns, and even worksheets. Although the contents of hidden cells cannot be seen, the data in those cells is still available for use in formulas and functions throughout the workbook.

Hiding removes a row or column from view while keeping it part of the worksheet. To hide a row or column, select the row or column heading, click the Format button in the Cells group on the Home tab, point to Hide & Unhide on the menu that appears, and then click Hide Rows or Hide Columns. The border of the row or column heading is doubled to mark the location of hidden rows or columns.

A worksheet often is hidden when the entire worksheet contains data that is not of interest to the reader and is better summarized elsewhere in the document. To hide a worksheet, make that worksheet active, click the Format button in the Cells group on the Home tab, point to Hide & Unhide, and then click Hide Sheet.

Unhiding redisplays the hidden content in the workbook. To unhide a row or column, click in a cell below the hidden row or to the right of the hidden column, click the Format button, point to Hide & Unhide, and then click Unhide Rows or Unhide Columns. To unhide a worksheet, click the Format button, point to Hide & Unhide, and then click Unhide Sheet. The Unhide dialog box opens. Click the sheet you want to unhide, and then click OK. The hidden content is redisplayed in the workbook.

Although hiding data can make a worksheet and workbook easier to read, be sure never to hide information that is important to the reader.

You will complete the miscellaneous expenses table by adding the account IDs for each expense. You can use Flash Fill to automatically create the account IDs.

Using Flash Fill

Flash Fill enters text based on patterns it finds in the data. As shown in Figure 1–33, Flash Fill generates names from the first and last names stored in the adjacent columns in the worksheet. To enter the rest of the names, press ENTER; to continue typing the names yourself, press ESC.

| Figure 1–33 | Text automatically entered with Flash Fill |

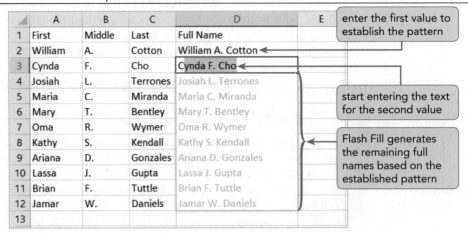

Flash Fill works best when the pattern is clearly recognized from the values in the data. Be sure to enter the data pattern in the column or row right next to the related data. The data used to generate the pattern must be in a rectangular grid and cannot have blank columns or rows.

MedIT account IDs combine the expense category and subcategory values. For example, an expense from the E2 expense category with a 9010 subcategory has the account ID of E2-9010. Rather than typing this information for every expense item, you will use Flash Fill to complete the data entry.

To enter the account IDs using Flash Fill:

1. Type **Account ID** in cell A14, and then press **ENTER**. The label is entered in cell A14, and cell A15 is the active cell.

2. Type **E2-9010** in cell A15, and then press **ENTER**. The first account ID is entered in cell A15, and cell A16 is the active cell.

3. Type **E2-9020** in cell A16. As soon as you complete those characters, Flash Fill generates the remaining entries in the column based on the pattern you entered. See Figure 1–34.

| Figure 1–34 | Account IDs generated by Flash Fill |

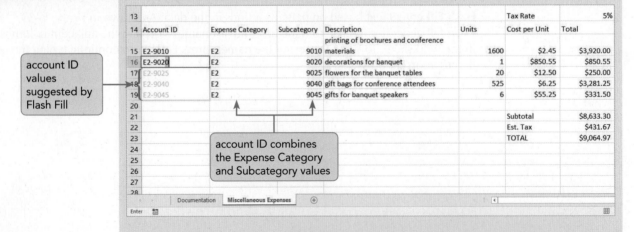

Trouble? If you pause for an extended time between entering text to establish the pattern, Flash Fill might not extend the pattern for you.

▶ **4.** Press **ENTER** to accept the suggested entries.

Note that Flash Fill generates text, not formulas. If you edit or replace the entry originally used to create the Flash Fill pattern, the other entries generated by Flash Fill in the column will not be updated.

Formatting a Worksheet

Formatting enhances the appearance of the worksheet data by changing its font, size, color, or alignment. Two common formatting changes are adding cell borders and changing the font size of text.

Adding Cell Borders

You can make spreadsheet content easier to read by adding borders around the worksheet cells. Borders can be added to the left, top, right, or bottom edge of any cell or range. You can set the color, thickness of and the number of lines in each border. Borders are especially useful when you print a worksheet because the gridlines that surround the cells in the workbook window are not printed by default. They appear on the worksheet only as a guide.

Carmen wants you to add borders around the cells that detail the miscellaneous expenses for the Boston conference to make that content easier to read when it's printed.

To add borders around the worksheet cells:

▶ **1.** Select the range **F13:G13**. You'll add borders to these cells.

▶ **2.** On the Home tab, in the Font group, click the **Borders arrow** ⊞ ▾, and then click **All Borders**. Borders are added around each cell in the selected range. The Borders button changes to reflect the last selected border option, which in this case is All Borders. The name of the selected border option appears in the button's ScreenTip.

▶ **3.** Select the nonadjacent range **A14:G19,F21:G23**.

▶ **4.** On the Home tab, in the Font group, click the **All Borders** button ⊞. Borders appear around all the cells in this range as well.

▶ **5.** Click cell **A24** to deselect the range. See Figure 1–35.

Figure 1–35   Borders added to cells

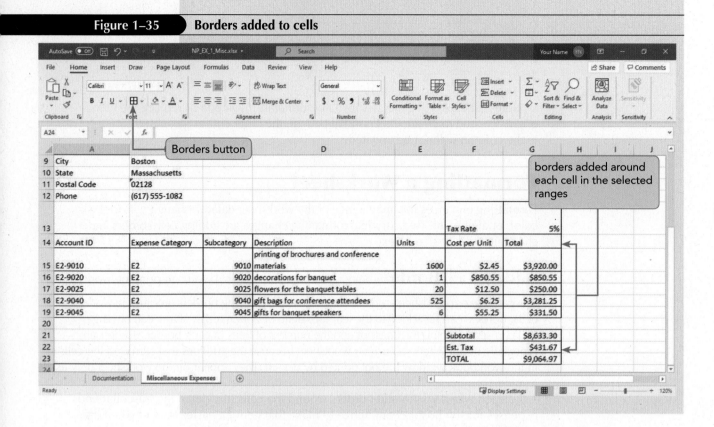

Changing the Font Size

Changing the size of text in a sheet provides a way to identify different parts of a worksheet, such as distinguishing a title or section heading from data. The size of the text is referred to as the font size and is measured in points. The default font size for worksheets is 11 points, but it can be made larger or smaller as needed. You can resize text in selected cells using the Font Size button in the Font group on the Home tab. You can also use the Increase Font Size and Decrease Font Size buttons to resize cell content to the next higher or lower standard font size.

Carmen wants you to increase the size of the worksheet title to 24 points to make it more visible and stand out from the rest of the worksheet content.

To change the font size of the worksheet title:

1. Scroll up the worksheet and click cell **A1** to select the worksheet title.

2. On the Home tab, in the Font group, click the **Font Size arrow** 11 ▾ to display a list of font sizes, and then click **24**. The worksheet title changes to 24 points. See Figure 1–36.

Figure 1–36	Font size increased in cell A1

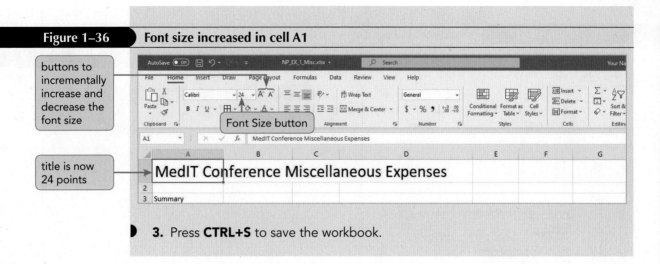

buttons to incrementally increase and decrease the font size

Font Size button

title is now 24 points

MedIT Conference Miscellaneous Expenses

3. Press **CTRL+S** to save the workbook.

Now that the worksheet content and formatting are final, you can print the worksheet.

Printing a Workbook

Excel has many tools to control the print layout and appearance of a workbook. Before printing a worksheet, you will want to preview the printout to make sure that it will print correctly.

Changing Worksheet Views

You can view a worksheet in three ways. Normal view, which you have been using throughout this module, shows the contents of the worksheet. Page Layout view shows how the worksheet will appear when printed. Page Break Preview displays the location of the different page breaks within the worksheet. This is useful when a worksheet will span several printed pages, and you need to control what content appears on each page.

Carmen wants you to preview the print version of the Miscellaneous Expenses worksheet. You will do this by switching between views.

To switch the Miscellaneous Expenses worksheet between views:

1. Click the **Page Layout** button 🔲 on the status bar. The page layout of the worksheet appears in the workbook window.

2. On the Zoom slider at the lower-right corner of the workbook window, click the **Zoom Out** button until the percentage is **60%**. The reduced magnification makes it clear that the worksheet will spread over two pages when printed. See Figure 1–37.

Figure 1–37 **Worksheet in Page Layout view**

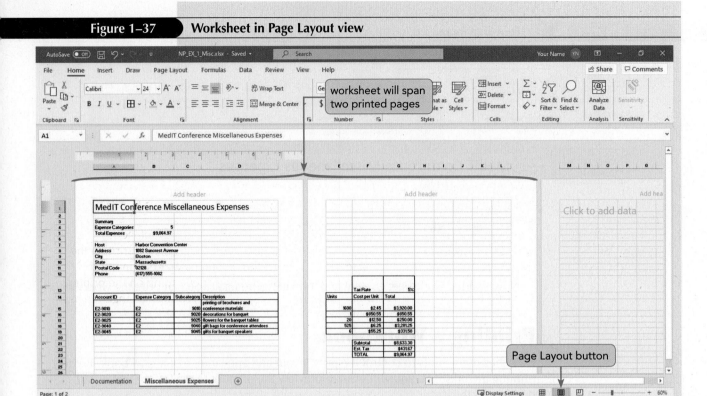

Tip

You can relocate a page break by dragging the dotted blue border in the Page Break Preview window.

3. Click the **Page Break Preview** button on the status bar. The view switches to Page Break Preview, which shows only those parts of the current worksheet that will print. A dotted blue border separates one page from another.

4. On the Zoom slider, drag the slider button to the right until the percentage is **80%**. You can now more easily read the contents of the worksheet. See Figure 1–38.

Figure 1–38 **Worksheet in Page Break Preview view**

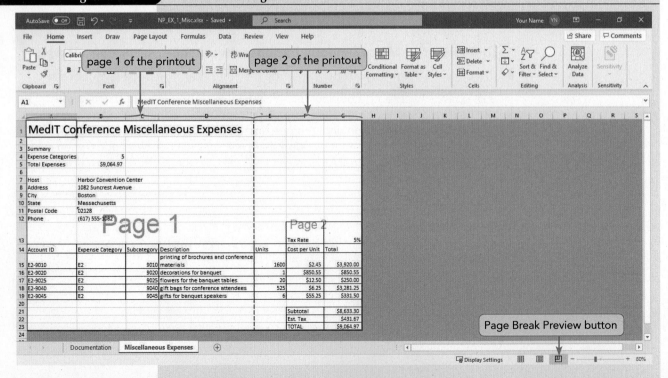

▶ **5.** Click the **Normal** button ⊞ on the status bar. The worksheet returns to Normal view. Notice that after viewing the worksheet in Page Layout or Page Break Preview, a dotted black line appears between columns D and E in Normal view to show where the page breaks occur.

Changing the Page Orientation

Page orientation specifies in which direction content is printed on the page. In **portrait orientation**, the page is taller than it is wide. In **landscape orientation**, the page is wider than it is tall. By default, Excel displays pages in portrait orientation. Changing the page orientation affects only the active sheet in the workbook and not the other, unselected, sheets.

As you saw in Page Layout view and Page Break Preview, the Miscellaneous Expenses worksheet will print on two pages—columns A through D will print on the first page, and columns E through G will print on the second page. Keep in mind that the columns that print on each page may differ slightly depending on the printer. Carmen wants the entire worksheet to print on a single page, so you'll change the page orientation from portrait to landscape.

To change the page orientation of the worksheet:

▶ **1.** On the ribbon, click the **Page Layout** tab. The tab includes options for changing how the worksheet is arranged.

▶ **2.** In the Page Setup group, click the **Orientation** button, and then click **Landscape**. The worksheet switches to landscape orientation, though you cannot see this change in Normal view.

▶ **3.** Click the **Page Layout** button ▣ on the status bar to switch to Page Layout view. The worksheet will still print on two pages.

Even with the landscape orientation the contents of the worksheet will still not fit on one page. You can correct this by scaling the page.

Setting the Scaling Options

Scaling resizes the worksheet to fit within a single page or set of pages. There are several options for scaling a printout of a worksheet. You can scale the width or the height of the printout so that all the columns or all of the rows fit on a single page. You can also scale the printout to fit the entire worksheet (both columns and rows) on a single page. If the worksheet is too large to fit on one page, you can scale the print to fit on the number of pages you select. You can also scale the worksheet to a percentage of its size. For example, scaling a worksheet to 50% reduces the size of the sheet by half when it is sent to the printer. When scaling a printout, make sure that the worksheet is still readable after it is resized. Scaling affects only the active worksheet, so you can scale each worksheet separately to best fit its contents.

Carmen asks you to scale the printout so that the Miscellaneous Expenses worksheet fits on one page in landscape orientation.

To scale the printout of the worksheet:

▶ **1.** On the Page Layout tab, in the Scale to Fit group, click the **Width arrow**, and then click **1 page** on the menu that appears. All the columns in the worksheet now fit on one page.

If more rows are added to the worksheet, Carmen wants to ensure that they still fit within a single sheet.

▶ **2.** In the Scale to Fit group, click the **Height** arrow, and then click **1 page**. All the rows in the worksheet will now always fit on one page. See Figure 1–39.

Figure 1–39	Printout scaled to fit on one page

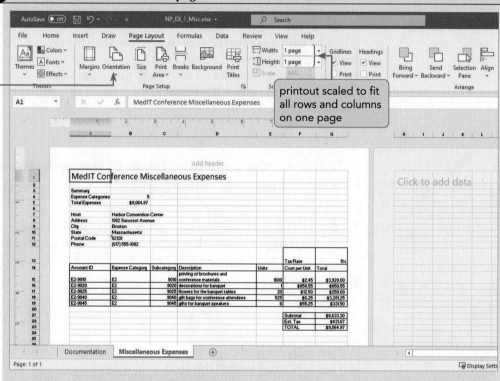

Orientation button to select portrait or landscape orientation

printout scaled to fit all rows and columns on one page

Setting the Print Options

You can print the contents of a workbook by using the Print screen in Backstage view. The Print screen provides options for choosing where to print, what to print, and how to print. For example, you can specify the number of copies to print, which printer to use, and what to print. You can choose to print only the selected cells, only the active sheets, or all the worksheets in the workbook that contain data. The printout will include only the data in the worksheet. The other elements in the worksheet, such as the row and column headings and the gridlines around the worksheet cells, will not print by default. The preview shows you exactly how the printed pages will look with the current settings. You should always preview before printing to ensure that the printout looks exactly as you intended and avoid unnecessary reprinting.

Carmen asks you to preview and print the workbook containing the estimates of miscellaneous expenses for the conference.

To preview and print the workbook:

▸ **1.** On the ribbon, click the **File** tab to display Backstage view.

▸ **2.** Click **Print** in the navigation bar. The Print screen appears with the print options and a preview of the printout of the Miscellaneous Expenses worksheet. See Figure 1–40.

| Figure 1–40 | Print screen in Backstage view |

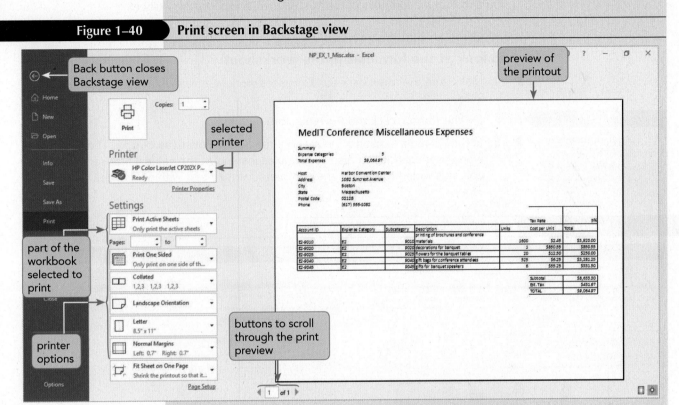

▸ **3.** Click the **Printer** button, and then click the printer you want to print to, if it is not already selected. By default, Excel will print only the active sheet.

▸ **4.** In the Settings options, click the top button, and then click **Print Entire Workbook** to print all of the sheets in the workbook—in this case, both the Documentation and the Miscellaneous Expenses worksheets. The preview shows the first sheet in the workbook—the Documentation worksheet. Note that this sheet is still in portrait orientation.

▸ **5.** Below the preview, click the **Next Page** button ▶ to view the print preview for the Miscellaneous Expenses worksheet, which will print on a single page in landscape orientation.

▸ **6.** If you are instructed to print, click the **Print** button to send the contents of the workbook to the specified printer. If you are not instructed to print, click the **Back** button ⬅ in the navigation bar to exit Backstage view.

Viewing Worksheet Formulas

Most of the time, you will be interested in only the final results of a worksheet, not the formulas used to calculate those results. However, in some cases, you might want to view the formulas used to develop the workbook. This is particularly useful when you encounter unexpected results and want to examine the underlying formulas, or you want to discuss the formulas with a colleague. You can display the formulas instead of the resulting values in cells.

If you print the worksheet while the formulas are displayed, the printout shows the formulas instead of the values. To make the printout easier to read, you should print the worksheet gridlines as well as the row and column headings so that cell references in the formulas are easy to find in the printed version of the worksheet.

You'll look at the formulas in the Miscellaneous Expenses worksheet.

To look at the formulas in the worksheet:

1. Make sure the Miscellaneous Expenses worksheet is displayed in Page Layout view.

2. On the ribbon, click the **Formulas** tab.

3. In the Formula Auditing group, click the **Show Formulas** button. The worksheet changes to display formulas instead of the values. Notice that the columns widen to display the complete formula text within each cell. See Figure 1–41.

Tip

You can also switch to the formula view by pressing CTRL+` (the grave accent symbol ` is usually located above TAB).

Figure 1–41   **Worksheet with formulas displayed**

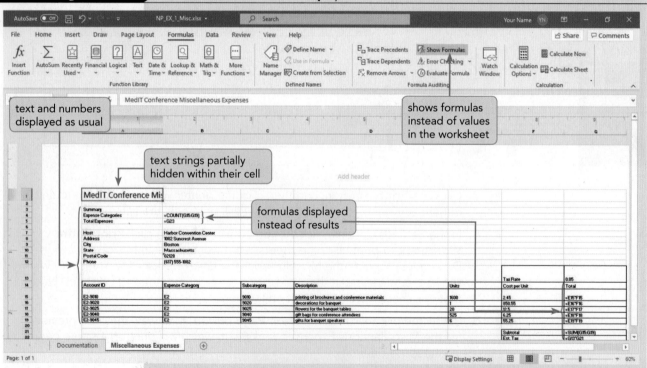

4. When you are done reviewing the formulas, click the **Show Formulas** button again to hide the formulas and display the resulting values.

5. Click the **Normal** button ⊞ on the status bar to return the workbook to Normal view.

6. On the Zoom slider, drag the slider button to the right until the percentage is **120%** (or the magnification you want to use).

7. **sam**⬆ Save the workbook, and then close it.

Carmen is pleased with the workbook you created and will use your estimates in the workbook she is using to track all of the cost estimates for the Boston conference. Carmen will continue to adjust the revenue and expense projections as the conference data approaches and will get back to you she needs to you to do additional analysis.

Review

Session 1.2 Quick Check

1. What is the formula to add values in cells A1, B1, and C1? What function will achieve the same result?
2. What is the formula to count the number of numeric values in the range A1:A30?
3. If you insert cells into the range C1:D10, shifting the cells to the right, what is the new location of the data that was previously in cell F4?
4. Cell E11 contains the formula =SUM(E1:E10). How is the formula adjusted when a new row is inserted above row 5?
5. In the following function, which arguments are required and which arguments are optional:

   AVERAGE(*number1*,[*number2*],[*number3*],…)

6. What is the formula to sum all the numeric values in column C.
7. Describe the four ways of viewing worksheet contents in Excel.
8. How are page breaks indicated in Page Break Preview?

1. =A1 + B1 + C1
2. =Count (A1:A30)
3. H4
4. ?
5. ?
6. =sum(c:c)
7. Normal veiw, Page layout, page break, formula veiw
8. blue dotted line

Practice

Review Assignments

There are no Data Files needed for the Review Assignments.

Carmen needs to estimate the total costs for supplying computers, audio/video equipment, and Internet access to the participants at the Boston conference. She has some documentation on the cost of different expense items. Carmen asks you to enter that information into a workbook and calculate the total cost of items in this expense category. Complete the following:

1. Create a new, blank workbook, and then save it as **NP_EX1_Equipment** in the location specified by your instructor.
2. Rename the Sheet1 worksheet using **Documentation** as the new name.
3. Enter the data shown in Figure 1–42 in the specified cells.

Figure 1–42   Documentation sheet data

Cell	Text
A1	MedIT
A3	Author
A4	Date
A5	Purpose
B3	*your name*
B4	*current date*
B5	To estimate the cost of renting computers, audio/video equipment, Internet access, and hiring technical support at the MedIT conference in Boston

4. Set the font size of the title text in cell A1 to 24 points.
5. Set the width of column B to 32 characters, and then wrap the contents of cell B5 within the cell.
6. Add borders around all of the cells in the range A3:B5.
7. Add a new worksheet after the Documentation sheet, and then rename the worksheet using **Equipment Expenses** as the new name.
8. In cell A1, enter **MedIT Conference Equipment Expenses** as the worksheet title. Set the font size of the title text in cell A1 to 20 points.
9. Enter the data summarizing the conference in the specified cells as shown in Figure 1–43. Make sure that the postal code value is treated as text rather than a number.

Figure 1–43   Conference Summary data

Cell	Text	Cell	Text
A4	Equipment Categories	A12	Phone
A5	Total Expenses	B7	Conference Connections
A7	Vendor	B8	480 Technology Lane
A8	Street Address	B9	Boston
A9	City	B10	Massachusetts
A10	State	B11	02155
A11	Postal Code	B12	(617) 555-7814

10. Enter the column titles and expenses for various equipment that will be used at the conference in the range A14:E20 as shown in Figure 1–44.

Figure 1–44	Equipment expenses

Expense Category	Subcategory	Description	Units	Cost per Unit
E2	5010	computer workstation rental	25	$105.00
E2	5020	audio/video rental	10	$85.00
E2	5030	screen projector rentals	10	$75.00
E2	5040	high-speed Internet access	1	$450.00
E2	5050	onsite wiring	1	$500.00
E2	5060	web hosting	1	$700.00

11. In cell F14, enter **Total** as the label. In the range F15:F20, calculate the total cost of each equipment item by entering formulas that return the value of the number of units ordered multiplied by the cost per unit.

12. In cell E22, enter **Subtotal** as the label, and then in cell F22, use the SUM function to calculate the sum of the values in the range F15:F20.

13. In cell E13, enter **Tax Rate** as the label, and then in cell F13, enter **3%** as the value.

14. In cell E23, enter **Est. Tax** as the label, and then in cell F23, calculate the estimated tax by entering a formula that multiplies the subtotal value in cell F22 by the tax rate in cell F13.

15. In cell E24, enter **TOTAL** as the label, and then in cell F24, use the SUM function to calculate the sum of the subtotal value in cell F22 and the estimated tax in cell F23.

16. Insert new cells in the range A13:A24, shifting the other cells to the right.

17. In cell A14, enter **Account ID** as the label. In cell A15, enter **E2-5010** as the first ID. In cell A16, enter **E2-5020** as the second ID, and allow Flash Fill to enter the remaining IDs.

18. Add borders around all of the cells in the range F13:G13,A14:G20,F22:G24.

19. Set the width of columns A and B to 22 characters. Set the width of columns C, E, F, and G to 13 characters. Set the width of column D to 24 characters. Set the height of row 13 to 30 points.

20. Wrap the text in the range D15:D20 so all of the content is visible.

21. In cell B4, use the COUNT function to count the number of numeric values in the range E15:E20. In cell B5, display the value of the total expenses that was calculated in cell G24.

22. Carmen wants to keep the equipment budget under $6,000. If the total cost of the equipment is less than $6,000, enter **within budget** in cell B3, otherwise enter **over budget** in the cell.

23. Change the page orientation of the Equipment Expenses worksheet to landscape orientation, and then scale the width and height of the Equipment Expenses worksheet to print on a single page.

24. Save the workbook. If you are instructed to print, then print the entire workbook.

25. Display the formulas in the Equipment Expenses worksheet. If you are instructed to print, then print the worksheet. Remove the worksheet from formula view.

26. Save the workbook, and then close it.

Apply

Case Problem 1

Data File needed for this Case Problem: NP_EX_1-2.xlsx

Cross State Trucking   Brian Eagleton is a dispatch manager at Cross State Trucking, a major freight hauler based in Chicago, Illinois. Brian needs to develop a workbook that will summarize the driving log of Cross State drivers. Brian has a month of travel data from one of the company's drivers and wants you to create a workbook that he can use to analyze this data. Complete the following:

1. Open the **NP_EX_1-2.xlsx** workbook located in the Excel1 > Case1 folder included with your Data Files. Save the workbook as **NP_EX_1_Trucking** in the location specified by your instructor.

2. Change the name of the Sheet1 worksheet using **Travel Log** as the name, and then move it to the end of the workbook. Rename the Sheet2 worksheet using **Documentation** as the name.

3. In the Documentation sheet, enter your name in cell B3 and the current date in cell B4.

4. Go to the Travel Log worksheet. Resize the columns so that all the data is visible in the cells.

5. Between the Odometer Ending column and the Hours column, insert a new column. Enter **Miles** as the column label in cell I4.

6. In the Miles column, in the range I5:I25, enter formulas to calculate the number of miles driven each day by subtracting the odometer beginning value from the odometer ending value.

7. Between the Price per Gallon column and the Seller column, insert a new column. Enter **Total Fuel Purchase** as the label in cell N4.

8. In the Total Fuel Purchase column, in the range N5:N25, enter formulas to calculate the total amount spent on fuel each day by multiplying the gallons value by the price per gallon value.

9. In cell B5, use the COUNT function to calculate the total number of driving days using the values in the Date column in the range D5:D25.

10. In cell B6, use the SUM function to calculate the total number of driving hours using the values in the Hours column in the range J5:J25.

11. In cell B7, enter a formula that divides the hours of driving value (cell B6) by the days of driving value (cell B5) to calculate the average hours of driving per day.

12. In cell B9, use the SUM function to calculate the driver's total expenses for the month for fuel, tolls, and miscellaneous expenditures using the nonadjacent range N5:N25,P5:Q25.

13. In cell B10, use the SUM function to calculate the total amount the driver spent on fuel using the range N5:N25. In cell B11, use the SUM function to calculate the total amount spent on tolls and miscellaneous expenses using the range P5:Q25.

14. In cell B13, use the SUM function to calculate the total gallons of gas the driver used during the month using the range L5:L25. In cell B14, use the SUM function to calculate the total number of miles driven that month using the range I5:I25.

15. In cell B15, enter a formula that divides the total miles (cell B14) by the total gallons (cell B13) to calculate the miles per gallon. In cell B16, enter a formula that divides the total expenses (cell B9) by the total miles driven (cell B14) to calculate the cost per mile.

16. Cross State Trucking wants to keep the cost of driving and delivering goods to less than 65 cents per mile. If the cost per mile is greater than 65 cents, enter **over budget** in cell B4, otherwise enter **on budget** in cell B4.

17. In cell A1, increase the font size of the text to 28 points. In cell D3 and cell L3, increase the font size of the Mileage Table and Expense Table labels to 18 points.

18. Change the worksheet to landscape orientation. Scale the printout so that the worksheet is scaled to 1 page wide by 1 page tall. If you are instructed to print, print the entire workbook.

19. Save the workbook, and then close it.

Create

Case Problem 2

Data File needed for this Case Problem: NP_EX_1-3.xlsx

Meucci Digital, Inc.   Travon Lee is a manager in the human resources department of Meucci Digital, a company that specializes in digital communications hardware and software. Travon wants to use a workbook to summarize employee data. The report will include the average employee's base salary, bonus salary, sick days, performance review, and the average number of years of employment at the company. You will add formulas and functions to the workbook to analyze the data. Because Travon may be adding data on other employees to the worksheet, all the calculations should be applied to entire columns of data rather than specified ranges within those columns. Complete the following:

1. Open the **NP_EX_1-3.xlsx** workbook located in the Excel1 > Case2 folder included with your Data Files. Save the workbook as **NP_EX_1_HRDepartment** in the location specified by your instructor.

2. In the Documentation sheet, enter your name in cell B3 and the current date in cell B4.

3. Add borders around the range A3:B5.

4. Go to the Sheet2 worksheet and rename it using **Employees** as the sheet name.

5. In cell I5 of the Employees worksheet, calculate the number of days that Clay Aaron has worked for the company by subtracting the hire date in cell H5 from the report date in cell G5. Copy the formula and then paste it to the range I6:I582.

6. Insert a new column between columns E and F. In the new cell F4, enter **Full Name** as the label. In cell F5, enter **Clay Aaron** as the first name, and in cell F6, enter **Angel Abarca** as the second name. Allow Flash Fill to enter the remaining full names of employees in the column.

7. In cell A1, enter **Meucci Digital, Inc.** as the title. In cell A2, enter **Employee Summary** as the label. Increase the font size of cell A1 to 22 points and increase the font size of cell A2 to 16 points.

8. Enter the labels shown in Figure 1–45 in the specified cells in preparation for adding a summary of the employee data.

Figure 1–45   Labels for employee information

Cell	Text
A4	Number of Employees
A6	Average Days of Employment
A7	Average Years of Employment
A9	Total Base Salary
A10	Average Base Salary
A11	Total Bonuses
A12	Average Bonuses
A13	Total Compensation
A14	Average Compensation
A16	Total Sick Days
A17	Average Sick Days
A19	Average Performance Rating

9. Resize the worksheet columns as necessary so that all of the cell content is visible.

Explore 10. Add the following calculations to the worksheet:

a. In cell B4, use the COUNT function to calculate the number of employees by counting the hiring dates in column I. (*Hint*: The column reference is I:I.)

b. In cell B6, calculate the average number of days of employment using the SUM function with the cells in column J (the column reference is J:J), and then dividing that sum by the number of employees reported in cell B4.

c. In cell B7, calculate the average years of employment by dividing the value in cell B6 by 365.25 (the number of days in a year).

d. In cell B9, calculate the total the company paid in base salaries by using the SUM function to sum the values in column K. In cell B10, calculate the average base salary by dividing the total value in cell B9 by the number of employees in cell B4.

e. In cell B11, calculate the total amount paid out in bonuses by summing the values in column L. In cell B12, calculate the average bonus per employee by dividing the total amount in bonuses by the total number of employees in cell B4.

f. In cell B13, calculate the total compensation the company paid by adding the values in cells B9 and B11. In cell B14, calculate the average compensation per employee by dividing cell B13 by cell B4.

g. In cell B16, sum the total number of sick days taken by employees of Meucci Digital. In cell B17, calculate the average number of sick days per employee.

h. In cell B19, calculate the average performance rating for the Meucci Digital employees.

✛ **Explore** 11. Insert a new row directly below row 432 (between the entry for Pamela Randazzo and George Raymond) containing the employee information shown in Figure 1–46. Have Excel automatically calculate the days of employment value when it inserts the formula directly into cell J431.

Figure 1–46 **New employee data for Meucci Digital**

Information	Value
First	Aditya
Last	Rao
Full Name	Aditya Rao
Department	Sales
Report Date	7/31/2025
Hire Date	7/1/2025
Base Salary	$32,200
Bonus	$0
Sick Days	0
Performance Rating	3

12. Verify that the summary statistics in column B automatically update to reflect the addition of the new employee and that the total number of employees in the report is 579.

13. Make sure the Employees worksheet is set to portrait orientation, and then scale its width to 1 page but leave the height set to automatic.

14. If you are instructed to print, print only the first page of the Employees worksheet.

15. Save the workbook, and then close it.

Module 2

Objectives

Session 2.1
- Change fonts, font style, and font color
- Add fill colors and a background image
- Create formulas to calculate sales data
- Format numbers as currency and percentages
- Format dates and times
- Align, indent, and rotate cell contents
- Merge a group of cells

Session 2.2
- Use the AVERAGE function
- Apply cell styles
- Copy and paste formats with the Format Painter
- Find and replace text and formatting
- Change workbook themes
- Highlight cells with conditional formats
- Format a worksheet for printing

Formatting Workbook Text and Data

Creating a Sales Report

Case | Bristol Bay

Stefan Novak is a sales manager for the Northwest region of the Bristol Bay department store chain. Stefan needs to create a report on sales data in the Home Furnishing department of 20 Bristol Bay stores in Washington, Oregon, and Idaho. The report will include summaries of the Home Furnishing department's gross revenue and net income over the current fiscal year compared to the same sales data from the previous year. The report will also track the sales data by store and month so that Stefan can view monthly sales trends and identify those stores that exceed expectations or are falling short of sales goals. Stefan asks you to enter the formulas needed to summarize the data and to format the report to make it easier to read and analyze the data.

Starting Data Files

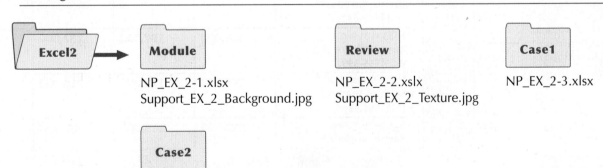

Excel2 → Module

NP_EX_2-1.xlsx
Support_EX_2_Background.jpg

Review

NP_EX_2-2.xslx
Support_EX_2_Texture.jpg

Case1

NP_EX_2-3.xlsx

Case2

NP_EX_2-4.xlsx

Session 2.1 Visual Overview:

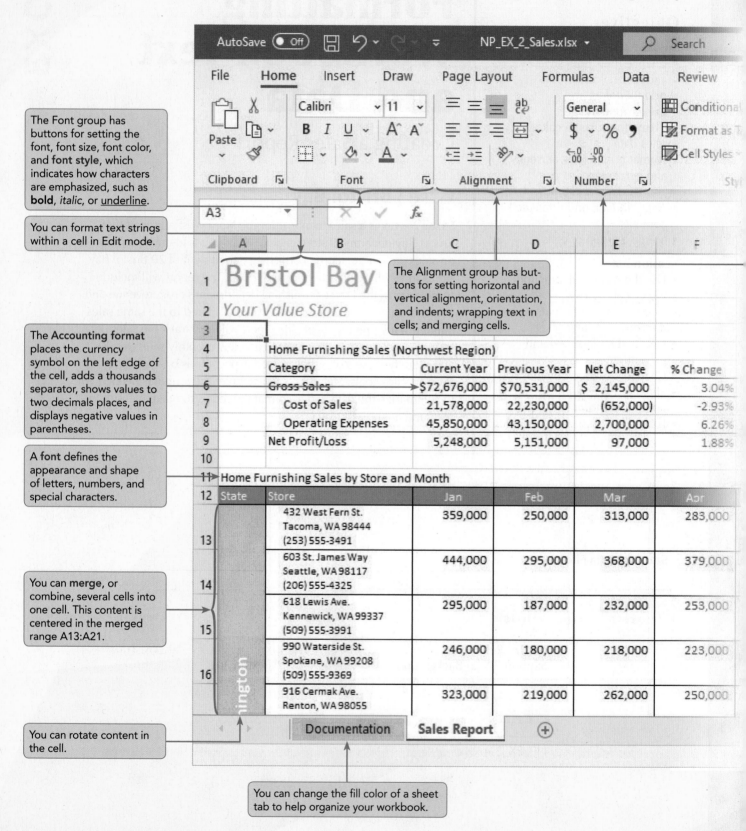

The Font group has buttons for setting the font, font size, font color, and **font style**, which indicates how characters are emphasized, such as **bold**, *italic*, or underline.

You can format text strings within a cell in Edit mode.

The **Accounting format** places the currency symbol on the left edge of the cell, adds a thousands separator, shows values to two decimals places, and displays negative values in parentheses.

A **font** defines the appearance and shape of letters, numbers, and special characters.

You can **merge**, or combine, several cells into one cell. This content is centered in the merged range A13:A21.

You can rotate content in the cell.

The **Alignment group** has buttons for setting horizontal and vertical alignment, orientation, and indents; wrapping text in cells; and merging cells.

You can change the fill color of a sheet tab to help organize your workbook.

	A	B	C	D	E	F
1	**Bristol Bay**					
2	*Your Value Store*					
3						
4		Home Furnishing Sales (Northwest Region)				
5		Category	Current Year	Previous Year	Net Change	% Change
6		Gross Sales	$72,676,000	$70,531,000	$ 2,145,000	3.04%
7		Cost of Sales	21,578,000	22,230,000	(652,000)	-2.93%
8		Operating Expenses	45,850,000	43,150,000	2,700,000	6.26%
9		Net Profit/Loss	5,248,000	5,151,000	97,000	1.88%
10						
11		Home Furnishing Sales by Store and Month				
12	State	Store	Jan	Feb	Mar	Apr
13		432 West Fern St. Tacoma, WA 98444 (253) 555-3491	359,000	250,000	313,000	283,000
14		603 St. James Way Seattle, WA 98117 (206) 555-4325	444,000	295,000	368,000	379,000
15		618 Lewis Ave. Kennewick, WA 99337 (509) 555-3991	295,000	187,000	232,000	253,000
16		990 Waterside St. Spokane, WA 99208 (509) 555-9369	246,000	180,000	218,000	223,000
		916 Cermak Ave. Renton, WA 98055	323,000	219,000	262,000	250,000

Documentation | **Sales Report**

Formatting a Worksheet

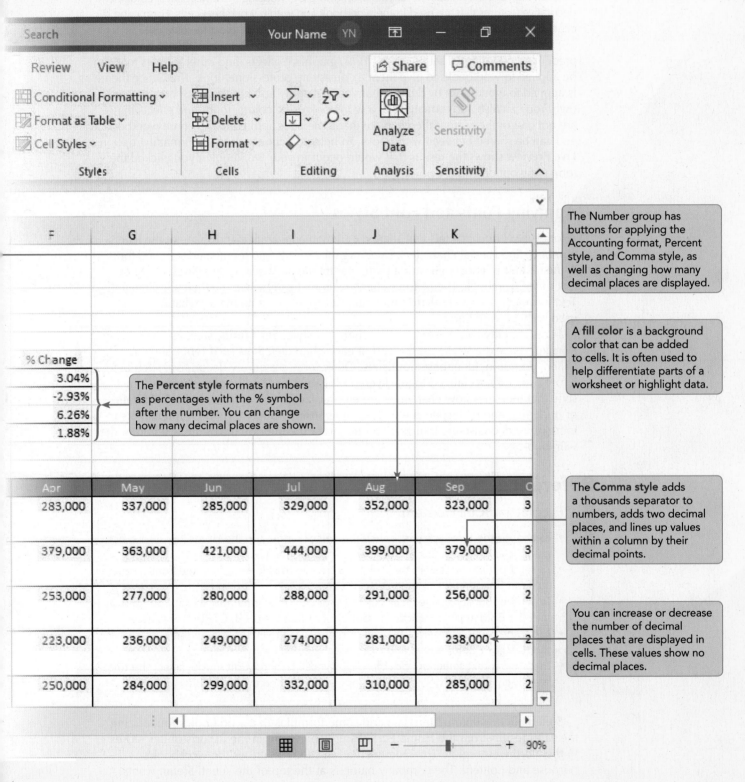

The Number group has buttons for applying the Accounting format, Percent style, and Comma style, as well as changing how many decimal places are displayed.

A **fill color** is a background color that can be added to cells. It is often used to help differentiate parts of a worksheet or highlight data.

The **Percent style** formats numbers as percentages with the % symbol after the number. You can change how many decimal places are shown.

The **Comma style** adds a thousands separator to numbers, adds two decimal places, and lines up values within a column by their decimal points.

You can increase or decrease the number of decimal places that are displayed in cells. These values show no decimal places.

% Change
3.04%
-2.93%
6.26%
1.88%

	Apr	May	Jun	Jul	Aug	Sep	O
	283,000	337,000	285,000	329,000	352,000	323,000	3
	379,000	363,000	421,000	444,000	399,000	379,000	3
	253,000	277,000	280,000	288,000	291,000	256,000	2
	223,000	236,000	249,000	274,000	281,000	238,000	2
	250,000	284,000	299,000	332,000	310,000	285,000	2

Formatting Cell Text

You can improve the readability of your workbooks by choosing the fonts, styles, colors, and decorative features that are used in the workbook and within worksheet cells. Formatting changes only the appearance of the workbook data—it does not affect the data itself.

Excel organizes complementary formatting options into themes. A **theme** is a predefined coordinated set of colors, fonts, graphical effects, and other formats that can be applied to workbooks to give them a consistent, professional look. The Office theme is applied to workbooks by default, but you can apply another theme or create your own. You can also add formatting to a workbook using colors, fonts, and effects that are not part of the current theme. Note that a theme is applied to the entire workbook and can be shared between workbooks. To help you choose the best formatting option, **Live Preview** shows the results that would occur in your workbook if you clicked the formatting option you are pointing to.

Applying Fonts and Font Styles

A font is a set of characters that share a common appearance and shape of the letters, numbers, and special characters. Excel organizes fonts into theme and standard fonts. A **theme font** is associated with a particular theme and used for headings and body text in the workbook. Theme fonts change automatically when the theme is changed. Text formatted with a **standard font** retains its appearance no matter what theme is used with the workbook.

Fonts are classified based on their character style. **Serif fonts**, such as Times New Roman, have extra strokes at the end of each character. **Sans serif fonts**, such as Calibri, do not include these flourishes. Other fonts are purely decorative, such as a font used for specialized logos. Every font can be further formatted with a font style that indicates how characters are emphasized, such as *italic*, **bold**, ***bold italic***, or <u>underline</u> and with special effects such as ~~strikethrough~~ and color. You can also increase or decrease the font size to emphasize the importance of the text within the workbook.

Reference

Formatting Cell Content

- To choose the font typeface, select the cell or range. On the Home tab, in the Font group, click the Font arrow, and then select a font name.
- To set the font size, select the cell or range. On the Home tab, in the Font group, click the Font Size arrow, and then select a size.
- To set the font style, select the cell or range. On the Home tab, in the Font group, click the Bold, Italic, or Underline button; or press CTRL+B, CTRL+I, or CTRL+U.
- To set the font color, select the cell or range. On the Home tab, in the Font group, click the Font Color arrow, and then select a color.
- To format a text selection, double-click the cell to enter Edit mode, select the text to format, change the font, size, style, or color, and then press ENTER.

Stefan already entered the data and some formulas in a workbook summarizing the sales results from the Home Furnishing department in the 20 Bristol Bay stores in the Northwest region. The Documentation sheet describes the workbook's purpose and content. The company name is at the top of the sheet. Stefan wants you to format the name in large, bold letters using the default heading font from the Office theme.

To format the company name:

1.  Open the **NP_EX_2-1.xlsx** workbook located in the **Excel2 > Module** folder included with your Data Files, and then save the workbook as **NP_EX_2_Sales** in the location specified by your instructor.

2. In the Documentation sheet, enter your name in cell B4 and the date in cell B5.

3. Click cell **A1** to make it the active cell.

4. On the Home tab, in the Font group, click the **Font arrow** to display a gallery of fonts available on your computer. Each name is displayed in its font typeface. The first two fonts listed are the theme fonts for headings and body text—Calibri Light and Calibri.

5. Scroll down the Fonts gallery until you see Arial Black in the All Fonts list, and then point to **Arial Black** (or a similar font). Live Preview shows the effect of the Arial Black font on the text in cell A1. See Figure 2–1.

Figure 2–1	Font gallery

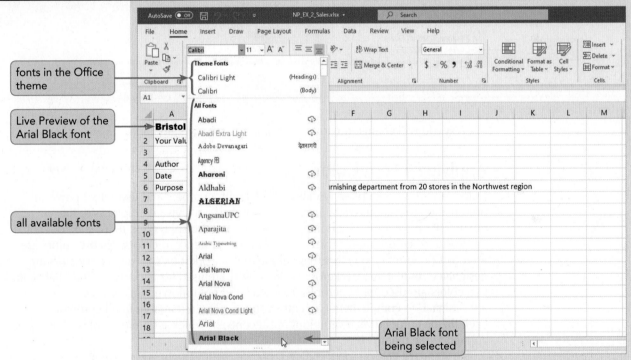

fonts in the Office theme

Live Preview of the Arial Black font

all available fonts

Arial Black font being selected

6. Point to three other fonts in the list to see the Live Preview of how the text in cell A1 appears in other fonts.

7. Click **Calibri Light** in the Theme Fonts list. The company name in cell A1 changes to the Calibri Light font, the default headings font in the current theme.

8. In the Font group, click the **Font Size arrow** to display a list of font sizes, point to **28** to preview the text in that font size, and then click **28**. The font size of the company name is now 28 points.

9. In the Font group, click the **Bold** button (or press **CTRL+B**). The text changes to a bold font.

10. Click cell **A2** to make it the active cell. The cell with the company slogan ("Your Value Store") is selected.

11. In the Font group, click the **Font Size arrow**, and then click **16**. The company slogan changes to 16 points.

12. In the Font group, click the **Italic** button I (or press **CTRL+I**). The company slogan is italicized.

13. Select the range **A4:A6**, and then press **CTRL+B**. The text in the selected range changes to bold.

14. Click cell **A7** to deselect the range. See Figure 2–2.

Figure 2–2 Formatted text in the Documentation sheet

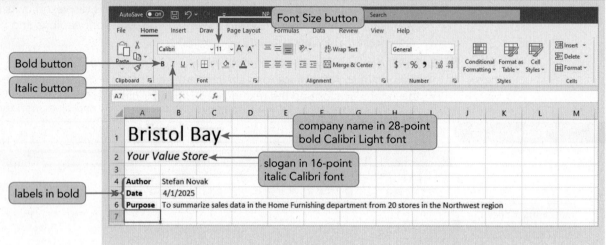

Next you will change the text color of the company name and slogan.

Applying a Font Color

Color can transform a plain workbook filled with numbers and text into a powerful presentation that captures the user's attention and adds visual emphasis to the document's most important points. By default, Excel displays text in a black font color.

Like fonts, colors are organized into theme and standard colors. **Theme colors** are a set of 12 coordinated colors that belong to the workbook's theme. Four colors are designated for text and backgrounds, six colors are used for accents and highlights, and two colors are used for hyperlinks (followed and not followed links). These 12 colors are designed to complement each other and to remain readable in all combinations. Each theme color has five variations, or accents, in which a different tint or shading is applied to the theme color.

Ten **standard colors**—dark red, red, orange, yellow, light green, green, light blue, blue, dark blue, and purple—are always available regardless of the workbook's theme. Beyond these easily accessible 10 standard colors, you can open an extended palette of 134 standard colors. You can also create a custom color by specifying a mixture of red, blue, and green color values, making available 16.7 million custom color combinations, which are more colors than the human eye can distinguish. Some dialog boxes have an automatic color option that uses your Windows default text and background colors, usually black text on a white background.

Insight

Creating Custom Colors

Custom colors let you add subtle and striking colors to a formatted workbook. To create custom colors, you use the **RGB Color model** in which each color is expressed with varying intensities of red, green, and blue. RGB color values are often represented as a set of numbers in the format

(*red*, *green*, *blue*)

where *red* is an intensity value assigned to red light, *green* is an intensity value assigned to green light, and *blue* is an intensity value assigned to blue light. The intensities are measured on a scale of 0 to 255—0 indicates no intensity (or the absence of the color) and 255 indicates the highest intensity. So, the RGB color value (255, 255, 0) represents a mixture of high-intensity red (255) and high-intensity green (255) with the absence of blue (0), creating the color yellow.

To create colors in Excel using the RGB model, click the More Colors option located in a color menu or dialog box to open the Colors dialog box. In the Colors dialog box, click the Custom tab, and then enter the red, green, and blue intensity values. A preview box shows the resulting RGB color.

Stefan wants the company name and slogan in the Documentation sheet to stand out by changing the font color in cells A1 and A2 to light blue.

To change the font color of the company name and slogan:

1. Select the range **A1:A2** containing the company name and slogan.

2. On the Home tab, in the Font group, click the **Font Color arrow**  to display the gallery of theme and standard colors.

3. In the Standard Colors section, point to the **Light Blue** color (the seventh color). The color name appears in a ScreenTip, and Live Preview shows the text with the light blue font color. See Figure 2–3.

| Figure 2–3 | **Font Color gallery** |

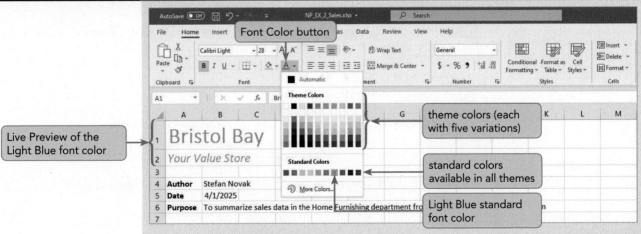

4. Click the **Light Blue** color. The company name and slogan change to that color.

Not all of the text within a cell has to have the same color. You can also format text strings within a cell.

Formatting Text Selections Within a Cell

In Edit mode, you can select and format selections of text within a cell. You can make these changes to selected text from the ribbon or from the Mini toolbar. The **Mini toolbar** is a small toolbar that appears next to selected content, containing the most frequently used formatting commands for that content.

Stefan asks you to format the company name in cell A1 so that the text "Bay" appears in light green.

To format part of the company name in light green:

1. Double-click cell **A1** to select the cell and enter Edit mode (or click cell **A1** and press **F2**). The status bar shows "Edit" to indicate that you are working with the cell in Edit mode. The pointer changes to the I-beam pointer over the cell that is in Edit mode.

2. Drag the pointer over the word **Bay** to select it. A Mini toolbar appears above the selected text with buttons to change the font, size, style, and color of the selected text in the cell. In this instance, you want to change the font color.

3. On the Mini toolbar, click the **Font Color arrow** $\boxed{\text{A}\;\cdot}$, and then point to the **Light Green** color (the fifth color) in the Standard Colors section. Live Preview shows the color of the selected text as light green. See Figure 2–4.

| **Figure 2–4** | **Mini toolbar in Edit mode** |

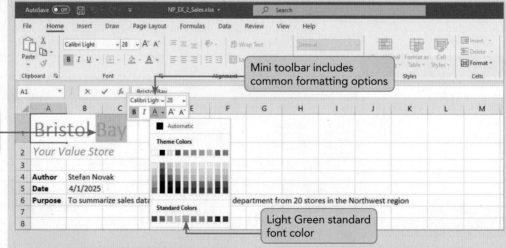

4. Click the **Light Green** standard color. The Mini toolbar closes and the selected text changes to light green.

In addition to font colors, you can also change the colors within cells.

Working with Fill Colors and Backgrounds

Another way to distinguish sections of a worksheet is by formatting the cell backgrounds. You can fill the cell background with color or with an image.

Changing a Fill Color

By default, worksheet cells do not include any background color. But filling a cell's background with color, also known as a fill color, can be helpful for highlighting data, differentiating parts of a worksheet, or adding visual interest to a report. The same selection of colors used to change the color of cell text can be used to change the cell background.

Insight

Using Color to Enhance a Workbook

When used wisely, color can enhance any workbook. However, when used improperly, color can distract the user, making the workbook more difficult to read. As you format a workbook, keep in mind the following tips:

- Use colors from the same theme to maintain a consistent look and feel across the worksheets. If the built-in themes do not fit your needs, you can create a custom theme.
- Use colors to differentiate types of cell content and to direct users where to enter data. For example, format a worksheet so that formula results appear in cells without a fill color and users enter data in cells with a light gray fill color.
- Avoid color combinations that are difficult to read.
- Print the workbook on both color and black-and-white printers to ensure that the printed copy is readable in both versions.
- Understand your printer's limitations and features. Colors that look good on your monitor might not look as good when printed.

Be sensitive to your audience. About 8% of all men and 0.5% of all women have some type of color vision deficiency and might not be able to see the text when certain color combinations are used. Red-green color vision deficiency is the most common, so avoid using red text on a green background or green text on a red background.

Stefan wants you to change the background color of the range A4:A6 in the Documentation sheet to light blue and the font color to white.

To change the font and fill colors in the Documentation sheet:

1. Select the range **A4:A6**.

2. On the Home tab, in the Font group, click the **Fill Color arrow** 🖌️▾ , and then click the **Light Blue** color (the seventh color) in the Standard Colors section.

3. In the Font group, click the **Font Color arrow** 🇦▾ , and then click the **White, Background 1** color (the first color in the first row) in the Theme Colors section. The labels are formatted as white text on a light blue background.

4. Select the range **B4:B6**, and then format the cells with the **Light Blue** standard font color and the **White, Background 1** theme fill color.

5. Increase the width of column B to **30** characters, and then wrap the text in the selected range.

6. Select the range **A4:B6**, and then add all borders around each of the selected cells.

7. Click cell **A7** to deselect the range. See Figure 2–5.

Figure 2–5   **Font and fill colors added to the Documentation sheet**

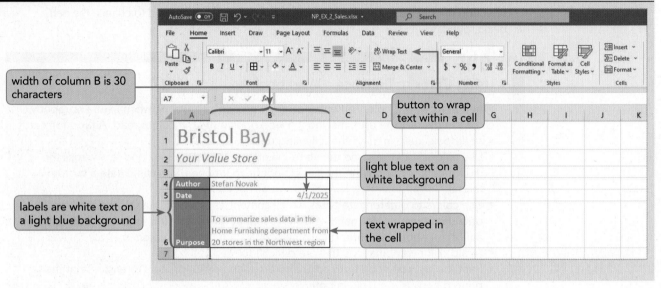

width of column B is 30 characters

button to wrap text within a cell

light blue text on a white background

labels are white text on a light blue background

text wrapped in the cell

Setting the Worksheet Tab Color

Fill colors can also be used with the sheet tabs. You can add the same tab color to sheets that share a common purpose to create a visual structure in the workbook. Stefan wants you to change the tab color of the Documentation sheet to gold.

To change the tab color of the Documentation sheet:

1. Right-click the **Documentation** sheet tab. A shortcut menu appears with options related to the sheet tab.

2. On the shortcut menu, point to **Tab Color** to display the palette of theme and standard colors.

3. In the Theme Colors section, click **Gold, Accent 4** (the eighth color in the first row). The Documentation sheet tab now has a gold fill. Because the Documentation sheet is the active sheet, its sheet tab shows a gold highlight.

4. Click the **Sales Report** tab to make it the active sheet. Now you can see the solid gold sheet tab color for the inactive Documentation sheet.

5. Click the **Documentation** sheet tab to make Documentation the active sheet.

Although you can change the sheet tab fill color, you cannot change its text color or text style.

Adding a Background Image

Another way to add visual interest to worksheets is with a background image. Many background images are based on textures such as granite, wood, or fibered paper. The image does not need to match the size of the worksheet. Instead, a smaller image can be repeated until it fills the entire sheet. Background images do not affect any cell's format or content. Fill colors added to cells appear on top of the image, covering that portion of the image.

Stefan provided the image that he wants you to use as the background of the Documentation sheet.

To add a background image to the Documentation sheet:

1. On the ribbon, click the **Page Layout** tab to display the page layout options.

2. In the Page Setup group, click the **Background** button. The Insert Pictures dialog box opens with options to search for an image from a file on your computer, from the Bing Image server, or on your OneDrive account.

3. Click the **From a file** option. The Sheet Background dialog box opens.

4. In the Sheet Background dialog box, navigate to the **Excel2 > Module** folder included with your Data Files, click the **Support_EX_2_Background.jpg** image file, and then click **Insert**. The image is added to the background of the Documentation sheet. See Figure 2–6.

Figure 2–6	Background image added to the Documentation sheet

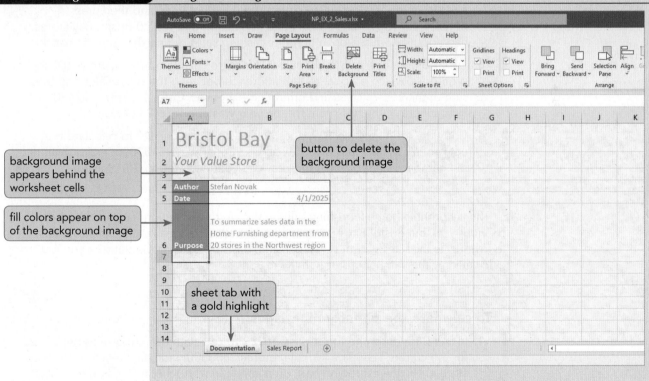

If you want to remove a background image from a worksheet, click the Delete Background button in the Page Setup group on the Page Layout tab.

You've completed the formatting the Documentation sheet. Next, you'll work on the Sales Report worksheet.

Using Functions and Formulas with Sales Data

In the Sales Report worksheet, you will format the data on the gross sales from each of Bristol Bay's 20 stores in the Northwest region. The worksheet is divided into two areas. The table at the bottom of the worksheet displays gross sales in the Home Furnishing department for the current year broken down by month and store. The section at the top of the worksheet compares sales from the current and previous year. Stefan has compiled the following sales data:

- **Gross Sales**—the total amount of sales incomes in the Home Furnishing department from the 20 stores in the Northwest region
- **Cost of Sales**—the cost to Bristol Bay for supplying the sales items in those 20 stores
- **Operating Expenses**—the cost of running the Home Furnishing department in those 20 stores
- **Net Profit/Loss**—the difference between the income from the gross sales and the total cost of sales and operating expenses
- **Items Sold**—the total number of home furnishing items sold by the 20 Bristol Bay stores

Stefan wants you to calculate these sales statistics for the 20 Bristol Bay stores in the Northwest region. First, you will calculate the gross sales from current year and the overall net profit and loss.

To calculate Bristol Bay's sales and profit/loss:

1. Click the **Sales Report** sheet tab to make the Sales Report worksheet active.

2. Click cell **C6**, type the formula **=SUM(C26:N45)** to calculate the total gross sales from the 20 Bristol Bay stores in the current year, and then press **ENTER**. Cell C6 displays 72676000, indicating that the 20 Bristol Bay stores had about $72.7 million in home furnishing sales during the current year.

3. In cell **C9**, enter the formula **=C6-(C7+C8)** to calculate the current year's net profit/loss, which is equal to the difference between the gross sales and the sum of the cost of sales and operating expenses. Cell C9 displays 5248000, indicating that the net profit for the year was about $5.25 million.

4. Copy the formula in cell **C9**, and then paste it into cell **D9** to calculate the net profit/loss for the previous year. Cell D9 displays 5151000, indicating that the company's net profit in the previous year was around $5.1 million.

The net profit in home furnishing sales in the Northwest region increased from the previous year, but Bristol Bay also opened a new store during that time. Stefan wants to investigate the sales statistics on a per-store basis by dividing the statistics you just calculated by the number of stores in the region.

To calculate the per-store statistics:

1. In cell **C15**, enter the formula **=C6/C22** to calculate the gross sales per store for the current year. The formula returns 3633800, indicating each Bristol Bay store in Northwest region had, on average, about $3.6 million in gross sales during the year.

2. In cell **C16**, enter the formula **=C7/C22** to calculate the cost of sales per store for the year. The formula returns the value 1078900, indicating each Bristol Bay store had a little more than $1 million in home furnishing sales cost.

▶ **3.** In cell **C17**, enter the formula **=C8/C22** to calculate the operating expenses per store for the year. The formula returns the value 2292500, indicating that annual operating expense of a typical store was about $2.3 million.

▶ **4.** In cell **C18**, enter the formula **=C9/C22** to calculate the net profit/loss per store for the year. The formula returns the value 262400, indicating that the net profit/loss in the Home Furnishing department of a typical Bristol Bay stores was $262,400.

▶ **5.** In cell **C20**, enter the formula **=C11/C22** to calculate the units sold per store for the year. The formula returns the value 70040, indicating that a typical store sold more than 70,000 units.

▶ **6.** Copy the formulas in the range **C15:C20** and paste them into the range **D15:D20**. The cell references in the formulas change to calculate the sales data for the previous year.

▶ **7.** Click cell **B4** to deselect the range. See Figure 2–7.

| Figure 2–7 | Overall and per-store sales |

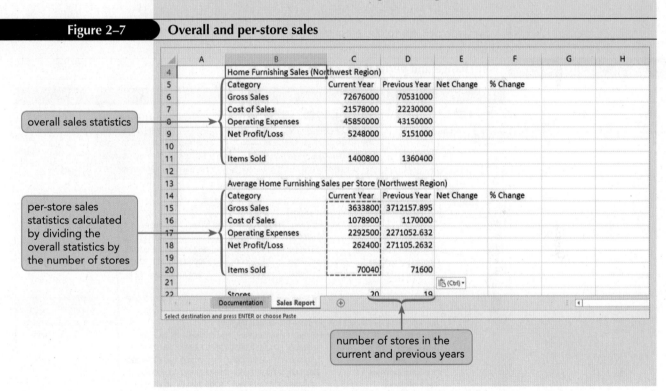

overall sales statistics

per-store sales statistics calculated by dividing the overall statistics by the number of stores

number of stores in the current and previous years

Stefan also wants to report how the company's sales and expenses have changed from the previous year to the current year. To do this, you will calculate the net change in the sales statistics as well as the percent change. The percent change is calculated using the following formula:

$$\text{percent change} = \frac{\text{current year value} - \text{previous year value}}{\text{previous year value}}$$

You will calculate the net change and percentage for all of the statistics in the Sales Report worksheet.

To calculate the net and percent changes:

1. In cell **E6**, enter the formula **=C6-D6** to calculate the difference in gross sales between the previous year and the current year. The formula returns 2145000, indicating that gross sales increased by about $2.15 million.

2. In cell F6, enter the formula =(C6-D6)/D6 to calculate the percent change in gross sales from the previous year to the current year. The formula returns 0.030412159, indicating an increase in gross sales of about 3.04%.

Next, you'll copy and paste the formulas in cells E6 and F6 to the rest of the sales data to calculate the net change and percent change from the previous year to the current year.

3. Select the range **E6:F6**, and then copy the selected range. The two formulas are copied to the Clipboard.

4. Select the nonadjacent range **E7:F9,E11:F11,E15:F18,E20:F20**, and then paste the formulas from the Clipboard into the selected range. The net and percent changes are calculated for the remaining sales data.

5. Click cell **A4** to deselect the range. See Figure 2–8.

> Be sure to include the parentheses as shown to calculate the percent change correctly.

Figure 2–8   **Net change and percent change in sales**

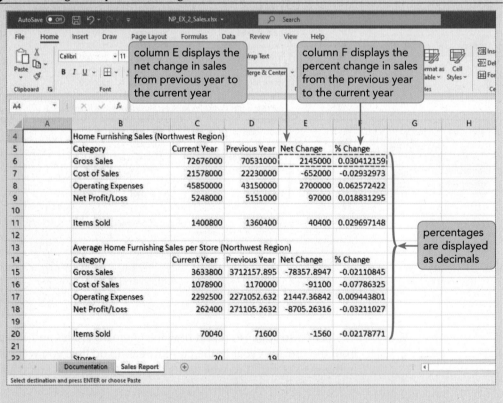

The bottom of the worksheet contains the home furnishing sales from each store during each month of the current year. You will use the SUM function to calculate the total gross sales for each store during the entire year, the total monthly sales of all 20 stores, and the total gross sales of all stores and months.

To calculate different subtotals of the gross sales:

▶ **1.** Scroll down and to the right, click cell **P25**, type **Yearly Totals** as the label, and then press **ENTER**. Cell P26 is the active cell.

▶ **2.** In cell **P26**, enter the formula =**SUM(C26:N26)** to calculate the total gross sales for the store located in Tacoma, Washington. Excel returns the value 3942000 indicating that the Tacoma store had total gross sales of $3.942 million in its Home Furnishing department during the current fiscal year.

▶ **3.** Copy the formula in cell **P26** to the range **P27:P45** to calculate the gross sales for all 20 Bristol Bay stores in the Northwest region.

Next, you will calculate the monthly gross sales across all stores.

▶ **4.** Click cell **B46**, enter **Monthly Totals** as the label, and then press **TAB**. Cell C46 is the active cell.

▶ **5.** Select the range **C46:N46**.

▶ **6.** On the Home tab, in the Editing group, click the **AutoSum** button to calculate the sum of the gross sales for each month. For example, the formula in cell N46 returns the value 7879000, indicating that across the 20 Northwest region stores, Bristol Bay had $7.879 million in gross sales from its Home Furnishing department in the month of December.

▶ **7.** Click cell **P46**, and then click the **AutoSum** button to insert the formula =SUM(P26:P45), and then press **ENTER**. This formula returns the value 72676000, the total gross sales for all Northwest stores for the entire year, matching the value shown earlier in cell C6.

▶ **8.** Click cell **P47** to deselect the range. See Figure 2–9.

Figure 2–9   **Gross sales by store and month**

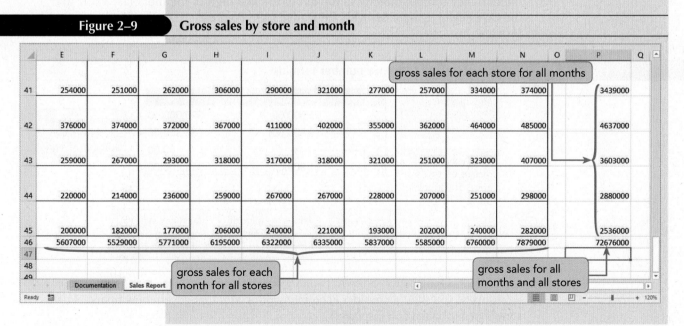

The Sales Report worksheet financial totals that are difficult to read in their current form. You can improve the readability of the data by adding number formats.

Formatting Numbers

You can make the financial figures in your workbooks easier to read by using commas to separate the thousands values. Other formatting options include setting the number of decimal places and using currency and percent symbols. Changing the number format does not affect the stored value, only how that value is displayed in the cell.

Applying Number Formats

Cells start out formatted with the **General format**, which, for the most part, displays numbers exactly as they are typed. If a value is calculated from a formula or function, the General format displays as many digits after the decimal point as will fit in the cell and rounds the last digit.

The General format is fine for small numbers, but some values require additional formatting to make the numbers easier to interpret. For example, you might want to:

- Change the number of digits displayed to the right of the decimal point
- Add commas to separate thousands in large numbers
- Include currency symbols to numbers to identify the monetary unit being used
- Identify percentages using the % symbol

Excel supports two monetary formats—Accounting and Currency. Both formats add thousands separators to the monetary values and display two digits to the right of the decimal point. The **Accounting format** places the currency symbol at the left edge of the column and displays negative numbers within parentheses and zero values with a dash. It also slightly indents the values from the right edge of the cell to allow room for parentheses around negative values. The **Currency format** places the currency symbol directly to the left of the first digit of the monetary value and displays negative numbers with a negative sign. Figure 2–10 compares the two formats.

Figure 2–10   Accounting and Currency number formats

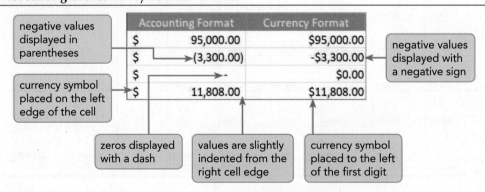

When choosing between the Accounting format and the Currency format for your worksheets, you should consider accounting principles that govern how financial data should be formatted and displayed.

Proskills

Written Communication: Formatting Monetary Values

Spreadsheets commonly include monetary values. To make these values simpler to read and comprehend, keep in mind the following guidelines when formatting the currency data in a worksheet:

- **Format for your audience.** For general financial reports, round values to the nearest hundred, thousand, or million. Investors are generally more interested in the big picture than in exact values. However, for accounting reports, accuracy is important and often legally required. So, for those reports, be sure to display the exact monetary value.

- **Use thousands separators.** Large strings of numbers can be challenging to read. For monetary values, use the thousands separator to make the amounts easier to comprehend.

- **Apply the Accounting format to columns of monetary values.** The Accounting format makes columns of numbers easier to read than the Currency format. Use the Currency format for individual cells that are not part of long columns of numbers.

- **Use only two currency symbols in a column of monetary values.** Standard accounting format displays one currency symbol with the first monetary value in the column and optionally displays a second currency symbol with the last value in that column. Use the Accounting format to fix the currency symbols, lining them up within the column.

Following these standard accounting principles will make your financial data easier to read both on the screen and in printouts.

Stefan wants you to format the gross sales values in the Accounting format so that they are easier to read.

To format the gross sales in the Accounting format:

1. Select the range **C6:E6** containing the gross sales for the current and previous year and the net change between the years.

2. On the Home tab, in the Number group, click the **Accounting Number Format** button $. The numbers are formatted in the Accounting format. You cannot see the format because the cells display ##########.

> **Tip**
>
> To choose a different currency symbol, click the Accounting Number Format arrow in the Number group on the Home tab and click a symbol.

The selected cells display ########## because the formatted numbers don't fit into the columns. One reason for this is that monetary values, by default, show both dollars and cents in the cell. However, you can increase or decrease the number of decimal places displayed in a cell. If you remove the cents value, the displayed values will be rounded to the nearest dollar so that a value such as 11.7 will be displayed as $12. Changing the number of decimal places displayed in a cell does not change the value stored in the cell.

Stefan suggests that you to hide the cents values in the report by decreasing the number of decimal places to zero.

To decrease the number of decimal places in the report:

1. Make sure the range **C6:E6** is still selected.

2. On the Home tab, in the Number group, click the **Decrease Decimal button** ⁰⁰⁄₀ twice. The cents are hidden for gross sales and the net change in sales.

3. Click cell **A3** to deselect the range. See Figure 2–11.

Figure 2–11 | **Formatted gross sales values**

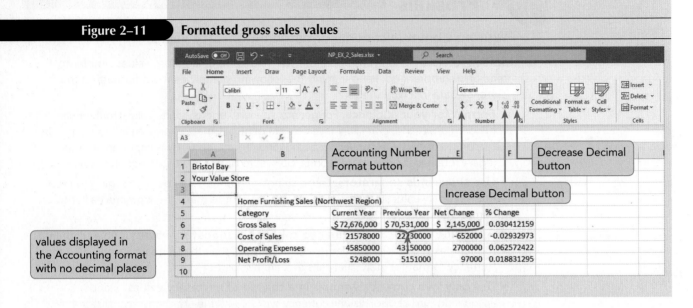

values displayed in the Accounting format with no decimal places

The Comma style is identical to the Accounting format except that it does not place a currency symbol on the left edge of the cell. The advantage of using the Comma style and the Accounting format together is that the numbers will be aligned in the column. Stefan asks you to apply the Comma style to the remaining sales statistics.

To apply the Comma style to a range of values:

1. Select the nonadjacent range **C7:E9,C11:E11** containing the sales figures for all stores in the current and previous year.

2. On the Home tab, in the Number group, click the **Comma Style** button 🔹. For some of the selected cells, the number is now too large to be displayed in the cell.

3. In the Number group, click the **Decrease Decimal** button twice to remove two decimal places. Digits to the right of the decimal point are hidden for all selected cells, and all of the numbers are now visible.

4. Click cell **A3** to deselect the range. See Figure 2–12.

Figure 2–12 | **Formatted sales values**

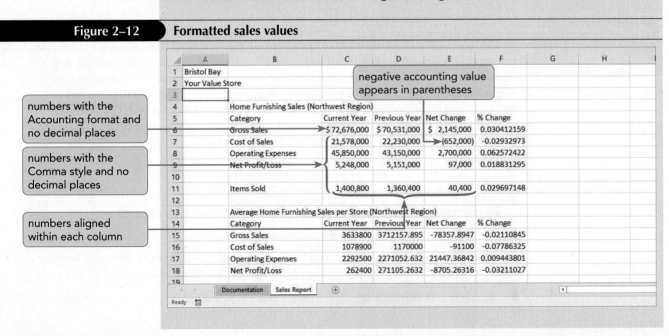

numbers with the Accounting format and no decimal places

numbers with the Comma style and no decimal places

numbers aligned within each column

Notice that the net change value in cell E7 is displayed as (652,000) with the parentheses indicating a negative net change so that the cost of sales decreased from the previous year into the current year.

Displaying Percentages

The Percent style formats numbers as percentages with no decimal places so that a number such as 0.124 appears as 12%. You can always change how many decimal places are displayed in the cell if that is important to show with your data.

Stefan wants you to display the percent change in sales and expenses between the previous year and the current year using the % symbol.

To format the percent change values as percentages:

1. Select the nonadjacent range **F6:F9,F11** containing the percent change values.

2. On the Home tab, in the Number group, click the **Percent Style** button % (or press **CTRL+SHIFT+%**). The values are displayed as percentages with no decimal places.

3. In the Number group, click the **Increase Decimal** button twice. The displayed number includes two decimal places.

4. Click cell **A3** to deselect the range. See Figure 2–13.

| Figure 2–13 | Formatted percent change values |

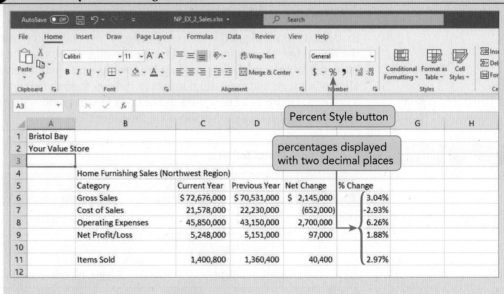

With the data reformatted, the worksheet clearly shows that the gross sales in home furnishing for the 20 Bristol Bay stores increased from the previous year to the current year by 3.04%, but the net profit on those sales increased by only 1.88% due to the large increase of 6.26% in operating expenses. This type of information is very important to the company executives planning for the upcoming year.

Formatting Dates and Times

Because Excel stores dates and times as numbers and not as text, you can apply different date formats without affecting the underlying date and time value. The abbreviated format, *mm/dd/yyyy*, entered in the Documentation sheet is referred to as the **Short Date format**. The **Long Date format** displays the day of the week and the full month name in addition to the day of the month and the year. Other built-in formats include formats for displaying time values in 12- or 24-hour time format.

Stefan asks you to change the date in the Documentation sheet to the Long Date format.

> **To format the date in the Long Date format:**
>
> **1.** Go to the **Documentation** sheet, and then select cell **B5**.
>
> **2.** On the Home tab, in the Number group, click the **Number Format arrow** to display a list of number formats, and then click **Long Date**. The date is displayed with the weekday name, month name, day, and year.

Tip

To view the underlying date and time value, apply the General format or display the formulas.

Notice that the date in the formula bar did not change because you changed only the display format, not the date value. Next, you will learn about other options for formatting cell content.

Formatting Worksheet Cells

You can format the appearance of individual cells by modifying the alignment of text within the cell, indenting cell text, or adding borders of different styles and colors.

Aligning Cell Content

By default, text is aligned with the left edge of the cell, and numbers are aligned with the right edge. You might want to change the alignment to make the text and numbers more readable or visually appealing. In general, you should center column titles, left-align other text, and right-align numbers to keep their decimal places lined up within a column. Figure 2–14 describes the buttons located in the Alignment group on the Home tab that you use to set these alignment options.

Figure 2–14   **Alignment group buttons**

Button	Name	Description
	Top Align	Aligns the cell content with the cell's top edge
	Middle Align	Vertically centers the cell content within the cell
	Bottom Align	Aligns the cell content with the cell's bottom edge
	Align Left	Aligns the cell content with the cell's left edge
	Align Center	Horizontally centers the cell content within the cell
	Align Right	Aligns the cell content with the cell's right edge
	Decrease Indent	Decreases the size of the indentation used in the cell
	Increase Indent	Increases the size of the indentation used in the cell
	Orientation	Rotates the cell content to any angle within the cell
	Wrap Text	Forces the cell text to wrap within the cell borders
	Merge & Center	Merges the selected cells into a single cell

The date in the Documentation sheet is right-aligned in cell B5 because Excel treats dates and times as numbers. Stefan wants you to left-align the date from the Documentation sheet and center the column titles in the Sales Report worksheet.

To left-align the date and center the column titles:

▶ **1.** In the Documentation sheet, make sure cell **B5** is still selected.

▶ **2.** On the Home tab, in the Alignment group, click the **Align Left** button ☰. The date shifts to the left edge of the cell.

▶ **3.** Go to the **Sales Report** worksheet.

▶ **4.** Select the range **C5:F5** containing the column titles.

▶ **5.** In the Alignment group, click the **Center** button ☰. The column titles are centered in the cells.

Indenting Cell Content

Sometimes you want a cell's content moved a few spaces from the cell's left edge. This is particularly useful to create subsections in a worksheet or to set off some entries from others. You can increase the indent to shift the contents of a cell away from the left edge of the cell, or you can decrease the indent to shift a cell's contents closer to the left edge of the cell.

Stefan wants you to indent the Cost of Sales and Operating Expenses labels in the sales statistics table from the other labels because they represent expenses to the company.

To indent the expense categories:

▶ **1.** Select the range **B7:B8** containing the expense categories.

▶ **2.** On the Home tab, in the Alignment group, click the **Increase Indent** button ☷ twice. Each label indents two spaces in its cell.

Another way to make financial data easier to read and interpret is with borders.

Adding Borders to Cells

Common accounting practices provide guidelines on when to add borders to cells. In general, a single black border should appear above a subtotal, a single bottom border should be added below a calculated number, and a double black bottom border should appear below the total.

Stefan wants you to follow common accounting practices in the Sales Report worksheet. You will add borders below the column titles and below the gross sales values. You will add a top border to the net profit/loss values and a top and bottom border to the Items Sold row.

To add borders to the sales statistics data:

▶ **1.** Select the range **B5:F5** containing the table headings.

▶ **2.** On the Home tab, in the Font group, click the **Borders arrow** ⊞▾, and then click **Bottom Border**. A border is added below the column titles.

▶ **3.** Select the range **B6:F6** containing the gross sales amounts.

▶ **4.** In the Font group, click the **Bottom Border** button ⊞. A border is added below the selected gross sales amounts.

▶ **5.** Select the range **B9:F9**, click the **Borders arrow** ⊞ ˅, and then click **Top Border**. A border is added above the net profit/loss amounts.

The Items Sold row does not contain monetary values as the other rows do. You will distinguish this row by adding a top and bottom border.

▶ **6.** Select the range **B11:F11**, click the **Borders arrow** ⊞ ˅, and then click **Top and Bottom Border**.

▶ **7.** Click cell **A3** to deselect the range. See Figure 2–15.

| Figure 2–15 | Borders, indents, and alignment added to cells |

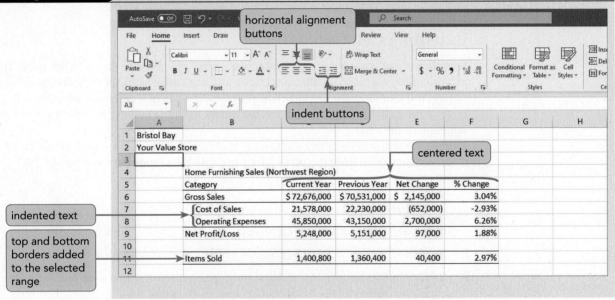

You can apply multiple formats to the same cell to create the look that best fits the data. For example, one cell might be formatted with a number format, alignments, borders, indents, fonts, font sizes, and so on. The monthly sales data needs to be formatted with number styles, alignments, indents, and borders. You'll add these formats now.

To format the monthly sales data:

▶ **1.** Select the range **C26:P46** containing the monthly gross sales by store.

▶ **2.** On the Home tab, in the Number group, click the **Comma Style** button ❯ to add the thousands separator to the values.

▶ **3.** In the Number group, click the **Decrease Decimal** button twice to hide the cents from the sales results.

▶ **4.** In the Alignment group, click the **Top Align** button to align the sales numbers with the top of each cell.

▶ **5.** Select the nonadjacent range **C25:N25,P25** containing the labels for the month abbreviations and the Yearly Totals column.

▶ **6.** In the Alignment group, click the **Center** button to center the column labels.

▶ **7.** Select the range **B26:B45** containing the store addresses.

▶ **8.** Reduce the font size of the store addresses to **9** points.

▶ **9.** In the Alignment group, click the **Increase Indent** button ⊞ twice to indent the store addresses.

▶ **10.** Select the range **B46:N46** containing the monthly totals.

▶ **11.** In the Font group, click the **Borders arrow** ⊞⌄, and then click **All Borders** to add borders around each monthly totals cell.

▶ **12.** Select the range **P25:P46** containing the annual totals for each restaurant, and then click the **All Borders** button ⊞ to add borders around each store total.

▶ **13.** Click cell **A23** to deselect the range. See Figure 2–16.

Figure 2–16	Formatted monthly gross sales

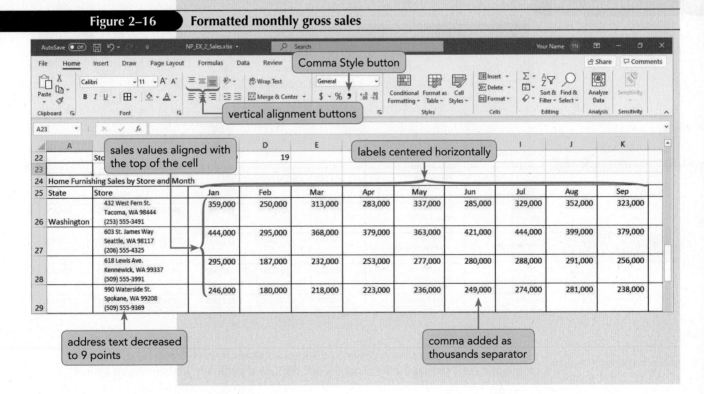

Merging Cells

You can merge, or combine, several cells into one cell. A merged cell contains two or more cells with a single cell reference. When you merge cells, only the content from the upper-left cell in the range is retained. The cell reference for the merged cell is the upper-left cell reference. So, if you merge cells A1 and A2, the merged cell reference is cell A1. After you merge cells, you can align the content within the merged cell. The Merge & Center button in the Alignment group on the Home tab includes the following options:

- **Merge & Center**—merges the range into one cell and horizontally centers the content
- **Merge Across**—merges each row in the selected range across the columns in the range
- **Merge Cells**—merges the range into a single cell but does not horizontally center the cell content
- **Unmerge Cells**—reverses a merge, returning the merged cell to a range of individual cells

Column A of the monthly sales data lists the states in Bristol Bay's Northwest region. You'll merge the cells for each state name into a single cell.

To merge the state name cells:

1. Select the range **A26:A34** containing the cells for the Washington stores. You will merge these cells into a single cell.

2. On the Home tab, in the Alignment group, click the **Merge & Center** button. The range A26:A34 merges into one cell with the cell reference A26, and the text is centered and bottom-aligned within the cell.

3. Select the range **A35:A42**, and then click the **Merge & Center** button. The cells for stores in the state of Oregon are merged and centered.

4. Select the range **A43:A45**, and then merge and center the cells for the Idaho stores. See Figure 2–17.

Figure 2–17	Merged cells

range A35:A42 merged into a single cell, cell A35

range A43:A45 merged into a single cell, cell A43

Merge & Center button

	A	B	C	D	E	F	G	H
41		117 Clyde St. Beaverton, OR 97006 (503) 555-2915	315,000	198,000	254,000	251,000	262,000	306,000
42	Oregon	406 Maple Ln. Portland, OR 97202 (503) 555-1881	408,000	261,000	376,000	374,000	372,000	367,000
43		66 Mango St. Boise, ID 83704 (208) 555-5417	309,000	220,000	259,000	267,000	293,000	318,000
44		758 Kent Ave. Idaho Falls, ID 83402 (208) 555-9701	258,000	175,000	220,000	214,000	236,000	259,000
45	Idaho	95 Laramie Way Nampa, ID 83651 (208) 555-1026	235,000	158,000	200,000	182,000	177,000	206,000
46		Monthly Totals	6,470,000	4,386,000	5,607,000	5,529,000	5,771,000	6,195,000

The merged cells make it easier to distinguish stores in each state. Next, you will rotate the cells so that the state names are displayed vertically in the merged cells.

Rotating Cell Contents

Text and numbers are displayed horizontally within cells. However, you can rotate cell text to any angle to save space or to provide visual interest to a worksheet. The state names at the bottom of the merged cells would look better and take up less room if they were rotated vertically within their cells. Stefan asks you to rotate the state names.

To rotate the state names:

1. Select the merged cell **A26**.

2. On the Home tab, in the Alignment group, click the **Orientation** button to display a list of rotation options, and then click **Rotate Text Up**. The state name rotates 90 degrees counterclockwise.

> **3.** In the Alignment group, click the **Middle Align** button ☰ to vertically center the rotated text in the merged cell.

> **4.** Repeat Steps 2 and 3 for the merged contents in cells A35 and A43.

> **5.** Reduce the width of column A to **7** characters because the rotated state names take up less horizontal space.

> **6.** Select cell **A46**. See Figure 2–18.

| Figure 2–18 | Rotated cell content |

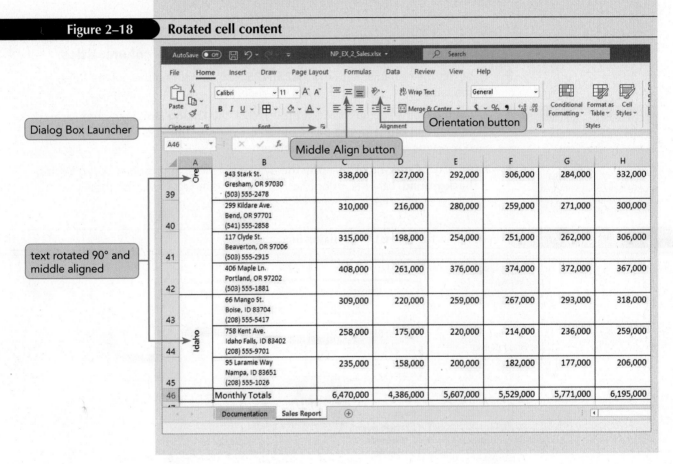

In addition to using the ribbon to apply formatting to a worksheet, you can also use the Format Cells dialog box to apply formatting.

Exploring the Format Cells Dialog Box

The buttons on the Home tab provide quick access to the most commonly used formatting choices. For more options, you can use the Format Cells dialog box. You can apply the formats in this dialog box to the selected worksheet cells. The Format Cells dialog box has six tabs, each focusing on a different set of formatting options, as described below:

- **Number**—options for formatting the appearance of numbers, including dates and numbers treated as text such as telephone or Social Security numbers
- **Alignment**—options for how data is aligned within a cell
- **Font**—options for selecting font types, sizes, styles, and other formatting attributes such as underlining and font colors

- **Border**—options for adding and removing cell borders as well as selecting a line style and color
- **Fill**—options for creating and applying background colors and patterns to cells
- **Protection**—options for locking or hiding cells to prevent other users from modifying their contents

Although you have applied many of these formats from the Home tab, the Format Cells dialog box presents them in a different way and provides more choices. You will use the Font and Fill tabs to format the column titles with a white font on a green background.

To use the Format Cells dialog box to format the column titles:

1. Select the nonadjacent range **A25:N25,P25** containing the column titles for the table.

Tip

Clicking the Dialog Box Launcher in the Font, Alignment, or Number group opens the Format Cells dialog box with that tab displayed.

2. On the Home tab, in the Font group, click the **Dialog Box Launcher** located to the right of the group name (refer to Figure 2–18). The Format Cells dialog box opens with the Font tab displayed.

3. Click the **Color** box to display the available colors, and then click the **White, Background 1** theme color (the first color in the first row). The font is set to white. See Figure 2–19.

Figure 2–19   **Font tab in the Format Cells dialog box**

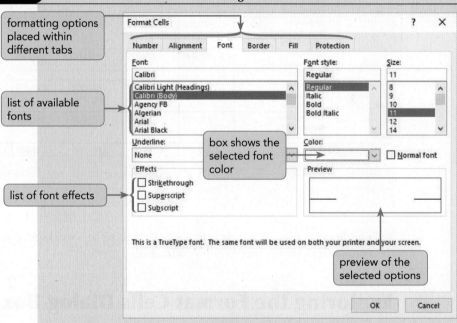

4. Click the **Fill** tab to display background options.

5. In the Background Color section, click the **Green, Accent 6** theme color (the last color in the first row). The background is set to green, as previewed in the Sample box.

6. Click **OK**. The dialog box closes, and the font and fill options you selected are applied to the selected cells.

You will also use the Format Cells dialog box to change the appearance of the row titles. You'll format them to be displayed in a larger white font on a gold background.

To format the row titles:

▶ **1.** Select the range **A26:A45** containing the rotated state names.

▶ **2.** Right-click the selected range, and then click **Format Cells** on the shortcut menu. The Format Cells dialog box opens with the last tab used displayed—in this case, the Fill tab.

▶ **3.** In the Background Color section, click the **Gold, Accent 4** theme color (the eighth color in the first row). Its preview is shown in the Sample box.

▶ **4.** Click the **Font** tab to display the font formatting options.

▶ **5.** Click the **Color** box, and then click the **White, Background 1** theme color to set the font color to white.

▶ **6.** In the Size box, click **16** to set the font size to 16 points.

▶ **7.** In the Font style box, click **Bold** to change the font to boldface.

▶ **8.** Click **OK**. The dialog box closes, and the font and fill formats are applied to the state names.

▶ **9.** Scroll up and click cell **A23** to deselect the range. See Figure 2–20.

Figure 2–20   **Formatted row and column titles**

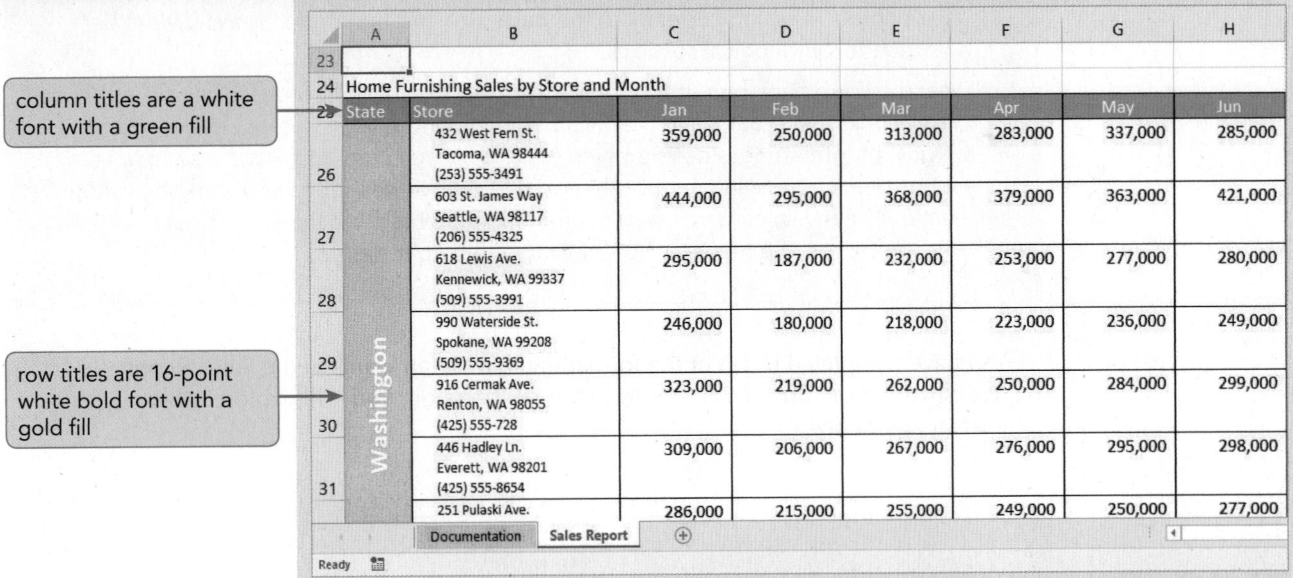

column titles are a white font with a green fill

row titles are 16-point white bold font with a gold fill

▶ **10.** Save the workbook.

With the formats you have added to the Sales Report worksheet, readers will be able to more easily read and interpret the large table of store sales.

Proskills

Written Communication: Formatting Workbooks for Readability and Appeal

Designing a workbook requires the same care as designing any written document or report. A well-formatted workbook is easy to read and establishes a sense of professionalism with readers. You can improve the readability of your worksheets with the following guidelines:

- **Clearly identify each worksheet's purpose.** Include column or row titles and a descriptive sheet name.

- **Include only one or two topics on each worksheet.** Don't crowd individual worksheets with too much information. Place extra topics on separate sheets. Readers should be able to interpret each worksheet with a minimal amount of horizontal and vertical scrolling.

- **Put worksheets with the most important information first in the workbook.** Place worksheets summarizing your findings near the front of the workbook. Place worksheets with detailed and involved analysis near the end as an appendix.

- **Use consistent formatting throughout the workbook.** If negative values appear in red on one worksheet, format them in the same way on all sheets. Also, be consistent in the use of thousands separators, decimal places, and percentages.

- **Pay attention to the format of the printed workbook.** Make sure your printouts are legible with informative headers and footers. Check that the content of the printout is scaled correctly to the page size and that page breaks divide the information into logical sections.

Excel provides many formatting tools. However, too much formatting can be intrusive, overwhelming your data, and making the document difficult to read. Remember that the goal of formatting is not simply to make a "pretty workbook" but also to accentuate important trends and relationships in the data. A well-formatted workbook should seamlessly convey information to the reader. If the reader is thinking about how your workbook looks, the reader is not thinking about your data.

You have completed much of the formatting that Stefan wants in the Sales Report worksheet for the Bristol Bay stores. In the next session, you will explore other formatting options.

Review

Session 2.1 Quick Check

1. What is the difference between a serif font and a sans serif font?
2. What is the difference between theme colors and standard colors?
3. A cell containing a number displays ######. Why does this occur, and what can you do to fix it?
4. How do you change the color of a worksheet tab?
5. What is the General format?
6. Describe the differences between the Accounting format and the Currency format.
7. The range B3:B13 is merged into a single cell. What is its cell reference?
8. How do you format text so that it is set vertically within the cell?

1. Serif has "feet" lines, and sans serif does not

2. theme is for overall workbook less options, and standard is the opposite

3. number doesn't fit in coloum.

4. tab color

5. defult number format

6. Curency format aligns the curency sign at left edge of cell value, Accounting does the same but near border

7. B3

8. ?

Session 2.2 Visual Overview:

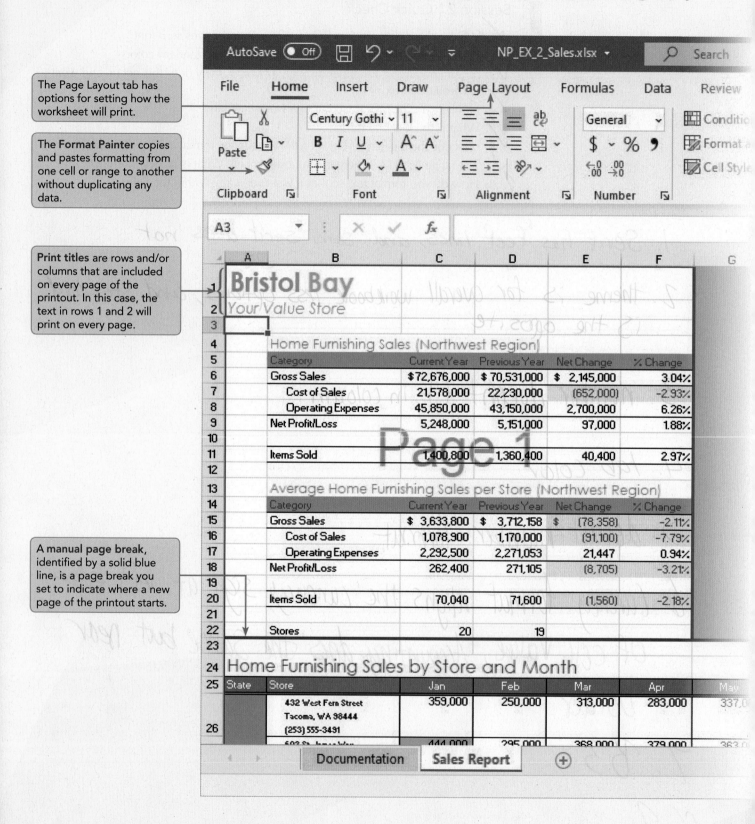

The Page Layout tab has options for setting how the worksheet will print.

The Format Painter copies and pastes formatting from one cell or range to another without duplicating any data.

Print titles are rows and/or columns that are included on every page of the printout. In this case, the text in rows 1 and 2 will print on every page.

A manual page break, identified by a solid blue line, is a page break you set to indicate where a new page of the printout starts.

Designing a Printout

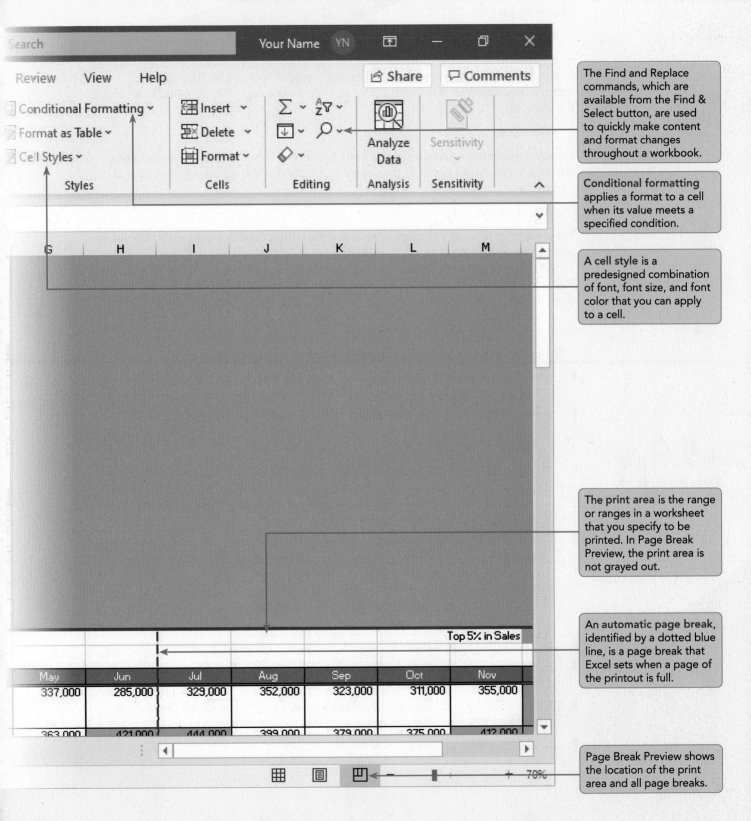

The Find and Replace commands, which are available from the Find & Select button, are used to quickly make content and format changes throughout a workbook.

Conditional formatting applies a format to a cell when its value meets a specified condition.

A cell style is a predesigned combination of font, font size, and font color that you can apply to a cell.

The print area is the range or ranges in a worksheet that you specify to be printed. In Page Break Preview, the print area is not grayed out.

An automatic page break, identified by a dotted blue line, is a page break that Excel sets when a page of the printout is full.

Page Break Preview shows the location of the print area and all page breaks.

Calculating Averages

The **AVERAGE function** calculates the average value from a collection of numbers. It has the syntax

    AVERAGE(*number1*,[*number2*],[*number3*],...)

where ***number1***, *number2*, *number3*, and so forth are either numbers or cell references to the cells or a range where the numbers are stored. For example, the following formula uses the AVERAGE function to calculate the average of 1, 2, 5, and 8, returning the value 4:

    =AVERAGE(1,2,5,8)

However, functions usually reference cells containing values entered in a worksheet. So, if the range A1:A4 contains the values 1, 2, 5, and 8, the following formula also returns the value 4:

    =AVERAGE(A1:A4)

The advantage of using cell references is that the values used in the function are visible and can be easily edited.

Stefan wants you to calculate the average monthly sales for each of the 20 Bristol Bay stores in the Northwest Region. You will use the AVERAGE function to calculate these values.

To calculate the average monthly sales for each store:

▶ **1.** If you took a break after the previous session, make sure the NP_EX_2_Sales.xslx workbook is open and the Sales Report worksheet is active.

▶ **2.** In cell **R25**, enter **Store Average** as the column title. The cell is automatically formatted with a white font color and green fill, matching the other column titles.

▶ **3.** In cell **R26**, enter the formula **=AVERAGE(C26:N26)** to calculate the average of the monthly gross sales values in the range C26:N26. The formula returns the value 328,500, which is the average monthly gross sales in home furnishing for the store in Tacoma, Washington.

▶ **4.** Copy the formula in cell **R26**, and then paste the copied formula in the range **R27:R46** to calculate the average monthly gross sales for each of the remaining Bristol Bay stores as well as the average monthly sales from all stores. The average monthly gross sales for individual stores range from $211,333 to $397,417. The monthly gross sales in home furnishing from all 20 stores in the Northwest region is $6,056,333.

▶ **5.** Select the range **R26:R46**. You will format this range of sales statistics.

▶ **6.** On the Home tab, in the Alignment group, click the **Top Align** button ⬒ to align each average value with the top edge of its cell.

▶ **7.** In the Font group, click the **Borders arrow** ⊞▾, then click **All Borders** to add borders around every cell in the selected range.

▶ **8.** Click cell **R26** to deselect the range. See Figure 2–21.

Figure 2–21 **Average sales results**

AVERAGE function used to calculate the average monthly sales

average monthly gross sales for each store

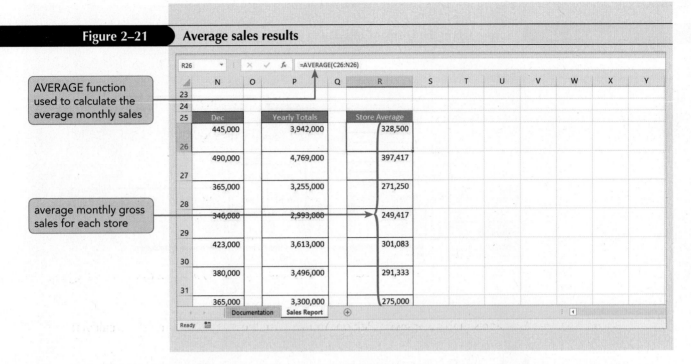

With so many values in the data, Stefan wants you to insert double borders around the sales values for each state. The Border tab in the Format Cells dialog box provides options for changing the border style and color and placement.

To add a double border to the state results:

1. Select the range **A26:N34** containing the Washington monthly gross sales totals.

2. Right-click the selection, click **Format Cells** on the shortcut menu to open the Format Cells dialog box, and then click the **Border** tab.

3. In the Line section, click the **double line** in the lower-right corner of the Style box.

4. In the Presets section, click the **Outline** option. The double border appears around the selected cells in the Border preview. See Figure 2–22.

Figure 2–22 **Border tab in the Format Cells dialog box**

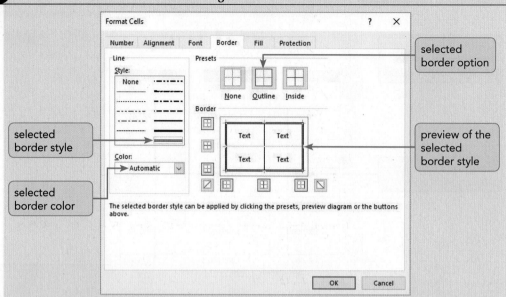

selected border option

selected border style

selected border color

preview of the selected border style

5. Click **OK**. The selected border is applied to the Washington monthly sales.

6. Repeat Steps 1 through 5 to apply double borders to the ranges **A35:N42** and **A43:N45**.

7. Click cell **A48** to deselect the range. See Figure 2–23.

Figure 2–23 **Worksheet with font, fill, and border formatting**

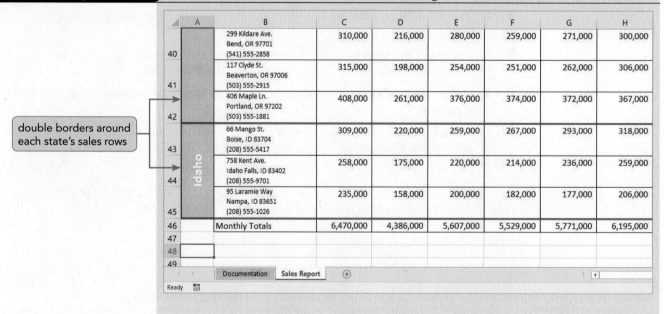

double borders around each state's sales rows

	A	B	C	D	E	F	G	H
40		299 Kildare Ave. Bend, OR 97701 (541) 555-2858	310,000	216,000	280,000	259,000	271,000	300,000
41		117 Clyde St. Beaverton, OR 97006 (503) 555-2915	315,000	198,000	254,000	251,000	262,000	306,000
42		406 Maple Ln. Portland, OR 97202 (503) 555-1881	408,000	261,000	376,000	374,000	372,000	367,000
43	Idaho	66 Mango St. Boise, ID 83704 (208) 555-5417	309,000	220,000	259,000	267,000	293,000	318,000
44		758 Kent Ave. Idaho Falls, ID 83402 (208) 555-9701	258,000	175,000	220,000	214,000	236,000	259,000
45		95 Laramie Way Nampa, ID 83651 (208) 555-1026	235,000	158,000	200,000	182,000	177,000	206,000
46		Monthly Totals	6,470,000	4,386,000	5,607,000	5,529,000	5,771,000	6,195,000
47								
48								
49								

Documentation Sales Report +

Ready

Applying Cell Styles

Cells throughout a workbook often store the same type of data. For example, a cell displaying the sheet title might appear on each worksheet, or cells containing totals and averages might appear several times within a range of financial data. It is good design practice to apply the same formatting to cells that contain the same type of data.

One way to ensure that similar data is displayed consistently is with cell styles. A **cell style** is a collection of formatting options—such as a specified font, font size, font styles, font color, fill color, and borders—that you can apply to cells. You can use the cell styles that come with Excel to format your workbooks. For example, you can use the built-in Heading 1 cell style to display sheet titles in a bold, blue-gray, 15-point Calibri font with no fill color and a blue bottom border. You can also create your own styles for each workbook.

All cell styles are listed in the Cell Styles gallery, which you access on the Home tab in the Styles group. The Cell Styles gallery also includes Accounting, Comma, and Percent number format styles that you already applied to the Sales Report worksheet using buttons in the Number group on the Home tab.

Reference

Applying a Cell Style

- Select the cell or range to which you want to apply a cell style.
- On the Home tab, in the Styles group, click the Cell Styles button.
- Point to each cell style in the Cell Styles gallery to see a Live Preview of that cell style on the selected cell or range.
- Click the cell style you want to apply to the selected cell or range.

Stefan wants you to add more color and visual interest to the Sales Report worksheet using cell styles in the Cell Styles gallery.

To apply cell styles to the Sales Report worksheet:

1. Scroll up and click cell **B4** containing the text "Home Furnishing Sales (Northwest Region)."

2. On the Home tab, in the Styles group, click the **Cell Styles** button. The Cell Styles gallery opens.

3. Point to the **Heading 1** cell style in the Titles and Headings section. Live Preview shows cell B4 in a 15-point, bold font with a solid blue bottom border. See Figure 2–24.

Figure 2–24   **Cell Styles gallery**

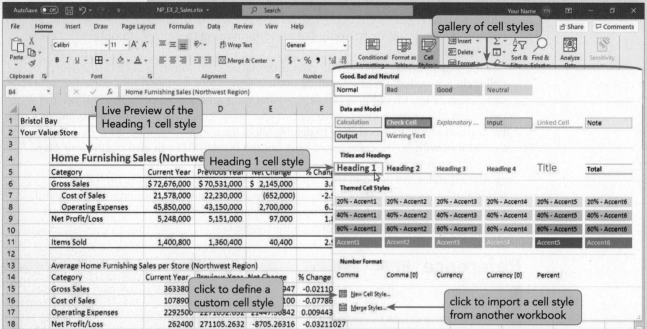

4. Move the pointer over different styles in the Cell Styles gallery to see cell B4 with a Live Preview of each cell style.

5. Click the **Title** cell style. The Title cell style—18-point, Blue-Gray, Text 2 Calibri Light font—is applied to cell B4.

6. Select the range **B5:F5** containing the column titles for the Sales Statistics data.

7. In the Styles group, click the **Cell Styles** button, and then click the **Accent4** cell style in the Themed Cell Styles section of the Cell Styles gallery.

8. Click cell **A24** containing the text "Home Furnishing Sales by Store and Month," and then apply the **Title** cell style to the cell.

9. Click cell **A3**. See Figure 2–25.

Figure 2–25   **Cell styles applied to the worksheet**

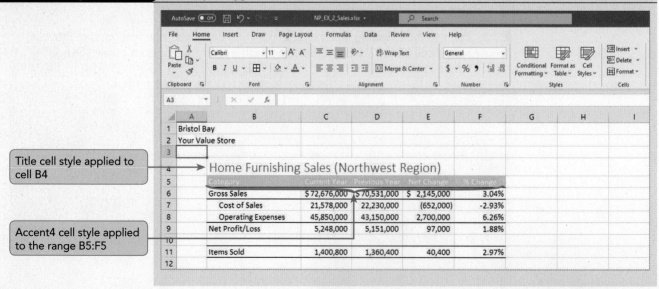

To remove all styles and formats, apply the Normal cell style to a selected cell or cell range.

Creating a Custom Cell Style

When you create a custom cell style, you select the font, font size, font styles, alignment, number format, borders, and fill you want to include in that cell style. You can base a new cell style on an existing cell style or on formatting that you applied to a cell. The custom cell style will then appear in the Cell Style gallery so you can apply it to any cell in your worksheet.

Stefan suggests that you create a custom cell style named "Bristol Bay Title" based on the Title cell style applied to cell B4. He wants you to reduce the font size and change the font color for the custom cell style.

To create the Bristol Bay Title custom cell style:

1. Click cell **B4** to select it. The Title cell style is applied to this cell.

2. Change the font size to **14** points and the font color to the **Blue, Accent 5** theme color (the ninth color in the first row).

3. On the Home tab, in the Styles group, click the **Cell Styles** button to display the Cell Styles gallery.

4. At the bottom of the Cell Styles gallery, click **New Cell Style** to open the Style dialog box.

5. In the Style name box, type **Bristol Bay Title** as name of the custom cell style. See Figure 2–26.

> **Tip**
>
> To apply only certain formatting options, click the check boxes of the format categories you want.

Figure 2–26   Style dialog box

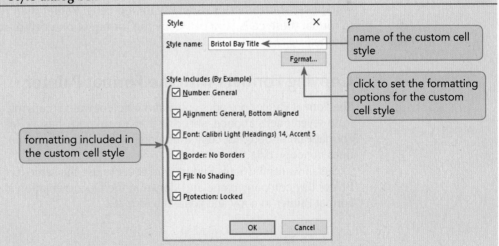

6. Click **OK**. The cell style applied to cell B4 is saved as the Bristol Bay Title custom cell style.

7. Click the **Cell Styles** button to open the Cell Styles gallery, and verify that the Bristol Bay Title custom cell style has been added to the Custom section at the top of the gallery.

8. Press **ESC** to close the Cell Styles gallery.

If you want to change the formatting included in a custom cell style, right-click the name of the custom cell style in the Cell Styles gallery and then click Modify on the shortcut menu. You can then change the formatting options specified in the Style dialog box.

Merging Custom Cell Styles

Custom cell styles are created in the current workbook. However, you can copy custom cell styles from one workbook to another so that you can use the same cell styles in multiple workbooks without recreating those cell styles. This is especially useful when a company or department wants to easily apply consistent formatting in all its workbooks.

Use the following steps to copy custom cell styles from one workbook to another:

1. Open the workbook containing the custom cell styles (the source workbook).
2. Open the workbook you want to copy the cell styles to (the destination workbook).
3. In the destination workbook, open the Cell Styles gallery, and then click Merge Styles at the bottom of the gallery.
4. Select the source workbook containing the custom cell styles, and then click OK.

All of the custom cell styles from the source workbook are copied into the destination workbook. Keep in mind that if you later modify a custom cell style in the source workbook, those changes will not appear in the destination workbook until you repeat the merge process.

Another way of repeating the same cell formats across a workbook is by copying and pasting.

Copying and Pasting Formats

Large workbooks often use the same formatting on similar data throughout the workbook, sometimes in widely scattered cells. Rather than repeating the same steps to format these cells, you can copy the format of one cell or range and paste it to another.

Copying Formats with the Format Painter

The Format Painter provides a fast and efficient way of copying and pasting formats from several cells at once, ensuring that a workbook has a consistent look and feel. The Format Painter does not copy formatting applied to selected text within a cell, and it does not copy data.

Stefan wants the Sales Report worksheet to use the same formats you applied to the Bristol Bay company name and slogan in the Documentation sheet. You will use the Format Painter to copy and paste the formats.

To use the Format Painter to copy and paste a format:

1. Go to the **Documentation** worksheet, and then select the range **A1:A2**.

2. On the Home tab, in the Clipboard group, click the **Format Painter** button. The formats from the selected cells are copied to the Clipboard, a flashing border appears around the selected range, and the pointer changes to the Format Painter pointer for cells ⊕🖌.

3. Go to the **Sales Report** worksheet, and then click cell **A1**. The formatting from the range A1:A2 in the Documentation worksheet is applied to the range A1:A2 in the Sales Report worksheet.

Tip

To paste the same format multiple times, double-click the Format Painter button. Click the button again or press ESC to turn it off.

Notice that green font color you applied to the text selection "Bay" was not included in the pasted formats because the Format Painter does not work with formats applied to text strings within cells.

4. Double-click cell **A1** to enter Edit mode, select **Bay**, and then change the font color to the **Light Green** standard color. The format for the company title now matches the company title in the Documentation sheet.

5. Press **ENTER** to exit Edit mode and select cell A2.

You can use the Format Painter to copy all formats within a selected range and then apply those formats to another range that has the same size and shape by clicking the upper-left cell of the range. Stefan wants you to copy all the formats that you applied to the Sales Statistics data to the sales statistics per store data.

To copy and paste multiple formats in the sales statistics data:

Tip

If you paste formats in a bigger range than the range you copied, Format Painter will repeat the copied formats to fill the pasted range.

1. Select the range **B4:F11** in the Sales Report worksheet.

2. On the Home tab, in the Clipboard group, click the **Format Painter** button.

3. Click cell **B13**. The number formats, cell borders, fonts, and fill colors are pasted in the range B13:F20.

4. Click cell **A21**. See Figure 2–27.

Figure 2–27	Formats copied and pasted between ranges

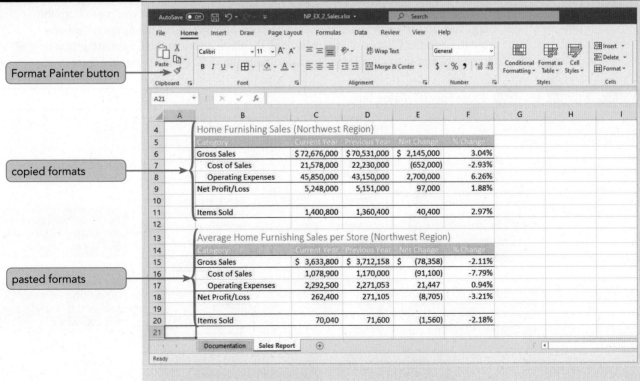

Copying Formats with the Paste Options Button

Another way to copy and paste formats is with the Paste Options button 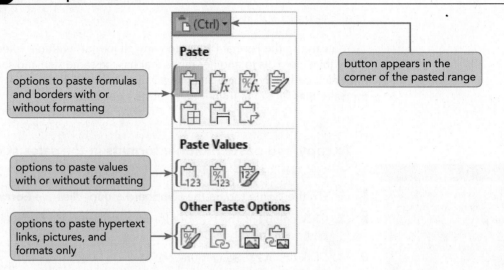(Ctrl) ▾, which provides options for pasting only values, only formats, or some combination of values and formats. Each time you paste, the Paste Options button appears in the lower-right corner of the pasted cell or range. You click the Paste Options button to open a list of pasting options, shown in Figure 2–28, such as pasting only the values or only the formatting.

Figure 2–28   Paste Options button

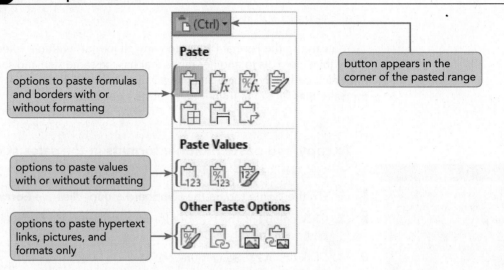

- options to paste formulas and borders with or without formatting
- options to paste values with or without formatting
- options to paste hypertext links, pictures, and formats only
- button appears in the corner of the pasted range

Copying Formats with Paste Special

The Paste Special command provides another way to control what you paste from the Clipboard. To use Paste Special, select and copy a range, select the range where you want to paste the Clipboard contents, click the Paste arrow in the Clipboard group on the Home tab, and then click Paste Special to open the dialog box shown in Figure 2–29.

Figure 2–29   Paste Special dialog box

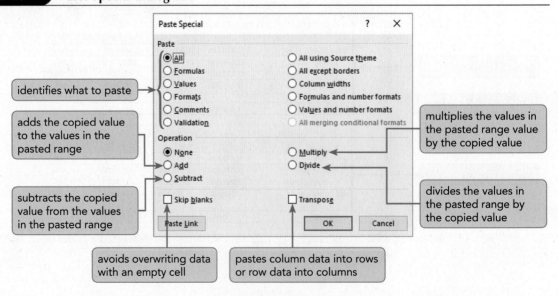

- identifies what to paste
- adds the copied value to the values in the pasted range
- subtracts the copied value from the values in the pasted range
- multiplies the values in the pasted range value by the copied value
- divides the values in the pasted range by the copied value
- avoids overwriting data with an empty cell
- pastes column data into rows or row data into columns

From the Paste Special dialog box, you can control exactly how to paste the copied range.

Insight

Performing Special Tasks with Paste Special

Excel has many options for copying and pasting data in different formats and layouts. The Paste Special dialog box provides access to these many different options. From the Paste Special dialog box, you can accomplish the following tasks in which you copy content from a selected source range and paste that content into a destination range:

- **Paste values only.** Rather than pasting both the cell values and formatting, you can paste only the values of selected cells by selecting the Values option in the Paste Special dialog box. Any formatting already applied to the cells in the destination range is unchanged when the values are pasted into the cells.
- **Paste column widths.** You can copy and paste column widths from one range to another. First, copy a range whose column widths you want to duplicate. Then, select the range whose columns you want to change. In the Paste Special dialog box, select the Column widths. No cell values are pasted.
- **Paste with no borders.** You can copy all formats applied to a cell *except* the cell borders by selecting the All except borders option in the Paste Special dialog box.
- **Skip blanks.** The source range may have empty or blank cells. If you want to copy only cells that contain content, use the Skip Blanks option in the Paste Special dialog box. This option prevents pasting over data in the destination range with blanks.
- **Perform a mathematical operation.** Rather than pasting a value, you can use the copied value in a mathematical operation that adds, subtracts, multiplies, or divides the values in the destination range by the copied value. For example, if you copy the number 2 from a cell and then choose the Multiply option in the Operation section of the Paste Special dialog box, all of the values in the destination range will be doubled in value.
- **Paste a link.** Rather than pasting a value, you can paste the cell references to the cells in the source range with the Paste Link button in the Paste Special dialog box. For example, copying cell A1 and then pasting a link in cell B4 enters the formula =A1 rather than the value in cell B4.

These paste special features help you work more efficiently as you develop large and complex worksheets.

Transposing Data

Data values are usually arranged in a rectangular grid. However, sometimes you might want to change the orientation of that rectangle, switching the rows and columns. You can easily do this with the Transpose option. Figure 2–30 shows a range of sales data that was copied and then pasted so that the rows and columns are transposed. As you can see, the store data switched from the rows to the columns and the month data switched from columns to rows. Both the cell values and cell formats are transposed in the pasted content.

Figure 2–30   Transposed pasted range

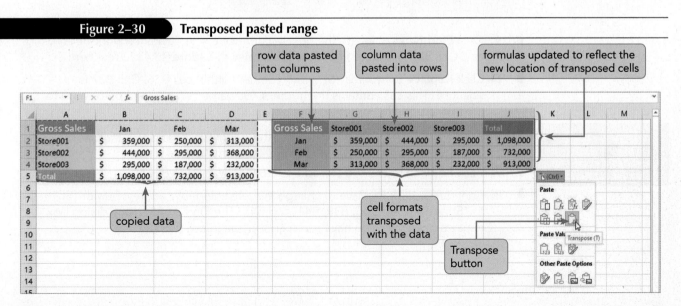

When you paste and transpose cells containing formulas, the cell references in those formulas are automatically updated to reflect the new layout of the data.

Finding and Replacing Text and Formats

The Find and Replace commands let you make content and design changes to a worksheet or the entire workbook quickly. The Find command searches through the current worksheet or workbook for the content or formatting you want to locate, and the Replace command then substitutes it with the new content or formatting you specify.

The Find and Replace commands are versatile. You can find each occurrence of the search text one at a time and decide whether to replace it. You can highlight all occurrences of the search text in the worksheet. Or, you can replace all occurrences at once without reviewing them.

Stefan wants you to replace all the street title abbreviations (such as St. and Ave.) in the Sales Report with their full names (such as Street and Avenue). You will use Find and Replace to make these changes.

To find and replace the street abbreviations:

1. On the Home tab, in the Editing group, click the **Find & Select** button, and then click **Replace** (or press **CTRL+H**). The Find and Replace dialog box opens.

2. Type **St.** in the Find what box.

3. Press **TAB** to move the insertion point to the Replace with box, and then type **Street** in the box. See Figure 2–31.

Figure 2–31	Find and Replace dialog box

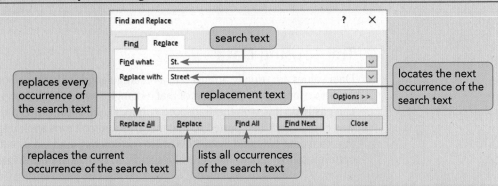

4. Click **Find Next** to locate the next occurrence of "St." within a worksheet cell. Cell B26 is selected because it contains the address "432 West Fern St."

5. Click **Replace** to replace "St." with "Street" within cell B26. Cell B27 is selected. This cell contains the address "St. James Way." You do not want to replace "St." with "Street" in this instance.

6. Click **Find Next** to go to the next occurrence of "St." in a cell. Cell B29 is selected containing the address "990 Waterside St."

7. Click **Replace** to change the address to 990 Waterside Street.

8. Continue to click **Replace** to change the remaining four addresses with "St." to "Street" in cells B35, B39, B41, and B43. The Find and Replace dialog box remains open after you have replaced the text in cell B43.

Always check the matched text so that you do not inadvertently replace text that should not be replaced.

Rather than reviewing each possible replacement, you can use the Replace All button in the Find and Replace dialog box to make all the replacements at once. You should do this only if you are sure there is no chance for a replacement error. You'll use the Replace All button to change all instances of "Ave." in the store addresses with "Avenue" and all instances of "Ln." with "Lane."

To replace all occurrences of "Ave." and "Ln.":

1. In the Find and Replace dialog box, type **Ave.** in the Find what box, and then type **Avenue** in the Replace with box.

2. Click **Replace All**. A dialog box appears, indicating Excel made seven replacements in the worksheet.

3. Click **OK** to return to the Find and Replace dialog box.

4. Type **Ln.** in the Find what box, and then type **Lane** in the Replace with box.

5. Click **Replace All**. A dialog box appears, indicating that Excel replaced Ln. with Lane five times in the worksheet.

6. Click **OK** to return to the Find and Replace dialog box.

> **Tip**
>
> All searches are case-insensitive. To include upper- and lowercase characters in the search, click the Options button and select the Match Case check box.

The Find and Replace dialog box can also be used with cell formatting, replacing both the content and the format of cells within the worksheet. Stefan wants you to replace all occurrences of the white text on a gold fill in the Sales Report worksheet with blue text on a gold fill. You'll do this using the Find and Replace dialog box.

To replace content based on formatting:

1. In the Find and Replace dialog box, click **Options** to expand the list of formatting options.

2. Delete the search text from the Find what and Replace with boxes, leaving those two boxes empty. By not specifying a text string to find and replace, the dialog box will search through all cells regardless of their content.

3. Click **Format** in the Find what row to open the Find Format dialog box, which is similar to the Format Cells dialog box you used earlier to format a range.

4. Click the **Font** tab to make it active, click the **Color** box, and then click the **White, Background 1** theme color.

5. Click the **Fill** tab, and then in the Background Color section, click the **gold** theme color (the eighth color in the first row).

6. Click **OK** to close the Find Format dialog box and return to the Find and Replace dialog box.

7. Click **Format** in the Replace with row to open the Replace Format dialog box.

8. On the Fill tab, click the **gold** theme color (the eighth color in the first row).

9. Click the **Font** tab, click the **Color** box, and then click the **Blue Accent 1** theme color (the fifth color in the first row).

10. Click **OK** to return to the Find and Replace dialog box. See Figure 2–32.

> **Tip**
>
> To search the entire workbook, select Workbook in the Within box.

Figure 2–32   **Expanded Find and Replace dialog box**

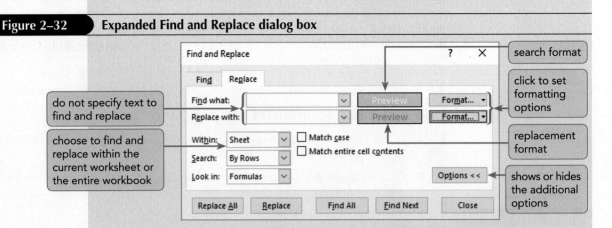

> ▶ **11.** Click **Replace All** to replace all occurrences of white text on a gold fill in the Sales Report worksheet with blue text on a gold fill. A dialog box opens, reporting that Excel made 13 replacements.

> ▶ **12.** Click **OK** to return to the Find and Replace dialog box.

It is a good idea to clear the find and replace formats after you are done so they won't affect any future searches and replacements. Stefan asks you to remove the formats from the Find and Replace dialog box.

To clear the options from the Find and Replace dialog box:

> ▶ **1.** In the Find and Replace dialog box, click the **Format arrow** in the Find what row, and then click **Clear Find Format**. The search format is removed.

> ▶ **2.** Click the **Format arrow** in the Replace with row, and then click **Clear Replace Format**. The replacement format is removed.

> ▶ **3.** Click **Close**. The Find and Replace dialog box closes.

The font color for cells in the range B5:F5,B14:F14,A26:A45 all changed to blue because of the cell format you found and replaced.

Working with Themes

Another way to make multiple changes to the formats used in your workbook is through themes. Recall that a theme is a predefined, coordinated set of colors, fonts, graphical effects, and other formats that are applied throughout a workbook to give them a consistent, professional look.

Applying a Theme

The Office theme is the default theme applied to workbooks. When you switch to a different theme, the theme-related fonts, colors, and effects change throughout the workbook to reflect the new theme. The appearances of standard fonts, colors, and effects remain unchanged no matter which theme is applied to the workbook.

Most of the formatting used in the Sales Report workbook is based on the Office theme. Stefan wants you to change the theme to see how it affects the workbook's appearance.

To change the workbook's theme:

1. Scroll up the worksheet and click cell **A1**.

2. On the ribbon, click the **Page Layout** tab.

3. In the Themes group, click the **Themes** button. The Themes gallery opens. Office—the current theme—is the default.

4. Point to different themes in the Themes gallery using Live Preview to preview the impact of each theme on the fonts and colors used in the worksheet.

5. Point to the **Ion** theme to see a Live Preview of that theme to the workbook. See Figure 2–33.

Figure 2–33	Live Preview of the Ion theme

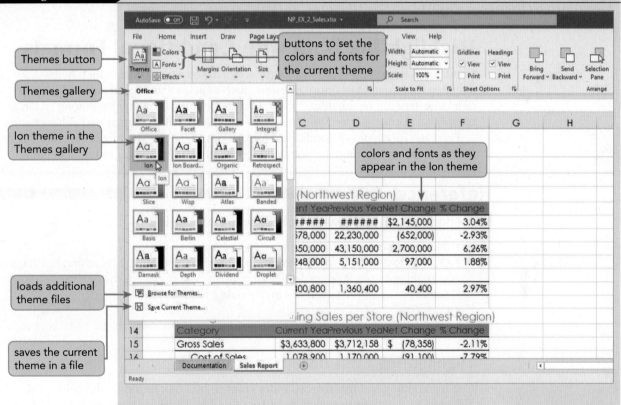

6. Click the **Ion** theme. The theme is applied to the workbook.

Changing the theme made a significant difference in the worksheet's appearance. The most obvious changes to the worksheet are the fill colors and the fonts. Only formatting options directly tied to a theme change when you select a different theme. Any formatting options you selected that are not theme-based remain unaffected by the change. For example, a standard color or font is not affected by the theme. That is why the standard colors used in cells A1 and A2 do not change when you change the theme.

Setting Theme Colors and Fonts

Businesses often use custom themes that match their company's logo colors and fonts. To change the theme colors, click the Colors button in the Themes group on the Page Layout tab, and then select one of the color palettes. To create your own color palette, click Customize Colors to open the Create New Theme Colors dialog box. In this dialog box, you can select colors for the text and background and the six accent colors used by that theme and save the custom colors with a name of your choosing.

To change the theme fonts, click the Fonts button in the Themes group on the Page Layout tab, and then select one of the font themes for heading and body text. To create your own theme fonts, click Customize Fonts to open the Create New Theme Fonts dialog box. From this dialog box, select the fonts for heading and body text and save the custom fonts under a new name.

Saving a Theme

Once you've changed a theme's colors or fonts, you can save the custom theme in its own theme file. You do this by clicking the Themes button in the Themes group on the Page Layout tab, and then clicking Save Current Theme. Theme files are stored in the Office Theme folder on your computer and are available to all Office applications, including Excel, Word, and PowerPoint.

Highlighting Data with Conditional Formats

Conditional formatting is used to format a cell based on its value, which helps draw attention to important or unusual results, such as sales that exceed a specified goal or a large expense on a balance sheet. Unlike the formatting you have done so far, a conditional format is based with the cell's value and will change as that value changes.

Excel has four types of conditional formatting—data bars, highlighting, color scales, and icon sets. In this module, you will use conditional formatting to highlight cells.

Reference

Highlighting Cells with Conditional Formatting

- Select the range in which you want to highlight cells.
- On the Home tab, in the Styles group, click the Conditional Formatting button, point to Highlight Cells Rules or Top/Bottom Rules, and then click the appropriate rule.
- Select the appropriate options in the dialog box.
- Click OK.

Highlighting Cells Based on Their Values

Cell highlighting changes the cell's font color or fill color based on the cell's value. Figure 2–34 describes the seven rules supported by Excel for choosing the cell value.

Figure 2–34   Highlight cells rules

Rule	Highlights Cell Values
Greater Than	Greater than a specified number
Less Than	Less than a specified number
Between	Between two specified numbers
Equal To	Equal to a specified number
Text that Contains	That contain specified text
A Date Occurring	That contain a specified date
Duplicate Values	That contain duplicate or unique values

Stefan wants to highlight important trends and sales values in the Sales Report worksheet by highlighting sales statistics that show a negative trend from the previous year to the current year. You will use conditional formatting to highlight the negative net change and percent change values in red.

To highlight negative values in red:

▶ **1.** In the Sales Report worksheet, select the range **E6:F20** containing the net and percent changes in sales from the previous year to the current year.

▶ **2.** On the ribbon, click the **Home** tab.

▶ **3.** In the Styles group, click the **Conditional Formatting** button, and then point to **Highlight Cells Rules** to display a menu of the available rules.

▶ **4.** Click **Less Than**. The Less Than dialog box opens so you can select the value and format to highlight negative values.

▶ **5.** Make sure the value in the first box is selected, and then type **0** so that cells in the selected range that contain values that are less than 0 are formatted with a light red fill and dark red text. Live Preview shows the conditional formatting applied to the cells with negative numbers. See Figure 2–35.

| Figure 2–35 | Live Preview of the Less Than conditional format |

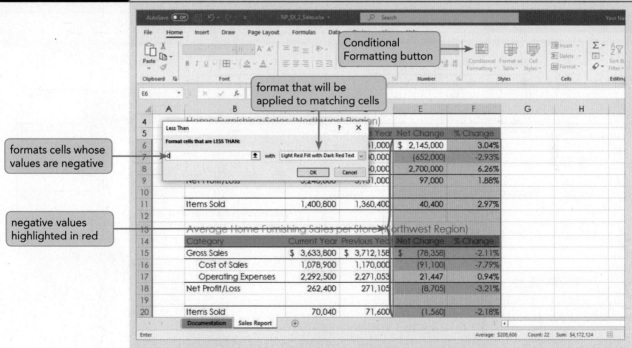

▶ **6.** Click **OK** to apply the highlighting rule.

Conditional formatting highlights some very important sales facts for Stefan. While the net profit for Northwest region stores increased by 1.88% (cell F9), this is not true when the data is adjusted for the number of stores. The net profit per store has decreased by 3.21% (cell F16). While the number of items sold in the Northwest region increased by 2.97% (cell F11), the items sold per store decreased by 2.18% (cell F20).

The net decline in the per-store statistics might be due to the new store that opened in the Northwest region still not finding its market. It also might be due to an overall decline in sales at brick-and-mortar stores over the past year. Stefan will need to do further research to determine the cause of the decline in per-store sales and profits.

Highlighting Cells with a Top/Bottom Rule

Another way of applying conditional formatting is with the Quick Analysis tool. The **Quick Analysis tool**, which appears whenever you select a range of cells, provides access to the most common tools for data analysis and formatting of the selected range. The Formatting category includes buttons for the Greater Than and Top 10% conditional formatting rules. You can highlight cells based on their values in comparison to other cells. For example, you can highlight cells with the 10 highest or lowest values in a selected range, or you can highlight the cells with above-average values in a range.

Stefan wants to know which stores and months rank in highest in sales. You will highlight the top 10% in monthly sales from all stores using the Quick Analysis tool.

To highlight the lowest-performing stores:

1. Select the range **C26:N45** containing the monthly sales from each of the 20 Bristol Bay stores in the Northwest region.

2. Click the **Quick Analysis** button 📊, and then point to **Top 10%**. Live Preview formats the cells in the top 10% with red font and a red fill. See Figure 2–36.

Figure 2–36	Quick Analysis tool applying a conditional format

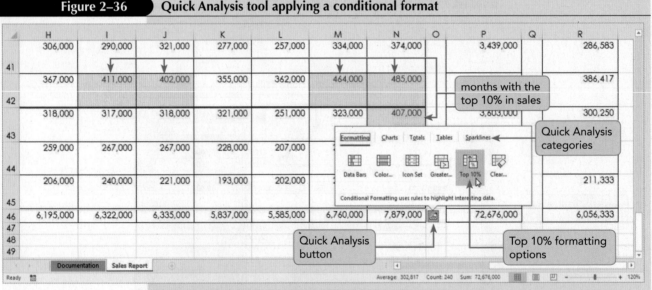

3. Click **Top 10%** to apply the conditional format.

4. Click cell **O46** to deselect the range.

A total of 24 cells are highlighted from the stores with the greatest monthly sales.

Editing a Conditional Formatting Rule

You can modify any conditional formatting rule to change what is being formatted, as well as change what formatting is applied. Stefan wants you to revise the conditional formatting rule you created with the Quick Analysis tool so that only the top 5% of monthly sales are highlighted and that the fill color is green rather than red. You will use the Manage Rules command to make this change.

To edit the Top 10% conditional formatting rule:

1. On the Home tab, in the Styles group, click the **Conditional Formatting** button and then click **Manage Rules**. The Conditional Formatting Rules Manager dialog box opens.

2. Click the **Show formatting rules for arrow**, and then click **This Worksheet** to list all conditional formatting rules in the current worksheet. See Figure 2–37.

Figure 2–37	Conditional Formatting Rules Manager

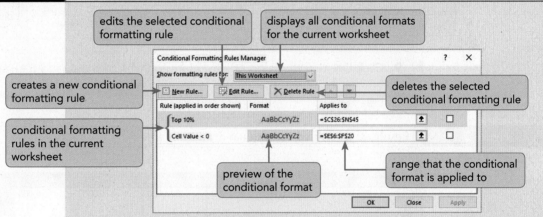

3. Make sure the **Top 10%** rule is highlighted, and then click **Edit Rule**. The Edit Formatting Rule dialog box opens.

4. In the Edit the Rule Description section, change the value in the box from 10 to **5**. This changes the rule to highlight only the top 5% of sales values.

5. Click **Format** to open the Format Cells dialog box.

6. On the Font tab in the dialog box, change the font color to the **Black, Text 1** theme color (the second color in the first row).

7. Click the **Fill** tab, change the background color to the **Light Green** standard color (the fifth standard color).

8. Click **OK** to return to the Edit Formatting Rule dialog box. See Figure 2–38.

Figure 2–38   **Edit Formatting Rule dialog box**

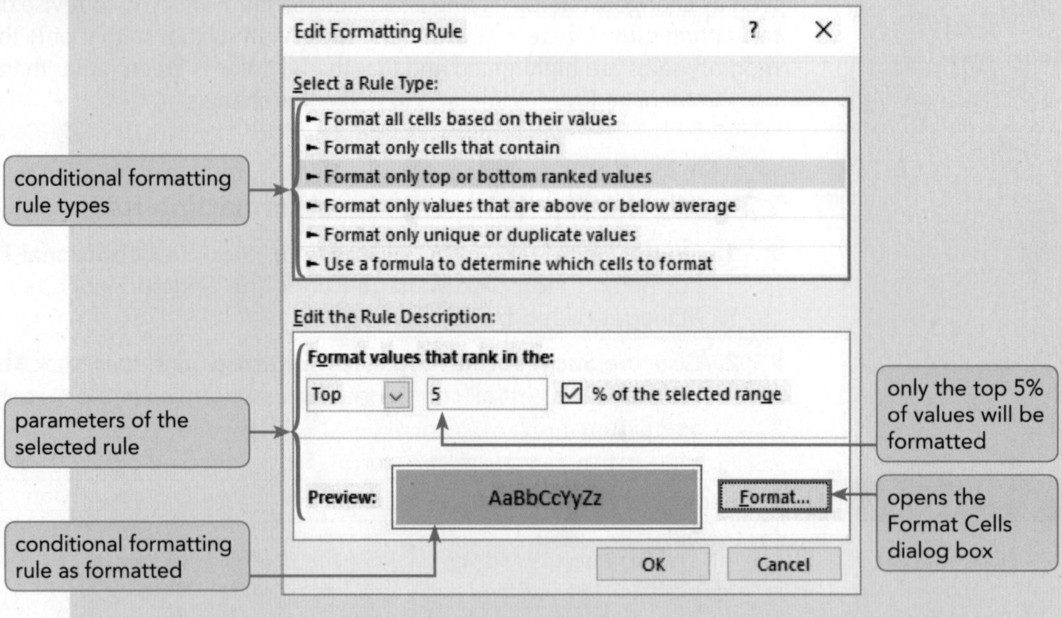

conditional formatting rule types

parameters of the selected rule

conditional formatting rule as formatted

only the top 5% of values will be formatted

opens the Format Cells dialog box

9. Click **OK** in each dialog box to return to the worksheet, and then scroll up to view the edited conditional formatting rule applied to the worksheet. See Figure 2–39.

Figure 2–39   **Results of the edited conditional formatting rule**

	H	I	J	K	L	M	N	O
25	Jun	Jul	Aug	Sep	Oct	Nov	Dec	
	285,000	329,000	352,000	323,000	311,000	355,000	445,000	
26								
	421,000	444,000	399,000	379,000	375,000	412,000	490,000	
27								
	280,000	288,000	291,000	256,000	254,000	277,000	365,000	
28								
	249,000	274,000	281,000	238,000	229,000	273,000	346,000	
29								
	299,000	332,000	310,000	285,000	293,000	333,000	423,000	
30								
	298,000	285,000	308,000	280,000	265,000	327,000	380,000	
31								

the top 5% of sales months are displayed with a green fill

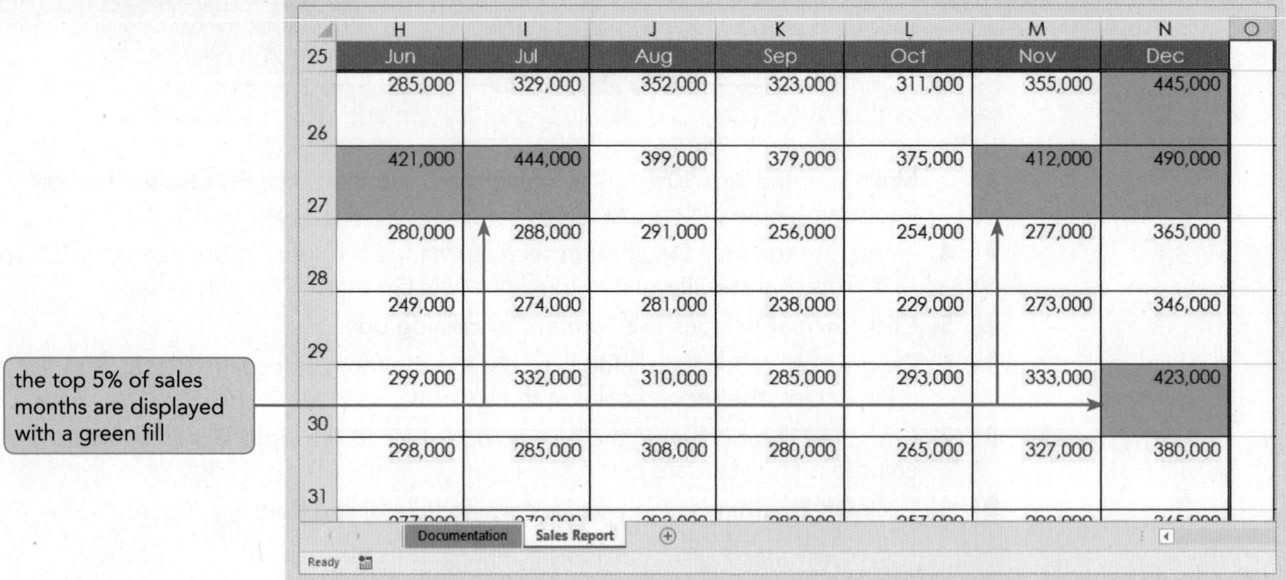

Stefan is not surprised that 7 of the 12 highlighted cells are in December when sales are always high because of the holiday season. However, Stefan is interested that the Seattle store accounts for five of the top-selling months, with large sales in January, June, July, November, and December. In fact, the June sales at the Seattle store exceed the December sales at 14 other stores.

Clearing Conditional Formatting Rules

You can remove a conditional format at any time without affecting the underlying data. Just select the range containing the conditional format, click the Conditional Formatting button in the Styles group on the Home tab, and then click the Clear Rules command. A menu opens, providing options to clear the conditional formatting rules from the selected cells or the entire worksheet. You can also click the Quick Analysis button that appears in the lower-right corner of the selected range, and then click the Clear Format button in the Formatting category. Note that you might see only "Clear..." as the button name.

Insight

Dynamic Conditional Formatting

Conditional formats can be static so that a specific value triggers the conditional format, such as highlighting monthly sales that exceed $400,000. Conditional formats can also be dynamic so that the conditional format is based on the value in a specified cell.

To create dynamic conditional formats that are based on a cell value, you enter a cell reference rather than a constant value in the dialog box when you create the conditional formatting rule. For example, you can highlight all cells whose value is greater than the value in cell B10 by entering the formula =$B$10 in the dialog box. Note that the $ character keeps the cell reference from changing if that formula moves to another cell. This lets you quickly change what is highlighted without having to continually edit the rule, making it easier to see different aspects of your data.

Documenting Conditional Formats

When you use conditional formatting to highlight cells in a worksheet, the purpose of the formatting is not always immediately apparent. To ensure that everyone knows why certain cells are highlighted, you should document the meaning of the format.

Stefan wants you to add text to the Sales Report worksheet to indicate that the green cells in the sales table represent the stores and months in the top 5% of all sales.

To document the top 5% conditional formatting rule:

1. In cell **M23**, enter **Top 5% in Sales** as the label, and then select cell **M23** again.

2. On the Home tab, in the Alignment group, click the **Align Right** button ≡ to right-align the contents of the selected cell. The cell entry now overlaps the blank cell L23.

3. In cell **N23**, type **green** to identify the conditional formatting color you used to highlight the values in the top 5%, and then select cell **N23** again.

4. In the Alignment group, click the **Center** button ≡ to center the contents of the cell.

   You will use a highlighting rule to format cell N23 using black text on a green fill.

5. On the Home tab, in the Styles group, click the **Conditional Formatting** button, point to **Highlight Cells Rules**, and then click **Text that Contains**. The Text That Contains dialog box opens. The text string "green" from the selected cell is already entered into the left input box.

6. In the right box, click the **arrow** button, and then click **Custom Format** to open the Format Cells dialog box.

7. Click the **Fill** tab, and then change the background fill color to the **Light Green** standard color.

8. Click the **Font** tab, and then change the font color to the **Black, Text 1** theme color to match the formatting used for sales in the top 5%.

9. Click **OK** in each dialog box to apply the conditional formatting to cell N23. See Figure 2–40.

| Figure 2–40 | Conditional formatting documented in worksheet |

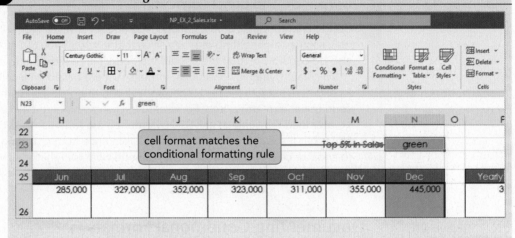

You've completed formatting the appearance of the workbook for the computer screen. Next, you will explore how to format the workbook for the printer.

Proskills

Written Communication: Using Conditional Formatting Effectively

Conditional formatting is an excellent way to highlight important trends and data values to clients and colleagues. However, be sure to use it judiciously. Overusing conditional formatting might obscure the very data you want to emphasize. Keep in mind the following tips as you make decisions about what to highlight and how it should be highlighted:

- **Document the conditional formats you use.** If a bold, green font means that a sales number is in the top 10% of all sales, document that information in the worksheet.

- **Don't clutter data with too much highlighting.** Limit highlighting rules to one or two per data set. Highlights are designed to draw attention to points of interest. If you use too many, you will end up highlighting everything—and, therefore, nothing.

- **Consider alternatives to conditional formats.** If you want to highlight the top 10 sales regions, it might be more effective to simply sort the data with the best-selling regions at the top of the list.

Remember that the goal of highlighting is to provide a strong visual clue to important data or results. Careful use of conditional formatting helps readers to focus on the important points you want to make rather than distracting them with secondary issues and facts.

Formatting a Worksheet for Printing

You should format any worksheets you plan to print so that they are easy to read and understand. You can do this using the print settings, which enable you to set the page orientation, the print area, page breaks, print titles, and headers and footers. Print settings can be applied to an entire workbook or to individual sheets. Because other people will likely see your printed worksheets, you should format the printed output as carefully as you format the electronic version.

Stefan wants you to format the printed version of the Sales Report worksheet to be distributed to the sales team at Bristol Bay.

Using Page Break Preview

Page Break Preview shows only those parts of the active sheet that will print and how the content will be split across pages. A dotted blue border indicates a page break, which separates one page from another. As you format the worksheet for printing, you can use this view to control what content appears on each page.

Stefan wants to know how the Sales Report worksheet would print in portrait orientation and how many pages would be required. You will look at the worksheet in Page Break Preview to find these answers.

To view the Sales Report worksheet in Page Break Preview:

 1. Scroll up the worksheet and click cell **A1**.

 2. Click the **Page Break Preview** button ⊞ on the status bar. The worksheet switches to Page Break Preview.

 3. Change the zoom level of the worksheet to **25%** so you can view the entire contents of this large worksheet. See Figure 2–41.

| Figure 2–41 | Sales Report worksheet in Page Break Preview |

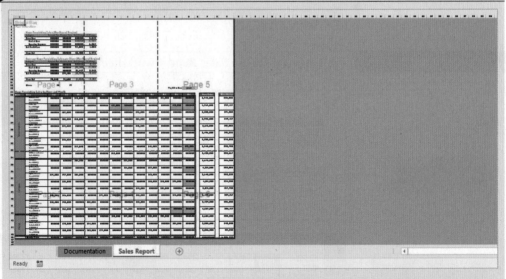

Trouble? If you see a different page layout or the worksheet is split onto a different number of pages, don't worry. Each printer is different, so the layout and pages might differ from what is shown in Figure 2–41.

Page Break Preview shows that a printout of the Sales Report worksheet requires six pages in portrait orientation and that pages 3 and 5 would be mostly blank. Note that each printer is different, so your Page Break Preview might show a different number of pages. With this layout, each page would be difficult to interpret because the data is separated from the descriptive labels. Stefan wants you to fix the layout so that the contents are easier to read and understand.

Defining the Print Area

By default, all cells in a worksheet containing text, formulas, or values are printed. If you want to print only part of a worksheet, you can set a print area, which is the region of the worksheet that is sent to the printer. Each worksheet has its own print area. Although you can set the print area in any view, Page Break Preview shades the areas of the worksheet that are not included in the print area, making it simple to confirm what will print.

Stefan doesn't want the blank cells in the range G1:R22 to be included in the printout, so you will set the print area to exclude those cells.

To set the print area of the Sales Report worksheet:

1. Change the zoom level of the worksheet to **80%** to make it easier to select cells and ranges.

2. Select the range **A1:F22**, hold down **CTRL**, select the range **A23:R46**, and then release **CTRL**. The nonadjacent range is selected.

3. On the ribbon, click the **Page Layout** tab.

4. In the Page Setup group, click the **Print Area** button, and then click **Set Print Area**. The print area changes to cover only the nonadjacent range A1:F22,A23:R46. The rest of the worksheet content is shaded to indicate that it will not be part of the printout.

5. Click cell **A1** to deselect the range.

6. Change the zoom level to **50%** so you can view more of the worksheet. See Figure 2–42.

| Figure 2–42 | Print area set for the Sales Report worksheet |

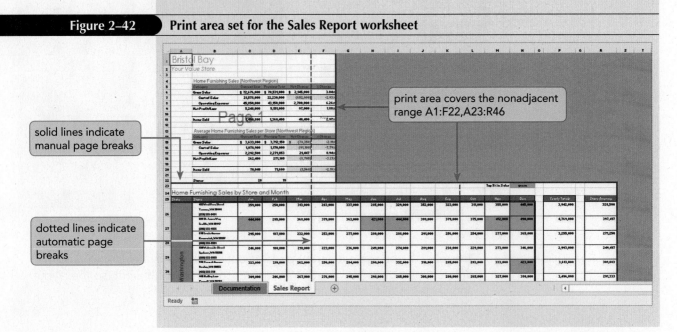

solid lines indicate manual page breaks

dotted lines indicate automatic page breaks

print area covers the nonadjacent range A1:F22,A23:R46

Inserting Page Breaks

Often, the contents of a worksheet will not fit onto a single printed page. When this happens, Excel prints as much of the content that fits on a single page without resizing, and then inserts automatic page breaks to continue printing the remaining worksheet content on successive pages. The resulting printouts might split worksheet content in awkward places, such as in the middle of a table of data.

To split the printout into logical segments, you can insert manual page breaks. Page Break Preview identifies manual page breaks with a solid blue line and automatic page breaks with a dotted blue line. When you specify a print area for a nonadjacent range, as you did for the Sales Report worksheet, manual page breaks are inserted around the adjacent ranges and appear in the print area you defined (refer again to Figure 2–42). You can remove a page break in Page Break Preview by dragging it out of the print area.

Tip

When you remove a page break, Excel rescales the printout to fit into the allotted pages.

Reference

Inserting and Removing Page Breaks

To insert a page break:
- Click the first cell below the row where you want to insert a page break, click a column heading, or click a row heading.
- On the Page Layout tab, in the Page Setup group, click the Breaks button, and then click Insert Page Break.

To remove a page break:
- Select any cell below or to the right of the page break you want to remove.
- On the Page Layout tab, in the Page Setup group, click the Breaks button, and then click Remove Page Break.

or

- In Page Break Preview, drag the page break line out of the print area.

The Sales Report worksheet has automatic page breaks along columns F and L. Stefan wants you to remove these automatic page breaks from the Sales Report worksheet.

To remove the automatic page breaks and insert manual page breaks:

1. Point to the **dotted blue page break** directly to the left of column L in Home Furnishing Sales by Store and Month table until the pointer changes to the double-headed horizontal pointer ↔.

   Trouble? If the dotted blue page break appears to the left of a different column, don't worry. Depending on your printer, the page breaks might be in a different column of the worksheet. Just point to the dotted blue page break that is closest to column L.

2. Drag the page break to the right and out of the print area. The page break is removed from the worksheet.

3. Point to the page break located in column F so that the pointer changes to the double-headed horizontal pointer ↔, and then drag the page break between column H and column I so that the first 6 months of sales are on one page and the last 6 months of sales data are on the next page.

   Trouble? If the dotted blue page break appears to the right of a different column, don't worry. Depending on your printer, the page breaks might be in a different column of the worksheet. Just drag the dotted blue page break that is closest to column F.

You will add a manual page break between columns N and O to place the total annual sales and store averages on their own pages.

▶ **4.** Click cell **O23**.

▶ **5.** On the Page Layout tab, in the Page Setup group, click the **Breaks** button, and then click **Insert Page Break**. A manual page break is added between columns N and O, forcing the total annual sales and average sales onto a fourth page. See Figure 2–43.

Figure 2–43   **Manual page breaks in the print area**

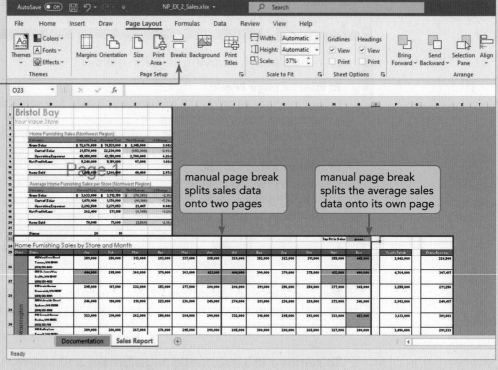

button to insert or remove page breaks

Adding Print Titles

It is a good practice to include descriptive information such as the company name, logo, and worksheet title on each page of a printout in case a page becomes separated from the other pages. You can repeat information, such as the company name, by specifying which rows or columns in the worksheet act as print titles. If a worksheet contains a large table, you can print the table's column headings and row headings on every page of the printout by designating those columns and rows as print titles.

In the Sales Report worksheet, the company name appears on the first page of the printout but does not appear on subsequent pages. Also, the descriptive row titles for the monthly sales table in column A do not appear on the third page of the printout. You will add print titles to fix these issues.

To set the print titles:

1. On the Page Layout tab, in the Page Setup group, click the **Print Titles** button. The Page Setup dialog box opens with the Sheet tab displayed.

2. In the Print titles section, click the **Rows to repeat at top** box, move the pointer over the worksheet, and then select rows **1** and **2**. A flashing border appears around the first two rows of the worksheet to indicate that the contents of the first two rows will be repeated on each page of the printout. The row reference $1:$2 appears in the Rows to repeat at top box.

3. Click the **Columns to repeat at left** box, move the pointer over the worksheet, and then select columns **A** and **B**. The column reference $A:$B appears in the Columns to repeat at left box. See Figure 2–44.

Tip

You can also open the Page Setup dialog box by clicking the Dialog Box Launcher in the Page Setup group on the Page Layout tab.

| Figure 2–44 | Sheet tab in the Page Setup dialog box |

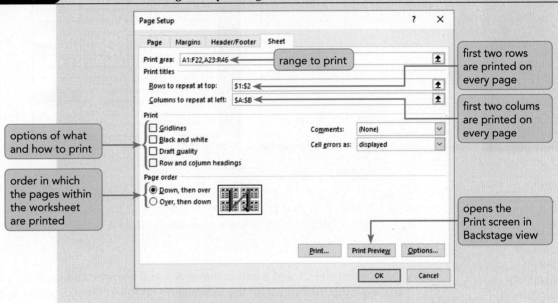

options of what and how to print

order in which the pages within the worksheet are printed

range to print

first two rows are printed on every page

first two colums are printed on every page

opens the Print screen in Backstage view

You will rescale the worksheet so that the cell values are easily readable in the printout.

To rescale the printout:

1. In the Page Setup dialog box, click the **Page** tab.

2. In the Scaling section, change the Adjust to amount to **70%** normal size.

3. Click the **Print Preview** button to preview the four pages of printed material on the Print screen in Backstage view.

4. Use the arrow buttons to scroll through the four pages of the report. Figure 2–45 shows a preview of the page three printout, containing the monthly sales from July to December of the current year.

Figure 2–45   **Print preview of page 3**

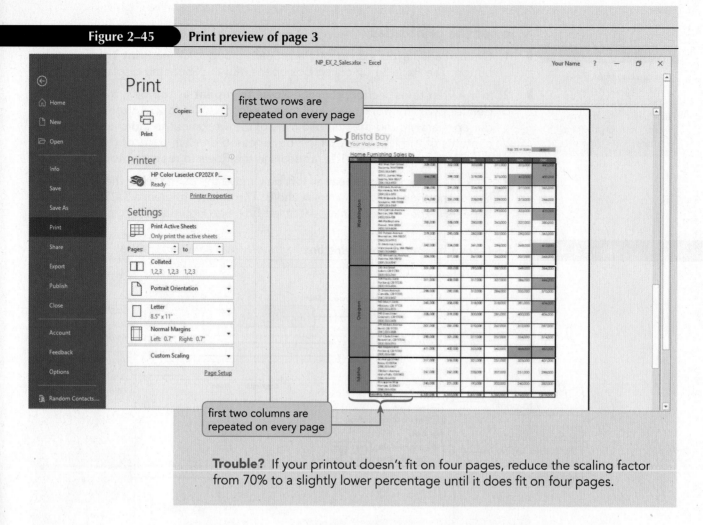

first two rows are repeated on every page

first two columns are repeated on every page

Trouble? If your printout doesn't fit on four pages, reduce the scaling factor from 70% to a slightly lower percentage until it does fit on four pages.

Notice that rows 1 and 2 and columns A and B are repeated on every page, providing valuable context for the information on the printout. Another way of repeating information on every page is with headers and footers.

Designing Headers and Footers

Headers and footers provide descriptive information on the printout. A **header** is information that appears at the top of each printed page, and a **footer** is the information that appears on the bottom of every page. Headers and footers are usually reserved for information that does not appear within the document. For example, the header might include the name of the document author and the date on which the document was printed. If the printout spans several pages, the page number and total number of pages might be displayed in the footer.

Headers and footers are divided into a left section, a center section, and a right section. In each section, you can insert elements with information about the workbook, worksheet, or general document properties, such as the worksheet name or the current date and time. These header and footer elements are dynamic; if you rename the worksheet, for example, the name is automatically updated in the header or footer. You can also type specific text that you want to appear in each section. The text you type doesn't change unless you edit the text in that section.

You can create multiple headers and/or footers in the printout. For example, you can create one header and footer for even pages and another for odd pages. You can also create one header and footer for the first page in the printout and a different header and footer for subsequent pages.

Stefan wants the printout to display the workbook's file name in the header's left section, and the current date in the header's right section. The center footer should display the page number and the total number of pages in the printout and the right footer should display your name as the workbook's author.

To set up the page header:

▶ **1.** Near the bottom of the Print screen, click the **Page Setup** link. The Page Setup dialog box opens.

▶ **2.** Click the **Header/Footer** tab to display the header and footer options.

▶ **3.** Click the **Different first page** check box to select it. This creates one set of headers and footers for the first page, and one set for the rest of the pages.

▶ **4.** Click the **Custom Header** button. The Header dialog box opens. Because you selected the Different first page option, the dialog box contains two tabs named Header and First Page Header.

▶ **5.** Click the **First Page Header** tab.

▶ **6.** On the Header tab, in the Left section box, type **File name:** and press **SPACEBAR**, and then click the **Insert File Name** button 📄. The code `&[File]`, which displays the file name of the current workbook, is added to the left section of the header.

▶ **7.** Press **TAB** twice to move to the right section of the header, and then click the **Insert Date** button 📅. The code `&[Date]` is added to the right section of the header. See Figure 2–46.

Tip

You can create or edit headers and footers in Page Layout view by clicking in the Header & Footer section and using the tools on the Design tab.

| Figure 2–46 | Header dialog box |

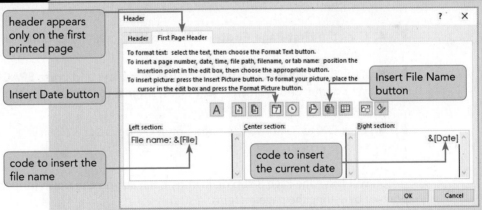

header appears only on the first printed page

Insert Date button

Insert File Name button

code to insert the file name

code to insert the current date

▶ **8.** Click **OK** to return to the Header/Footer tab in the Page Setup dialog box.

The header text you just created will appear only on the first page of the printout; subsequent pages will not display that header information. Stefan wants a footer to appear on all pages of the printout. Because you selected different headers and footers for the first page, you will create one footer for the first page and another footer for subsequent pages.

To create the page footer:

▶ 1. On the Header/Footer tab of the Page Setup dialog box, click the **Custom Footer** button. The Footer dialog box opens.

▶ 2. On the Footer tab, click the **Center** section box, type **Page** and press **SPACEBAR**, and then click the **Insert Page Number** button 📄. The code &[Page], which inserts the current page number, appears after the label "Page."

▶ 3. Press **SPACEBAR**, type **of** and press **SPACEBAR**, and then click the **Insert Number of Pages** button 📄. The code &[Pages], which inserts the total number of pages in the printout, is added to the Center section box. See Figure 2–47.

Figure 2–47 **Footer dialog box**

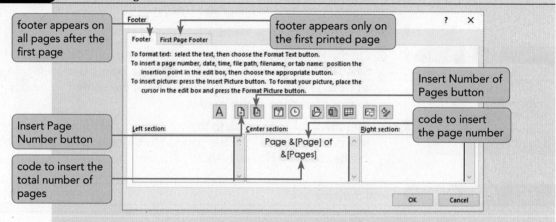

▶ 4. Click the **First Page Footer** tab so you can create the footer for the first page of the printout.

▶ 5. Click the **Right** section box, type **Prepared by:** and press **SPACEBAR**, type your name, and then type **(&[Pages] pages)** to indicate the total number of pages in the printed report.

▶ 6. Click **OK** to return to the Page Setup dialog box.

You will leave the Page Setup dialog box open so you can finish formatting the printout by setting the page margins.

Setting the Page Margins

A **margin** is the space between the page content and the edges of the page. By default, Excel sets the page margins to 0.7 inch on the left and right sides, and 0.75 inch on the top and bottom; and it allows for 0.3-inch margins around the header and footer. You can reduce or increase these margins as needed by selecting predefined margin sizes or setting your own.

Stefan's reports need a wider margin along the left side of the page to accommodate a binder, so you will increase the left margin for the printout from 0.7 inch to 1 inch.

To set the left margin:

1. Click the **Margins** tab in the Page Setup dialog box to display options for changing the page margins.

2. Double-click the **Left** box to select the setting, and then type **1** to increase the size of the left margin to 1 inch. See Figure 2–48.

Figure 2–48   Margins tab in the Page Setup dialog box

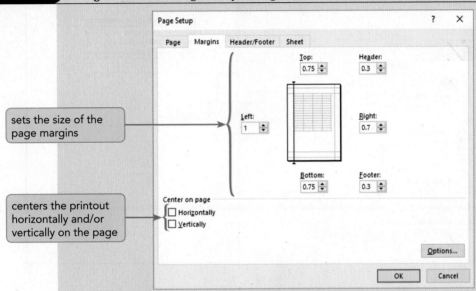

sets the size of the page margins

centers the printout horizontally and/or vertically on the page

3. Click **OK** to close the Page Setup dialog box. In the preview, the left margin shifts to reflect the new margin setting.

You can also center the worksheet contents both horizontally and vertically within the margins by selecting the Horizontally and Vertically check boxes on the Margins tab in the Page Setup dialog box.

Now that you have formatted the printout, you can print the final version of the worksheet.

To preview, print, and save the workbook:

▶ **1.** On the Print screen in Backstage view, preview the final version of the printed report. Figure 2–49 shows a preview of page 1 of the printout.

Figure 2–49	Preview of the completed first page

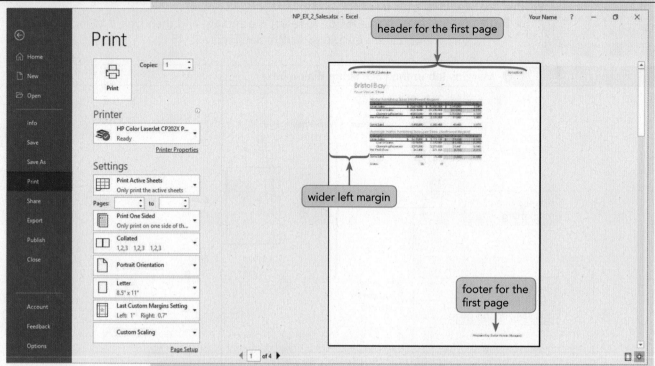

▶ **2.** On the Print screen, in the Settings section, click the first box, and then click **Print Entire Workbook**. The printout will include five pages—one page for the Documentation sheet and four pages for the Sales Report sheet.

▶ **3.** If you are instructed to print, click the **Print** button to print the entire workbook. If you are not instructed to print, click the **Back** button ⬅ on the Backstage view navigation bar to return to the workbook window.

▶ **4.** Click the **Normal** button ▦ on the status bar to return the view of the workbook to normal.

▶ **5.** Increase the zoom level to **120%** (or whatever zoom level you have been using).

▶ **6.** **sam** ⬆ Save the workbook, and then close it.

Stefan is pleased that your work on formatting the workbook has made the sales report easier to read and interpret. Stefan will get have future projects for you to complete using what you've learned about formatting data in Excel.

Review

Session 2.2 Quick Check

1. Describe two methods of applying the same format to different ranges.
2. Red is a standard color. What happens to red text when you change the workbook's theme?
3. What is a conditional format?
4. How would you highlight the top 10% values in the range A1:C20?
5. How do you insert a manual page break in a worksheet?
6. What is a print area?
7. What are print titles?
8. Describe how to add the workbook file name to the center section of the footer on every page of the printout.

2. Red doesn't change

3. makes it easy to highlight certain values or make particular cells easy to identify.

5. Insert > Page break

7. Allows you to designate certain rows and coloums to repeat on every printed page

Practice

Review Assignments

Data Files needed for the Review Assignments: NP_EX_2-2.xlsx, Support_EX_2_Texture.jpg

Stefan has another workbook for you to work on. This report will also deal with home furnishing sales in the Northwest region; but rather than breaking down the sales figures by store, Stefan wants to analyze the data by product to determine whether specific product categories have seen an increase or decrease in sales from the previous year. Stefan already compiled the data in a workbook but needs you to develop a finished report that will be distributed among the sales team. Complete the following:

1. Open the **NP_EX_2-2.xlsx** workbook located in the Excel2 > Review folder included with your Data Files, and then save the workbook as **NP_EX_2_Products** in the location specified by your instructor.

2. In the Documentation sheet, enter your name in cell B4 and the date in cell B5. Format the date in cell B5 with the Long Date cell format and left-align the date in the cell.

3. Set the background of the Documentation sheet to the **Support_EX_2_Texture.jpg** image file located in the Excel2 > Review folder included with your Data Files, and then change the fill color of the range B4:B6 to white.

4. In the Product Sales worksheet, enter formulas to make the following calculations:

   a. In cell B6, use the SUM function to calculate the total of the Decorative sales for the current year using the values in the range C31:N35.

   b. In cell B7, use the SUM function to calculate the sum of the Living sales using the values in the range C36:N40.

   c. In cell B8, calculate the sum of the Utility sales using the values in the range C41:N44.

   d. In cell B9, calculate the total sales from all three categories in the current year by adding the values in the range B6:B8.

   e. In cell C9, add the total sales from all three categories in the previous year.

   f. In the range D6:D9, calculate the net change in sales by subtracting the previous year values in column C from the current year values in column B for all three product categories and overall.

   g. In the range E6:E9, calculate the percent change in sales for the three categories and total sales by dividing the net change values in column D by the previous year's sales values in column C.

5. Apply the following formats to the data:

   a. Format the range B6:D9 with Accounting style and no decimal places.

   b. Format the range E6:E9 in Percent style showing two decimal places.

   c. Format cell A4 with the Title cell style.

   d. Format the range A5:E5 with the Heading 3 cell style.

   e. Format the range A9:E9 with the Total cell style.

6. Complete the following calculations for the Sales by Product Type data using the monthly sales data for each product:

   a. In cell B13, use the SUM function to calculate the total sales for Home Decorations from the range C31:N31, and then copy that formula into the range B14:B26.

   b. In cell B27, use the SUM function to calculate the sum of the values in the range B13:B26. Copy your formula and paste it into cell C27. Verify that the values in the range B27:C27 equal the values in the range B9:C9.

   c. In cell D13, calculate the difference between the value in cell B13 and cell C13. Copy the formula to the range D14:D27.

   d. In cell E13, divide the value in cell D13 by the value in cell C13. Copy the formula to the range E14:E27.

7. Use Format Painter to do the following:

   a. Copy the formatting from cell A4 to cell A11.

   b. Copy the formatting from the range A5:E5 to the range A12:E12.

   c. Copy the formatting from the range A6:E6 to the range A13:E26.

   d. Copy the formatting from the range A9:E9 to the range A27:E27.

8. Add conditional formatting that displays negative values in the nonadjacent range D6:E9,D13:E27 in a dark red font on a light red background to highlight sales categories and product types that show a decrease in sales from the previous year.

9. In the range C45:N45, use the SUM function to calculate the sum of monthly sales across all product types.

10. In the range O31:O45, use the SUM function to calculate the sum of sales for each product category and across all product types. Verify that the value in cell O45 equals the value in cells B9 and B27.

11. Format the monthly sales data as follows:
    a. In the range C31:N44, format the sales data in Comma style with no decimal places.
    b. In the nonadjacent range C45:N45,O31:O45, format the calculated values in Accounting format with no decimal places.
    c. Format cell A29 with the Title cell style.
    d. Format the range A30:O30 with the 60% - Accent6 cell style.
    e. Format the range A31:A45 with the 60% - Accent3 cell style.
    f. Format the range B31:B45 with the 40% - Accent3 cell style.
    g. Format B45:O45 using the Total cell style.

12. Add a left border to the monthly totals in the range O31:O45.

13. Merge and center the cells in the range A31:A35. In the merged cell, rotate the text up, and then middle-align the text in the cell. Bold the text within the merged cell. Repeat for the ranges A36:A40 and A41:A44. Reduce the width of column A to 16 characters.

14. Add thick outside borders around the ranges A31:O35, A36:O40, and A41:O44.

15. Do the following to highlight the top-selling product types in the report:
    a. In the range O31:O44, use conditional formatting to highlight the top three selling product types in dark green text on a green fill.
    b. In cell O29, enter the text **Top 3 Sellers** and use the Text That Contains conditional format to change the format of this cell to a dark green text on a green fill to match the conditional formatting you added to the top three product types.

16. Change the theme of the workbook to Wisp.

17. Change the tab color of the Documentation sheet tab to the Brown, Accent 3 theme color. Change the tab color of the Product Sales sheet tab to the Olive Green, Accent 5 theme color.

18. Make the following format changes to the printed version of the Product Sales worksheet:
    a. Set the print area to the nonadjacent range A1:E28,A29:O45.
    b. Insert page breaks below rows 9 and 28 and to the right of columns H and N. Remove any automatic page breaks that were added to the sheet.
    c. Set the print titles to repeat rows 1 and 2 and columns A and B on every page.
    d. Set the size of the left margin to 1 inch.
    e. Scale the printout to 60% of its normal size.
    f. Add a different first page for headers and footers. On the first page header, display your name in the left section, display the file name in center, and display the date in the right section.
    g. For the first page footer and subsequent page footers, enter the code **Page &[Page] of &[Pages]** in the center section.

19. Preview the workbook. The printout should have only five pages. If you are instructed to print, print the entire workbook.

20. Save the workbook, and then close it.

Apply

Case Problem 1

Data File needed for this Case Problem: NP_EX_2-3.xlsx

Vestis Wholesale Suppliers   Jacinta Safar is an inventory manager at Vestis Wholesale Suppliers, a major clothing supplier for stores and vendors across the United States. Every week Jacinta compiles an inventory report for different warehouses, detailing the contents in the warehouse, the value of those contents, and the anticipated time until those contents need to be restocked. Jacinta wants you to make workbook containing the weekly report for the Akron, Ohio, warehouse easier to read and understand. Complete the following:

1. Open the **NP_EX_2-3.xlsx** workbook located in the Excel2 > Case1 folder included with your Data Files, and then save the workbook as **NP_EX_2_Inventory** in the location specified by your instructor.

2. In the Documentation sheet, enter your name in cell B4 and the date in cell B5.

3. Change the theme of the workbook to View.

4. In the Documentation sheet, make the following formatting changes:

   a. In cell A1, change the font to Impact, increase the font size to 20 points, and change the font color to Brown, Accent 6.

   b. Change cell A2 to a 14-point bold font.

   c. Add borders around the cells in the range A4:B6.

   d. In the range A4:A6, change the fill color to Brown, Accent 6, Lighter 60% and top-align the cell contents.

5. Use the Format Painter to copy the formatting from the range A1:A2 in the Documentation sheet to the range A1:A2 in the Inventory worksheet.

6. In the Inventory worksheet, add borders around the cells in the range A4:B7 and change the fill color of the range A4:A7 to Brown, Accent 6, Lighter 60%.

7. Enter formulas to add the following calculations to the Inventory worksheet:

   a. In the range G10:G391, calculate the value of each item in the warehouse inventory by multiplying the item's unit price by the quantity in stock.

   b. In the range I10:I391, calculate the difference between the Quantity in Stock values in column F and the Reorder at Quantity values in column H to determine whether items have dropped below the automatic reorder level.

   c. In cell B5, use the COUNT function to count the values in column F to calculate the total number of items in the warehouse. Use the range reference F:F to reference the entire column.

   d. In cell B6, use the SUM function to sum the values in column G to calculate the total inventory value.

   e. In cell B7, use the AVERAGE function to average the values in column J to determine the average days to reorder new items.

8. Add the following formats to the worksheet:

   a. Format cell B6 with the Currency style.

   b. Format cell B7 to show one decimal place.

   c. Format the nonadjacent range E10:E391,G10:G391 in Currency style.

   d. Format the range A9:J9 with the Accent3 cell style.

9. Display the inventory table with banded rows of alternating colors by setting the fill color of the range A10:J10 to Olive Green, Accent 3 - Lighter 80%, and then using the Format Painter to copy the formatting in the range A10:J11 to the range A12:J391.

10. Use conditional formatting to highlight all of the values in the range I10:I391 that are less than 0 in a light red fill and dark red text to make inventory items that must be immediately reordered stand out.

11. Format the Inventory worksheet for printing as follows:

    a. Set the print area to the range A9:J391 so only the inventory table will print.

    b. Remove the column page breaks that would divide the inventory table into separate pages.

c. Set the print titles so that rows 1 through 9 of the worksheet print on every page.

d. Set the header of the first page to display the file name in the left section and your name and the date on separate lines in the right section.

e. For the first page and all subsequent pages, display a center footer that shows **Page** followed the page number followed by **of** followed by the number of pages in the printout.

12. Preview the workbook. If you are instructed to print, print the entire workbook.

13. Save the workbook, and then close it.

Create

Case Problem 2

Data File needed for this Case Problem: NP_EX_2-4.xlsx

TechMasters   Javon Lee is the customer service manager at TechMasters, an electronics and computer firm located in Scottsdale, Arizona. Javon is analyzing the records for technical support calls to TechMasters to determine which times are understaffed, resulting in unacceptable wait times. Javon has compiled several months of data and calculated the average wait times in one-hour intervals for each day of the week. You will format Javon's workbook to make it easier to determine when TechMasters should hire more staff to assist with customer support requests. Complete the following:

1. Open the **NP_EX_2-4.xlsx** workbook located in the Excel2 > Case2 folder included with your Data Files, and then save the workbook as **NP_EX_2_Support** in the location specified by your instructor.

2. In the Documentation sheet, enter your name in cell B3 and the current date in cell B4.

3. Apply the Vapor Trail theme to the workbook.

4. Apply the following formats to the Documentation sheet:

   a. Format the title in cell A1 using a 36-point Impact font with the Bright Green, Accent 5 font color.

   b. Format the range A3:A5 with the Accent5 cell style.

   c. Add a border around the cells in the range A3:B5. Wrap the text within each cell, and top-align the cell text.

Explore 5. Click cell A1, and then save the format you applied to that cell as a new cell style using **TechMasters Title** as the cell style name.

6. Go to the Wait Times worksheet and apply the TechMasters Title cell style to cell A1.

Explore 7. Change the font color in cell A2 to Bright Green, Accent 5 and increase the font size to 12 points. Save the format used in this cell as a new cell style using **TechMasters Subtitle** as the cell style name.

8. Format the average customer wait time values in the range A14:H39 as follows:

   a. Merge and center the range A14:H14, and then apply the Heading 2 cell style to the merged contents.

   b. Format the data in the range B16:H39 to show one decimal place.

   c. Format the column and row labels in the nonadjacent range A15:H15,A16:A39 with the Light Yellow, 60% - Accent3 cell style.

   d. Center the column headings in the range B15:H15.

9. In cell B5, enter **22** as an excellent wait time. In cell B6, enter **28** as a good wait time. In cell B7, enter **47** as an acceptable wait time. In cell B8, enter **69** as a poor wait time. In cell B9, enter **84** as a very poor wait time. In cell B10, enter **90** as an unacceptable wait time.

10. Merge and center the range A4:C4 and apply the Heading 2 cell style to the merged cell. Add borders around all of the cells in the range A5:C10.

11. Do the following to create a table summarizing the wait time data that has been collected:

   a. In cell E4, enter **Average Wait Time (All Days)** as the label. In cell E7, enter **Average Wait Time (Weekdays)** as the label. In cell E10, enter **Average Wait Time (Weekends)** as the label.

   b. In cell H4, enter a formula to calculate the average of the wait times in the range B16:H39. In cell H7, calculate the average weekday wait times in the range C16:G39. In cell H10, calculate the average weekend rate times in the nonadjacent range B16:B39,H16:H39.

12. Apply the following formats to the data in the range E4:H12:

   a. Merge and center the range E4:G6, wrap the text in the merged cell, center the cell content both horizontally and vertically, and then apply the Light Yellow, 60% - Accent3 cell style to the merged cell.

   b. Merge and center the range H4:H6, and then center the averaged value in the merged cell H4 both horizontally and vertically.

   c. Add borders around the cells in the range E4:H6.

   d. Copy the formatting in the range E4:H6 and apply them to the range E7:H12.

13. Apply the following formats to the wait time categories in the range A5:C10 to color code the different wait times:

   a. Change the fill color of the range A5:C5 to the standard green color and the font color to white.

   b. Change the fill color of the range A6:C6 to the standard light green color.

   c. Change the fill color of the range A7:C7 to the standard yellow color.

   d. Change the fill color of the range A8:C8 to the standard orange color.

   e. Change the fill color of the range A9:C9 to the standard red color and the font color to white.

   f. Change the fill color of the range A10:C10 to black and the font color to white.

14. Apply the following conditional formats in the specified order to the nonadjacent range H4:H12,B16:H39:

   a. Highlight values less than 22 with a standard green fill and white font. (*Hint:* When applying the conditional format, use the Custom Format option and choose the fill and font colors from the Format Cells dialog box.)

   b. Highlight values greater than 90 with black fill and white font.

   c. Highlight values between 22 and 34 with a standard light green fill.

   d. Highlight values between 34 and 60 with a standard yellow fill.

   e. Highlight values between 60 and 78 with a standard orange fill.

   f. Highlight values between 78 and 90 with a standard red fill and white font.

15. Create a cell to record wait time results as follows:

   a. In cell A41, enter **Notes** as the label, and then format it with the TechMasters Subtitle cell style.

   b. Merge the range A42:H50. Top- and left-align the contents of the merged cell, turn on text wrapping, and then add a thick outside border in the Blue, Accent 6 color to the merged cell.

16. In cell A42, summarize your conclusions about the wait times. Answer whether the wait times are within acceptable limits on average for the entire week, on weekdays, and on weekends. Also indicate whether there are times during the week that customers experience very poor to unacceptable delays.

17. Indent your comments in the merged cell to the right twice to provide additional space between your comment text and the border.

18. Change the tab color of the Documentation sheet tab to Bright Green, Accent 5. Change the tab color of the Wait Times sheet tab to Gold, Accent 3.

19. Format the printed version of the Wait Times worksheet as follows:

   a. Scale the sheet so that it fits on a single page in portrait orientation.

   b. Center the sheet on the page horizontally and vertically.

   c. In the right section of the header, type **Prepared by** followed by your name and the date on a separate line.

   d. In the left section of the footer, insert the file name. In the right section of the footer, insert the worksheet name.

20. Preview the workbook. If you are instructed to print, print the entire workbook.

21. Save the workbook, and then close it.

Objectives

Session 3.1
- Translate an equation into a function
- Do calculations with dates and times
- Extend data and formulas with AutoFill
- Use the Function Library
- Calculate statistics

Session 3.2
- Using the Quick Analysis tool
- Use absolute and relative cell references
- Use a logical function
- Retrieve data with lookup tables
- Do what-if analysis with Goal Seek

Performing Calculations with Formulas and Functions

Staffing a Call Center

Case | Evergreen Fidelity Insurance

Kiara Patel is the manager of the call center for Evergreen Fidelity Insurance. The call center, which handles customer queries and new applications, is open Monday through Friday from 8 a.m. to 6 p.m., Central Time. Part of Kiara's responsibility is to hire operators to answer the calls that come into the center and maintain quality customer support. Good customer support includes handling calls promptly with a minimum of time spent on hold waiting for the next available operator. To do this, Kiara needs enough operators to handle the call volume. But with a fixed budget, the call center has a limited number of operators it can hire.

You will work with Kiara to develop an Excel worksheet that will analyze the call center's current response times and make recommendations on the correct number of operators for the company to hire to handle the work.

EXCEL

Starting Data Files

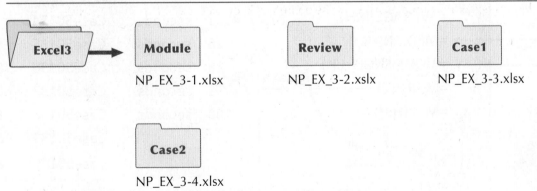

Excel3 → Module
NP_EX_3-1.xlsx

Review
NP_EX_3-2.xslx

Case1
NP_EX_3-3.xlsx

Case2
NP_EX_3-4.xlsx

Session 3.1 Visual Overview:

Functions are organized by category in the Function Library group. When you select a function, the Function Arguments dialog box opens.

The Insert Function button opens the Insert Function dialog box from which you can select a function.

The **AVERAGE function** returns the average of values in the range.

The **MEDIAN function** returns the middle value in the range.

The **MODE.SNGL function** returns the single value that is repeated most often in the range.

The **MAX function** returns the highest (maximum) value in the range.

The **MIN function** returns the lowest (minimum) value in the range.

AutoFill extends patterns of data.

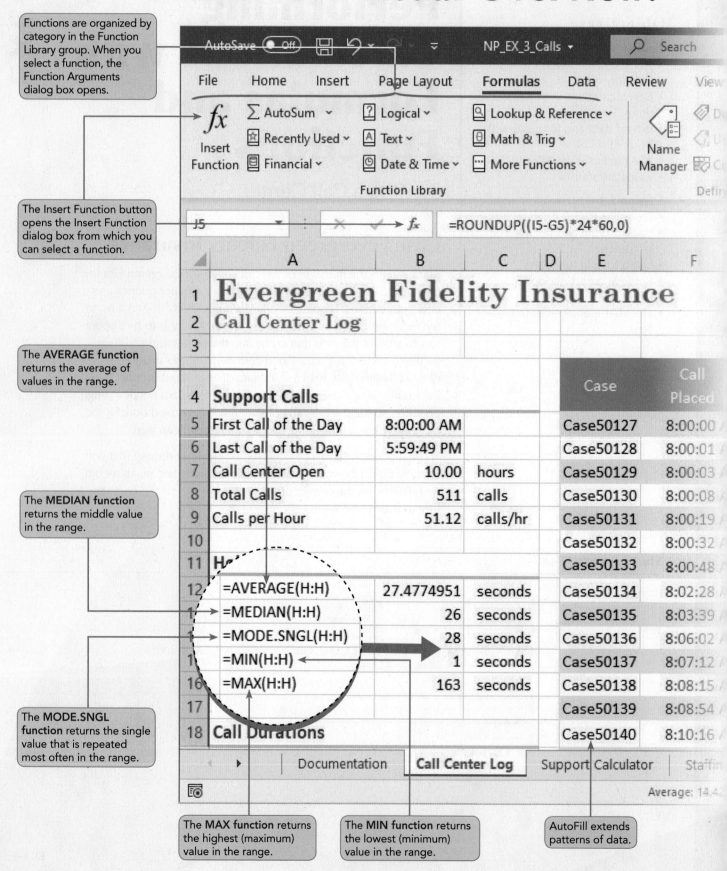

	A	B	C	D	E	F
1	**Evergreen Fidelity Insurance**					
2	**Call Center Log**					
3						
4	**Support Calls**				Case	Call Placed
5	First Call of the Day	8:00:00 AM			Case50127	8:00:00 A
6	Last Call of the Day	5:59:49 PM			Case50128	8:00:01 A
7	Call Center Open	10.00	hours		Case50129	8:00:03 A
8	Total Calls	511	calls		Case50130	8:00:08 A
9	Calls per Hour	51.12	calls/hr		Case50131	8:00:19 A
10					Case50132	8:00:32 A
11	H				Case50133	8:00:48 A
12	=AVERAGE(H:H)	27.4774951	seconds		Case50134	8:02:28 A
13	=MEDIAN(H:H)	26	seconds		Case50135	8:03:39 A
14	=MODE.SNGL(H:H)	28	seconds		Case50136	8:06:02 A
15	=MIN(H:H)	1	seconds		Case50137	8:07:12 A
16	=MAX(H:H)	163	seconds		Case50138	8:08:15 A
17					Case50139	8:08:54 A
18	**Call Durations**				Case50140	8:10:16 A

Cell reference box: **J5**

Formula bar: =ROUNDUP((I5-G5)*24*60,0)

Ribbon: AutoSave Off · NP_EX_3_Calls · Search

File | Home | Insert | Page Layout | **Formulas** | Data | Review | View

fx Insert Function · Σ AutoSum · ☆ Recently Used · 📄 Financial · ? Logical · A Text · 🕑 Date & Time · 🔍 Lookup & Reference · 🔢 Math & Trig · More Functions

Function Library

Name Manager · Defi

Sheet tabs: Documentation | **Call Center Log** | Support Calculator | Staffi

Average: 14.4

Formulas and Functions

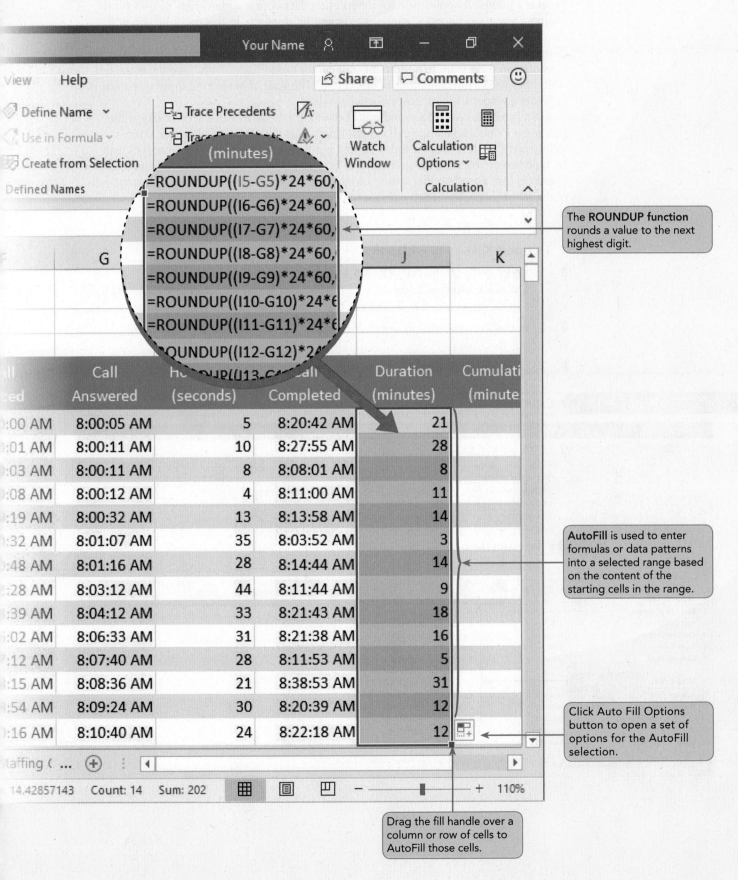

The **ROUNDUP function** rounds a value to the next highest digit.

AutoFill is used to enter formulas or data patterns into a selected range based on the content of the starting cells in the range.

Click Auto Fill Options button to open a set of options for the AutoFill selection.

Drag the fill handle over a column or row of cells to AutoFill those cells.

Designing a Workbook for Calculations

Excel is a powerful application for interpreting data with a wide variety of uses from business reports to financial analyses to scientific research. In this module, you will create a workbook to analyze data from a call center. Call center science is a rich field of research that uses many mathematical tools to answer questions such as "How many operators are necessary to handle the call center traffic?" and "What are the expected wait times with a given number of operators?" The goal of answering these questions is to create a responsive and cost-effective service.

Kiara Patel has created a workbook containing raw data from a typical day at the Evergreen Fidelity Insurance call center. You will use the Excel mathematical tools to interpret this data. This includes finding out how long a typical customer will wait on hold before reaching an operator and how long conversations with call center operators last. Based on that information you can then make predictions about the size of the staff Kiara will need to effectively handle the call center traffic.

To open Kiara's workbook:

1. **sam** ⬇ Open the **NP_EX_3-1.xlsx** workbook located in the **Excel3 > Module** folder included with your Data Files, and then save the workbook as **NP_EX_3_Calls** in the location specified by your instructor.

2. In the Documentation sheet, enter your name in cell B3 and the date in cell B4.

3. Go to the **Call Center Log** worksheet. See Figure 3–1.

Figure 3–1	Call Center Log worksheet

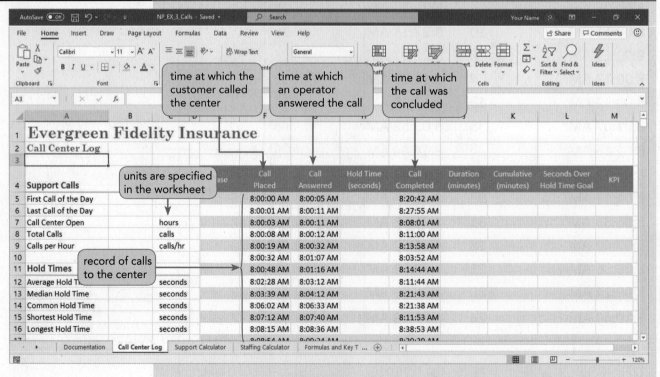

The Call Center Log worksheet contains the call records from a typical workday. Kiara has entered the time each call was received, the time an operator answered the call, and the time the call with the operator ended. Other information, such as how long the customer was on hold and the length of each conversation with the operator, are not included in the call log and need to be calculated.

Documenting Calculations

A workbook with many calculations can be challenging for the author to write and for others to use. To help everyone, it is important to list the formulas used in the workbook and to explain the assumptions behind those formulas. The workbook documentation should also include the definitions of key terms to make it clear what is being calculated and why.

Kiara included a worksheet containing explanations of the equations and key terms used in this workbook. Before you start creating the formulas, you will review this worksheet.

To review the workbook's formulas and key terms:

▶ **1.** Go to the **Formulas and Key Terms** worksheet.

▶ **2.** Review the worksheet contents, paying attention to the equations and key terms that you will be using in this workbook.

▶ **3.** Go to the **Call Center Log** worksheet.

Constants and Units

One skill you need when working with Excel is the ability to translate an equation into an Excel formula. Some equations use **constants**, which are terms in an equation whose values don't change. For example, the following equation converts a duration value measured in days to a duration value measured in seconds by multiplying the *day* value by three constants—24, 60, and 60, because there are 24 hours in a day, 60 minutes in each hour, and 60 seconds in each minute:

$$seconds = day \times 24 \times 60 \times 60$$

It is good practice in worksheets to include the units in any calculation. In some situations, the unit is obvious, such as when a currency value is formatted with the appropriate currency symbol. In other situations, such as reporting time intervals, the unit is unknown unless you include it (hours, minutes, or seconds) as text in the worksheet.

Insight

Deciding Where to Place a Constant

Constants can be placed in an Excel formula or in a worksheet cell that is referenced by the formula. Which approach is better?

The answer depends on the constant being used, the purpose of the workbook, and the intended audience. Placing constants in separate cells that you reference in the formulas can help users better understand the worksheet because no values are hidden within the formulas. Also, when a constant is entered in a cell, you can add explanatory text next to each constant to document how it is being used in the formula. On the other hand, you don't want a user to inadvertently change the value of a constant and alter the formula result. You will need to evaluate how important it is for other people to immediately see the constant and whether the constant requires any explanation for other people to understand the formula.

In general, if the constant is a common one, such as the constant 60 used to multiply an hour value into a minute value, you can place the constant directly in a formula. However, if the constant is less well-known, it is better to place the constant in its own cell, making it more visible. If you decide to place a constant in a cell, you can lock that cell value, to prevent users from changing the constant without permission. This ensures that the constant value remains unchanged.

You will use constants to calculate each customer's hold time during their calls to center.

Calculating with Dates and Times

Excel stores dates and times as the number of days since January 0, 1900. Full days are a whole number and partial days are a fraction such as 0.5 for a half day or 12 hours. Storing dates and times as numbers makes it easier to calculate time and date intervals.

Kiara wants you to calculate the amount of time the first customer in the call log spent on hold and the length of the conversation with the Evergreen Fidelity Insurance operator.

To calculate the first customer's hold time and call duration:

▶ 1. In cell **H5**, enter the formula **=G5-F5** to calculate the hold time of the first call, which is equal to difference between the time when the call was placed and when the call was answered. The time value 12:00:05 AM appears in cell H5.

▶ 2. In cell **J5**, enter the formula **=I5-G5** to calculate the length of time of the first conversation, which is equal to the difference between the time the call was answered and the time the conversation was concluded. The time value 12:20:37 AM appears in cell J5.

The results of the two formulas are not what you might have expected. The issue is that the Excel applies the same number format to a formula result as was used in the cells referenced by the formula. In this case, cells H5 and J5 are formatted to appear as time values.

Kiara wants these time differences formatted as seconds and minutes. You'll remove the date/time format applied to cells H5 and J5 to view their underlying numeric values, and change the formulas to convert those time differences as seconds and minutes.

To convert the first customer's hold time and call duration to seconds and minutes:

1. Click cell **H5** containing the calculated hold time for the first customer.

2. Change the formula to **=(G5-F5)*24*60*60** to multiply the hold time by the number of seconds in one day and then press **ENTER**.

3. Click cell **J5** containing the call duration for the first customer.

4. Change the formula to **=(I5-G5)*24*60** to multiply the call duration by the number of minutes in one day and then press **ENTER**.

5. Select the nonadjacent range **H5,J5** and on the Home tab, in the Number group, click the **Number Format arrow**, and then click **General**.

   The values 5 and 20.6166667 appear in the cells, indicating that the first customer was on hold for 5 seconds with a call length of 20 minutes plus a fraction of a minute.

6. Click cell **K5**. See Figure 3-2.

Figure 3–2   **First hold time and call length calculations**

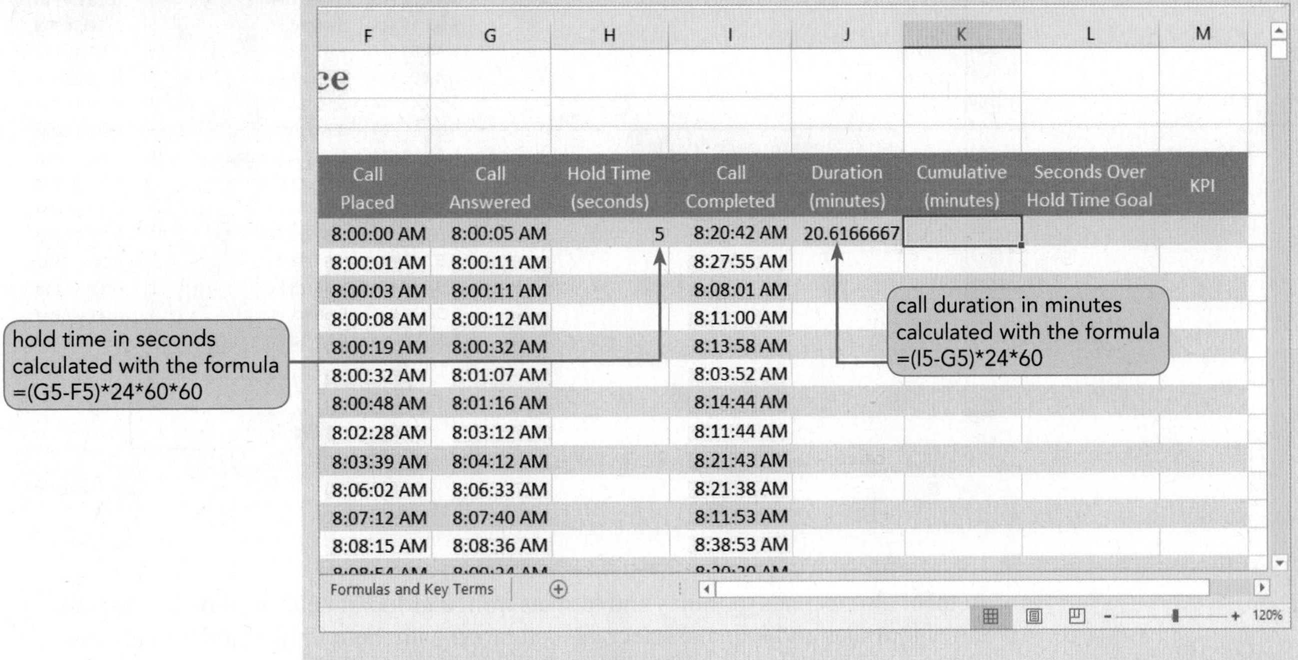

Now that you have calculated the hold time and call duration for the first customer, you will apply these formulas to the remaining entries in the call log.

AutoFilling Formulas and Data Patterns

One way to efficiently enter long columns or rows of formulas and data values is with AutoFill. AutoFill extends a formula or a pattern of data values into a selected range and is often faster than copying and pasting, which requires two distinct actions on the part of the user.

AutoFilling a Formula

Tip

You can also select a range, click the Fill button in the Editing group on the Home tab, and then select the direction to fill.

To extend a formula into range with AutoFill, you select the cell containing the formula to be extended. When the cell is selected, the **fill handle** appears as a green square in the lower-right corner of the cell. Dragging the fill handle down or across extends the formula and the cell formats into a new range.

You will use AutoFill to extend the formula in cell H5 over the entire call log in the range H5:H515.

To use AutoFill to extend the formula in cell H5:

1. Click cell **H5** to select it. The fill handle, the small green square, appears in the lower-right corner of the selected cell.

2. Drag the **fill handle** over the range **H5:H515**. The worksheet window will scroll as you drag the fill handle down to cell H515. See Figure 3–3.

| Figure 3–3 | Formula extended with AutoFill |

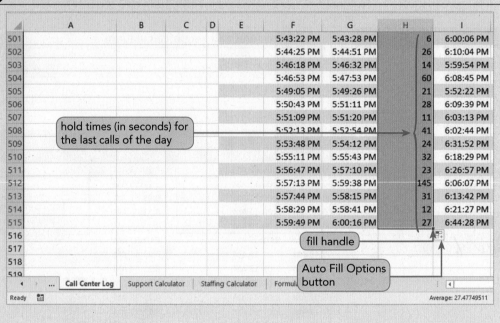

AutoFill also extends formulas and formats from a group of cells. To repeat the same group of formulas and formats, select the cell range with the formulas and formats you want to extend, and then drag the fill handle over the range that you want to fill.

Exploring Auto Fill Options

By default, AutoFill extends both the formulas and the formatting of the initial cell or cells. However, you might want to extend only the formulas or only the formatting. The Auto Fill Options button that appears after you release the mouse button lets you specify what part of the initial cells should be extended. Figure 3–4 shows the menu of AutoFill options.

Figure 3–4   Auto Fill Options menu

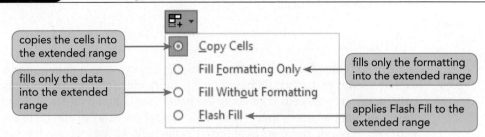

copies the cells into the extended range

fills only the data into the extended range

fills only the formatting into the extended range

applies Flash Fill to the extended range

- ⊙ Copy Cells
- ○ Fill Formatting Only
- ○ Fill Without Formatting
- ○ Flash Fill

Kiara used banded rows to make the call log easier to read. By extending cell H5 into the range H5:H515, you copied cell H5's format as well as its formula, removing the banded row effect for the entries in column H. You'll use the Auto Fill Options button to restore the banded row effect to the table.

To use the Auto Fill Options button to copy only formulas:

1. Click the **Auto Fill Options** button. A menu of AutoFill options appears.

2. Click the **Fill Without Formatting** option button. The original formatting of the range is restored without affecting the copied formulas.

3. Click cell **J5** to select it.

4. Drag the **fill handle** down over the range **J5:J515**. Both the formulas and formatting are copied.

5. Click the **Auto Fill Options** button, and then click the **Fill Without Formatting** option button to restore the original formatting.

6. Scroll up the worksheet and click cell **D3** to deselect the range. Figure 3–5 shows the hold time and call duration for the first several customers in the call log.

Figure 3–5   Hold time and call duration formulas extended

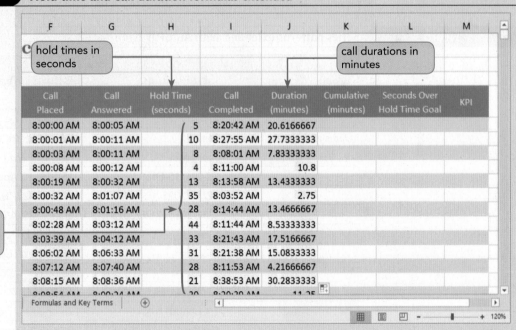

hold times in seconds

call durations in minutes

calculated values filled without formatting

Call Placed	Call Answered	Hold Time (seconds)	Call Completed	Duration (minutes)	Cumulative (minutes)	Seconds Over Hold Time Goal	KPI
8:00:00 AM	8:00:05 AM	5	8:20:42 AM	20.6166667			
8:00:01 AM	8:00:11 AM	10	8:27:55 AM	27.7333333			
8:00:03 AM	8:00:11 AM	8	8:08:01 AM	7.83333333			
8:00:08 AM	8:00:12 AM	4	8:11:00 AM	10.8			
8:00:19 AM	8:00:32 AM	13	8:13:58 AM	13.4333333			
8:00:32 AM	8:01:07 AM	35	8:03:52 AM	2.75			
8:00:48 AM	8:01:16 AM	28	8:14:44 AM	13.4666667			
8:02:28 AM	8:03:12 AM	44	8:11:44 AM	8.53333333			
8:03:39 AM	8:04:12 AM	33	8:21:43 AM	17.5166667			
8:06:02 AM	8:06:33 AM	31	8:21:38 AM	15.0833333			
8:07:12 AM	8:07:40 AM	28	8:11:53 AM	4.21666667			
8:08:15 AM	8:08:36 AM	21	8:38:53 AM	30.2833333			

Formulas and Key Terms

The call log should display the case number for each call. You can also enter this information with AutoFill.

Filling a Series

AutoFill can extend any data pattern involving dates, times, numbers, and text. To extend a series of data values based on a pattern, enter enough values to establish the pattern, select those cells containing the pattern, and then drag the fill handle extending the pattern into a larger range. Figure 3–6 shows how AutoFill can be used to extend an initial series of odd numbers established in the cells A2 and A3 into the range A2:A9.

Figure 3–6   **AutoFill used to extend a series**

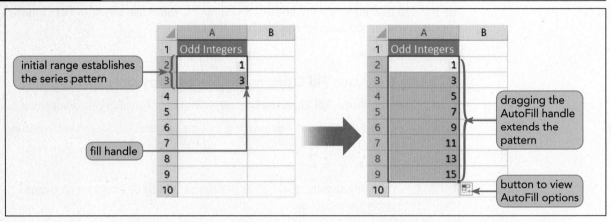

Figure 3–7 shows other extended patterns created with AutoFill. In each case, you must provide enough information for AutoFill to identify the pattern. AutoFill recognizes some patterns from only a single entry—such as Jan or January to create a series of month abbreviations or names, and Mon or Monday to create a series of the days of the week. A text pattern that includes text and a number such as Region 1, Region 2, and so on can also be automatically extended using AutoFill. You can start the series at any point, such as Weds, June, or Region 10, and AutoFill will continue with the next days, months, or text.

Figure 3–7   **Series patterns extended with AutoFill**

Type	Initial Value(s)	Extended Values
Numbers	1, 2, 3	4, 5, 6, ...
	2, 4, 6	8, 10, 12, ...
Dates and Times	Jan	Feb, Mar, Apr, ...
	January	February, March, April, ...
	15-Jan, 15-Feb	15-Mar, 15-Apr, 15-May, ...
	12/30/2025	12/31/2025, 1/1/2025, 1/2/2025, ...
	1/31/2025, 2/28/2025	3/31/2025, 4/30/2025, 5/31/2025, ...
	Mon	Tue, Wed, Thu, ...
	Monday	Tuesday, Wednesday, Thursday, ...
	11:00 AM	12:00 PM, 1:00 PM, 2:00 PM, ...
	11:58 AM, 11:59 AM	12:00 PM, 12:01 PM, 12:02 PM, ...
Patterned Text	1st period	2nd period, 3rd period, 4th period, ...
	Region 1	Region 2, Region 3, Region 4, ...
	Quarter 3	Quarter 4, Quarter 1, Quarter 2, ...
	Qtr3	Qtr4, Qtr1, Qtr2, ...

AutoFill can extend patterns either horizontally across columns within a single row or vertically across rows within a single column.

Reference

Extending a Series with AutoFill

- Enter the first few values of the series into a range.
- Select the range, and then drag the fill handle over the cells you want to fill.
- To copy only the formats or only the formulas, click the Auto Fill Options button and select the appropriate option.

or

- Enter the first few values of the series into a range.
- Select the entire range into which you want to extend the series.
- On the Home tab, in the Editing group, click the Fill button, and then click Down, Right, Up, Left, Series, or Justify.

At Evergreen Fidelity Insurance, calls are automatically assigned a sequential case number following the general pattern Case*number*, where *number* is an integer that increases by 1 with each new call. In this call log, the first case number assigned on this day is Case50127, the case number for the second call is Case50128, and so forth. You will use AutoFill to insert of all the case numbers in column E of the call log.

To extend the case number series in the call log:

1. In cell **E5**, enter the text **Case50127** as the first case number for the day.

2. Click cell **E5** again to select the cell, and then drag the fill handle down over the range **E5:E515**. Case numbers are entered sequentially into the extended range, ending with Case50637 in cell E515.

3. Click the **Auto Fill Options** button, and then click the **Fill Without Formatting** option button to retain the banded rows design used in the table.

Another way of defining a series is with the Series dialog box shown in Figure 3–8. To access the Series dialog box, select the range in which you want to place a series of values, click the Fill button in the Editing group on the Home tab, and then select Series. You can specify a linear or growth series for numbers; a date series for dates that increase by day, weekday, month, or year; or an AutoFill series for patterned text. With numbers, you can also specify the step value (how much each number increases over the previous entry) and a stop value (the endpoint for the entire series).

Figure 3–8   Series dialog box

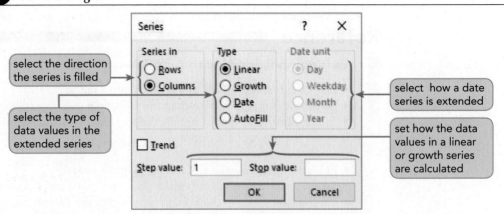

select the direction the series is filled

select the type of data values in the extended series

select how a date series is extended

set how the data values in a linear or growth series are calculated

You have finished with using AutoFill to enter formulas and data patterns. Next, you will analyze the call data using Excel functions.

Applying Excel Functions

Excel supports several hundred functions covering a wide range of topics, including finance, statistics, and engineering. With so many functions, it can be challenging to find the function you need to accomplish a specific task. To make it easier to find a specific function, Excel organizes the functions into a function library with the 13 categories described in Figure 3–9.

Figure 3–9   Function library categories

Category	Description
Compatibility	Functions from Excel 2010 or earlier, still supported to provide backward compatibility
Cube	Retrieve data from multidimensional databases involving online analytical processing (OLAP)
Database	Retrieve and analyze data stored in databases
Date & Time	Analyze or create date and time values and time intervals
Engineering	Analyze engineering problems
Financial	Analyze information for business and finance
Information	Return information about the format, location, or contents of worksheet cells
Logical	Return logical (true-false) values
Lookup & Reference	Look up and return data matching a set of specified conditions from a range
Math & Trig	Perform math and trigonometry calculations
Statistical	Provide statistical analyses of data sets
Text	Return text values or evaluate text
Web	Provide information on web-based connections

You can access the function library from the Function Library group on the Formulas tab or from the Insert Function dialog box. The Insert Function dialog box includes a search tool to find a function based on a general description. It also displays the function syntax, making it easier to enter a function without syntax errors. You'll use the library to find a function to round the call duration values to whole minutes.

Rounding Data Values

Excel supports three rounding functions: ROUND, ROUNDDOWN, and ROUNDUP. The **ROUND function** rounds a value to the nearest digit, the **ROUNDDOWN function** rounds the value to the next lowest digit, and the **ROUNDUP function** rounds the value to the next highest digit. These functions use the same arguments in their syntax

```
ROUND(number, Num_digits)
ROUNDDOWN(number, Num_digits)
ROUNDUP(number, Num_digits)
```

where **number** is the number to be rounded and **Num_digits** is the digit to round the number to—0 rounds the number to the nearest integer, 1 rounds the number to the nearest tenth, 2 rounds the number to the nearest hundredth and so forth. For example, the following expression returns a value of 132.44:

```
ROUND(132.438, 2)
```

But when you change the *Num_digits* value from 2 to 1, as in the following expression, the returned value is 132.4:

```
ROUND(132.438, 1)
```

A negative *Num_digits* value rounds the number to a power of 10. For example, the *Num_digits* value of -1 rounds the number to the nearest power of ten. So, the expression

```
ROUND(132.438, -1)
```

returns the value 130.

Reference

Using Functions to Round Values

- To round a number to the nearest digit, use

  ```
  ROUND(number, Num_digits)
  ```

  where **number** is the numeric value and **Num_digits** is the number of digits to which the numeric value is rounded.
- To round a number down to the next lowest digit, use

  ```
  ROUNDDOWN(number, Num_digits)
  ```

- To round a number to the next highest digit, use

  ```
  ROUNDUP(number, Num_digits)
  ```

- To round a number to nearest integer, use

  ```
  INT(number)
  ```

- To round a number to nearest multiple of a value, use

  ```
  MROUND(number, multiple)
  ```

  where **multiple** is a multiple to be rounded to.

Kiara wants the call durations in column J displayed as whole minutes with any fraction of a minute rounded up to the next minute. For example, a call duration of 2.3 minutes should be rounded up to 3 minutes. You will use the Insert Function dialog box to locate and apply the ROUNDUP function to the call duration data.

To use the Insert Function dialog box with the ROUNDUP function:

▶ **1.** Click cell **J5**, and then press **DELETE** to remove the formula stored in the cell.

▶ **2.** On the ribbon, click the **Formulas** tab to access the Function Library.

▶ **3.** In the Function Library group, click the **Insert Function** button. The Insert Function dialog box opens.

▶ **4.** In the Search for a function box, type **round** to describe the function you want to find, and then click **Go**. Functions that deal with rounding appear in the search results. See Figure 3–10.

Figure 3–10   Insert Function dialog box

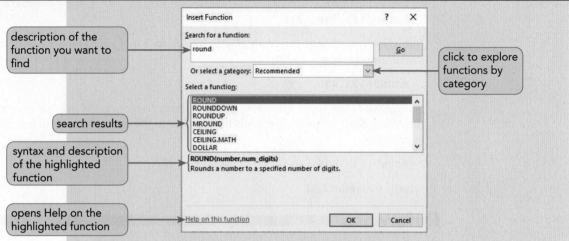

5. In the Select a function box, click **ROUNDUP** from the search results, and then click **OK**. The Function Arguments dialog box opens, describing the arguments used by the function.

▶ **6.** In the Number box, type the formula **(I5-G5)*24*60** to calculate the duration of the first call in minutes. The value 20.61666667, which is the unrounded value of this calculation, appears next to the Number box.

▶ **7.** Press **TAB**, and then type **0** in the Num_digits box to round up the calculated value to the next highest integer. In this case, the formula result 20.61666667 will be rounded up to 21. See Figure 3–11.

Figure 3–11   Function Arguments dialog box

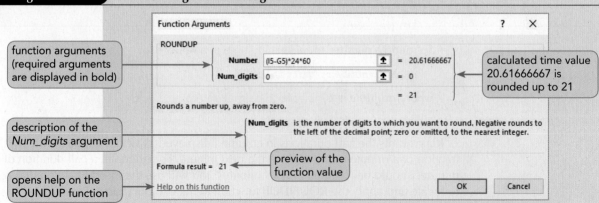

▶ **8.** Click **OK** to close the dialog box and insert the formula. The value 21 appears in cell J5, indicating that the first call required about 21 minutes of the operator's time.

▶ **9.** Drag the **fill handle** down over the range **J5:J515** to extend the formula to the rest of the entries in the call log.

▶ **10.** Click the **Auto Fill Options** button, and then click the **Fill Without Formatting** option button to retain the banded rows.

▶ **11.** Scroll up the worksheet and click cell **J5** to deselect the range. See Figure 3-12.

| Figure 3-12 | Rounded up call duration values |

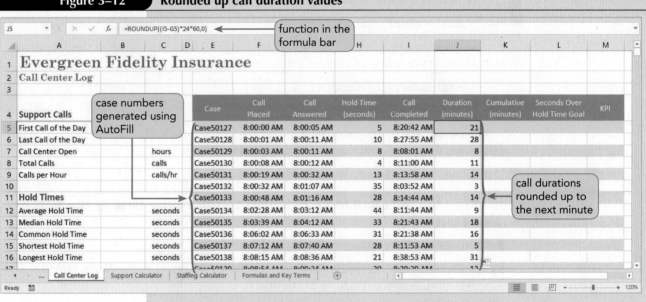

The ROUND, ROUNDDOWN, and ROUNDUP functions all round values to the nearest power of 10 such as 1/100, 1/10, 1, 10, 100, and so forth. To round values to powers other than 10, use the following **MROUND function**

MROUND(*number*, *multiple*)

where **number** is the number to be rounded and **multiple** is a multiple of a value to be rounded to. For example, the following function rounds 5241 to the nearest multiple of 25, returning 5250 :

MROUND(5241, 25)

To always rounds a value down to the next lowest integer, use the **INT function**:

INT(*number*)

For example, the following expression returns a value of 52:

INT(52.817)

You can learn more about the rounding functions available in Excel using Excel Help.

Calculating Minimums and Maximums

The MIN and MAX functions return the smallest and largest values from a specified set of numbers:

MIN(*number1*, [*number2*], …)
MAX(*number1*, [*number2*], …)

where *number1, number2,* and so on are the numbers or cell ranges from which to find the smallest or largest value.

Reference

Using Functions to Find Minimums and Maximums

- To return the smallest value from a data series, use

    MIN(**number1**, [*number2*], …)

    where **number1**, *number2*, and so on are the cell ranges or numbers in the data series.
- To return the largest value from a data series, use

    MAX(**number1**, [*number2*], …)

Kiara wants you to determine the times of the first and last calls made to the call center. You will use the MIN and MAX functions to do this.

To use the MIN and MAX functions to return the time of the first and last calls:

1. Click cell **B5** to select it.

2. On the Formulas tab, in the Function Library group, click the **More Functions** button, and then point to **Statistical** to display a list of all the statistical functions.

3. Scroll down the list, and then click **MIN**. The Function Arguments dialog box for the MIN function opens.

4. In the Number1 box, type **F:F** to find the smallest value from all of the time values in column F. You won't enter anything in the Number2 box because you want to search only this range of cells.

5. Click **OK**. The function returns 0.3333333, which is the numeric value of the minimum time value in column F.

6. On the ribbon, click the **Home** tab. In the Number group, click the **Number Format arrow**, and then click **Time**. The value displayed in cell B5 changes to 8:00:00 AM (the time of the first call).

7. Click cell **B6**, and then repeat Steps 2 through 6, clicking the **MAX** function in Step 3 to return the time of the last call of the day. Cell B6 displays 5:59:49 PM, indicating that the last call was placed just before the call center closed.

The Call Center Log worksheet should also display the total hours the call center was open, the number of calls received during that time and the number of calls per hour. You'll add these calculations to the worksheet.

To calculate the total call center hours, calls, and calls per hour:

▶ **1.** In cell **B7**, enter the formula **=(B6-B5)*24** to calculate the difference between the last call and first call.

▶ **2.** Click cell **B7** to select it, and then on the Home tab, in the Number group, click the **Number Format arrow**, and then click **Number**. A time interval of 10 hours is displayed in the cell.

▶ **3.** In cell **B8**, enter the formula **=COUNT(F:F)** to count all of the cells in column F containing numeric values. Cell B8 displays 511, indicating that 511 calls were placed during the day.

▶ **4.** In cell **B9**, enter the formula **=B8/B7** to calculate the number of calls per hour.

▶ **5.** Click cell **B9** to select it, and then in the Number group, click the **Number Format arrow**, and then click **Number** to display the value to two decimal places. Cell B9 displays 51.12, indicating that the call center received more than 51 calls every hour. See Figure 3–13.

| Figure 3–13 | Completed support calls data |

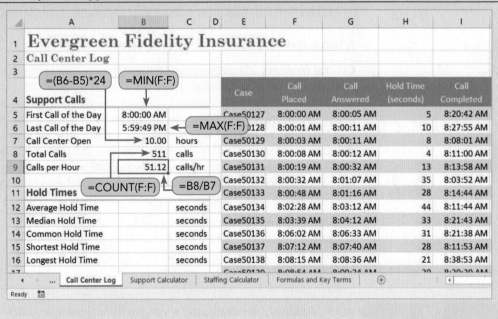

Kiara now has a better picture of the level of traffic at the call center. Next, you will calculate how long a typical caller waits before reaching an operator.

Proskills

Written Communication: Displaying Significant Digits

Excel stores numbers with a precision up to 15 digits and displays as many digits as will fit into the cell. So even the result of a simple formula such as =10/3 will display 3.33333333333333 if the cell is wide enough.

A number with 15-digit accuracy is difficult to read, and calculations rarely need that level of precision. Many scientific disciplines, such as chemistry or physics, have rules specifying exactly how many digits should be displayed with any calculation. These digits are called **significant digits** because they indicate the accuracy of the measured and calculated values. For example, the value 19.32 has four significant digits.

The rules for determining the number of significant digits reported in a calculation vary between disciplines. Generally, a calculated value should display no more digits than are found in any of the values used in the calculation. For example, because the input value 19.32 has four significant digits, any calculated value based on that input should have no more than four significant digits. Showing more digits would be misleading because it implies a level of accuracy beyond what was measured.

Because Excel displays calculated values with as many digits as can fit into a cell, you need to know the standards that your profession uses for reporting significant digits and format the results accordingly.

Measures of Central Tendency

Central tendency is a single measurement from a data series that returns the most typical or "central" data value. There are several measures of central tendency. This module focuses on the three most commonly used measures—average, median, and mode. The **average**, also known as the **mean**, is equal to the sum of the data values divided by the number of values in the data series. The **median** is the central value of the data series so that half of the values are less than the median and half are greater. Finally, the **mode** is the value repeated most often in the data series. A data series can have several modes if different values are repeated the same number of times. These three measures are calculated using the following functions:

```
AVERAGE(number1, [number2], …)
MEDIAN(number1, [number2], …)
MODE.SNGL(number1, [number2], …)
MODE.MULT(number1, [number2], …)
MODE(number1, [number2], …)
```

Tip

If there are several possible modes, both the MODE.SNGL and MODE functions return the first mode value listed in the data series.

where **number1**, **number2**, and so on are the values from a data series. Notice that Excel includes three different mode functions. The MODE.SNGL function returns a single value representing the mode from the data series. The **MODE.MULT function** returns either a single value or a list of values if more than one value is repeated the same number of times. The MODE function is the older version of the function for calculating modes and is equivalent to the MODE.SNGL function.

The average, while the most commonly used measure of central tendency, can be adversely effected by extreme values. Consider an exam in which every student receives a 90 except one student who receives a zero. That single zero value will cause the class average to drop, making it appear that students did worse on the exam than all but one actually did. On the other hand, the median and mode will both be 90, providing a more accurate assessment of a typical student's performance. However, the median and mode are also limited because they obscure information that might be useful. The instructor might want to know that one student did extremely poorly on the exam, which only the average indicates. For these reasons, it's often best to compare the results of all three measures.

Reference

Calculating Measures of Central Tendency

- To calculate the average from a data series, use

  AVERAGE(***number1***, [***number2***], …)

- To calculate the median or midpoint from a data series, use

  MEDIAN(***number1***, [***number2***], …)

- To return a single value that is repeated most often in a data series, use

  MODE.SNGL(***number1***, [***number2***], …)

- To return the value or list of values that is repeated most often in a data series, use

  MODE.MULT(***number1***, [***number2***], …)

Kiara wants to know the typical hold time that customers will experience at the call center based on the average, median, and mode measures of the hold-time data. Kiara also wants to know the shortest and longest hold times that customers experienced during the day. You'll calculate these measures using the AVERAGE, MEDIAN, MODE.SNGL, MIN, and MAX functions.

To calculate the average, median, and mode hold times:

▶ 1. Click cell **B12**, and then click the **Formulas** tab on the ribbon.

▶ 2. In the Function Library group, click the **More Functions** button, and then point to **Statistical** in the list of function categories. A list of statistical functions appears.

▶ 3. In the Statistical functions list, click **AVERAGE** to open the Function Arguments dialog box.

▶ 4. In the Number1 box, type **H:H** as the range reference, and then click **OK**. The cell displays 27.477495, indicating that the average time spent on hold was about 27 and a half seconds.

▶ 5. Click cell **B13**, and then repeat Steps 2 through 4, selecting **MEDIAN** as the statistical function in Step 3. The cell displays a median value of 26.

▶ 6. Click cell **B14**, and then repeat Steps 2 through 4, selecting **MODE.SNGL** as the statistical function in Step 3. The cell displays a mode value of 28.

▶ 7. In cell **B15**, enter the formula = **MIN(H:H)** to calculate the minimum hold-time value in column H. The shortest hold time was 1 second.

▶ 8. In cell **B16**, enter the formula =**MAX(H:H)** to calculate the maximum hold-time value in column H. The longest hold time was 163 seconds. See Figure 3–14.

| Figure 3–14 | Completed customer hold-times data |

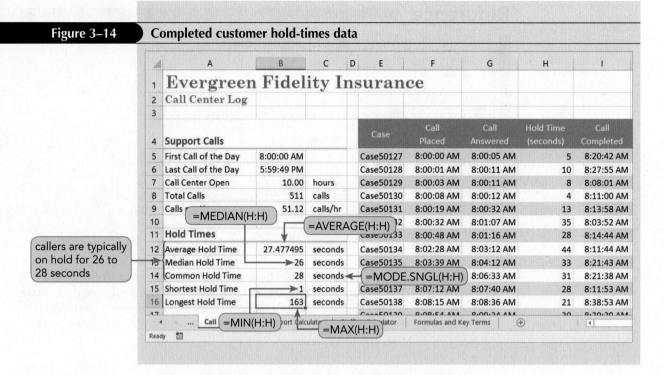

The average, median, and mode values all indicate that the typical caller waits on hold for about 26 to 28 seconds. Kiara wants you to do a similar analysis for the length of each customer conversation with an operator.

To calculate the typical length of the support conversations:

1. In cell **B19**, enter the formula **=AVERAGE(J:J)** using whatever method you prefer. The average conversation is 16.154599 minutes.

2. In cell **B20**, enter the formula **=MEDIAN(J:J)** to calculate the middle value. The median conversation is 13 minutes.

3. In cell **B21**, enter the formula **=MODE.SNGL(J:J)** to calculate the most common value. The most common conversation lasts 6 minutes.

4. In cell **B22**, enter the formula **=MIN(J:J)** to calculate the smallest value. The shortest conversation lasted 1 minute.

5. In cell **B23**, enter the formula **=MAX(J:J)** to calculate the largest value. The longest conversation was 73 minutes. See Figure 3–15.

| Figure 3–15 | Completed call duration data |

The three measures of central tendency for the length of the conversations show distinctly different values. The average conversation with the operator lasts a little over 16 minutes, but the most common length, as indicated by the mode, is 6 minutes with a median of 13 minutes. It would seem that many calls could be dealt with in a short time, although some longer calls (up to 73 minutes) require more operator time, bringing up the average. This information tells Kiara that the call center might handle calls more efficiently by sending more difficult, time-consuming calls to the most experienced operators and having all other calls handled by the rest of the operators.

Nesting Functions

Functions can be placed inside, or **nested**, within other functions. When functions are nested, Excel evaluates the innermost function first and then moves outward to evaluate the remaining functions with the inner function acting as an argument for the next outer function. For example, the following expression nests the AVERAGE function within the ROUND function. In this expression, the average of the values in the range A1:A100 is calculated first, and then that average is rounded to the nearest integer:

```
ROUND(AVERAGE(A1:A100),0)
```

Formulas that involve several layers of nested functions can be challenging to read. The more nested functions there are, the more difficult it becomes to associate each set of arguments with its corresponding function. To help interpret nested functions, Excel displays the opening and closing parentheses of each function level in a different color. If a syntax error occurs, Excel offers suggestions for rewriting the formula.

The last part of the Call Durations section in the Call Center Log worksheet calculates the total amount of time operators spent on the phone throughout the day. Knowing how long operators are actively engaged with customers is important to determining the call center's staffing needs. Kiara wants the total support time rounded to the nearest hour. To do that, you will use both the SUM function and the ROUND function nested in a single formula. Kiara also wants to know the total operator time per hour, rounded to the nearest tenth of an hour. You'll calculate this value by dividing the total operator time by the total number of hours the call center was open.

To calculate and round the total operator time and the operator time per hour:

▶ 1. Click cell **B24** to make it the active cell.

▶ 2. Type **=ROUND(** to begin the formula. As you type the formula, the syntax of the ROUND function appears in a ScreenTip. The number argument is in bold to indicate that you are entering this part of the function.

▶ 3. Type **SUM(J:J)** to include the nested SUM function as part of the number argument in the ROUND function. The ScreenTip shows the syntax of the SUM function. Typing the closing parenthesis of the SUM function returns the ScreenTip returns to the ROUND function syntax.

▶ 4. Type **/60** to convert the sum of the values in column J from minutes to hours. The number argument of the ROUND function is complete.

Make sure the formula contains two sets of parentheses—one for the SUM function and the other for the ROUND function.

▶ 5. Type **, 0)** to enter the number of decimal places to include in the results. The formula with nested functions =ROUND(SUM(J:J)/60, 0) is complete. Notice that the color for the parentheses of the SUM function differs from the color of the parentheses for the ROUND function.

▶ 6. Press **ENTER**. Cell B24 displays 138, indicating that the call center operators spend around 138 hours on the phone with customers during the day.

▶ 7. In cell **B25**, type the formula **=ROUND(B24/B7, 1)** to divide the total operator time in cell B24 by the total number of hours the call center was open in cell B7 and round the total to the nearest tenth of an hour, and then press **ENTER**. Cell B25 displays 13.8, which is the workload per hour rounded to tenths. See Figure 3–16.

Figure 3–16	Using nested functions to calculate operator time

◢	A	B	C	D	E	F	G	H	I
18	Call Durations				Case50140	8:10:16 AM	8:10:40 AM	24	8:22:18 AM
19	Average Duration	16.154599	minutes		Case50141	8:10:46 AM	8:11:31 AM	45	8:29:25 AM
20	Median Duration	13	minutes		Case50142	8:11:12 AM	8:11:45 AM	33	8:35:39 AM
21	Common Duration	6	minutes		Case50143	8:13:08 AM	8:13:31 AM	23	8:34:30 AM
22	Shortest Duration	1	minutes		Case50144	8:15:45 AM	8:16:09 AM	24	8:20:17 AM
23	Longest Duration	73	minutes		Case50145	8:17:13 AM	8:17:40 AM	28	8:30:14 AM
24	Total Operator Time	138	hours◄— =ROUND(SUM(J:J)/60, 0)				8:40:56 AM	28	8:40:49 AM
25	Workload per Hour	13.8	hours◄— =ROUND(B24/B7, 1)				8:20:00 AM	16	8:52:44 AM
26					Case50148	8:20:33 AM	8:20:53 AM	20	8:56:44 AM
27	Key Performance Indicator (KPI)				Case50149	8:22:04 AM	8:22:20 AM	16	8:43:10 AM
28	Hold Time Goal		seconds		Case50150	8:24:16 AM	8:24:41 AM	25	8:30:15 AM
29	Hold Times Above Goal		calls		Case50151	8:25:49 AM	8:26:00 AM	11	8:30:04 AM
30	Hold Time Failure Rate				Case50152	8:27:33 AM	8:28:03 AM	30	8:49:02 AM
31					Case50153	8:28:37 AM	8:29:12 AM	35	8:44:48 AM
32					Case50154	8:30:25 AM	8:30:55 AM	30	8:51:54 AM
33					Case50155	8:31:41 AM	8:32:11 AM	30	8:49:08 AM
34					Case50156	8:32:39 AM	8:33:04 AM	25	8:53:50 AM
35					Case50157	8:33:43 AM	8:34:05 AM	22	8:52:22 AM

◀ ▶ ...   Call Center Log   Support Calculator   Staffing Calculator   Formulas and Key Terms   ⊕   ⁝   ◀

Ready   🖬

The value in cell B25 shows that each hour the call center is open requires 13.8 hours of operator time. In other words, the call center needs about 14 operators every hour to keep up with the traffic. Fewer than 14 operators will result in a backlog that will only get worse as the day progresses.

The Role of Blanks and Zeroes

The functions you've entered were applied to whole columns of data even though those columns contained empty cells and cells with text strings. Mathematical and statistical functions like SUM, COUNT, AVERAGE, and MEDIAN include only numeric data in their calculations, ignoring empty cells and text entries. A blank cell is considered a text entry and is not treated as the number zero. Figure 3–17 shows how the results differ when a blank replaces a zero in a data series.

| Figure 3–17 | Calculations with blank cells and zeroes |

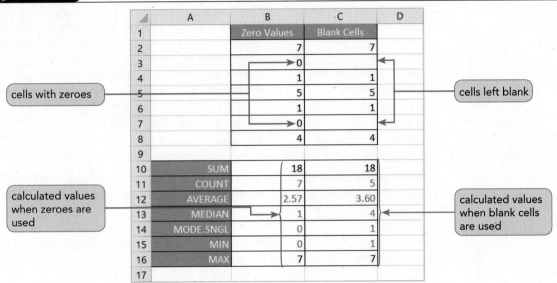

Whether you use a blank cell or a zero in a data series depends on what you are trying to measure. For example, to calculate the average number of hours per day that the call center is open, Kiara could enter 0 for holidays in which the call center is closed or leave the cell blank. Using a zero returns the average hours worked across all calendar days and gives a good overall summary of the company's annual staffing needs. Using a blank cell would summarize staffing needs only for the days that the call center is open. Both approaches have their uses. So consider the ultimate goal of any calculation and choose the approach that best achieves your goal.

Date and Time Functions

Excel supports a large collection of date and time functions. Figure 3–18 summarizes some of the most useful ones.

Figure 3-18   **Date and time functions**

Function	Description
DATE(*year*,*month*,*day*)	Creates a date value for the date represented by the *year*, *month*, and *day* arguments
DAY(*serial_number*)	Extracts the day of the month from a date value stored as *serial_number*
MONTH(*serial_number*)	Extracts the month number from a date value stored as *serial_number*, where 1=January, 2=February, and so on
YEAR(*serial_number*)	Extracts the 4-digit year value from a date value stored as *serial_number*
NETWORKDAYS(*start_date*, *end_date*,[*holidays*])	Calculates the number of whole working days between *start_date* and *end_date*; to exclude holidays, add the optional holidays argument containing a list of holiday dates to skip
WEEKDAY(*serial_number*, [*return_type*])	Calculates the weekday from a date value stored as *serial_number*, where 1=Sunday, 2=Monday, and so forth; to choose a different numbering scheme, set *return_type* to 1 (1=Sunday, 2=Monday, ...), 2 (1=Monday, 2=Tuesday, ...), or 3 (0=Monday, 1=Tuesday, ...)
WORKDAY(*start_date*, *days*,[*holidays*])	Returns the workday after *days* workdays have passed since the *start_date*; to exclude holidays, add the optional holidays argument containing a list of holiday dates to skip
NOW( )	Returns the current date and time
TODAY( )	Returns the current date

Many workbooks include the current date so that any reports generated by the workbook are identified by date. To display the current date, you can use the following **TODAY function**:

```
TODAY ( )
```

The date displayed by the TODAY function is updated automatically whenever you enter a new formula or reopen the workbook.

You'll use the TODAY function to display the current date.

To display the current date:

1. Go to the **Documentation** sheet.

2. In cell **B4**, enter the formula **=TODAY()** to display the current date in the cell. The date displayed in cell B4 will be updated every time you reopen the workbook.

To display the current date and the current time, use the NOW function. The NOW function, like the TODAY function, is automatically updated whenever you add a new calculation to the workbook or reopen the workbook.

Insight

Date Calculations with Working Days

Businesses are often more interested in workdays rather than calendar days. For example, to estimate a delivery date in which packages are not shipped or delivered on weekends, it is more useful to know the date of the next weekday rather than the date of the next day.

To display the date of a working day that is a specified number of workdays past a start date, use the **WORKDAY function**

```
WORKDAY(start_date, days, [holidays])
```

where **start_date** is the starting date, **days** is the number of workdays after that starting date, and *holidays* is an optional list of holiday dates to skip. For example, if cell A1 contains the date 12/23/2025, a Tuesday, the following formula displays the date 1/5/2026, a Monday that is nine working days later:

```
WORKDAY(A1,9)
```

The optional *holidays* argument references a series of dates that the WORKDAY function will skip in performing its calculations. So, if both 12/25/2025 and 1/1/2026 are entered in the range B1:B2 as holidays, the following function will return the date 1/7/2026, a Thursday that is nine working days, excluding the holidays, after 12/23/2025:

```
WORKDAY(A1,9,B1:B2)
```

To reverse the process and calculate the number of working days between two dates, use the following **NETWORKDAYS function**

```
NETWORKDAYS(start_date, end_date, [holidays])
```

where **start_date** is the starting date, **end_date** is the ending date, and *holidays* is an optional list of holiday dates to skip. So, if cell A1 contains the date 12/23/2025 and cell A2 contains the date 1/3/2026, the following function returns the value 6, indicating that there are six working days between the start and ending date, excluding the holidays specified in the range B1:B2:

```
NETWORKDAYS(A1,A2,B1:B2)
```

For international applications, which might have a different definition of working day, Excel supports the WORKDAY.INTL function. See Excel Help for more information.

Interpreting Error Values

It's easy to mistype a formula. When you make a mistake writing a formula, Excel returns an **error value** indicating that some part of a formula was entered incorrectly. Figure 3–19 lists the common error values you might see in place of calculated values from formulas and functions. For example, the error value #VALUE! indicates that the wrong type of value is used as an argument for an Excel function or formula.

Figure 3–19   Common error values

Error Value	Description
#DIV/0!	The formula or function contains a number divided by 0.
#NAME?	Excel doesn't recognize text in the formula or function, such as when the function name is misspelled.
#N/A	A value is not available to a function or formula, which can occur when a workbook is initially set up prior to entering actual data values.
#NULL!	A formula or function requires two cell ranges to intersect, but they don't.
#NUM!	Invalid numbers are used in a formula or function, such as text entered in a function that requires a number.
#REF!	A cell reference used in a formula or function is no longer valid, which can occur when the cell used by the function was deleted from the worksheet.
#VALUE!	The wrong type of argument is used in a function or formula. This can occur when you reference a text value for an argument that should be strictly numeric.

Error values by themselves might not be particularly descriptive or helpful. To help you locate the error, an error indicator appears in the upper-left corner of the cell with the error value. When you point to the error indicator, a ScreenTip appears with more information about the error. Although the ScreenTips provide hints as to the reason for the error, you will usually need to examine the formulas in the cells with error values to determine exactly what went wrong.

Kiara wants you to test the workbook to verify that it will catch common arithmetic errors. You will change the value of cell B7 from its current calculated value of 10 hours to a blank cell to see its impact on other cells in the worksheet.

To create an error value:

1. Go to the **Call Center Log** sheet in the workbook.

2. Click cell **B7**, and then press **DELETE** to remove the formula from the cell. Cell B7 is now blank.

3. Verify that both cells B9 and B25 show the error value #DIV/0! indicating that the formulas in those cells contain expressions in which a value is divided by zero.

4. Click cell **B9**, and then point to the **Error** button that appears to the left of the cell. A ScreenTip appears, providing information about the cause of the error value. In this case, the ScreenTip "The formula or function used is dividing by zero or empty cells." appears. See Figure 3–20.

Figure 3–20	Error value in the worksheet

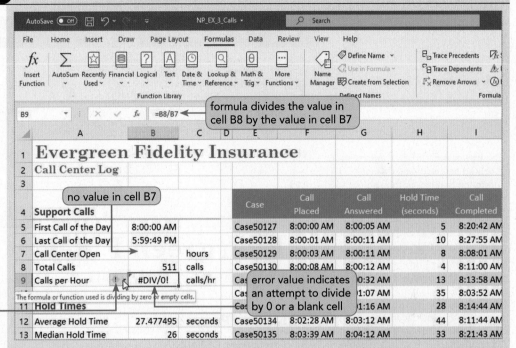

5. On the Quick Access Toolbar, click the **Undo** button ↺ to restore the original formula in cell B7. The cell again displays 10 hours as the formula result.

6. Verify that no error values appear in the worksheet, and then save the workbook.

You've completed your initial work in using Excel formulas and functions to analyze the call center data that Kiara compiled. In the next session, you will continue your analysis and use it to determine the optimal number of operators required to provide fast and efficient service for Evergreen Fidelity Insurance customers.

Review

Session 3.1 Quick Check

1. Write a formula to convert the number of days entered in cell B10 to seconds.
2. If 4/30/2025 and 5/31/2025 are the initial values in a range, list the next two values that AutoFill will insert.
3. Write a formula to round the value in cell A5 to the nearest multiple of 1000.
4. Write a formula to return the single value that is repeated the most times in the range Y1:Y100.
5. The range of values is defined as the maximum value minus the minimum value. Write a nested formula that calculates the range of values in the range Y1:Y100 and then rounds that value to the nearest integer.
6. Houses in a neighborhood usually sell for between $250,000 and $350,000 except for a large mansion that sold for $1,200,000. Which best expresses the typical home sales price: Average or median? Why?
7. Stephen is entering hundreds of temperature values into a worksheet for a climate research project, and wants to speed up data entry by leaving freezing point values as blanks rather than typing zeroes. Explain why this will cause complications in the calculation of the average temperature.
8. Cell B2 contains the formula =SUME(A1:A100) with the name of the SUM function misspelled as SUME. What error value will appear in the cell?

Session 3.2 Visual Overview:

A **mixed cell reference** is a cell reference that has both absolute and relative components in the reference. For example, B$8 is a mixed cell reference.

An **absolute cell reference** is a cell reference that does not change when the formula containing that reference is moved to a new location. Absolute references have "$" before the row and column components. For example, $B$5 is an absolute cell reference.

A **relative cell reference** is a cell reference that changes when the formula containing that reference is moved to a new location. For example, B11 and B6 are both relative cell references.

The **VLOOKUP function** returns values from a vertical lookup table by specifying the value to be matched, the location of the lookup table, and the column containing the return values.

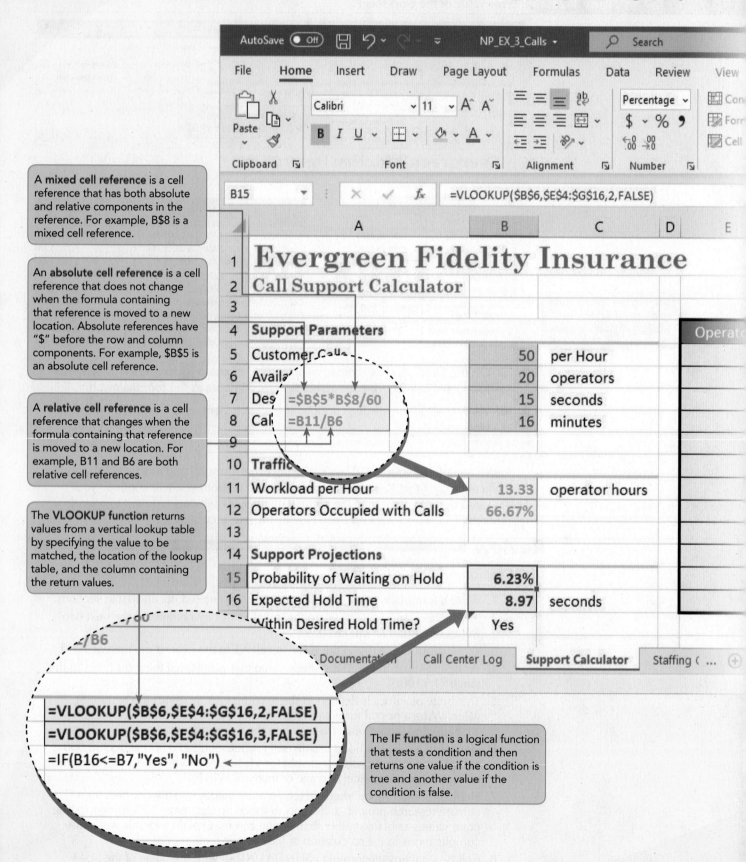

The **IF function** is a logical function that tests a condition and then returns one value if the condition is true and another value if the condition is false.

```
=VLOOKUP($B$6,$E$4:$G$16,2,FALSE)
=VLOOKUP($B$6,$E$4:$G$16,3,FALSE)
=IF(B16<=B7,"Yes", "No")
```

Lookup Tables and Logical Functions

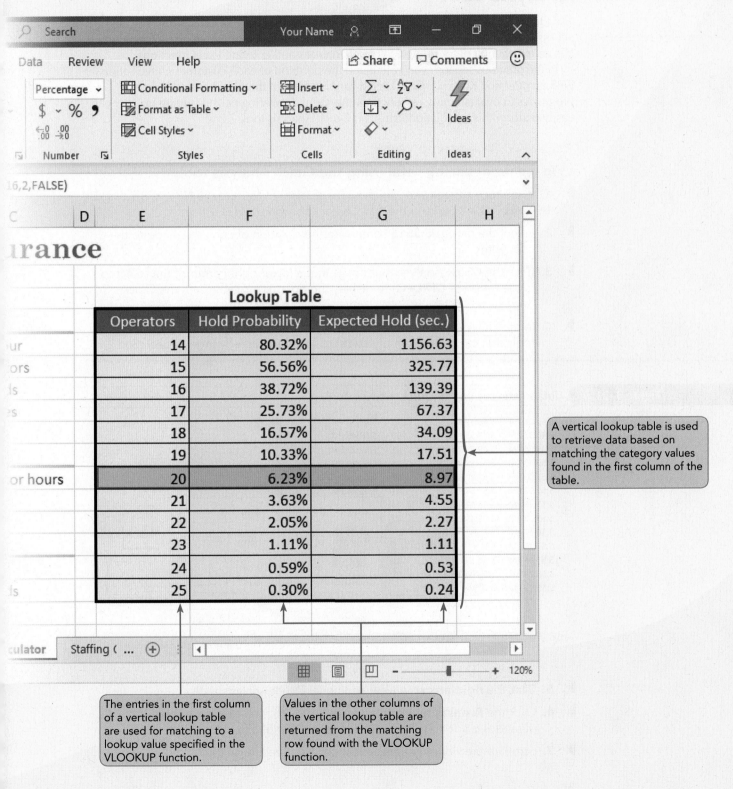

Lookup Table

Operators	Hold Probability	Expected Hold (sec.)
14	80.32%	1156.63
15	56.56%	325.77
16	38.72%	139.39
17	25.73%	67.37
18	16.57%	34.09
19	10.33%	17.51
20	6.23%	8.97
21	3.63%	4.55
22	2.05%	2.27
23	1.11%	1.11
24	0.59%	0.53
25	0.30%	0.24

A vertical lookup table is used to retrieve data based on matching the category values found in the first column of the table.

The entries in the first column of a vertical lookup table are used for matching to a lookup value specified in the VLOOKUP function.

Values in the other columns of the vertical lookup table are returned from the matching row found with the VLOOKUP function.

Calculating Running Totals with the Quick Analysis Tool

The Quick Analysis tool appears whenever you select a range of cells, providing easy access to the most common tools for data analysis, chart creation, and data formatting. It is an excellent tool for doing useful calculations and entering Excel functions.

In the previous session, you calculated the duration of each customer conversation with an operator. Kiara wants to keep a running total of that number as the day progresses to evaluate how rapidly the time spent answering calls is adding up. You can easily perform this calculation using the Quick Analysis tool.

To create a running total using the Quick Analysis tool:

1. If you took a break after the previous session, make sure the NP_EX_3_Calls.xlsx workbook is open and the Call Center Log worksheet is active.

2. Select the range **J5:J515** containing the duration of each call made to the call center.

3. Click the **Quick Analysis** button 🖺 in the lower-right corner of the selected range (or press **CTRL+Q**) to display the options available with the Quick Analysis tool.

4. In the Quick Analysis tool categories, click **Totals**. The Quick Analysis tools that calculate summary statistics for the selected range appear. See Figure 3–21.

| Figure 3–21 | Totals category on the Quick Analysis tool |

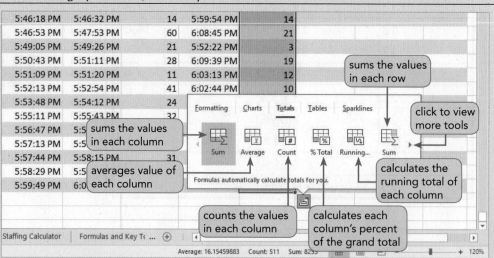

5. Click the **right arrow** to view additional Quick Analysis tools.

6. Click the **Running** tool (the last icon in the list). The running total of call durations is added to the adjacent range K5:K515.

7. Scroll up the worksheet and select cell **K5**. See Figure 3–22.

Figure 3–22   **Running total of the call durations**

	F	G	H	I	J	K	L	M
	.ce							
						=SUM($J$5:J5)		
	Call Placed	Call Answered	Hold Time (seconds)	Call Completed	Duration (minutes)	Cumulative (minutes)	Seconds Over Hold Time Goal	KPI
	8:00:00 AM	8:00:05 AM	5	8:20:42 AM	21	21		
	8:00:01 AM	8:00:11 AM	10	8:27:55 AM	28	49		
	8:00:03 AM	8:00:11 AM	8	8:08:01 AM	8	57		
	8:00:08 AM	8:00:12 AM	4	8:11:00 AM	11	68		
	8:00:19 AM	8:00:32 AM	13	8:13:58 AM	14	82		
	8:00:32 AM	8:01:07 AM	35	8:03:52 AM	3	85		
	8:00:48 AM	8:01:16 AM	28	8:14:44 AM	14	99		
	8:02:28 AM	8:03:12 AM	44	8:11:44 AM	9	108		
	8:03:39 AM	8:04:12 AM	33	8:21:43 AM	18	126		
	8:06:02 AM	8:06:33 AM	31	8:21:38 AM	16	142		
	8:07:12 AM	8:07:40 AM	28	8:11:53 AM	5	147		
	8:08:15 AM	8:08:36 AM	21	8:38:53 AM	31	178		
	8·08·54 AM	8·00·24 AM	20	8·20·20 AM	12	100		

running total of call minutes created using the Quick Analysis tool

Staffing Calculator | Formulas and Key To ... ⊕

120%

Column K now shows the running total of call duration in minutes. The first two calls required a combined 49 minutes of operator time. The first three calls required a combined 57 minutes—nearly an hour—of operator time. With each call added to the previous sum, Kiara can track how total operator time grows throughout the day. For example by 9 AM, operators have logged 980 minutes of customer support time (cell K56) or the equivalent of more than 16 hours of support within the first hour that call center was open.

By default, Quick Analysis summary statistics are displayed in bold. You'll remove the bold formatting so that the values in column K have same formatting as column J.

To remove the bold formatting from the running total:

1. Select the range **K5:K515**.

2. On the ribbon, click **Home** tab, and then in the Font group, click the **Bold** button B to remove bold formatting from the selected text.

3. Click cell **K5** to deselect the range K5:K515.

To create the running totals in column K, the Quick Analysis tool first adds the following formula to cell K5:

`=SUM($J$5:J5)`

When that formula is extended down the column, the formula changes in cell K6 to

`=SUM($J$5:J6)`

and the formula changes in cell K7 to

`=SUM($J$5:J7)`

As the formula is extended through the range K5:K515, the SUM function covers a longer and longer range of cells. By cell K515, the formula is =SUM($J$5:J515). To make those changes to the argument of the SUM function, the Quick Analysis tool used a mixture of relative and absolute cell references.

Exploring Cell References

Excel has three types of cell references: relative, absolute, and mixed. Each type of cell reference is affected differently when a formula or function is copied and pasted to a new location.

Relative Cell References

Excel interprets a relative cell reference relative to the position of the cell containing the formula. For example, if cell A1 contains the formula =B1+B2, Excel interprets that formula as "Add the value of the cell one column to the right (B1) to the value of the cell one column to the right and one row down (B2)." This relative interpretation of the cell reference is retained when the formula is copied to a new location. If the formula in cell A1 is copied to cell A3 (two rows down in the worksheet), the relative references also shift two rows down, resulting in the formula =B3+B4.

Figure 3–23 shows another example of how relative references change when a formula is pasted to new locations in the worksheet. In this figure, the formula =A3 entered in cell D6 displays 10, which is the number entered in cell A3. When pasted to a new location, each of the pasted formulas contains a reference to a cell that is three rows up and three rows to the left of the current cell's location.

Figure 3-23	Formulas using relative references

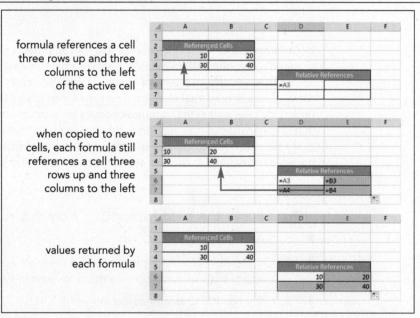

Relative references are why you can copy the same formula down a column or across a row. As long as the relative location of the referenced cells remains the same, the formula can be applied anywhere in the worksheet.

Absolute Cell References

An absolute cell reference remains fixed even when a formula or function is copied to a new location. Absolute references include $ (a dollar sign) before each column and row designation. For example, B8 is a relative reference to cell B8, while $B$8 is an absolute reference to that cell.

Figure 3–24 shows how copying a formula with an absolute reference results in the same cell reference being pasted in different cells regardless of their position compared to the location of the original copied cell. In this example, the formula =$A$3 will always reference cell A3 no matter where the formula is copied to.

Figure 3–24   **Formulas using absolute references**

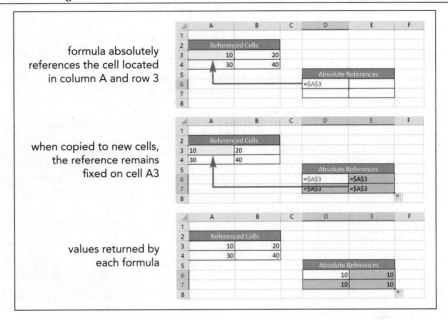

formula absolutely references the cell located in column A and row 3

when copied to new cells, the reference remains fixed on cell A3

values returned by each formula

The running total formula, =SUM($J$5:J5) from cell K5 in the Call Center Log worksheet uses the absolute cell reference $J$5 so that the first cell in the SUM function always points to cell J5, no matter where the formula is copied to. However, the relative portion of that formula, J5, will move down as the location of the formula moves down so that when the formula is copied to cell K6, it then becomes =SUM($J$5:J6) expanding to =SUM($J$5:J515) for cell K515.

Mixed Cell References

A mixed cell reference contains both relative and absolute components. For example, a mixed cell reference for cell A2 can be either $A2 where the column is the absolute component and the row is the relative component, or it can be entered as A$2 with a relative column component and a fixed row component. A mixed cell reference "locks" only one part of the cell reference. When copied to a new location, the absolute portion of the cell reference remains fixed but the relative portion shifts.

Figure 3–25 shows mixed cell references used to complete a multiplication table. The first cell in the table, cell B3, contains the formula =$A3*B$2, which multiplies the first column entry (cell A3) by the first-row entry (cell B2), returning 1. When this formula is copied to another cell, the absolute portions of the cell references remain unchanged, and the relative portions of the references change. For example, if the formula is copied to cell E6, the first mixed cell reference changes to $A6 because the column reference is absolute and the row reference is relative, and the second cell reference changes to E$2 because the row reference is absolute and the column reference is relative. The result is that cell E6 contains the formula =$A6*E$2 and returns a value of 16. Other cells in the multiplication table are similarly modified so that each entry returns the multiplication of the intersection of the row and column headings.

Figure 3-25   **Formulas using mixed references**

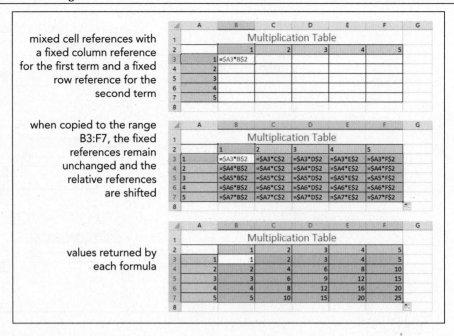

mixed cell references with a fixed column reference for the first term and a fixed row reference for the second term

when copied to the range B3:F7, the fixed references remain unchanged and the relative references are shifted

values returned by each formula

You will use relative and absolute references when you enter a formula in the Call Center Log worksheet.

 Proskills

Problem Solving: When to Use Relative, Absolute, and Mixed Cell References

Part of effective workbook design is knowing when to use relative, absolute, and mixed cell references. Use relative references when you want to apply the same formula with input cells that share a common layout or pattern. Relative references are commonly used when copying a formula that calculates summary statistics across columns or rows of data values. Use absolute references when you want your copied formulas to always refer to the same cell. This usually occurs when a cell contains a constant value, such as a tax rate, that will be referenced in formulas throughout the worksheet. Mixed references are seldom used other than when creating tables of calculated values such as a multiplication table in which the values of the formula or function can be found at the intersection of the rows and columns of the table.

Entering an Absolute Cell Reference

Kiara's goal for the call center is to have every call answered within 15 seconds. To analyze how well the call center is meeting this goal, you will determine by how much each call meets or exceeds the 15-second goal.

To calculate the difference between the hold times and the 15-second goal:

▶ 1. In cell **B28**, enter **15** as the hold-time goal.

▶ 2. Scroll up the worksheet and in cell **L5**, enter the formula **=H5-$B$28** to subtract 15 seconds from the hold time, and then press **ENTER**. The cell displays −10, indicating that the customer was on hold for 10 seconds less than the 15-second goal.

3. Drag the **fill handle** over the range **L5:L515** to extend the formula through the rest of the call log. The final call has a value of 12, indicating that the caller was on hold for 12 seconds more than the hold-time goal that Kiera established.

4. Click the **Auto Fill Options** button, and then click the **Fill Without Formatting** option button to retain the banded rows.

5. Scroll up the worksheet, and then click cell **L5** to deselect the range. See Figure 3–26.

Figure 3–26   **Formulas with absolute references**

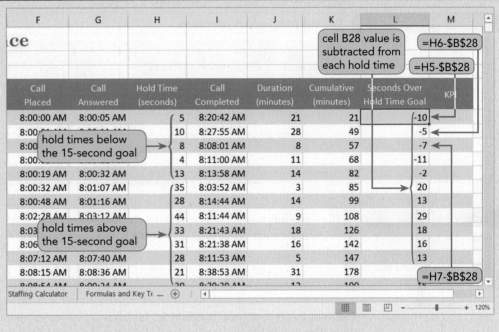

Because the formula uses an absolute reference to cell B28, it will always point to cell B28 even as it's extended through the range L5:L515. Thus, the formula in cell L6 is =H6-$B$28, the formula in L7 is =H7-$B$28, and so forth.

You can easily cycle between relative, absolute, and mixed cell references in formulas by selecting the cell reference in the formula and pressing F4 while in Edit mode. For example, if you type the formula =A4 and then press F4, the formula changes to =$A$4. Pressing F4 again changes the formula to =A$4. Pressing F4 a third time changes the formula to =$A4. Pressing F4 a fourth time returns the formula to =A4 where the cycle begins again.

Kiera wants to know how many calls were on hold for longer than 15 seconds. One way of answering this question is with a logical function.

Working with the IF Logical Function

A **logical function** is a function that returns one of two possible values depending on whether a given condition is true or false. The condition is entered as an expression, such as A5=3. If cell A5 is equal to 3, the condition is true; if cell A5 is not equal to 3, the condition is false.

You use conditional expressions in logical functions like the IF function

`IF(logical_test, value_if_true, [value_if_false])`

Tip

If no *value_if_false* argument is provided, the IF function returns the value FALSE if the condition is false.

where ***logical_test*** is a condition that is either true or false, ***value_if_true*** is the value returned by the function if the condition is true, and *value_if_false* is an optional argument containing the value if the condition is false. For example, the following function returns a value of 100 if A1=B1, otherwise it returns a value of 50:

```
IF(A1=B1, 100, 50)
```

The *value_if_true* and the *value_if_false* in the IF function can also be cell references. For example, the following function returns the value of cell C1 if the condition is true, otherwise it returns the value of cell D1:

```
IF(A1=B1, C1, D1)
```

The = symbol in IF function is a **comparison operator**, which is an operator expressing the relationship between two values. Figure 3–27 describes other comparison operators that can be used with logical functions.

Figure 3–27	Logical comparison operators

Operator	Expression	Tests
=	A1 = B1	If value in cell A1 is equal to the value in cell B1
>	A1 > B1	If the value in cell A1 is greater than the value in cell B1
<	A1 < B1	If the value in cell A1 is less than the value in cell B1
>=	A1 >= B1	If the value in cell A1 is greater than or equal to the value in cell B1
<=	A1 <= B1	If the value in cell A1 is less than or equal to the value in cell B1
<>	A1 <> B1	If the value in cell A1 is not equal to the value in cell B1

Tip

To apply multiple logical conditions, you can nest one IF function within another.

Thus, the following function returns the text string "goal met" if the value in cell A1 is less than or equal to the value of cell B1; otherwise, it returns the text string "goal failed":

```
IF(A1 <= B1, "goal met", "goal failed")
```

Kiara wants a quick way to tell whether a customer was on hold longer than 15 seconds. You'll use the IF function to test each call. If a customer's hold time is greater than zero, the IF function will return a value of 1 (a long hold time); otherwise, it will return a value of 0 (a short hold time).

To use the IF function to indicate if a call exceeds the hold-time goal:

1. Click cell **M5** to select it.

2. On the ribbon, click the **Formulas** tab, and then in the Function Library group, click the **Logical** button to display a list of all of the logical functions.

3. Click **IF** to open the Function Arguments dialog box for the IF function.

4. In the Logical_test box, type the expression **L5>0** to test whether the value in cell L5 is greater than 0.

5. Type **1** in the Value_if_true box, and then type **0** in the Value_if_false box.

6. Click **OK** to enter the formula **=IF(L5>0, 1, 0)** into cell M5. The value 0 appears in cell M5, indicating that this first call was within the 15-second hold-time goal.

7. Drag the **fill handle** over the range **M5:M515** to extend the formula through the rest of the call log.

8. Click the **Auto Fill Options** button, and then click the **Fill Without Formatting** option button to retain the banded rows.

9. Scroll up the worksheet and click cell **M5** to deselect the range. See Figure 3–28.

Figure 3–28   **IF function that evaluates customer hold time**

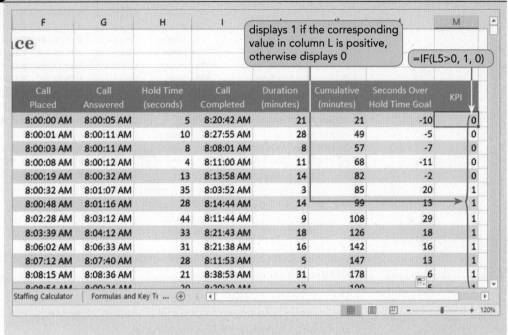

Businesses often report success in terms of a **key performance indicator (KPI)**, which measures the achievement of a specific goal. The percentage of customers experiencing long hold times is one KPI that Kiara uses to measure the success of the call center. A high percentage would indicate that the call center needs to improve its service.

You can count the number of calls that exceeded the 15-second goal by summing up the values in column M, because every call is graded as either a 0 (success) or 1 (failure). You'll use the SUM function to determine how many calls placed to the call center get a failing grade.

To sum the number of failed calls:

1. Scroll the worksheet down and in cell **B29**, enter the formula **=SUM(M:M)** to add all the values in column M. Cell B29 displays 441, indicating that 441 customers had hold times longer than 15 seconds.

2. In cell **B30**, enter the formula **=B29/B8** to calculate the percentage of calls with long hold times by dividing the number of failed calls by the total number of calls.

3. Click cell **B30**, and then on the Home tab, in the Number group, click the **Percent Style** button % (or press **CTRL+SHIFT+%**) to display the value as a percentage. The cell shows that 86% of the calls failed the 15-second hold-time goal. See Figure 3–29.

Figure 3–29 Calls that fail the hold-time goal

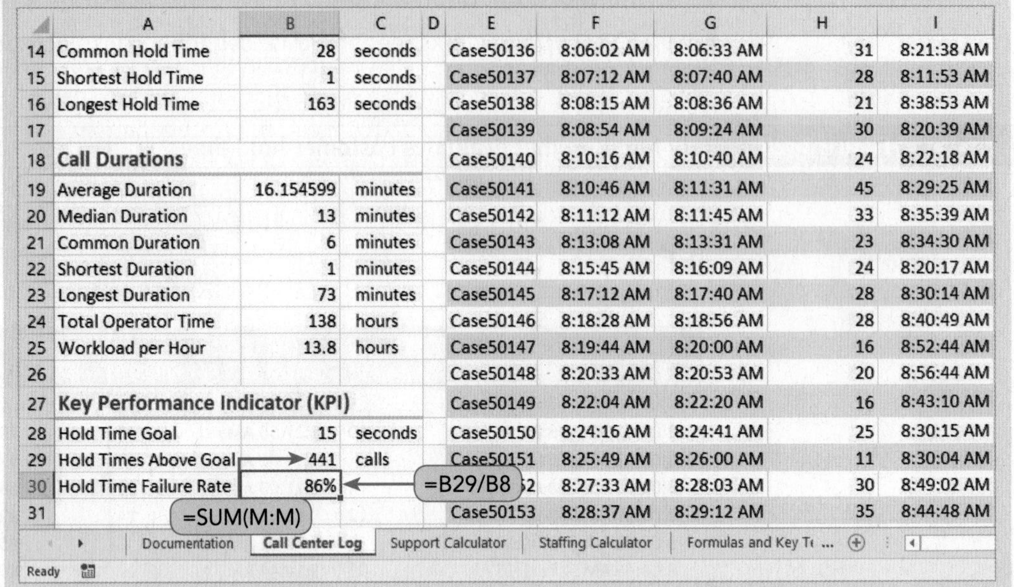

You have compiled a lot of useful information for Kiara. Based on your analysis, you know the following information:

- The call center receives about 50 calls per hour.
- The average hold time for each call is around 27 seconds, and 86% of calls are not answered within Kiara's 15-second goal.
- Conversations last around 6 minutes, but can sometimes take over an hour. The average conversation lasts around 16 minutes.
- It takes about 14 hours of operator time every hour to handle the call center traffic.

Kiara wants to know whether customer support can be improved by increasing the number of available operators. And, if so, how many operators are needed to provide effective and efficient service? You will answer those questions next.

Insight

Using the IFERROR Function to Catch Error Values

An error value does not mean that your formula is wrong. Some errors appear simply because you have not yet entered any data into the workbook. For example, if you apply the AVERAGE function to range that does not yet contain any data values, the #DIV/0! error value appears because Excel cannot calculate averages without data. However, as soon as you enter your data, the #DIV/0! error value disappears, replaced with the calculated average.

Error values of this type can make your workbook confusing and difficult to read. One way to hide them is with the following **IFERROR function**

    IFERROR (*Value*, *Value_if_error*)

where **Value** is the value to be calculated and **Value_if_error** is the value returned by Excel if any error is encountered in the function. For example, the following IFERROR function returns the average of the values in column F, but if no values have yet been entered in that column, it returns a blank text string (""):

    IFERROR(AVERAGE(F:F),"")

Using this logical function results in a cleaner workbook that is easier to read and use without distracting error values.

Formatting Input, Calculated, and Output Values

It's important in your worksheets to identify which cells contain input values for formulas and functions, which cells contain calculations, and which cells contain primary output values. Formatting cells based on their purpose helps others correctly use and interpret your worksheet. The Cell Styles gallery includes cell styles to format cells containing input, calculation, and output values.

You will use these styles in the Support Calculator worksheet in which you will estimate the number of operators that the call center needs to provide good customer service. Before entering any values or formulas in the Support Calculator worksheet, you'll format the purpose of each cell using built-in cell styles in the Cell Styles gallery.

To apply cell styles to input, calculated, and output values:

▶ **1.** Go to the **Support Calculator** worksheet.

▶ **2.** Select the range **B6:B9**. You will format this range as input cells.

▶ **3.** On the Home tab, in the Styles group, click the **Cell Styles** button to open the Cell Styles gallery.

▶ **4.** In the Data and Model section, click the **Input** cell style. The selected cells are formatted with light blue font on a light orange background, identifying these cells as containing input values for the Support Calculator.

▶ **5.** Select the nonadjacent range **B10,B13:B15**. These cells will contain calculations that will be entered later.

▶ **6.** Format the selected cells with the **Calculation** cell style located in the Data and Model section of the Cell Styles gallery. The cells with the calculated values are formatted with a bold orange font on a light gray background.

▶ **7.** Select the range **B18:B21**. These cells will contain the primary output measures used to predict the efficiency of the call center.

▶ **8.** Format the selected range with the **Output** cell style located in the Data and Model section of the Cell Styles gallery. The cells with the calculated values are formatted with a bold dark gray font on a light gray background.

Now that the different types of cells in the Support Calculator worksheet are formatted distinctly, it is easier to enter the data about the call center in the correct cells. You'll enter the input and calculated values.

To enter the input values and calculated values:

▶ **1.** In cell **B6**, enter the input value **50** as the anticipated calls per hour to the center.

▶ **2.** In cell **B7**, enter the input value **14** as number of operators available to answer calls.

▶ **3.** In cell **B8**, enter the input value **15** as the desired hold time in seconds.

▶ **4.** In cell **B9**, enter the input value **16** as the average call duration in minutes.

5. In cell **B10**, enter the formula **=B9/60** to calculate the average call duration in hours. The formula returns the value 0.27 hours.

6. In cell **B13**, enter the formula **=B6*B10** to calculate the number of operator hours required each hour to handle the call traffic. The formula returns 13.33 operator hours.

7. In cell **B14**, enter the formula **=B13/B7** to calculate the anticipated percentage of operators who will be occupied with calls at any one time. At the current workload, 95.24% of the operators will be occupied.

8. In cell **B15**, enter the formula **=1-B14** to display the percentage of operators who will be free at any one time. In this case, 4.76% of the operators will be free. See Figure 3–30.

Figure 3–30   Formatted input and calculated values

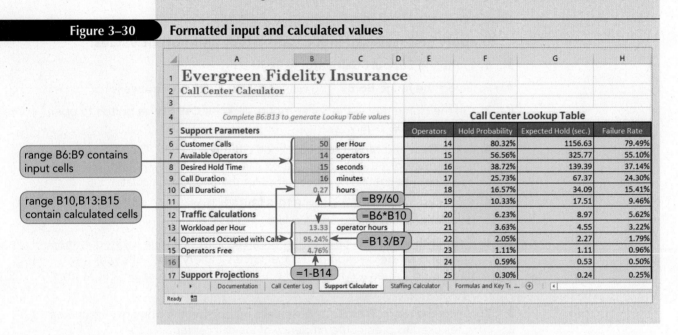

range B6:B9 contains input cells

range B10,B13:B15 contain calculated cells

With the input and calculated values entered into the worksheet, you will next determine the optimal number of operators to handle the call volume. To do that analysis, you will use a lookup function.

Looking Up Data

A **lookup function** retrieves a value matching a specified condition from a table of data. For example, a lookup function can be used to retrieved a tax rate from a tax table for a given annual income or to retrieve a shipping rate for a specified delivery date.

The table storing the data to be retrieved is called a **lookup table**. The first row or column of the table contains the **lookup values**, which are the values that are being looked up. If the lookup values are in the first row, the table is a horizontal lookup table; if the values are in the first column, the table is a vertical lookup table. The remaining rows or columns contain the data values retrieved by the lookup function, known as **return values**.

Figure 3–31 displays a vertical lookup table for retrieving data about Evergreen Fidelity Insurance employees. The first column contains the lookup value (Employee ID) and the other columns contain return values (First Name, Last Name,

Department). In this example, the Employee ID "E54-0-2138" corresponds to the entry in the fifth row of the table and the employee's last name found in the third column is returned.

| Figure 3–31 | Exact match returned from a lookup table |

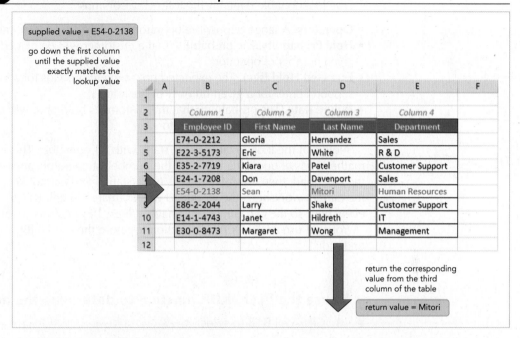

Lookup tables can be constructed for exact match or approximate match lookups. In an **exact match lookup**, like the one shown in Figure 3–31, the lookup value must exactly match one of the values from the table's first column (or first row for a horizontal lookup table). An **approximate match lookup** is used when the lookup value falls within a range of values in the first column or row. You will work only with exact match lookups in this module.

Finding an Exact Match with the VLOOKUP Function

To retrieve a return value from a vertical lookup table, you use the VLOOKUP function

VLOOKUP(***lookup_value***,***table_array***,***col_index_num***,[*range_lookup*=TRUE])

where ***lookup_value*** is the lookup value to find in the first column of the lookup table, ***table_array*** is the reference to the lookup table, and ***col_index_num*** is the number of the column in the lookup table that contains the return value. Keep in mind that ***col_index_num*** refers to the number of the column within the lookup table, not the worksheet column. So, a ***col_index_num*** of 2 refers to the lookup table's second column no matter where the lookup table is located within the worksheet.

Finally, *range_lookup* is an optional argument that specifies whether the lookup should be done as an exact match or an approximate match. The default value of *range_lookup* is TRUE, creating an approximate match. To create an exact match, enter a value of FALSE for the *range_lookup* argument.

The following VLOOKUP function performs the exact match lookup shown in Figure 3–31 with "E54-0-2138" as the lookup value, returning the value from the third column of the table:

VLOOKUP("E54-0-2128", B3:E11, 3, FALSE)

Tip

If the VLOOKUP function cannot find a match in the lookup table, it returns the #N/A error value.

Kiara included a lookup table in the range E5:H55 of the Support Calculator worksheet. The table was generated by Evergreen Fidelity Insurance statisticians using a branch of mathematics called "queuing theory" to predict call center performance assuming a given number of operators. A study of queueing theory is beyond the scope of this module, but you can use the results shown from the lookup table in your report.

The lookup table contains the following columns:

- **Operators.** A range of possible operators available to answer calls.
- **Hold Probability.** The probability that a customer will be placed on hold assuming a given number of operators.
- **Expected Hold (sec).** The expected hold time in seconds for a customer calling the support center for a given number of operators.
- **Failure Rate.** The probability that the customer's hold time will exceed the hold-time goal for a given number of operators.

Note that the lookup table value starts with 14 operators. This is due to the mathematics of queueing theory. If the number of operators answering calls is less than the workload, then the call center is understaffed and cannot keep up with demand. In the current worksheet, the workload was estimated in cell B13 as 13.33 operator hours every hour so the call center must have at least 14 operators on hand at all times.

You will use the VLOOKUP function to return the probability of a customer waiting on hold.

To use the VLOOKUP function to determine the hold probability:

1. Click cell **B18** to select it.

2. On the ribbon, click the **Formulas** tab, and then in the Formula Library group, click the **Insert Function** button. The Insert Function dialog box opens.

3. Click the **Or select a category** box, and then click **Lookup & References** in the list of function categories.

4. Scroll down the Select a function box, and then double-click **VLOOKUP**. The Function Arguments dialog box opens.

5. In the Lookup_value box, type **$B$7** to reference the number of operators entered in cell B7.

6. In the Table_array box, type **$E$5:$H$32** to reference the vertical lookup table containing the queueing theory predictions.

7. In the Col_index_num box, type **2** to return a matching value from the lookup table's second column.

Be sure to use FALSE to do an exact match lookup.

8. In the Range_lookup box, type **FALSE** to do an exact match lookup. You have entered all of the arguments for the VLOOKUP function. See Figure 3–32.

Figure 3–32   **Function Arguments dialog box for the VLOOKUP function**

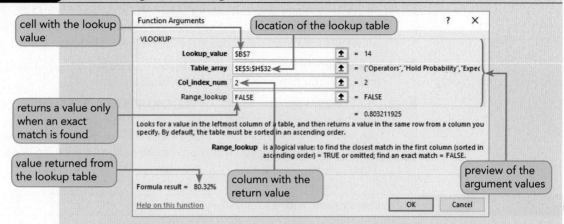

cell with the lookup value

location of the lookup table

returns a value only when an exact match is found

value returned from the lookup table

column with the return value

preview of the argument values

▶ **9.** Click **OK**. The formula =VLOOKUP($B$7, $E$5:$H$32, 2, FALSE) is entered into cell B18, returning a value of 80.32%. See Figure 3–33.

Figure 3–33   **VLOOKUP function results**

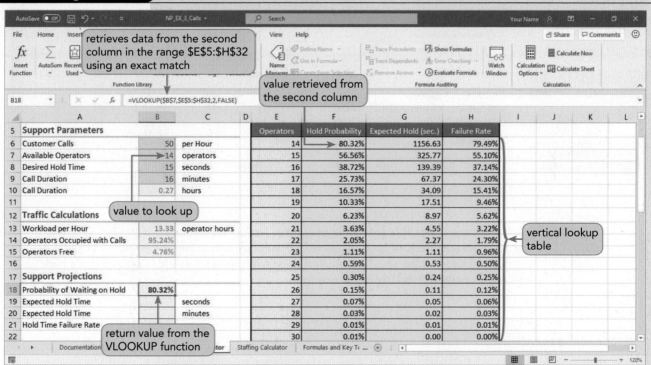

retrieves data from the second column in the range $E$5:$H$32 using an exact match

value retrieved from the second column

value to look up

vertical lookup table

return value from the VLOOKUP function

Trouble? If you cannot select or view the formulas in the lookup table, don't worry. The cells in the range E5:H55 have been locked and protected to prevent users from inadvertently changing their contents.

Based on the result of the VLOOKUP function, queueing theory estimates that 80.32% of the customers will have to wait on hold if only 14 operators are working the call center. You'll use the VLOOKUP function again to retrieve other call center predictions assuming only 14 available operators.

To use the VLOOKUP function for the other output cells:

▶ 1. In cell **B19**, enter the formula **=VLOOKUP($B$7, $E$5:$H$32, 3, FALSE)** to retrieve the value from the third column of the lookup table. Excel returns the value 1156.63 indicating that the expected hold time is 1156.63 seconds.

▶ 2. In cell **B20**, enter the formula **=B19/60** to convert the expected hold time to minutes. The expected hold time is 19.28 minutes.

▶ 3. In cell **B21**, enter the formula **=VLOOKUP($B$7, $E$5:$H$32, 4, FALSE)** to retrieve the value from the fourth column of the lookup table. Excel returns the value 79.49%, indicating that almost 80% of the customers will be on hold longer than the hold-time goal of 15 seconds, entered in cell B8. See Figure 3–34.

Figure 3–34   **Predicted results with 14 operators**

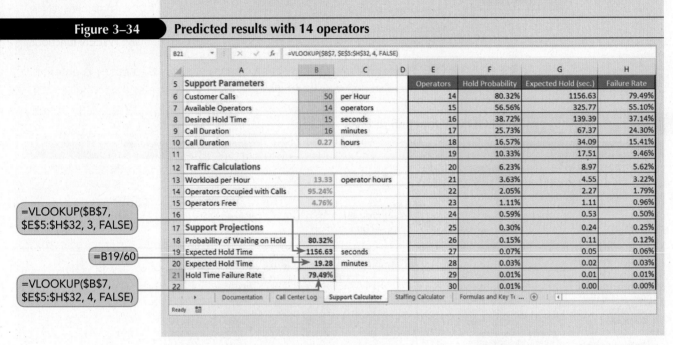

Fourteen operators are barely enough to handle the expected workload, resulting in unacceptable hold times of almost 20 minutes. Increasing the number of operators should improve the situation. You will next explore what would happen if Kiara had more operators working the phone lines.

Insight

Generating Random Data

For some projects you will want to simulate scenarios using randomly generated data. Excel provides the following RAND( ) function to create a random decimal between 0 and 1:

```
RAND()
```

To convert this random number to any decimal within a given range, apply the formula:

```
(top-bottom)*RAND()+bottom
```

where *bottom* is the bottom of the range and *top* is the top of the range. For example, the following expression generates a random decimal number between 10 and 50:

```
(50-10)*RAND()+10
```

To limit the random numbers to integers, apply the following RANDBETWEEN function:

```
RANDBETWEEN(bottom, top)
```

For example, to generate a random integer between 10 and 50, use the formula:

```
RANDBETWEEN(10, 50)
```

Random number functions are **volatile functions** in that they will automatically recalculate their values every time Excel does any calculation in the workbook. This means you will see a different set of random numbers with every new calculation in the workbook.

Performing What-If Analyses with Formulas and Functions

A **what-if analysis** explores the impact that changing input values has on calculated values and output values. By exploring a wide range of different input values, you will achieve a better understanding of your data and its implications.

Using Trial and Error

One way to perform a what-if analysis is by **trial and error** where you change one or more of the input values to see how they affect other cells in the workbook. Trial and error requires some guesswork as you estimate which values to change and by how much. You'll use trial and error to investigate how changing values such as the average call duration or number of operators impacts the call center operation.

To investigate call center scenarios using trial and error:

▶ 1. In cell **B9**, enter **11** to change the average call duration from 16 minutes to 11 minutes. With a shorter average call duration, the probability of waiting on hold drops to 10.06% (cell B18) and the expected hold time drops to 13.74 seconds (cell B19). Handling calls more efficiently will greatly improve the customer experience with the call center.

▶ 2. In cell **B9**, restore the value to **16** minutes because Kiara believes that the operators cannot successfully wrap up calls faster than the 16-minute average.

▶ 3. In cell **B7**, enter **18** to increase the number of operators at the call center. With 18 operators and average call durations of 16 minutes, the probability of callers waiting for an operator is 16.57% with an expected hold time of 34.09 seconds. Kiara thinks this might still be too long, but additional operators would improve the situation markedly.

4. In cell **B7**, enter **25** to further increase the number of operators. With even more operators, the probability of customers being put on hold drops to 0.30% with expected hold time of 0.24 seconds. In other words, with 25 operators calls to support center will be almost always answered immediately. See Figure 3–35.

| Figure 3–35 | Increased number of operators |

number of operators set to 25

revised predictions for the call center

	A	B	C	D	E	F	G	H
5	**Support Parameters**				Operators	Hold Probability	Expected Hold (sec.)	Failure Rate
6	Customer Calls	50	per Hour		14	80.32%	1156.63	79.49%
7	Available Operators	25	operators		15	56.56%	325.77	55.10%
8	Desired Hold Time	15	seconds		16	38.72%	139.39	37.14%
9	Call Duration	16	minutes		17	25.73%	67.37	24.30%
10	Call Duration	0.27	hours		18	16.57%	34.09	15.41%
11					19	10.33%	17.51	9.46%
12	**Traffic Calculations**				20	6.23%	8.97	5.62%
13	Workload per Hour	13.33	operator hours		21	3.63%	4.55	3.22%
14	Operators Occupied with Calls	53.33%			22	2.05%	2.27	1.79%
15	Operators Free	46.67%			23	1.11%	1.11	0.96%
16					24	0.59%	0.53	0.50%
17	**Support Projections**				25	0.30%	0.24	0.25%
18	Probability of Waiting on Hold	0.30%			26	0.15%	0.11	0.12%
19	Expected Hold Time	0.24	seconds		27	0.07%	0.05	0.06%
20	Expected Hold Time	0.00	minutes		28	0.03%	0.02	0.03%
21	Hold Time Failure Rate	0.25%			29	0.01%	0.01	0.01%
22					30	0.01%	0.00	0.00%

| | Documentation | Call Center Log | **Support Calculator** | Staffing Calculator | Formulas and Key T ... ⊕ | ◄ |

Ready

At some point, increasing the number of operators will no longer be cost effective as more operators will be idle waiting for the next call. Kiara believes having 25 operators on call at all hours provides the right balance of customer support and busy operators. Kiara wants to determine how many staff members are needed to ensure that 25 operators are available for every shift.

Staff size is affected by what is known in business as "shrinkage" in which the number of available employees to perform a task is reduced due to illness, vacations, and competing duties like staff meetings. For example, if half of the company's operators are absent due to shrinkage, to get 25 operators working the phones Kiara would have to hire a staff of 50. The general formula to calculate the size of the staff for a given level of shrinkage is

$$staff\ size = \frac{required\ employees}{1 - \%absent}$$

where *required employees* is the number of employees needed at any one time and *%absent* is the percentage of available employees that will be absent due to shrinkage. To determine the value of *%absent*, you calculate the total hours in which a typical employee is absent divided by the total hours of work that need to be covered.

Kiara created a Staffing Calculator worksheet to calculate the shrinkage factor for the operator staff and determine the staff size needed to compensate for shrinkage. First, you'll calculate the total hours that a typical operator works during the year and the number of working hours that operator will spend not answering customer support calls.

To calculate the total hours a typical operator works:

▶ 1. Go to the **Staffing Calculator** worksheet.

▶ 2. In cell **B9**, enter the formula **=B5*B6-B7** to calculate the total working days per year less days in which the call center is closed for holidays. The formula returns 253.5, indicating the call center is open 253 and half days per year.

▶ 3. In cell **B10**, enter the formula **=B9*B8** to multiply the number of days in which the call center is open by the number of hours per working day. The formula returns 2028, indicating that the call center is open 2028 hours per year.

▶ 4. In cell **B15**, enter the formula **=(B13+B14)*B8** to multiply the number of days allotted for vacation and sick leave by the number of hours per working day. The formula returns 160 hours, indicating that 160 working hours will be lost to vacation and sick leave.

▶ 5. In cell **B20**, enter the formula **=B9*(B18+B19)** to multiply the number of days in which the center is open by the number of hours spent on breaks and staff meetings. The formula returns 570.375 hours, indicating that 570.375 hours will be lost per year to duties that do not involve answering customer calls. See Figure 3–36.

Figure 3–36 | **Total operator hours**

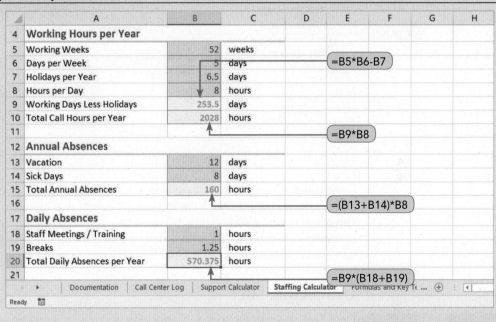

Next, you will calculate the shrinkage factor for staffing call center operators.

To calculate the shrinkage factor:

▶ 1. In cell **B23**, enter **25** as the number of operators Kiara wants available to answer calls.

▶ 2. In cell **B24**, enter the formula **=B15+B20** to add the total hours lost each year to absences to the total hours lost to daily tasks. The formula returns 730.375 hours, indicating that 730.375 hours will be lost each year to things not involved with answering customer calls.

3. In cell **B25**, enter the formula **=B24/B10** to divide the total hours lost by the total hours the call center will be open. The formula returns 36%, indicating that 36% of the available hours will not be spent on answering customer calls.

4. In cell **B26**, enter the formula **=B23/(1-B25)** to calculate the total staff required for shrinkage factor. The formula returns 39.07, indicating that Kiara would need a staff of 39 or 40 employees to cover the call center at the desired level of efficiency. See Figure 3–37.

Figure 3–37   **Staff shrinkage calculations**

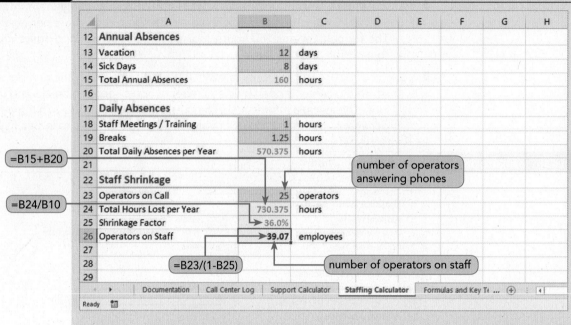

Although having 39 or 40 operators on staff will allow 25 operators to handle calls at any time, Kiara does not have the budget to hire that many people. The company can afford to hire a staff of only 30 operators. Kiara wants you to determine how many operators would be on call with a staff of 30 assuming the 36% shrinkage factor. You can answer that question with Goal Seek.

Using Goal Seek

Tip

Goal Seek can be used only with calculated numbers, not with text.

Goal Seek reverses the trial-and-error process by specifying an output value and working backward to find the input value needed to reach that goal. The output is always a calculated value and the input is always a constant that can be changed using the Goal Seek tool.

Reference

Performing What-If Analysis and Goal Seek

To perform a what-if analysis by trial and error:
- Change the value of a worksheet cell (the input cell).
- Observe its impact on one or more calculated cells (the result cells).
- Repeat until the desired results are achieved.

To perform a what-if analysis using Goal Seek:
- On the Data tab, in the Forecast group, click the What-If Analysis button, and then click Goal Seek.
- Select the result cell in the Set cell box, and then specify its value (goal) in the To value box.
- In the By changing cell box, specify the input cell.
- Click OK. The value of the input cell changes to set the value of the result cell.

In this situation, the output value is cell B26, which calculates the total staff size for the given shrinkage factor. The input value is the number of operators available at any one time to answer calls. You'll use Goal Seek to determine how many operators will be on call if the staff size is limited to 30 employees.

To use Goal Seek to set the staff size to 30 employees:

▶ 1. On the ribbon, click the **Data** tab.

▶ 2. In the Forecast group, click the **What-If Analysis** button, and then click **Goal Seek**. The Goal Seek dialog box opens.

▶ 3. In the Set cell box, type **B26** to specify the output cell whose value you will set using Goal Seek.

▶ 4. In the To value box, type **30** to set the value of cell B26 to 30.

▶ 5. In the By changing cell box, type **B23** to specify in the cell containing the input value that will be changed in order to reach your goal. See Figure 3–38.

| **Figure 3–38** | **Goal Seek dialog box** |

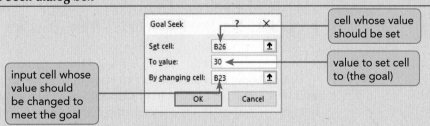

▶ 6. Click **OK**. The Goal Seek dialog box closes and the Goal Seek Status dialog box opens, indicating that Goal Seek has found a solution.

▶ 7. Click **OK**. The value in cell B23 changes to 19.1956361 and the value in cell B26 changes to goal value, 30. See Figure 3–39.

Figure 3–39	Staff shrinkage calculated by Goal Seek

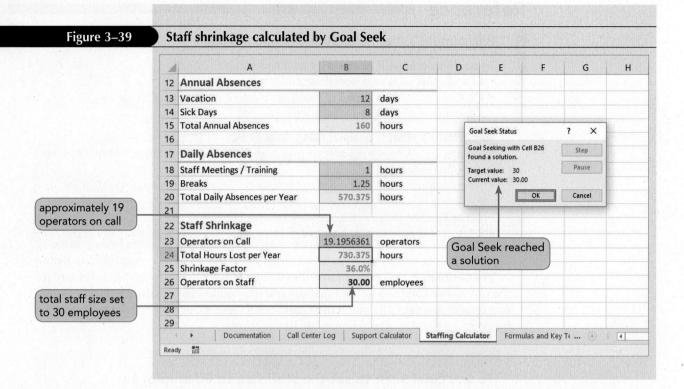

This analysis shows that with a staff of 30, Kiara will have approximately 19 operators available to answer calls at any time. Kiara wants to know whether 19 operators will be enough. To complete this analysis, you'll return to the Support Calculator worksheet and rerun the numbers to find the impact of limiting the call center to 19 available operators.

To calculate the performance of 19 operators:

▶ **1.** Go to the **Support Calculator** worksheet.

▶ **2.** In cell **B7**, enter **19** to set the number of call center operators. The results show that 10.33% of the customers will probably wait on hold (cell B18) for 17.51 seconds.

▶ **3.** **sam**⬆ Save the workbook, and then close it.

With 30 operators on staff and 19 operators on call at any time, a 17- to 18-second wait time is still a bit longer than Kiara's 15-second wait-time goal. But given the budget constraints, this is a reasonable compromise. Kiara will review your analysis and consider other ways of improving the call center's performance while staying within budget.

Review

Session 3.2 Quick Check

1. Explain how to use the Quick Analysis tool to calculate a running total of the values in the range D1:D10.

2. You need to reference cell Q57 in a formula. What is its relative reference? What is its absolute reference? What are the two mixed references?

3. If cell R10 contains the formula =R1+R2 that is then copied to cell S20, what formula is entered in cell S20?

4. If cell R10 contains the formula =$R1+R$2 that is then copied to cell S20, what formula is entered in cell S20?

5. If cell Q3 is greater than cell Q4, you want to display the text "OK"; otherwise, display the text "RETRY". Write the formula that accomplishes this.

6. Write the formula to perform an exact match lookup with the lookup value from cell G5 using a vertical lookup table located in the range A1:F50. Return the value from the third column of the table.

7. What is the difference between a what-if analysis by trial and error and by Goal Seek?

2. Q57, $Q$57, $Q57 and Q$57

3. =S11 + S12

4. =$R1 + S$2

7.

Practice

Review Assignments

Data File needed for the Review Assignments: NP_EX_3-2.xlsx

Kiara has been asked to manage staffing for the claims center. The claims center manages requests from across the country, so its daily call volume is quite large. Kiara wants to determine the optimal number of agents to staff the claims center. You will examine sample data on the number of calls made to the claims center, the duration of each call, and the length of time customers will be put on hold before speaking to an agent. Complete the following:

1. Open the **NP_EX_3-2.xlsx** workbook located in the Excel3 > Review folder included with your Data Files. Save the workbook as **NP_EX_3_Claims** in the location specified by your instructor.

2. In the Documentation sheet, enter your name in cell B3 and the date in cell B4.

3. In cell B4, use the TODAY function to display the current date.

4. Claims are labeled sequentially according to the pattern Claim*number* where *number* is an integer that increases by 1 for each new claim. In the Claims Center Log worksheet, in cell E5, enter **Claim22515** and then use AutoFill to fill in the rest of the claim numbers. Fill in the values without formatting.

5. Enter the following calculations in the claims log (retaining the banded rows effect when you AutoFill formulas over rows):

   a. In column H, display the hold time in seconds for each call made to the claims center by calculating the difference between the column G and column F values and multiplying that difference by 24*60*60. Check your formula by verifying that the first hold time is 29 seconds.

   b. In column I, use the IF function to return the value **1** if the hold time from column H is greater than the hold-time goal in cell B10; otherwise, return the value **0**.

   c. In column K, calculate the length of the call with the agent in minutes by subtracting the values in column J from the values of column G, and then multiplying the difference by 24*60. Use the ROUNDUP function to round the value to the next highest integer. Check your formula by verifying that the first call duration is 21 minutes.

   d. In column L, use the Quick Analysis tool to calculate the running total of the call duration values in minutes. Remove the boldface font from the values. Check your work by verifying that the value in cell L1287 is 32597.

6. Enter formulas to calculate the following summary statistics:

   a. In cell B6, calculate the total number of calls to the claims center by using the COUNT function to count the values in column F. (Use the column reference F:F in the function.)

   b. In cell B7, divide the value in B6 by the value in B5 to calculate the calls per hour.

   c. In the range B11:B13, use the AVERAGE, MEDIAN, and MODE.SNGL functions to calculate the average, median, and mode of the hold times in column H.

   d. In cells B14 and B15, apply the MIN and MAX function to the values in column H to display the minimum and maximum hold times in seconds.

   e. In the range B18:B20, use the AVERAGE, MEDIAN, and MODE.SNGL functions to calculate the average, median, and mode of the call durations in column K.

   f. In cells B21 and B22, use the MIN and MAX functions to display the shortest and longest calls in minutes in column K.

   g. In cell B25, use the SUM function to calculate the total amount of agent time on the phone in column K, and then divide that value by 60 to express the total as hours. Use the ROUND function to round the total to the nearest whole hour.

   h. In cell B26, divide the value in B25 by the value in B5 to calculate the number of agent hours per hour. Use the ROUND function to round this calculation to the nearest tenth.

   i. In cell B27, determine the hold time failure rate by using the SUM function to total the values in column I and then dividing that sum by the total number of calls overall in cell B6.

7. Format the Claims Center Log worksheet as follows:
   a. Apply the Input cell style to cells B5 and B10.
   b. Apply the Calculation cell style to the nonadjacent range B6:B7,B11:B15,B18:B22.
   c. Apply the Output cell style to the range B25:B27.

8. In the Staffing Calculator worksheet, use Goal Seek to determine how many agents will be on call (cell B23) if the staff size is set to 92 agents (cell B26).

9. In the Claims Conclusion worksheet, enter the following constant values as integers (you do not have to use formulas):
   a. In cell B5, enter the expected calls per hour based on the calculated value in cell B7 on the Claims Center Log worksheet rounded up to the next highest integer.
   b. In cell B6, enter the number of available agents based on the calculation in cell B23 on the Staffing Calculator worksheet.
   c. In cell B7, enter **20** as the hold-time goal in seconds.
   d. In cell B8, enter the expected duration of the calls using the average value calculated in cell B18 of the Claims Center Log worksheet rounded up to the next highest integer.

10. In the Claims Conclusion worksheet, enter the following calculations to evaluate whether the number of agents on call will be sufficient to provide good customer service:
    a. In cell B9, divide the value in cell B8 by 60 to calculate the expected call duration in hours.
    b. In cell B12, calculate the Workload per Hour by multiplying the value in cell B5 by the value in cell B9.
    c. In cell B13, divide cell B12 by cell B6 to calculate the percent of agents occupied with calls.

11. Use the lookup table to the display the expected results from the claims center calls based on the number of operators and the call traffic:
    a. In cell B16, use the VLOOKUP function with cell B6 as the lookup value, the range E5:H32 as the reference to the lookup table, 2 as the column index, and FALSE as range_lookup type to return the hold probability for the given number of agents on call.
    b. In cell B17, enter the same VLOOKUP function but return the third column from the lookup table to show the expected hold time in seconds for the given number of agents on call (cell B6).
    c. In cell B18, divide the value in cell B17 by 60 to display the expected hold time in minutes.
    d. In cell B19, enter the same VLOOKUP function but return the fourth column from the lookup table to show the expected failure rate for the given number of agents.

12. In cell B22, write a short summary of your conclusions, answering the question: Is the number of agents that will be available on call sufficient to meet the demands of the claims center without sacrificing customer support performance?

13. Save the workbook, and then close it.

Apply

Case Problem 1

Data File needed for this Case Problem: NP_EX_3-3.xlsx

Multex Digital   Liana Bonnet is a production quality control engineer for Multex Digital, a manufacturer of computer components. Part of Liana's job is to analyze batches of semiconductor wafers to ensure that the wafers are within design specifications. Wafers have to have a thickness of around 625 microns but that thickness will vary due to the inherit inaccuracy of the machines creating the wafers. Liana needs to ensure that machines are operating correctly because a machine that is constantly creating wafers that are too thin or too thick will have to be removed from the assembly line and retuned.

Liana will suspect a machine is out-of-alignment when the average wafer size of batch of wafers taken from that machine that operates beyond quality control limits. Control limits are established according to the following two equations:

$$Lower\ Control\ Limit\ (LCL) = Xbar - A_2 \times Rbar$$

$$Upper\ Control\ Limit\ (UCL) = Xbar + A_2 \times Rbar$$

where *Xbar* is the average wafer thickness from all sample batches, *Rbar* is the average range of wafer thickness from all sample batches, and A_2 is a constant that depends on the batch sample size.

Liana has recorded data from 50 machine batches with the sample size of each batch varying from 3 to 10 wafers. Liana wants you to report which of the 50 machines are no longer operating within control limits. Complete the following:

1. Open the **NP_EX_3-3.xlsx** workbook located in the Excel3 > Case1 folder included with your Data Files, and then save the workbook as **NP_EX_3_Quality** in the location specified by your instructor.

2. In the Documentation sheet, enter your name in cell B3. Use an Excel function to display the current date in cell B4.

3. In the Control Data worksheet, in the range A6:A55, use AutoFill to enter the text strings **Batch-1** through **Batch-50**. In the range B5:K5, use AutoFill to enter the text strings **Wafer-1** through **Wafer-10**.

4. Enter the following summary statistics to the worksheet:

   a. In cell M6, use the COUNT function to the count of number of values in the range B6:K6.

   b. In cell N6, calculate the difference between the maximum value in the range B6:K6 (using the MAX function) and the minimum value in the range B6:K6 (using the MIN function).

   c. In cell O6, use the AVERAGE function to calculate the average wafer size in the range B6:K6.

   d. Use AutoFill to extend the formulas in the range M6:O6 through the range M6:O55.

5. Calculate the following quality control statistics:

   a. In cell V5, display the value of *Xbar* by using the AVERAGE function to calculate the average of the values in column O.

   b. In cell V6, display the value of *Rbar* by using the AVERAGE function to calculate the average of the values in column N.

6. Do the following to complete a lookup table that you will use to calculate the lower and upper control limits for batch samples sizes of 2 up to 25:

   a. In cell W10, calculate the lower control limit by returning the value of cell V5 minus the value of cell V10 times cell V6. Use absolute references for cells V5 and V6 and a relative reference for cell V10. Check your formula by verifying that cell W10 shows the value 598.45.

   b. In cell X10, calculate the upper control limit by returning the value of cell V5 plus the value of cell V10 times cell V6. Once again, use absolute references for cells V5 and V6 and a relative reference for cell V10. Check your formula by verify that cell X10 shows the value 651.61.

   c. Use AutoFill to extend the formulas in the range W10:X10 over the range W10:X33 to show the lower and upper control limits for batch sizes ranging from 2 up to 25.

7. In cell P6, use the VLOOKUP function to display the lower control limit for the first batch from the assembly line using cell M6 as the lookup value, the range $U$9:$X$33 as the lookup table, 3 as the column index number, and FALSE for the range_lookup value. Extend the formula in cell P6 over the range P6:P55.

8. Repeat Step 7 in cell Q6 using 4 as the column index number in the VLOOKUP function to retrieve the upper control limit for the first batch and then extend the formula over the range Q6:Q55.

9. Determine whether a batch is not in control because the batch average falls below the lower control limit. In cell R6, use an IF function to test whether the value of sample average in cell O6 is less than the value of lower control limit in cell P6. If the condition is true, display "Out of Control"; otherwise, display "In Control" in the cell. Extend the formula over the range R6:R55 to indicate which batches are falling below the lower control limit for the machinery.

10. Repeat Step 9 for cell S6 except test for the condition that sample average in cell O6 is greater than the value of the upper control limit in cell Q6. Extend the formula over the range S6:S55 to indicate which batches are operating above the upper control limit.

11. Add conditional formatting to the range R6:S55, displaying any cell containing the text "Out of Control" in a red font on a light red background.

12. In cell A58, write your conclusions indicating which of the 50 machines on the assembly line are not within the control parameters set by Liana and indicate in what ways those machines are failing.

13. Save the workbook, and then close it.

Challenge

Case Problem 2

Data File needed for this Case Problem: NP_EX_3-4.xlsx

Canvas Scribe   Michael Feinbaum is a production manager for Canvas Scribe, a manufacturer of digital games. To produce and release a quality game requires a team of programmers, animators, writers, and testers. Typically a game will take a year to develop from its initial planning stages to final release. Michael wants to create a production schedule for a new game called *Escape from Dunkirk*, to be released in time for holiday sales. To create this production schedule, you will use the WORKDAY and NETWORKDAYS functions described in Figure 3–18 and in the InSight box, "Date Calculations with Working Days." Complete the following:

1. Open the **NP_EX_3-4.xlsx** workbook located in the Excel3 > Case2 folder included with your Data Files, and then save the workbook as **NP_EX_3_Schedule** in the location specified by your instructor.

2. In the Documentation sheet, enter your name in cell B3. Use a function to enter the current date in cell B4.

3. In the Production Schedule worksheet, in cell B4, enter **9/12/2025** as an initial proposed start date for the project.

4. In cell B10, enter the formula **=B4** to reference the start date you entered in cell B4.

⊕ **Explore** 5. In cell C10, calculate the date on which the Idea Development phase ends using the WORKDAY function. Use cell B10 as the starting date, cell D10 as the number of workdays, and the range $H$10:$H$29 as the reference to the holiday dates.

6. Use AutoFill to extend the formula in cell C10 to the range C10:C28 but do not extend the formatting.

7. In cell B5, enter the formula **=B28** to display the date on which the game will be released.

⊕ **Explore** 8. In cell B6, use the NETWORKDAYS function to calculate the total number of working days that will be devoted to creating the *Escape from Dunkirk* game. Use cell B4 as the start_date, cell B5 as the end_date, and the range $H$10:$H$29 as the holidays argument.

9. In cell B7, calculate the total number of calendar days devoted to the project by taking the difference between the release date and the start date.

10. The game must be released no later than 10/12/2026 to take advantage of holiday sales. Use Goal Seek to determine the starting date that will meet this goal by entering cell B5 in the Set cell box, the date 10/12/2026 in the To value box, and cell B4 in the By changing cell box.

11. In cell D4, write a summary of your findings in developing this production schedule.

12. Save the workbook, and then close it.

Objectives

Session 4.1
- Create a pie chart
- Format chart elements
- Create a line chart
- Work with chart legends
- Create a combination chart

Session 4.2
- Create a scatter chart
- Edit a chart data source
- Create a data callout
- Insert shapes and icons into a worksheet
- Create and edit a data bar
- Create and edit a group of sparklines

EXCEL

Analyzing and Charting Financial Data

Preparing an Investment Report

Case | Philbin Financial Group

Hideki Eto is an analyst for the Philbin Financial Group, a financial investment firm located in Phoenix, Arizona. Hideki needs to prepare financial reports that the company's clients will receive at meetings with a Philbin Financial Group advisor. One of the funds handled by the company is the Sunrise Fund, a large growth/large risk investment fund. Hideki needs you to summarize the fund's financial holdings as well as document its recent and long-term performance. Hideki has already entered the financial data into a workbook but wants you to finish the report. Because many clients are overwhelmed by tables of numbers, you will summarize the data using Excel financial charts and graphics.

Starting Data Files

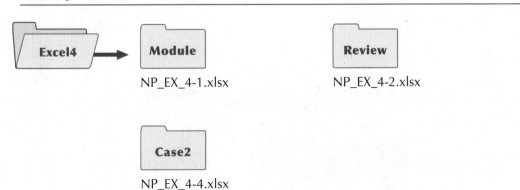

Excel4 →	Module	Review	Case1
	NP_EX_4-1.xlsx	NP_EX_4-2.xlsx	NP_EX_4-3.xlsx

Case2
NP_EX_4-4.xlsx

Session 4.1 Visual Overview:

A **chart legend** identifies the data markers associated with each data series.

The **chart title** is a descriptive label or name for the chart.

A **pie chart** presents data in the shape of a circle divided into slices with each slice representing a single data category.

A **data label** is text associated with an individual data marker, such as the percentage value next to a pie slice.

A **line chart** displays data values using a connected line rather than columns or bars.

Chart **gridlines** extend the values of the major or minor tick marks across the plot area.

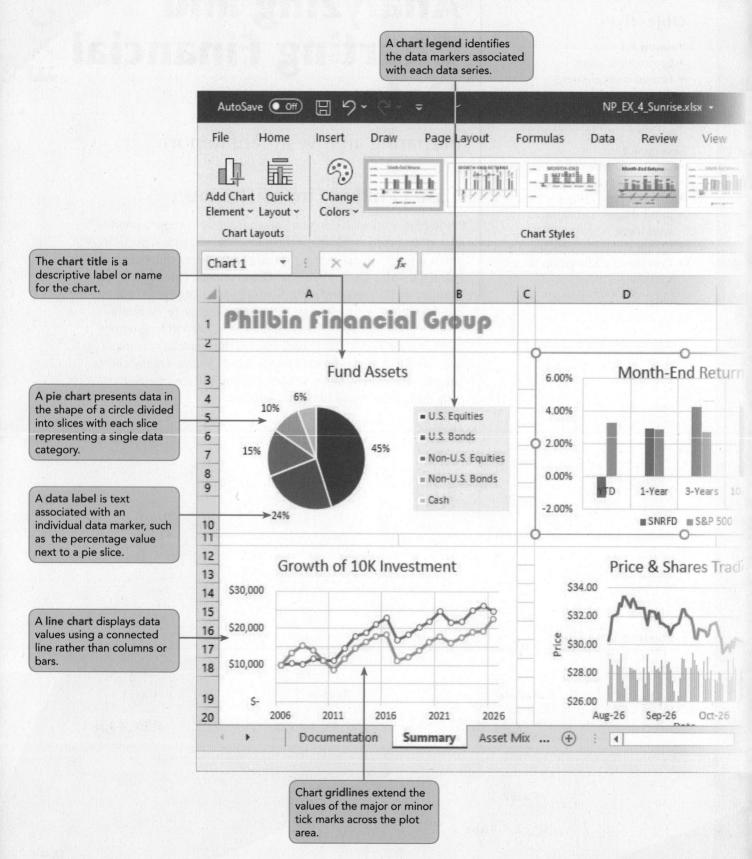

Chart Elements

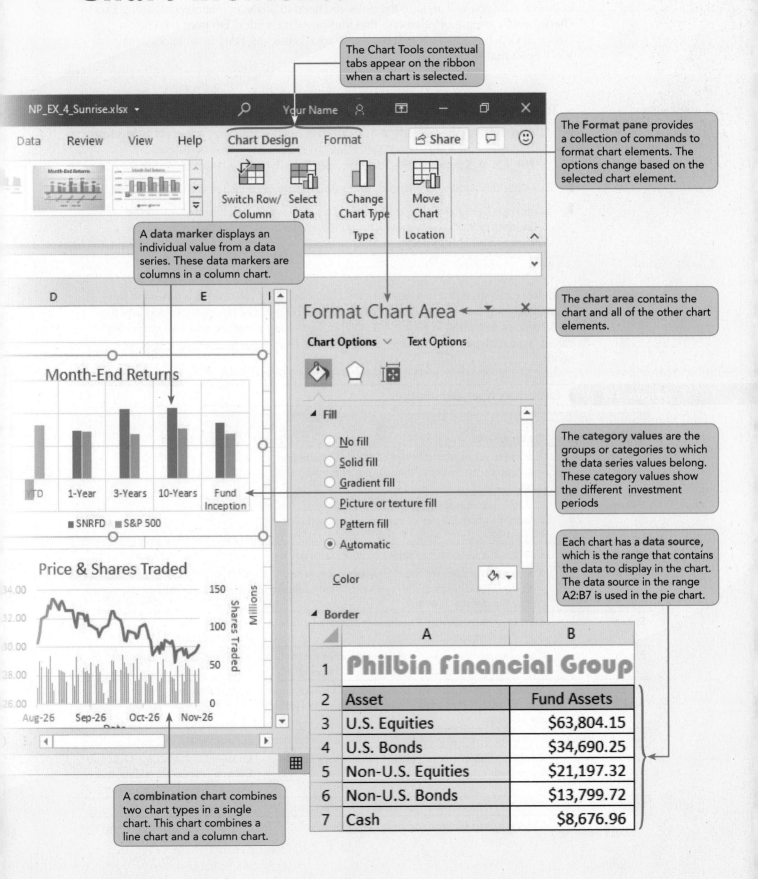

The Chart Tools contextual tabs appear on the ribbon when a chart is selected.

The Format pane provides a collection of commands to format chart elements. The options change based on the selected chart element.

A data marker displays an individual value from a data series. These data markers are columns in a column chart.

The chart area contains the chart and all of the other chart elements.

The category values are the groups or categories to which the data series values belong. These category values show the different investment periods

Each chart has a data source, which is the range that contains the data to display in the chart. The data source in the range A2:B7 is used in the pie chart.

A combination chart combines two chart types in a single chart. This chart combines a line chart and a column chart.

NP_EX_4_Sunrise.xlsx

Your Name

Data   Review   View   Help   Chart Design   Format   Share

Switch Row/ Column   Select Data   Change Chart Type   Move Chart

Type   Location

Format Chart Area

Chart Options   Text Options

◢ Fill

○ No fill
○ Solid fill
○ Gradient fill
○ Picture or texture fill
○ Pattern fill
● Automatic

Color

◢ Border

Month-End Returns

YTD   1-Year   3-Years   10-Years   Fund Inception

■ SNRFD ■ S&P 500

Price & Shares Traded

Shares Traded   Millions

Aug-26   Sep-26   Oct-26   Nov-26

	A	B
1	**Philbin Financial Group**	
2	Asset	Fund Assets
3	U.S. Equities	$63,804.15
4	U.S. Bonds	$34,690.25
5	Non-U.S. Equities	$21,197.32
6	Non-U.S. Bonds	$13,799.72
7	Cash	$8,676.96

Getting Started with Excel Charts

In this module you will acquire the skills you need to analyze financial data using Excel **charts**, which are graphic elements that illustrate data. Hideki Eto from the Philbin Financial Group has already entered the financial data you need in an Excel workbook. You'll open that workbook now.

To open Hideki's workbook:

▶ **1.** sam↓ Open the **NP_EX_4-1.xlsx** workbook located in the **Excel4 > Module** folder included with your Data Files, and then save the workbook as **NP_EX_4_Sunrise** in the location specified by your instructor.

▶ **2.** In the Documentation sheet, enter your name in cell B3 and the date in cell B4.

▶ **3.** Review the financial data stored in the workbook and then return to the **Summary** worksheet in which you'll summarize data stored in the other sheets of the workbook.

In data analysis, a properly constructed chart can be as valuable as a thousand lines of financial facts and figures. Excel has more than 60 types of charts organized into the 10 categories described in Figure 4–1. Within each chart category are chart variations called chart subtypes. You can also design custom chart types to meet your specific needs.

Figure 4–1   Excel chart types and subtypes

Chart Category	Description	Chart Subtypes
Column or Bar	Compares values from different categories. Values are indicated by the height of the columns or the length of a bar.	2-D Column, 3-D Column, 2-D Bar, 3-D Bar
Hierarchy	Displays data that is organized into a hierarchy of categories where the size of the groups is based on a number.	Treemap, Sunburst
Waterfall or Stock	Displays financial cash flow values or stock market data.	Waterfall, Funnel, Stock
Line or Area	Compares values from different categories. Values are indicated by the height of the lines. Often used to show trends and changes over time.	2-D Line, 3-D Line, 2-D Area, 3-D Area
Statistic	Displays a chart summarizing the distribution of values from a sample population.	Histogram, Pareto, Box and Whisker
Pie	Compares relative values of different categories to the whole. Values are indicated by the areas of the pie slices.	2-D Pie, 3-D Pie, Doughnut
X Y (Scatter) or Bubble	Shows the patterns or relationship between two or more sets of values. Often used in scientific studies and statistical analyses.	Scatter, Bubble
Surface or Radar	Compares three sets of values in a three-dimensional chart.	Surface, Radar
Combo	Combines two or more chart types so the data can be compared.	Clustered Column-Line, Clustered Column-Line on Secondary Axis, Stacked Area-Clustered Column
Map	Compares data values across geographical regions.	Filled Map
PivotChart	Creates a chart summarizing data from a PivotTable.	PivotChart, PivotChart & PivotTable

Each chart type provides a different insight into your data. Figure 4–2 presents the same financial data displayed in pie chart, column chart, treemap chart, and a map chart. The chart you choose depends on what aspect of the data you are trying to highlight.

Figure 4–2	Data displayed with different Excel chart types

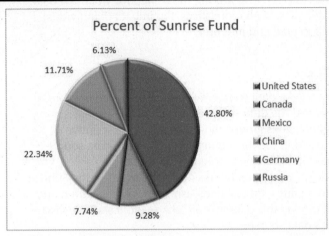

pie chart

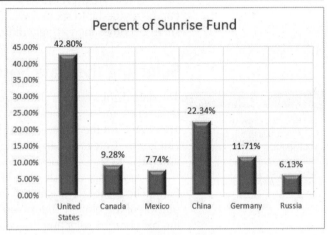

column chart

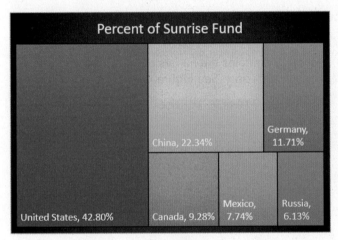

treemap chart

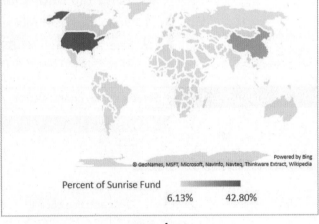

map chart

Creating a chart is a multistep process involving selecting the data to display, choosing the chart type best suited to that data, and finally formatting the chart's appearance to maximize the chart's impact. The first chart you will create for the Sunrise Fund report is a pie chart providing a visual breakdown of the fund's assets.

Reference

Creating a Chart

- Select the range containing the data you want to chart.
- On the Insert tab, in the Charts group, click the Recommended Charts button or a button representing the general chart type, and then click the chart you want to create; or click the Quick Analysis button, click the Charts category, and then click the chart you want to create.
- On the Chart Design tab, in the Location group, click the Move Chart button, select whether to embed the chart in a worksheet or place it in a chart sheet, and then click OK.
- Use the chart tools to format the appearance of individual chart elements.

Creating a Pie Chart

A pie chart presents data in a circle graph divided into slices with each slice representing a single data category. Categories whose data values take up larger percentages of the whole are represented with larger slices; categories that take up a smaller percentage of the whole are presented as smaller slices. Pie charts are most effective when the data can be divided into six or fewer categories. With more slices, the impact of individual slices becomes increasingly difficult to read and interpret.

Selecting the Data Source

Tip

Don't include row or column totals in the pie chart data because Excel will treat those totals as another category.

The data displayed in a chart come from a data source, which includes one or more data series and a set of category values. The **data series** is the actual values that are plotted on the chart. The category values groups those values into descriptive categories. Categories are usually listed in the first column or row of the data source and the data series values are placed in subsequent columns or rows.

The Asset Mix worksheet in Hideki's workbook breaks down the assets in the Sunrise Fund. The assets are organized into equities, bonds, and cash from sources within and outside of the United States. You'll display this data in a pie chart. You'll start creating the pie chart by selecting the chart's data source.

To select the data source for the pie chart:

1. Go to the **Asset Mix** worksheet.

2. Select the range **A4:B9**. This range contains the names of the assets and the amount invested within each asset category. See Figure 4–3.

Figure 4–3   Selected chart data source

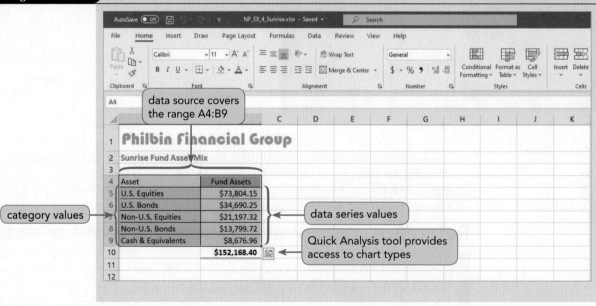

The selected data source covers two columns. The categories in the first column (Asset) will identify each pie slice and the data series in the second column (Fund Assets) will set the size of each slice.

Charting with the Quick Analysis Tool

After you select a data source, the Quick Analysis tool appears in the lower-right corner of the selection. The Charts category in the Quick Analysis tool displays chart types that are appropriate for the selected data source. For this data source, a pie chart provides a good way to compare the relative amount that the Sunrise Fund invests in five asset categories. You'll use the Quick Analysis tool to generate the pie chart for Hideki.

To create a pie chart with the Quick Analysis tool:

▶ **1.** With the range A4:B9 still selected, click the **Quick Analysis** button 🖾 in the lower-right corner of the selected range (or press **CTRL+Q**) to open the Quick Analysis tool.

▶ **2.** Click the **Charts** category. The chart types you will most likely want to use with the selected data source are listed.

▶ **3.** Point to each chart type to see a preview and a description of the data rendered as that chart. See Figure 4–4.

Figure 4–4	Charts category of the Quick Analysis tool

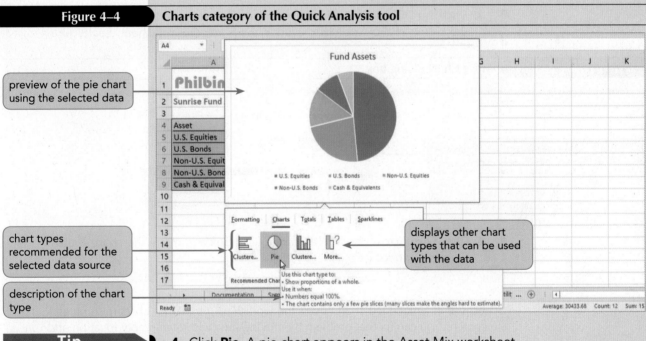

preview of the pie chart using the selected data

chart types recommended for the selected data source

description of the chart type

displays other chart types that can be used with the data

▶ **4.** Click **Pie**. A pie chart appears in the Asset Mix worksheet.

Excel automatically identifies the slice categories and the slice values from the data source. When the selected range is taller than it is wide, Excel assumes that the category values and data series are laid out in columns. Conversely, a data source that is wider than it is tall is assumed to have the category values and data series laid out in rows. The biggest slice in this pie chart represents the amount of the fund invested in U.S. equities, the smallest slice represents the amount invested in cash and equivalents. Slices start at the 12 o'clock position and are added clockwise around the pie.

Each new chart is given a reference name viewed in the Reference box. The default names are Chart 1, Chart 2, and so forth. When a chart is selected, two chart contextual tabs appear on the ribbon. The Chart Design tab is used to modify the chart's overall design and its data source, while the Format tab is used to format the individual parts of the chart, such as the chart's border or the slices from a pie chart. When the chart is not selected, the contextual tabs disappear.

Moving and Resizing a Chart

Tip

You can print an embedded chart with its worksheet, or you can print only the selected embedded chart without its worksheet.

A chart is placed either within its own chart sheet or embedded within a worksheet. The advantage of an embedded chart is that it can be displayed alongside relevant text and tables in the worksheet. Chart sheets are best used for charts that occupy a single page in a report or printout. In this report, all your charts will be embedded within the Summary worksheet. You'll move the pie chart you created in the Asset Mix worksheet to that sheet.

To move the embedded chart to the Summary worksheet:

1. Make sure the pie chart is selected, and then, on the ribbon, click the **Chart Design** tab, if necessary, to display it.

2. In the Location group, click the **Move Chart** button. The Move Chart dialog box opens.

3. Click the **Object in** arrow, and then click **Summary** in the list to indicate that the pie chart should be displayed in the Summary worksheet. See Figure 4–5.

Figure 4–5 Move Chart dialog box

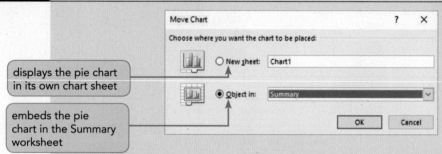

displays the pie chart in its own chart sheet

embeds the pie chart in the Summary worksheet

4. Click **OK** to close the Move Chart dialog box and move the chart to the Summary worksheet.

Because an embedded chart covers the worksheet grid, it can obscure some of the content. You can fix that problem by moving the chart to an empty location and resizing it. To move and resize a chart, the chart must be selected, which adds a selection box around the chart. The selection box has sizing handles to change the chart's width and height. As you move and resize a chart, holding down ALT snaps the chart to the worksheet grid. If you do not hold down ALT, you can move and resize the chart to any location on the grid.

Hideki wants the pie chart to cover the range G7:H14 in the Summary worksheet. You'll move and resize the chart to fit this space.

To move and resize the pie chart:

Make sure the ScreenTip shows "Chart Area" so the entire chart moves when you drag.

1. Move the pointer over an empty part of the chart so that the pointer changes to the Move pointer ✛ and the ScreenTip displays "Chart Area."

2. Hold down **ALT**, drag the chart to cell **G7** until its upper-left corner snaps to the upper-left corner of the cell, and then release the mouse button and **ALT**.

The upper-left corner of the chart now aligns with the upper-left corner of cell G7.

Trouble? If the pie chart resizes or does not move to the new location, you probably didn't drag the chart from an empty part of the chart area. Press CTRL+Z to undo your last action, and then repeat Steps 1 and 2, being sure to drag the pie chart from the chart area.

3. Point to the sizing handle in the lower-right corner of the selection box until the pointer changes to the Resizing pointer ⬉.

4. Hold down **ALT**, drag the sizing handle up to the lower-right corner of cell **H14**, and then release the mouse button and **ALT**, resizing the chart. The chart resizes to cover the range G7:H14 and remains selected. See Figure 4–6.

Figure 4–6	Moved and resized pie chart

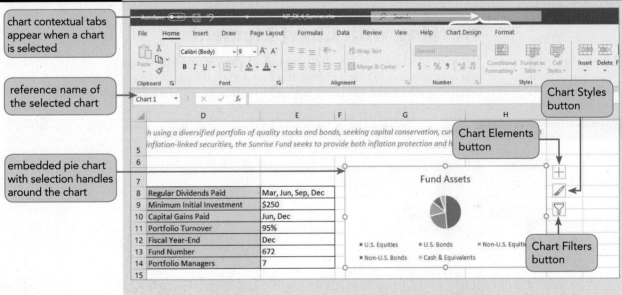

chart contextual tabs appear when a chart is selected

reference name of the selected chart

embedded pie chart with selection handles around the chart

Chart Styles button

Chart Elements button

Chart Filters button

Another way of moving a chart is by cutting and pasting. Select the chart, click the Cut button in the Clipboard group on the Home tab, and then select the cell you want to place the chart. Click the Paste button to paste the chart at the new location.

Even though a chart is not part of the worksheet grid, it resizes with the grid. So if you change a column width or row height, the chart's width and height will also change. This ensures that an embedded chart always stays in the same relative location within the worksheet even as rows and columns are resized.

Insight

Exploding a Pie Chart

Pie slices do not need to be fixed within the pie. An **exploded pie chart** moves one slice away from the others as if someone were taking the piece away from the pie. Exploded pie charts are useful for emphasizing one category above the others. For example, to emphasize the fact that Sunrise Fund invests heavily in U.S. equities, you could explode that single slice, moving it away from the other slices.

To explode a pie slice, first click the pie to select it, and then click the single slice you want to move. Make sure that a selection box appears around only that slice. Drag the slice away from the pie, offsetting it from the others. You can explode multiple slices by selecting each slice in turn and dragging them away. To explode all the slices, select the entire pie and drag the pointer away from the pie's center. Although you can explode more than one slice, the resulting pie chart is rarely effective as a visual aid to the reader.

Working with Chart Elements

The individual parts of the chart are called **chart elements**. Figure 4–7 shows elements that are common to many charts. You can access the properties of these chart elements by clicking the Chart Elements button ⊞ that appears to the right of the chart.

Figure 4–7   **Common chart elements**

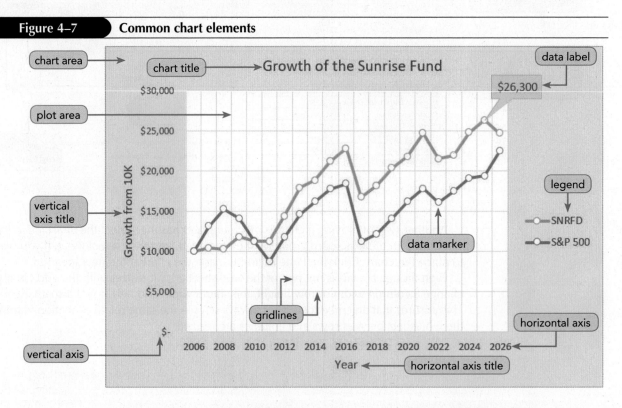

The pie chart you created does not contain any data labels. Hideki thinks showing the data values associated with each pie slice would make the chart easier to interpret. You will use the Chart Elements button ⊞ to add that element to the pie chart.

To add the data labels chart element to the pie chart:

1. With the pie chart still selected, click the **Chart Elements** button ⊞. A menu of chart elements associated with the pie chart opens. As the checkmarks indicate, only the chart title and the chart legend are displayed in the pie chart.

2. Point to the **Data Labels** check box. Live Preview shows how the chart will look when the data labels show the dollar amount (in millions) invested within each category.

3. Click the **Data Labels** check box to select it. The data labels are added to the chart. See Figure 4–8.

Figure 4–8 | **Common chart elements**

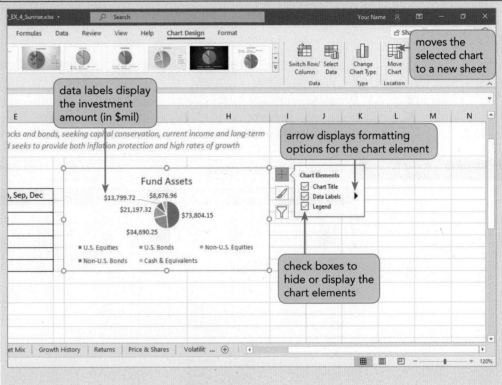

Hideki does not want the data labels to show the amount invested in each asset, but rather the percentage of the total invested in each asset. You can make that change by editing the properties of the Data Labels element.

Formatting a Chart Element

Each element listed in the Chart Elements button contains a submenu of common formatting choices, such as the placement of data labels relative to the position of the data marker or pie slice. From within that submenu, you can also open a formatting pane that has an extensive menu of formatting options. You'll explore the formatting choices available with the pie slice labels now.

To format a data label:

▶ 1. With the pie chart still selected, click the **Chart Elements** button ⊞ if necessary to display the submenu, point to **Data Labels**, and then click the **right arrow** icon ▶ to view the list of common formatting choices for data labels.

▶ 2. Point to each of the following options to get a Live Preview of data labels positioned at different locations around the pie chart: **Center**, **Inside End**, **Outside End**, **Best Fit**, and **Data Callout**.

▶ 3. Click **More Options** to view the extensive menu of formatting options for data labels in the Format Data Labels pane. The Format Data Labels pane is divided into different sections indicated by the icons near the top of the pane. The formatting options for the data labels ⏸ is selected by default.

▶ 4. Click the **Percentage** check box to add percentages to the data labels for each pie slice.

▶ 5. Click the **Value** check box to deselect it, removing those data value from the data labels.

▶ 6. Scroll down the Format Data Labels pane, and then click the **Outside End** option button in the Label Position section to always place the data labels outside and at the end of each pie slice. See Figure 4–9.

Figure 4–9   **Format Data Labels pane**

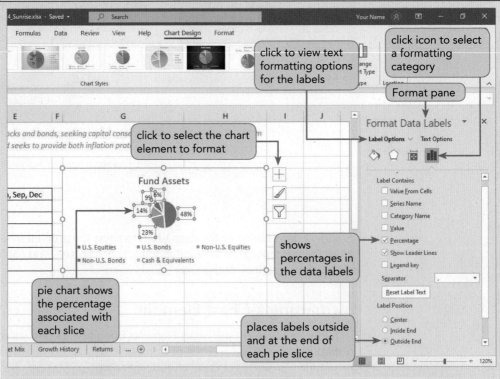

The Format pane is attached, or docked, to the right side of the workbook window. You can undock the pane so that it floats free above the worksheet grid by pointing to a blank area of the pane until the pointer changes to the Move pointer ⊹ and then clicking and dragging the pane over the worksheet grid. To redock the pane, point to the floating pane until the pointer changes to the Move pointer ⁺↕⃗ and then drag to the right until the pane reattaches to the workbook window.

From the Format pane, you can format other chart elements. For example, Hideki thinks the pie chart would look better if the legend were aligned with the right edge of the chart area rather than its current position at the bottom. Hideki also wants the background of the legend to change to a light gold color. You'll use the Format pane to make those changes now.

To move and format the pie chart legend:

1. In the Format Data Labels pane, click the **Label Options arrow** directly below the Format Data Labels title, and then click **Legend** in the list of chart elements. The name of the Format pane changes to Format Legend and options for formatting the pie chart legend appear in the pane.

2. In the Legend Options section, click the **Right** option button to place the pie chart legend on the right side of the chart area. See Figure 4–10.

Figure 4–10 **Chart legend in chart area**

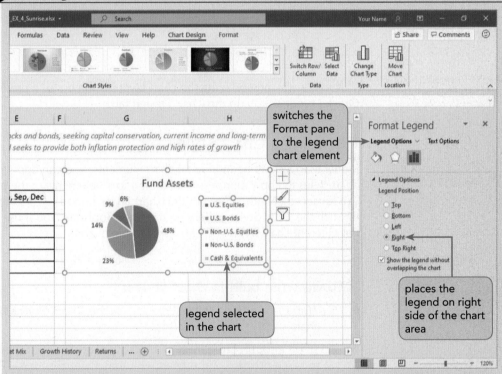

3. Click the **Fill & Line** icon ◇, and then click the **Fill** heading to view the fill options for the legend.

4. Click the **Solid fill** option button, and then click the **Fill Color** button 🎨▾ and select **Gold, Accent 5, Lighter 80%** (the ninth theme color in the second row) in the color palette. See Figure 4–11.

Figure 4–11 Fill color for the chart legend

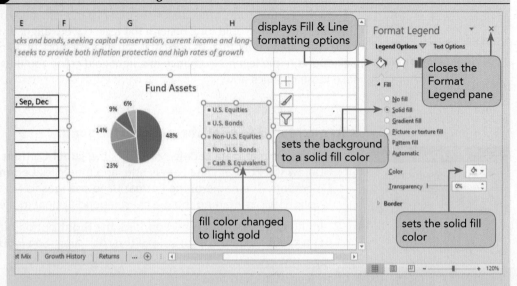

5. Click the **Close** button [X] in the upper-right corner of the Format Legend pane to close the pane.

Another way of modifying the chart layout is to choose a predefined layout from the Quick Layout button on the Chart Design tab.

Choosing a Chart Style

Rather than formatting individual chart elements, you can apply one of the built-in chart styles to apply a professional design to all elements of the chart. Chart styles can be accessed either through the Chart Styles button 🖌 next to a selected chart or through the Chart Styles gallery on the Chart Tools tab. You'll use Live Preview to view the different chart styles you can apply to pie charts.

To view the built-in chart styles:

1. With the pie chart still selected, click the **Chart Styles** button 🖌 next to the chart.

2. Scroll through the gallery of chart styles, pointing to each entry in the gallery to see a preview of the chart with that style. Figure 4–12 shows a preview of design of the Style 6 chart style applied to the Asset Mix pie chart.

Figure 4–12	Preview of a chart style

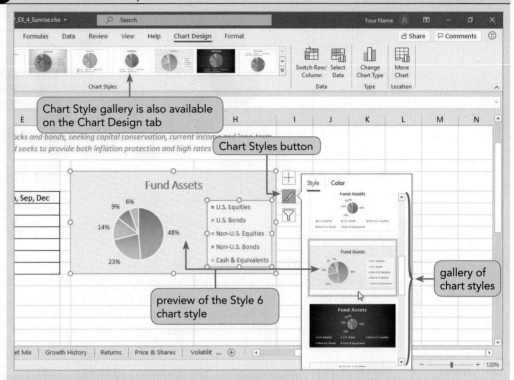

3. Press **ESC** to close the chart style gallery without changing the style of the Asset Mix pie chart.

> **Trouble?** If you accidentally apply a chart style, click the Undo button ↶ on the Quick Access Toolbar to restore the chart to its previous style.

While Hideki doesn't want you to change the chart style of the Asset Mix pie chart, another concern is that the pie chart is difficult to interpret with its mix of colors. You can correct this problem by choosing a different color scheme.

Changing the Color Scheme

Each chart has a color scheme. By default, Excel applies the theme colors to the pie chart slices. You can select a different color scheme from the Chart Styles button in the Colors submenu. Hideki wants you to use colors in the same blue hue but with different levels of saturation so that the largest slice is displayed in dark blue and the smallest slice displayed in a light blue. You'll apply this color scheme to the Asset Mix pie chart.

To change the pie slice colors:

1. Click the **Chart Styles** button 🖌 to reopen the gallery of chart styles.

2. Click the **Color** tab to display a gallery of possible color schemes.

3. Select the blue monochromatic color scheme labeled **Monochromatic Palette 1**. See Figure 4–13.

Tip

You can also use the Change Colors button in the Chart Styles group on the Chart Design tab.

Figure 4–13   Color schemes for the chart

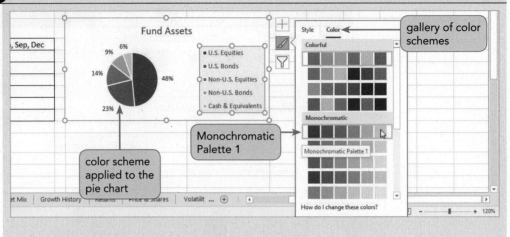

Because the color schemes are based on the theme colors, you can change the color schemes by selecting new theme colors from the Colors box in the Themes group on the Page Layout tab. If you don't want to change the workbook's color theme, you can change the color of individual pie slices. To change a pie slice to another color, double-click the slice to select only that slice (and no other elements on the chart) and then choose a color from the Fill Color button in the Font group on the Home tab.

Insight

Overlaying Chart Elements

An embedded chart takes up less space than a chart sheet. However, it can be challenging to fit all the chart elements into that smaller space. One solution is to overlay one element on top of another. The most commonly overlaid elements are the chart title and the chart legend. To overlay the chart title, click the Chart Title arrow in the Chart Elements list and select Centered Overlay as the position option. Excel will place the chart title on top of the plot area, freeing up more space for other chart elements. Chart legends can also be overlaid by opening the Format pane for the legend and deselecting the Show the legend without overlapping the chart check box in the Legend Options section. Other chart elements can be overlaid by dragging them to new locations in the chart area and then resizing the plot area to recover the empty space.

Don't overuse the technique of overlaying chart elements. Too much overlaying of chart elements can make a chart difficult to read.

Performing What-If Analyses with Charts

Because a chart is linked to its data source, any changes in the data source values will be reflected in the chart. This link between a chart and its data source provides a powerful tool for data exploration. For the Asset Mix pie chart, the chart title is linked to the text in cell B4 of the Asset Mix worksheet, the size of the pie slices is based on values in the range B5:B9 and the category names are linked to the category values in the range A4:A9.

Hideki notes that the value in cell B5 for the amount invested in U.S. Equities should be $63,804.15 instead of $73,804.15. You will change the value in the cell and change the category name in cell B9 from "Cash & Equivalents" to simply "Cash."

To modify the pie chart's data:

▶ **1.** Go to the **Asset Mix** worksheet, and then in cell **B5**, change the value to **$63,804.15** to reflect the correct amount invested in U.S. Equities.

▶ **2.** In cell **A9**, change the text to **Cash** to update the label.

▶ **3.** Go to the **Summary** worksheet and confirm that the percent of assets invested in U.S. equities has decreased to 45% and that the last legend entry changed to "Cash."

If you want a chart to focus on fewer categories, you can filter the chart by removing one or more categories. Removing a category has no impact on the data source. To focus on U.S. investments, you'll filter the pie chart to show the breakdown of assets between U.S. equities and U.S. bonds.

To filter the pie chart:

▶ **1.** Select the pie chart if it is not already selected and then click the **Filter** button 🔽 next to the chart, opening a list of data categories.

Tip
When you point to a category, Live Preview highlights the pie slice corresponding to that category.

▶ **2.** Click the **Non-U.S. Equities**, **Non-U.S. Bonds**, and **Cash** check boxes to remove the checkmarks from those boxes.

▶ **3.** Click **Apply** to apply the filters to the chart. The pie chart shows that 65% of the non-cash U.S. investments are in equities and 35% are in bonds. See Figure 4–14.

Figure 4–14	Filtered pie chart

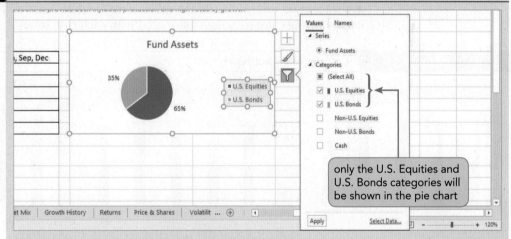

▶ **4.** Double-click the **(Select All)** check box to select all chart categories, and then click **Apply** to return the pie chart to its former state.

The pie chart revealed some important information about the assets of the Sunrise Fund. Next, you will use a column chart to explore the level of returns that the fund has provided for investors over the past ten years.

Creating a Column Chart

A **column chart** displays data values as columns with the height of each column based on the data value. A column chart turned on its side is called a **bar chart**, with the length of the bar determined by the data value. It is better to use column and bar charts than pie charts when the number of categories is large, or when the data categories are close in value. Figure 4–15 displays the same data as a pie chart and a column chart. As you can see, it's difficult to determine which pie slice is biggest and by how much. It is much simpler to make those comparisons in a column or bar chart.

| Figure 4–15 | Data displayed as different chart types |

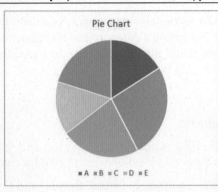 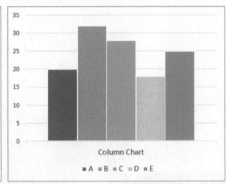

Comparing Column Chart Subtypes

Unlike pie charts, which can show only one data series, column and bar charts can display multiple data series. Figure 4–16 shows three examples of column charts in which five data series (U.S. Equities, U.S. Bonds, Non-U.S. Equities, Non-U.S. Bonds, and Cash) are plotted against one category series (Years). Column charts are plotted against a **value axis** displaying the values from the data series and a **category axis** displaying the category values associated with each data series.

| Figure 4–16 | Column chart subtypes |

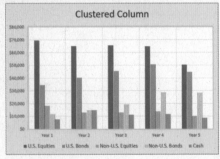 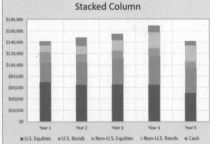 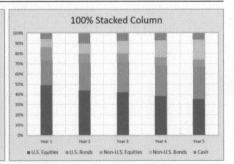

A **clustered column chart** displays the data series values in separate columns side by side so that you can compare the relative heights of values across categories. The clustered column chart in Figure 4–16 compares the amount invested in each category in year 1 through year 5. Note that the amount invested in U.S. equities steadily declines as the amount invested in U.S. bonds and non-U.S. bonds increases.

A **stacked column chart** combines the data series values within a single column to show how much of the total is contributed by each item. The stacked column chart in Figure 4–16 gives information on the total amount invested each year in the fund and how each year's investment is split among five investment categories. This chart makes it clear that the total investment in fund dropped between the fourth and fifth year.

Finally, a **100% stacked column chart** makes the same comparison as the stacked column chart except that the stacked sections are expressed as percentages of the whole. As you can see from the 100% stacked column chart in Figure 4–16, the investment in U.S. equities and bonds starts out at over 70% in the first year and steadily decreases to about 65% by the fifth year as more of the fund is invested in non-U.S. bonds. Each chart, while working with the same data source, reveals something different about the activity of the investment fund over the 5-year period.

Creating a Clustered Column Chart

The process for creating a column chart is the same as for creating a pie chart: Select the data source and then choose a chart type and subtype. After the chart is embedded in the worksheet, you can move and resize the chart as well as change the chart's design, layout, and format.

Hideki wants a column chart showing the returns of the Sunrise Fund adjusted over 1-year, 3-year, and 10-year periods, as well as year-to-date (YTD) and since the fund's inception. The column chart will include the returns from the Standard & Poor's 500 index (S&P 500) to indicate how the fund compares to an industry standard. You'll create that chart now.

To create a clustered column chart:

1. Go to the **Returns** worksheet containing the returns based on month-end values.

2. Select the range **A4:C9** containing the categories and values to chart.

3. On the ribbon, click the **Insert** tab, and then in the Charts group, click the **Recommended Charts** button. The Insert Chart dialog box opens to the Recommended Charts tab. From this tab, you can preview and select a chart best suited to the data source. See Figure 4–17.

Figure 4–17   Recommended Charts tab in the Insert Chart dialog box

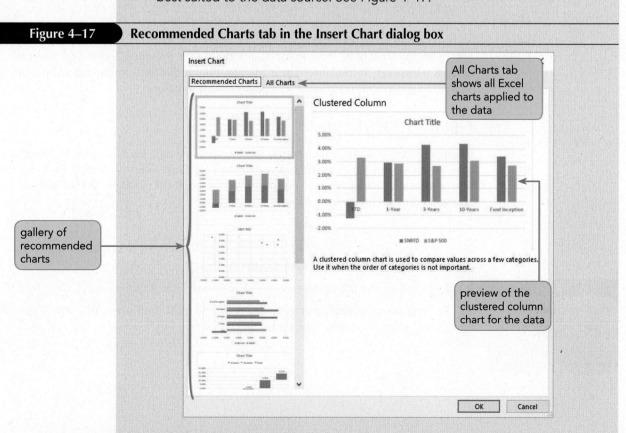

gallery of recommended charts

All Charts tab shows all Excel charts applied to the data

preview of the clustered column chart for the data

4. Confirm that the **Clustered Column** chart is selected, and then click **OK**.

5. On the Chart Design tab, in the Location group, click the **Move Chart** button.

6. From the Object in box, click **Summary** and then click **OK** to move the column chart to the Summary worksheet.

7. In the Summary worksheet, hold down **ALT** as you move and resize the chart to cover the range **A17:B28**, and then release **ALT**. The chart snaps to the grid. See Figure 4–18.

Figure 4–18   Column chart of return data

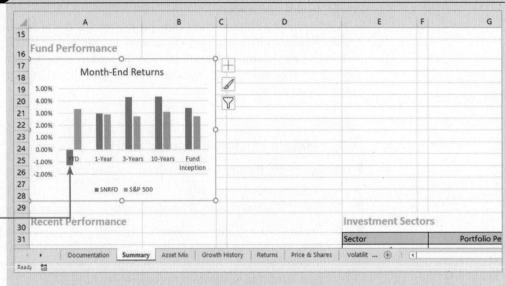

negative return value for the SNRFD fund in the year-to-date

The column chart shows that the Sunrise Fund has generally outperformed the S&P 500 index for most of its life and especially during the previous 3-year and 10-year periods. However, in the current year-to-date, the fund is performing worse than the S&P 500 and, in fact, is showing a negative return in value.

Editing a Chart Title

When a chart has a single data series, the name of the data series is used for the chart title. When a chart has more than one data series, "Chart Title" is used as the temporary title of the chart. Hideki wants you to change the chart title to "Month-End Returns." You will edit the chart title now.

To change the title of the column chart:

1. At the top of the column chart, click **Chart Title** to select it.

2. Type **Month-End Returns** as the new title, and then press **ENTER**. The new title is inserted into the chart.

Note that because the chart title is not linked to any worksheet cell, it will not be updated if changes are made to the data source.

Setting the Gap Width

Excel automatically sets the space between the data series in a column chart as well as the gap width between one category value and the next. If the column chart contains several data series, there might be too little room between the categories, making it difficult to know when one category ends and the next begins. You can modify the space between the data series and gap width using the Format pane.

Hideki wants you to reduce the space between the two data series and increase the interval width between the Year categories.

To set the column chart gap and interval widths:

1. Double-click any column in the column chart to display the Format Data Series pane with the Series Options section already selected.

2. Select the **Series Overlap** box, and then change the space between the data series to **-10%**.

3. Select the **Gap Width** box and increase the value of the gap between the category values to **300%**. See Figure 4–19.

| Figure 4–19 | Series overlap and gap width values |

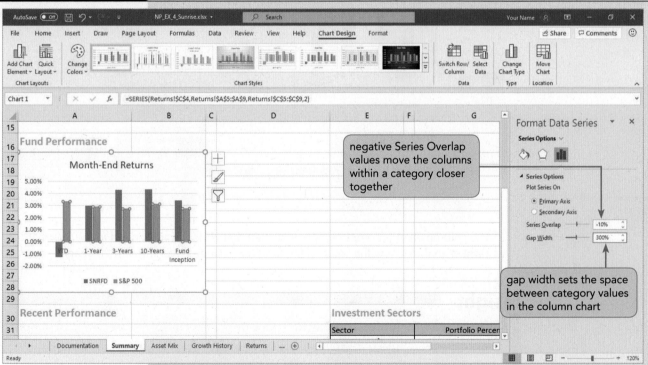

4. Close the Format Data Series pane.

Adding Gridlines to a Chart

Another way of distinguishing columns in separate categories is with gridlines. A gridline is a line that extends from the chart's horizontal and vertical axis into the plot area, making it easier to identify the values or categories associated with the chart's data markers. For example, the horizontal gridlines in Month-End Returns chart make it easier to see where the return from the Sunrise Fund exceeds 4% growth, as it did for the 3-year and 10-year time periods.

Hideki wants you to add vertical gridlines to provide an additional visual aid for separating the time intervals from each other.

To add vertical gridlines to the chart:

1. With the column chart still selected, click the **Chart Elements** button ⊞ to the right of chart to display the list of chart elements associated with column charts.

2. Click the **arrow** ▶ to the right of Gridlines, and then click **Primary Major Vertical** to add vertical gridlines to the chart. See Figure 4–20.

Figure 4–20 | Gridlines added to the column chart

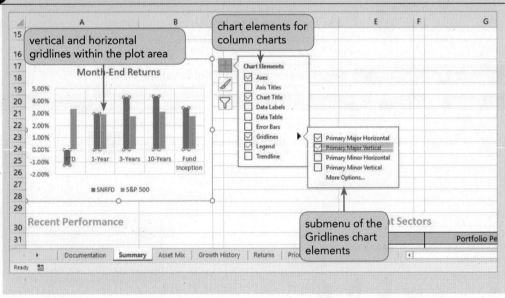

The column chart is complete. The next chart that Hideki wants added to the Summary worksheet analyzes how the value of the fund has changed over the past 20 years.

Insight

Adding Data Tables to Charts

You can use data labels to add data directly to a chart. Another way of viewing the data values associated with a chart is by adding a data table. The data table will be inserted within the chart area directly below the plot area. Each data series will appear as a separate row within the data table with category values placed in the first column of the table.

Creating a Line Chart

A line chart uses lines to plot one or more data series against a set of categories. The categories should follow a sequential order that is evenly spaced. For example, if the categories represent calendar months the space between one month and the next must be constant. Otherwise, the line chart will give an inaccurate depiction of change over time.

Hideki wants a line chart that compares the growth of an investment in the Sunrise Fund over the past 20 years to the same investment in the Standard & Poor's 500 index. You'll create this line chart using the data in the Growth History worksheet.

To create the growth history line chart:

1. Go to the **Growth History** worksheet, and then select the range **A4:C25** containing the growth of the Sunrise Fund and the S&P 500 index from a hypothetical $10,000 initial investment.

2. On the ribbon, click the **Insert** tab, and then in the Charts group, click the **Recommended Charts** button. The Insert Chart dialog box opens to the Recommended Charts tab.

3. Confirm that the **Line** chart type is selected, and then click **OK** to insert the line chart into the Growth History worksheet.

4. Move the chart to the Summary worksheet.

5. Move and resize the line chart so that it covers the range **D17:E28**, holding down **ALT** to snap the chart to the worksheet grid.

6. In the chart, click **Chart Title** to select it, type **Growth of 10K Investment** as the title, and then press **ENTER**. Figure 4–21 shows the appearance of the line chart.

| Figure 4–21 | Line chart of the fund value over time |

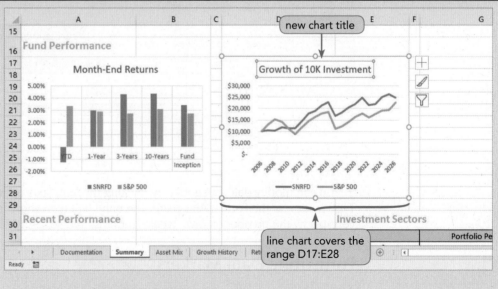

The line chart shows that the value of the Sunrise Fund exceeds the S&P 500 index for most of the past 20 years. Only in its early history did the fund fall below the S&P 500 in value. However, Hideki also notes that in the last year the Sunrise Fund has lost value, though it is still slightly above the value of the S&P 500 index.

Editing the Category Axis

You can modify the axis labels and tick marks to change which category values are displayed in the chart. Hideki doesn't like how crowded the year values are displayed in the horizontal axis. You'll revise the axis so that it lists years in 5-year increments.

To format the horizontal axis:

▶ 1. Double-click one of the years on the horizontal axis to open the Format Axis pane.

▶ 2. At the top of the Format pane, click the **Axis Options** button 📊.

▶ 3. Scroll down and click **Tick Marks** to view options for modifying the tick marks on the category axis.

▶ 4. In the Interval between marks box, change the value to **5** so that the tick marks are laid out in 5-year intervals.

▶ 5. Click the **Major type** arrow, and then click **Cross** so that the tick marks are displayed as crosses.

▶ 6. Click **Labels** to expand that section, click the **Specify interval unit** option button, enter **5** in the box next to the option button to display the year labels at 5-year intervals, and then press **ENTER**. See Figure 4–22.

| Figure 4–22 | New category intervals for the horizontal axis |

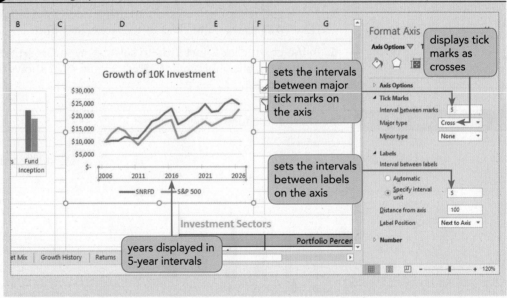

You can modify date categories by clicking the Date axis option button in the Axis Type section of the Format Axis pane. The pane will then show input box from which you specify the number of days, weeks, months, and so forth between date values.

Formatting Data Markers

Each value from a data series is represented by a data marker. In pie charts, the data markers are the individual pie slices. In column charts, the columns are the data markers. In a line chart, the data markers are the points connected by the line. Depending on the line chart style, these data marker points can be displayed or hidden.

In the line chart you created, the data marker points are hidden, and only the line connecting those markers is visible. Hideki wants you to display those data markers and change their fill color to white so that they stand out, making it easier to view the data values.

To display and format the line chart data markers:

1. Within the line chart, double-click the blue line for the Sunrise Fund (SNRFD) to display the Format Data Series pane.

2. At the top of the Format pane, click the **Fill & Line** button ⬨.

3. Scroll to the top of the pane, click **Marker**, and then click **Marker Options** to display options specific to data markers.

4. Click the **Automatic** option button to automatically display the markers along with the line for the Sunrise Fund data series. The data markers are now visible in the line chart, but they have a blue fill color. You will change this fill color to white.

5. In the Fill section, click the **Solid fill** option button, and then click the **Color** button and select the **White, Background 1** theme color. The fill color for the data markers for the Sunrise Fund line changes to white.

6. Repeat Steps 1 through 5 for the green line representing the S&P 500 index. See Figure 4–23.

Figure 4–23   Formatted data markers in a line chart

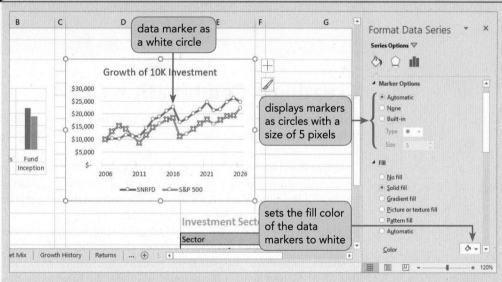

7. Close the Format Data Series pane.

By adding the data markers, you now have a better view of individual values in plotted in the line chart.

Proskills

Written Communication: Communicating Effectively with Charts

Studies show that people more easily interpret information when it is presented as a graphic rather than in a table. As a result, charts can help communicate the real story underlying the facts and figures you present to colleagues and clients. A well-designed chart can illuminate the bigger picture that might be hidden by viewing only the numbers. However, poorly designed charts can mislead readers and make it more difficult to interpret data.

   To create effective and useful charts, keep in mind the following tips as you design your charts:

- **Keep it simple.** Do not clutter a chart with too many graphical elements. Focus attention on the data rather than on decorative elements that do not inform.
- **Focus on the message.** Design the chart to highlight the points you want to convey to readers.
- **Limit the number of data series.** Most charts should display no more than four or five data series. Pie charts should have no more than six slices.
- **Choose colors carefully.** Display different data series in contrasting colors to make it easier to distinguish one series from another. Modify the default colors as needed to make them distinct on the screen and in the printed copy.
- **Limit your chart to a few text styles.** Use a maximum of two or three different text styles in the same chart. Having too many text styles in one chart can distract attention from the data.

The goal of written communication is always to inform the reader in the simplest, most accurate, and most direct way possible. Everything in your workbook should be directed toward that end.

Creating a Combination Chart

So far, the charts you created have only one chart type. A combination chart combines two chart types enabling you to display each data series using the chart type best suited for it.

   When the data series values cover vastly different ranges, you can plot one data series against the **primary axis**, the vertical axis appearing along the left edge of the chart, and the other data series against the **secondary axis**, the vertical axis on the chart's right edge.

   The next chart that Hideki wants added to the Summary worksheet will display the recent performance of the Sunrise Fund, showing its daily selling price and the number of shares traded over the past three months. You will display the daily selling price in a line chart plotted against the primary axis and the number of shares traded in a column chart plotted against the secondary axis.

To create the combination chart:

▶ 1. Go to the **Price & Shares** worksheet and select the range **A4:C69**.

▶ 2. On the ribbon, click the **Insert** tab, and then in the Charts group, click the **Recommended Charts** button. The Insert Chart dialog box opens showing the recommended Line chart.

▶ 3. Click the **All Charts** tab to see previews of all Excel chart types.

▶ 4. In the list of chart types, click **Combo**.

5. Click the **Custom Combination** chart subtype (the last subtype listed for the Combo chart). At the bottom of the dialog box, the "Choose the chart type and axis for your data series" box lists two data series in the selected data. First you need to select the chart type to display the Price data.

6. In the "Choose the chart type and axis for your data series" box, click the **Price** Chart Type box arrow, and then click **Line**. Now you need to select the chart type for the Shares Traded data series.

7. Click the **Shares Traded** Chart type box arrow, and then click **Clustered Columns** from list of chart types.

8. In the Shares Traded row, click the **Secondary Axis** check box to plot the Shares Traded values on the secondary axis. See Figure 4–24.

Figure 4–24	Combination chart preview

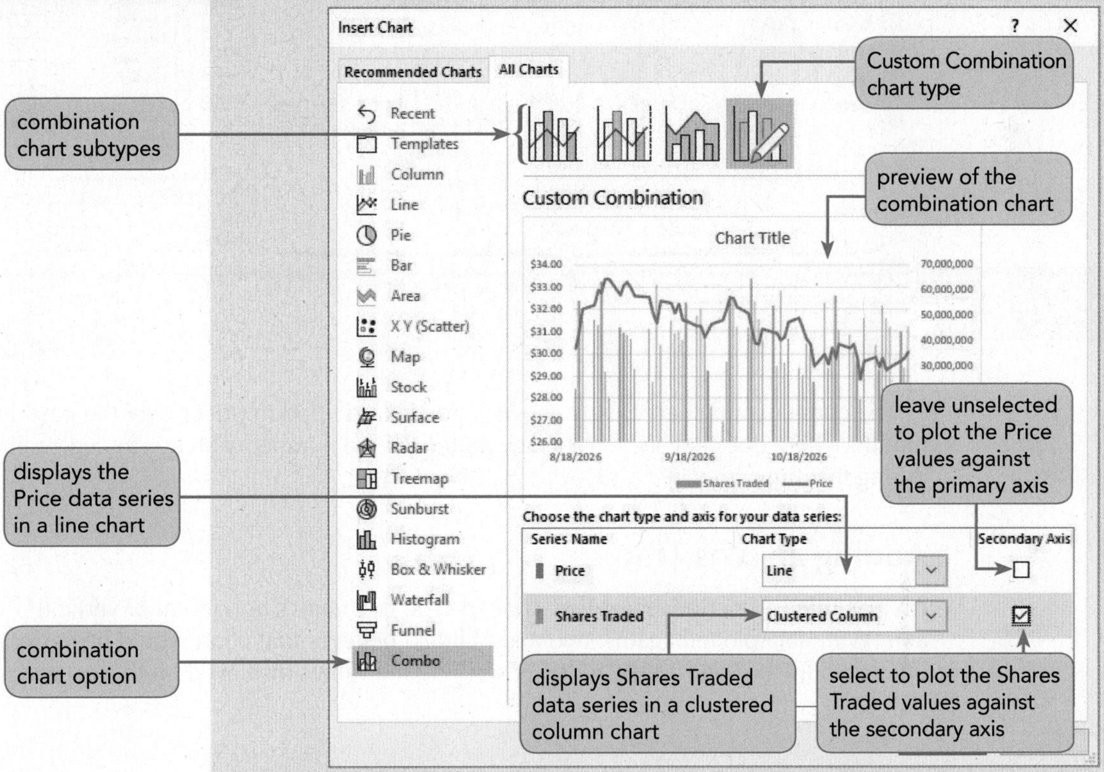

9. Click **OK** to embed the chart into the Price & Shares worksheet.

Next, you'll move the combination chart to the Summary worksheet and format it.

To move and format the combination chart:

Tip
To retain the chart's proportions as it is resized, hold down SHIFT as you drag the resizing handle.

1. Move the combination chart to the Summary worksheet, and then move and resize the chart to cover the range **A31:D43**, holding down the **ALT** key to snap the worksheet to the grid. You may have to scroll through the worksheet to find the chart.

2. Click **Chart Title** in the combination chart to select it, type **Price & Shares Traded** as the new title, and then press **ENTER** to insert the new chart title.

3. Click the **Chart Elements** button ⊞ and then click the **arrow** ▶ next to the Legend entry in the list of chart elements to display a submenu of formatting choices for the chart legend.

4. Click **Right** to move the legend to the right of the chart area. See Figure 4–25.

| Figure 4–25 | Combination chart of Price and Shares traded |

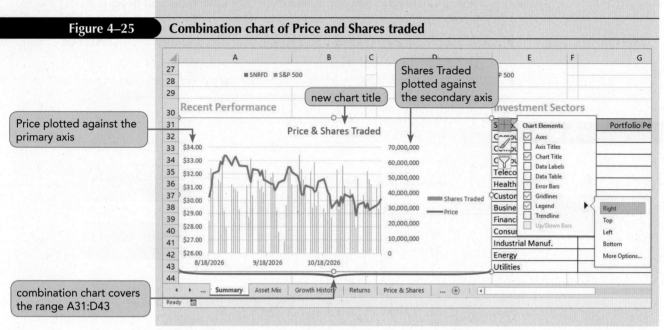

The combination chart clearly shows a downward trend in prices over the past three months. There does not seem to be any pattern in the number of shares traded each day during that time.

Adding an Axis Title

An **axis title** is descriptive text that appears next to a chart's horizontal or vertical axis. With data plotted against two axes, Hideki believes that chart would be easier to understand if axis titles were added describing the values displayed on those axes.

To add axis titles to the chart:

1. With the combination chart still selected, click the **Chart Elements** button ⊞ and then click the **Axis Titles** check box to select it. Titles are added to all three axes.

2. Click **Axis Title** next to the primary axis (on the left side of the chart), type **Price** as the axis title, and then press **ENTER**. The primary axis title is changed.

3. Click **Axis Title** along the category (bottom) axis, type **Date** as the axis title, and then press **ENTER**. The horizontal axis title is changed.

4. Click **Axis Title** next to the secondary axis (on the right side of the chart), type **Shares Traded** as the axis title, and then press **ENTER**. The secondary axis title is changed.

5. With the Shares Traded title still selected, click the **Home** tab on the ribbon, and then in the Alignment group, click the **Orientation** button and click **Rotate Text Down**. The axis title is rotated for better visibility. See Figure 4–26.

| Figure 4–26 | Axis titles added to a chart |

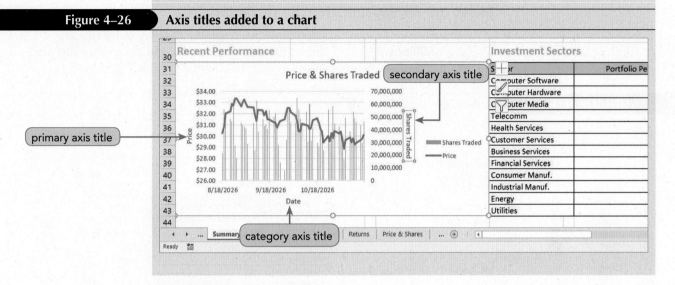

Editing a Value Axis Scale

Excel automatically chooses the range of values, or **scale**, used on the value primary and secondary axes. For the Price data series, the scale ranges from $26 to $34 and for the Shares Traded data series, the scale ranges from 0 to 70,000,000.

Excel automatically divides the scale into regular intervals, marked on the axis with tick marks and labels. **Major tick marks** identify the main units on the chart axis while **minor tick marks** identify the smaller intervals between the major tick marks. The major tick marks for the Price series are placed at intervals of $1 and the major tick marks for the Shares Traded Series are placed at intervals of 10,000,000 shares. There are no minor tick marks in combination chart. Tick marks placed so close together so that the tick mark labels overlap can make the chart difficult to read. On the other hand, increasing the gap between tick marks could make the chart less informative.

You'll use the Format Axis pane to specify a different scale for the secondary axis, changing the size of the scale used with the Shares Traded data. Hideki also wants you to expand the scale of the secondary axis so that the data markers for the column chart don't overlap the contents of the line chart.

To set the scale of the secondary axis:

1. Double-click the secondary axis values to open the Format Axis pane.

2. Click the **Axis Options** button if necessary, and then click the **Axis Options** label.

3. In the Bounds section at the top of the list of Axis Options, click the **Maximum** box and enter **1.6E08** (representing 160,000,000 in exponential notation) as the top-end of the scale for the secondary axis.

4. Press **TAB** to enter the new scale value. The scale of the secondary axis expands so that the column chart is displayed below the line chart.

When the range of the axis covers values of a large magnitude, you can simplify the axis labels by including the units as part of the scale. Hideki thinks the secondary axis numbers will look better without all the zeros in the axis values. You will display the secondary axis values in units of one million.

To set the display units for the secondary axis:

▶ **1.** In the Format Axis pane, scroll down and click the **Display units** box and select **Millions**. The Unit Label "Millions" is added to the secondary axis and the axis displays the axis values in units of one million. See Figure 4–27.

| Figure 4–27 | Scale of the secondary axis |

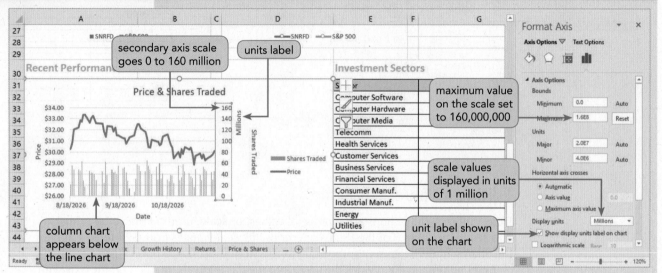

▶ **2.** Close the Format Axis pane, and then save the workbook.

The combination chart comparing the yearly value of the Sunrise Fund to the S&P 500 index is complete. In the next session, you will create other charts and graphics that reveal valuable information about the Sunrise Fund.

Review

Session 4.1 Quick Check

1. In a chart's data source, where does Excel assume that category values are placed?
2. What three chart elements are included in a pie chart?
3. A data series contains values grouped into 12 categories. Would this data be better displayed as a pie chart or a column chart? Explain why.
4. A research firm wants to display the population of a state organized into five geographic locations. Which chart should it use? Explain why.
5. If the firm wants to display the total population growth of a state over a 10-year period organized by those five geographic locations, which chart type best displays this information? Explain why.
6. If the firm wants to display how the population of the geographic locations within the state changes over time as a percentage of the whole population, which chart type should it use? Explain why.
7. If the firm wants to display both the average annual income and the total population of the state over the 10-year period, what chart should it use and why?
8. What are major tick marks and minor tick marks?

1. In the first coloum or first row

2. title, axis labels, a legend, gridline.

3.

Session 4.2 Visual Overview:

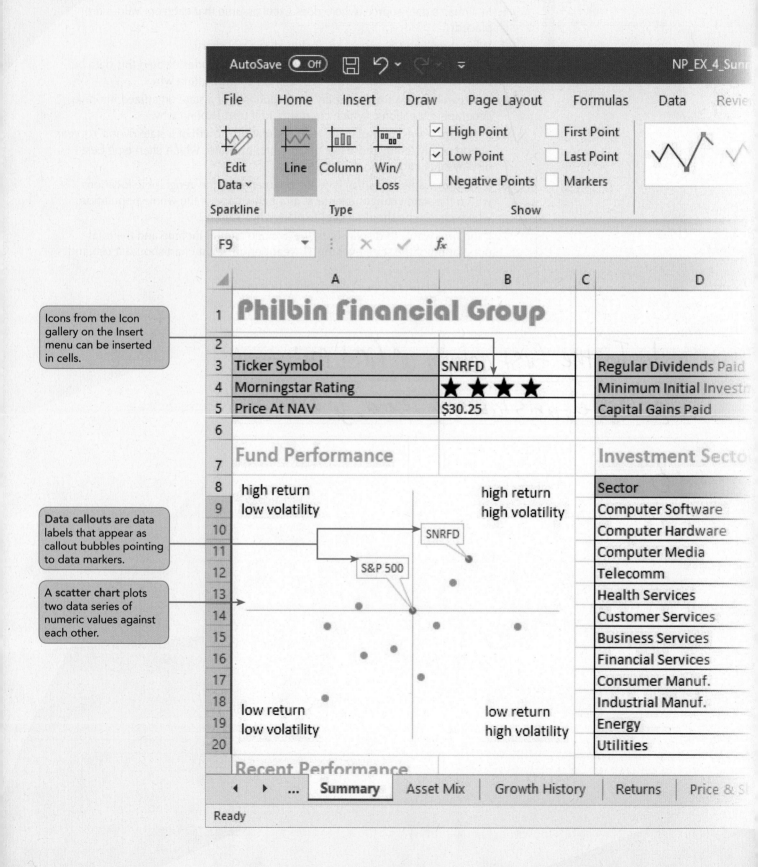

Icons from the Icon gallery on the Insert menu can be inserted in cells.

Data callouts are data labels that appear as callout bubbles pointing to data markers.

A scatter chart plots two data series of numeric values against each other.

Scatter Charts, Data Bars, and Sparklines

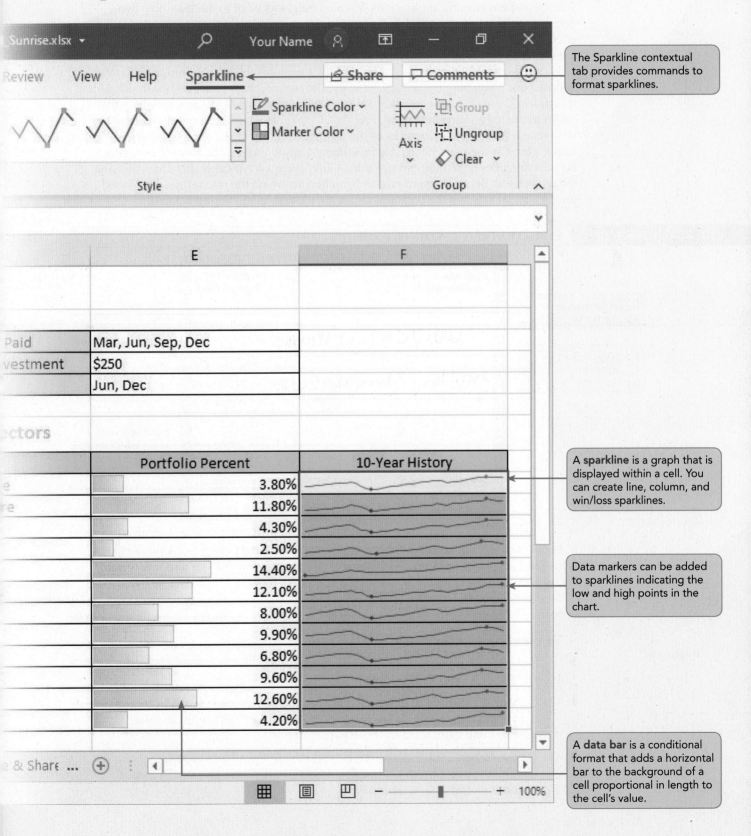

The Sparkline contextual tab provides commands to format sparklines.

A **sparkline** is a graph that is displayed within a cell. You can create line, column, and win/loss sparklines.

Data markers can be added to sparklines indicating the low and high points in the chart.

A **data bar** is a conditional format that adds a horizontal bar to the background of a cell proportional in length to the cell's value.

Creating a Scatter Chart

The charts you created in the previous session all involve plotting numeric data against categorical data. Another important type of chart is the scatter chart, which plots two data series of numeric values against each other. Scatter charts are widely used in science and engineering applications when investigators want to discover how two numeric variables are related. For example, an economist might want to investigate the effect of high tax rates on tax revenue or the effect of increasing the minimum wage on the unemployment rate.

Hideki wants you to create a scatter chart that explores the relationship between the Sunrise Fund's rate of return and its volatility. The rate of return indicates how much an investment can earn for the investor while volatility measures the degree by which that return estimate can vary. In general, investments that have high rates of return are often very volatile so that the investor faces the prospect of either making a lot of money or losing a lot. On the other hand, safe investments, while usually not very volatile, also do not often offer high return rates. Figure 4–28 presents a typical scatter chart showing the relationship between return rate and volatility in which the return rates are plotted on the vertical axis and the volatility values are plotted on the horizontal axis.

Figure 4–28   Scatter chart of return rate vs. volatility

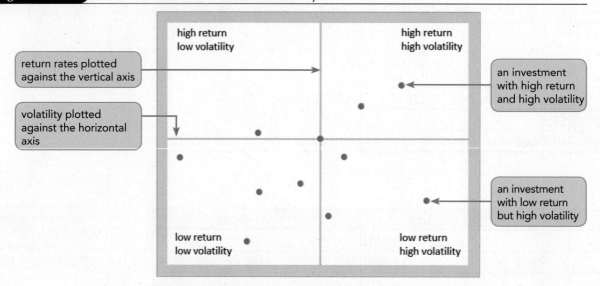

Hideki's clients will want to know where the Sunrise Fund falls in that kind of chart. Is the fund a high risk/high reward venture or does it offer low risk but also low reward? You will explore this question by creating a scatter chart of those two data series.

To create a scatter chart:

1. If you took a break at the end of the previous session, make sure the NP_EX_4_Sunrise workbook is open.

2. Go to the **Volatility & Return** worksheet and select the range **B5:C7** containing the volatility and return rates for the S&P 500 index and the Sunrise Fund calculated over a 10-year interval.

3. On the ribbon, click the **Insert** tab, and then in the Charts group, click the **Recommended Charts** button. The Insert Chart dialog box opens to the Recommended Charts tab.

4. In the gallery of recommended chart types, select **Scatter**. See Figure 4–29.

Figure 4–29 Scatter chart preview

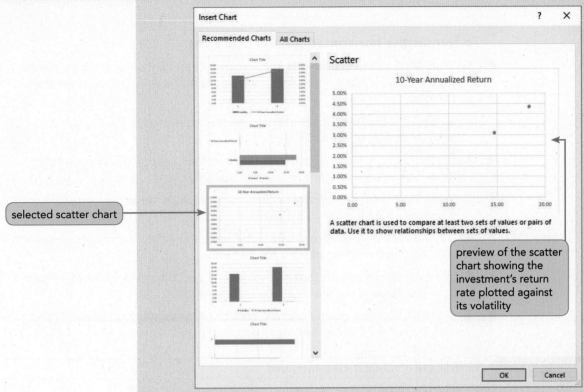

selected scatter chart

preview of the scatter chart showing the investment's return rate plotted against its volatility

5. Click **OK** to insert the scatter chart.

6. Click the **Move Chart** button, select **Summary** from the Object in box, and then click **OK** to move the scatter chart to the Summary worksheet.

7. Move and resize the scatter chart to cover the range **G17:H28**, holding down the **ALT** key to snap the chart to the worksheet grid. See Figure 4–30.

Figure 4–30 Scatter chart

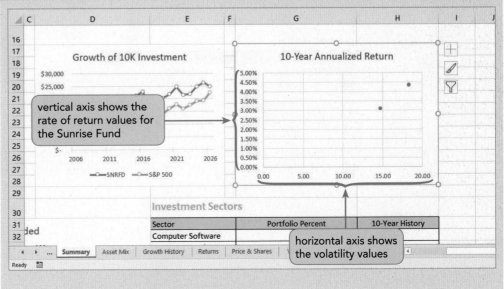

vertical axis shows the rate of return values for the Sunrise Fund

horizontal axis shows the volatility values

Scatter charts comparing rates to volatility are usually centered at a point representing a balance between the two. In most cases, this is an investment standard such as the S&P 500 index. To center the chart at that point you will modify the properties of both the vertical and horizontal axis so that those axes cross at the chart coordinates (0.031, 14.71), which is the return rate and volatility of the S&P 500 index. You'll format these axes now.

To format the horizontal and vertical axes:

1. Double-click the **vertical axis** in the scatter chart containing the rate of return percent values. The Format Axis pane opens to the Axis Options formatting choices.

   Trouble? If the Axis Options button ▥ is not selected in the Format Axis pane, click it to select it.

2. Set the value of the Minimum box to **0** and then set the Maximum box to **0.06**. The axis will range from 0.00% to 6.00%.

3. In the Horizontal axis crosses section, click the **Axis value** option button, and then enter **0.031** in the Axis value box.

4. Double-click the **horizontal axis** in the scatter chart to open the Format Axis pane to the formatting options for that axis.

5. In the Minimum box, change the value to **4**, and then click in the Maximum box. The value in the Maximum box changes to 24.

6. In the Vertical axis crosses section, click the **Axis value** option button, and then enter **14.71** in the Axis value box. See Figure 4–31.

Figure 4–31   **Vertical and horizontal axes formatted**

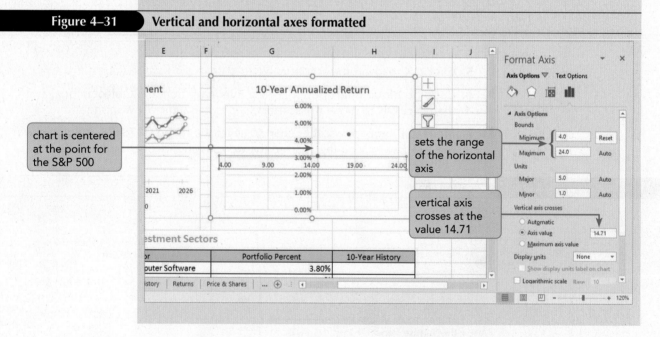

Hideki wants you to clean up the scatter chart by removing the axis labels, chart title, and gridlines, leaving only the axis lines and the data markers.

To remove elements from the scatter chart:

▶ **1.** Scroll down the Format Axis pane for the horizontal axis, click the **Labels** section head, and then in the Label Position box, select **None** to remove the axis labels from the chart.

▶ **2.** Double-click the labels for the vertical axis to display the Format Axis pane for the vertical axis.

▶ **3.** Scroll down to the Labels section for that axis, and then select **None** from the Label Position box to remove the vertical axis labels.

▶ **4.** On the Chart Design tab, in the Chart Layouts group, click the **Add Chart Element** button, point to **Chart Title**, and then click **None** to remove the chart title.

▶ **5.** Click the **Add Chart Element** button, point to **Gridlines**, and then click **Primary Major Horizontal** and **Primary Major Vertical** to deselect those two options, removing them from the scatter chart.

▶ **6.** Close the Format pane.

The scatter chart now contains only the two data points and the two axes lines. But with only two data markers in the chart, there's not a lot of basis for comparison with other investments. Hideki asks you to add data markers representing other funds to the scatter chart.

Insight

Copying and Pasting Chart Formats

You will often want to repeat the same design for the charts in your worksheet. Rather than rerun the same commands, you can copy the formatting from one chart to another. To copy a chart format, first select the chart with the existing design that you want to replicate, and then click the Copy button in the Clipboard group on the Home tab (or press CTRL+C). Next, select the chart that you want to format, click the Paste arrow in the Clipboard group, and then click Paste Special to open the Paste Special dialog box. In the Paste Special dialog box, select the Formats option button, and then click OK. All the copied formats from the original chart—including fill colors, font styles, axis scales, and chart types—are then pasted into the new chart. Be aware that the pasted formats will overwrite any formats previously used in the new chart.

Editing the Chart Data Source

Excel automates most of the process of assigning a data source to the chart. However, sometimes the completed chart is not what you want, and you need to edit the chart's data source. At any time, you can modify the chart's data source to add more data series or change the current data series in the chart.

Reference

Modifying a Chart's Data Source

- Select the chart to make it active.
- On the Chart Design tab, in the Data group, click the Select Data button.
- In the Legend Entries (Series) section of the Select Data Source dialog box, click the Add button to add another data series to the chart or click the Remove button to remove a data series from the chart.
- Click the Edit button in the Horizontal (Category) Axis Labels section to select the category values for the chart.
- Click OK.

Hideki wants you to add a data series containing information from other funds to the scatter chart of returns vs. volatility. You'll edit the chart's data source definition to make that change.

To edit the chart's data source:

▶ **1.** With the scatter chart still selected, on the Chart Design tab, in the Data group, click the **Select Data** button. The Select Data Source dialog box opens. See Figure 4–32.

Figure 4–32	Select Data Source dialog box

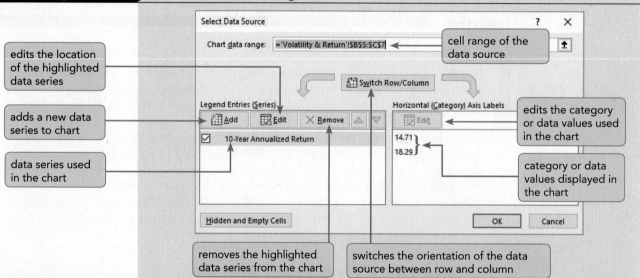

Tip

To organize a chart's data source by rows rather than columns (or vice-versa), click the Switch Row/Column button in the Select Data Source dialog box.

▶ **2.** Click **Add** to open the Edit Series dialog box. You can add another data series to the chart from here.

▶ **3.** With the insertion point in the Series name box, click the **Volatility & Return** sheet tab, and then click cell **G5** in that worksheet. The expression ='Volatility & Return'!$G$5 is entered into the Series name box.

▶ **4.** Click the **Series X values** box, click the **Volatility & Return** sheet tab if necessary, and then select the range **F6:F14** to enter the expression ='Volatility & Return'!$F$6:$F$14.

Values or expressions might already be entered into the Edit Series dialog box, so you must delete any expressions before inserting a new reference.

▶ **5.** Click the **Series Y values** box, delete any expression in that box, and then select the range **G6:G14** in the Volatility & Return worksheet, inserting the expression ='Volatility & Return!'$G$6:$G$14 into the box. See Figure 4–33.

Figure 4–33	Edit Series dialog box

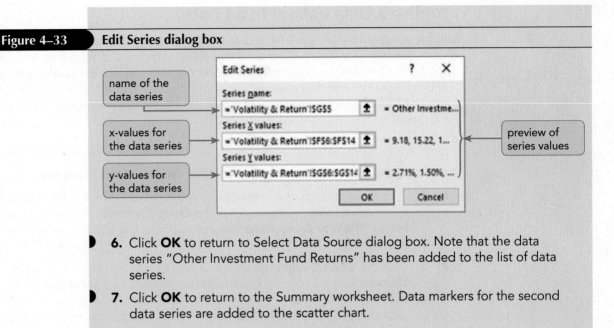

6. Click **OK** to return to Select Data Source dialog box. Note that the data series "Other Investment Fund Returns" has been added to the list of data series.

7. Click **OK** to return to the Summary worksheet. Data markers for the second data series are added to the scatter chart.

You've simplified the scatter chart by removing elements that Hideki feels will not be of interest to the company's investors (such as the exact values of the stock's volatility). However, the chart still needs some descriptive information to aid in its interpretation. You'll add this additional text and graphics to the chart and worksheet next.

Insight

Adding Trendlines to Charts

Scatter charts are often used in statistical analysis and scientific studies in which the researcher attempts to find a relationship between one variable and another. For that purpose, Excel includes several statistical tools to augment scatter charts. One of these tools is a **trendline**, which is a line representing the general direction in a data series. Excel supports several different kinds of trendlines, include linear (or straight) lines, exponential curves, power curves, and logarithmic curves. Excel draws the trendline to best fit the data in the scatter chart.

You can add a trendline to any scatter chart by right-clicking the data series in the chart, and then clicking Add Trendline on the shortcut menu to open the Format Trendline pane. From the Format Trendline pane, you can select the trendline type. If the scatter chart plots a data series against a time variable, you can also extend the trendline to project future values, as might be done if a company wanted to project future earnings based on the trend of current earnings. Excel also provides summary statistics indicating how well the trendline fits the data.

Adding Graphic Objects to a Workbook

Another way of enhancing your workbooks is with graphic art. Excel supports a large gallery of clip art and icons to supplement your charts and worksheet data. One graphic feature you can add to charts is a data callout.

Adding a Data Callout to a Chart

In the previous session, you used a data label to display percentage values in a pie chart. Another type of data label is a **data callout**, which is a label that appears as a text bubble attached to a data marker. Hideki suggests you add data callouts to S&P 500 and Sunrise Fund data markers. The data callouts should contain the abbreviated names of those two investments so that they can be easily identified by clients viewing the report.

To add a data callout to the scatter chart's data markers:

▶ **1.** With the scatter chart still selected, on the ribbon, click the **Format** tab. In the Current Selection group, click the **Chart Elements arrow**, and then click **Series "10-Year Annualized Return"** to select the two data makers for that data series.

▶ **2.** Click the **Chart Design** tab. In the Chart Layouts group, click the **Add Chart Element** button, point to **Data Labels**, and then click **Data Callout** to add callouts to the two data makers in the series. Excel inserts the volatility and return values into the two data callouts. You will change those values, so they reference the abbreviated names of the two investments.

▶ **3.** Right-click either of the two data labels, and then click **Format Data Labels** on the shortcut menu. The Format Data Labels pane opens.

Tip

You can change the shape of the callout by right-clicking the data callout, clicking Change Data Label Shapes, and choosing a callout shape.

▶ **4.** Click the **Value from Cells** check box. The Data Label Range dialog box opens.

▶ **5.** Click the **Volatility & Return** sheet tab, and then select the range **A6:A7** to enter the expression `='Volatility & Return!'$A$6:$A7` into the Select Data Label Range box.

▶ **6.** Click **OK**.

▶ **7.** Click the **X Value** and **Y Value** check boxes to deselect them. See Figure 4–34.

Figure 4–34   **Data callouts added to the scatter chart**

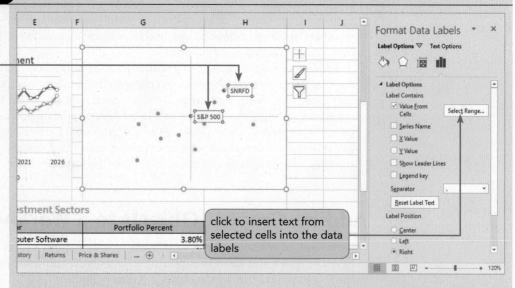

data callouts showing the abbreviated names of the Sunrise Fund and S&P 500 index

click to insert text from selected cells into the data labels

▶ **8.** Close the Format Data Labels pane.

Inserting a Graphic Shape

Microsoft Office supports a gallery of over 160 shapes that can be added to any workbook or other Office document. The shape gallery includes rectangles, circles, arrows, stars, flow chart symbols, and text boxes. Each shape can be resized and formatted with a wide selection of colors, line styles, and special effects such as drop shadows and glowing borders. You can insert text strings, including numbered and bulleted lists, to any graphic shape.

Hideki asks you to complete the return rate/volatility scatter chart by inserting text boxes in the four corners of the chart, indicating which chart quadrant corresponds to high or low return rates and high or low volatility. You will insert the text box from the shape gallery.

To insert a text box:

1. With the scatter chart still selected, click the **Insert** tab on the ribbon.

2. In the Illustrations group, click the **Illustrations** button, and then click the **Shapes** button. The Shapes gallery opens, organized into the categories of Recently Used Shapes, Lines, Rectangles, Basic Shapes, Block Arrows, Equations Shapes, Flowchart, Stars and Banners, and Callouts.

   Trouble? Depending on your monitor and settings, you may not see the Illustrations button. In that case, click the Shapes button in the Illustrations group.

3. In the Basic Shapes group, click the **Text Box** shape Ⓐ.

4. Click near the upper-left corner of the scatter chart. A box opens in which the text box will be entered.

5. Type **high return** as the first line of text in the text box, press **ENTER**, and then type **low volatility** as the second line of text in the text box.

6. Click and drag the **sizing handles** around the selected text box as needed to reduce the text box to fit the text.

7. Point to the text box border so the pointer changes to the Move pointer ⊹, and then drag the text box so that it aligns with the upper-left corner of the scatter chart.

8. Repeat Steps 2 through 7 to insert a text box containing **high return** and **high volatility** (placing the return and volatility text strings on different lines) in the upper-right corner of the chart.

9. Repeat Steps 2 through 7 to insert a text box containing **low return** and **low volatility** on separate lines in the lower-left corner of the chart.

10. Repeat Steps 2 through 7 to insert a text box containing **low return** and **high volatility** on separate lines in the lower-right corner of the chart. See Figure 4–35, which shows the final design of the scatter chart of return rate versus volatility.

Figure 4–35   Text boxes added to a scatter chart

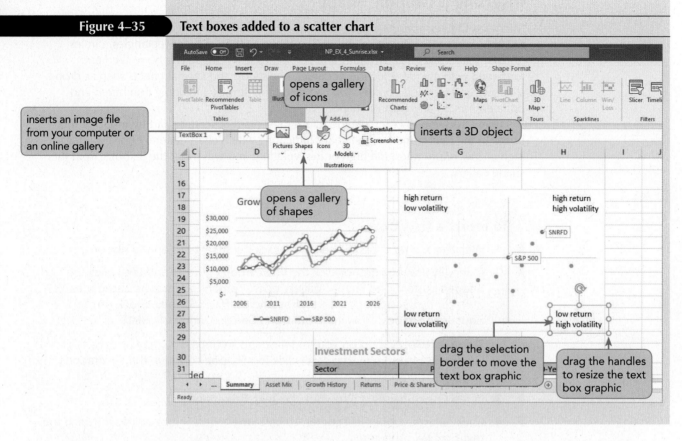

With the final version of the scatter chart, Hideki's clients can quickly identify the Sunrise Fund as a high return, high volatility investment, particularly when compared to the S&P 500 index and other sample investments.

Inserting Graphic Icons

Graphic icons, another type of graphic object supported by Microsoft Office, are common symbols often found in signs and posters. Like shapes, icons can be resized and reformatted to meet a variety of design needs. Office organizes icons in a wide range of categories from icons used for business to icons of animals to icons with a sports theme.

In cell B9 of the Summary worksheet, Hideki entered the rating of the Sunrise Fund given by Morningstar, an investment research firm that rates investments and funds. Ratings range from 1 star (poor) to 5 stars (the best). Morningstar has given the Sunrise Fund a 4-star rating. Hideki wants to replace the text "4 stars" with four star icons. You'll use the icon gallery to insert those images into cell B9.

To insert the star icons from the icon gallery:

1. In the Summary worksheet, select cell **B9**, and then press **DELETE** to delete the contents of the cell.

2. On the Insert tab, in the Illustrations group, click the **Illustrations** button, and then click **Icons**. The Insert Icons dialog box opens.

   Trouble? Depending on your monitor and settings, you may not see the Illustrations button. In that case, click the Icons button in the Illustrations group.

3. Type **Celebration** in the Search box, press **ENTER**, and then click the **star** icon to select it. See Figure 4–36.

Tip

You can also insert star images using the star shape from the Shapes gallery.

Figure 4–36   **Insert Icons dialog box**

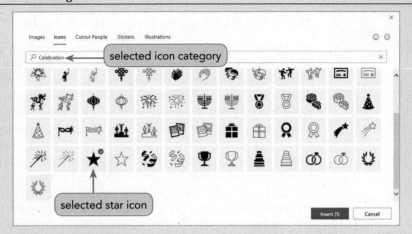

4. Click **Insert** to insert the icon into cell B9. Because the icon is selected, the Graphics Format tab appears on the ribbon.

5. On the Graphics Format tab, in the Size group, click the **Height** box, type **0.25**, and then press **ENTER**. Both the height and width change to 0.25 inches.

6. With the star icon still selected, press **CTRL+C** to copy the icon, and then press **CTRL+V** three times to paste three more star icons into the worksheet.

7. Click and drag each of the four icons so that they are aligned in cell B9. Don't worry about exactly arranging the icons within the cell. See Figure 4–37.

Figure 4–37   **Icons in the worksheet**

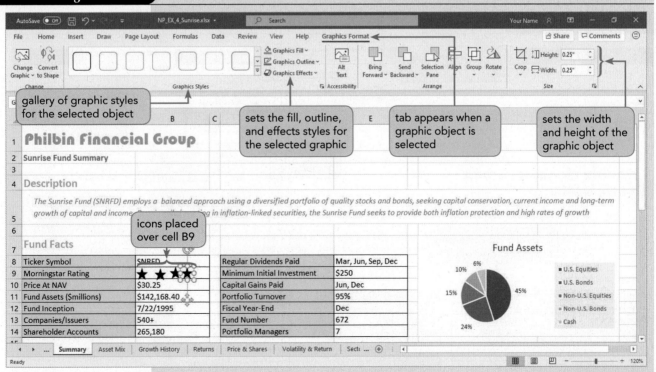

The star icons appear in cell B9 but note that they are not part of the cell's content. Like embedded charts, a graphic shape icon is placed on top of the worksheet grid.

Tools for Managing Graphic Objects

You can use the drag-and-drop technique to place your graphic objects, but it can be hard to get objects exactly where you want them. For more precise placement of objects, Excel provides commands to align graphics within a row or column, distribute them evenly across a horizontal or vertical space, or stack graphics on top of each other. You can also group images together, creating new classes of graphic objects.

To select graphics embedded in the workbook, you can open the Selection pane, which is a pane providing access to all graphics and charts embedded in the current workbook. From the Selection pane, you can select individual or groups of graphic objects. The Selection pane can also be used to hide graphic objects or reveal hidden graphics.

Hideki wants the star icons from cell B9 to be precisely aligned and evenly distributed across the cell. You'll use the Selection pane to select those icons and then use commands on the Graphics Format tab to align and distribute the icons.

To select and place icons within the worksheet:

▶ 1. On the Graphics Format tab, in the Arrange group, click the **Selection Pane** button. A list of graphics and charts in the current worksheet appears in the Selection pane.

▶ 2. Hold down **CTRL** and click the names of the four graphics listed in the Selection pane so that all four are selected in both the pane and the worksheet.

▶ 3. On the Graphics Format tab, in the Arrange group, click the **Align** button, and then click **Align Middle** so that the icons are aligned through their middles.

▶ 4. Click the **Align** button again, and then click **Distribute Horizontally** so that the icons are evenly distributed in the horizontal direction. See Figure 4–38.

Figure 4–38   **Graphics aligned in the worksheet**

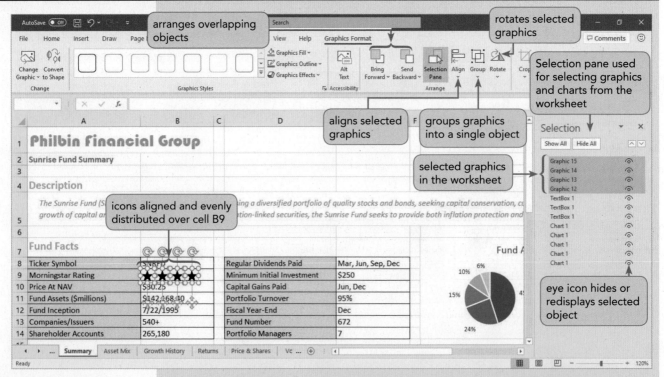

Trouble? Depending on how you created your graphics and charts, you might have different names assigned to the graphic and chart objects in the Selection pane.

5. Click the **Close** button ☒ in the upper-right corner of the Selection pane to close it.

You can also use your mouse to select graphic objects, but first you must switch to Select Object mode by clicking the Find & Select button in the Editing group on the Home tab and then clicking the Select Object command. The pointer will switch to a mode for selecting objects rather than worksheet cells. To turn off the Select Object mode so the mouse can select cells again, click the Select Object command on the Find & Select button, disabling Select Object mode.

Exploring Other Chart Types

At this point, you've used only a few of the many Excel chart types. Excel has other chart types that are useful for financial and scientific research, which you can access from the Charts group on the Insert tab. If you want to change the chart type of an existing chart, click the Change Chart Type button in the Type group on the Chart Design tab and then select the new chart type from the dialog box.

Hierarchy Charts

Hierarchy charts are like pie charts in that they show the relative contribution of groups to a whole. Unlike pie charts, a hierarchy chart also shows the organizational structure of the data with subcategories displayed within main categories. Excel supports two types of hierarchy charts: treemap charts and sunburst charts.

In a **treemap chart**, each category is placed within a rectangle, and subcategories are nested as rectangles within those rectangles. The rectangles are sized to show the relative proportions of the two groups based on values from a data series. The treemap chart in Figure 4–39 shows the investor sectors of the Sunrise Fund broken down by group and category. You can create a treemap chart by clicking the Recommended Charts button and then selecting Treemap from the list of chart types on the All Charts tab.

Figure 4–39   **Treemap and Sunburst charts**

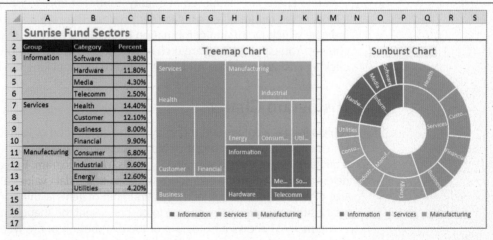

A **sunburst chart** organizes hierarchical data through a series of concentric rings with the innermost rings showing the highest category levels and the outer rings showing categories from lower levels. The size of the rings indicates the relative proportions of the different groups and categories within groups. See Figure 4–39. Sunburst charts are better than treemap charts at conveying information from multiple levels of nested groups. But treemaps are better at displaying the relative sizes of the categories within each group level. You can create a sunburst chart by clicking the Recommended Charts button and then selecting Sunburst from the list of chart types on the All Charts tab.

Pareto Charts

A special kind of combination chart is the **Pareto chart**, which combines a column chart and a line chart to indicate which factors are the largest contributors to the whole. Figure 4–40 shows a Pareto chart of investment categories. The categories are sorted in descending order of importance so that the largest investment category, Health, is listed first followed by Energy, Customer, Hardware, and so forth. The line chart provides a running total of the percentage that each category adds to the overall total. Roughly 50% of the Sunrise Fund is invested in the first four categories listed in the chart.

Figure 4–40	Pareto chart

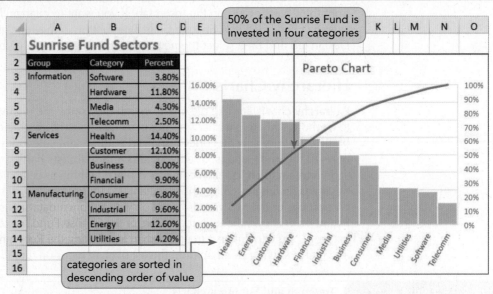

Pareto charts are often used in quality control studies to isolate the most significant factors in the failure of a manufacturer process. They are also in market research to indicate which factor and combination of factors are the most crucial in consumer choices. You can create a Pareto chart by clicking the Recommended Charts button, clicking Histogram on the All Charts tab, and then clicking the Pareto chart type.

Histogram Charts

A **histogram** is a column chart displaying the distribution of values from a single data series. For example, a professor might create a histogram to display the distribution of scores from a midterm exam. There is no category series for a histogram. Instead, the categories are determined based on the data series values with the data values allocated to **bins** and the size of the columns determined by the number of items within each bin. The number of bins is arbitrary and can be chosen to best represent the shape of the distribution.

Figure 4–41 shows a histogram of the distribution of the weekly price of the Sunrise Fund over a 15-month period. From the histogram it's clear that the price of the Sunrise Fund most often falls between $29 and $30 (the bin with the most values), but there are a few values as low as $23 to $24 and as high as $36 to $37. You can create a Histogram by clicking the Recommended Charts button, clicking Histogram on the All Charts tab, and then selecting the Histogram chart type.

| Figure 4–41 | Histogram chart |

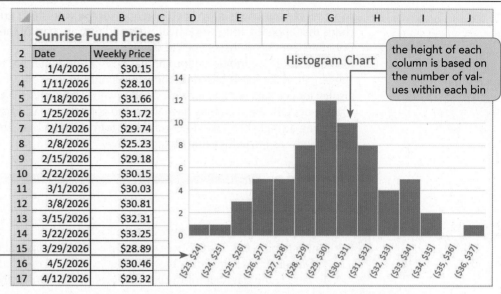

To modify the bins used in the histogram, double-click the horizontal axis to open the Format Axis pane and then set the bin size or the number of bins in the Bins section of the Axis Options section.

Waterfall Charts

A **waterfall chart** tracks the addition and subtraction of values within a sum. Figure 4–42 shows a waterfall chart of the value of an investment in the Sunrise Fund over five years. The initial and final value of the fund are shown in red. Positive changes in the fund's value are shown in green. Years in which the fund decreased in value are shown in dark gray. The waterfall chart is so named because the increasing and decreasing steps in the graph resemble a waterfall.

| Figure 4–42 | Waterfall chart |

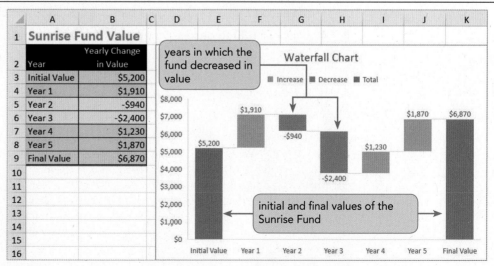

Waterfall charts are often used with Profit and Loss statements to track the impact of revenue and expenses on a company's net profit.

Creating Data Bars

So far all of your charts have been placed over the worksheet grid. You can also create charts that appear within worksheet cells and that are part of the worksheet grid itself. Data bars are one of these types of charts.

A data bar is a conditional format that adds a horizontal bar to a cell background. The length of the bar is based on the value stored in the cell. Cells storing larger values display longer data bars; cells with smaller values have shorter bars. When applied to a range of cells, the data bars have the same appearance as a bar chart, with each cell displaying a single bar. Like all conditional formats, data bars are dynamic, changing their lengths as the cell's value changes.

Reference

Creating Data Bars

- Select the range containing the data to be charted.
- On the Home tab, in the Styles group, click the Conditional Formatting button, point to Data Bars, and then click the data bar style you want to use.
- To modify the data bar rules, click the Conditional Formatting button, and then click Manage Rules.

Hideki inserted data on the economic sectors in which the Sunrise Fund invests in the range E31:G43 on the Summary worksheet. You'll display the percentage figures in the range G32:G43 with data bars.

To add data bars to the portfolio percentages in the worksheet:

▶ **1.** On the Summary worksheet, select the range **G32:G43**.

▶ **2.** On the ribbon, click the **Home** tab. In the Styles group, click the **Conditional Formatting** button, and then click **Data Bars**. A gallery of data bar styles opens.

▶ **3.** In the Gradient Fill section, click the **Orange Data Bar** style (the first style in the second row). Orange data bars are added to the selected cells.

▶ **4.** Click cell **E30** to deselect the range. See Figure 4–43.

Figure 4–43   **Data bars added to the Summary worksheet**

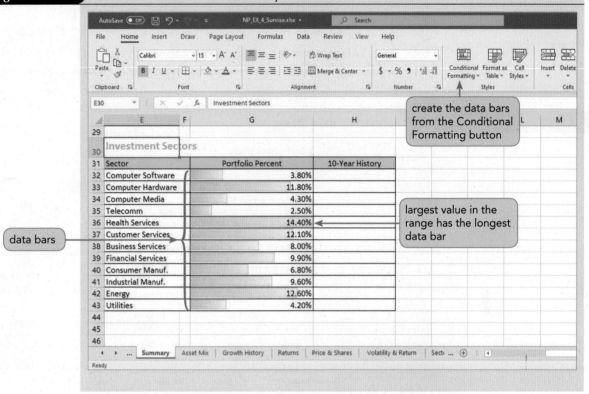

The data bars allow comparison of the relative size of the investment sectors for the Sunrise Fund. However, some of the data bars cover their cell value. Hideki wants you to shorten the length of the bars so that there is no overlap.

Modifying a Data Bar Rule

By default, the cell with the largest value in the range will have a data bar that stretches across the width of the cell. You can modify the length of the data bars by altering the rules of the conditional format.

The longest data bar is in cell G36, representing the amount of the fund invested in health services (14.40%). You'll modify the conditional format rule for the data bar, setting the maximum length to 0.25 so that the longest bar doesn't overlap the value in its cell.

Tip

When the range contains negative values, the data bars originate from the center of the cell—negative bars extend to the left, and positive bars extend to the right.

To modify the data bar conditional formatting rule:

▶ **1.** On the Home tab, in the Styles group, click the **Conditional Formatting** button, and then click **Manage Rules**. The Conditional Formatting Rules Manager dialog box opens, displaying all the rules applied to any conditional format in the workbook.

▶ **2.** In the Show formatting rules for box, select **This Worksheet** to show all the conditional formatting rules for the current sheet.

3. With the Data Bar rule selected, click the **Edit Rule** button. The Edit Formatting Rule dialog box opens.

4. In the Type row, click the **Maximum arrow**, and then click **Number**.

5. Press **TAB** to move the insertion point to the Maximum box in the Value row, and then type **0.25**. All data bar lengths will then be defined relative to this value. See Figure 4–44.

Figure 4–44   **Edit Formatting Rule dialog box**

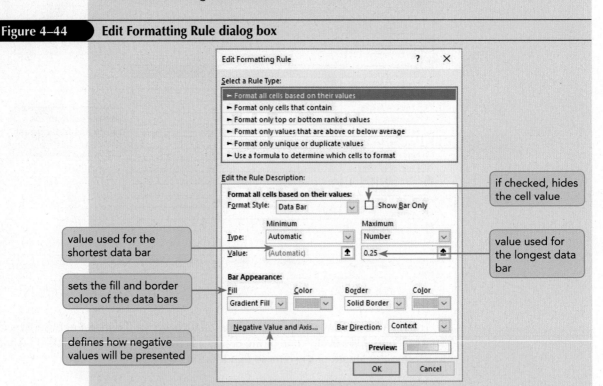

6. Click **OK** in each dialog box to return to the worksheet, and then verify that the data bars no longer span the width of the selected cells.

Creating Sparklines

Another way of adding a chart to a cell is with a sparkline, which is a small chart completely confined to the borders of a single cell. Because of their small size, sparklines don't include chart elements such as legends, titles, or gridlines. The goal of a sparkline is to display the maximum amount of information in the smallest amount of space. As a result, sparklines are useful when you only need to convey a general impression of the data without any distracting detail.

Excel supports three types of sparklines: line sparklines, column sparklines, and win/loss sparklines. Figure 4–45 shows an example of each type in which the price history, shares traded, and increases and declines of 10 investments are displayed within a worksheet.

Figure 4–45   **Sparklines types**

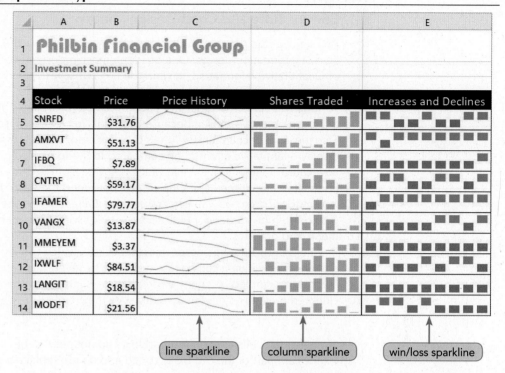

The line sparkline indicates the daily fluctuation in the selling price of each investment. While the sparkline does not provide specific prices, it's clear that the selling price of the Sunrise Fund (SNRFD) has seen an increase followed by a decline over its history, with prices rebounding in the last few days. Other investments such as the IFBQ stock (cell C7) have shown a steady decline in price while the IFAMER stock (cell C9) has shown a steady increase.

The column sparkline indicates the volume of shares traded. Once again, specific details are not provided, but an investor can see that the trading volume for the Sunrise Fund has generally increased over the last several days (cell D5).

Finally, the win/loss sparkline displays a green block for positive values on those days in which the investment's selling price increased and a red block for days in which the selling price declined. The selling price of an investment like MMEYEM (cell E11) is quickly seen to have declined every day, while the IFAMER investment (cell E9) showed an increase in its selling price every day except the first.

The range C5:E14 displays 30 different charts. Although these charts show only general trends, they give the investor a quick and easily interpreted snapshot of the 10 investments and their recent performance. More details can always be provided elsewhere with more informative Excel charts.

Insight

Edward Tufte and Chart Design Theory

Any serious study of charts will include the works of Edward Tufte, who pioneered the field of information design. One of Tufte's most important works is The Visual Display of Quantitative Information, in which he laid out several principles for the design of charts and graphics.

Tufte was concerned with what he termed as "chart junk," in which a proliferation of chart elements—chosen because they look "nice"—confuse and distract the reader. One measure of chart junk is Tufte's data-ink ratio, which is the amount of "ink" used to display quantitative information compared to the total ink required by the chart. Tufte advocated limiting nondata ink, which is any part of the chart that does not convey information about the data. One way of measuring the data-ink ratio is to determine how much of the chart you can erase without affecting the user's ability to interpret your data. Tufte argued for high data-ink ratios with a minimum of extraneous elements and graphics.

To this end, Tufte helped develop sparklines, which convey information with a high data-ink ratio within a compact space. Tufte believed that charts that can be viewed and comprehended at a glance have a greater impact on the reader than large and cluttered graphs, no matter how attractive they might be.

Note that the cells containing sparklines do not need to be blank because the sparklines are part of the cell background and do not replace any content.

Reference

Creating and Editing Sparklines

- On the Insert tab, in the Sparklines group, click the Line, Column, or Win/Loss button to open the Create Sparklines dialog box.
- In the Data Range box, enter the range for the data source of the sparkline.
- In the Location Range box, enter the range into which to place the sparkline.
- Click OK.
- On the Sparkline tab, in the Show group, click the appropriate check boxes to specify which markers to display on the sparkline.
- In the Group group, click the Axis button, and then click Show Axis to add an axis to the sparkline.

Hideki wants you to use line sparklines in the range H32:H43 of the Summary worksheet to display the general trend of the growth of the Sunrise Fund's investment into 12 economic sectors.

To create the line sparklines showing the sector history growth trends:

1. Select the range **H32:H43** in the Summary worksheet.

2. On the ribbon, click the **Insert** tab, and then in the Sparklines group, click the **Line** button. The Create Sparklines dialog box opens.

3. Make sure the insertion point is in the Data Range box, click the **Sector History** sheet tab, and then select the range **B6:M45** on the Sector History

worksheet. This range contains the growth of investments in 12 economic sectors given a hypothetical $10,000 initial investment.

4. Verify that the range **$H$32:$H$43** is entered in the Location Range box. See Figure 4–46.

Figure 4–46   Create Sparklines dialog box

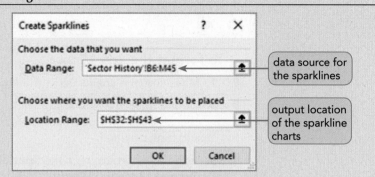

5. Click **OK** to insert the sparklines into the range H32:H43 of the Summary worksheet. See Figure 4–47.

Figure 4–47   Line sparklines in the Summary worksheet

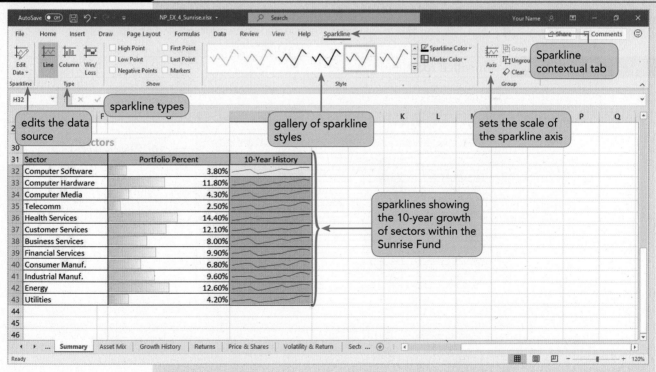

The Sparkline contextual tab appears on the ribbon when a sparkline is selected. From this tab, you can change the sparkline type, edit the sparkline's data source, and format the sparkline's appearance.

Formatting a Sparkline

Because of their compact size, sparklines have fewer formatting options than other Excel charts. You can add data markers to highlight low and high values, initial and ending values, and negative values. From the Style gallery on the Sparkline tab, you can apply built-in styles to the sparklines. From the Sparkline Color and Marker Color buttons in the Style group, you can set the color of the sparklines and their data markers.

Hideki wants you to add data markers identifying the low and high points within the time interval to each sparkline and to change the sparkline color to dark orange.

To format the sparklines:

▶ **1.** Make sure the sparklines in the range H32:H43 are still selected.

▶ **2.** On the Sparkline tab, in the Show group, click the **High Point** and **Low Point** check boxes. Two data markers appear on each sparkline identifying the low and high points.

▶ **3.** In the Style group, click the **Sparkline Color** button, and then click the **Orange, Accent 3, Darker 25%** theme color (the seventh theme color in the fifth row) in the color palette. The sparkline colors change to orange.

▶ **4.** In the Style group, click the **Marker Color** button, click **High Point**, and then click the **Green** standard color. The high point data marker color changes to green.

▶ **5.** Click the **Marker Color** button, click **Low Point**, and then click the **Red** standard color. The low point data marker color changes to red.

▶ **6.** Click cell **I30** to deselect the sparklines. See Figure 4–48.

Figure 4–48   **Formatted sparklines**

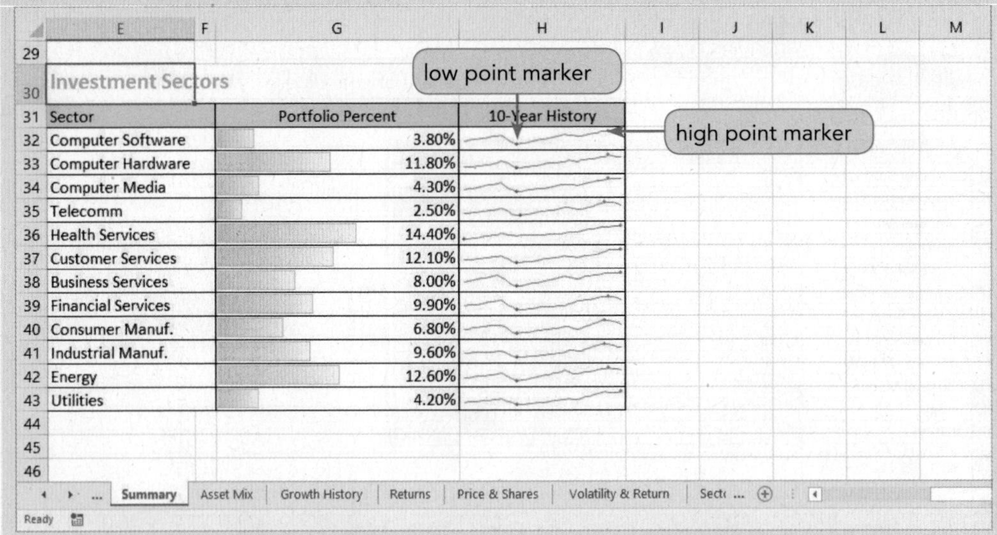

▶ **7.** sam↑ Save the workbook, and then close it.

The sparklines show that the 12 economic sectors experienced the same general growth trend over the previous 10 years with negative growth occurring around years 3 and 4 followed by steady growth thereafter. The lowest for all sectors seem to come around the fourth year.

Sparkline Groups and Sparkline Axes

Sparklines are grouped together by default so that the format choices are applied to every sparkline chart in the group. Grouping ensures that sparklines for related data series are formatted consistently. To format a single sparkline, click the cell containing the sparkline and then click the Ungroup button in the Group group on the Sparkline tab. The selected sparkline is split from the rest of the sparkline group. You can then apply a unique format to it. To regroup the sparklines, select all the cells containing the sparklines, and then click the Group button in the Group group.

Excel displays each sparkline on its own vertical axis ranging from the data series' low point and high point. That means comparing one sparkline to another can be misleading if they are all plotted on a different scale. You can modify the vertical axes by clicking the Axis button in the Group group on the Sparkline tab. To ensure that the vertical scale is the same for all charts in the sparkline group, click the Same for All Sparklines option for both the minimum and maximum scale values. To explicitly define the scale of the vertical axis, click the Custom Value option and specify the minimum and maximum values.

Proskills

Written Communication: Honesty in Charting

One of the great challenges in chart design is to not mislead your audience by misrepresenting the data. Here are a few of the ways in which a chart, created even with the best of intentions, can mislead the viewer:

- **Improper scaling.** This is a very common mistake in which the range of the data scale is set so narrow that even small changes seem large or so wide that all values appear to be the same. For example, a 1% change in a data value will appear large if the scale goes from 0% to 2% and it will appear insignificant if the scale goes from 0% to 100%.

- **Scaling data values differently.** If improper scaling can exaggerate or minimize differences, the problem can be compounded with combination charts in which two data series that should be plotted on the same scale are instead plotted against vastly different scales. For example, one data series might appear to show a significant trend while the other shows none and yet the only difference is the scale on which the values have been plotted.

- **Truncating the vertical axis.** You can make trends appear more significant than they are if you cut off what might appear to be irrelevant information. Is an increase in the interest rate from 4% to 4.05% a significant jump? If you set the scale of the vertical axis to cover the range from 0% to 4.1% it will not appear to be. However, if your chart only covers the range from 4% to 4.1% it will appear to be significant jump.

- **3-D distortions.** Displaying charts in 3D can be eye-catching, but the effect of perspective in which objects appear to recede into the distance can exaggerate or minimize important differences that would be more apparent with a 2D chart.

To be fair, one should not assume that a misleading chart was designed with malicious intent. Because Excel and other software packages include charting, they can lead to the kinds of mistakes discussed above. To avoid misleading the audience, check your assumptions and verify that you are not altering your chart to make it appear more dramatic or interesting. View your charts under different formatting options to confirm that it is truly the data that is telling the story.

You have finished creating charts and graphics to summarize the history and performance of the Sunrise Fund. Hideki is pleased that so much information fits on a single worksheet. Figure 4–49 shows a preview of the printed worksheet containing all the charts and graphics you have created for the report.

Figure 4–49   Final Summary report

Philbin Financial Group

Sunrise Fund Summary

Description

The Sunrise Fund (SNRFD) employs a balanced approach using a diversified portfolio of quality stocks and bonds, seeking capital conservation, current income and long-term growth of capital and income. By primarily investing in inflation-linked securities, the Sunrise Fund seeks to provide both inflation protection and high rates of growth

Fund Facts

Ticker Symbol	SNRFD	Regular Dividends Paid	Mar, Jun, Sep, Dec
Morningstar Rating	★★★★	Minimum Initial Investment	$250
Price At NAV	$30.25	Capital Gains Paid	Jun, Dec
Fund Assets ($millions)	$142,168.40	Portfolio Turnover	95%
Fund Inception	7/22/1995	Fiscal Year-End	Dec
Companies/Issuers	540+	Fund Number	672
Shareholder Accounts	265,180	Portfolio Managers	7

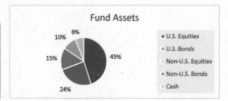

Fund Performance

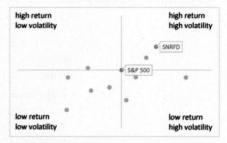

Recent Performance

Investment Sectors

Sector	Portfolio Percent	10-Year History
Computer Software	3.80%	
Computer Hardware	11.80%	
Computer Media	4.30%	
Telecomm	2.50%	
Health Services	14.40%	
Customer Services	12.10%	
Business Services	8.00%	
Financial Services	9.90%	
Consumer Manuf.	6.80%	
Industrial Manuf.	9.60%	
Energy	12.60%	
Utilities	4.20%	

Hideki will continue to study the workbook and get back to you with future reports for the Philbin Financial Group clients.

Review

Session 4.2 Quick Check

1. A researcher wants to plot weight vs. blood pressure. Should the researcher use a line chart or a scatter chart? Explain why.
2. How would you select multiple graphic objects within a worksheet?
3. When would you use a Pareto chart?
4. When would you use a histogram?
5. Describe the three types of sparklines.
6. Under what circumstances would you use sparklines in a report?
7. Why would you not use a sparkline?
8. What are data bars? How do data bars differ from sparklines?

Practice

Review Assignments

Data File needed for the Review Assignments: NP_EX_4-2.xlsx

Hideki wants you to develop another investment report for a Philbin Financial Group client on the Ortus Fund. As with the report you generated for the Sunrise Fund, this workbook will include a worksheet that uses Excel charts and graphics to summarize financial data about the fund. Complete the following:

1. Open the **NP_EX_4-2.xlsx** workbook located in the Excel4 > Review folder included with your Data Files, and then save the workbook as **NP_EX_4_Ortus** in the location specified by your instructor.

2. In the Documentation sheet, enter your name and the date in the range B3:B4.

3. Hideki wants a pie chart that breaks down the allocation of the assets in the Ortus Fund. Do the following:

   a. In the Allocation worksheet, create a pie chart from the data in the range A4:B8.

   b. Move the pie chart to the range D7:E14 in the Prospectus worksheet.

   c. Place the legend on the right side of the chart area.

   d. Change the color scheme to the Monochromatic Palette 5.

   e. Add data labels showing the percentage allocated to each category, positioning the label on the outside end of each pie slice.

4. Hideki wants the report to display a column chart of the month-end returns for the Ortus Fund and the S&P 500 over different time intervals. Do the following:

   a. In the Returns worksheet, create a clustered column chart from the data in the range A4:C9.

   b. Move the chart to the range F7:H14 of the Prospectus worksheet.

   c. Change the chart title to **Month-End Returns**.

   d. Place the legend on the right side of the chart area.

5. Hideki wants a line chart comparing the growth of a theoretical investment of $10,000 in the Ortus Fund and the S&P 500 over the past 10 years. Do the following:

   a. In the Growth worksheet, create a line chart of the data in the range A4:C25, showing the Year value on the horizontal axis.

   b. Move the chart to the range D15:E24 of the Prospectus worksheet.

   c. Change the chart title to **Growth of 10K Investment**.

   d. Add primary major vertical gridlines to the chart.

   e. Place the legend on the right side of the chart area.

   f. Change the interval between the major tick marks and between labels on the category axis to 5 units so that the years 2005, 2010, 2015, 2020, and 2025 appear on the horizontal axis.

6. Hideki wants the report to show the recent selling price and shares traded of the Ortus Fund in a combination chart. Do the following:

   a. In the Recent History worksheet, create a combination chart of the data in the range A4:C58. Display the price data as a line chart plotted on the primary axis and the shares traded data as a clustered column chart plotted on the secondary axis.

   b. Move the chart to the range A26:D38 of the Prospectus worksheet.

   c. Change the chart title to **Recent History**.

   d. Display axis titles on the chart. Change the primary vertical axis title to **Price**, the secondary vertical axis title to **Shares Traded**, and the category axis title to **Date**. Change the angle of rotation of the Shares Traded axis title to Rotate Text Down.

   e. Place the legend on the right side of the chart area.

   f. Change the scale of the secondary axis to go from 0 to 1.6E08 and display the scale in units of 1 million with the units label displayed on the chart.

7. Hideki needs to compare the return rate and volatility of the Ortus Fund to other investment vehicles. Do the following:

   a. In the Performance worksheet, create a scatter chart from the data in the range B5:C7 using the scatter chart from the list of recommended charts.

   b. Move the chart to the range F15:H24 of the Prospectus worksheet.

   c. Remove the chart title and the gridlines from the chart.

   d. Rescale the vertical axis to go from 0.0 to 0.06 with the horizontal axis crossing at 0.031. Rescale the horizontal axis to go from 4 to 24 with the vertical axis crossing at 14.71.

   e. Set the label position to none for both the vertical and horizontal axis labels.

   f. Add data callouts to the data markers in the data series showing only the text from the range A6:A7 in the Performance worksheet.

   g. Complete the scatter chart by adding a new data series to the chart with cell G5 in the Performance worksheet as the series name, the range F6:F15 in the Performance worksheet as the Series X values, and the range G6:G15 in the Performance worksheet as the Series Y values.

8. Add the four text boxes shown earlier in Figure 4–28 to the scatter chart, placing the return and volatility descriptions on separate lines. Resize and move the text boxes so that they align with the chart corners.

9. On the Prospectus worksheet, replace the text in cell B9 with three star icons from the Celebration group in the icon gallery. Set the height and width of each icon 0.20". Align and evenly distribute the icons within cell B9.

10. Add solid blue data bars to the values in the range G28:G38. Keep the data bars from overlapping the values in those cells by modifying the conditional formatting rule so that the maximum length of the data bar corresponds to a value of 0.30.

11. Add line sparklines to the range H28:H38 using the data values from the range B5:L44 of the Sectors worksheet. Add data markers for the high and low points of each sparkline using the Red standard color.

12. Save the workbook, and then close it.

Apply

Case Problem 1

Data File needed for this Case Problem: NP_EX_4-3.xlsx

Certus Car Rental John Tretow is an account manager for Certus Car Rental, an industry-leading car rental firm that serves customers across the United States and overseas. John is developing a market report for an upcoming sales conference and needs your assistance in summarizing market information into a collection of Excel charts and graphics. Complete the following.

1. Open the **NP_EX_4-3.xlsx** workbook located in the Excel4 > Case1 folder included with your Data Files. Save the workbook as **NP_EX_4_Certus** in the location specified by your instructor.

2. In the Documentation sheet, enter your name and the date in the range B3:B4.

3. John wants the report to include pie charts that break down the current year's revenue in terms of market (Airport vs. Off-Airport), car type (Leisure vs. Commercial), and location (Americas vs. International). In the Rentals by Type worksheet, do the following:

   a. Create a pie chart of the data in the range A6:B7. Move the chart cover the range D5:F9 in the Analysis worksheet.

   b. Remove the chart title from the pie chart.

   c. Add data labels to the outside end of the two slices showing the percentage of the Airport vs. Off-Airport sales.

4. Repeat Step 3 for the data in the range A11:B12 of the Rentals by Type worksheet, placing the pie chart comparing Leisure and Commercial sales in the range H5:H9 of the Analysis worksheet.

5. Repeat Step 3 for the data in the range A16:B17 of the Rentals by Type worksheet, placing the pie chart comparing revenue between the Americas and International sales in the range J5:J9 of the Analysis worksheet.

6. John wants to present the company revenue broken down by car type. In the Car Models worksheet, create a clustered bar chart of the data in the range A4:B9. Move the bar chart to the range B11:F21 of the Analysis worksheet. Remove the chart legend if it exists. Add data labels to the end of the data markers showing the revenue for each car model.

7. John also wants to track revenue for each car model over the years to determine whether certain car models have increased or decreased in popularity. In the Revenue by Year worksheet, create a line chart of the data in the range A4:F15. Move the chart to the range H11:J21 in the Analysis worksheet.

8. Apply the following formats to the line chart you created in Step 7:
   a. Remove the chart title.
   b. Add major gridlines for the primary vertical and horizontal axes.
   c. Move the chart legend to the right side of the chart area.
   d. Add axis titles to the chart. Set the vertical axis title to the text **Revenue ($bil)** and the horizontal axis title to **Year**.
   e. Set the interval between tick marks and between the labels on the category (horizontal) axis to 2 units so that the category labels are Y2015, Y2017, Y2019, Y2021, Y2023, and Y2025.

9. John wants to compare the Certus brand to competing car rental companies. In the range F25:F29, insert line sparklines showing the trend in market share percentages using the data from the range B19:F29 on the Market Share worksheet.

10. Add green data bars with a gradient fill to the data values in the range E25:E29.

11. In the range F32:F36, insert line sparklines showing the trend in revenue using the data from the range B5:F15 on the Market Share worksheet.

12. Add orange data bars with a gradient fill to the data values in the range E32:E36.

13. John wants to present a more detailed chart of the revenue values from the five competing rental car agencies over the past several years. In the Market Share worksheet, create a Stacked Column chart from the data in the range A4:F15. Move the chart over the range H24:J36 in the Analysis worksheet.

14. Apply the following formatting to the column chart you created in Step 13:
   a. Remove the chart title
   b. Add axis titles to the chart. Set the vertical axis title to the text **Revenue ($bil)** and the horizontal axis title to **Year**.
   c. Move the legend to the right side of the chart area.
   d. Set the interval between tick marks and between the labels on the category (horizontal) axis to 2 units to display the category values Y2015, Y2017, Y2019, Y2021, Y2023, and Y2025.
   e. Set the gap width between the bars in the chart to 30%.

15. The company revenue decreased in the past year. John wants you to highlight this fact by adding a down-arrow shape from the Shape gallery to the right side of the merged cell B5 on the Analysis worksheet. Set the height of the down arrow to 1" and the width to 0.5".

16. While the company revenue has decreased in the last year, its market share has increased. Add an up-arrow shape to the right side of the merged cell B25. Set the arrow to be 1" high and 0.5" wide.

17. Save the workbook, and then close it.

Challenge

Case Problem 2

Data File needed for this Case Problem: NP_EX_4-4.xlsx

Spirit Care Hospital & Clinic   Dakota Kohana is the site coordinator for the Spirt Care Hospital & Clinic on the Pine Ridge reservation in South Dakota. As part of an annual report for the clinic's trustees, Dakota needs to document patient care at the clinic including inpatient and outpatient admissions, length of stay, and average waiting time. Dakota has asked your help in supplementing the report with informative charts and graphics. Complete the following.

1. Open the **NP_EX_4-4.xlsx** workbook located in the Excel4 > Case2 folder included with your Data Files. Save the workbook as **NP_EX_4_Spirit** in the location specified by your instructor.

2. In the Documentation sheet, enter your name in cell B3. Use an Excel function to enter the current date in cell B4.

3. In the Summary worksheet, in the range D5:D11, Dakota has broken down the number of inpatient admissions by department. Add solid green data bars to the range, setting to maximum length of the data bars to 8000.

4. Repeat Step 3 for the outpatient admissions in the range E5:E11, using solid blue data bars.

Explore 5. In the Patients by Month worksheet, create a Sunburst chart of the data in the nonadjacent range A4:C4,A17:C17. Move the chart to the Summary worksheet covering the range G4:J11.

6. Apply the following formatting to the Sunburst chart you created in Step 5:
   a. Remove the chart title.
   b. Display the chart legend at the top of the chart.
   c. Change the data labels to show the values only and not the category names.

Explore 7. Dakota also wants to view the admission data by month. In the Patients by Month worksheet, create a Stacked Area chart of the data in the range A4:C16. Move the chart to the Summary worksheet covering the range L4:P11.

8. Apply the following formats to the Stacked Area chart you created in Step 7.
   a. Remove the chart title.
   b. Add primary major vertical gridlines to the chart.

Explore 9. The report will also include an analysis of the length of inpatient stays. Dakota has retrieved length of stay data for 300 randomly selected patients and wants you to display the distribution of those stays in a histogram chart. In the Length of Stay worksheet, create a histogram of the data in the range A4:A304. Move the chart to the range C13:E25 in the Summary worksheet. (Note: If the chart is placed at the bottom of the worksheet, you can quickly move the chart to the top by selecting the chart, and then cutting and pasting the chart to a cell near the top of the worksheet.)

10. Apply the following formatting options to the histogram chart you created in Step 9:
    a. Change the chart title to **Length of Stay (Days)**.
    b. Double-click the histogram categories along the horizontal axis to display the Format Axis pane. Change the Bin Width value to **1**. Change the Overflow Bin value to 10 so that length of stay values larger than 10 are pooled together in a single category.

11. When patients are admitted to the hospital and then discharged, they might be readmitted within 30 days. Dakota wants the report to include the inpatient admission totals and the 30-day readmission rates for each quarter of the past year. In the Readmission worksheet, create a combination chart of the data in the range A4:C8. Display the Inpatient Admissions data series as a clustered column chart. Display the Readmission Rate data series as a line chart on the secondary axis. Move the chart to the range G13:J25 of the Summary worksheet.

12. Apply the following formatting options to the combination chart you created in Step 11:
    a. Change the chart title to **Admissions and 30-Day Readmission Rate**.
    b. Add axis titles to the chart. Name the primary vertical axis **Inpatient Admissions**. Name the secondary vertical axis **Readmission Rate** and rotate the text down. Name the category axis **Quarter**.
    c. Change the scale of the secondary axis to go from 0.1 to 0.3.

Explore 13. Dakota's report needs to break down admissions by payer (Medicare, Medicaid, Private Insurance, or Uninsured). Dakota thinks this data would be best presented in a Pareto chart. In the Payer worksheet, create a Pareto chart of the data in the range A4:B8. Move the chart to range L13:P25 in the Summary worksheet and change the chart title to **Admissions by Payer**.

14. Monitoring the length of time that patients must wait before being treated is an important task for Dakota. On the Summary worksheet, add solid red data bars to range D29:D35 containing the wait times for different departments. Set the maximum length of the data bars to 40.

15. Dakota wants to track how wait times within each department have changed over the past year. Add line sparklines to the range E29:E35 using the data from the range B5:H16 of the Waiting Times worksheet. Mark the high and low point within each sparkline using the Red standard color.

16. Trustees want to track the nurse-to-patient ratio during both the day and the night shifts. Dakota included this information in the Summary worksheet and augmented it with graphic icons, but the alignment is off and wants you to fix it. Do the following:

   a. Open the Selection pane and select the Graphic 1 through Graphic 3 icons in cell I29 and align them along their middle positions.

   b. Use the Selection pane to select the Graphic 4 through Graphic 7 icons in cell I33 and distribute them evenly in the horizontal direction.

17. Save the workbook, and then close it.

Generating Reports from Multiple Worksheets and Workbooks

Summarizing Profit and Loss Statements

Objectives

Session 5.1
- Copy worksheets between workbooks
- View a workbook in multiple windows
- Organize worksheets in a worksheet group
- Write a 3-D reference

Session 5.2
- Write an external reference
- Manage the security features of linked documents
- Create a hyperlink to a document source
- Link to an email address

Session 5.3
- Create and apply a named range
- Work with the scope of named ranges
- Create a workbook template

Case | Tibetan Grill

Gail Bailey is a financial officer for Tibetan Grill, a popular chain of Indian restaurants located across the country. As a financial officer, Gail needs to retrieve and combine financial statements from individual Tibetan Grill franchises into summary reports to be analyzed by the Board of Directors. Gail is currently working on an annual report of financial statements from eight Tibetan Grill restaurants located in Illinois and Iowa. You will help her combine data from multiple worksheets and workbooks into one workbook.

Starting Data Files

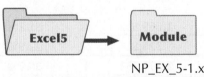

Excel5 → **Module**

NP_EX_5-1.xlsx
NP_EX_5-2.xlsx
Support_EX_5_2020.xlsx
Support_EX_5_2021.xlsx
Support_EX_5_2022.xlsx
Support_EX_5_2023.xlsx
Support_EX_5_Grill08.xlsx

Review

NP_EX_5-3.xlsx
Support_EX_5_Peoria.xlsx
Support_EX_5_Region1.xlsx
Support_EX_5_Region2.xlsx
Support_EX_5_Region3.xlsx
Support_EX_5_Region4.xlsx

Case1

NP_EX_5-4.xlsx

Case2

NP_EX_5-5.xlsx
Support_EX_5_Fund01.xlsx
Support_EX_5_Fund02.xlsx
Support_EX_5_Fund03.xlsx
Support_EX_5_Fund04.xlsx
Support_EX_5_Fund05.xlsx

Session 5.1 Visual Overview:

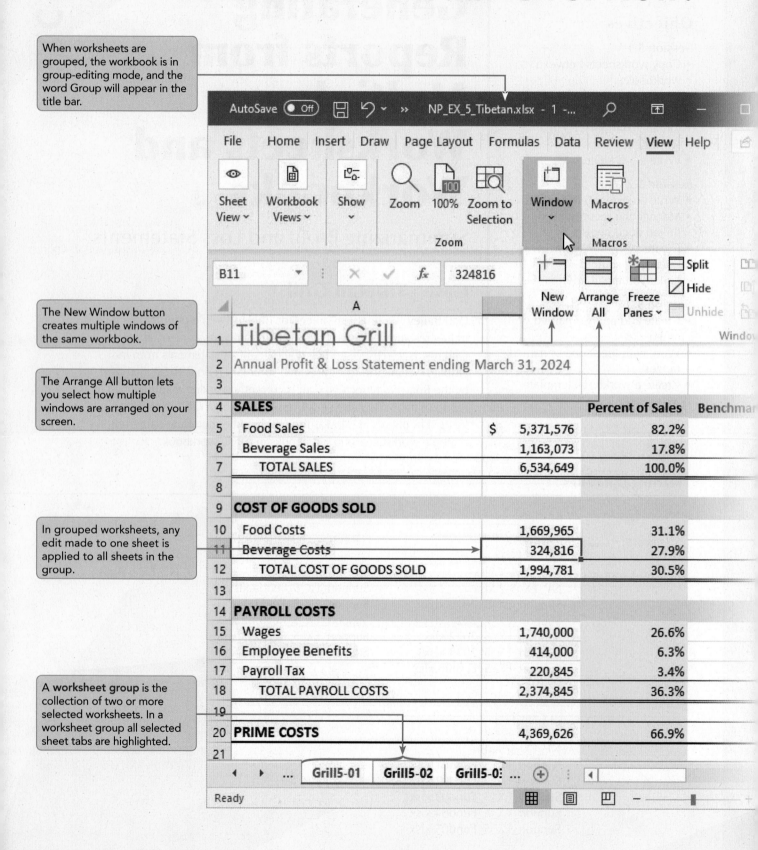

When worksheets are grouped, the workbook is in group-editing mode, and the word Group will appear in the title bar.

The New Window button creates multiple windows of the same workbook.

The Arrange All button lets you select how multiple windows are arranged on your screen.

In grouped worksheets, any edit made to one sheet is applied to all sheets in the group.

A **worksheet group** is the collection of two or more selected worksheets. In a worksheet group all selected sheet tabs are highlighted.

AutoSave ● Off · NP_EX_5_Tibetan.xlsx - 1 -...

File Home Insert Draw Page Layout Formulas Data Review View Help

Sheet View · Workbook Views · Show · Zoom 100% Zoom to Selection Window · Macros ·

Zoom Macros

New Window Arrange All Freeze Panes · Split Hide Unhide

B11 · fx 324816

	A			
1	Tibetan Grill			
2	Annual Profit & Loss Statement ending March 31, 2024			
3				
4	**SALES**		**Percent of Sales**	**Benchmar**
5	Food Sales	$ 5,371,576	82.2%	
6	Beverage Sales	1,163,073	17.8%	
7	TOTAL SALES	6,534,649	100.0%	
8				
9	**COST OF GOODS SOLD**			
10	Food Costs	1,669,965	31.1%	
11	Beverage Costs	324,816	27.9%	
12	TOTAL COST OF GOODS SOLD	1,994,781	30.5%	
13				
14	**PAYROLL COSTS**			
15	Wages	1,740,000	26.6%	
16	Employee Benefits	414,000	6.3%	
17	Payroll Tax	220,845	3.4%	
18	TOTAL PAYROLL COSTS	2,374,845	36.3%	
19				
20	**PRIME COSTS**		4,369,626	66.9%
21				

◄ ► ... | Grill5-01 | Grill5-02 | Grill5-0: | ... ⊕

Ready

Worksheet Groups and 3-D References

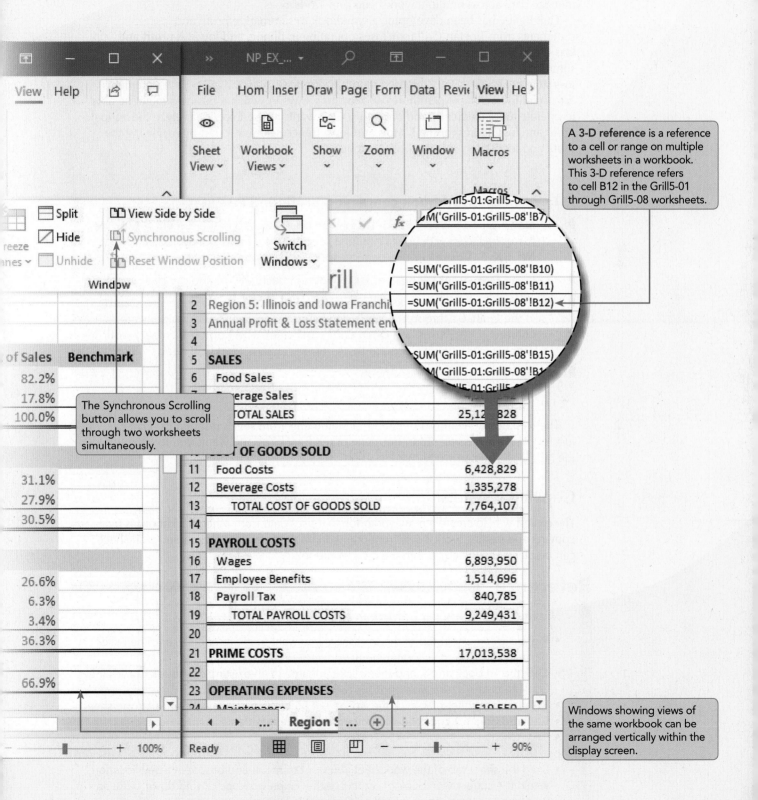

A **3-D reference** is a reference to a cell or range on multiple worksheets in a workbook. This 3-D reference refers to cell B12 in the Grill5-01 through Grill5-08 worksheets.

The Synchronous Scrolling button allows you to scroll through two worksheets simultaneously.

Windows showing views of the same workbook can be arranged vertically within the display screen.

Working with Multiple Worksheets

So far, you have worked with formulas and functions that referenced cells in a single worksheet within a single workbook. However, data is often stored across several worksheets and workbooks. In this module you'll learn the skills you need to effectively manage data across multiple worksheets and workbooks.

Gail Bailey has been developing a workbook to summarize profit and loss statements from Tibetan Grill franchises operating in Illinois and Iowa. A **profit and loss (P&L) statement**, also called an **income statement**, is a financial statement that summarizes the income and expenses incurred during a specified interval. Profit and loss statements are usually released monthly, quarterly, and annually. Such statements are useful in tracking expenditures and locating ways in which a business might be able to operate more efficiently and profitably. Gail wants to use Excel to analyze the annual profit and loss figures for the Illinois and Iowa franchises. You'll start by reviewing the profit and loss statements for those franchises.

To open the workbook containing profit and loss statements:

1. **sam** ⬇ Open the **NP_EX_5-1.xlsx** workbook located in the **Excel5 > Module** folder included with your Data Files, and then save the workbook as **NP_EX_5_Tibetan** in the location specified by your instructor.

2. In the **Documentation** sheet, enter your name in cell B3 and the date in cell B4.

3. Review each of the worksheets in the workbook. P&L statements are stored in the Grill5-01 through Grill5-07 worksheets and financial definitions are entered in the Terms and Definitions worksheet. The Region Summary worksheet is where you will create the summary analysis that Gail needs.

4. Go to the **Grill5-01** worksheet.

The workbook contains profit and loss statements from seven restaurants. Gail has just received the missing report from one of the franchises and wants you to copy it into the NP_EX_5_Tibetan workbook.

Copying a Worksheet

The easiest way to create a new workbook that uses data from other workbooks is by copying and pasting worksheets from one workbook to another. The copied worksheet can be placed anywhere within the new workbook.

Reference ▬▬▬▬▬▬▬▬▬▬▬

Moving and Copying a Worksheet

- Right-click the sheet tab of the worksheet you want to move or copy, and then click Move or Copy on the shortcut menu.
- Click the To book arrow, and then click the name of an existing workbook or click (new book) to create a new workbook for the sheet.
- In the Before sheet box, click the worksheet before which you want to insert the sheet.
- Click the Create a copy check box to copy the sheet rather than moving it.
- Click OK.

or

- Drag the sheet tab of the worksheet you want to move and drop it in a new location within the current workbook or within another open workbook. Hold down CTRL as you drag and drop the sheet tab to copy rather than move the sheet.

Gail has provided you with a workbook showing the profit and loss statement from the Tibetan Grill franchise in Peoria, Illinois. You'll copy the worksheet in that workbook to the NP_EX_5_Tibetan workbook.

To open the Peoria workbook:

1. Open the **Support_EX_5_Grill08.xlsx** workbook located in the **Excel5 > Module** folder included with your Data Files.

2. Go to the **Grill5-08** worksheet.

3. Right-click the **Grill5-08** sheet tab, and then click **Move or Copy** on the shortcut menu. The Move or Copy dialog box opens.

4. Click the **To book arrow**, and then click **NP_EX_5_Tibetan.xlsx** in the list.

5. In the Before sheet box, scroll down and click **Terms and Definitions** to place the Grill5-08 worksheet before the Terms and Definitions worksheet.

6. Click the **Create a copy** check box to place a copy of the Grill5-08 worksheet in the NP_EX_5_Tibetan workbook. See Figure 5–1.

Tip

You can create a new workbook and move or copy a sheet into that workbook by clicking (new book) in the To book list.

Be sure to click the Create a copy check box to copy, not move, the worksheet.

| Figure 5–1 | Move or Copy dialog box |

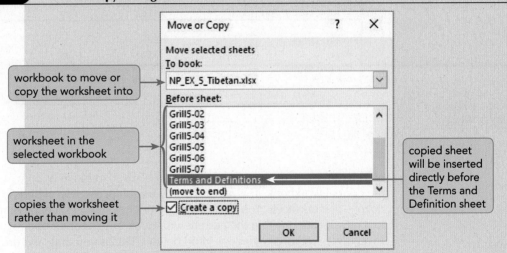

workbook to move or copy the worksheet into

worksheet in the selected workbook

copies the worksheet rather than moving it

copied sheet will be inserted directly before the Terms and Definition sheet

7. Click **OK**. The Grill5-08 worksheet is copied into the Tibetan workbook.

8. Close the **Support_EX_5_Grill08** workbook without saving changes.

9. Return to the **NP_EX_5_Tibetan** workbook and scroll through the sheets and verify that the Grill5-08 worksheet appears directly after the Grill5-07 sheet. See Figure 5–2.

Figure 5–2   **Grill5-08 worksheet copied to the Tibetan workbook**

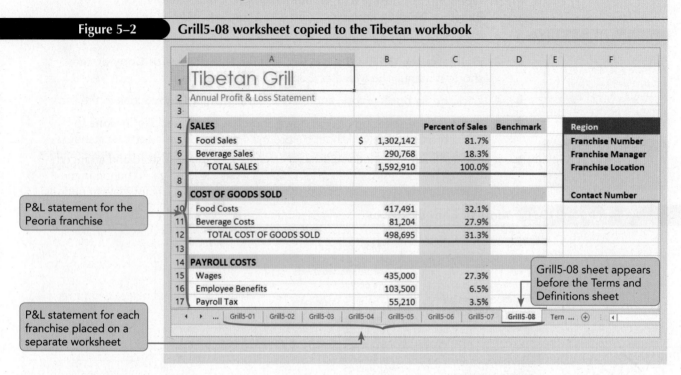

P&L statement for the Peoria franchise

P&L statement for each franchise placed on a separate worksheet

Grill5-08 sheet appears before the Terms and Definitions sheet

The Move or Copy dialog box can also be used to move or copy worksheets within the current workbook. This is particularly useful for large workbooks that contain dozens of worksheets. You can also move or copy a worksheet by dragging its sheet tab to a new location within the current workbook or to another open workbook displayed in a visible workbook window. Hold down CTRL as you drag and drop the sheet tab to create a copy of the sheet rather than moving it. Once you copy a worksheet into a different workbook, any changes you make to the copied worksheet do not appear in the original worksheet.

Viewing a Workbook in Multiple Windows

When a workbook has several worksheets, you might find yourself constantly switching between sheets to compare data from different sheets. Instead, you can work on different parts of the workbook at the same time by displaying different sheets in separate windows. You do this with the New Window button in the Window group on the View tab.

Gail wants to compare all the franchises' income and expenses to determine whether any franchises are underperforming or exceeding expectations. Because each franchise's profit and loss statement is on a separate worksheet, Gail would have to switch between eight sheets to complete this analysis. Instead, you can create separate windows for different sheets.

To create a new viewing window for the workbook:

1. On the ribbon, click the **View** tab to display the commands for viewing the workbook's contents.

2. In the Window group, click the **New Window** button. A second window displaying the same workbook opens.

Two windows now display the same workbook. Excel distinguishes the different windows by adding a number after the file name in the title bar. In this case, the two windows for the NP_EX_5_Tibetan.xlsx workbook include the numbers 1 and 2. If you opened a third workbook window, the number 3 would appear after the file name, and so forth.

Arranging Multiple Workbook Windows

When you have multiple windows, you can change how they are sized and arranged so you can see all windows at one time. When you use the Arrange All button in the Window group on the View tab, you can choose from the following four layout options, shown in Figure 5–3.

- **Tiled.** Resizes the height and width of windows to fill the screen in both horizontal and vertical directions likes floor tiles.
- **Horizontal.** Expands the width of the windows to fill the screen and places them in a single column.
- **Vertical.** Expands the height of the windows to fill the screen and places them in a single row.
- **Cascade.** Layers the windows in an overlapping stack.

Figure 5–3	Workbook window layouts

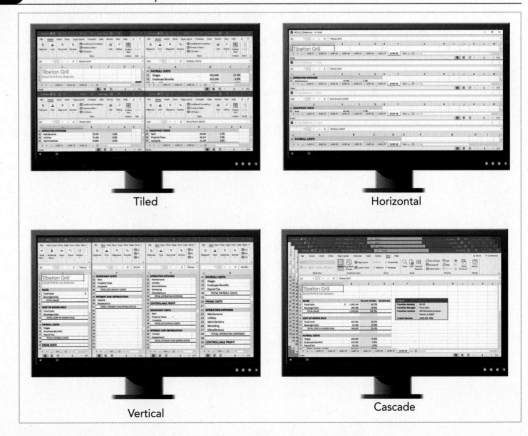

Tiled

Horizontal

Vertical

Cascade

Generally, you do not want to tile more than four windows at a time. With more windows, the contents become small and difficult to view. You'll use the Arrange All command to display the two windows of the NP_EX_5_Tibetan workbook in a vertical layout.

To view the Tibetan workbook windows in a vertical layout:

1. On the ribbon, click the **View** tab and then in the Window group, click the **Arrange All** button. The Arrange Windows dialog box opens.

2. Click the **Vertical** option button to select a vertical layout for the workbook windows.

3. Click the **Windows of active workbook** check box to select it. Now, only windows for the active workbook, and not any other open workbooks, will be arranged. See Figure 5–4.

| Figure 5–4 | Arrange Windows dialog box |

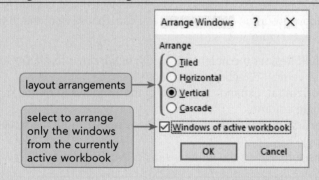

4. Click **OK**. The windows of the current workbook change to a vertical layout with one window on the left and another on the right.

5. Click the **title bar** of left workbook window to select it, and then click the **Grill5-01** sheet tab to display the profit and loss statement for the Chicago franchise.

6. Increase the zoom level of the worksheet to **120%**.

7. Click the title bar of the right workbook window to select it, and then click the **Grill5-02** sheet tab to display the profit and loss statement for the Des Moines franchise.

8. If necessary, increase the zoom level of the worksheet to **120%**. See Figure 5–5.

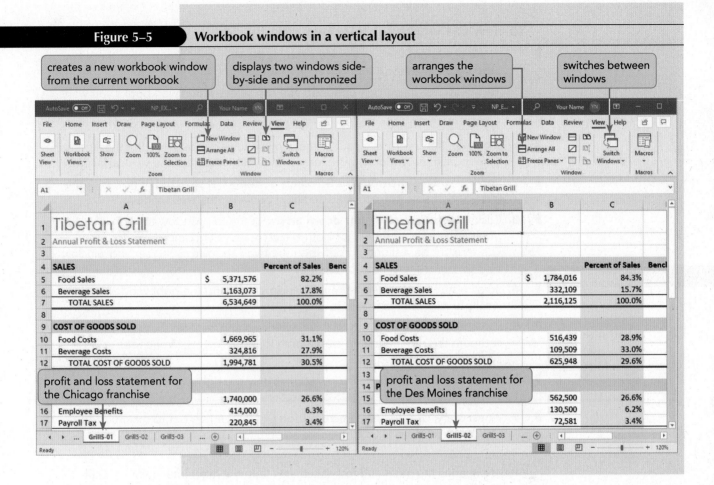

Figure 5-5   **Workbook windows in a vertical layout**

The two workbook windows allow you to compare the contents of one sheet with another. Because the windows are not maximized, more of the sheet contents area are hidden. You can deal with that problem with synchronized scrolling.

Reference

Arranging Multiple Workbook Windows

- To create a new window for the current workbook, on the View tab, in the Window group, click the New Window button.
- To arrange multiple workbook windows, on the View tab, in the Window group, click the Arrange All button, click an arrangement option button, click the Windows of active workbook check box to arrange only windows for the current workbook, and then click OK.
- To view two workbook windows side-by-side, on the View tab, in the Window group, click the View Side by Side button and select the workbook window to view along with the current window. If necessary, select the Synchronized Scrolling button to scroll both windows simultaneously.

Using Synchronized Scrolling Between Windows

You can use synchronized scrolling in two windows that are viewed side by side. As you scroll the worksheet contents in one window, the scrolling is mirrored in the other window. Synchronized scrolling lets you more easily compare two worksheets whose contents extend beyond the workbook window. You'll use synchronized scrolling to review the two windows of the NP_EX_5_Tibetan workbook.

To view the workbook windows side-by-side:

▸ **1.** In the active window, on the View tab, in the Windows group, click the **View Side by Side** button 🕮.

   Trouble? If a dialog box opens so you can select which workbooks you want to view side-by-side, you have multiple workbooks open. Select the window for NP_EX_5_Tibetan.xlsx - 2 workbook as the other window.

   Trouble? If the vertical layout of the two windows disappears, click the Arrange All button in the Window group on the View tab to restore the vertical layout.

▸ **2.** Verify that the **Synchronized Scrolling** button 🔲 is selected. If not, click the button to enable synchronized scrolling between the two windows.

▸ **3.** Click the **vertical scroll bar down arrow** of the left window to verify that the profit and loss statements for both franchises scroll up and down together. There might be a slight lag between the two windows as the second window tries to mirror the actions of the first.

▸ **4.** Scroll horizontally through the left window, verifying the right window also scrolls horizontally to match it.

▸ **5.** View other worksheets with the two windows and confirm that you can compare the profit and loss statements for other pairs of franchises using synchronized scrolling.

▸ **6.** Close the left workbook window so that only the right workbook window is visible for the workbook.

▸ **7.** If necessary, click the **Maximize** button 🔲 on the title bar to maximize the workbook window, filling the entire screen.

After comparing the profit and loss statements from the different franchises, Gail sees several errors. Each statement needs a subtitle specifying the end date on which the profit and loss numbers are calculated as well as a calculation of pretax profit for the year. Rather than fixing each worksheet individually, you can edit all the sheets simultaneously by grouping them.

Working with Worksheet Groups

You can edit several worksheets simultaneously by grouping the worksheets. In a worksheet group, any changes made to one worksheet are automatically applied to all sheets in the group, including entering formulas and data, changing row heights and widths, applying conditional formats, inserting or deleting rows and columns, defining page layouts, and setting view options. Worksheet groups save time and improve consistency because identical actions are performed within several sheets at the same time.

Reference

Grouping and Ungrouping Worksheets

- To select an adjacent group, click the sheet tab of the first worksheet in the group, press and hold SHIFT, click the sheet tab of the last worksheet in the group, and then release SHIFT.
- To select a nonadjacent group, click the sheet tab of one worksheet in the group, press and hold CTRL, click the sheet tabs of the remaining worksheets in the group, and then release CTRL.
- To ungroup the worksheets, click the sheet tab of a worksheet that is not in the group; or right-click the sheet tab of one worksheet in the group, and then click Ungroup Sheets on the shortcut menu.

You'll group the profit and loss statements for the eight Tibetan Grill franchises.

To group the Grill5-01 through Grill5-08 worksheets:

1. Click the **Grill5-01** sheet tab to select that worksheet.

2. Scroll the sheet tabs to the right until you see the sheet tab for the Grill5-08 worksheet.

3. Hold down **SHIFT**, click the **Grill5-08** sheet tab, and then release **SHIFT**. All of the worksheets from the Grill5-01 worksheet and the Grill5-08 worksheet are selected. The sheet tab names are in bold and the word "Group" is added to the title bar as a reminder that you selected a worksheet group.

4. Scroll the sheet tabs back to the front of the workbook, displaying the contents of the Grill5-01 worksheet. See Figure 5–6.

Figure 5–6	Grouped worksheets

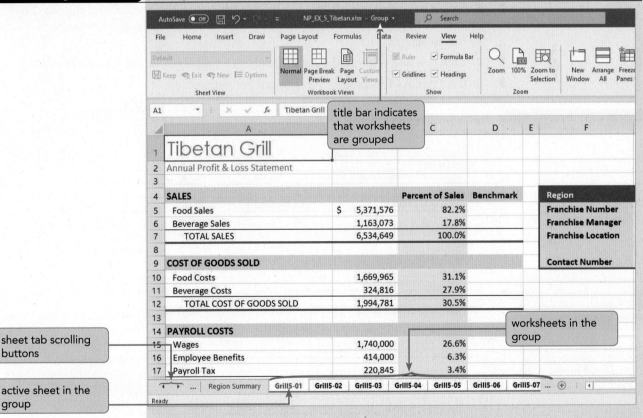

Trouble? If the sheets ungrouped, you probably clicked a sheet tab outside of the group. Repeat Steps 1 through 4 to regroup the sheets.

Editing a Worksheet Group

With the worksheets selected as a single group, you can now edit all of them at the same time. Remember, any changes you make to one worksheet will be made to all sheets in the group. You will edit all of the sheets in the group now, adding a new subheading to each sheet and calculating the pretax profit for each franchise.

To edit the worksheet group:

▶ 1. Make sure the **Grill5-01** worksheet is still the active sheet in the group, and then click cell **A2**. Cell A2 is selected in all the worksheets in the group.

▶ 2. In cell A2, change the subheading to **Annual Profit & Loss Statement ending March 31, 2024** to add the ending date, and then press **ENTER**. The subheading is updated for all worksheets in the group.

▶ 3. Scroll down and click cell **A43**, type **PRETAX PROFIT** as the label, and then press **TAB**. The label is added to all sheets in the group.

▶ 4. In cell **B43**, enter the formula **=B30-B36-B41** to subtract the total occupancy costs, interest, and depreciation from the franchise's controllable profit, and then press **TAB**. The pretax profit is $418,881.

▶ 5. In cell **C43**, enter the formula **=B43/B7** to calculate pretax profit divided by total sales, and then press **ENTER**. The pretax profit expressed as a percentage of total sales is 0.06410153.

▶ 6. Select the range **A29:D30**, click the **Home** tab on the ribbon, and then in the Clipboard group, click the **Format Painter** button to copy the format from the selected range.

▶ 7. Click cell **A42** to paste the copied format to the pretax figures you just calculated.

▶ 8. Click cell **A44** to deselect the range. See Figure 5–7.

Figure 5–7	Pretax profit calculations

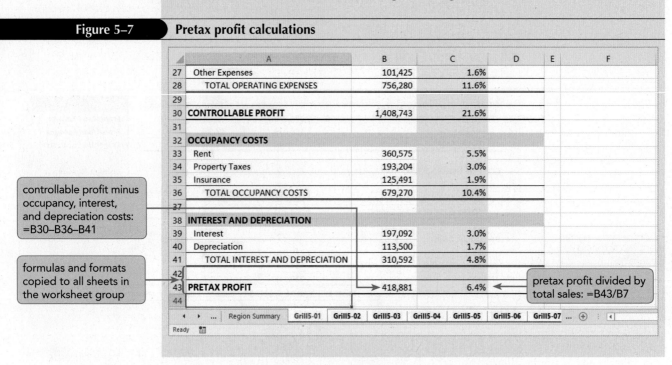

controllable profit minus occupancy, interest, and depreciation costs: =B30–B36–B41

formulas and formats copied to all sheets in the worksheet group

pretax profit divided by total sales: =B43/B7

The Chicago franchise's pretax profit as a percent of total sales is 6.4%, which is a good profit margin in the restaurant industry. Because you made these edits in a worksheet group, the text, data, and formulas you entered in the Grill5-01 worksheet also appear in the other sheets of the worksheet group. You'll review those other sheets to see the pretax profits and percentages in the other franchises.

To view the pretax profits and percentages in the other sheets in the group:

▶ 1. Click the **Grill5-02** sheet tab to view the profit and loss statement for the Des Moines franchise.

▶ 2. Scroll up the worksheet and verify that the subheading in cell A2 includes the date for the profit and loss statement.

▶ 3. Scroll down to row **43** and verify that the pretax profit for the Des Moines franchise is $179,261 with a percent of total sales value of 8.5%.

▶ 4. Click each of the other sheet tabs in the worksheet group to verify that the subheading in cell A2 was updated and the pretax profit and percentage appear in row 43.

As you can see from the different sheets in the worksheet group, only the franchise in Rockford, Illinois, showed a net loss for the last fiscal year. The other franchises showed pretax profits ranging from 1.4% to 8.5% of total sales.

Ungrouping a Worksheet Group

Once you are finished with a worksheet group, you should ungroup the selected sheets so that all sheets start acting independently again. To ungroup worksheets, click the sheet tab of any sheet that is not part of the group. If the group includes all sheets in the workbook, clicking any sheet tab will ungroup the worksheets. You can also right-click any sheet tab in the selected group and click Ungroup Sheets on the shortcut menu.

You will ungroup the selected sheets in the worksheet group.

To ungroup the sheets in the worksheet group:

▶ 1. Right-click any **sheet tab** in the worksheet group to display the shortcut menu.

▶ 2. Click **Ungroup Sheets** on the shortcut menu.

▶ 3. Verify that the sheets are ungrouped and the word "Group" no longer appears in the title bar.

Be cautious when editing a worksheet group. If the layout and structure of the sheets are not the same, you might inadvertently overwrite important data in one of the worksheets. Also, remember to ungroup the worksheet group after you finish editing it. Otherwise, changes you intend to make to only one worksheet will be made to all the sheets in the group, potentially producing incorrect results.

Insight

Printing a Worksheet Group

Page layouts can be duplicated across multiple sheets. By grouping the worksheets, any of your choices for page orientation, margins, headers, footers, and other layout options will be applied to every other sheet in the group.

You can also print a worksheet group. To print a worksheet group, first group the sheets to be printed. Next, on the ribbon, click File to open Backstage view, and then click Print in the navigation bar. Then, on the Print screen, in the Settings section, verify that the Print Active Sheets option is selected. Finally, click the Print button to send the contents of all the worksheets in the group to the printer.

Gail reviewed the financial information from the eight Tibetan Grill franchises in Illinois and Iowa, and wants you to summarize the data from all of the franchises in a single worksheet.

Writing 3-D References

So far, all the formulas and functions you created have used data stored on the same sheet. But as workbooks get larger and more complex, data can be spread across many sheets within the workbook. To analyze the data, you need to reference that data in other places.

Referencing Cells in Other Worksheets

Formulas with references to cells on the same sheet can be thought of as 2-D (or 2-dimensional) references because they involve only the row address and the column address. A 3-D reference includes the row address, the column address, and the worksheet address, expressed within a single reference as:

    Sheet!*Range*

where *Sheet* is the worksheet name and *Range* is the 2-D cell reference within that worksheet. The following expression references cell B10 on the Summary worksheet:

    `Summary!B10`

If the worksheet title contains spaces, enclose the sheet name within a set of single quotation marks. The following expression uses this form to reference cell B10 on the Summary Report worksheet.

    `'Summary Report'!B10`

The reference to a cell within a worksheet can be relative, absolute, or mixed so that the expression `'Summary Report'!$B$10` provides an absolute reference to cell B10 in the Summary Report worksheet.

Applying 3-D References to Formulas and Functions

3-D cell references can be used within any Excel formula and function. For example, the following formula calculates the combined total of cell B10 from the Jan, Feb, Mar, Apr, and May worksheets.

    `=Jan!B10+Feb!B10+Mar!B10+Apr!B10+May!B10`

Another way to reference several worksheets is to treat them as worksheet group starting from the group's first sheet and ending at the last sheet. The syntax of the worksheet group reference is

    FirstSheet:*LastSheet*!*Range*

where *FirstSheet* is the first sheet in the group, *LastSheet* is the last sheet in the group, and *Range* is a cell range common to all sheets in the group. The following expression references cell B10 from all sheets in a group starting with the Jan worksheet and ending with the May worksheet:

    `Jan:May!B10`

Any worksheet placed between the Jan and May sheets is part of the group reference. The following formula calculates the total of the B10 cells within the group:

    `=SUM(Jan:May!B10)`

So, if the Feb, Mar, and Apr sheets are placed between the Jan and May worksheets in the workbook, they will be included in the calculation.

Proskills

Problem Solving: Managing 3-D Group References

Worksheet group references are based on the *current order* of worksheets in the workbook. Rearranging the worksheets will affect what values are included in the calculation. Here are some tips to keep in mind when you revised the structure of a workbook containing a reference to a worksheet group:

- If you insert a new sheet between the first and last sheets of the group, it automatically becomes part of the worksheet group reference.
- If you move a worksheet out from between the first and last sheets, it is no longer part of the worksheet group reference.
- If you move the positions of the first or last sheets, the worksheet group will automatically refer to the new position of the group within the workbook.
- If the first sheet in the group is deleted, the sheet to the right of the first sheet becomes the new first sheet in the worksheet group reference.
- If the last sheet in the group is deleted, the sheet to the left of the last sheet becomes the new last sheet in the worksheet group reference.

Keep in mind that relative references within the worksheets will not update if you change the structure of the sheets. For example, if you insert a new column B in the Jan through May worksheets, which moves cell B10 to cell C10 in those sheets, the formula remains =SUM(Jan:May!B10).

It's a good practice to use formulas that include a worksheet group reference only when you are confident that the sheet order and the row/column structure of the worksheets within the group will not change.

A 3-D reference can be used with most statistical functions, including the MIN, MAX, COUNT, AVERAGE, and MEDIAN functions. You can easily insert a 3-D reference in a formula by using your mouse to select the worksheet and then the cell range within the worksheet group.

Reference

Entering a 3-D Reference

- To create a 3-D reference to a range within a worksheet, enter

    Sheet!Range

    where *Sheet* is the worksheet name and *Range* is the cell address within that worksheet (enclose worksheet names that include spaces within a set of single quotes).
- To insert a 3-D reference in a formula, click the sheet tab of the worksheet, click the cell range in that worksheet, and then press ENTER.
- To copy the range from the worksheet, on the Home tab, in the Clipboard group, click the Paste arrow, and then click the Paste Link button.
- To create a 3-D reference to a range within a worksheet group, enter

    FirstSheet:LastSheet!Range

    where *FirstSheet* is the first sheet in the group, *LastSheet* is the last sheet in the group, and *Range* is a cell range common to all sheets in the group.
- To insert a 3-D reference to a range in a worksheet group, click the sheet tab of the first worksheet in the worksheet group, hold down SHIFT, click the tab for the last sheet in the group, release SHIFT, select the cell range in the selected worksheet group, and then press ENTER.

Gail wants you to determine the total food sales for all eight Tibetan Grill franchises. You will calculate that value using the SUM function with a 3-D cell reference.

To calculate total food sales using a 3-D cell reference:

▶ 1. Go to the **Region Summary** worksheet, and then click cell **B6** to select it.

▶ 2. Type **=SUM(** to begin the SUM function.

▶ 3. Click the **Grill5-01** sheet tab. The formula displayed in the formula bar is =SUM('Grill5-01'! showing the first worksheet used in the 3-D reference.

▶ 4. Scroll the sheet tabs until the Grill5-08 sheet tab is visible.

▶ 5. Press and hold **SHIFT**, click the **Grill5-08** sheet tab, and then release **SHIFT**. The formula changes to =SUM('Grill5-01:Grill5-08'! showing the entire worksheet group used in the reference.

▶ 6. Click cell **B5** to complete the 3-D reference. The formula changes to =SUM('Grill5-01:Grill5-08'!B5 in the formula bar.

▶ 7. Type **)** to complete the formula, and then press **ENTER**. The formula returns the value $20,599,586, which is the sum of food sales from all eight Tibetan Grill franchises in Illinois and Iowa.

▶ 8. Click cell **B6** to select it. See Figure 5–8.

Figure 5–8	**3-D reference in the SUM function**

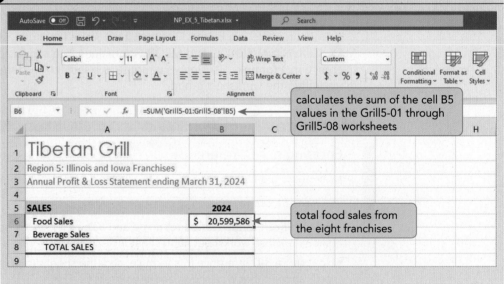

Rather than typing the SUM formula for the rest of the cells in the Region Summary worksheet, you can use AutoFill to copy the formula you created in cell B6. You will use AutoFill now to complete the summary statistics in the Region Summary worksheet.

To calculate the totals for the rest of the worksheet:

▶ **1.** With cell B6 still selected, drag the fill handle down to cell **B44**. The 3-D formula is copied down through the range B7:B44.

▶ **2.** Click the **Auto Fill Options** button ⊞, and then click the **Fill Without Formatting** option button. The cells return to their original formatting. Some cells that were blank now display the value 0.

▶ **3.** In the range B6:B44, select all of the cells displaying 0 or -, and then press **DELETE** to clear the formulas from those cells.

▶ **4.** Click cell **B44** to select it. The total pretax profit from all eight stores is $1,193,864. See Figure 5–9.

Figure 5–9   **3-D cell reference copied through Region Summary worksheet**

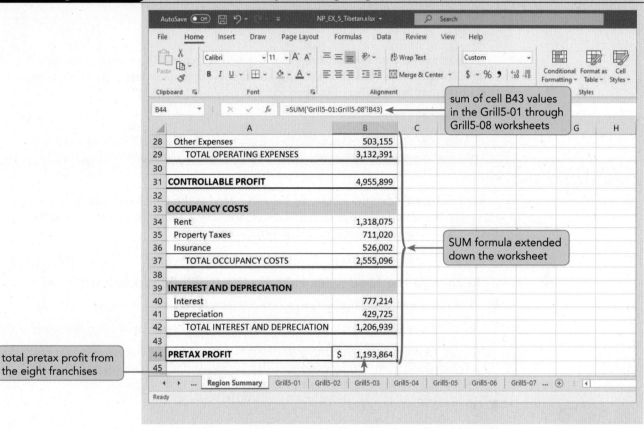

As with 2-D cell references, formulas with 3-D cell references update automatically when any of the values in a referenced worksheet cell change, making 3-D cell references a dynamic tool for analyzing data scattered across a workbook.

Insight

Wildcards and 3-D References

You can create flexible 3-D references by using wildcards. A **wildcard** is a symbol that represents any character, much as wildcards in poker can take on any card value. Two useful wildcards are the question mark (?) wildcard, which represents any single character and the asterisk (*) wildcard, which represents any string of characters. For example, to sum the value of cell B5 from all worksheets beginning with the text string "Grill", you could use the formula

```
=SUM('Grill*'!B5)
```

which would include worksheets named Grill5-01, Grill5-02, and so on in the calculation. If that wildcard expression includes worksheets you don't want to include, you can use the ? wildcard to narrow down the list of matching worksheets. In the following formula, only sheets that have names starting with 'Grill5-0' and followed by a single character would be included in the sum:

```
=SUM('Grill5-0?'!B5)
```

You can also omit any text string and use only wildcards. The following formula calculates the sum of cell B5 from any worksheet with three letters in its name, such as sheet names like Jan, Feb, Mar, and so forth:

```
=SUM('???'!B5)
```

When Excel encounters a wildcard in a worksheet reference, it automatically converts the reference to one in which the sheet name is explicitly entered.

Gail discovered that the food sales values entered in the Grill5-08 worksheet are incorrect. You'll update the data in that sheet, and then confirm that the values in the Region Summary worksheet updated automatically.

To change the food sales value in the Grill5-08 worksheet:

1. Click the **Grill5-08** sheet tab to make Grill5-08 worksheet the active sheet.

2. Click cell **B5**, and then enter **1,322,142** as the correct value for food sales.

3. Go to the **Region Summary** worksheet and verify that the value in cell B6 increased from $20,599,586 to $20,619,586 and that the total pretax profit in cell B44 has increased from $1,193,864 to $1,213,864.

4. Save the workbook.

Gail now has a summary of the profit and losses for the restaurants in the Illinois/Iowa region over the past year. But how do those values compare to previous years? You will answer that question in the next session when you compare the profit and loss values in this workbook to profit and loss statements from other workbooks created over the past several years.

Review

Session 5.1 Quick Check

1. How do you create a worksheet group consisting of sheets that are not adjacent in a workbook?
2. Can a workbook have only one window?
3. How do you ungroup a worksheet group that consists of all the sheets in the workbook?
4. What is the 3-D cell reference to cell C20 in the Monday worksheet?
5. What is the absolute 3-D cell reference to cell C20 in the Monday worksheet?
6. What is the 3-D cell reference to cell C20 in the Monday through Friday worksheet group?
7. Write a formula that uses the MAX function to calculate the maximum value of cell C20 of the Monday through Friday worksheet group.

Session 5.2 Visual Overview:

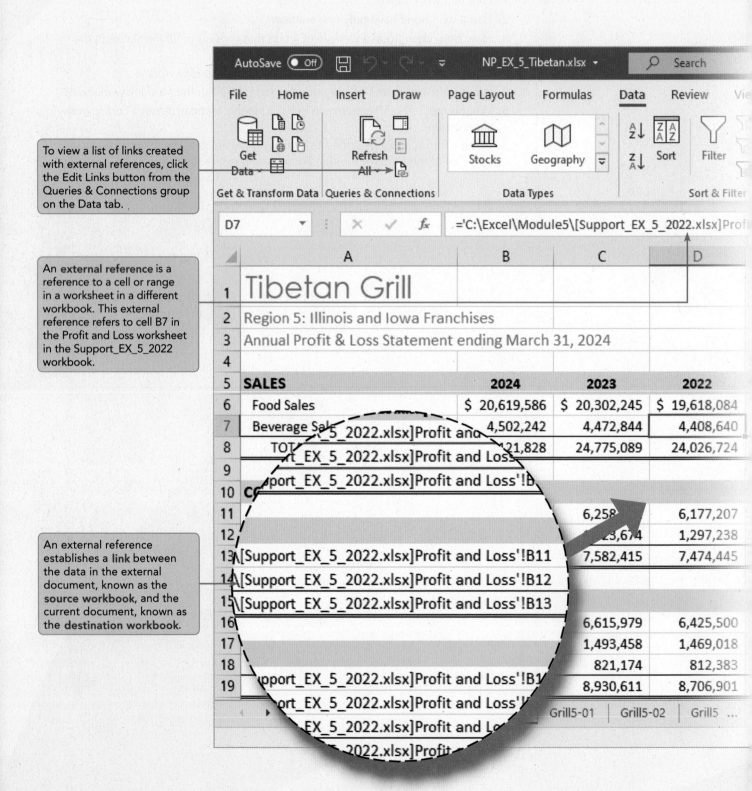

To view a list of links created with external references, click the Edit Links button from the Queries & Connections group on the Data tab.

An **external reference** is a reference to a cell or range in a worksheet in a different workbook. This external reference refers to cell B7 in the Profit and Loss worksheet in the Support_EX_5_2022 workbook.

An external reference establishes a **link** between the data in the external document, known as the **source workbook**, and the current document, known as the **destination workbook**.

External References and Links

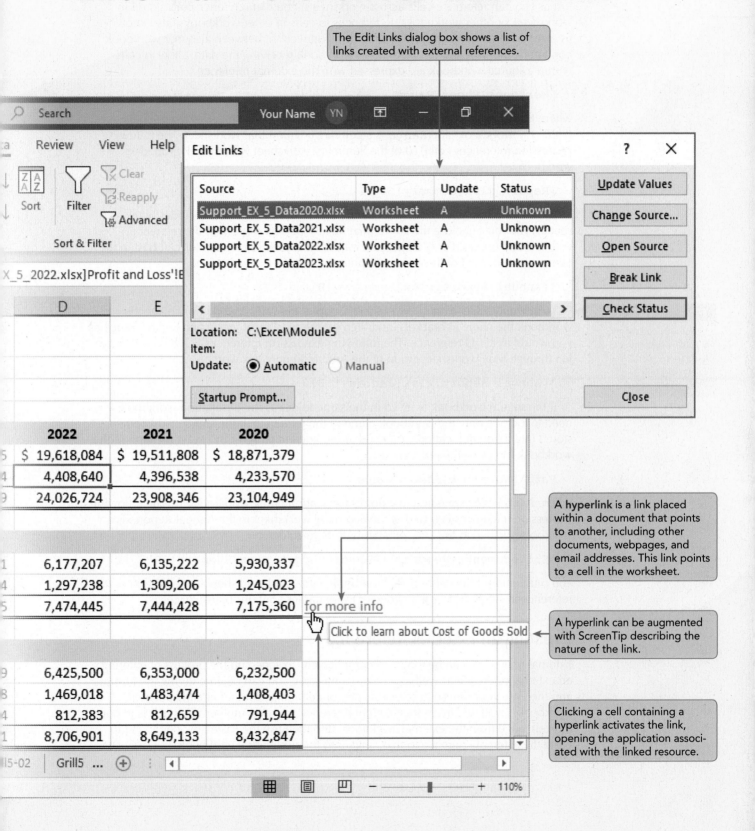

The Edit Links dialog box shows a list of links created with external references.

A **hyperlink** is a link placed within a document that points to another, including other documents, webpages, and email addresses. This link points to a cell in the worksheet.

A hyperlink can be augmented with ScreenTip describing the nature of the link.

Clicking a cell containing a hyperlink activates the link, opening the application associated with the linked resource.

Linking to External Workbooks

Just as you can reference cells across worksheets, you can reference cells stored in worksheets of other workbooks. References to cells in other workbooks, also known as external references, establish a link, or a connection, between a source workbook containing the data and the destination workbook receiving the data. Links to cells within a source workbook are expressed with the external reference

`[Workbook]Sheet!Range`

where `Workbook` is the file name of the source workbook, `Sheet` is a worksheet within the workbook, and `Range` is a cell range within that worksheet. The following expression references cell B10 of the Summary worksheet within the Report.xlsx workbook.

`[Report.xlsx]Summary!B10`

If either the source workbook file name or the worksheet name includes blank spaces, you must enclose the entire `[Workbook]Sheet` portion of the reference within single quotes. For example, the following expression references cell B10 in the Summary worksheet of the Annual Report.xlsx file.

`'[Annual Report.xlsx]Summary'!B10`

> **Tip**
>
> Unlike with worksheets, there's no such thing as a workbook group. You can specify only one workbook at a time.

To reference cells within a worksheet group of the source workbook, place the workbook file name in brackets, and then list the worksheet group and cell reference as you would in a 3-D reference. The following expression references cell B10 within the Jan through May worksheet group of the Annual Report.xlsx workbook:

`'[Annual Report.xlsx]Jan:May'!B10`

If the source workbook is saved in the same folder as the destination workbook, you need to include only the workbook name in the reference. If the source workbook is stored in a different location, you need to include the **path**, or the exact location of the workbook file using the expression

`Path\[Workbook]Sheet!Range`

where `Path` is an expression that points to location of the workbook file. The following expression references cell B10 of the Summary worksheet in the Annual Report.xlsx workbook located in the C:\Documents\Reports folder:

`'C:\Documents\Reports\[Annual Report.xlsx]Summary'!B10`

You must enclose the entire path, workbook name, and worksheet name portion of the reference in single quotes if any one of those names contains blank spaces.

Creating an External Reference

External references can be long and complicated. To speed up the process of entering an external reference as well as to avoid a mistake, you can begin entering the formula and then use your mouse to select the cell or cell range from an already opened workbook. Excel will insert the external reference for you. Another approach is to copy the cell range from the external workbook, and then use the Paste Link command to paste the external reference to that range into the destination workbook.

Reference

Entering an External Reference

- To create an external reference to a range from another workbook, enter

  [*Workbook*]*Sheet*!*Range*

  where *Workbook* is the file name of an Excel workbook, *Sheet* is a worksheet within that workbook, and *Range* is a cell range within that worksheet (enclose workbook or worksheet names that include spaces within a set of single quotes).
- To insert the external reference into a formula as you type, click the cell range from the source workbook and press ENTER.
- To enter the external reference into a formula, copy the range from the source workbook, in the destination workbook, on the Home tab, in the Clipboard group, click the Paste arrow, and then click the Paste Link button.
- To create an external reference to a source workbook stored at a different location than the destination workbook, enter

  Path\[*Workbook*]*Sheet*!*Range*

  where *Path* is the location of the folder containing the source workbook (enclose the path, workbook, or worksheet names that include spaces within a set of single quotes).

Gail wants you to create a link to the profit and loss statement in the previous year's report. You will use the Paste Link feature to insert this external reference.

To insert an external reference to the previous year's data:

1. If you took a break after the previous session, make sure that the NP_EX_5_Tibetan workbook is open and the Region Summary worksheet is active.

2. Open the **Support_EX_5_2023.xlsx** workbook located in the **Excel5 > Module** folder included with your Data Files.

3. In the Profit and Loss worksheet, select the range **B5:B44** containing the previous year's profit and loss values.

4. On the Home tab, in the Clipboard group, click the **Copy** button to copy the data.

5. Return to the **NP_EX_5_Tibetan** workbook, and then click cell **C5** in the Region Summary worksheet to select it.

6. On the Home tab, in the Clipboard group, click the **Paste arrow** to open the Paste gallery, and then in the Other Paste Options section, click the **Paste Link** button 📋. Excel inserts links to the cells in the Support_EX_5_Data2023 workbook, starting with the formula =`'[Support_EX_5_Data2023.xlsx] Profit and Loss'!B5` in cell C5 and extending down through cell C44 showing the pretax profit from 2023.

7. Click the **column B** header to select the entire column, and then in the Clipboard group, click the **Format Painter** button to copy the format from that column.

8. Click the **column C** header to paste the copied formats.

9. Click cell **C5** to select it. See Figure 5–10.

> Make sure to use the Paste Link option so you paste the reference to the copied cells rather than pasting the cell values.

Figure 5–10   **Formula with an external reference**

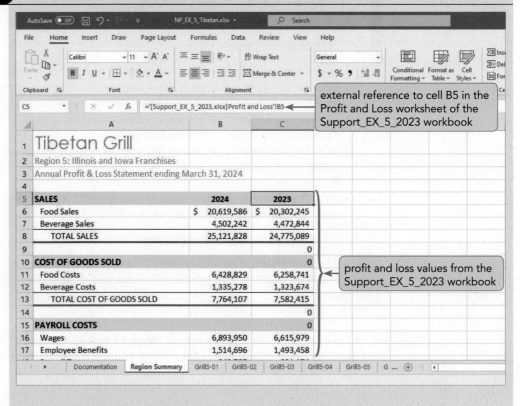

You learn that there has been an increase in total sales from the previous year, but there has also been an increase in the total cost of goods sold. Is this part of a trend? To find out, you'll retrieve more data from other years of profit and loss statements.

To insert internal references to more years of data:

1. Repeat the previous set of steps, using the Paste Link command to create external references to the profit and loss values in the **Support_EX_5_2022.xlsx**, **Support_EX_5_2021.xlsx**, and **Support_EX_5_2020.xlsx** workbooks, placing the linked data in columns D through F. Several rows show zero or - because they contain formulas the reference empty cells in the source documents. You will remove those formulas.

2. Use **DELETE** on your keyboard to clear the zeros or - from rows 9, 10, 14, 15, 20, 22, 23, 30, 32, 33, 38, 39, and 43 in columns C through F of the Region Summary worksheet.

3. Scroll up the worksheet and click cell **F5** to select it. See Figure 5–11.

Figure 5–11   Profit and loss values from 2020 through 2024

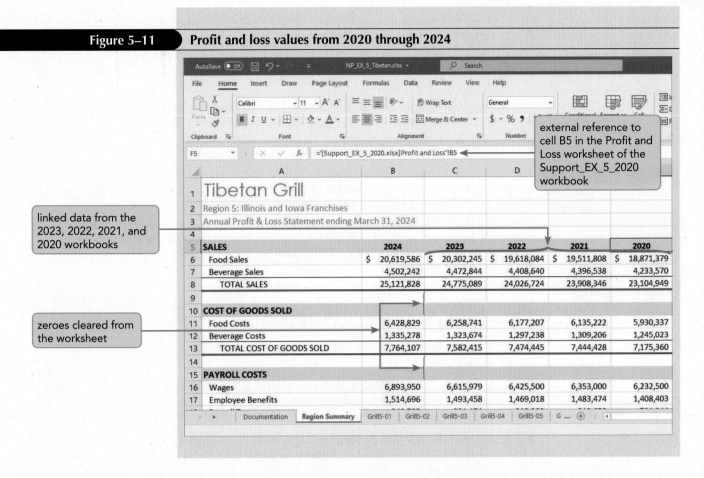

linked data from the 2023, 2022, 2021, and 2020 workbooks

external reference to cell B5 in the Profit and Loss worksheet of the Support_EX_5_2020 workbook

zeroes cleared from the worksheet

The annual profit and loss values show an interesting trend. Total sales have increased every year from the eight Illinois/Iowa franchises, rising from $23,104,949 in 2020 to $25,121,828 in 2024 (the range B8:F8). But pretax profits have decreased in the last year, dropping from $1,416,783 in 2023 (cell C44) to $1,213,864 in 2024 (cell B44). The decreased profit margin in the face of increasing sales indicates that rising costs are eating into profits. Gail also notices that payroll costs have increased by almost $320,000 from $8,930,611 in 2023 (cell C19) to $9,249,431 in 2024 (cell B19), which might be the important factor in the declining in profits. These are the types of insights that a workbook combining data from multiple worksheets and workbooks can provide.

Updating Workbook Links

If both the destination and source workbooks are currently open, any changes you make to data in the source workbook will also be reflected in the destination workbook. Gail has a correction for the food sales value in the 2023 data. You'll make this edit in the source workbook.

To edit the food sales value in the 2023 data source workbook:

▶ **1.** Go to the **Support_EX_5_2023** workbook.

▶ **2.** Make sure the **Profit and Loss** worksheet is the active sheet, and then in cell **B6**, change the entry from $20,302,245 to **$20,102,245** to correct the food sales value.

◗ **3.** Return to the **NP_EX_5_Tibetan** workbook and verify that cell C6 in the Region Summary worksheet displays the value $20,102,245.

Next you will explore how to manage the links created by your external references.

External References and Security Concerns

Tip

You can view and edit the Excel security settings by clicking the File on the ribbon, clicking Options in Backstage view, and then clicking Trust Center in the Excel Options dialog box.

There are security issues involved with the linking to external source documents. It is possible you could open a workbook that contains links to malicious software. For that reason, Excel disables links to source documents unless you explicitly indicate that you trust the data source. Once you have indicated that you trust the source, Excel will add the source document to its list of trusted documents and you will not be prompted again.

You will explore how to work with the Excel security measures as you work with the NP_EX_5_Tibetan workbook.

To open the linked Tibetan Grill workbooks:

◗ **1.** Save the **NP_EX_5_Tibetan** and **Support_EX_5_2023** workbooks, and then close them.

◗ **2.** Close the **Support_EX_5_2022**, **Support_EX_5_2021**, and **Support_EX_5_2020** workbooks, but do *not* save any changes that you may have inadvertently made during this session.

◗ **3.** Reopen the **NP_EX_5_Tibetan** workbook. Excel shows a status message requesting confirmation that the links in this workbook are from known and trusted data sources.

◗ **4.** Click the **Enable Content** button.

◗ **5.** Close the **NP_EX_5_Tibetan** workbook without saving any changes you may have inadvertently made to the workbook.

◗ **6.** Reopen the **NP_EX_5_Tibetan** workbook. Because you've already indicated that this is a trusted data source, you are not prompted to enable the external content. Instead the dialog box shown in Figure 5–12 opens.

Figure 5-12	Dialog box prompting for action on links to external files

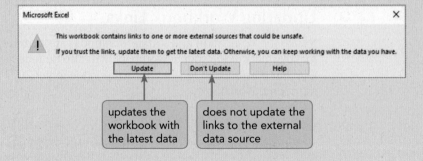

◗ **7.** Click **Update** to update the links.

Excel prompts you to update the links every time you open the workbook to ensure that you are working with the most current data. But what happens after you open the document? If several people are working with a source document at the same time, the data might change from the time you first opened the workbook so that you are no longer working with the most current data. To deal with that problem, you can review and update all of the links currently active in your workbook.

Reviewing Links Within a Workbook

A list of all links in your workbook is available in the Edit Links dialog box. For each link, the Edit Links dialog box shows the following information:

- **Source.** Indicates the source file for a given link
- **Type.** Identifies the type of source file, such as an Excel worksheet, a Word document, or a PowerPoint slideshow
- **Update.** Specifies how values are updated from the linked data source, where the letter *A* indicates the link is updated automatically upon opening the workbook, and *M* indicates that the link is updated manually in response to your request
- **Status.** Shows whether the data source has been accessed during the current session and if so, whether the link has been updated

Within the Edit Links dialog box, you can manually update each link, change a link's data source, open a link's data source, break the connection to the link's data source, or check the status of the link. You'll review the links in the NP_EX_5_Tibetan workbook.

To review the links in the NP_EX_5_Tibetan workbook:

1. On the ribbon, click the **Data** tab to access commands for working with data.

2. In the Queries and Connections group, click the **Edit Links** button. The Edit Links dialog box opens, showing the four links in the workbook, their source file, the type of data source, how the data source is updated, and whether the link has been accessed during this session.

3. Click **Support_EX_5_2023.xlsx** (the last link) in the list.

4. Click **Update Values** to connect to the data source and update the values displayed in the workbook. The status for the Support_EX_5_2023.xlsx workbook changes from Unknown to OK, indicating that Excel has successfully accessed and updated it. See Figure 5–13.

Figure 5–13 Edit Links dialog box

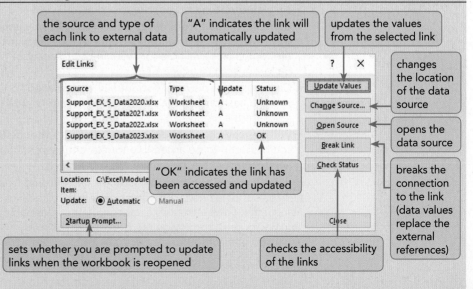

the source and type of each link to external data

"A" indicates the link will automatically updated

updates the values from the selected link

changes the location of the data source

changes the location of the data source

opens the data source

breaks the connection to the link (data values replace the external references)

"OK" indicates the link has been accessed and updated

sets whether you are prompted to update links when the workbook is reopened

checks the accessibility of the links

> **5.** Click **Check Status** to check the accessibility of all listed links. That status of the other links changes from Unknown to OK, indicating that they have also been accessed and updated.

> **6.** Click **Close** to close the dialog box and return to the workbook.

Managing Workbook Links

In some cases, you want to display only a "snapshot" of the data source at a single moment in time, as with financial statements that show final sales and expense figures at the end of the current month or year. To prevent a workbook from updating its content with data you don't want, you can break its link to the data source by clicking the Break Link button in the Edit Links dialog box. Breaking the link will remove the external references from your workbook, replacing them with the data values themselves.

Sometimes the source workbook that a workbook is linked to is renamed or moved. Such a situation can occur for organizations that are restructuring their file system or switching to a new file server. To keep workbook links active and updateable, click the Change Source button in the Edit Links dialog box, and then replace the link to the old location with a link to the data in its new location or with its new name. You do not need to use the Change Source button if the destination and source workbooks both move to a new location and their relative positions within the folder structure are unchanged. Using the Change Source button is necessary only if the location of the source workbook alone is changed.

Proskills

Decision Making: Deciding When to Link Workbooks

At most businesses, a team works together to assemble data used in formulating policy and making decisions. Linked workbooks provide one way to make information compiled by different people or departments accessible to the decision-makers. When choosing whether to create a structure of linked workbooks, consider the following questions:

- **Is a large workbook too difficult to use?** While it may appear simpler to just keep everything within a single file, such workbooks can quickly become large and unwieldy. It is often better to divide information among several workbooks, allowing teams to focus on their own areas of expertise. However, keep in mind that a workbook with many links can also take a long time to open and update.

- **Can separate workbooks share a common design and structure?** Workbooks from different stores, branches, or departments need to have a uniform structure to avoid errors in data entry and analysis. Someone needs to be responsible for ensuring that all related documents adhere to a shared layout and structure.

- **Can information from different workbooks be summarized?** Is there an obvious way to summarize data from several source files within a single workbook, leaving the source files available for more in-depth analysis? Would important information be lost in such a summary?

- **Can source workbooks continually be updated?** Users of the summary workbook will often assume that the information is current and accurate. Are mechanisms in place for the timely update of key data?

- **Will the source workbooks be available to the destination workbook?** Data sources need to be accessible to relevant users so that links can be updated as needed and so the data itself can be reviewed for accuracy and completeness.

If you can answer yes to these questions, then linked workbooks might be the solution to your data needs. Creating a system of linked files can lead to more reliable data management and ultimately better and more informed decisions. A system of linked workbooks can also provide the company with flexibility as data sources become more expansive and complex.

An external reference is only one type of link supported by Excel. You can create links to a wide variety of data sources.

Creating Hyperlinks

Another type of link supported by Excel is a hyperlink, which is a text string or graphic image connected to a wide variety of resources, including:

- Websites
- Files on your computer, such as Word documents, PowerPoint presentations, text files, and PDF documents
- Cells and cell ranges within the current workbook
- Email addresses
- New documents created specifically as the source of the hyperlink

Clicking a hyperlink opens its linked resource using the application associated with that resource. So clicking a cell with a hyperlink to a website opens the website in your default browser; a hyperlink to a Word document opens the document file in Microsoft Word, and so forth. Hyperlinks are helpful in providing users with additional information not found in your workbook. For example, Gail can use hyperlinks to connect her workbook to Tibetan Grill's website or to an operation manual for franchise managers.

Excel recognizes website addresses and email addresses as links. So if you enter a website or email address into a cell, Excel will automatically convert that text into a hyperlink. For other types of links, you must manually define the type of link and its location.

> **Tip**
>
> You can create a hyperlink using the HYPERLINK function in which you specify the text of the link and the link's source.

Linking to a Location Within a Workbook

You can manually create a link within a worksheet cell. Select the cell where you want to place the link. On the ribbon, click the Insert tab, and then in the Links group, click the Link button. The Insert Hyperlink dialog box opens. From the Insert Hyperlink dialog box, specify the type of resource to link to and the hyperlink text associated with that link. You can provide additional information about the hyperlink by adding a ScreenTip.

Reference

Working with Hyperlinks

- To create a hyperlink, select the text, graphic, or cell in which you want to insert the hyperlink. On the Insert tab, in the Links group, click the Hyperlink button. In the Insert Hyperlink dialog box, specify the link's location and the text as needed. Click the ScreenTip button to add a ScreenTip. Click OK.
- To create a hyperlink to a website or email address, type the address in a cell, and then press ENTER or TAB to convert the text into a hyperlink.
- To use a hyperlink, click the text, graphic, or cell containing the hyperlink; or right-click the hyperlink, and then click Open Hyperlink on the shortcut menu.
- To remove a hyperlink, right-click the hyperlink, and then click Remove Hyperlink on the shortcut menu.
- To edit a hyperlink, right-click the hyperlink, and then click Edit Hyperlink on the shortcut menu.

Gail thinks that some of the terms in the profit and loss statement might not be familiar to users. She asks you to create a hyperlink between those terms and their definitions on the Terms and Definitions worksheet. You'll create some of these hyperlinks now.

To create hyperlinks to the Prime Costs and Controllable Profits entries in the Region Summary worksheet:

1. On the Region Summary worksheet, click cell **G21**, which is next to the data on prime costs.

2. On the ribbon, click the **Insert** tab, and then in the Links group, click the **Link** button. The Insert Hyperlink dialog box opens.

3. In the Text to display box, type **for more info** as the text of the hyperlink.

4. In the Link to section, click **Place in This Document** to display a list of places in the workbook you can link to.

5. In the Type the cell reference box, type **C16** as the cell reference, and then in the Or select a place in this document list, click **Terms and Definitions** to specify that the link be created to cell C16 in the Terms and Definitions worksheet. See Figure 5–14.

| Figure 5–14 | Insert Hyperlink dialog box |

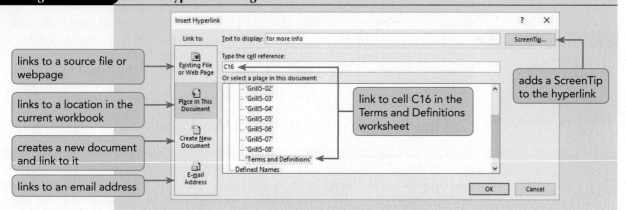

links to a source file or webpage

links to a location in the current workbook

creates a new document and link to it

links to an email address

link to cell C16 in the Terms and Definitions worksheet

adds a ScreenTip to the hyperlink

6. Click **ScreenTip** to open the Set Hyperlink ScreenTip dialog box.

7. In the ScreenTip text box, type **Click to learn more about Prime Costs** as the ScreenTip text, and then click **OK** to return to the Insert Hyperlink dialog box.

8. Click **OK** to insert the hyperlink into cell G21. The text "for more info" appears in cell G21, underlined and in green.

9. Repeat Steps 2 through 8 to link cell **G31** in the Region Summary worksheet to cell **C18** in the **Terms and Definitions worksheet** using **Click to learn more about Controllable Profit** as the ScreenTip text.

Excel indicates hyperlinked text by displaying the text in a green font and underlined. To use a link, click the cell containing the hyperlink. Excel will then jump to the linked location in the workbook. You will test the hyperlinks you created in cells G21 and G31 now.

To use the hyperlinks you created:

1. Point to cell **G21** to view the ScreenTip for that hyperlink. See Figure 5–15.

Figure 5–15 **Hyperlink text within a worksheet**

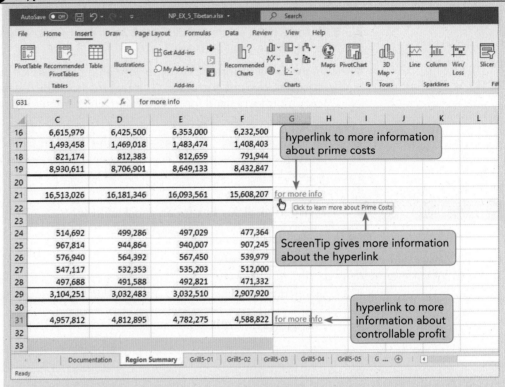

Tip

Only linked text within a cell is treated as a hyperlink; text extending beyond the cell's borders is not.

2. Click cell **G21** to make cell C16 in the Terms and Definitions worksheet the active cell.

3. Read the definition of the Prime Costs definition entered in cell C16.

4. Return to the **Region Summary** worksheet and click cell **G31** to make cell C18 in the Terms and Definitions worksheet the active cell.

5. Read the definition of Controllable Profit and return to the **Region Summary** worksheet.

If you need to edit an existing hyperlink, right-click the cell, text, or graphic containing the link, and then click Edit Hyperlink on the shortcut menu to open the Edit Hyperlink dialog box. To remove a hyperlink, right-click the link, and then click Remove Hyperlink on the shortcut menu.

Linking to an Email Address

You can make it easier for users to send you messages about your workbook by adding a hyperlink to your email address. Clicking a linked email address automatically opens the user's email program to a new message with your email address and a preset subject line already inserted. Gail wants you to add an email address to the Documentation sheet of the NP_EX_5_Tibetan workbook so users can easily submit questions and queries about the workbook's contents. You'll create this email link now.

To link to an email address:

1. Go to the **Documentation** sheet, and then click cell **B3** containing your name.

2. On the Insert tab, in the Links group, click the **Link** button. The Insert Hyperlink dialog box opens.

3. In the Link to section, click **E-mail Address** to display the options for creating a link to an email address.

4. In the E-mail address box, type your email address (or the email address specified by your instructor). The text *mailto:*, which is an Internet communication protocol used for linking to email addresses, appears before the email address.

5. In the Subject box, type **Regarding the Tibetan Grill Profit and Loss Statement** as the subject line of any email created using this link. See Figure 5–16.

Figure 5–16	Insert Hyperlink dialog box for an email address

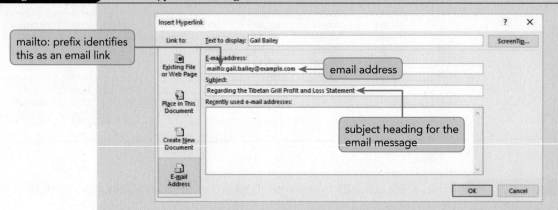

mailto: prefix identifies this as an email link

email address

subject heading for the email message

6. Click the **ScreenTip** button, type **Email me for questions about the workbook** in the Set Hyperlink ScreenTip dialog box, and then click **OK**.

7. In the Insert Hyperlink dialog box, click **OK** to insert the hyperlink in cell B3 of the Documentation sheet.

8. Click cell **B3** and verify that your email program opens to a new message with your email address and the subject line already filled in.

9. Close the email message without sending it.

10. Save the workbook.

Tip

To select a cell containing a hyperlink without activating the link, right-click the cell.

Note that the hyperlinks you added are part of the workbook, but they won't appear in the Edit Links dialog box. That dialog box is used only for data values retrieved from external sources.

You've completed your work on external reference and links. In the next session, you will learn how to assign names to references to make it easier to write and understand formulas.

Review

Session 5.2 Quick Check

1. What is the external reference to cell C20 of the Final Report worksheet located in the Annual Statement.xlsx workbook?

2. What is the external reference to cell D10 of the Sunday worksheet located in the Weekly Report.xlsx workbook that is stored in the C:\Documents\ Reports folder?

3. When would you paste a copied cell using the Paste Link option?

4. How do you check the status of a link within the current workbook to determine whether the link's source file is accessible and up-to-date?

5. How does Excel indicate that a cell contains linked text?

6. What does Excel do when a hyperlink is clicked by the user?

Session 5.3 Visual Overview:

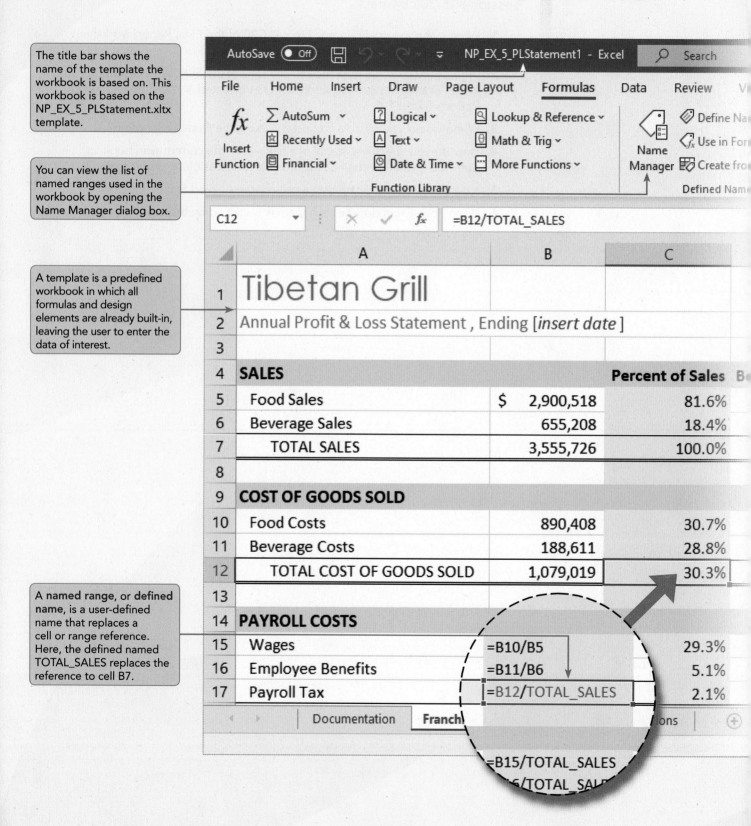

The title bar shows the name of the template the workbook is based on. This workbook is based on the NP_EX_5_PLStatement.xltx template.

You can view the list of named ranges used in the workbook by opening the Name Manager dialog box.

A template is a predefined workbook in which all formulas and design elements are already built-in, leaving the user to enter the data of interest.

A named range, or defined name, is a user-defined name that replaces a cell or range reference. Here, the defined named TOTAL_SALES replaces the reference to cell B7.

AutoSave ● Off · 🖫 · ↺ · ↻ · ⩫ · NP_EX_5_PLStatement1 - Excel · 🔍 Search

File · Home · Insert · Draw · Page Layout · **Formulas** · Data · Review

Insert Function · Σ AutoSum ˅ · ⭐ Recently Used ˅ · Financial ˅ · ? Logical ˅ · Text ˅ · Date & Time ˅ · Lookup & Reference ˅ · Math & Trig ˅ · More Functions ˅ · Name Manager · Define Na... · Use in For... · Create fro...

Function Library · Defined Name...

C12 · fx · =B12/TOTAL_SALES

	A	B	C
1	Tibetan Grill		
2	Annual Profit & Loss Statement , Ending [*insert date*]		
3			
4	**SALES**		**Percent of Sales**
5	Food Sales	$ 2,900,518	81.6%
6	Beverage Sales	655,208	18.4%
7	TOTAL SALES	3,555,726	100.0%
8			
9	**COST OF GOODS SOLD**		
10	Food Costs	890,408	30.7%
11	Beverage Costs	188,611	28.8%
12	TOTAL COST OF GOODS SOLD	1,079,019	30.3%
13			
14	**PAYROLL COSTS**		
15	Wages	=B10/B5	29.3%
16	Employee Benefits	=B11/B6	5.1%
17	Payroll Tax	=B12/TOTAL_SALES	2.1%

Documentation | **Franch**... | ...ons | ⊕

=B15/TOTAL_SALES
...5/TOTAL_SAL...

Named Ranges and Templates

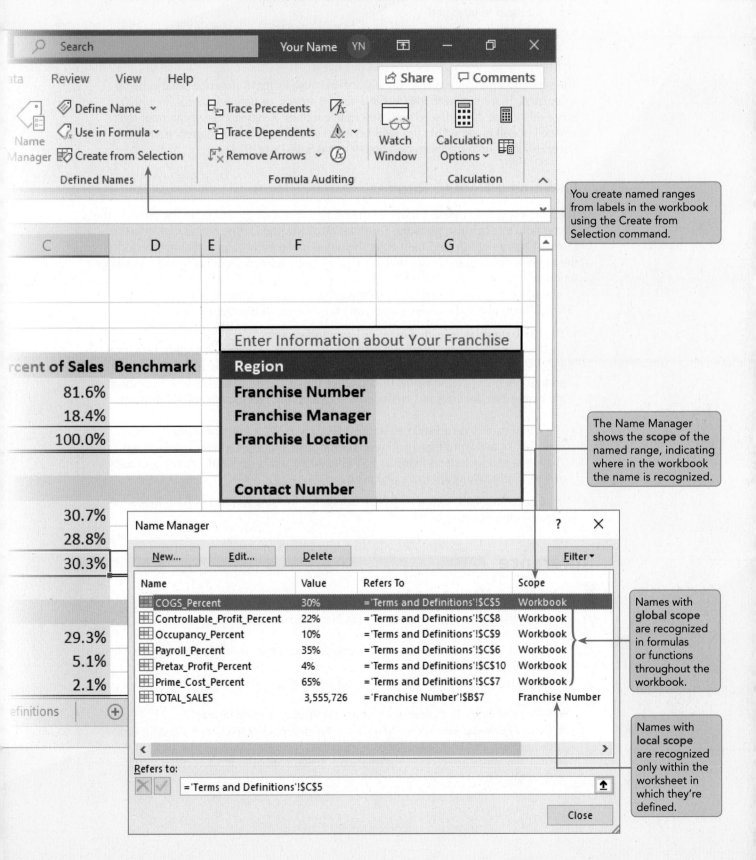

You create named ranges from labels in the workbook using the Create from Selection command.

The Name Manager shows the scope of the named range, indicating where in the workbook the name is recognized.

Names with global scope are recognized in formulas or functions throughout the workbook.

Names with local scope are recognized only within the worksheet in which they're defined.

Simplifying Formulas with Named Ranges

If you are showing your workbook to other people, which of the following formulas is easier for them to interpret?

```
=B7 - B28

=Income - Expenses
```

The second formula is easier to understand because its terms describe what is being calculated. That's the basic idea behind named ranges, or defined names, in which range references are replaced with descriptive names. A named range can refer to any cell or cell range within the workbook, so you can replace a reference such as Sheet1!B7:B43 with the more descriptive name SalesData2024.

Defining a Named Range

The simplest way to define a named range is to select a range and enter the name in the Name box. You can also go to the Formulas tab, click the Define Name button in the Defined Names group, and then enter the name in the New Names dialog box. Once the name is defined, it can be used in place of range references in any Excel formula or function.

The name you use should be short, meaningful, and descriptive of the range being defined. Keep in mind that any name you choose must follow these rules:

- The name must begin with a letter or _ (an underscore).
- The name can include letters and numbers as well as periods and underscores, but it cannot include other symbols or spaces. To distinguish multiword names, use an underscore between the words or capitalize the first letter of each word. For example, the names Net_Income and NetIncome are valid, but Net Income and Net-Income are not.
- The name cannot be a valid cell address (such as A20), a function name (such as Average), or any word that Excel reserves for other purposes (such as Print_Area).
- The name can include as many as 255 characters, although short, meaningful names of 5 to 15 characters are more practical.

Names are not case sensitive, so the named range Sales and SALES both reference the same cell address.

Reference

Defining a Named Range

- Select the range, type the name in the Name box, and then press ENTER.
  or
- Select the range, and then on the Formulas tab, in the Defined Names group, click the Define Name button.
- Type a name in the Name box, and then click OK.
  or
- Select the data values and labels you want used as named ranges.
- On the Formulas tab, in the Defined Names group, click the Create from Selection button.
- Click the check box to indicate where the labels appear in the selection.
- Click OK.

You will use named ranges as you analyze the profit and loss statements from the eight Tibetan Grill franchises. In the restaurant industry, incomes and expenses are often expressed in terms of their percent of total sales. For example, instead of only noting that the Chicago franchise has total payroll costs of $2,374,845, a profit and loss statement would also include the fact that Chicago's payroll costs were 36.3% of its total sales. This is done to compare restaurants operating in differently sized markets. The Tibetan Grill operating in Chicago should show a larger income, expense, and hopefully, profit, than a franchise operating in a smaller market like Rockford. But that doesn't mean the Chicago franchise is better managed. Expressing the profit and loss figures as a percent of total sales provides a way of determining whether the franchise is adequately managing its expenses regardless of the size of its market.

Gail entered industry benchmarks for different parts of the profit and loss statement in the Terms and Definitions worksheet. The worksheet shows a benchmark percentage for payroll costs of 35%, meaning that, regardless of the size of the market, a restaurant should spend no more than about 35% of its total sales income on payroll. You will create named ranges for these benchmark values so that you can display their values in the profit and loss statements for the eight franchises.

To define a named range using the Name box:

▶ **1.** If you took a break at the end of the previous session, make sure the NP_EX_5_Tibetan workbook is open.

▶ **2.** Go to the **Terms and Definitions** worksheet, and then click cell **C5** containing 30% as the benchmark for cost of goods as a percentage of total sales.

▶ **3.** Click the **Name box** to select the cell reference.

▶ **4.** Type **COGS_Percent** as the name of the defined range, and then press **ENTER**. The COGS_Percent named range now points to cell C5 of the Terms and Definitions worksheet. See Figure 5–17.

Figure 5–17	Named range defined in the Name box

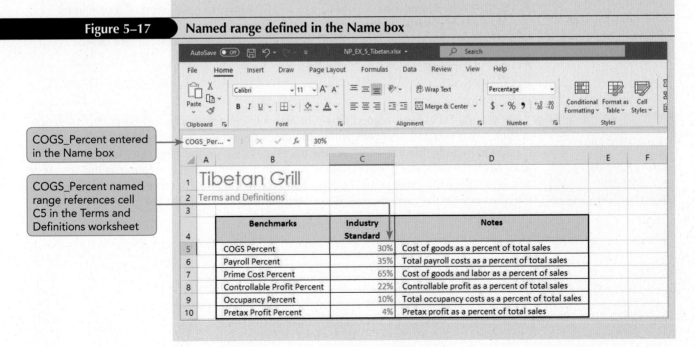

COGS_Percent entered in the Name box

COGS_Percent named range references cell C5 in the Terms and Definitions worksheet

If you have many names to define, a more efficient approach is to use labels entered in the cells adjacent to the data cells as your names. The Create from Selection button in the Defined Names group on the Formulas tab automatically generates the named ranges based on the label text. In the Terms and Definitions worksheet, range B6:B10 contains other labels for the industry benchmarks, and the range C6:C10 contains the benchmark percent figures. You will use those labels to define named ranges for the values in the range C6:C10.

To define named ranges using labels in adjacent cells:

1. In the Terms and Definitions worksheet, select the range **B6:C10** containing the industry benchmark labels and their associated values.

Tip

You can also press CTRL+SHIFT+F3 to open the Create Names from Selection dialog box.

2. On the ribbon, click the **Formulas** tab, and then in the Defined Names group, click the **Create from Selection** button. The Create Names from Selection dialog box opens.

3. If necessary, click the **Left column** check box to insert a checkmark, leaving the other check boxes unselected. See Figure 5–18.

Figure 5–18 Create Names from Selection dialog box

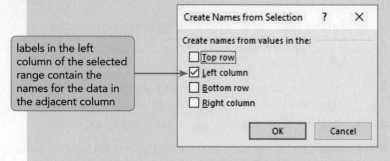

labels in the left column of the selected range contain the names for the data in the adjacent column

4. Click **OK** to define the named ranges.

5. Click the **Name box arrow** to see all six named ranges listed. These names match the labels in the range B5:B10. Because the names cannot contain spaces, the underscore (_) replaced the spaces in the benchmark labels.

6. Press **ESC** to close the Name box.

Tip

You can select a named range in the Name box to jump to its location wherever it is in the workbook and select it.

By default, Excel treats named ranges as absolute cell references. However, the reference is dynamic. If you add new cells within the range the reference for the range name will expand to include the new cells and contract if cells within the range are deleted. If you remove all the cells, the named range will lose its reference and any formulas that invoke it will return the #REF error value. Finally, if you move the referenced cells to a new location, the reference for the named range is updated automatically so that the name will always point to your data.

Proskills

Written Communication: Saving Time with Defined Names

Words can be more descriptive than numbers. This is especially true with cell references. Compared to the letter and number references for cells, a named range provides a more intuitive reference, which is increasingly important as the workbook becomes longer and more complex. Other advantages of named ranges are:

- Names such as TaxRate and TotalSales are more descriptive than cell references and are easier to remember and apply.
- Names in formulas clearly show users exactly what is being calculated. For example, a formula like =GrossPay−Deductions is more easily interpreted than =C15−C16.
- Names remain associated with their range. If a range is moved within the workbook, its name moves with it. Any formulas that contain the name automatically reference the new location.
- Named ranges operate like absolute cell references. If a formula containing a named range is moved or copied, the reference remains pointed to the correct range.

Using defined names saves time and gives everyone reviewing the worksheet a clearer understanding of what that worksheet is doing and what the results mean.

Using Named Ranges in Formulas

A named range can be used in place of a cell reference in any Excel formula or function. So, the 3-D reference in the formula

```
=SUM('Sales Data'!E4:E20)
```

can be replaced with

```
=SUM(salesFigures)
```

where `salesFigures` refers to the 'Sales Data'!E4:E20 location.

You can insert names into a formula by typing them directly in the formula or by clicking the Use in Formula button in the Defined Names group on the Formulas tab.

Gail wants you to display the benchmark values within each franchise's profit and loss statement. To enter the formulas at the same time across all eight worksheets, you will group the eight worksheets and then create formulas using the named ranges you defined.

To create formulas for the benchmark values:

▶ 1. Click the **Grill5-01** sheet tab, hold down **SHIFT**, click the **Grill5-08** sheet tab, and then release **SHIFT** to make the Grill5-01 through Grill5-08 worksheets a worksheet group.

▶ 2. Click cell **D12**, and then type **=** to begin the formula.

▶ 3. Type **cog** as the first letters of the COGS_Percent named range. As you type, a list of functions and named ranges that start with those letters appear. See Figure 5–19.

Figure 5–19   **Named range being added to a formula**

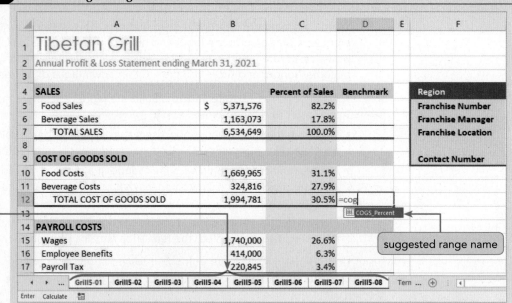

worksheets are grouped

suggested range name

Tip

You can also click the Use in Formula button in the Defined Names group on the Formulas tab and select the name from a list of available named ranges.

4. Press **TAB** to complete the formula **=COGS_Percent**, and then press **ENTER**. The value 30.0% is displayed in cell D12, which is also the value of C5 in the Terms and Definitions worksheet.

5. In cell **D18**, enter **=Payroll_Percent** as the formula. The value 35.0% is displayed in the cell.

6. In cell **D20**, enter **=Prime_Cost_Percent** as the formula. The value 65.0% is displayed in the cell.

7. In cell **D30**, enter **=Controllable_Profit_Percent** as the formula. The value 22.0% is displayed in the cell.

8. In cell **D36**, enter **=Occupancy_Percent** as the formula. The value 10.0% appears in the cell.

9. In cell D43, enter **=Pretax_Profit_Percent** as the formula. The value 4.0% appears in the cell. See Figure 5–20.

Figure 5–20   Named ranges used in formulas

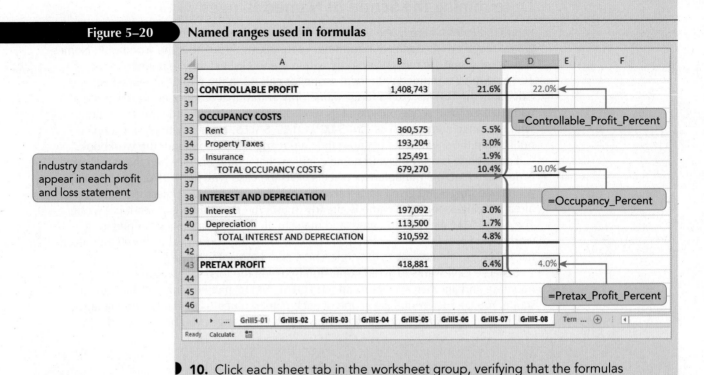

industry standards appear in each profit and loss statement

▶ **10.** Click each sheet tab in the worksheet group, verifying that the formulas containing named ranges are duplicated on every sheet in the group.

Comparing the franchise figures with the industry benchmarks helps Gail locate possible sources of trouble. For example, the Rockford franchise (Grill5-04), which showed a net loss during the past year, also spent 43% of its total sales on payroll, far exceeding the recommended 35% goal (cell D18).

Because total sales are involved in so many calculations in the profit and loss statements, Gail wants you to create a named range for total sales in each of the eight franchise profit and loss worksheets.

To define a named range for total sales:

▶ **1.** In the worksheet group, click the **Grill5-01** sheet tab to make it the active sheet within the group.

▶ **2.** Select the range **A7:B7**. This selects the range in each worksheet in the group.

▶ **3.** On the ribbon, click the **Formulas** tab, and then in the Defined Names group, click the **Create from Selection** button. The Create Names from Selection dialog box opens.

▶ **4.** Make sure only the **Left column** check box is selected, and then click **OK**. The named range TOTAL_SALES associated with cell B7 is created for each worksheet in the group.

▶ **5.** On the formula bar, click the **Name box arrow** to display a list of defined names and verify that the new defined name TOTAL_SALES appears in the list of names.

Because the worksheets were grouped when you used the Create from Selection commands, the action of creating the named range TOTAL_SALES was duplicated on each of the grouped worksheets. So how does Excel manage eight TOTAL_SALES named ranges? That question brings up the issue of scope.

Determining the Scope of Named Ranges

Scope indicates where in the workbook the named range is recognized. Names with global scope are recognized in formulas or functions throughout the workbook. Names with local scope are recognized only within the worksheet they're defined in. So, if TOTAL_SALES is defined with local scope for cell B7 in the Grill5-02 worksheet, you can apply the TOTAL_SALES range name only within that worksheet. To reference a name with a local scope outside of its worksheet, you must include the sheet along with the range name, such as Grill5-02!TOTAL_SALES. Names with global scope do not require the sheet name because they are recognized throughout the workbook.

Local scope is used to avoid name conflicts that would occur when the same name is duplicated across multiple worksheets, as is the case with the TOTAL_SALES name. All named ranges are given global scope when they are created unless that name is already being used. If the name is already in use, the new name is given local scope. The Name Manager lets you view and manage all the named ranges defined for a workbook. From the Name Manager, you can learn the current value stored with each named range, the cell range they reference, and the name's scope.

Because Gail wants to avoid confusion between the total sales value for one franchise and another, she wants all the TOTAL_SALES named ranges to have local scope. You can determine the scope of each named range using the Name Manager. You'll open the Name Manager to review the named ranges you have created.

To open the Name Manager:

▶ **1.** If necessary, click the **Formulas** tab on the ribbon.

▶ **2.** In the Defined Names group, click the **Name Manager** button (or press **CTRL+F3**). The Name Manager dialog box opens. See Figure 5–21.

Figure 5–21   **Name Manager dialog box**

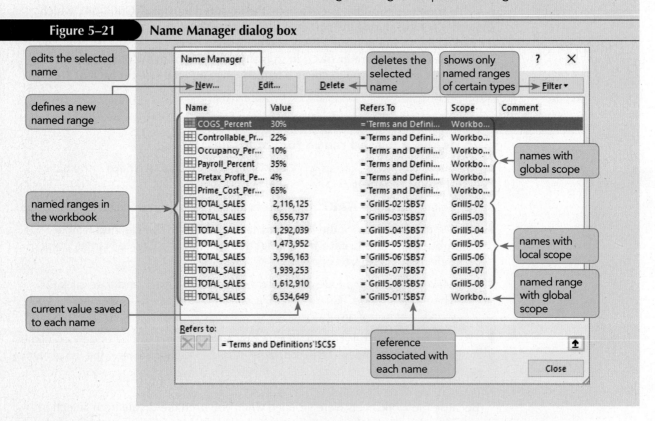

- edits the selected name
- defines a new named range
- named ranges in the workbook
- current value saved to each name
- deletes the selected name
- shows only named ranges of certain types
- names with global scope
- names with local scope
- named range with global scope
- reference associated with each name

The Name Manager lists the 14 names defined for the workbook. The first six have global scope and point to ranges in the Terms and Definitions worksheet. The next eight are all named TOTAL_SALES and have local scope, confining them to use within the Grill5-02 through Grill5-08 worksheet. Only the TOTAL_SALES name from the Grill5-01 worksheet has global scope and can be referenced anywhere within the workbook.

The TOTAL_SALES name for the Grill5-01 worksheet has global scope because it was the first TOTAL_SALES name created when you were defining names in the worksheet group (Grill5-01 was the active sheet in that group). Once that named range had global scope, the other TOTAL_SALES names were forced to have local scope because the same name cannot be used more than once if it has global scope. If it did, Excel would have no way of resolving the conflict.

Gail wants the TOTAL_SALES name for the Grill5-01 worksheet to also have local scope to avoid confusion. You can't change the scope of a named range once it's created. Instead, you must delete and recreate the name using the Name Manager. You will use the Name Manager to delete and recreate the TOTAL_SALES name as a name with local scope for the Grill5-01 worksheet.

To delete and recreate the TOTAL_SALES defined name:

1. In the Name Manager dialog box, click the **TOTAL_SALES** named range that references cell B7 in the Grill5-01 worksheet and has a current value of 6,534,649.

2. Click **Delete** to delete the TOTAL_SALES name, and then click **OK** in the dialog box that appears to confirm the deletion. The TOTAL_SALES name for the Grill5-01 worksheet no longer appears in the Name list.

3. Click **New** to open the New Name dialog box.

4. In the Name box, type **TOTAL_SALES** as the name for the new defined name, and then press **TAB**.

> Make sure you select the worksheet from the Scope list box to create a named range of local scope.

5. In the Scope list, select **Grill5-01** as the worksheet. This specifies that scope of the TOTAL_SALES named range you are creating will be restricted to the Grill5-01 worksheet.

6. Press **TAB** twice to move to the Refers to box.

7. Click cell **B7** in the Grill5-01 worksheet. The reference ='Grill5-01'$B$7 appears in the Refers to box. See Figure 5–22.

Figure 5–22	New Name dialog box

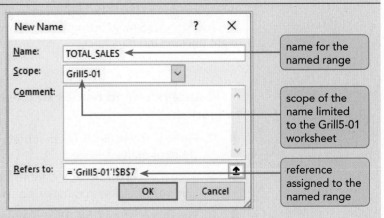

◗ **8.** Click **OK** to close the New Name dialog box and return to the Name Manager dialog box.

◗ **9.** Verify that the TOTAL_SALES name with the Scope value set to Grill5-01 appears in the list of named ranges.

◗ **10.** Click **Close** to close the Name Manager dialog box.

Next you will use the TOTAL_SALES range names in the calculations from the eight profit and loss statements.

Insight

Naming Constants

In addition to referencing ranges in a workbook, names can also store specific values. If you commonly use constants in your formulas, you can name the constant by completing the following steps:

1. In the Name Manager dialog box, click the New button. The New Name dialog box opens.
2. In the New name box, enter a name for the defined name.
3. In the Refers to box, enter the expression =*value* where *value* is the constant value stored in the defined name.
4. Click OK.

Once the constant is named, it can be used in any formula or function. For example, you can create a constant named salesTax that stores the value 0.05. Then the formula =B10*salesTax would multiply the value in cell B10 by 0.05. By storing named constants rather than using a worksheet cell, you can simplify your workbook and make it easier to write meaningful formulas and functions.

Using Defined Names in Existing Formulas

Once you have defined a named range, you can have Excel replace all cell references in formulas and functions with the equivalent name. One advantage of such a substitution is that it makes your code easier to interpret.

To apply names to an existing set of formulas click the Apply Names command in the Defines Name button on the Formulas tab. This command cannot be used with a worksheet group. It can be applied only to ranges within individual sheets. You'll apply the TOTAL_SALES range names in formulas from the profit and loss statement from the eight Tibetan Grill franchises.

To apply defined names to existing formulas in the profit and loss worksheets:

◗ **1.** Right-click the **Grill5-01** sheet tab, and then click **Ungroup Sheets** on the shortcut menu.

◗ **2.** Save the workbook. You want to save before using the Apply Names command in case you make a mistake in the substitution.

◗ **3.** Select the range **C5:C43** containing the formulas that calculate the percent of total sales values.

◗ **4.** On the Formulas tab, in the Defined Names group, click the **Define Name arrow**, and then click **Apply Names**. The Apply Names dialog box opens.

5. In the Apply names list, make sure **TOTAL_SALES** is selected. You want to replace every reference to cell B7 in the current worksheet with the TOTAL_SALES name.

6. Verify that the **Ignore Relative/Absolute** check box is selected so that the name is applied whether cell B7 is referenced using an absolute or relative reference. See Figure 5–23.

Figure 5–23   Apply Names dialog box

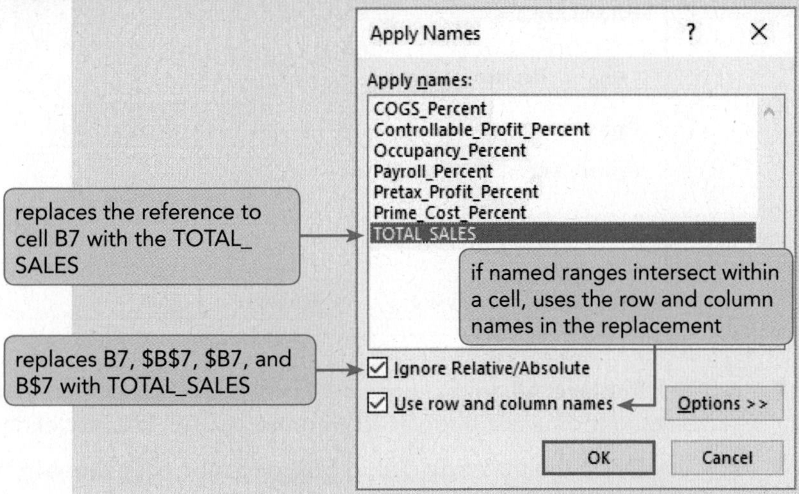

replaces the reference to cell B7 with the TOTAL_SALES

replaces B7, $B$7, $B7, and B$7 with TOTAL_SALES

if named ranges intersect within a cell, uses the row and column names in the replacement

7. Click **OK** to apply the named range to formulas in the selected cells.

8. Click each cell in the range C5:C43 of the Grill5-01 worksheet, verifying that references to cell B7 have been replaced with TOTAL_SALES.

Trouble? If the replacement was not made, you may have made a mistake when using the Apply Names command. Close the workbook without saving changes, reopen the workbook, and repeat Steps 3 through 7.

You cannot use the Apply Names command for worksheet groups. But, you can use the Find and Replace command to replace every occurrence of a cell reference with its equivalent defined name within a worksheet group. You'll use this technique to replace every reference to cell B7 with TOTAL_SALES in the remaining franchise profit and loss statements.

To replace cell references with the TOTAL_SALES defined name:

1. Save the workbook so that if you make a mistake, you can close the workbook without saving changes and then reopen the workbook and repeat this set of steps.

2. Click the **Grill5-02** sheet tab, hold down **SHIFT**, click the **Grill5-08** sheet tab, and then release **SHIFT**. The Grill5-02 through Grill5-08 sheets are selected in a worksheet group.

▶ **3.** In the worksheet group, select the range **C5:C43**.

▶ **4.** On the ribbon, click the **Home** tab, in the Editing group, click the **Find & Select** button, and click **Replace**. The Find and Replace dialog box opens.

▶ **5.** Type **B7** in the Find what box, press **TAB**, and then type **TOTAL_SALES** in the Replace with box. See Figure 5–24.

Figure 5–24   **Find and Replace dialog box**

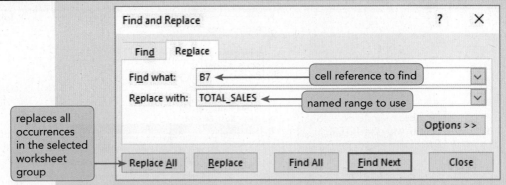

▶ **6.** Click **Replace All**. In the worksheet group, 161 occurrences of B7 in the selected formulas are replaced with the TOTAL_SALES defined name.

▶ **7.** Click **OK** in the message dialog box, and then click **Close** in the Find and Replace dialog box to return to the workbook.

▶ **8.** Examine the formulas in the C5:C43 range and verify that the references to cell B7 in the worksheet group have been replaced with the TOTAL_SALES name.

   Trouble? If the cell references weren't changed to the defined name, you made a mistake in the steps. Close the workbook without saving changes, reopen the workbook, and then repeat Steps 2 through 7.

▶ **9.** **sam**⬆ Ungroup the selected worksheets, and then save and close the workbook.

    If a workbook has a lot of defined names, you might want a way to easily see all of the defined names. In addition to viewing the list of names in the Name Manager, you can paste a list of the defined names into a worksheet table. To create a list of defined names, click the Use in Formula arrow in the Defined Names group on the Formulas tab, and then click Paste Names. In the Paste Names dialog box that opens, click Paste List to paste a list of all the names and the ranges they reference. The pasted list will not be updated as you add, modify, or delete the names. So, be sure to paste the list of defined names only when your workbook is complete.

Insight

Indirect Referencing

A cell reference tells a formula or function exactly where to find the data it needs. However, some formulas need to retrieve data from several possible locations. An application might need the same SUM function to calculate the sum of values from the range C1:C10 in one case and from the range D1:D10 in another. Being able to change a cell reference without having to rewrite a formula is the purpose of **indirect referencing** in which the reference itself is a calculated value. Indirect references are created with the INDIRECT function

```
INDIRECT(ref_text, [a1])
```

where *ref_text* is a text string that specifies the reference address and *a1* is an optional argument specifying how that reference is written. For example, if cell A1 contains the text string C1:C10, then the expression

```
INDIRECT(A1)
```

is equivalent to typing the range reference C1:C10. So, nesting the INDIRECT function in the formula

```
=SUM(INDIRECT(A1))
```

is the equivalent to the formula =SUM(C1:C10). If the value of A1 is changed to the text string D1:D10, then the formula becomes the equivalent of =SUM(D1:D10), and so forth. You can also use a named range so that if the value of cell A1 is changed to TotalExpenses, the formula becomes the equivalent of =SUM(TotalExpenses), calculating the sum of the values referenced by named range TotalExpenses.

Using the INDIRECT function, you can make the same formula calculate the sum of any range in the workbook by changing the text string stored in cell A1. Paired with named ranges, indirect referencing can be used to create dynamic Excel applications in which the formulas themselves are modified even by users who have no training in writing Excel formulas and functions.

Exploring Workbook Templates

This module began by looking at ways of collecting data from several workbooks. Now it examines how to ensure that those source workbooks employ an identical structure and design. Templates, or predesigned workbooks in which all the formulas and design elements are already built-in, are an easy way to ensure that a consistent design among workbooks. An additional advantage is that the end user will only focus on data entry because all of the structure, formatting, and formulas are already in place.

Proskills

Teamwork: Using Excel Templates

A team working together will often need to create the same types of workbooks. Rather than each person or group designing a different workbook, each team member should create a workbook from the same template. The completed workbooks will then all have the same structure with identical formatting and formulas. Not only does this ensure consistency and accuracy, it also makes it easier to compile and summarize the results. Templates help teams work better together and avoid misunderstandings.

For example, a large organization may need to collect the same information from several regions. By creating and distributing a workbook template, each region knows what data to track and where to enter it. The template already includes the formulas, so the results are calculated consistently.

The following are just some of the advantages of using a template to create multiple workbooks with the same features:

- Templates save time and ensure consistency in the design and content of workbooks because all labels, formatting, and formulas are entered once.
- Templates ensure accuracy because formulas can be entered and verified once, and then used with confidence in all workbooks.
- Templates standardize the appearance and content of workbooks.
- Templates prevent data from being overwritten when an existing workbook is inadvertently saved with new data rather than saved as a new workbook.

If you are part of a team that needs to create the same type of workbook repeatedly, it's a good idea to use a template to both save time and ensure consistency in the design and content of the workbooks.

Setting Up a Workbook Template

Any workbook can be turned into a template by just deleting all of the current data, leaving only the formulas and design elements. The data is left blank for end users to fill in at a later date when they start creating their own documents.

Gail is concerned that all of the franchise managers didn't complete their Profit and Loss reports in the same way, which made it more difficult to combine their results in a summary workbook. Gail has already created a workbook to use as a model for future reports and wants you to convert that workbook into a template. You'll open Gail's workbook now.

To open Gail's workbook:

1. Open the **NP_EX_5-2.xlsx** workbook located in the **Excel5 > Module** folder included with your Data Files.

2. Review the **Documentation**, **Franchise Number**, and **Terms and Definitions** worksheets. Do not make any changes to the contents of those sheets. Figure 5–25 shows the contents of the Franchise Number worksheet.

Figure 5–25 **Template for profit and loss statements**

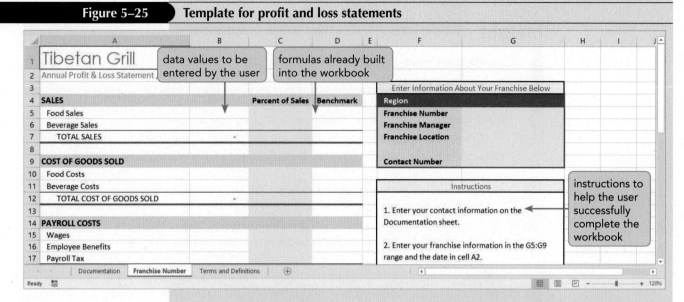

3. In each worksheet, scroll up to the top of the worksheet and click cell **A1**.

4. Click the **Documentation** sheet tab to make it the active sheet.

> **Tip**
>
> Good template designs assume users are not Excel experts and make it easy to fill out the workbook correctly.

The Franchise Number worksheet contains the framework Gail wants all franchises to use for their profit and loss reports. It does not include data values because those will be entered by the franchise managers. However, the worksheet does include all the formulas required to calculate sales and expense totals as well as percentages. The formulas in the worksheet use the TOTAL_SALES defined name to make the formulas easier to understand. Gail added detailed instructions about how the workbook should be filled out. Gail's email address is included as a hyperlink in case users want help completing the workbook.

Gail wants you to convert this workbook into a template. When you save the workbook as a template, Excel will save the file to the user's Custom Office Templates folder. An icon for the template will appear in the New screen in Background view so users can easily create workbooks based on the template design. However, you can save a template to any folder you choose. You'll save Gail's workbook as a template to a different folder.

To save Gail's workbook as a template:

1. On the ribbon, click the **File** tab to open Backstage view, and then in the navigation bar, click **Save As**. The Save As screen appears.

2. Click the **More options** link. The Save As dialog box opens.

3. In the File name box, type **NP_EX_5_PLStatement** as the file name for the template.

> **Tip**
>
> Excel template files have the .xltx file extension.

4. Click the **Save as type arrow**, and then click **Excel Template (*.xltx)** to save the file as a template. The default location for Excel templates, the Custom Office Templates folder, is displayed.

5. Navigate to the **Excel5 > Module** folder.

6. Click **Save** to save the template, and then close the file.

Now that you have created the template file, your next step is to create a new workbook based on this template design.

Insight

Creating a Chart Template

Templates can also be created for Excel charts. These chart templates store customized chart designs that can be added as a new type in the chart gallery. Complete the following steps to save a chart template on your computer:

1. Create a chart, choosing the chart type and design of the chart elements.
2. Right-click the completed chart, and click Save as Template on the shortcut menu.
3. Enter a name for the chart template file. All chart template files have the *.crtx file extension.
4. Save the chart template file. All chart templates are saved in the Microsoft > Templates > Charts folder within your user account on your computer.

Once you've saved the chart template file, it will appear as an option in the Recommended Charts dialog box, under the All Charts tab in the Templates folder. Select the chart template to apply it to the next chart you create.

Creating a Workbook Based on a Template

The great advantage of templates is that new workbooks are created based on the template design without altering the template file itself. As shown in Figure 5–26, each new workbook is a copy of the template design. Just as a blank workbook is named Book1, Book2, etc. based on the default "Book" template for new workbooks, files based on customized template are named *template*1, *template*2, etc. where *template* is the file name of the original template file.

Figure 5–26   **Workbooks created from a template**

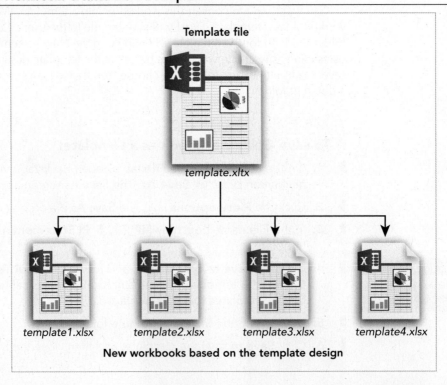

New workbooks based on the template design

There are two ways to create a workbook based on a template. If you save the template file to the Custom Office Templates folder, the template is always available to you from the New screen in Backstage view, placed within the Personal section of the gallery of new file designs. Figure 5–27 shows how the NP_EX_5_PLStatement would appear in Backstage view.

Figure 5–27   **New screen with templates**

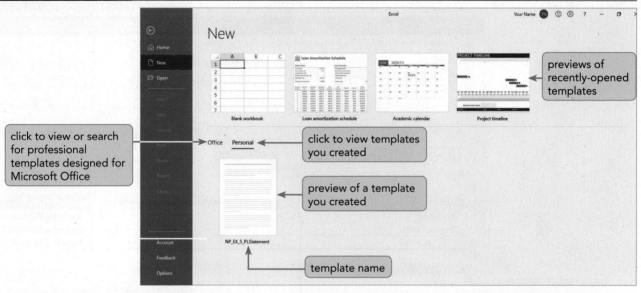

click to view or search for professional templates designed for Microsoft Office

click to view templates you created

preview of a template you created

template name

previews of recently-opened templates

Clicking the template's icon in the gallery creates a new workbook based on the template design. You can also use one of the built-in templates displayed in the Featured gallery or use the Search box to search online for other templates created by professional designers.

When the template file is *not* stored in the Custom Office Templates folder, you can create a new workbook based on the template design by opening the template file from the File Explorer. You cannot use the Open screen in Backstage view of Excel because that would reopen the actual template file. Remember, you don't want users editing the template file, you only want to create new workbooks based on the template design.

You'll create a new workbook from the NP_EX_5_PLStatement template, and then enter some test data into it.

To create a new workbook based on a PLStatement template:

1. Open **File Explorer** and navigate to the **Excel5 > Module** folder containing your Data Files.

2. Double-click the **NP_EX_5_PLStatement** template file. A workbook named NP_EX_5_PLStatement1 opens in the workbook window.

3. Go to the **Franchise Number** worksheet.

4. In cell **B5**, enter **820,000** for the food sales, and then in cell **B6**, enter **210,000** for the beverage sales.

5. In cell **B10**, enter **210,000** for the food costs, and then in cell **B11**, enter **58,000** for the beverage costs.

6. In cell **B15**, enter **255,000** for wages, in cell **B16**, enter **52,000** for employee benefits, and then in cell **B17**, enter **24,000** for payroll tax. The worksheet automatically calculates the total sales, the total cost of goods sold, the total payroll costs, and the percent of total sales for each number. See Figure 5–28.

Figure 5–28   New workbook based on a template

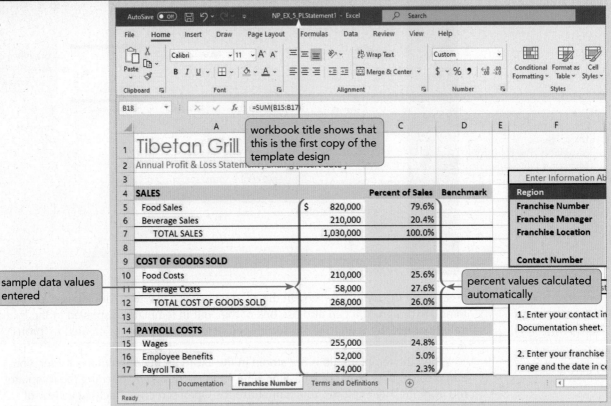

7. Save the workbook as **NP_EX_5_Franchise** in the location specified by your instructor, and then close the workbook.

If you want to edit the template file, you can reopen the file from the Open screen in Backstage view. Any changes you make to the template file will not be reflected in workbooks already created based on earlier versions of the template.

Insight

Copying Styles Between Templates

Consistency is a hallmark of professional documents. If you want to reuse the styles that you created for the workbook but don't want to recreate the entire workbook, you can copy only the styles from that template. To copy styles from one template to another:

1. Open the template with the styles you want to copy.
2. Open the workbook or template in which you want to place the copied styles.
3. On the Home tab, in the Styles group, click the Cell Styles button, and then click Merge Styles. The Merge Styles dialog box opens, listing the currently open workbooks and templates.
4. Select the workbook or template with the styles you want to copy, and then click OK to copy those styles into the current workbook or template.
5. If a dialog box opens, asking if you want to "Merge Styles that have the same names?", click YES.
6. Save the workbook with the new styles as the Excel Template file type.

Copying template styles is much faster and more accurate than trying to recreate all those styles in a new workbook document. However, the styles are not linked, so if you modify your design, you will have to recopy all the styles again.

Gail appreciates your work on the template and will forward the template to the franchise managers so that they can base their next profit and loss statements on its design.

Review

Session 5.3 Quick Check

1. Why is Report-Date not a valid named range?
2. What happens when you select a defined name in the Name box?
3. What is the difference between a defined name with global scope and one with local scope?
4. What is the expression to reference the local scope defined name TotalSales from the Final Report worksheet?
5. When would you create a template rather than just providing a coworker with the copy of your workbook?
6. What is displayed in the title bar for a workbook created from the EmployeeList.xltx template file?
7. By default, where does Excel store workbook templates?

Practice

Review Assignments

Data Files needed for the Review Assignments: NP_EX_5-3.xlsx, Support_EX_5_Peoria.xlsx, Support_EX_5_Region1.xlsx, Support_EX_5_Region2.xlsx, Support_EX_5_Region3.xlsx, Support_EX_5_Region4.xlsx

Gail wants to get a monthly sales and expense report from each franchise so that the company can catch issues early and offer suggestions to franchises that are underperforming. Gail started a summary workbook that will contain the collected data. She needs you to finalize the workbook. Complete the following:

1. Open the **NP_EX_5-3.xlsx** workbook located in the Excel5 > Review folder included with your Data Files. Save the workbook as **NP_EX_5_Report** in the location specified by your instructor.

2. In the Documentation sheet, in the range B3:B4, enter your name and the date.

3. Change your name to a hyperlink pointing to your email address using the subject heading **Monthly Sales and Expenses Report** for the message and **Email me for more info** as the ScreenTip text.

4. Open the **Support_EX_5_Peoria.xlsx** workbook located in the Excel5 > Review folder. Copy the Grill5-08 worksheet into the NP_EX_5_Report workbook, placing the worksheet at the end of the workbook.

5. Create a worksheet group from the Grill5-01 through Grill5-08 worksheets. In the worksheet group, select the nonadjacent range A7:B7,A11:B11,A16:B16, and then create named ranges from the selection using the labels in the left column.

6. Use the Name Manager to change the TOTAL_COST_ OF_ GOODS_SOLD, TOTAL_PAYROLL_COSTS, and TOTAL_SALES named ranges for the Grill5-01 worksheet from global scope to local scope by deleting those names and recreating them, limiting them to the scope of the Grill5-01 worksheet. Verify in the Name Manager that all the defined names in the workbook have local scope.

7. In the range B5:C17 of the Grill5-01 through Grill5-08 worksheets, replace the cell references to cells B7, B11, and B16 with the TOTAL_SALES, TOTAL_COST_OF_GOODS_SOLD, and TOTAL_PAYROLL_COSTS defined names. You can either use the Apply Names command or find and replace the cell reference with the range name.

8. In the Region Report worksheet, in cell F5, use the SUM function to calculate the sum of cell B5 in the Grill5-01 through Grill5-08 worksheet group, displaying the total income from food sales.

9. Use AutoFill to extend the formula in cell F5 through the range F5:F17. Fill without formatting in the range. Delete the zeros in cells F8 and F12.

10. Open the **Support_EX_5_Region1.xlsx** file located in the Excel5 > Review folder. Copy the range B5:B17 of the Region 1 worksheet, and then use the Paste Link command to paste the external reference to the copied cells in the range B5:B17 of the Region Report worksheet. Delete the zeroes in cells B8 and B12.

11. Repeat Step 10 for the Region 2 through Region 4 data located in the **Support_EX_5_Region2.xlsx** through **Support_EX_5_Region4.xlsx** workbooks, pasting their external references in the ranges C5:C17, D5:D17, and E5:E17, respectively. Delete the zeroes in rows 8 and 12.

12. Copy the Grill5-01 worksheet to a new workbook so you can create a template of the Sales and Expenses worksheet with all the data removed, but the formulas and formatting retained.

13. Save the NP_EX_5_Report workbook, and then close it.

14. In the new workbook you created in Step 12, make the following changes to the Grill5-01 worksheet:

    a. Change the worksheet name to **Franchise**.

    b. Change the text of cell A2 to **[Region] Monthly Sales and Expenses**.

    c. Delete the data in the nonadjacent range **B5:B6, B9:B10, B13:B15, F4:F9**.

15. Save the workbook as a template with the file name **NP_EX_5_Sales.xltx** in the location specified by your instructor.

16. Save and close all the workbooks you used in the Review Assignments.

Apply

Case Problem 1

Data File needed for this Case Problem: NP_EX_5-4.xlsx

Medicina Medical Software   Imani Emeka is the Social Media Manager for Medicina Medical Software, a tech company specializing in medical software for managing patient enrollments and hospital staffing. Imani is working on improving the company's visibility on social media and wants your help in maintaining a workbook tracking the company's monthly social media posts. Imani wants metrics on the number of posts made to social media, including the number of retweets, likes, mentions, clicks, and followers. Imani wants to determine whether the efforts to expand and improve the company's media presence are showing results. Complete the following.

1. Open the **NP_EX_5-4.xlsx** workbook located in the Excel5 > Case1 folder included with your Data Files. Save the workbook as **NP_EX_5_Medicina** in the location specified by your instructor.

2. In the Documentation sheet, in the range B3:B4, enter your name and the date.

3. The January through June worksheets contain the monthly social media logs. In each worksheet, change the entries in column C to hyperlinks by double-clicking each cell, and then pressing ENTER. (Note that you cannot make this change in a worksheet group.) Excel will automatically convert the cells to hyperlinks using the addresses stored into the cells. (Note that these fictional web addresses will not open real pages if clicked.)

4. One important social media metric is the number of engagements for each post where an individual is actively engaged in the post by retweeting the post, liking the post, mentioning the post in other forums, or clicking links within the post. In column I of the January through June worksheets, use the SUM function to calculate the total number of retweets, likes, mentions, and clicks. Do not include the number of followers in the total.

5. Another important social media metric is the Engagement Rate, which is the percentage of followers that are actively engaged with the post. In column J of the January through June worksheets, calculate the Engagement Rate by dividing the number of engagements by the number of followers for each post.

6. In the Metrics worksheet, calculate the following summary statistics:

   a. In cell C5, use the COUNT function to count the number of data values in column B of the January worksheet.

   b. In cell D5, use the SUM function to sum the total retweets in column D of the January worksheet.

   c. In cell D6, use the AVERAGE function to calculate the average number of retweets in column D of the January worksheet.

   d. Use AutoFill to copy the formulas from the range D5:D6 over the range D5:H6.

   e. In cell I5, use the AVERAGE function to calculate the average Engagement Rate from column J of the January worksheet.

7. Repeat Step 6 for February through June rows in the table to calculate summary statistics of the media metrics for each month.

8. Calculate summary statistics of the media metrics across all months by doing the following:

   a. In cell C19, use the COUNT function applied to column B of the January:June worksheet group to calculate the total number of posts made over the six month period.

   b. In cell D19, use the SUM function to sum up the total retweets in column D of January through June worksheets.

   c. In cell D20, use the AVERAGE function to average the number of retweets from column D of the January through June worksheets.

    d. Use AutoFill to extend the formulas from the range D19:D20 over the range D19:H20.

    e. In cell I19, use the AVERAGE function to calculate the average Engagement Rate from column J in the January through June worksheets.

9. Change the entries in cells B5, B7, B9, B11, B13, and B15 into hyperlinks that point to cell A1 of their respective monthly worksheets. For each hyperlink, add **View monthly posts** as the ScreenTip message.

10. Save the workbook, and then close it.

Challenge

Case Problem 2

Data Files needed for this Case Problem: NP_EX_5-5.xlsx, Support_EX_5_Fund01.xlsx, Support_EX_5_Fund02.xlsx, Support_EX_5_Fund03.xlsx, Support_EX_5_Fund04.xlsx, Support_EX_5_Fund05.xlsx

Templeton Investments   John Riegel is an accounts manager at Templeton Investments. John wants your help in creating an Excel workbook that can retrieve fund data from external workbooks and display summary statistics about those funds. The workbook should be accessible to non-Excel users. You'll use the INDIRECT function so that the user needs to enter only the symbol for the fund to get a summary report. The INDIRECT function is discussed in the "Indirect Referencing" InSight box. Complete the following.

1. Open the **NP_EX_5-5.xlsx** workbook located in the Excel5 > Case2 folder included with your Data Files. Save the workbook as **NP_EX_5_Templeton** in the location specified by your instructor.

2. In the Documentation sheet, enter your name in cell B3. Use an Excel function to enter the current date in cell B4.

3. Go to the Fund Lookup worksheet. In this sheet, you will create a lookup table with data drawn from external workbooks.

4. Open the **Support_EX_5_Fund01.xlsx** file located in the Excel5 > Case2 folder. Copy the data from the range E2:P2 of the Summary worksheet.

5. In the NP_EX_5_Templeton workbook, in the Fund Lookup worksheet, in the range A4:L4, paste a link to the data you copied.

6. Repeat Steps 4 and 5 using the data in the **Support_EX_5_Fund02.xlsx**, **Support_EX_5_Fund03.xlsx**, **Support_EX_5_Fund04.xlsx**, and **Support_EX_5_Fund05.xlsx** workbooks, pasting links to the copied data in the ranges A5:L5, A6:L6, A7:L7, and A8:L8 of the Fund Lookup worksheet.

7. Assign the named range **Fund_Lookup** to lookup table in the range A3:L8 of the Fund Lookup worksheet.

8. Copy the data in the range A2:C32 of the Summary worksheet in the Support_EX_5_Fund01 workbook. In the NP_EX_5_Templeton workbook, paste a link to the copied data in the range A3:C33 of the 30-Day Data worksheet.

9. Repeat Step 8 using data from Support_EX_5_Fund02, Support_EX_5_Fund03, Support_EX_5_Fund04, and Support_EX_5_Fund05 workbooks, pasting links to the copied data in the ranges D3:F33, G3:I33, J3:L33, and M3:O33 of the 30-Day Data worksheet.

10. Select the range A3:O33, and then create named ranges from the selection, using the labels in the top row. (*Hint*: Make sure only the Top row check box is selected.)

11. Go to the Statistics worksheet. In this worksheet, you will display information and summary statistics on a selected fund. In cell B4, enter the text **ORTFD** for the Ortus fund.

12. Select cell B4 and define a named range using **Symbol** as the name.

13. In cell B5, enter the VLOOKUP function to retrieve the name of the fund. Use the Symbol named range as the lookup value, the Fund_Lookup named range as the lookup table, 2 as the column to look up, and FALSE as the type of look up (exact match).

14. In the range B6:B15, repeat Step 13, inserting VLOOKUP functions for the remaining information on the selected fund, entering the next higher value as the column to look up (from 3 up to 12).

⊕ **Explore** 15. In cell B18, display the 30-day high value for the selected fund using the MAX function. Nest the INDIRECT function within the MAX function, using the named range Symbol as the input value for the INDIRECT function.

16. Repeat Step 15 using the MIN function in cell B19 to return the 30-day low of the selected fund and using the AVERAGE function in cell B20 to return the 30-day average of the selected fund.

⊕ **Explore** 17. In cell B21, calculate the average shares traded per day using the AVERAGE function. Nest the INDIRECT function within the AVERAGE function, using the argument **Symbol&"_Shares"** to reference the named range of shares traded for the selected fund.

18. Test the formulas you created by changing the value in cell B4 to **SNRFD**, **AIF**, **LTDX**, and then **IHGF**, verifying that a different set of information and summary statistics appears for each symbol.

⊕ **Explore** 19. In the Documentation sheet, in the range A8:B24, paste a list of the defined names used in the workbook. On the Formulas tab, in the Defined Names group, click the Use in Formula button, and then click Paste Names. In the Paste Name dialog box, click Paste List.

20. Save the NP_EX_5_Templeton workbook, and then close it. Close all other open workbooks without saving any changes.

Module **6**

Objectives

Session 6.1
- Split a workbook window into panes
- Highlight and remove duplicate values in a data range
- Sort a data range by one or more fields
- Add subtotals to a data range

Session 6.2
- Find and select workbook cells
- Filter data based on one or more fields
- Create an advanced filter
- Convert a data range to an Excel table
- Work with table styles and table elements

Session 6.3
- Create and apply a slicer
- Calculate summary statistics with the SUBTOTAL function
- Design and create an interactive dashboard

Managing Data with Data Tools

Analyzing Employment Data

Case | Orthographic

Jacek Baros is a Human Resources (HR) analyst for Orthographic, a company that produces 3-D imaging hardware and software with offices in Boston, Chicago, Denver, San Francisco, and Dallas. As an HR analyst, Jacek prepares employment reports and summaries. In doing these analyses, Jacek must deal with large amounts of employee data. You'll help Jacek complete a workbook that will provide an overview of the employee situation at Orthographic.

Starting Data Files

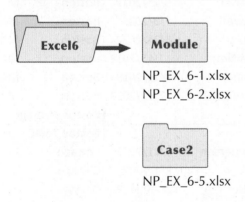

Excel6 → Module

NP_EX_6-1.xlsx
NP_EX_6-2.xlsx

Review

NP_EX_6-3.xlsx

Case1

NP_EX_6-4.xlsx

Case2

NP_EX_6-5.xlsx

Session 6.1 Visual Overview:

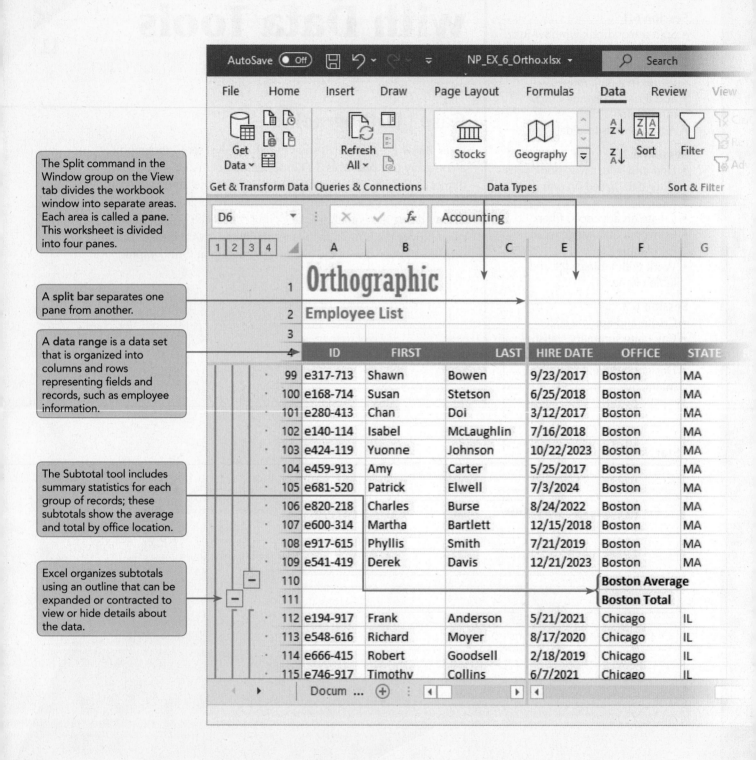

The Split command in the Window group on the View tab divides the workbook window into separate areas. Each area is called a **pane**. This worksheet is divided into four panes.

A split bar separates one pane from another.

A data range is a data set that is organized into columns and rows representing fields and records, such as employee information.

The Subtotal tool includes summary statistics for each group of records; these subtotals show the average and total by office location.

Excel organizes subtotals using an outline that can be expanded or contracted to view or hide details about the data.

	ID	FIRST	LAST	HIRE DATE	OFFICE	STATE
99	e317-713	Shawn	Bowen	9/23/2017	Boston	MA
100	e168-714	Susan	Stetson	6/25/2018	Boston	MA
101	e280-413	Chan	Doi	3/12/2017	Boston	MA
102	e140-114	Isabel	McLaughlin	7/16/2018	Boston	MA
103	e424-119	Yuonne	Johnson	10/22/2023	Boston	MA
104	e459-913	Amy	Carter	5/25/2017	Boston	MA
105	e681-520	Patrick	Elwell	7/3/2024	Boston	MA
106	e820-218	Charles	Burse	8/24/2022	Boston	MA
107	e600-314	Martha	Bartlett	12/15/2018	Boston	MA
108	e917-615	Phyllis	Smith	7/21/2019	Boston	MA
109	e541-419	Derek	Davis	12/21/2023	Boston	MA
110					Boston Average	
111					Boston Total	
112	e194-917	Frank	Anderson	5/21/2021	Chicago	IL
113	e548-616	Richard	Moyer	8/17/2020	Chicago	IL
114	e666-415	Robert	Goodsell	2/18/2019	Chicago	IL
115	e746-917	Timothy	Collins	6/7/2021	Chicago	IL

Data Ranges, Workbook Panes, and Subtotals

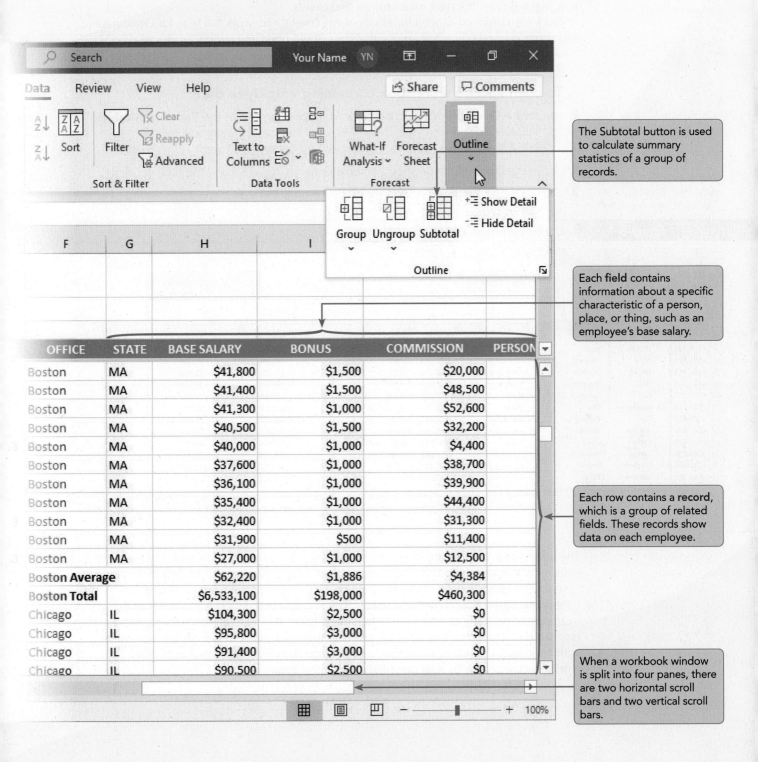

The Subtotal button is used to calculate summary statistics of a group of records.

Each field contains information about a specific characteristic of a person, place, or thing, such as an employee's base salary.

Each row contains a record, which is a group of related fields. These records show data on each employee.

When a workbook window is split into four panes, there are two horizontal scroll bars and two vertical scroll bars.

OFFICE	STATE	BASE SALARY	BONUS	COMMISSION	PERSON
Boston	MA	$41,800	$1,500	$20,000	
Boston	MA	$41,400	$1,500	$48,500	
Boston	MA	$41,300	$1,000	$52,600	
Boston	MA	$40,500	$1,500	$32,200	
Boston	MA	$40,000	$1,000	$4,400	
Boston	MA	$37,600	$1,000	$38,700	
Boston	MA	$36,100	$1,000	$39,900	
Boston	MA	$35,400	$1,000	$44,400	
Boston	MA	$32,400	$1,000	$31,300	
Boston	MA	$31,900	$500	$11,400	
Boston	MA	$27,000	$1,000	$12,500	
Boston **Average**		$62,220	$1,886	$4,384	
Boston **Total**		$6,533,100	$198,000	$460,300	
Chicago	IL	$104,300	$2,500	$0	
Chicago	IL	$95,800	$3,000	$0	
Chicago	IL	$91,400	$3,000	$0	
Chicago	IL	$90,500	$2,500	$0	

Handling Data in Excel

Excel is a popular application for storing data and includes tools for managing and exploring that data. In this module, you will learn how to use Excel to handle large data sets, highlighting important relationships and trends.

Jacek has compiled data on hundreds of employees who work full time for Orthographic and wants your help in summarizing that data. You'll open and review Jacek's workbook.

To open Jacek's workbook containing employee data:

▶ **1.** sam↓ Open the **NP_EX_6-1.xlsx** workbook located in the **Excel6 > Module** folder included with your Data Files, and then save the workbook as **NP_EX_6_Ortho** in the location specified by your instructor.

▶ **2.** In the Documentation sheet, enter your name in cell B3 and the date in cell B4.

▶ **3.** Go to the **Employees** worksheet. See Figure 6–1.

Figure 6–1	Employees worksheet

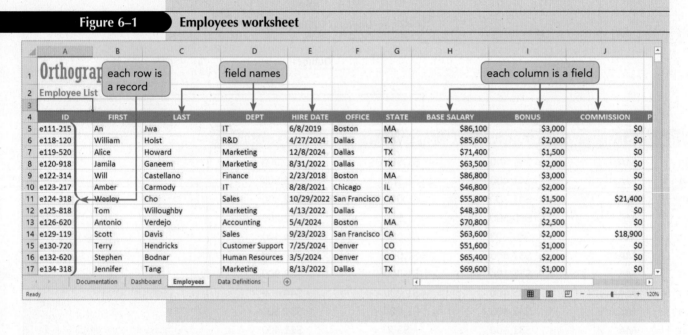

The information in the Employees worksheet is organized into a rectangular range of cells, or data range. In a data range, each column stores information known as a field describing a characteristic of a person, place, or thing and each row stores a record containing a group of related field values. The first row of a data range, known as the **header row**, typically contains the field names. Excel automatically recognizes data organized in this format and uses the labels in the header row to identify the columns within the range. To avoid confusion, a data range should be separated from other worksheet content by at least one blank row and column.

The field names for the employee data are in columns A through M of row 4 in the Employees worksheet. Jacek included fields for employee IDs, names, departments, dates of hire, office locations, wages (base salaries, bonuses, and commissions), personal days, sick days, and evaluation scores. Rows 5 through 538 contain 534 records providing detailed information on each employee.

With any data range, it's excellent practice to provide a **data definition table**, which lists the fields included with each record, the type of data stored in each field (such as numbers, text, or dates), and a short description of each field. A data definition table is useful for planning the kinds of data needed for an analysis and helping others who will use that data.

Jacek already entered a data definition table for the employee data. You will review that table to learn more about the data in the Employees worksheet.

To view the data definition table for the Employees data:

▶ **1.** Go to the **Data Definitions** worksheet containing the data definition table. See Figure 6–2.

Figure 6–2   **Data Definitions worksheet**

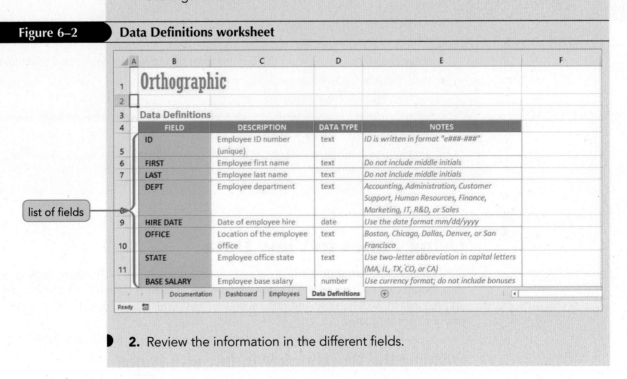

list of fields

▶ **2.** Review the information in the different fields.

Next, you will study the contents of the Employees worksheet.

Proskills

Written Communication: Planning for Data Entry

Before entering data, you should plan how that data should be structured to best achieve your goals. Those goals help to determine the fields needed for each record. Consider each of the following:

- Who can view the data, and which fields contain confidential information available to a select few
- What questions you want answered, and what fields are required to generate those answers
- What reports you want generated for different audiences (supervisors, customers, directors, etc.)
- How often the data needs to be updated, and who is responsible for ensuring data accuracy

After you have identified the data needed and how it should be organized, you can set up your worksheet. Keep in mind the following guidelines:

- Use short, descriptive field names that reflect the content and fit more fields in the window without scrolling.
- Distinguish field names from the data records with different colors and font styles.
- Break fields into single units of information, such as one field for the city name and another field for the state name.
- Separate the data range from other information in the worksheet with at least one blank row and one blank column.

With careful and thorough planning, you will avoid having to redesign your worksheet after you start entering data.

Using Panes to View Data

Data ranges can span thousands of records with dozens of fields. Because such large data ranges extend beyond the workbook window, it can be difficult to compare fields and records in widely separated columns and rows. One way of dealing with this problem is with panes.

Dividing the Workbook Window into Panes

Excel can split the workbook window in up to four sections called panes with each pane offering a separate view into the worksheet. By scrolling through the contents of individual panes, you can compare cells from different sections of the worksheet side-by-side within the workbook window. To split the workbook window into four panes, select any cell or range in the worksheet, and then on the View tab, in the Window group, click the Split button. Split bars divide the workbook window along the top and left border of the selected cell or range. To split the window into two vertical panes displayed side-by-side, select any cell in the first row of the worksheet and then click the Split button. To split the window into two stacked horizontal panes, select any cell in the first column and then click the Split button.

Reference

Splitting the Workbook Window into Panes

- To split the workbook window into four panes, click any cell or range, and then click the Split button in the Window group on the View tab.
- To split the window into two vertical panes, select a cell in the first row, and then click the Split button.
- To split the window into two horizontal panes, select a cell in the first column, and then click the Split button
- To close the panes and return to one window, click the Split button again.

Jacek wants you to split the Employees worksheet into fours panes so you can more easily compare different parts of the worksheet.

To split the Employees worksheet into four panes:

1. Go to the **Employees** worksheet and click cell **D5** to select it.

2. On the ribbon, click the **View** tab, and then in the Window group, click the **Split** button (or press **ALT,W,S**). Two split bars divide the workbook window into four panes with two sets of scroll bars along the horizontal and vertical edges of the workbook window.

3. Drag the **lower vertical scroll bar** down until row 70 is aligned with the horizontal split bar. Notice that scrolling is synchronized between the lower-left and lower-right panes so that both panes show the same rows.

4. Drag the **right horizontal scroll bar** until column H is aligned with the vertical split bar. Scrolling between the upper-right and lower-right panes is also synchronized so that both panes show the same columns. See Figure 6–3.

Tip

To resize the panes, point to a pane split bar, and then use the double-headed split arrow to drag the split bar to a new location.

Figure 6–3   **Workbook window split into four panes**

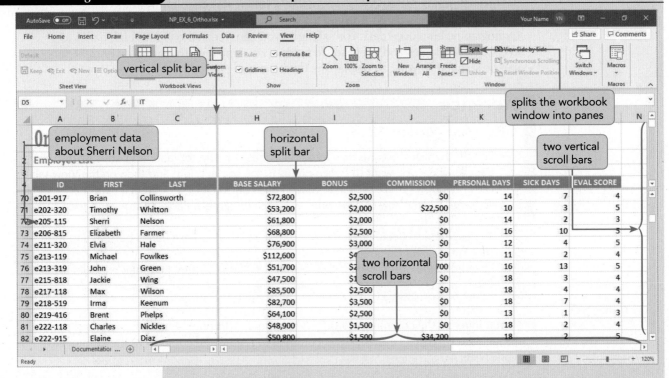

▶ 5. Continue to drag the **lower vertical scroll bar** down until you can see row 538 in the workbook window. As you can see, you can view widely spaced areas in the different panes of the workbook window.

With the workbook window split into four panes, it is easy to read information about individual employees. For example, as you can see in Figure 6–3, Sherri Nelson is paid a base salary of $61,800 with a yearly bonus of $2,000. Reading this information without panes would be much more difficult because scrolling through the workbook window would have hidden those field names and values from view.

Splitting the workbook window affects only the active sheet or worksheet group. Other worksheets will remain unaffected. To return a worksheet to one pane, you remove the split. You'll change the Employees worksheet back to a single pane.

To remove the split bars from the worksheet:

▶ 1. Drag the **lower vertical scroll bar** up until you can see row 1 in the bottom two panes.

▶ 2. On the View tab, in the Window group, click the **Split** button. The panes are removed, and the worksheet is again displayed within a single window.

Tip

You can also remove panes by double-clicking the split bar.

Freezing Panes

Another way of viewing different sections of a worksheet is by freezing the split panes. When you **freeze** a pane, its contents are always visible though you cannot scroll within it. You can freeze the panes located to the top and left of a selected cell, allowing scrolling within the lower-right pane. You can freeze the top row of the worksheet, allowing scrolling for all rows in the pane below it. You can also freeze the first column of the worksheet, allowing scrolling for all columns in the pane to the right. Freezing panes is useful for worksheets with large data ranges like the Orthographic employee data. For example, you can freeze the top and left panes to keep the field names and a few select fields always in view. Then, the lower-right pane can be scrolled so you can display the data.

Reference ▬▬▬▬▬▬▬▬▬▬▬

Freezing Window Panes

- To split the workbook window into four panes with the top and left panes frozen, click the cell where you want to freeze panes to the top and left, and then on the View tab, in the Window group, click the Freeze Panes button and click Freeze Panes.
- To freeze the top row of the worksheet, click the Freeze Panes button, and then click Freeze Top Row.
- To freeze the first column of the worksheet, click the Freeze Panes button, and then click Freeze First Column.
- To remove the frozen panes, click the Freeze Panes button, and then click Unfreeze Panes.

You'll freeze the columns A through C and rows 1 through 4 to make scrolling through the worksheet easier as you continue to review the contents of the Employees worksheet.

To freeze rows and columns in the Employees worksheet:

1. Scroll up the Employees worksheet so that cell A1 is visible in the upper-left corner of the worksheet.

2. Click cell **D5** to select it.

3. On the View tab, in the Window group, click the **Freeze Panes** button, and then click **Freeze Panes** on the menu that appears below the button. Narrow dividing lines appear between columns C and D and rows 4 and 5. Note that the worksheet has only one set of scrolling bars to scroll the contents in the lower-right pane.

4. Scroll down to row 210 and scroll to the right so that column H is displayed next to column C. Note that as you scroll through the worksheet, the contents of the first four rows and first three columns are locked in place.

5. Click cell **H210** to select the cell containing the base salary for Angeline Glover. See Figure 6–4.

| Figure 6–4 | Employees worksheet with frozen panes |

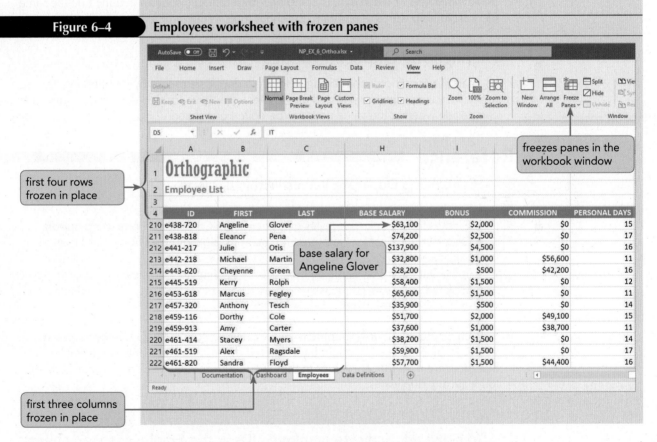

After you freeze the panes, the first option on the Freeze Panes button menu changes to Unfreeze Panes which releases the frozen panes and removes the panes from the workbook window. Now that you have viewed the contents of the Employees worksheet using panes, you will unfreeze and remove the panes.

To unfreeze the panes in the workbook window:

▶ **1.** On the View tab, in the Window group, click the **Freeze Panes** button. The first option is now Unfreeze Panes.

▶ **2.** Click **Unfreeze Panes** to remove the frozen panes from the workbook window.

▶ **3.** Scroll through the worksheet to verify that there are no frozen panes within the workbook window.

Locating Duplicate Records

When a worksheet has a lot of data, data entry errors are almost sure to occur. One common error is creating a duplicate record in which the same record appears multiple times in the worksheet. Duplicate records can happen when several people enter data into a worksheet or when data is combined from multiple sources that include the same records. To help with this problem, Excel has tools to find and remove duplicated data.

Highlighting Duplicate Values

You can use conditional formatting to locate a duplicate record by highlighting duplicate values within a selected range. Once you have located duplicate values, you can decide whether the value needs to be edited or deleted.

Reference ▬▬▬▬▬▬▬▬▬▬▬▬▬▬

Highlighting Duplicate Values Within a Range

- Select the range you want to locate duplicate values within.
- On the Home tab, in the Styles group, click the Conditional Formatting button.
- On the conditional formatting menu, point to Highlight Cells Rules, and then click Duplicate Values.
- In the Duplicate Values dialog box, specify the highlighting style for duplicate values.
- Click OK.

Each employee at Orthographic is given a unique employee ID number. Jacek is worried that duplicate IDs might have entered by mistake and wants you to make sure that there are no duplicate values in the ID column. You will use conditional formatting to locate any duplicates.

To highlight duplicate employee IDs in the Employees worksheet:

▶ **1.** Click the **Name** box, type **A5:A538** as the range to select, and then press **ENTER**. All the ID values in column A are selected.

▶ **2.** On the ribbon, click the **Home** tab. In the Styles group, click the **Conditional Formatting** button, point to **Highlight Cell Rules**, and then click **Duplicate Values**. The Duplicate Values dialog box opens.

▶ **3.** Click **OK**. Cells that contain duplicate values are formatted with a light red fill with dark red text.

▶ **4.** Scroll down the worksheet until you can see rows 38 and 39. The red formatting in cells A38 and A39 highlight that these two employees have duplicate ID numbers. See Figure 6–5.

Figure 6–5   **Conditional formatting highlights cells with duplicate values**

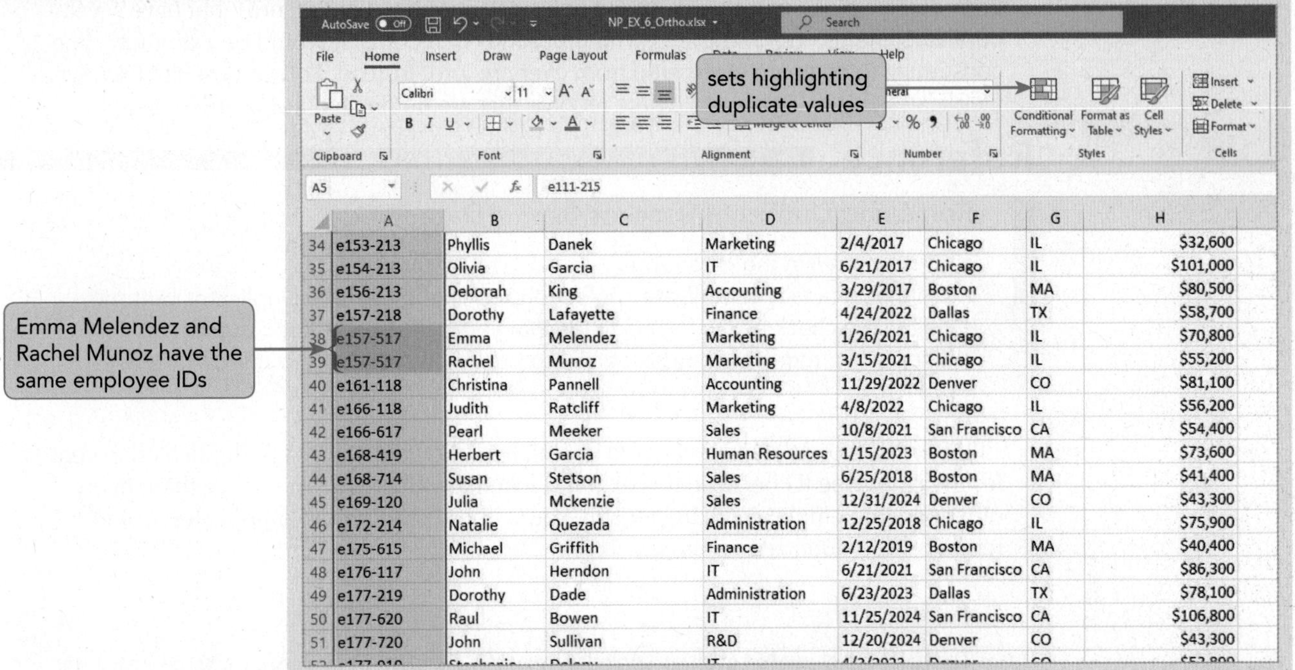

Emma Melendez and Rachel Munoz have the same employee IDs

	A	B	C	D	E	F	G	H
34	e153-213	Phyllis	Danek	Marketing	2/4/2017	Chicago	IL	$32,600
35	e154-213	Olivia	Garcia	IT	6/21/2017	Chicago	IL	$101,000
36	e156-213	Deborah	King	Accounting	3/29/2017	Boston	MA	$80,500
37	e157-218	Dorothy	Lafayette	Finance	4/24/2022	Dallas	TX	$58,700
38	e157-517	Emma	Melendez	Marketing	1/26/2021	Chicago	IL	$70,800
39	e157-517	Rachel	Munoz	Marketing	3/15/2021	Chicago	IL	$55,200
40	e161-118	Christina	Pannell	Accounting	11/29/2022	Denver	CO	$81,100
41	e166-118	Judith	Ratcliff	Marketing	4/8/2022	Chicago	IL	$56,200
42	e166-617	Pearl	Meeker	Sales	10/8/2021	San Francisco	CA	$54,400
43	e168-419	Herbert	Garcia	Human Resources	1/15/2023	Boston	MA	$73,600
44	e168-714	Susan	Stetson	Sales	6/25/2018	Boston	MA	$41,400
45	e169-120	Julia	Mckenzie	Sales	12/31/2024	Denver	CO	$43,300
46	e172-214	Natalie	Quezada	Administration	12/25/2018	Chicago	IL	$75,900
47	e175-615	Michael	Griffith	Finance	2/12/2019	Boston	MA	$40,400
48	e176-117	John	Herndon	IT	6/21/2021	San Francisco	CA	$86,300
49	e177-219	Dorothy	Dade	Administration	6/23/2023	Dallas	TX	$78,100
50	e177-620	Raul	Bowen	IT	11/25/2024	San Francisco	CA	$106,800
51	e177-720	John	Sullivan	R&D	12/20/2024	Denver	CO	$43,300

Rachel Munoz's ID should have been entered as e157-617 and not e157-517. You'll correct this mistake now.

5. Click cell **A39**, and then enter **e157-617** as the ID value. Highlighting disappears from cells A38 and A39 because those IDs are no longer duplicates.

6. Scroll down the worksheet until you see duplicates highlighted. In rows 86 through 88, the employee record for Jennifer Rizzo is repeated three times. Jacek wants only one record per employee.

7. Drag the pointer over the **row 87** and **row 88** row headers to select both rows.

8. Right-click the selected rows, and then click **Delete** on the shortcut menu to remove these rows from the worksheet.

9. Scroll down the worksheet to rows 295 and 296. The employee record for Carmen Casares is duplicated.

10. Right-click the **row 296** row header, and then click **Delete** on the shortcut menu to remove row 296 from the worksheet.

11. Scroll down the worksheet to verify no other IDs are as duplicated.

12. Scroll back up to row 296, and then click cell **A295** to select it.

Tip

The conditional formatting rule will highlight duplicate values even if they are not adjacent to each other.

Carmen Casares is listed in both row 295 and row 296, although each listing has a different ID. Although it's not uncommon in a large company to have employees with the same name, these two records are completely identical except for the IDs. It would be extremely unlikely for two Carmen Casares to be hired on the same date in the same department at the same location for the same pay, not to mention reporting the same amount of personal and sick days and receiving the same employee evaluation score. Obviously, these are duplicate records in which the wrong ID was entered at some point, resulting in two records for the same employee. Jacek tells you that the second record has the incorrect employee ID and should be deleted. However, Jacek is concerned that the worksheet may contain other data entry errors like this.

Removing Duplicate Records

One limit of using conditional formatting to locate duplicate records is that the process finds duplicate values only in a single field. It cannot highlight records that have several duplicated fields. In a worksheet with thousands of records, it would be extremely time-consuming to compare every field from every record. Instead, you can use the Remove Duplicates tool to locate and delete records that are duplicated across multiple fields.

Reference

Removing Duplicate Records from a Data Range

- Click any cell in the data range.
- On the Data tab, in the Data Tools group, click the Remove Duplicates button.
- Select the check boxes for the fields that you want to check for duplicates.
- Click OK to remove records containing duplicates of all of the selected fields.

Jacek asks you to remove records in which *all* the field values are duplicated except for the employee ID because it is extremely unlikely that two employees share every other possible employee characteristic. You will use the Remove Duplicates tool to remove those duplicate records.

To find and delete duplicate records in the Employees worksheet:

1. On the ribbon, click the **Data** tab, and then in the Data Tools group, click the **Remove Duplicates** button. The Remove Duplicates dialog box opens. All the employee data in the Employees worksheet is selected, and the dialog box lists the column labels in the first row of the range to identify the field names (ID through Eval Score).

   Trouble? If Excel shows the Remove Duplicates Warning dialog box, verify that the Expand the selection option button is selected and click the Remove Duplicates button.

2. Click the **ID** check box to deselect it, and then verify that every other field check box is selected. You deselected the ID field because you want to locate any delete duplicate records in which only the ID value is different while all other field values are identical. See Figure 6–6.

Figure 6–6   **Remove Duplicates dialog box**

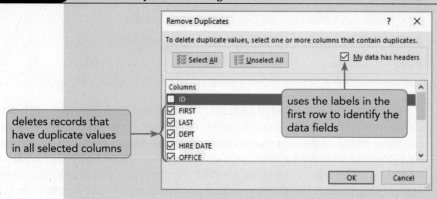

deletes records that have duplicate values in all selected columns

uses the labels in the first row to identify the data fields

3. Click **OK** to remove the duplicate records. A dialog box opens, indicating that 1 duplicate record was found and deleted, leaving 530 unique records in the data range.

4. Click **OK** to close the dialog box and return to the worksheet.

5. Scroll to row **295** and verify that only one record exists for Carmen Casares.

Tip

If you delete records you did not intend to, click the Undo button on the Quick Access Toolbar (or press CTRL+Z).

Be *extremely cautious* when using the Remove Duplicates tool. You are *not* prompted to confirm deletion of duplicate records. Instead, Excel keeps the first instance of any duplicates it finds and deletes subsequent records. Make sure that you are deleting records based only on fields that should *never* be duplicated. For example, you wouldn't want to delete records in which the employee's first and last names are the same, because two people can share the same name.

Because you've found and corrected the duplicate records and IDs, you can remove the conditional formatting rule from the worksheet.

To remove the Duplicate Values conditional formatting rule:

1. On the ribbon, click the **Home** tab, and then in the Styles group, click the **Conditional Formatting** button.

2. At the bottom of the menu, click **Manage Rules**. The Conditional Formatting Rules Manager opens.

3. Click the **Show formatting rules for** box, and then click **This Worksheet** to show all of the conditional formats in the current sheet.

4. Click the **Duplicate Values** entry (the only conditional format in the worksheet), and then click **Delete Rule**. No rules appear in the dialog box.

5. Click **OK** to close the dialog box and return to the worksheet.

The data in the Employees worksheet is listed by the employee ID number. Jacek wants to arrange the data values in a different order. You can do that by sorting.

Sorting Records in a Data Range

By default, records appear in the order in which they're entered. However, you can gain valuable insights into your data by arranging the records by one or more chosen fields. You can sort those fields in **ascending order** so that text entries are arranged alphabetically from A to Z, numeric values are sorted from smallest to largest, and date and time values are sorted from oldest to most recent. Excel can also sort the records in **descending order** so that text entries are sorted from Z to A, numeric values are sorted from largest to smallest, and dates and times are sorted from most recent to oldest.

Sorting by a Single Field

You can sort any data range by any field in ascending or descending order. To sort data in ascending order by a single field or column, select any cell in that field or column. On the Data tab, in the Sort & Filter group, click the Sort A to Z button ⬇. To sort in descending order, click the Sort Z to A button ⬇.

Reference

Sorting Records in a Data Range

To sort by a single field:
- Click any cell in the field you want to sort by.
- On the Data tab, in the Sort & Filter group, click the Sort A to Z button or click the Sort Z to A button.

To sort records by multiple fields:
- Click any cell in the data range you want to sort.
- On the Data tab, in the Sort & Filter group, click the Sort button to open the Sort dialog box.
- Click the Sort by arrow and select a field to sort by. Click the Order arrow and select how the field should be sorted.
- For each additional field you want to sort by, click the Then by arrow to add a new row, click the Sort arrow and select a field, and then click the Order arrow and select how the field should be sorted.
- Click OK.

Jacek wants to know which employees have been with the company the longest. You will sort the data in the Employees worksheet in ascending order of the Hire Date field to answer that question.

To sort the Employee data in ascending order by the Hire Date field:

Tip

You can click the Sort & Filter button in the Editing group on the Home tab to sort records by values in a single column.

1. Scroll up the worksheet and click cell **E5** to select a cell in the Hire Date column.

2. On the ribbon, click the **Data** tab.

3. In the Sort & Filter group, click the **Sort A to Z** button [A/Z↓]. The records are rearranged by the date the employees were hired with the earliest hire dates shown first. See Figure 6–7.

Figure 6–7   **Data sorted based on a single column**

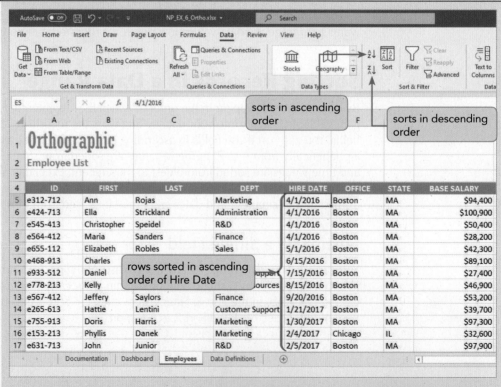

4. Scroll down the worksheet to verify that the values in the Hire Date column appear in ascending order, ending with the most recent hiring dates.

This sort shows that employees who have been with Orthographic the longest were all hired in 2012 in Boston, which isn't surprising given that the company was formed in Boston that year and expanded over the next several years to offices across the country. Next, Jacek wants you to sort the data to find out which employee has the highest base salary and which employee received the largest end-of-year bonus.

To sort the employee data by the Base Salary and Bonus fields:

1. Click cell **H5** to select a cell in the Base Salary field.

2. On the Data tab, in the Sort & Filter group, click the **Sort Z to A** button to sort the employee records from the largest base salary to the smallest. The employee with the largest base salary is Paula Bernardi, an administrator from the San Francisco office, followed by Julie Otis, an administrator in the Chicago office.

3. Click cell **I5** to select a value in the Bonus field, and then click the **Sort Z to A** button to sort the records in descending order of the Bonus field. Bennie Treadwell of the Chicago office IT department received the largest bonus with $5,000. Four employees received bonuses of $4,500.

The Sort A to Z and Sort Z to A buttons provide a fast way to sort your data. But they are limited to sorting by one field at a time. When you want to sort by multiple fields, you can use the Sort dialog box.

Sorting by Multiple Fields

Sometimes you will want to sort by multiple levels of fields. For example, you might want to sort by base salary within a particular department to find the highest paid employees within that department. With sorts that involve multiple fields or columns, you identify one field as the **primary sort field** by which to initially sort the data and a second field as the **secondary sort field** for sorting data within the primary sort field. You can continue this process by identifying a third sort field for values within values of the first two fields and so forth.

Jacek wants to identify the highest-paid employees within each department at each office location. To retrieve that information, you will sort the employee data first by the Office field, then by Department within Office, and finally by Base Salary within Department.

To sort the employee data by the Office, Dept, and Base Salary fields:

1. On the Data tab, in the Sort & Filter group, click the **Sort** button. The Sort dialog box opens. The selected data range is currently set to sort in descending order of the Bonus field. You will change that that first sort field the Office field.

2. Click the **Sort by arrow** to display a list of fields in the data range, and then click **OFFICE** in the list. The first sort is now set the Office field.

3. Click the **Order arrow** to display the sort order options, and then click **A to Z** to sort the data in ascending order of office name. The first sort level is complete.

4. Click the **Add Level** button. A second sort level is added to the sort.

5. Click the **Then by arrow**, and then click **DEPT** to sort the values by department within office location. The sort order is already ascending, so you don't need to change it.

6. Click the **Add Level** button to add a third sort level, click its **Then by arrow** and click **BASE SALARY** to add the Base Salary as the third sort field, and then click its **Order arrow** and click **Largest to Smallest** to change the sort order to descending. See Figure 6–8.

Figure 6–8	Sort dialog box with three sorted fields

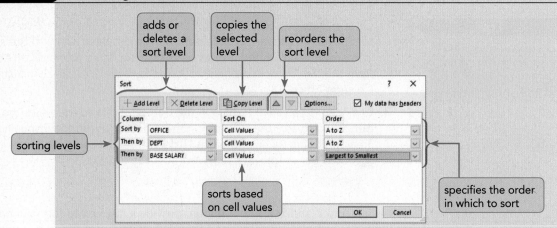

7. Click **OK** to sort the data in the Employees worksheet.

8. Scroll down the worksheet and verify that the data is sorted in ascending order by Office, then ascending order by department name within each office, and finally in descending order by base salary within each department. See Figure 6–9.

Figure 6–9	Employees sorted by the Office, Dept, and Base Salary fields

	A	B	C	D	E	F	G	H	I	J	P
1	**Orthographic**										
2	Employee List										
3											
4	ID	FIRST	LAST	DEPT	HIRE DATE	OFFICE	STATE	BASE SALARY	BONUS	COMMISSION	P
5	e674-714	Jean	Branch	Accounting	4/25/2018	Boston	MA	$92,900	$2,500	$0	
6	e468-520	Cheryl	Burnett	Accounting	5/21/2024	Boston	MA	$85,200	$2,500	$0	
7	e289-115	James	Mccoy	Accounting	10/27/2019	Boston	MA	$84,800	$3,000	$0	
8	e848-816	Walter	Henderson	Accounting	3/4/2020	Boston	MA	$83,200	$2,500	$0	
9	e156-213	Deborah	King	Accounting	3/29/2017	Boston	MA	$80,500	$1,500	$0	
10	e375-419	William	Nix	Accounting	7/30/2023	Boston	MA	$76,300	$3,000	$0	
11	e563-213	Jean	Rakes	Accounting	9/24/2017	Boston	MA	$70,800	$2,500	$0	
12	e126-620	Antonio	Verdejo	Accounting	5/4/2024	Boston	MA	$70,800	$2,500	$0	
13	e670-620	Charles	Parvin	Accounting	8/17/2024	Boston	MA	$67,400	$2,000	$0	
14	e425-617	Clifton	Howton	Accounting	2/2/2021	Boston	MA	$57,900	$1,500	$0	
15	e565-815	Matthew	Trinidad	Accounting	5/1/2019	Boston	MA	$49,000	$1,500	$0	
16	e577-119	Devon	Andersen	Accounting	7/31/2023	Boston	MA	$48,200	$1,500	$0	
17	e147-616	Shelley	Baker	Accounting	10/14/2020	Boston	MA	$43,700	$1,500	$0	

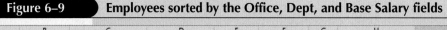

Documentation   Dashboard   **Employees**   Data Definitions   ⊕

120%

Excel supports 64 levels of sort fields, so you can continue to add more sorting levels as needed. However, you probably won't use more than three for most reports.

Insight

Choosing Sort Options

Typically, you sort a data range based on field values. You can also arrange data based on the formats applied to the cell, sorting the cells by the fill color, font color, and conditional formatting icon. To choose a different way of sorting, click the Sort On arrow in the Sort dialog box and select how you want the cells sorted.

All sorts assume that records are in rows and sort the data from top to bottom. If the records are in columns, you can change the sort orientation to sort the records from left to right. To do this, click the Options button in the Sort dialog box and change the orientation.

The default option for sorting text fields is to ignore capitalization so that values like "Chicago" and "CHICAGO" are sorted the same. To make the sort see different capitalization as unique entries, click the Options button in the Sort dialog box, and then click the Case Sensitive check box. If the records are sorted in ascending order, lowercase letters will be displayed first. For example, Chicago will come before CHICAGO.

Sorting with a Custom List

So far, you have sorted data in ascending or descending order. However, some types of text data have their own special sort order. For example, the months of the year—January, February, March, and so on—and the days of week—Sunday, Monday, Tuesday, and so on—have a sort order that is neither alphabetical nor numeric. The Sort dialog box includes sort order options for month name and day name. But, for other sort orders, you can create a **custom list** that arranges the field values in the order you specify.

Jacek wants you to sort the Orthographic offices in the order they opened rather than alphabetically. Each office opened in a different year: Boston in 2016, Chicago in 2017, Denver in 2018, San Francisco in 2020, and Dallas in 2022. You'll create a custom list of those city names in that order and use it in your sort of the employee data.

To create and apply a custom list to sorting:

1. On the Data tab, in the Sort & Filter group, click the **Sort** button. The Sort dialog box opens.

2. In the Office field row, click the **A to Z** box, and then click **Custom List**. The Custom Lists dialog box opens.

3. Click **Add** to begin a new custom list.

4. In the List Entries box, type **Boston** and press **ENTER**. Boston is added to the List Entries box.

5. Type the following city names, pressing **ENTER** after each name: **Chicago**, **Denver**, **San Francisco**, and **Dallas**. See Figure 6–10.

> **Tip**
>
> Any custom list can be sorted in either ascending or descending order.

Figure 6-10   **Custom Lists dialog box**

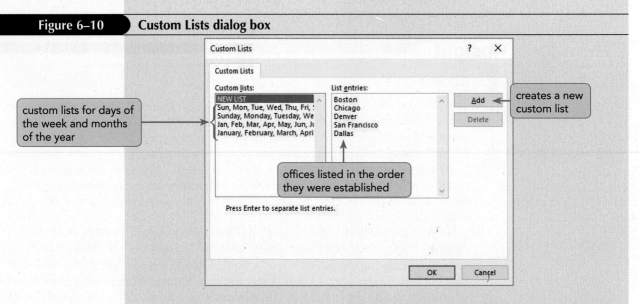

custom lists for days of the week and months of the year

offices listed in the order they were established

creates a new custom list

6. Click **OK** to create the list and return to the Sort dialog box. The Order box for the Office field shows the custom sort order: Boston, Chicago, Denver, San Francisco, and Dallas.

7. Click **OK** to apply this sort order to the employee data.

8. Scroll down the Employees worksheet and verify that employees are sorted in the new order with Boston employees listed first and Dallas employees listed last.

Tip

Any custom lists you create are available to and used by AutoFill.

Any custom list you create will remain part of your Excel settings and available to all other workbooks. If you want to remove a custom list, select the custom list in the Custom Lists dialog box, and click Delete. You will remove this custom list from your Excel settings.

To delete a custom list:

1. On the Data tab, in the Sort & Filter group, click the **Sort** button. The Sort dialog box opens.

2. In the Office field row, click the **Boston**, **Chicago**, **Denver**, **San Francisco**, **Dallas** box, and then click **Custom List**. The Custom Lists dialog box opens.

3. In the Custom lists box, click **Boston**, **Chicago**, **Denver**, **San Francisco**, **Dallas**. The offices appear in the List entries box. You could edit the list entries if needed. Instead you want to delete the entire list.

4. Click **Delete** to delete the custom list, and then click **OK** in the dialog box that opens to confirm that you want to permanently delete this custom list.

5. Click **OK** in each dialog box to return to the Employees worksheet.

Even though you removed this custom list, the employee data is still sorted in the order that the Orthographic offices opened. The sort order will remain unchanged until you sort the data in a different way.

Calculating Subtotals

Analyzing a large data range usually includes making calculations on the data. You can summarize the data by applying summary functions such as COUNT, SUM, and AVERAGE to the entire data range.

Creating a Subtotal Row

Some analysis requires calculations on sections of a data range. To do this, you can add **subtotals**, which are summary functions that are applied to a part of a data range. For example, you can calculate a sum of the base salary for employees from each department or office. To calculate a subtotal, the data must first be sorted by a field, such as the Office or Dept field. Then the Subtotal tool will insert a new row wherever the field changes value and display the subtotal for the previous group of records.

Reference

Adding a Subtotal to a Data Range

- Sort the data range by the field where you want to place the subtotal values.
- On the Data tab, in the Outline group, click the Subtotal button.
- Click the At each change in arrow and select the field where the subtotals will be added to the data range.
- Click the Use function arrow and select the summary function to use in the subtotal calculation.
- In the Add subtotal to box, select the fields for which the subtotal will be calculated.
- Click OK to generate the subtotals.
- Use the outline buttons on the worksheet to expand and collapse groups within the data range.

Jacek wants you to calculate the total spent by each of the five offices on base salaries, bonuses, and commissions. You'll use the Subtotal button to add subtotal rows containing those statistics.

To calculate the salary subtotal for each office:

▶ **1.** On the Data tab, in the Outline group, click the **Subtotal** button. The Subtotal dialog box opens.

▶ **2.** Click the **At each change in arrow**, and then click **OFFICE** in the list of fields to specify adding a subtotal for each Office field value.

▶ **3.** If necessary, click the **Use function arrow**, and then click **Sum** to calculate the sum at each change in the Office field.

▶ **4.** In the Add subtotal to box, click the **BASE SALARY**, **BONUS**, and **COMMISSION** check boxes to select them, and if necessary, click the **EVAL SCORE** check box to deselect it.

▶ **5.** Verify that the **Replace current subtotals** and **Summary below data** check boxes are selected. See Figure 6–11.

Figure 6–11   Subtotal dialog box

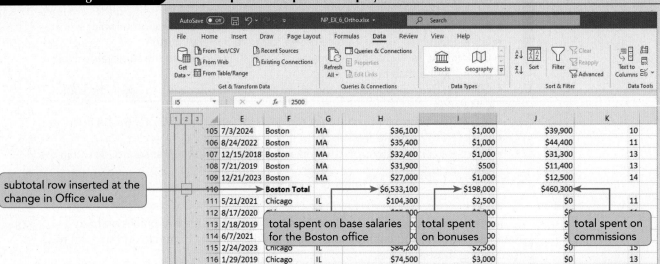

adds a subtotal row at each change in Office

calculates the sum of base salaries, bonuses, and commissions within each office

removes all subtotal rows from the data range

calculates the sum within each office

replaces any previous subtotals in the data range

adds a row containing the grand total across all offices

6. Click **OK** to generate the subtotal rows.

7. Scroll down to row 110 to view the total spent on base salaries, bonuses, and commissions at the Boston office. See Figure 6–12.

Figure 6–12   Total compensation spent on employees in the Boston office

subtotal row inserted at the change in Office value

total spent on base salaries for the Boston office

total spent on bonuses

total spent on commissions

8. Continue to scroll down the worksheet to view the subtotals for offices in Chicago, San Francisco, Denver, and Dallas. Row 540 at the bottom of data range shows the grand total spent on commissions for all five offices.

The subtotal rows show that the Boston office spent $6,533,100 on base salaries, $198,000 on bonuses, and $460,300 on commissions. Other offices have similar totals. The grand total in row 540 shows that the entire company spent $32,803,000 on base salaries, $985,500 on bonuses, and $2,413,900 in commissions.

You can include several summary statistics in the subtotals row. Jacek wants this report to also include the average employee compensation in each office and across all offices. You'll add the AVERAGE function to the subtotal report.

To add a second summary statistic to the employees subtotals:

▶ **1.** On the Data tab, in the Outline group, click the **Subtotal** button. The Subtotal dialog box opens.

▶ **2.** Click the **Use function arrow**, and then click **Average** in the list of summary statics.

▶ **3.** Click the **Replace current subtotals** check box to deselect it. This ensures that the averages are added to the current subtotal values instead of replacing them.

▶ **4.** Click **OK** to add an average calculation to the subtotals.

▶ **5.** Scroll down the worksheet and verify that each office shows the average and the total amount Orthographic spends on employee compensation. See Figure 6–13.

Uncheck the Replace current subtotals check box so new statistics don't overwrite the current ones.

Figure 6–13	Sums and averages for the subtotal rows

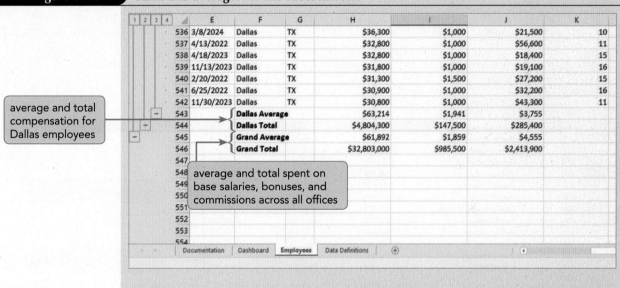

average and total compensation for Dallas employees

average and total spent on base salaries, bonuses, and commissions across all offices

▶ **6.** Scroll back up to the top of the worksheet.

This report tells Jacek that across all offices, Orthographic pays its employees an average of $61,892 in base salary, $1,859 in bonuses, and $4,555 in commissions.

Using the Subtotal Outline View

Rather than view detailed information on every field, you might want to view only summary statistics. The outline tool lets you control the level of detail displayed in the worksheet. The Employees worksheet has four levels in the outline of its data range. The topmost level, or Level 1, displays only the grand totals. Level 2 displays the total spent at each office. Level 3 displays both the total and average spent at each office. Finally, the bottommost level, Level 4, displays individual records. Clicking the outline buttons located to the left of the row numbers lets you choose how much detail you want to see in the worksheet. You will use the outline buttons to expand and collapse different sections of the data range.

To expand and collapse the employee data outline:

▶ 1. Click the **Level 1 Outline** button ①　to collapse the outline. All of the rows between row 4 and row 545 are hidden. Only the grand average and grand total values for all offices are visible.

▶ 2. Click the **Level 2 Outline** button ②　to expand the outline to the second level. The totals for all offices as well as grand average and grand total are visible.

▶ 3. Click the **Level 3 Outline** button ③　to show the averages and totals for each office and for all offices. See Figure 6–14.

Figure 6–14　　**Sums and averages for each office and across offices**

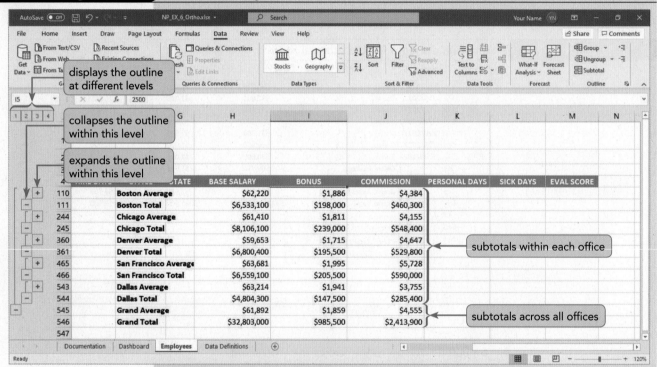

▶ 4. Click the **Show Detail** button ⊞ by row 465 to display employee records for only the San Francisco office. The outline expands to show rows 362 through 464. This lets you display select sections of the outline.

▶ 5. Click the **Hide Detail** ⊟ by row 465 to hide the rows 362 through 464 in the worksheet. The employee records from the San Francisco office are again hidden.

▶ 6. Click the **Level 4 Outline** button ④　to display all of the employee records. All of the rows from the data range are visible in the worksheet.

You have finished reviewing the employee records and the subtotals, so you can remove the subtotals from the worksheet. You will remove the subtotals now.

To remove the subtotals from the Employees worksheet:

▶ **1.** On the Data tab, in the Outline group, click the **Subtotal** button. The Subtotal dialog box opens.

▶ **2.** Click **Remove All**. The subtotals and the outline groups are removed from the worksheet.

▶ **3.** Save the workbook.

If at any time you wish to display the subtotals again or calculate different subtotals, you can rerun the Subtotal command.

Insight

Creating Manual Outlines

You can create outlines with any data range. Outlines can be applied to the range's rows or columns. To outline data, select the rows or columns you want to group and then click the Group button in the Outline group on the Data tab. Outline buttons appear in the worksheet. You can use these buttons to expand or collapse the outline. To remove the outlining, click the Ungroup button in the Outline group on the Data tab, and then click Clear Outline.

Many financial statements, such as profit and loss statements, already have subtotals. If you want to add outlining to a long and complicated financial statement, select anywhere within the statement and click the Group button and then click Auto Outline. The financial statement will automatically be grouped and outlined at each location of a subtotal.

You've completed your initial work with the employee records. In the next session, you will learn how to show subsets of the data range and how to convert a data range into an Excel table.

Review

Session 6.1 Quick Check

1. What is a field? What is a record?
2. If you split the worksheet into panes at cell E3, how many panes are created?
3. What are the three freeze pane options?
4. When highlighting duplicate values with a conditional format, do the duplicate values have to be adjacent to each other?
5. Why is it *not* a good idea for a company to treat employee records with duplicate first and last names as duplicate records?
6. When an ascending sort order is used, how is a date-time field sorted?
7. If you want to sort employees by the value of the Hire Date field within each value of the Dept field, which field is the primary sort field? Which is the secondary sort field?
8. Before you can add subtotals to a data range, what must you first do with the data?

Session 6.2 Visual Overview:

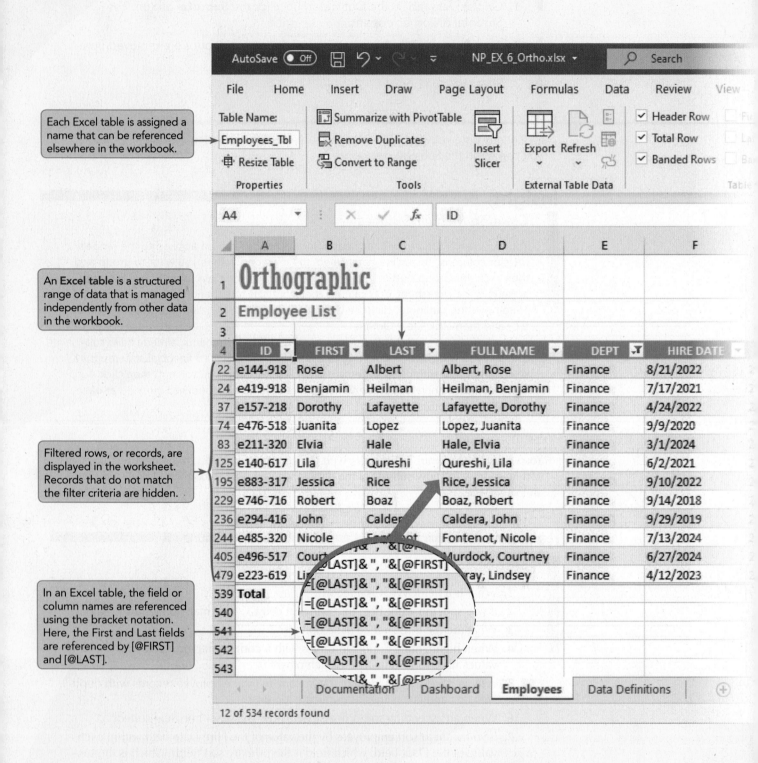

Each Excel table is assigned a name that can be referenced elsewhere in the workbook.

An **Excel table** is a structured range of data that is managed independently from other data in the workbook.

Filtered rows, or records, are displayed in the worksheet. Records that do not match the filter criteria are hidden.

In an Excel table, the field or column names are referenced using the bracket notation. Here, the First and Last fields are referenced by [@FIRST] and [@LAST].

Filters and Excel Tables

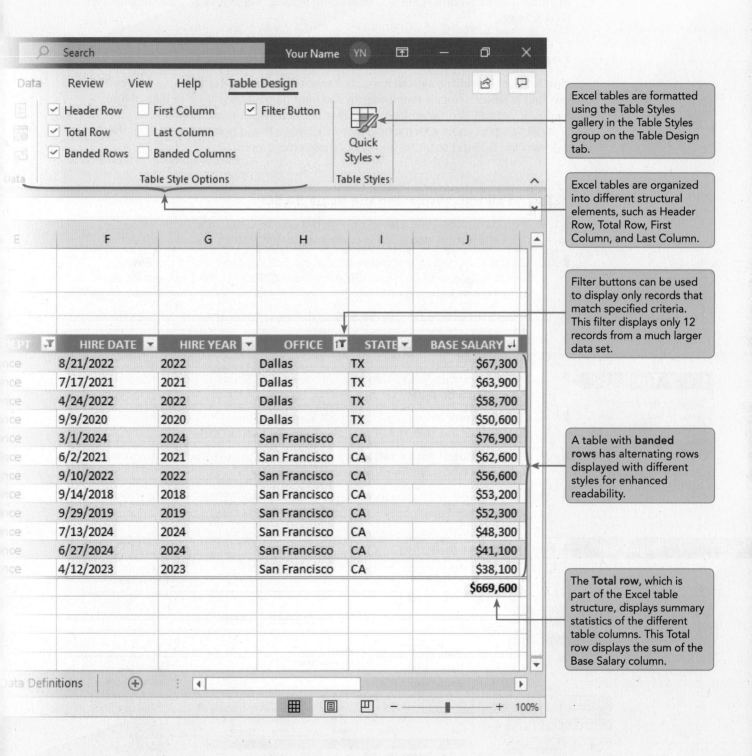

Excel tables are formatted using the Table Styles gallery in the Table Styles group on the Table Design tab.

Excel tables are organized into different structural elements, such as Header Row, Total Row, First Column, and Last Column.

Filter buttons can be used to display only records that match specified criteria. This filter displays only 12 records from a much larger data set.

A table with **banded rows** has alternating rows displayed with different styles for enhanced readability.

The **Total row**, which is part of the Excel table structure, displays summary statistics of the different table columns. This Total row displays the sum of the Base Salary column.

DEPT	HIRE DATE	HIRE YEAR	OFFICE	STATE	BASE SALARY
nce	8/21/2022	2022	Dallas	TX	$67,300
nce	7/17/2021	2021	Dallas	TX	$63,900
nce	4/24/2022	2022	Dallas	TX	$58,700
nce	9/9/2020	2020	Dallas	TX	$50,600
nce	3/1/2024	2024	San Francisco	CA	$76,900
nce	6/2/2021	2021	San Francisco	CA	$62,600
nce	9/10/2022	2022	San Francisco	CA	$56,600
nce	9/14/2018	2018	San Francisco	CA	$53,200
nce	9/29/2019	2019	San Francisco	CA	$52,300
nce	7/13/2024	2024	San Francisco	CA	$48,300
nce	6/27/2024	2024	San Francisco	CA	$41,100
nce	4/12/2023	2023	San Francisco	CA	$38,100
					$669,600

Locating Cells Within a Worksheet

As the number of records grows within a data range, it becomes increasingly difficult to locate specific records. One way of locating records within a large data range is with Find & Select.

Finding and Selecting Multiple Cells

Find & Select can locate cells that match a specified criterion. For example, you can use Find & Select to locate employees by their last name, base salary, or date of hire. Find & Select can also list multiple cells that satisfy the specified criterion.

Jacek wants to know which employees received year-end bonuses of $4,500. You will use Find & Select to locate and select those employees.

To find all cells displaying the value $4,500:

1. If you took a break at the end of the previous session, make sure the NP_EX_6_Ortho workbook is open and the Employees worksheet is active.

2. On the ribbon, click the **Home** tab. In the Editing group, click the **Find & Select** button, and then click **Find** (or press **CTRL+F**). The Find and Replace dialog box opens.

3. In the Find what box, type **$4,500** as the value to locate.

4. Click **Options** if necessary to display an expanded list of find and replace options.

5. If necessary, click the **Within** box, and then click **Sheet** to limit the search to the current worksheet.

6. Click the **Look in** box, and then click **Values** to search based on the values displayed in the cells rather than the formulas used in those cells.

7. Click the **Match entire cell contents** check box to limit the search only to those cells whose entire displayed value is $4,500.

8. Click **Find All**. Four cells in the Employees worksheet match the specified criterion. See Figure 6–15.

Tip

To make a search sensitive to upper- and lower-case letters, click the Match Case check box.

Figure 6–15   Find and Replace dialog box

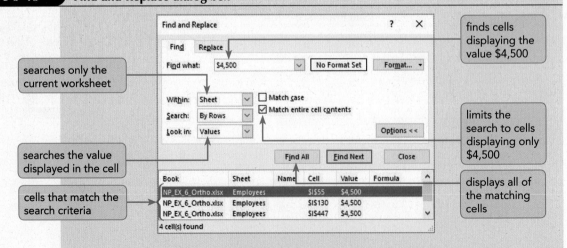

searches only the current worksheet

finds cells displaying the value $4,500

searches the value displayed in the cell

limits the search to cells displaying only $4,500

cells that match the search criteria

displays all of the matching cells

▶ **9.** Click the first entry in the list. Excel selects cell I55, the record for Rita Roden of the IT department in the Boston Office.

▶ **10.** Click each of the other three entries in the list to view the records for Julie Otis, Paula Bernardi, and Michael Fowlkes, who each received a $4,500 end-of-the year bonus.

▶ **11.** Click **Close** to close the Find and Replace dialog box.

The Find & Select command will select any cell that displays the value $4,500. It does not distinguish between fields.

Finding Cells by Type

Find & Select can also locate cells based on criteria other than cell value, such as whether the cell contains a formula, constant, blank, or conditional formatting rule. To locate cells of a specific type, click the Find & Select button in the Editing group on the Home tab, and then click Go To Special. The Go To dialog box shown in Figure 6–16 opens.

Figure 6–16 Go To Special dialog box

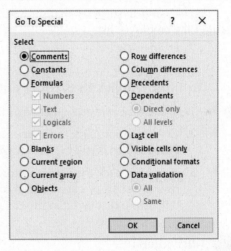

The dialog box includes many ways to locate cells by types. For example, to select all of the records in a data range, click any cell in the data range, open the Go To Special dialog box, click the Current region option button, and then click OK. This approach is a big time-saver if you are working with a data range composed of thousands of records and dozens of fields.

Filtering Data

Find & Select is a quick way of locating cells of a specific type within a worksheet and across worksheets. But, it does not search based on multiple criteria. To find records based on search criteria that involve multiple fields, you must filter the data.

Filtering Based on One Field

Filtering data hides the rows whose values do not match the search criteria. Those rows are not removed from the worksheet. They can be redisplayed by removing the filter or applying a new filter. When you create a filter, Excel displays a filter button alongside each field name. By clicking the filter button, you can choose which values in that field to display, hiding the rows or records that do not match that value.

Reference

Filtering Data

- To add filter buttons to a data range or table, on the Data tab, in the Sort & Filter group, click the Filter button.
- To filter by a single field, click its filter button, click the check boxes for the values to include in the filter, and then click OK.
- To filter by a numeric field, click the filter button, click Number Filters, click the filter to apply, and then click OK.
- To filter by a date field, click the filter button, click Date Filters, click the filter to apply, and then click OK.
- To filter by a text field, click the filter button, click Text Filters, click the filter to apply, and then click OK.

Jacek wants to see a list that shows only employees in the Chicago office. You will filter the employee list.

To filter the list to display only the Chicago records:

1. In the Employees worksheet, click cell **A5** to select a cell in the data range.

2. On the ribbon, click the **Data** tab, and then in the Sort & Filter group, click the **Filter** button. Filter buttons appear next to each field name in the range A4:M4.

3. In cell F4, click the **filter** button next to the Office field name. The filter menu opens, listing the five unique office values within the Office field. Currently all offices are displayed in the data range. See Figure 6–17.

Tip

Select any cell within a data range to enable the Filter command for the entire range.

Figure 6–17   Filter criteria

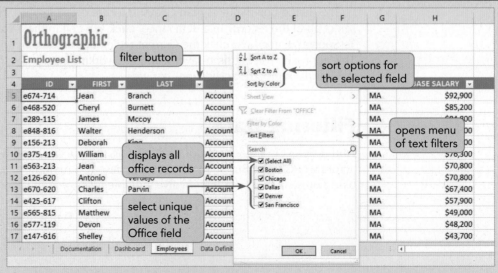

▶ **4.** Click the **Select All** check box to deselect all the check boxes, and then click the **Chicago** check box. Only the Chicago office is selected.

▶ **5.** Click **OK** to apply the filter. Only employees from the Chicago office appear in the worksheet. The records for other employees are hidden. See Figure 6–18.

Figure 6–18   **Employee records for the Chicago office**

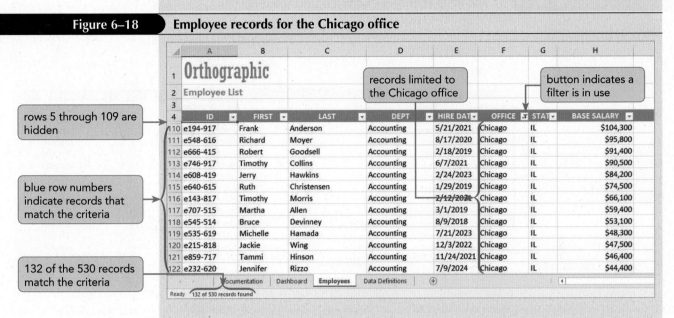

rows 5 through 109 are hidden

blue row numbers indicate records that match the criteria

132 of the 530 records match the criteria

▶ **6.** Scroll down the worksheet to verify that only employees from the Chicago office are listed.

When a field or column is filtered, the filter button changes from ▾ to ▼ as a visual reminder that some of the data records are hidden because of the filter. The status bar also indicates the number of records that match the filter criteria. In this case 132 of the 530 records in the data range match the filter. Row numbers for records that match the criteria are displayed in blue.

Filtering Based on Multiple Fields

You can filter a data range based on criteria from multiple fields. Each additional filter reduces the number of records displayed since a record has to fulfill all filter criteria to be selected. To use filters from multiple fields, select the filter button from other column headers in the data range.

Jacek wants you to add a filter to display only those Chicago employees working in the IT or R&D departments. You'll add that filter to the employees list.

To add a second filter to the employee lists:

▶ **1.** In cell **D4**, click the **filter** button next to the Dept field name. The filter menu opens.

▶ **2.** Click the **Select All** check box to deselect all the department check boxes.

▶ **3.** Click the **IT** and **R&D** check boxes to select only those two departments from the list.

4. Click **OK** to add this filter to the data range. The number of records found reduces to 35, which is the number of people employed in the IT or R&D departments of Chicago. See Figure 6–19.

Figure 6–19   IT and R&D employees from the Chicago office

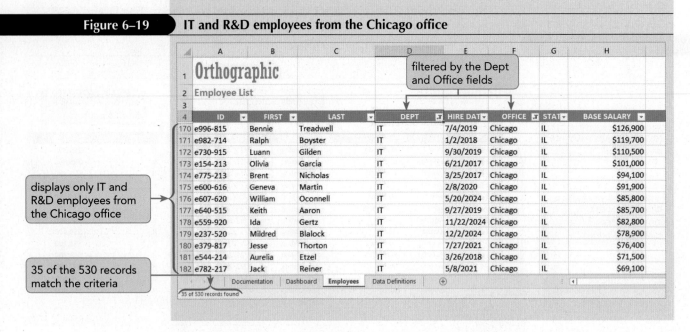

displays only IT and R&D employees from the Chicago office

35 of the 530 records match the criteria

filtered by the Dept and Office fields

The two filters you've applied have selected records based on field categories. You can also filter data based on date and time, numbers, and text.

Using Criteria Filters

The filters created are limited to selecting records for fields matching a specific value or set of values. For more general criteria, you can create **criteria filters**, which are expressions involving dates and times, numeric values, and text strings. For example, you can filter the employee data to show only those employees hired within a specific date range or who receive a base salary above a certain amount. Figure 6–20 describes some of the criteria filters that you can apply to your data.

| Figure 6–20 | Text, number, and date criteria filters |

Filter	Criteria	Records Displayed
Text	Equals	Exactly match the specified text
	Does Not Equal	Do not exactly match the specified text
	Begins With	Begin with the specified text
	Ends With	End with the specified text
	Contains	Have the specified text anywhere
	Does Not Contain	Do not have the specified text anywhere
Number	Equals	Exactly match the specified number
	Greater Than or Equal to	Are greater than or equal to the specified number
	Less Than	Are less than the specified number
	Between	Are greater than or equal to and less than or equal to the specified numbers
	Top 10	Are the top or bottom 10 (or the specified number)
	Above Average	Are greater than the average
Date	Today	Have the current date
	Last Week	Are in the prior week
	Next Month	Are in the month following the current month
	Last Quarter	Are in the previous quarter of the year (quarters defined as Jan, Feb, Mar; Apr, May, June; and so on)
	Year to Date	Are since January 1 of the current year to the current date
	Last Year	Are in the previous year (based on the current date)

Jacek wants to further limit the employees list to include only those employees hired during 2024 and who have a base salary of at least $90,000 per year. You will use criteria filters now to add those two conditions to the worksheet.

To filter the employee list for dates and values:

1. In cell **E4**, click the **filter** button next to the Hire Date field name.

2. On the filter menu, point to **Date Filters**, and then click **After** in the date filter menu. The Custom AutoFilter dialog box opens.

3. Click the upper-left **arrow**, click **is after or equal to**, press **TAB**, and then type **1/1/2024** as the first date in the filter.

4. Verify the **And** option button is selected.

5. Click the bottom-left **arrow**, click **is before or equal to**, press **TAB**, and then type **12/31/2024** as the last date in the filter. See Figure 6–21.

Tip

You can also enter a date by clicking the calendar icon next to the input box and selecting a date from the calendar.

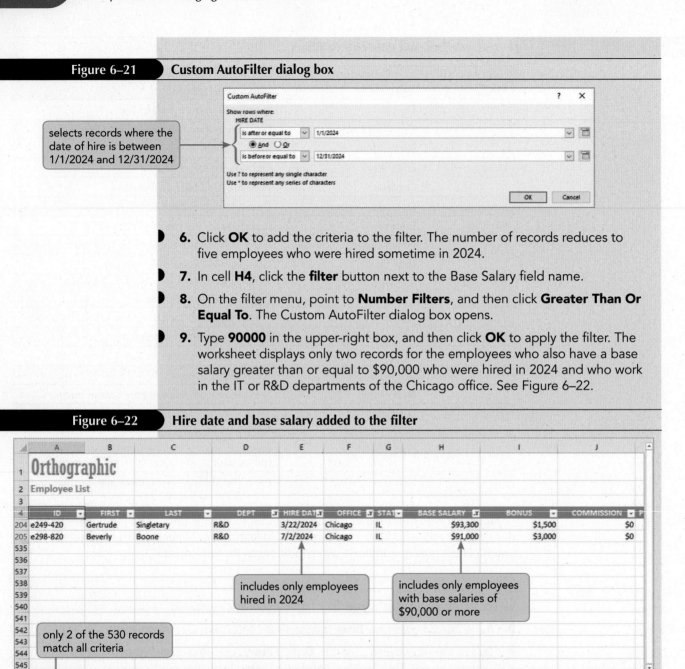

Figure 6–21   **Custom AutoFilter dialog box**

selects records where the date of hire is between 1/1/2024 and 12/31/2024

6. Click **OK** to add the criteria to the filter. The number of records reduces to five employees who were hired sometime in 2024.

7. In cell **H4**, click the **filter** button next to the Base Salary field name.

8. On the filter menu, point to **Number Filters**, and then click **Greater Than Or Equal To**. The Custom AutoFilter dialog box opens.

9. Type **90000** in the upper-right box, and then click **OK** to apply the filter. The worksheet displays only two records for the employees who also have a base salary greater than or equal to $90,000 who were hired in 2024 and who work in the IT or R&D departments of the Chicago office. See Figure 6–22.

Figure 6–22   **Hire date and base salary added to the filter**

ID	FIRST	LAST	DEPT	HIRE DATE	OFFICE	STATE	BASE SALARY	BONUS	COMMISSION	P
e249-420	Gertrude	Singletary	R&D	3/22/2024	Chicago	IL	$93,300	$1,500	$0	
e298-820	Beverly	Boone	R&D	7/2/2024	Chicago	IL	$91,000	$3,000	$0	

includes only employees hired in 2024

includes only employees with base salaries of $90,000 or more

only 2 of the 530 records match all criteria

Ready   2 of 530 records found

Through the use of criteria filters, you can report to Jacek that only Gertude Singletary and Bevery Boone of the Chicago R&D department were hired during 2024 at base salaries greater than or equal to $90,000.

Insight

Exploring Text Filters

Text filters are useful for locating records based on all or part of a specified text string. If you want to match a certain pattern of characters within a text string, use the text filter options Begins With, Ends With, or Contains operators to filter a text field based on the characters the string starts with, ends with, or includes. The following are some text fields that can be applied to names and addresses:

- To match names like Smith, Smithe, or Smythe, use the Begins With text filter, matching all names which start with "Sm."
- To match names like Robertson, Anderson, Dawson, or Gibson, apply the Ends With text filter, matching all names that end with "son."
- To match addresses that share a common street name like 101 East Main St., 45B West Main St., or 778 West Main St., apply the Contains text filter, matching all street address containing "Main."

For more advanced text filters, you can use wildcard characters, which are symbols that match a character pattern. The ? character represents any single character and the * character represents any series of characters. For example, a text filter based on the criteria "Will?" will match any name starting with "Wil" followed by 0 or 1 character, like Will, Wills, or Wille, but not Williams. A text file based on the criteria "Wil*son" will match any name that starts with "Wil" and ends with "son" and has 0 or more characters in-between such as Wilson, Wilkerson, and Williamson.

Clearing Filters

After you have narrowed down a data range to a select few records, you can copy the data in the data range by selecting the visible rows and columns and pasting the selection to a new worksheet or workbook. This pastes only the selected records, ignoring any hidden rows or columns in the selection.

Once you have the information you need from the filtered data range, you can clear all the filters, revealing any hidden rows and columns. You'll clear the date filters from the employees list.

To clear all the filters from the employees list:

▶ **1.** On the Data tab, in the Sort & Filter group, click the **Clear** button to remove all the filters. All the records are redisplayed in the worksheet.

▶ **2.** In the Sort & Filter group, click the **Filter** button. The filter buttons are removed from the field name cells in the worksheet.

If you want to clear only one filter out of multiple filters, click the filter button for that field, and then click Clear Filter on the filter menu.

Applying an Advanced Filter

Filter buttons are limited to combining fields using the AND logical operator. For example, you searched records for employees in the Chicago office AND working in the IT or R& D departments AND hired during 2024 AND having a base salary of at least $90,000. If any one of those conditions is not met, the record fails the search criteria. You cannot use the filter buttons to create filters that combine fields with the OR logical operator, such as a filter that shows employees who work in the Chicago office (regardless of salary) OR make at least $90,000 a year (regardless of location).

Advanced filtering provides a way of writing more complicated filter criteria that involve expressions that combine fields using the AND and OR logical operators. To write an advanced filter, you must define a **criteria range** that lays out the specifications of the filter. Criteria ranges are placed in a table with the following structure:

1. Field names are listed in the first row of the table and must exactly match the field names from the data range. A field name can be repeated in the table.

2. Criteria for each field are listed in subsequent rows of the table.

3. Criteria within the same row are combined using the AND logical operator.

4. Criteria in different rows are combined using the OR logical operator.

Figure 6–23 show an example of a criteria range that contains three criteria entered in three rows.

Figure 6–23   **Criteria range with three conditions**

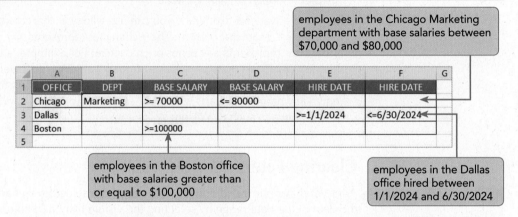

employees in the Chicago Marketing department with base salaries between $70,000 and $80,000

employees in the Dallas office hired between 1/1/2024 and 6/30/2024

employees in the Boston office with base salaries greater than or equal to $100,000

Three groups of employees would be matched by this advanced filter:

1. Employees in the Chicago Marketing department with base salaries between $70,000 and $80,000.

2. Employees in the Dallas office hired between 1/1/2024 and 6/30/2024.

3. Employees in the Boston office with a base salary of $100,000 or more.

Advanced filters can filter the data records in place as was done with the filter buttons or they can be used to copy records matching the filter criteria to a new location. If you copy the filtered records, all the columns from the data range satisfying the criteria will be copied in their current order and format. The copied values are not linked to the original values, so if you change your data values or the search criteria, you will have to copy the values again.

Reference

Applying an Advanced Filter

- Create a criteria range in which the field names are in the first row, criteria for each field are listed in subsequent rows, criteria within the same row are combined with the AND operator, and criteria in different rows are combined with the OR operator.
- On the Data tab, in the Sort & Filter group, click the Advanced button.
- Specify whether to filter the data in place or copy to another location.
- In the List range box, specify the range containing the data values. In the Criteria range box, specify the range containing the criteria.
- Click OK to apply the advanced filter.

Jacek has a colleague who wants a list of the employees in the Dallas accounting department with base salaries between $60,000 and $70,000 or employees in the Denver accounting department with base salaries between $80,000 and $90,000. You will use an advanced filter to find records satisfying either of these criteria.

To enter the criteria range for an advanced filter:

▶ 1. Open the **NP_EX_6-2.xlsx** workbook located in the **Excel6 > Module** folder included with your Data Files and then save the workbook as **NP_EX_6_Filters** in the location specified by your instructor.

▶ 2. In the **Documentation** sheet, enter your name in cell B3 and the date in cell B4.

▶ 3. Go to the **Filters** worksheet. Jacek has already entered the field names for this advanced filter in this sheet.

▶ 4. In cell **A6**, type **Dallas** as the office to include in the filter, press **TAB**, type **Accounting** in cell B6 as the department to include, press **TAB**, type **>=60000** in cell C6 as the minimum base salary to include, press **TAB**, type **<=70000** in cell D6 as the maximum base salary to include, and then press **ENTER**. The first row of the criteria range will filter the employee records to display only employees in the Dallas office who work in the Accounting department and have a base salary between $60,000 and $70,000.

▶ 5. In the second row of the criteria range, type **Denver** in cell A7, press **TAB**, type **Accounting** in cell B7, press **TAB**, type **>=80000** in cell C7, press **TAB**, type **<=90000** in cell D7, and then press **ENTER**. See Figure 6–24.

| Figure 6–24 | Criteria range for matching accounting employees |

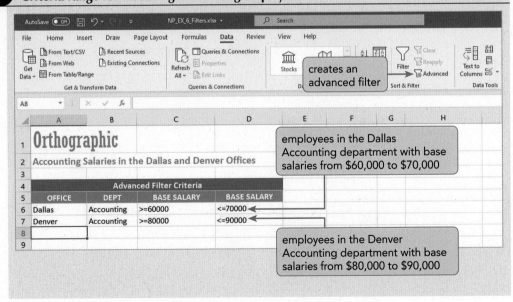

Next you will use an advanced filter to copy the records that match these criteria from the Employees worksheet in the NP_6_Ortho workbook to the Filters worksheet in the NP_6_Filters workbook.

To copy the employee data with an advanced filter:

▶ **1.** On the ribbon, click the **Data** tab, and then in the Sort & Filter group, click the **Advanced** button. The Advanced Filter dialog box opens.

▶ **2.** Click the **Copy to another location** option button to copy matching records from the data range, and then press **TAB** to make the List range box active.

▶ **3.** Go to the **Employees** worksheet in the **NP_EX_6_Ortho** workbook, click cell **A4**, and then press **CTRL+SHIFT+SPACEBAR** to select the entire data range. The external reference [NP_EX_6_Ortho.xlsx]Employees!$A$4:$M$534 appears in the List range box.

▶ **4.** Press **TAB** to make the Criteria Range box active.

▶ **5.** Select the range **A5:D7** containing the advanced filter criteria. The 3-D reference Filters!$A$5:$D$7 appears in the Criteria range box.

▶ **6.** Press **TAB** to make the Copy to box active, and then click cell **A9** to specify the location for inserting the copied records. See Figure 6–25.

Figure 6–25   Advanced Filter dialog box

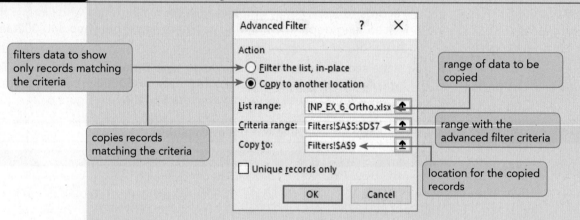

▶ **7.** Click **OK** to copy the records that match the advanced filter criteria. See Figure 6–26.

| Figure 6–26 | Advanced filter results |

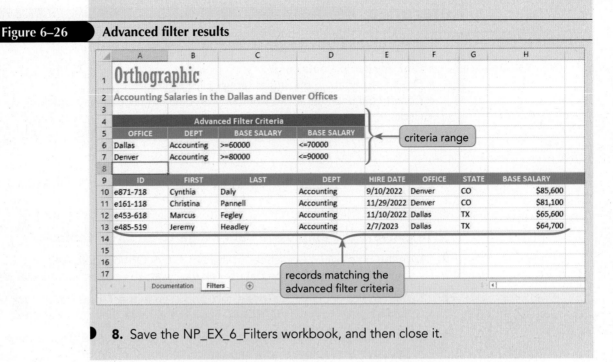

8. Save the NP_EX_6_Filters workbook, and then close it.

Four employees match the specified criteria: Marcus Fegley and Jeremy Headley in the Dallas Accounting department, and Cynthia Daly and Christina Pannell in the Denver Accounting department.

Creating an Excel Table

So far, you have relied on Excel to recognize that a range of cells with labels in the first row and data values in subsequent rows contained fields and records to be analyzed. To explicitly indicate that a range contains fields and records, you can create a structured range of data also known as an Excel table.

Converting a Range to a Table

An Excel table is a range of data that is treated by Excel as a single object that can be managed independently from other data in the workbook. Excel tables support several features that are not available with data ranges, including:

- Sorting and filtering tools built into the table itself
- Table styles to format different features of the table, including banded rows and columns
- Automatic insertion of a totals row containing summary statistics for each field, which update as records are inserted or deleted
- Calculated values that use field names rather than cell references to make formulas easier to write and understand
- Named references to different parts of the table structure, including table columns, total rows, and header rows

Almost anything you can do with a data range, such as filtering and sorting, you can do with an Excel table. The main exception is that you *cannot* add subtotals to an Excel table because the table structure of field and records must be preserved, which doesn't allow for the insertion of subtotal rows.

Reference

Converting a Data Range to an Excel Table

- Click any cell in a data range.
- On the Insert tab, in the Tables group, click Tables.
- Confirm the data range and whether your data range contains headers.
- Click OK to create the Excel table.

Jacek asks you to convert the employee data to an Excel table. You'll do that now.

To convert the employee data range to an Excel table:

1. In the Employees worksheet of the NP_EX_6_Ortho workbook, click cell **A4** to select a cell within the data range you want to convert to an Excel table.

2. On the ribbon, click the **Insert** tab, and then in the Tables group click the **Table** button (or press **CTRL+T**). The Create Table dialog box opens.

3. Verify that **=$A$4:$M$534** is specified as the data range. This range contains all the employee data and the column headers.

4. Verify that the **My tables has headers** check box is selected. This generates field names based on the labels in the first row of the selected range.

5. Click **OK** to convert the data range to a table. Filter buttons are added to each field name and banded rows distinguish one row from the next. The Table Design tab appears on the ribbon, which includes commands for formatting and analyzing the Excel table.

6. Click cell **A4** to remove highlighting from the entire table. See Figure 6–27.

Figure 6–27   **Employees data converted to an Excel table**

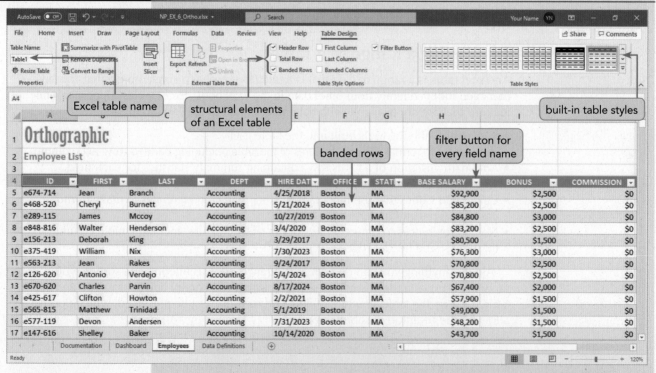

7. Scroll down the Employees worksheet. As you scroll further down the list, the field names replace the column letters, eliminating the need for freeze panes to keep the field names in view.

An Excel table has the following structural elements:

- **Header row**—The first row of the table containing the field names
- **Total row**—A row at the bottom of the table containing summary statistics for selected fields
- **First column**—The leftmost column of the table
- **Last column**—The rightmost column of the table
- **Banded rows**—The odd- and even-numbered rows of the table formatted differently to make records easier to distinguish
- **Banded columns**—The odd- and even-numbered columns of the table formatted differently to make fields easier to distinguish
- **Filter buttons**—Buttons next to each field name for filtering and sorting the table data

An Excel table is automatically assigned a name that can be referenced in any formula. The first table is named Table1, the next is named Table2, and so forth. You can rename any table with a more meaningful and descriptive name. Table names must start with a letter or an underscore but can use any combination of letters, numbers, and underscores for the rest of the name. Table names cannot include spaces.

Jacek wants a more descriptive name for this table. You will rename Table1 as Employees_Tbl.

To rename the Table1 Excel table:

1. With the table still selected, on the ribbon, click the **Table Design** tab, if necessary.

2. In the Properties group, click the **Table Name** box.

3. Type **Employees_Tbl** as the new name, and then press **ENTER**. The Excel table is renamed.

An Excel table name is added to the Name box with global scope, so you can go to an Excel table from any location in the workbook by selecting the table's name from the Name box just as you would for global named ranges. To convert an Excel table back to a data range, click the Convert to Range button in the Tools group on the Table Design tab.

Using Table Styles

Because an Excel table is composed of structural elements, you can apply styles to different parts of the table. For example, you can create a special style for the table's first or last columns or the header row containing the field names. Excel also includes a gallery of built-in table styles that can be used to apply a professional look to the table. Jacek wants you to change the Excel table style to make it easier to read.

To apply styles to the Employees_Tbl table:

1. On the Table Design tab, in the Table Style Options group, click the **First Column** and **Last Column** check boxes to select those table elements.

2. Scroll through the worksheet and verify that values for the ID field in column A and the Eval Score field in column M are displayed in bold.

3. In the Table Style Options group, click the **First Column** and **Last Column** check boxes to deselect them. The boldface style applied to those two columns is removed.

4. In the Table Style Options group, click the **Banded Rows** check box to deselect it, and remove banded rows from the table. The table is harder to read this way, so Jacek wants you to add the banded rows back to the table.

5. Click the **Banded Rows** check box again to select it and add banded rows back to the table.

6. Click the **Filter Button** check box to remove the filter buttons from the Excel table, and then click the **Filter Button** check box again to redisplay them.

Tip

To remove table styles, click Clear in the Table Styles gallery.

7. In the Table Styles group, click the **More** button in the Table Styles gallery to display different styles that can be applied to the table.

8. Point to different styles in the Table Styles gallery. Live Previews shows how the Employees_Tbl table appears with those styles. See Figure 6–28.

Figure 6–28   Live Preview of the Employees_Tbl table with a table style

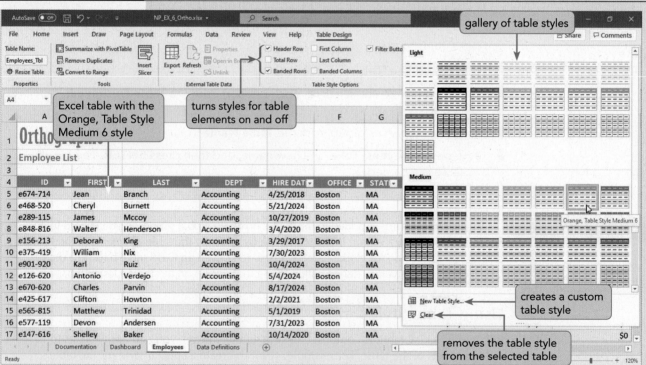

9. In the Table Styles gallery, click **Orange, Table Style Medium 6** to apply it to the Employees_Tbl table.

Table styles do not, by default, override the formatting applied to individual cells. So, if you format a cell or range those formats will be unaffected by your choice of table styles. To override a cell format with the table style, right-click the table style in the gallery, and then click Apply and Clear Formatting on the shortcut menu.

Adding a Total Row

A useful table element for data analysis is the Total row, which is added to the end of the table after the last data record. The Total row calculates summary statistics, including the average, sum, minimum, and maximum of select fields within the table. The Total row is formatted with values displayed in bold and a double border line separating the data records from the Total row.

Jacek wants you to add summary statistics to the Employees_Tbl table. You'll calculate those statistics by adding a Total row.

To add a Total Row to the Employees Excel table:

▶ 1. On the Table Design tab, in the Table Style Options group, click the **Total Row** check box to select it (or press **CTRL+SHIFT+T**). The Total row is added at the bottom of the table. Excel has already calculated the sum of the values in the Eval Score field.

▶ 2. Click the cell in the Total row for the BASE SALARY column. An arrow button appears. You use this button to select a summary statistic.

▶ 3. Click the **arrow**, and then click **Sum** in the list of summary statistics. The cell displays $32,803,000, which is the amount that company spent on base salaries.

▶ 4. Press **TAB** to move to the Bonus column in the Total row, click the **arrow**, and then click **Sum** in the list of statistics. The cell displays $985,500, which is the amount that Orthographic spent on bonuses.

▶ 5. Press **TAB** to move to the Commission column, click the **arrow**, and then click **Sum**. The cell displays $2,413,900, which is the amount the company spent on commissions.

▶ 6. Press **TAB** to move to the Personal Days column, click the **arrow**, and then click **Average**. The cell displays about 13.978 as the average number of personal days claimed by the employees.

▶ 7. In the Total row, for the Sick Days field, select **Average** from the list of statistics. The cell displays about 6.213 as the average number of sick days.

The Total row already includes the sum of the Eval Score values, but that does not provide any relevant information to Jacek. Instead, Jacek wants to see the average evaluation score employees received.

▶ 8. In the Total row, change the Eval Score column to show **Average** as the statistic. The cell displays about 3.964 as the average evaluation score. See Figure 6–29.

Figure 6–29   **Total row added to the Employees_Tbl table**

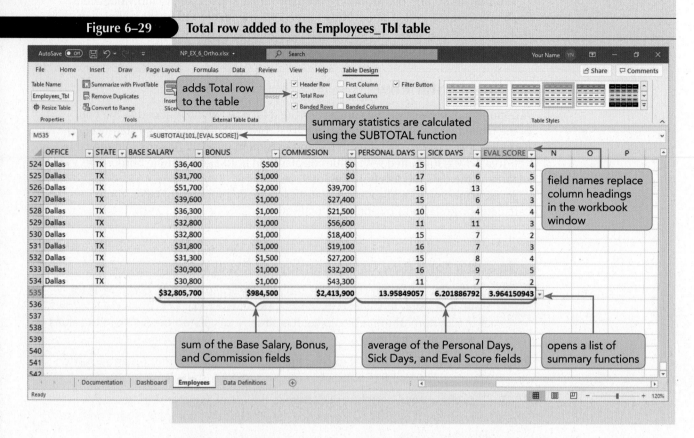

The values in the Total row automatically update to reflect any filters applied to the table. For example, if you filter the table to show only records from the Boston office, the Total row will show the sums and averages of employees from Boston.

Adding and Deleting Records

When you add or delete records within an Excel table, the table adjusts to the new contents. The format applied to the banded rows updates to accommodate the new data set size. The calculations in the Total row reflect the new data.

Jacek wants you to edit the records in the Employees worksheet. Jean Rakes of the Accounting department in Boston is no longer with the company and Karl Ruiz has taken over that position. So you'll remove the record for Jean Rakes and replace it with a new record for Karl Ruiz.

To modify the Employees_Tbl table by adding and deleting records:

1. Scroll up the worksheet, click the **row 11** header containing the record for Jean Rakes.

2. On the ribbon, click the **Home** tab, and then in the Cells group, click the **Delete** button. The record for Jean Rakes is deleted from the table.

3. With row 11 still selected, in the Cells group, click the **Insert** button. A new row is added to the worksheet.

4. In row 11, enter the following information to create the record for Karl Ruiz: **e901-920** in the ID field, **Karl** in the First field, **Ruiz** in the Last field, **Accounting** in the Dept field, **10/4/2024** in the Hire Date field, **Boston** in the Office field, **MA** in the State field, **$73,500** in the Base Salary field, **$1,500** in Bonus field, **$0** in the Commission field, **10** in the Personal Days field, **0** in the Sick Days field, and **4** in the Eval Score field.

In addition to adding or deleting table records, you can also add or delete table fields. You will modify the Employees_Tbl table by adding new fields containing formulas.

Creating a Calculated Field

So far, all of the fields in the table contain entered values. A field can also contain a formula that references other fields in the table. Such a field is called a **calculated field**, and it updates automatically as other field values in the table change. Instead of cell references, formulas in a calculated field use field names enclosed in brackets as follows:

```
[field]
```

For example, the following formula adds the values of the Base Salary, Bonus, and Commission fields from all records in a table:

```
=[Base Salary]+[Bonus]+[Commission]
```

A formula can also include the name of the table by prefacing the field name with the table name as follows:

```
table[field]
```

The following formula returns the sum of the Base Salary values from all records in the Employees_Tbl table:

```
=SUM(Employees_Tbl[Base Salary])
```

With Excel tables, you enter the formula in only one record and it automatically applies to all records. This is faster than adding a formula to a data range, in which you copy and paste the formula across a range of cells.

An important symbol in calculated fields is the @ symbol, which refers to the current record or row within the table. The @ symbol is used in formulas that calculate values for each table record. For example, the following formula multiplies the value of the SalesPrice field by the UnitSold field within the table's current row:

```
=[@SalesPrice]*[@UnitsSold]
```

Jacek wants to add the Full Name field to the Employees_Tbl table. The Full Name field will display each employee's full name in the format *Last, First* using the formula:

```
=[@Last] & ", " & [@First]
```

The & symbol combines two text strings into one. You'll create the calculated field.

To add the Full Name calculated field to the Employees_Tbl table:

1. Scroll up to the top of the worksheet, click the **Column D** header.

2. On the Home tab, in the Cells group, click the **Insert** button. A new field named "Column1" is added to the table between the Last and Dept fields.

3. Click cell **D4**, type **FULL NAME** as the descriptive name of this field, and then press **ENTER**.

Be sure to enclose references to field or column names of an Excel table in square brackets.

4. In cell **D5**, type **=[@** to begin the structural reference. One advantage of Excel tables is that a list of field names appears as you type a formula. See Figure 6–30.

Figure 6–30   **Field name being entered in a structural reference**

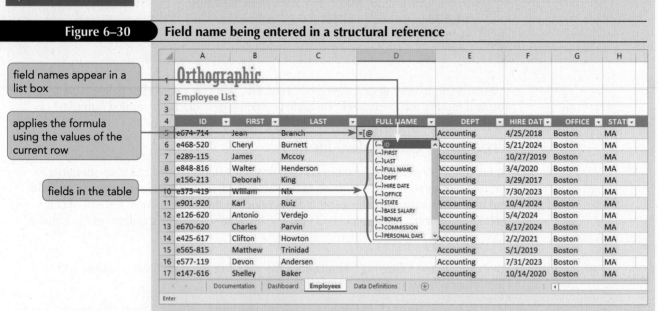

field names appear in a list box

applies the formula using the values of the current row

fields in the table

5. Press **DOWN ARROW** to highlight LAST in the list of field names, and then press **TAB**. The field name is added the structural reference.

6. Type **]** to close the reference to the Last field, press **SPACEBAR**, and then type **& ", " & [@** to enter the next part of the formula. Make sure you include a space directly after the comma. The list of field names in the table appears again after you type the bracket symbol.

7. Select **FIRST** in the list, press **TAB**, and then type **]** to finish the field reference.

8. Press **ENTER** to insert the formula. The formula applies to all the table records within Full Name field. See Figure 6–31.

Figure 6–31   **Values displayed for the Full Name calculated field**

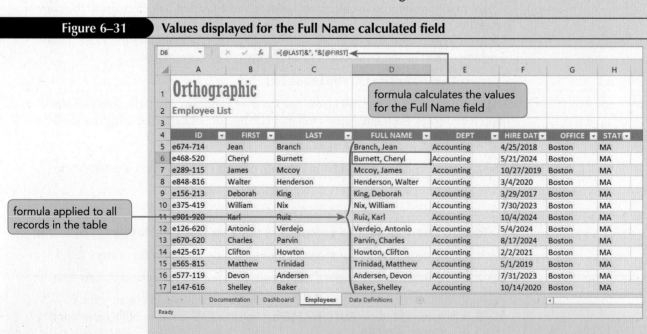

formula calculates the values for the Full Name field

formula applied to all records in the table

Jacek wants you to create a calculated field to display the year the employee was hired. You can extract the year value from a date using the YEAR function.

To add the Hire Year field to the Employees_Tbl table:

▶ 1. Click the **Column G** header, and then on the Home tab, in the Cells group, click the **Insert** button.

▶ 2. Click cell **G4**, type **HIRE YEAR** as the field name, and then press **ENTER**.

▶ 3. In cell **G5**, enter the formula **=YEAR([@[HIRE DATE]])** to extract the year value from the current row's Hire Date field, and then press **ENTER**. Excel displays the year values in date format, so they erroneously appear as 1905 dates. You'll reformat the values using the General format.

▶ 4. Press **CTRL+SPACEBAR** to select all the data records in the HIRE YEAR column.

▶ 5. On the Home tab, in the Number group, click the **Number Format arrow**, and then click **General**. The year value appears for each record.

▶ 6. Scroll back to the top of the worksheet and click cell **G5**.

> **Tip**
>
> You can select all the fields within a data row by pressing SHIFT+SPACEBAR.

Structural References and Excel Tables

References to fields and elements in an Excel table are called **structural references** and are enclosed within square brackets [ ]. You've already seen a single field entered using the structural reference [*field*]. Structural references also exist for other parts of the table. For example, the header row is referenced with the expression [#Headers] and the Totals row is referenced with the expression [#Totals]. Structural references can also be nested inside one another. This expression uses nested structural references to reference a group of fields in the current row of the Excel table

[@[*fieldFirst*]:[*fieldLast*]]

where *fieldFirst* is the first field in the group and *fieldLast* is the last. For example, you can calculate the sum of the values in the Base Salary through Commission fields for the current row, including any fields between these two, with the formula

=SUM([@[Base Salary]:[COMMISSION]])

If you omit the @ symbol, the SUM function calculates the sum of the fields across all rows in the table.

Structural references are a powerful feature of Excel tables, but the syntax can be challenging. A simple way to enter a formula involving structural references is to select the fields with your mouse and let Excel enter the formula for you.

Jacek wants you to create a calculated field named Wages that calculates the sum of the Base Salary, Bonus, and Commission field for each employee record.

To add the Wages field to the Employees_Tbl table:

▶ 1. Click the **Column M** header, and then on the Home tab, in the Cells group, click the **Insert** button.

▶ 2. Click cell **M4**, type **WAGES** as the new field name, and then press **ENTER**.

▶ 3. In cell **M5**, type **=SUM(** to begin the formula.

▶ 4. Use your mouse to select the range **J5:L5**. Excel inserts the structural reference Employees_Tbl[@[BASE SALARY]:[COMMISSION]] to reference the Base Salary through Commission fields for the current employee record.

5. Type **)** to end the formula, and then press **ENTER**. The formula =SUM(Employees_Tbl[@[BASE SALARY]:[COMMISSION]]) is entered for every record, calculating every employees total wages. See Figure 6–32.

Figure 6–32   Calculated fields added to the Employees table

| M6 | | fx | =SUM(Employees_Tbl[@[BASE SALARY]:[COMMISSION]]) | | | | | | |

> year extracted from the Hire Date field using =YEAR([@[HIRE DATE]])

> formula calculates the values for the Wages field

> sum of the Base Salary through Commission fields calculated for each record

	HIRE DATE	HIRE YEAR	OFFICE	STATE	BASE SALARY	BONUS	COMMISSION	WAGES	PERSONAL DAYS	SICK DAYS
5	4/25/2018	2018	Boston	MA	$92,900	$2,500	$0	$95,400	15	6
6	5/21/2024	2024	Boston	MA	$85,200	$2,500	$0	$87,700	15	4
7	10/27/2019	2019	Boston	MA	$84,800	$3,000	$0	$87,800	17	3
8	3/4/2020	2020	Boston	MA	$83,200	$2,500	$0	$85,700	18	6
9	3/29/2017	2017	Boston	MA	$80,500	$1,500	$0	$82,000	13	9
10	7/30/2023	2023	Boston	MA	$76,300	$3,000	$0	$79,300	10	3
11	10/4/2024	2024	Boston	MA	$73,500	$1,500	$0	$75,000	10	0
12	5/4/2024	2024	Boston	MA	$70,800	$2,500	$0	$73,300	10	4
13	8/17/2024	2024	Boston	MA	$67,400	$2,000	$0	$69,400	13	7
14	2/2/2021	2021	Boston	MA	$57,900	$1,500	$0	$59,400	12	5
15	5/1/2019	2019	Boston	MA	$49,000	$1,500	$0	$50,500	13	7
16	7/31/2023	2023	Boston	MA	$48,200	$1,500	$0	$49,700	10	6
17	10/14/2020	2020	Boston	MA	$43,700	$1,500	$0	$45,200	15	8

Documentation | Dashboard | **Employees** | Data Definitions | +

Ready

6. Save the workbook.

Excel automatically updates formulas that involve structural references to reflect any changes made to the workbook. For example, if you change a field name any formula referencing that field will update automatically to use the new name.

Proskills

Problem Solving: Data Ranges vs. Excel Tables

As you've seen, you can do a great deal with data entered as either a data range or an Excel table. For managing a data set, Excel tables are much better than data ranges. Almost everything you can do with a data range, you can do with an Excel table. The only exception is subtotal rows, which you cannot add to an Excel table.

But Excel tables do even more than data ranges. In Excel tables, you can work with the structure of the data itself rather than with individual cells. This lets you create formulas that are easy to interpret because they use field names rather than cell references. Also, you can format different parts of the table with styles that update automatically as you add and delete rows in the table structure. The table structure itself helps to ensure data accuracy by preventing common data entry errors such as mistyping a cell reference. Finally, Excel tables are more easily read by other applications such as the Microsoft Access database program and the Microsoft Power BI data analytics service.

Despite these advantages, you do not want to replace every data range with an Excel table. Some data cannot be laid out in a table format and lack the structure that Excel tables require. You may find it more comfortable to work with data ranges and references, at least until you are more familiar with the table structure. But don't overlook Excel tables as a solution for data management challenges. The more Excel tools you master, the more you can accomplish for your company and organization.

In this session, you worked with Excel tables to analyze employee data for Jacek. In the next session, you will use slicers to create an interactive dashboard that Jacek can use to quickly and easily generate reports on the employee data.

Review

Session 6.2 Quick Check

1. What happens to worksheet rows that do not match the filter criteria? What happens to the data they contain?
2. When multiple filter buttons are used with a data range, how are criteria in different fields combined?
3. When would you use an advanced filter in place of the filter buttons?
4. What happens to banded rows in an Excel table when you insert or delete a row?
5. What is the reference to the Income field from the Employees table?
6. What is the formula to calculate the average of the Income field from the Employees table?
7. What is the structural reference to the table header row?

Session 6.3 Visual Overview:

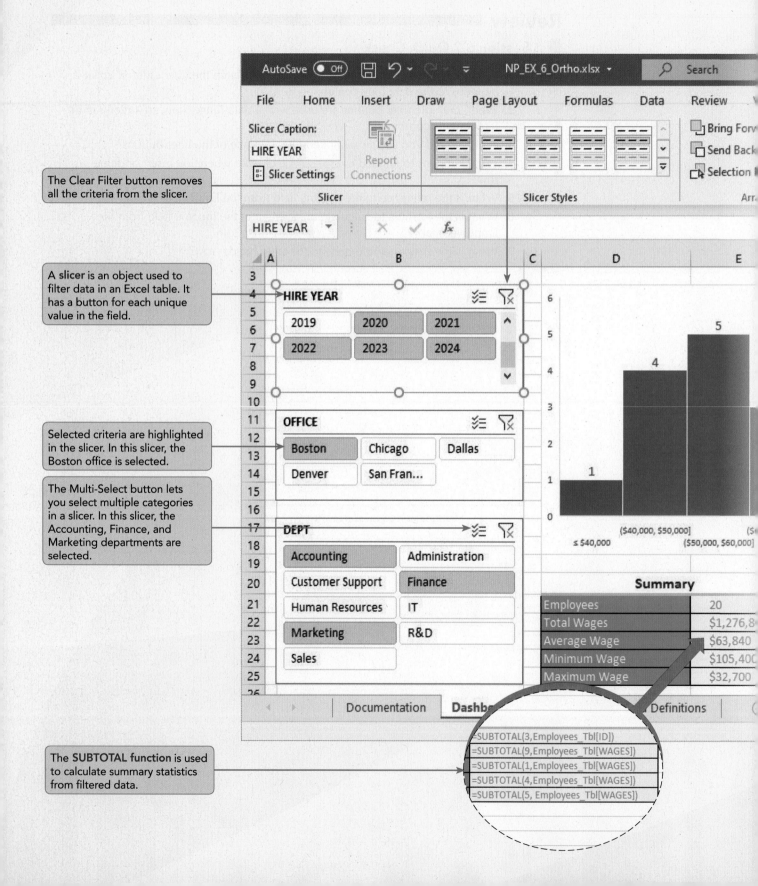

The Clear Filter button removes all the criteria from the slicer.

A **slicer** is an object used to filter data in an Excel table. It has a button for each unique value in the field.

Selected criteria are highlighted in the slicer. In this slicer, the Boston office is selected.

The Multi-Select button lets you select multiple categories in a slicer. In this slicer, the Accounting, Finance, and Marketing departments are selected.

The **SUBTOTAL** function is used to calculate summary statistics from filtered data.

Slicers and Dashboards

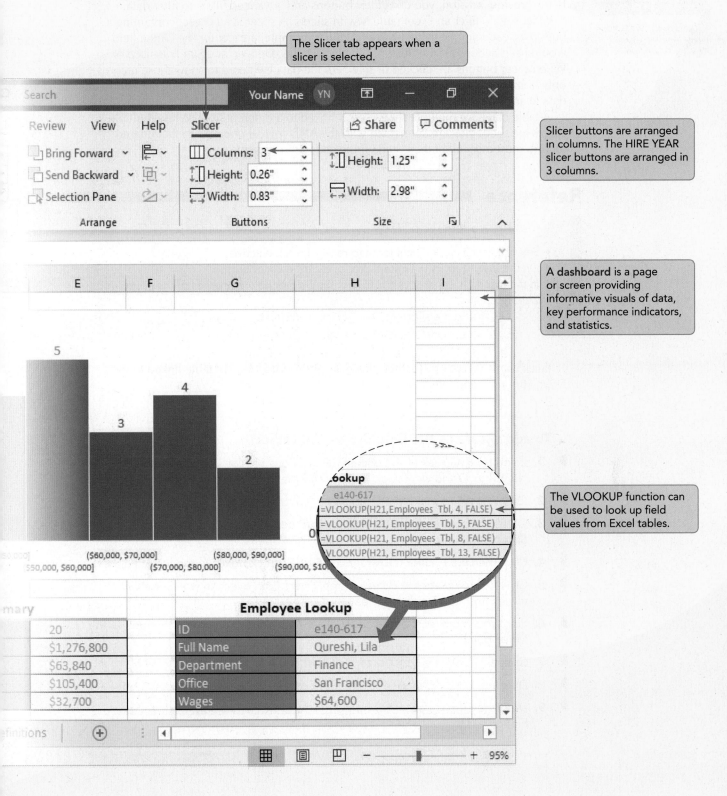

The Slicer tab appears when a slicer is selected.

Slicer buttons are arranged in columns. The HIRE YEAR slicer buttons are arranged in 3 columns.

A dashboard is a page or screen providing informative visuals of data, key performance indicators, and statistics.

The VLOOKUP function can be used to look up field values from Excel tables.

Filtering Data with Slicers

In the previous session, you used filter buttons and advanced filters to filter data. Another way to filter an Excel table is with slicers. A slicer is an object containing a button for each unique value from a field. For example, a slicer for the Office field would have buttons for the Boston, Chicago, Dallas, Denver, and San Francisco offices. When slicer buttons are clicked or selected, the data is filtered to show those records only from the selected buttons. Slicers make it clear what filters are being applied to the data at any moment.

A table can have multiple slicers, each linked to a different field. When multiple slicers are used, they are connected with the AND logical operator so that filtered records must meet all of the criteria indicated in the slicers.

Reference

Creating a Slicer

- Select any cell in the Excel table to make the table active.
- On the Insert tab, in the Filters group, click the Slicer button.
- In the Insert Slicers dialog box, select the field or column names of the slicers you want to create.
- Click OK to add the slicers to the current worksheet.

Jacek wants you to create three slicers for the Employees_Tbl table linked to the Dept, Hire Year, and Office fields.

To add slicers to the Employees_Tbl table:

1. If you took a break at the end of the previous session, make sure the NP_EX_6_Ortho workbook is open and the Employees worksheet is active.

2. Click cell **A4** to make the Employees_Tbl table active.

3. On the ribbon, click the **Insert** tab, and then in the Filters group, click the **Slicer** button. The Insert Slicers dialog box opens.

4. Click the **DEPT**, **HIRE YEAR**, and **OFFICE** check boxes in the list of fields.

5. Click **OK** to create the slicers. Three slicers float over the worksheet with values from the Dept, Hire Year, and Office fields.

6. Point to a blank part of the DEPT slicer to change the pointer changes to the Move pointer ⇱.

7. Click and drag the DEPT slicer cell over cell **A1**.

8. Drag the HIRE YEAR slicer to the right of the DEPT slicer over cell **C1**.

9. Drag the OFFICE slicer to the right side of the workbook window. See Figure 6–33.

| Figure 6–33 | Slicers added to the Employees_Tbl table |

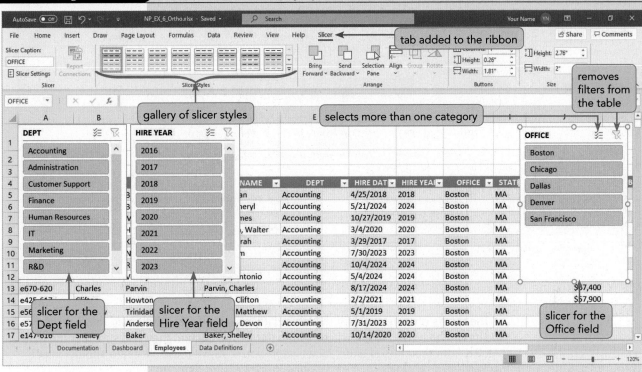

Each slicer shows the unique values for the selected field. The field name appears in the slicer title bar along with two buttons. The Multi-Select button 📋 lets you select multiple slicer buttons. The Clear Filter button 🔽 clears the slicer filters from the table. When a slicer is selected, the Slicer tab appears on the ribbon. You use this tab to format slicers.

Jacek wants to see only those employees hired in the Denver Customer Support department from 2021 through 2024. You will use the three slicers to filter the Employees_Tbl table.

To filter the Employees_Tbl table using slicers:

▶ 1. In the DEPT slicer, click **Customer Support** to show only those employee records from the Customer Support department. Only 27 of the 530 records match this criterion.

▶ 2. In the HIRE YEAR slicer, click the **Multi-Select** button 📋 (or press **ALT+S**) so you can select multiple field categories.

▶ 3. Click the **2016**, **2017**, **2018**, **2019**, and **2020** buttons to deselect them from the filter, leaving the 2021 through 2024 buttons selected. The number of found records reduces to 21.

▶ 4. In the Office slicer, click the **Denver** button. Six employees match the filter criteria. Notice that the 2016 through 2019 buttons in the HIRE YEAR slicer are grayed out because they have no matching records in the table. The Denver office opened in 2020, so no employee records exist before that year. See Figure 6–34.

Figure 6–34   Multiple slicers created to filter the Employees_Tbl table data

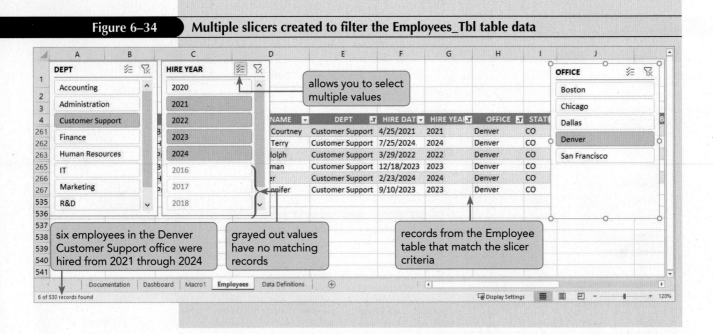

Figure 6–34   Multiple slicers created to filter the Employees_Tbl table data

The slicers obscure much of the table data, making it difficult to read the records. Slicers can be moved to anywhere within the workbook and they will still filter the data records from their linked table. Jacek wants you to move these slicers to another sheet to create a dashboard.

Insight

Choosing Between Slicers and Filter Buttons

Slicers and filter buttons are two ways to filter data in an Excel table. Use slicers when data has a few distinct values that can be easily listed within the slicer. Also, use slicers when you want to perform data from a table on another worksheet.

Use filter buttons when you need to use criteria filters involving text, date, or numeric values. For example, use filter buttons to filter for records that fall within a specified time interval or for a specific range of incomes or expenses.

Creating a Dashboard

A dashboard is a page or screen providing informative visuals of data, key performance indicators, and statistics. Most dashboards contain interactive tools to help users explore data under different conditions and assumptions. The term *dashboard* evokes the idea of an automobile dashboard that presents important information to the driver that can be quickly interpreted. Slicers are often used in dashboards because they provide a quick way to filter data.

Jacek included a Dashboard worksheet in the workbook. He wants you to place the three slicers you created in the Employees worksheet on this sheet. You'll cut and paste those slicers now.

To move the slicers for the Employees_Tbl table to the Dashboard worksheet:

1. Click the **HIRE YEAR** slicer to select it. Sizing handles in the corners and along the sides of the selected object.

2. On the ribbon, click the **Home** tab, and then in the Clipboard group, click the **Cut** button (or press **CTRL+X**).

3. Go to the **Dashboard** worksheet, click cell **B4** as the location for pasting the slicer, and then in the Clipboard group, click the **Paste** button (or press **CTRL+V**). The HIRE YEAR slicer is pasted into the worksheet.

Tip

You can cut and paste slicers between worksheets; you cannot cut and paste slicers between workbooks.

4. Hold down **ALT** as you drag the lower-right sizing handle of the slicer to the lower-right corner of cell **B9**. The slicer resizes to cover the range B4:B9.

5. Repeat Steps 1 through 4 to cut and paste the **OFFICE** slicer to cover the range **B11:B15** on the Dashboard worksheet.

6. Repeat Steps 1 through 4 to cut and paste the **DEPT** slicer to cover the range **B17:B25** on the Dashboard worksheet. See Figure 6–35.

Figure 6–35	Slicers pasted onto the Dashboard worksheet

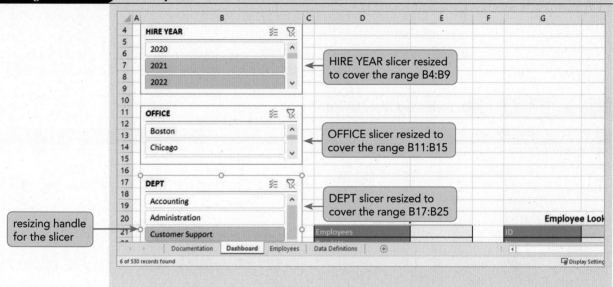

Even though the slicers are on a different worksheet, they will still filter the data in the Employees_Tbl table. Jacek wants you to test the slicers in their new location.

To test the Employees_Tbl table slicers on the Dashboard worksheet:

1. In the HIRE YEAR slicer, select **2024** to limit the filter to employees hired in 2024.

2. In the OFFICE slicer, select **Chicago** to further limit the filter to employees hired at the Chicago office.

3. In the DEPT slicer, select **Accounting**. The message in the status bar indicates that 4 of 530 records were found.

4. Go to the **Employees** worksheet to view the records for the four employees who were hired in the Chicago Accounting department in 2024.

5. Return to the **Dashboard** worksheet.

Formatting a Slicer

By default, slicer buttons are arranged in a single column. You can increase the number of the columns by formatting the slicer. Jacek suggest you increase the number of columns for the Hire Year, Office, and Dept slicers so that all of the buttons can be viewed together without needing to use the scroll bar. You will increase the number of columns now.

To change the number of columns in the slicers:

▶ **1.** Click the title bar of the HIRE YEAR slicer to select it.

▶ **2.** On the ribbon, click the **Slicer** tab, and then in the Buttons group, click the **Columns** box.

▶ **3.** In the Columns box, change the value to **3**. The buttons in the HIRE YEAR slicer are laid out in three columns and three rows.

▶ **4.** Click the title bar of the OFFICE slicer to select it, and then enter **3** in the Columns box in the Buttons group.

▶ **5.** Click the title bar of the DEPT slicer, and then enter **2** in the Columns box. The three slicers now have all buttons visible without scrolling. See Figure 6-36.

Figure 6-36   **Formatted slicer layout**

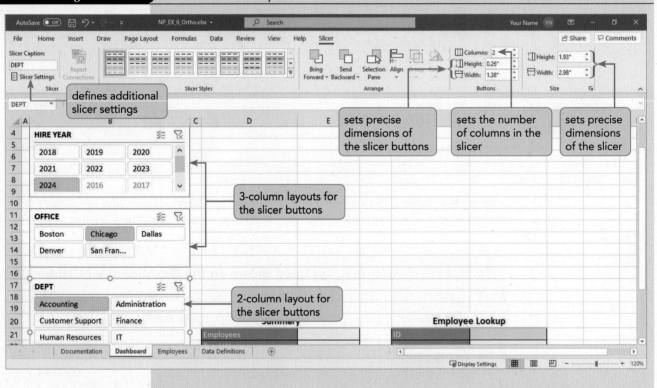

There are other ways to format a slicer's appearance using tools on the Slicer tab. You can set the exact size of the slicer and its buttons using the Height and Width boxes in the Buttons and Size groups. You can change the color scheme by selecting a slicer style from the Slicer Styles gallery. You can change the button order by clicking the Slicer Settings button in the Slicer group and then choosing the button sorting order (or create a custom sorting list) in the Slicer Settings dialog box. You can also change the slicer's title bar text from the field name to one of your own choosing by entering text in the Slicer Caption box in the Slicer group of the Slicer tab.

Proskills

Written Communication: Designing a Dashboard

A dashboard is designed to tell a story. It can be a springboard to reports providing more in-depth analysis, but fundamentally a dashboard needs to present useful information at a glance. As you create dashboards, keep in mind the following design tips:

- **Go Big. Go Bold.** Don't be afraid to use extremely large fonts and bright colors for important results. You want the viewer's eyes to be attracted to those results first, and you want those results to be remembered.
- **Start from the Upper-Left Corner.** Most people read from the top to the bottom and left to right, so put your most important information in the upper-left corner where it will be noticed first.
- **Keep It Simple.** Focus on a few key points, and keep the clutter of charts, graphics, and text to a minimum. You can always create additional dashboards.
- **Don't Let Color Overwhelm.** Keep the design of charts and graphics to a few complementary colors and be consistent in their use. Adding too many colors is distracting and reduces the impact of the dashboard.
- **Make It User Friendly.** The use and purpose of interactive tools like slicers and drop-down menus should be clear. You may not have room to explain how to use the dashboard.
- **Be Focused.** Settle on a few key points. If a chart or graphic doesn't relate to that idea, remove it or place it in a different dashboard.

As you design a dashboard, always keep your audience in mind. What are they looking for? The dashboard you present to a sales director might be very different from one you present to a marketing manager or an HR executive. A dashboard is most useful and has the greatest impact when it is tailored to the needs of your audience.

Using the SUBTOTAL Function

Jacek wants the dashboard to display summary statistics on the employees matched by the slicers. The first summary statistic will count the number of employees listed in the filtered table. You'll use the COUNTA function to count the number of entries in the ID field of the Employees_Tbl table.

To use the COUNTA function in the dashboard:

1. In each slicer's title bar, click the **Clear Filter** button to clear the filters. All 530 records are displayed in the Employees_Tbl table.

2. Click cell **E21**, and type the formula **=COUNTA(Employees_Tbl[ID])** to count the number of entries in the ID field. As you type the formula, the name of the Excel table and a list of fields within that table appear. You can use the TAB key to select the highlighted names provided by Excel.

3. Press **ENTER**. The formula returns 530, which is the number of records in the Employees_Tbl table.

4. In the OFFICE slicer, click **Boston**. The status bar indicates 105 employee records for the Boston office. However, the value in cell E21 is unchanged and still shows 530 as the number of employees.

Why does the dashboard show the same number of employees after limiting the employee list to the Boston office? The reason is that statistical functions like the COUNTA, AVERAGE, SUM, MAX, and MIN functions are applied to the *entire table*, regardless of any filter criteria. To count only records that match the filter criteria, you use the SUBTOTAL function

SUBTOTAL(*Function_Num, ref1,* [*ref2*], [*ref3*], …)

where *Function_Num* is the number corresponding to a statistical function, *ref1* is a reference to the data to be analyzed, and *ref2*, *ref3*, and so on are optional arguments for additional data references. Figure 6–37 lists some of the function numbers recognized by the SUBTOTAL function.

Figure 6–37   **Function numbers of the SUBTOTAL function**

Function Number	Function	Function Number	Function
1	AVERAGE	6	PRODUCT
2	COUNT	7	STDEV
3	COUNTA	8	STDEVP
4	MAX	9	SUM
5	MIN	10	VAR

Tip

To apply the SUBTOTAL function to data with manually hidden rows, add 100 to the function number.

The following formula uses the SUBTOTAL function with function number 3 to apply the COUNTA function only to records in the Employees_Tble table whose ID values match whatever filter criteria has been applied to the table:

=SUBTOTAL(3, Employees_Tbl[ID])

You've already worked with the SUBTOTAL function without realizing it when you had Excel calculate subtotals (refer back to Figure 6–12) and totals (refer back to Figure 6–29) in the Employees_Tbl table. Both calculations used the SUBTOTAL function.

Reference

Applying the SUBTOTAL Function

- To apply summary statistics records that match a filter criteria, apply the function

  SUBTOTAL(*Function_Num, ref1,* [*ref2*], [*ref3*], …)

  where *Function_Num* is an integer representing a statistical function to use in the subtotal calculation, *ref1* is a reference to the data to be analyzed, and *ref2*, *ref3*, etc. are optional arguments for additional data references.
- To calculate SUM from the filtered records of a table, set *Function_Num* to 9.
- To calculate AVERAGE from the filtered records, set *Function_Num* to 1.
- To calculate COUNT from the filtered records, set *Function_Num* to 2.
- To calculate COUNTA from the filtered records, set *Function_Num* to 3.

You'll use the SUBTOTAL function to calculate summary statistics from the Employees_Tbl table based on whatever records are selected the slicers on the dashboard.

To apply the SUBTOTAL function:

1. Click cell **E21**, and then type **=SUBTOTAL(** to begin the formula. A list of function numbers for statistical functions appears.

2. Press **DOWN ARROW** to select 3. - COUNTA from the list, and then press **TAB** to insert 3 into the formula.

> Use the arrow keys or mouse to select the function number to ensure that you use the correct summary statistic.

3. Type **, Employees_Tbl[ID])** to complete the formula, and then press **ENTER**. The formula returns 105, which is the number of records that match the filter criteria in the slicers.

4. In cell **E22**, enter the formula **=SUBTOTAL(9, Employees_Tbl[WAGES])** to calculate the sum that Orthographic spends on wages for the 105 employees. The formula returns $7,193,100 as the total wages paid to the 105 employees.

5. In cell **E23**, enter the formula **=SUBTOTAL(1, Employees_Tbl[WAGES])** to calculate the average of those wages. The formula returns $68,506 as the average wage for Boston employees.

6. In cell **E24**, enter the formula **=SUBTOTAL(5, Employees_Tbl[WAGES])** to calculate the minimum wage paid to Boston employees. The formula returns $28,400 as the minimum wage.

7. In cell **E25**, enter the formula **=SUBTOTAL(4, Employees_Tbl[WAGES])** to calculate the maximum wage paid to Boston employees. The formula returns a maximum wage of $120,000. See Figure 6–38.

Figure 6–38   **Summary statistics for Boston employees**

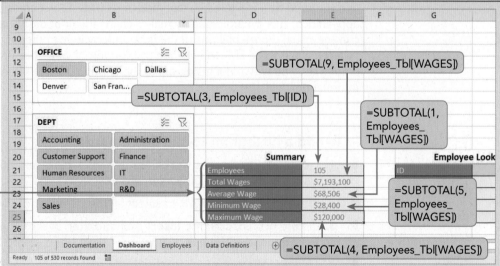

8. In the DEPT slicer, click **Accounting** to limit the report to only those employees in the Boston Accounting department. Because they use the SUBTOTAL function, the summary statistics in the range E21:E25 update to reflect the new filter criteria. See Figure 6–39.

| Figure 6–39 | Summary of employee wages for the Boston Accounting department |

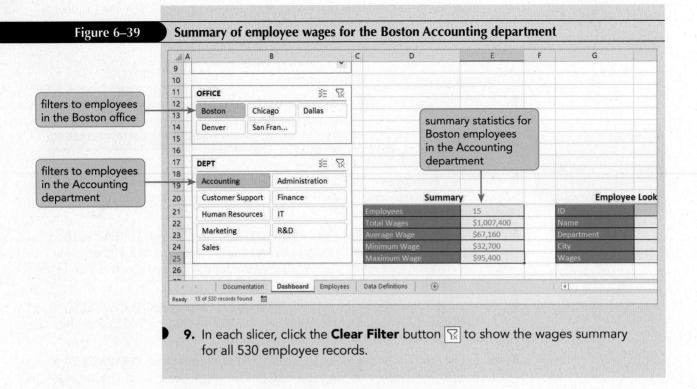

9. In each slicer, click the **Clear Filter** button to show the wages summary for all 530 employee records.

In addition to the summary statistics, dashboards often contain informative charts. You will add charts to the dashboard next.

Creating Dynamic Charts

Charts based on Excel tables are dynamic, which means they update automatically as the source data is filtered so that hidden records do not contribute to the chart's appearance. This dynamic quality makes charts ideal for dashboards, because the users can see visual representations of the data under varying criteria.

Jacek wants to be able to view the distribution of wages for different groups of employees. You will add a histogram to the Dashboard worksheet to show this information.

To add a histogram to the dashboard:

1. Go to the **Employees** worksheet, and then click cell **M5** containing the wages in the first employee record.

2. Press **CTRL+SPACEBAR** to select all the data in the Wages column.

3. On the ribbon, click the **Insert** tab, and then in the Charts group, click the **Recommended Charts** button. The Insert Chart dialog box opens.

4. Click the **Histogram** chart, the third item displayed in the list of recommended charts, and then click **OK**. The histogram chart is created on the Employees worksheet.

5. On the ribbon, click the **Home** tab, and then in the Clipboard group, click the **Cut** button (or press **CTRL+X**).

6. Return to the **Dashboard** worksheet, click cell **D4**, and then in the Clipboard group, click the **Paste** button (or press **CTRL+V**) to paste the chart.

7. In the Dashboard worksheet, hold down **ALT** as you move and resize the histogram chart so it covers the range D4:H18. See Figure 6–40.

Figure 6–40   **Histogram chart of the distribution of employee wages**

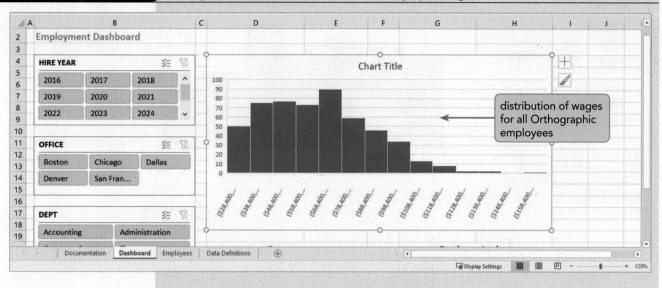

Jacek asks you to remove the chart title and gridlines and to change the bin intervals for the histogram chart. You'll change the axis scale to group the wages in intervals of $10,000 from $40,000 up to $100,000. Wages below or above that interval will be grouped together in the histogram.

To format the histogram chart:

1. With the chart still selected, click the **Chart Elements** button ⊞, and then click the **Chart Title** and **Gridlines** check boxes to deselect them. The chart title and horizontal gridlines disappear from the chart.

2. Click the **Data Labels** check box to add show the number employees in each wage group on the chart.

3. Double-click the labels in the horizontal axis. The Format Axis pane opens.

4. In the Axis Options section, click the **Bin width** option button to set a bin width for the histogram intervals and, if necessary, type **10000** in the Bin width box.

5. Click the **Overflow bin** check box, and then type **100000** in the Overflow bin box.

6. Click the **Underflow bin** check box, and then type **40000** in the Underflow bin box.

7. On the ribbon, click the **Home** tab, and then in the Font group, click the **Font Size arrow** and click **8** to reduce the font size of the horizontal labels to 8 points. See Figure 6–41.

Figure 6–41   Formatted histogram chart

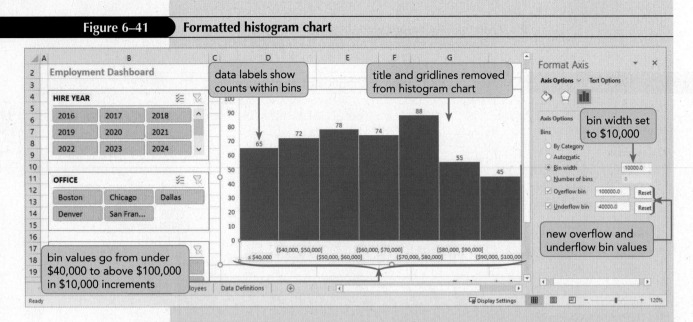

8. In the Format Axis pane, click the **Close** button ⊠ to close the pane, and then click cell **A2** to deselect the chart.

The histogram chart you created is dynamic and will show the distribution for employees based on the selected criteria. Jacek wants to view the distribution of wages for employees hired in the Finance department of any office in 2024.

To view the distribution of wages for Finance department employees hired in 2024:

1. In the HIRE YEAR slicer, click the **2024** button to select that year. Only employees hired in 2024 are included in the chart.

2. In the DEPT slicer, click the **Finance** button to select only that category. Only the eight employees hired in 2024 that work in the Finance department are included in the chart. The summary statistics show that the average wage for these eight employees is $56,763. The histogram chart shows that one employee received less than $40,000 in wages and that three employees received from $70,000 to $80,000. The grayed-out Dallas button in the Office slicers indicates that the Dallas office did not hire anyone in its Finance department during 2024. See Figure 6–42.

Figure 6–42   Distribution of wages for Finance department employees hired in 2024

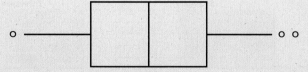

3. In each slicer, click the **Clear Filter** button ▽ to display results for all Orthographic employees.

Using the slicers on the Dashboard worksheet Jacek can continue to explore the distribution of wages for different groups of employees at Orthographic.

Insight

Exploring Boxplots

Another way of showing the distribution of data values is with a boxplot. A boxplot is a schematic diagram of the distribution in which the location of the central 50% of the data is displayed as a box with edges at the 25th and 75th percentiles. Extending beyond the 25th and 75th percentiles are straight lines, or whiskers, that indicate the range of the data values. The median of the data set is displayed as a central line within the box. Extremely small or large values are displayed as open circles beyond the whiskers. A typical boxplot would appear as follows:

Boxplots are extremely useful charts for statisticians who want a quick overview of the data and as a way of identifying unusually small or large data values. You can create a boxplot from the Insert Chart dialog box by selecting the Box and Whisker chart type.

Looking Up Data with Tables

Excel tables work well as lookup tables for the VLOOKUP function. As you add more records to the lookup table, the VLOOKUP function will automatically include the additional rows. If you filter the data, the lookup table will be restricted only to those rows that match filter criteria. Also, you can use the table name as the lookup table reference rather than referencing a range.

Jacek wants to be able to retrieve information about specific employees using their employee ID number right from the dashboard. You will add VLOOKUP functions to the Dashboard worksheet to retrieve this information.

To look up data from the Employees_Tbl table from the dashboard:

1. Click cell **H21**, type the employee ID **e850-316** as the lookup entry, and then press **ENTER**.

2. In cell **H22**, type **=VLOOKUP(H21, Employees_Tbl, 4, FALSE)** to locate the record with the ID e850-316 from the Employees_Tbl table and retrieve the data from the fourth column (the Full Name column).

3. Press **ENTER**. The full name of the employee with the ID e850-316, Baros, Jacek, appears in cell H22.

4. In cell **H23**, enter the formula **=VLOOKUP(H21, Employees_Tbl, 5, FALSE)** to retrieve data from the fifth column (Dept) of the Employees_Tbl table for the employee with the ID e850-316. Human Resources is displayed in cell H23.

5. In cell **H24**, enter the formula **=VLOOKUP(H21, Employees_Tbl, 8, FALSE)** to retrieve data from the eighth column (Office) of the Employees_Tbl table for the employee with the ID e850-316. Denver is displayed in cell H24.

6. In cell **H25**, enter the formula **=VLOOKUP(H21, Employees_Tbl, 13, FALSE)** to retrieve data from the thirteenth column (Wages) of the Employees_Tbl table for the employee with the ID e850-316. The value $83,300 is displayed in cell H25. See Figure 6–43.

Figure 6–43 — **Data retrieved for a single employee**

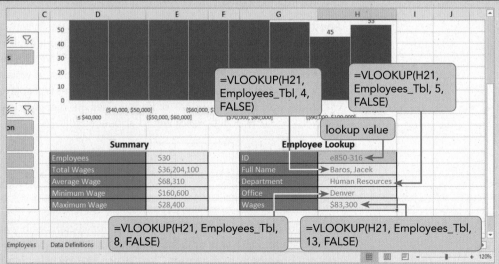

7. In cell **H21**, enter the employee ID **e140-617** to view information on Lila Qureshi and further test the VLOOKUP.

> **Trouble?** If the lookup fails to retrieve the employee record, you probably mistyped the employee ID. Re-enter the value in cell H21 making sure you enter the ID correctly.
>
> ▶ **8. sam** ⬆ Save the workbook, and then close it.

You've completed your work on the Employee dashboard. With this dashboard, Jacek can quickly retrieve payroll information for different groups of employees. By inserting even more slicers, Jacek can add more factors and depth to that analysis.

Review

Session 6.3 Quick Check

1. What are two reasons for using slicers rather than filter buttons to filter data?
2. What are two reasons for using filter buttons rather than slicers to filter data?
3. Can slicers be used with both data ranges and Excel tables?
4. Can slicers be moved to any worksheet or external workbook?
5. Write a formula to calculate the sum of the filtered values from the Sales Price field in the Sales_Result table.
6. Write a formula to calculate the average of the filtered values from the Sales Price field in the Sales_Result table.
7. Write a formula to retrieve the value from the third field in the Sales_Result table that exactly matches the lookup value in cell B10.

Practice

Review Assignments

Data File needed for the Review Assignments: NP_EX_6-3.xlsx

Jacek in the Human Resources department of Orthographic needs to track the hiring process for new recruits, from the initial application stage, through the interview stages, and culminating in a final offer of employment. Jacek compiled information on current candidates for positions in the soon-to-be-opened Atlanta office and wants you to develop reports and summaries of the recruitment efforts. Complete the following:

1. Open the **NP_EX_6-3.xlsx** workbook located in the Excel6 > Review folder included with your Data Files. Save the workbook as **NP_EX_6_Recruits** in the location specified by your instructor.

2. In the Documentation sheet, enter your name and the date in the range B3:B4.

3. Go to the Applications worksheet containing a list of applications made to the Atlanta office for 12 positions. The worksheet lists the dates that each applicant completed each stage of the recruitment process from the date the application was received, through the phone screening, manager interview, onsite interview, offer date, and acceptance date. The value #N/A indicates that the applicant did not pass to that recruitment stage. See the Table Data worksheet for a description of each field.

4. Use conditional formatting to locate records that have a duplicate Applicant ID in the range A5:A1043. Delete the second duplicate record. Do not remove the conditional formatting rule when you are finished.

5. One applicant record is duplicated for all fields except for the Applicant ID field. Use the Remove Duplicates command to remove the duplicate.

6. In the Applications worksheet, show how applicants are tracked through the recruitment process by sorting the data range by the Position field in A to Z order and then by Acceptance Date, Offer Date, Onsite Date, Manager Date, and finally Phone Date fields, with all dates sorted from newest to oldest. The sorted data should show applicants for each position that went farthest last.

7. Filter the data in the Applications worksheet to show only those records for which the value of the Hired field is Yes.

8. Copy the filtered values and paste them into the Hires worksheet starting at cell A4.

9. In the Hires worksheet, do the following:

   a. Sort the data in ascending order of the Position field.

   b. Add subtotal rows at each change in the value of the Position field, showing the average of the Base Salary field within each Position.

   c. Freeze panes at cell F5 so that you can scroll vertically and horizontally while keeping the data labels in view.

10. Return to the Applications worksheet and clear the filter from the data.

11. A colleague of Jacek's wants specific information about five hires to the IT and Marketing departments. Go to the IT and Marketing Hires worksheet and complete the following advanced filter:

   a. Complete the criteria range to create a list of new hires from the IT department with base salaries greater than $70,000 or from the Marketing department with base salaries greater than $60,000.

   b. Run the Advanced Filter using the copy data to another location option. Use the data in the range A4:N1041 of the Applications worksheet as the list range, the range A4:B6 in the IT and Marketing worksheet as criteria range, and cell D4 of the IT and Marketing Hires worksheet as the Copy to cell.

12. Return to the Applications worksheet, convert the data range to an Excel table, and then rename the table using **Recruits** as the name.

13. In the Recruits table, do the following:

   a. Insert a new field named **Full Name** between the Last Name and Position fields.

   b. In the Full Name field, enter the formula **=[@Last Name] & ", " & [@First Name]** to insert the applicants' full names.

   c. Insert a new field after the Base Salary field named **Days to Hire** by entering the field name in cell P4.

   d. In the Days to Hire field, use your mouse to enter a formula calculating the value of the Acceptance Date field in cell M5 minus the Application Date field in cell G5.

   e. Apply the General number format to the result so that the values appear as days rather than dates and then resize the column to make the field name visible.

14. Insert a slicer for the Position field. Move the slicer to the Metrics worksheet and resize it to fit in the range B4:B13. Display the slicer buttons in two columns.

15. In the range E5:E10 of the Metrics worksheet, do the following to count the number of applicants who reach each stage of the recruitment process:

   a. In cell E5, use the SUBTOTAL function with the COUNTA function to count the number of entries in the Applicant ID field of the Recruits table.

   b. In cell E6, use the SUBTOTAL function with the COUNT function to count the number of values in the Phone Date field.

   c. In cell E7, use the SUBTOTAL function with the COUNT function to count the number of values in the Manager Date field.

   d. In cell E8, use the SUBTOTAL function with the COUNT function to count the number of values in the Onsite Date field.

   e. In cells E9 and E10, use the SUBTOTAL function with the COUNT function to count the number of values in the Offer Date and Acceptance Date fields, respectively.

16. Jacek wants to track certain Key Performance Indexes (KPIs) that indicate the efficiency of the recruitment process. Calculate the following values:

   a. In cell E11, calculate the number of applicants for each hire by dividing the value in cell E5 by the value in cell E10.

   b. In cell E12, calculate the number of interviews for each hire by dividing the sum of the values in cells E7 and E8 by the value in cell E10.

   c. In the range F6:F10, calculate the percent of the original applicants that survive to each step in the process by dividing the number of applicants that made it to each step by the value in cell E5.

   d. In the range E5:E10, use conditional formatting to add orange data bars with a gradient fill to the values to show how the number of applicants is trimmed during recruitment.

17. In the Applications worksheet, create a Histogram chart of the data in the range P4:P1041 to the view the distribution of the number of days required for hiring new employees.

18. Do the following to the chart:

   a. Move the chart to the Metrics worksheet, and then resize the chart to cover the range H4:M13.

   b. Change the chart title to **Days to Hire** and add data labels to the bars in the histogram.

   c. In the axis options, change the histogram's Bin width to 5 with an Overflow bin value of 50 and an Underflow bin value of 25.

19. Test the dashboard you created by showing the recruitment statistics for the Programmer, Systems Analyst, and Website Designer positions. The KPIs updated to reflect this subset of the data and the histogram changes to show the distributions of the number of days required to fill those three positions.

20. Save the workbook, and then close it.

Apply

Case Problem 1

Data File needed for this Case Problem: **NP_EX_6-4.xlsx**

Seacation Alana Ngata is an inventory manager for Seacation, a major manufacturer and distributor of boating parts and tools. Alana uses Excel to help manage the inventory at Seacation warehouses, ensuring that products remain stocked and resupplied on a timely basis. At the Seacation warehouses, the products are located by row number and bin number. Alana wants a report that indicates how many of the warehouse items need restocking and at what cost. The report also must track restocking needs by row number and bin number. You will create a dashboard that will display the answers that Alana needs. Complete the following:

1. Open the **NP_EX_6-4.xlsx** workbook located in the Excel6 > Case1 folder included with your Data Files. Save the workbook as **NP_EX_6_Seacation** in the location specified by your instructor.

2. In the Documentation sheet, enter your name and the date in the range B3:B4.

3. Alana is concerned that the list of inventory items contains duplicate records. In the Inventory worksheet, use the Remove Duplicates tool to remove records for which every field value is duplicated. Verify that Excel reports that five duplicates are removed.

4. Convert the data range in the Inventory worksheet to an Excel table. Rename the table using **Inventory_Tbl** as the table name.

5. Sort the table by ascending order of the Warehouse, Bin, and Part ID fields.

6. Insert a new field named **Inventory Value** between the Stock Qty and Reorder Qty fields. Calculate the inventory value by using your mouse to enter the formula that multiplies the Unit Cost field (cell E5) by the Stock Qty field (cell F5). If necessary, format the values using the Currency format and resize the column to fit the data.

7. Click cell J4 and add a new field named **Restock** that you'll use to determine which items need to be restocked. Use your mouse to enter an IF function that displays a value of "Yes" if the Stock Qty field (cell F5) is less than or equal to the Reorder Qty field (cell H5) and "No" if it is not.

8. Click cell K4 and add the **Restock Indicator** field. Use your mouse to enter a formula that uses the IF function to display the value 1 if the Restock field (cell J5) equals "Yes" and the value 0 otherwise. Resize the column to fit the data.

9. Click cell L4 and add the **Restock Qty** field. In this field, determine the number of items to order for products that need to be restocked. Use your mouse to enter a formula equal to the Restock Indicator field (cell K5) times the difference between the Restock Level and Stock Qty fields (I5 – F5). Resize the column to fit the data.

10. Click cell M4 and add a new field named **Restock Cost** to calculate how much it will cost to restock the items that need restocking. Use your mouse to enter a formula that multiplies the Restock Qty field (cell L5) by the Unit Cost field (cell E5). Format the calculated values as currency and resize the column to fit the data.

11. Filter the Inventory_Tbl table to show only records where the Restock field equals "Yes." Copy the filtered table and paste it into the Restock List worksheet at cell A4.

12. In the Restock List worksheet, add subtotal rows at each change in the Warehouse field, showing the sum of the Restock Qty and Restock Cost fields.

13. Add a freeze pane to the Restock List worksheet at cell E5.

14. Return to the Inventory worksheet and clear the filter to redisplay all the records in the table.

15. Insert slicers for the Warehouse and Bin fields. Move the slicers to the Report worksheet. Place the Warehouse slicer over the range A4:A7 with 4 columns in the button layout. Place the Bin slicer in the range A9:A16 with 3 columns in the button layout.

16. Calculate the following summary statistics for the inventory data:

    a. In cell D5, apply the SUBTOTAL with the COUNTA function to count the number of records in the Part ID field of the Inventory_Tbl table.

    b. In cell D6, apply the SUBTOTAL function with the SUM function to the Stock Qty field to calculate the quantity of items in the warehouse.

c. In cell D7, apply the SUBTOTAL function with the SUM function to the Inventory Value field to calculate the total value of items in the warehouse.

d. In cell D8, apply the SUBTOTAL function with the SUM function to the Restock Indicator field to calculate the number of items requiring restocking.

e. In cell D9, calculate the difference between cells D5 and D8, returning the total number of items that do not require restocking.

f. In cell D10, apply the SUBTOTAL function with the SUM function to the Restock Cost field to calculate the total cost of restocking items that have low inventory.

17. Insert a pie chart of the data in the range C8:D9 and resize it to cover the range C11:D18. Remove the chart title and add data labels to the pie slices showing the percentage of items that need restocking.

18. Use the slicers to show results for items only in warehouse row 1 and bin 9.

19. Save the workbook, and then close it.

Challenge

Case Problem 2

Data File needed for this Case Problem: NP_EX_6-5.xlsx

Mercy Field Clinic   Craig Manteo is the Quality of Care manager at Mercy Field Clinic located in Knoxville, Tennessee. Craig wants to use Excel to monitor daily clinic appointments, looking at how many patients a doctor sees per day and how much time is spent with each patient. Craig is also interested in whether patients are experiencing long wait times within particular departments or with specific doctors. You've been given a worksheet containing the scheduled appointments from a typical day. Craig wants you to create a dashboard that can be used to summarize the appointments from that day. Complete the following.

1. Open the **NP_EX_6-5.xlsx** workbook located in the Excel6 > Case2 folder included with your Data Files. Save the workbook as **NP_EX_6_Mercy** in the location specified by your instructor.

2. In the Documentation sheet, enter your name and the date.

3. The Patient Log worksheet lists the entire day's appointments, from 8 am to 5 pm at four departments. Convert this data range into an Excel table using **Appointments** as the table name. Turn off the banded rows style.

4. In the Dept Lookup, Physician Lookup, and Patient Lookup worksheets, convert each data range to a table, naming them **Dept_Lookup**, **Physician_Lookup**, and **Patient_Lookup**, respectively. You'll use these tables to display names instead of IDs in the Appointments table.

5. In the Patient Log worksheet, use your mouse to enter formulas for the following calculated fields (resize the columns as needed):

   a. Between the Dept ID and Physician ID fields, insert the **Department** field, and then create an exact match lookup with the VLOOKUP function using the value of the Dept ID field in the Appointments table to retrieve the department name from column 2 of the Dept_Lookup table. (*Hint*: Remember with an exact match lookup to set the range_lookup argument to FALSE.)

   b. Between the Physician ID and Patient ID fields, insert the **Physician** field, and then create an exact match lookup with the VLOOKUP function using the Physician ID field to retrieve the physician name from column 2 of the Physician_Lookup table.

   c. Between the Patient ID and Patient Check In fields, insert the **Patient** field, and then create an exact match lookup using the Patient ID field to retrieve the patient name from column 2 of the Patient_Lookup table.

6. Insert the **Patient Wait** field in column K to calculate whether a patient had to wait past the scheduled appointment time. Use your mouse to enter the IF function to test whether the value of the Exam Start field (cell I5) is greater than the Appt Time Field (cell A5); if it is, return the value 1; otherwise, return the value 0. Format the calculated values with the General cell format.

7. Insert the **Wait Time** field in column L. Calculate how many minutes each patient had to wait by using your mouse to enter a formula that multiplies the value of the difference between the Exam Start (cell I5) and Appt Time (cell A5) fields by 24*60 (to express the difference in minutes). Format the calculated values with the General cell format.

8. Insert the **Visit Length** field in column M. Calculate the visit length in minutes by using your mouse to enter a formula that multiplies the difference between the Exam End and Exam Start fields by 24*60. Format the calculated values with the General cell format.

9. Insert slicers for the Department and Physician fields, and then move those slicers to the **Dashboard** worksheet. Resize the Department slicer to cover the merged range A4:D7. Resize the Physician slicer to cover the merged range A8:D16. Set the layout of both slicers to 5 columns.

⊕ **Explore** 10. On the Slicer tab, in the Slicer group, in the Slicer Caption box, change the caption of the Department slicer to **Treating Department** and the caption of the Physician slicer to **Examining Physician**.

⊕ **Explore** 11. Select the Department slicer, and then click the Slicer Settings button in the Slicer group to open the Slicer Settings dialog box. Click the Hide Items with no data check box to hide department names when they are not relevant to the dashboard report. Repeat for the Physician slicer.

12. Calculate the following summary statistics in the Dashboard worksheet:

   a. In the merged cell A19, show the number of appointments behind schedule by applying the SUBTOTAL function with the SUM function to the Patient Wait field of the Appointments table.

   b. In the merged cell B19, show the number of appointments that were on time by applying the SUBTOTAL function with the COUNT function to the Appt Time field of the Appointments table and subtracting the value of cell A19.

   c. In the merged cell C19, use the SUBTOTAL function to calculate the average value of the Wait Time field in the Appointments table.

   d. In the merged cell D19, use the SUBTOTAL function to calculate the average value of the Visit Length field in the Appointments table.

13. Insert a pie chart of the data in the range A18:B23, move the chart to cover the range A25:B34. Remove the chart legend but add Data Callouts data labels showing the percent of each category. (*Hint*: If you don't see two categories in the pie chart, on the Chart Design tab, in the Data group click the Switch Row/Column button.)

14. Create a histogram of the data in the Wait Time column in the Patient Log worksheet. Move the histogram to the Dashboard worksheet and then resize the chart to fit in the range C25:C34. Change the chart title to **Waiting Time**. Add data labels. Set the bin width to **5**, the Overflow bin value to **10**, and the Underflow bin value to **0**.

15. Create a histogram of the data in the Visit Length column in the Patient Log worksheet. Move the histogram to the Dashboard worksheet and resize it to fit in the range D25:D34. Change the chart title to **Length of Visit** and add data labels. Set the bin width to **10**, the Overflow bin value to **60**, and the Underflow bin value to **20**.

16. Test the slicer buttons by showing the results for Dr. Jacob Leiva of the Internal Medicine department.

17. Save the workbook, and then close it.

Summarizing Data with PivotTables

EXCEL

Objectives

Session 7.1
- Do approximate match lookups
- Work with logical functions
- Calculate statistics with summary IF functions

Session 7.2
- Create a PivotTable
- Change a PivotTable layout
- Format a PivotTable

Session 7.3
- Create a PivotChart
- Apply a slicer to multiple PivotTables
- Create a timeline slicer

Preparing a Social Media Marketing Report

Case | Syrmosta

Claire Christos is the social media marketing manager for the clothing company Syrmosta. Part of Claire's job is evaluating the impact of the company's presence on popular social media sites like Facebook, Twitter, and Instagram. Over the past 12 months, Syrmosta has instituted an ad campaign to increase its visibility on social media sites. Claire has received a workbook detailing the public's response to its social media posts. You'll help Claire summarize and analyze that market data.

Starting Data Files

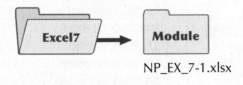

Excel7 →

Module	Review	Case1
NP_EX_7-1.xlsx	NP_EX_7-2.xlsx	NP_EX_7-3.xlsx

Case2

NP_EX_7-4.xlsx

Session 7.1 Visual Overview:

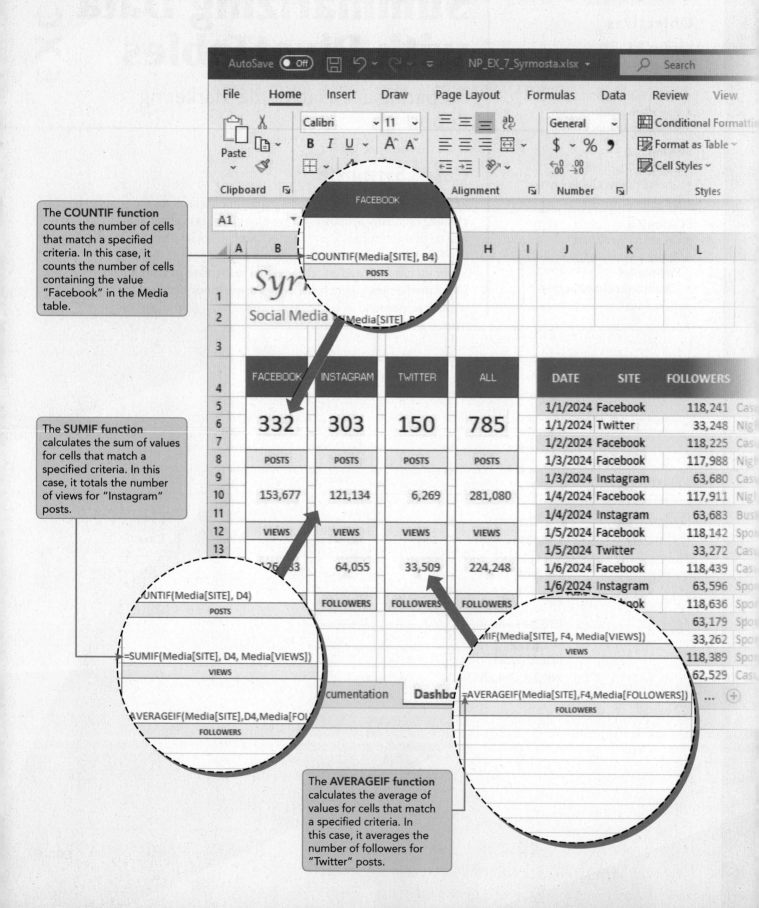

The **COUNTIF** function counts the number of cells that match a specified criteria. In this case, it counts the number of cells containing the value "Facebook" in the Media table.

=COUNTIF(Media[SITE], B4)

The **SUMIF** function calculates the sum of values for cells that match a specified criteria. In this case, it totals the number of views for "Instagram" posts.

=SUMIF(Media[SITE], D4, Media[VIEWS])

The **AVERAGEIF** function calculates the average of values for cells that match a specified criteria. In this case, it averages the number of followers for "Twitter" posts.

=AVERAGEIF(Media[SITE],F4,Media[FOLLOWERS])

Summary IF Functions and VLOOKUP

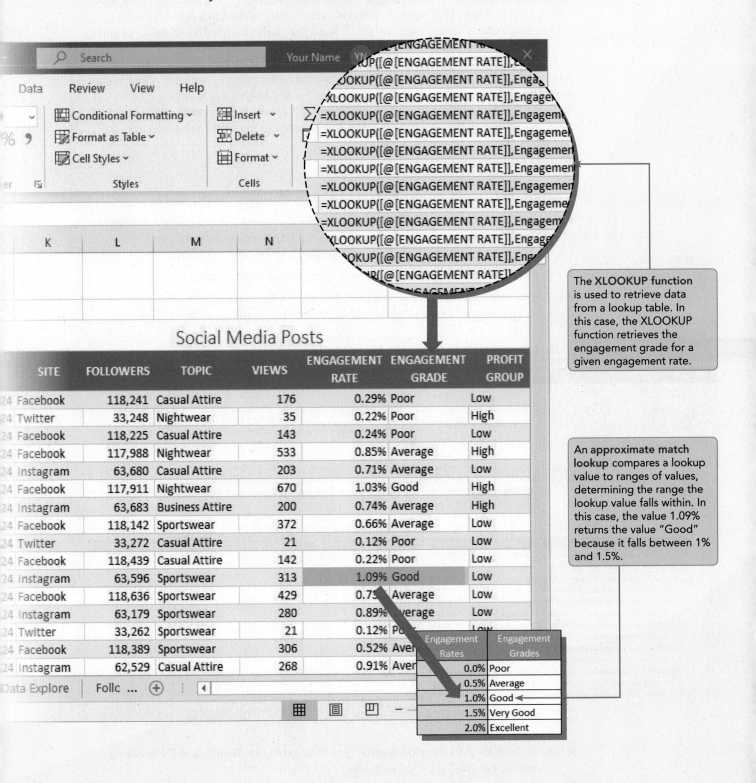

The XLOOKUP function is used to retrieve data from a lookup table. In this case, the XLOOKUP function retrieves the engagement grade for a given engagement rate.

An **approximate match lookup** compares a lookup value to ranges of values, determining the range the lookup value falls within. In this case, the value 1.09% returns the value "Good" because it falls between 1% and 1.5%.

Social Media Posts

SITE	FOLLOWERS	TOPIC	VIEWS	ENGAGEMENT RATE	ENGAGEMENT GRADE	PROFIT GROUP
Facebook	118,241	Casual Attire	176	0.29%	Poor	Low
Twitter	33,248	Nightwear	35	0.22%	Poor	High
Facebook	118,225	Casual Attire	143	0.24%	Poor	Low
Facebook	117,988	Nightwear	533	0.85%	Average	High
Instagram	63,680	Casual Attire	203	0.71%	Average	Low
Facebook	117,911	Nightwear	670	1.03%	Good	High
Instagram	63,683	Business Attire	200	0.74%	Average	High
Facebook	118,142	Sportswear	372	0.66%	Average	Low
Twitter	33,272	Casual Attire	21	0.12%	Poor	Low
Facebook	118,439	Casual Attire	142	0.22%	Poor	Low
Instagram	63,596	Sportswear	313	1.09%	Good	Low
Facebook	118,636	Sportswear	429	0.75%	Average	Low
Instagram	63,179	Sportswear	280	0.89%	Average	Low
Twitter	33,262	Sportswear	21	0.12%	Poor	Low
Facebook	118,389	Sportswear	306	0.52%	Average	
Instagram	62,529	Casual Attire	268	0.91%	Average	

Engagement Rates	Engagement Grades
0.0%	Poor
0.5%	Average
1.0%	Good
1.5%	Very Good
2.0%	Excellent

Using Lookup Functions

Often data analysts receive large data sets with hundreds or even thousands of records and dozens of fields. They must then reduce that wealth of data to a few important statistics and charts. In this module, you'll learn the skills you need to reveal facts and trends hidden within a mass of information.

Claire has a workbook containing results of a social media marketing survey. The raw data is stored in an Excel table named "Media" containing records from 785 social media posts made to Facebook, Instagram, and Twitter. Within each record, Claire included the date of the post, the post's general topic, and the response it received. You need to summarize the social media data to evaluate the impact of the company's ad campaign on its social media presence.

To open Claire's workbook containing the marketing data:

▶ 1. **sam** ↓ Open the **NP_EX_7-1.xlsx** workbook located in the **Excel7 > Module** folder included with your Data Files, and then save the workbook as **NP_EX_7_Syrmosta** in the location specified by your instructor.

▶ 2. In the **Documentation** sheet, enter your name and the date.

▶ 3. Go to the **Media Log** worksheet. The Media Excel table on this sheet contains Syrmosta's social media posts from the past year. See Figure 7–1.

Figure 7–1	Media Excel table in the Media Log worksheet

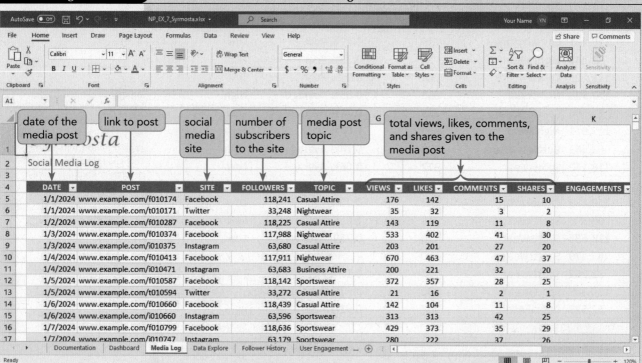

▶ 4. Review each of the worksheets, and then go to the **Terms and Definitions** worksheet to study the fields used with this data table.

▶ 5. Go to the **Media Log** worksheet.

Successful social media marketing is all about getting the user engaged. An engaged user is more likely to turn into a loyal customer. There are four general types of social media engagement with increasing levels of user involvement: (1) The user has viewed the social media post. (2) The user has indicated approval or "like" of the post. (3) The user has taken the time and effort to comment on the post. (4) The user has shared the post with others.

In the Media table, Claire recorded the total number of views, likes, comments, and shares for each social media post made in the last year. You will add another field that calculates the sum of these engagements for each post.

To calculate the total engagements per post:

▶ **1.** In the Media Log worksheet, click cell **K5** to select it.

▶ **2.** Type **=SUM(** to begin the SUM function.

▶ **3.** Use your mouse to select the range **G5:J5**. The field reference Media[@[VIEWS]:[SHARES]] is added to the formula to reference the Views through Shares field in the current row of the Media table.

▶ **4.** Type **)** to complete the SUM function, and then press **ENTER**. Excel calculates the sum of the engagements for each post, returning a total of 343 engagements for the first post. See Figure 7–2.

| Figure 7–2 | Engagements calculated field added to the Media table |

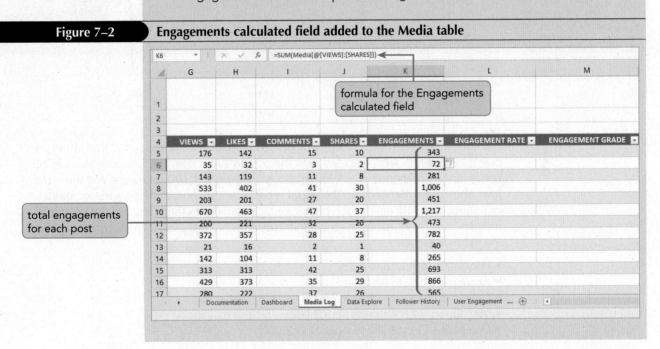

Claire is also interested in the engagement rate, which is the percentage of followers that engage with each post. The number of followers tells Claire how many subscribers a post might have, but the engagement rate shows how often they respond to the post's contents. You will calculate the engagement rate for each post by dividing the total engagements by total followers at the time the post was uploaded.

To calculate the engagement rate per post:

▶ **1.** In the Media Log worksheet, click cell **L5** to select it.

▶ **2.** Type **=** to begin the formula, click cell **K5** to select the Engagements field, type **/** for division, click cell **E5** to select the Followers field, and then press **ENTER**. The formula =[@ENGAGEMENTS]/[@FOLLOWERS] is entered in the Engagement Rate column. See Figure 7–3.

Figure 7–3   **Engagement rate per post**

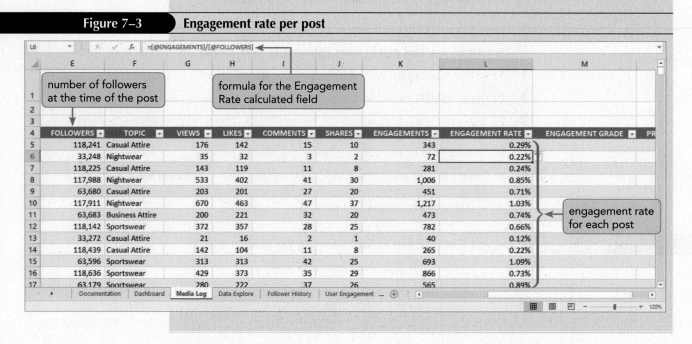

The first post, in row 5, has an engagement rate of 0.29% indicating that about 29 out of 10,000 followers engaged with the post in some way. The last post, in row 789, has an engagement rate of 2.49% or about 2.5 users per 100 followers. Are these rates low? The answer depends on the social media content. Social media sites for sports or politics typically have much higher engagements rates than this, but the fashion industry must work harder to engage its followers. Claire grades engagement rates at the following levels:

- Poor—0% to less than 0.5%
- Average—0.5% to less than 1.0%
- Good—1.0% to less than 1.5%
- Very Good—1.5% to less than 2.0%
- Excellent—Greater than or equal to 2.0%

Claire wants to show the engagement grade for each post. You will display the grade using an approximate match lookup.

Creating Approximate Match Lookups

An approximate match lookup compares a lookup value to a range of values rather than a single, specific value. For example, an engagement rate of 0.38% would receive a "Poor" grade from Claire because it falls between 0% and 0.5%, and a value of 1.83% would receive a "Very Good" grade because it falls between 1.5% and 2.0%.

Approximate match lookups use a vertical lookup table or a horizontal lookup table. In a vertical lookup table, the range of values are in one column of the table and the return values are retrieved from another column. In a horizontal lookup table, the compare values are in one row of the table and the return values are retrieved from another row.

Claire wants to see the engagement grade for each post. You will add a vertical lookup table to the workbook that lists the ranges of engage rates in the first column and engagement grades in the second column.

To create the vertical lookup table of engagement rates and grades:

1. Go to the **Lookup Tables** worksheet.

2. In the range **B5:B9**, enter the values **0.0%, 0.5%, 1.0%, 1.5%, and 2.0%** representing the lower end of each range of engagement rates in ascending order.

> Be sure to enter the approximate match lookup table values in ascending order using the lower end of each interval.

3. In the range **C5:C9**, enter **Poor, Average, Good, Very Good,** and **Excellent** as the grades for each interval of engagement rates. See Figure 7–4.

| Figure 7–4 | Vertical lookup table for the engagement rate |

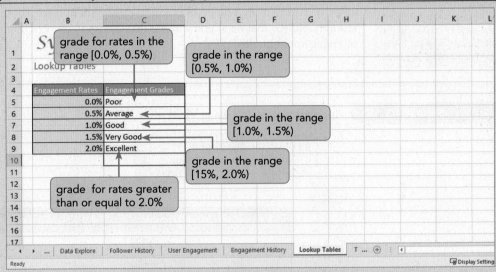

4. Select the range **B4:C9**.

5. On the ribbon, click the **Formulas** tab, and then in the Defined Names group, click the **Create from Selection** button.

6. Click the **Right column** check box to deselect it. Only the Top row check box is selected.

7. Click **OK**. The range names Engagement_Rates and Engagement_Grades are added to the workbook.

Once you have created a lookup table, you can use a lookup function to retrieve a value from that table using an approximate match lookup. Two lookup functions commonly found in Excel workbook are VLOOKUP and HLOOKUP.

The VLOOKUP function uses a vertical lookup table. The first column of the table contains the range of lookup values in ascending order. Each value listed is the *lower* end of the interval. The VLOOKUP function makes an approximate match by going down the first column to locate the cell containing the largest value that is less than or equal to the supplied value. Then the VLOOKUP function retrieves the value from a different column in the same row.

The HLOOKUP function uses a horizontal lookup table. The first row of the table contains the range of lookup values in ascending order. Like the vertical lookup table, each value listed is the *lower* end of the interval. An approximate match is made going left to right across the row until a cell containing the largest value that is less than or equal to the supplied value is found. The HLOOKUP function retrieves the value from another row in the same column.

The VLOOKUP and HLOOKUP functions have similar syntax:

```
VLOOKUP(lookup, array, col, [range_lookup=TRUE])

HLOOKUP(lookup, array, row, [range_lookup=TRUE])
```

where `lookup` is the value to look up, `array` references the cell range containing the lookup table, `col` and `row` are index numbers representing the column or row containing the values returned by the function, and `range_lookup` specifies whether to do an approximate match lookup (TRUE) for a range of values, or an exact match lookup (FALSE) to match a single specific value. If you do not specify a `range_lookup` value, an approximate match lookup is performed by default.

Figure 7–5 shows the VLOOKUP function finding an approximate match for a lookup value of 1.83% from a range of possible engagement rates listed in the table's first column. Notice that each entry in the first column contains the lower value of the range of engagement grades.

> **Tip**
>
> With exact match lookups, the data in the first column or row of the lookup table can be placed in any order.

Figure 7–5 **Approximate match using VLOOKUP**

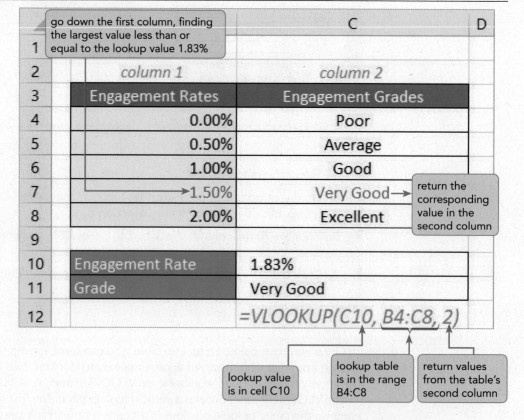

The HLOOKUP function would return the same result with the engagement rates placed in the first row of the lookup table and the grades placed in another row. The HLOOKUP function goes across the row of engagement rates, finding the largest rate that is less than or equal to 1.83%.

Another Excel lookup function is the XLOOKUP function. The XLOOKUP function has the following advantages over the VLOOKUP and HLOOKUP functions:

- Lookup tables can be arranged in either the vertical or horizontal direction.

- Lookup values can be in any column or row, not just the first column or row.

- Lookup values can be arranged in any order and not just ascending order.

- If no match is found, the XLOOKUP function can return a user-specified value instead of the default #N/A error value.

The syntax of the XLOOKUP function is:

```
XLOOKUP(lookup, array, return, [not_found], [match], [search])
```

where *lookup* is the value to look up, *array* is the column or row containing the lookup values, *return* is the column or row containing the return values, *not_found* is an optional value returned by the function if no match is found, *match* is the match mode used by the function, and *search* is the search mode used by the function. For example, the following XLOOKUP function searches the values in the range C1:C10, looking for a match to the value in cell A1. If a match is found, it returns the value in the corresponding row in the range E1:E10.

```
XLOOKUP(A1, C1:C10, E1:E10)
```

If no match is found, the function returns the error value #N/A. To provide a more friendly message, the following function displays the text string "no match" if no match is found:

```
XLOOKUP(A1, C1:C10, E1:E10, "no match")
```

By default, the XLOOKUP function searches for exact matches. If you don't want an exact match, you choose one of the following values for the optional *match* argument:

- *match* = 0   (default) Exact match; if none is found, returns #N/A, unless a value is specified by the *not_found* argument
- *match* = −1   Exact match; if none is found, returns the next smaller value (like approximate match lookups with the VLOOKUP and HLOOKUP functions)
- *match* = 1   Exact match; if none is found, returns the next larger value
- *match* = 2   Wildcard match using the *, ? and ~ symbols to locate a match

By default, XLOOKUP starts the search with the first entry in the column or row of lookup values and then proceeds down or to the right. You can specify a different direction for the search by adding one of the following optional *search* argument values to the function:

- *search* = 1   (default) Search starting from the first entry in the column or row of lookup values
- *search* = −1   Reverse search, starting from the last entry in the column or row of lookup values
- *search* = 2   Binary search using lookup values sorted in ascending order; returns invalid results if not sorted
- *search* = −2   Binary search using lookup values sorted in descending order; returns invalid results if not sorted

If you do not include values for the *match* and *search* arguments, the XLOOKUP function assumes the defaults and performs an exact match lookup starting with the first value in the specified lookup row or column. Figure 7–6 shows the XLOOKUP function performing an approximate match lookup in a vertical lookup table of engagement rates and grades.

Tip

If you don't specify a *not_found* value, include a comma placeholder (, ,) to include values for the *match* or *search* arguments of the XLOOKUP function.

Figure 7-6   **Approximate match using XLOOKUP**

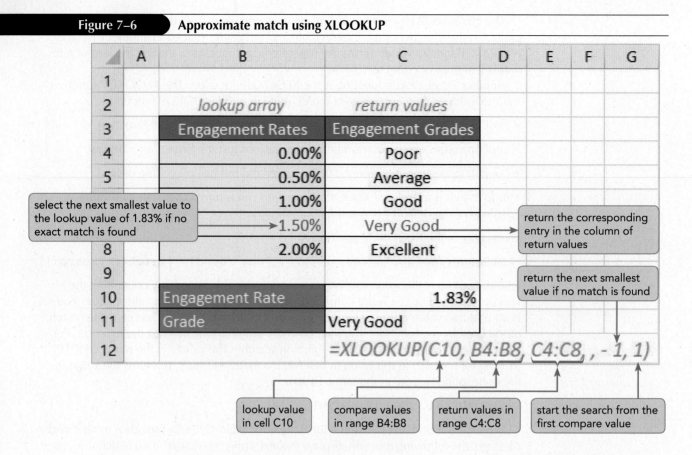

Because of its greater flexibility and power, you will use the XLOOKUP function to grade every social media post in the Media Log worksheet based on its engagement rate.

To perform an approximate match lookup with the XLOOKUP function:

1. Go to the **Media Log** worksheet and click cell **M5**.

2. On the Formulas tab, in the Function Library group, click the **Lookup & Reference** button, scroll down the list of functions, and then click **XLOOKUP**. The Function Arguments dialog box opens.

3. Make sure the insertion point is in the Lookup_value box, and then click cell **L5** in the Media table. The cell reference [@[ENGAGEMENT RATE]] references the value of the Engagement Rate field in the current row.

4. Press **TAB** to move to the Lookup_array box, and then type **Engagement_ Rates** to reference to lookup column contain the engagements rate you defined in the last set of steps.

5. Press **TAB** to move to the Return_array box, and then type **Engagement_ Grades** to reference the column of grades associated with the range of engagement rates.

6. Press **TAB** twice to move to the Match_mode box, and then type **–1** to specify that XLOOKUP will return the next smallest value from the lookup table if no match is found. You will not specify a value for the Search_mode box, accepting the default method of a search starting with the first entry in the column of lookup values. See Figure 7–7.

Figure 7–7	Function arguments for an approximate match XLOOKUP function

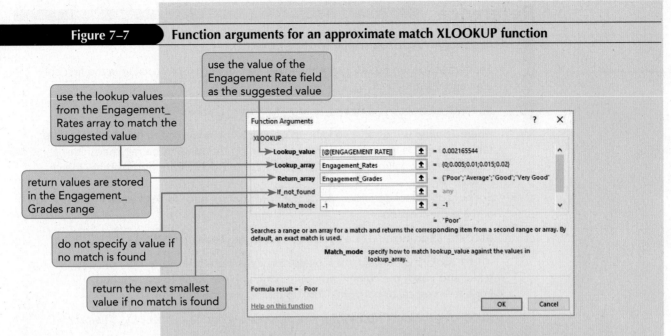

use the lookup values from the Engagement_Rates array to match the suggested value

use the value of the Engagement Rate field as the suggested value

return values are stored in the Engagement_Grades range

do not specify a value if no match is found

return the next smallest value if no match is found

7. Click **OK** to close the dialog box and apply the XLOOKUP function to the Engagement Grades field for all records in the table. See Figure 7–8.

Figure 7–8	Engagement grades retrieved by the XLOOKUP function

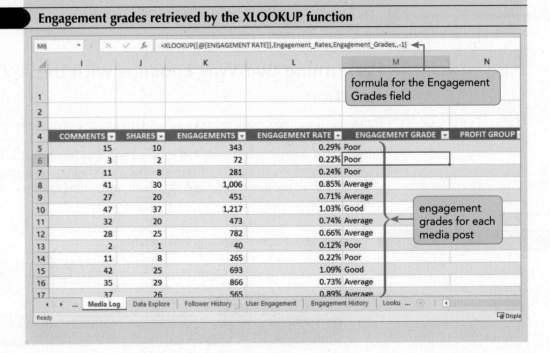

formula for the Engagement Grades field

engagement grades for each media post

A grade appears alongside each post based on the value of the engagement rate. Later, you'll explore how these grades differ based on the social media site and the content of post.

Reference

Creating an Approximate Match Lookup

- For vertical lookup tables, place the lower part of each lookup value in the first column and use the function

    VLOOKUP(*lookup*, *array*, *col*, [*range_lookup*=TRUE])

    where **lookup** is the value to look up, **array** is the reference to the vertical lookup table, and **col** is the column number containing the value to be returned. The **range_lookup** value is optional, but must be set to TRUE for approximate match lookups.
- For horizontal lookup tables, place the lower part of each lookup value in the first row and use the function

    HLOOKUP(*lookup*, *array*, *row*, [*range_lookup*=TRUE])

    where **lookup** is the value to look up, **array** is the reference to the horizontal lookup table, and **row** is the column number containing the value to be returned.
- For either vertical or horizontal lookup tables, use the function

    XLOOKUP(*lookup*, *array*, *return*, [*not_found*], [*match*], [*search*])

    where **lookup** is the value to look up, **array** is the column or row containing the lookup values, **return** is the column or row containing the return values, **not_found** is an optional value returned by the function if no match is found, **match** is the match mode used by the function, and **search** is the search mode used by the function.

Performing Two-Way Lookups with the XLOOKUP Function

Sometimes you might need to find a value that occurs where a row and a column cross. A **two-way lookup table** has lookup values in both a row and a column with the return value at their intersection. Figure 7–9 shows a two-way lookup table that lists media sites in the first column and months in the first row. Looking up Instagram as the media site and MAR as the month returns 824, which is the number of social media shares on Instagram during March.

Figure 7–9 **Value retrieved from a two-way lookup table**

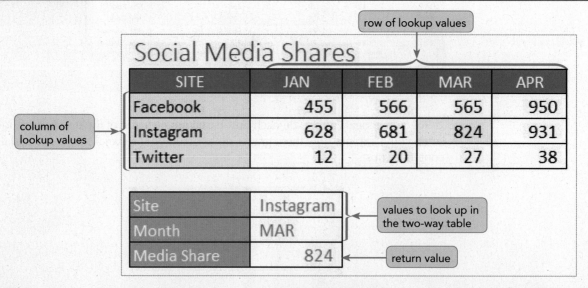

A useful feature of the XLOOKUP function is that it can return an array of values matching a given lookup value. For example, in Figure 7–10, the XLOOKUP function searches across the lookup table's first row and returns the monthly media shares that match the Instagram media site.

Figure 7–10   **Array of values returned using XLOOKUP**

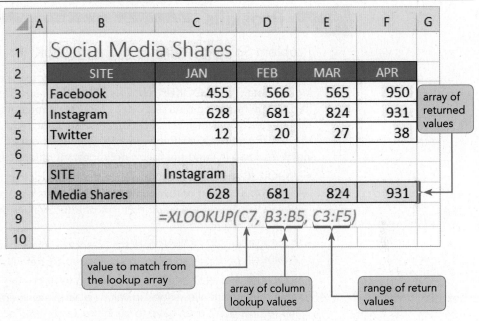

This XLOOKUP feature is useful with two-way tables because the array of return values can act as a lookup table for another XLOOKUP function by nesting one XLOOKUP function within another. The general syntax for returning a value from a two-way table using nested XLOOKUP functions is

`XLOOKUP(value1, column, XLOOKUP(value2, row, return))`

where *value1* is the value to be matched in the column of the two-way table, *value2* is the value to be matched in the row, *column* and *row* reference the column and row containing the lookup values, and *return* references the array of return values from the two-way table. Figure 7–11 shows how to apply nested XLOOKUP functions to retrieve media shares based on the name of the media site and the month. Notice that the array of values returned by the XLOOKUP function in Figure 7–10 appears as the lookup table in the outer XLOOKUP function.

Figure 7–11   **Two-way lookup with nested XLOOKUP functions**

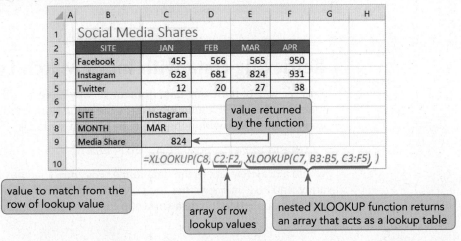

This process of nesting one XLOOKUP function within another can also be used with approximate match lookups in which the two-way table's row and column contain ranges of values rather than specific categories. For those types of tables, you will need to include argument values specifying how the XLOOKUP functions will search through the lookup values to find an approximate match.

 Proskills

Problem Solving: Transitioning to XLOOKUP

The VLOOKUP and HLOOKUP functions are older Excel standards for retrieving lookup data. The XLOOKUP function is the newer standard and provides greater flexibility in retrieving data, especially for approximate match lookups. Because of the advantages associated with the XLOOKUP function, you might want to transition any VLOOKUP and HLOOKUP functions in your workbooks to the XLOOKUP function. However, keep in mind the following important differences between them:

- VLOOKUP and HLOOKUP reference the entire lookup table and retrieve values based on a column or row number. XLOOKUP references the column or row of lookup values and the column or row of return values. XLOOKUP does not use column or row numbers.

- VLOOKUP and XLOOKUP perform an approximate match lookup by default. XLOOKUP performs an exact match lookup by default.

- VLOOKUP and HLOOKUP require lookup values in the first column or row of the table. XLOOKUP allows lookup values placed anywhere. In fact, the lookup values and returns don't even have to be in the same table or in the same worksheet.

- VLOOKUP and HLOOKUP for approximate match lookups require lookup values sorted in ascending order with each value representing the lower end of a numeric interval. XLOOKUP allows lookup values to be arranged in any order with the $match$ argument determining what constitutes a matching value.

- VLOOKUP or HLOOKUP do not support two-way lookups; instead you use the INDEX and MATCH functions. XLOOKUP supports two-way lookups using nested XLOOKUP functions.

- VLOOKUP and HLOOKUP must be edited if you revise the structure of a lookup table by inserting rows and columns. XLOOKUP automatically adjusts if you add or remove table rows and columns.

- VLOOKUP and HLOOKUP return the #N/A error value in the case of a failed match. XLOOKUP can return any specified value.

While XLOOKUP can do everything the VLOOKUP and HLOOKUP can do and more, the experienced Excel user should be comfortable with both approaches as they will both be encountered in many workbooks.

Retrieving Data with Index Match Lookups

Another way of retrieving data from a two-way table is with the INDEX and MATCH functions. The INDEX function returns the value from a table by specifying a row index and column index within that table. Its general syntax is

    INDEX(array, row_num, col_num)

where $array$ references the data range, row_num specifies the row number within that array, and col_num specifies the column number. For example, the following INDEX function applied to the data shown in Figure 7–11 returns a value of 950, which is the number of media shares for Facebook during April located at the first row and fourth column of the array of media shares:

```
INDEX(C3:F5, 1, 4)
```

The MATCH function returns the position of a value found within a row or column. Its syntax is

```
MATCH(lookup_value, array, [match = 1])
```

where *lookup_value* is the value to locate, *array* is the row or column in which to search, and *match* is an optional argument specifying how the search should be conducted. The *match* argument has three values, similar to the *match* argument in the XLOOKUP function:

- *match* = 1   (default) An approximate match lookup that finds the largest value less than or equal to lookup value. The values must be arranged in ascending order.
- *match* = 0   An exact match. If none is found, returns #N/A.
- *match* = −1   An approximate match lookup that finds the smallest value greater than or equal to *lookup_value*. The values must be arranged in descending order.

For example, using the table shown in Figure 7–11, the following two expressions return values of 1 and 4, respectively, indicating the exact positions of the "Facebook" and "APR" values in the table's first column and first row:

```
MATCH("Facebook", B3:B5, 0)
```

```
MATCH("APR", C2:F2, 0)
```

You can nest the MATCH function within the INDEX function to return a specific value from a two-way lookup table. The general syntax is

```
INDEX(array, columnMatch, rowMatch)
```

where *array* is the array of return values, *columnMatch* is the MATCH function applied to the lookup values in the table's first column and *rowMatch* is a MATCH function applied to lookup values in the table's first row. For example, the following expression combines the INDEX and MATCH functions retrieve the return value for Facebook media posts in April:

```
INDEX(C3:F5, MATCH("Facebook", B3:B5, 0), MATCH("APR", C2:F2, 0))
```

Nested XLOOKUP functions and nested INDEX MATCH functions can both be used to retrieve values from a two-way table. Which approach you use is often a matter of personal preference.

Insight

Performing Partial Lookups with Wildcards

Partial lookups can be helpful when you're working with large data sets. A **partial lookup** matches a character pattern rather than a specific value. You use wildcards to create the character pattern for the lookup. For example, the following XLOOKUP function uses the * wildcard to match any string of characters that start with letters "WIL" using the lookup values in the LastNames array and returning values from the FirstNames array. If no match is found, the text string "No Name" is returned. The *match* argument value must equal 2 for XLOOKUP to interpret the wildcard symbols within the lookup value.

```
XLOOKUP("WIL*", LastNames, FirstNames, "No Name", 2)
```

Because XLOOKUP ignores case, values such as William, Willet, Will, or Willey would be matched by this function. Excel will choose the first match it encounters in the table even if other entries would match the wildcard pattern. To combine a wildcard character with a cell value, use the & character. For example, the following function looks up values starting with the text stored in cell B10:

```
XLOOKUP(B10&"*", LastNames, FirstNames, "No Name", 2)
```

Partial lookups can also be done with VLOOKUP or HLOOKUP by adding wildcard characters within the lookup value. The following VLOOKUP function uses wildcards to retrieve values of the second column in the UserNames table in which the values in the lookup column starts with the text string "WIL":

```
XLOOKUP("WIL*", UserNames, 2, FALSE)
```

Note that partial matches in VLOOKUP and HLOOKUP can be done only with exact match lookups, so the range_lookup argument must be set to FALSE.

Exploring Logical Functions

Logical functions are used to set data values based on whether a condition is true or false. So far, you've only used the IF function

```
IF(logical_test, value_if_true, [value_if_false])
```

where **logical_test** is the condition that is either true or false, **value_if_true** is the value returned by the IF function if **logical_test** is true, and *value_if_false* is the function's value if **logical_test** is false. The IF function is limited to returning one of two possible results. To test for multiple conditions, returning different values for each condition, you can nest one IF function within the other, replacing the *value_if_false* argument with another IF function. For example, the following function uses two nested IF function to test the value of cell A1:

```
IF(A1 < 0.5%, "Poor", IF(A1 < 1%, "Average", "Good"))
```

If A1 is less than 0.5%, the function returns the value "Poor." Otherwise, the function tests for whether A1 is less than 1%. If that condition is true, the function returns the value "Average." And if that condition is false, the function returns the value "Good." By adding more nested IF functions, you can test for as many possible conditions as you want. However, at some point the collection of nested IF functions will become so convoluted that you're better off using a lookup table to match each condition to a different value.

Reference

Applying a Logical Function

- To test one condition against two possible outcomes, use

  IF(*logical_test*, *value_if_true*, [*value_if_false*])

  where ***logical_test*** is the condition that is either true or false, ***value_if_true*** is the value returned by the IF function if ***logical_test*** is true, and *value_if_false* is the function's value if ***logical_test*** is false.

- To test for multiple possible outcomes, use

  IF(*logical_test1*, *value_if_true1*, *logical_test2*, *value_if_true2*, …)

  where ***logical_test1***, ***logical_test2***, and so on are the different logical conditions, and *value_if_true1*, *value_if_true2*, and so on are the values associated with each condition, if true.

- To return a true value if any one of multiple conditions are true, use

  OR(*logical1*, [*logical2*], [*logical3*], …)

  where ***logical1***, *logical2*, *logical3*, and so on are conditions which are either true or false.

- To return a true value only if all conditions are true, use

  AND(*logical1*, [*logical2*], [*logical3*], …)

Using the IFS Function

Another way of working with multiple IF conditions is with the IFS function. The **IFS function** tests for multiple conditions without nesting and has the syntax

IFS(*logical_test1*, *value_if_true1*, *logical_test2*, *value_if_true2*, …)

where ***logical_test1***, ***logical_test2***, and so on are logical conditions, and *value_if_true1*, *value_if_true2*, and so on are the values associated with each condition, if the condition is true. This means that you could rewrite the nested IF function from earlier using the following IFS function that specifies three possible conditions for the value of cell A1:

IFS(A1 < 0.5%, "Poor", A1 < 1%, "Average", A1 >= 1%, "Good")

The IFS function doesn't include a default value if all the conditions are false. However, you can add a default condition to the end of the list by setting the final logical test to the value TRUE, as in the following expression:

IFS(A1 < 0.5%, "Poor", A1 < 1%, "Average", TRUE, "Good")

This IFS function will return a value of "Poor" if A1 is less than 0.5%. Otherwise, the function will return a value of "AVERAGE" if A1 is less than 1. But if neither of those conditions is met, the function will return a value of "Good."

Combining Conditions with the OR and AND Functions

Another way of combining multiple conditions is with the OR function or the AND function. The **OR function** combines multiple conditions, returning a value of TRUE if *any* of the conditions are true. The **AND function** returns a value of TRUE if *all* of the conditions are true. The two functions have a similar syntax:

OR(*logical1*, [*logical2*], [*logical3*], …)
AND(*logical1*, [*logical2*], [*logical3*], …)

where *logical1*, *logical2*, *logical3*, and so on are conditions that are either true or false. For example, the following expression returns a value of TRUE if cell A1 equals 2 *or* if cell B1 equals 4 *or* if cell C1 equals 10:

```
OR(A1=2, B1=4, C1=10)
```

However, the following expression returns the value TRUE only if A1 equals 2 *and* B1 equals 4 *and* C1 equals 10:

```
AND(A1=2, B1=4, C1=10)
```

Tip

To switch a logical value between TRUE and FALSE, enclose the logical value within the NOT function.

The OR and AND functions can be nested within an IF function to provide a test involving multiple conditions. The following IF function tests three conditions enclosed within the AND function, returning the value "Pass" if A1 = 2 *and* B1 = 4 *and* C1=10; otherwise, it returns the value "Fail":

```
IF(AND(A1=2, B1=4, C1=10), "Pass", "Fail")
```

Claire wants to know whether the clothing product discussed in the media post is a high-profit or low-profit item. Clothes from the Business Attire or Nightwear categories are considered high-profit items for the company, and clothes from the Casual Attire or Sportswear categories are considered low-profit items. You'll add a field named Profit Group to the Media table, and then nest an OR function within an IF function to calculate the value of the Profit Group field for each record in the table.

To nest the OR in an IF function to display the product's profitability:

▶ 1. In the Media Log worksheet, click cell **N5** to select it.

   Because this will be a complicated nested function, you will enter the formula starting with the innermost function.

▶ 2. On the Formulas tab, in the Function Library group, click the **Logical** button, and then click **OR**. The Function Arguments dialog box opens.

▶ 3. With the insertion point in the Logical1 box, click cell **F5** to enter the reference [@TOPIC] in the box, type **="Business Attire"** as the first logical condition, and then press **TAB** to go to the Logical2 box.

▶ 4. In the Logical2 box, click cell **F5** to enter the reference[@TOPIC], type **="Nightwear"** as the second logical condition.

▶ 5. Click **OK**. The formula is entered in the Profit Group column. Each record in the Profit Group column displays either TRUE or FALSE. FALSE appears in cell N5, TRUE appears in cell N6, FALSE appears in cell N7, and so forth.

▶ 6. Double-click cell **N5** to enter Edit mode. You will enclose the OR function in cell N5 within an IF function.

▶ 7. Click between the = symbol and OR, and then type **IF(** to begin inserting the IF function before the OR function.

▶ 8. Click the end of the formula, and then type **, "High", "Low")** to specify the two possible values that can appear depending on the value returned by OR function.

▶ 9. Press **ENTER**. The formula =IF(OR([@TOPIC]="Business Attire",[@TOPIC]="Nightwear"), "High", "Low") is added to every record in the Profit Group column. See Figure 7–12.

| Figure 7–12 | OR function nested within an IF function |

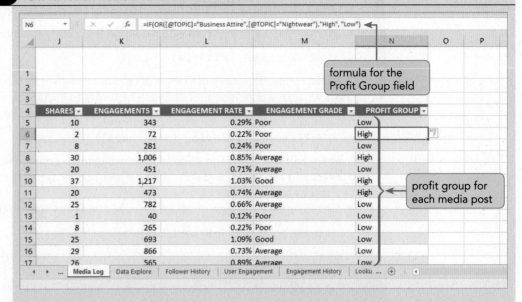

formula for the Profit Group field

profit group for each media post

Trouble? If Excel reports a syntax error, you made a mistake when typing the formula. Clear the formulas from the Profit Group column, and then repeat Steps 1 through 9. Before pressing ENTER, make sure you have closed all quotation marks and matched opening and closing parentheses and brackets.

If you are still having trouble, clear the formulas from the Profit Group column, and then go to the Terms and Definitions worksheet. Copy cell G18, go back to the Media Log worksheet, and paste the formula into cell N5. Double-click cell N5, and then press ENTER to enter the formula for every record in the Media table.

The Media table is complete. Next, you will analyze the data in the table, starting by calculating summary statistics that tally the number of posts made to each social media site.

Applying Summary IF Functions

Excel supports several functions that combine statistics like AVERAGE, SUM, and COUNT, with logical expressions, so that you calculate statistics only on those cells that match the logical condition.

Reference

> ## Using a Summary IF Function
>
> - To count the number of cells within a range that satisfy specified criteria, use
>
>   `COUNTIF(range, criteria)`
>
>   where **range** references the range of cells or table field to be counted and **criteria** is a value or a condition that defines which cells to include in the count.
> - To calculate the sum of values for cells that satisfy specified criteria, use
>
>   `SUMIF(range, criteria, [sum_range])`
>
>   where **range** is the range of cells to be evaluated by the criteria specified in the **criteria** argument, and *sum_range* is an optional argument that specifies the range of values to sum.
> - To calculate the average of values for cells that satisfy specified criteria, use
>
>   `AVERAGEIF(range, criteria, [average_range])`
>
>   where *average_range* is an optional argument that specifies the range of values to average.
> - For conditions that involve multiple criteria ranges, use the COUNTIFS, SUMIFS, AVERAGEIFS, MAXIFS, and MINIFS functions.

Conditional Counting with COUNTIF

Claire wants to know how many posts over the past year were made to Facebook, Instagram, and Twitter. You can use the COUNT function to count the number of social media posts, but that would include all records, regardless of the social media site. To count only those records that match a specified condition, you can create a **conditional count** using the COUNTIF function

`COUNTIF(range, criteria)`

where **range** references the range of cells or table field to be counted and **criteria** is a value or a condition that defines which cells to include in the count. For example, the following expression counts the number of cells in the range D5:D789 whose value equals "Facebook":

`COUNTIF(D5:D789, "Facebook")`

Rather than explicitly entering the criteria value, you can reference a cell containing that value. The following formula counts the numbers of cells in the range D5:D789 whose values equal the value stored in cell B10:

`COUNTIF(D5:D789, B10)`

Figure 7–13 provides examples of other ways the COUNTIF function can be used for conditional counting.

Figure 7–13	Conditional counting with the COUNTIF function

Formula	Description
=COUNTIF(A1:A100, "Twitter")	Counts the cells in the A1:A100 range with the text, "Twitter"
=COUNTIF(Media[SITE], "Twitter")	Counts the records in the Media table whose Platform field value equals the text, "Twitter"
=COUNTIF(B1:B100, 25)	Counts the cells in the B1:B100 range that have a value of 25
=COUNTIF(C1:C100, D10)	Counts the cells in the C1:C100 range with values equal to the value stored in cell D10
=COUNTIF(E1:E100, "> 50")	Counts the cells in the E1:E100 range with values greater than 50
=COUNTIF(Media[SHARES], ">=50")	Counts the records in the Media table whose Shares value is greater than or equal to 50
=COUNTIF(F1:F100, ">=" & G10)	Counts the cells in the F1:F100 range with values greater than or equal to the value in cell G10
=COUNTIF(Media[VIEWS], "> " & Popular)	Counts the records in the Media table where the value of the Views field is greater than the value stored in the Popular defined name

Note that you can use the ampersand character (&) to combine text strings with cell values. For example, if cell A1 contains the value 50, then the expression "<=" & A1 is equivalent to the text string "<= 50". By storing conditional values within cells, you can use the COUNTIF function to calculate different conditions by changing those cell's values.

You will use the COUNTIF function to count the number of posts from each social media site, placing the formulas in the Dashboard worksheet.

To do conditional counting with the COUNTIF function:

1. Go to the **Dashboard** worksheet and click cell **B11**.

2. Type **=COUNTIF(Media[SITE], B10)** to count the number of records in Media table where the value of the Site field equals the value stored in cell B10 (Facebook).

3. Press **ENTER**. The formula returns 332, indicating that 332 posts were made to Facebook over the past 12 months.

4. Copy the formula in cell **B11** and paste it into cells **D11** and **F11** to count the number of posts made to the Instagram and Twitter sites. There were 303 posts to Instagram and 150 posts to Twitter.

5. In cell **H11**, enter the formula **=COUNTA(Media[SITE])** to calculate the total posts from all sites. The formula returns 785, which is also equal to the sum of cells B11, D11, and F11. See Figure 7–14.

Tip

When entering the formula, use AutoComplete to select the table name (Media) and the field name (SITE) from the list.

| Figure 7–14 | COUNTIF function applied to the Media table |

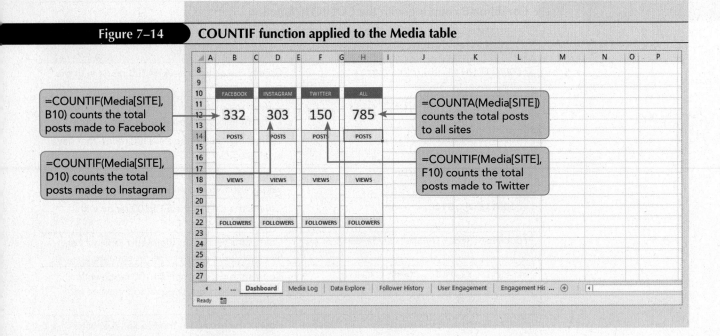

=COUNTIF(Media[SITE], B10) counts the total posts made to Facebook

=COUNTIF(Media[SITE], D10) counts the total posts made to Instagram

=COUNTA(Media[SITE]) counts the total posts to all sites

=COUNTIF(Media[SITE], F10) counts the total posts made to Twitter

Note that the COUNTIF function makes no distinction between text values and numeric values unlike the COUNT function, which does not count text values.

Calculating Conditional Sums with SUMIF

The SUMIF function calculates the sum of values that match specified criteria, creating a **conditional sum**. The syntax of the SUMIF function is

```
SUMIF(range, criteria, [sum_range])
```

where **range** is the range of cells to be evaluated by the criteria specified in the **criteria** argument, and *sum_range* is an optional argument that specifies the values to sum. The following expression uses the SUMIF function to calculate the sum of values in the range A1:A100, but only those cells whose value is greater than 50:

```
SUMIF(A1:A100, "> 50")
```

Tip

For the SUMIF function, the criteria and sum ranges can cover multiple rows and columns.

If you include the *sum_range* argument, the selected cells in that range will correspond to the selected cells in the criteria range. Figure 7–15 shows an example of using the SUMIF function to sum the values in the range E3:E12 whose cells correspond to cells in the criteria range (range C3:C12) with the value "Twitter."

Figure 7–15   **Conditional sums with the SUMIF function**

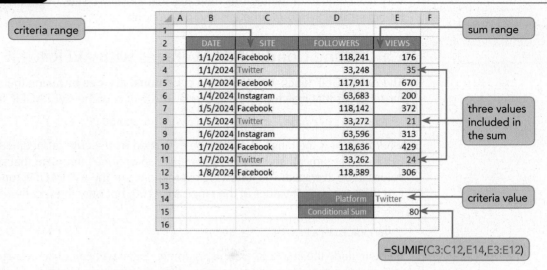

You will use the SUMIF function to calculate the total number of views for each social media site in Media table. You will use the SITE field as the criteria range and the VIEWS field as the sum range.

To calculate a conditional sum with the SUMIF function:

1. In the Dashboard worksheet, click cell **B15**.

2. Type **=SUMIF(Media[SITE], B10, Media[VIEWS])** to sum the values from the Views field for records whose Site field value equals "Facebook" (cell B10).

3. Press **ENTER**. The formula returns 153,677, which is the total number of views from posts made to Facebook over the past year.

4. Copy the formula in cell **B15** and paste it into cells **D15** and **F15** to find the total views from posts made to Instagram and Twitter. The values 121,134 and 6,269 appear in cells D15 and F15, respectively.

5. In cell **H15**, enter the formula **=SUM(Media[VIEWS])** to calculate the total views from all sites. The formula returns 281,080. See Figure 7–16.

Figure 7–16   **SUMIF function applied to the Media table**

=SUMIF(Media[SITE], B10,Media[VIEWS]) sums views from Facebook

=SUMIF(Media[SITE], D10, Media[VIEWS]) sums views from Instagram

=SUM(Media[VIEWS]) sums views across sites

=SUMIF(Media[SITE], F10,Media[VIEWS]) sums views from Twitter

	FACEBOOK	INSTAGRAM	TWITTER	ALL
	332	303	150	785
	POSTS	POSTS	POSTS	POSTS
	153,677	121,134	6,269	281,080
	VIEWS	VIEWS	VIEWS	VIEWS
	FOLLOWERS	FOLLOWERS	FOLLOWERS	FOLLOWERS

Dashboard   Media Log   Data Explore   Follower History   User Engagement   Engagement His

Tip

For more general matches, use wildcards in the criteria expression.

These calculations reveal that most views come from Facebook and Instagram, and very few come from Twitter. This indicates that those two sites might be better platforms for advertising Syrmosta products and promotions.

Calculating Conditional Averages with AVERAGEIF

The AVERAGEIF function calculates a **conditional average** by taking the average only of those values that match specified criteria. The syntax of the AVERAGEIF function is

    AVERAGEIF(*range*, *criteria*, [*average_range*])

where *range* is the range of cells to be evaluated by the criteria specified in the *criteria* argument, and *average_range* is an optional argument that specifies the values to be averaged. The following expression uses the AVERAGEIF function to calculate the sum of values in the range A1:A100, but only those cells whose value is greater than 50:

    AVERAGEIF(A1:A100, "> 50")

If you include the *average_range* argument, Excel will calculate averages for cells in that range corresponding to values in the criteria range. Figure 7–17 shows how to apply the AVERAGEIF function to calculate the average of the values in the range D3:D12 but only for followers of the Facebook site.

Figure 7–17   **Conditional averages with the AVERAGEIF function**

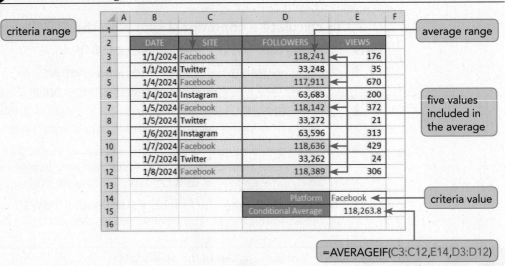

The number of followers for each social media site varies from day-to-day throughout the year. Claire wants you to calculate the average number of followers per post. You will use the AVERAGEIF function to calculate the average number of followers broken down by the social media site.

To calculate a conditional average with the AVERAGEIF function:

1. In the Dashboard worksheet, click cell **B19**.

2. Type **=AVERAGEIF(Media[SITE], B10, Media[FOLLOWERS])** to calculate the average number of followers for the Facebook posts over the past year.

3. Press **ENTER**. The formula returns 126,683, which is the average formatted to the nearest integer.

> **4.** Copy the formula in cell **B19** and paste it into cells **D19** and **F19** to calculate the average followers per post for Instagram and Twitter. The formulas return 64,055 and 33,509, respectively.

> **5.** In cell **H19**, enter the formula **=B19+D19+F19** to calculate the sum of the three averages. The average for all the three sites is 224,248. See Figure 7–18.

| Figure 7–18 | **AVERAGEIF function applied to the Media table** |

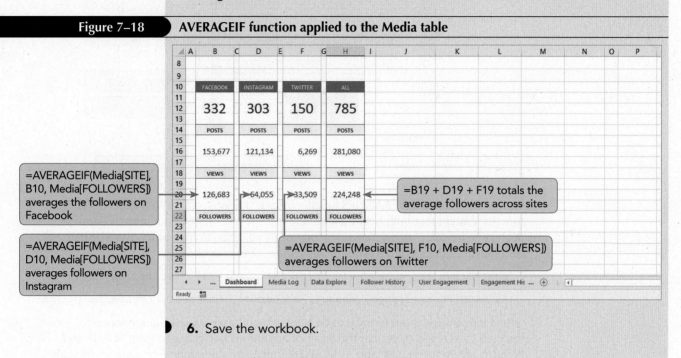

> **6.** Save the workbook.

Facebook is the most popular social media site for following news about Syrmosta. Your calculations show that an average post has almost 127,000 followers on Facebook, 64,000 followers on Instagram, and more than 33,000 followers on Twitter. The total number of followers is about 224,000.

Using Summary IFS Functions

The COUNTIF, SUMIF, and AVERAGEIF functions support a single criteria argument. Excel also supports summary functions that allow for multiple criteria—COUNTIFS, SUMIFS, and AVERAGEIFS. To apply multiple criteria for a conditional count, use the **COUNTIFS function**

```
COUNTIFS(range1, criteria1, [range2], [criteria2] …)
```

where *range1* is the range in which to count cells indicated in *criteria1*; the optional arguments *range2*, *criteria2*, and so on are additional ranges and criteria for choosing which cells to count. You can include up to 127 range/criteria pairs. Each additional range must have the same number of rows and columns as *range1* and *criteria1*, though the ranges do not have to be adjacent.

Figure 7–19 shows conditional counting with two range/criteria pairs. Notice that the count includes only those records that satisfy *both* criteria.

Figure 7–19   Conditional counting with the COUNTIFS function

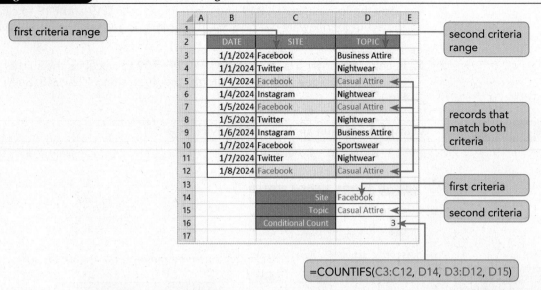

The SUMIFS and AVERAGEIFS functions have similar syntaxes to the COUNTIFS function except that both begin with a reference to the range containing the sum or average to be calculated followed by one or more criteria/range pairs. The **SUMIFS function** and **AVERAGEIFS function** have the syntax

```
SUMIFS(sum_range, range1, criteria1, [range2], [criteria2] …)

AVERAGEIFS(avg_range, range1, criteria1, [range2], [criteria2] …)
```

where **sum_range** is a reference to cells to sum and **avg_range** is a reference to the cells to average. Note that the order of arguments has changed from SUMIF and AVERAGEIF. In the SUMIF and AVERAGEIF functions, the range to be calculated is an optional argument listed last. With the SUMIFS and AVERAGEIFS functions, the range to be calculated is listed first and is required.

Figure 7–20 shows how to calculate conditional sums and averages using multiple range/criteria pairs. Once again, only those cells that match *all* criteria are included in the calculated result.

Figure 7–20   Sums and averages with multiple criteria

Finally, to calculate the minimum and maximum value in a range under multiple criteria, use the **MINIFS function** and the **MAXIFS function**, which have the syntax

MINIFS(*min_range, range1, criteria1*, [*range2*], [*criteria2*] …)

MAXIFS(*max_range, range1, criteria1*, [*range2*], [*criteria2*] …)

where *min_range* and *max_range* reference the cells in which to find the minimum and maximum value, subject to constraints specified in the range/criteria pairs.

The summary IFS functions calculate summary statistics based on several criteria. But that approach becomes cumbersome as you add more criteria ranges to the function. A better approach in those situations is to construct a PivotTable. You'll work with PivotTables in the next session.

Review

Session 7.1 Quick Check

1. A school gives out grades in the following ranges: F: 0 – < 60; D: 60 – < 70; C: 70 – < 80; B: 80 – < 90; A: 90 – 100. Create a vertical lookup table for this grade scale with the range values in the first column and the letter grades in the second.

2. What is the VLOOKUP function to perform an approximate match lookup for a test score of 83? Assume the lookup table is named GradeScale and the grades are in the second column.

3. What is the XLOOKUP function to perform an approximate match lookup for a test score of 83? Assume the column containing the lower end of the range of test scores is named TestScores and the range containing the grades is named Grades.

4. How does XLOOKUP differ from VLOOKUP in the placement of the column of lookup values?

5. How does XLOOKUP differ from VLOOKUP in how it handles failed matches?

6. What is the function to count the number of cells in the range B1:B50 that equal "B"?

7. What is the function to calculate the average of the cells in the range C1:C50 for which the adjacent cell in the range B1:B50 equals "B"?

8. What is the function to calculate the sum of the values in the range D1:D50 for which the adjacent value in the range A1:A50 equals "Senior" and the adjacent value in the range B1:B50 equals "B"?

Session 7.2 Visual Overview:

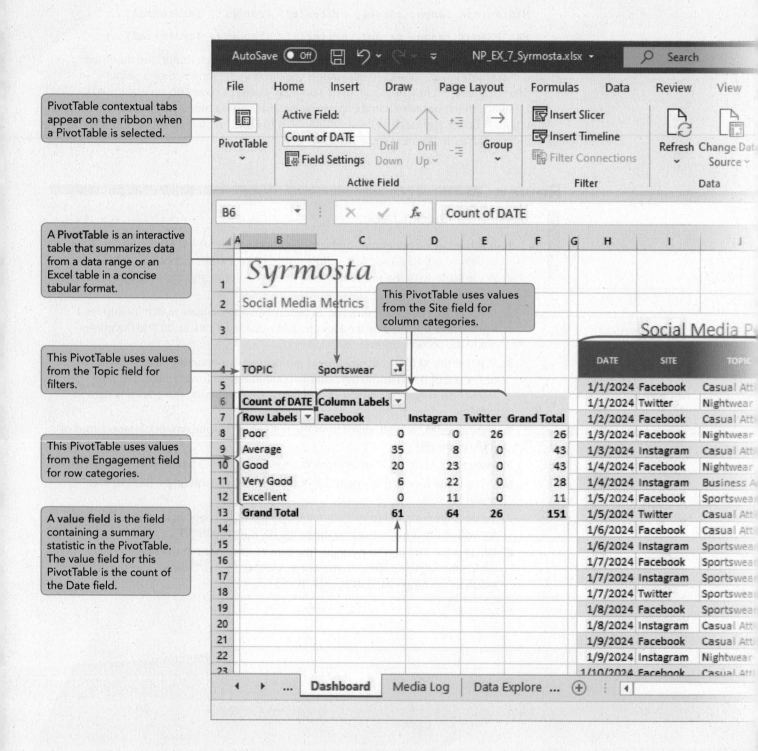

PivotTable contextual tabs appear on the ribbon when a PivotTable is selected.

A **PivotTable** is an interactive table that summarizes data from a data range or an Excel table in a concise tabular format.

This PivotTable uses values from the Site field for column categories.

This PivotTable uses values from the Topic field for filters.

This PivotTable uses values from the Engagement field for row categories.

A value field is the field containing a summary statistic in the PivotTable. The value field for this PivotTable is the count of the Date field.

PivotTables

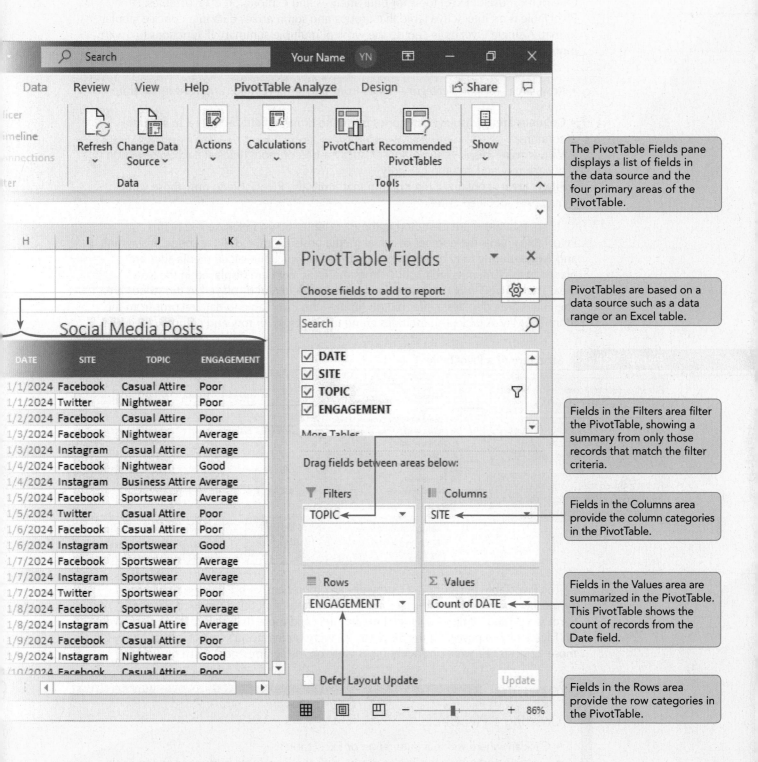

The PivotTable Fields pane displays a list of fields in the data source and the four primary areas of the PivotTable.

PivotTables are based on a data source such as a data range or an Excel table.

Fields in the Filters area filter the PivotTable, showing a summary from only those records that match the filter criteria.

Fields in the Columns area provide the column categories in the PivotTable.

Fields in the Values area are summarized in the PivotTable. This PivotTable shows the count of records from the Date field.

Fields in the Rows area provide the row categories in the PivotTable.

Creating PivotTables

One of most useful Excel tools for data analysis and exploration is PivotTables. A PivotTable is an interactive table that groups and summarizes data in a concise tabular format. A single PivotTable can do the work of multiple summary IF functions but with more ease and flexibility.

Every PivotTable includes the following four primary areas:

- **Rows area**—displays category values from one or more fields arranged in separate rows
- **Columns area**—displays categories from one or more fields arranged in separate columns
- **Values area**—displays summary statistics for one or more fields at each intersection of each row and column category
- **Filters area**—contains a filter button that limits the PivotTable to only those values matching specified criteria

These four areas are identified in the PivotTable shown in Figure 7–21. This PivotTable counts the number of social media posts submitted to Facebook, Instagram, and Twitter during May broken down by the post topic. The social media sites are placed in the Columns area. Values from the Topic field are displayed in the Rows area. The COUNT function is applied to the Post field and displayed in the Values area. The Filters area displays a filter button limiting the PivotTable to data records from the month of May. A table also includes grand totals across all row and column categories.

Figure 7–21 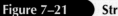 **Structure of a PivotTable**

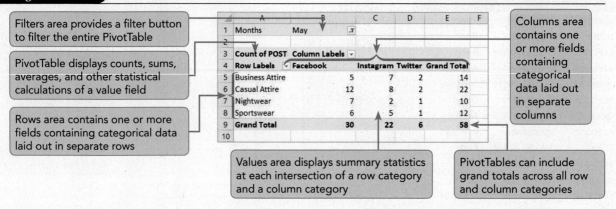

Filters area provides a filter button to filter the entire PivotTable

PivotTable displays counts, sums, averages, and other statistical calculations of a value field

Rows area contains one or more fields containing categorical data laid out in separate rows

Columns area contains one or more fields containing categorical data laid out in separate columns

Values area displays summary statistics at each intersection of a row category and a column category

PivotTables can include grand totals across all row and column categories

The PivotTable in Figure 7–21 provides a comprehensive breakdown of where Syrmosta is posting their messages and for what line of clothing products. In May, Syrmosta posted 58 times on social media sites, and more than half of those posts were on Facebook (30 posts). Of the 58 posts, 22 were on Syrmosta's line of casual attire. Of those 22 posts, 12 were on Facebook, 8 were on Instagram, and 2 were on Twitter.

Reference

Creating a PivotTable

- Click anywhere within a data range or Excel table.
- On the Insert tab, in the Tables group, click the PivotTable button; or on the Table Design tab, in the Tools group, click the Summarize with PivotTable button.
- Specify whether to insert the PivotTable in a new worksheet or at a cell location within an existing worksheet.
- Click OK.
- Drag fields from the field list on the PivotTable Fields pane and drop them on the Filters, Columns, Rows, or Values area boxes.

Inserting a PivotTable

You can create a PivotTable from any data range or Excel table and insert the PivotTable within a new worksheet or an existing worksheet. To create a PivotTable, click in a data range or an Excel table, and then click the PivotTable button in the Tables group on the Insert tab. Excel reserves a space 3 columns wide by 18 rows tall for the initial PivotTable report. If the worksheet does not have enough empty space, you'll be prompted to overwrite the cell content.

Claire wants to analyze social media posts by site and product line. You'll create a PivotTable from the data in the Media table for this purpose.

To create a PivotTable from the Media table:

1. If you took a break at the end of the previous session, make sure the NP_EX_7_Syrmosta workbook is open.

2. Go to the **Media Log** worksheet and click cell **B4** to select a cell in the Media table.

> **Tip**
>
> You can also click the Summarize with PivotTable button in the Tools group on the Table Design tab to open the Create PivotTable dialog box.

3. On the ribbon, click the **Insert** tab, and then in the Tables group, click the **PivotTable** button. The Create PivotTable dialog box opens.

4. Verify that **Media** appears in the Table/Range box. This specifies the Media table as the source for the PivotTable.

5. Click the **Existing Worksheet** option button, and then press **TAB** to move the insertion point into the Location box. You want to insert the PivotTable into the Data Explore worksheet starting at cell B6.

6. Click the **Data Explore** sheet tab, and then in the Data Explore worksheet, click cell **B6**. The 3-D reference 'Data Explore'!$B$6 is entered into the Location box. See Figure 7–22.

| Figure 7–22 | Create PivotTable dialog box |

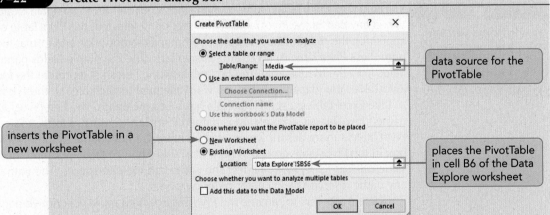

- inserts the PivotTable in a new worksheet
- data source for the PivotTable
- places the PivotTable in cell B6 of the Data Explore worksheet

7. Click **OK**. The empty PivotTable report appears in the Data Explore worksheet. See Figure 7–23.

Figure 7–23   **Empty PivotTable report**

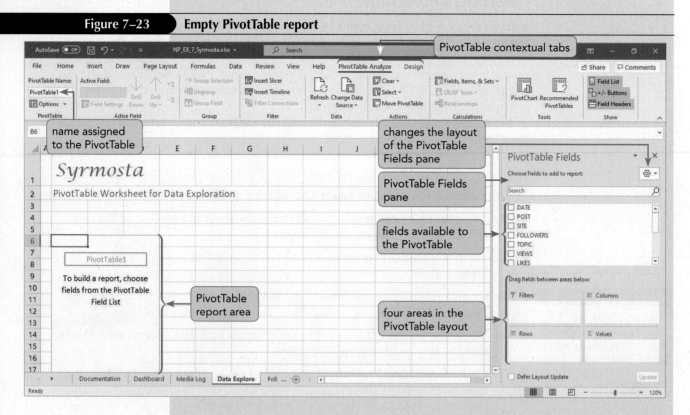

Trouble? If you do not see the PivotTable Fields pane, you need to display it. Click the PivotTable Analyze tab, and then in the Show group, click the Field List button.

The empty PivotTable report section starts from cell B6 in the Data Explore worksheet. When any part of the PivotTable report section is selected, the PivotTable contextual tabs appear on the ribbon. You can select commands to populate and format the PivotTable from these PivotTable Analyze and Design tabs. The PivotTable Fields pane shows the fields from the Media table. The boxes below the fields list represent the four areas of the PivotTable. You place the fields you want assigned to each area in these boxes.

Like Excel tables, each PivotTable has a unique name. The first PivotTable created is named PivotTable1, the second is named PivotTable2, and so forth. You can give each PivotTable a more descriptive name by entering a new name in the PivotTable Name box in the PivotTable group on the PivotTable Analyze tab. PivotTable names have the same rules as Excel table names: The name can include spaces. The name cannot be any name reserved by Excel for other purposes.

Claire wants you to rename the PivotTable with a more descriptive name. You will change the name now.

To change the PivotTable name:

1. On the PivotTable Analyze tab, in the PivotTable group, double-click the **PivotTable Name** box. The default name "PivotTable1" is selected.

2. Press **DELETE**, and then type **Explore PivotTable** as the new name.

3. Press **ENTER**. The PivotTable is renamed.

Next you will begin populating the PivotTable with the fields from the Media table.

Creating a PivotTable Layout

The PivotTable layout is created by dragging fields from the field list into one of the four area boxes. This determines the basic structure of the PivotTable. There is no particular order that the areas of the table need to be filled in. Although it's often best to start with the field containing the data you want to summarize and then expand the PivotTable from there. Excel updates the PivotTable in the report area and does all the calculations to match your selections. Once the PivotTable layout is in place, you can fine-tune its format and appearance.

Claire wants this PivotTable to count the number of posts made to the different social media sites broken down by topic. You will start by placing the Post field in the Values area box, followed by the Site field in the Columns areas and the Topic field in the Rows area.

To place fields in the Values, Columns, and Rows areas:

▶ **1.** In the PivotTable Fields pane, point to **POST** in the field list to highlight it, and then drag the Post field into the Values areas box. "Count of POST" appears in the Values box and the PivotTable shows the count of the Posts field. See Figure 7–24.

Figure 7–24   **Post field added to the Values area**

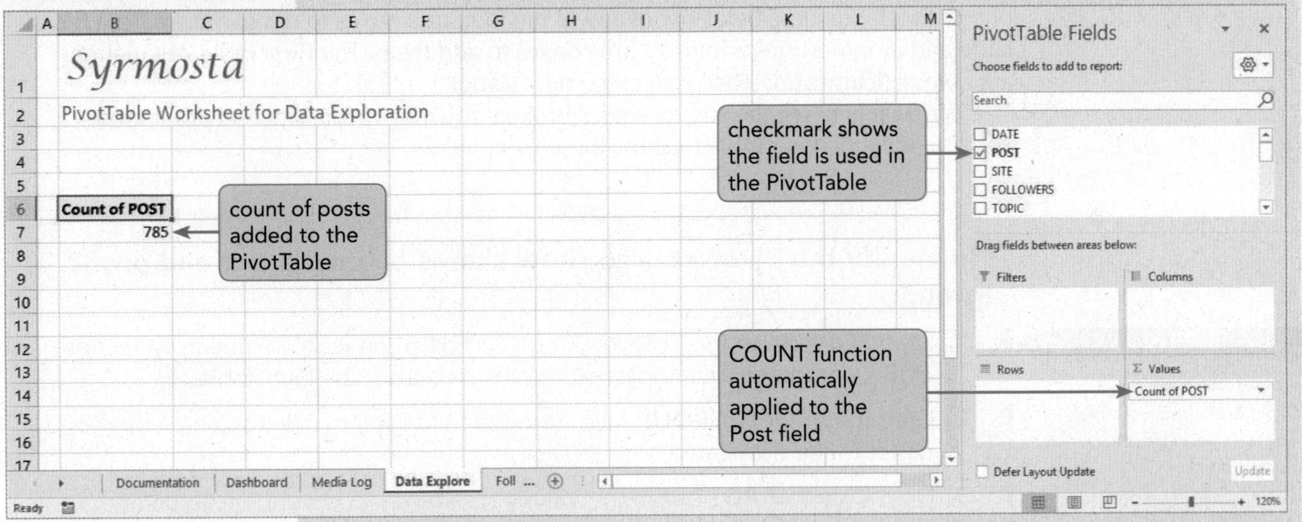

Tip

PivotTables by default use the COUNT function for non-numeric data placed in the Values area.

▶ **2.** Drag the **Site** field into the Columns area box. The number of posts is broken down by social media site, showing 332 posts made to Facebook, 303 posts made to Instagram, and 150 posts made to Twitter. These are the same numbers you calculated with the COUNTIF function (refer back to Figure 7–14), but the PivotTable does all those calculations for you.

▶ **3.** Drag the **Topic** field onto the Rows area box. The number of posts for each social media site is now broken out by topic. See Figure 7–25.

Figure 7–25   **Fields added to the Rows and Columns areas**

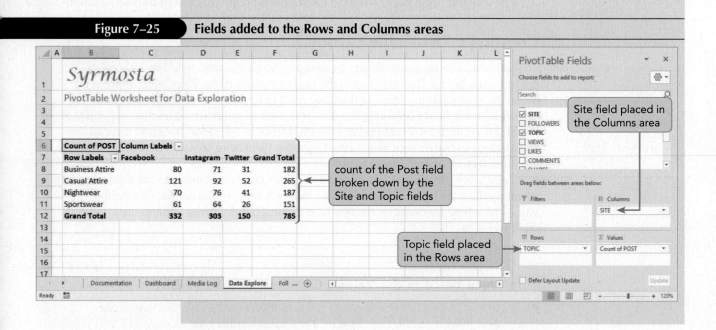

Modifying the PivotTable Layout

PivotTables are excellent for data exploration because you can quickly change the PivotTable layout to view your data from many different angles. To change the content of the PivotTable, drag fields out of any of the four area boxes to remove them from the table and drop new fields into the area boxes to add them. The PivotTable calculations are automatically updated to reflect the new layout.

Claire wants to see the sum of shares broken down by media site and profit group. You'll modify the PivotTable to show these calculations.

To modify the PivotTable to show shares by media site and profit group:

1. Drag **TOPIC** from the Rows area box and drop the icon on an empty section of the worksheet. The Topic field is removed from the PivotTable.

2. Drag the **PROFIT GROUP** field from the field list into the Rows area box to add it to the PivotTable.

3. Drag **Count of POST** from the Values area box and drop the icon on an empty section of the worksheet. The Post field is removed from the PivotTable.

4. Drag the **SHARES** field from the field list into the Values area box. The sum of the Shares field is added to the PivotTable. PivotTables by default use the SUM function for numeric data placed in the Values area. See Figure 7–26.

> **Tip**
>
> You can also remove a field from the PivotTable by deselecting its check box in the field list.

| Figure 7-26 | Modified PivotTable |

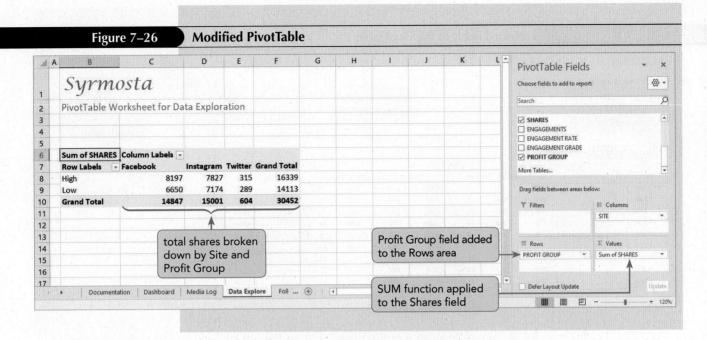

Over the past year, there was a total of 30,452 shares of Syrmosta social media posts. The row totals show the media shares were fairly evenly split between the high-profit and low-profit items, with high-profit items receiving slightly more shares across all media sites.

Adding Multiple Fields to a Row or Column

PivotTables are not limited to a single field in the Rows or Columns area. You can place additional fields in each area, nesting one field within another. For example, placing the Profit Group field and then Site field in the Columns area would show values for each profit group divided into different media sites. The PivotTable will include subtotals for each profit group, so you can view summary statistics within and across the group levels.

Excel automatically provides subgroups for date fields. If values from a date field span several years, the dates are grouped by years and by quarters within years. If the dates cover a single year, the dates are automatically grouped by months.

Claire wants you to modify the PivotTable to show the Profit Group and Site fields in the Columns area and the Date field in the Rows area. You'll make these changes now.

To nest fields within a PivotTable:

▶ 1. Drag **PROFIT GROUP** from the Rows area box and drop it into the Columns area box directly above the SITE field. Both the Profit Group field and the Site field appear in the PivotTable columns. Subtotals appear for each profit group and site.

▶ 2. Drag the **DATE** field from the field list and drop it into the Rows area box to add it to the PivotTable. A new field named Months is added to the PivotTable, which groups the dates in the PivotTable by month. See Figure 7-27. You can expand any month to view daily statistics.

Figure 7–27   Nested fields in the PivotTable

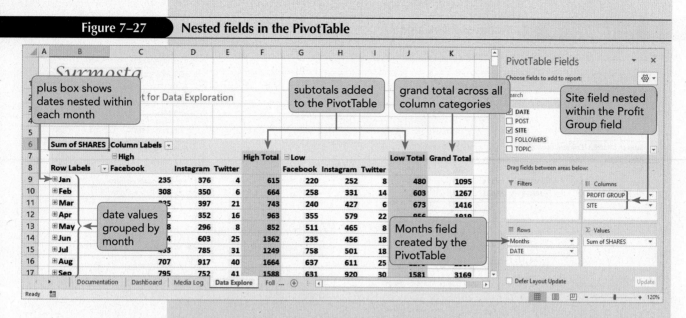

3. In the Rows area of the PivotTable, to the left of the Jan entry, click the **plus box** to expand the January group. The posts made for dates in January are displayed. Depending on your computer's configuration, dates might appear as 01-Jan, 02-Jan, and so forth. See Figure 7–28.

Figure 7–28   Grouped field expanded

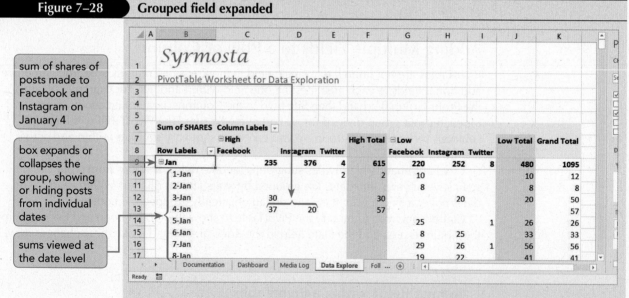

4. Click the **minus box** to left of the Jan entry to collapse the group, showing only the month totals.

5. Click the **Date** check box in the field list. The Date field is deselected, removing it from the PivotTable. The Months field remains, leaving only the monthly totals.

6. Click the **Profit Group** check box in the field list to remove that field from the PivotTable.

The PivotTable now shows the sum of the Shares field broken down by media site and month. Next you will explore how to filter the PivotTable data.

Filtering a PivotTable

The Filters area is a quick way to filter PivotTable data. When you add a field to the Filters area, a filter button appears two rows above the upper-left corner of the table. You can then use the button to choose a value to filter the entire PivotTable by. For example, you can add a filter button for the Topic field, and then use the button to filter the PivotTable by one of the Topic values, such as Sportswear. Like the Columns and Rows area, the Filters area can contain multiple fields.

Claire wants the PivotTable to show a summary of the posts about Syrmosta's line of sportswear. You'll add the Topic field to the Filters area, and then use the filter button to show only posts dealing with sportswear.

Tip

To select multiple items, click the Select Multiple Items check box and then click each item to include in the filter.

To add the Topic field to the Filters area:

1. Drag the **TOPIC** field from the field list and drop it in the Filters area box. A label and filter button are added to the range B4:C4.

2. Click the **filter** button in cell C4, and then click **Sportswear** from the list of topics.

3. Click **OK** to apply the filter to the PivotTable. See Figure 7–29.

Figure 7–29   **Filtered PivotTable**

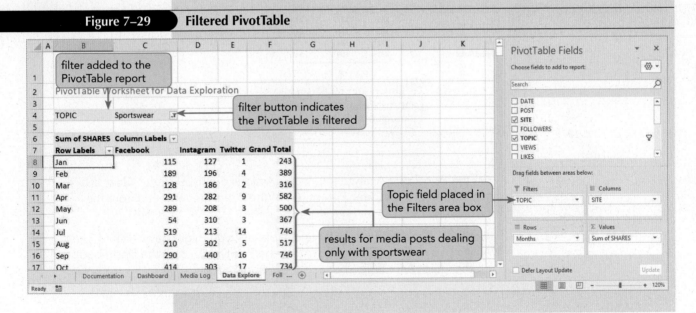

For more filter options, you can use the filter buttons next to the row and column labels in the PivotTable, choosing which row or column categories to include in the PivotTable. Claire wants you to limit the PivotTable to show only Facebook and Instagram posts for the months of January through March. You'll use the column and row labels filter buttons to do this.

To filter the column and row categories:

▶ **1.** In cell C6, click the **Column Labels filter** button. The filter menu opens.

▶ **2.** Click the **Select All** check box to deselect it, and then click the **Facebook** and **Instagram** check boxes to select them.

▶ **3.** Click **OK** to apply the filter to the column categories. Only Facebook and Instagram posts appear in the PivotTable.

▶ **4.** In cell B7, click the **Row Labels filter** button. The filter menu opens.

▶ **5.** Click the **Select All** check box to deselect it, and then click the **Jan**, **Feb**, and **Mar** check boxes to select them.

▶ **6.** Click **OK** to apply the filter to the row categories. Only January, February, and March posts appear in the PivotTable. See Figure 7–30.

Figure 7–30   Filtered column and row categories

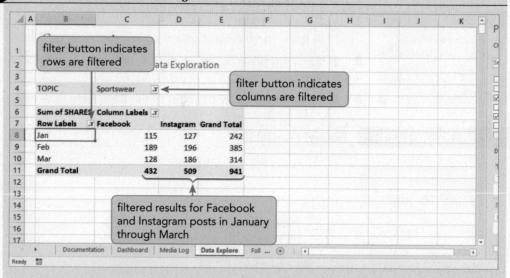

▶ **7.** On the PivotTable Analyze tab, in the Actions group, click the **Clear** button, and then click **Clear Filters**. All of the filters are removed from the PivotTable.

Trouble? If the entire PivotTable disappears, you might have clicked Clear All instead of Clear Filters. To restore the PivotTable, click the Undo button on the Quick Access Toolbar and then repeat Step 7.

As you've seen, PivotTables are extremely flexible. With them you can quickly explore data from a variety of views without writing a single formula.

Insight

Choosing a Recommended PivotTable

If you're not sure what to include in a PivotTable or how to structure it, you can use the Recommend PivotTables tool. To use the tool, select any cell within a data range or Excel table, and then click the Recommended PivotTables button in the Tables group on the Insert tab. A gallery of PivotTable layouts suitable for that data opens. Choose the one you find most useful and relevant. The PivotTable is inserted on a new sheet in the workbook using the layout you selected.

Formatting a PivotTable

You can format PivotTables to make them more visually appealing and the results easier to read. You should format a PivotTable after you have decided on its structure, layout, and content.

Claire wants PivotTables added to the Dashboard worksheet that provide a concise summary of Syrmosta's social media history. The first PivotTable will display the total number of views, likes, comments, shares, and engagements for Syrmosta social media posts. You'll add this table now.

To create a PivotTable that summarizes social media engagement:

1. Go to the **Media Log** worksheet and click cell **B4** if necessary to select it.

2. On the ribbon, click the **Insert** tab, and then in the Tables group, click **PivotTable**. The Create PivotTable dialog box opens.

3. Click the **Existing Worksheet** option button, press **TAB**, click the **Dashboard** sheet tab, click cell **J11** on the Dashboard worksheet, and then click **OK**. A blank PivotTable Report is added to the Dashboard worksheet starting from cell J11.

4. On the PivotTable Analyze tab, in the PivotTable group, click the **PivotTable Name** box, type **Engagement Pivot**, and then press **ENTER**. The PivotTable is renamed.

5. Drag the **VIEWS**, **LIKES**, **COMMENTS**, **SHARES**, and **ENGAGEMENTS** fields from the field list into the Values area box in the order listed. The sum of each field is displayed in the PivotTable.

   When a PivotTable contains multiple value fields, Excel organizes those fields into an item called ∑Values, so you can place all value fields within a single location in the PivotTable. In this PivotTable, the ∑Values item is added to the Columns area so that each of the fields appears in a separate column.

6. Drag **∑Values** from the Columns area box and drop it in the Rows area box. The five fields are now placed in separate rows.

7. Drag the **SITE** field from the field list into the Columns area box to add the sums for each field by media site. The PivotTable shows the total number of views, likes, comments, shares, and engagements for Facebook, Instagram, and Twitter. See Figure 7–31.

Figure 7–31 | **Sum of social media engagements**

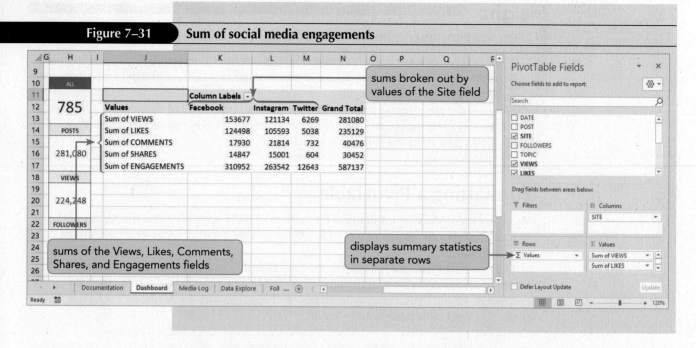

Next, you will format the contents of the PivotTable.

Changing Labels and Number Formats

The label for each value field contains the summary function followed by the field name. For example, the first label in the Engagement Pivot PivotTable is "Sum of VIEWS," the second is "Sum of LIKES," and so forth. You can change these labels to any text except the name of a field used by the PivotTable. You can also modify the appearance of the summary statistics by changing the number format.

Claire wants the PivotTable labels changed to Viewed, Liked, Commented, Shared and Engaged. Claire also wants a thousands separator added to the calculated results to make the numbers easier to read. You will make these changes to the format of the five value fields now.

To format the five PivotTable calculated value fields:

1. In cell J13 of the PivotTable, double-click the **Sum of VIEWS** label. The Value Field Settings dialog box opens so you can set the options for this value field.

2. Click the **Number Format** button. The Format Cells dialog box opens and contains only the Number tab.

3. In the Category box, click **Number**, enter **0** in the Decimal places box, click the **Use 1000 Separator (,)** check box, and then click **OK** to return to the Value Field Settings dialog box.

4. In the Custom Name box, change the text to **Viewed**. See Figure 7–32.

Figure 7-32   **Value Field Settings dialog box**

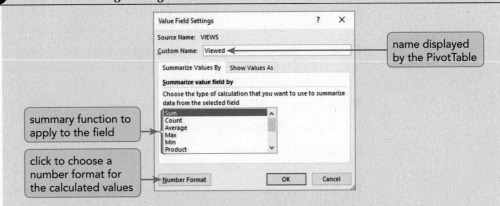

5. Click **OK**. The title in the PivotTable's first row changes to Viewed and the calculated sums in the first row have a thousands separator and no decimal places.

6. Repeat Steps 1 through 5 for the Sum of LIKES, Sum of COMMENTS, Sum of SHARES, and Sum of ENGAGEMENTS value fields, changing their names to **Liked**, **Commented**, **Shared**, and **Engaged** and changing the number formats to display zero decimal places and include a thousands separator. See Figure 7-33.

Figure 7-33   **PivotTable with custom labels and number formats**

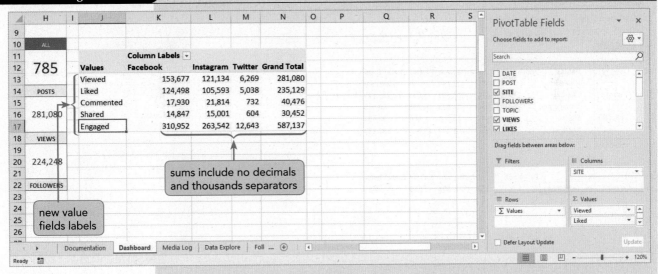

Although you can format PivotTable values using the formatting commands on the Home tab, this formatting is lost if the PivotTable layout changes. Instead, you should format values using the Value Field Settings dialog box, which maintains the formats even when the PivotTable layout changes.

The next PivotTable Claire wants added to the dashboard will count the number of posts by social media site. You'll create and format this PivotTable, changing the label to "Total Posts." Rather than creating a new PivotTable from the Media table, you can copy the PivotTable that already exists on the Dashboard worksheet and then edit that new PivotTable.

To create a PivotTable counting the number of social media posts:

1. In the Dashboard worksheet, copy the range **J11:N17** and paste it into cell **J20**. The Engagement Pivot PivotTable is duplicated.

2. On the ribbon, click the **PivotTable Analyze** tab, in the Actions group, click the **Clear** button, and then click **Clear All** to remove all the fields from the pasted PivotTable. If prompted, click the **Clear PivotTable** button.

3. Place the **SITE** field into the Columns area of the PivotTable.

4. Place the **POST** field in the Values area.

5. Double-click cell **J22** containing the label "Count of Post" to open the Value Field Settings dialog box.

6. In the Custom Name box, type **Total Posts** to revise the field label, and then click **OK**.

7. On the PivotTable Analyze tab, from the PivotTable group, click the **PivotTable Name** box, type **Total Posts Pivot** as the new name, and then press **ENTER**. See Figure 7–34.

Figure 7–34   Total posts by media site

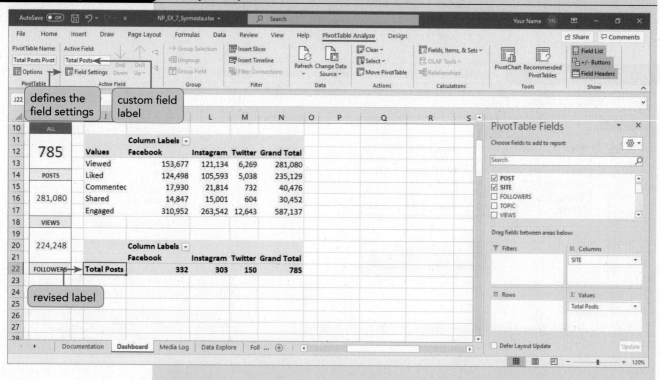

Choosing a PivotTable Summary Function

By default, Excel uses the COUNT function to summarize non-numeric data and the SUM function for numeric data. However, sometimes you'll want to use different statistics in your analysis. You can choose a different summary function, such as AVERAGE, MIN, and MAX, from the Value Field Settings dialog box.

Claire wants to see a PivotTable showing the average engagement rate for each social media site added to the dashboard. You'll create that PivotTable now.

To create a PivotTable of average engagement rates:

▶ 1. In the Dashboard worksheet, copy the range **J20:N22** and paste it into cell **J25**. The Total Posts Pivot PivotTable is duplicated.

▶ 2. Drag **Total Posts** out of the Values area, and then drag the **ENGAGEMENT RATE** field into the Values area.

▶ 3. On the ribbon, click the **PivotTable Analyze** tab, and then in the PivotTable Name box, enter **Engagement Rate Pivot** as the PivotTable name.

▶ 4. Double-click cell **J27** containing the "Sum of ENGAGEMENT RATE" label. The Value Field Settings dialog box opens.

▶ 5. In the list of summary statistics, click **Average**.

▶ 6. In the Custom Name box, type **Engaged Rate** as the new name.

▶ 7. Click the **Number Format** button. The Format Cells dialog box opens.

▶ 8. In the Category box, click **Percentage**, and then click **OK** in each dialog box to return to the worksheet. See Figure 7–35.

Figure 7–35	Average engagement rate by media site

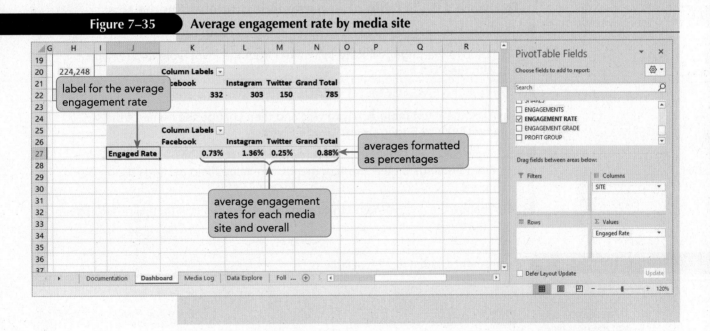

The Engagement Rate Pivot PivotTable shows that the highest average engagement rates are associated with posts on Instagram (1.36%) followed by Facebook (0.73%). Twitter has the lowest average engagement rate with 0.25%.

Insight

Moving a PivotTable

You can move any PivotTable to a new location in the workbook. To move a PivotTable within its current worksheet, select the entire PivotTable range and then drag the table to a new location, being careful not to overwrite other content in the process. To move a PivotTable to a different worksheet, click anywhere within the PivotTable to select it, and then click the Move PivotTable button in the Actions group on the PivotTable Analyze tab. The Move PivotTable dialog box opens so you can choose the new location for the PivotTable. You can create a new worksheet for the PivotTable or choose an existing worksheet in the workbook. You can also select the entire PivotTable and then use the Cut and Paste buttons in the Clipboard group on the Home tab to move the PivotTable within the workbook.

The last PivotTable Claire wants added to the dashboard will summarize the media posts by values of the Engagement Grade field. You will create this PivotTable now.

To create a PivotTable of engagement grade vs. media site:

1. Copy the range **J25:N27** and paste it into cell **J30**.

2. Remove the **Engaged Rate** value field from the PivotTable and replace it with the **Post** field.

3. Place the **ENGAGEMENT GRADE** field in the Rows area.

4. Click the **PivotTable Analyze** tab, and then change the name of the PivotTable to **Engagement Grade Pivot**.

5. Right-click cell **J30** containing the label "Count of POST," and click **Value Field Settings** on the shortcut menu. The Value Field Settings dialog box opens.

6. Change the custom name to **Engagement Grades** and then click **OK**. See Figure 7–36.

| Figure 7–36 | Engagement Grade Pivot PivotTable |

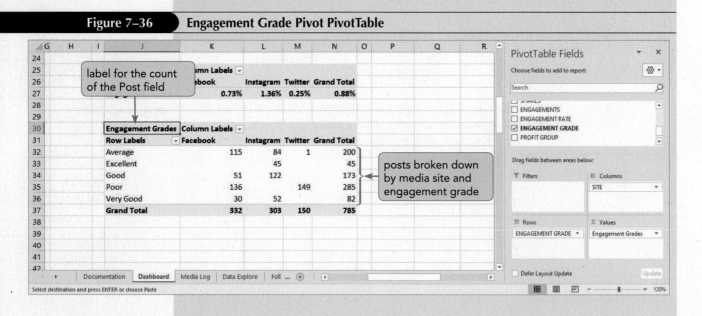

All of the posts that had an excellent grade of user engagement (where the engagement rate is above 2%) were on Instagram. On the other hand, of the 150 posts made on Twitter, 149 had poor engagement grades (an engagement rate less than 0.5%). The PivotTable contains several blank cells where there is no count of media posts. For example, no post made to Facebook had an excellent engagement response, so cell K33 is blank.

Reordering PivotTable Categories

The categories listed in a PivotTable row or column follow a predefined order. Text categories are listed alphabetically. Date categories are arranged from the earliest date to the latest. If a custom list has been defined for the field, the categories appear in the order of the custom list. However, you can change the order of the categories at any point by typing the category names in whatever order you choose.

The categories for the Engagement Grade Pivot PivotTable are difficult to interpret because they are arranged alphabetically rather than in the order of user engagement. Claire wants them sorted from Poor up to Excellent. You'll rearrange the categories.

To rearrange the Engagement Grade categories:

Make sure you type the category name exactly so the PivotTable can match it to the correct category.

1. Click cell **J32** containing the Average category value.

2. Type **Poor** as the category name, and then press **ENTER**. The values for the Poor category are displayed in row 32 and the other categories are shifted down.

3. Click cell **J36** containing the Very Good category value.

4. Type **Excellent** as the category name, and then press **ENTER**. The Engagement Grade values are now listed in the order Poor, Average, Good, Very Good, and Excellent.

Once you define the category order, that order becomes part of the **PivotTable cache**, which stores information about the PivotTable. If you move the Engagement Grade field to another area of the table or remove it and add it back in later, Excel will remember your preferred category order, so you will not have to redefine it.

Insight

Choosing a Report Layout

In addition to changing the structure of a PivotTable by moving fields into the different areas, you can change the overall table layout. PivotTables have possible three report layouts:

- **Compact Form**—(the default layout) places all fields from the Rows area in a single worksheet columns and indents values to distinguish nested fields from other fields.

- **Outline Form**—places each field in the Rows area in its own column and includes subtotals above every field category group.

- **Tabular Form**—places each field in the Rows area in its own column and includes subtotals below every group.

To switch between PivotTable layouts, click the Report Layout button from the Layout group on the Design tab. Choose the PivotTable layout that presents your data in the informative and effective format.

Setting PivotTable Options

Several default values and behaviors are associated with PivotTables. For example, Excel automatically sorts the row and column categories and displays missing combinations within the PivotTable as blank cells. You can modify these defaults in the PivotTable Options dialog box.

Claire wants the Engagement Grade Pivot PivotTable to display zeros in place of blank cells to prevent confusion about the PivotTable values. Claire also doesn't want the PivotTable to display a Grand Total row because that information already appears in another PivotTable. Finally, Claire wants all the PivotTables in the Dashboard worksheet to maintain a constant width. Right now, the width of column J has varied with the addition of each PivotTable. You'll change these settings now.

To set the PivotTable options:

▶ 1. On the PivotTable Analyze tab, in the PivotTable group click the **Options** button. The PivotTable Options dialog box opens.

▶ 2. On the Layout & Format tab, verify that the **For empty cells show** check box is selected, and then type **0** as the value to display for blank PivotTable cells.

▶ 3. Click the **Autofit column widths on update** check box to remove the checkmark. The row will remain the same width no matter how the PivotTables might change. See Figure 7–37.

Figure 7–37   PivotTable Options dialog box

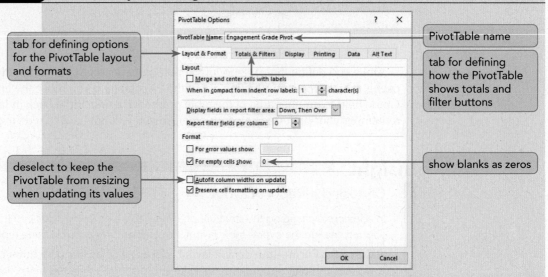

tab for defining options for the PivotTable layout and formats

PivotTable name

tab for defining how the PivotTable shows totals and filter buttons

show blanks as zeros

deselect to keep the PivotTable from resizing when updating its values

▶ 4. Click the **Totals & Filters** tab to display options for PivotTable totals and filters.

▶ 5. Click the **Show grand totals for columns** check box to deselect it.

▶ 6. Click **OK** to return to the worksheet and verify that the grand total row has been removed and blank cells are displayed as zeros.

▶ 7. Click cell **J25** to select the Engagement Rate Pivot PivotTable.

▶ 8. On the PivotTable Analyze tab, in the PivotTable group, click the **Options** button, click the **Autofit column widths on update** check box to deselect it, and then click **OK**. The PivotTable will not be resized.

> **9.** Click cell **J20** to select the Total Posts Pivot PivotTable and then repeat Step 8 so the PivotTable will not resize.

> **10.** Click cell **J11** to select the Engagement Pivot PivotTable, and then repeat Step 8 so that the PivotTable will not resize.

You can also remove grand total rows and columns by clicking the Grand Totals button in the Layout group on the Design tab, and selecting an option turn grand totals on or off for the rows and columns.

 Proskills

Written Communication: Making PivotTables Accessible

Many companies and government agencies require documents to be accessible to users with visual impairments and special needs. Excel provides support for those users by making objects such as charts, graphics, and PivotTables accessible through alternate text.

To add alternate text to a PivotTable, open the PivotTable Options dialog box, and go to the Alt Text tab. On the Alt Text tab, you can specify a title for the alternate text. The title provides a brief description of the alternate text so that the user can decide whether to continue to review the PivotTable content. Below the title box, you can insert a description of the PivotTable. The description can be a general overview of the table's contents or a detailed summary of the PivotTable numbers and summary statistics. There is no character limit on alternate text, though a general guideline is to limit the summary to about 160 characters.

If you have to add alternate text to many objects in your workbooks, you can add the Alt Text command to the Quick Access Toolbar. For information on modifying the Quick Access Toolbar, refer to Excel Help.

Setting the PivotTable Design

Just as you can apply built-in styles to Excel tables, there are built-in styles that you can apply to PivotTables. These styles are available in the PivotTable Styles gallery, which includes a variety of column and row colors. You can also set options such as adding banded rows and banded columns to the PivotTable design and whether to include column and row headings.

Another design feature you might want to remove are the filter buttons from the PivotTable's row and column areas. If you are preparing a final report in which you no longer need to filter the PivotTable data, you can hide this feature, giving your PivotTable a more compact and clean design.

Claire wants you to format the PivotTables on the Dashboard worksheet in preparation for the final report.

To apply a design style to a PivotTable:

> **1.** In cell **J10**, enter **USER RESPONSES** to label the top PivotTable, and then apply the **Accent3** cell style to cell J10.

> **2.** Click cell **J11** to select the Engagement Pivot PivotTable.

Tip

You can hide the PivotTable Field pane by deselecting the Field List button in the Show group on the PivotTable Analyze tab.

3. On the ribbon, click the **PivotTables Analyze** tab, and then in the Show group, click the **Field Headers** button to deselect it. The Column Labels filter button disappears from the PivotTable.

4. Click the **Design** tab to display commands related to the layout and design of the PivotTable.

5. In the PivotTable Styles group, click the **More** button to open the PivotTable Styles gallery, and then in the Medium section, click the **Light Yellow, Pivot Style Medium 4** style located in the first row and fourth column of the Medium section.

6. In the PivotTable Style Options group, click the **Banded Rows** and **Banded Columns** check boxes to add gridlines to the PivotTable. See Figure 7–38.

Figure 7–38 PivotTable with style and options

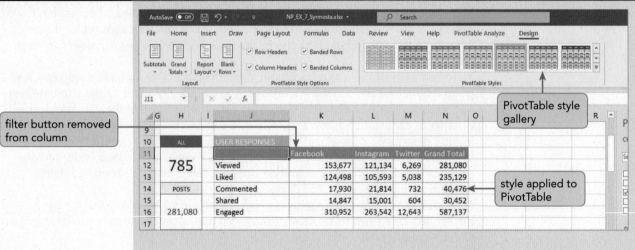

Claire wants all the PivotTables on the Dashboard worksheet to have the same look and design. You will repeat the formatting for the remaining PivotTables on the Dashboard worksheet.

To complete the designs of the remaining PivotTables:

1. In cell **J19**, enter **MEDIA POSTS** as the label, and then format that cell using the **Accent2** cell style.

2. Click cell **J20** to select the Total Posts Pivot PivotTable.

3. On the ribbon, click the **PivotTable Analyze** tab, and then in the Show group, click the **Field Headers** button to remove the Column Labels filter button.

4. On the ribbon, click the **Design** tab, in the PivotTable Styles group, click the **More** button, and then in the Medium section, click the **Light Orange, Pivot Style Medium 3** style in the gallery.

5. In the PivotTable Styles Options group, click the **Banded Rows** and **Banded Columns** check boxes to select them.

6. Repeat Steps 1 through 5 for the Engagement Rate Pivot PivotTable, inserting **ENGAGEMENTS** in cell J24 with the **Accent4** cell style and applying the **Lavender, Pivot Style Medium 5** style to the PivotTable.

7. Repeat Steps 1 through 5 for the Engagement Grade Pivot PivotTable, insert-ing **USER RESPONSES** in cell J29 with the **Accent6** cell style and applying the **Ice Blue, Pivot Style Medium 7** style to the PivotTable. See Figure 7–39.

Figure 7–39	Completed PivotTables in the Dashboard worksheet

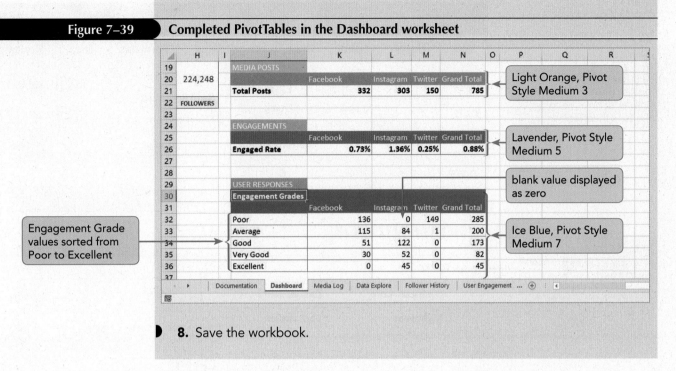

8. Save the workbook.

You've finished adding PivotTables to the dashboard. In the next session, you will complete the dashboard by adding PivotCharts and slicers to create a dashboard that users can interact with to explore Syrmosta's social media presence.

Review

Session 7.2 Quick Check

1. What is a PivotTable?
2. What are the four primary areas of a PivotTable?
3. What default statistic is used for non-numeric data in the Values area of the PivotTable?
4. What default statistic is used for numeric data in the Values area of the PivotTable?
5. By default, how does a PivotTable arrange the categories in a row or column?
6. What happens when you place a date field in a row or column area?
7. What are two ways of filtering a PivotTable?

Session 7.3 Visual Overview:

The Report Connections button is used to connect a slicer or timeline to multiple PivotTables.

This slicer is used to filter PivotTables to show results from only posts about sportswear.

These PivotTables show filtered results.

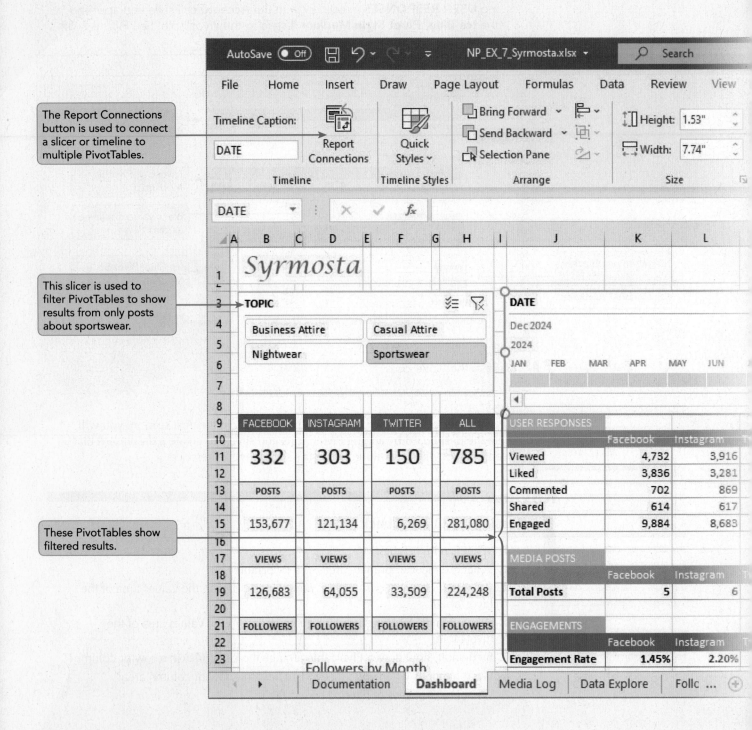

PivotCharts and Slicers

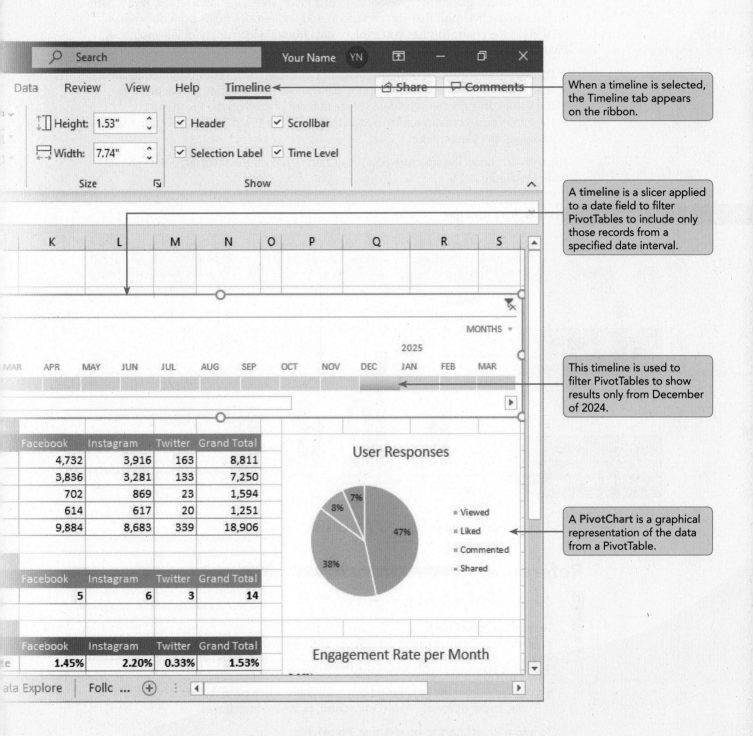

When a timeline is selected, the Timeline tab appears on the ribbon.

A **timeline** is a slicer applied to a date field to filter PivotTables to include only those records from a specified date interval.

This timeline is used to filter PivotTables to show results only from December of 2024.

A **PivotChart** is a graphical representation of the data from a PivotTable.

Introducing PivotCharts

A PivotChart is a graphical representation of a PivotTable. Like PivotTables, PivotCharts include interactive tools that you can use to add and remove fields from different sections of the chart. This lets you explore data from a wide variety of viewpoints. A PivotChart has four primary areas:

- The Axis (Category) area displays categories that each data series is plotted against.
- The Legend (Series) area breaks up the data values into separate data series.
- The Values area contains the data values that are plotted on the PivotChart.
- The Filters area contains a filter button that limits the PivotChart to only those values satisfying specified criteria.

Figure 7–40 shows the structure of a PivotChart based on the PivotTable data shown earlier in Figure 7–21.

Figure 7–40 **PivotChart structure**

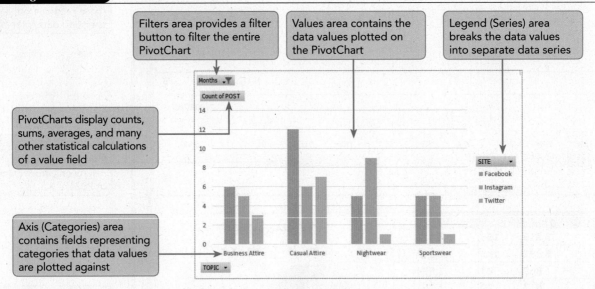

A PivotChart is always linked to a PivotTable.

Reference

Creating a PivotChart

To insert a PivotChart:
- On the Insert tab, in the Charts group, click the PivotChart button.
- Specify whether to insert the PivotChart in a new worksheet or at a cell location within an existing worksheet.
- Drag fields from the field list on the PivotChart Fields pane and drop them on the Filters, Legend (Series), Axis (Categories), or Values area boxes.

To add a PivotChart to an existing PivotTable:
- Select a PivotTable from the workbook.
- On the PivotTable Analyze tab, in the Tools group, click the PivotChart button.
- Select the PivotChart chart type.
- If necessary, move the PivotChart to a different worksheet than the PivotTable.

Creating a PivotChart

A PivotChart is either created from an existing PivotTable or created at the same time as its PivotTable. The layouts of a PivotTable and PivotChart always mirror one another. Any changes you make to the structure and layout of a PivotTable affect the PivotChart, and vice versa.

Claire wants you to create a PivotChart using data from the Media table on the Media Log worksheet.

To begin building a PivotChart:

▶ 1. If you took a break at the end of the previous session, make sure the NP_EX_7_Syrmosta workbook is open.

▶ 2. Go to the **Media Log** worksheet and click cell **B4** if necessary to select the Media table.

▶ 3. On the ribbon, click the **Insert** tab, and then in the Charts group, click the **PivotChart** button. The Create PivotChart dialog box opens.

▶ 4. Click the **Existing Worksheet** option button, press **TAB** to move to the Location box, click the **Follower History** sheet tab, and then click cell **B4** in the Follower History worksheet. The reference 'Follower History'!$B$4 appears in the Location box.

▶ 5. Click **OK**. An empty PivotTable report and an empty PivotChart appear in the worksheet. See Figure 7–41.

| Figure 7–41 | Empty PivotTable report and PivotChart |

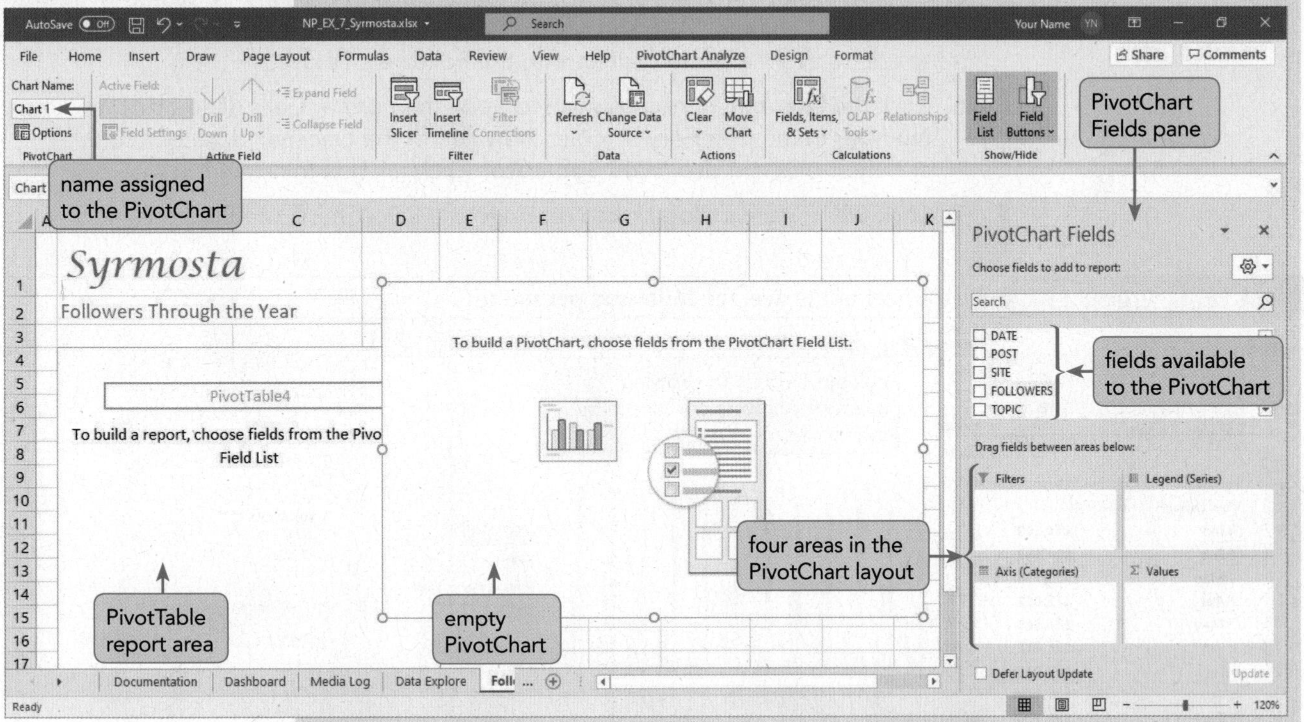

When a PivotChart is selected, the PivotChart Analyze, Design, and Format tabs appear on the ribbon. The Design and Format tabs include the same commands you've seen for working with other Excel charts. The PivotChart Analyze tab includes many of the same commands you've seen for working with PivotTables. So, once you know how to work with PivotTables and charts, you've already mastered many of the tools applicable to PivotCharts.

PivotCharts are built the same way as PivotTables: by choosing fields from the field list and dropping them into one of four PivotChart areas. Claire wants you to create a PivotChart line chart showing the average number of followers for each media site per month to determine whether the number of followers has increased over the past year. You will create this PivotChart layout now.

To lay out the PivotChart contents:

1. Drag the **FOLLOWERS** from the field list into the Values area box. The PivotChart becomes a column chart showing the sum of the Followers field. The PivotTable is also updated to show the value of that sum.

2. Drag the **SITE** field from the field list into the Legend (Series) area box. The column PivotChart and PivotTable update to show the sum of the Followers broken down by media site.

3. Drag the **DATE** field from the field list into the Axis (Categories) area box. The column PivotChart and PivotTable show the sum of the Followers field for each month of the year. The Date field is grouped, so you can ungroup individual months to view day-to-day values of the Followers field.

4. In the upper-left corner of the PivotChart, right-click the **Sum of FOLLOWERS** cell, and then click **Value Field Settings** on the shortcut menu. The Value Field Settings dialog box opens. Claire wants to the view the average of the Followers field.

5. Click **Average** in the list of statistical functions, and then in the Custom Name box, change "Average of Followers" to **Followers** followed by a blank space (to avoid a name conflict with the Followers field.

6. Click the **Number Format** button to open the Format Cells dialog box, click **Number** in the Category box, set the value of the Decimal place box to **0**, and then click the **Use 1000 Separator (,)** check box to select it.

7. Click **OK** in each dialog box to return to the PivotChart. See Figure 7–42.

| Figure 7–42 | PivotChart of the average followers per month |

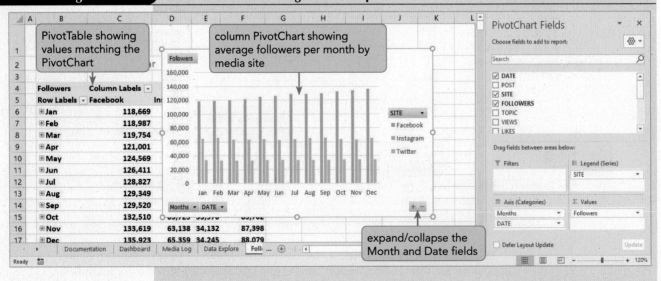

Tip

To use a chart type that is not a PivotChart, copy and paste the data from a PivotTable into a new data range and then create a regular chart from the pasted values.

Not every Excel chart type can be created as a PivotChart. You can create PivotCharts from only the Column, Line, Pie, Bar, Area, Surface, Radar chart types, and from Combo charts created from the preceding chart types. Claire thinks this data would be better displayed as a line chart. You'll change the chart type now.

To change the chart type:

▶ 1. On the ribbon, click the **Design** tab to show commands for changing the design of the selected PivotChart.

▶ 2. In the Type group, click the **Change Chart Type** button. The Change Chart Type dialog box opens.

▶ 3. Click **Line** in the list of chart types, and then click **OK**. The PivotChart changes from a column chart to a line chart.

▶ 4. Next to the chart, click the **Chart Elements** button ⊞, click the **Chart Title** check box, type **Followers by Month** as the chart title, and then press **ENTER**. The chart title appears at the top of the chart.

▶ 5. Click the **Chart Elements** button ⊞, click the **Gridlines arrow**, and then click the **Primary Major Vertical** check box. Vertical gridlines appear on the chart.

▶ 6. In the Chart Elements menu ⊞, click the **Legend arrow**, and then click **Bottom**. The legend moves to the bottom of the chart. See Figure 7–43.

| Figure 7–43 | Line PivotChart showing average followers per month |

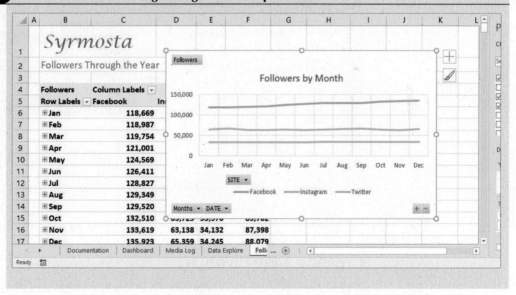

Moving a PivotChart to Another Worksheet

The PivotTable and PivotChart do not need to be on the same worksheet (though they must be in the same workbook). Claire wants the PivotChart moved to the Dashboard worksheet to be displayed alongside other summary tables and charts. Before moving the chart, Claire wants you to give the PivotTable a descriptive name to distinguish it from other PivotTables you've already created for your workbook.

To name and move the PivotChart:

▶ **1.** Click cell **B4** to make the PivotTable the active object in the workbook.

▶ **2.** On the ribbon, click the **PivotTable Analyze** tab, and then in the PivotTable group, click the **PivotTable Name** box and enter **Followers by Month Pivot** as the name of the PivotTable.

▶ **3.** Click the PivotChart to select it, click the **PivotChart Analyze** tab on the ribbon, and then in the Actions group, click the **Move Chart** button. The Move Chart dialog box opens.

▶ **4.** Verify that the **Object in** option button is selected, click the **Object in** box, click **Dashboard** as the worksheet to place the PivotChart in, and then click **OK**. The PivotChart moves to the Dashboard worksheet.

▶ **5.** In the Dashboard worksheet, move and resize the PivotChart to cover the range **B24:H36**. Claire is not going to revise the layout of this PivotChart, so you can hide the field buttons.

▶ **6.** On the PivotChart Analyze tab, in the Show/Hide group, click the **Field Buttons** button to hide the field buttons. See Figure 7–44.

Figure 7–44   **Line PivotChart moved to the Dashboard worksheet**

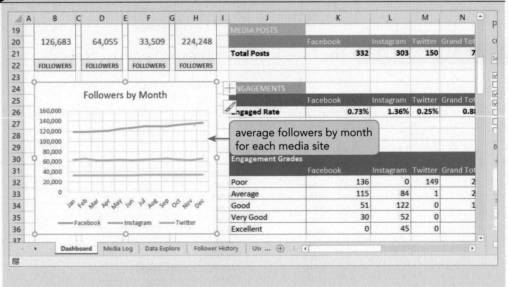

Creating a Pie PivotChart

A media post is more successful when it elicits comments and shares, so Claire wants the dashboard to include a pie chart breaking down total user engagements by views, likes, comments, and shares. You'll create a PivotChart showing this information as a pie chart.

To create the pie PivotChart showing the breakdown of user engagements:

▶ **1.** Go to the **Media Log** worksheet, click the **Insert** tab on the ribbon, and then in the Charts group, click the **PivotChart** button. The Create PivotChart dialog box opens.

2. Place the PivotChart on the existing **User Engagement** worksheet in cell **B4**, and then click **OK**. A blank PivotTable and a PivotChart appear on the User Engagement worksheet.

3. In the field list, click the **Views**, **Likes**, **Comments**, and **Shares** check boxes to add those fields to the Values area box.

4. Drag the **∑Values** item from the Legend (Series) box to the Axis (Categories) box.

5. On the ribbon, click the **Design** tab, and then in the Type group, click the **Change Chart Type** button. The Change Chart Type dialog box opens.

6. Click **Pie** as the chart type, and then click **OK**. The PivotChart changes to a pie chart.

7. Double-click cell **B5**, change the value in the Custom Name box to **Viewed**, and then click **OK**.

8. Repeat Step 7 to change the label in cell **B6** to **Liked**, the label in cell **B7** to **Commented**, and the label in cell **B8** to **Shared**. See Figure 7–45.

Figure 7–45	Pie PivotChart of the engagement totals

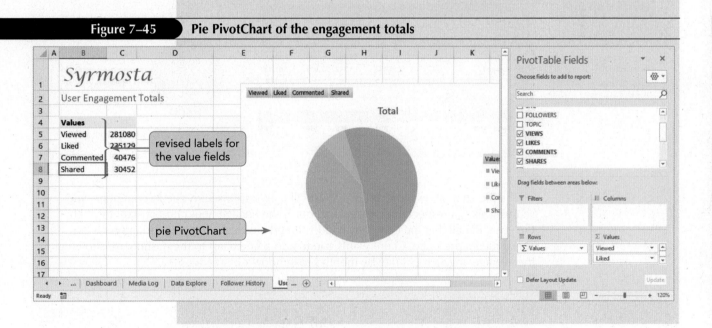

You'll move the pie chart to the Dashboard sheet and format it for Claire's report.

To format the pie chart PivotChart:

1. Click the **PivotTable Analyze** tab, in the PivotTable group, click the **PivotTable Name** box, type **Engagement Pie Pivot** as the PivotTable name, and then press **ENTER**.

2. Click the Engagement Pie Pivot PivotChart to select it, click the **PivotChart Analyze** tab on the ribbon, in the Actions group, click the **Move Chart** button.

3. Move the PivotChart to the **Dashboard** worksheet, and then move and resize the Engagement Pie Pivot PivotChart to cover the range **P11:S21**.

4. On the ribbon, click the **PivotChart Analyze** tab, and then in the Show/Hide group, click the **Field Buttons** button to hide the field buttons on the chart.

5. Change the chart title to **User Responses**.

6. Click the **Design** tab, in the Chart Layouts group, click the **Quick Layout** button, and then click **Layout 6** to add data callouts to the pie chart.

7. In the Chart Styles group, click **Style 1** to add a white border around each slice. See Figure 7–46.

Figure 7–46 | Formatted pie chart on the dashboard

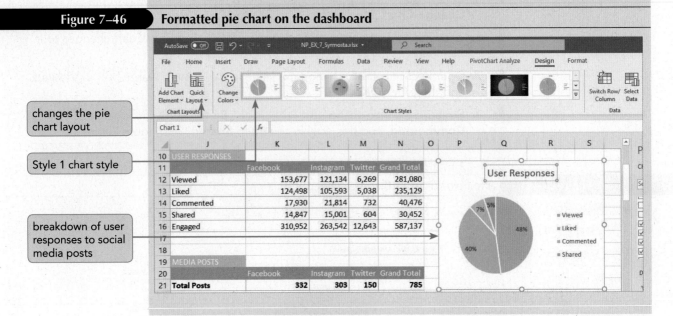

changes the pie chart layout

Style 1 chart style

breakdown of user responses to social media posts

The pie chart shows that about 12% of all user response are due to comments and shares. This is a respectable percentage, but is the engagement rate constant through the year? Recall that the company had instituted a new ad campaign to improve its social media presence. Claire wants you to add a line chart to the dashboard, showing the average engagement rate by month broken down by media site.

To create a PivotChart of engagement rate per month:

1. Go to the **Media Log** worksheet, click the **Insert** tab on the ribbon, and then in the Charts group, click the **PivotChart** button.

2. Place the PivotTable/PivotChart on the **Engagement History** worksheet starting at cell **B4**.

3. Place the **SITE** field in the Legend (Series) area box, place the **DATE** field in the Axis (Categories) area box, and then place the **ENGAGEMENT RATE** field in the Values area box.

4. Change the PivotChart chart type to a **Line** chart.

5. Right-click cell **B4**, and then click **Value Field Settings** on the shortcut menu. The Value Field Settings dialog box opens.

6. Click **Average** in the list of functions.

7. Click the **Number Format** button, click **Percentage** in the Category box, and then click **OK** in each dialog box to return to the worksheet.

8. On the ribbon, click the **PivotTable Analyze** tab, and then in the PivotTable group, enter **Engagement Rate per Month Pivot** in the PivotTable Name box.

You'll move the line chart to the Dashboard worksheet and finish formatting it.

To place the line chart in the Dashboard worksheet:

1. Move the line PivotChart to the Dashboard worksheet, and then resize the chart to cover the range **P23:S36**.

2. On the PivotChart Analyze tab, in the Show/Hide group, click the **Field Buttons** button to hide the field buttons.

3. Click the **Design** tab, in the Chart Layouts group, click the **Quick Layout** button, and then click the **Layout 3** layout to place the legend at the bottom of the chart.

4. Change the chart title to **Engagement Rate per Month**.

5. Close the PivotChart Fields pane. See Figure 7–47.

| Figure 7–47 | Chart of engagement rate per month |

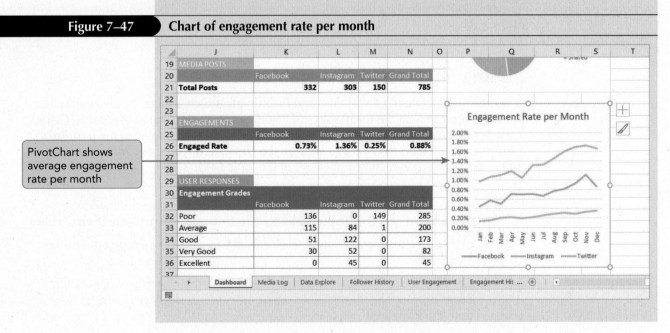

PivotChart shows average engagement rate per month

The line chart shows that average engagement rates generally increased throughout the year for all three media sites, except for a decrease in the last month Facebook posts. This favorable trend indicates to Claire that the ad campaign has increased customer interest and engagement.

Insight

Dynamic Referencing with the OFFSET Function

In working with data ranges and Excel tables, you referenced a range whose size and location were defined and static. In some Excel applications, you might need to reference a range whose size and location changes based on the need of the application. For example, a formula might need to reference data in the range A1:A10 on one occasion and the range C11:E15 on another occasion.

You can create references whose location and size change by using the OFFSET function

```
OFFSET(reference, rows, cols, [height], [width])
```

where *reference* points to cells in the workbook, *rows* and *cols* are the number of rows and columns to shift that reference, and *height* and *width* set the size of the new reference in terms of rows and columns. For example, the following expression shifts the A1:A10 reference 10 rows down and 2 columns across to point the range C11:C20:

```
OFFSET(A1:A10, 10, 2)
```

To resize the range to cover C11:E15, you specify the size of the new reference to be 5 rows high and 3 columns wide in the following expression:

```
OFFSET(A1:A10, 10, 2, 5, 3)
```

By modifying the parameters of the OFFSET argument, you can reference ranges of any location and size in a workbook, creating dynamic ranges that can change with your application.

Using Slicers and PivotTables

Another way of filtering PivotTables and PivotCharts is with a slicer. By clicking a slicer button, you can limit the PivotTable and PivotChart to a select group of records. Claire wants to explore whether user engagement varies based on the topic of the post. To answer this question, you'll add a slicer to the Dashboard worksheet and use it to filter the PivotTable based on different values of the Topic field.

To add a slicer for the Topic field to the Engagement Pivot PivotTable:

1. On the Dashboard worksheet, click cell **J11** to select the Engagement Pivot PivotTable.

2. On the ribbon, click the **Insert** tab, and then in the Filters group, click the **Slicer** button. The Insert Slicers dialog box opens, displaying a list of fields from the PivotTable.

3. Click the **TOPIC** check box, and then click **OK**. The TOPIC slicer appears on the Dashboard worksheet.

4. Move and resize the TOPIC slicer to cover the range **B4:H7**.

5. On the Slicer tab, in the Buttons group, change the value in the Columns box to **2** to arrange the slicer buttons in two rows and two columns.

6. In the TOPIC slicer, click the **Business Attire** button to filter the Engagement Pivot PivotTable to show only posts regarding business attire. The filtered PivotTable shows there were 100,603 engagements for posts dealing with business attire. See Figure 7–48.

Figure 7–48   Business Attire posts

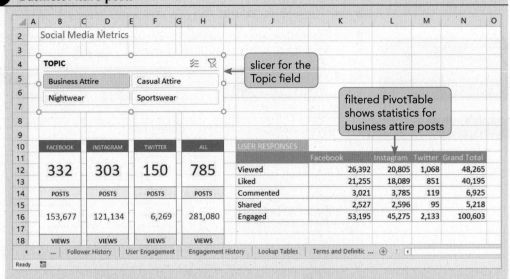

7. Click the **Nightwear**, **Casual Attire**, and **Sportswear** slicer buttons to filter the summary statistics for the other topic categories in the PivotTable.

8. Click the **Clear Filter** button ⧩ (or press **ALT+C**) to clear the filters and redisplay summary statistics for all topics.

The slicer made it possible to compare engagements across values of the Topic field. The highest number of total engagements occurs with posts on nightwear, which had 215,426 engagements. Claire wants to see how the other PivotTables and PivotCharts on the dashboard are affected by a change in topic.

Applying a Slicer to Multiple PivotTables

The same slicer can be applied to multiple PivotTables (and their associated PivotCharts), allowing you to filter the entire dashboard based on criteria you choose. The PivotTables do not need to be in the same worksheet, only the same workbook. Note that a slicer is not applied directly to a PivotChart, only the PivotTable that PivotChart is based on.

Reference

Applying a Slicer to Multiple PivotTables

- Click the PivotTable slicer to select it.
- On the Slicer tab, in the Slicer group, click the Report Connections button.
- Click the check boxes for all the PivotTables to be associated with the slicer.
- Click OK.

Claire wants you to apply the slicer you created for the Topic field to all PivotTables and PivotCharts in the Dashboard worksheet.

To apply a slicer to all the PivotTables in the dashboard:

▶ **1.** Click in the **TOPIC** slicer to make sure it is selected.

▶ **2.** On the Slicer tab, in the Slicer group, click the **Report Connections** button. The Report Connections (TOPIC) dialog box opens.

▶ **3.** Click the check box for every PivotTable listed *except* the Explore PivotTable from the Data Explore worksheet. See Figure 7–49.

Select the PivotTables associated with the PivotCharts to filter both table and chart.

Figure 7–49   **Report Connections (TOPIC) dialog box**

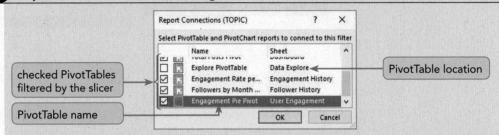

checked PivotTables filtered by the slicer

PivotTable name

PivotTable location

▶ **4.** Click **OK** to apply the slicer to all selected PivotTables.

▶ **5.** In the TOPIC slicer, click the **Business Attire**, **Casual Attire**, **Nightwear**, and then **Sportswear** buttons, and then confirm that all of the PivotTables and PivotCharts displayed in the Dashboard worksheet are filtered by the slicer.

▶ **6.** Click the **Clear Filter** button 🔽 (or press **ALT+C**) to clear the filters from all the PivotTables and PivotCharts on the dashboard.

Your analysis shows that the highest engagement rates and the greatest increase in engagement rates occur with media posts on nightwear and sportswear. The engagements rates for business and casual attire are much lower. Although posts on business and casual attire show an increase in user engagement over the past 12 months, the increase is not as great as for nightwear and sportswear.

Proskills

Problem Solving: Consolidating Data from Multiple Worksheets

This module worked with PivotTables whose data is stored within a single data range or Excel table. However, some projects require PivotTables that analyze data spread across several worksheets.

One way of summarizing, or consolidating, data from multiple worksheets is with the Consolidate Data command. Click the Consolidate button in the Data Tools group on the Data tab to open the Consolidate dialog box. From the Consolidate dialog box, first choose the function for consolidating the data, such as average, count, minimum, and maximum, among others. Then, select a list of ranges from different worksheets containing the data to be consolidated, including any row or column labels to identify the data. Excel will generate a table containing the statistical summary for the data from multiple worksheets.

Unlike PivotTables, the Consolidate command does not create an interactive table, so you must recreate the table each time you want to analyze your data from a different point of view. The consolidation table also does not interact with slicers or timelines, so you cannot filter the results. You can learn more about the Consolidate command in Excel Help.

Tip

Timeline slicers can be applied only to PivotTables and not to Excel tables.

Creating a Timeline Slicer

Another type of slicer is a timeline slicer, which filters a PivotTable to include only those records from a specified date interval. For example, you can limit the PivotTables only to those results between January and April or for an interval of specific years.

Reference

Filtering a PivotTable with a Timeline Slicer

- Click anywhere in the PivotTable to select it.
- On the Insert tab, in the Filters group, click the Timeline button.
- Click the check boxes of the fields containing date values which you want to create timelines.
- Click OK.
- Format the size, position, and appearance of the timeline.
- Select intervals within the timeline to filter the PivotTable.

Claire is interested not just in the engagement rate, but also in the quality of the engagements. Are more users commenting on and sharing posts at the end of the year than at the beginning? To answer that question, you will add a timeline slicer to the dashboard and examine the number of views, likes, comments, and shares from different time intervals.

To create the Date timeline slicer:

1. In the Dashboard worksheet, click cell **J11** to select the first PivotTable.

2. On the ribbon, click the **Insert** tab, and then in the Filters group, click the **Timeline** button. The Insert Timelines dialog box opens. There is only one field that contains date information.

3. Click the **DATE** check box, and then click **OK**. The DATE timeline slicer is inserted in the dashboard.

4. Move and resize the timeline slicer to cover the range **J4:S9**.

5. On the Timeline tab, in the Timeline group, click the **Report Connections** button. The Report Connections (DATE) dialog box opens.

6. Click the **Engagement Grade Pivot, Engagement Rate Pivot, Total Posts Pivot**, and **Engagement Pie Pivot** check boxes to select those PivotTables, and then click **OK**. See Figure 7–50.

Figure 7–50 **Timeline connected to all PivotTables**

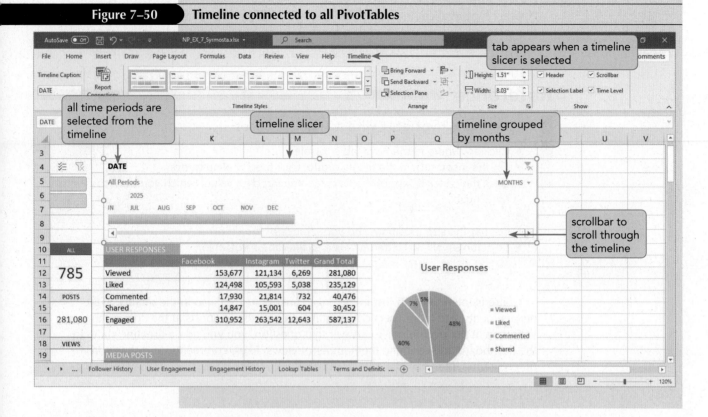

The timeline is laid out as a horizontal scroll bar grouped by months. You can filter the dashboard to show values only for specified time periods by selecting data ranges from the timeline. You'll filter the data on the dashboard by viewing the results for January 2024, and then you'll compare those values to the results for December 2024.

To filter the timeline by dates:

1. Drag the timeline scroll bar to the left until you see JAN 2024 in the timeline slicer.

2. Click the **JAN** box located directly below JAN 2024, deselecting all the other months in the timeline. The PivotTables and PivotCharts show the January results. During the month of January 2024, there were 30,973 user engagements (cell N16), a total of 65 posts (cell N21), and an average engagement rate of 0.59% (cell N26). The pie chart shows that 5% of the engagements involved user comments and 4% involved user shares.

3. Click the **DEC** box from 2024 to select only that month. In that month, there were 65,594 engagements (cell N16), 73 posts (cell N21), and an average engagement rate of 1.02% (cell N26). The pie chart shows that 8% of the engagements involved user comments and 7% involved user shares. See Figure 7–51.

Tip

To select a range of months, click the selection box in the timeline and drag the left or right selection handles over the range of months you want to cover.

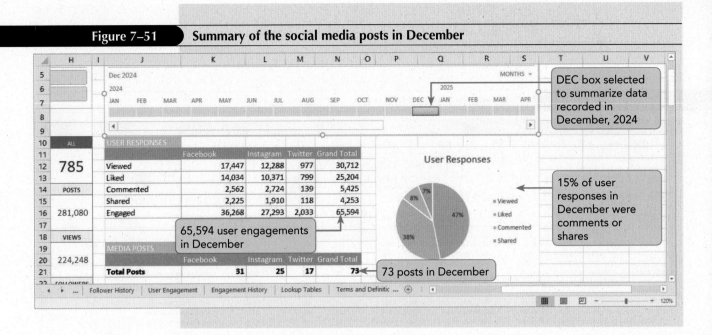

Figure 7–51   **Summary of the social media posts in December**

Comparing the January and December figures reveals that by the end of the year, more users were engaging with the company's social media posts and there were a higher percentage of active engagements in which users either commented on the posts or shared them with others. Claire can report that the ad campaign has had a positive impact on the company's social media presence.

Drilling Down a PivotTable

A PivotTable summarizes data, but sometimes you will want to examine the data records themselves. You can do this by **drilling down** the PivotTable to display the records responsible for the PivotTable calculations. To drill down a PivotTable, double-click any cell within the table. Excel then opens a new sheet displaying the records used to calculate that PivotTable value.

From the filtered values on the dashboard, Claire has learned that in December there were nine posts in which user engagement was graded as excellent. Claire wants to study those posts to discover what might have made them so appealing to users. You will drill down the PivotTable to display those records.

To drill down the Engagement Grade Pivot PivotTable:

▶ **1.** In the Dashboard worksheet, scroll down to the Engagement Grade Pivot PivotTable.

▶ **2.** Double-click cell **L36** containing the value 9, which is the number of Instagram posts that had an excellent grade of user engagement in December 2024. A new worksheet opens, containing the 9 relevant records. Some of the data is not visible in the columns.

▶ **3.** On the Home tab, in the Cells group, click the **Format** button, and then click **AutoFit Column Width**. The column widths expand to show all the data within each column.

▶ **4.** Rename the worksheet **Excellent Posts** and then move the sheet to be the second to last worksheet in the workbook, directly before the Terms and Definitions worksheet. See Figure 7–52.

Figure 7–52   **Drilling into PivotTable data**

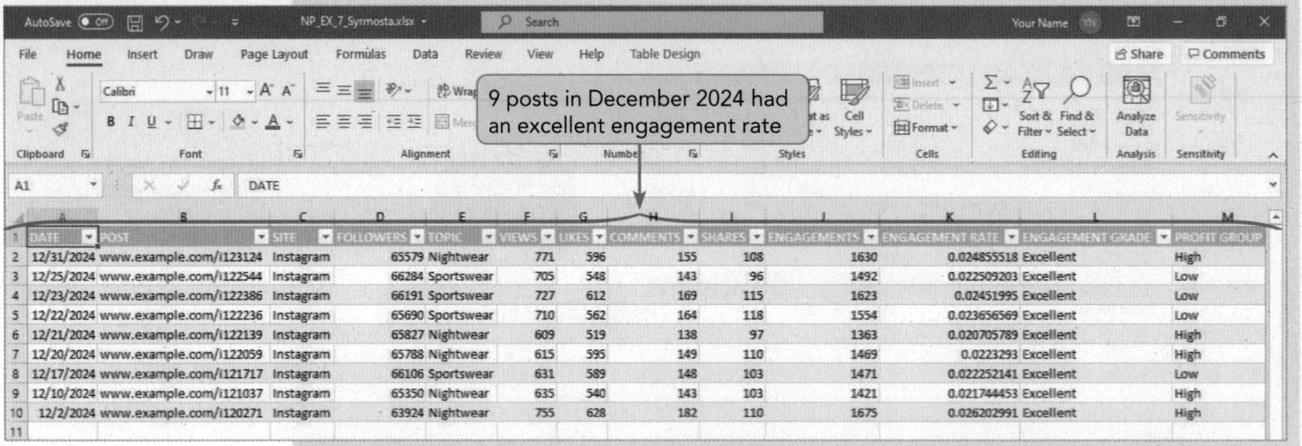

▶ **5.** sam↑ Save the workbook, and then close it.

Claire can use the contents of the Excellent Posts worksheet to further study what makes an effective media post. Note that the data retrieved through drilling down is not linked to the source data, so any changes made to the values in the data source, will not be reflected in the worksheet.

Insight

Refreshing PivotTable Data

The information in a PivotTable is connected to a data source, which can be a data range or Excel table. As you add more data to the data source or revise the data, the PivotTable is not updated to show the most current results. The PivotTable is not updated until you **refresh** it, forcing Excel to recreate the table using new data. To refresh the PivotTable, click the Refresh button in the Data group on the PivotTable Analyze tab.

You can modify the PivotTable settings to have Excel automatically update a PivotTable every time the workbook is opened. Select the PivotTable and then click the Options button in the PivotTable group on the PivotTable Analyze tab to open the PivotTable Options dialog box. On the Data tab, click the Refresh data when opening the file check box. Excel will then refresh the PivotTable each time the workbook is reopened. Note that whenever you refresh a PivotTable, *all* PivotTables that rely on the same data source get updated.

You've completed your work on the social media report. Using the interactive dashboard you created, Claire can quickly analyze social media metrics for any topic within any timeframe.

Review

Session 7.3 Quick Check

1. What are the four areas of a PivotChart?
2. Can you create a PivotChart without a PivotTable?
3. Can any Excel chart type be turned into a PivotChart?
4. How do you apply the same slicer to multiple PivotTables?
5. Can a timeline slicer be used with Excel tables as well as PivotTables?
6. When you do you need to refresh a PivotTable?

Practice

Review Assignments

Data File needed for the Review Assignments: NP_EX_7-2.xlsx

Claire continues to analyze social media metrics and needs to evaluate what factors might result in a successful Facebook post. Claire has compiled a list of Facebook posts that advertise company specials and business news. Claire wants to know whether user engagement is higher when the posts include photos and coupon offers. She also wants to determine whether certain days of the week are better than others to engage the user. Finally, Claire is mindful that users might ignore long posts and wants to examine whether word count has an impact on user engagement. Claire grades post length according to the table in Figure 7–53.

Figure 7–53   **Lengths of Facebook posts**

Character Count	Post Size
0 – < 80 characters	short
80 – < 160 characters	medium
160 – < 240 characters	long
>= 240 characters	very long

Complete the following:

1. Open the **NP_EX_7-2.xlsx** workbook located in the Excel7 > Review folder included with your Data Files. Save the workbook as **NP_EX_7_Facebook** in the location specified by your instructor.

2. In the Documentation sheet, enter your name and the date.

3. In the Lookup Tables worksheet, use the data in Figure 7–53 to complete the lookup table in the range B4:C8. Give the first column of values the defined name **Character_Lookup** and give the second column of values the defined name **Post_Lookup**.

4. In the Media Posts worksheet, in column G of the Facebook table, apply the XLOOKUP function to categorize the size of each post, using the value of the Characters field for the lookup value, the Character_Lookup range as the lookup array, and the Post_Lookup range as the return array. Do not specify the if_not_found argument, and use −1 for the match_mode argument.

5. In the Report worksheet, count the number of posts with and without photos and coupons as follows:

   a. In cell C15, use the COUNTIF function to count the number of records in the Photo field of the Facebook table equal to the "Photo" field value.

   b. In cell C16, calculate the difference between cell C14 and C15.

   c. In cell C18, count the number of records in the Coupon field equal to the "Coupon" field value.

   d. In cell C19 calculate the difference between cell C14 and C18.

6. Calculate the average engagement rate for posts with and without photos and coupons as follows:

   a. In cell C23, calculate the average engagement rate for posts with photos by using the AVERAGEIF function with the *Range* argument equal to Facebook[PHOTO], the *Criteria* argument equal to "Photo", and the *Average_Range* argument equal to Facebook[ENGAGEMENT RATE].

   b. In cell C24, calculate the average engagement rate for posts without posts by copying the formula in C23 and change the value of the **Criteria** argument to "No Photo".

   c. In cell C26, calculate the average engagement rate for posts with coupons by using the AVERAGEIF function with the **Range** argument equal to Facebook[COUPON], the *Criteria* argument equal to "Coupon", and the *Average_Range* argument equal to Facebook[ENGAGEMENT RATE].

d. In cell C27, calculate the average engagement rate for posts without coupons by copying the formula in C26 and change the value of the *Criteria* argument to "No Coupon".

7. Create a PivotTable of the data in the Media Posts worksheet, placing the PivotTable in cell E12 of the Report worksheet.

8. Make the following changes to the PivotTable:

a. Rename the PivotTable as **Day Pivot**.

b. Place the Day field in the Rows area of the table, and then place the Post and Engagement Rate fields in the Values area. (Posts are in the left column of the PivotTable.)

c. Change the label for the Count of Posts value field to **Posted**. Change the label for the Sum of Engagement Rate value field to **Engagement Rates** and display the average engagement rate as a percentage formatted to two decimal places.

d. Apply the Light Green, Pivot Style Medium 7 to the PivotTable and turn on Banded Rows and Banded Columns.

e. Modify the PivotTable options so that the Excel does *not* AutoFit column widths on update.

9. Copy the PivotTable in the range E12:G20 and paste it in cell E22, and then make the following changes to the PivotTable:

a. Rename the PivotTable as **Size Pivot**.

b. Replace the Day field in the Rows area with the Post Size field.

c. Reorder the categories in the Rows area to the following order: short, medium, long, very long.

10. In the Media Posts worksheet, create a PivotChart from the data, placing the PivotTable/ PivotChart in the Engagement Types worksheet in cell B4, and then do the following:

a. Rename the PivotTable as **Engaged Pivot**.

b. Place the Clicks, Likes, Comments, and Shares field in the Values area box.

c. Rename the value fields as **Clicked**, **Liked**, **Commented**, and **Shared**.

d. Move the ΣValues item into the Rows area box so that all values fields are displayed in separate rows.

11. Make the following changes to the PivotChart:

a. Move the PivotChart to the Report worksheet, and then resize it to cover the range I12:L18.

b. Change the chart type to a pie chart.

c. Remove the field buttons and the chart title from the chart.

d. Change the chart style to Style 8.

12. Create another PivotChart from the data in the Facebook table, place it in the Engagement History worksheet in cell B4, and then make the following changes:

a. Rename the PivotTable as **History Pivot**.

b. Place the Date field in the Rows area and the Engagement Rate field in the Values areas.

c. Change the Engagement Rate value field settings to display the average of the Engagement Rate field as a percentage to two decimal places using **Engagement Rates** as the label.

d. Change the PivotChart to a line chart. Remove the legend and field buttons from the PivotChart. Change the chart title to **Engagement Rates**.

e. Move the PivotChart to the Report worksheet and resize it to cover the range I19:L27.

13. Click cell E12 to select the first PivotTable, add slicers for the Photo and Coupon fields, and then do the following:

a. Move and resize the PHOTO slicer to cover the range B4:C6.

b. Move and resize the COUPON slicer to cover the range B8:C11.

c. Display both slicers with two columns.

d. Set the report connections of both slicers to connect to every PivotTable in the workbook.

14. Click cell E12 to select the first PivotTable, insert a timeline using the Date field, and then do the following:

   a. Resize the timeline to cover the range E4:L10.

   b. Set the report connections of the slicer to connect to the Engaged Pivot, Day Pivot, and Size Pivot PivotTables.

15. Use the slicers to filter the Report worksheet to show only the social media metric for posts that involved photos and coupons and were posted in December 2024.

16. Display the posts that match these conditions by double-clicking cell G20 to drill down into the PivotTable. Rename the worksheet containing the drilled-down data **Drilled Data** and move the sheet after the Media Posts worksheet. Resize the column widths so that all of the data is visible.

17. Save the workbook, and then close it.

Apply

Case Problem 1

Data File needed for this Case Problem: NP_EX_7-3.xlsx

STEM Mentors   Robert Harshaw is an Events Coordinator for STEM Mentors, a company specializing in education software for high school STEM teachers. Every July, the company sponsors a conference to showcase its wares and provide informative speakers and workshops on technology in science and math education. After the conference, Robert compiles results from a survey to act as a guide for the next conference. You'll help Robert generate a report on the conference response. In the Survey Results worksheet, the answers to seven survey questions have been entered in an Excel table named Survey. The responses for the first four questions are the letters a through d, which represent responses from "very satisfied" to "very dissatisfied." The text of the survey questions is on the Survey Questions worksheet. Complete the following.

1. Open the **NP_EX_7-3.xlsx** workbook located in the Excel7 > Case1 folder included with your Data Files, and then save the workbook as **NP_EX_7_STEM** in the location specified by your instructor.

2. In the Documentation sheet enter your name and the date.

3. In the Survey Results worksheet, in the Workshops column, display text associated with answers to Q1 by clicking cell I6 and inserting the XLOOKUP function to do an exact match lookup with the Q1 field as the lookup value, the survey_lookup range as the lookup array, and the rating_lookup range as the return array.

4. Repeat Step 3 for the Speakers through Meals field, using values of the Q2 through Q4 fields. (*Hint:* You can use AutoFill to quickly enter the formulas for the Speakers through Meals fields.)

5. In the School column, display the type of school of each attendee (Public, Private, Online, or Tutor) by clicking cell M6 and inserting the XLOOKUP function to do an exact match lookup of values in the Q5 field from the school_lookup range, and returning values from the type_lookup range.

6. In the Prior Conferences column, indicate the number of conferences previously attended (0, 1, 2, and 3+) by clicking cell N6 and inserting the XLOOKUP function to do an approximate match lookup of the values in the Q6 field using the conference_lookup range as the lookup array and returning the value from the prior_lookup range. Set the match_mode value to −1.

7. In the Report worksheet, do the following:

   a. In cell B14, use the COUNTIF function to count the number of records in the Return field from the Survey table that equal "will return."

   b. In cell B15, calculate the difference between cell B11 and B14.

   c. In the range B18:B21, use the COUNTIF function to count the number of records of the School field in the Survey table that equal Public, Private, Online, and Tutor.

   d. In the range B24:B27, use the COUNTIF function to count the number of records in the Prior Conferences field of the Survey table that equal 0, 1, 2, and 3+.

    e. In cells C14, C15, C18:C21, and C24:C27, divide the counts you calculated for each response group by the total number of responses shown in cell B11 to express the values as percentages.

8. In the Survey Results worksheet, create a PivotChart, placing it in cell A4 of the PivotTables worksheet, and then do the following to analyze what factors might have contributed to a person deciding against returning to next year's conference:

    a. Name the PivotTable as **workshop pivot**.

    b. Place the Workshops field in the Columns area, the Return field in the Rows area, and the ID field in the Values area.

9. Make the following changes to the PivotChart:

    a. Move the chart to the Report worksheet to cover the range E7:I17.

    b. Change the chart type to the 100% Stacked Column chart.

    c. Remove the chart legend and field buttons from the chart.

    d. Add the chart title **Workshop Satisfaction** to the chart.

    e. Display the table associated with this chart by clicking the Data Tables check box in the Chart Elements menu. Verify that data table rows are arranged from top to bottom in the order Very Satisfied, Satisfied, Dissatisfied, and Very Dissatisfied.

10. Repeat Steps 8 and 9 to create a 100% Stacked column chart plotting the Speakers field against the Return field. Place the PivotTable in cell A10 on the PivotTables worksheet. Enter **speaker pivot** as the PivotTable name. Place the PivotChart in the range K7:O17 on the Report worksheet and add **Speaker Satisfaction** as the chart title.

11. Repeat Steps 8 and 9 to create a 100% Stacked column chart plotting the Facilities field against the Return field. Place the PivotTable in cell A16 on the PivotTables worksheet. Enter **facility pivot** as the PivotTable name. Place the PivotChart in the range E19:I29 on the Report worksheet and add **Facility Satisfaction** as the chart title.

12. Repeat Steps 8 and 9 to create a 100% Stacked column chart plotting the Meals field against the Return field. Place the PivotTable in cell A22 on the PivotTables worksheet. Enter **meal pivot** as the PivotTable name. Place the PivotChart in the range K19:O29 on the Report worksheet and add **Meal Satisfaction** as the chart title.

13. Click the first PivotChart to select it and then create a slicer for the School field. Move and resize the slicer to cover the range E2:O5 and then arrange the buttons in 4 columns. Connect the slicer to all four PivotTables in the workbook.

14. Use the School slicer to filter the PivotCharts to show only the summaries of the public school attendees.

15. Save the workbook, and then close it.

Challenge

Case Problem 2

Data File needed for this Case Problem: NP_EX_7-4.xlsx

Blue Star Grocery   Gina Ndaw, as a fleet manager for Blue Star Grocery, is responsible for managing the trucks and drivers that make deliveries to grocery stores in Colorado. Gina wants to analyze shipping data and track the delivery times and accumulated mileage of the company drivers. Gina has compiled a shipping log detailing the routes of four drivers from the past three months and needs your help creating the PivotTables and PivotCharts to analyze the data. Complete the following:

1. Open the **NP_EX_7-4.xlsx** workbook located in the Excel7 > Case2 folder included with your Data Files. Save the workbook as **NP_EX_7_Driving** in the location specified by your instructor.

2. In the Documentation sheet, enter your name and the date.

3. The Driving Log worksheet contains driving records of four Blue Star Grocery drivers. Each record in the Log table contains a separate segment of a daily trip by a driver and provides the date and times for each segment. In the Driving Time field, determine the time required for each

segment in hours by calculating the difference between the End Time field and the Start Time field and multiplying that difference by 24. (*Hint*: You can find the formula for this field in the Terms and Definitions worksheet.)

Explore 4. In the Time Goal field of the Log table, you will display the time it should take a driver to drive between cities (as determined by the company). To display that time value, use a nested XLOOKUP function. XLOOKUP should first use the value in the Start City field as the lookup value, and then search the Time_Start range in the Travel Times worksheet as the lookup array. For the return array, include a nested XLOOKUP function that uses the value in the End City field as its lookup value and searches the Time_End range as its lookup array. Finally, the nested XLOOKUP function returns the value in the Travel_Times range at the intersection of the start city and end city being looked up. (*Hint*: See the Terms and Definitions worksheet for help in constructing the function.)

5. In the Time Over field, calculate the amount by which the driver was over the recommended travel time in minutes by calculating the difference between the Driving Time field and the Time Goal field, and then multiplying that difference by 60.

Explore 6. In the Mileage field, use a nested XLOOKUP function to calculate the mileage for each segment driven. Refer to Step 4 as you create the function to first look for the Start City field value in the Distance_Start range in the Travel Distances worksheet. The nested XLOOKUP function should look for the End City field value in the Distance_End range and return the value at the intersection of the two in the Travel_Distances range. (*Hint*: You can refer to the Terms and Definitions worksheet if you need help in constructing the function.)

7. In the Driving Summary worksheet, Gina entered a formula in cell C10 to calculate the average daily mileage for the first driver. Copy the formula in cell C10 into the range C11:C13 to calculate the average daily mileage for the other three drivers.

8. In cell C16 of the Driving Summary worksheet, Gina has entered a formula to calculate the average daily driving time for the first driver. Copy the formula in cell C16 into the range C17:C19 to calculate the average daily driving times for the other drivers.

9. Gina wants to track the number of minutes the drivers are over their scheduled driving times. Use data in the Driving Log worksheet to create a PivotTable/PivotChart in the Driver Times worksheet in cell B4. Rename the PivotTable as **Driving Times Pivot**. Place the Time Over field in the Values area, place the Date field in the Rows area, and then remove the Months field from the Rows area.

10. Move the PivotChart to the Driving Summary worksheet, placing it in the range E9:G19. Change the chart type to a line chart. Remove the field buttons and the legend from the chart. Change the chart title to **Minutes Over Time Goal**.

11. Gina wants to track the daily distance driven by the drivers. In the Driving Log worksheet, create another PivotTable/PivotChart from the Log table, placing them in the Driver Miles worksheet in cell B4. Rename the PivotTable using **Driving Miles Pivot** as the name. Place the Mileage field in the Values area, place the Date field in the Rows area, and remove the Months field.

12. Move the PivotChart to the Driving Summary worksheet in the range I9:K19. Change the chart type to a line chart. Remove the field buttons and the chart legend. Change the title to **Distance in Miles**.

13. Insert a slicer for the Driver field in the range E4:K7. Display the slicer buttons in 4 columns and connect the slicer to both PivotTables.

14. Click each slicer button to verify that you can view time and distance charts for each individual driver over the past three months.

15. Driver D600-622 is new to the job, and Gina wants to know whether that driver's travel times have improved in the last three months. Use the slicer to display the charts for only that driver, displaying the general trend of the minutes over the company's time goals each day.

16. Save the workbook, and then close it.

Module **8**

Objectives

Session 8.1
- Explore the principles of cost-volume-profit relationships
- Create a one-variable data table
- Create a two-variable data table

Session 8.2
- Create and apply different Excel scenarios with the Scenario Manager
- Generate a scenario summary report
- Generate a scenario PivotTable report

Session 8.3
- Explore the principles of a product mix
- Run Solver to calculate optimal solutions
- Create and apply constraints to a Solver model
- Save and load a Solver model

Performing What-If Analyses

Maximizing Profits with the Right Product Mix

Case | **Athena Cycles**

Roy Lockley is a sales analyst for Athena Cycles, a manufacturer of high-end bicycles for triathletes and cycling enthusiasts. Roy wants to use Excel to analyze the profitability of the company's line of bicycles to determine the number of each model the company must produce and sell to be profitable. Roy is interested in whether the company can increase its net income by reducing the selling price of the bikes to increase the sales volume or by increasing the sales price even if it means less sales. Roy also wants to determine whether the company can increase profits by promoting one model over another. To answer these questions, you will use the Excel what-if tools.

Starting Data Files

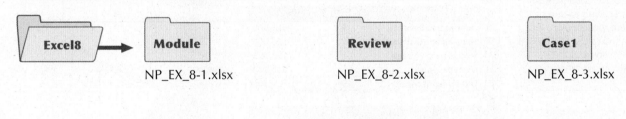

Excel8 →	Module	Review	Case1
	NP_EX_8-1.xlsx	NP_EX_8-2.xlsx	NP_EX_8-3.xlsx

Case2

NP_EX_8-4.xlsx

Session 8.1 Visual Overview:

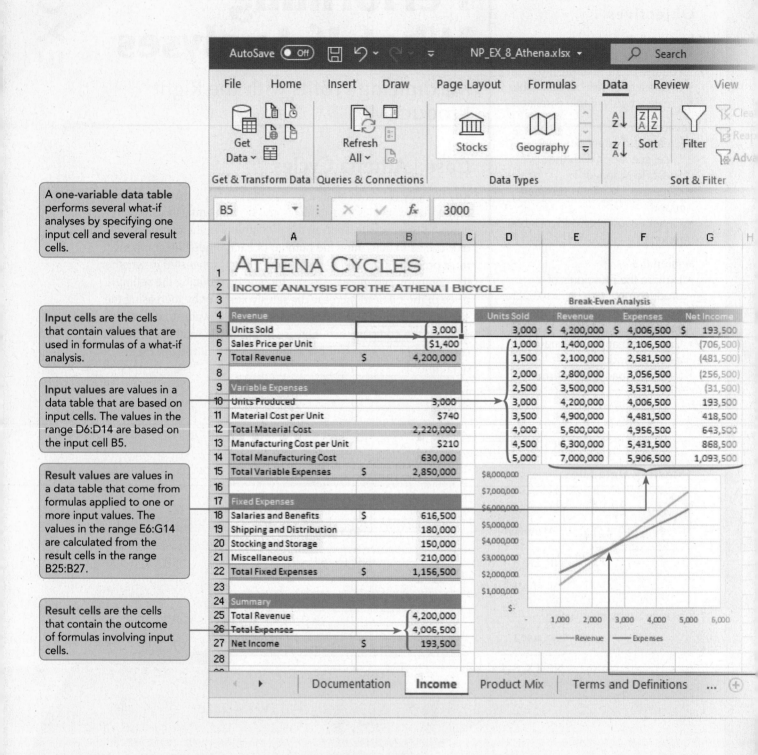

A one-variable data table performs several what-if analyses by specifying one input cell and several result cells.

Input cells are the cells that contain values that are used in formulas of a what-if analysis.

Input values are values in a data table that are based on input cells. The values in the range D6:D14 are based on the input cell B5.

Result values are values in a data table that come from formulas applied to one or more input values. The values in the range E6:G14 are calculated from the result cells in the range B25:B27.

Result cells are the cells that contain the outcome of formulas involving input cells.

B5   fx   3000

ATHENA CYCLES
INCOME ANALYSIS FOR THE ATHENA I BICYCLE

Break-Even Analysis

			Units Sold	Revenue	Expenses	Net Income
Revenue			3,000	$ 4,200,000	$ 4,006,500	$ 193,500
Units Sold		3,000	1,000	1,400,000	2,106,500	(706,500)
Sales Price per Unit		$1,400	1,500	2,100,000	2,581,500	(481,500)
Total Revenue	$	4,200,000	2,000	2,800,000	3,056,500	(256,500)
			2,500	3,500,000	3,531,500	(31,500)
Variable Expenses			3,000	4,200,000	4,006,500	193,500
Units Produced		3,000	3,500	4,900,000	4,481,500	418,500
Material Cost per Unit		$740	4,000	5,600,000	4,956,500	643,500
Total Material Cost		2,220,000	4,500	6,300,000	5,431,500	868,500
Manufacturing Cost per Unit		$210	5,000	7,000,000	5,906,500	1,093,500
Total Manufacturing Cost		630,000				
Total Variable Expenses	$	2,850,000				
Fixed Expenses						
Salaries and Benefits	$	616,500				
Shipping and Distribution		180,000				
Stocking and Storage		150,000				
Miscellaneous		210,000				
Total Fixed Expenses	$	1,156,500				
Summary						
Total Revenue		4,200,000				
Total Expenses		4,006,500				
Net Income	$	193,500				

Documentation | **Income** | Product Mix | Terms and Definitions

Data Tables and What-If Analysis

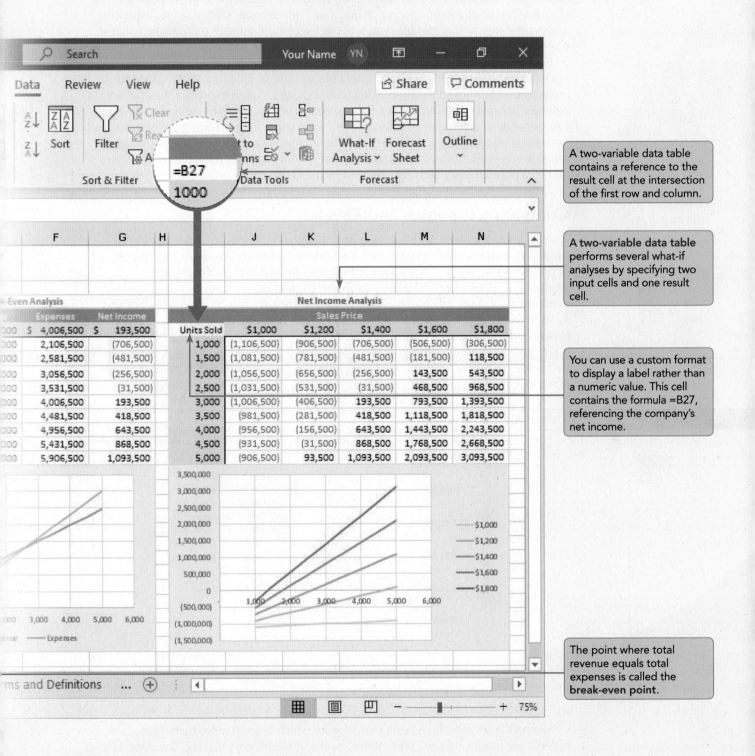

A two-variable data table contains a reference to the result cell at the intersection of the first row and column.

A two-variable data table performs several what-if analyses by specifying two input cells and one result cell.

You can use a custom format to display a label rather than a numeric value. This cell contains the formula =B27, referencing the company's net income.

The point where total revenue equals total expenses is called the break-even point.

Net Income Analysis

Units Sold	$1,000	$1,200	$1,400	$1,600	$1,800
1,000	(1,106,500)	(906,500)	(706,500)	(506,500)	(306,500)
1,500	(1,081,500)	(781,500)	(481,500)	(181,500)	118,500
2,000	(1,056,500)	(656,500)	(256,500)	143,500	543,500
2,500	(1,031,500)	(531,500)	(31,500)	468,500	968,500
3,000	(1,006,500)	(406,500)	193,500	793,500	1,393,500
3,500	(981,500)	(281,500)	418,500	1,118,500	1,818,500
4,000	(956,500)	(156,500)	643,500	1,443,500	2,243,500
4,500	(931,500)	(31,500)	868,500	1,768,500	2,668,500
5,000	(906,500)	93,500	1,093,500	2,093,500	3,093,500

Understanding Cost-Volume Relationships

One of the most powerful features of Excel is the ability to explore the impact of changing financial conditions on outcomes such as revenue, sales volume, expenses, and profitability. In this module, you will use Excel to investigate a variety of "what-if" scenarios. You will begin by exploring Cost-Volume-Profit analysis.

Cost-Volume-Profit (CVP) analysis is a branch of financial analysis that studies the relationship between expenses, sales volume, and profitability. CVP analysis is an important business decision-making tool because it can help predict the effect of cutting overhead or raising prices on a company's net income. For example, Athena Cycles needs to determine a reasonable price to charge for the company's bicycles and how much added profit could be realized by increasing (or even decreasing) the sales price. In this session, you will focus on the sales and expenses related to the Athena I model, a popular entry-level bicycle sold by the company.

Comparing Expenses and Revenue

The first component of CVP analysis is cost, or expense. There are three types of expenses—variable, fixed, and mixed. **Variable expenses** are expenses that change in proportion to production volume. For each additional bicycle the company produces, it spends more on parts, raw materials, and other expenses associated with manufacturing. Each Athena I produced by the company costs $740 in materials and $210 in manufacturing, for a total cost of $950 per unit. The company's total variable expenses are equal to the cost of producing each Athena I multiplied by the total number of bikes produced. Figure 8–1 shows a line graph of the total variable expense as it relates to production volume. From this graph, you learn that Athena Cycles will incur $4.75 million in variable expenses if it produces 5,000 Athena I bicycles.

| Figure 8–1 | Chart of variable expenses |

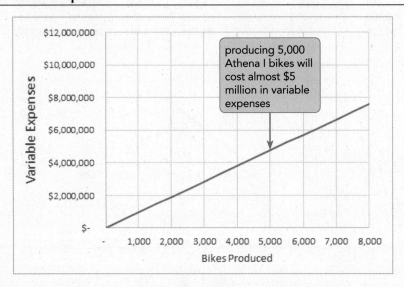

Athena Cycles sells the Athena I for $1,400, which is $450 more than the variable expense for producing each unit. At first glance, it might seem that the company earns a $450 profit on each sale, but that is incorrect. The sales price must also cover the company's fixed expenses. A **fixed expense** is an expense that must be paid regardless of sales volume. For example, the company must pay salaries and benefits for its employees as well as insurance, maintenance fees, and administrative overhead. Roy tells you that the Athena I model costs the company more than $1 million in fixed expenses that must be paid even if the company doesn't sell a single bike.

You can estimate total expense by adding variable and fixed expenses. The graph in Figure 8–2 shows the company's total expenses for a given number of Athena I bicycles produced each year. From this chart, you learn that if the company produces 5,000 Athena I bicycles, its total expense would be about $5.9 million. Of this, about $4.75 million represents variable expenses and about 1.15 million is from fixed expenses.

Figure 8–2   **Chart of total expenses**

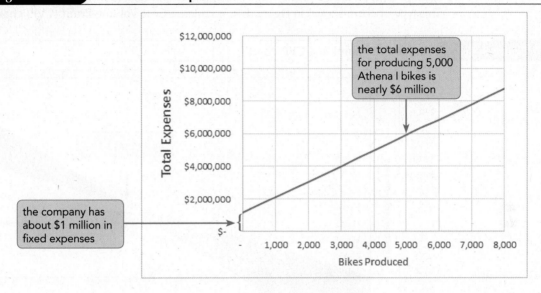

A third type of expense is a **mixed expense**, which is an expense that is part variable and part fixed. For example, if the salespeople at Athena Cycles receive commissions based on sales volume, their total compensation would be a mixed expense to the company because each salesperson has a fixed salary but also earns extra income as sales volume increases. You will not consider any mixed expenses in the analysis you'll prepare for Roy.

Because Athena Cycles is a highly specialized company with a select but loyal clientele, Athena Cycles sells almost all of what it produces. So, the company should bring in more revenue as it increases production. Figure 8–3 shows the increase in revenue in relation to the increase in sales volume. For example, selling 5,000 Athena I bicycles at an average price of $1,400 per bike would generate about $7 million in revenue.

Figure 8–3   **Chart of revenue**

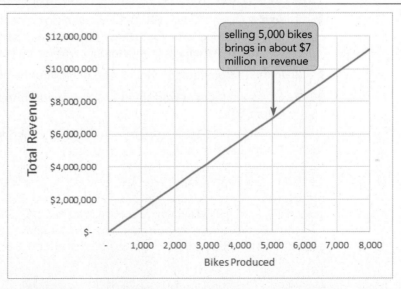

Exploring the Break-Even Point

The point where total revenue equals total expenses is called the break-even point. For this reason, CVP analysis is sometimes called **break-even analysis**. The more bicycles Athena Cycles sells above the break-even point, the greater its profit. Conversely, when sales levels fall below the break-even point, the company loses money.

You can illustrate the break-even point by graphing revenue and total expenses against sales volume on the same chart. The break-even point occurs where the two lines cross. This type of chart, shown in Figure 8–4, is called a **Cost-Volume-Profit (CVP) chart**.

Figure 8–4	Break-even point in a CVP chart

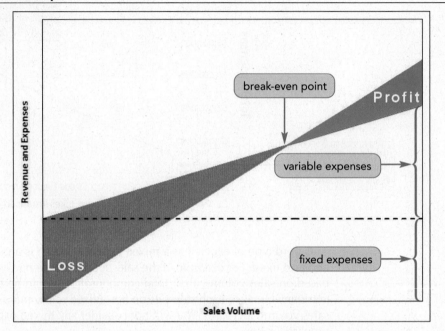

Roy prepared an income statement for the Athena I model that projects the revenue, variable expenses, and fixed expenses for next year's sales. You'll review Roy's data now. Later, you will use Roy's projections to calculate the break-even point for sales of the Athena I model.

To review the income statement for the Athena I:

1. **sam** ↓ Open the **NP_EX_8-1.xlsx** workbook located in the **Excel8 > Module** folder included with your Data Files, and then save the workbook as **NP_EX_8_Athena** in the location specified by your instructor.

2. In the Documentation worksheet, enter your name and the date.

3. Go to the **Income** worksheet and review its contents and formulas. See Figure 8–5.

Figure 8–5	Income statement for the Athena I bicycle

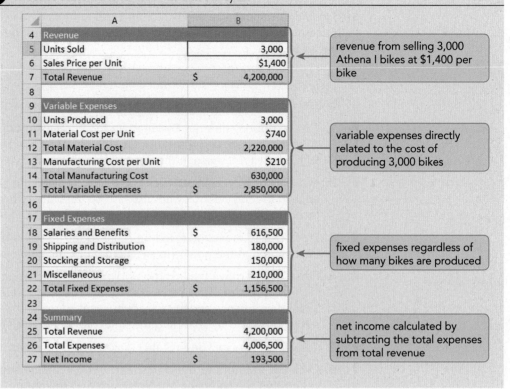

	A	B
4	Revenue	
5	Units Sold	3,000
6	Sales Price per Unit	$1,400
7	Total Revenue	$ 4,200,000
8		
9	Variable Expenses	
10	Units Produced	3,000
11	Material Cost per Unit	$740
12	Total Material Cost	2,220,000
13	Manufacturing Cost per Unit	$210
14	Total Manufacturing Cost	630,000
15	Total Variable Expenses	$ 2,850,000
16		
17	Fixed Expenses	
18	Salaries and Benefits	$ 616,500
19	Shipping and Distribution	180,000
20	Stocking and Storage	150,000
21	Miscellaneous	210,000
22	Total Fixed Expenses	$ 1,156,500
23		
24	Summary	
25	Total Revenue	4,200,000
26	Total Expenses	4,006,500
27	Net Income	$ 193,500

revenue from selling 3,000 Athena I bikes at $1,400 per bike

variable expenses directly related to the cost of producing 3,000 bikes

fixed expenses regardless of how many bikes are produced

net income calculated by subtracting the total expenses from total revenue

As itemized in the Income worksheet, the company projects that it will sell 3,000 Athena Is for $1,400 each, generating $4.2 million in revenue. The variable expenses involved in producing those bicycles is $2.85 million and the company's fixed expenses are about $1.16 million. Based on this sales volume, the company would generate $193,500 in net income.

Finding the Break-Even Point with What-If Analysis

What-if analysis lets you explore the impact of changing different values in a worksheet. You can use such an analysis to explore the impact of changing financial conditions on a company's profitability. Roy wants to know what the impact would be if the number of Athena I bicycles the company produces and sells rises to 4,000 or falls to 2,000.

To perform what-if analysis for different sales volumes:

▶ 1. In cell **B5**, enter **4000** to change the units produced and sold value. Increasing the sales volume to 4,000 units, the net income of the company shown in cell B27 increases to $643,500.

▶ 2. In cell **B5**, enter **2000**. If the units produced and sold drop to 2,000, the net income shown in cell B27 becomes –$256,500. The company will lose money with that low of a sales volume.

▶ 3. In cell **B5**, enter **3000** to return to the original units produced and sold projection.

Roy wants to know how low sales can go and still maintain a profit. In other words, what is the sales volume for the break-even point? One way of finding the break-even point is to use Goal Seek. Recall that Goal Seek is a what-if analysis tool that can be used to find the input value needed for an Excel formula to match a specified value. In this case, you'll find out how many Athena I bicycles must be sold to set the net income to $0.

To use Goal Seek to find the break-even point for the Athena I:

▶ **1.** On the ribbon, click the **Data** tab. In the Forecast group, click the **What-If Analysis** button, and then click **Goal Seek**. The Goal Seek dialog box opens with the cell reference in the Set cell box selected.

▶ **2.** In the Income worksheet, click cell **B27** to replace the selected cell reference in the Set cell box with $B$27. The absolute reference specifies the Net Income cell as the cell whose value you want to set.

▶ **3.** Press **TAB** to move the insertion point to the To value box, and then type **0** indicating that the goal is to set the net income value in cell B27 to 0.

▶ **4.** Press **TAB** to move the insertion point to the By changing cell box, and then click cell **B5** in the Income worksheet to enter the cell reference $B$5. The absolute reference specifies that you want to reach the goal of setting the net income to 0 by changing the units produced and sold value in cell B5.

▶ **5.** Click **OK**. The Goal Seek Status dialog box opens once Excel finds a solution.

▶ **6.** Click **OK** to return to the worksheet. The value 2,570 appears in cell B5, indicating that the company must produce and sell about 2,570 Athena I bicycles to break even. See Figure 8–6.

Figure 8–6	Sales required to break even

	A	B	
4	Revenue		
5	Units Sold	2,570	← Goal Seek solution
6	Sales Price per Unit	$1,400	
7	Total Revenue	$ 3,598,000	
8			
9	Variable Expenses		
10	Units Produced	2,570	
11	Material Cost per Unit	$740	
12	Total Material Cost	1,901,800	
13	Manufacturing Cost per Unit	$210	
14	Total Manufacturing Cost	539,700	
15	Total Variable Expenses	$ 2,441,500	
16			
17	Fixed Expenses		
18	Salaries and Benefits	$ 616,500	
19	Shipping and Distribution	180,000	
20	Stocking and Storage	150,000	
21	Miscellaneous	210,000	
22	Total Fixed Expenses	$ 1,156,500	
23			
24	Summary		
25	Total Revenue	3,598,000	
26	Total Expenses	3,598,000	
27	Net Income	$ -	

producing and selling about 2,570 Athena I bikes results in a net income of $0 with total revenue balanced against total expenses

▶ **7.** Click cell **B5** and enter **3000** to return to the original units produced and sold projection.

Roy wants to continue to analyze the company's net income under different sales assumptions. For example, what would happen to the company's net income if sales increased to 5,000 bicycles? How much would the company lose if the number of sales fell to 1,500? How many bicycles must the company sell to reach a net income of exactly $500,000? You could continue to use Goal Seek to answer each of these questions in turn, but a more efficient approach is to use a data table.

Working with Data Tables

A **data table** is an Excel table that displays the results from several what-if analyses. The table consists of input cells and result cells. The input cells contain the constants to be changed in a what-if analysis. The result cells contain calculated values that are impacted by the changing input values. In Excel, you can use one-variable data tables and two-variable data tables.

Creating a One-Variable Data Table

A one-variable data table contains one input cell and any number of result cells. The range of possible values for the input cell is entered in the first row or column of the data table, and the corresponding result values appear in the subsequent rows or columns. One-variable data tables are particularly useful in business to explore how changing a single input value can impact several financial measures.

Reference

Creating a One-Variable Data Table

- In the upper-left cell of the table, enter a formula that references the input cell.
- In either the first row or the first column of the table, enter input values.
- For input values in the first row, enter formulas referencing result cells in the table's first column; for input values in the first column, enter formulas referencing result cells in the table's first row.
- Select the table (excluding any row or column headings).
- On the Data tab, in the Forecast group, click the What-If Analysis button, and then click Data Table.
- If the input values are in the first row, enter the cell reference to the input cell in the Row input cell box; if the input values are in the first column, enter the cell reference to the input cell in the Column input cell box.
- Click OK.

Figure 8–7 shows a one-variable data table for calculating the total revenue, expenses, and net income for units sold values that range from 2,000 up to 3,000 units in increments of 100 units. In this worksheet, cell B4 is the input cell and cells B13 through B15 contain the results cells. These cells correspond to columns D through G in the one-variable data table. With this table, you can, at a glance, compare the financial outcomes for different amounts of bicycles sold by the company. For example, you can see that between 2,500 and 2,600 units sold the net income goes from positive to negative. You've already determined that the break-even point occurs at around 2,570 units sold, but the one-variable data table gives you a broader picture.

Figure 8–7	One-variable data table example

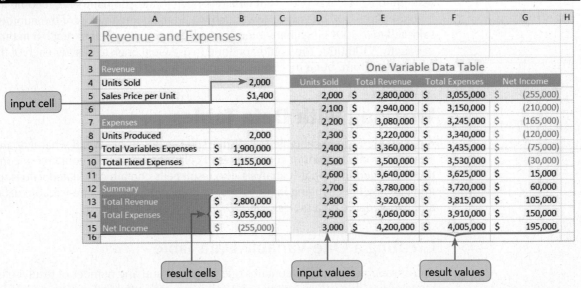

input cell → (points to Sales Price per Unit)

result cells

input values

result values

Roy wants to add a one-variable data table to the Income worksheet, with the units sold values going from 1,000 to 5,000 units in 500-unit increments. The first step is to set up the data table so that the first row of the table starts with a reference to the input cell in the worksheet, followed by references to one or more result cells.

To set up the one-variable data table to examine the impact of changing sales volume:

1. In cell **D3**, enter **Break-Even Analysis** as the table label, merge and center the range **D3:G3**, and then format the text with the **Heading 3** cell style.

2. In the range **D4:G4**, enter **Units Sold**, **Revenue**, **Expenses**, and **Net Income** as the labels, center the text in the selected cells, and then apply the **Accent 2** cell style to the cells.

3. In cell **D5**, enter the formula **=B5** to reference the input cell to be used in the data table.

4. In cell **E5**, enter the formula **=B25** to reference the result cell that displays the total revenue.

5. In cell **F5**, enter the formula **=B26** to reference the total expenses.

6. In cell **G5**, enter the formula **=B27** to reference the company's net income.

7. Format the range **E5:G5** using the **Accounting** format with no decimal places.

8. Format the range **D5:G5** with the **40% - Accent1** cell style and add a bottom border.

9. In the range **D6:D14**, enter Units Sold values from **1000** to **5000** in 500-unit increments, and then format the selected cells with the **Comma** style and no decimal places.

10. Select cell **D5**. See Figure 8–8.

Figure 8–8   Setup for the one-variable data table

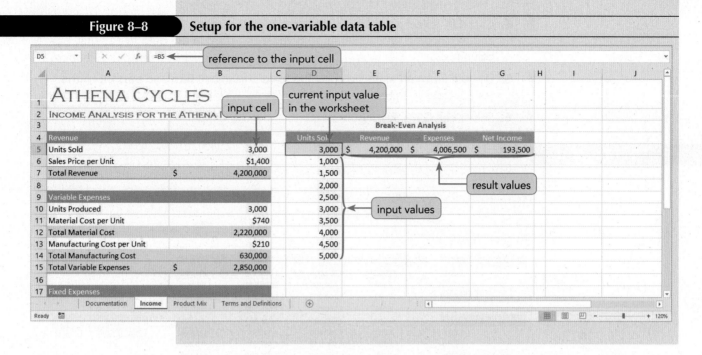

A one-variable data table is based on either a row input cell matching the values placed in the first row of the data table or a column input cell matching the values in the data table's first column. You want to find the revenue, expenses, and net income values for different units sold figures, so you will match the value from cell B5 to the units sold values in the first column of the data table.

To complete the one-variable data table:

1. Select the range **D5:G14** containing the cells for the data table.

2. On the Data tab, in the Forecast group, click the **What-If Analysis** button, and then click **Data Table**. The Data Table dialog box opens.

3. Press **TAB** to move the insertion point to the Column input cell box, and then click cell **B5** in the Income worksheet to indicate that all the result values in the data table first column should be matched with cell B5. The absolute reference $B$5 appears in the Column input box. See Figure 8–9.

Figure 8–9   Data Table dialog box

Data Table   ?   ×

Row input cell: ⬚   ⬆

Column input cell: $B$5 ⬆   ← input cell for the values in the first column of the data table

OK   Cancel

4. Click **OK**. Excel completes the data table by entering the revenue, expenses, and net income for each units sold value specified in the data table's first column.

5. Use the Format Painter to copy the format from cell **B25** and apply it to the result values in the range **E6:G14**.

6. Select cell **G14**. See Figure 8–10.

Figure 8–10   **Completed one-variable data table**

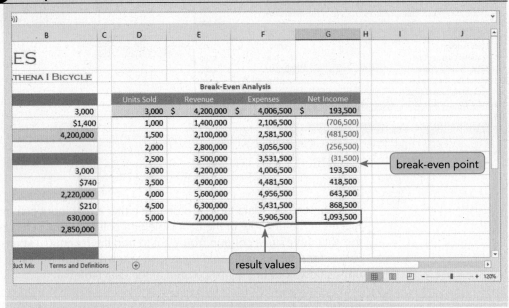

The data table shows the results of several what-if analyses simultaneously. For example, if 4,500 Athena I bicycles are sold, the revenue would be $6,300,000, but the total expenses would be $5,431,500, yielding a net income of $868,500.

Charting a One-Variable Data Table

The one-variable data table provides the results of several what-if analyses, but the results are often clearer if you include a CVP chart along with the table. The chart gives a better picture of the relationship between sales volume, revenue, and expenses. You'll use a scatter chart to map out the revenue and total expenses against the total number of units sold.

To create the CVP chart of the data table:

1. Select the range **D4:F14** containing the data you want to chart.

2. On the ribbon, click the **Insert** tab.

3. In the Charts group, click the **Insert Scatter (X, Y) or Bubble Chart** button, and then click **Scatter with Straight Lines** (the second option in the second row of the Scatter section). Each point in the data table is plotted on the chart and connected with a line. The break-even point occurs where the two lines cross.

4. Move and resize the chart so that it covers the range **D15:G27**.

5. Remove the chart title from the chart.

6. Change the fill color of the chart area to **Ice Blue, Accent 1, Lighter 80%**, and then change the fill color of the plot area to **White, Background 1**. See Figure 8–11.

Figure 8–11   Completed CVP chart

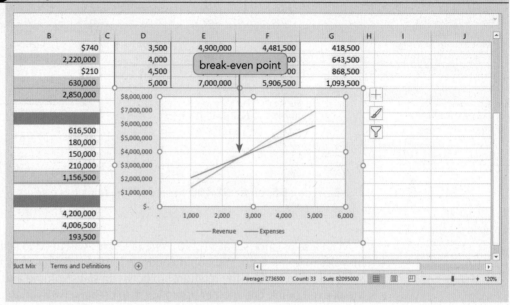

The line chart provides a visual representation of the break-even point that Roy can use in reports that he presents to other members of the Athena Cycles sales team.

Modifying a Data Table

Data tables are dynamic, which means that changes in the worksheet data are automatically reflected in the data table result values. This includes changes to cells that are displayed in data table but are involved in the results calculations. Athena Cycles is considering lowering its prices to be more competitive with other manufacturers. Roy wants you to perform another what-if analysis that examines the effect of reducing sales price of the Athena I from $1,400 to $1,250. Changing the value in the Income worksheet will affect other results in the sheet, including the what-if analysis displayed in the one-variable data table and the break-even chart.

To view the impact of changing the sales price:

1. In cell **B6**, enter **$1,250** to reduce the sales price of the Athena I. At this lower sales price, the break-even point moves to somewhere between 3,500 and 4,000 units—a fact reflected in both the data table and the CVP chart. See Figure 8–12.

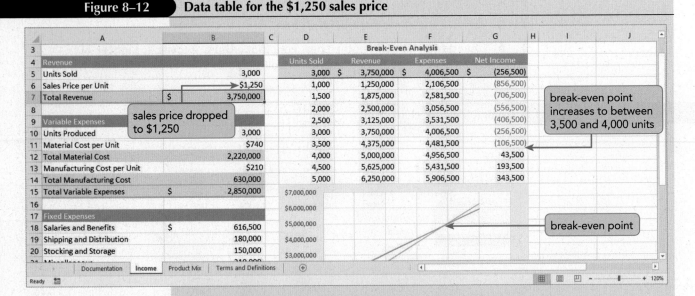

Figure 8–12   Data table for the $1,250 sales price

2. In cell **B6**, enter **$1,400** to return the sales price to its original value.

With a sales price set at $1,250, Athena Cycles will need to sell about 4,000 Athena I bicycles to break-even. You could continue to perform what-if analyses with different sales prices to explore the relationship between sales volume and sales price on the break-even point, but another approach is to create a two-variable data table.

Insight

Directly Calculating the Break-Even Point

A CVP chart is a useful visual tool for displaying the break-even point. You can also calculate the break-even point directly by using the following formula:

$$break\text{-}even\ point = \frac{fixed\ expenses}{sales\ price\ per\ unit - variable\ expenses\ per\ unit}$$

For example, with a sales price of $1,250, fixed expenses of $1,156,500, and variable expenses of $950 per unit, the following equation calculates the break-even point:

$$break\text{-}even\ point = \frac{1,156,500}{1,250 - 950} = 3,855$$

Athena Cycles would have to sell 3,855 Athena I bikes to break-even. If the company sells more than that number, the company will show a profit.

Creating a Two-Variable Data Table

A two-variable data table lets you view the relationship between two input cells and one result cell. Figure 8–13 shows a two-variable data table that examines the impact of sales price and sales volume on the company's net income.

Figure 8–13   Two-variable data table example

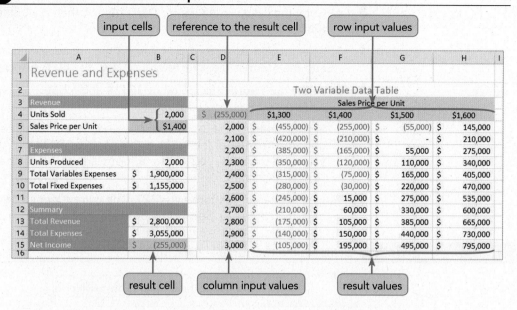

The two input cells are cell B4 and cell B5, containing the units sold and the sales price per unit. The first column of the data table displays a range of possible values for the first input cell (units sold) and the first row contains possible values for the second input cell (sales price). The result cell is cell D4—net income—and references the value in cell B15. The data table shows the net income for each combination of input values. For example, selling 2,200 bikes at $1,500 each will result in a net income of $55,000 (cell G7).

Reference

Creating a Two-Variable Data Table

- In the upper-left cell of the table, enter a formula that references the result cell.
- In the first row and first column of the table, enter input values.
- Select the table (excluding any row or column headings).
- On the Data tab, in the Forecast group, click the What-If Analysis button, and then click Data Table.
- Enter the cell reference to the first row input values in the Row input cell box, and then enter the cell reference to the first column input values in the Column input cell box.
- Click OK.

Roy wants you to examine the impact of the sales price and the yearly sales volume on the net income from selling the Athena I. You'll create a two-variable data table to do this.

To set up the two-variable data table:

1. In cell **I3**, enter **Net Income Analysis**, merge and center the range **I3:N3**, and then format the merged range with the **Heading 3** cell style.

2. In cell **I4**, enter **Sales Price**, and then merge and center the range **I4:N4**.

3. In the range **J5:N5**, enter the possible sales prices **$1,000** through **$1,800** in increments of $200.

4. Copy the values in the range **D6:D14**, and then paste them into the range **I6:I14**.

5. Select the two sets of input values in the nonadjacent range **J5:N5, I6:I14**, and then format the selected range with the **40% - Accent1** cell style.

6. Add a right border to the range **I6:I14** and a bottom border to the range **J5:N5**.

   In two-variable data tables, the reference to the result cell is placed in the upper-left corner of the table at the intersection of the row and column input values. In this case, you'll enter a formula in cell I5 that references the company's net income.

7. In cell **I5**, enter the formula **=B27**. The current net income value $193,500 is displayed in cell I5. See Figure 8–14.

Figure 8–14	Setup for the two-variable data table

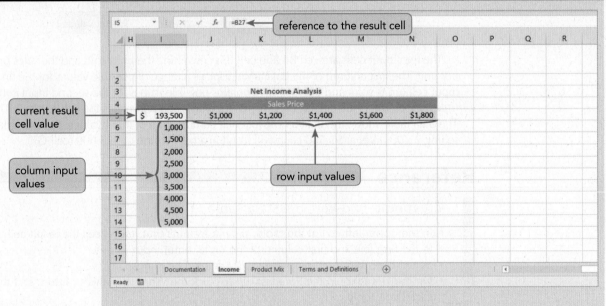

The two-variable data table is generated using the same Data Table command used with the one-variable data table, except that you specify both the row input cell (matched to the values in the first row of the table) and the column input cell (matched to the values in the table's first column).

To generate the result values:

1. Select the range **I5:N14** containing the row input values, the column input values, and the reference to the result cell.

2. On the ribbon, click the **Data** tab. In the Forecast group, click the **What-If Analysis** button, and then click **Data Table**. The Data Table dialog box opens.

3. In the Row input cell box, type **B6** to reference the sales price from the income statement.

4. In the Column input cell box, type **B5** to reference the number of units sold from the income statement.

5. Click **OK**. The data table values appear in the range J6:N14.

6. Use the Format Painter to copy the formatting from cell **G14** to the range **J6:N14**.

7. Click cell **J6** to deselect the highlighted range. See Figure 8–15.

| Figure 8–15 | Completed two-variable data table |

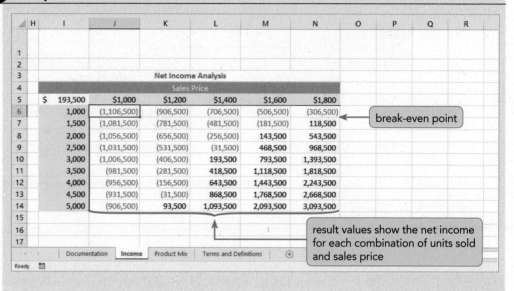

The break-even points for different combinations of price and units sold are easy to track because negative net income values are displayed in red and positive net income values are displayed in black. For example, if the sales price is set at $1,600, Athena Cycles must sell between 1,500 and 2,000 Athena I bicycles to break even. However, if the price is decreased to $1,000, no break-even point appears in the table, indicating that the company must sell much more than 5,000 Athena I bicycles to break even.

Formatting the Result Cell

The reference to the result cell in the table's upper-left corner might confuse some users. To prevent that, you can hide the cell value using the custom cell format "*text*", where *text* is the text you want to display in place of the cell value. In this case, Ron wants you to use a custom format to display "Units Sold" instead of the value in cell I5.

To apply a custom format to cell I5:

1. Right-click cell **I5**, and then click **Format Cells** on the shortcut menu (or press **CTRL+1**). The Format Cells dialog box opens.

2. If necessary, click the **Number** tab, and then in the Category box, click **Custom**.

> Be sure to use opening and closing quotation marks around the custom text.

3. In the Type box, select the format code text, and replace it with the text string **"Units Sold"** (including the quotation marks) as the custom text to display in the cell. See Figure 8–16.

Figure 8–16 Format Cells dialog box

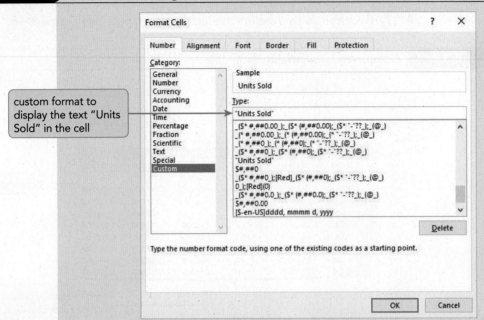

custom format to display the text "Units Sold" in the cell

> **Tip**
>
> You can also hide the reference to the result cell by applying the same font and fill color to the cell.

4. Click **OK**. The text "Units Sold" appears in cell I5 even though the cell's underlying formula is =B27.

Trouble? If "Units Sold" does not appear in cell I5, you probably didn't include the quotation marks in the custom format. Repeat Steps 1 through 4, making sure that you include both opening and closing quotation marks.

Charting a Two-Variable Data Table

You can chart the values from a two-variable data table using lines to represent the different columns of the table. Roy wants you to create a scatter chart based on the two-variable data table you just created.

To create a chart of the two-variable data table:

1. Select the range **I6:N14**. You'll plot this range on a scatter chart. You did not select the unit prices in row 5 because Excel would interpret these values as data values to be charted, not as labels.

2. On the ribbon, click the **Insert** tab. In the Charts group, click the **Insert Scatter (X, Y) or Bubble Chart** button , and then click the **Scatter with Straight Lines** chart subtype (the second chart in the second row of the Scatter section).

3. Move and resize the chart so that it covers the range **I15:N27**.

4. Remove the chart title, and then position the chart legend to the right of the chart.

5. Change the fill color of the chart area to **Ice Blue, Accent 1, Lighter 80%**, and then change the fill color of the plot area to **White, Background 1**. See Figure 8–17.

| Figure 8–17 | Chart of net income values |

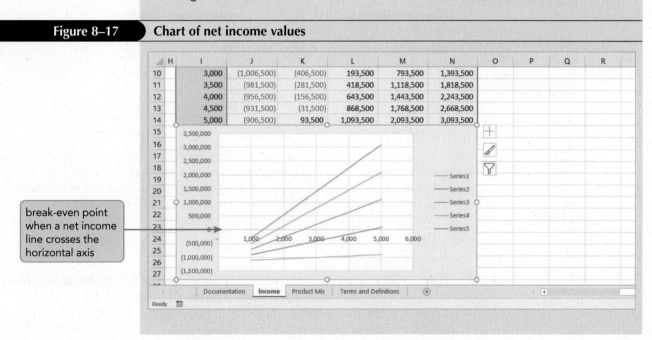

The chart shows a different trend line for each of the five possible values for unit price. However, the prices are not listed in the chart, and Excel uses generic series names (Series1, Series2, Series3, Series4, and Series5). To display the unit prices rather than the generic names in the chart, you must add the unit price values as series names.

To edit the chart series names:

1. On the Chart Design tab, in the Data group, click the **Select Data** button. The Select Data Source dialog box opens.

2. In the Legend Entries (Series) box, click **Series1**, and then click **Edit**. The Edit Series dialog box opens.

3. With the insertion point in the Series name box, click cell **J5** to insert the reference =Income!$J$5, and then click **OK**. The Select Data Source dialog box reappears with the Series1 name changed to $1,000. See Figure 8–18.

Figure 8–18   Select Data Source dialog box

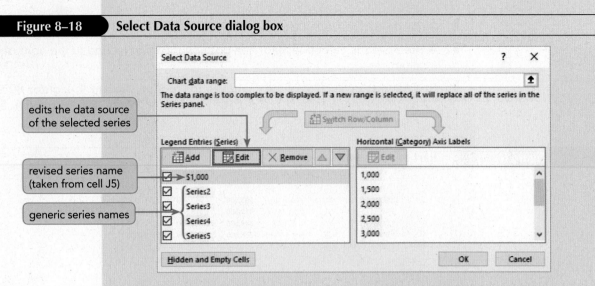

edits the data source
of the selected series

revised series name
(taken from cell J5)

generic series names

4. Repeat Steps 2 and 3 to edit Series2 to use cell **K5** as the series name, edit Series3 to use cell **L5** as the series name, edit Series4 to use cell **M5** as the series name, and edit Series5 to use cell **N5** as the series name. All the chart series are renamed to match the sales price values in row 5 of the two-variable data table.

5. Click **OK**. The Select Data Source dialog box closes, and the legend shows the renamed series.

6. On the Chart Design tab, in the Chart Styles group, click the **Change Colors** button, and then click **Monochromatic Palette 10** in the Monochromatic section. The line colors change to shades of olive green, reflecting the increasing value of the unit price. See Figure 8–19.

Figure 8–19   Final chart of net income values

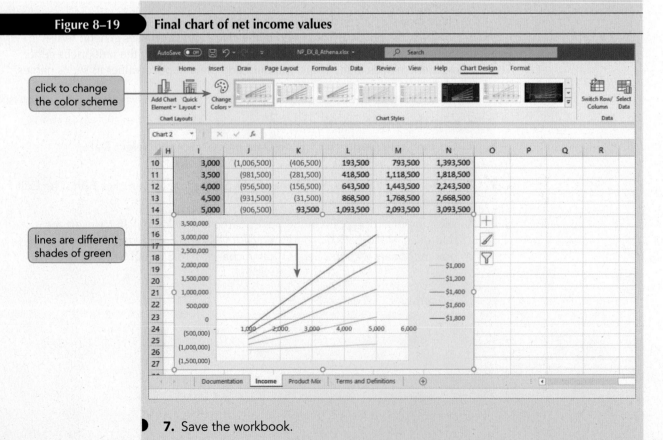

click to change
the color scheme

lines are different
shades of green

7. Save the workbook.

The chart shows how different unit prices will affect the relationship between sales volume and net income; where each line crosses the horizontal axis indicates the break-even point for that sales price. For example, the $1,600 line (the second highest of the five lines) crosses the horizontal axis near 1,800 units, indicating that with sales price of $1,600, the company will have to sell about 1,800 Athena I bicycles to break even.

Insight

Data Tables and Arrays

If you examine the cells in the two-variable data table you just created, you can see that every cell displays a different value even though it has the same formula: `{=TABLE(B6, B5)}`. This formula is an **array formula**, which performs multiple calculations in a single step, returning either a single value to one cell or multiple values to several cells. Array formulas are always enclosed within curly braces.

An array formula that returns a single value is `{=SUM(B1:B10*C1:C10)}`. This formula multiplies each cell in the range B1:B10 by the matching cell in the same row of the range C1:C10. The sum of those 10 products is then calculated and returned. To create this array formula, enter the formula `=SUM(B1:B10*C1:C10)` in the formula bar and then press CTRL+SHIFT+ENTER. Excel treats the formula as an array formula, adding the curly braces for you.

The TABLE function is an array function that returns multiple values to multiple cells. Other such functions include the TREND, MINVERSE, MMULT, and TRANSPOSE functions. To calculate multiple cell values, select the range, type the array formula, and then press CTRL+SHIFT+ENTER to enter the formula. Excel applies the array formula to all the selected cells.

Array formulas are a powerful feature of Excel. They can perform complex calculations within a single expression and extend a single formula over a range of cells. Use Excel Help to learn more about array formulas and the functions that support them.

So far, you have used what-if analysis with Goal Seek and data tables to analyze how the number of Athena I bikes sold and the sales price impact the company's net income. In the next session, you will use other what-if analysis tools to examine the impact of more than two input values on multiple result values.

Review

Session 8.1 Quick Check

1. Describe the difference between a variable expense and a fixed expense.
2. When does the break-even point occur?
3. What is a data table? What is an input cell? What is a result cell?
4. What is a one-variable data table? What is a two-variable data table?
5. How many result cells can you display with a one-variable data table? How many result cells can you display with a two-variable data table?
6. Cell E5 contains the formula =B10. You want to display the text "Profits" instead of the formula's value. What custom format would you use?
7. What is an array formula?

Session 8.2 Visual Overview:

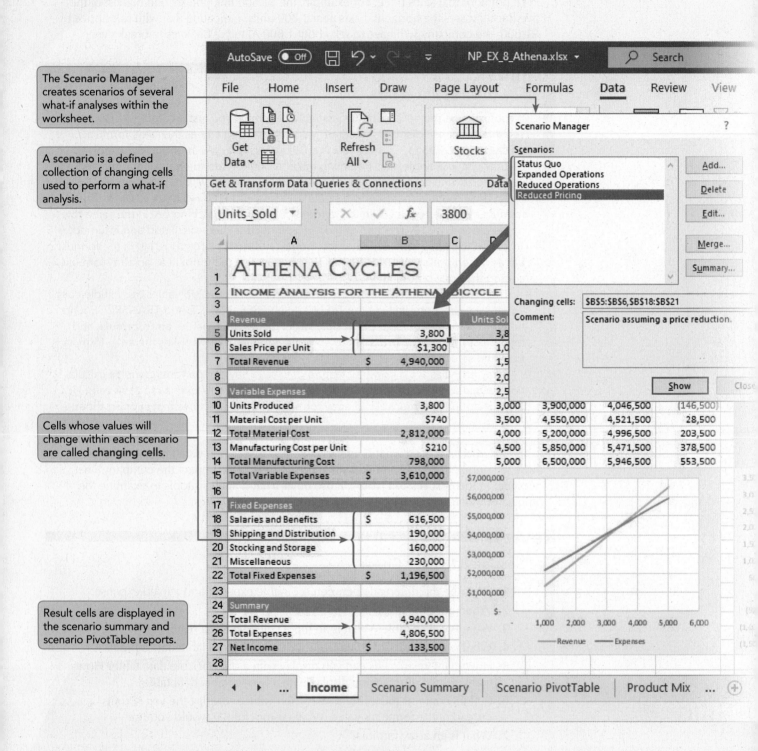

The Scenario Manager creates scenarios of several what-if analyses within the worksheet.

A scenario is a defined collection of changing cells used to perform a what-if analysis.

Cells whose values will change within each scenario are called changing cells.

Result cells are displayed in the scenario summary and scenario PivotTable reports.

What-If Scenarios

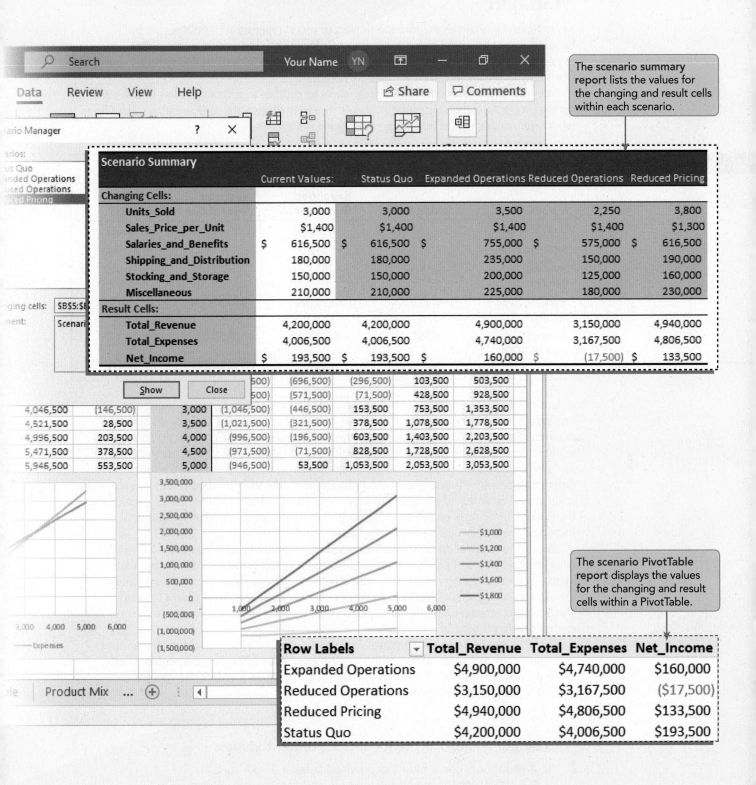

The scenario summary report lists the values for the changing and result cells within each scenario.

The scenario PivotTable report displays the values for the changing and result cells within a PivotTable.

Scenario Summary

	Current Values:	Status Quo	Expanded Operations	Reduced Operations	Reduced Pricing
Changing Cells:					
Units_Sold	3,000	3,000	3,500	2,250	3,800
Sales_Price_per_Unit	$1,400	$1,400	$1,400	$1,400	$1,300
Salaries_and_Benefits	$ 616,500	$ 616,500	$ 755,000	$ 575,000	$ 616,500
Shipping_and_Distribution	180,000	180,000	235,000	150,000	190,000
Stocking_and_Storage	150,000	150,000	200,000	125,000	160,000
Miscellaneous	210,000	210,000	225,000	180,000	230,000
Result Cells:					
Total_Revenue	4,200,000	4,200,000	4,900,000	3,150,000	4,940,000
Total_Expenses	4,006,500	4,006,500	4,740,000	3,167,500	4,806,500
Net_Income	$ 193,500	$ 193,500	$ 160,000	$ (17,500)	$ 133,500

Row Labels	Total_Revenue	Total_Expenses	Net_Income
Expanded Operations	$4,900,000	$4,740,000	$160,000
Reduced Operations	$3,150,000	$3,167,500	($17,500)
Reduced Pricing	$4,940,000	$4,806,500	$133,500
Status Quo	$4,200,000	$4,006,500	$193,500

Exploring Financial Scenarios with Scenario Manager

Many financial analyses explore the impact of several factors on a final result, but because data tables are limited to at most two input cells, you must create a scenario to perform a what-if analysis that involves more than two factors. In this session, you'll learn how to create scenarios for a financial analysis.

After reviewing your data tables, Roy wants to explore four other models or scenarios for the production and sale of the Athena I. Figure 8–20 lists the four scenarios, detailing what input values would be changed under each scenario.

Figure 8–20   What-if scenarios

Input Cells	Status Quo	Expanded Operations	Reduced Operations	Reduced Pricing
Units Sold (B5)	3,000	3,500	2,250	4,000
Sales Price (B6)	$1,400	$1,400	$1,400	$1,300
Salaries and Benefits (B18)	$616,500	$755,000	$575,000	$616,500
Shipping and Distribution (B19)	$180,000	$235,000	$150,000	$190,000
Stocking and Storage (B20)	$150,000	$200,000	$125,000	$160,000
Miscellaneous (B21)	$210,000	$225,000	$180,000	$230,000

Under the Status Quo scenario, Roy assumes that the fixed expenses, units sold, and unit prices remain unchanged for the coming year. The Expanded Operations scenario assumes that the company will increase the total number of bikes produced and sold while at the same time increasing its expenditures on salaries and benefits, shipping and distribution, stocking and storage, and miscellaneous expenses. The Reduced Operations scenario foresees a gradual phase-out of the Athena I model with fewer units produced and sold accompanied by lower fixed costs for all categories. Finally, the Reduced Pricing scenario proposes cutting the sales price by $100, resulting in increased sales with slightly more fixed costs.

You cannot analyze these scenarios using a data table because you need six input cells. Instead, you will create the scenarios using the Scenario Manager. Rather than manually changing every input cell value, the Scenario Manager defines input values for each scenario, allowing you to switch the workbook from one scenario to another. The Scenario Manager can also be used to create reports summarizing the impact of each scenario on a set of result cells.

Before using the Scenario Manager, Roy wants you to define names for all the input and result cells that you will use in this what-if analysis. Although not a requirement, using defined names makes it easier to work with scenarios and for other people to understand the scenario reports.

To define names for the income statement values:

1. If you took a break after the previous session, make sure the NP_EX_8_Athena workbook is open, and the Income worksheet is the active sheet.

2. In the Income worksheet, select the range **A5:B6,A18:B21,A25:B27**. You'll define names for each of these cells.

3. On the ribbon, click the **Formulas** tab, and then in the Defined Names group, click the **Create from Selection** button. The Create Names from Selection dialog box opens.

4. Click the **Left column** check box to insert a checkmark, if necessary, and then click any other check box that has a checkmark to deselect it.

5. Click **OK**. The cell values in column B are named using the labels in the corresponding cells in column A.

6. Click cell **A1** to deselect the range.

Defining a Scenario

Now that you've defined the names used in the worksheet, you'll use the Scenario Manager to create scenarios based on the values shown in Figure 8–20. Each scenario includes a scenario name, a list of input or changing cells, and the values of each input cell under the scenario. The number of scenarios you can create is limited only by your computer's memory.

Reference

Defining a Scenario

- Enter the data values in the worksheet for the scenario.
- On the Data tab, in the Forecast group, click the What-If Analysis button, and then click Scenario Manager.
- Click Add in the Scenario Manager dialog box.
- In the Scenario name box, type a name for the scenario.
- In the Changing cells box, specify the changing cells.
- Click OK.
- In the Scenario Values dialog box, specify values for each input cell, and then click Add.
- Click OK.

You'll start by creating the Status Quo scenario, whose values match those currently entered in the workbook.

To add the Status Quo scenario:

1. On the ribbon, click the **Data** tab. In the Forecast group, click the **What-If Analysis** button, and then click **Scenario Manager**. The Scenario Manager dialog box opens. No scenarios are defined yet.

2. Click **Add**. The Add Scenario dialog box opens.

3. In the Scenario name box, type **Status Quo**, and then press **TAB**. The cell reference in the Changing cells box is selected.

Tip

Scenarios are limited to a maximum of 32 changing cells.

The Scenario Manager refers to input cells as "changing cells" because these worksheet cells contain values that are changed under the scenario. Changing cells can be located anywhere in the current worksheet. You can type the range names or locations of changing cells, but it's faster and more accurate to select them with the mouse.

The changing cells for each of the four scenarios are:

- Cell B5: Units Sold
- Cell B6: Sales Price per Unit
- Cell B18: Salaries and Benefits
- Cell B19: Shipping and Distribution
- Cell B20: Stocking and Storage
- Cell B21: Miscellaneous

You'll specify these cells as the changing cells for the Status Quo scenario.

To specify the changing cells for the Status Quo scenario:

1. With the Changing cells box still active, select the nonadjacent range **B5:B6,B18:B21**. Absolute references for the range appear in the Changing cells box. These are the input cells.

2. Press **TAB** to select the default text in the Comment box, and then type **Scenario assuming no change in values** in the Comment box. See Figure 8–21.

Figure 8–21	Edit Scenario dialog box

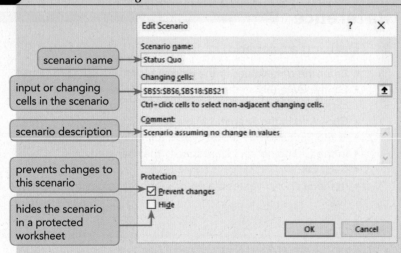

3. Click **OK**. The Scenario Values dialog box opens so you can enter values for each changing cell you entered in the Changing cells box in the Edit Scenario dialog box. The Status Quo scenario values already appear in the dialog box because these are the current values in the workbook. See Figure 8–22.

Figure 8–22	Scenario Values dialog box

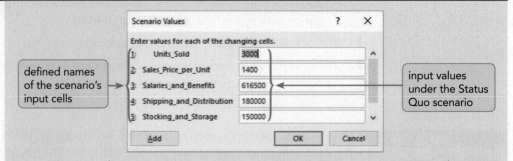

4. Click **OK**. The Scenario Manager dialog box reopens with the Status Quo scenario listed in the Scenarios box. See Figure 8–23.

Figure 8–23   Scenario Manager dialog box

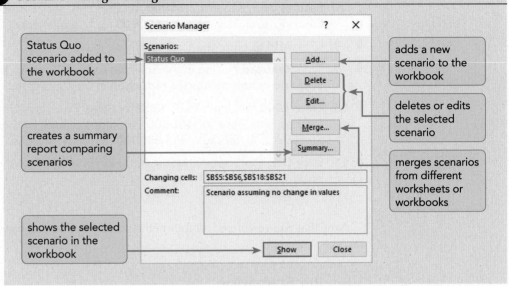

You'll use the same process to add the remaining three scenarios on Roy's list—Expanded Operations, Reduced Operations, and Reduced Pricing.

To add the remaining scenarios:

1. Click **Add**. The Add Scenario dialog box opens.

2. In the Scenario name box, type **Expanded Operations**, press **TAB** twice to go the Comment box, and then type **Scenario assuming expanded operations** in the Comment box.

   Note that the nonadjacent range you selected for the Status Quo scenario appears in the Changing cells box. Because you want to use the same set of changing cells, you didn't edit the range.

3. Click **OK**. The Scenario Values dialog box for the Expanded Operations scenario opens.

> Be sure you enter the values for the scenario; do not simply accept the default values currently in the worksheet.

4. Enter the following values, pressing **TAB** to move from one input box to the next: **3500** for Units_Sold, **1400** for Sales_Price_per_Unit, **755000** for Salaries_and_Benefits, **235000** for Shipping_and_Distribution, **200000** for Stocking_and_Storage, and **225000** for Miscellaneous.

   Trouble? If the Scenario Manager dialog box reopens, you probably pressed ENTER instead of TAB. Make sure that the Expanded Operations scenario is selected in the Scenarios box, click Edit, and then click OK to return to the Scenario Values dialog box. Enter the remaining values in the scenario, being sure to press TAB to move to the next input box.

5. Click **Add**. The Add Scenario dialog box reopens so you can enter the next scenario.

   Trouble? If the Scenario Manager dialog box reopens, you clicked OK instead of Add. Click Add in the Scenario Manager dialog box to return to the Add Scenario dialog box, and then continue with Step 6.

6. Type **Reduced Operations** in the Scenario name box, press **TAB** twice, type **Scenario assuming reduced operations** in the Comment box, and then click **OK**.

▶ 7. Enter **2250** for Units_Sold, **1400** for Sales_Price_per_Unit, **575000** for Salaries_and_Benefits, **150000** for Shipping_and_Distribution, **125000** for Stocking_and_Storage, and **180000** for Miscellaneous.

▶ 8. Click **Add** to enter the final scenario.

▶ 9. Type **Reduced Pricing** in the Scenario name box, press **TAB** twice, type **Scenario assuming a price reduction** in the Comment box, and then click **OK**.

▶ 10. Enter **4000** for Units_Sold, **1300** for Sales_Price_per_Unit, **616500** for Salaries_and_Benefits, **190000** for Shipping_and_Distribution, **160000** for Stocking_and_Storage, and **230000** for Miscellaneous.

▶ 11. Click **OK**. The Scenario Manager dialog box reappears with all four scenarios listed.

Now that you've entered all four of the scenarios, you can view their impact on the income statement.

Viewing Scenarios

You can view the effect of each scenario by selecting that scenario in the Scenario Manager dialog box. You switch from one scenario to another by clicking Show in the Scenario Manager dialog box. You do not have to close the dialog box to switch scenarios. You'll start by viewing the results of the Expanded Operations scenario.

To view the impact of the Expanded Operations scenario:

▶ 1. In the Scenario Manager dialog box, in the Scenarios box, click **Expanded Operations**. The changing cells and the comment for the selected scenario appear at the bottom of the Scenario Manager dialog box.

Tip

You can double-click a scenario name in the Scenario Manager dialog box to view that scenario.

▶ 2. Click **Show**. The values in the Income worksheet change to reflect the scenario.

▶ 3. Click **Close**. The Scenario Manager dialog box closes. The income statement for is updated to show expanded operations with increased fixed expenses. See Figure 8–24.

Figure 8–24   **Income statement under the Expanded Operations scenario**

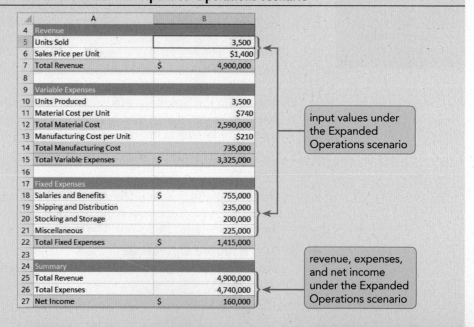

	A	B
4	Revenue	
5	Units Sold	3,500
6	Sales Price per Unit	$1,400
7	Total Revenue	$ 4,900,000
8		
9	Variable Expenses	
10	Units Produced	3,500
11	Material Cost per Unit	$740
12	Total Material Cost	2,590,000
13	Manufacturing Cost per Unit	$210
14	Total Manufacturing Cost	735,000
15	Total Variable Expenses	$ 3,325,000
16		
17	Fixed Expenses	
18	Salaries and Benefits	$ 755,000
19	Shipping and Distribution	235,000
20	Stocking and Storage	200,000
21	Miscellaneous	225,000
22	Total Fixed Expenses	$ 1,415,000
23		
24	Summary	
25	Total Revenue	4,900,000
26	Total Expenses	4,740,000
27	Net Income	$ 160,000

input values under the Expanded Operations scenario

revenue, expenses, and net income under the Expanded Operations scenario

Trouble? If the values in your income statement do not match those in the figure, you probably entered the values for the scenario incorrectly. You'll learn how to edit a scenario shortly, and can then enter the correct values.

Excel automatically changes the values of the six input cells to match the scenario. Under the Expanded Operations scenario, the company's net income in cell B7 declines from the current value of $193,500 to $160,000. You'll review the other scenarios.

To view the impact of the remaining scenarios:

1. On the Data tab, in the Forecast group, click the **What-If Analysis** button, and then click **Scenario Manager**. The Scenario Manager dialog box opens.

2. In the Scenarios box, double-click **Reduced Operations** to update the worksheet, and then click **Close** to close the Scenario Manager dialog box. Under the Reduced Operations scenario, the company will show a net loss of $17,500 in the sales of Athena I bikes.

3. Repeat Steps 1 and 2 to update the worksheet with the **Reduced Pricing** scenario. Under that scenario, the company would generate a net income of $203,500. Figure 8–25 shows the income statements under both scenarios.

Figure 8–25	Income statements under the Reduced Operations and Reduced Pricing scenarios

Reduced Operations

	A	B
4	Revenue	
5	Units Sold	2,250
6	Sales Price per Unit	$1,400
7	Total Revenue	$ 3,150,000
8		
9	Variable Expenses	
10	Units Produced	2,250
11	Material Cost per Unit	$740
12	Total Material Cost	1,665,000
13	Manufacturing Cost per Unit	$210
14	Total Manufacturing Cost	472,500
15	Total Variable Expenses	$ 2,137,500
16		
17	Fixed Expenses	
18	Salaries and Benefits	$ 575,000
19	Shipping and Distribution	150,000
20	Stocking and Storage	125,000
21	Miscellaneous	180,000
22	Total Fixed Expenses	$ 1,030,000
23		
24	Summary	
25	Total Revenue	3,150,000
26	Total Expenses	3,167,500
27	Net Income	$ (17,500)

Reduced Pricing

	A	B
4	Revenue	
5	Units Sold	4,000
6	Sales Price per Unit	$1,300
7	Total Revenue	$ 5,200,000
8		
9	Variable Expenses	
10	Units Produced	4,000
11	Material Cost per Unit	$740
12	Total Material Cost	2,960,000
13	Manufacturing Cost per Unit	$210
14	Total Manufacturing Cost	840,000
15	Total Variable Expenses	$ 3,800,000
16		
17	Fixed Expenses	
18	Salaries and Benefits	$ 616,500
19	Shipping and Distribution	190,000
20	Stocking and Storage	160,000
21	Miscellaneous	230,000
22	Total Fixed Expenses	$ 1,196,500
23		
24	Summary	
25	Total Revenue	5,200,000
26	Total Expenses	4,996,500
27	Net Income	$ 203,500

When you substitute a new scenario for the Status Quo scenario, all the worksheet values and charts are automatically updated. For example, under the Reduced Pricing scenario, the one-variable and two-variable data tables changed to reflect the new values of the input and result cells. The break-even point for the Reduced Pricing scenario is close to 3,500 units.

Editing a Scenario

After you create a scenario, you can edit its assumptions to view other possible outcomes. When you edit a scenario, the worksheet calculations are automatically updated to reflect the revised input values.

The Reduced Pricing scenario results in the highest net income, but it relies on the company selling 4,000 Athena I bikes for $1,300 per model to generate a net income of $203,500. Roy is unsure whether the company can meet that sales goal at that sales price. He asks you to modify the Reduced Pricing scenario, reducing the total sales to 3,800 units to see how this impacts the company's profitability.

To edit the Reduced Pricing scenario:

▶ **1.** On the Data tab, in the Forecast group, click the **What-If Analysis** button, and then click **Scenario Manager**. The Scenario Manager dialog box opens.

▶ **2.** In the Scenarios box, click **Reduced Pricing** if it is not already selected, and then click **Edit**. The Edit Scenario dialog box opens. You don't need to make any changes in this dialog box.

▶ **3.** Click **OK**. The Scenario Values dialog box opens.

▶ **4.** Change the Units_Sold value from 4000 to **3800**, and then click **OK** to return to the Scenario Manager dialog box.

▶ **5.** Click **Show**, and then click **Close**. The Income worksheet updates to reflect the revised scenario, which results in net income decreasing from $203,500 to $133,500—a decline of $70,000. See Figure 8–26.

Figure 8–26   **Revised Reduced Pricing scenario**

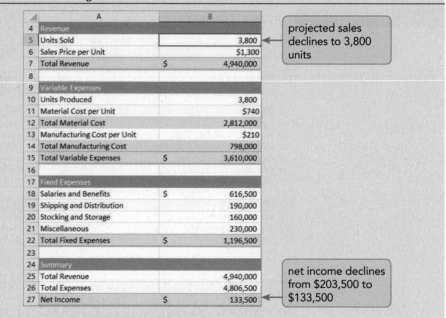

	A	B
4	Revenue	
5	Units Sold	3,800
6	Sales Price per Unit	$1,300
7	Total Revenue	$ 4,940,000
8		
9	Variable Expenses	
10	Units Produced	3,800
11	Material Cost per Unit	$740
12	Total Material Cost	2,812,000
13	Manufacturing Cost per Unit	$210
14	Total Manufacturing Cost	798,000
15	Total Variable Expenses	$ 3,610,000
16		
17	Fixed Expenses	
18	Salaries and Benefits	$ 616,500
19	Shipping and Distribution	190,000
20	Stocking and Storage	160,000
21	Miscellaneous	230,000
22	Total Fixed Expenses	$ 1,196,500
23		
24	Summary	
25	Total Revenue	4,940,000
26	Total Expenses	4,806,500
27	Net Income	$ 133,500

projected sales declines to 3,800 units

net income declines from $203,500 to $133,500

▶ **6.** Open the Scenario Manager dialog box, and then double-click **Status Quo** in the Scenarios box to return the Income worksheet to the original values. Leave the Scenario Manager dialog box open.

Creating Scenario Summary Reports

Although scenarios can help you make important business decisions, repeatedly switching between scenarios can become time-consuming. You can summarize all your scenarios in a single report, either as an Excel table or PivotTable. Roy wants you to create both types of reports with the four scenarios you generated for the company, starting with a summary report that appears as an Excel table.

Reference

Creating a Scenario Summary Report or a Scenario PivotTable Report

- On the Data tab, in the Forecast group, click the What-If Analysis button, and then click Scenario Manager.
- Click Summary.
- Click the Scenario summary or Scenario PivotTable report option button.
- Select the result cells to display in the report.
- Click OK.

To create a scenario summary report, you must identify which result cells you want to include in the report. Roy is interested in the following result cells—cell B25 (Total Revenue), cell B26 (Total Expenses), and cell B27 (Net Income). You'll display these values along with the values of the input cell defined by the scenario in your report.

To create the scenario summary report:

▶ 1. In the Scenario Manager dialog box, click **Summary**. The Scenario Summary dialog box opens, allowing you to create a scenario summary report or a scenario PivotTable report. You want to create a scenario summary report.

▶ 2. Verify that the **Scenario summary** option button is selected.

▶ 3. Make sure that the reference in the Result cells box is selected, and then in the Income worksheet, select the range **B25:B27** to enter the range reference for the result cells you want to display in the report.

▶ 4. Click **OK**. The scenario summary report is inserted in the workbook as a new worksheet.

▶ 5. Move the Scenario Summary worksheet directly after the Income worksheet.

▶ 6. Increase the Zoom factor of the worksheet to **120%** to better view its contents. See Figure 8–27.

Figure 8–27	Scenario summary report

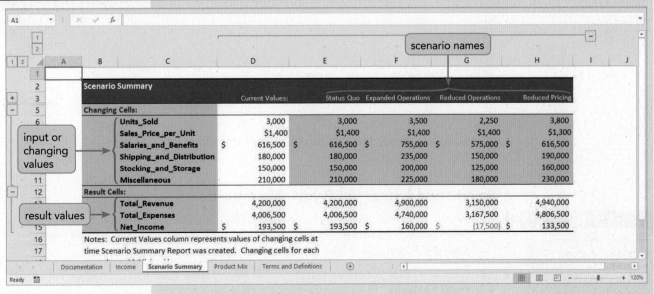

The scenario summary report displays the values of the changing cells and result cells under each scenario. Each scenario is listed by name, and the current worksheet values are also displayed. The report uses the defined names you created earlier to identify the changing and result cells, making the report simpler to interpret. The report also includes outline buttons to allow you expand and collapse different sections of the report, a useful feature when the scenarios involve many different input and result values.

Next, Roy wants you to compare the scenarios using a PivotTable report. As the name implies, a Scenario PivotTable report displays the results from each scenario as a PivotTable field within a PivotTable.

To create the Scenario PivotTable report:

1. Go to the **Income worksheet** and open the Scenario Manager dialog box.

2. Click **Summary** to open the Scenario Summary dialog box, and then click the **Scenario PivotTable report** option button. You'll use the same result cells for this report.

3. Click **OK**. The Scenario PivotTable sheet is inserted in the workbook and contains the scenario values in a PivotTable.

4. Move the Scenario PivotTable worksheet after the Scenario Summary worksheet, and then change the zoom level of the worksheet to **120%**. See Figure 8–28.

Figure 8–28   Scenario PivotTable report

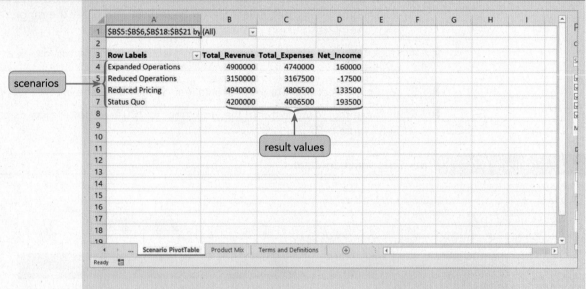

Roy wants you to edit the scenario PivotTable to make it easier to read.

To edit and format the PivotTable report:

1. In the PivotTable Fields pane, in the FILTERS area box, click the **$B$5:$B$6,$B$18:$B...** button, and then click **Remove Field**. You will not filter the PivotTable.

2. Click the **Total_Revenue** button in the Values area box, and then click **Value Field Settings**. The Value Field Settings dialog box opens.

3. Click **Number Format** to open the Format Cells dialog box, click **Currency** in the Category box, change the number of decimal places to **0**, and then click the last entry **($1,234)** in the Negative numbers box to display negative currency values in a red font enclosed in parentheses.

4. Click **OK** in each dialog box to return to the worksheet. The currency format is applied to the Total_Revenue cells.

5. Repeat Steps 2 through 4 for the **Total_Expenses** and the **Net_Income** buttons in the Values box to apply the same currency format.

6. In cell A1, enter **Scenario PivotTable**, and then format the text with the **Title** cell style. See Figure 8–29.

| Figure 8–29 | Formatted PivotTable report |

Row Labels	Total_Revenue	Total_Expenses	Net_Income
Expanded Operations	$4,900,000	$4,740,000	$160,000
Reduced Operations	$3,150,000	$3,167,500	($17,500)
Reduced Pricing	$4,940,000	$4,806,500	$133,500
Status Quo	$4,200,000	$4,006,500	$193,500

The Scenario Summary report and the Scenario PivotTable report are both static reports. If you alter the source data or the terms of the scenarios, those changes will not be reflected in either report. You will have to recreate the reports to view the impact of your edits.

Roy wants you to augment the Scenario PivotTable report with a chart of the scenario results. You'll add a PivotChart to the worksheet now.

To create a PivotChart with the scenario results:

1. Click cell **A3** to select the PivotTable.

2. On the ribbon, click the **PivotTable Analyze** tab, and then in the Tools group, click the **PivotChart** button. The Insert Chart dialog box opens.

3. On the All Charts tab, click the **Combo** chart type to create a combination chart.

4. Verify that the **Total_Revenue** and **Total_Expenses** series are displayed as clustered column charts and the **Net_Income** series is displayed as a line chart.

5. Click the **Secondary Axis** check box for the Net_Income series to chart those data values on a secondary axis.

▶ **6.** Click **OK** to create the chart.

▶ **7.** Move and resize the PivotChart to cover the range **A8:D19**.

▶ **8.** On the ribbon, click the **PivotChart Analyze** tab, and then in the Show/
Hide group, click the **Field Buttons** button. The field buttons in the chart are
hidden.

▶ **9.** Position the chart legend at the bottom of the chart. See Figure 8–30.

Figure 8–30	**Scenario PivotChart**

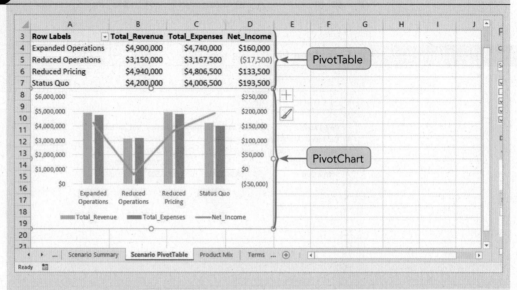

▶ **10.** Save the workbook.

Roy can now present an informative summary to the financial team at Athena
Cycles. Using that report the team can determine whether other scenarios need to be
explored. However, at the current time, the status quo appears to still offer the best
outcome in terms of net income.

Proskills

Teamwork: Merging Scenarios

In many businesses, several workbooks often track the same set of figures and evaluate the same set of scenarios. Colleagues can share scenarios by merging the scenarios from multiple workbooks into one workbook. The Scenario Manager dialog box includes a Merge button that you can use to merge scenarios from different workbooks. The scenarios will be merged into the active sheet, so they can be compared within a single document. It's easier to merge scenarios if all the what-if analyses on the different worksheets and workbooks are identical. All the changing cells from the merged scenario must correspond to changing cells in the active workbook and worksheet.

Once the scenarios are merged, they can be analyzed using a Scenario PivotTable report. One of the advantages of the Scenario PivotTable report over the Scenario Summary report is that you can use it with merged scenarios created by different users. For example, each member of the financial analysis team might propose different numbers for the various scenarios being considered. A Scenario PivotTable report can filter the four scenarios by user or show the average results across all users, giving the team a broader understanding of the various financial scenarios.

By sharing and merging scenarios, the team can more easily explore the impact of different financial situations, ensuring that everyone is always working from a common set of assumptions and goals.

In this session, you used scenarios to examine the impact of different financial scenarios on the profitability of the Athena I. However, the Athena I is just one of many models sold by Athena Cycles. In the next session, you'll explore how by promoting different models within its lineup, Athena Cycles can increase the profitability of its entire operation.

Review

Session 8.2 Quick Check

1. What is one advantage of scenarios over data tables?
2. What should you do before creating a scenario report to make the entries on the report easier to interpret?
3. What are changing cells in a scenario?
4. Where are the result cells in a scenario?
5. What are the two types of scenario reports?
6. When would you use the filter button in a Scenario PivotTable report?

Session 8.3 Visual Overview:

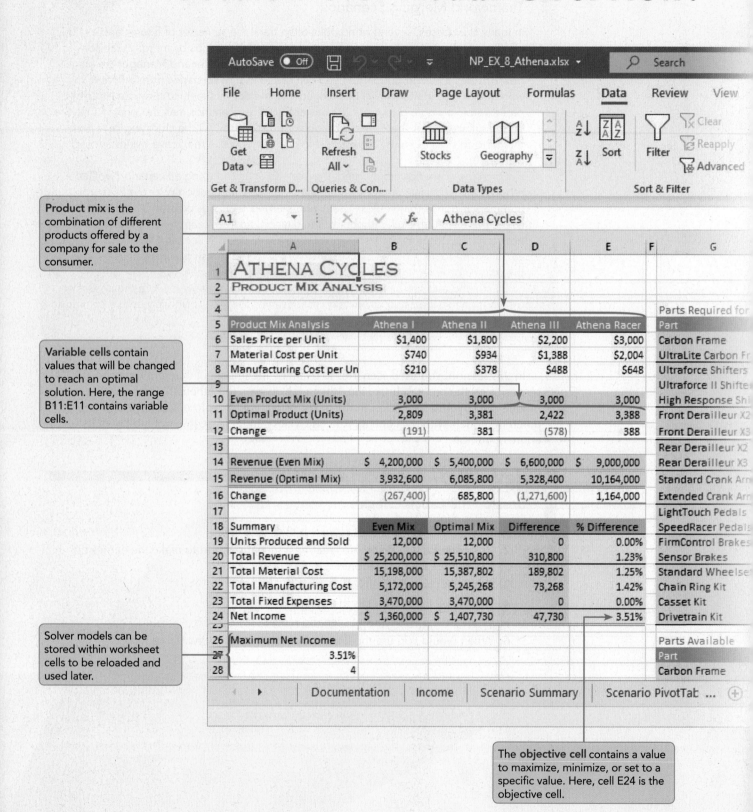

Product mix is the combination of different products offered by a company for sale to the consumer.

Variable cells contain values that will be changed to reach an optimal solution. Here, the range B11:E11 contains variable cells.

Solver models can be stored within worksheet cells to be reloaded and used later.

The **objective cell** contains a value to maximize, minimize, or set to a specific value. Here, cell E24 is the objective cell.

Optimal Solutions with Solver

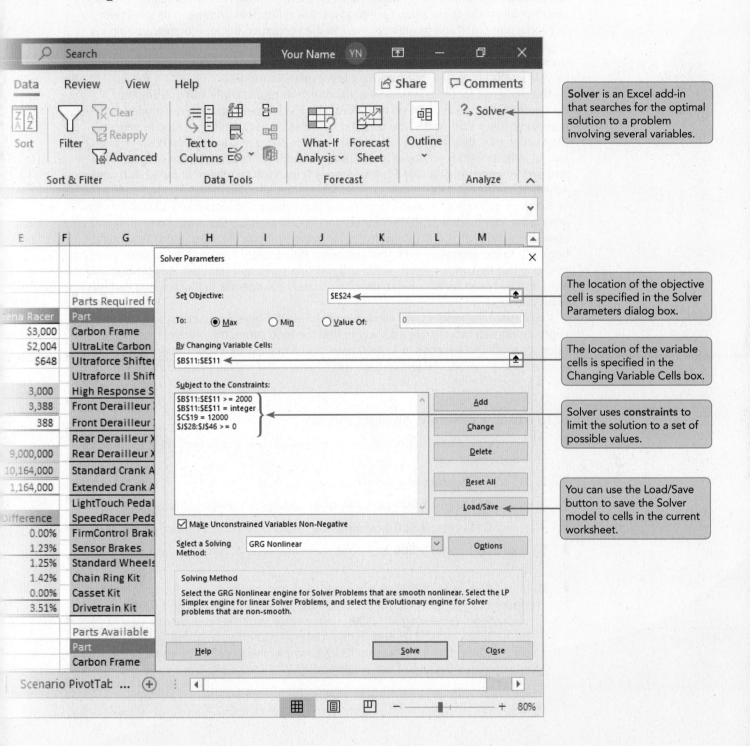

Optimizing a Product Mix

The combination of products offered by a company is known as the company's product mix. Not all products are alike. One product may differ from another in its sales price, its production costs, and its attractiveness to the consumer. Because of this, a company might find that it is profitable to devote more of its resources to selling one product over another. For example, Athena Cycles might make a larger profit on each high-end bicycle it sells compared to its profit on less expensive models.

The challenge for the company is to maximize its profits while still meeting the demands of the market. So even though Athena Cycles might make more money from some bikes than others, the demand for those bikes might be smaller. In general, companies want their product mix to cover a wide range of consumer needs. For that reason, Athena Cycles produces and sells four road bike models of increasing quality and performance: Athena I for $1,400, Athena II for $1,800, Athena III for $2,200, and Athena Racer for $3,000.

Based on sales projections, Roy estimates that Athena Cycles can sell 12,000 bicycles among the four models. If all the models are equally popular, that would mean that the company would sell 3,000 of each type. However, splitting the sales in that way might not result in the greatest profit to the company. Roy wants you to find the optimal product mix, one that maximizes profits while still meeting consumer demand. Any product mix must also be based on the availability of parts and resources for manufacturing that mix of bicycle models.

Roy created the Product Mix worksheet that lists the sales price, costs, and variable expenses of each bicycle. He asks you to find the most profitable product mix if total sales across all models stays at 12,000 units. You'll first explore how changing the number of bikes produced within each model affects the overall profitability of the line.

To explore different product mixes:

1. If you took a break after the previous session, make sure the NP_EX_8_Athena workbook is open.

2. Go to the **Product Mix** worksheet.

3. In cell **B11**, enter **1,500** as the number of Athena I bikes produced and sold.

4. In cell **C11**, enter **2,500** as the number of Athena II bikes produced and sold.

5. In cell **D11**, enter **3,500** as the number of Athena III bikes produced and sold.

6. In cell **E11**, enter **4,500** as the number of Athena Racers produced and sold. Under this product mix, the total number of bikes produced and sold is unchanged, remaining at 12,000 units overall, but the revenue has increased by 10.32% (cell E20). However, the material and manufacturing costs have also increased by 13.97% and 13.77%, respectively (cells E21 and E22), resulting in a decline of net income of 17.28% (cell E24). See Figure 8–31.

Figure 8–31   **Product mix assuming increasing sales for higher-end models**

bicycle models

	A	B	C	D	E
5	Product Mix Analysis	Athena I	Athena II	Athena III	Athena Racer
6	Sales Price per Unit	$1,400	$1,800	$2,200	$3,000
7	Material Cost per Unit	$740	$934	$1,388	$2,004
8	Manufacturing Cost per Unit	$210	$378	$488	$648
9					
10	Even Product Mix (Units)	3,000	3,000	3,000	3,000
11	Optimal Product (Units)	1,500	2,500	3,500	4,500
12	Change	(1,500)	(500)	500	1,500
13					
14	Revenue (Even Mix)	$ 4,200,000	$ 5,400,000	$ 6,600,000	$ 9,000,000
15	Revenue (Optimal Mix)	2,100,000	4,500,000	7,700,000	13,500,000
16	Change	(2,100,000)	(900,000)	1,100,000	4,500,000
17					
18	Summary	Even Mix	Optimal Mix	Difference	% Difference
19	Units Produced and Sold	12,000	12,000	0	0.00%
20	Total Revenue	$ 25,200,000	$ 27,800,000	2,600,000	10.32%
21	Total Material Cost	15,198,000	17,321,000	2,123,000	13.97%
22	Total Manufacturing Cost	5,172,000	5,884,000	712,000	13.77%
23	Total Fixed Expenses	3,470,000	3,470,000	0	0.00%
24	Net Income	$ 1,360,000	$ 1,125,000	(235,000)	(17.28%)

sales price and cost for each model

product mix in which an equal number of model types are produced

product mix in which more higher-end models are produced and sold

revenue for each model under the two product mixes

results under the even product mix

results under the optimal product mix

net income decreases by 17.28%

total revenue increases by 10.32%

Next, you'll try a different product mix to see if you can increase the company's net income by producing more of the low-end models.

7. In the range **B11:E11**, enter the following values: **3,500**, **3,500**, **2,500**, and **2,500**. Under this product mix, even though the revenue declines by 3.97% (cell E20), the material and manufacturing costs decline even more (cells E21 and E22). resulting in an increase of net income by 9.78% (cell E24). See Figure 8–32.

Figure 8–32	Product mix assuming lower sales for higher-end models

	A	B	C	D	E
5	Product Mix Analysis	Athena I	Athena II	Athena III	Athena Racer
6	Sales Price per Unit	$1,400	$1,800	$2,200	$3,000
7	Material Cost per Unit	$740	$934	$1,388	$2,004
8	Manufacturing Cost per Unit	$210	$378	$488	$648
9					
10	Even Product Mix (Units)	3,000	3,000	3,000	3,000
11	Optimal Product (Units)	3,500	3,500	2,500	2,500
12	Change	500	500	(500)	(500)
13					
14	Revenue (Even Mix)	$ 4,200,000	$ 5,400,000	$ 6,600,000	$ 9,000,000
15	Revenue (Optimal Mix)	4,900,000	6,300,000	5,500,000	7,500,000
16	Change	700,000	900,000	(1,100,000)	(1,500,000)
17					
18	Summary	Even Mix	Optimal Mix	Difference	% Difference
19	Units Produced and Sold	12,000	12,000	0	0.00%
20	Total Revenue	$ 25,200,000	$ 24,200,000	(1,000,000)	(3.97%)
21	Total Material Cost	15,198,000	14,339,000	(859,000)	(5.65%)
22	Total Manufacturing Cost	5,172,000	4,898,000	(274,000)	(5.30%)
23	Total Fixed Expenses	3,470,000	3,470,000	0	0.00%
24	Net Income	$ 1,360,000	$ 1,493,000	133,000	9.78%

product mix in which sales are greater for lower-end models

net income increases by 9.78%

total revenue decreases by 3.97%

A trial-and-error approach gives a quick financial picture under different scenarios, but it doesn't really get you any closer to answering the fundamental question, "Which product mix is the best?" Keep in mind that "best" doesn't simply mean the most profitable because the company still must meet consumer demand and be capable of manufacturing what has been ordered. To find the best solution to this problem, you need to use Solver.

Finding the Optimal Solution with Solver

Solver is an **add-in**, which is a program that adds commands and features to Microsoft Office applications such as Excel. Solver works to find a numeric solution to a problem involving several input values, such as the problem of finding a product mix that maximizes profits. It can also be used for other problems such as scheduling employees subject to their availability or finding a travel route that minimizes time or distance traveled. Before you can use Solver, it must be activated.

Reference

Activating Solver

- On the Data tab, confirm whether Solver appears in the Analyze group. If it appears, Solver is already active. If it does not appear, continue with these steps.
- On the ribbon, click the File tab, and then click Options in the navigation bar.
- Click Add-ins in the left pane, click the Manage arrow, and then click Excel Add-ins.
- Click Go to open the Add-Ins dialog box.
- Click the Solver Add-in check box, and then click OK.
- Follow the remaining prompts to install Solver, if it is not already installed.

Activating Solver

Solver is supplied with every desktop version of Microsoft Excel, but it might not be "turned on" or activated. You need to check whether Solver is already active on your version of Excel. If the Solver button does not appear in the Analyze group on the Data tab, the Solver add-in needs to be activated. If you are working on a network, you might need your instructor or network administrator to activate Solver for you. If you are working on a stand-alone PC, you can activate Solver yourself.

To activate the Solver add-in:

1. On the ribbon, click the **Data** tab, and then look for the Analyze group and the Solver button. If you see the Solver button, as shown in Figure 8–33, Solver is active and you should read but not perform the rest of the steps in this section. If you don't see the Solver button, continue with Step 2.

| Figure 8–33 | Solver button in the Analyze group on the Data tab |

Solver is installed and active

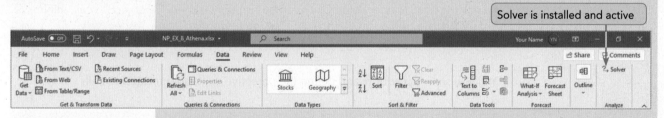

Tip

You can also open the Excel Options dialog box by right-clicking the ribbon, and then clicking Customize the Ribbon on the shortcut menu.

2. On the ribbon, click the **File** tab, and then click **Options** at the bottom of the navigation bar. The Excel Options dialog box opens.

3. In the left pane, click **Add-ins**. Information about all the add-ins currently installed within Excel appears in the right pane.

4. If necessary, click the **Manage arrow** at the bottom of the dialog box, and then click **Excel Add-ins**.

5. Click **Go**. The Add-ins dialog box opens and displays a list of all the available Excel add-ins. Although these add-ins are available, they might not have been activated.

6. Click the **Solver Add-in** check box to insert a checkmark.

   Trouble? If you don't see Solver in the list of available add-ins, you may have to reinstall Excel on your computer. See your instructor or technical resource person for help.

7. Click **OK**. Solver is activated, and its button is added on the Data tab in the Analyze group.

Now that Solver is activated, you can use it to find the optimal product mix.

Insight

Excel Add-Ins

Solver is only one of many available Excel add-ins. Other add-ins provide the ability to perform statistical analyses, generate business reports, and produce interactive maps. You can also create your own add-ins using the Visual Basic for Applications (VBA) macro language. The process for activating other add-ins is the same as the process you used to activate the Solver add-in. Most third-party add-ins provide detailed instructions for their installation and use.

Setting the Objective Cell and Variable Cells

Every Solver model needs an objective cell and one or more variable cells. An objective cell is a result cell that is maximized, minimized, or set to a specific value. A variable cell is an input cell that changes so that the objective cell can meet its defined goal.

In the Product Mix worksheet, cell E24, which displays the percent change in net income, is the objective cell whose value you want to maximize. The cells in the range B11:E11, which contain the number of bicycles of each model produced and sold by the company, are the variable cells whose values you want Solver to change to achieve an optimal result.

Reference

Setting Solver's Objective and Variable Cells

- On the Data tab, in the Analyze group, click the Solver button.
- In the Set Objective box, specify the cell whose value you want to set to match a specific objective.
- Click the Max, Min, or Value Of option button to maximize the objective cell, minimize the objective cell, or set the objective cell to a specified value, respectively.
- In the By Changing Variable Cells input box, specify the changing cells.

You will start Solver now and define the objective cell and the variable cells.

To set up the Solver model:

1. On the Data tab, in the Analyze group, click the **Solver** button. The Solver Parameters dialog box opens with the insertion point in the Set Objective box.

2. Click cell **E24** in the Product Mix worksheet. The absolute reference to the cell appears in the Set Objective box.

3. Verify that the **Max** option button is selected. This option tells Solver to find the maximum value possible for cell E24.

Tip

Changing cells can contain only constant values, not formulas.

4. Click the **By Changing Variable Cells** box, and then select the range **B11:E11** in the Product Mix worksheet. The absolute reference to this range tells Solver to modify the product mix values stored in these cells to maximize the value in cell E24. See Figure 8–34.

Figure 8–34   Solver Parameters dialog box

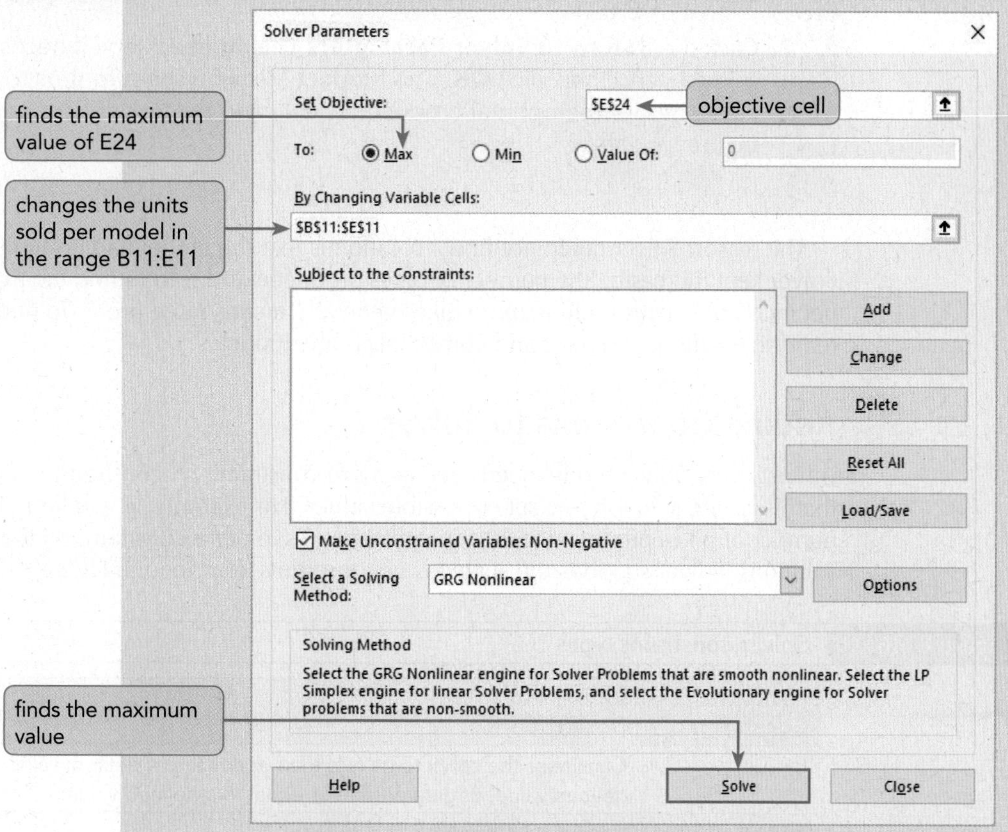

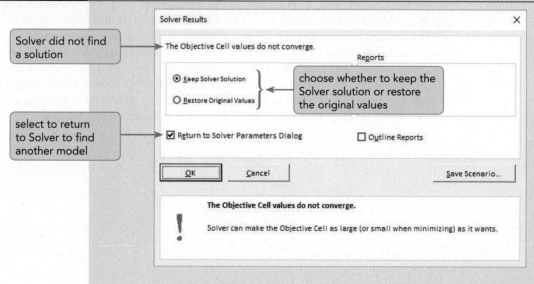

finds the maximum value of E24

changes the units sold per model in the range B11:E11

objective cell

finds the maximum value

5. Click **Solve**. Solver finds the optimal product mix by evaluating different product mix combinations. The Solver Results dialog box opens, reporting that Solver was not able to arrive at a solution. See Figure 8–35.

Figure 8–35   Solver Results dialog box

Solver did not find a solution

choose whether to keep the Solver solution or restore the original values

select to return to Solver to find another model

6. Click the **Restore Original Values** option button to reset the original product mix numbers.

7. Click the **Return to Solver Parameters Dialog** check box if necessary to select it, and then click **OK**. The Product Mix worksheet returns to the original values for the optimal product mix cell, and the Solver Parameters dialog box reappears.

The reason Solver could not find a solution is that the model had no limits. So, Solver kept increasing the number of bikes produced and sold to find the maximum net income, because selling more bikes generally means more profit. To find a more realistic solution, you must add constraints to the model.

Adding Constraints to Solver

Almost every Solver model needs one or more constraints. A constraint is a condition that limits the solution to a set of possible values. For example, if you limit the total number of bikes produced to 12,000 units, you have put a constraint on the possible solutions. Solver supports the six types of constraints described in Figure 8–36.

| Figure 8–36 | Solver constraint types |

Constraint	Description
<= , = , >=	Constrains the cell(s) to be less than or equal to a defined value, equal to a defined value, or greater than or equal to a defined value
int	Constrains the cell(s) to be integers
bin	Constrains the cell(s) to binary values (0 or 1)
dif	Constrains the cells to be different integers within the range 1 to n, where n is the number of cells in the constraint

You can use the <= constraint to limit the total number of bikes produced and sold to a reasonable number, or you can use the = constraint to specify the exact number of bikes produced and ultimately sold. Other constraints are used for special types of data.

The bin, or binary, constraint limits a cell value to 0 or 1 and is often used to indicate the presence or absence of a property. For example, a binary constraint could be used in a work schedule to indicate whether an employee can work a particular shift or not. Finally, the dif, or All Different, constraint is used to limit cells to different integer values within the range of 1 to n and is often applied for factors that need to follow a defined order when 1 is assigned to the first factor and n is assigned to the last one.

Reference

Setting Constraints on the Solver Solution

- In the Solver Parameters dialog box, click Add.
- Enter the cell reference of the cell or cells containing the constraint.
- Select the constraint type (<=, =, >=, int, bin, or dif).
- Enter the constraint value in the Constraint box.
- Click OK to add the constraint and return to the Solver Parameters dialog box.
- Repeat for each constraint you want to add to the model.

Roy wants to set the total number of bikes produced and sold to exactly 12,000 units because that is the limit of the company's production capacity and what the market will bear. You will add an = constraint to Solver.

To add the units sold constraint to Solver:

Tip

Constraints can be applied only to adjacent ranges. For a nonadjacent range, apply separate constraints to each part of the range.

1. In the Solver Parameters dialog box, click **Add**. The Add Constraint dialog box opens with the insertion point in the Cell Reference box.

2. Click cell **C19** in the Product Mix worksheet to enter the absolute cell reference to the Optimal Units Produced and Sold value.

3. Click the **arrow** next to the constraint type box (the center box), and then click **=** in the list to specify an equal to constraint.

4. In the Constraint box, type **12000**. This constraint limits cell C19 to be equal to 12,000. See Figure 8–37.

Figure 8–37   **Add Constraint dialog box**

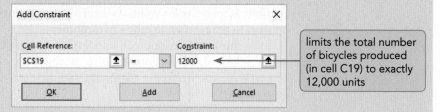

limits the total number of bicycles produced (in cell C19) to exactly 12,000 units

5. Click **OK**. The Solver Parameters dialog box reappears with the constraint $C$19 = 12000 added to the Subject to the Constraints box.

6. Click **Solve**. The Solver Results dialog box opens, indicating that the solution that Solver found satisfies the objective and constraints. Solver's solution, shown in the Product Mix worksheet, is that the company should produce only Athena II bicycles. See Figure 8–38.

Figure 8–38	Solver results with one constraint

	A	B	C	D	E
5	Product Mix Analysis	Athena I	Athena II	Athena III	Athena Racer
6	Sales Price per Unit	$1,400	$1,800	$2,200	$3,000
7	Material Cost per Unit	$740	$934	$1,388	$2,004
8	Manufacturing Cost per Unit	$210	$378	$488	$648
9					
10	Even Product Mix (Units)	3,000	3,000	3,000	3,000
11	Optimal Product (Units)	-	12,000	-	-
12	Change	(3,000)	9,000	(3,000)	(3,000)
13					
14	Revenue (Even Mix)	$ 4,200,000	$ 5,400,000	$ 6,600,000	$ 9,000,000
15	Revenue (Optimal Mix)	-	21,600,000	-	-
16	Change	(4,200,000)	16,200,000	(6,600,000)	(9,000,000)
17					
18	Summary	Even Mix	Optimal Mix	Difference	% Difference
19	Units Produced and Sold	12,000	12,000	0	0.00%
20	Total Revenue	$ 25,200,000	$ 21,600,000	(3,600,000)	(14.29%)
21	Total Material Cost	15,198,000	11,208,000	(3,990,000)	(26.25%)
22	Total Manufacturing Cost	5,172,000	4,536,000	(636,000)	(12.30%)
23	Total Fixed Expenses	3,470,000	3,470,000	0	0.00%
24	Net Income	$ 1,360,000	$ 2,386,000	1,026,000	75.44%

under this solution, all of the production is used to create the Athena II model

total number of bikes produced is fixed at 12,000 units

Roy has several problems with this solution. First, the company cannot limit its production to only the Athena II because there is not enough demand for that model. Second, Athena Cycles wants to diversify its offerings by producing and selling a variety of bikes to attract a wide range of customers.

To fix this problem, you will add the constraint that the company must produce at least 2,000 units of each model. Also, because the company cannot produce a fraction of a bicycle, you'll add the constraint that the number of bikes produced and sold must be an integer value.

To add more constraints to the model:

1. Click the **Restore Original Values** option button, verify that the **Return to Solver Parameters Dialog** check box is selected, and then click **OK** to return to the Solver Parameters dialog box.

2. Click **Add**. The Add Constraint dialog box opens with the insertion point in the Cell Reference box.

3. Select the range **B11:E11** in the Product Mix worksheet, select **>=** as the constraint type, and then enter **2000** in the Constraint box. This specifies that each value in the range B11:E11 must be greater than or equal to 2,000.

4. Click **Add** to add the constraint to the Solver model. The Add Constraint dialog box remains open, so you can create another constraint.

5. Select the range **B11:E11** in the Product Mix worksheet, and then select **int** as the constraint type. The word "integer" is added to the Constraint box, specifying that each value in the range B11:E11 must be an integer.

6. Click **OK** to add the constraint to the model and return to the Solver Parameters dialog box. The Subject to the Constraints box now lists three constraints.

7. Click **Solve**. Solver reports that it has found a solution that satisfies all of the constraints.

8. Click the **Return to Solver Parameters Dialog** check box to remove the checkmark.

9. Click **OK**. The Solver Results dialog box closes, and the Solver solution remains in the worksheet. See Figure 8–39.

| Figure 8–39 | Solver results with three constraints |

the company must produce at least 2,000 units of each model

	A	B	C	D	E
5	Product Mix Analysis	Athena I	Athena II	Athena III	Athena Racer
6	Sales Price per Unit	$1,400	$1,800	$2,200	$3,000
7	Material Cost per Unit	$740	$934	$1,388	$2,004
8	Manufacturing Cost per Unit	$210	$378	$488	$648
9					
10	Even Product Mix (Units)	3,000	3,000	3,000	3,000
11	Optimal Product (Units)	2,000	6,000	2,000	2,000
12	Change	(1,000)	3,000	(1,000)	(1,000)
13					
14	Revenue (Even Mix)	$ 4,200,000	$ 5,400,000	$ 6,600,000	$ 9,000,000
15	Revenue (Optimal Mix)	2,800,000	10,800,000	4,400,000	6,000,000
16	Change	(1,400,000)	5,400,000	(2,200,000)	(3,000,000)
17					
18	Summary	Even Mix	Optimal Mix	Difference	% Difference
19	Units Produced and Sold	12,000	12,000	0	0.00%
20	Total Revenue	$ 25,200,000	$ 24,000,000	(1,200,000)	(4.76%)
21	Total Material Cost	15,198,000	13,868,000	(1,330,000)	(8.75%)
22	Total Manufacturing Cost	5,172,000	4,960,000	(212,000)	(4.10%)
23	Total Fixed Expenses	3,470,000	3,470,000	0	0.00%
24	Net Income	$ 1,360,000	$ 1,702,000	342,000	25.15%

net income increases by 25.15% under this solution

Solver's solution is a product mix in which 6,000 Athena IIs are produced and sold with 2,000 each of the other three models. Under this product mix, the company will show a net income of $1,702,000, which is a 25.15% increase over a product mix that has equal numbers of the four models.

Although this product mix is the most profitable to the company, production is limited by the number of available parts. In the range G27:J46, Roy included a table that tracks the parts each model requires, the quantity of each part currently available, and the number of parts remaining after the proposed production run. Figure 8–40 shows the parts usage under the optimal product mix you just found using Solver.

Figure 8–40   **Parts remaining after the proposed product mix**

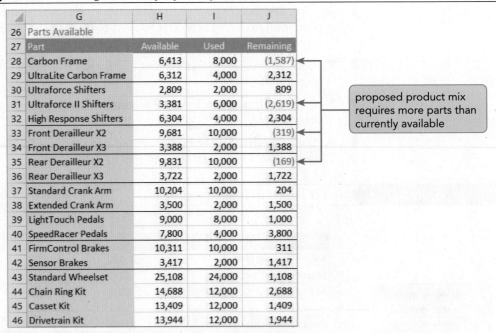

Part	Available	Used	Remaining
Carbon Frame	6,413	8,000	(1,587)
UltraLite Carbon Frame	6,312	4,000	2,312
Ultraforce Shifters	2,809	2,000	809
Ultraforce II Shifters	3,381	6,000	(2,619)
High Response Shifters	6,304	4,000	2,304
Front Derailleur X2	9,681	10,000	(319)
Front Derailleur X3	3,388	2,000	1,388
Rear Derailleur X2	9,831	10,000	(169)
Rear Derailleur X3	3,722	2,000	1,722
Standard Crank Arm	10,204	10,000	204
Extended Crank Arm	3,500	2,000	1,500
LightTouch Pedals	9,000	8,000	1,000
SpeedRacer Pedals	7,800	4,000	3,800
FirmControl Brakes	10,311	10,000	311
Sensor Brakes	3,417	2,000	1,417
Standard Wheelset	25,108	24,000	1,108
Chain Ring Kit	14,688	12,000	2,688
Casset Kit	13,409	12,000	1,409
Drivetrain Kit	13,944	12,000	1,944

proposed product mix requires more parts than currently available

Athena Cycles simply does not have the parts in stock to manufacture the bicycles in the proposed product mix. It lacks enough carbon frames, Ultraforce II Shifters, Front Derailleur X2s, and Rear Derailleur X2s. Roy asks you to add one more constraint that would limit the product mix only to those models for which Athena Cycles is equipped to produce in the specified quantities.

To add a constraint limiting the product mix to the available parts:

1. On the Data tab, in the Analyze group, click the **Solver** button. The Solver Parameters dialog box opens showing the current Solver model.

2. Click **Add** to open the Add Constraint dialog box.

3. Select the range **J28:J46**, which contains the number of parts remaining after the production run, select **>=** as the constraint type, and then type **0** in the Constraint box to force all the values in the range J28:J46 to be greater than or equal to 0.

4. Click **OK**. The complete Solver model appears in the Solver Parameters dialog box. See Figure 8–41.

Figure 8–41   Final Solver model

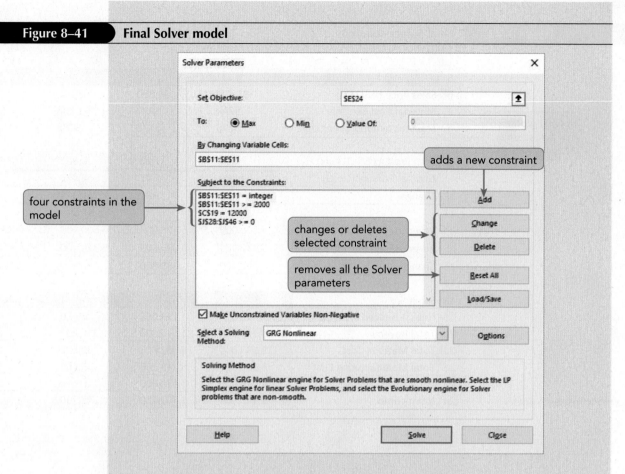

five. **5.** Click **Solve**, and then click **OK** in the Solver Results dialog box to accept the Solver solution and return to the worksheet.

6. Scroll to the top of the Product Mix worksheet to see the Solver results. See Figure 8–42.

Figure 8-42   **Final Solver solution**

	A	B	C	D	E
5	Product Mix Analysis	Athena I	Athena II	Athena III	Athena Racer
6	Sales Price per Unit	$1,400	$1,800	$2,200	$3,000
7	Material Cost per Unit	$740	$934	$1,388	$2,004
8	Manufacturing Cost per Unit	$210	$378	$488	$648
9					
10	Even Product Mix (Units)	3,000	3,000	3,000	3,000
11	Optimal Product (Units)	2,809	3,381	2,422	3,388
12	Change	(191)	381	(578)	388
13					
14	Revenue (Even Mix)	$ 4,200,000	$ 5,400,000	$ 6,600,000	$ 9,000,000
15	Revenue (Optimal Mix)	3,932,600	6,085,800	5,328,400	10,164,000
16	Change	(267,400)	685,800	(1,271,600)	1,164,000
17					
18	Summary	Even Mix	Optimal Mix	Difference	% Difference
19	Units Produced and Sold	12,000	12,000	0	0.00%
20	Total Revenue	$ 25,200,000	$ 25,510,800	310,800	1.23%
21	Total Material Cost	15,198,000	15,387,802	189,802	1.25%
22	Total Manufacturing Cost	5,172,000	5,245,268	73,268	1.42%
23	Total Fixed Expenses	3,470,000	3,470,000	0	0.00%
24	Net Income	$ 1,360,000	$ 1,407,730	47,730	3.51%

optimal product mix that satisfies all constraints

under the optimal product mix, net income increases by 3.51%

> **7.** Scroll through the worksheet to verify that all four constraints are met, including the constraint that manufacturing the bicycles in the proposed product mix will not exceed the number of available parts.

Based on the Solver results, Athena Cycles can increase its profits by 3.51% and satisfy all of the constraints related to customer demand and available parts, by producing and selling 2,809 Athena Is, 3,381 Athena IIs, 2,422 Athena IIIs, and 3,388 Athena Racers. This is the best outcome in terms of maximizing profits that Roy can report to the company.

Exploring the Iterative Process

Solver arrives at optimal solutions through an **iterative process**, in which Solver starts with an initial solution and uses that as a basis to calculate a new solution. If that solution improves the value of the objective cell, it will be used to generate the next solution; if it doesn't, Solver tries a different set of values as the starting point for the next step. Each step, or iteration, in this process improves the solution until Solver reaches the point where the new solutions are not significantly better than the solution from the previous step. At that point, Solver will stop and indicate that it has found an answer.

One way to think about this process is to imagine a terrain in which you want to find the highest point. The iterative process accomplishes this by following the terrain upward until the highest peak is scaled. The challenge with this approach is that you might simply find a nearby peak that is not the overall high point in the area. Solver refers to the overall high point as the **global optimum** and a nearby high point, which is not necessarily the highest overall point, as the **local optimum**.

To find the global optimum, you may want to rerun Solver using different initial values and then compare the solutions to determine which result represents the overall best solution. Solver also supports the following iterative methods:

Tip

For simple expressions, the Simplex LP method will always find the global optimum solution; that may not be the case with more complex expressions.

- The **Simplex LP method** is used for simple linear expressions involving only the operations of addition, subtraction, multiplication, and division.
- The **GRG Nonlinear method** is used for complicated expressions involving nonlinear functions such as some exponential and trigonometric functions.
- The **Evolutionary method** is used for complicated expressions that involve discontinuous functions that jump from one value to another.

If Solver fails to find a solution or you are not sure if its solution is the global optimum, you can try each method and compare the results to determine which solution is the best.

Creating a Solver Answer Report

Tip

You cannot display sensitivity and limits reports when the Solver model contains integer constraints.

You can evaluate the solution the Solver produced through three different reports—an answer report, a sensitivity report, and a limits report. The **answer report** is probably the most useful because it summarizes the results of a successful solution by displaying information about the objective cell, changing cells, and constraints as well as the initial and final values in the worksheet. The **sensitivity report** and **limits report** are often used in science and engineering to investigate the mathematical aspects of the Solver result, allowing you to quantify the reliability of the solution.

As part of documenting the Solver solution, Roy wants you to create an answer report providing information on the process used to determine the optimal product mix. To ensure that the answer report includes information on the entire process, you'll change the current values in the range B11:E11 to assume a product mix with 3,000 of each model produced and sold.

To create an answer report for the optimal product mix:

1. In the range **B11:E11**, enter **3,000** for each bike to set the product mix to an even distribution of production and sales among the four models.

2. On the Data tab, in the Analyze group, click the **Solver** button to open the Solver Parameters dialog box, and then click **Solve** to run Solver using the conditions you specified earlier.

3. In the Solver Results dialog box, click **Answer** in the Reports box, and then verify that the **Keep Solver Solution** option button is selected.

4. Click the **Outline Reports** check box so that Solver returns its report using the outline tools. See Figure 8–43.

Figure 8–43   Solver Results dialog box with the answer report selected

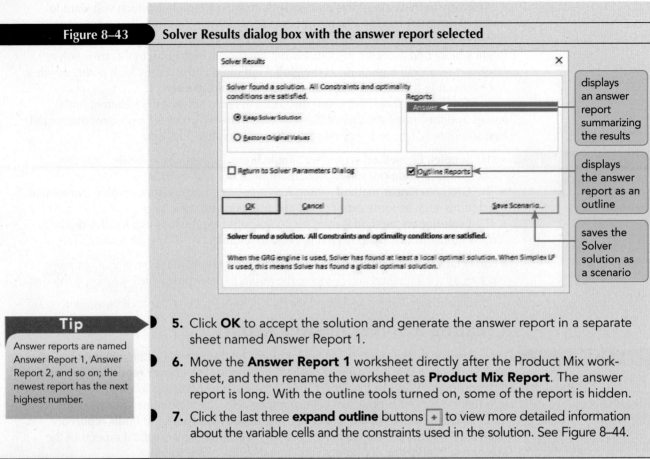

displays an answer report summarizing the results

displays the answer report as an outline

saves the Solver solution as a scenario

Tip

Answer reports are named Answer Report 1, Answer Report 2, and so on; the newest report has the next highest number.

5. Click **OK** to accept the solution and generate the answer report in a separate sheet named Answer Report 1.

6. Move the **Answer Report 1** worksheet directly after the Product Mix worksheet, and then rename the worksheet as **Product Mix Report**. The answer report is long. With the outline tools turned on, some of the report is hidden.

7. Click the last three **expand outline** buttons ⊞ to view more detailed information about the variable cells and the constraints used in the solution. See Figure 8–44.

Figure 8–44   Solver answer report

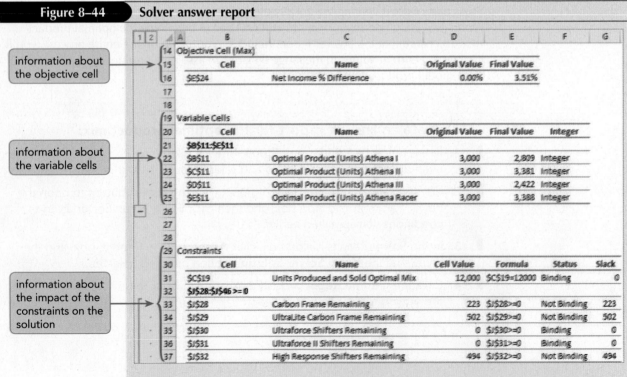

information about the objective cell

information about the variable cells

information about the impact of the constraints on the solution

The answer report is divided into the following sections:

• The Title section (not shown in Figure 8–44) identifies the worksheet containing the Solver model, the date on which the report was created, and whether Solver found a solution.

- The Solver Engine section (not shown) provides technical information about how long Solver took to find a solution.
- The Solver Options section (not shown) lists the technical options used by Solver in arriving at a solution.
- The Objective Cell section provides the original and final value of the objective cell.
- The Variable Cells section lists the original and final values of the variable cells used in the solution.
- The Constraints section lists the constraints imposed on the solution by Solver.

The status of each constraint is listed as either Binding or Not Binding. A **binding constraint** is a constraint that must be included in the Solver model because it is a limiting factor in arriving at the solution. A **nonbinding constraint** is a constraint that did not need to be included as part of the Solver model. For example, the constraint that the number of units produced and sold be equal to 12,000 is a binding constraint that limited the solutions available to Solver. On the other hand, the constraint that the company produce and sell at least 2,000 of each type of bike turned out to be nonbinding. Once the company was limited to producing exactly 12,000 bicycles and was limited by the available parts on hand, the optimal product mix would have resulted in the company producing at least 2,000 units of each model anyway.

The last column in the Constraints section shows the slack for each constraint. The **slack** is the difference between the value in the cell and the value at the limit of the constraint, showing how close the constraint came to be a binding constraint. A binding constraint always shows a slack of 0, while nonbinding constraints show a nonzero value. For example, the slack for cell J28, the number of carbon frames remaining in stock, is 223, indicating that when Solver found the optimal product mix, there were still carbon frames left, ready to be used if needed. As a result, the availability of carbon frames was not a limiting factor in the solution.

Proskills

Decision Making: Choosing a What-If Analysis Tool

Part of performing an effective what-if analysis is deciding which what-if analysis tool to use. Each tool has its own set of advantages and disadvantages. Data tables are best used when you want to perform several what-if analyses involving one or two input cells and you need to display the analysis in a tabular format. Data tables can also be easily displayed as charts, providing a visual picture of the relationship between the input values and the result values. For what-if analyses involving more than two input cells, you must create a scenario. Scenario summary tables and scenario PivotTables can be used to obtain a quick snapshot of several possible outcomes, and scenarios can be merged and shared among several workbooks. Data tables and scenarios can provide a lot of information, but they cannot easily deliver a single solution or "best outcome." If you need to maximize or minimize a value, you must use Solver. You can also use Solver to set a calculated cell to a specific value. However, if you don't need to specify any constraints on your solution, it is generally quicker and easier to use Goal Seek.

Saving and Loading Solver Models

You might want to apply different Solver models to the same data. For example, in addition to knowing what product mix maximizes the company's net income, Roy wants to know what product mix minimizes the company's total cost spent on materials. To determine this, you would create another Solver model, but creating a new model in the worksheet overwrites the previous model. You can save the Solver parameters within the worksheet to be retrieved later if needed.

Reference

Saving and Loading a Solver Model

- Open the Solver Parameters dialog box.
- Click Load/Save.
- Select an empty range containing the number of cells specified in the dialog box, and then click Save.
- Select the range containing the saved model, and then click Load.

Before running the second Solver problem for Roy, you'll store the parameters of the current model that maximizes the company's net income.

To save the current Solver model:

1. Go to the **Product Mix** worksheet.

2. On the Data tab, in the Analyze group, click the **Solver** button. The Solver Parameters dialog box opens.

3. Click **Load/Save**. The Load/Save Model dialog box opens, specifying that you need to select an empty range with eight cells to store the model.

4. Select the range **A27:A34** in the Product Mix worksheet. You'll store the Solver parameters in this range.

5. Click **Save**. The information about the Solver model is entered in the range A27:A34, and the Solver Parameters dialog box reappears.

6. Click **Close** to close the Solver Parameters dialog box.

7. In cell **A26**, enter **Maximum Net Income** and then format that cell with the **40% - Accent 4** cell style. See Figure 8–45.

> Be sure the range of cells you select to save the Solver parameters is empty so you don't over-write other information on the worksheet.

| Figure 8–45 | Saved Solver model |

current value of the objective cell

logical values indicating whether the four constraints are met

number of changing cells in the model

Solver iterative options saved as an array of numbers

	A	B	C	D	E	F	G
18	Summary	Even Mix	Optimal Mix	Difference	% Difference		SpeedRacer Pedals
19	Units Produced and Sold	12,000	12,000	0	0.00%		FirmControl Brakes
20	Total Revenue	$ 25,200,000	$ 25,510,800	310,800	1.23%		Sensor Brakes
21	Total Material Cost	15,198,000	15,387,802	189,802	1.25%		Standard Wheelset
22	Total Manufacturing Cost	5,172,000	5,245,268	73,268	1.42%		Chain Ring Kit
23	Total Fixed Expenses	3,470,000	3,470,000	0	0.00%		Casset Kit
24	Net Income	$ 1,360,000	$ 1,407,730	47,730	3.51%		Drivetrain Kit
25							
26	Maximum Net Income						Parts Available
27		3.51%					Part
28		4					Carbon Frame
29	TRUE						UltraLite Carbon Frame
30	TRUE						Ultraforce Shifters
31	TRUE						Ultraforce II Shifters
32	TRUE						High Response Shifters
33		32767					Front Derailleur X2
34		0					Front Derailleur X3
35							Rear Derailleur X2
36							Rear Derailleur X3

... | Income | Scenario Summary | Scenario PivotTable | **Product Mix** | Product Mix Report | Terms ...

Ready

The first parameter in cell A27 displays 3.51%, which is the value of the objective cell under this model. The second parameter in cell A28 displays 4, indicating the number of variable cells in the model. The next four cells display TRUE, indicating that the four constraints in the model are all satisfied in the Solver solution. If you later change some of the worksheet data so that it violates a constraint, the Solver parameter cells will display FALSE. These cells provide a quick visual check that all the model's conditions are still being met as the worksheet is modified. The final two cells, cells A27 and A28, are used to store the technical options for the iterative process by which Solver arrives at a solution (refer to the section titled, "Exploring the Iterative Process").

Now that you have saved this Solver model, you can create a second model to determine the product mix that minimizes the material cost of producing and selling these bicycles. Roy wants to know what product mix would result in the lowest material cost given that the company still wants to produce 12,000 bicycles and still wants to make at least 2,000 of each model. The objective cell for this model is cell C21 instead of cell E24.

To determine the product mix that minimizes the total material cost:

1. In the range **B11:E11**, change the value of each cell to **3,000**.

2. Open the Solver Parameters dialog box.

3. With the Set Objective box selected, click cell **C21** in the Product Mix worksheet. This cell contains the total material cost under the Optimal product mix.

4. Click the **Min** option button. You want Solver to find the minimum value for cell C21. The changing cells and constraints you used to find the maximum net income remain unchanged for this model.

5. Click **Solve**. Solver finds the product mix that minimizes the total material cost.

6. Click **OK** to close the Solver Results dialog box and view the solution. See Figure 8–46.

Figure 8–46 Solution to minimizing total material costs

	A	B	C	D	E
5	Product Mix Analysis	Athena I	Athena II	Athena III	Athena Racer
6	Sales Price per Unit	$1,400	$1,800	$2,200	$3,000
7	Material Cost per Unit	$740	$934	$1,388	$2,004
8	Manufacturing Cost per Unit	$210	$378	$488	$648
9					
10	Even Product Mix (Units)	3,000	3,000	3,000	3,000
11	Optimal Product (Units)	2,809	3,381	3,491	2,319
12	Change	(191)	381	491	(681)
13					
14	Revenue (Even Mix)	$ 4,200,000	$ 5,400,000	$ 6,600,000	$ 9,000,000
15	Revenue (Optimal Mix)	3,932,600	6,085,800	7,680,200	6,957,000
16	Change	(267,400)	685,800	1,080,200	(2,043,000)
17					
18	Summary	Even Mix	Optimal Mix	Difference	% Difference
19	Units Produced and Sold	12,000	12,000	0	0.00%
20	Total Revenue	$ 25,200,000	$ 24,655,600	(544,400)	(2.16%)
21	Total Material Cost	15,198,000	14,729,298	(468,702)	(3.08%)
22	Total Manufacturing Cost	5,172,000	5,074,228	(97,772)	(1.89%)
23	Total Fixed Expenses	3,470,000	3,470,000	0	0.00%
24	Net Income	$ 1,360,000	$ 1,382,074	22,074	1.62%

product mix that minimizes the total material costs

minimum total material cost based on the constraints

material costs decline 3.08% from the Even product mix model

The minimum material cost to the company is $14,729,298, which is $468,702 less than the material cost under the Even product mix. This is the optimal solution based on the constraints that the company must produce exactly 12,000 bicycles with 2,000 units of each model, and not exceed the available parts. You will save this model in the Product Mix worksheet.

To save the model to minimize material costs:

▶ **1.** In cell **A36**, enter **Minimum Material Cost** and then format that cell with the **40% - Accent2** cell style.

▶ **2.** Open the Solver Parameters dialog box, and then click **Load/Save**. The Load/Save Model dialog box opens.

▶ **3.** Select the range **A37:A44** in the Product Mix worksheet to specify the eight cells in which to save the model.

▶ **4.** Click **Save**. The current Solver model is saved in the Product Mix worksheet.

▶ **5.** Click **Close** to close the Solver Parameters dialog box.

You have two Solver models saved in the Product Mix worksheet—the Maximum Net Income model and the Minimum Material Cost model. You can quickly reload each of these Solver models in the worksheet from the Solver Parameters dialog box.

Roy wants the final version of the worksheet to use the Solver model that maximizes net income for the company. You'll load and run the Maximum Net Income model.

To load the Maximum Net Income model and run it:

▶ **1.** In the range **B11:E11**, change the values in each cell to **3,000** as the initial product mix.

▶ **2.** Open the Solver Parameters dialog box, and then click **Load/Save**. The Load/Save Model dialog box opens.

▶ **3.** In the Product Mix worksheet, select the range **A27:A34** containing the parameters of the Maximum Net Income model.

Tip
To combine the Solver model with the model currently used in the worksheet, click the Merge button.

▶ **4.** Click **Load** to load the Solver parameters from the worksheet. The Load Model dialog box opens, asking whether you want to replace the current model or merge the new model with the current model.

▶ **5.** Click **Replace**. The Solver Parameters dialog box appears. The parameters for the Maximum Net Income model have replaced the parameters for the Minimum Material Cost model with the objective cell set once again to cell E24 and the Max option button selected in the dialog box.

▶ **6.** Click **Solve**. Solver runs the Maximum Net Income model, and then the Solver Results dialog box opens.

▶ **7.** Click **OK** to keep the Solver solution and return to the Product Mix worksheet.

▶ **8.** sam↑ Save the workbook, and then close it.

By saving the Solver model parameters to cells on the worksheet, you can create as many models as you need to effectively analyze the data. You can then load and apply these different models to your analysis as new data is entered.

You have finished analyzing how Athena Cycles can maximize its profits from its line of road bicycles by modifying the product mix. Using data tables, Excel scenarios, and Solver models, you provided Roy with several pricing and production options to increase the company's net income or minimize material costs for the upcoming year.

Review

Session 8.3 Quick Check

1. What is an add-in?
2. What are three options for the objective cell using Solver?
3. What is an objective cell? What is a variable cell?
4. What are the six types of constraints you can put on a cell in a Solver model?
5. What is an iterative process?
6. What is the difference between a binding constraint and a nonbinding constraint?
7. In the Solver report, what is meant by the term "slack"?

Practice

Review Assignments

Data File needed for the Review Assignments: NP_EX_8-2.xlsx

Athena Cycles is planning to start a new line of mountain bikes. As you did with the company's line of road bikes, Roy wants you to perform a what-if analysis on the company's income statement for its mountain bike line, creating one-variable and two-variable data tables to determine the break-even point for sales. Roy also wants you to use Scenario Manager to explore the impact on the profitability of the line under different possible scenarios. Finally, you will calculate the product mix, among four different mountain bike models, that will result in the maximum net income to the company. Complete the following:

1. Open the **NP_EX_8-2.xlsx** workbook located in the Excel8 > Review folder included with your Data Files. Save the workbook as **NP_EX_8_Bikes** in the location specified by your instructor.
2. In the Documentation sheet, enter your name and the date.
3. In the Income Statement worksheet, in the range D5:G5, enter formulas that reference Units Sold value in cell B5 and the Revenue, Expenses, and Net Income values from the cells B25, B26, and B27.
4. In the range D6:D13, enter Units Sold values from 250 to 2,000 in 250-unit increments.
5. Create a one-variable data table in the range D5:G13 with cell B5 as the column input cell.
6. Create a Cost-Volume-Profit chart of the revenue and expenses values in the range D4:F13 of the one-variable data table. Resize the chart to cover the range D14:G27. Change the chart title to **CVP Analysis**.
7. Copy the Units Sold values from the range D6:D13 into the range I6:I13. In the range J5:N5, enter Sales Price values from $800 to $1,200 in $100 increments. In cell I5, enter a formula that references the net income value stored in cell B27. Format the value in cell I5 to display the text **Units Sold** rather than the net income value.
8. Create a two-variable data table in the I5:N13 range using cell B6 and the row input cell and cell B5 as the column input cell.
9. Select the range I6:N13 and create a scatter chart with straight lines of the data. Move and resize the chart to cover the range I14:N27. Format the chart as follows:
    a. Change the chart title to **Break-Even Analysis**.
    b. Change the name of each of the five data series from their default names to the Sales Price values in the cells J5 through N5.
    c. Move the chart legend to the right of the chart.
    d. Change the scale of the horizontal axis to go from 0 to 2,000 in 500-unit increments.
10. Use the Scenario Manager to store the three scenarios listed in Figure 8–47.

Figure 8–47   Mountain bike what-if scenarios

Input Cells	Status Quo	Increased Production	Decreased Production
Units Sold	1,200	1,500	1,000
Sales Price	$900	$800	$950
Salaries and Benefits	$175,000	$175,000	$145,000
Shipping and Distribution	$72,000	$90,000	$60,000
Stocking and Storage	$65,000	$75,000	$55,000
Miscellaneous	$55,000	$70,000	$40,000

11. Create a scenario summary report of the three scenarios, displaying their impact on total revenue, total expenses, and net income. Move the worksheet directly after the Income Statement worksheet.

12. Create a Scenario PivotTable report of the three scenarios displaying the total revenue, total expenses, and net income under each scenario. Make the following changes to the PivotTable:

    a. Display Total Revenue, Total Expenses, and Net Income in Currency style with no decimals places and negative values displayed in red, enclosed within parentheses.

    b. Remove the filter from the PivotTable.

    c. Enter **Scenario Report** in cell A1 and format that cell with the Title cell style.

13. Add a PivotChart of the PivotTable displaying the data as combination chart positioned over the range A8:D20. Display the Total_Revenue and Total_Expenses fields as clustered columns, display the Net_Income field as a line chart on the secondary axis. Remove the field buttons from the chart and move the legend below the chart.

14. Move the Scenario PivotTable worksheet after the Scenario Summary worksheet.

15. The Product Line worksheet lists four mountain bikes produced and sold by Athena Cycles. Use Solver to find the product mix that maximizes the value in cell E24 by changing the values in the range B11:E11 under the following constraints:

    a. The total mountain bikes produced and sold as indicated in cell C19 must be exactly 5,000.

    b. The company needs to produce 1,000 or more of each model type, so the values in the range B11:E11 must be at least 1,000.

    c. The values in the range B11:E11 must be integers.

    d. The values in the range J28:J46 must be greater than or equal to zero because Athena Cycles cannot produce more mountain bikes than the available parts.

16. Save the Solver model you just created to the range A27:A34.

17. Change the values in the range B11:E11 to 1,000 units of each model, and then rerun Solver to find the product mix that minimizes the total material cost in cell C21 subject to the same constraints you used for the Maximum Net Income model.

18. Save the Solver model to the range A37:A44.

19. Restore the values in the range B11:E11 to 1,000 units of each model. Load the Maximum Net Income model into Solver, and then run Solver. Create an answer report with outline buttons enabled, and then move the Answer Report 1 worksheet after the Product Line worksheet.

20. Save the workbook, and then close it.

Apply

Case Problem 1

Data File needed for this Case Problem: NP_EX_8-3.xlsx

Granite Life   Brenda Castro is an Events Coordinator for the Granite Life insurance company. One event that the company sponsors is a three-day educational seminar on insurance and investing, which will take place in Provo, Utah, this year. Brenda wants to estimate the number of attendees and predict the net income from the event. Complete the following:

1. Open the **NP_EX_8-3.xlsx** workbook located in the Excel8 > Case1 folder included with your Data Files. Save the workbook as **NP_EX_8_Seminar** in the location specified by your instructor.

2. In the Documentation sheet, enter your name and the date.

3. Brenda wants to calculate a budget that assumes **200** people will attend the seminar at a cost of **$500** per person. In the Budget worksheet, enter these values in the range B5:B6. In cell B7, calculate the total revenue from attendance at the seminar by multiplying the number of attendees and the registration fee per attendee.

4. Each attendee will receive training materials costing **$150** and supplementary materials costing **$75**. Enter these values into the range B10:B11. In cell B12, calculate the total variable costs by multiplying the cost of the materials by the number of attendees.

5. In the range B15:B19, enter the fixed costs associated with the seminar. Providing computers and networking support for the entire seminar will cost **$1,400**. The speakers at the seminar will cost **$2,400** for their fees, **$2,000** for their travel, and **$950** for their lodging. Brenda estimates **$5,000** in miscellaneous expenses. In cell B20, calculate sum of these fixed costs.

6. The company must rent conference rooms large enough to accommodate the number of attendees. The lookup table in the range D5:E11 contains the room charges for seminars of in groups of 100 from 0 up to 500 or more. For example, to accommodate 0 to 100 people will cost the company $1,500. In cell B23, calculate the room costs by looking up the room rental fee based on the number of attendees (cell B5). (*Hint*: Use the XLOOKUP function to perform an approximate match lookup using the value in cell B5, the list of attendees in the AttendeeLookup range, the room fees in the RoomFees range, and the match mode set to −1.)

7. The more attendees, the less the hotel will charge per person to cater the seminar meals. In cell B24, calculate the total catering charge by using the XLOOKUP function to do an approximate match lookup with the value in B5, the lookup values in the AttendeeLookup range, the return values in the MealCatering range, and the match mode set to −1. Multiply the returned value by the value in B5.

8. The company also pays for seminar support staff. The larger the seminar, the higher the support staff fee. The lookup table in the range D23:E29 contains the staff fees for groups of different sizes. For example, a seminar of 0 to 100 people will incur a $150 staff fee. In cell B25, calculate the support cost by doing an approximate match lookup with the XLOOKUP function, using cell B5 as the lookup value, AttendeeLookup as the lookup range, SeminarSupport as the return range, and −1 as the match mode value.

9. In cell B26, calculate the total mixed costs by adding the room, meal, and support costs.

10. In cell B28, calculate the cost per attendee by dividing the sum of the variable costs (cell B12), fixed costs (cell B20), and mixed costs (cell B26) by the number of attendees (cell B5).

11. In cell B29, calculate the balance from the conference by subtracting the sum of the variable, fixed, and mixed costs from the total revenue (cell B7).

12. Create a one-variable data table of different seminar budgets. In cell G6, display the value of cell B5. In cell H6, display the value of B7. In cell I6, display the sum of cells B12, B20, and B26. In cell J6, display the value of cell B29. In the range G7:G16, enter the number of possible attendees ranging from 50 to 500 in increments of 50. Complete the data table with cell B5 as the column input cell, showing the total revenue, total costs, and balance under different numbers of attendees.

13. Create a CVP chart of the Total Revenue and Total Costs values using the data from the range G5:I16, the one-variable table, and then format the chart as follows:

   a. Move and resize the chart to cover the range G18:J29.

   b. Change the chart title to **CVP Analysis**.

   c. Change the scale of the horizontal axis to go from 0 to 500 in 100-unit increments.

14. Brenda wants to investigate the impact of different registration fees and number of attendees on the seminar balance. In cell L6, display the value of cell B29 formatted to display the text **Attendees**. In the range L7:L16, enter attendee values ranging from 50 to 500 in increments of 50. In the range M6:P6, enter registration fees of **$200**, **$300**, **$400**, and **$500**.

15. Create a two-variable data table in the range L6:P16, using cell B6 as the row input cell and cell B5 as the column input cell.

16. Create a scatter chart with straight lines of the data in the range L7:P16, and then make the following changes to the chart:

   a. Move and resize the chart to cover the range L18:P29.

   b. Change the chart title to **Balance Analysis**.

   c. Change the name of the four data series to match the registration fee values in cells M6, N6, O6, and P6.

   d. Change the scale of the horizontal axis to go from 0 to 500 in 100-unit increments.

17. Create scenarios for the other possible values for the input cells listed in Figure 8–48.

| Figure 8–48 | Seminar what-if scenarios |

Changing Cell	Seminar 1	Seminar 2	Seminar 3
Attendees	200	300	150
Registration Fee	$500	$400	$600
Training Materials	$150	$175	$135
Supplemental Materials	$75	$100	$55
Computing Costs	$1,400	$1,200	$1,600
Speaker Fees	$2,400	$2,800	$2,600
Speaker Travel	$2,000	$2,200	$1,600
Speaker Lodging	$950	$1,200	$1,000
Miscellaneous	$5,000	$4,500	$4,800

18. Create a scenario summary report of the Seminar 1, Seminar 2, and Seminar 3 scenarios, show-ing the cost per person and balance from each seminar as the result. Move the sheet to the end of the workbook.

19. Show the results of Seminar 3 in the Budget worksheet.

20. Experience has taught Brenda that as the registration fee for the seminar increases, the number of attendees willing to pay decreases. Based on data from other seminars, Brenda has defined a relationship between attendance and registration fee, shown in the range R4:X21 on the Budget worksheet. In cell B5 of the Budget worksheet, change the number of attendees from a constant value to the following formula that projects the number of attendees for a given registration fee based on the value in cell B6. (*Hint:* Look at the formulas in the range S6:S21 to learn how to translate this equation into an Excel formula.)

$$Attendees = 1000 \times e^{-(fee/500)}$$

21. Use Solver to determine the registration fee in cell B6 that will maximize the balance value in cell B29 with the constraint that the registration fee should be an integer. Run Solver with an initial registration fee of $1,000.

22. Save the workbook, and then close it.

Challenge

Case Problem 2

Data File needed for this Case Problem: NP_EX_8-4.xlsx

Hardin Medical Clinic   Catherine Smythe is a personnel manager for Hardin Medical Clinic in Toledo, Ohio. Part of Catherine's job is to manage the weekly nursing schedule. The clinic employs 20 nurses—16 full-time and 4 part-time. The clinic needs 12 nurses on weekdays and 10 on week-ends. Catherine is working on the schedule for an upcoming week and is trying to accommodate all the vacation and sick-leave requests, while maintaining the required level of on-duty nurses. Catherine asks you to develop a schedule that meets the needs of the clinic and the requests of the nurses. Complete the following:

1. Open the **NP_EX_8-4.xlsx** workbook located in the Excel8 > Case2 folder included with your Data Files. Save the workbook as **NP_EX_8_Clinic** in the location specified by your instructor.

2. In the Documentation sheet, enter your name and the date.

3. In the Schedule worksheet, in the range D5:J24, enter **0** in all the cells. In this sheet, 0s and 1s indicate whether an employee is scheduled for a shift that day (0 indicates an employee is not scheduled, and 1 indicates an employee is scheduled).

4. In the range K5:K24, enter formulas to sum the total number of shifts worked by each employee from Monday through Sunday.

5. In the range L5:L24, calculate the total number of hours worked by each employee during the week by multiplying the number of shifts worked by 8 (each shift is eight hours long).

6. In the range D26:J26, enter the required shifts per day. The clinic requires 12 nurses on the weekdays, and 10 nurses on Saturday and Sunday.

7. In the range D27:J27, enter formulas to sum the total number of shifts scheduled for nurses on each day.

8. In the range D28:J28, enter formulas to calculate the difference between the number of nurses scheduled and the number of nurses required. A negative value indicates that not enough nurses are scheduled to cover that day's shifts.

9. In cell D30, calculate the total shortfall for the week by summing the daily shortfall values in the range D28:J28.

⊕ **Explore** 10. Create a Solver model that sets the value of cell D30 to 0 (indicating that all shifts are covered for every day of the week) by changing the values in the range D5:J24 under the following constraints:

    a. Add a binary constraint to force every value in the range D5:J24 to be either a 0 or a 1.

    b. Add a constraint to limit the total hours worked by each full-time employee to less than or equal to 40.

    c. Add a constraint to limit the total hours worked by each part-time employee to less than or equal to 24.

    d. Add a constraint to require that the difference values in the range D28:J28 all equal 0.

    e. Add more constraints based on the schedule requests in the range C5:C24 so that nurses are not scheduled to work shifts on days they have requested off. If a nurse has requested a day off, the cell corresponding to that day for that nurse must equal 0.

⊕ **Explore** 11. Run the Solver model using the Evolutionary method. (Solver might take a minute to arrive at a solution.) Confirm that the schedule generated by Solver fulfills all the requirements—all shifts are covered each day, no full-time nurse works more than 40 hours, no part-time nurse works more than 24 hours, and no nurse works on a requested day off.

12. Save the workbook, and then close it.

Module 9

Objectives

Session 9.1
- Work with financial functions to analyze loans and investments
- Create an amortization schedule
- Calculate interest and principal payments for a loan or investment

Session 9.2
- Perform calculations for an income statement
- Interpolate and extrapolate a series of values
- Calculate a depreciation schedule

Session 9.3
- Determine a payback period
- Calculate a net present value
- Calculate an internal rate of return
- Trace a formula error to its source

Exploring Financial Tools and Functions

Analyzing a Business Plan

Case | Holoease

Asli Kaplan is a financial analyst for Holoease, a startup tech company based in Athens, Georgia, that is introducing a new product: holographic printers for companies, small businesses, and individuals. Because of technological breakthroughs, the Holoease line of printers is more affordable and easier-to-use than previous models produced by other companies. The problem that still needs to be overcome is financial.

To obtain the capital that Holoease will need to start production, Asli must create a business plan that details the financial challenges the company will face and the likely return investors can expect within the next five years of operation. Asli needs your help in projecting future revenue, expenses, and cash flow. To do those calculations, you will rely on the Excel library of financial tools and functions.

Starting Data Files

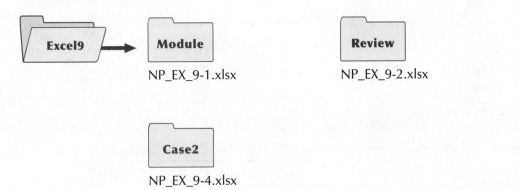

Excel9 → Module
NP_EX_9-1.xlsx

Review
NP_EX_9-2.xlsx

Case1
NP_EX_9-3.xlsx

Case2
NP_EX_9-4.xlsx

Session 9.1 Visual Overview:

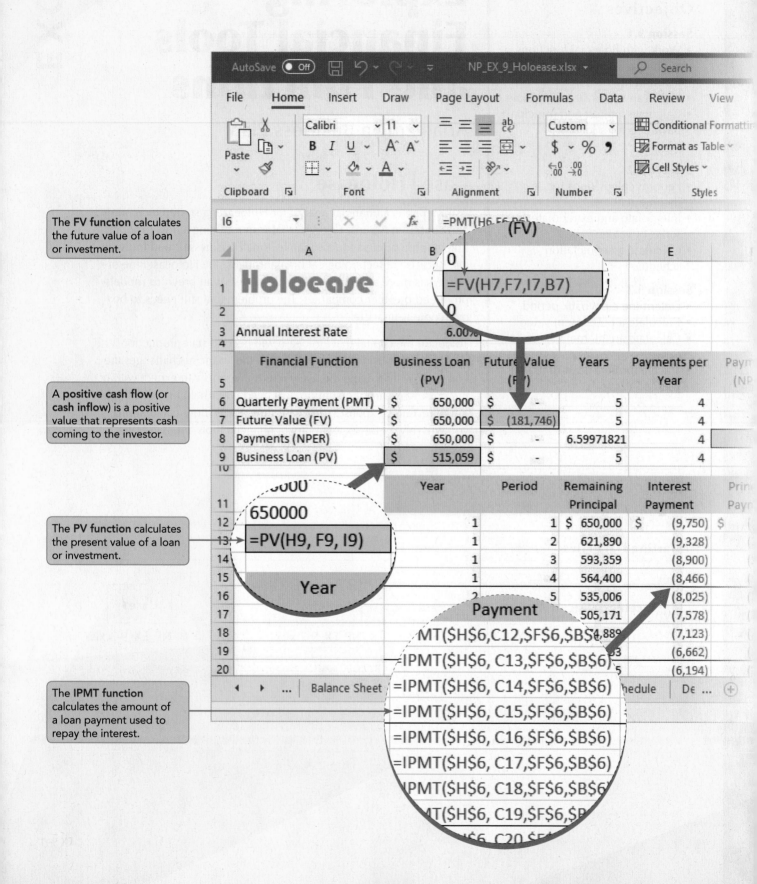

The FV function calculates the future value of a loan or investment.

A positive cash flow (or **cash inflow**) is a positive value that represents cash coming to the investor.

The PV function calculates the present value of a loan or investment.

The IPMT function calculates the amount of a loan payment used to repay the interest.

(FV)

=FV(H7,F7,I7,B7)

=PMT(H6,F6,B6)

Holoease

	A	B		E	
1			0		
2			0		
3	Annual Interest Rate	6.00%			
5	Financial Function	Business Loan (PV)	Future Value (FV)	Years	Payments per Year	Paym (NP
6	Quarterly Payment (PMT)	$ 650,000	$ -	5	4	
7	Future Value (FV)	$ 650,000	$ (181,746)	5	4	
8	Payments (NPER)	$ 650,000	$ -	6.59971821	4	
9	Business Loan (PV)	$ 515,059	$ -	5	4	

650000

=PV(H9, F9, I9)

Year

	Year	Period	Remaining Principal	Interest Payment	Prin Payn
12	1	1	$ 650,000	$ (9,750)	$
13	1	2	621,890	(9,328)	
14	1	3	593,359	(8,900)	
15	1	4	564,400	(8,466)	
16	2	5	535,006	(8,025)	
17			505,171	(7,578)	
18			4,889	(7,123)	
19			3	(6,662)	
20			5	(6,194)	

Payment

MT($H$6,C12,$F$6,$B$6)

=IPMT($H$6, C13,$F$6,$B$6)

=IPMT($H$6, C14,$F$6,$B$6)

=IPMT($H$6, C15,$F$6,$B$6)

=IPMT($H$6, C16,$F$6,$B$6)

=IPMT($H$6, C17,$F$6,$B$6)

IPMT($H$6, C18,$F$6,$B$6)

MT($H$6, C19,$F$6,$B

6, C20 $F

Balance Sheet ... hedule De ...

Loan and Investment Functions

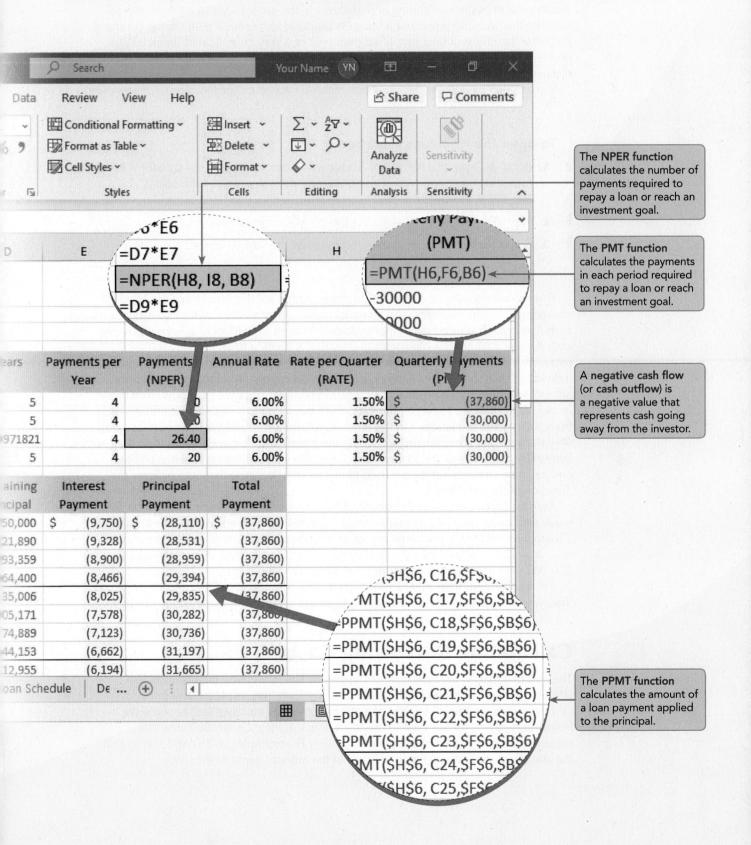

The NPER function calculates the number of payments required to repay a loan or reach an investment goal.

The PMT function calculates the payments in each period required to repay a loan or reach an investment goal.

A negative cash flow (or cash outflow) is a negative value that represents cash going away from the investor.

The PPMT function calculates the amount of a loan payment applied to the principal.

Introducing Financial Functions

In this module, you will learn the Excel skills you need to calculate important financial results used in business planning and analysis. In the process, you'll explore how to evaluate the financial aspects of a business proposal to finance a tech startup company. Be aware that this will be a simplified treatment of a very complicated financial problem that usually involves dozens of pages of financial reports and in-depth discussions with a team of accountants and lawyers.

You will start by opening the workbook that Asli created for the Holoease business plan.

To open the Holoease workbook:

▶ 1. **sam** ⬇ Open the **NP_EX_9-1.xlsx** workbook located in the **Excel9 > Module** folder included with your Data Files, and then save the workbook as **NP_EX_9_Holoease** in the location specified by your instructor.

▶ 2. In the Documentation worksheet, enter your name and the date.

▶ 3. Go to each worksheet in the workbook and review its contents.

This module focuses on **financial functions**, which are the Excel functions used for analyzing loans, investments, and financial metrics. Many financial functions deal with **cash flow**, which is direction of money to and from an individual or group. A positive cash flow, or cash inflow, represents money that is coming to an individual (cash received). A negative cash flow, or cash outflow, represents money that is leaving the individual (cash spent). For example, if you borrow money by taking out a loan, the amount you borrow is a positive cash flow to you but a negative cash flow from the lender. When you start to repay the loan, the repayments are negative cash flows away from you back to the lender. On the other hand, money you invest is a negative cash flow because you are spending money on the investment, but any returns from that investment back to you are positive cash flows. Pay close attention to when positive and negative currency values are used in this module because they will indicate the direction of the cash flow.

Another important concept in financial functions is the difference between present value and future value. As the names imply, **present value** refers to the current value of a loan or investment, whereas **future value** references that loan or investment's value at a future date. For example, if you take out a loan for $50,000, its present value is $50,000, and if you repay the entire loan, its future value is $0.

Asli wants to estimate the costs associated with business loans to the company. To do that, you will use the Excel financial functions associated with loans and investments.

Calculating Borrowing Costs

The cost of a loan to an individual or business is based on three factors: principal, interest, and time. **Principal** is the amount of the loan. **Interest** is the amount added to the principal by the lender. You can think of interest as a "user fee" because the borrower is paying for the right to use the lender's money. Generally, interest is expressed as an annual percentage rate, or APR. For example, an 8% APR means that the annual interest rate on the loan is 8% of the amount owed to the lender.

An annual interest rate is divided by the number of payments per year (often monthly or quarterly). So, if the 8% annual interest rate is paid monthly, the resulting monthly interest rate is 1/12 of 8%, or about 0.67% per month. If payments are made quarterly, then the interest rate per quarter would be 1/4 of 8%, or 2% per quarter.

The third factor in calculating the loan cost is the time required to repay the loan, which is specified as the number of payment periods. The number of payment periods is based on the length of the loan multiplied by the number of payments per year. For example, a 10-year loan that is paid monthly has 120 payment periods. If that same 10-year loan is repaid quarterly, it has 40 payment periods.

Excel calculates five values associated with loans and investments:

- The required payment for each period of the loan or investment (PMT)
- The future value of the loan or investment (FV)
- The total number of payments (NPER)
- The present value of the loan or investment (PV)
- The interest rate of the loan or investment (RATE)

Knowing four of these values, you can use a financial function to calculate the fifth. You will start by exploring how to calculate the payment required for each period.

Calculating Payments with the PMT Function

To determine the size of payments made periodically to either repay a loan or reach an investment goal, use the PMT or payment function

```
PMT(Rate, Nper, Pv, [Fv=0], [Type=0])
```

where **Rate** is the interest rate per period, **Nper** is the total number of payment periods, **Pv** is the present value of the loan or investment, and **Fv** is the future value of the loan or investment after all the scheduled payments have been made. The **Fv** argument is optional and has a default value of 0. Finally, the optional **Type** value specifies whether payments are made at the end of each period (**Type**=0) or at the beginning (**Type**=1). The default is to assume that payments are made at the end of each period.

For example, if Asli's company borrows $500,000 at 6% annual interest to be repaid quarterly over a five-year period, the **Rate** value would be 6%/4, or 1.5%, because the 6% annual interest rate is divided into four quarters. The **Nper** value is 4×5 (four payments per year for five years), resulting in 20 payments over the five-year period. The PMT function for this loan would be entered as

```
PMT(6%/4, 4*5, 500000)
```

returning the negative cash flow value –$29,122.87, indicating that the company must pay almost $30,000 each quarter to entirely repay the $500,000 loan in five years at 6% annual interest. Note that you enter the loan amount ($500,000) as a positive cash flow value because it represents money to the company. Also note that a default value of 0 is assumed for the **Fv** argument because the loan will be completely repaid and thus have a future value of 0. If you were to use the PMT function to calculate payments made toward an investment, you would use a negative **Pv** value and Excel would return a positive value since the investment is money being returned to you.

Reference

Working with Loans and Investments

- To calculate the size of the monthly or quarterly payments required to repay a loan or meet an investment goal, use PMT function

  PMT(*Rate*, *Nper*, *Pv*, [*Fv*=0], [*Type*=0])

  where **Rate** is the interest rate per period, **Nper** is the total number of payment periods, **Pv** is the present value, *Fv* is the future value, and *Type* specifies whether payments are made at the end of each period (*Type*=0) or at the beginning (*Type*=1).

- To calculate the future value of a loan or an investment, use the FV function

  FV(*Rate*, *Nper*, *Pmt*, [*Pv*=0], [*Type*=0])

- To calculate the number of payments required to repay a loan or meet an investment goal, use the NPER function

  NPER(*Rate*, *Pmt*, *Pv*, [*Fv*=0], [*Type*=0])

- To calculate the present value of a loan or an investment, use the PV function

  PV(*Rate*, *Nper*, *Pmt*, [*Fv*=0], [*Type*=0])

- To calculate the interest rate on a loan or an investment, use the RATE function

  RATE(*Nper*, *Pmt*, *Pv*, [*Fv*=0], [*Type*=0], [*Guess*=0.1])

  where the optional *Guess* argument provides an initial guess of the interest rate value.

Holoease plans to take out a business loan of $650,000 to cover some of the costs for the first few years of business. Asli wants you to calculate the quarterly payment on a $650,000 loan at 6% annual interest to be completely repaid in five years. A good practice is to enter the loan conditions into separate cells rather than including them in the PMT function. This makes the loan conditions visible and allows them to be changed in a what-if analysis. You will enter the loan conditions in the workbook Asli created, and then use the PMT function to calculate the quarterly payment.

To calculate a quarterly payment with the PMT function:

1. Go to the **Loan Analysis** worksheet. Asli has already entered and formatted much of the content in this worksheet.

2. In cell **B4**, enter **6%** as the annual interest rate of the loan.

3. In cell **B7**, enter **$650,000** as the amount of the business loan.

4. In cell **C7**, enter **0** for the future value of the loan because the loan will be completely repaid by the company.

5. In cell **D7**, enter **5** as the length of the loan in years.

6. In cell **E7**, enter **4** as the number of payments per year, which is quarterly.

7. In cell **F7**, enter the formula **=D7*E7** to calculate the total number of loan payments. In this case, four loan payments per year for five years is 20.

8. In cell **G7**, enter the formula **=$B$4** to display the annual interest rate specified in cell B4.

9. In cell **H7**, enter the formula **=G7/E7** to calculate the interest rate for each payment. In this case, the annual interest rate divided by quarterly payments returns 1.5% as the interest rate per quarter.

Be sure to use the interest rate for that payment period rather than the annual interest rate to apply the PMT function correctly.

▶ **10.** In cell **I7**, enter the formula **=PMT(H7,F7,B7)** to calculate the payment due each quarter based on the rate value in cell H7, the number of payments specified in cell F7, and the amount of the loan in cell B7. The formula returns ($37,860), a negative value that indicates the company will need to make payments of $37,860 each quarter to pay off the loan in five years. See Figure 9–1.

Figure 9–1	Quarterly payment required to repay a loan

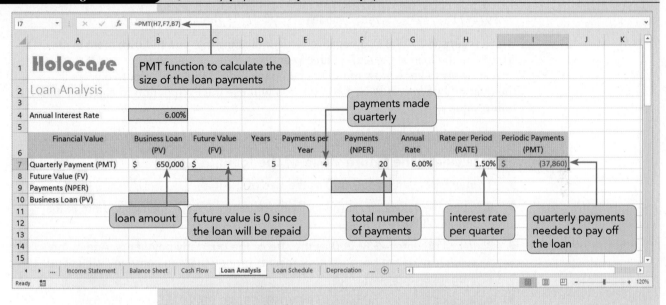

The $37,860 quarterly payments are higher than Asli anticipated. Asli was hoping for payments closer to $30,000 and asks you to determine how much of the loan would be unpaid after five years with quarterly payments of $30,000. You can calculate the amount left on the loan using the FV function.

Calculating a Future Value with the FV Function

So far, you have used the default value of 0 for the future value because the intent was to completely repay the loan. However, when a loan will not be completely repaid, you use the FV function to calculate the loan's future value after a specified number of periods. The future value will be the amount that still needs to be repaid to the lender. The syntax of the FV function is

```
FV(Rate, Nper, Pmt, [Pv=0], [Type=0])
```

where the **Rate**, **Nper**, **Pmt**, and **Type** values still represent the interest rate per period, the number of payments, the payment each period, and when the payment is due (beginning or end of the period). The **Pv** argument is optional and represents the present value of the loan or investment, which is assumed to be 0 by default.

The FV function is often used with investments to calculate the future value of a series of payments. For example, if you deposit $100 per month in a new savings account that has a starting balance of $0 and pays 1% interest annually, the FV function to calculate the future value of that investment after 10 years or 120 months is

```
FV(1%/12, 10*12, -100)
```

which returns $12,614.99. The extra $614.99 above the total amount of $12,000 you deposited is the interest earned from the money during that 10-year period. Note that the payment value is –100 because it represents the monthly deposit (negative cash flow), and the value returned by the FV function is positive because it represents money returned to the investor (positive cash flow). The *Pv* value in this example is assumed to be 0 because no money was in the savings account before the first deposit.

When used with a loan, a positive payment value is included as the present value of the loan. For example, if you borrow $10,000 at 4% annual interest and repay the loan at a rate of $250 per month, you would calculate the amount remaining on the loan after three years or 36 months as the future value

```
FV(4%/12, 12*3, -250, 10000)
```

which returns ($1,727.33), a negative value indicating that you still owe more than $1,700 on the loan at the end of three years.

Asli wants to know how much the company would still owe after five years if the quarterly payments were $30,000. You will use the FV function to calculate this future value.

To calculate the future value of the loan:

1. In cell **B8**, enter **$650,000** as the size of the loan.

2. Copy the values and formulas from the range **D7:H7** and paste them in the range **D8:H8**.

3. In cell **I8**, enter **–$30,000** as the size of the quarterly payments. Again, the value is negative because it represents money that the company will spend (negative cash flow).

4. In cell **C8**, enter the formula **=FV(H8, F8, I8, B8)** to calculate the future value of the loan based on the rate value in cell H8, the number of payments specified in cell F8, the quarterly payments specified in cell I8, and the present value of the loan entered in cell B8. The formula returns ($181,746), a negative value that indicates the company will still owe the lender more than $180,000 at the end of the five-year period. See Figure 9–2.

Figure 9–2   Future value of a loan

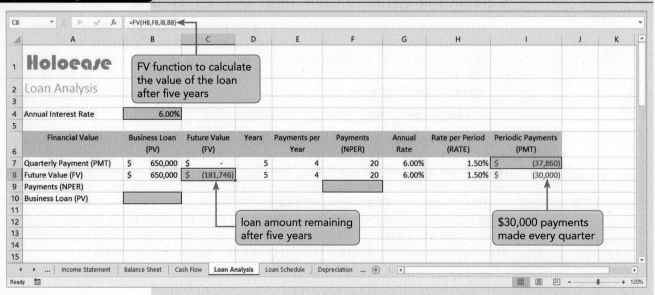

At 6% annual interest, about 27% of the original $650,000 loan will still need to be repaid at the end of five years if the quarterly payments are limited to $30,000.

Insight

Calculating Inflation with the FV Function

You can use the FV function to calculate future costs, adjusting for the effects of inflation. To project a future value of an item, use

```
FV(Rate, Years, 0, Present)
```

where *Rate* is the annual inflation rate, *Years* is the number of years in the future for which you want to project the cost of the item, and *Present* is the present-day cost. For example, if an item currently costs $15,000 and the inflation rate is 2.3%, the cost of the item in eight years is calculated using

```
FV(2.3%, 8, 0, 15000)
```

which returns –$17,992.70. The negative value is based on how Excel handles the FV function with positive and negative cash flows. For the purposes of predicting an inflated value, you can ignore the minus sign and use a value of $17,992.70 as the future cost of the item. Notice that you enter 0 for the value of the *Pmt* argument because you are not making payments toward inflation.

The FV function can also be used to express today's dollars in terms of yesterday's dollars by entering a negative value for the *Years* value. For example, the following function uses a value of –8 for years

```
FV(2.3%, -8, 0, 15000)
```

returning the value –$12,505.07, indicating that at an annual inflation rate of 2.3%, $15,000 today is equivalent to about $12,500 eight years ago.

Because a significant amount of the original loan would still be unpaid after five years, Asli wants to know how much more time would be required to repay the $650,000 loan assuming quarterly payments of $30,000. You can calculate the length of the payment period using the NPER function.

Calculating the Payment Period with the NPER Function

The NPER function calculates the number of payments required either to repay a loan or to reach an investment goal. The syntax of the NPER function is

```
NPER(Rate, Pmt, Pv, [Fv=0], [Type=0])
```

where the *Rate*, *Pmt*, *Pv*, *Fv*, and *Type* arguments are the same as described with the PMT and FV functions. For example, the following function calculates the number of $20 monthly payments needed to repay a $1,000 loan at 4% annual interest:

```
NPER(4%/12, -20, 1000)
```

The formula returns 54.7875773, indicating that the loan and the interest will be completely repaid in about 55 months.

To use the NPER function for investments, you define a future value of the investment along with the investment's present value and the periodic payments made to the investment. If you placed $200 per month in an account that pays 3% interest compounded monthly, the following function calculates the number of payments required to reach $5,000:

```
NPER(3%/12, -200, 0, 5000)
```

The formula returns 24.28, which is just over two years. Note that the *Pv* value is set to 0 based on the assumption that no money was in the account before the first deposit.

Tip
The NPER function returns the number of payments, not necessarily the number of years.

You will use the NPER function to calculate how long it will take to repay a $650,000 loan at 6% interest with quarterly payments of $30,000.

To calculate the number of payments for the loan:

1. Copy the present and future values of the loan in the range **B7:C7** and paste them into the range **B9:C9**.

2. In cell **E9**, enter **4** to specify that payments are made quarterly.

3. Copy the annual interest rate, rate per quarter, and size of the quarterly payments values and formulas in the range **G8:I8** and paste them in the range **G9:I9**.

4. In cell **F9**, enter the formula **=NPER(H9, I9, B9)** to calculate the required number of payments based on the interest rate per quarter in cell H9, the quarterly payments value in cell I9, and the present value of the loan in cell B9. The formula returns 26.40, indicating that about 27 payments are required to fully repay the loan.

5. In cell **D9**, enter the formula **=F9/E9** to divide the total number of payments by the number of payments per year, which determines the number of years needed to repay the loan. The formula returns 6.599718, indicating that the loan will be repaid in about 6.6 years.

6. Select cell **F9**. See Figure 9–3.

Tip

If the NPER function returns #NUM!, the loan cannot be repaid because the payments for each period are less than the interest due.

Figure 9–3	Payments required to repay the loan

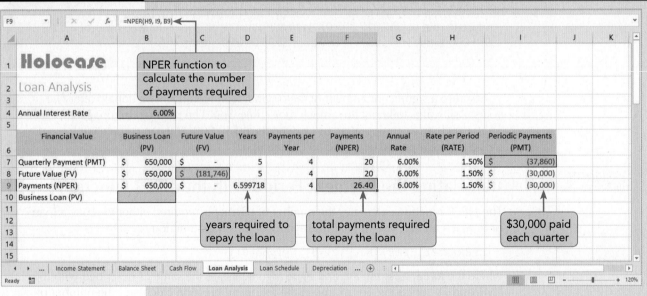

The company doesn't want to take more than six years to repay a business loan, so Asli suggests that you calculate the size of the loan that could be repaid within five years at $30,000 per quarter.

Calculating the Present Value with the PV Function

The PV function calculates the present value of a loan or an investment. For a loan, the present value would be the current size of the loan. For an investment, the present value is the amount of money initially placed in the investment account. The syntax of the PV function is

```
PV(Rate, Nper, Pmt, [Fv=0], [Type=0])
```

where the *Rate*, *Nper*, *Pmt*, *Fv*, and *Type* arguments have the same meanings they had for the other financial functions. You can use the PV function to calculate the loan amount that you can afford given a set number of payments and an annual interest rate. For example, if you make $100 monthly payments at 4% annual interest for four years (or 48 months), the function to calculate the largest loan you can afford is

```
PV(4%/12, 48, -100)
```

which returns $4,428.88. Note that because you are paying $100 per month for 48 months, the total amount paid back to the lender is $4,800. The $371.12 difference between the total amount paid and the loan amount represents the cost of the loan in terms of the total amount of interest paid.

You can also use the PV function with investments to calculate the initial payment required to reach a savings goal. For example, if you add $100 per month to a college savings account that grows at 4% annual interest and you want the account to reach a future value of $25,000 in 10 years (or 120 months), the following function returns the size of the initial payment:

```
PV(4%/12, 120, -100, 25000)
```

The function returns –$6,892.13, indicating you must start with almost $6,900 in the account to reach the $25,000 savings goal at the end of 10 years. You will use the PV function to determine the largest loan that Holoease can afford if the company pays back the loan with quarterly payments of $32,000 made over a five-year period at 6% annual interest.

To apply the PV function to calculate the loan size:

1. Copy the loan condition values and formulas in the range **C7:H7** and paste them in the range **C10:H10**.

2. In cell **I10**, enter **–$32,000** as the quarterly payment amount.

3. In cell **B10**, enter **=PV(H10, F10, I10)** to calculate the size of the loan based on the interest rate per quarter value in cell H10, the number of payments specified in cell F10, and the size of the quarterly payments in cell I10. The formula results specify a loan amount of $549,396. See Figure 9–4.

| Figure 9–4 | Present value of the loan |

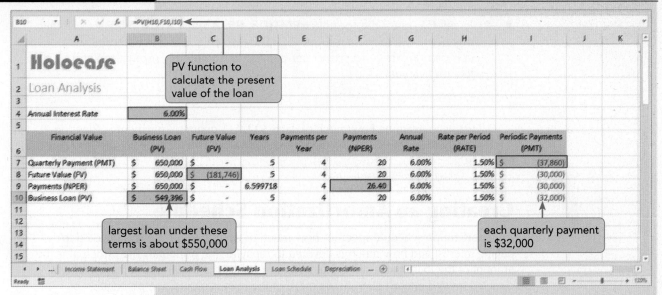

Asli will recommend a loan amount of $550,000 to be repaid at 6% interest in quarterly payments over the first five years of the company's operation. You will enter this loan amount in the Startup worksheet, which contains the company's startup costs and assets.

To enter the loan amount:

1. Go to the **Startup** worksheet.

2. In cell **B26**, enter **550,000** as the loan amount.

3. Review the Startup worksheet, noting the expenses and assets for starting up the company as well as other sources of funding. You will use some of these values later.

Asli wants you to provide more detailed information about the proposed business loan in the Loan Schedule worksheet. You'll start by entering the terms of the loan and calculate the exact value of each loan payment.

To calculate the size of the loan payments:

1. Go to the **Loan Schedule** worksheet.

2. In cell **A5**, type **=** to begin the formula, go to the **Startup** worksheet, click cell **B26**, and then press **TAB**. The formula **=Startup!B26** entered in cell A5 displays the loan amount of $550,000 from cell B26 in the Startup worksheet.

3. In cell **B5**, enter **6.00%** as the annual interest rate.

4. In cell **C5**, enter **4** as the number of payments per year because the company plans to make quarterly payments.

5. In cell **D5**, enter the formula **=B5/C5** to calculate the interest rate per quarter. The formula returns 1.50% as the interest rate.

6. In cell **E5**, enter **5** to indicate that the loan will be repaid in five years.

7. In cell **F5**, enter the formula **=C5*E5** to calculate the total number of payments, which is 20 payments in this case.

8. In cell **G5**, enter the formula **=PMT(D5, F5, A5)** to calculate the size of each payment. The formula returns −$32,035, which is the exact amount the company will have to spend per quarter to completely repay the $550,000 loan in five years.

Asli wants to examine how much of each $32,035 quarterly payment is spent on interest charged by the lender. To determine that value, you'll create an amortization schedule.

Creating an Amortization Schedule

An amortization schedule specifies how much of each loan payment is devoted to paying interest and how much is devoted to repaying the principal. The principal is the amount of the loan that is still unpaid. In most loans, the initial payments are usually directed toward interest charges. As more of the loan is repaid, the percentage of each payment devoted to interest decreases (because the interest is being applied to a smaller and smaller principal) until the last few payments are almost entirely devoted to repaying the principal. Figure 9–5 shows a typical relationship between the amount paid toward interest and the amount paid toward the principal plotted against the number of payments.

Figure 9–5   **Interest and principal payments**

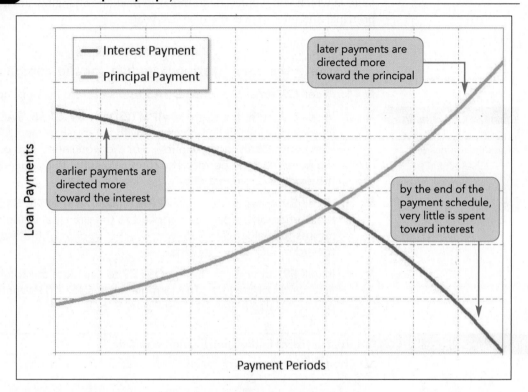

Calculating Interest and Principal Payments

To calculate the amount of a loan payment devoted to interest and to principal, use the IPMT and PPMT functions. The IPMT function returns the amount that each payment is directed toward paying the interest on the loan. It has the syntax

```
IPMT(Rate, Per, Nper, Pv, [Fv=0], [Type=0])
```

where the **Rate**, **Nper**, **Pv**, **Fv**, and **Type** arguments have the same meaning as they do for the PMT and other financial functions. The **Per** argument indicates the payment period for which the interest is due. For example, the following function calculates how much interest is due in the third payment of the company's $550,000 loan at 6% interest paid quarterly over five years:

```
IPMT(6%/4, 3, 20, 550000)
```

returning a value of –$7,531.09, indicating that the company will owe about $7,500 in interest in the third payment. The PPMT function calculates the amount used to repay the principal and has a similar syntax:

```
PPMT(Rate, Per, Nper, Pv, [Fv=0], [Type=0])
```

 The function to calculate the amount of the third payment that is devoted to principal is

```
PPMT(6%/4, 3, 20, 550000)
```

returning a value –$24,504.06. Note that the sum of the interest payment and the principal payment is –$32,035.15, which is the quarterly payment amount returned by the PMT function in cell G5 of the Loan Schedule worksheet. The total amount paid to the bank each quarter doesn't change—the only change is how that amount is allocated between interest and principal.

Asli asks you to use the IPMT and PPMT functions to complete an amortization schedule for the proposed loan. The Loan Schedule worksheet already contains the table in which you'll enter the formulas to track the changing amounts spent on principal and interest over the next five years.

To create the amortization schedule for the company's loan:

▶ **1.** In cell **C9**, enter the formula **=A5** to display the initial principal of the loan.

▶ **2.** In cell **D9**, enter the formula **=IPMT($D$5, B9, $F$5, $A$5)** to calculate the interest due for the first payment, with $D$5, $F$5, and $A$5 referencing the loan conditions specified in row 5 of the worksheet, and cell B9 referencing the number of the period. The formula returns the value –$8,250, which is the amount of interest due in the first payment.

▶ **3.** In cell **E9**, enter the formula **=PPMT($D$5, B9, $F$5, $A$5)** to calculate the portion of the payment applied to the principal in the first period. Excel returns the value –$23,785, which is the amount of the first payment directed toward reducing the principal.

▶ **4.** In cell **F9**, enter the formula **=D9+E9** to calculate the total payment for the first period of the loan. The formula returns –$32,035, matching the quarterly payment value in cell G5. See Figure 9–6.

Tip

Use absolute references to apply the same loan conditions to every payment period when you copy the formulas to the rest of the amortization schedule.

| Figure 9–6 | Initial payment in the amortization schedule |

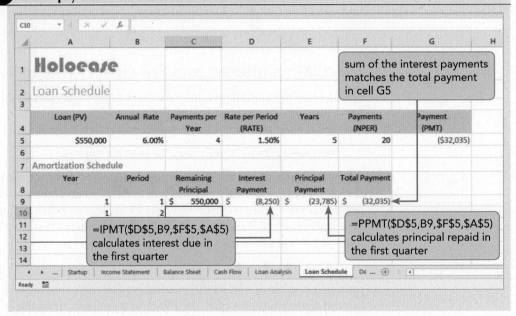

The formulas for the rest of the amortization schedule are like those used for the first quarter except that the remaining principal in column C must be reduced by the amount paid toward the principal from the previous quarter.

To complete the amortization schedule:

1. In cell **C10**, enter the formula **=C9+E9** to add the remaining principal at the start of the first quarter to the first quarter principal payment. The remaining principal at the start of the second quarter is $526,215.

2. Copy the formulas in the range **D9:F9** and paste them in the range **D10:F10** to calculate the interest, principal, and total payment for the second quarter. The interest paid drops to –$7,893 because the interest is charged on a smaller principal, while the amount paid toward the principal increases to –$24,142. The total payment remains $32,035, a valuable check that the formulas are correct.

3. Use the fill handle to extend the formulas in the range **C10:F10** to the range **C11:F28**. The formulas are copied into the rest of the rows of the amortization schedule to calculate the remaining principal, interest payment, principal payment, and total payment for each of the remaining 18 quarters of the loan.

4. Click the **Auto Fill Options** button 🖳, and then click the **Fill Without Formatting** option button. The formulas are entered without overwriting the existing worksheet formatting. Notice that in the last quarterly payment at the end of the fifth year, only $473 of the $32,035 payment is used to pay the interest on the loan. The remaining $31,562 is used to pay off the principal.

5. In cell **C29**, enter the formula **=C28+E28** to calculate the final balance of the loan after the final payment. The final balance is $0.00, verifying that the loan is completely repaid at the end of the five-year period. See Figure 9–7.

Figure 9–7	Completed amortization schedule

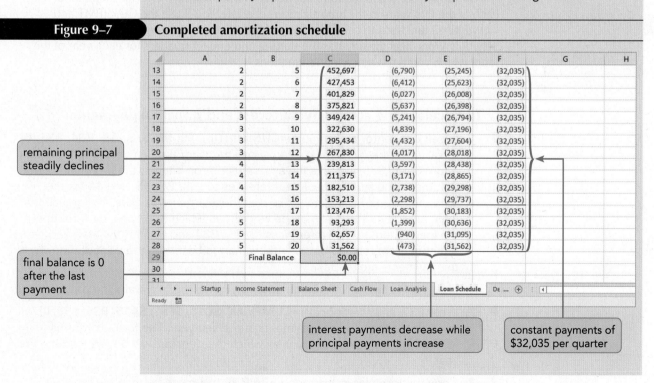

	A	B	C	D	E	F	G	H
13	2	5	452,697	(6,790)	(25,245)	(32,035)		
14	2	6	427,453	(6,412)	(25,623)	(32,035)		
15	2	7	401,829	(6,027)	(26,008)	(32,035)		
16	2	8	375,821	(5,637)	(26,398)	(32,035)		
17	3	9	349,424	(5,241)	(26,794)	(32,035)		
18	3	10	322,630	(4,839)	(27,196)	(32,035)		
19	3	11	295,434	(4,432)	(27,604)	(32,035)		
20	3	12	267,830	(4,017)	(28,018)	(32,035)		
21	4	13	239,813	(3,597)	(28,438)	(32,035)		
22	4	14	211,375	(3,171)	(28,865)	(32,035)		
23	4	15	182,510	(2,738)	(29,298)	(32,035)		
24	4	16	153,213	(2,298)	(29,737)	(32,035)		
25	5	17	123,476	(1,852)	(30,183)	(32,035)		
26	5	18	93,293	(1,399)	(30,636)	(32,035)		
27	5	19	62,657	(940)	(31,095)	(32,035)		
28	5	20	31,562	(473)	(31,562)	(32,035)		
29		Final Balance	$0.00					
30								
31								

remaining principal steadily declines

final balance is 0 after the last payment

interest payments decrease while principal payments increase

constant payments of $32,035 per quarter

Startup | Income Statement | Balance Sheet | Cash Flow | Loan Analysis | **Loan Schedule** | De ...

Ready

Asli finds it helpful to see how much interest the company is paying each quarter. However, many financial statements also show the amount paid toward interest and principal over the whole year because this information is used when creating annual budgets and calculating taxes.

Calculating Cumulative Interest and Principal Payments

Cumulative totals of interest and principal payments can be calculated using the CUMIPMT and CUMPRINC functions. The **CUMIPMT function** calculates the sum of several interest payments and has the syntax

    CUMIPMT(*Rate*, *Nper*, *Pv*, *Start*, *End*, *Type*)

where *Start* is the starting payment period for the interval you want to sum and *End* is the ending payment period. This function does not specify a future value because the assumption is that loans are always completely repaid. Also, note that the *Type* argument is not optional. You must specify whether the payments are made at the end of the period (*Type*=0) or at the start (*Type*=1). For example, to calculate the total interest paid in the second year of the company's loan (at the end of quarters 5 through 8), you would enter the function

    CUMIPMT(6%/4, 20, 550000, 5, 8, 0)

which returns –$24,867.01 as the total spent on interest in the second year of the loan.

To calculate the cumulative total of payments made toward the principal, you use the **CUMPRINC function**, which has a similar syntax:

    CUMPRINC(*Rate*, *Nper*, *Pv*, *Start*, *End*, *Type*)

The following function calculates the total amount spent on reducing the principal of the loan during the fifth to eighth quarters

    CUMPRINC(6%/4, 20, 550000, 5, 8, 0)

returning a value of –$103,273.61, indicating that the amount remaining on the loan is reduced by more than $100,000 during the second year.

Asli wants you to add the total interest and principal payments for the loan for each of the five years in the amortization schedule. You'll use the CUMIPMT and CUMPRINC functions to calculate these values. The table at the bottom of the Loan Schedule worksheet already has the starting and ending quarters for each year of the loan, which you'll reference in the functions.

To calculate the cumulative interest and principal payments:

1. In cell **B36**, enter the formula **=CUMIPMT($D$5, $F$5, $A$5, B34, B35, 0)** to calculate the cumulative interest payments for the first year. The formula returns –$30,838, which is the amount spent on interest the first year. Notice that the formula uses absolute references to cells D5, F5, and A5 for the *Rate*, *Nper*, and *Pv* arguments so that these arguments always reference the loan conditions at the top of the worksheet, which don't change throughout the loan schedule. The references to cells B34 and B35 for the start and end arguments are relative because they change based on the period over which the payments are made.

   Next you'll calculate the cumulative payments made toward the principal.

2. In cell **B37**, enter the formula **=CUMPRINC($D$5, $F$5, $A$5, B34, B35, 0)** to calculate the principal payments in the first year. The formula returns –$97,303, which is the amount by which the principal will be reduced the first year.

3. Copy the formulas in the range **B36:B37** and paste them in the range **C36:F37** to calculate the cumulative interest and principal payments for each of the next four years.

4. Click cell **F37**. See Figure 9–8.

Figure 9–8   **Annual cumulative interest and principal payments**

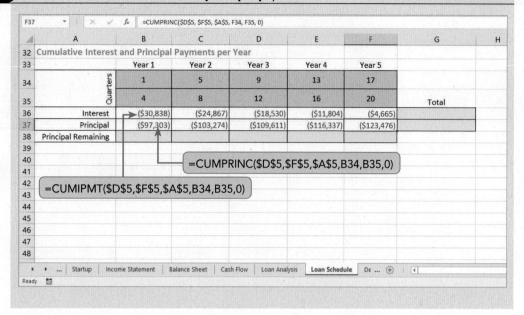

Each year, more money is spent reducing the principal. For example, in Year 5, the company will spend $4,665 on interest payments and will reduce the loan principal by $123,476. Next you will calculate the total paid on interest and principal through the five years of the loan and the principal remaining at the end of each year.

To complete the cumulative payment table:

1. Select the range **G36:G37**.

2. On the Home tab, in the Editing group, click the **AutoSum** button to calculate the total interest and principal payments over the five years of the loan, which are $90,703 and $550,000, respectively.

   Finally, you will calculate the principal remaining at the end of each of the five years of the loan.

3. In cell **B38**, enter the formula **=$A$5+B37** to add the cumulative principal payment to the initial amount of the loan in cell A5. The formula returns $452,697, which is the amount of the loan remaining to be paid after the first year.

4. In cell **C38**, enter the formula **=B38+C37** to calculate the remaining principal at the end of Year 2 by adding the Year 1 principal to the Year 2 principal payments. The formula returns $349,424.

5. Copy the formula in cell **C38** and paste it in the range **D38:F38** to calculate the remaining principal at the end of each of the next three years. Note that at end of the fifth year, the principal remaining is zero since the entire loan is paid off.

6. Select cell **A31** to deselect the table. Figure 9–9 shows the final table of cumulative interest and principal payments.

Figure 9–9 | **Total loan payments**

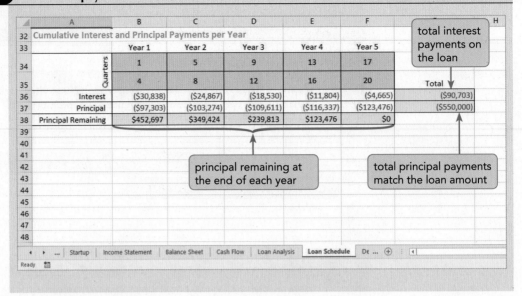

		Year 1	Year 2	Year 3	Year 4	Year 5	Total
Cumulative Interest and Principal Payments per Year							
	Quarters	1	5	9	13	17	
		4	8	12	16	20	Total
Interest		($30,838)	($24,867)	($18,530)	($11,804)	($4,665)	($90,703)
Principal		($97,303)	($103,274)	($109,611)	($116,337)	($123,476)	($550,000)
Principal Remaining		$452,697	$349,424	$239,813	$123,476	$0	

total interest payments on the loan

principal remaining at the end of each year

total principal payments match the loan amount

The Loan Schedule worksheet shows that the company will spend more than $90,000 in interest payments to finance this loan. Calculating the total principal payment lets you verify that the loan conditions are set up correctly. If the total payment on the principal does not match the initial amount of the loan, there must be a mistake in the calculations used in the loan schedule.

Proskills

Written Communication: Writing a Financial Workbook

A properly written financial workbook should communicate key pieces of information in a way that is concise and quickly grasped. It should also be editable to allow exploration of what-if scenarios that analyze the impact of different assumptions on the financial bottom line. To help ensure that any financial workbook you create meets these goals, keep in mind the following principles:

- Place all important financial variables at or near the top of a worksheet so that they are visible to others. For example, place the interest rate you use in calculations in a clearly labeled worksheet cell.

- Use defined names with the financial variables to make it easier to apply them in formulas and functions.

- Clearly identify the direction of the cash flow in all your financial calculations by expressing the cash value as negative or positive. Using the wrong sign will turn the calculation of a loan payment into an investment deposit or vice versa.

- Place argument values in worksheet cells where they can be viewed and changed. Never place these values directly into a financial formula.

- When values are used in more than one calculation, enter them in a cell that you can reference in all formulas rather than repeating the same value throughout the workbook.

- Use the same unit of time for all the arguments in a financial function. For example, when using the PMT function to calculate monthly loan payments, the interest rate and the number of payments should be based on the interest rate per month and the total months to repay the loan.

A financial workbook that is easy to read and understand is more useful to yourself and others when making business decisions.

You have finished analyzing the conditions for the company's business loan. In the next session, you'll make projections about the company's future earnings by developing projection of the company's income statement over the next five years.

Review

Session 9.1 Quick Check

1. Explain the difference between positive and negative cash flow. If you borrow $20,000 from a bank, is that a positive or negative cash flow? Explain your answer.

2. What is the formula to calculate how much a savings account would be worth if the initial balance is $1,000 with monthly deposits of $75 for 10 years at 4.3% annual interest compounded monthly? What is the formula result?

3. You want a savings account to grow from $1,000 to $5,000 within two years. Assume the bank provides a 3.2% annual interest rate compounded monthly. What is the formula to calculate how much you must deposit each month to meet your savings goal? What is the formula result?

4. A business takes out a loan for $250,000 at 4.8% interest compounded monthly. If the business can afford to make monthly payments of only $1,500 on the loan, what is the formula to calculate the number of months required to repay the loan completely? What is the formula result?

5. Rerun your calculations from Question 4 assuming that the business can afford only a $1,000 monthly payment. What is the revised formula and resulting value? How do you explain the result?

6. A business takes out a 10-year loan for $250,000 at 5.3% interest compounded monthly. What is the formula to calculate the monthly payment and what is the resulting value?

7. For the loan conditions specified in Question 6, provide formulas to calculate the amount of the first payment used for interest and the amount of the first payment used to repay the principal. What are the resulting values?

8. For the loan conditions specified in Question 6, what are the formulas to calculate how much interest the business will pay in the first year and how much the business will repay toward the principal? What are the resulting values?

9. For the loan conditions in Question 6, calculate the total cost of the loan in terms of the total interest paid through the 10 years of the loan.

Session 9.2 Visual Overview:

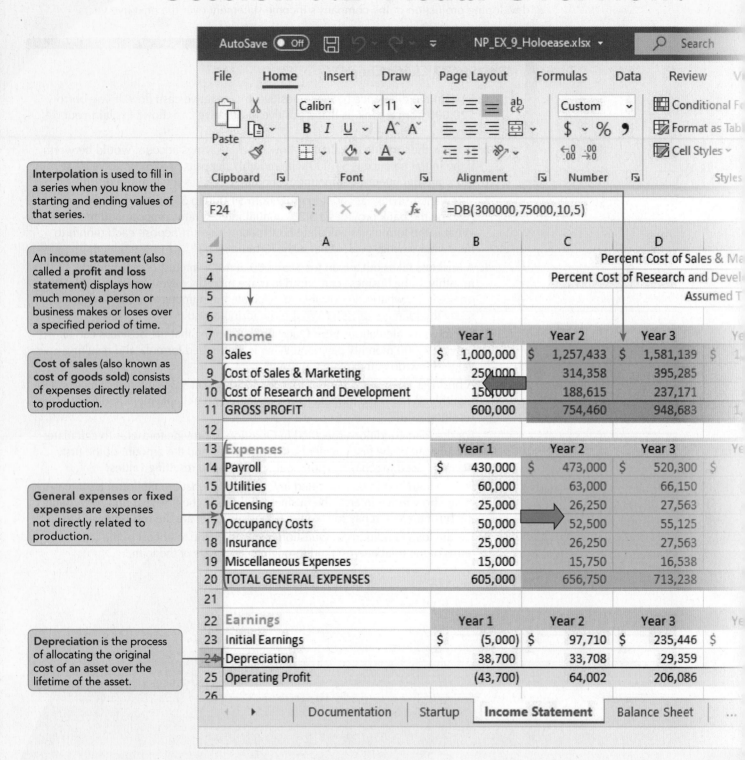

Interpolation is used to fill in a series when you know the starting and ending values of that series.

An **income statement** (also called a **profit and loss statement**) displays how much money a person or business makes or loses over a specified period of time.

Cost of sales (also known as **cost of goods sold**) consists of expenses directly related to production.

General expenses or **fixed expenses** are expenses not directly related to production.

Depreciation is the process of allocating the original cost of an asset over the lifetime of the asset.

AutoSave ⦿ Off   NP_EX_9_Holoease.xlsx ▾   🔍 Search

File   Home   Insert   Draw   Page Layout   Formulas   Data   Review

F24   fx   =DB(300000,75000,10,5)

	A	B	C	D
3			Percent Cost of Sales & Ma	
4			Percent Cost of Research and Devel	
5			Assumed T	
6				
7	Income	Year 1	Year 2	Year 3	Ye
8	Sales	$ 1,000,000	$ 1,257,433	$ 1,581,139	$ 1,
9	Cost of Sales & Marketing	250,000	314,358	395,285	
10	Cost of Research and Development	150,000	188,615	237,171	
11	GROSS PROFIT	600,000	754,460	948,683	1,
12					
13	Expenses	Year 1	Year 2	Year 3	Ye
14	Payroll	$ 430,000	$ 473,000	$ 520,300	$
15	Utilities	60,000	63,000	66,150	
16	Licensing	25,000	26,250	27,563	
17	Occupancy Costs	50,000	52,500	55,125	
18	Insurance	25,000	26,250	27,563	
19	Miscellaneous Expenses	15,000	15,750	16,538	
20	TOTAL GENERAL EXPENSES	605,000	656,750	713,238	
21					
22	Earnings	Year 1	Year 2	Year 3	Ye
23	Initial Earnings	$ (5,000)	$ 97,710	$ 235,446	$
24	Depreciation	38,700	33,708	29,359	
25	Operating Profit	(43,700)	64,002	206,086	
26					

◄ ► | Documentation | Startup | **Income Statement** | Balance Sheet | ...

Income Statements and Depreciation

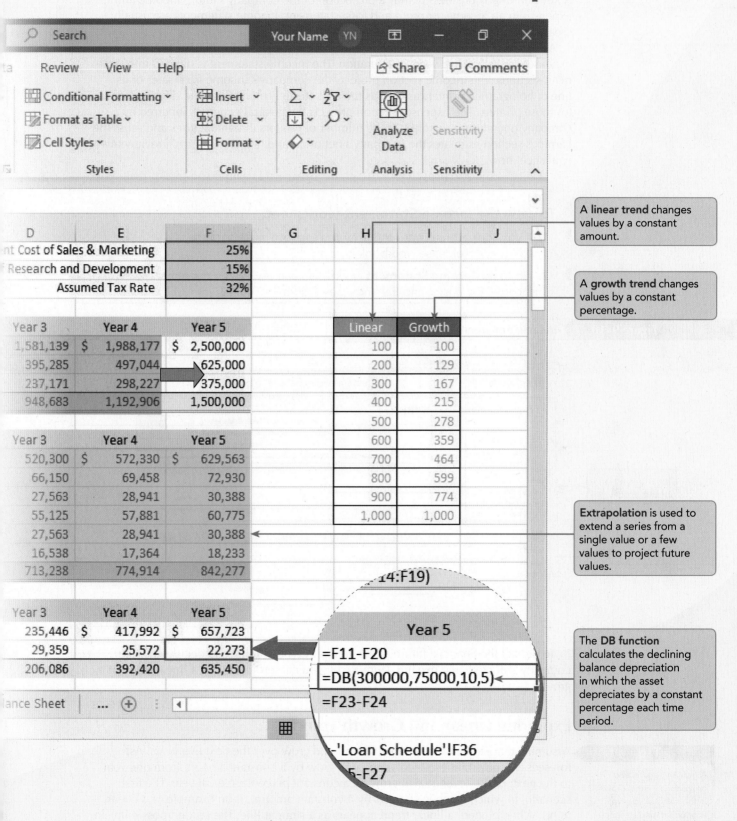

A **linear trend** changes values by a constant amount.

A **growth trend** changes values by a constant percentage.

Extrapolation is used to extend a series from a single value or a few values to project future values.

The **DB function** calculates the declining balance depreciation in which the asset depreciates by a constant percentage each time period.

D	E	F
nt Cost of **Sales & Marketing**		25%
Research and Development		15%
Assumed Tax Rate		32%

Year 3	Year 4	Year 5
1,581,139	$ 1,988,177	$ 2,500,000
395,285	497,044	625,000
237,171	298,227	375,000
948,683	1,192,906	1,500,000

Year 3	Year 4	Year 5
520,300	$ 572,330	$ 629,563
66,150	69,458	72,930
27,563	28,941	30,388
55,125	57,881	60,775
27,563	28,941	30,388
16,538	17,364	18,233
713,238	774,914	842,277

Linear	Growth
100	100
200	129
300	167
400	215
500	278
600	359
700	464
800	599
900	774
1,000	1,000

Year 3	Year 4	Year 5
235,446	$ 417,992	$ 657,723
29,359	25,572	22,273
206,086	392,420	635,450

14:F19)

Year 5

=F11-F20

=DB(300000,75000,10,5)

=F23-F24

-'Loan Schedule'!F36

5-F27

lance Sheet

Projecting Future Income and Expenses

A key part of any business plan is a projection of the company's future income and expenses in an income, or profit and loss, statement. Income statements are usually created monthly, semiannually, or annually.

Asli created the Income Statement worksheet to project the company's income and expenses for its first five years of operation. The income statement is divided into three main sections. The Income section projects the company's income from sales of its line of holographic printers as well as the cost of sales, marketing, and development for those printers. The Expenses section projects the general expenses incurred by company operations regardless of the number of printers it manufactures and sells. The Earnings section estimates the company's net profit and tax liability. You'll review this worksheet now.

To view the Income Statement worksheet:

1. If you took a break after the previous session, make sure the NP_EX_9_Holoease workbook is open.

2. Go to the **Income Statement** worksheet, and review the three main sections—Income, Expenses, and Earnings. See Figure 9–10.

Figure 9–10	Income Statement worksheet

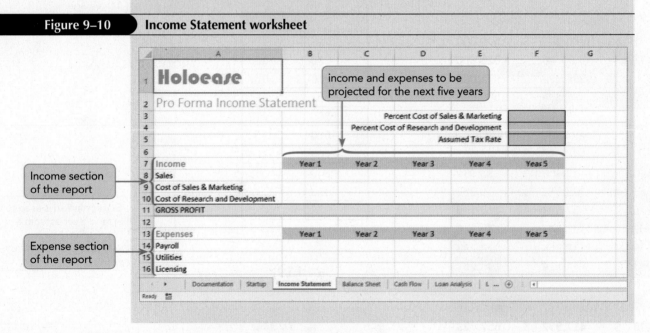

To project the financial future of the company, you will have to decide how the company will grow and expand. With Excel, you can project either a linear trend or a growth trend.

Exploring Linear and Growth Trends

> **Tip**
>
> A growth trend is also called exponential growth in the fields of science, economics, and statistics.

Assuming that Holoease will be successful and grow over the next five years, Asli foresees two possibilities: (1) Revenue will grow by a constant amount from one year to the next; or (2) Revenue will grow by a constant percentage each year. The first scenario, in which revenue changes by a constant amount, is an example of a linear trend. When plotted, a linear trend appears as a straight line. The second possibility, in which revenue changes by a constant percentage rather than a constant amount, is an example of a growth trend. For example, each value in a growth trend might be 15%

higher than the previous year's value. When plotted, a growth trend appears as a curve with the greatest numerical differences occurring near the end of the series.

Figure 9–11 shows a linear trend and a growth trend for revenue that starts at $1,000,000 in Year 1 increasing to $2,500,000 by Year 5. The growth trend lags behind the linear trend in the early stages but reaches the same revenue value at the end of the time period.

| Figure 9–11 | Linear and growth trends |

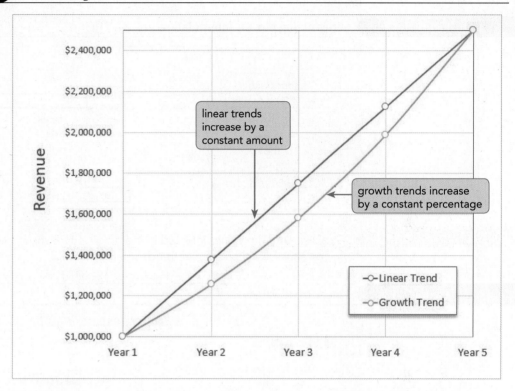

To fill in the data from a linear trend or a growth trend, you can use interpolation.

Interpolating from a Starting Value to an Ending Value

Interpolation is the process that estimates values that fall between a starting point and an ending point. You can use AutoFill to interpolate values for both linear and growth trends. Asli wants you to estimate revenues for each of the company's first five years, assuming that the company's revenue will grow from $1,000,000 in Year 1 to $2,500,000 in Year 5. Asli first wants to determine how much revenue will be generated each year if the revenue grows by a constant amount. You'll interpolate the company's revenue for Year 2 through Year 4 using a linear trend.

To project future revenue based on a linear trend:

▶ **1.** In cell **B8**, enter **$1,000,000** as the Year 1 revenue.

▶ **2.** In cell **F8**, enter **$2,500,000** as the Year 5 revenue.

▶ **3.** Select the range **B8:F8**, which includes the starting and ending revenue values.

▶ **4.** On the Home tab, in the Editing group, click the **Fill** button, and then click **Series**. The Series dialog box opens.

5. Verify that the **Rows** option button in the Series section and the **Linear** option button in the Type section are selected. Excel will fill the series within the same rows using a linear trend.

6. Click the **Trend** check box to insert a checkmark and apply a trend that interpolates between the starting and ending values in the selected range. See Figure 9–12.

Figure 9–12	Series dialog box for interpolation

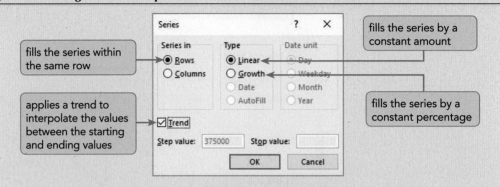

7. Click **OK**. The values inserted in the range C8:E8 show the company's projected revenue based on a linear trend. See Figure 9–13.

Figure 9–13	Linear trend values

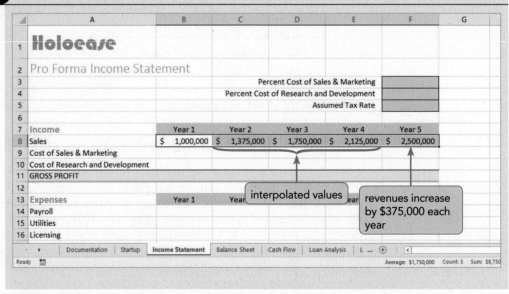

The linear trend projects an increase in the company's revenue of $375,000 per year. Next, you'll fill in the revenue values in Year 2 through Year 4 assuming a growth trend. To interpolate the growth trend correctly, you first must remove the Year 2 through Year 4 values, leaving those cells blank.

To project future revenue assuming a growth trend:

You must leave the middle cells in the range blank to interpolate new values.

1. Select the range **C8:E8**, and then press **DELETE** on your keyboard to clear the contents of those cells.

2. Select the range **B8:F8**.

3. On the Home tab, in the Editing group, click the **Fill** button, and then click **Series**. The Series dialog box opens.

4. In the Type section, click the **Growth** option button, and then click the **Trend** check box to select it, applying a growth trend to the interpolated values.

5. Click **OK**. The Year 1 through Year 5 revenue projections are now based on a growth trend. See Figure 9–14.

| Figure 9–14 | Growth trend values |

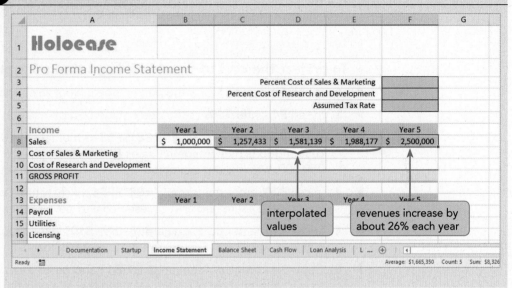

In a growth trend, the values change by a constant percentage each year. You can determine the percentage change by dividing one year's revenue value by the previous year's revenue. For the projected revenue values, the values grow at a constant rate of about 25.74% per year. The largest revenue increase occurs at the end of the five-year period. For example, revenue grows by $257,433 from Year 1 to Year 2, but by $511,823 from Year 4 to Year 5.

Insight

Interpolating and Extrapolating in Charts

You can add interpolated values to any scatter chart by adding a trendline to the chart. To add a trendline, select the chart, click the Chart Elements button for the chart, and then click the Trendline check box. Excel supports trendlines for exponential (or growth) trends, linear (straight line) trends, logarithmic trends, polynomial trends, power trends, and moving averages. All these options can be found in the Format Trendline pane of the chart.

Trendlines can be extrapolated forward or backward from the points in the scatter chart by setting the forecast options in the Format Trendline pane. Again, these extrapolated values can be based on a wide variety of functions including linear and exponential functions. For more information, you can display the equation of the trendline on the chart itself.

Calculating the Cost of Goods Sold

The next part of the worksheet displays the cost of sales, also known as the cost of goods sold. Holoease needs to purchase the raw material to create the printers, and it also must invest time into the development and upgrade of the software used to generate the holographic images. Asli has estimated for every dollar of sales revenue, the company will need to spend 25 cents on sales and marketing and 15 cents on research and development. As the company's revenue increases, these costs will also increase. The difference between the company's sales revenue and the cost of goods sold is the company's **gross profit**.

Asli wants you to project the cost of goods sold and the company's gross profit for each of the next five years using those estimates.

To project the cost of goods sold and the gross profit:

▶ **1.** In cell **F3**, enter **25%** as the percentage cost of sales and marketing.

▶ **2.** In cell **F4**, enter **15%** as the percentage cost of research and development.

▶ **3.** In cell **B9**, enter the formula **=B8*$F$3** to multiply the Year 1 revenue by the cost of goods percentage for sales and marketing. Excel returns a value of 250,000, which is the estimated cost of sales and marketing for Year 1.

▶ **4.** In cell **B10**, enter the formula **=B8*$F$4**. Excel returns a value of 150,000, which is the estimated cost of research and development in Year 1.

▶ **5.** In cell **B11**, enter the formula **=B8–(B9+B10)**. Excel returns a value of 600,000, which is the estimated gross profit in Year 1.

▶ **6.** Copy the formulas in the range **B9:B11** and paste them in the range **C9:F11** to calculate the cost of goods sold and the gross profit for Year 2 through Year 5. See Figure 9–15.

Figure 9–15	Cost of goods sold and gross profit

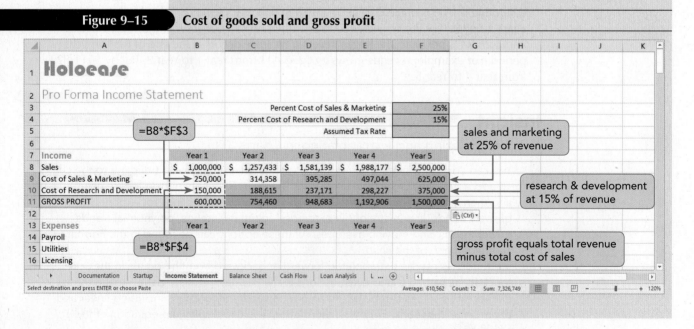

Based on these calculations, the company's gross profit is projected to increase from $600,000 in Year 1 to $1,500,000 in Year 5.

Reference

Interpolating and Extrapolating a Series

To interpolate a series of values between starting and ending values:
- Select the range with the first cell containing the starting value, blank cells for middle values, and the last cell containing the ending value.
- On the Home tab, in the Editing group, click the Fill button, and then click Series.
- Select whether the series is organized in rows or columns, select the type of series to interpolate, and then check the Trend check box.
- Click OK.

To extrapolate a series from a starting value:
- Select a range with the first cell containing the starting value followed by blank cells to store the extrapolated values.
- On the Home tab, in the Editing group, click the Fill button, and then click Series.
- Select whether the series is organized in rows or columns, select the type of series to extrapolate, and then enter the step value in the Step value box.
- Click OK.

The next section of the income statement contains the projected general expenses for the company. These expenses are not directly related to production. For example, the company must purchase insurance, provide for general maintenance, and pay for office space, regardless of the number of products it sells. You'll add the Year 1 general expenses to the Income Statement worksheet.

To enter the Year 1 expenses:

▶ **1.** In the range **B14:B19**, enter the following general expense values: **$430,000** in cell B14 for payroll, **60,000** in cell B15 for utilities, **25,000** in cell B16 for licensing, **50,000** in cell B17 for occupancy costs, **25,000** in cell B18 for insurance, and **15,000** in cell B19 for miscellaneous expenses.

▶ **2.** In cell **B20**, enter the formula **=SUM(B14:B19)** to calculate the total expenses for Year 1. The formula returns the value 605,000.

The total expenses for the first year will be $5,000 greater than the gross profit, so the company will lose money, whether this is true for the remaining four years depends in part on how fast expenses will grow relative to gross profit.

Extrapolating from a Series of Values

Extrapolation differs from interpolation in that only a starting value is provided; the succeeding values are estimated by assuming that the values follow a trend. As with interpolation, Excel can extrapolate a data series based on either a linear trend or a growth trend. With a linear trend, the data values are assumed to change by a constant amount. With a growth trend, they are assumed to change by a constant percentage. To extrapolate a data series, you must provide a step value representing the amount by which each value is changed as the series is extended. You do not have to specify a stopping value.

Asli estimates that the company's payroll will increase by 10% per year. The other costs will increase by 5% per year. These increases are equivalent to multiplying each year's expenses by 1.10 and 1.05, respectively. Rather than writing this formula into the worksheet, you'll extrapolate the expenses using the Fill command.

To extrapolate the Year 1 expenses:

▶ 1. Select the range **B14:F14** containing the cells in which the Year 1 through Year 5 payroll expenses will be entered.

▶ 2. On the Home tab, in the Editing group, click the **Fill** button, and then click **Series**. The Series dialog box opens.

▶ 3. In the Type section, click the **Growth** option button, and then type **1.10** in the Step value box. See Figure 9–16.

| Figure 9–16 | Series dialog box for extrapolation |

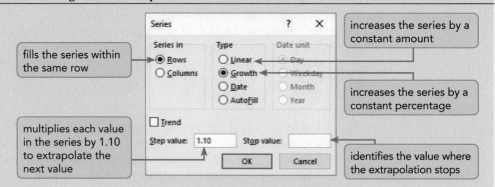

▶ 4. Click **OK**. The payroll expenses are extrapolated into Year 2 through Year 5, culminated in a Year 5 payroll of $629,563.

Next, you will extrapolate the other general expenses assuming a growth rate of 5%.

▶ 5. Select the range **B15:F19**. Do not select the row containing the total general expenses.

▶ 6. In the Editing group, click the **Fill** button, and then click **Series**. The Series dialog box opens.

▶ 7. Click the **Growth** option button, and then type **1.05** in the Step value box to increase the expenses by 5% per year.

Tip

To extrapolate a decreasing trend, use a negative step value for a decreasing linear trend, and a step value between 0 and 1 for a decreasing growth trend.

▶ 8. Click **OK**. The expense values from Year 1 are extrapolated into the Year 2 through Year 5 columns. For example, the expense for utilities increases to $72,930 in Year 5.

▶ 9. Copy the formula in cell **B20** and paste it in the range **C20:F20** to calculate the total general expenses for the company for each of the five years.

The calculations show that the projected general expenses will rise from $605,000 in Year 1 to $842,277 by the end of Year 5. Next, you want to calculate the company's earnings during each of the next five years. The initial earnings estimate is equal to the company's gross profit minus the total general expenses.

To calculate the company's initial earnings:

▶ 1. In cell **B23**, enter the formula **=B11–B20** to subtract the total general expenses from the gross profit for Year 1. The estimate of earnings for the first year is a loss of $5,000.

▶ 2. Copy the formula in cell **B23** and paste it in the range **C23:F23** to project yearly earnings through Year 5. See Figure 9–17.

| Figure 9–17 | Projected general expenses and earnings |

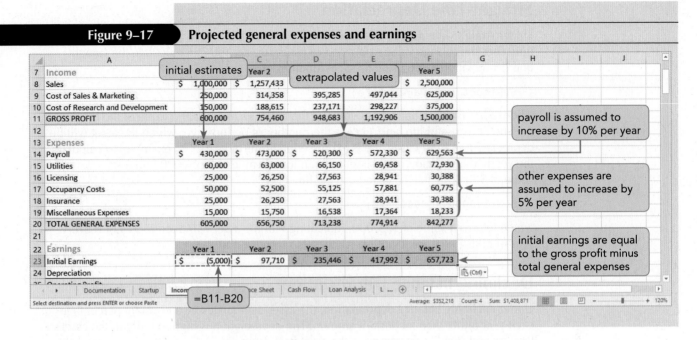

The calculations project that the company's annual earnings will increase from $5,000 loss in Year 1 to a net gain of $657,723 in Year 5.

Calculating Depreciation of Assets

The financial status of a company is not determined solely by its revenue, expenses, or annual earnings. Its wealth is also tied up in noncash assets such as equipment, land, buildings, and vehicles. These assets are known as **tangible assets** because they are long-lasting material assets not intended for sale but for use only by the company. Not all material assets are tangible assets. For example, assets such as the ingredients a restaurant uses when preparing its dishes are not considered tangible assets because although they are used in the cooking process, they are sold indirectly to the consumer in the form of a finished meal. However, items such as the cooking stove, refrigeration units, deep fryers, and so forth are tangible assets for that restaurant.

Tangible assets wear down over time and lose their value and thus reduce the company's overall worth. Tax laws allow companies to deduct this loss from reported earnings on the company's income statement, reducing the company's tax liability. The loss of the asset's original value doesn't usually happen all at once but is instead spread out over several years in a process known as depreciation. For example, an asset whose original value is $200,000 might be depreciated to $50,000 after 10 years of use. Different types of tangible assets have different rates of depreciation. Some items depreciate faster than others, which maintain their value for longer periods. In general, to calculate the depreciation of an asset, you need to know the following:

- The asset's original cost
- The length of the asset's useful life
- The asset's salvage value, which is the asset's value at the end of its useful life
- The rate at which the asset is depreciated over time

There are several ways to depreciate an asset. This module focuses on straight-line depreciation and declining balance depreciation.

Straight-Line Depreciation

Under **straight-line depreciation**, an asset loses value by equal amounts each year until it reaches the salvage value at the end of its useful life. You can calculate the straight-line depreciation value using the SLN function

```
SLN(cost, salvage, life)
```

where **cost** is the initial cost or value of the asset, **salvage** is the value of the asset at the end of its useful life, and **life** is the number of periods over which the asset will be depreciated. In most cases, life is expressed in terms of years. For example, to calculate the yearly depreciation of an asset with an initial value of $200,000 and a salvage value of $50,000 after 10 years, use the function

```
SLN(200000, 50000, 10)
```

which returns a value of $15,000, indicating that the asset will decline $15,000 every year from its initial value until it reaches its salvage value.

Declining Balance Depreciation

Under **declining balance depreciation**, the asset depreciates by a constant percentage each year rather than a constant amount. The depreciation is highest early in the asset's lifetime and steadily decreases as the asset itself loses value. Figure 9–18 compares the yearly straight-line and declining balance depreciation over a 10-year lifetime as an asset declines from its initial value of $300,000 down to $75,000.

| Figure 9–18 | Straight-line and declining-balance depreciation |

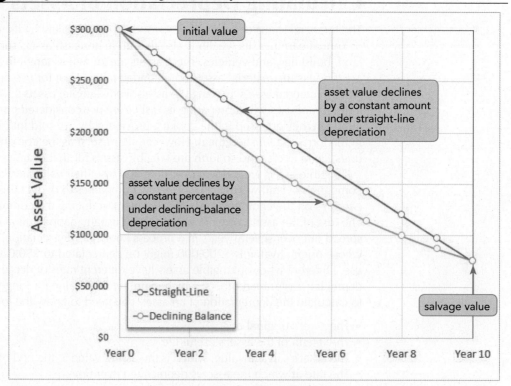

An asset shows a greater initial decline under declining balance depreciation than under straight-line depreciation. Declining balance depreciation is another example of a negative growth trend in which the asset decreases in value by a constant percentage rather than by a constant amount, as is the case with straight-line depreciation.

You can calculate the declining balance depreciation with the DB function

DB(*cost*, *salvage*, *life*, *period*, [*month=12*])

where *cost*, *salvage*, and *life* are again the initial value, salvage value, and lifetime of the asset, respectively, and *period* is the period for which you want to calculate the depreciation. If you are calculating depreciation on a yearly basis, then period would contain the year value of the depreciation. For example, to calculate the fourth year of depreciation of a $200,000 asset that declines to a salvage value of $50,000 after 10 years, you would use the function

DB(200000, 50000, 10, 4)

which returns $17,048.03, indicating that the asset declines in value more than $17,000 during its fourth year of use. By contrast, the asset's depreciation in its fifth year is

DB(200000, 50000, 10, 5)

which returns $14,848.83. The depreciation is smaller in the fifth year because the asset has a lower value later into its useful life.

The DB function also supports an optional *month* argument, which is needed when the asset is used for only part of the first year. For example, if you are depreciating the $200,000 asset after using it for only two months in Year 1, you would calculate its depreciation in the fifth year as

DB(200000, 50000, 10, 5, 2)

which returns $16,681.50. The depreciated value is higher because the asset has not been subjected to wear and tear for a full five years, making it more valuable going into Year 5.

Asli estimates that Holoease will have $300,000 in tangible assets at its startup. The useful life of these assets is estimated at 10 years with a salvage value of $75,000. You will add this information to the company's startup figures and then apply it to the Depreciation worksheet.

To specify the values of the tangible assets:

▶ **1.** Go to the **Startup** worksheet.

▶ **2.** In cell **B13**, enter **300,000** as the value of the long-term assets.

▶ **3.** Go to the **Depreciation** worksheet.

▶ **4.** In cell **B4**, type **=** to begin the formula, go to the **Startup** worksheet, click cell **B13**, and then press **ENTER**. The formula =Startup!B13 is entered in cell B4, displaying the $300,000 long-term assets value from the Startup worksheet.

▶ **5.** In cell **B5**, enter **$75,000** as the asset's estimated salvage value.

▶ **6.** In cell **B6**, enter **10** as the useful life of the asset.

Next, you'll calculate the depreciation of the company equipment using straight-line depreciation.

To calculate the straight-line depreciation:

▶ **1.** In cell **B10**, enter the formula **=SLN($B$4, $B$5, $B$6)** to calculate the straight-line depreciation in Year 1 based on the cost value in cell B4, the salvage value in cell B5, and the life value in cell B6. The formula returns a depreciation value of $22,500, indicating the asset will decline in value by $22,500 in Year 1.

▶ **2.** Copy the formula in cell **B10** and paste it in the range **C10:F10** to calculate the straight-line depreciation for the remaining years. Because the straight-line depreciation is a constant amount every year, the formula returns a depreciation value of $22,500 for Year 2 through Year 5.

   Next, you will calculate the cumulative depreciation of the asset from Year 1 through Year 5.

▶ **3.** In cell **B11**, enter the formula **=B10** to display the depreciation for the first year.

▶ **4.** In cell **C11**, enter the formula **=B11+C10** to add the Year 2 depreciation to the depreciation from Year 1. The total depreciation through the first two years is $45,000.

▶ **5.** Copy the formula in cell **C11** and paste it in the range **D11:F11** to calculate cumulative depreciation through the first five years. By Year 5, the asset's value will have declined by $112,500.

▶ **6.** In cell **B12**, enter the formula **=$B$4–B11** to calculate the depreciated asset's value after the first year. The asset's value is $277,500.

▶ **7.** Copy the formula in cell **B12** and paste it in the range **C12:F12**. By Year 5, the asset's value has been reduced to $187,500.

▶ **8.** Click cell **B10** to deselect the copied range. See Figure 9–19.

Figure 9–19	Straight-line depreciation of the asset

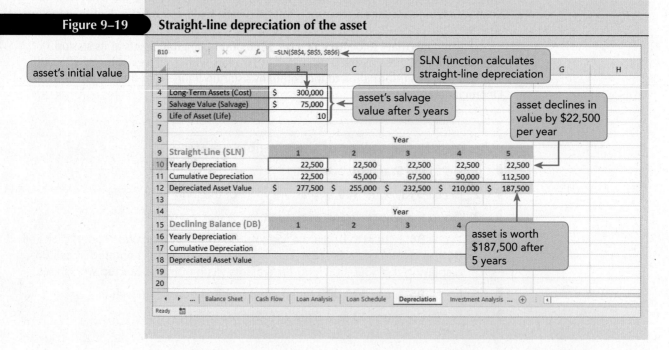

Asli also wants to explore the depreciation of the company's tangible assets under the declining balance depreciation method.

To calculate the declining balance depreciation:

1. In cell **B16**, enter the formula **=DB($B$4, $B$5, $B$6, B15)** to calculate the declining balance depreciation for Year 1 based on the initial cost of the asset in cell B4, the salvage value in cell B5, the life of the asset in cell B6, and the current period (or year) in cell B15. The formula returns 38,700, which is the amount that the assets will depreciate in Year 1.

2. Copy the formula in cell **B16** and paste it in the range **C16:F16** to calculate the depreciation in each of the remaining four years. The depreciation amount decreases each year under the declining balance schedule, dropping to $22,273 in Year 5.

3. Copy the formulas in the range **B11:F12** and paste it in the range **B17:F18** to calculate the cumulative depreciation and depreciated value of the asset.

4. Click cell **B16** to deselect the copied range. See Figure 9–20.

Figure 9–20	Declining-balance depreciation of the asset

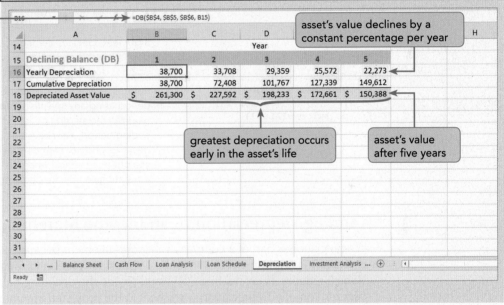

DB function calculates declining-balance depreciation

asset's value declines by a constant percentage per year

greatest depreciation occurs early in the asset's life

asset's value after five years

Based on the declining balance depreciation method, the value of the asset declines to $150,388 by the end of Year 5, which is lower than the Year 5 value under the straight-line depreciation model. Figure 9–21 describes several other depreciation functions that can be used to satisfy specialized accounting needs.

Figure 9–21   **Excel depreciation functions**

Function	Description
SLN(*cost*, *salvage*, *life*)	Returns the straight-line depreciation in which the asset declines by a constant amount each year, where *cost* is the initial cost of the asset, *salvage* is the salvage value, and *life* is the useful lifetime of the asset.
DB(*cost*, *salvage*, *life*, *period*, [*month*])	Returns the declining balance depreciation in which the asset declines by a constant percentage each year, where *period* is the year of the depreciation and *month* is an optional argument that defines the number of months that the asset was owned during Year 1.
SYD(*cost*, *salvage*, *life*, *period*)	Returns the sum-of-years' digit depreciation that results in a more accelerated depreciation than straight-line depreciation, but a less accelerated depreciation than declining balance depreciation.
DDB(*cost*, *salvage*, *life*, *period*, [*factor*=2])	Returns the double-declining balance depreciation that doubles the depreciation under the straight-line method and applies that accelerated rate to the original asset value minus the cumulative depreciation. The *factor* argument specifies the factor by which the straight-line depreciation is multiplied. If no factor is specified, a factor of 2 (for doubling) is assumed.
VDB(*cost*, *salvage*, *life*, *start*, *end*, [*factor*=2], [*no_switch*=FALSE])	Returns a variable declining depreciation for any specified period using any specified depreciation method, where *start* is the starting period of the depreciation, *end* is the ending period, *factor* is the rate at which the depreciation declines, and *no_switch* specifies whether to switch to the straight-line method when the depreciation falls below the estimate given by the declining balance method.

Adding Depreciation to an Income Statement

Depreciation is part of a company's income statement because even though the company is not losing actual revenue, it is losing value as its tangible assets depreciate, which reduces its tax liability. Asli wants to add the declining balance depreciation figures from the Depreciation worksheet to the projected income statement to project the company's operating profit, which represents the company's profits before taxes.

To add depreciation to the income statement:

1. Go to the **Income Statement** worksheet.

2. In cell **B24**, type **=** to begin the formula, go to the **Depreciation** worksheet, click cell **B16**, and then press **ENTER**. The formula =Depreciation!B16 is entered and displays the depreciation value 38,700 for Year 1.

3. Copy the formula in cell **B24** and paste it in the range **C24:F24** to show the annual depreciation for Year 2 through Year 5.

4. In cell **B25**, enter the formula **=B23−B24** to subtract the depreciation from the company's initial earnings. The projection shows a loss in operating profit for the company in the first year of $43,700.

5. Copy the formula in cell **B25** and paste it in the range **C25:F25** to calculate the operating profit for Year 2 through Year 5.

Even when depreciation of its assets is included, the company's operating profit increases throughout the five-year period, culminating in a Year 5 operating profit of $635,450.

Proskills

Decision Making: Choosing a Depreciation Schedule

How do you decide which method of depreciation is the most appropriate? The answer depends on the type of asset being depreciated. Tax laws allow different depreciation methods for different kinds of assets and different situations. In general, you want to choose the depreciation method that most accurately describes the true value of the asset and its impact on the company's financial status.

In tax statements, depreciation appears as an expense that is subtracted from the company's earnings. So, if you accelerate the depreciation of an asset in the early years of its use, you might be underestimating the company's profits, making it appear that the company is less profitable than it is. On the other hand, depreciating an asset slowly could make it appear that the company is more profitable than it really is. For this reason, the choice of a depreciation method is best made in consultation with an accountant who is fully aware of the financial issues and tax laws.

Adding Taxes and Interest Expenses to an Income Statement

Interest expenses are also part of a company's income statement. You have already projected the annual interest payments the company will have to make on its $550,000 loan (shown earlier in row 36 of Figure 9–9). Rather than reenter these values, you can reference the calculated values from that worksheet in the income statement. Because those values were displayed as negative numbers, you'll change the sign to match the format of the Income Statement worksheet in which those interest expenses are entered as positive values.

To include the interest expense in the income statement:

1. In cell **B27**, type **=–** (an equal sign followed by a minus sign) to begin the formula.

2. Go to the **Loan Schedule** worksheet, click cell **B36**, which contains the total interest payments in Year 1, and then press **ENTER**. The formula = –'Loan Schedule'!B36 is entered in the cell, returning the value 30,838.

3. In cell **B28**, enter the formula **=B25–B27** to subtract the interest expense from the operating profit for Year 1. Excel returns a value of –74,538, indicating that the company will lose almost $75,000 pretax for the first year.

4. Copy the formulas in the range **B27:B28** and paste them in the range **C27:F28** to calculate the interest payments and pretax profits for the remaining years.

Despite losing almost $75,000 in the first year, by the fifth year when interest payments are included, the company's projected pretax profit is $630,785.

Finally, you need to account for the taxes that the company will pay on the money it makes. Asli estimates that the company will be subject, in general, to a 32% tax rate on its pretax income. You will add this tax rate to the Income Statement worksheet and then calculate the company's tax liability. The company will pay taxes only if it makes money, so you will use an IF function to test whether the pretax income is positive before calculating taxes. If the pretax profit is negative, the tax will be zero.

To calculate the company's tax liability:

▶ 1. In cell **F5** of the Income Statement worksheet, enter **32%** as the assumed tax rate.

▶ 2. In cell **B30**, enter the formula **=IF(B28>0, B28*$F$5, 0)** to test whether the pretax income in Year 1 is greater than 0. If it is, then the pretax income will be multiplied by the tax rate in cell F5; otherwise, the formula will return 0. Because the company will show a net loss in its first year of operation, the formula should return a value of 0.

▶ 3. In cell **B31**, enter the formula **=B28−B30** to subtract the taxes owed for Year 1 from the pretax income.

▶ 4. Copy the formulas in the range **B30:B31** and paste them in the range **C30:F31** to calculate the tax liability and after-tax profit for the remaining years. After accounting for taxes, Holoease will show an after-tax profit of $428,934 by the end of its fifth year.

▶ 5. Click cell **B30** to deselect the copied formulas. See Figure 9–22.

Figure 9–22	Revised income statement

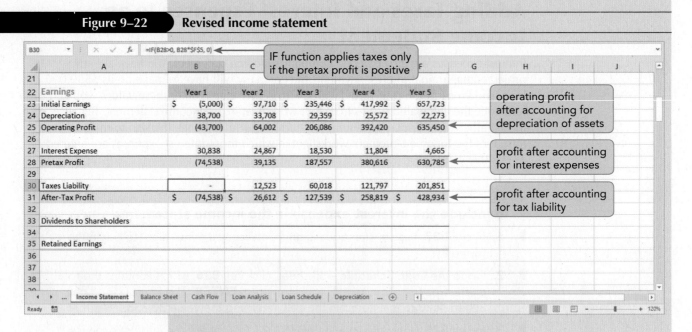

▶ 6. Save the workbook.

With the initial financial planning laid out, the company needs to attract some investors. In the next session, you will evaluate the return on investment that the company will be able to offer investors and the impact it will have on the company's profitability.

Review

Session 9.2 Quick Check

1. The first value in a linear trend is 50 and the fifth value is 475. What are the values of the second, third, and fourth items?

2. The first value in a growth trend is 50 and the fifth value is 475. What are the values of the second, third, and fourth items?

3. By what percentage do the values in Question 3 grow?

4. The first value in a series is 100. Extrapolate the next four values assuming a linear trend with a step size of 125.

5. The first value in a series is 100. Extrapolate the next four values if each value grows by 18% over the previous value.

6. A new business buys $20,000 worth of computer equipment. If the useful life of the equipment is 10 years with a salvage value of $3,000, provide the formula to determine the depreciation during the first year assuming straight-line depreciation. What is the formula result?

7. Provide the value of the asset in Year 1 through Year 5 using the depreciation schedule in Question 6.

8. Assume a declining balance depreciation for the computer equipment described in Question 6 and provide the formula and result to determine the depreciation in the first year.

9. Provide the value of the asset in Year 1 through Year 5 using the declining balance depreciation schedule in Question 8.

Session 9.3 Visual Overview:

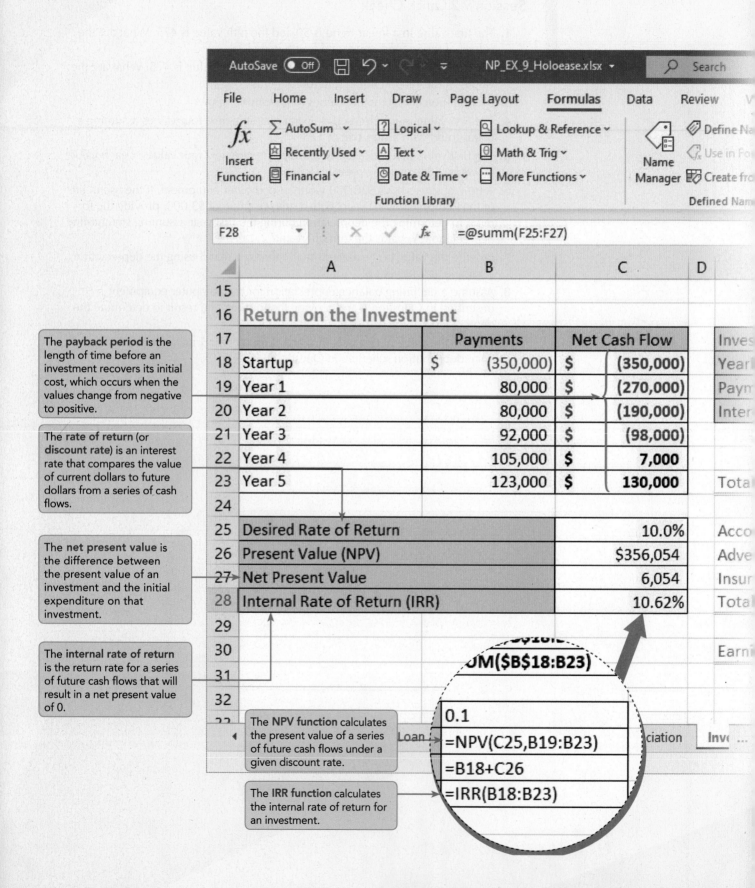

The payback period is the length of time before an investment recovers its initial cost, which occurs when the values change from negative to positive.

The rate of return (or discount rate) is an interest rate that compares the value of current dollars to future dollars from a series of cash flows.

The net present value is the difference between the present value of an investment and the initial expenditure on that investment.

The internal rate of return is the return rate for a series of future cash flows that will result in a net present value of 0.

The NPV function calculates the present value of a series of future cash flows under a given discount rate.

The IRR function calculates the internal rate of return for an investment.

F28   =@summ(F25:F27)

	A	B	C	D
15				
16	**Return on the Investment**			
17		**Payments**	**Net Cash Flow**	Inves
18	Startup	$ (350,000)	$ (350,000)	Yearl
19	Year 1	80,000	$ (270,000)	Paym
20	Year 2	80,000	$ (190,000)	Inter
21	Year 3	92,000	$ (98,000)	
22	Year 4	105,000	$ 7,000	
23	Year 5	123,000	$ 130,000	Total
24				
25	Desired Rate of Return		10.0%	Acco
26	Present Value (NPV)		$356,054	Adve
27	Net Present Value		6,054	Insur
28	Internal Rate of Return (IRR)		10.62%	Total
29				
30				Earni
31				
32				

JM($B$18:B23)

0.1
=NPV(C25,B19:B23)
=B18+C26
=IRR(B18:B23)

NPV and IRR Functions and Auditing

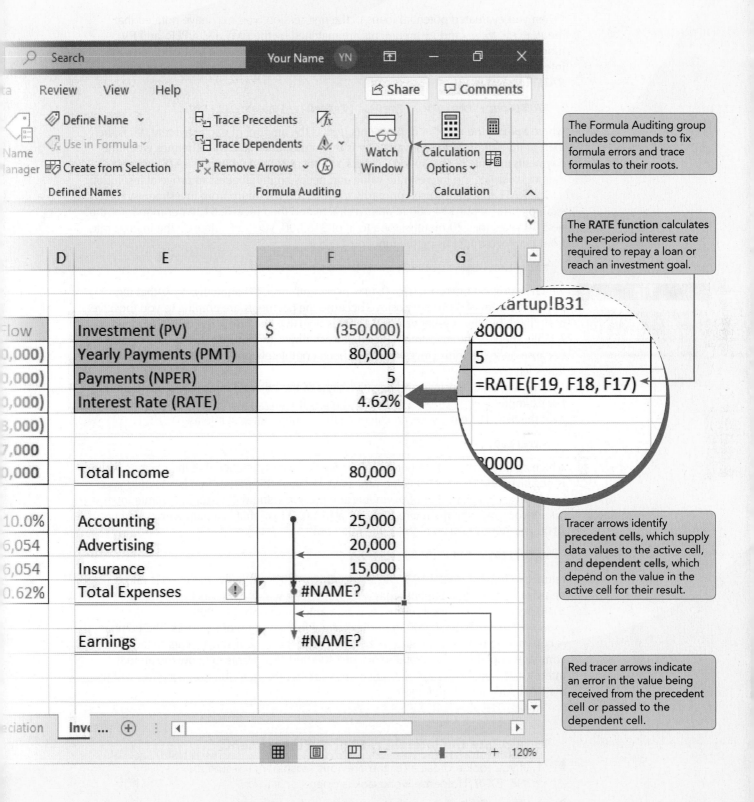

The Formula Auditing group includes commands to fix formula errors and trace formulas to their roots.

The **RATE function** calculates the per-period interest rate required to repay a loan or reach an investment goal.

Tracer arrows identify **precedent cells**, which supply data values to the active cell, and **dependent cells**, which depend on the value in the active cell for their result.

Red tracer arrows indicate an error in the value being received from the precedent cell or passed to the dependent cell.

Calculating Interest Rates with the RATE Function

When you evaluated potential loans in the first session, you may have noticed that the *Pmt*, *Fv*, *Nper*, and *Pv* arguments are matched by the PMT, FV, NPER, and PV functions. The *Rate* argument also has a matching RATE function that calculates the interest rate based on the values of the other financial arguments. The syntax of the RATE function is

```
RATE(Nper, Pmt, Pv, [Fv=0], [Type=0], [Guess=0.1])
```

where *Nper* is the number of payments, *Pmt* is the amount of each payment, *Pv* is the loan or investment's present value, *Fv* is the future value, and *Type* defines when the payments are made. The optional *Guess* argument is used when the RATE function cannot calculate the interest rate value and needs an initial guess to arrive at a solution.

The RATE function is used primarily to calculate the return from investments. For example, if you put $14,000 in an investment and then receive $150 per month for the next 10 years (or 120 months) for a total of $18,000, you can calculate the interest rate from that investment using the function

```
RATE(120, 150, -14000)
```

Tip

Always multiply the RATE function results by the number of payments per year. For monthly payments, multiply the rate value by 12.

which returns an interest rate of 0.43% per month or 5.2% annually. Note that the payment values of $150 are positive because the payments are coming to you (positive cash flow), but the present value –14,000 is negative because it represents money initially spent in the investment (negative cash flow). The future value is 0 by default because once the initial investment has been completely paid back to you, there are no funds left.

With loans, the positive and negative signs of the *Pmt* and *Pv* values are switched. For example, if you borrow $14,000 and repay it with payments of $150 per month over the next 10 years, you can calculate the monthly interest rate as

```
RATE(120, -150, 14000)
```

which again returns 0.43% per month or 5.2% annually. Notice that the payment value is negative, and the present value is positive because this transaction is a loan to you.

Not every combination of payments and present value will result in a viable interest rate. If you calculate the interest rate for a $14,000 loan that is repaid with payments of $100 per month for 120 months, the function

```
RATE(120, -100, 14000)
```

returns an interest rate of –0.25% per month or –3.0% annually. The interest rate is negative because you cannot repay a $14,000 loan within 10 years by paying only $100 per month. The total payments would amount to only $12,000.

Holoease needs $350,000 in startup capital from a group of investors. The company is considering repaying the group $80,000 per year for the first five years of the company's operation for a total return of $400,000. Asli wants to know the annual interest rate that this repayment schedule would represent to the investors. You will use the RATE function to find out.

To calculate the interest rate of the investment:

▶ **1.** If you took a break after the previous session, make sure the NP_EX_9_Holoease workbook is open.

▶ **2.** Go to the **Startup** worksheet, and then in cell **B31**, enter **350,000** as the amount contributed by investors.

▶ **3.** Go to the **Investment Analysis** worksheet, which you'll use to analyze the value of investing in the company.

> **4.** In cell **B6**, type **=–** (an equal sign followed by a minus sign), go to the **Startup** worksheet, click cell **B31**, and then press **ENTER**. The formula =–Startup!B31 is entered in the cell.

   The formula displays the negative value $(350,000) in the cell. You want to use a negative value because you are examining this investment from the point of view of the group of investors, who are making an initial startup payment of $350,000 to the company (a negative cash flow).

> **5.** In cell **B7**, enter **80,000** as the annual payment. The value is positive because this money is being repaid to the investors each year (a positive cash flow from their point of view).

> **6.** In cell **B8**, enter **5** as the total number of payments made to the investors.

> **7.** In cell **B9**, enter the formula **=RATE(B8, B7, B6)** to calculate the interest rate of this repayment schedule based on the number of payments in cell B8, the size of each payment in cell B7, and the present value of the investment in cell B6. See Figure 9–23.

Figure 9–23   **Interest rate of the investment**

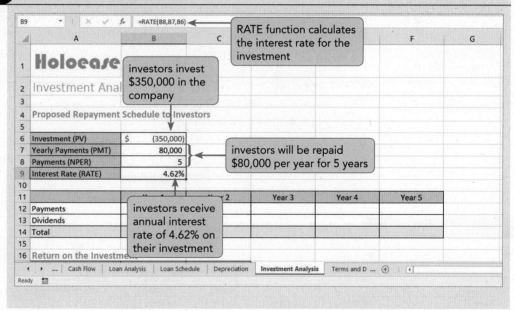

Based on these calculations, the annual interest rate to the investors for this repayment schedule is 4.62%. One way to interpret this value is that it is like to placing $350,000 in a savings account that pays 4.62% annual interest. Is this a good investment? There are several ways of making that determination. One way is the payback period.

Viewing the Payback Period of an Investment

The payback period is the length of time required for an investment to recover its initial cost. For example, a $400,000 investment that returns $25,000 per year would take 16 years to repay the initial cost of the investment.

The company doesn't believe it can attract investors if all it can promise is a 4.62% annual interest rate. Another possibility is to augment the $80,000 per year with dividends taken from the company's annual profits. Because the company will not show much profit initially, leaving less cash to pay dividends, Asli is examining the following schedule of dividend payments: Year 1—$0; Year 2—$0; Year 3—$12,000;

Year 4—$25,000; and Year 5—$43,000 for a total of $80,000 spread over the company's first five years, resulting in a grand total of $480,000 repaid to investors for their $350,000 initial investment.

Asli wants you to add these dividends to the repayment of the investors' original $350,000 investment and then calculate the payback period.

To determine the payback period for the investment:

▶ **1.** In cell **B12**, enter the formula **=$B$7** to reference the annual loan repayment to the investors.

▶ **2.** Copy the formula in cell **B12** and paste it in the range **C12:F12** to apply the same $80,000 loan repayment to each year.

▶ **3.** In the range **B13:F13**, enter the following dividends: **0** in cell B13, **0** in cell C13, **12,000** in cell D13, **25,000** in cell E13, and **43,000** in cell F13.

▶ **4.** Select the range **B14:F14**, and then use AutoSum to calculate the total reimbursement to the investor group for each of the first five years. The total values range from $80,000 in Year 1 to $123,000 in Year 5.

Next, you'll add these totals to the initial investment to view the cumulative total payments made to the investors.

▶ **5.** In cell **B18**, enter the formula **=B6** to reference the initial investment value.

▶ **6.** In the range **B19:B23**, enter the following formulas to reference the annual payments made to the investors: **=B14** in cell B19 for the Year 1 repayment, **=C14** in cell B20 for the Year 2 repayment, **=D14** in cell B21 for the Year 3 repayment, **=E14** in cell B22 for the Year 4 repayment, and **=F14** in cell B23 for the Year 5 repayment.

▶ **7.** Select the range **B18:B23**, click the **Quick Analysis** button 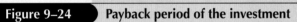, click **Totals**, scroll right to the end of the Totals tools, and then click **Running Total** to calculate a column of running totals for the net cash flow to investors. See Figure 9–24.

Figure 9–24	Payback period of the investment

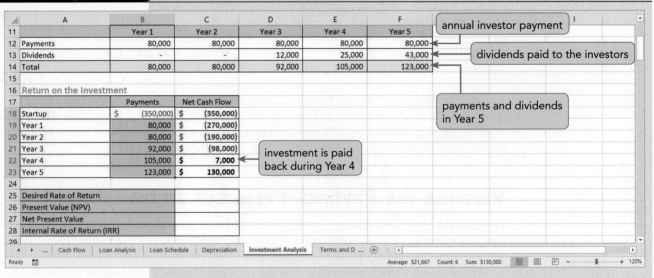

Based on these calculations, the investors will be repaid for their investments during the fourth year (when the value of the cumulative net cash flow changes to positive). By the end of the fifth year, investors will see a profit of $130,000 on their original investments.

Calculating Net Present Value

The payback period is a quick method of assessing the long-term value of an investment. The major drawback of the payback period is that it does not consider the time value of money. To understand why, you must explore how time impacts financial decisions.

The Time Value of Money

The **time value of money** is based on the observation that money received today is often worth more than the same amount received later because you can always invest the money you receive today and earn interest on that investment. The time value of money can be expressed by what represents a fair exchange between current dollars and future dollars.

For example, is it better to get $100 today or $105 one year from now? The answer depends on what you could do with that $100 during the year. If you could invest it in an account that pays 6% interest per year, the $100 would turn into $106 in one year, making it better to receive the $100 now and invest it; but, if you could earn only 4% interest on the $100, it would be better to wait a year and receive the $105.

The interest rate you assume for the present value of your investment is known as the rate of return, or the discount rate. The rate of return defines the time value of money and provides a method of comparing present value to future value.

You can use the PV function to calculate the time value of money under different rates of return. For example, the following PV function calculates the present value of receiving $100 per year for the next five years at a 6% annual rate of return:

```
PV(6%, 5, 100)
```

The function returns a negative value of –$421.24, indicating that it would be a fair exchange to spend $421.24 today to receive $100 per year for each of the next five years. In other words, $421.24 today is worth the same as $500 spread out over $100 annual payments if the discount rate is 6%.

For investments that pay off at the end without any intermediate payments, enter 0 for the payment value and enter the amount returned by the investment as the future value. So, to calculate the present value of receiving $500 at the end of five years at a 6% rate of return, enter the PV function

```
PV(6%, 5, 0, 500)
```

which returns –$373.63, indicating that it would be a fair exchange to spend $373.63 today to receive $500 five years from now.

You also can use the FV function to estimate how much a dollar amount today is worth in terms of future dollars. For example, to determine the future value of $100 in two years when the rate of return is 5%, enter

```
FV(5%, 2, 0, -100)
```

which returns a value of $110.25. The positive cash flow indicates that spending $100 today is a fair exchange for receiving $110.25 two years from now.

Using the NPV Function

The PV function assumes that all future payments are equal. If the future payments are not equal, you must use the NPV function to determine the present value of the investment. The syntax of the NPV function is

```
NPV(Rate, value1, [value2, value3,…])
```

where **Rate** is the rate of return, and **value1**, **value2**, **value3**, and so on are the values of future payments. The NPV function assumes payments occur at the end of each payment period and the payment periods are evenly spaced.

For example, to calculate the present value of a three-year investment that pays $100 at the end of the first year, $200 at the end of the second year, and $500 at the end of the third year with a 6% annual rate of return, you would apply the NPV function

```
NPV(6%, 100, 200, 500)
```

which returns a value of $692.15, indicating that this repayment schedule is equivalent to receiving $692.15 today if the discount rate is 6%.

Unlike the PV function, which returns a negative value for the investment's present value, the NPV function returns a positive value. This occurs because the PV function returns a cash flow value that indicates how much you need to invest now (a negative cash flow) to receive money later (a positive cash flow); whereas the NPV function calculates the value of those payments in today's dollars based on your chosen rate of return.

You can receive surprising results examining the time value of money. Consider an investment that has a 6% rate of return with these transactions: Year 1—investor receives $250; Year 2—investor receives $150; Year 3—investor receives $100; Year 4—investor pays $150; and Year 5—investor pays $400.

At first glance, this seems to be a bad investment. The investor receives $500 in the first three years but spends $550 in the last two years, for a net loss of $50. However, that analysis doesn't consider the time value of money. When the present value of this transaction is calculated using the NPV function

```
NPV(6%, 250, 150, 100, -150, -400)
```

the present value of the investment is $35.59, a positive result. The investment is profitable because the investor receives the money early and pays it back later using dollars of lesser value.

Choosing a Rate of Return

Whether an investment is profitable or not often depends on what value is used for the rate of return. The rate of return is related to the concept of risk—the possibility that the entire transaction will fail, resulting in a loss of the initial investment. Investments with higher risks generally should have higher rates of return. If an investor places $350,000 in a simple bank account (a low-risk venture), the investor would not expect a high rate of return; on the other hand, investing the $350,000 in a startup company like Holoease is riskier and merits a higher rate of return.

After discussing the issue with financial analysts, the company has settled on a 10% rate of return, meaning that Holoease will return to the investors at least as much as they would get if they had invested $350,000 in an account paying 10% annual interest over five years. You'll use that rate of return in the NPV function as you calculate the present value of the proposal that Asli will make to the group of investors.

To calculate the present value of the investment:

▶ 1. In cell **C25**, enter **10.0%** as the desired rate of return.

▶ 2. In cell **C26**, enter **=NPV(C25, B19:B23)** to calculate the present value of the investment based on the rate value in cell C25 and the return paid to the investors for Year 1 through Year 5 in the range B19:B23. The formula returns $356,054 which is the present value of the investment to the investor group. You will add this present value to the cost initial investment in order to calculate the net present value.

▶ 3. In cell **C27**, enter **=B18+C26** to add the initial investment to the present value of the investment over the next five years. The net present value is $6,054.

▶ 4. Select cell **C26**. See Figure 9–25.

Be sure to add the initial case flow value to the value return by the NPV function to get the net present value.

| Figure 9–25 | Net present value of the investment |

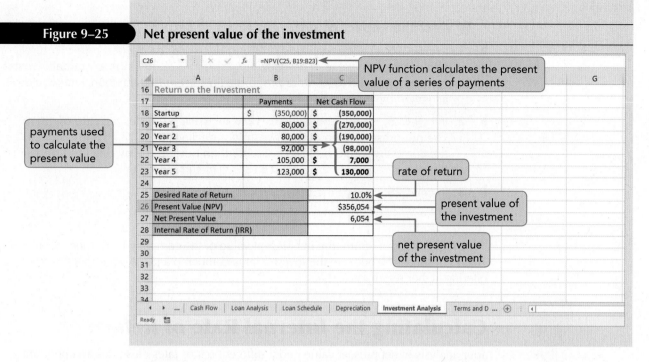

According to these results, the $350,000 investment in the company is worth $6,054 more than placing the same amount in a different investment paying 10% annual interest. Of course, that assumes Holoease will be as profitable as Asli hopes and will be able to honor the terms of the investor agreement over the next five years.

Insight

Understanding Net Present Value and the NPV Function

Net present value is the difference between the present value of a series of future cash flows and the current value of the initial investment. One source of confusion for Excel users is that despite its name, the NPV function does not actually return the net present value of an investment. Instead, it returns the investment's present value based on the returns that the investment will provide in the future.

To calculate the net present value in Excel, the initial cost of the investment must be added to the present value of the returns from the investment using the formula

```
=initial investment + NPV value
```

where *initial investment* is the initial cost of the investment and *NPV value* is the value of the NPV function applied to future returns. The initial investment is assumed to have a negative cash flow because that investment is being purchased, and it is assumed to be based on current, not future, dollars.

The exception to this formula occurs when the initial investment also takes place in the future. For example, if the initial investment takes place in one year and the returns occur annually after that, then the NPV function will return the net present value without having to be adjusted because the initial investment is also paid with discounted dollars.

In any financial analysis, it is a good idea to test other values for comparison. You will rerun the analysis using return rates of 8% and 12%.

To view the impact of different rates of return:

▶ **1.** In cell **C25**, change the value to **8%** to decrease the desired rate of return. The net present value in cell C27 increases to $26,584 indicating that investment is about $27,000 more profitable (in current dollars) than what could be achieved by an account bearing 8% annual interest.

▶ **2.** In cell **C25**, change the value to **12%**, increasing the desired rate of return. The net present value of the investment declines to –$12,789. Investing in the company would be less profitable than putting the money in an account bearing 12% interest by almost $13,000 in current dollars.

▶ **3.** In cell **C25**, change the value back to **10%**.

At higher rates of return, the net present value of the company investment decreases. That's not surprising because the investment is compared against other investments offering higher return rates.

Calculating the Internal Rate of Return

Your analysis of net present value under different return rates illustrates an important principle: At some return rate, the net present value of an investment switches from positive (profitable) to negative (unprofitable). Figure 9–26 shows the change in net present value for the Holoease investment under different rates of return.

Figure 9–26   **Net present value and internal rate of return**

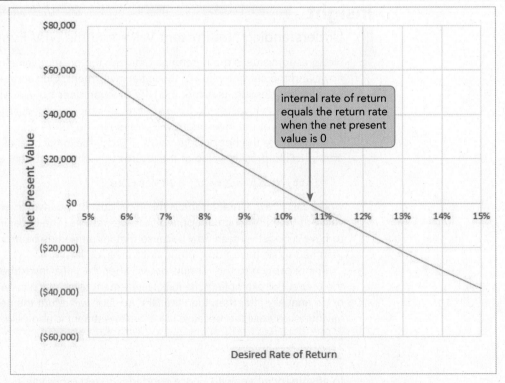

The point at which the net present value of an investment equals 0 is called the internal rate of return (IRR) of the investment. The internal rate of return is another popular measure of the value of an investment because it provides a basis of comparison between investments. Investments with higher internal rates of return are preferred to those with lower IRRs.

Using the IRR Function

The IRR function calculates the internal rate of return for an investment. Its syntax is

```
IRR(values, [guess=0.1])
```

where **values** are the cash flow values from the investment, and **guess** is an optional argument in which you provide a guess for the IRR value. A guess is needed for financial transactions that have several possible internal rates of return. This can occur when the investment switches between negative and positive cash flows several times during its lifetime. For those types of transactions, an initial guess helps Excel locate the final value for the IRR. Without the guess, Excel might not be able to calculate the IRR. If you don't include a guess, Excel will use an initial guess of 10% for the IRR and proceed from there to determine the answer.

For example, the internal rate of return for a $500 investment that pays $100 in the first year, $150 in the second and third years, and $200 in the fourth year is calculated using the IRR function

```
IRR({-500, 100, 150, 150, 200})
```

which returns a value of 6.96% indicating that the return for this investment is equally profitable as an account that pays 6.96% annual interest.

The order of payments affects the internal rate of return. In the above example, the total amount of money paid back on the investment is $600. However, if the payments were made in the opposite order—$200, $150, $150, and $100—the internal rate of return would be calculated as

```
IRR({-500, 200, 150, 150, 100})
```

which returns a value of 8.64%. The increased rate of return is due to the larger payments made earlier with dollars of greater value.

The list of values in the IRR function must include at least one positive cash flow and one negative cash flow, and the order of the values must reflect the order in which the payments are made and the payoffs are received. Like the NPV function, the IRR function assumes that the payments and payoffs occur at evenly spaced intervals. Unlike the NPV function, you include the initial cost of the investment in the values list.

Reference

Calculating the Value of an Investment

- To calculate the net present value when the initial investment is made immediately, use the NPV function with the discount rate and the series of cash returns from the investment. Add the cost of the initial investment (negative cash flow) to the value returned by the NPV function.
- To calculate the net present value when the initial investment is made at the end of the first payment period, use the NPV function with the discount rate and the series of cash returns from the investment. Include the initial cost of the investment as the first value in the series.
- To calculate the internal rate of return, use the IRR function with the cost of the initial investment as the first cash flow value in the series. For investments that have several positive and negative cash flow values, include a guess to aid Excel in finding a reasonable internal rate of return value.

You will calculate the internal rate of return that can be quoted to the investor group for Holoease.

To calculate the internal rate of return for the investment:

▶ **1.** In cell **C28**, enter the formula **=IRR(B18:B23)** to calculate the internal rate of return, where the range B18:B23 contains the initial investment and the returns that investors can expect. The internal rate of return is 10.62%.

▶ **2.** Select cell **C28**. See Figure 9–27.

Figure 9–27	Internal rate of return

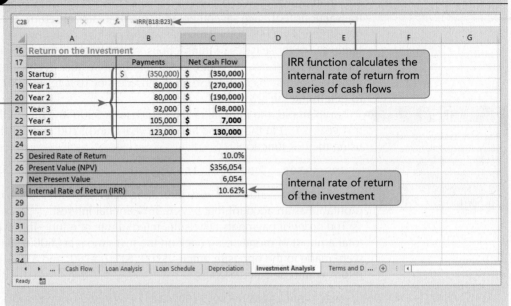

cash flow values used to calculate the internal rate of return

IRR function calculates the internal rate of return from a series of cash flows

internal rate of return of the investment

Based on the IRR calculation, Asli can tell potential investors that they will receive a 10.62% return on their investments if the financial projections for the company are met.

 Proskills

Decision Making: Using NPV and IRR to Compare Investments

Investors will always have several investment options. In comparing two investments, investors usually want to select the investment with the higher net present value or the higher internal rate of return. However, if investors rely solely on the net present value, they can receive contradictory results depending on the value specified for the desired rate of return.

For example, consider the following two returns from an initial investment of $1,000. Option 1 has a higher net present value when discount rates are greater than 9%, while Option 2 has a higher net present value when the discount rate is 9% or less.

Option	Investment	Year 1	Year 2	Year 3	Year 4
Option 1	–$1,000	$350	$350	$350	$350
Option 2	–$1,000	$0	$0	$0	$1,600

Using the internal rate of return instead of the net present value can also lead to contradictory results. This often occurs when an investment switches several times between positive and negative cash flows during its history. In those situations, more than one internal rate of return value could fit the data.

To choose between two or more investments, it is a good idea to graph the net present value for each investment against different possible rates of return. By comparing the graphs, you can reach a decision about which investment is the most profitable and under what conditions.

Exploring the XNPV and XIRR Functions

Both the NPV and IRR functions assume that the cash flows occur at evenly spaced intervals such as annual payments in which the cash receipts from an investment are returned at the end of the fiscal year. For cash flows that appear at unevenly spaced intervals, Excel provides the XNPV and XIRR functions.

The **XNPV function**, which calculates the net present value of a series of cash flows at specified dates, has the syntax

XNPV(*Rate*, *Values*, *Dates*)

where *Rate* is the desired rate of return, *Values* is the list of cash flows, and *Dates* are the dates associated with each cash flow. The series of values must contain at least one positive and one negative value. The cash flow values are discounted starting after the first date in the list, with the first value not discounted at all. Figure 9–28 shows an investment in which the initial deposit of $300,000 on September 8, 2021 is repaid with eight payments totaling $340,000 spaced at irregular intervals over the next two years. The net present value of this investment is $7,267.04 based on a 7.2% rate of return. Note that the net present value is not $40,000 (the difference between the initial deposit and the total payments) because the investment is paid back over time with dollars of lesser value.

Figure 9–28   Net present value calculated over irregular intervals

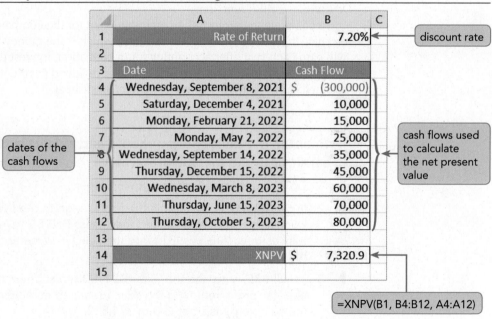

Likewise, the following **XIRR function** calculates the internal rate of return for a series of cash flows made at specified dates

XIRR(*Values*, *Dates*, [*Guess*=0.1])

where *Values* is the list of cash flow values, *Dates* are the dates of each cash flow, and *Guess* is an optional argument that guesses at the internal rate of return when you have a complicated set of cash flows with multiple possible return rates. Figure 9–29 shows the internal rate of return for the transaction presented in Figure 9–28. This investment's internal rate of return is 9.01%.

| Figure 9–29 | Internal rate of return calculated over irregular intervals |

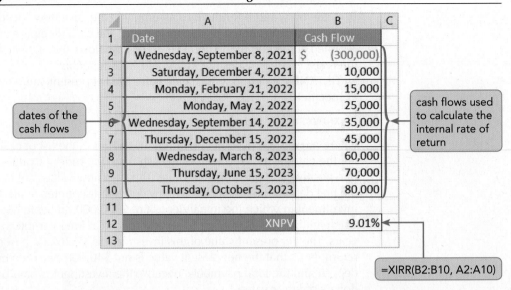

dates of the cash flows

cash flows used to calculate the internal rate of return

=XIRR(B2:B10, A2:A10)

In the Holoease business plan, all payments to the investors are to be made at regular intervals, at the end of the upcoming fiscal years, so you do not need to use either the XNPV or the XIRR function.

To complete the projected income statement for the company, Asli wants you to estimate the company's retained earnings, which is the money that the company will earn each year after accounting for depreciation, interest expenses, taxes, and dividends to shareholders. You will enter the dividend payments and calculate the retained earnings in the Income Statement worksheet.

To enter the dividend payments and calculate the retained earnings in the income statement:

▶ 1. Go to the **Income Statement** worksheet.

▶ 2. In cell **B33**, type **=** to begin the formula, go to the **Investment Analysis** worksheet, click cell **B13,** and then press **ENTER** to insert the formula ='Investment Analysis'!B13 into the cell. No value appears in the cell because there are no dividends in the first year.

▶ 3. In cell **B35**, enter the formula **=B31–B33** to subtract the dividends from the after-tax profit, returning the Year 1 retained earnings. At the end of Year 1, the company has a net loss of $74,538.

   Next, you will calculate the net earnings for the remaining four years.

▶ 4. Copy the range **B33:B35** and paste it in the range **C33:F35**.

▶ 5. Click cell **F35** to deselect the copied range. Figure 9–30 shows the projected retained earnings for Holoease from Year 1 through Year 5.

Figure 9-30   Final income statement

	A	B	C	D	E	F	G
22	Earnings	Year 1	Year 2	Year 3	Year 4	Year 5	
23	Initial Earnings	$ (5,000)	$ 97,710	$ 235,446	$ 417,992	$ 657,723	
24	Depreciation	38,700	33,708	29,359	25,572	22,273	
25	Operating Profit	(43,700)	64,002	206,086	392,420	635,450	
26							
27	Interest Expense	30,838	24,867	18,530	11,804	4,665	
28	Pretax Profit	(74,538)	39,135	187,557	380,616	630,785	
29							
30	Taxes Liability	-	12,523	60,018	121,797	201,851	
31	After-Tax Profit	$ (74,538)	$ 26,612	$ 127,539	$ 258,819	$ 428,934	
32							
33	Dividends to Shareholders	-	-	12,000	25,000	43,000 ←	
34							
35	Retained Earnings	$ (74,538)	$ 26,612	$ 115,539	$ 233,819	$ 385,934	
36							
37							
38							
39							

retained earnings after dividends

dividends paid to shareholders

Income Statement | Balance Sheet | Cash Flow | Loan Analysis | Loan Schedule | Depreciation ...

Ready

Based on Asli's projections, the annual retained earnings of the company will grow to $385,934 by Year 5 after accounting for all expenses, depreciation, interest payments, taxes, and owed dividends. At the end of the fifth year, the company has completely repaid its $550,000 startup loan and its investors.

Auditing a Workbook

In designing this workbook, Asli created several worksheets with interconnected values and formulas. The initial financial conditions entered in the Startup worksheet impact the company's loan repayment schedule. The values in the Depreciation worksheet are used in the Income Statement to access the company's yearly pretax profits. The dividends in the Investment Analysis worksheet are used to calculate the annual retained earnings. This interconnectedness gives Asli the ability to view the impact of changing one or more financial assumption on a wide variety of financial statements.

Two of these statements are stored in the Balance Sheet and the Cash Flow worksheets. The Balance Sheet worksheet projects what the company will own in both cash and tangible assets and what it will owe to banks and investors for each of the next five years. The Cash Flow worksheet projects the cash the company will have on hand through in its first five years of operation. You will view the contents of these worksheets now.

To review the Balance Sheet and Cash Flow worksheets:

▶ **1.** Go to the **Balance Sheet** worksheet. Many cells display the #NAME? error value. See Figure 9–31.

Figure 9–31   Error values in the Balance Sheet worksheet

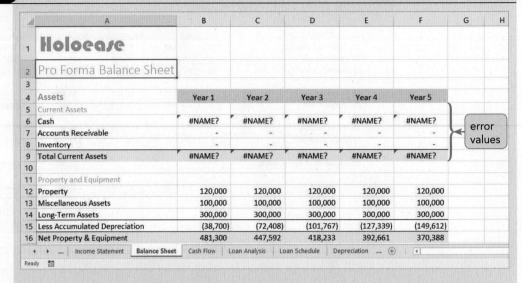

2. Go to the **Cash Flow** worksheet and scroll to the bottom of the worksheet. Note that several other cells also display the #NAME? error value.

The downside of a workbook with many interconnected worksheets and formulas is that an error in one cell can propagate throughout the entire workbook. Does the error displayed in the Balance Sheet originate in that worksheet or is it somewhere else? Asli wants you to locate the source of the #NAME error. To do that, you will use auditing tools.

Tracing an Error

One of most useful tools in fixing an error-filled workbook is the Trace Error tool. In tracing an error value to its source, you need to work with dependent and precedent cells. A dependent cell is one whose value depends on the values of other cells in the workbook. A precedent cell is one whose value is used by other cells. For example, if cell C15 contains the formula =C13+C14, then cell C15 is a dependent cell because it relies on cells C13 and C14 for its value. This makes cells C13 and C14 precedent cells. Any error values in cell C13 or cell C14 would propagate to cell C15. A cell can be both a dependent and precedent. For example, if cell C15 is used by another cell in the workbook, then it becomes the precedent to that cell.

To locate the source of an error value, you select any cell containing the error value and trace that error back through the line of precedent cells. If any of the precedent cells displays an error value, you need to trace that cell's precedents and so on until you reach an error cell that has no precedents. That cell is the source of the error. After correcting the error, if other errors still exist, repeat this process until you have removed all the errors from the workbook.

Reference

Tracing Error Values

- Select the cell containing an error value.
- On the Formulas tab, in the Formula Auditing group, click the Error Checking arrow, and then click Trace Error.
- Follow the tracer arrows to a precedent cell containing an error value.
- If the tracer arrow is connected to a worksheet icon, double-click the tracer arrow, and open the cell references in the worksheet.
- Continue to trace the error value to its precedent cells until you locate a cell containing an error value that has no precedent cells with errors.

You will use the auditing tools to trace the #NAME? error values in the Balance Sheet worksheet back to their source or sources, and then correct the errors.

To trace the errors in the Balance Sheet worksheet:

1. Go to the **Balance Sheet** worksheet, and then click cell **F9**. You'll start tracing the error from this cell.

2. On the ribbon, click the **Formulas** tab.

3. In the Formula Auditing group, click the **Error Checking arrow**, and then click **Trace Error**. A tracer arrow is attached to cell F9. See Figure 9–32.

Figure 9–32 **Error value being traced**

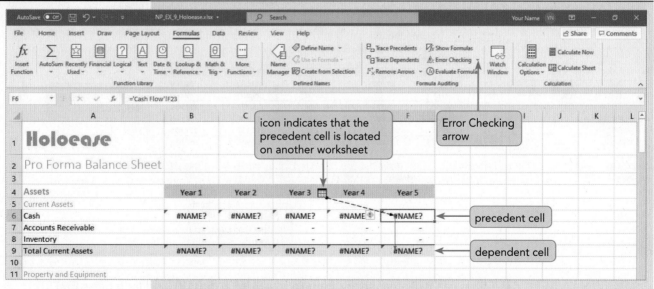

The tracer arrow provides a visual clue to the source of the error. A blue tracer arrow indicates that no error has been received or passed. A red tracer arrow indicates that an error has been received from the precedent cell or passed to the dependent cell. In this case, a red tracer arrow points from cell F6 to cell F9, indicating that cell F6 is the source of the error in cell F9. However, cell F6 also has a precedent cell. A black dashed tracer arrow points from a worksheet icon ▦, indicating that the precedent cell for the value in cell F6 is in another worksheet in the workbook. You'll follow the tracer arrow to that sheet.

To continue tracing the error to its source:

1. Double-click the **tracer arrow** that connects the worksheet icon ▦ to cell F6. The Go To dialog box opens, listing a reference to cell F23 in the Cash Flow worksheet.

2. In the Go to box, click the reference to cell **F23**, and then click **OK**. Cell F23 in the Cash Flow worksheet is now the active cell.

3. On the Formulas tab, in the Formula Auditing group, click the **Error Checking arrow**, and then click **Trace Error** to trace the source of the error in cell F23.

   The tracer arrows pass through several cells in row 23 before going to cell B23 and settling on cell B20. Cell B20 has a single precedent indicated by the blue arrow and the blue box, which surrounds the range that is the precedent to the formula in cell B20. Because blue is used to identify precedent cells that are error free, the source of the error must be in cell B20 of the Cash Flow worksheet, which is selected.

4. Review the formula for cell B20 in the formula bar. Notice that the function name in the formula is entered incorrectly as SUMM, which is why the #NAME? error code appears in cell B20. See Figure 9–33.

Figure 9–33	Source of the error value

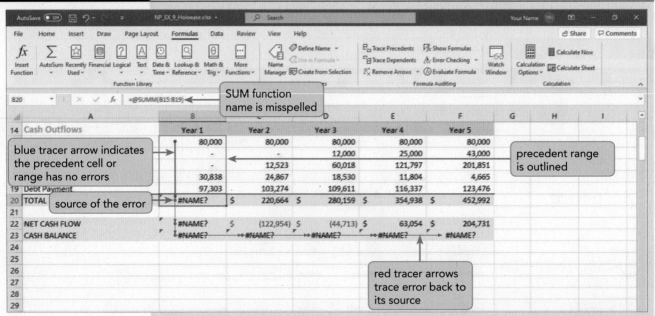

5. In cell **B20**, change the formula to **=SUM(B15:B19)**, and then press **ENTER**. After you edit the formula, the #NAME? error values disappear from the worksheet. If a dialog box opens asking if you want to see an explanation of @, press **Enter**. If a dialog opens saying this formula is not supported by older Excel versions, press **Enter** to insert the formula.

Tip

To restore tracer arrows that have disappeared, retrace the formulas in the workbook.

6. On the Formulas tab, in the Formula Auditing group, click the **Remove Arrows** button if necessary to remove all the tracer arrows from the worksheet.

7. Return to the **Balance Sheet** worksheet and verify that no error values appear on that sheet.

8. Click the **Remove Arrows button**, if necessary, to remove the tracer arrows from the worksheet.

Trouble? If the tracer arrows already disappeared from your workbook, it's not a problem. Excel removes tracer arrows automatically after a few seconds.

You can use the auditing tools to track any cell formula whether or not it contains an error. To trace the precedents of the active cell, click the Trace Precedents button in the Formula Auditing group on the Formulas tab (or press CTRL+[). To locate cells that are dependent upon the active cell, click the Trace Dependents button (or press CTRL+]).

Evaluating a Formula

Another way to explore the relationship between cells in a workbook is by evaluating formulas using the Evaluate Formula tool. From the Evaluate Formula dialog box, you can display the value of different parts of the formula or display other formulas in the cell references in the formula to discover the source of the formula's value. This is helpful for subtle worksheet errors that are not easily seen and fixed.

On a balance sheet, the value of the company's total assets should equal the value of the total liabilities and equity. Checking that these totals match is a basic step in auditing any financial report. In the Balance Sheet worksheet, the total assets in row 18 are equal to the total liabilities and equity in row 34 for Year 1 through Year 4. However, in Year 5 these values do not match. The company's Year 5 total assets shown in cell F18 are $637,366, but the Year 5 total liabilities and equity shown in cell F34 is $760,841. Because the values differ, an error must occur somewhere in the workbook. You'll use the Evaluate Formula tool to evaluate the formula in cell F34 to locate the source of the error.

To evaluate the formula in cell F34 of the Balance Sheet worksheet:

1. Select cell **F34**, which contains the total liabilities and equity value for Year 5.

2. On the Formulas tab, in the Formula Auditing group, click the **Evaluate Formula** button. The Evaluate Formula dialog box opens with the formula in cell F34 displayed. See Figure 9–34.

Figure 9–34	**Evaluate Formula dialog box**

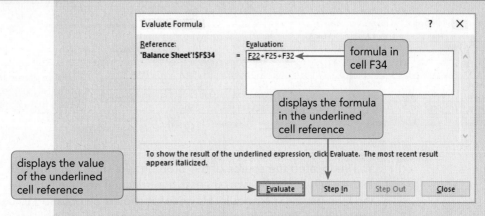

From this dialog box, you can evaluate each component of the formula in cell F34. To display the value of the underlined cell reference, click Evaluate. If the underlined part of the formula is a reference to another formula located elsewhere in the workbook, click Step In to display the other formula. Likewise, click Step Out to hide the nested formula.

▶ 3. Click **Evaluate**. The selected cell reference F22 is replaced with the current liabilities for Year 5 (0). Cell F25 is now the underlined reference.

▶ 4. Click **Step In** to view the formula in cell F25. Below the original formula, the formula ='Loan Schedule'!E38 appears, indicating that cell F25 gets its value from cell E38 in the Loan Schedule worksheet. See Figure 9–35.

Figure 9–35	Stepping into a formula

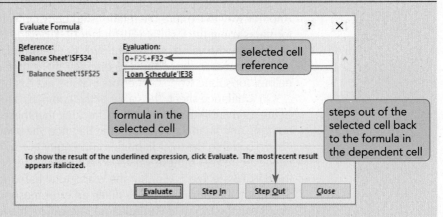

▶ 5. Click **Step In** to evaluate the formula in cell E38 of the Loan Schedule worksheet. See Figure 9–36.

Figure 9–36	Source of the error found

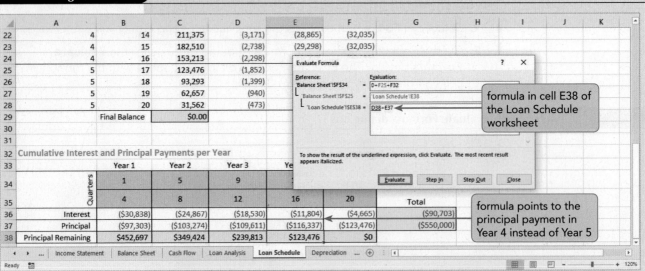

You've located the source of the problem. As shown in Figure 9–36, cell E38 in the Loan Schedule worksheet is the Principal Remaining value for Year 4 of the loan payment schedule. However, it should be pointing to cell F38, which contains the Year 5 value, because you are examining liabilities and assets for Year 5.

6. Click **Step Out** to hide the nested formula and redisplay the Balance Sheet worksheet.

7. Click **Close** to close the Evaluate Formula dialog box and return to the Balance Sheet worksheet with cell F25 selected.

8. In cell **F25**, change the formula to **='Loan Schedule'!F38** to change the cell reference from cell E38 to cell F38. The total liabilities and equity value in cell F34 changes to $637,366 matching the total assets value in cell F18. The balance sheet is in balance again.

Using the Watch Window

Workbooks can contain dozens of worksheets with interconnected formulas. When you change a value in one worksheet, you may want to view the impact of that change on cell values in other worksheets. Moving among worksheets can be slow and clumsy if the values you want to follow are spread across many worksheets. Rather than jumping to different worksheets, you can create a **Watch Window**, which is a window that displays values of cells located throughout the workbook. When you change a cell's value, a Watch Window allows you to view the impact of the change on widely scattered dependent cells. The window also displays the workbook, worksheet, defined name, cell value, and formula of each cell being watched.

Asli wants to know the financial impact of a government tax rate increase from 32% to 38%. You'll create a Watch Window to display the company's Year 5 retained earnings, the Year 5 net worth value, and the Year 5 cash balance value.

To use the Watch Window to display values from multiple cells:

1. Go to the **Income Statement** worksheet and scroll to the top of the sheet.

2. On the Formulas tab, in the Formula Auditing group, click the **Watch Window** button. The Watch Window opens.

3. Click **Add Watch**. The Add Watch dialog box opens.

4. Click cell **F35** in the Income Statement worksheet, and then click **Add**. The Year 5 retained earnings value in cell F35 of the Income Statement worksheet is added to the Watch Window.

5. Click **Add Watch**, go to the **Balance Sheet** worksheet, click cell **F36**, and then click **Add**. The Year 5 net worth value from cell F36 of the Balance Sheet worksheet is added to the Watch Window.

> **Tip**
>
> You can assign defined names to watched cells to make the Watch Window easier to interpret.

6. Click **Add Watch**, go to the **Cash Flow** worksheet, click cell **F23**, and then click **Add**. The Year 5 cash balance in cell F23 of the Cash Flow worksheet is added to the Watch Window.

Now you can see the impact on these three values when the tax rate changes from 32% to 38%.

To modify the tax rate value:

1. In the Income Statement worksheet, click cell **F5**. This cell contains the assumed tax rate.

2. Change the assumed tax rate value from 32% to **38%**. The Watch Window shows the impact of increasing the tax rate. See Figure 9–37.

Figure 9–37   Watch Window under 38% tax rates

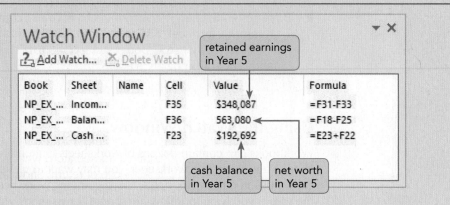

From the Watch Window, you can observe the effect of the revised tax rate by the end of the company's first five years. The Year 5 retained earnings amount in the Income Statement worksheet drops about $40,000 from $385,934 to $348,087; the Year 5 net worth value in the Balance Sheet worksheet falls about $75,000 from $637,366 to $563,080. Finally, the Year 5 balance in the Cash Flow worksheet also drops about $75,000 from $266,978 to $192,692. With operating margins so tight in the tech field, those losses are a great concern. Asli will study this more closely and perhaps revise the business plan to deal with this possibility. You will restore the tax rate to its original values.

To restore the tax rate:

1. In cell **F5**, change the tax rate value back to **32%**.

2. Close the Watch Window.

3. sam↑ Save the workbook, and then close it.

You have completed the initial financial analysis of Asli's business plan for Holoease. This is, of course, a preliminary rough estimate of the factors and issues involved with providing a 5-year projection of the company's financial future. More in-depth analysis in consultation with financial analysts, lawyers, and other interested parties, will still be required before going forward.

Review

Session 9.3 Quick Check

1. If you take out a loan for $200,000 that must be repaid in 10 years with quarterly payments of $7,200, what is the formula to calculate the annual interest rate of the loan? What is the result?

2. If the annual rate of return is 5%, is $95 today worth more than, less than, or the same as $100 a year from now? Show the formula and formula results you used to answer this question.

3. You receive $50 at the end of Year 1 from an investment, $75 at the end of Year 2, and $100 at the end of Year 3. If the rate of return is 6%, what is the present value of this investment? Show the formula and formula results you used to answer this question.

4. You spend $350 on an investment that pays $75 per year for the next six years. If you make the investment immediately, what is the net present value of the investment? Assume a 6% rate of return. Show the formula and formula results you used to answer this question.

5. Suppose that instead of spending $350 immediately on an investment, you spend $350 one year from now and then receive $75 per year for the next six years after that. What is the net present value assuming a 6% rate of return? Show the formula and formula results you used to answer this question.

6. Calculate the internal rate of return for the investment in Question 4. If another investment is available that pays a 7.3% rate of return, should you take it? Show the formula and formula results you used to answer this question.

7. When tracing an error with the auditing tools, what do red tracer arrows indicate?

8. What is the purpose of the Watch Window?

Practice

Review Assignments

Data File needed for the Review Assignments: NP_EX_9-2.xlsx

After consulting with financial analysts and accountants, Asli has some new figures for the Holoease business plan. The company can get slightly better conditions on the business loan, which means that Holoease needs less money from investors to fund the company. Asli has also modified the depreciation schedule for the business's tangible assets. Asli wants you to make the necessary changes in the workbook to calculate the company's financial data for the next five years. Complete the following:

1. Open the **NP_EX_9-2.xlsx** workbook located in the Excel9 > Review folder included with your Data Files. If a dialog box opens, asking whether you want to update links, click Don't Update. Save the workbook as **NP_EX_9_Plan** in the location specified by your instructor.

2. In the Documentation sheet, enter your name and the date.

3. In the Loan Scenarios worksheet, in cell B4, enter **5.75%** as the annual interest rate that the company will secure for a business loan of $750,000.

4. Complete the calculations for the Loan Scenarios worksheet, which includes the constants you will need:

   a. In cell I7, use the PMT function to calculate the size of the quarterly payments for the $750,000 loan. Use cell H7 for the Rate argument, cell F7 for the Nper argument, and cell B7 for the Pv argument.

   b. In cell C8, use the FV function to calculate the future value of the loan assuming that quarterly payments are limited to $22,000. Use cell H8 for the Rate argument, cell F8 for Nper argument, cell I8 for the Pmt argument, and cell B8 for the Pv argument.

   c. In cell F9, use the NPER function to calculate the total number of payments required to repay a $750,000 loan with quarterly payments of $22,000. Use cell H9 for the Rate argument, cell I9 for the Pmt argument, cell B9 for the Pv argument, and cell C9 for the Fv argument.

   d. In cell D9, calculate the payback period in years by dividing the value in cell F9 by the value in cell E9.

   e. In cell B10, use the PV function to calculate the present value of the loan the company can afford if quarterly payments are limited to $22,000 over a 10-year period. Use cell H10 for the Rate argument, cell F10 for Nper argument, and cell I10 for the Pmt argument.

5. In the Startup Plan worksheet, in cell B25, enter **660,000** as the size of the loan that Holoease will take out to fund its startup costs.

6. Create an amortization schedule for the business loan in the Amortization Schedule worksheet. In cell G5, calculate the payment per quarter by using the PMT function with cell D5 as the Rate argument, cell F5 as the Nper argument, and cell A5 as the Pv argument.

7. Calculate the quarterly payments made to interest and principal:

   a. In cell D9, use the IPMT function to calculate the interest payment for the first quarter. In cell E9, use PPMT function to calculate the principal payment for the first quarter. Use cell $D$5 for the Rate argument, cell B9 for the Per argument, cell $F$5 for the Nper argument, and cell $A$5 for the Pv argument.

   b. AutoFill the formulas in the range D9:E9 to the range D10:E48 to calculate the payments for the remaining quarters. Fill the formulas without formatting.

   c. Verify that the loan is completely repaid by checking that the value in cell C49 is equal to $0.00.

8. Complete the Amortization Schedule worksheet by calculating the cumulative interest and principal payments per year:

   a. In cell B55, use the CUMPRINC function to calculate the principal paid for the first year. In cell B56, use the CUMIPMT function to calculate the interest paid for the first year. Use cell $D$5 used for the Rate argument, cell $F$5 for the Nper argument, cell $A$5 for the Pv argument, cell B53 for the Start argument, cell B54 for the End argument, and 0 for the Type argument.

   b. Copy the range B55:B56 and paste it in the range C55:F56.

9. Project future income statements under this new business plan. In the Profit and Loss worksheet, in the range C8:E8, project the company's revenue for the next five years by interpolating the Year 2 through Year 4 revenue assuming a growth trend. The costs of marketing and R&D as well as gross profit will be calculated for you.

10. In the range C14:F14, extrapolate the Year 2 through Year 5 payroll expenses by assuming the payroll will grow by 12% per year. In C15:F17, extrapolate the other expenses by assuming they grow by 5% per year from the initial Year 1 values. The range C18:F18 automatically calculates the total expenses for Year 2 through Year 5.

11. Calculate depreciation of the company's tangible assets. In the Startup Plan worksheet, in cell B12, enter **350,000** as current value of the long-term tangible assets.

12. Asli estimates that the long-term tangible assets will depreciate to a salvage value of $50,000 in 15 years. In the Depreciation worksheet, in the range B10:F10, calculate the yearly straight-line depreciation of the long-term assets using the SLN function with absolute references to the Cost, Salvage, and Life values in the range B4:B6.

13. In the range B16:F16, use the DB function to calculate the yearly declining balance of the assets using absolute references to the Cost, Salvage, and Life values in the range B4:B6 and relative references to the Period values in the cells B15 through F15.

14. In the Profit and Loss worksheet, in the range B22:F22, enter formulas to reference the declining balance depreciation values in the range B16:F16 of the Depreciation worksheet.

15. In the range B25:F25, enter formulas to reference the cumulative interest payments in the range B56:F56 of the Amortization Schedule worksheet. Enter the interest expenses as positive values by changing the sign of the interest value.

16. In the range B28:F28, use an IF function to calculate the company's taxes for each year. If the company's pretax profit in row 26 is negative, set the tax to 0; otherwise, multiply the assumed tax rate in cell F5 by the pretax profit.

17. Calculate the value of the company to potential investors. In the Startup Plan worksheet, in cell B30, enter **$250,000** as the amount the company hopes to attract from investors.

18. Calculate the rate of return if the investor group is paid $55,000 per year for the next five years on the $250,000 investment. In the Investment worksheet, in cell B9, use the RATE function to calculate the interest of the proposed repayment schedule using the corresponding values in the range B6:B8.

19. The company will also offer investors dividends on their investment. In cell B13, enter **$0** for the Year 1 dividend. In cells C13 and D13, enter **$6,000** as the Year 2 and Year 3 dividends. In cells E13 and F13, enter **$25,000** for the Year 4 and Year 5 dividends.

20. In the range C18:C23, calculate the payback period of the investment by calculating a running total of the values in the range B18:B23.

21. Determine the profitability of the investment to the investors:

    a. In cell C25, enter **12%** as the desired rate of return for the investors.

    b. In cell C26, use the NPV function to calculate the present value of the investment using the desired rate of return in cell C25 and the payments in the range B19:B23.

    c. In cell C27, calculate the net present value by adding to the cost of the initial investment in cell B18 to the present value in cell C26.

    d. In cell C28, use the IRR function to calculate the internal rate of return for this investment using the cash flow values in the range B18:B23.

22. In the Profit and Loss worksheet, in the range B31:F31, enter formulas to reference the yearly dividend values paid to the shareholders in the range B13:F13 of the Investment worksheet.

23. An error is somewhere in the workbook. Starting with cell F18 in the Balance sheet, trace the #REF error in the workbook back to its source, and correct it.

24. Save the workbook, and then close it.

Apply

Case Problem 1

Data File needed for this Case Problem: NP_EX_9-3.xlsx

Eagle Manufacturing   Jim Helt is a financial manager at Eagle Manufacturing, a steel manufacturer specializing in construction projects ranging from support structures used in large buildings and highways to decorative railings for new homes and apartments. For each piece of industrial equipment the company needs, Jim must evaluate whether it is better to purchase the equipment or to lease the equipment for several years before replacing it with newer models. Currently, Jim must choose between buying a large-capacity hydraulic steel metal press for $35,000 or leasing that machinery for three years for $500 a month. You'll use the Excel financial functions to compare the cost of buying versus leasing. Complete the following:

1. Open the **NP_EX_9-3.xlsx** workbook located in the Excel9 > Case1 folder included with your Data Files. Save the workbook as **NP_EX_9_Eagle** in the location specified by your instructor.

2. In the Documentation worksheet, enter your name and the date.

3. In the Buy vs. Lease worksheet, in cell B4, enter **$35,000** as the purchase price of the sheet metal press.

4. The sheet metal press has a salvage value of $15,000 after 120 months, or 10 years. In the range B5:B6, enter the salvage value and the salvage time (in months).

5. If the company does opt to buy the sheet metal press, the company will purchase a service maintenance contract that will cover maintenance costs for the next three years. In cell B9, enter **$950** as the cost of this contract.

6. If the company buys the sheet metal press it will also have to pay sales tax on the purchase. In cell B10, enter **3.25%** as the sales tax rate. In cell B11, enter a formula to calculate the amount of sales tax by multiplying the sales tax rate by the current price of the equipment.

7. If the company decides to buy the sheet metal press, Jim believes that it can be sold after three years for 90% of its depreciated value. In cell B12, enter **90%** as the resale percentage.

8. If the company decides to lease this equipment, Eagle Manufacturing will have to pay a $2,500 security deposit and a monthly payment of $500. Enter these values in the range B15:B16.

9. The table in columns D through G will be used to track the monthly cost of buying versus leasing over the next 36 months. In cell E4, enter a formula that shows the current price of the equipment entered in cell B4.

10. Calculate the value of the equipment as it depreciates each year as follows:

    a. In cell E5, calculate the difference between the value in cell E4 and the depreciation of the sheet metal press in the first month of use using the DB function. Use cells $B$4, $B$5, and $B$6 for the Cost, Salvage, and Life arguments and use cell D5 for the Period argument.

    b. Use AutoFill to fill the formula in cell E5 through the range E6:E40. Fill the formulas without formatting.

11. In cell F4, enter as a negative cash flow the initial cost of purchasing the sheet metal press by adding the cost of the equipment in cell B4, the cost of the service contract in cell B9, and the cost of the sales tax in cell B11.

12. For Month 1 through Month 36, the company will not have to make any payments on the sheet metal press. Enter **0** as the cash flow values in the range F5:F40.

13. After Month 36, the company will sell sheet metal price at a reduced value. In cell F41, enter as a positive cash flow the final depreciated value of the equipment in cell E40 multiplied by the resale percentage in cell B12.

14. If the company chooses to lease the sheet metal press it must first pay the security deposit. In cell G4, enter as a negative cash flow the cost of the security deposit on the digital equipment entered in cell B15.

15. Every month Eagle Manufacturing must pay the leasing fee. In the range G5:G40, enter as a negative cash flow the monthly lease payment from cell B16.

16. After the term of the lease is over, the company will return the sheet metal press and receive the security deposit back. In cell G41, enter the value of the security deposit from cell B15 as a positive cash flow.

17. To assess the time value of money, Jim will assume a **5.25%** discount rate. Enter this value into cell B19. To express this as a monthly percentage, in cell B20, enter a formula to divide the value of cell B19 by 12.

18. Calculate the net present value of buying the sheet metal press. In cell B21, add the initial investment in cell F4 to the present value of owning and then reselling the equipment after three years. To determine the present value of owning the equipment, use the NPV function with the monthly discount rate in cell B20 as the rate of return and the values in the F5:F41 as the cash flows for owning and using the equipment.

19. Calculate the cost leasing the sheet metal press in current dollars. In cell B22, calculate the net present value by adding the initial cost of the security deposit in cell G4 to the value returned by the NPV function for the discount rate in cell B20 and the cash flows in the range G5:G41.

20. Determine whether buying is less expensive than leasing. In cell B23, enter an IF function that displays the text **BUY** if the net present value of buying the equipment is greater than the net present value of leasing the equipment; otherwise display the text **LEASE**.

21. Save the workbook.

22. The decision to buy versus lease is closely related to the time value of money. If the discount rate is high, then Eagle Manufacturing will be selling the sheet metal press in three years for dollars of substantially reduced value. Redo your analysis by changing the discount rate in cell B19 to **6.50%**.

23. Save the workbook as **NP_EX_9_Eagle2** in the location specified by your instructor, and then close it.

Challenge

Case Problem 2

Data File needed for this Case Problem: NP_EX_9-4.xlsx

Midwest Copper   Linda Rubin is a project analyst at Midwest Copper, a mining company in northern Minnesota. The company is considering investing in a copper mine near Spirit River. Linda wants you to help develop a financial workbook that analyzes the cost of opening the mine, running it for 25 years, and then cleaning up the mine site after its useful life is over. Complete the following:

1. Open the **NP_EX_9-4.xlsx** workbook located in the Excel9 > Case2 folder included with your Data Files. Save the workbook as **NP_EX_9_Mine** in the location specified by your instructor.

2. In the Documentation worksheet, enter your name and the date.

3. In the Project Analysis worksheet, enter the following initial assumptions for the project:

   a. In cell B5, enter **$12.30** as the startup costs for the project (in millions).

   b. In cell B6, enter **32.0%** as operation costs as a percentage of the mine's revenue.

   c. In cell B7, enter **$13.25** as the cleanup cost in current dollars (in millions).

   d. In cell B8, enter **25** as the years of operation of the proposed copper mine.

   e. In cell B9, enter **3.4%** as the projected annual inflation rate over the course of the mine's existence.

✛ **Explore** 4. In cell B12, use the FV function to calculate the cleanup cost in 25 years, using the inflation rate in cell B9, the number of years in cell B8, a payment value of 0, and the present value of the cleanup cost in cell B7. Change the sign of the result so it appears as a positive value.

5. In cell G6, enter the startup cost of the mine using the value in cell B5.

6. Enter the following projected annual income values that the mine will generate:

   a. In cell E7, enter **$0.75** as the projected earnings for Year 1 (in millions).

   b. In cell E16, enter **$18.00** as the projected earnings for Year 10 (in millions).

   c. In cell E26, enter **$4.00** as the projected earnings for Year 20 (in millions).

   d. In cell E31, enter **$1.00** as the projected earnings for Year 25 (in millions).

7. Fill in the missing income values in column E:

   a. Interpolate the rising income values between cells E7 and E16 assuming a growth trend.

   b. Interpolate the declining income values between cells E16 and E26 assuming a growth trend.

   c. Interpolate the declining income values between cells E26 and E31 assuming a linear trend.

8. In the range F7:F31, calculate the annual operational costs of the mine by multiplying the income value for each year by the operational cost percentage in cell B6.

9. Linda estimates the copper mine will have $1.80 million in fixed costs in Year 1. Enter **$1.80** in cell G7.

10. Linda projects that fixed costs will initially grow at a rate of 4% per year. Extrapolate the Year 1 fixed cost value through Year 20 in the range G8:G26.

11. From Year 21 to Year 25, Linda projects that fixed costs will decline by 10% per year (so that each year's fixed cost is 90% of the previous year). Extrapolate the Year 21 fixed-cost values through Year 25 in the range G27:G31 using a growth value of **0.9**.

12. In cell G32, enter the cleanup cost using the value in cell B12.

13. In the range H6:H32, calculate the copper mine's gross profit by subtracting the sum of the annual cost of goods and fixed costs from the mine's annual income. AutoFill the values without formatting.

14. In the range I6:I32, calculate the running total of gross profit for each year.

15. Create a line chart of the range D5:D32,I5:I32 to show the cumulative profit of the mine. Move and resize the chart to cover the range K5:Q20. The payback period is indicated where the line chart crosses the horizontal axis.

16. In cell B13, calculate the total income from the copper mine by adding all the values in column E. In cell B14, calculate the total cost of the mine by adding all the values in columns F and G. Note that by the raw totals, the mine appears to lose money because the total expenses are greater than the total income.

⊕ **Explore** 17. Because the cash flow from the mine changes between positive and negative several times during its 25-year projected history, there are different possible internal rates of return. Calculate two possible rates of return from the copper mine:

   a. In cell A17, enter **1.0%** as your guess for the rate of return. In cell B17, calculate the internal rate of return using the profit values in the range H6:H32 and your guess in cell A17.

   b. In cell A18, enter **10.0%** as your guess for the rate of return. In cell B18, calculate the internal rate of return using the cash flow values in the range H6:H32 and your guess in cell A18.

18. Supplement your calculations of the internal rate of return with calculations of the net present value of the copper mine investment under different discount rates:

   a. In the range A21:A39, enter the discount rates from 1% to 10% in steps of 0.5%.

   b. In the range B21:B39, add the value of cell $H$6 to the present value of the cash flows in the range $H$7:$H$32 using the NPV function with the corresponding discount rate in column A.

19. Create a scatter chart with smooth lines of the data in the range A20:B39. Move and resize the chart to cover the range K22:Q32. Note that the chart crosses the horizontal axis twice indicating that there are two possible rates of return.

20. Save the workbook, and then close it.

EXCEL

Objectives

Session 10.1
- Retrieve data with the Query Editor
- Create and edit a query
- Chart trends and forecast future values

Session 10.2
- Add data to the Excel Data Model
- Manage table relations in Power Pivot
- Create PivotTables drawing data from several connected tables

Session 10.3
- Drill through a hierarchy of fields
- Create maps with the map chart type
- Create map presentations with 3D Maps

Analyzing Data with Business Intelligence Tools

Presenting Sales and Revenue Data

Case | Cup and Platter

Dmitry Kovan is an account manager at Cup and Platter, a consumer retail chain that specializes in home furnishings and kitchen products. Dmitry is developing a sales report that analyzes sales data on select products and product categories sold on the company's website and five Cup and Platter stores located in Brooklyn, Chicago, Indianapolis, Philadelphia, and Washington, D.C. The report needs to analyze consumer preferences and project future sales revenue based on thousands of sales transactions. This large volume of data will be retrieved from a variety of data sources, including text files and external databases. You will help Dmitry by accessing and analyzing the data using Excel data tools.

Starting Data Files

Excel10 →

Module

NP_EX_10-1.xlsx
Support_EX_10_Data.accdb
Support_EX_10_History.csv
Support_EX_10_TwoYear.csv

Review

NP_EX_10-2.xlsx
Support_EX_10_Sales01.csv
Support_EX_10_Sales02.csv
Support_EX_10_Sales03.accdb

Case1

NP_EX_10-3.xlsx
Support_EX_10_Yogurt.accdb

Case2

NP_EX_10-4.xlsx.
Support_EX_10_Turkeys.csv
Support_EX_10_Migration.csv

Session 10.1 Visual Overview:

The **Power Query Editor** is an Office tool used to write queries.

A **query** is a request for information from a data source. This query retrieves information from the Year, Business Year, and Revenue ($mil) fields.

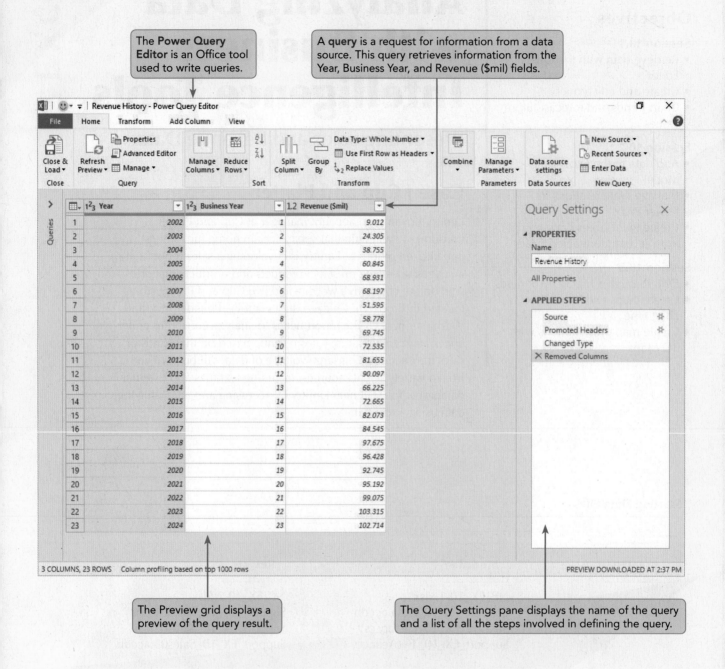

The Preview grid displays a preview of the query result.

The Query Settings pane displays the name of the query and a list of all the steps involved in defining the query.

Queries and Trendlines

To create a query, you click commands in the Get & Transform Data group on the Data tab and select the data source.

To create a worksheet containing forecasted values, including values that follow a seasonal pattern, you click the Forecast Sheet button.

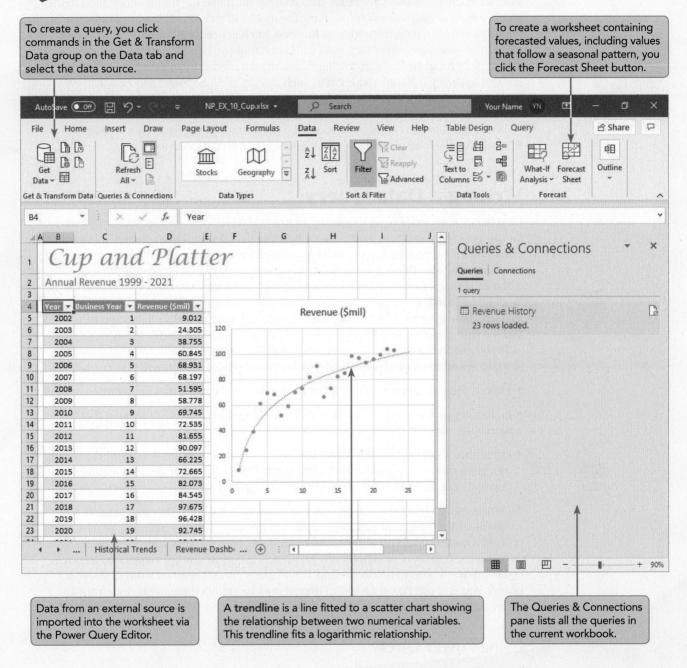

Data from an external source is imported into the worksheet via the Power Query Editor.

A **trendline** is a line fitted to a scatter chart showing the relationship between two numerical variables. This trendline fits a logarithmic relationship.

The Queries & Connections pane lists all the queries in the current workbook.

Introducing Business Intelligence

With so much information available, data analysts must find the useful information hidden within a mass of data values and sources. The tools and techniques used to extract useful information from data is referred to as **Business Intelligence** (or **BI**). Business Intelligence seeks to answer questions of fact, such as *What happened?* and *When did it happen?* and *Where did it happen?* Business Intelligence is often paired with **analytics**, which seeks answers to strategic planning questions, such as *Why did it happen?* and *How can we make it happen again?* Properly applied, Business Intelligence accelerates and improves decision making, resulting in a competitive advantage in the marketplace.

In this module, you'll learn the tools you need to turn Excel into an effective Business Intelligence platform. That process starts with data queries.

Writing a Data Query

Data being analyzed is often located in an external file or data source. To access that data for use in Excel, you create a data query. Because data sources often contain thousands or even millions of records, a query will typically include commands to reduce the data to a manageable size. This lets you import only those items of interest to you. For example, a human resources manager might construct a query to retrieve company salary records, limiting the search to employees from a particular department who were hired within a specified time interval. Queries can also be used to create new data fields and records so that the data imported into Excel is "cleaned up" and ready for study.

In the process of creating a query, you establish a connection between the Excel workbook and the data source. A connection does one of the following:

- Imports the data once, creating a "snapshot" of the data at a specific moment in time

- Establishes a "live connection" that will be updated periodically, ensuring that the workbook contains the most current data

- Establishes a connection but leaves the data residing within the data source, creating a smaller, more manageable workbook and avoiding the confusion of creating duplicate copies of the data across multiple locations

A climatologist might be interested only in temperature values from past epochs and would need to import that data only once. On the other hand, a financial analyst would probably want to establish a live connection between a workbook and a stock market data source so that the workbook always reflects the most current values and trends.

Dmitry wants you to report on Cup and Platter's annual revenue from its 23-year history. You will use Power Query to import the company's financial history from an external data source.

Using Power Query

Power Query is a BI tool that writes queries for almost any kind of data source, from text files to websites to large data structures. With Power Query, you can specify which parts of the data you want to import and how that data should be formatted. You can even modify the structure of the data prior to bringing it into Excel.

Text files are the simplest and one of the most widely used data storage formats, containing only text and numbers without any internal coding, formulas, or graphics. The data are usually organized in columns separated by a character known as a **delimiter**. The most commonly used delimiters are commas and tabs. Text files with comma delimiters are known as **Comma Separated Values (CSV) files**.

Figure 10–1 shows some lines from the CSV text file Dmitry wants you to use. The data are arranged in five columns separated by commas. The column titles, shown in the first line of the figure, are Year, Business Year, Revenue ($mil), Units Sold, and Notes. The remaining lines of the file contain the annual sales figures and commentary for the 23 years of sales data.

| Figure 10–1 | Data arranged in a CSV file |

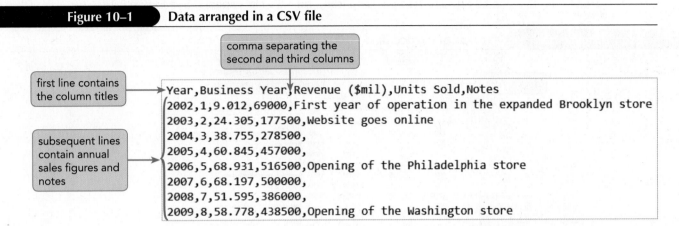

You want to be careful saving financial data in a CSV file because commas within currency totals will be interpreted as column separators. If your data requires commas, use a text file in which a tab character separates one column from another.

Reference

Constructing a Query

- On the Data tab, in the Get & Transform Data group, click the Get Data button.
- On the Get Data menu, select a data source category, click the type of file or the data source, and then import the data source file.
- Click Transform Data, and then in the Power Query Editor, click toolbar commands to transform the data from the data source.
- In the Query Settings pane, edit the steps in the query.
- On the Home tab, in the Close group, click the Close & Load arrow, and then click Close & Load To.
- In the Load To dialog box, select how to load the data, and then click Load.

You will create a query to retrieve the data values from the CSV file shown in Figure 10–1.

To create a query to the revenue history data:

1. **sam**↓ Open the **NP_EX_10-1.xlsx** workbook located in the **Excel10 > Module** folder included with your Data Files, and then save the workbook as **NP_EX_10_Cup** in the location specified by your instructor.

2. In the Documentation worksheet, enter your name and the date.

3. Go to the **Company History** worksheet. You will place the revenue data that Dmitry has compiled in this worksheet.

4. On the ribbon, click the **Data** tab, and then in the Get & Transform Data group, click the **From Text/CSV** button. The Import Data dialog box opens.

Tip

You can also open CSV files directly in Excel using the Open command in Backstage view.

5. Navigate to the **Excel10 > Module** folder included with your Data Files, if necessary, click the **Support_EX_10_History.csv** file, and then click **Import**. A preview of the data from the CSV file appears. See Figure 10–2.

Figure 10–2   **Preview of queried data**

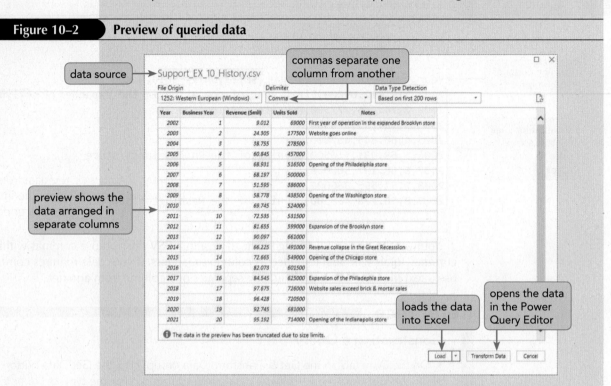

6. Click **Edit** or **Transform Data**. The Power Query Editor window for this data source opens. See Figure 10–3.

Figure 10–3   **Power Query Editor window**

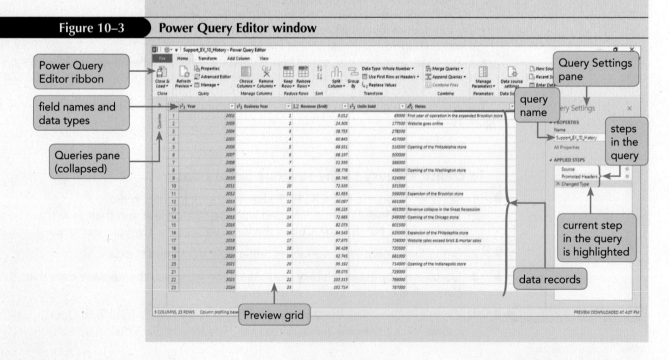

Power Query assigns each query a name. The default is the name of the data source, which in this case is the Support_EX_10_History file. You will change the name of the query to Revenue History.

To set the query name:

▶ **1.** Click the **Name** box located near the top of the Query Settings pane.

▶ **2.** Select the default name assigned to the query, and then press **DELETE**.

▶ **3.** Type **Revenue History** as the query name, and then press **ENTER**. The query is renamed.

A query is entered as a list of commands appearing in the APPLIED STEPS box of the Query Settings pane. Power Query entered three commands to import the data from the CSV file. To better understand what Power Query is doing, you will view the impact of each step on the data query by viewing the status of the data in the Preview grid.

To view the first three steps of the query:

▶ **1.** In the Query Settings pane, in the APPLIED STEPS box, click **Source**. The Source step establishes the connection to the Support_EX_10_History.csv file. The Preview grid displays the appearance of the data after this step but before the next step. At this point in the query process, the default column names are Column1 through Column5, and all fields are treated as containing only text values, as indicated by A^B_C.

▶ **2.** In the APPLIED STEPS box, click **Promoted Headers**. In this step, Power Query uses the first line in the CSV file as a header row and assigns field names to the five columns of data.

▶ **3.** In the APPLIED STEPS box, click **Changed Type**. The Changed Type step applies data types to the values in the five columns, with the Year, Business Year, and Unit Sold fields defined as containing whole numbers 1^2_3, the Revenue ($mil) field as containing decimal numbers 1.2, and the Notes field as containing text A^B_C.

You can modify a query step by selecting the step in the APPLIED STEPS box and clicking the Gear icon ⚙ to the right of the step title. You can also delete a step by clicking the Delete button ✕ that appears to the left of the selected step title. Be aware, however, that editing or deleting a query step might cause subsequent steps to fail.

Insight

M: The Language of Power Query

All steps in Power Query are written in the language **M**, which is a **mashup query language** that extracts and transforms data from a data source. Each expression in M is applied as a function that creates or acts upon the connection to the data source. For example, the following Csv.Document() function from the M language retrieves the contents of the revenue.csv file located in the Excel folder of the user's MAIN computer, using a comma symbol as the delimiter to separate one column of data from the next:

```
=Csv.Document(File.Contents("\\MAIN\Excel\Revenue.csv"),
[Delimiter=",",Encoding=1252])
```

As you progress in your understanding of Power Query, you may find it more efficient to write your own commands in M rather than letting the Power Query Editor do it for you. You can view and edit all the M commands in a query by clicking the Advanced Editor button in the Query group on the Home tab of the Power Query Editor window.

Retrieving Data into an Excel Table

Once the data is in the form you want, you can load the data into your Excel workbook. Queried data can be imported into an Excel table, PivotTable, or PivotChart. You can also just create a connection to the data source and load the actual data later. Dmitry wants you to load the financial history data into an Excel table on the Company History worksheet. You'll import the data now.

To load the query data into an Excel table:

> Be sure to click the Close & Load arrow so you can choose where to place the imported data.

1. On the Home tab, in the Close group, click the **Close & Load arrow**, and then click **Close & Load To**. The Import Data dialog box opens.

   Trouble? If Excel loaded the data into a new worksheet, you clicked the Close & Load button. Cut and paste the Excel table into cell A3 in the Company History worksheet and then read but do not perform Steps 2 through 4.

2. Verify that the **Table** option button is selected, and then click the **Existing worksheet** option button.

3. If necessary, click cell **B4** to enter the expression =$B$4 in the cell reference box.

4. Click **OK**. After a few seconds, the data is loaded into a new table on the Company History worksheet. See Figure 10–4.

Figure 10–4	Queried data loaded into an Excel table

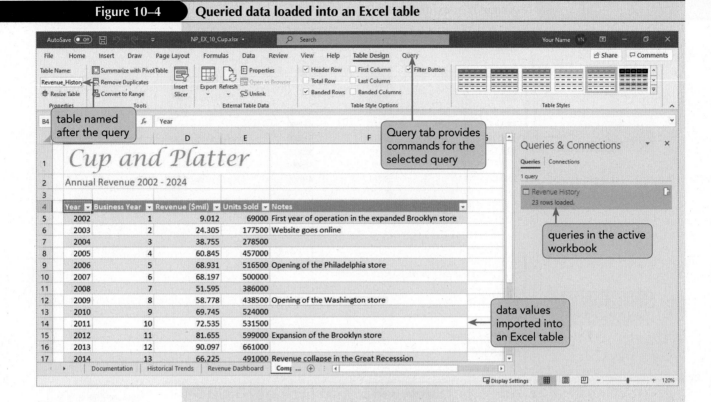

Excel assigns the new table the same name as the query that generated it. When the Revenue_History table is selected, the ribbon includes the Table Design tab and the Query tab, which contains commands for editing the selected query. The Queries & Connections pane also appears, listing all the queries in the active workbook.

Editing a Query

Dmitry wants you to edit the Revenue History query, removing the Units Sold and Notes columns so the table focuses only the revenue data. To edit a query, point to that query in the Queries & Connections pane. A dialog box opens, displaying information about the selected query and options for modifying the query. You'll edit the Revenue History query now.

To edit the existing Revenue History query:

1. In the Queries & Connections pane, point to **Revenue History**. A dialog box appears with information about the query. See Figure 10–5.

Figure 10–5	Revenue History dialog box

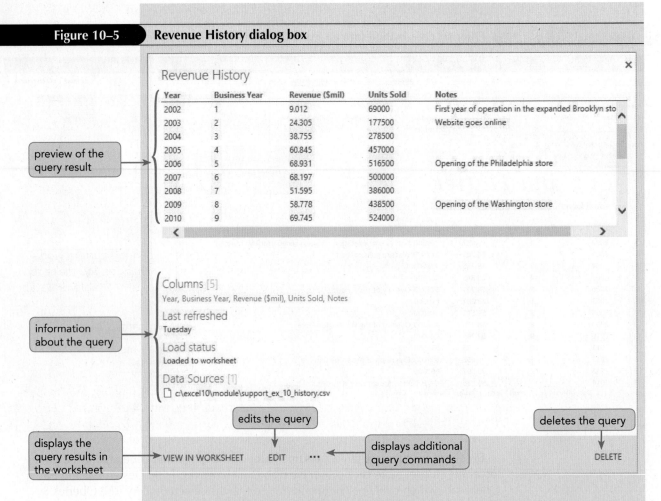

Revenue History

Year	Business Year	Revenue ($mil)	Units Sold	Notes
2002	1	9.012	69000	First year of operation in the expanded Brooklyn sto
2003	2	24.305	177500	Website goes online
2004	3	38.755	278500	
2005	4	60.845	457000	
2006	5	68.931	516500	Opening of the Philadelphia store
2007	6	68.197	500000	
2008	7	51.595	386000	
2009	8	58.778	438500	Opening of the Washington store
2010	9	69.745	524000	

preview of the query result

Columns [5]
Year, Business Year, Revenue ($mil), Units Sold, Notes

Last refreshed
Tuesday

information about the query

Load status
Loaded to worksheet

Data Sources [1]
c:\excel10\module\support_ex_10_history.csv

edits the query

deletes the query

displays the query results in the worksheet

VIEW IN WORKSHEET   EDIT   •••   displays additional query commands   DELETE

2. At the bottom of the box, click **EDIT**. The Power Query Editor window for the Revenue History query opens.

3. Click the **Units Sold** column header, hold down **CTRL**, click the **Notes** column header to select both columns, and then release the CTRL key.

4. On the Home tab, in the Manage Columns group, click the **Remove Columns** button. The Units Sold and Notes columns are removed from the query, leaving only the Year, Business Year, and Revenue ($mil) columns.

5. On the Home tab, in the Close group, click the **Close & Load** button. The edited query is loaded, and the Revenue History table now shows only the first three columns from the data source.

Note that removing columns from a query does not affect the data in the data source. It affects only the data that was imported into Excel.

Refreshing Query Data

Tip

To load a query to a different location, click the Load To button in the Load group on the Query tab, and specify a new location in the Import Data dialog box.

Loading data from a query into Excel creates a snapshot of that data. If the values in the data source change, the connection can be refreshed to show the most current information. You can refresh a query by clicking the Refresh button in the Load group on the Query tab.

To automatically refresh a data query, click the Refresh All arrow in the Queries & Connections group on the Data tab, and then click Connection Properties. The Query Properties dialog box opens to the Usage tab. From that tab, you can view controls for the connection to the query's data source. You can have Excel automatically refresh external data on a periodic schedule or whenever the workbook is opened. In this way, you can ensure the workbook contains timely and accurate information.

Insight

Excel Tables as Data Sources

An Excel table or a data range can be a data source for other Excel workbooks. To create a query to an Excel table or data range, select the table or data range, and then click the From Table/Range button in the Get & Transform Data group on the Data tab.

One advantage of using Power Query for tables and data ranges is that you then have access to all the unique tools and commands in Power Query. You can filter, reorder, and transform the table or data range for use in the current workbook or in other workbooks. However, like all queries, any changes you make to the data in the query do not impact the content or structure of the table or data range itself.

Transforming Data with Queries

A data source is often not organized in the way you need it for your report. As you have seen, you can use Power Query to remove columns from the data source. Power Query also includes tools to create new columns, group data values, and calculate summary statistics. This capability is particularly useful for large datasets in which the analyst is interested in only overall measures and not individual values.

Dmitry has another CSV file with two years of daily revenue totals for Cup and Platter. Dmitry wants a query that totals this data by month. You will use Power Query to group and summarize the data from the CSV file. First, you'll access the data source.

To write a query to access the Two Year Revenue data source:

1. Go to the **Recent History** worksheet.

2. On the Data tab, in the Get & Transform Data group, click the **From Text/ CSV** button. The Import Data dialog box opens.

3. If necessary, navigate to the **Excel10 > Module** folder included with your Data Files, click the **Support_EX_10_TwoYear.csv** file, and then click **Import**. The preview box for the CSV file opens.

4. Click **Edit** or **Transform Data** to open the Power Query Editor.

5. In the Query Settings pane, in the Name box, change the name of the query from Support_EX_10_TwoYear to **Recent History**. See Figure 10–6.

| Figure 10–6 | Initial preview of the Recent History query |

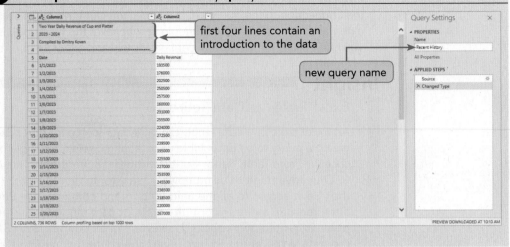

It is not uncommon for text files to include a few lines of descriptive text prior to the data. However, the inclusion of an introduction means that Power Query cannot automatically set up the data query. You must do that manually. You will indicate that the data begins on the fifth row of the file and then establish the data types of column headers for the two data fields in the CSV file.

To set up the data query:

1. On the Home tab, in the Reduce Rows group, click the **Remove Rows** button, and then click **Remove Top Rows**. The Remove Top Rows dialog box opens.

2. In the Number of rows box, type **4** and then click **OK**. The first four rows are removed from the data.

3. On the Home tab, in the Transform group, click the **Use First Row as Headers** button. The top row is used as the column headers for the two data columns.

Excel creates the Date and Daily Revenue fields, assigning the Date data type ⊞ to the Date field and the Whole Number data type 1^2_3 to the Daily Revenue field. Next, you will add a new column to the data query.

Adding a New Column

Dmitry wants to know the monthly revenue totals, not the daily revenue totals shown in the data file. Because revenue figures are tallied at the end of each month, you will add a new column named Month displaying the date of the last day in each month—that is, 1/31/2024 for January, 2/29/2024 for February, and so forth.

To create a new column with the end-of-month dates:

1. If necessary, click the **Date** column heading to select that column.

2. On the ribbon, click the **Add Column** tab, and then in the From Date & Time group, click the **Date** button. A menu opens with date options.

3. On the menu, point to **Month**, and then click **End of Month**. The End of Month column is added to the data.

4. Double-click the **End of Month** column heading to select the current column name, type **Month** as the new column name, and then press **ENTER**. The column is renamed and resized. See Figure 10–7.

Figure 10–7	Month column added to the data query

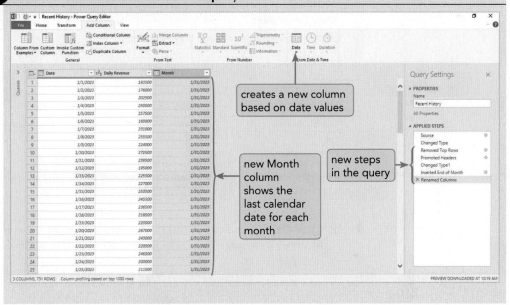

You will complete the query by grouping revenue values within the same month.

Grouping Values in a Query

You can group the data in a query by the values within one or more of its columns. When you create a grouping, Power Query adds a new column that summarizes the numeric values within each group by calculating statistics such as the sum, average, median, minimum, maximum, or count of those values.

Dmitry wants the query to return the total revenue within each month. You will group the query by the values in the Month column and create a new column containing the sum of the Revenue field.

To calculate the monthly revenues:

1. On the ribbon, click the **Transform** tab, and then in the Table group, click the **Group By** button. The Group By dialog box opens.

2. If necessary, click the **Group by** box, and then click **Month** to group the values by the dates in the Month column.

3. In the New column name box, double-click **Count**, and then type **Monthly Revenue** as the name of the new column to be added to the query, and then press **TAB**.

4. In the Operation box, select **Sum** to apply the sum function to the column, and then press **TAB**.

5. In the Column box, select **Daily Revenue** as the column to sum within the Month group. See Figure 10–8.

Figure 10–8   **Group By dialog box**

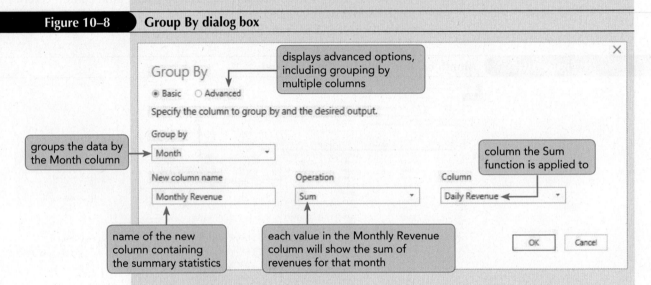

You can now load queried data into an Excel table.

6. Click **OK**. The values in the data query are grouped in a new column named Monthly Revenue. The Daily Revenue column is removed from this new grouping.

To close and load the Monthly Revenue query:

1. On the ribbon, click the **Home** tab. In the Close group, click the **Close & Load arrow**, and then click **Close & Load To**. The Import Data dialog box opens.

2. Verify that the **Table** option button is selected.

3. Click the **Existing worksheet** option button, and then click cell **B4** in the Recent History worksheet to load the Excel table containing the query data into that location.

4. Click **OK**. The 24 monthly revenue values appear in an Excel table in the Recent History worksheet.

5. Select the range **C5:C28**, and then format the selected cells with the **Currency** number format with no decimal places. See Figure 10–9.

Figure 10–9	Imported monthly revenue values

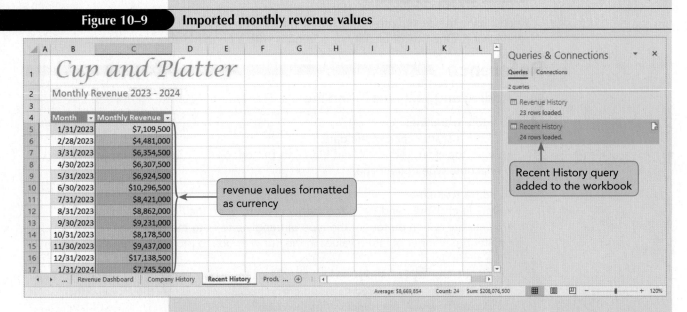

6. Close the Queries & Connections pane.

The contents of the Recent_History table provides Dmitry with valuable insight into how Cup and Platter's sales vary throughout the year. For example, the lowest revenue total occurred in February 2023 in which Cup and Platter gained $4,481,000 in revenue (cell C6). The highest occurred in December 2024 in which the total revenue was $18,007,500 (cell C28). Can these numbers provide information for projecting revenue totals in future months? You will do that analysis shortly.

Insight

Moving a Query's Data Source

The connection between a workbook and a data source is lost when one or the other is moved to a new location. If the files are no longer stored in the original location, the data can no longer be refreshed. To update the path between the workbook and the data source, do the following:

1. Open the query in the Power Query.
2. Double-click the Source step from the list of query steps in the APPLIED STEPS box.
3. Specify the new location of the data source in the File path box.
4. Click OK to save the query with the new location of the data source.

After saving the query, you can refresh the query within Excel and verify that it can again connect to the data source without error.

Charting Trends

Recognizing trends and projecting future values is an important goal of Business Intelligence. One way of identifying a trend is with a trendline added to a chart.

Reference

Adding and Editing a Trendline

To add a trendline:
- Create a scatter chart of the data.
- Select the chart, click the Chart Elements button, click the Trendline arrow, and then select the type of trendline.

To edit a trendline:
- Double-click the trendline in the scatter chart to open the Format Trendline pane.
- Select the option button for the type of trendline to fit to the data.
- Enter the number of future values in the Forward box to project future values along the same trend.
- Click the Display Equation on chart check box to display the equation of the trendline.
- Click the Display R-squared value on chart check box to display the R^2 value that indicates how well the trendline fits the data.

Dmitry wants you to create a scatter chart showing the company's annual revenue from the past 23 years with trendline indicating the general pattern of revenue growth. Dmitry is interested in learning whether revenues have grown by a constant amount each year or are showing signs of leveling off.

To create a scatter chart of the company's annual revenue:

1. Go to the **Company History** worksheet, and then select the range **C4:D27**.

2. Click the **Insert** tab. In the Charts group, click the **Insert Scatter (X, Y) or Bubble Chart** button, and then click **Scatter** (the first chart in the gallery). A scatter chart plotting Revenue vs. Business Year appears in the worksheet.

3. Move the chart to the **Historical Trends** worksheet, and then move and resize it to cover the range **B4:H16**.

4. Add the title **Annual Revenue ($mil)** to the vertical axis and the title **Business Year** to the horizontal axis.

5. Change the chart title to **Trend in Annual Revenue**.

6. Click the **Chart Elements** button, and then click the **Trendline** check box. A straight line is added to the chart showing a general upward trend in the revenue figures over the past 23 years. See Figure 10–10.

| Figure 10–10 | Linear trendline added to a scatter chart |

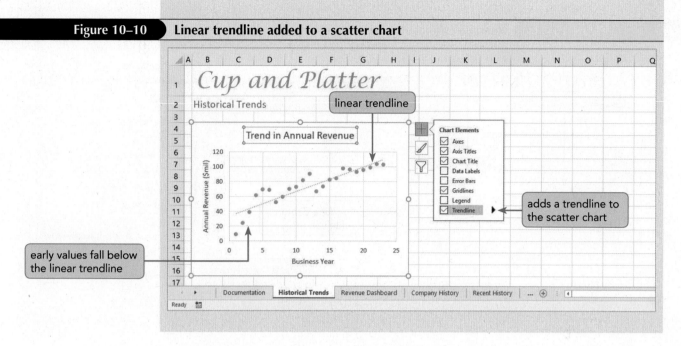

Excel scatter charts support the following trendline types:

- **Linear** for straight-line trends that increase or decrease by a constant amount (the default)
- **Exponential** for data values that rise or fall at increasingly higher rates
- **Logarithmic** for trends that increase or decrease quickly and then level out
- **Moving Average** to smooth out data by charting the average of consecutive data points
- **Polynomial** for trends that fluctuate between peaks and valleys
- **Power** for trends that increase or decrease by a constant multiple

Tip

Power and Exponential trendlines cannot be used if the data contains zero or negative values.

The straight line in the chart you created for Dmitry is for a linear trend, based on the assumption that revenue increases by a constant amount each year. However, the linear trendline overestimates the revenue in the early years. Dmitry thinks that a logarithmic trendline would be more appropriate because revenues grew rapidly at the beginning and then leveled off in later years. Dmitry also wants the logarithmic trendline extended two years into the future so that the company can estimate future revenue.

To change the trendline to logarithmic and project future values:

1. With the chart still selected, click the **Chart Elements** button ⊞, and then click the **Trendline** check box. The linear trendline disappears from the chart.

2. Click the **Trendline arrow** to display a menu of trendline options, and then click **More Options**. The Format Trendline pane opens.

3. In the Trendline Options section, click the **Logarithmic** option button. The logarithmic trendline appears on the chart.

4. Scroll down the Format Trendline pane to the Forecast options, type **2** in the Forward box, and then press **ENTER**. The trendline extends to forecast the company's annual revenue for the next two periods, or years. See Figure 10–11.

Figure 10–11	Revenue estimated using a logarithmic trend

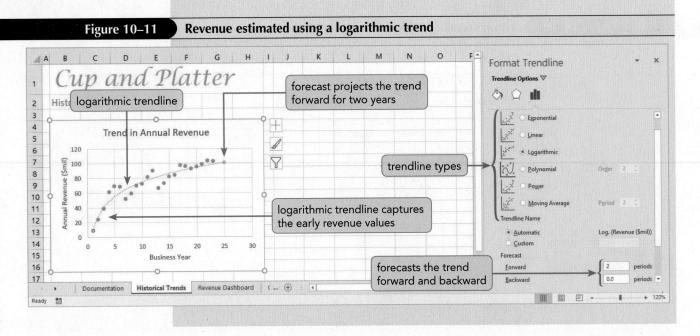

The logarithmic trendline follows the general growth of the company's annual revenue better than the linear trend though slightly underestimate revenues of the past three years. Dmitry will use the logarithmic trendline going forward, which indicates that the company's annual revenue should be at or above $100 million for each of the next two years.

Insight

Judging a Trendline with R^2

How well a trendline fits the data can be evaluated using the **R^2 statistic**, which measures what percentage of the variability in the data can be explained by the trendline. The R^2 statistic is expressed as a decimal between 0 and 1 where an R^2 value such as 0.85 indicates that 85% of the variability of the data can be accounted for by the trendline. R^2 values close to 1 indicate much of the data can be fitted by the trendline. On the other hand, R^2 values close to 0 indicate there is little evidence of a trend in the data based on the fitted line. You can display the R^2 value for an Excel trendline by clicking the Display R-squared value on chart check box in the Format Trendline pane.

Creating a Forecast Sheet

Forecast sheets are another Excel tool used for displaying trends and projecting future values. One advantage of forecast sheets is that they can be used to analyze **seasonal data** in which the values follow a periodic pattern during the calendar year.

Reference

Creating a Forecast Sheet and Setting the Forecast Options

- Select the data range containing the date values and numeric values to be forecasted.
- On the Data tab, in the Forecast group, click the Forecast Sheet button.
- In the Create Forecast Worksheet dialog box, click Options.
- To add a seasonal trend to the forecasts, in the Seasonality group, click the Set Manually option, and then enter the number of periods in one season.
- To set the confidence interval for the forecasted values, enter a value in the Confidence Interval input box.
- To set the extent of the forecast, enter the ending date in the Forecast End box.
- Click Create.

Dmitry wants to create a forecast sheet to track the seasonal changes in monthly revenue and project next year's monthly revenue.

To generate a forecast sheet of the monthly revenue:

1. Go the **Recent History** worksheet, and select the range **B4:C28**.

2. On the ribbon, click the **Data** tab, and then in the Forecast group, click the **Forecast Sheet** button. The Create Forecast Worksheet dialog box opens, showing a preview of the forecasted values. See Figure 10–12.

| Figure 10–12 | Create Forecast Worksheet dialog box |

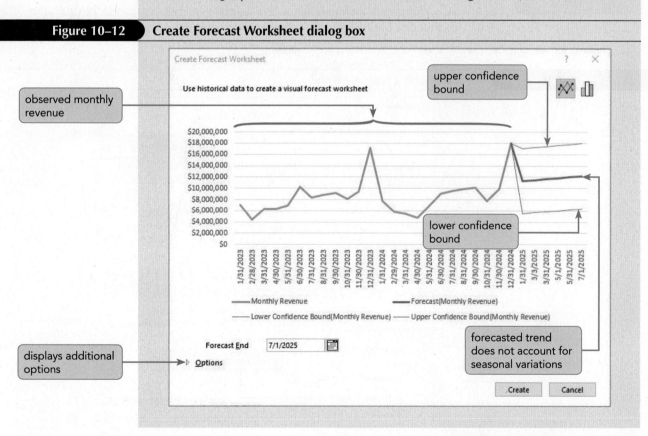

Tip

To change the confidence interval percentage, click Options in the Create Forecast Worksheet dialog box, and then enter a new value in the Confidence Interval box.

Excel uses two years of monthly revenue figures to project the revenue trend up to July 1, 2025. The trend is bracketed by upper and lower **confidence bounds**, which provide a measure of the uncertainty of the forecast by indicating within what range the forecasted values will lie. The default is to create 95% confidence bound for a region in which one is 95% confident that the actual values will appear. Thus, if the 95% confidence bound for a forecasted revenue ranges from $10 million to $15 million, you would be 95% confident that the eventual revenue will be not less than $10 million and not greater than $15 million. The fact that the upper and lower bounds are so far apart in Figure 10–12 indicates a large measure of uncertainty in the projected monthly revenue.

However, Dmitry notes that revenue follows a seasonal pattern with the highest sales totals occurring in November and December and low sales in January through March. The forecasted values have not picked up this trend. You will revise the forecast to account for seasonal variability.

To create a seasonal forecast of the monthly revenue:

1. In the lower-left corner of the Create Forecast Worksheet dialog box, click **Options**. The dialog box expands to display the forecast options.

Tip

You need at least two complete years of data to project a seasonal trend for the next year.

2. In the Seasonality group, click the **Set Manually** option button, and then enter **12** in the Set Manually box. This specifies a seasonal pattern that will repeat itself every 12 months.

3. In the Forecast End box, change the date to **12/31/2025** to forecast a year of monthly revenue. When the revenue follows a seasonal pattern, the confidence bands are much smaller than when no seasonality was assumed. See Figure 10–13.

Figure 10–13   **Forecasts with a seasonal trend**

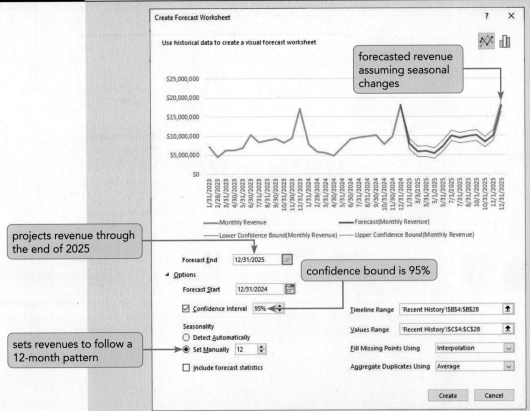

projects revenue through the end of 2025

confidence bound is 95%

sets revenues to follow a 12-month pattern

4. Click **Create**. A new worksheet containing the forecasted values is added to the workbook. The forecasted values have been placed within an Excel table.

5. If the Forecast Sheet dialog box opens, read the message, and then click **Got it!**

6. Rename the forecast worksheet as **Monthly Revenue Forecasts** and then move the sheet directly before the Data Sources worksheet near the end of the workbook.

7. Click the **Table Design** tab, and then in the Properties group, click the **Table Name** box and change the table name to **Forecast_Table**.

8. Scroll down to the bottom of the worksheet to view the projected revenue totals. See Figure 10–14.

Figure 10–14	Forecast worksheet

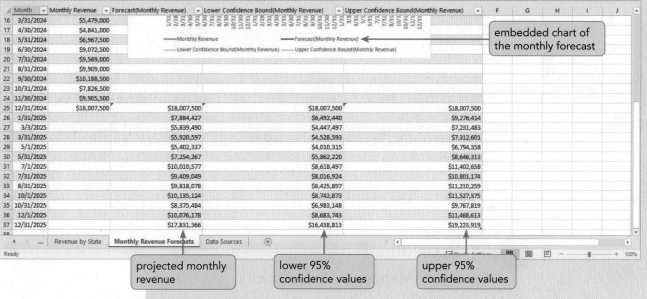

From the forecasted values, Dmitry projects the December 2025 revenue to be about $17.83 million (cell C37) and is 95% confident that the revenue will be at least about $16.438 million (cell D37) but not more than about $19.223 million (cell E37).

You will complete this part of the report by moving the forecast chart into the Historical Trends worksheet.

To move the monthly revenue chart:

1. Move the embedded chart on the Monthly Revenue Forecasts worksheet to the **Historical Trends** worksheet.

2. Move and resize the chart to cover the range **J4:R16**.

3. Remove the chart legend.

4. Add the chart title **Trend in Monthly Revenue**.

5. Add the axis titles **Monthly Revenue** and **Date** to the vertical and horizontal axes.

6. Close any open worksheet panes. See Figure 10–15.

Figure 10–15 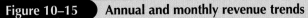 Annual and monthly revenue trends

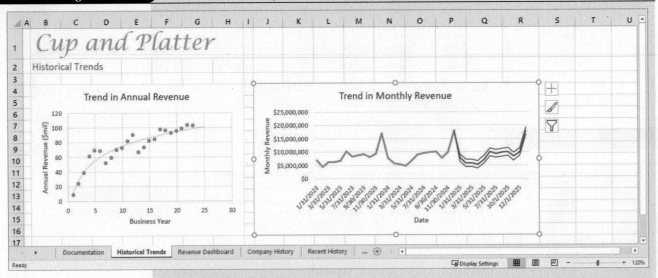

7. Save the workbook.

Dmitry will include both charts in a report projecting future revenue for the company.

 Proskills

Teamwork: Maintaining Data Security

Data security is essential for any business to maintain the integrity of its data and retain the trust of its colleagues and customers. It is critical to secure data to prevent lapses in security. If your workbooks are connected to external data sources, keep in mind the following tips:

- **Apply data security controls.** Make sure your data files are set up with password controls to prohibit unauthorized access.

- **Keep software updated.** Be sure to diligently update the software that stores your data with the latest security patches.

- **Closely monitor data copying.** Have only one source of your data. When multiple copies of the data exist, data security, consistency, and integrity are compromised.

- **Encrypt your data.** Use data encryption to prevent hackers from gaining unauthorized access to sensitive information.

Maintaining data security requires that everyone with access to your data files knows how to retrieve and process that data appropriately. In the end, your data will be only as secure as the work habits of the people who access it.

You have completed the revenue estimates and projections using data retrieved with the Power Query Editor. In the next session, you'll perform analyses that involve combining data from several data sources within a single PivotTable and PivotChart.

Review

Session 10.1 Quick Check

1. What is Business Intelligence?
2. What is a query?
3. What is a delimiter?
4. What is a CSV file?
5. How do you undo an action in the Power Query Editor?
6. What trendline should you add to a chart for data that increases or decreases quickly and then levels out?
7. What does a 95% confidence bound tell you about forecasted values?

Session 10.2 Visual Overview:

The Power Pivot add-in provides access to the **Data Model**, which is a database attached to an Excel workbook.

A database is a highly structured collection of data values organized into separate tables. This database has five tables.

You can click the Diagram View button in Power Pivot to view the structure and relationships of the tables in the Data Model.

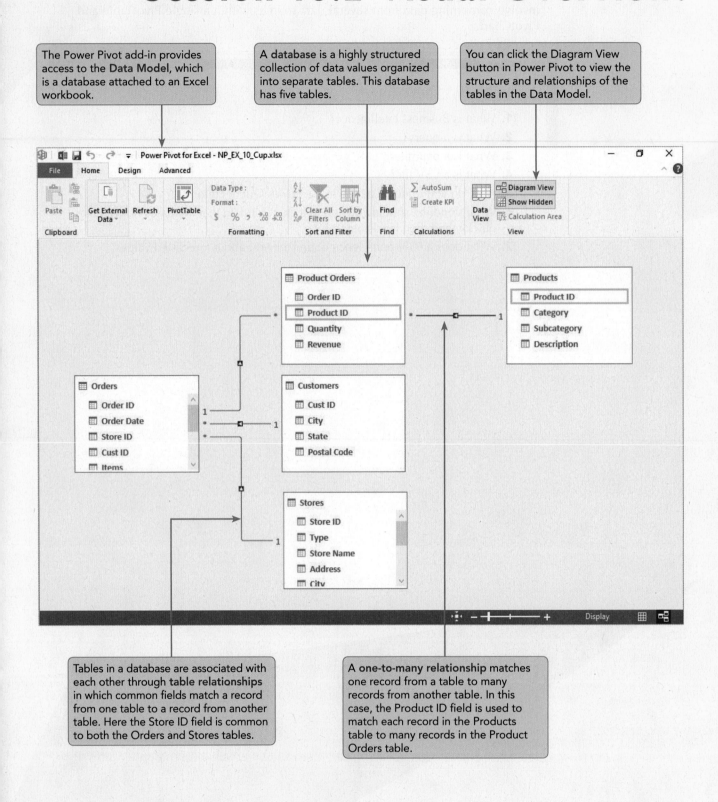

Tables in a database are associated with each other through **table relationships** in which common fields match a record from one table to a record from another table. Here the Store ID field is common to both the Orders and Stores tables.

A **one-to-many relationship** matches one record from a table to many records from another table. In this case, the Product ID field is used to match each record in the Products table to many records in the Product Orders table.

Power Pivot and the Data Model

You click the Manage button to manage the contents of the Data Model.

When the Power Pivot add-in is activated, the Power Pivot tab appears on the ribbon.

PivotTables can retrieve data from multiple fields in different tables in the Data Model.

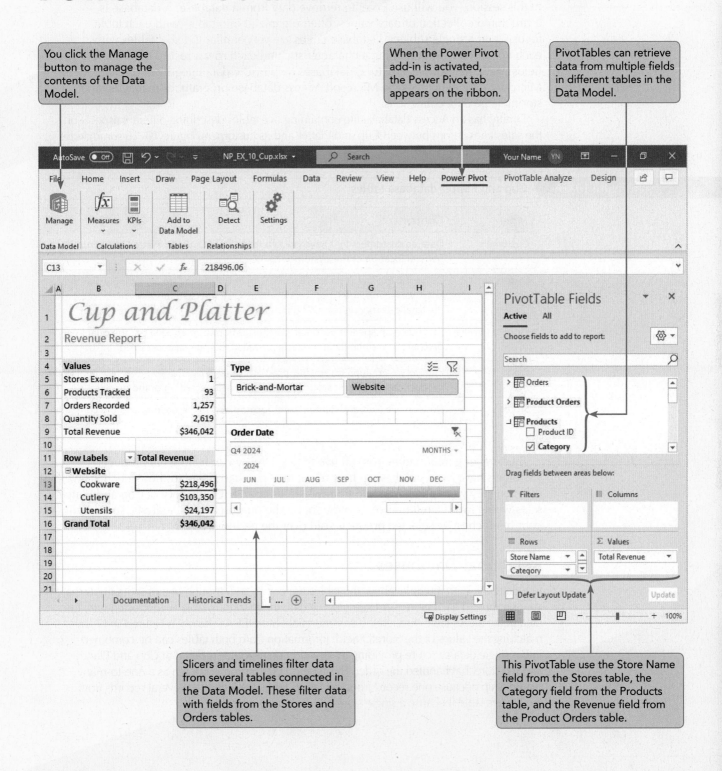

Slicers and timelines filter data from several tables connected in the Data Model. These filter data with fields from the Stores and Orders tables.

This PivotTable use the Store Name field from the Stores table, the Category field from the Products table, and the Revenue field from the Product Orders table.

Introducing Databases

In this session, you will use Excel to retrieve data from a database. A database is a structured collection of data values, often organized into tables with each table focusing on a single subject. Database tables are very similar to Excel tables with each column a field describing a characteristic and each row a record of multiple fields. With their formal structure, databases help insure data integrity and reliability. Microsoft Office includes the Microsoft Access database program for managing and storing large data collections.

Dmitry has an Access database file containing five tables describing different aspects of the sales transactions between Cup and Platter and its customers. Figure 10–16 summarizes the contents of these tables.

Figure 10–16	Cup and Platter database tables

Table	Contains
Customers	Data on customers that have bought items from Cup and Platter, including the general location of the customer
Orders	Data on customer orders made at a Cup and Platter store, including when the order was made, the ID of the store, the ID of the customer who made the order, the total quantity of items, and the costs associated with the order
Product Orders	Sales data on specific products purchased from Cup and Platter, the quantity purchased, and the ID of the order in which the purchase occurred
Products	Product information on specific products offered by Cup and Platter including the product category, subcategory, and a general description of the product
Stores	Data on five Cup and Platter stores located across the country and the company website

By extracting information from all five tables, Dmitry can learn what products customers have been purchasing, how many they purchased and for how much, as well as when they were purchased and from where. A complete inventory of Cup and Platter sales would involve millions of records, so, for the purpose of this analysis, you'll limit your research to 93 selected products sold over the past two years.

Relational Databases

In a database with multiple tables, the tables are connected through one or more fields that are common to each table. For example, the data in the Orders table is connected with the data in the Stores table through the common field StoreID. As shown in Figure 10–17, by matching the values of the StoreID field, information from both tables can be combined into a single data structure providing information on products ordered at Cup and Platter and the store that handled the order. This type of relationship is known as a one-to-many relationship because one record from the Stores table is matched to several records from the Orders table (because a single store handles many orders).

| Figure 10–17 | Tables related by a common field |

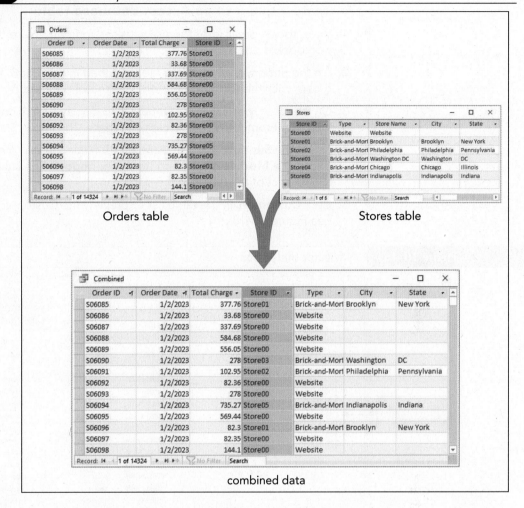

Orders table   Stores table

combined data

Another type of relationship is the **one-to-one relationship** in which one record from the first table can be matched to only one record from the second table. If the Cup and Platter database had a table with information about the head manager of each store, it would have a one-to-one relationship with the Stores table because each store would have only one head manager.

Databases in which tables can be joined through the use of common fields are known as **relational databases**. Because the tables can be joined through common fields, it is unnecessary to duplicate the same piece of information in multiple tables. Information about Cup and Platter stores needs to be entered in only one table and then connected to other tables via a table relationship. Removing duplication makes it easier to manage large datasets and improves data quality and integrity.

Querying an Access Database

Power Query supports almost all the popular database applications, including Microsoft Access, SQL Server, Oracle, IBM DB2, and MySQL. You then use the Query Editor to create a query that extracts data from any one table within those databases, or you can create a query that extracts data from several tables. You will access the tables stored in the Cup and Platter Access database file.

To create a query to an Access database table:

▶ 1. If you took a break after the previous session, make sure the NP_EX_10_Cup workbook is open.

▶ 2. On the ribbon, click the **Data** tab, and then in the Get & Transform Data group, click the **Get Data** button. A menu of data options appears.

▶ 3. On the menu, point to **From Database** to display a list of database sources, and then click **From Microsoft Access Database**. The Import Data dialog box opens.

▶ 4. Select the **Support_EX_10_Data.accdb** file located in the **Excel10 > Module** folder, and then click **Import**. The Navigator dialog box shows a list of the tables in the database.

▶ 5. Click **Customers** in the table list to preview the Customer table contents. See Figure 10–18.

Figure 10–18   Navigator dialog box

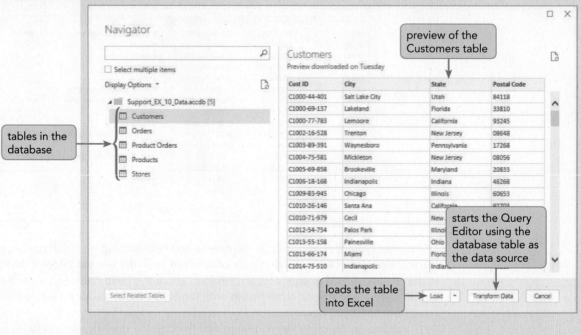

The Customers table has four fields. The Cust ID field uniquely identifies a Cup and Platter customer, and the City, State, and Postal Code fields specify the customer's location. Though not shown in the dialog box, the Customers table has 7,734 records. With so many records, Dmitry doesn't want to create a large Excel table to hold all the customer data. An alternative is to use the Excel Data Model.

Exploring the Data Model

The Data Model is a database attached to an Excel workbook that provides many of the tools found in database programs such as Microsoft Access. Because the Data Model is part of the workbook, its contents are immediately available to PivotTables, PivotCharts, and other Excel tools. One advantage of storing data in the Data Model rather than in a worksheet is that data stored in the Data Model are compressed, resulting in a smaller file size. Compressing the data also means that queries run faster, and PivotTables load quicker. The drawback is that Data Model contents are not visible in the workbook. To view them, you must use Power Pivot, an Excel add-in for managing the Data Model contents.

Data are placed into the Data Model using the same Power Query application used for retrieving data from CSV files and other data sources. Once placed in the Data Model, Excel establishes a connection between the Data Model contents and the workbook. Essentially, it's like having a connection to an external data source even though the Data Model is saved within the workbook file.

You will load the contents of the Customers table into the Data Model.

To load the Customers table into the Data Model:

▶ **1.** With the Navigator dialog box still open and the Customers table still selected, click the **Load arrow**, and then click **Load To**. The Import Data dialog box opens.

▶ **2.** Click the **Only Create Connection** option button. This option establishes a connection between the Data Model contents and the workbook without loading the data in to an Excel table, PivotTable, or PivotChart.

▶ **3.** Click the **Add this data to the Data Model** check box. See Figure 10–19.

Be sure to only create a connection; don't load the data into an Excel table, PivotTable, or PivotChart.

Figure 10–19	Import Data dialog box to load data into the Data Model

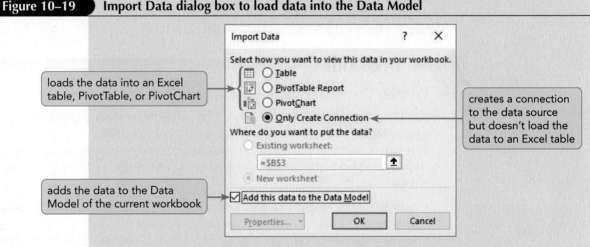

loads the data into an Excel table, PivotTable, or PivotChart

creates a connection to the data source but doesn't load the data to an Excel table

adds the data to the Data Model of the current workbook

▶ **4.** Click **OK** to establish the connection to the Data Model. When the data loading is complete, the Customers query appears in the Queries & Connection pane indicating that 7,734 rows have been loaded.

Trouble? If you see an Excel table containing the Items Purchased data, delete the table and the query, repeat the previous set of steps to recreate the query, and then repeat Steps 1 through 4, making sure to load the table only to the Data Model and not to an Excel table.

You will add the remaining tables from the database to the workbook's Data Model. Because the data have been structured within the Access database, you will not need to edit the data contents with Power Query. You'll load the remaining four tables in the Data Model.

To load the remaining database tables:

▶ **1.** On the Data tab, in the Get & Transform Data group, click the **Get Data** button, point to **From Database**, and then click **From Microsoft Access Database** to select the database source. The Import Data dialog box opens.

▶ **2.** Select the **Support_EX_10_Data.accdb** file, and then click **Import**. The Navigator dialog box opens.

▸ 3. Click the **Select multiple items** check box so you can select more than one table from the database. Check boxes appear before each table name.

▸ 4. Click the **Orders**, **Product Orders**, **Products**, and **Stores** check boxes to select those tables. As you select a check box, a preview of that table's contents appears in the Navigator dialog box.

▸ 5. Click the **Load arrow**, and then click **Load To**. The Import Data dialog box opens.

▸ 6. Make sure the **Only Create Connection** option button and the **Add this data to the Data Model** check box are selected to load the tables without placing them in Excel tables, PivotTables, or PivotCharts.

▸ 7. Click **OK** to load the four tables into the Data Model.

After several seconds, the four tables will be listed as queries in the Queries & Connections pane. There are 14,324 rows are loaded from the Orders table, 21,418 rows from the Product Orders table, 93 rows from the Products table, and 6 rows from the Stores table. Later, Dmitry might perform a more complete analysis involving the entire sales lineup, but even this sample of a few products results in a large dataset to manage.

Proskills

Written Communication: Designing a Database

Databases are great tools to organize information, track statistics, and generate reports. When used with Excel, a properly designed database can provide valuable information and help you make informed financial decisions. Whether you are creating a database in the Data Model or Microsoft Access, keep in mind the following guidelines:

- **Split data into multiple tables.** Keep each table focused on a specific topical area. Link the tables through one or more common fields.
- **Avoid redundant data.** Key pieces of information, such as a customer's address or phone number, should be entered in only one place in your database.
- **Use understandable field names.** Avoid using acronyms or abbreviations that may be unclear or confusing.
- **Maintain consistency in data entry.** Include validation rules to ensure that rules such as abbreviating titles (for example, Mr. instead of Mister) are always followed.
- **Test the database on a small subset of data before entering all the data.** The more errors you eliminate early, the sooner your database will be ready for use.

A badly designed or improperly used database will end up creating more problems rather than solving them.

With all the tables loaded into the Data Model, you can view their contents with Power Pivot.

Transforming Data with Power Pivot

Tip

Excel tables can be added to the Data Model by selecting the table and clicking the Add to Data Model button in the Tables group on the Power Pivot tab.

Power Pivot is a BI tool built into Excel used for managing data from multiple sources in a single data structure. With Power Pivot you can define table relationships, reorganize and regroup your data, and create new columns from calculations on existing fields. Many of the skills used with Excel tables and data ranges can also be applied to the tables in Power Pivot, but Power Pivot offers even more commands and options to manage your data.

Because Power Pivot is an add-in, you must install it before using it to work with the contents of the Data Model. You can have Excel install the Power Pivot add-in by attempting to view the contents of the Data Model. If Power Pivot is not already installed, Excel will install it for you.

To install Power Pivot:

▶ **1.** On the Data tab, in the Data Tools group, click the **Manage Data Model** or **Go to the Power Pivot Window** button. If Power Pivot is not installed, a dialog box opens, prompting you to enable the Data Analysis add-ins.

▶ **2.** If prompted, click **Enable**. If it is not already present, the Power Pivot tab appears on the ribbon, and the Power Pivot window opens showing the contents of the Data Model.

▶ **3.** If necessary, maximize the window to fill the entire screen. See Figure 10–20.

| Figure 10–20 | **Power Pivot window** |

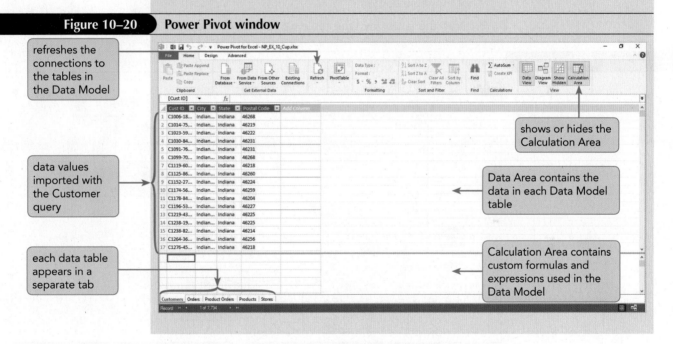

The Power Pivot window places each table in the Data Model on a separate tab. The Data Area displays the contents of each table. Below the table grid is the Calculation Area used for writing customized functions and expressions.

To view the contents of the Data Model:

▶ **1.** Use the top vertical scroll bar to scroll up and down the rows of the Customers tab to view other customer records.

▶ **2.** Click the **Orders** tab to view the contents of the Orders table.

▶ **3.** Click the **Product Orders** tab to review records from the Product Orders table.

▶ **4.** Click the **Products** tab to view information about select products sold by Cup and Platter.

▶ **5.** Click the **Stores** tab to view information and the five brick-and-mortar Cup and Platter stores as well as the company's website.

▶ **6.** Return to the **Customers** tab.

Exploring the Data Model in Diagram View

So far, you have looked at the Data Model in **Data view**, which shows the contents of each table in a separate tab. You can also examine the Data Model in **Diagram view**, which lists the fields within each table. Diagram view is useful when you want to work with the general structure of the Data Model. From Diagram view, you can quickly define the relationships that connect the tables. You will switch to Diagram view now.

To switch to Diagram view and arrange the tables:

 1. On the Home tab, in the View group, click the **Diagram View** button. Power Pivot displays each table in a separate box with the table name and a list of fields. Power Pivot initially lines up all the tables horizontally in the Diagram view window.

 2. If necessary, use the scroll bars to scroll through Diagram view to review all of the table contents.

 3. Drag the tables by their table names to arrange them as shown in Figure 10–21.

Figure 10–21   Power Pivot in Diagram view

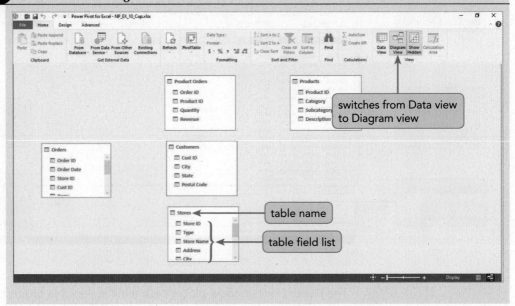

Managing Table Relationships

Table relationships are defined in Diagram View by dragging a common field between two tables. In a one-to-many relationship one of the tables acts as a lookup table for the other. For example, the Stores table acts as a lookup table for the Orders table, providing specific information about the store in which the purchase was made. Diagram View indicates the existence of a relationship by a line connecting the two tables.

Dmitry wants you to establish the following relations between the five tables:

• Orders table to the Customers table through the Cust ID field, matching every order with a customer

• Orders table to the Stores table through the Store ID field, matching every order with a store

• Orders table to the Product Orders table through the Order ID field, matching every order with products purchased on that order
• Product Orders table to the Products table through the Product ID field, matching every product order with information about that product

You'll establish these relationships between the tables in the Data Model now.

To define table relationships in Diagram View:

1. Click the **Orders** table to select it.

2. Drag the **Store ID** field from the Orders table and drop it onto the Store ID field in the Stores table. Power Pivot connects the two tables with a line. A "1" appears where the line connects to the Stores table and a "*" appears next to connection to the Orders table, indicating that this is a one-to-many relationship in which one store can be matched to many orders.

3. Drag the **Cust ID** field from the Orders table and drop it onto the Cust ID field in the Customers table. Power Pivot establishes another one-to-many relationship between the Orders table (many) and the Customers table (one) because one customer can be matched to several orders.

4. Drag the **Order ID** field from the Orders table and drop it onto the Order ID field in the Product Orders table. This establishes another one-to-many relationship. In this case, the Orders table is the "one" and the Product Orders table is the "many" because a single order might include several products.

5. Drag the **Product ID** field from the Product Orders table and drop it onto the Product ID field in the Products table, creating a one-to-many relationship between the two tables. See Figure 10–22.

> **Tip**
>
> You can also drag the field from the Stores table to the Orders table and Power Pivot will establish the same relationship.

| Figure 10–22 | Table relationships defined in Power Pivot |

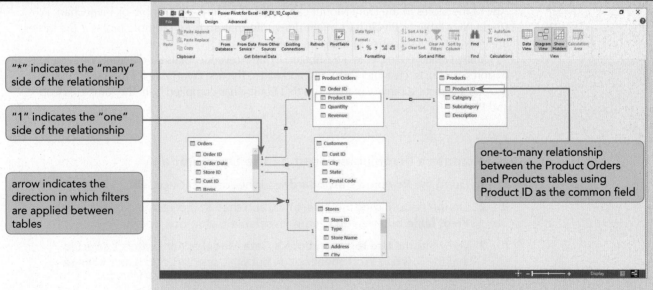

"*" indicates the "many" side of the relationship

"1" indicates the "one" side of the relationship

arrow indicates the direction in which filters are applied between tables

one-to-many relationship between the Product Orders and Products tables using Product ID as the common field

Arrows in the connecting lines indicate the direction in which filters propagate between tables. The arrow in the Stores and Orders table relation in Figure 10–22 points from Stores to Orders so that filtering the Stores table (perhaps to show records from a single store) also filters records in the Orders table. However, the reverse is not possible: Filtering the Orders table will not affect the Stores table. The arrow points in one direction only.

You can determine how a filter will affect other tables in the Data Model by following the arrows. The Orders table is connected to the Product Orders table, so that any filtering done to the Stores table will also pass through the Orders table to the Product Orders table. In this way, filters applied to one table will propagate through the Data Model wherever there exists a connected path pointing from one table to the next.

You will close Power Pivot now and return to the Excel workbook.

Tip

You can also define table relationships in an Excel workbook by clicking the Relationships button in the Data Tools group on the Data tab.

To return to the Excel workbook:

▶ **1.** Close the Power Pivot window. Power Pivot saves the table relationships you've defined.

▶ **2.** If a Security Warning bar appears indicating that external connections have been disabled, click **Enable Content**, and then click **Yes** to enable the connections to the Access database and the Data Model.

▶ **3.** Close the Queries & Connections pane.

With the table relationships defined, you are ready to analyze the Cup and Platter sales data, pulling information from any of the five tables in the Data Model.

Creating a PivotTable from the Data Model

Any of the tables in the Data Model can be analyzed in a PivotTable or PivotChart. A single PivotTable or PivotChart might draw information from multiple tables if the tables are connected via a series of table relationships.

Dmitry wants you to create a dashboard to view revenue totals for different combinations of stores, products, customer locations, and dates. The first PivotTable for this dashboard will provide a general summary of the items that Dmitry has compiled from the sample of Cup and Platter products.

To create a PivotTable based on the Data Model:

▶ **1.** Go to the **Revenue Dashboard** worksheet and click cell **B4**.

▶ **2.** On the ribbon, click the **Insert** tab, and then in the Tables group, click the **PivotTable** button. The Create PivotTable dialog box opens.

▶ **3.** Verify that the **Use this workbook's Data Model** option button is selected, that the **Existing Worksheet** option button is selected, and that **'Revenue Dashboard'!$B$4** appears in the Location box. See Figure 10–23.

Figure 10–23	Create PivotTable dialog box

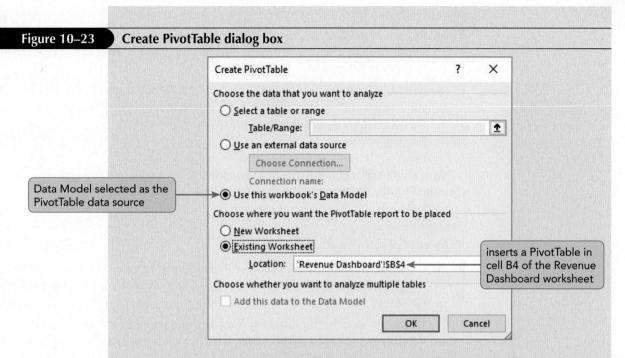

Data Model selected as the PivotTable data source

inserts a PivotTable in cell B4 of the Revenue Dashboard worksheet

▶ **4.** Click **OK** to insert the PivotTable. The five tables from the Data Model are listed in the PivotTable Fields pane along with the three Excel tables also present in the workbook.

▶ **5.** On the PivotTable Analyze tab, in the PivotTable group, click the **PivotTable Name** box and enter **Summary** as the PivotTable name.

▶ **6.** In the PivotTable group, click the **Options** button. The PivotTable Options dialog box opens.

▶ **7.** Click the **Autofit columns widths on update** check box to deselect it. This prevents the column widths in the PivotTable from resizing.

▶ **8.** Click **OK**.

Dmitry wants you to add summary calculations to the PivotTable showing the number of stores examined, the number of products tracked, the number of customer orders placed, the total number of items ordered, and finally the total revenue generated. You will start with the count of the number of stores, the number of products, and the number of orders.

To display the summary calculations:

▶ **1.** In the PivotTable Fields pane, scroll down the list of tables, and then click the **Stores** table. The list of fields in the table appears.

▶ **2.** Drag the **Store ID** field into the Values area box, change the label "Count of Store ID" to **Stores Examined**, and then display the field using the Number format with no decimal places and a thousands separator.

▶ **3.** Repeat Steps 1 and 2 for the **Product ID** field in the Products table, placing the Product ID field after the Stores Examined field and changing the label name to **Products Tracked**.

▶ **4.** Repeat Steps 1 and 2 for the **Order ID** field from the Orders table, placing Order ID field after the Products Tracked field and changing the label name to **Orders Recorded**.

▶ **5.** Drag the **ΣValues** icon from the Columns area box to the Rows area box. The summary statistics are displayed in a single column on different rows. The report tracks 6 stores, 93 products, and 14,324 orders.

Next, you'll add a count of the total quantity of items sold and the total revenue generated for the company to the PivotTable.

To complete the PivotTable:

▶ **1.** Click the **Product Orders** table in the table list to view its contents, and then drag the **Quantity** field into the Values area box, placing it below the Orders Recorded value field.

   Trouble? To drag the Quantity field to the bottom of the entries in the Values area box, you might need to scroll down the area box first.

▶ **2.** Change the label name from "Sum of Quantity" to **Quantity Sold** and display the field value in the Number format with a thousands separator and no decimal places. The value 29,979 appears in cell C8.

▶ **3.** Drag the **Revenue** field from Product Orders table in to the Values area box after the Quantity Sold value field.

▶ **4.** Change the name of the field from "Sum of Revenue" to **Total Revenue** and display the value in the Currency format with no decimal places. See Figure 10–24.

Figure 10–24   PivotTable with data from the Data Model

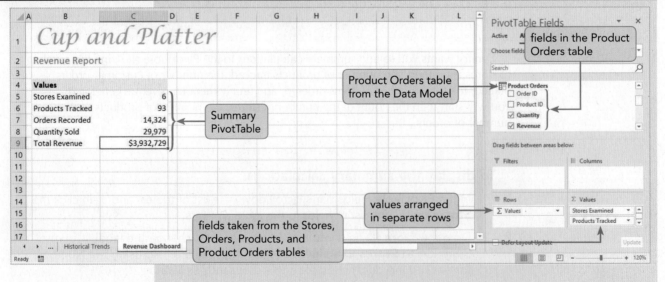

Tabulating Across Fields from Multiple Tables

PivotTables can also tabulate values from different tables so that the row and columns of the table involves categories from different tables in the Data Model. You'll add another PivotTable to the worksheet showing the revenue totals organized by store and product category.

To show revenue by store and product category:

1. Click cell **B11**, click the **Insert** tab on the ribbon, and then in the Tables group, click the **PivotTable** button. The Create PivotTable dialog box opens.

2. Click **OK** to insert the PivotTable. The PivotTable Fields pane opens.

3. On the PivotTable Analyze tab, in the PivotTable group, click the **PivotTable Name** box and change the PivotTable name to **Product by Store**.

4. In the PivotTable group, click the **Options** button. The PivotTable Options dialog box opens.

5. Click the **Autofit column widths on update** check box to deselect it, and then click **OK**.

6. In the PivotTable Fields pane, click the **Stores** table from the list of tables, and then drag the **Store Name** field into the Rows area box.

7. Click the **Products** table, and then drag the **Category** field into the Rows area box directly below the Store Name field.

8. Click the **Product Orders** table, and then drag the **Revenue** field into the Values area box.

9. Change the field name from "Sum of Revenue" to **Total Revenue** and display the values in Currency format with no decimal places. See Figure 10–25.

Figure 10–25   Total revenue displayed by store and product category

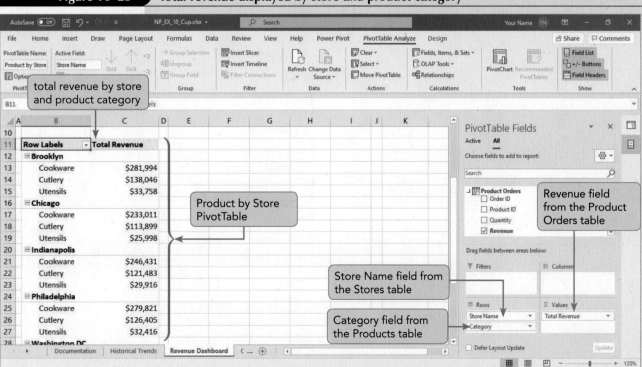

Trouble? If your PivotTable is showing blanks for the Store or Category fields, check your table relations in Power Pivot, verifying that you are connecting the tables through a common field.

From the PivotTable report, Dmitry learns that Cup and Platter gets more of its revenue from its cookware products, followed by cutlery, and then utensils. Cup and Platter sells most of its wares online. For example, the website brought in about $1.29 million in cookware sales (cell C33) compared to the brick-and-mortar stores, which brought in about $168,000 at the Washington D.C. store (cell C29) and almost $282,000 at the Brooklyn store (cell C13). The other product categories show a similar range of revenue figures.

Applying Slicers and Timelines from the Data Model

Slicers and timelines can be applied across multiple tables if the tables are connected through a common field. Dmitry wants you to add a slicer to the dashboard that filters the PivotTables by company website and brick-and-mortar stores.

To add a slicer to the dashboard:

1. With the Product by Store PivotTable still selected, click the **Insert** tab on the ribbon, and then in the Filters group, click the **Slicer** button. The Insert Slicers dialog box opens.

2. On the Active tab, scroll down to the Stores table, and then click the **Type** check box. See Figure 10-26.

Figure 10-26   **Insert Slicers dialog box**

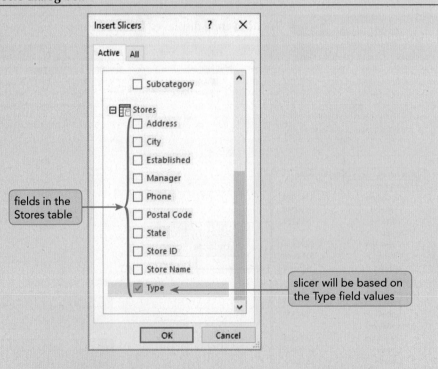

fields in the Stores table

slicer will be based on the Type field values

3. Click **OK** to insert the slicer.

4. Move and resize the slicer to cover the range **E4:I7**.

5. On the Slicer tab, in the Buttons group, change the Columns box to **2** columns. See Figure 10–27.

Figure 10–27   **Type slicer from the Stores table**

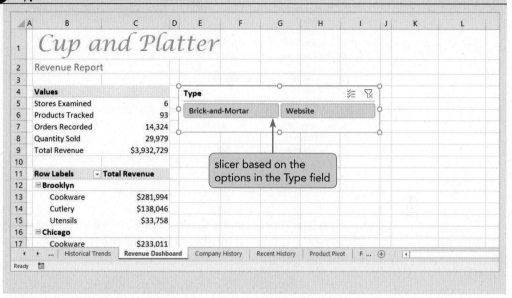

Dmitry also wants to filter the sales values by date. You will add a timeline slicer to the dashboard, basing it on the Order Date field from the Orders table.

To add the Order Date timeline to the dashboard:

1. On the ribbon, click the **Insert** tab, and then in the Filters group, click the **Timeline** button. The Existing Connections dialog box opens.

2. Click the **Data Model** tab, and then click **Open** to access the Data Model tables. The Insert Timelines dialog box opens.

3. Go to the **Orders** table, and then click the **Order Date** check box.

4. Click **OK** to insert the timeline.

5. Move and resize the slicer to cover the range **E9:I16**. See Figure 10–28.

Figure 10–28   Order Date timeline from the Orders table

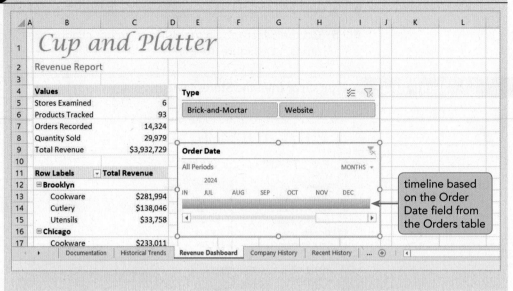

timeline based on the Order Date field from the Orders table

Next, you'll connect the slicer and the timeline to the two PivotTables on the dashboard. Then you'll use them to display revenue figures for the website in the fourth quarter of 2024.

To connect the slicer and timeline to the PivotTables:

1. With the timeline still selected, on the ribbon, click the **Timeline** tab.

2. In the Timeline group, click the **Report Connections** button. The Report Connections (Order Date) dialog box opens.

3. Click the **Product by Store** and **Summary** check boxes to apply the timeline to both PivotTables in the dashboard, and then click **OK**.

4. Click the **Type** slicer to select it, click the **Slicer** tab on the ribbon, and then in the Slicer group, click the **Report Connections** button. The Report Connections (Type) dialog box opens.

5. Click the **Summary** check box, and then verify that the check boxes for both PivotTables are selected.

6. Click **OK**.

7. In the Type slicer, click **Website** to filter the dashboard, showing results only from the company website.

8. In the Order Date timeline, click **OCT** from 2024, and then drag over **NOV** and **DEC** to filter the dashboard for orders placed in Q4 2024, from October through December 2024. See Figure 10–29.

Tip

You can also select the 4th quarter of 2024 by changing the time scale of the timeline to QUARTERS and clicking Q4 from 2024.

Figure 10–29 Dashboard filtered by store type and order date

summary statistics from orders placed on the website in 4th quarter of 2024

filters the dashboard to show only website sales

changes the timescale to years, quarters, months, or days

filters the dashboard to show only 2024 Q4 sales

▶ **9.** Click the **Clear Filter** button ⧖ in the slicer and timeline to show results from all the records in the Data Model.

▶ **10.** Save the workbook.

Based on the filters applied through the Type slicer and the Order Date timeline, Dmitry learns that in the 4th quarter of 2024, the website generated about $346,000 in revenue from the 93 selected products with about $218,000 coming from cookware sales, $103,000 from cutlery sales, and $24,000 from sales of cooking utensils. The fact that filtering field values from one table affected the summary statistics of fields in the other tables is a consequence of the relationships you set up in Figure 10–22.

In this session, you loaded data from an Access database into the Data Model and then analyzed data from fields spread across multiple tables in a PivotTable. In the next session, you'll continue to explore Business Intelligence tools by learning how to organize fields into a hierarchy and how to display data in geographic maps.

Review

Session 10.2 Quick Check

1. What is a relational database?

2. What is a one-to-many relationship?

3. What is the advantage of placing large tables in the Data Model rather than in an Excel table that is visible in the workbook?

4. What is Power Pivot?

5. Describe how to create a table relationship in Power Pivot Diagram view.

6. In Diagram view, what does the arrow on the line connecting two tables indicate?

7. What is the advantage of using table relationships when creating a PivotTable report?

Session 10.3 Visual Overview:

Quick Explore is a feature of PivotTables and PivotCharts for drilling into a hierarchy or to explore the impact of other fields on your data outcomes.

A **hierarchy** is an organization of fields that start with the most general and go down to the most specific; the Product List hierarchy includes three fields.

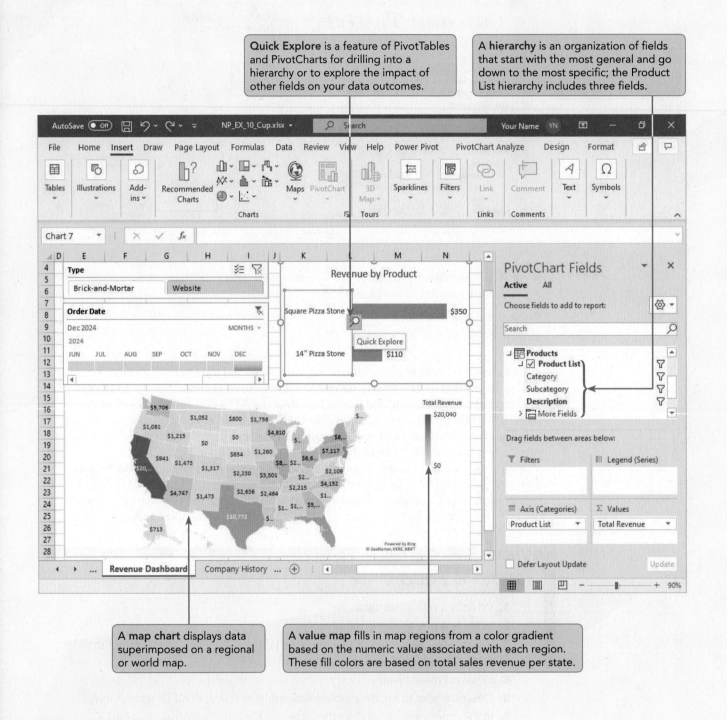

A **map chart** displays data superimposed on a regional or world map.

A **value map** fills in map regions from a color gradient based on the numeric value associated with each region. These fill colors are based on total sales revenue per state.

Hierarchies and Maps

3D Maps is an Excel tool that presents data geographically on a virtual 3-D globe.

The height of each column is based on the value of the Revenue field.

Map data is placed in **layers**, which are superimposed on the map.

The location of each marker is determined by the customer's postal code.

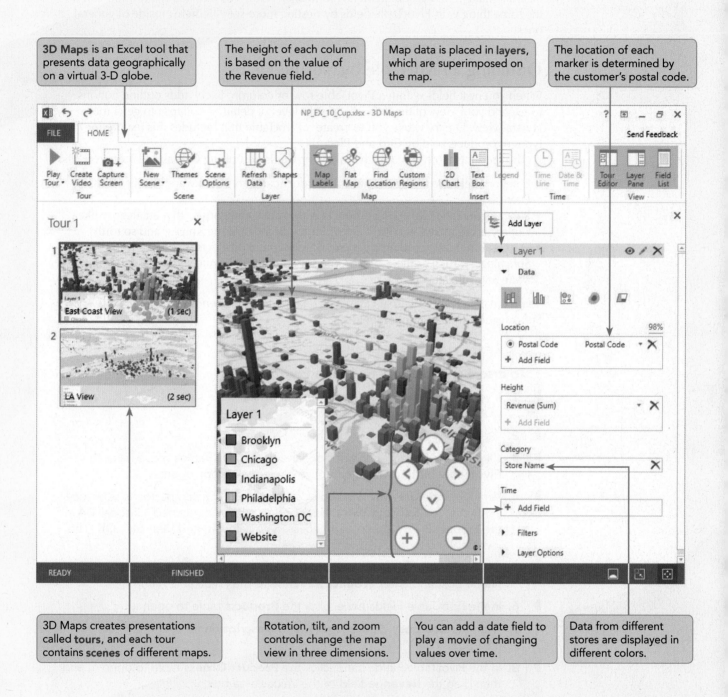

3D Maps creates presentations called **tours**, and each tour contains **scenes** of different maps.

Rotation, tilt, and zoom controls change the map view in three dimensions.

You can add a date field to play a movie of changing values over time.

Data from different stores are displayed in different colors.

Working with Outlines and Hierarchies

Often in data analysis, you want to drill into the data, going from a general overview down to a more detailed view. Timelines provide this feature by allowing you to examine data across years, quarters, months, and down to individual days. You can do the same thing with PivotTable fields by nesting more specific fields inside of general ones.

Outlining a PivotTable by Nested Fields

When you nest fields within a PivotTable row or column, Excel adds outline buttons to expand your view of the data at a greater level of detail or collapse to get a more general view. Dmitry wants you to create a PivotTable that includes this feature for the types of products sold by Cup and Platter.

The Products table contains the following fields describing Cup and Platter products:

- Category field specifying the general product category (Cookware, Cutlery, and Utensils)
- Subcategory field classifying products within each category so that a category like Cutlery is organized into Knife Sets, Cutting Boards, Paring Knives, and so forth
- Description field providing a general description of products within each Subcategory, such as the 7-piece knife sets and 8-piece knife sets sold within the Knife Sets subcategory

You'll create a PivotTable that calculates total revenue broken down by the Category, Subcategory, and Description fields.

To insert the Product Revenue PivotTable:

1. If you took a break after the previous session, make sure the NP_EX_10_Cup workbook is open.

2. Go to the **Product Pivot** worksheet.

3. Click the **Insert** tab on the ribbon, and then in the Tables group, click the **PivotTable** button. The Create PivotTable dialog box opens.

4. Verify that the **Use this workbook's Data Model** option button is selected, verify that the **Existing Worksheet** option button is selected, click cell **B4** in the Product Pivot worksheet if necessary to select it, and then click **OK**. The PivotTable form is added to the worksheet.

5. On the PivotTable Analyze tab, in the PivotTable group, click the **PivotTable Name** box, and enter **Product Revenue** as the PivotTable name.

6. In the PivotTable Fields pane, click the **Products** table to open it.

7. Drag the **Category**, **Subcategory**, and **Description** fields to the Rows area box.

8. In the PivotTable Fields pane, click the **Product Orders** table to open it, and then drag the **Revenue** field to the Values area box.

9. Change the value field name from "Sum of Revenue" to **Total Revenue** and change the number format to Currency with no decimal places. See Figure 10–30.

Figure 10–30   **Total Revenue by product fields**

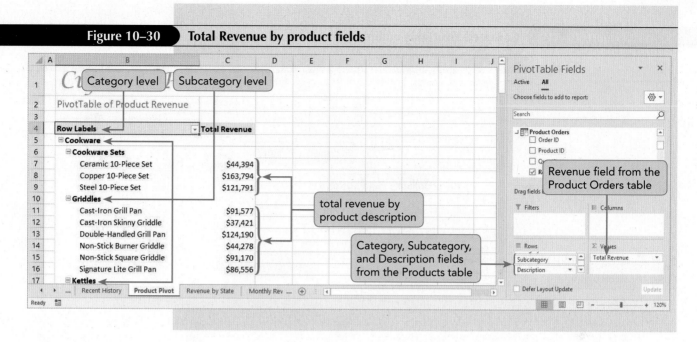

The PivotTable opens in an expanded view, showing total revenue across the lowest field level, which in this case is the Description field. You can collapse the fields to show data at the highest level, which is the Category field for these tabulations. You can also expand and collapse individual items within each field to view some with more detail and others with less detail. You'll expand and collapse the fields in the row area of the PivotTable now.

To collapse and expand the categories in the PivotTable:

1. In front of Cookware Sets, click the **Collapse Outline** button ⊟. The Cookware Sets subcategory collapses and the PivotTable shows $329,979 as the total revenue for all cooking sets.

2. In front of Cookware, click the **Collapse Outline** button ⊟. The Cookware category collapses and the PivotTable shows $2,503,562 as the total revenue for all cookware.

3. On the PivotTable Analyze tab, in the Active Field group, click the **Collapse Field** button. The entire PivotTable collapses to display revenue totals at the Category level. See Figure 10–31.

Figure 10–31   **Collapsed PivotTable outline**

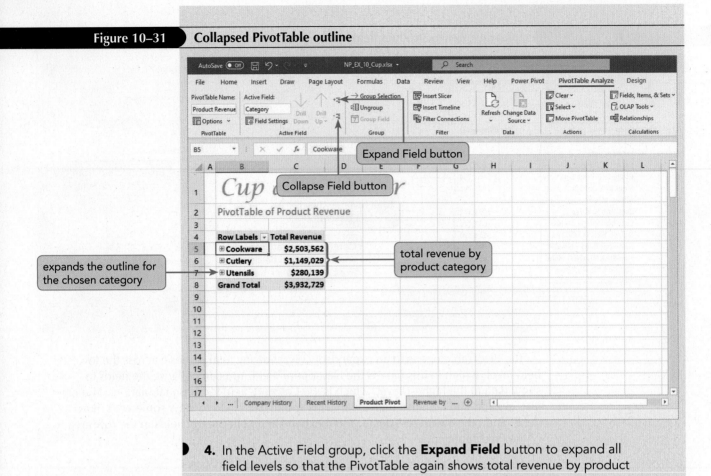

4. In the Active Field group, click the **Expand Field** button to expand all field levels so that the PivotTable again shows total revenue by product description.

In this way, you can display revenue totals at any level of specificity. However, a PivotTable outline can be unwieldy if the table contains a lot of categories or nested levels. If you're interested only in the total revenue generated by, say, pizza stone sales, you would have to go down several field levels and in the process the table would show results for other categories you're not interested in. To limit the view to only those categories of interest, you can create a hierarchy.

Drilling Down a Field Hierarchy

A hierarchy is named set of fields organized from the most general down to the most specific. Unlike outlines involving multiple fields nested within one another, a hierarchy displays only one field level at a time. To switch the PivotTable view from one field level to the next lower level, you drill down into the hierarchy. Thus, you can drill down into a hierarchy of product fields, displaying revenue totals from all product categories and then revenue from all cookware products and, finally, revenue from all types of pressure cookers. To go from the most specific field to the most general, you **drill up** the hierarchy; going up from pressure cooker sales to cookware sales to sales of all products.

Reference

Creating a Hierarchy of Fields

- View the Data Model in Diagram view in the Power Pivot window.
- Click the Create Hierarchy button in the table box to create a hierarchy for the table.
- Specify a name for the hierarchy.
- Drag fields into the hierarchy, arranged in order from the most general down to the most specific.

Hierarchies are defined within Power Pivot, becoming part of the data structure of their tables. Once defined, a hierarchy is treated as any other PivotTable field and can be moved to different sections of the PivotTable. Dmitry wants you to create a hierarchy named "Product List" containing the Category, Subcategory, and Description fields from the Products table. You'll return to Power Pivot now to create this hierarchy.

To create a hierarchy of the fields in the Products table:

1. On the ribbon, click the **Power Pivot** tab, and then in the Data Model group, click the **Manage** button. The Power Pivot window opens.

2. On the Home tab, in the View group, click the **Diagram View** button, if necessary, to switch Power Pivot to Diagram view.

3. Point to the bottom border of the **Products** table box until the pointer changes to a double arrow pointer ↕, and then drag the bottom border until the table box is twice as high.

4. Point to the upper-right corner of the table box, and then click the **Create Hierarchy** button ▣. A new entry named "Hierachy1" appears in the Products field list.

5. With the name selected, type **Product List** as the hierarchy name, and then press **ENTER**.

6. Click the **Category** field, hold down **SHIFT** and click the **Description** field to select the Category, Subcategory, and Description fields, and then release SHIFT.

7. Drag the select fields on top of the Product List hierarchy, placing the three fields into that hierarchy. See Figure 10–32.

Figure 10–32   Fields in the Product List hierarchy

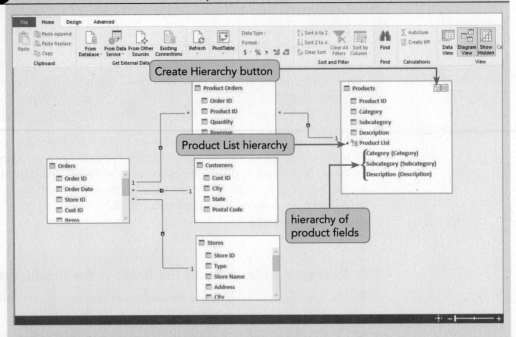

8. Close Power Pivot to return to the Excel workbook.

The Product List hierarchy is now part of the Products table and appears within the PivotTable Fields pane. You will replace the Category, Subcategory, and Description fields displayed in the PivotTable row with the Product List hierarchy, which contains all those fields.

To add the Product List hierarchy to the PivotTable:

1. Drag the **Category**, **Subcategory**, and **Description** fields out of the Rows area box, removing them from the PivotTable.

2. If necessary, click the **Products** table in the PivotTable Fields pane to display its contents.

3. Drag the **Product List** hierarchy from the field list and drop it into the Rows area box to add it to the PivotTable. The PivotTable displays the total revenue broken down by the Category field. The Expand Outline button ⊞ appears to the left of each product category (Cookware, Cutlery, and Utensils).

Though it looks like nothing has changed in the PivotTable, you can now drill down into the Product List hierarchy, viewing the revenue totals within each category, subcategory, and description group. Dmitry wants you to use the Product List hierarchy to show the total revenue from sales of Cup and Platter's line of pressure cookers.

To drill down and up the Product List hierarchy:

▶ **1.** Click cell **B5**, containing the Cookware label. You want to drill down this product category.

▶ **2.** On the ribbon, click the **PivotTable Analyze** tab, and then in the Active Field group, click the **Drill Down** button. The column labels change, displaying the subcategories within the Cookware category, starting with Cookware Sets and ending with Woks.

▶ **3.** In cell **B10**, click the **Pressure Cookers** label, and then click the **Drill Down** button to view revenue totals of the pressure cooker line. Cup and Platter sells three pressure cookers with revenues ranging from about $69,000 to $164,000. See Figure 10–33.

Figure 10–33 PivotTable drilled down the Product List hierarchy

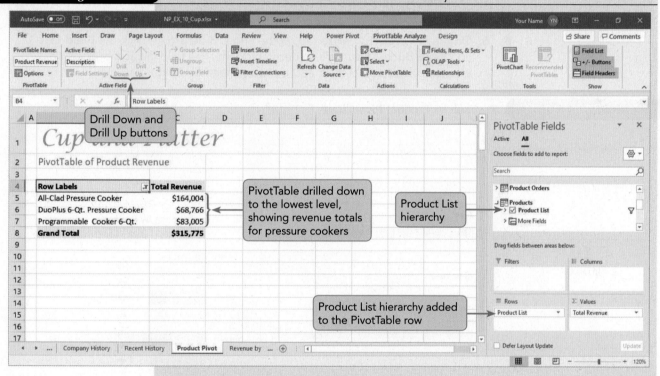

Next, you'll drill up the Product List hierarchy moving from the most specific categories to the most general.

▶ **4.** Click cell **B5** to select the "All-Clad Pressure Cooker" label.

▶ **5.** Click the **Drill Up** button twice to go up the hierarchy and back to the level containing the Category field. At each step in the process the labels in the PivotTable row are replaced with categories of the next highest level in the Product List hierarchy.

Using a hierarchy creates a simpler and cleaner PivotTable that focuses your attention on those details of most interest to you. However, you can always use the Expand Outline and Collapse Outline buttons to view the table outline.

Dmitry wants you to add this product revenue information to the dashboard as a clustered bar chart. You'll create the PivotChart based on this table and add it to the Revenue Dashboard worksheet.

To create a PivotChart of product revenue:

1. With the PivotTable still selected, click the **PivotTable Analyze** tab on the ribbon, and then in the Tools group, click the **PivotChart** button. The Insert Chart dialog box opens.

2. On the All Charts tab, click **Bar** as the chart type, click **Clustered Bar** as the chart subtype, and then click **OK**. The bar chart is added to the worksheet.

3. Move the chart to the **Revenue Dashboard** worksheet, and then move and resize it to cover the range **K4:N16**.

4. Change the chart title to **Revenue by Product**, add data labels to the chart showing revenue totals for each category, and remove the chart legend and chart gridlines.

5. Click the **Chart Elements** button ⊞, click the **Axes arrow**, and then click the **Primary Horizontal** check box to remove the horizontal axis from the chart.

6. On the PivotChart Analyze tab, in the Show/Hide group, click the **Field List** and **Field Buttons** buttons to deselect them. The field list and buttons no longer appear on the chart and the worksheet. See Figure 10–34.

Figure 10–34   **Revenue by Product PivotChart**

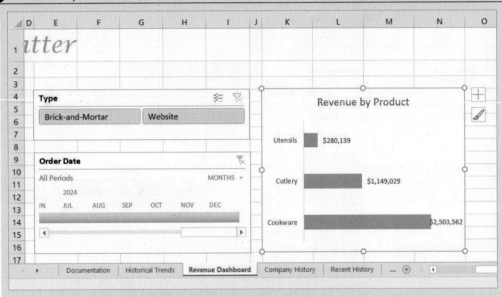

Finally, you'll connect the Product Revenue PivotTable to both the slicer and the timeline on this worksheet.

7. Click the **Type** slicer to select it, click the **Slicer** tab on the ribbon, and then in the Slicer group, click the **Report Connections** button. The Report Connections (Type) dialog box opens.

8. Click the **Product Revenue** check box to add it to the list of connected PivotTables for the slicer, and then click **OK**.

9. Click the **Order Date** timeline, click the **Timeline** tab, and then in the Timeline group, click the **Report Connections** button. The Report Connections (Type) dialog box opens.

10. Click the **Product Revenue** check box to add it to the list of connected PivotTables for the timeline, and then click **OK**.

11. In the Type slicer, click **Website**, and then in the Order Date timeline, click **Dec 2024**. The PivotChart filters to show the website revenue for December 2024, matching the results shown in the range B13:C14. Almost $11,000 of the revenue comes from sales of utensils, more than $50,000 from cutlery, and more than $100,000 from cookware.

The process of drilling down and drilling up through a hierarchy can be done with PivotCharts using the Quick Explore Tool.

Viewing Data with the Quick Explore Tool

The Quick Explore Tool is a feature of PivotTables and PivotCharts used to drill into data at any level of specificity or to explore the impact of other fields on your analysis. As with PivotTables, drilling down or up a PivotChart replaces the categories from one field with those of another. You'll use the Quick Explore tool to drill down the Revenue by Product PivotChart to view sales data on Cup and Platter cooking thermometers.

To drill down the Revenue by Product PivotChart using the Quick Explore tool:

1. Click the **Utensils** category in the Revenue by Product PivotChart. The Quick Explore button 🔎 appears below the label.

   Trouble? If the Quick Explore button does not appear, right-click the Utensils category and click Quick Explore on the shortcut menu in Step 2.

2. Click the **Quick Explore** button 🔎. The Explore box appears with options to drill down the Products table to the Subcategory field or to choose a different field to display in the PivotChart. See Figure 10–35.

Figure 10–35   Quick Explore button

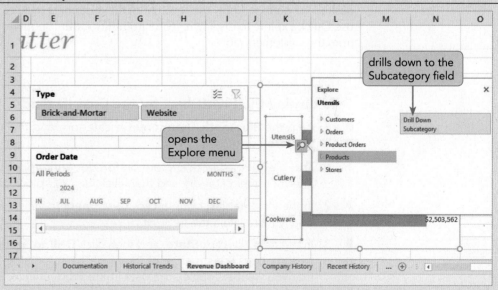

Tip

You can drill up the PivotChart by clicking Drill Up Category in the Explore box.

3. In the Explore box, click **Drill Down Subcategory**. The horizontal axis labels are replaced with Subcategory values ranging from Zesters to Colanders.

4. In the PivotChart, click the **Thermometers** subcategory, click the **Quick Explore** button 🔍 that appears, and then click **Drill Down Description** in the Explore box. The PivotChart displays revenue totals for three types of cooking thermometers. See Figure 10–36.

Figure 10–36   Cooking thermometer sales

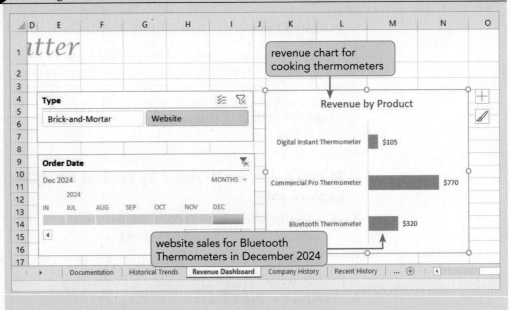

Drilling into the data, Dmitry learns that in December 2024, website sales were $320 in Bluetooth Cooking Thermometers, $770 in Commercial Pro Thermometers, and $105 in Digital Instant Thermometers. A customer support specialist using Dmitry's dashboard wants to know the location of the customers making these purchases. You'll use Quick Explore to display revenue from Bluetooth Thermometers by the State field from the Customers table.

To display the PivotChart by the Cust ID field:

1. Click the **Bluetooth Thermometer** category, and then click the **Quick Explore** button 🔍.

   Trouble? If the Quick Explore button does not appear, right-click the Blue Thermometer category and then click Quick Explore on the shortcut menu.

2. In the list of tables, double-click **Customers** to view the field list. You can drill to any field within the field list.

3. In the field list, click **State**, and then click **Drill to State**. Drilling to a new field changes the structure of the PivotChart. A dialog box opens to confirm that you want to replace the data in the Product Pivot PivotTable.

4. Click **OK**. The $320 in website sales of Bluetooth Thermometers in December 2024 was divided between $240 in Florida and $80 in Arizona. See Figure 10–37.

Figure 10–37   **Bluetooth thermometer revenue by state**

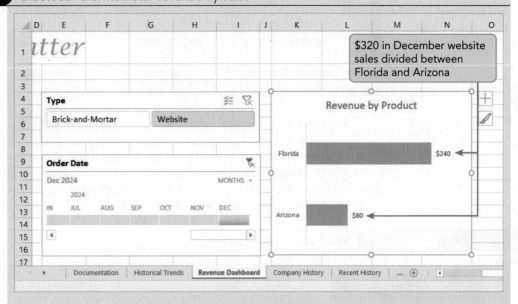

5. On the ribbon, click the **PivotChart Analyze** tab, and then in the Show/Hide group, click the **Field List** button. The PivotTable Fields pane opens. As you can see from the Filters area box, the PivotChart shows data from the Product List hierarchy.

6. Drag the **State** field out of the Axis (Categories) box to remove it, and then move the **Product List** hierarchy from the Filters box to the Axis (Categories) box. The PivotChart is restored to its original structure, showing total revenue charted against product category.

7. Close the PivotChart Fields pane.

8. Clear the filters from both the Type slicer and Order Date timeline to show revenue from all store types and all order dates.

The Quick Analysis Tool is useful for displaying important pieces of information such as who bought what products, when, and where. However, because it can change the PivotTable structure, you should be prepared to reorganize the PivotTable and PivotChart layouts when you are done using it.

Viewing Data with Map Charts

Location is another important aspect of data analysis. Financial analysts at Cup and Platter want to know what products are generating revenue for the company. The Advertising department wants to know who is buying those products so that it can target advertising dollars to specific regions and the country. The Shipping department wants customer location data to better predict shipping expenses. If the company opens another brick-and-mortar store, it can use location data to place the new store in a region filled with customers already supportive of the Cup and Platter brand.

Reference

Creating a Map Chart

- Create a data source with the first column or columns containing region names from countries down to states and counties.
- Enter data values in the last column of the data source.
- On the Insert tab, in the Charts group, click the Maps button.

You can create a map chart to plot data by location. Map chart data must be organized with the first column or columns indicating the map location and the last column containing the values to be charted. Excel supports two types of map charts. In a **value map**, regions are filled with a color gradient based on the numeric value associated with each region. In a **category map**, regions belonging to the same category share the same color. See Figure 10–38.

Figure 10–38	Value and category maps

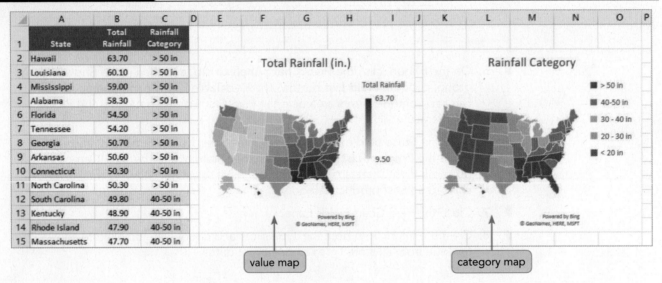

Colors are always applied at the region level, filling in entire counties, states, or countries.

Creating a Value Map Chart

Dmitry wants you to add a value map to the dashboard showing revenue totals from each state. One challenge in creating a map chart based on data in the Data Model is that map is not a PivotChart type. To get around that problem, you'll first create a PivotTable of revenue broken down by state and then copy those PivotTable values into a data range, which *can* be mapped.

To create a PivotTable of revenue by state:

1. Go to the **Revenue by State** worksheet.

2. On the Insert tab, in the Tables group, click the **PivotTable** button.

3. In cell **B4** of the Revenue by State worksheet, insert a PivotTable using the workbook's Data Model.

4. Rename the PivotTable as **State Revenue**.

5. Drag the **State** field from the Customers table into the Rows area box.

6. Drag the **Revenue** field from the Product Orders table into the Values area box.

Next, you will copy the contents of the PivotTable to a data range using Paste Link so that any changes to the PivotTable values will be reflected in the data range.

To create a PivotTable of revenue by state:

1. Select the range **B4:C55**, and then on the Home tab, in the Clipboard group, click the **Copy** button.

2. Click cell **E4**, and then in the Clipboard group, click the **Paste arrow** and click **Paste Special**. The Paste Special dialog box opens.

> Be sure to use Paste Link so that the data range always updates as the PivotTable updates.

3. In the Paste Special dialog box, click the **Paste Link** button. The pasted PivotTable is linked to the original PivotTable.

4. In cell **E4**, enter **State** as the column label, and then in cell **F4**, enter **Total Revenue** as the label.

5. Select the range **F5:F55** and format the selection as **Currency** with no decimal places. See Figure 10–39.

Figure 10–39   **PivotTable data pasted using Paste Link**

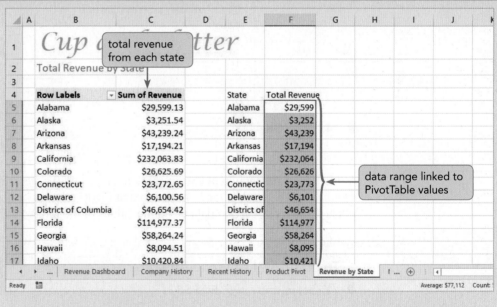

You can use this Paste Link technique with other chart types that are not supported by PivotCharts. For example, you can link PivotTable results to a data range for use in creating a histogram or scatter chart.

Be careful about the effect of filters. Some states might not be represented under some filters and thus would not be listed in the PivotTable. For example, a filter that limits the PivotTable to sales from the Chicago store might not show any revenue from customers who live outside the state of Illinois. However, Dmitry wants all states represented in the data, even if their revenue is zero. You can set the PivotTable options so that the PivotTable always displays every state, even when there is no data for that state.

To display all state categories:

▶ **1.** Right-click cell **B4**, and then click **PivotTable Options** on the shortcut menu. The PivotTable Options dialog box opens.

▶ **2.** Click the **Display** tab.

▶ **3.** Click the **Show items with no data on rows** and **Show items with no data on columns** check boxes so that the PivotTable always shows all rows and categories even when there is no data. See Figure 10–40.

Figure 10–40	PivotTable Options dialog box

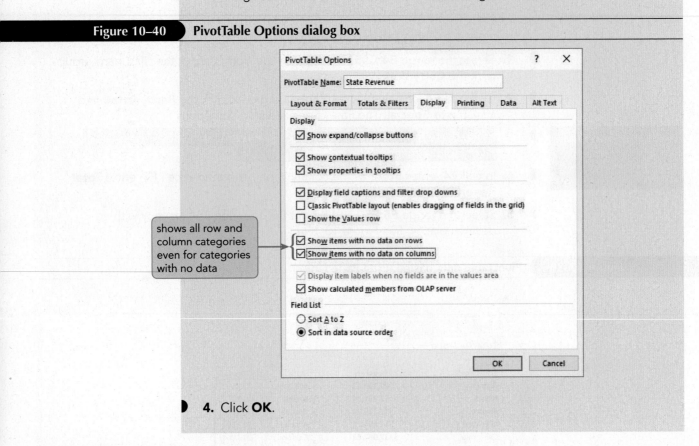

shows all row and column categories even for categories with no data

▶ **4.** Click **OK**.

The PivotTable now will always show data for all 50 states, no matter how it is filtered, as will the data range linked to that PivotTable. You will now create a map chart of the total revenue data using the values in the range E4:F55.

To map total revenue by state:

▶ **1.** Select the range **E4:F55**.

▶ **2.** On the ribbon, click the **Insert** tab, and then in the Charts group, click the **Recommended Charts** button. The Insert Chart dialog box opens.

▶ **3.** Verify that the **Filled Map** chart type is selected, and then click **OK**. The map chart is inserted into the workbook.

Trouble? If you are prompted to send your data to Bing to create the map chart, click I Accept or OK to retrieve location data from Bing.

4. Move the chart to the **Revenue Dashboard** worksheet, and then move and resize the chart to cover the range **E18:N32**.

5. Remove the chart title, and then add data labels to chart that will display total revenue superimposed over the state regions. See Figure 10–41.

Figure 10–41   **Revenue totals on the value map chart**

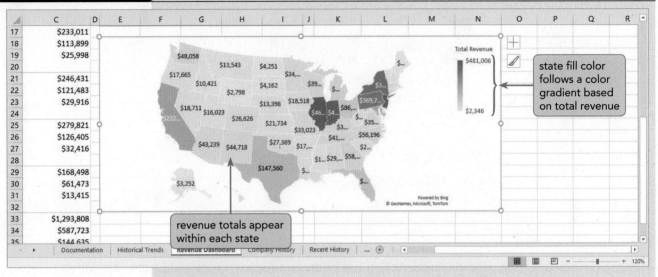

The darkest colors are found in or near the locations of Cup and Platter stores (Brooklyn, Chicago, Indianapolis, Philadelphia, and Washington D.C.). Dmitry wants to filter the map chart so that it shows only the state revenue totals for website sales from December 2024. You'll connect the slicer and timeline to the State Revenue PivotTable and then use them to filter the map.

To connect the map chart to the slicer and timeline filters:

1. Scroll up the worksheet and click the **Type** slicer to select it.

2. On the Slicer tab, in the Slicer group, click the **Report Connections** button, add the **State Revenue** PivotTable to the list of connected tables, and then click **OK**.

3. Click the **Order Date** timeline to select it.

4. On the Timeline tab, in the Timeline group, click the **Report Connections** button, connect the timeline to the **State Revenue** PivotTable, and then click **OK**.

5. On the Type slicer, click the **Website** button, and then on the Order Date timeline, click **DEC 2024**.

6. Verify that the map chart shows revenue totals only for orders placed on the company website during December 2024. See Figure 10–42.

Figure 10–42	Revenue totals from the website in December 2024

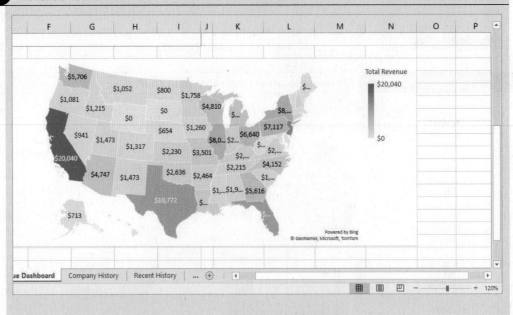

From the map chart, Dmitry learns that the largest website sales occur in California, Texas, and Florida. As Cup and Platter considers where to build a new store, those states would be logical places for the location.

Proskills

Problem Solving: Specifying a Map Location

The map chart uses location names from the search site Bing to determine where to place data values. However, this can result in misplacing map locations when several regions share the same name. Does "Georgia" mean the state of Georgia within the United States or the county of Georgia located north of Turkey? Does "Norfolk" refer to the county in Massachusetts or the county in England? There are 31 different counties named "Washington" alone. Bing will use the context of other regions in your data list to decide on a location, but it can make mistakes.

To avoid confusion, include several columns in your data source: one to specify the country, another to specify the state, and a third to specify the county (if needed). You can also include a detailed region name such as "Georgia, United States" rather than "Georgia" to indicate that the location is a state within the United States and not an Eastern European country. Finally, avoid abbreviations when possible. Spell out state names like Indiana rather than using the two-letter abbreviation IN. Many regions share the same abbreviation. If your data is not mapped correctly, try different combinations of names and locations to correct the problem.

Formatting a Map Chart

Excel supports several formatting options specific to map charts. To access the map formatting options, right-click any of the map regions and click Format Data Series on the shortcut menu. In the Format Data Series pane, you can set the map projection; define the scope of the mapped area; add labels identifying counties, states, and countries; and define the fill colors used by the map.

The default map format uses a map projection that preserves the relative size of regions on the globe with the map area set just large enough to incorporate all regions listed in the data. Figure 10–43 shows a map chart using the Mercator map projection with the map area set to the entire world, adding labels as country names where they would fit.

| Figure 10–43 | Map chart formatting options |

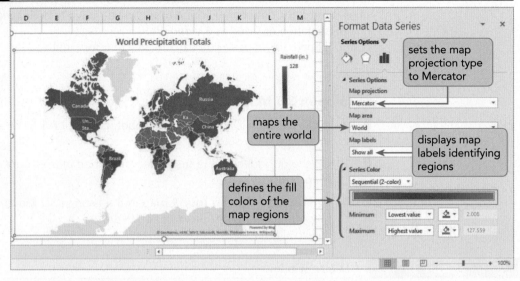

Map charts have several limitations: They cannot be used directly with PivotTables. They can plot only high-level regions like counties, states, and countries, but not map points like cities, postal codes, or latitude and longitude. They cannot be zoomed in to smaller regional areas.

Dmitry wants to focus a revenue map on one region of the country such as the southwestern United States. Because of the map chart limitations, you'll need to use 3D maps.

Insight

Using Linked Data Types

When analyzing geographic data, you will often want to include information about the regions being studied. For example, if you are reporting total sales revenue by state, it might be helpful to compare the revenue totals to state populations. **Linked data types** are data types linked to resources on the Internet. At the time of this writing, Excel supports two linked data types: Stocks for stock market information and Geography for geographic data. Microsoft plans to add more linked data types as it refines this Excel feature.

To retrieve data from a Linked Data Type, enter your stock symbols or map names into a worksheet, select the range containing those values, and then on the Data tab, in the Data Types group, click the Stocks or Geography linked data type. If Excel finds a match between your data and its online resources, it will convert your data to a Stocks or Geography data type. When you select your data, the Insert Data command appears, which you can use to choose the relevant stock market or geographic information you want to download from the Internet and add to your worksheet.

The linked data type feature is not available with every version of Excel, so check Excel Help to determine whether you have access to this feature.

Visualizing Data with 3D Maps

3D Maps is an Excel tool for creating map presentations. The presentations are not displayed within the workbook but instead open in a separate window with a different set of ribbon tabs and commands. Map presentations are called tours, and each tour contains one or more map scenes that can be played as a movie with one map scene transitioning into another. For example, Dmitry could create a tour with a first scene displaying sales data from one region of the country and a second scene displaying sales data from a different region. A tour can be shown to colleagues and clients as part of a presentation or saved as a video file.

You'll open 3D Maps so you can create a tour for Dmitry.

To open 3D Maps:

1. In the Revenue Dashboard worksheet, click cell **A1** to deselect any charts or slicers currently selected.

2. On the ribbon, click the **Insert** tab, and then in the Tours group, click the **3D Map** button.

3. If necessary, click the **Tour 1** map in the Launch 3D Maps dialog box. The 3D Maps window opens. See Figure 10–44.

Figure 10–44   3D Map window

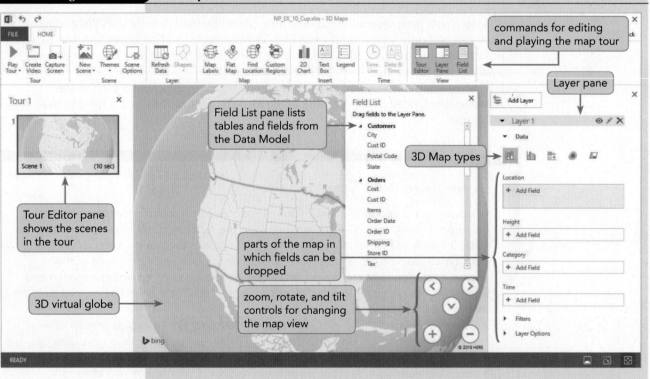

The 3D map window is organized into four sections: The Tour Editor pane lists the map scenes in the current tour. A map of the data is displayed in 3D view. The Field List pane shows tables and fields from the current workbook and Data Model. The Layer pane defines where and how data will be used in the map. A single map can contain multiple overlapping layers. You add data to a map scene by dragging fields onto area boxes in the Layer pane.

Tip

To rotate and tilt the map, press SHIFT+arrow in the direction you want the map to move. To zoom the map, press SHIFT+ + to zoom in and SHIFT+− to zoom out.

Superimposed on the map are controls for changing the map view. The Zoom in control ⊕ focuses on specific regions in the map. The Zoom out control ⊖ gives a wider view of the map. The Tilt up control ⊼ tilts the map and the Tilt down control ⊻ tilts the map down. The Rotate Left control ⊲ and the Rotate Right control ⊳ rotates the map from side to side. You can also use your mouse pointer to drag the virtual 3D globe into a new view of the data.

Dmitry wants a map showing the location of Cup and Platter customers by their postal code. You'll create this map scene using the Postal Code field from the Customers table.

To map the location of Cup and Platter customers:

1. In the Tour Editor pane, click the **Close** button ☒ to make more screen space for the 3D map you will create.

2. In the Field List box, drag the **Postal Code** field from the Customers table into the Location box in the Layer pane. Markers appear on the map at every location of a Cup and Platter customer.

   Trouble? If you don't see all the markers plotted on the map, be patient. Depending on your connection speed, it might take several seconds for all the markers to be plotted on the map.

3. Click the **Zoom out** control ⊖ (or press **SHIFT+−**) until the entire continental United States is in view.

4. Drag the globe to the left, moving your view.

5. On the Home tab, in the Map group, click the **Map Labels** button. Descriptive labels appear on the map. See Figure 10–45.

Figure 10–45   **Customers mapped by postal code**

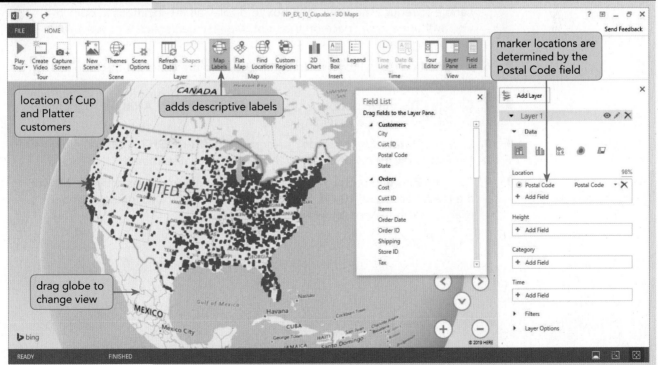

Once you have the general view of the map, you can set how you want the data displayed.

Choosing a Map Style

There are five ways of plotting data on a 3D map: The Stacked Column map 📊 displays data values as column markers divided into categories. The Clustered Column map 📊 displays data values as column markers with separate columns for each category value. The Bubble map 📊 displays markers as bubbles with bubble sizes determined by the values of a numeric field. The Heat map ⦿ displays markers with colors of increasing intensity determined by the values of a numeric field. Finally, the Region map ▱ fills in regions such as states and countries with colors determined by the values of a numeric or categorical field.

Dmitry wants you to create a Clustered Column map with the column heights determined by the Revenue field and the categories determined by the Store Name field. You'll modify the map now.

To create the Clustered Column map:

▶ **1.** At the top of the Layer pane, click the **Clustered Column** icon 📊.

▶ **2.** Drag the **Revenue** field from the Product Orders table and drop it in the Height box in the Layer pane. The columns heights change to reflect how much money each customer spent.

▶ **3.** Drag the **Store Name** field from the Stores table and drop it in the Category box in the Layer pane. The columns change colors to reflect which location each customer purchased from.

▶ **4.** In the Field List pane, click the **Close** button ✕ to view more of the 3D map.

▶ **5.** Click the **Layer 1** legend box to select it, and then drag the lower-right sizing handle to reduce the size of the box to display all the locations in one column without excess space on the right. More screen space is now available to view the map.

▶ **6.** Use your mouse to move Washington D.C. into the center of the Map window.

▶ **7.** Click the **Tilt down** button ⊙ (or press **SHIFT+DOWN ARROW**) eight times to view the map at a lower angle.

▶ **8.** Click the **Rotate Right** button ⊙ (or press **SHIFT+RIGHT ARROW**) eight times to show a view of the data above the Eastern seaboard.

▶ **9.** Click the **Zoom in** button ⊕ (or press **SHIFT++**) twice to magnify the view of the map. See Figure 10–46. Note that the rendering of your map might not exactly match the one shown in the figure.

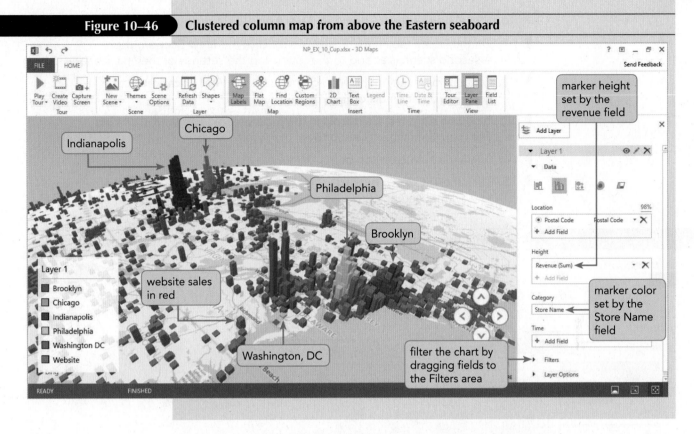

Figure 10–46   **Clustered column map from above the Eastern seaboard**

Cup and Platter is considering opening a new store in Los Angeles. As part of a presentation on this proposal, Dmitry wants another scene showing total revenue from potential store customers already living in the Los Angeles area.

Insight

Using Dates and Times in 3D Maps

If your data contains a date and time field like the date of a customer order, you can add that field to the Time box in the Layer pane. Adding a date/time field creates a play button on the map that you can use to view how the mapped data changes over time. For example, Dmitry could use the Order Date field to view changing revenue totals throughout the year in different regions of the country.

Creating New Scenes

New scenes can be created using an empty world map as the background—as you did when creating the first scene in this tour—or you can copy a current scene as the starting point for the next map. You can also create customized scenes with backgrounds of your choosing. For this new scene, you will copy the current scene and then change the view to show revenue in the Los Angeles area.

To add a new scene showing Los Angeles revenue to the tour:

▶ 1. On the Home tab, in the Scene group, click the **New Scene** button. A second scene is added to the tour using the settings of the first scene.

▶ 2. On the Home tab, in the Map group, click the **Find Location** button. The Find Location dialog box opens.

▶ 3. Type **Los Angeles, California** in the location box, and then click **Find**. The map view shifts to a spot over Los Angles.

▶ 4. Close the Find Location box.

▶ 5. Click the **Tilt down button** ⊙ (or press **SHIFT+DOWN ARROW**) ten times to view the map at a lower angle. See Figure 10–47.

Figure 10–47 **Tour with two scenes**

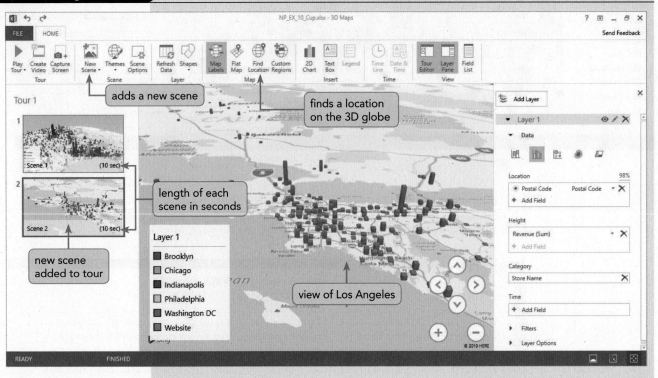

You will complete this tour by adding the transition timing between Scene 1 and Scene 2.

Setting Scene Options

Each scene in a tour has a duration measured in the seconds. The default duration is 10 seconds, but you can change the duration by modifying the scene options. You can also change the length of time required to transition from one scene to the next. During the transition, the 3D maps tool gradually changes the values and styles associated with one scene to match the values associated with the next scene. For example, with the two scenes you created, the transition will gradually change from a view of the United

States along the East Coast to a new view along the West Coast. You can enhance the transition with the following effects:

- Circle and Figure 8 effects add a repetitive circular motion to transition
- Dolly and Rotate Globe effects move the map clockwise in a straight line
- Push In effect zooms in on the scene
- Fly Over effect moves the map from top to bottom mimicking a camera flying over the object

You'll set the scene options of the two scenes in the tour.

To set the scene options:

1. With the second scene still selected in the Tour Editor, on the Home tab, in the Scene group, click the **Scene Options** button. The Scene Options dialog box opens. Because the second scene is selected, the changes you make in the Scene Options box affect that scene.

2. In the Scene duration (sec) box, change the value to **2** so that the second scene lasts two seconds.

3. In the Scene Name box, type **LA View** to rename the scene.

<table>
<tr><td>**Tip**
Transition durations are always measured from the previous scene; no transition is applied to the first scene in the tour.</td></tr>
</table>

4. In the Transition duration (sec) box, change the value to **4** so that the length of transition from Scene 1 to Scene 2 is 4 seconds.

5. Click the **Effect** button, and then click **Push In**. The Push In effect is added to the transition. Do not make any change to the effect speed. See Figure 10–48.

Figure 10–48   Scene Options dialog box

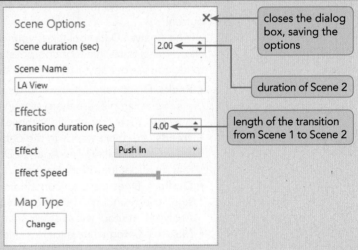

6. In the Tour Editor pane, click **Scene 1** to select it. Now you can set options for the first scene.

7. Change the Scene duration to **1** second, change the Scene Name to **Northeast View**, and then close the Scene Options dialog box. The Scene 1 options are saved and applied.

Playing a Tour

Playing a tour presents all the scenes of the tour in order using the scene options you set. You will play the tour to view a presentation of revenue totals from across the United States on a 3D map.

To play the tour:

1. On the Home tab, in the Tour group, click the **Play Tour** button. The tour plays with the camera moving from the Northeast to Los Angeles over the United States. By default, tours are played in full screen view.

2. Press **ESC** to return to the 3D Maps window.

3. In 3D Maps window, click the **Close** button ☒. All changes are saved automatically, and you are returned to the workbook.

4. sam↑ Save the workbook, and then close it.

Tip

To revise the tour and add new scenes, click the 3D Maps button in the Tours group on the Insert tab.

Dmitry appreciates the tour you've created and will use it in a report on Cup and Platter revenue and the prospects of opening a new store in the Los Angeles area.

Insight

Getting Ideas for Analysis

If you want ideas on how to present the information in a dataset, you can use the Excel Analyze Data tool, which examines data and uncovers trends and associations that you might want to highlight. To use the Analyze Data tool, place your data in an Excel table or data range, and then on the Home tab, in the Analysis group, click the Analyze Data button.

The Analyze Data tool takes your data and previews several charts in an Analyze Data (Ideas) pane, highlighting possibly interesting trends and factors you might want to include in your analysis. Some of the things the Ideas tool looks for are:

- **Ranks.** Do certain data categories result in outcomes significantly larger than others? For example, are there stores that are high sellers? The Analyze Data tool will preview charts that highlight those stores for further analysis.
- **Trends.** Are there trends in the data? Are sales increasing, decreasing, or showing seasonal variability? The Analyze Data tool will preview scatter charts with trendlines that highlight important trends.
- **Outliers.** Does the data contain unusual values or outliers? Is there a store that is significantly underperforming or a product that is exceeding expected sales? The Analyze Data tool will suggest charts that focus on those unusual outcomes.
- **Majority Categories.** Is there a single factor that contributes to most of the outcomes? Are most of the sales associated with one store or one product line? The Analyze Data tool will preview charts that showcase those important factors in your data.

Once you've reviewed the suggested charts from the Analyze Data (Ideas) pane, you can select and insert those charts directly into your workbook to be used in any reports or dashboards you create. Remember, the Analyze Data tool should be the beginning of your analysis, providing you with insights and motivation to further pursue the stories hidden in your data.

You've completed analyzing the large amount of data Dmitry had on the Cup and Platter company sales. In the process, you've retrieved data from a variety of data sources, combined data from different sources in a single report, and presented that data using tables, charts, maps, and tours. This just touches on the power of Power Query, Power Pivot, and 3D maps. If you explore these BI tools in greater depth, you'll find they are powerful tools with many useful features.

Review

Session 10.3 Quick Check

1. What is a hierarchy? How do you create a hierarchy?
2. What is the advantage of a hierarchy over an outline in a PivotTable design?
3. What are the two types of map charts?
4. Name three limitations of map charts.
5. What is a map tour?
6. Which 3D map type should you use to display locations with higher-sale totals in colors of greater intensity?
7. What is the Analyze Data tool?

Practice

Review Assignments

Data Files needed for the Review Assignments: NP_EX_10-2.xlsx, Support_EX_10_Sales01.csv, Support_EX_10_Sales02.csv, Support_EX_10_Sales03.accdb

Dmitry has another set of sales data for you to analyze. This time, you will look at the short- and long-term trends in sales from Cup and Platter's website. This data has been stored in a pair of CSV files. Dmitry has also compiled sample data on revenue generated from electric items, bakeware, and dinnerware. You will use that data to generate a revenue report and display the data on a map chart and 3D Maps tour. Complete the following:

1. Open the **NP_EX_10-2.xlsx** workbook located in the Excel10 > Review folder included with your Data Files. Save the workbook as **NP_EX_10_StoresReport** in the location specified by your instructor.

2. In the Documentation sheet, enter your name and the date.

3. Dmitry wants to view how website sales have increased over the year. Create a query to retrieve data from the **Support_EX_10_Sales01.csv** file. Use Power Query to remove the first four rows of the text file and use the titles in the fifth row as column headers. Load the three columns of data into an Excel table in cell B4 of the Website History worksheet.

4. Create a scatter chart of the data stored the range C4:D26. Move the chart to the Summary Report worksheet in the range B4:H16. Add a polynomial trendline of order 2 to the chart. (Use the Format Trendline pane and choose the Polynomial option.) Forecast the trendline forward 2 periods (or years).

5. Dmitry wants to view monthly website sales from the past two years. Create a query to retrieve data from the **Support_EX_10_Sales02.csv** file. Load the data as an Excel table to cell B4 in the Recent Website Sales worksheet. Format the data in the range C5:C28 as currency with no decimal places.

6. Using the data in the range B4:C28 of the Recent Website Sales worksheet, create a Forecast sheet, forecasting website revenue through 12/31/2025. Assume a seasonality in the data of 12 periods (or months). Name the Forecast sheet as **Forecasts**.

7. Move the forecast chart to the Summary Report worksheet in the range B18:H29. Remove the chart legend and add the chart title **Two-Year Forecast**.

8. Dmitry has a sampling of product sales from three Cup and Platter classes. Create a query that retrieves the Customers, Customer Orders, Items, Item Sales, and Stores tables from the **Support_EX_10_Sales03.accdb** Access database. Create a connection to the database file and add the tables in the Excel Data Model. Do not load any tables in an Excel table, PivotTable, or PivotChart.

9. Go to Power Pivot and create the following table relations between the five database tables:
   - Connect the Customer Orders and Customers tables through the Cust ID field.
   - Connect the Customer Orders and Stores tables through Store ID field.
   - Connect the Customer Orders and Item Sales tables through the Order ID field.
   - Connect the Item Sales and Items tables through the Item ID field.

10. Add a hierarchy to the Items table named **Item Tree** and add the Class, Subclass, and Group fields to it in that order.

11. Close Power Pivot and return to the workbook. In the Items Pivot worksheet, in cell B4, insert a PivotTable from the Data Model. Rename the table as **Items Pivot**. Add the Item Tree hierarchy from the Items table to the Rows area box, add the Type field from the Stores table to Columns area box, and add the Revenue field from the Item Sales table to the Values area box (displaying the revenue sum).

12. Create a clustered bar PivotChart from the Items Pivot PivotTable. Move the chart to the Summary Report worksheet in the range J11:P29. Remove the field buttons, primary horizontal axis, and gridlines from the chart. Move the chart legend to the bottom of the chart area. Add data labels to the chart.

13. Dmitry wants to examine revenue from coffee maker sales. Use the Quick Explore tool to drill down the bar chart categories through the Electrics class and the Coffee Makers subclass down to the group level, displaying total revenue of three coffee maker types.

14. Dmitry wants to view sales by state. In the State Revenue worksheet, add a PivotTable from the Data Model to cell B4. Name the PivotTable as **State Revenue**. Place the State field from the Customers table in the Rows area and the Revenue field from the Item Sales table in the Values area. In the PivotTable Options dialog box, on the Display tab, click the check boxes to show items with no data on the rows and columns.

15. Copy the data in the range B5:C55. Use Paste Link to paste references to the data values in the range E5:F55. Format the values in the range F5:F55 as currency. Enter **State** in cell E4 and enter **Revenue** in cell F4.

16. Create a Map chart of the data in the range E4:F55. Move the map to the Summary Report worksheet in the range R11:X29. Remove the chart title, add data labels to the chart, and then move the legend to the bottom of the chart area.

17. In the Summary Report worksheet, create a timeline using the Date field from the Customer Orders table. Place the timeline across the range J4:X10. Create connections between the timeline and the Items Pivot and State Revenue PivotTables. Use the timeline to filter the PivotTables to show data only from July 2024 through December 2024.

18. Dmitry wants a 3D Map presentation of this data. Insert a 3D Map. In scene 1, place the Postal Code field from the Customers table in the Location area, the Revenue field from the Items Sales table in the Height area, and the Store Name field from the Stores table in the Category area. Add map labels to the map.

19. Change the view of the globe to a location above Minnesota, looking down and to the east.

20. Create a second scene of this data positioned above Cuba looking northwest.

21. Change the durations of Scene 1 and Scene 2 to 1 second and play the tour verifying that your viewpoint moves across the United States from northwest of Chicago around to south of Florida.

22. Return to the workbook, save the workbook, and then close it.

Apply

Case Problem 1

Data Files needed for this Case Problem: NP_EX_10-3.xlsx, Support_EX_10_Yogurt.accdb

Umai Frozen Yogurt   Joan Amari is a sales executive for Umai Frozen Yogurt, a chain of frozen yogurt stores. Joan is responsible for overseeing 20 franchises in California. Joan wants to compare average customers per day at the franchises over the past three years and determine whether factors such as location, date, and weather play a significant role in the volume of customer traffic. She has data that contains over 21,000 records from the daily sales in the 20 stores from the past three years. Complete the following:

1. Open the **NP_EX_10-3.xlsx** workbook located in the Excel10 > Case1 folder included with your Data Files. Save the workbook as **NP_EX_10_Umai** in the location specified by your instructor.

2. In the Documentation sheet, enter your name and the date.

3. Use Power Query to access the **Support_EX_10_Yogurt.accdb** Access database, creating a connection to the Sales and Stores tables into the workbook's Data Model. You do not have to edit the query for these tables.

4. Open Power Pivot to view the Data Model in Diagram View. Create a relationship between the Sales and Stores table through the Store ID field.

5. In the Sales table, create a hierarchy named **Calendar** containing the Year, Month, and Weekday fields in that order.

6. Joan wants to analyze the number of customers served by the Umai Frozen Yogurt. Return to the workbook, and then insert a PivotTable in cell B4 of the Customer Calendar worksheet using the Data Model. Name the PivotTable **Customer Calendar**. Place the Calendar hierarchy from the Sales table in the Rows area of the PivotTable. Place the Customers field from the Sales table in the Values area. Change the field settings of the Sum of Customers value field to display the average of the Customers field with no decimal places.

7. Create a Line PivotChart from the PivotTable data. Move the PivotChart into the Sales Report worksheet, covering the range B14:I29. Remove the field buttons and the legend from the chart. Change the chart title to **Average Customers per Day**. Add data labels to the chart showing the value of each data marker.

8. Joan wants to know whether days of intense rainfall cause a decline in customer traffic. In the Rain Table worksheet, in cell B4, insert a PivotTable using the Data Model. Rename the PivotTable as **Rain Table**. Place the Rainy field from the Sales table in the Rows area. Display the average of the Customers field from the Sales table in the Values area. Display the average in the Number format with no decimal places.

9. Create a Clustered Column PivotChart of the Rain Table PivotTable. Move the PivotChart to cover the range K4:Q15 of the Sales Report worksheet. Remove the legend and the field buttons from the PivotChart. Change the chart title to **Average Customers per Day during Rainfall**. Add data labels to the chart.

10. Joan wants to examine the relationship between temperature and customer sales. In the Temperature Table worksheet, in cell B4, insert a PivotTable using the Data Model. Rename the PivotTable as **Temperature Table**. Place the Month field from the Sales table in the Rows area of the table. Display the average of the High Temp and Customers fields in the Values area of the table, in that order, to display the average high temperature and customers per month.

11. Joan wants to create a scatter chart of the relationship between average high temperature and average number of customers. Because PivotCharts cannot be created as scatter charts, you need to prepare the data to create a scatter chart of the relationship between average high temperature and average number of customers. Copy the range C4:D16 and use Paste Link to paste a link to the copied cells in the range F4:G16. Change the text in cell F4 to **Temperature** and change the text in cell G4 to **Customers**. Format the values in the range F5:G16 in the Number format with no decimal places.

12. Create a scatter chart of the data in the range F4:G16. Move the chart to the range K17:Q29 of the Sales Report worksheet. Change the chart title to **Customers vs. Temperature**. Add the axis titles to the chart, using **Average Customers per Day** for the Primary Vertical axis and **Average Temperature** for the Primary Horizontal axis. Change the scale of the vertical axis to go from 50 to 350. Change the scale of the Temperature axis to go from 50 to 110. Add a linear trendline to the chart.

13. Joan wants to view the charts on the Sales Report worksheet filtered by city. In the range B4:I12 of the Sales Report worksheet, insert a slicer using the City field from the Stores table. Lay out the slicer buttons in 4 columns and 5 rows. Connect the slicer to the three PiovtTables in the workbook.

14. Joan wants to show monthly results for the Malibu store from 2024. In the Sales Report worksheet, use the City slicer to show results for the Malibu store. In the Average Customers per Day chart, drill down into the 2024 Year category to the level of month.

15. As part of a presentation, Joan wants a map showing the locations of the stores with the highest average customers per day. Click cell A1 in the Sales Report worksheet, and then open a 3D Maps tour. Do the following to create a map showing the locations of the stores with the highest average customers per day:

a. Place the City field from the Stores table in the Location box.

b. Place the Customers field from the Sales table in the Height box. In the Height box, point to Customers (Sum), click the arrow, and then click Average on the menu to display the Customers (Average) instead of Customers (Sum).

c. Change the map style to a heat map.

d. Zoom into the state of California map to better view the average intensity of customer traffic in the 20 cites.

e. Display the map labels.

16. Close the 3D Map tour, save the workbook, and then close it.

Challenge

Case Problem 2

Data Files needed for this Case Problem: NP_EX_10-4.xlsx, Support_EX_10_Turkeys.csv,
Support_EX_10_Migration.csv

Department of Ornithology Karen Hatch is a professor in the Department of Ornithology at the
University of West Hilton in Florida. Professor Hatch is examining the migratory habits of turkey vultures and has compiled tracking data on seven birds. Professor Hatch wants you to complete a workbook that displays the turkey's migratory pattern and analyzes the relationship between each bird's
physical characteristics and the total distance they traveled. Complete the following:

1. Open the **NP_EX_10-4.xlsx** workbook located in the Excel10 > Case2 folder included with your
   Data Files. Save the workbook as **NP_EX_10_Ornithology** in the location specified by your
   instructor.
2. In the Documentation sheet, enter your name and the date.
3. Use Power Query to access the **Support_EX_10_Turkeys.csv** file, opening the file in the Power
   Query Editor, and then doing the following:
   a. Rename the query as **Turkeys**.
   b. Remove the summary text in the first three rows of the query.
   c. Use the text in the new first row as column headers.
   d. Remove the Species, Tracking Type, and Tracker columns from the query.
   e. Close and load the query to establish a connection to the Turkeys query and load it into the
      Data Model. Do not load the data into an Excel table, PivotTable, or PivotChart.
4. Use Power Query to access the **Support_EX_10_Migration.csv** file, and then edit the query as
   follows:
   a. Rename the query as **Migration**.
   b. Remove the first three rows from the query and use the new first row as column headers.
   c. Select the DateTime column; on the Add Column tab, in the From Date & Time group, click
      the Date button; and then click Date Only to create a new column named Date that contains
      only the date from the DateTime column.
   d. Remove the DateTime column from the query.
   e. Select the Date column and create a new column showing the End of Month date. Rename
      the column as **YearMonth**.
   f. Close and load the query to establish a connection to the Migration query and load it into the
      Data Model. Do not load the data into an Excel table, PivotTable, or PivotChart.
5. Use Power Pivot to create a relation between the Turkeys and Migration tables through the Tag field.
6. Karen wants to track the monthly distance traveled by each turkey vulture throughout the years.
   In the Migration Pivot worksheet, in cell B4, insert a PivotTable to track the monthly distance
   and average speed by each turkey vulture throughout the years.
   a. Rename the PivotTable as **Migration Pivot**.
   b. Move the Distance field from the Migration table to the Values area to calculate the sum of
      the Distance field. Rename the value field **Miles Traveled**.
   c. Move the YearMonth field to the Rows area. Remove the YearMonth (Year), YearMonth
      (Quarter), and YearMonth (Month) fields generated by Excel, leaving only the YearMonth
      field.
7. Karen wants a scatter chart of the data in the PivotTable. Copy the data in the range B4:C16
   and paste a link to those copied cells in the range E4:F16 to set up the data for a scatter chart.
   Format the data in the range E5:E16 using the Short Date format. Format the Miles Traveled data
   in the range F5:F16 using the Number format with a thousands separator and no decimal places.

✛ **Explore** 8. Create a scatter chart with smooth lines using the data in the range E4:F16. Complete the scatter chart as follows:

    a. Move the chart to cover the range B12:H27 on the Migration Dashboard worksheet.

    b. Change the chart title to **Turkey Vulture Monthly Migration**.

    c. Add the axis title **Miles Traveled** to the vertical axis and **Date** to the horizontal axis.

    d. Select the data labels on the horizontal axis and use the Orientation button in the Alignment group on the Home tab to angle the date text counterclockwise to fit within the chart area space.

9. In the range B6:H10, add a slicer for the Tag field from the Turkeys table. Lay out the slicer in 4 columns and connect it to the Migration Pivot PivotTable. Filter the chart to show the migration results from tag B45664.

10. Karen wants to investigate whether a relationship exists between migration distance and the bird's weight. In the Weight Analysis worksheet, in cell B4 insert a PivotTable with the Weight field from the Turkeys table in the Rows area and the sum of the Distance field from the Migration table in the Values area. You'll use this to investigate whether a relationship exists between migration distance and the bird's weight.

11. Copy the data in the range B4:C12 and paste a link in the range E4:F12. Display the values in the range F5:F12 as numbers with a thousands separator and no decimal places. Create a scatter chart of the data in the range E4:F12. Add a linear trendline to the chart and change the chart title to **Miles Traveled vs. Weight (oz)**. Move the chart to the range J4:O11 in the Migration Dashboard worksheet.

12. Karen wants to see whether length is related to migration distance. In the Length Analysis worksheet, repeat Steps 10 and 11 comparing the migration distance to the bird's length. Place the chart in the range J12:O19 of the Migration Dashboard worksheet and change the chart title to **Miles Traveled vs. Length (in)**.

13. In the Wingspan Analysis worksheet, repeat Steps 10 and 11 to compare migration distance to the bird's wingspan. Place the chart in the range J20:O27 of the Migration Dashboard worksheet with the chart title **Miles Traveled vs. Wingspan (in)**. Set the scale of vertical axis to go from 0 to 20,000 in 5,000 unit increments to match the other charts on the dashboard.

14. Karen wants to display the route that the eight turkey vultures followed. Insert a 3D Map, and then do the following:

    a. Add map labels to the 3D globe.

    b. Drag the Latitude and Longitude fields from the Migration table to the Location area to show the path of the migration.

    c. Drag the Speed field from the Migration table to the Height area so that the height of the data markers is proportional to the bird's speed.

    d. Drag the Tag field from the Turkeys table to the Category area to identify each bird's migration route.

    e. Resize the Layer 1 box so that you can see all of the legend entries.

✛ **Explore** 15. Do the following to see the turkey vulture migration in action:

    a. Drag the Date field from the Migration table to the Time area.

    b. Above and to the right of the Time area box, click the Clock button and click "Data shows for an instant" to have each marker replaced by the subsequent location of the bird in its migration.

    c. Click the Play button below the map to view the migration of the eight birds in action.

16. Close the 3D Map window, save the workbook, and then close it.

Exploring PivotTable Design

Summarizing Sales and Revenue Data

EXCEL

Objectives

Session 11.1
- Change a PivotTable layout
- Display and hide PivotTable grand totals and subtotals
- Sort PivotTable contents
- Filter PivotTable contents
- Group items within a PivotTable field

Session 11.2
- Apply calculations to a PivotTable
- Create PivotTable conditional formats
- Manage the PivotTable cache
- Create calculated items and calculated fields

Session 11.3
- Analyze PivotTables based on the Data Model
- Create a table measure using DAX
- Retrieve PivotTable data with the GETPIVOTDATA function
- Explore Excel Database functions

Case | QC Inn

Anna Fischer is a regional manager for QC Inn, a nationwide chain of affordable motels for vacationing families and business travelers. Anna is preparing the year-end report for 24 QC Inn franchises located in the Nebraska/South Dakota region. Anna's report will explore how revenue and occupancy rates have changed over the past two years and highlight those motels and regions that are performing below or above expectations. To create this report, you'll help Anna summarize daily motel data with a variety of PivotTable designs.

Starting Data Files

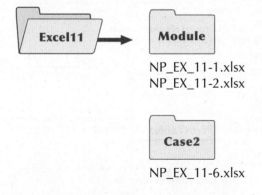

Excel11 → **Module**
NP_EX_11-1.xlsx
NP_EX_11-2.xlsx

Review
NP_EX_11-3.xlsx
NP_EX_11-4.xlsx

Case1
NP_EX_11-5.xlsx

Case2
NP_EX_11-6.xlsx

Session 11.1 Visual Overview:

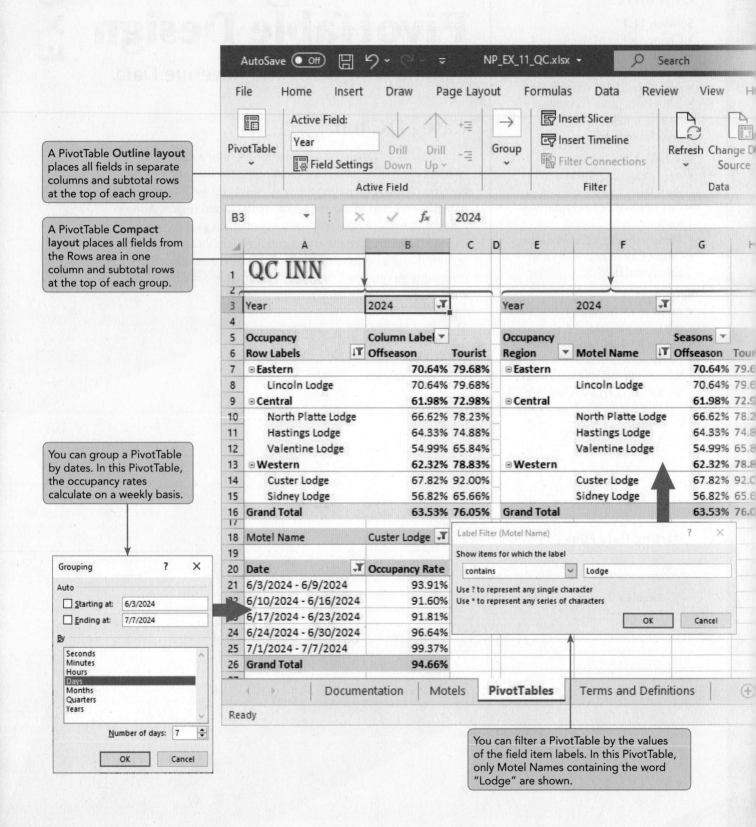

A PivotTable **Outline layout** places all fields in separate columns and subtotal rows at the top of each group.

A PivotTable **Compact layout** places all fields from the Rows area in one column and subtotal rows at the top of each group.

You can group a PivotTable by dates. In this PivotTable, the occupancy rates calculate on a weekly basis.

You can filter a PivotTable by the values of the field item labels. In this PivotTable, only Motel Names containing the word "Lodge" are shown.

Layouts, Sorting, Filtering, and Grouping

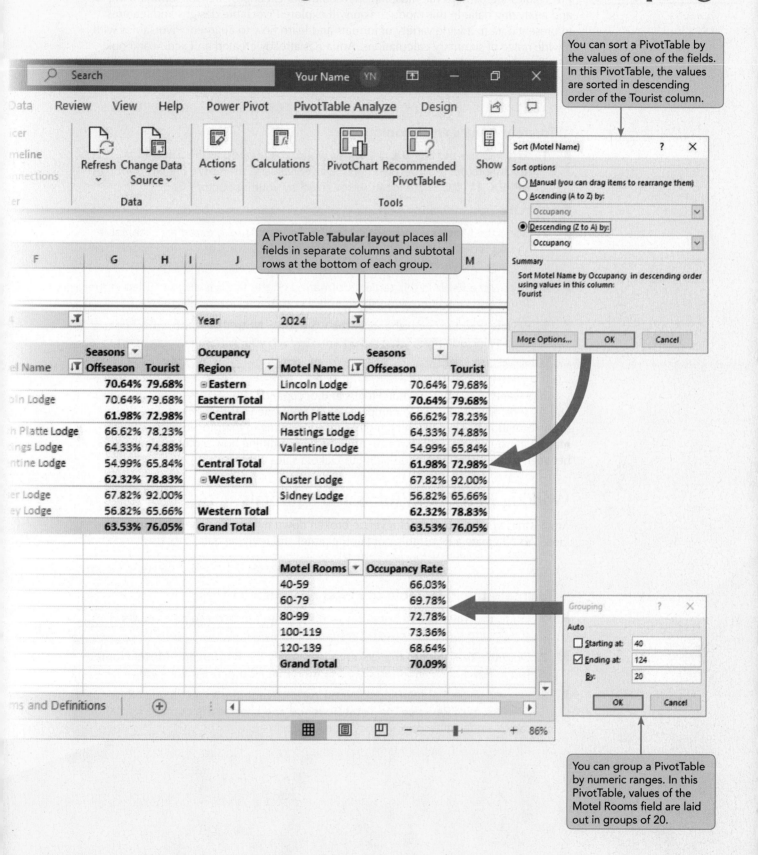

You can sort a PivotTable by the values of one of the fields. In this PivotTable, the values are sorted in descending order of the Tourist column.

Sort (Motel Name)

Sort options
- ○ Manual (you can drag items to rearrange them)
- ○ Ascending (A to Z) by:
  - Occupancy
- ● Descending (Z to A) by:
  - Occupancy

Summary

Sort Motel Name by Occupancy in descending order using values in this column:
Tourist

More Options...   OK   Cancel

A PivotTable **Tabular layout** places all fields in separate columns and subtotal rows at the bottom of each group.

	Seasons	
el Name	Offseason	Tourist
	70.64%	79.68%
oln Lodge	70.64%	79.68%
	61.98%	72.98%
h Platte Lodge	66.62%	78.23%
ings Lodge	64.33%	74.88%
ntine Lodge	54.99%	65.84%
	62.32%	78.83%
er Lodge	67.82%	92.00%
ey Lodge	56.82%	65.66%
	63.53%	76.05%

Year   2024

Occupancy Region	Motel Name	Seasons	
		Offseason	Tourist
⊟ Eastern	Lincoln Lodge	70.64%	79.68%
Eastern Total		70.64%	79.68%
⊟ Central	North Platte Lodg	66.62%	78.23%
	Hastings Lodge	64.33%	74.88%
	Valentine Lodge	54.99%	65.84%
Central Total		61.98%	72.98%
⊟ Western	Custer Lodge	67.82%	92.00%
	Sidney Lodge	56.82%	65.66%
Western Total		62.32%	78.83%
Grand Total		63.53%	76.05%

Motel Rooms	Occupancy Rate
40-59	66.03%
60-79	69.78%
80-99	72.78%
100-119	73.36%
120-139	68.64%
Grand Total	**70.09%**

Grouping

Auto
- ☐ Starting at: 40
- ☑ Ending at: 124
- By: 20

OK   Cancel

You can group a PivotTable by numeric ranges. In this PivotTable, values of the Motel Rooms field are laid out in groups of 20.

Laying Out a PivotTable

PivotTables are perhaps the most indispensable tool Excel provides for summarizing and analyzing data. In this module, you will explore PivotTable designs and features to present data in a wide variety of formats and learn how to augment PivotTables with a wide range of summary calculations. Anna has already created an Excel workbook detailing daily usage numbers from the past two years at 24 QC Inn motels located in Nebraska and South Dakota. You'll start by reviewing her workbook.

> **To view Anna's workbook:**
>
> ▶ 1. sam ↓ Open the **NP_EX_11-1.xlsx** workbook located in the **Excel11 > Module** folder included with your Data Files, and then save the workbook as **NP_EX_11_QC** in the location specified by your instructor.
>
> ▶ 2. In the Documentation worksheet, enter your name and the date.
>
> ▶ 3. Go to the **Motels** worksheet. In this worksheet, Anna created an Excel table named Motels containing 17,544 records of daily stays at QC Inn motels from the past two years.
>
> ▶ 4. Review the fields in this table. Information on the fields is also included in the Terms and Definitions worksheet at the end of the workbook.
>
> ▶ 5. Review the other worksheets in the workbook. Note that some worksheets already include PivotTable report areas, which you will use in your report.

Anna wants to examine revenue totals and occupancy rates across motels, months, and seasons. She also wants to compare values from one year to the next. She'll use this information to identify which motels are succeeding in their location and which may be in trouble. You will start your analysis by examining how motel revenue varies between locations in the Nebraska/South Dakota sales territory.

Working with Grand Totals and Subtotals

Anna wants you to show motel revenue broken down by year and the location of the motel. You'll create a PivotTable containing motel and revenue data.

> **To create the PivotTable of motel revenue:**
>
> ▶ 1. Go to the **Revenue vs Location** worksheet, and then make sure cell **B4** is selected to make the PivotTable report area active.
>
> ▶ 2. Drag the **Year** field to the Columns area, drag the **Region** and **Motel Name** to the Rows area, and then drag the **Revenue** field to the Values area.
>
> ▶ 3. Use the Value Field Settings dialog box to change the value field for Revenue from "Sum of Revenue" to **Total Revenue** and change the number format of the revenue values to Currency. See Figure 11–1.

Figure 11–1	PivotTable of Revenue by Location

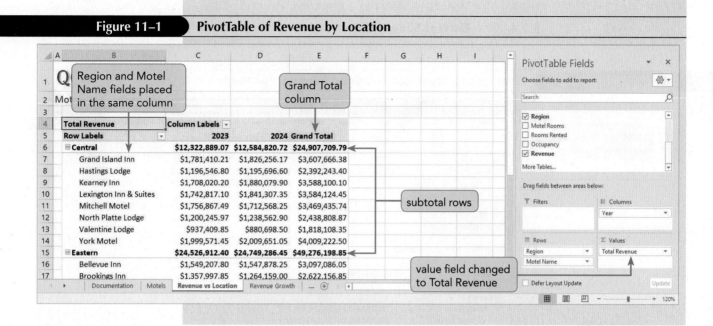

PivotTables, by default, include grand totals across all columns and rows. The grand totals in column E in this table provide the total revenue from 2023 and 2024 for each of the 24 motels and the grand totals in row 33 display the totals across all motels for each year. Based on this information, Anna can report that the chain had almost $100 million in total revenue (cell E33) with revenue totals slightly higher in 2024 than in 2023. Many individual motels saw their revenues increase. For example, the Grand Island Inn increased its annual revenue from $1.781 million in 2023 to $1.826 million in 2024 for a total of $3.608 million across the two years (row 7). Some motels saw revenue declines. The Valentine Lodge (row 13) saw its revenue decline from about $937,400 to about $880,700 for a two-year grand total of almost $1,818 million.

Subtotals appear for each of the three geographic regions. The motels in the Central region had about $24.9 million in revenue from the past two years (cell E6), while the Eastern and Western regions had two-year revenue totals of about $49.3 million (cell E15) and $25.2 million (cell E26), respectively.

If the grand totals and subtotals are not of interest, you can remove those totals from the report.

To remove the grand totals and subtotals from the PivotTable:

1. On the ribbon, click the **Design** tab to view commands for setting the appearance of your PivotTable, and then in the Layout group, click the **Grand Totals** button. A menu of options appears. You can turn off grand totals for the PivotTable rows and columns, keep the grand total values on for either rows or columns, or keep grand totals on for both (the default).

2. Click **Off for Rows and Columns**. The Grand Totals disappear from column E and row 33.

3. In the Layout group, click the **Subtotals** button. You have the option of removing all subtotal calculations or moving the location of the subtotal rows to either the top of each group or the bottom.

▶ **4.** Click **Do Not Show Subtotals** to remove the subtotals from the PivotTable. The subtotal calculations disappear from the PivotTable. See Figure 11–2.

Figure 11–2	Grand total and subtotals removed from the PivotTable

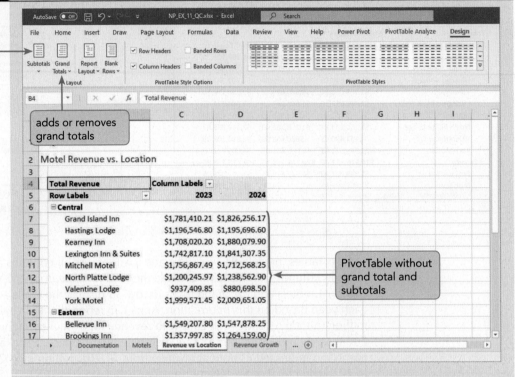

▶ **5.** Click the **Subtotals** button, and then click **Show All Subtotals at Top of Group** to restore the subtotal values.

You will next explore how to change the layout of a PivotTable report.

Insight

Displaying Multiple Subtotal Functions

The PivotTable default is to base subtotals on the same summary function that is applied to the individual table rows. So, a subtotal row will use the SUM function if the value field is summarized with sums and the AVERAGE function if the PivotTable shows averages of the value field. If you want to show the results of more than one summary function, you can add multiple subtotal rows with different calculations to a PivotTable. First, open the Field Settings dialog box for the field over which the summary statistics are calculated. In the Field Settings dialog box, go to the Subtotal & Filters tab, and then click the Custom option button. Select one or more functions from the list of summary functions, which includes Sum, Count, Average, Max, Min, and Product. Click OK to close the Field Settings dialog box. The PivotTable will now show multiple summary statistics in each subtotal row.

Changing the PivotTable Layout

You can lay out PivotTables in one of three ways: Compact (the default shown in Figure 11–1), Outline, and Tabular. The three layouts differ mainly in how they arrange multiple fields placed in the Rows area and where they display subtotal rows. Figure 11–3 summarizes these differences.

Figure 11–3	PivotTable layout options	

Layout	Fields in the Rows Area	Subtotals
Compact	Placed together in the first column, separated by outlining buttons	Placed at the top of each row group
Outline	Placed in separate columns	Placed at the top of each row group
Tabular	Placed in separate columns	Placed at the bottom of each row group

Tip

Subtotals for a Tabular layout can only be placed at the bottom of a row group.

An advantage of the Compact layout is that it reduces PivotTable width by placing all fields from the Rows area in one column. The Outline and Tabular layouts are best if you want to use values from the PivotTable in a subsequent analysis by placing each field value in its own PivotTable cell. You can also repeat field values in the Outline and Tabular layouts so that every row shows a field value.

Reference

Choosing a PivotTable Layout

- On the Design tab, in the Layout group, click the Report Layout button.
- Choose the Compact form to place all fields in the Rows area within a single column; choose the Outline or Tabular forms to place the fields in separate columns.
- To repeat item labels within a field, click the Report Layout button, and then click Repeat All Item Labels.

You'll change the layout of the Revenue PivotTable to the Tabular form and repeat the field values within each row.

To display a PivotTable in Tabular layout:

1. On the Design tab, in the Layout group, click the **Report Layout** button, and then click **Show in Tabular Form**. The PivotTable changes to the Tabular layout.

2. In the Layout group, click the **Report Layout** button again, and then click **Repeat All Item Labels**. The name of the region is repeated for each row.

3. In the Layout group, click the **Blank Rows** button, and then click **Insert Blank Line After Each Item**. The PivotTable is easier to read now that each row group is separated with a blank row. See Figure 11–4.

Figure 11–4   **PivotTable in a Tabular layout**

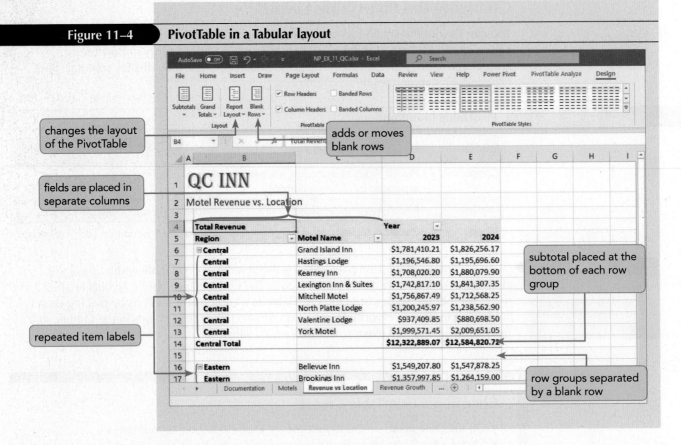

Anna finds the Tabular layout more readable for this data and more useful in the Revenue report.

Proskills

Written Communication: Setting Default PivotTable Options

Some professions have design standards that all reports must follow. The default Compact layout might not be one that you need use. Rather than changing the PivotTable layout every time you create a report, you can set your own preferred layout options.

To define your PivotTable defaults, click Options in Backstage view to open the Options dialog box. In the Options dialog box, click the Data tab, and then click the Edit Default Layout button in the Data options section to make changes to the default layout of PivotTables. In the Edit Default Layout dialog box, specify whether to show subtotals and, if so, where they should be placed, whether to show grand totals for PivotTable rows and/or columns, and finally whether new PivotTables should be created using the Compact, Outline, or Tabular layouts. To save time, you can select a cell from an existing PivotTable and then click Import to use all the layout choices from that PivotTable as the defaults going forward. To set defaults for PivotTable options other than layouts, click the PivotTable Options button in the Edit Default Layout dialog box. In the PivotTable Options dialog box, you can set all the other PivotTable options for any new PivotTables you create.

By defining your own PivotTable options, you can reduce the time required to create a finished report and make your reports more consistent in design and appearance.

Sorting a PivotTable

PivotTables labels are automatically sorted in alphabetical order if they contain text or chronological order if they contain date/time values. Thus, both the region names and the motel names within region shown in Figure 11–4 are sorted alphabetically. Anna wants to change that order so that the regions are listed in geographic order going east to west and then within each region, the busiest motels are listed first.

Manually Sorting a Field

To change the order of the field items, you can use your mouse to drag and drop the item labels in your preferred order. A quicker approach is to select each item label and retype its name. The items will then be automatically resorted to match the names you enter. You'll use the typing approach to reorder the Region field, arranging the items in the order of Eastern, Central, and then Western.

To manually sort the Region field:

1. Click cell **B6** containing the text Central.

2. Type **Eastern** to specify the first item you want to appear in the field, and then press **ENTER**. The Central and Eastern categories switch position. The motels in the Eastern region are listed first in the table, starting with the Bellevue Inn. The motels for the Central and Western regions follow.

    Trouble? If the category is renamed but not reordered, you probably mistyped the category name. Undo that action, and then repeat Steps 1 and 2, being sure to type the name of the category correctly.

Excel remembers your chosen order so that if you recreate this PivotTable or create another PivotTable with the Region field, you will not have to reorder the items again.

Reference

Sorting PivotTables

- To manually sort the items within a PivotTable field, drag the field items or type the item labels in the order you prefer.
- To sort the items in ascending or descending order, click the Filter button next to the field name, and then click Sort A to Z or Sort Z to A on the menu.
- To sort a field based on values from another field in the PivotTable, click the Filter button next to the field name, click More Sort Options, select the field the sorting is based on, specify the sorting options, and then click OK.

Sorting by Value

You can have Excel automatically sort a field by clicking the Filter button next to the field name and selecting a sorting option from the menu. Anna wants you to sort the motels within each region so that the motels with the highest revenue appear at the top of the list. You will sort the values of the Motel Name field in descending order of the 2024 revenue.

To sort the motel names in descending order of revenue:

▶ **1.** Click the **Filter button** in cell C5 of the PivotTable to open the filter menu.

▶ **2.** Click **More Sort Options**. The Sort (Motel Name) dialog box opens.

▶ **3.** Click the **Descending (Z to A) by** option button, click the **Descending (Z to A) by** box, and then click **Total Revenue**. See Figure 11–5.

Figure 11–5   Sort (Motel Name) dialog box

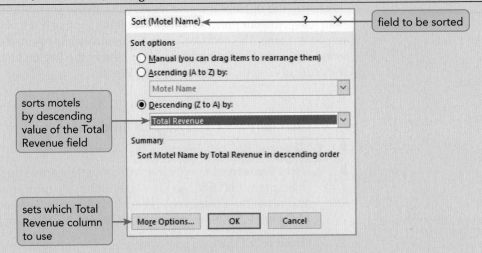

sorts motels by descending value of the Total Revenue field

sets which Total Revenue column to use

field to be sorted

You can sort the motels by the 2023 revenue total, the 2024 total, or the grand total across both years. The default is to use the grand total, even if that grand total doesn't appear in the PivotTable. Anna wants the motels within each region sorted in descending order of the 2024 revenues.

▶ **4.** Click **More Options**. The More Sort Options (Motel Name) dialog box opens.

▶ **5.** Click the **Values in selected column** option button, and then press **TAB** to select the cell reference.

Make sure you select a cell from the column containing the values used for sorting.

▶ **6.** Click cell **E6** to replace the cell reference. This will sort the motel names by the 2021 revenue values in column E. See Figure 11–6.

Figure 11–6   More Sort Options (Motel Name) dialog box

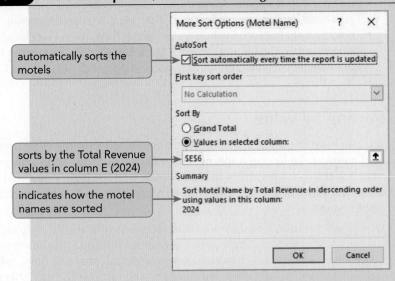

automatically sorts the motels

sorts by the Total Revenue values in column E (2024)

indicates how the motel names are sorted

> **7.** Click **OK** in each dialog box to return to the workbook. The motel names within each region are sorted in descending order of the 2024 revenue totals. See Figure 11–7.

Figure 11–7	Motels sorted by 2024 revenue

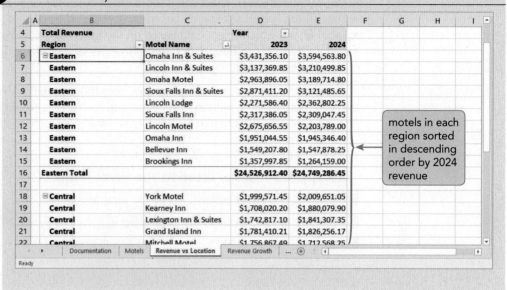

	B	C	D	E
4	**Total Revenue**		Year	
5	**Region**	Motel Name	2023	2024
6	⊟ **Eastern**	Omaha Inn & Suites	$3,431,356.10	$3,594,563.80
7	**Eastern**	Lincoln Inn & Suites	$3,137,369.85	$3,210,499.85
8	**Eastern**	Omaha Motel	$2,963,896.05	$3,189,714.80
9	**Eastern**	Sioux Falls Inn & Suites	$2,871,411.20	$3,121,485.65
10	**Eastern**	Lincoln Lodge	$2,271,586.40	$2,362,802.25
11	**Eastern**	Sioux Falls Inn	$2,317,386.05	$2,309,047.45
12	**Eastern**	Lincoln Motel	$2,675,656.55	$2,203,789.00
13	**Eastern**	Omaha Inn	$1,951,044.55	$1,945,346.40
14	**Eastern**	Bellevue Inn	$1,549,207.80	$1,547,878.25
15	**Eastern**	Brookings Inn	$1,357,997.85	$1,264,159.00
16	**Eastern Total**		$24,526,912.40	$24,749,286.45
17				
18	⊟ **Central**	York Motel	$1,999,571.45	$2,009,651.05
19	**Central**	Kearney Inn	$1,708,020.20	$1,880,079.90
20	**Central**	Lexington Inn & Suites	$1,742,817.10	$1,841,307.35
21	**Central**	Grand Island Inn	$1,781,410.21	$1,826,256.17
22	**Central**	Mitchell Motel	$1,756,867.49	$1,712,568.25

motels in each region sorted in descending order by 2024 revenue

Documentation | Motels | **Revenue vs Location** | Revenue Growth

The PivotTable now effectively shows the information that Anna needs for the report. The top-selling motel in the Eastern region for 2024 is the Omaha Inn & Suites with $3.594 million in revenue, followed by the Lincoln Inn & Suites and then the Omaha Motel with $3.210 million and $3.189 million, respectively. The top-selling motel for the Central region is the York Motel with over $2 million in 2024 revenue (cell E18), and the top-selling motel for the Western region is the Rapid City Inn with about $3.585 million in 2024 revenue (cell E28).

Insight

Sorting PivotTables by a Custom List

PivotTables can be automatically sorted alphabetically, by numeric value, or by date, in ascending or descending order. However, in some situations, you will want PivotTables automatically sorted based on a custom list. For example, Anna might want to always list motels based geographic location, going from east to west.

To create a custom list, click Options in Backstage view to open the Excel Options dialog box. Click the Advanced tab, scroll down to the General section, and then click the Edit Custom Lists button. The Custom Lists dialog box opens, from which you can create lists of items in any order to use with your PivotTables.

If later you want to prevent Excel from automatically sorting based on custom lists, go to the PivotTable Analyze tab, and then in the PivotTable group, click the Options button. In the PivotTable Options dialog box, on the Totals & Filters tab, deselect the Use Custom Lists when sorting check box, and then click OK.

The motels in the QC Inn chain are often built with different clientele in mind. For example, the line of Inn & Suites motels, such as the Omaha Inn & Suites, provides more spacious rooms and meeting facilities, perfect for the needs of business travelers and conferences. The success of those motels is of special interest to Anna, who wants to limit the PivotTable to those motels. You can narrow the scope of a PivotTable report using filters.

Filtering a PivotTable

Excel provides several ways of filtering PivotTables. You can add fields to the Filters area to give users the ability to select field values from a drop-down list. You can also connect slicers or timelines to the PivotTable. Finally, you can apply filters directly to the fields within the PivotTable. The four types of filters that can be applied directly to PivotTable fields are:

- **Manual filters**, which select values from check boxes listing all of the unique field values
- **Date filters**, which select data based on specific dates or date ranges
- **Label filters**, which select data based on the labels of the items in the field
- **Value filters**, which filter data based on values of a numeric field elsewhere in the PivotTable

Anna wants the Revenue table to show only those motels of the Inn & Suites line that had more than $3 million in revenue during 2024. To modify the report, you will first use a manual filter to narrow the focus of the PivotTable to 2024 revenue totals.

To apply a manual filter to the PivotTable:

▶ 1. Click the **Filter button** in cell D4 next to the Year label.

▶ 2. Click the **2023** check box to deselect it, leaving only the 2024 check box selected.

▶ 3. Click **OK**. The 2023 revenue column is removed from the PivotTable, leaving only the 2024 revenue totals displayed in column D.

Tip

You can reduce the filter values by entering a search string in the Search box directly above the list of field item values.

Manual filters are a quick way to filter data. However, if data contains a lot of field values, the list of filter values will be extremely long. Another approach is to use the Label filter in which you limit the field to only those labels whose value matches specified criteria. You will narrow the PivotTable so that it only shows results from motels with the word "Suites" in their name. You'll filter the PivotTable now.

To apply a Label filter to the PivotTable:

▶ 1. Click the **Filter button** in cell C5 next to the Motel Name label.

▶ 2. Click **Label Filters** on the menu. A list of criteria that can be applied to the labels of the selected field appears.

▶ 3. Click **Contains** from the list of filter options. The Label Filter (Motel Name) dialog box opens with "contains" already selected in the left box and the insertion point in the input box on the right.

▶ 4. In the input box, type **Suites** to limit the PivotTable to only those motels with the word "Suites" in their name. See Figure 11–8.

Figure 11–8   **Label Filter (Motel Name) dialog box**

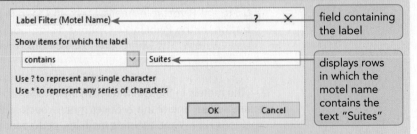

▶ 5. Click **OK**.

The PivotTable is filtered to show 2024 revenue from five Inn & Suites motels located in Omaha, Lincoln, Sioux Falls, Lexington, and Deadwood. Note that Label filters can also be applied to labels that have numeric values. For example, a field specifying the number of rooms in the motel could be filtered to show only those motels with more than 100 rooms or between 50 and 75 rooms. Label filters, whether used with text strings or numeric values, always apply the filter to the field associated with the filter button. To filter a field based on the values from another field in the PivotTable, use a Value filter.

Anna wants to filter this PivotTable to show only those Inn & Suites motels with 2024 revenues of $3 million or greater. However, there is a problem. By default, only one filter can be applied to a field at a time: You can apply a Label filter or a Value filter to the Motel Name field, but not both. To apply multiple filters to a single field, you must first modify the PivotTable properties.

To allow multiple filters within the same field:

▶ **1.** Make sure the Revenue Location PivotTable is still selected.

▶ **2.** On the ribbon, click the **PivotTable Analyze** tab, and then, in the PivotTable group, click the **Options** button. The PivotTable Options dialog box opens.

▶ **3.** Click the **Totals & Filters** tab to view options for totals and filters.

▶ **4.** In the Filters section, click the **Allow multiple filters per field** check box. See Figure 11–9.

Figure 11–9   **PivotTable Options dialog box**

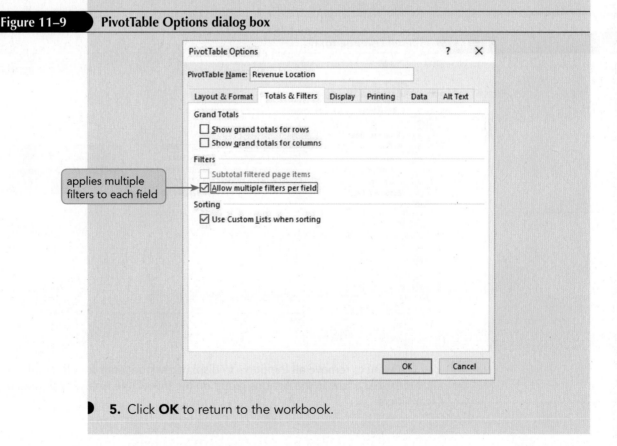

▶ **5.** Click **OK** to return to the workbook.

Next, you'll add a second filter that limits the PivotTable to only those motels with a total of revenue of $3 million or more.

To apply a Value filter to the PivotTable:

1. Click the **Filter button** in cell C5 next to the Motel Name label.

2. On the menu, click **Values Filters**. A submenu of filter options that can be applied to numeric values appears.

3. Click **Greater Than Or Equal To**. The Value Filter (Motel Name) dialog box opens with Total Revenue already chosen as the numeric field that "is greater than or equal to" a specified value.

4. In the input box on the right, type **3,000,000** to limit the PivotTable to those Inn & Suites motels with a total 2024 revenue of $3 million or greater. See Figure 11–10.

> **Tip**
>
> Unlike sorting, filters cannot be based on specific columns within a field.

Figure 11–10 Value Filter (Motel Name) dialog box

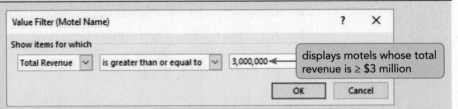

5. Click **OK**. The Value filter is applied to the table. Three motels satisfy all the filter criteria. See Figure 11–11.

Figure 11–11 Filtered revenue totals

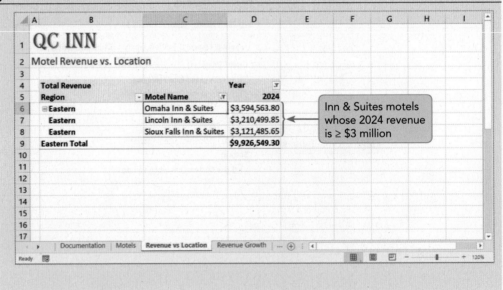

If you want to remove all the filters to display revenue totals for all motels, you can click the Clear arrow in the Actions group on the PivotTable Analyze tab, and then click Clear Filters.

Insight

Generating Multiple PivotTables with Show Report Filter Pages

You can create multiple copies of a PivotTable with the **Show Report Filters Pages** tool. To apply the tool, first place a field in the Filters area of the PivotTable. Then, rather than using the Filter button to switch the PivotTable between values of the filter, do the following:

1. Click the PivotTable Analyze tab.
2. In the PivotTable group, click the Options arrow, and then click Show Report Filter Pages.
3. In the Show Report Filter Pages dialog box, select the field from which to generate the filter pages.
4. Click OK.

Excel will generate new worksheets with each sheet containing a copy of the original PivotTable, filtered to show a different field value and the sheets automatically named for their field value. The PivotTables are not linked to the original table so any changes you make to the original PivotTable will not be reflected in the copies. The Show Report Filter Pages tool is a great way of quickly generating reports for specific stores, regions, or time periods in data.

Grouping PivotTable Fields

Total revenue is one metric to gauge the success or failure of a motel. Another is the average occupancy rate, which measures the percentage of available rooms being rented on average per night. A motel might not return a lot in revenue because of the size of its market, yet still be successful if it constantly rents out most of its rooms. On the other hand, a motel in a large market might be underutilized even if it is bringing in a large amount of revenue.

Anna is interested in exploring how occupancy rates in the Nebraska/South Dakota motels vary throughout the year. You'll create a new PivotTable report to calculate the average occupancy rate for each of the 24 motels from January through December in 2024.

To report on average occupancy rates:

1. Go to the **Seasonal Occupancy** worksheet.

2. Drag the **Year** field into the Filters area, drag the **Month** field into the Columns area, drag the **Motel Name** field into the Rows area, and drag the **Occupancy** field into the Values area. By default, Excel displays the sum of the occupancy rates, but Anna wants to analyze the average occupancy rate.

3. Modify the Value Field Settings for the Sum of Occupancy so that the PivotTable displays the average occupancy as percentages with two decimal places and change the name from "Sum of Occupancy" to **Occupancy Rate**. The PivotTable now shows the average occupancy rate.

4. On the ribbon, click the **Design** tab. In the Layout group, click the **Report Layout** button, and then click **Show in Tabular Form** to apply the Tabular layout to the PivotTable.

5. On the Design tab, in the Layout group, click the **Grand Totals** button, and then click **On for Columns Only** to display the average occupancy rate for each month but not across all months. Anna wants to focus on occupancy rates for 2024.

6. Click the **Filter button** in cell C4, **2024** on the submenu, and then click **OK** to display the occupancy rates for only 2024. See Figure 11–12.

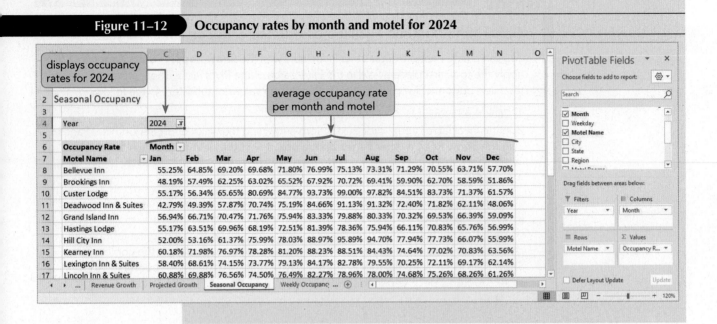

Figure 11-12 Occupancy rates by month and motel for 2024

The size of this PivotTable is 12 columns by 24 rows, not including the grand total row. As a PivotTable grows, the sheer number of cells of data can be overwhelming. In those cases, you can reduce the PivotTable size by grouping common categories. For example, a PivotTable containing monthly sales data might be better understood if the months were grouped into quarters.

However, with the motel business, Anna is not really interested in quarterly reports as much as the comparison between the tourist season and the offseason. For motels in the Nebraska/South Dakota sales territory, tourist season lasts from May through September. Anna wants those months grouped together. The remaining months should be grouped together to constitute the motel's off season.

Reference

Grouping PivotTable Fields

- To manually group items within a PivotTable field, select individual items, and then on the PivotTable Analyze tab, in the Group group, click the Group Selection button, and then enter a name for the group in the Active Field box.
- To group a date field, select the field, and then on the PivotTable Analyze tab, in the Group group, click the Group Selection button, and then in the Grouping dialog box, specify starting and ending dates for the field and select the levels from Seconds up to Years in which the dates should be grouped.
- To group a numeric field, select the field, and then on the PivotTable Analyze tab, in the Group group, click the Group Selection button, and then in the Grouping dialog box, specify the numeric intervals on which the groups are based.

Manual Grouping

One way of creating a PivotTable group is through a **manual group** in which items within a field are combined to create a new group that appears as a new field within the PivotTable. You will use manual grouping to create a group of tourist season months and a group of offseason months.

To create a manual group:

▶ 1. Click cell **C7** containing the Jan label, hold down **SHIFT**, click cell **F7**, and then release SHIFT to select the range C7:F7.

▶ 2. Hold down **CTRL** and click cells **L7**, **M7**, and **N7**, and then release CTRL. The nonadjacent range C7:F7,L7:N7 is selected.

▶ 3. On the ribbon, click the **PivotTable Analyze** tab, and then in the Group group, click the **Group Selection** button. A new grouped field named Month2 is added to the PivotTable.

▶ 4. On the PivotTable Analyze tab, in the Active Field group, click the Active Field box, and then change the name from Month2 to **Season**.

▶ 5. Drag the **Month** field out of the Columns area. Only the Season field remains in the Columns area of the PivotTable.

Next, you will group the five remaining months, which make up the tourist season for the motels.

▶ 6. Click cell **D7**, hold down **SHIFT** and click cell **H7**, and then release SHIFT. The range D7:H7 is selected.

▶ 7. In the Group group, click the **Group Selection** button to group these months together. There are two group categories named Group1 and Group2.

▶ 8. Click cell **C7** and enter **Offseason** as the label for Group1, and then click cell **D7** and enter **Tourist Season** as the label for Group2. These categories now have more descriptive names.

▶ 9. Increase the width of column D to display the complete text of the field item label. See Figure 11–13.

Figure 11–13	Occupancy rates by season for 2024

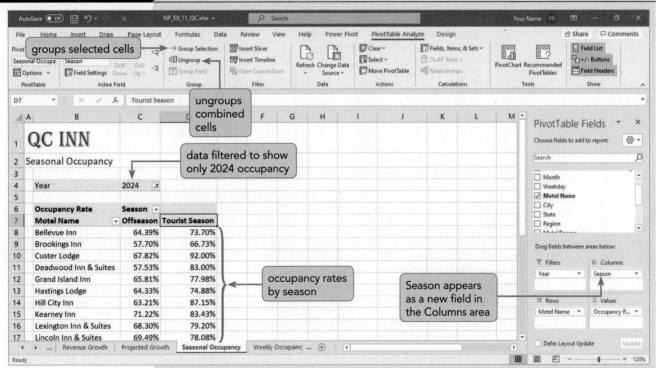

Not surprisingly, the occupancy rates during tourist season are higher than offseason. For example, the Bellevue Inn rents out on average 64.39% of its rooms each night during the offseason, a figure that rises to 73.70% during tourist season (row 8). Other motels show even greater improvement. The Deadwood Inn & Suites jumps from a 57.53% occupancy rate in the offseason to 83.00% during tourist season—an increase of more than 25% (row 11).

Anna wants a better view of the top-performing motels, so you will sort the PivotTable in descending order of occupancy rate during the tourist season.

To sort in descending order of the tourist season occupancy:

1. Click the **Filter button** in cell B7 next to the Motel Name label.

2. Click **More Sort Options** from the menu. The Sort (Motel Name) dialog box opens.

3. Click the **Descending (Z to A) by** option button, and then select **Occupancy Rate** from the accompanying box.

4. Click the **More Options** button. The More Sort Options (Motel Name) dialog box opens.

5. Click the **Values in selected column** option button, press **TAB**, and then click cell **D8**.

6. Click **OK** in each dialog box to return to the workbook. See Figure 11–14.

Figure 11-14	Sorted occupancy rates

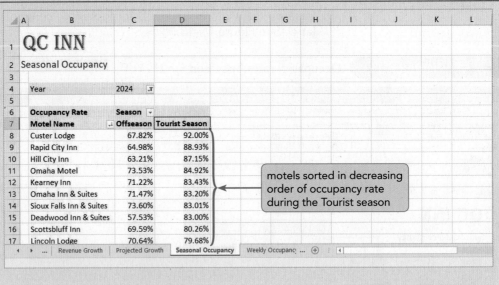

The busiest motel in the tourist season is Custer Lodge with an average daily occupancy rate during tourist season of 92%. In fact, the top three motels—Custer Lodge, Rapid City Inn, and Hill City Inn—are all located near Mount Rushmore and the Black Hills, which are prime tourism spots during the summer. Once you have manually created a group, it will be available to other PivotTables based on the same data source. For example, the Season group you created can be used again with other PivotTables in this workbook.

Grouping by Dates

Even within a season, Anna knows that some weeks are busier than others. She wants you to break down the data by date. You'll begin creating the PivotTable to do that now.

To create a PivotTable of occupancy rate vs. date:

▶ **1.** Go to the **Weekly Occupancy** worksheet.

▶ **2.** Drag the **Occupancy** field to the Values area and drag the **Motel Name** field to the Filters area.

▶ **3.** Change the summary function for the Occupancy field from calculating the sum to calculating the average.

▶ **4.** Change the number format to display the averages as a percentage to two decimal places, and then change the Value field name to **Occupancy Rate**. The overall occupancy rate for all the motels is 70.09%.

▶ **5.** Drag the **Date** field to the Rows area. Excel creates an outline of nested fields, grouping the dates by year, quarter, and month. You want to view the nested fields.

▶ **6.** Click the **Design** tab. In the Layout group, click the **Report Layout** button, and then click **Show in Tabular Form**. Three columns labeled Years, Quarters, and Date appear.

▶ **7.** Click the **expand outline** button ⊞ in cell B8 to expand the 2024 Year field into its subgroups consisting of quarters.

▶ **8.** Click the **expand outline** button ⊞ in cell C8 to expand the Qtr1 field into its subgroups consisting of the months of Jan through Mar. See Figure 11–15.

| Figure 11–15 | Occupancy rates by year, quarters, and months |

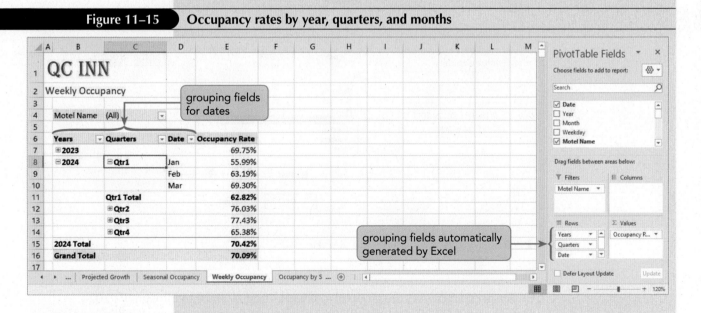

Tip

To remove automatic date groups, click any date field in the grouping and then click the Ungroup button in the Group group on the PivotTable Analyze tab.

When Excel encounters a date field that spans more than one year, it automatically groups the date values into quarters, months, and years. The grouping ends at the month level, so under the current grouping there is no way to view individual dates unless you regroup the data.

To group the dates in a different way, you can modify the group selection using the Grouping dialog box. You can regroup the dates to span any time interval from years down to seconds. You will use the Grouping dialog box to group the dates to show weekly occupancy rates during the summer of 2024 between Memorial Day and Labor Day.

To group the occupancy data by weeks:

▶ **1.** Click cell **B8** to select it.

▶ **2.** On the ribbon, click the **PivotTable Analyze** tab, and in the Group group, click the **Group Selection** button. The Grouping dialog box opens.

   Currently, the dialog box covers dates starting with 1/1/2023 through 1/1/2025. The Months, Quarters, and Years options are selected to group the date values from months, quarters, and years.

▶ **3.** In the Starting at input box, change the starting date to **5/27/2024**, which is Memorial Day in 2024.

▶ **4.** Press **TAB** twice, and change the ending date to **9/2/2024**, which is Labor Day in 2024.

▶ **5.** In the By box, click **Days** to select it and add it as a date grouping level.

▶ **6.** In the By box, click **Months**, **Quarters**, and **Years** to deselect and remove them as grouping levels.

▶ **7.** In the Number of days box, enter **7** so that you group the Date by 7-day weeks. See Figure 11–16.

Figure 11–16 ▶ **Grouping dialog box**

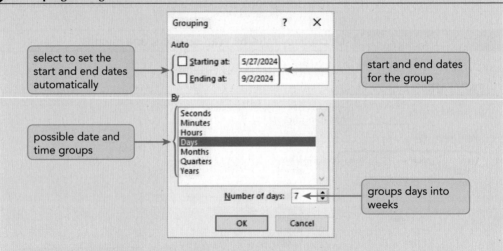

▶ **8.** Click **OK** to return to the workbook.

The occupancy rates are grouped into weeks from 5/27/2024 through 9/2/2024. Dates before 5/27/2024 or after 9/2/2024 constitute their own groups. You'll use a Date filter now to filter out those date ranges, focusing the PivotTable on the weeks during the summer of 2024. Then you'll view the weekly occupancy rates for select motels.

To apply a Date filter for dates:

▶ **1.** Click the **Filter button** in cell B6.

▶ **2.** On the Filter menu, click **Date Filters** to display a list of date filters that can be applied to the field.

▶ **3.** Click **Between**. The Date Filter (Date) dialog box opens.

▶ **4.** Enter **5/27/2024** in the first calendar box and then enter **9/2/2024** in the second calendar box. See Figure 11–17.

Figure 11–17   Date Filter dialog box

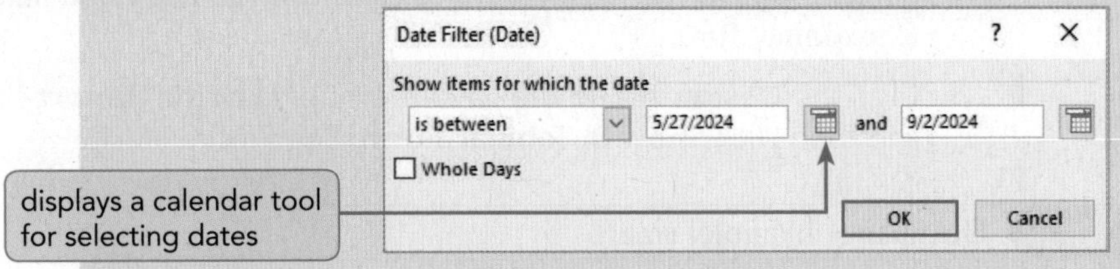

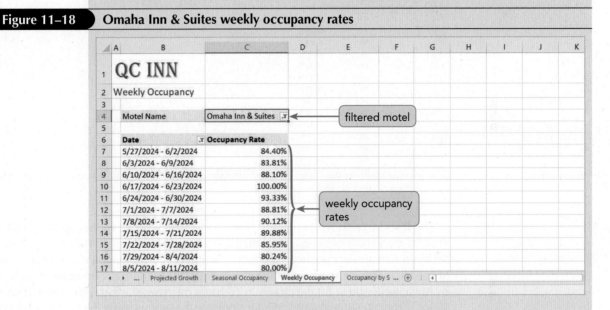

5. Click **OK** to return to the workbook.

6. Click the **Filter button** in cell C4, click **Omaha Inn & Suites**, and then click **OK** to view the average weekly occupancy rate for that motel. See Figure 11–18.

Figure 11–18   Omaha Inn & Suites weekly occupancy rates

The weekly average occupancy rate for Omaha Inn & Suites consistently stays between 80% and 90%, except for the week of 6/17/2024 to 6/23/2024 during which the motel was filled. Upon further investigation, Anna learns that during that week Omaha was hosting the annual College World Series, which brought a lot of college baseball fans into the area, occupying many of the motels in Omaha.

Using the PivotTable, Anna can study the weekly occupancy rates for the other 23 motels in the Nebraska/South Dakota sales territory, learning when those motels were at their most busy during the summer of 2024.

Grouping by Numeric Fields

Anna wants to explore whether occupancy rates are related to the size of the motel. Are larger motels less likely to have high occupancy rates or are they large because they attract more customers and thus rarely have vacancies? To answer that question, you will create another PivotTable comparing average occupancy to motel size, where size is measured by the number motel rooms.

To apply a Label filter for dates:

1. Go to the **Occupancy by Size** worksheet.

2. Drag the **Occupancy** field to the Values area, and then drag the **Motel Rooms** field to the Rows area.

3. Change the Sum of Occupancy to display the average occupancy rate as percentages to two decimal places and change the Value field name to **Occupancy Rate**.

4. Click the **Design** tab. In the Layout group, click the **Report Layout** button, and then click **Show in Tabular Form**. See Figure 11–19.

Figure 11–19 Occupancy by motel size

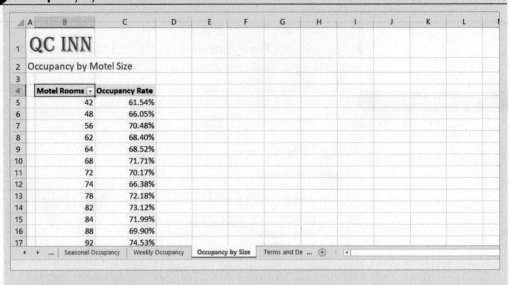

The PivotTable shows occupancy rates for motels with 42 rooms up to 124 rooms. With so many possible sizes, it's difficult to get a clear picture of the relationship between size and occupancy. To create a simpler PivotTable, you can group the values of the Motel Rooms field with each group category spanning an interval of motel sizes.

Anna wants you to list the motels in 20-room intervals, starting with motels containing 40 to 59 rooms. You will automatically generate the groups using the Grouping dialog box.

To group by number:

1. Click cell **B4** containing the Motel Rooms label to select it.

2. Click the **PivotTable Analyze** tab, and then in the Group group, click the **Group Field** button. The Grouping dialog box opens.

3. In the Starting at input box, enter the value **40**.

4. Press **TAB** three times, and then in the By input box, enter **20** as the group size. See Figure 11–20.

Figure 11–20 Grouping dialog box

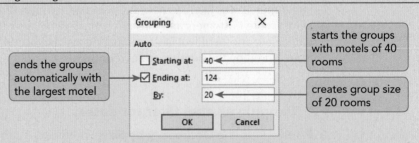

5. Click **OK** to return to the workbook. See Figure 11–21.

| Figure 11–21 | Motels grouped by size |

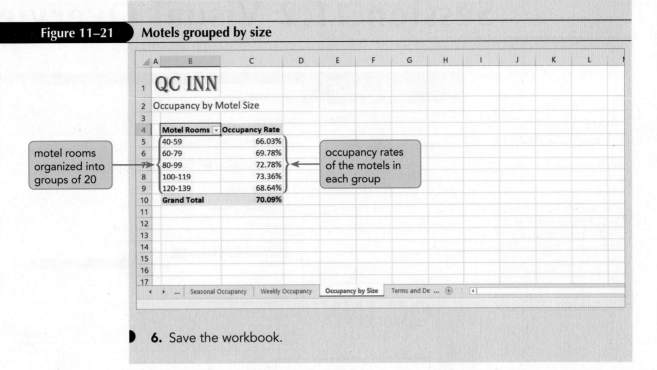

6. Save the workbook.

Grouping motel rooms in groups of 20 gives a clearer picture of the relationship between motel size and occupancy. The lowest occupancy rates occur for the smallest and largest hotels with rates below 70%, and the mid-sized motels with 80 to 119 rooms typically fill about 73% of their rooms. It appears the motels that are most difficult to fill are either small (and presumably found in smaller markets) or large (and might be in more competitive markets).

The groups you create either manually or through the Grouping dialog box are retained with the PivotTable and available to all future PivotTables that share the same data source. Note that groups created through manual selection are stored as new fields, whereas groups created automatically or through the Grouping dialog box replace the PivotTable field that they group. That means that once you group the Date field by weeks, all future uses of the Date field will be grouped in that fashion.

You've finished your initial analysis of the motel data for the QC Inn chain, learning what factors have contributed to successful motels as well as when and where those motels will be the busiest. In the next session, you'll use PivotTables to perform other calculations on this motel data.

Review

Session 11.1 Quick Check

1. How does the Compact layout differ from the Tabular layout?
2. What are two ways of manually sorting a PivotTable field?
3. When sorting a PivotTable by values in a field, how are the field values sorted by default?
4. When would you use a Label filter in a PivotTable?
5. When would you use a Value filter in a PivotTable?
6. How do you allow a PivotTable field to include both a Date filter and a Value filter?
7. When a PivotTable field is manually grouped, how does Excel treat the grouped items?
8. What does Excel do to date fields that are added to a PivotTable?

Session 11.2 Visual Overview:

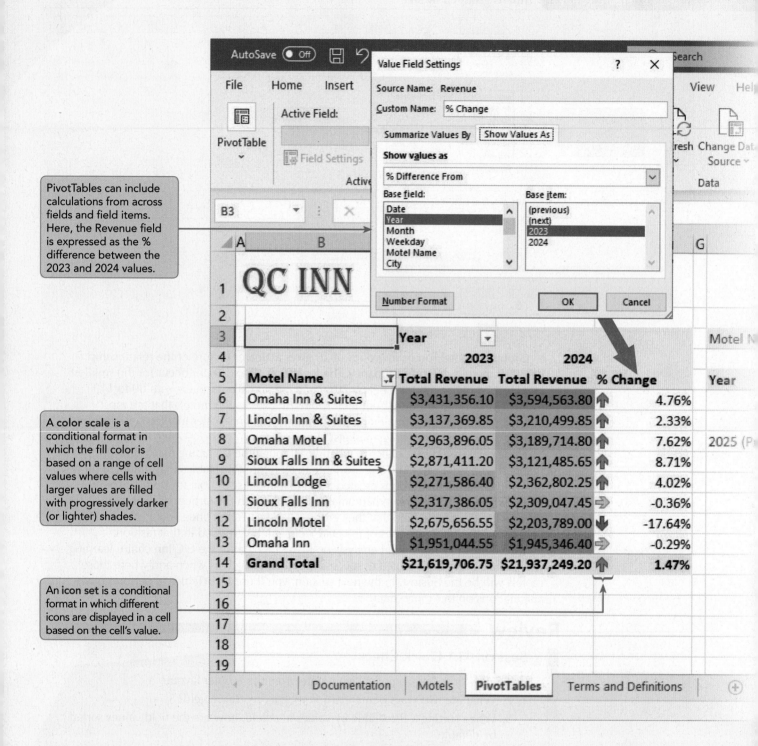

PivotTables can include calculations from across fields and field items. Here, the Revenue field is expressed as the % difference between the 2023 and 2024 values.

A color scale is a conditional format in which the fill color is based on a range of cell values where cells with larger values are filled with progressively darker (or lighter) shades.

An icon set is a conditional format in which different icons are displayed in a cell based on the cell's value.

Value Field Settings

Source Name: Revenue

Custom Name: % Change

Summarize Values By   Show Values As

Show values as

% Difference From

Base field:
Date
Year
Month
Weekday
Motel Name
City

Base item:
(previous)
(next)
2023
2024

Number Format   OK   Cancel

Motel Name	Year 2023 Total Revenue	2024 Total Revenue	% Change
Omaha Inn & Suites	$3,431,356.10	$3,594,563.80	4.76%
Lincoln Inn & Suites	$3,137,369.85	$3,210,499.85	2.33%
Omaha Motel	$2,963,896.05	$3,189,714.80	7.62%
Sioux Falls Inn & Suites	$2,871,411.20	$3,121,485.65	8.71%
Lincoln Lodge	$2,271,586.40	$2,362,802.25	4.02%
Sioux Falls Inn	$2,317,386.05	$2,309,047.45	-0.36%
Lincoln Motel	$2,675,656.55	$2,203,789.00	-17.64%
Omaha Inn	$1,951,044.55	$1,945,346.40	-0.29%
Grand Total	**$21,619,706.75**	**$21,937,249.20**	**1.47%**

Documentation   Motels   **PivotTables**   Terms and Definitions

Conditional Formats and Calculations

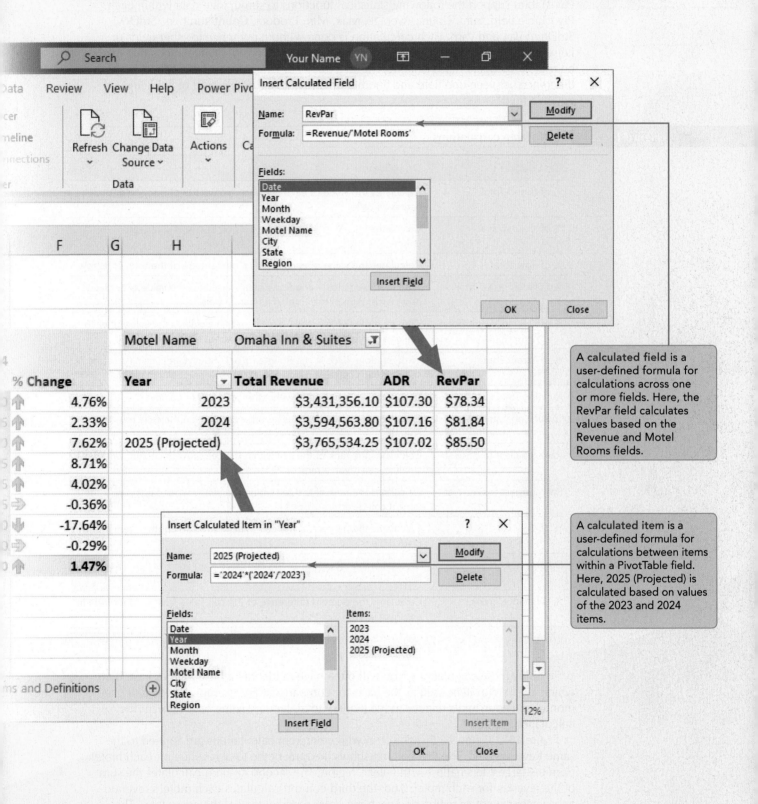

A calculated field is a user-defined formula for calculations across one or more fields. Here, the RevPar field calculates values based on the Revenue and Motel Rooms fields.

A calculated item is a user-defined formula for calculations between items within a PivotTable field. Here, 2025 (Projected) is calculated based on values of the 2023 and 2024 items.

Insert Calculated Field

Name: RevPar

Formula: =Revenue/'Motel Rooms'

Fields:
Date
Year
Month
Weekday
Motel Name
City
State
Region

Motel Name   Omaha Inn & Suites

% Change	Year	Total Revenue	ADR	RevPar
4.76%	2023	$3,431,356.10	$107.30	$78.34
2.33%	2024	$3,594,563.80	$107.16	$81.84
7.62%	2025 (Projected)	$3,765,534.25	$107.02	$85.50
8.71%				
4.02%				
-0.36%				
-17.64%				
-0.29%				
1.47%				

Insert Calculated Item in "Year"

Name: 2025 (Projected)

Formula: ='2024'*('2024'/'2023')

Fields:
Date
Year
Month
Weekday
Motel Name
City
State
Region

Items:
2023
2024
2025 (Projected)

Calculations with PivotTables

PivotTables support the following statistical functions to summarize data within each PivotTable field: Sum, Count, Average, Max, Min, Product, CountNumbers, StdDev, StdDevP, Var, and Varp. Each calculation is done without reference to other fields or items in the PivotTable. Figure 11–22 describes other PivotTable calculations that can be used to compare fields or items within a field. For example, you can calculate the difference between one field and another or calculate a running total of the items within a field.

| **Figure 11–22** | **PivotTable calculations** |

Calculation	Description
% of Grand Total	Calculates the value of each cell as a percentage of the grand total across all cells
% of Column Total	Calculates the value of each cell as a percentage of the total of its column
% of Row Total	Calculates the value of each cell as a percentage of the total of its row
% of Parent Row Total	With multiple fields in the Rows area, calculates the value of each cell as a percentage of the total of its parent field
% of Parent Column Total	With multiple fields in the Columns area, calculates the value of each cell as a percentage of the total of its parent field
% of Parent Total	With multiple fields in the Rows and/or Columns area, calculates the value of each cell as a percentage of its row and column parent
Running Total In	Calculates a running total within the cell's row or column
% Running Total In	Calculates a running total as a percentage within the cell's row or column
Rank Smallest to Largest	Calculates the rank of the cell within the cell's row or column with the smallest cell given a rank of "1"
Rank Largest to Smallest	Calculates the rank of the cell within the cell's row or column with the largest cell given a rank of "1"
% of	Calculates the percent of the cell value relative to another item in the PivotTable
Difference from	Calculates the difference of the cell value from another item in the PivotTable
% Difference From	Calculates the percent difference of the cell value from another item in the PivotTable
Index	Calculates the relative importance of the cell within the PivotTable

To apply these calculations, you will often have to identify a **base field** or **base item**, which is a field or item used as the basis for comparison. For example, if you calculate monthly revenue totals relative to the January total, January is the base item for the calculation.

Figure 11–23 shows a PivotTable in which different calculations are applied to the same Revenue field. The first column shows the rank of the total revenue for each motel from the largest to smallest within each region. The second column calculates the sum of the revenue for each motel. And, the third column calculates each motel's revenue as a percentage of its region and each region as a percentage of the grand total. This table provides a clear picture of how revenue totals are related across motels and regions.

Figure 11–23   Calculated ranks and percentage of parent row totals

Region	Motel Name	Rank Largest to Smallest	Sum	% of Parent Row Total
⊟ Central	Grand Island Inn	2	$903,704.57	33.35%
	Kearney Inn	1	$931,528.45	34.38%
	Lexington Inn & Suites	3	$874,507.60	32.27%
Central Total			**$2,709,740.62**	**16.27%**
⊟ Eastern	Bellevue Inn	6	$791,470.90	9.34%
	Brookings Inn	7	$603,661.10	7.12%
	Lincoln Inn & Suites	3	$1,545,787.85	18.24%
	Omaha Inn	5	$980,493.10	11.57%
	Omaha Inn & Suites	1	$1,814,091.40	21.41%
	Sioux Falls Inn	4	$1,175,380.70	13.87%
	Sioux Falls Inn & Suites	2	$1,562,503.15	18.44%
Eastern Total			**$8,473,388.20**	**50.88%**
⊟ Western	Deadwood Inn & Suites	3	$1,072,043.35	19.59%
	Hill City Inn	2	$1,426,482.70	26.07%
	Rapid City Inn	1	$2,023,142.29	36.98%
	Scottsbluff Inn	4	$949,639.80	17.36%
Western Total			**$5,471,308.14**	**32.85%**
Grand Total			**$16,654,436.96**	**100.00%**

subtotals show the percent of each region's total revenue compared to the grand total

revenue rank within each region

total revenue by motel

percent of total revenue within or across regions

Figure 11–24 shows a PivotTable with 2024 monthly revenue totals for the Rapid City Inn. The columns show the total revenue per month, a running total of monthly revenue, the difference in revenue from one month and the next, and the monthly revenue as a percentage of June's total revenue.

Figure 11–24   Monthly revenue calculations

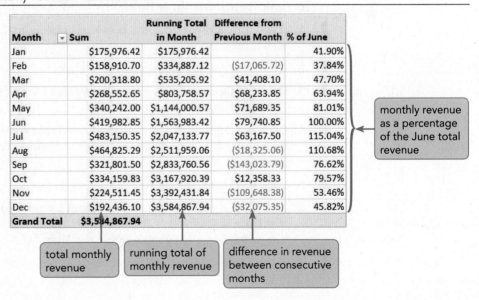

Month	Sum	Running Total in Month	Difference from Previous Month	% of June
Jan	$175,976.42	$175,976.42		41.90%
Feb	$158,910.70	$334,887.12	($17,065.72)	37.84%
Mar	$200,318.80	$535,205.92	$41,408.10	47.70%
Apr	$268,552.65	$803,758.57	$68,233.85	63.94%
May	$340,242.00	$1,144,000.57	$71,689.35	81.01%
Jun	$419,982.85	$1,563,983.42	$79,740.85	100.00%
Jul	$483,150.35	$2,047,133.77	$63,167.50	115.04%
Aug	$464,825.29	$2,511,959.06	($18,325.06)	110.68%
Sep	$321,801.50	$2,833,760.56	($143,023.79)	76.62%
Oct	$334,159.83	$3,167,920.39	$12,358.33	79.57%
Nov	$224,511.45	$3,392,431.84	($109,648.38)	53.46%
Dec	$192,436.10	$3,584,867.94	($32,075.35)	45.82%
Grand Total	**$3,584,867.94**			

monthly revenue as a percentage of the June total revenue

total monthly revenue

running total of monthly revenue

difference in revenue between consecutive months

Each column provides a different insight into the motel's monthly revenue. The running total shows how quickly revenue is generated through the year and can aid in developing the motel's budget. The column showing the differences from one month to the next is useful for planning future expenditures. A hotel manager can quickly see that expenses will have to be cut in September to make up for a $143,000 drop in revenue that month.

Reference

Calculating Values for a PivotTable Field

- Open the Value Field Settings dialog box for the field and click the Show Values As tab.
- To show ranks of items within a field, choose Rank Smallest to Largest or Rank Largest to Smallest.
- To calculate a running total of items within a field, choose Running Total In or % Running Total In.
- To calculate the change from one field item to another, choose Difference From or % Difference From.
- To calculate percentages of PivotTable totals, choose % of Column Total, % of Row Total, or % of Grand Total.
- To calculate percentages of a parent item in the table, choose % Of, % of Parent Column Total, % of Parent Row Total, or % Parent Total.
- Click OK.

Calculating Ranks

In the previous session, you created a PivotTable showing weekly occupancy during the summer of 2024. You will supplement this table now by ranking those weeks in order from most busy to least busy.

To rank items within a field:

1. If you took a break after the previous session, make sure the NP_EX_11_QC workbook is open.

2. Go to the **Weekly Occupancy** worksheet.

3. Drag the **Occupancy** field into the Values area box directly below the Occupancy Rate value.

4. Click cell **D6** to select it, click the **PivotTable Analyze** tab on the ribbon, and then in the Active Field group, click the **Field Settings** button. The Value Field Settings dialog box opens.

5. Click the **Show Values As** tab.

6. In the Show values as box, select **Rank Largest to Smallest** and then verify that **Date** is selected as the Base field because all ranks are determined relative to the occupancy rates within the Date field.

7. In the Custom name box, enter **Rank** as the name. See Figure 11–25.

Figure 11–25   **Ranks for the occupancy field calculation**

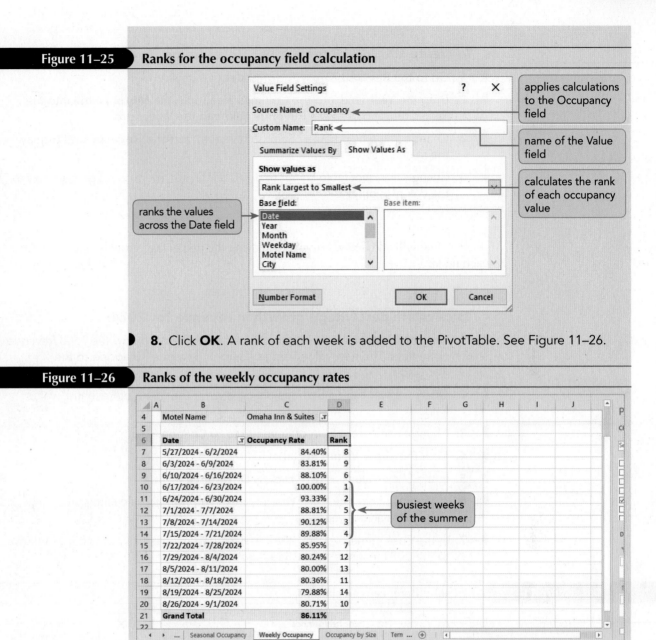

8. Click **OK**. A rank of each week is added to the PivotTable. See Figure 11–26.

Figure 11–26   **Ranks of the weekly occupancy rates**

Date	Occupancy Rate	Rank
Motel Name	Omaha Inn & Suites	
Date	Occupancy Rate	Rank
5/27/2024 - 6/2/2024	84.40%	8
6/3/2024 - 6/9/2024	83.81%	9
6/10/2024 - 6/16/2024	88.10%	6
6/17/2024 - 6/23/2024	100.00%	1
6/24/2024 - 6/30/2024	93.33%	2
7/1/2024 - 7/7/2024	88.81%	5
7/8/2024 - 7/14/2024	90.12%	3
7/15/2024 - 7/21/2024	89.88%	4
7/22/2024 - 7/28/2024	85.95%	7
7/29/2024 - 8/4/2024	80.24%	12
8/5/2024 - 8/11/2024	80.00%	13
8/12/2024 - 8/18/2024	80.36%	11
8/19/2024 - 8/25/2024	79.88%	14
8/26/2024 - 9/1/2024	80.71%	10
Grand Total	86.11%	

busiest weeks of the summer

Adding the ranks makes it more evident that the highest occupancy occurs during the middle of the summer starting with the week of 6/17/2024 and going through the end of the week of 7/21/2024.

Calculating Percent Differences

Anna has collected two years of data to identify which motels are increasing their business and which are losing customers. You will create a PivotTable that compares annual revenue by year and motel and display the percentage growth of each motel's revenue from 2023 to 2024. First, you'll create the PivotTable of Total Revenue vs. Motel Name.

To create the Total Revenue vs. Motel Name PivotTable:

▶ **1.** Go to the **Revenue Growth** worksheet.

▶ **2.** Drag the **Year** field into the Columns area, drag the **Motel Name** into the Rows area, and drag the **Revenue** field into the Values area.

▶ **3.** Change Value field name "Sum of Revenue" to **Total Revenue** and display the revenue totals as currency.

▶ **4.** Change the PivotTable layout to a Tabular layout and turn on grand totals for the columns only.

Next, you will add a new column displaying the percentage growth in revenue for each motel.

To calculate percentage growth in revenue for 2024:

▶ **1.** Drag the **Revenue** field into the Values area directly below the Total Revenue value field. The new value field as "Sum of Revenue" is added to the PivotTable.

▶ **2.** Open the Value Field Settings dialog box for the "Sum of Revenue" value field.

▶ **3.** Change name from Sum of Revenue to **% Change**.

▶ **4.** Click the **Show Values As** tab.

▶ **5.** In the Show Values as box, click **% Difference From**.

▶ **6.** In the Base field box, click **Year** because you want to calculate percentage differences across years.

▶ **7.** In the Base item box, click **2023**, if necessary, to base all percentages relative to the 2023 revenue totals. See Figure 11–27.

Figure 11–27   **Percent differences calculations**

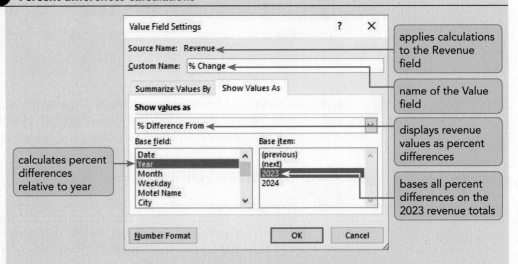

Tip

A hidden column is not removed from the worksheet, but instead is given a width of 0 pixels, effectively hiding it from the user.

8. Click **OK** to calculate the percent change from 2023 revenues to 2024. Two new columns appear on the PivotTable. Column F shows the percent change in revenue from 2023 to 2024 for each motel. Column D does the same calculation, but the column is blank because there is no percent change in 2023 revenue totals from themselves. To avoid confusing the reader, you will hide this column.

9. Right-click the **column D** heading, and then click **Hide** on the shortcut menu. Column D is hidden in the workbook. See Figure 11–28.

Figure 11–28   **Monthly revenue calculations**

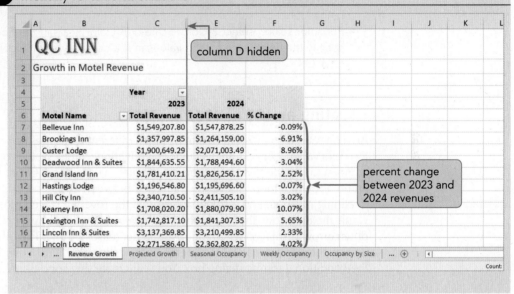

Overall, the motels in the QC Inn chain saw a revenue increase of 1.72% (cell F31), but this result was not uniform across motels. The revenue of the Lincoln Motel decreased by 17.64% (cell F18), while the annual revenue of Custer Lodge increased by 8.96% (cell F9). With so many numbers and calculations, the PivotTable can be difficult to read. You can correct that problem by adding a conditional format.

Displaying PivotTables with Conditional Formats

PivotTables do a great job of summarizing large amounts of data, but sometimes it can be overwhelming to wade through all those numbers. One way of making PivotTables more accessible is with a conditional format that highlights key values, painting a visual picture of the data. You can apply a conditional format to the following parts of a PivotTable:

- **Selected Cells.** The conditional format is applied directly to cells selected from the PivotTable.
- **All Cells Showing a Field Value.** The conditional format is associated with a specific field, wherever that field is located within the PivotTable.
- **All Cells Showing Multiple Field Values.** The conditional format is applied to cells where multiple fields intersect, such as the cells representing revenue totals from motels in each month.

The conditional format is applied within a PivotTable structure. If you alter the table's layout, the conditional format adapts to the new layout, following the new location of the field values wherever they end up.

You will explore two conditional formats that are well suited to PivotTables: icon sets and color scales.

Reference

Creating Icon Sets and Color Scales

- To display a conditional format with icon sets or color scales, select the data range or PivotTable, and then on the Home tab, in the Styles group, click the Conditional Formatting button.
- Click New Rule on the Conditional Formatting menu.
- For PivotTables, select which part of the PivotTable the rule should be applied to.
- For icon sets, select Icon Sets in the Format Style box and specify the value or percent ranges for each icon.
- For color scales, select 2-Color Scale or 3-Color Scale in the Format Style box and specify the color scale for the values in the data range or PivotTable field.
- Click OK.

Creating an Icon Set

An icon set is a conditional format in which different icons are displayed in a cell based on the cell's value. Icon sets are useful for highlighting extreme values or trends in your data.

Anna thinks the PivotTable you just created would benefit from icon sets that show an up arrow if a motel's revenue increased between 2023 and 2024, a down arrow for declining revenue, and a sideways arrow if the revenue stayed mostly the same. Anna wants the up arrow displayed when the revenue increases by more than 1% and the down arrow displayed when the revenue decreases by 1%. The other values should display the sideways arrow. For percentage values, you must enter decimals numbers in the conditional format dialog box. You will create this conditional format now.

To create the icon set conditional format:

1. Click cell **F7** to select a cell in the % Change column.

2. On the ribbon, click the **Home** tab. In the Styles group, click the **Conditional Formatting** button, and then click **New Rule**. The New Formatting Rule dialog box opens.

3. Click the **All cells showing "% Change" values** option button. This applies the conditional format to every cell in the % Change column, including the cell displaying the grand total across all motels.

4. In the Edit the Rule Description section, click the **Format Style arrow**, and then click **Icon Sets**.

Tip

To change or remove an icon in an icon set click the drop-down list arrow next to the icon image.

5. Click the **Icon Style arrow**, and then click the three-arrow icon set with the red arrow pointing down, the yellow arrow pointing sideways, and a green arrow pointing up.

6. Click the upper **Type** box, select **Number** and then enter **0.01** in the Value box. The up arrow will appear for motels that gained more than 1% in revenue.

7. Click the lower **Type** box, select **Number**, and then enter **–0.01**. The down arrow will appear for motels that lost more than 1% in revenue. See Figure 11–29.

Figure 11–29   New Formatting Rule dialog box

applies only to selected cells in the PivotTable

applies to all cells with a motel name and a year

appears when % change is ≥1%

appears when % change is between 1% and −1%

appears when % change is < −1%

applies to all cells in the % Change column

percentages entered as decimals

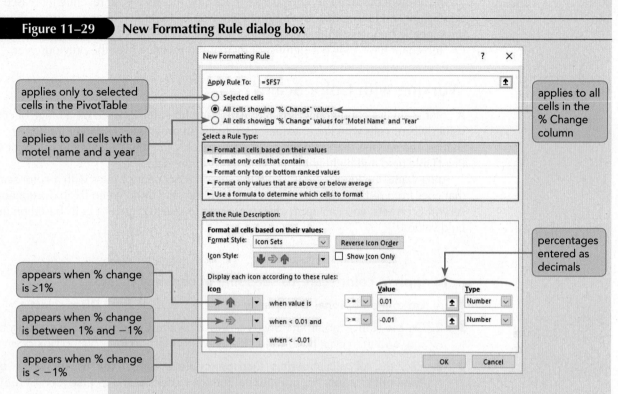

8. Click **OK** to apply the icons to all the values in the % Change column. See Figure 11–30.

Figure 11–30   Icons added to the % Change column

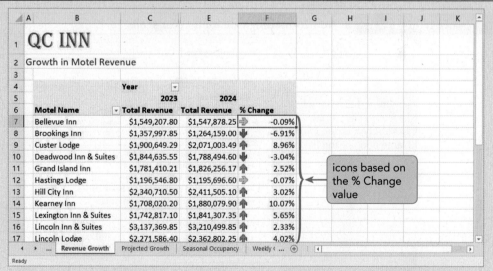

icons based on the % Change value

Trouble? If your icons are different, you probably mistyped something in the Conditional Formatting Rules Manager. Click the Conditional Formatting button, click Modify Rules, select the conditional format for the Icon Set, click Edit Rule, check the settings in your dialog box against those shown in Figure 11–29, correct any mistakes, and then click OK.

The arrow icons make it much easier to identify motels whose revenue increased significantly and those that saw a significant drop in revenue. Green up arrows figure prominently throughout the worksheet so it is quickly apparent that most motels in the QC Inn chain have shown a significant increase in revenue over the previous year.

Working with Color Scales

A color scale is a conditional format in which the fill color is based on a range of cell values where cells with larger values are filled with progressively darker (or lighter) shades. The varying shades in the color scale quickly identify the extreme values of the PivotTable field and highlight important trends in the data.

Anna wants the PivotTable to show the seasonal occupancy rates with a color scale that goes from red (low occupancy) through yellow and up to green (high occupancy). As with icon sets, you can apply the color scale to selected cells or cells based on their field values.

To apply a color scale to seasonal occupancy rates:

▶ **1.** Go to the **Seasonal Occupancy** worksheet and click cell **D8** to select it.

▶ **2.** On the Home tab, in the Styles group, click the **Conditional Formatting** button, and then click **New Rule**. The New Formatting Rule dialog box opens.

▶ **3.** Click the **All cells showing 'Occupancy Rate' values for 'Motel Name' and 'Season'** to apply the conditional format to cells at the intersection of the Motel Name and Season field values.

▶ **4.** In the Format Style box, click **3-Color Scale** to choose a color gradient going from red up to green. See Figure 11–31.

Figure 11–31   **New formatting rule for a color scale**

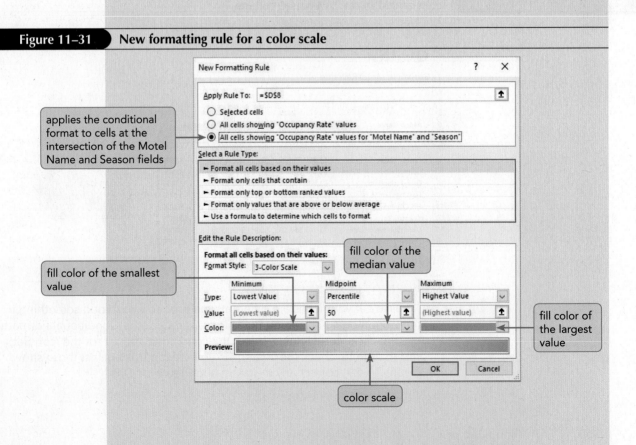

applies the conditional format to cells at the intersection of the Motel Name and Season fields

fill color of the smallest value

fill color of the median value

fill color of the largest value

color scale

5. Click **OK**. A color scale is added to all the seasonal occupancy rates in the PivotTable. See Figure 11–32.

Figure 11–32 **Color scales applied to the seasonal occupancy rates**

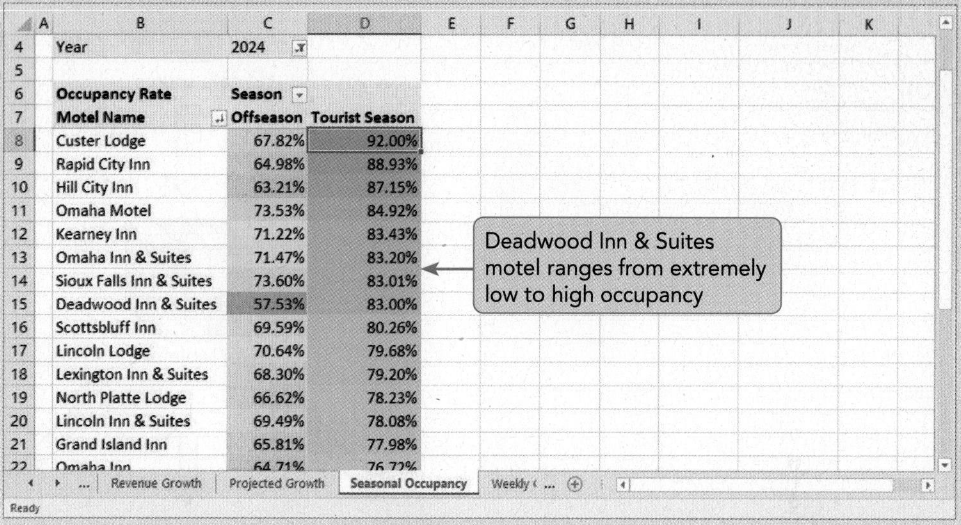

The color scale highlights trends in the data that might have gone unnoticed. Of interest to Anna is the performance of the Deadwood Inn & Suites motel, which goes from an extremely low occupancy rate during the offseason to a very high rate during tourist season. Anna might use this information to suggest to the motel manager ways that the Deadwood Inn & Suites could improve its profile in the offseason to take advantage of a potentially larger customer base.

Exploring the PivotTable Cache

The information used to create a PivotTable is stored within a data structure called the **PivotTable cache**. The cache contains an exact copy of the PivotTable's data source optimized for size and speed, which makes PivotTables very responsive to changes in content and layout. When you modify a PivotTable layout, Excel retrieves the data from the cache, not the original data source. In fact, if the data has been finalized and will not change, you could even delete the data source and work entirely from the information stored in the cache. (*Be sure you no longer need the data source before doing that!*) The existence of the cache is also why you must refresh your PivotTables whenever the data changes. Refreshing the PivotTable regenerates the cache so that it reflects the most recent version of the data source.

Sharing a Cache Between PivotTables

The price of speed and responsiveness is an increased file size because the same data is duplicated in both the workbook and the cache. Excel mitigates this problem by having all PivotTables operate from the same cache. This means that all PivotTables share the same fields and groups because that information is part of the cache. See Figure 11–33.

Figure 11–33   **PivotTable cache shared by multiple PivotTables**

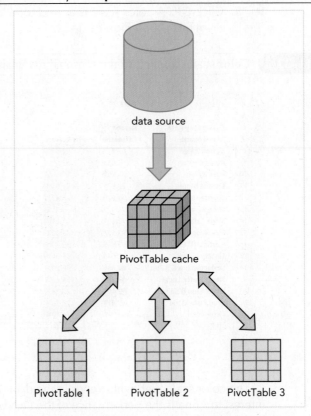

A consequence of sharing the same cache is that anything you do in one PivotTable becomes part of the cache and is instantly applied to the other PivotTables. For example, if you group the Date field by weeks in one table, the Date field will be grouped by weeks for every other PivotTable. You can't show weekly revenue figures in one PivotTable and then monthly revenue totals in a different PivotTable. If you regroup the dates in the second PivotTable to show monthly totals, the first table will be automatically regrouped to match.

One solution to this problem is to create separate caches for different PivotTables so that you can change the structure and contents of one PivotTable without affecting the others. Both caches connect to the same data source, so that the impact of refreshing the data source will still be reflected in both caches but changing one cache has no impact on the other. A separate cache will increase the size of your workbook file, but it will give you more flexibility in designing your PivotTables. See Figure 11–34.

Figure 11–34   **Multiple PivotTable caches**

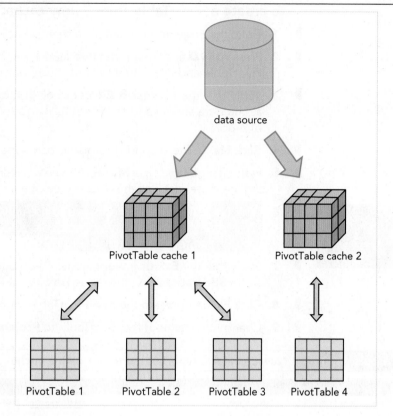

Creating a New Cache

To create a separate cache, you will use a tool that was available in older versions of Excel. Prior to Excel 2016, PivotTables were created using a tool called the **PivotTable Wizard**. Part of the PivotTable Wizard in versions of Excel 2007 and earlier was an option to create a PivotTable from an existing cache or to create a new cache. The PivotTable Wizard is still available, though not directly accessible from the ribbon.

Reference

Creating a PivotTable from a New Cache

- Press ALT+D and then press P to open the PivotTable Wizard.
- Specify the type of data and the type of report to create in Step 1 of the wizard.
- Specify the data source in Step 2 of the wizard.
- Click No to create the report using a new PivotTable cache.
- Specify the location of the PivotTable report in Step 3 of the wizard.
- Click Finish to insert the PivotTable report.

Anna wants you to create a new PivotTable that will project future performance of the motels in the QC Inn chain. Because the structure of this PivotTable will be different from the PivotTables you've already created, you will use a separate cache for it. You'll create this PivotTable using the PivotTable Wizard.

To create a PivotTable from a new cache:

1. Go to the **Projected Growth** worksheet and click cell **B6** to select it, if necessary.

2. Press **ALT+D** and then press **P** to launch the PivotTable Wizard. The PivotTable and PivotChart Wizard dialog box opens to the Step 1 of 3.

3. Verify that the **Microsoft Excel list or database** option button is selected as the data source and the **PivotTable** option button is selected as the type of report.

4. Click **Next**. The second step dialog box appears.

5. In the Range box, type **Motels** (the name assigned to the Excel table containing the motel data) as the data source of the PivotTable, and then click **Next**.

6. Click **No** when Excel prompts you to use an existing cache for the new PivotTable. This puts the new PivotTable you are creating in its own, separate cache. The Step 3 dialog box appears.

> You must click No or else Excel will not base the new PivotTable on its own separate cache.

7. Verify that the **Existing worksheet** option button is selected and the expression **=$B$6** appears in the range box.

8. Click **Finish** to create the new PivotTable report.

9. Change the name of the PivotTable to **Projected Growth**. See Figure 11–35.

Figure 11–35   New PivotTable report based on a separate cache

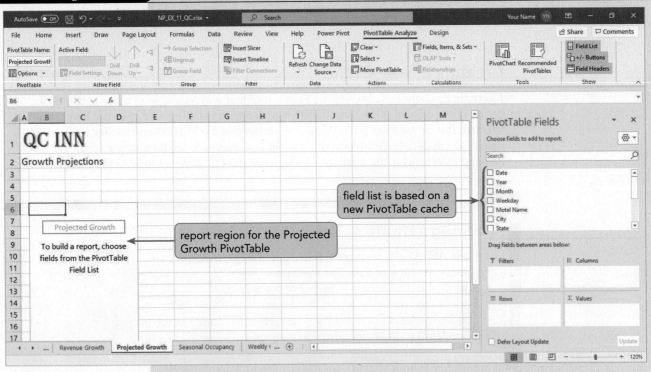

With the Projected Growth PivotTable generated from a new cache, you are ready to create a PivotTable projecting future revenue. That table will involve using calculated items and calculated fields.

Insight

Counting Your Caches

In a workbook with multiple PivotTables and multiple caches, you might want to know exactly how many caches are in use. Excel does not provide a direct way to get that information, but you can view it using the Excel programming language, Visual Basic for Applications (VBA). To view the total number of caches in your workbook at any given time, do the following:

1. Press ALT+F11 to open the Visual Basic Editor window.
2. Press CTRL+G to open a window in which you can immediately enter VBA commands.
3. Type `?ActiveWorkbook.PivotCaches.Count` and press ENTER. Excel returns a count of caches in the workbook.
4. Press ALT+Q to close the Visual Basic editor and return to the workbook.

Each PivotTable cache is given an index number. The first PivotTable cache is given an index of 1, the second an index of 2, and so forth. To identify the index number of the cache used for a specific PivotTable, select any cell in the PivotTable and then press ALT+F11, press CTRL+G, and enter the command `?ActiveCell.PivotTable.CacheIndex`. Excel will return the index number of the cache. Press ALT+Q to close the editor and return to your PivotTable.

Working with Calculated Items and Calculated Fields

PivotTables are not limited to the list of calculations supplied by Excel. You can enter your own formulas to create calculated items and calculated fields. First, you'll explore how to create a calculated item.

Creating a Calculated Item

A **calculated item** is a user-defined formula for calculations between items within a PivotTable field. For example, within the Motel Name field, you could create a calculated item that calculates the difference between the revenue of one group of motels and another. A calculated item appears as a new item within the field and can be moved, sorted, and filtered just like any other items. However, because it's a calculated item, any changes to the data are automatically reflected in its value.

Calculated items are part of the PivotTable cache. This means that a calculated item in one PivotTable is available to all PivotTables using the same cache. Be aware that calculated items cannot be shared between PivotTables that use different caches.

Reference

Creating a Calculated Item or Calculated Field

- Select any cell in a PivotTable field.
- On the PivotTable Analyze tab, in the Calculations group, click the Fields, Items, & Sets button.
- Click Calculated Item or click Calculated Field.
- Enter a name for the calculated item or field.
- In the Formula box, for a calculated item enter a formula that performs calculations on items within a field or for a calculated field, enter a formula that performs calculations between fields in the PivotTable's data source.
- Click OK.

You will create a PivotTable now that shows the revenue generated for each year and motel. Then, you will create a calculated item that projects next year's values.

To create a PivotTable of 2023 and 2024 performance:

▶ **1.** With the Projected Growth PivotTable still selected, drag the **Motel Name** field to the Filters area box, drag the **Year** field to the Rows area box, and then drag the **Revenue** field to the Values area box.

▶ **2.** Change Value field name from "Sum of Revenue" to **Total Revenue** and display the revenue totals as currency.

▶ **3.** Change the PivotTable layout to a Tabular layout and remove all grand totals from the table. See Figure 11–36.

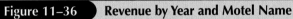

Figure 11–36   Revenue by Year and Motel Name

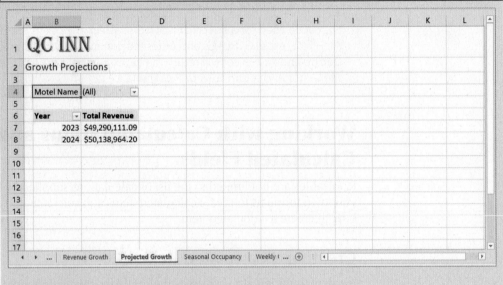

To project next year's revenue based on the 2023 and 2024 values, Anna assumes that revenues will increase at the same rate they increased between 2023 and 2024. The formula to calculate the 2025 revenue is:

$$2025\ revenue = (2024\ revenue) \times \frac{2024\ revenue}{2023\ revenue}$$

You'll create a calculated item based on this formula and add it to the PivotTable.

To create a calculated item that calculates the 2025 revenue:

▶ **1.** Click cell **B6** to select a cell in the Year column.

▶ **2.** On the ribbon, click the **PivotTable Analyze** tab. In the Calculations group, click the **Fields, Items, & Sets** button, and then click **Calculated Item**. The Insert Calculated Item in "Year" dialog box opens.

▶ **3.** Type **2025 (Projected)** in the Name box to change the name from Formula1, and then press **TAB** to go the Formula box.

▶ **4.** Type **=** to begin the formula, click **2024** in the Items box, and then click **Insert Item**.

5. Type ***(** to continue the formula, click **2024** in the Items box, and then click **Insert Item**.

6. Type **/** for the division operator, click **2023** in the Items box, click **Insert Item**, and then type **)** to finish the formula. The complete formula `='2024'*('2024'/'2023')` is entered the Formulas box. See Figure 11–37.

Figure 11–37   **Insert Calculated Item in "Year" dialog box**

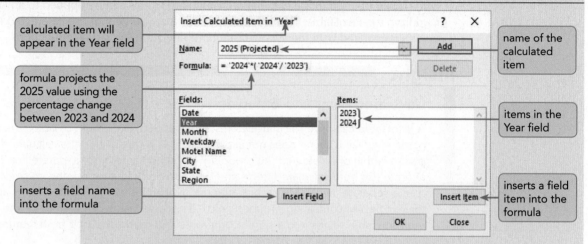

7. Click **OK**. The 2025 (Projected) formula is entered as a calculated item into the PivotTable and projected total revenue for all motels is displayed in cell C9. See Figure 11–38.

Figure 11–38   **Projection of 2025 total revenue**

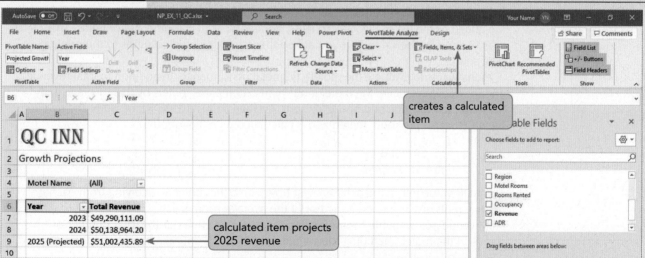

Next, you'll view projected revenues for individual motels within the QC Inn chain.

8. Click the **Filter** button in cell C4, select **Rapid City Inn** from the list of motels, and then click **OK**. The 2025 revenue for this motel is calculated in cell C9 as $3,752,993.55, which is a projected increase of about $168,000.

9. Click the **Filter** button in cell C4, click **Lincoln Motel** in the motel list, and then click **OK** to view the projected income for the Lincoln Motel.

If 2025 continues the trend shown in 2024, this motel's revenue will drop to $1,815,138.03, which is a decrease of almost $390,000.

▶ **10.** Click the **Filter** button in cell C4, select **(All)** to remove the filter, and then click **OK**. The PivotTable again shows projected revenue across all motels.

Note that in the formula for the calculated item, you never specified that the revenue field should be used in the calculation. Calculated items can be applied to any numeric field from the PivotTable. The only exception is that you cannot use calculated items for fields summarized with the average, standard deviation, or variance functions.

Insight

Calculated Items and Grouping

A PivotTable can have calculated items and grouped fields, but not both. The structure of the PivotTable cache does not allow for it. This is true even if the calculated item is placed within one field and the grouping is done on an entirely separate field. If you need to use both calculated items and grouped fields in a report, the best option is to create separate PivotTable caches: one for PivotTables with calculated items and one for PivotTables containing grouped fields. If necessary, you can then copy and paste the PivotTable values into a single comprehensive report showing both features.

Creating a Calculated Field

Where a calculated item performs calculations on items within a field, a **calculated field** is a user-defined formula for calculations across one or more fields. For example, a calculated field could multiply the value of a Rooms Rented field and a Price per Room field to return the total income generated from all the room rentals. Calculated fields are added to the list of PivotTable fields, appearing as just another set of fields. The effect would be the same as if you added them as calculated columns to the original data source.

Anna wants to evaluate the motel's financial performance. In addition to total revenue and the occupancy rate, the motel industry also compares motels by their average daily rate and their revenue per available room. Average daily rate (ADR) measures the revenue the motel earns per room rented and is calculated with the formula:

$$ADR = \frac{Revenue}{Rooms\ Rented}$$

The ADR value tells a financial analyst how much the motel is receiving from each room it rents and is a good indicator of the average room price.

Revenue per available room (RevPar) measures revenue per the total number of rooms in the motel (including the vacant rooms) and is calculated with the formula:

$$RevPar = \frac{Revenue}{Motel\ Rooms}$$

The RevPar value tells an analyst how the average price per room is affected by vacancies. A motel might have a very high ADR value if its rooms are expensive but a low RevPar value if it can't fill those rooms. Such a situation might lead a motel owner to reduce prices to attract more business and increase total revenue even though the revenue per rented room is lower.

The Motels data source doesn't include an ADR or RevPar field. Anna wants you to add these to the PivotTable as calculated fields, showing values for 2023 and 2024 and projecting those values into 2025. You will start by creating a calculated field to calculate ADR.

To create a calculated field for ADR:

1. On the PivotTable Analyze tab, in the Calculations group, click **Fields, Items, & Sets**, and then click **Calculated Field**. The Insert Calculated Field dialog box opens.

2. Enter **ADR** in the Name box, and then press **TAB**.

3. In the Formula box, type **=** to begin the formula, click **Revenue** in the Fields list, and then click **Insert Field**.

4. Type **/** for the division operator, click **Rooms Rented** in the Fields list, and then click **Insert Field**. The formula =Revenue/'Rooms Rented' appears in the Formula box. See Figure 11–39.

Figure 11–39   Insert Calculated Field dialog box

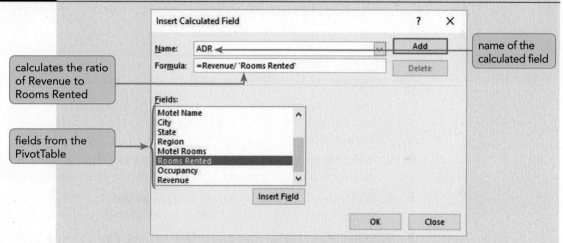

calculates the ratio of Revenue to Rooms Rented

fields from the PivotTable

name of the calculated field

5. Click **OK**. The Sum of ADR is added to the PivotTable with ADR calculations based on all the motels in the data source.

6. Click cell **D6** to select it, and then in the Active Field group, change the value of the Active Field box from Sum of ADR to **ADR** followed by a blank space to avoid conflict with the calculated field name. See Figure 11–40.

Figure 11–40   Calculated ADR values

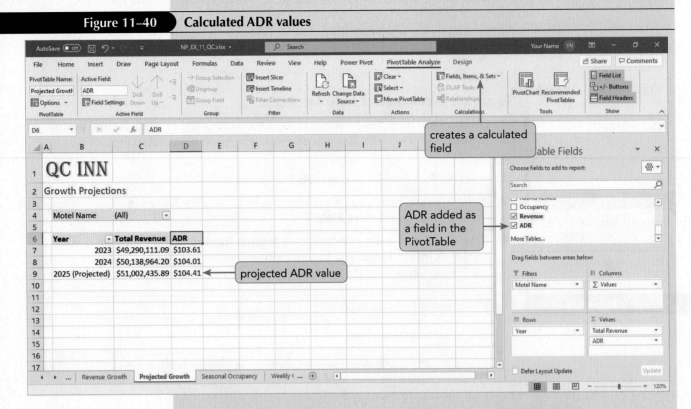

The average price of a rented room across all motels is currently about $104 and rising slightly in the upcoming year. You'll see how individual motels compare to this.

7. In the Motel Name filter, select **Rapid City Inn**. The ADR value for a rented room at the motel is nearly $111, projected to drop slightly in 2025.

8. In the Motel Name filter, select **Lincoln Motel**. The average price of a rented room at that motel is about $86, projected to drop slightly as well in 2025.

9. In the Motel Name filter, select **(All)** to once again show the ADR values from across all motels in the QC Inn chain.

You'll use the same process to add RevPar as a calculated field to the PivotTable.

To create a calculated field for RevPar:

1. On the PivotTable Analyze tab, in the Calculations group, click the **Fields, Items, & Sets** button, and then click **Calculated Field**. The Insert Calculated Field dialog box opens.

2. In the Name box Enter **RevPar** as the field name, and then press **TAB**.

3. In the Formula box, enter **=Revenue/'Motel Rooms'** as the formula, using the Fields box and the Insert Field button.

4. Click **OK** to create the calculated field and return to the workbook.

5. Click cell **E6** and change the value the Active Fields box from Sum of RevPar to **RevPar** followed by a blank space. See Figure 11–41.

Figure 11–41	Calculated RevPar values

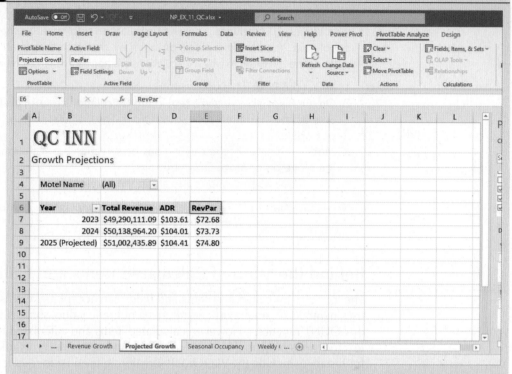

For all motels in the QC Inn chain, the revenue per room is projected to increase from $73.73 in 2024 to $74.80 in 2025. Again, you'll compare this to individual motels.

6. In the Motel Name filter, select **Rapid City Inn**. The RevPar value for that motel is $83.01 in the current year and is projected to rise by more than $3 to $86.66, indicating that the motel is becoming more profitable to the chain.

7. In the Motel Name filter, select **Lincoln Motel**. RevPar values for that motel have steadily declined from $59.12 in 2023 to $48.56 in 2024 and projected to drop further to $39.89 in 2025.

8. In the Motel Name filter, select **(All)** to return to the RevPar values for all motels in the chain.

9. Save the workbook, and then close it.

The RevPar numbers for the Lincoln Motel are particularly concerning to Anna. The low RevPar score indicates that the motel might be having problems getting business and that the motel might want to lower its prices to attract more customers and fill more rooms. The other alternatives are to attract more customers through customer incentives and reward programs, upgrading the facilities, and flexible pricing models that will take advantage of periods of high customer demand.

Insight

Setting the Solve Order for Calculated Items

The value shown in a PivotTable cell might be the result of applying several calculated items and fields. If you find that a cell is displaying an unexpected or wrong value, it could be a problem with the order of calculations. Excel has rules that determine which calculations are done first. But in some situations, performing the calculations in different orders produces different results. For example, doubling a cell's value and then adding 10 produces a different result than adding 10 to the cell's value and then doubling it. You can correct this problem by changing the default order.

To define the order in which calculations are applied within a PivotTable, do the following:

1. Select the PivotTable you want to reorder calculations for.
2. On the PivotTable Analyze tab, in the Calculations group, click the Fields, Items & Sets button, and then click Solve Order. The Calculated Item Solve Order dialog box opens.
3. Modify the order of the calculations by selecting a calculation formula and clicking the Move Up or Move Down buttons.
4. Click Close when the formulas are in the correct order.

Note that when you change the order of the formulas, the new order will be applied to all calculated items in that PivotTable.

Behind the Math of Calculated Items and Fields

The formulas for calculated items and fields can accept any worksheet function that uses numbers as arguments and returns a numeric value, such as the AVERAGE, SUM, or COUNT functions. However, calculated items and calculated formulas cannot use text functions nor can they reference data outside of the PivotTable. You could not, for instance, include the VLOOKUP function in formula for a calculated item or field because it will reference data outside of the PivotTable. Only data residing within another PivotTable field or entered explicitly as a constant is available.

The other important factor to consider is that calculated fields are always based on sums of fields. For example, the ADR calculations shown in Figure 11–40 are the equivalent of taking the sum of the revenue from all the motels and dividing that sum by the total number of rented rooms. But because calculated fields are limited to sums, you could not, for example, create a calculated field from an average value, such as the average occupancy rate.

The fact that calculated fields are limited only to sums can lead to incorrect results. Figure 11–42 shows a PivotTable that multiplies the value of the Rooms Rented field by the value of the Price per Room field to create the Total Income calculated field.

Figure 11–42	Calculated formulas applied to grand totals

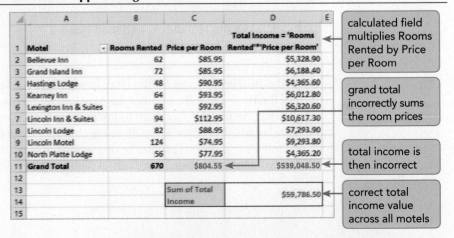

	Motel	Rooms Rented	Price per Room	Total Income = "Rooms Rented"*"Price per Room"	
1					
2	Bellevue Inn	62	$85.95	$5,328.90	
3	Grand Island Inn	72	$85.95	$6,188.40	
4	Hastings Lodge	48	$90.95	$4,365.60	
5	Kearney Inn	64	$93.95	$6,012.80	
6	Lexington Inn & Suites	68	$92.95	$6,320.60	
7	Lincoln Inn & Suites	94	$112.95	$10,617.30	
8	Lincoln Lodge	82	$88.95	$7,293.90	
9	Lincoln Motel	124	$74.95	$9,293.80	
10	North Platte Lodge	56	$77.95	$4,365.20	
11	Grand Total	670	$804.55	$539,048.50	
12					
13			Sum of Total Income	$59,786.50	
14					
15					

calculated field multiplies Rooms Rented by Price per Room

grand total incorrectly sums the room prices

total income is then incorrect

correct total income value across all motels

The total income calculations are fine and reasonable for individual motels but make no sense when applied to the grand total because you would not sum the price of individual rooms to calculate total income across all rooms. You always want to confirm that the values a calculated field is summing should, in fact, be summed. It many cases, you will want to avoid displaying subtotals and grand totals for tables that involve calculated fields. Another way to solve this problem is to create a calculated measure, which you'll do in the next session.

Proskills

Written Communication: Documenting PivotTables

As PivotTables grow in size and complexity, it is helpful to document your work for others. You should always give PivotTable fields and calculations clear and descriptive names. Choose formats that are appropriate for the type of data you are displaying and apply conditional formats if possible to highlight key features in your tables.

You should document any customized calculations used in a PivotTable somewhere in the workbook. You can create the documentation sheet, or you can have Excel create a list of calculated items and fields by doing the following:

1. Select the PivotTable whose calculated items and fields you want to document.
2. On the PivotTable Analyze tab, in the Calculations group, click the Fields, Items, & Sets button, and then click List Formulas.

Excel will create a new worksheet describing all the calculated items and fields, including the name of the items and the fields, the formulas involved, and the solution order. This is a static list, so if you add to or edit your calculated items and fields, you must regenerate the list of formulas.

You have finished designing PivotTables for the data in the Motels table. In the next session, you will explore design issues involved with creating PivotTables from data stored in an Excel Data Model.

Review

Session 11.2 Quick Check

1. How do you display the rank (smallest to largest) of a PivotTable field?
2. Conditional formats can be applied to which parts of a PivotTable?
3. What is the PivotTable cache?
4. If motels are grouped by size in one PivotTable, how are they displayed in other PivotTables sharing the same cache?
5. How do you create a PivotTable with its own cache?
6. What is the difference between a calculated item and a calculated field?
7. How is the value of a calculated field summarized within a PivotTable?
8. What is a potential mistake you could make with calculated fields?

Session 11.3 Visual Overview:

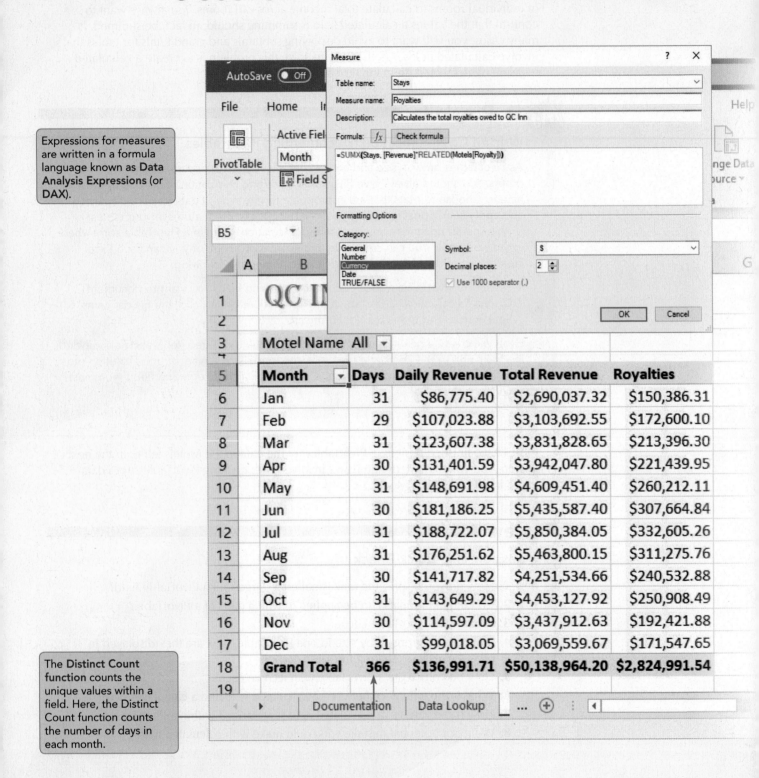

Expressions for measures are written in a formula language known as **Data Analysis Expressions (or DAX).**

Measure ? ✕

Table name: Stays

Measure name: Royalties

Description: Calculates the total royalties owed to QC Inn

Formula: *fx* | Check formula

=SUMX(Stays, [Revenue]*RELATED(Motels[Royalty]))

Formatting Options

Category:
General
Number
Currency
Date
TRUE/FALSE

Symbol: $

Decimal places: 2

☑ Use 1000 separator (,)

OK | Cancel

QC IN

Motel Name All ▾

Month ▾	Days	Daily Revenue	Total Revenue	Royalties
Jan	31	$86,775.40	$2,690,037.32	$150,386.31
Feb	29	$107,023.88	$3,103,692.55	$172,600.10
Mar	31	$123,607.38	$3,831,828.65	$213,396.30
Apr	30	$131,401.59	$3,942,047.80	$221,439.95
May	31	$148,691.98	$4,609,451.40	$260,212.11
Jun	30	$181,186.25	$5,435,587.40	$307,664.84
Jul	31	$188,722.07	$5,850,384.05	$332,605.26
Aug	31	$176,251.62	$5,463,800.15	$311,275.76
Sep	30	$141,717.82	$4,251,534.66	$240,532.88
Oct	31	$143,649.29	$4,453,127.92	$250,908.49
Nov	30	$114,597.09	$3,437,912.63	$192,421.88
Dec	31	$99,018.05	$3,069,559.67	$171,547.65
Grand Total	**366**	**$136,991.71**	**$50,138,964.20**	**$2,824,991.54**

Documentation | Data Lookup | ... ⊕

The **Distinct Count** function counts the unique values within a field. Here, the Distinct Count function counts the number of days in each month.

PivotTable Measures

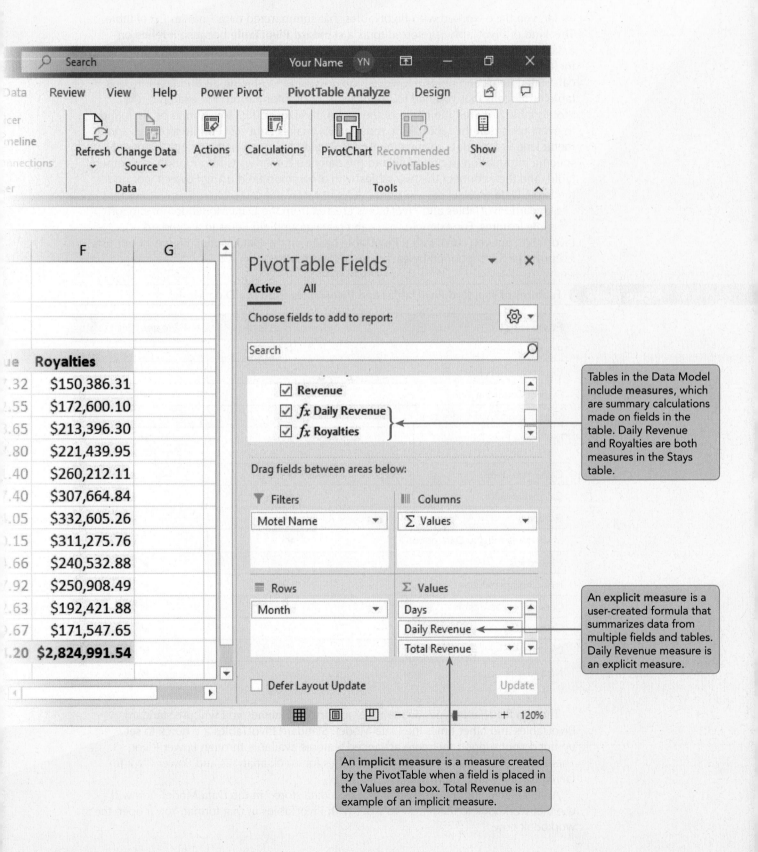

Tables in the Data Model include measures, which are summary calculations made on fields in the table. Daily Revenue and Royalties are both measures in the Stays table.

An explicit measure is a user-created formula that summarizes data from multiple fields and tables. Daily Revenue measure is an explicit measure.

An implicit measure is a measure created by the PivotTable when a field is placed in the Values area box. Total Revenue is an example of an implicit measure.

Introducing PivotTable Design Under the Data Model

So far, you have worked with PivotTables that summarized data from an Excel table. This kind of PivotTable is referred to as a **standard PivotTable** because it relies on a data source within the workbook, such as an Excel table or a data range, and includes many standard tools such as automatic sorting of dates, grouping, and calculated items and fields. However, the downside to placing all the data into one table or range is that you had to duplicate a lot of information. For example, the Motels table required the name of the motel, its size, and its location to be included in every record in the table. Such redundancy makes data susceptible to errors and is inefficient. From a data management perspective, it's much better to put the motel-specific information in one table and the daily customer visits information in another table, and then connect the two tables with a common field using Power Pivot under the Excel Data Model.

Standard PivotTables and PivotTables created from the Data Model do not support the same features. For example, you can create group field items in a standard PivotTable, but you can't with a PivotTable based on the Data Model. Figure 11–43 lists features that are supported by each type of PivotTable.

Figure 11–43 | **Features of standard PivotTables and PivotTables from the Data Model**

Feature	Standard PivotTable	Data Model PivotTable
Product function	✔	
Count Numbers function	✔	
Distinct Count function		✔
Show Report Filter Pages tool	✔	
Drill into a PivotTable cell	✔	✔ (first 1000 rows)
Calculated items	✔	
Calculated fields	✔	
Grouping	✔	
Show Items with No Data option	✔	
Hierarchies		✔
Including filtered items in totals		✔
Connect multiple tables		✔
Calculated measures		✔
DAX functions		✔
Named sets		✔

The two PivotTable types are complementary: Sometimes you will use standard PivotTables and other times the Data Model. Standard PivotTables are quick to set up but do not support the more advanced features available through Power Pivot. Therefore, you might use standard PivotTables for quick analyses and Power Pivot for large projects with custom applications.

Anna created another workbook that uses data stored in the Data Model. You will use that workbook to learn how to work with PivotTables in that format. You'll open the workbook now.

To open the Data Model workbook:

▶ **1.** Open the **NP_EX_11–2.xlsx** workbook located in the **Excel11 > Module** folder included with your Data Files, and then save the workbook as **NP_EX_11_Inn** in the location specified by your instructor.

▶ **2.** In the Documentation worksheet, enter your name and the date.

▶ **3.** On the ribbon, click the **Power Pivot** tab, and then in the Data Model group, click the **Manage** button. Power Pivot opens.

▶ **4.** On the Home tab, in the View group, click the **Diagram View** button to display the relationship between the Motels and Stays tables.

▶ **5.** Close Power Pivot and return to the workbook.

The Motels table contains information about the 24 QC Inn motels in Nebraska and South Dakota. The Stays table describes daily stays at the motels during 2024. The Motels and Stays tables are connected via the common field Motel ID in a one-to-many relationship.

Insight

Named Sets and the Data Model

In a standard PivotTable, the combination of fields is repeated for every PivotTable level. For example, you can't choose to display one set of months for one year in your PivotTable and a different set of months for a different year. You must display the same set of months for both years.

PivotTables based on the Data Model allow for **named sets** to define which fields are displayed within each part of the PivotTable. The named set feature allows for asymmetric PivotTables in which the list of fields can differ within the same PivotTable. This means you could display one set of financial calculations for one year and a different set for another year.

To create a named set, on the PivotTable Analyze tab, in the Calculations group, click the Field, Items, & Sets button. You can then choose to define sets based on items in the PivotTable rows or PivotTable columns. Named sets are very useful in removing extraneous or irrelevant data from a final PivotTable report.

Calculating Distinct Counts

A distinct count is a count of the unique values from a field, which is different from the COUNT function which counts both unique values and duplicates. The DISTINCT COUNT function is available in PivotTables created from the Data Model.

You will use distinct counts in a PivotTable that analyzes daily sales across all the motels in the Nebraska/South Dakota sales territory. You'll begin creating this PivotTable by calculating the number of days within each month that the motels were open.

To begin creating the PivotTable:

▶ **1.** Go to the **Daily Revenue** worksheet. A PivotTable report area named "Daily Revenue" has already been set up in this worksheet.

▶ **2.** Drag the **Month** field from the Stays table into the Rows area box, drag the **Date** field from the Stays table into the Values area box, and then drag the **Motel Name** field from the Motels table into the Filters area box.

▶ **3.** Change the format of the Count of Date field to a number value with no decimal places.

With Data Model PivotTables, month names are not automatically sorted in chronological order. You'll apply the custom sort list that Excel provides for sorting by month.

▶ **4.** Click the **Filter** button in cell B6, and then click **More Sort Options**. The Sort (Month) dialog box opens.

▶ **5.** Click the **Ascending (A to Z) by** option button and verify that **Month** appears in the box.

▶ **6.** Click **More Options**. The More Sort Options (Month) dialog box opens.

▶ **7.** Click the **Sort automatically every time the report is updated** check box to deselect it.

▶ **8.** Click the **First key sort order** box and click the **Jan, Feb, Mar…** custom list.

▶ **9.** Click **OK** in each dialog box to return to the workbook. Figure 11–44 shows the current PivotTable.

Figure 11–44	PivotTable of Count of Date

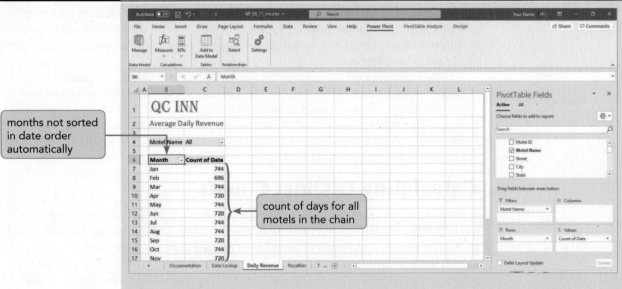

months not sorted in date order automatically

count of days for all motels in the chain

The PivotTable shows a count of days from every motel within every month. For example, the day count in January is 744 because there are 31 days in January multiplied by 24 motels, which equals 744 days. However, because Anna wants to count the number of days across all motels and doesn't want to count the same day more than once, you will replace the COUNT function in the PivotTable with the DISTINCTCOUNT function.

To calculate the distinct count of days:

▶ **1.** Click cell **C6** containing the Count of Date label to select it.

▶ **2.** On the ribbon, click the **PivotTable Analyze** tab, and then in the Active Field group, click the **Field Settings** button. The Value Field Settings dialog box opens.

▶ **3.** Scroll down the list of summary functions and select **Distinct Count**.

▶ **4.** In the Custom Name box, change the label from "Distinct Count of Date" to **Days**.

▶ **5.** Click **OK** to return to the workbook. The number of days in each month is now shown in column C.

You will use the distinct count of the days to determine the average number of customers per day at all of the QC Inn motels in the Nebraska/South Dakota sales territory. You can do this calculation by creating a measure.

Creating a Measure

Because PivotTables based on the Power Pivot Data Model do not support calculated fields, you must define a measure, which is a calculation that summarizes data from a Data Model table. PivotTables use two types of measures: implicit and explicit.

An implicit measure is a measure created by the PivotTable when a field is placed in the Values area box. For example, placing the Revenue field in the Values area creates the implicit measure "Sum of Revenue" to calculate a total revenue for each cell in the PivotTable. Implicit measures are limited to the standard summary functions: SUM, COUNT, MIN, MAX, AVG, and DISTINCTCOUNT and can be used only within a PivotTable or PivotChart.

An explicit measure is a user-created formula that summarizes data from multiple fields and tables. Measures become part of a data table's structure and are available to PivotTables, PivotCharts, and any application that can access the Data Model.

A crucial point to understand is that a measure provides the formula for summarizing data, but the data is determined by the PivotTable. Just like an implicit measure that calculates an average can be applied across different cells within a PivotTable, an explicit measure acts the same way. In writing a measure, you are telling Excel how to calculate a value; the PivotTable determines where it's applied.

Introducing DAX

An explicit measure is written in the formula language Data Analysis Expressions, or more commonly known as DAX. It's beyond the scope of this module to go deeply into the syntax of DAX. However, DAX uses many of the same functions used with Excel worksheets and Excel tables, so you can apply what you've learned about those topics to get started in writing your own measures in DAX.

For example, a reference to the Rooms Rented field would be written as `[Rooms Rented]`. To create a measure that calculates the sum of the Rooms Rented field, apply the formula `=SUM([Rooms Rented])`. If you need to specify the table, insert the table name prior to the field name, as in the expression `=SUM(Stays[Rooms Rented])` which calculates the sum of the Room Rented field from the Stays table.

Reference

Adding a Measure to a Data Model table

- On the Power Pivot tab, in the Calculations group, click the Measures button, and then click New Measure.
- In the Measures dialog box, specify the table that will contain the measure and the name of the measure.
- Enter the DAX formula for the measure.
- Specify the output format of the measure.
- Click OK to apply the measure to the table.

DAX is a powerful language. As you develop your Excel skills, knowledge of DAX and its uses will be essential for creating powerful and sophisticated Excel reports and applications. In this session, you'll just get started.

Adding a Measure to a Table

Measures are always associated with a table in the Data Model, and they become part of that table's definition. Anna wants you to create a measure for the Stays table that calculates the average number of motel rooms rented each day across the QC Inn chain. To calculate that value, you will divide the sum of the Rooms Rented field by a distinct count of the number of days. The measure formula written in DAX is:

`=SUM([Rooms Rented])/DISTINCTCOUNT([Date])`

You will create this measure the Measure dialog box.

To create a measure calculating the daily average motel rooms rented:

1. On the ribbon, click the **Power Pivot** tab. In the Calculations group, click the **Measures** button, and then click **New Measure**. The Measure dialog box opens.

2. Click the **Table Name arrow**, and then click **Stays** to add this measure to the Stays table.

> You must select the Stays table so that the measure is associated with the correct table in the Data Model.

3. Press **TAB**, and then type **Daily Rentals** in the Measure name box.

4. Press **TAB**, and then type **Average rooms rented daily at QC Inn motels** in the Description box.

5. Click after the = symbol in the Formula box, and then type **SUM(** to begin the formula. Note that as you type, Excel provides a list of functions, tables, and fields you can insert into the formula.

6. Double-click **[Rooms Rented]** from the field list to insert this field into the formula, and then type **)** to complete the SUM function.

> **Tip**
>
> You can check for errors in a formula by clicking the Check formula button.

7. Type **/DISTINCTCOUNT(** as the next part of the formula, double-click **[Date]** in the fields list, and then type **)** to complete the formula. The formula `=SUM([Rooms Rented])/DISTINCTCOUNT([Date])` appears in the Formula box.

8. Click **Number** in the Category box and change the number of decimals displayed by the measure to **0**. See Figure 11–45.

Figure 11–45   Measure dialog box

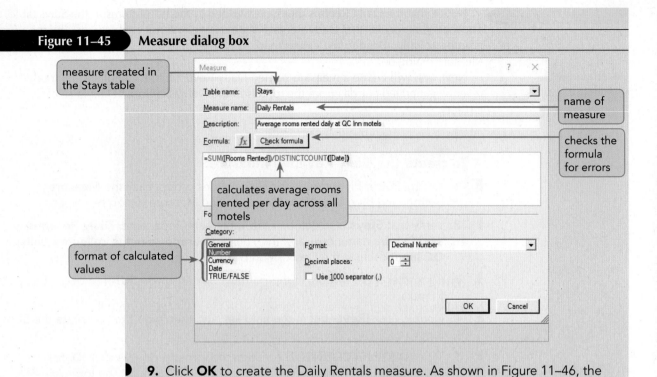

9. Click **OK** to create the Daily Rentals measure. As shown in Figure 11–46, the measure is added as a new column to the PivotTable.

Figure 11–46   PivotTable of the Daily Rentals measure

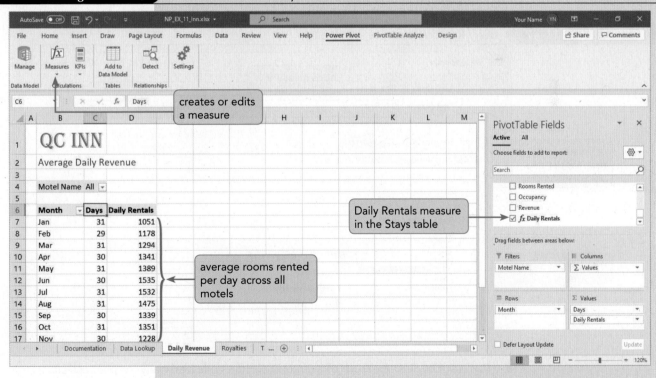

Based on the Daily Rentals measure, you learn that on a typical day in January 2024 that 1,051 rooms are rented from all the motels in the Nebraska/South Dakota sales territory. That number rises by almost 500 to 1,535 on a typical day in June. Overall in 2024, the Nebraska/South Dakota sales territory was hosting about 1,317 customers per day (cell D19).

Tip

Measures become part of the table structure and are available to any new PivotTable that uses that table.

Notice that the Daily Rentals measure is added to the list of items in the Stays table. The icon f_x indicates that Daily Rentals is a measure and not a table field. The measure is automatically added to the Values field, using the label name you specified in the Measure dialog box.

Next, you will create a measure named Daily Revenue that calculates the total revenue generated per day from the motels in the Nebraska/South Dakota sales territory.

To create the Daily Revenue measure:

▶ 1. On the Power Pivot tab, in the Calculations group, click the **Measures** button, and then click **New Measure**. The Measure dialog box opens.

▶ 2. Verify that **Stays** is selected in the Table name box, enter **Daily Revenue** in the Measure name box, and then enter **Average revenue collected daily at QC Inn motels** in the Description box.

▶ 3. Click after the = symbol in the Formula box and type **SUM(** to begin the formula.

▶ 4. Double-click **[Revenue]** in the field list, and then type **)** to complete the SUM function.

▶ 5. Type **/DISTINCTCOUNT(** to continue the formula, double-click **[Date]** in the fields list, and then type **)** to complete the formula. The formula =SUM([Revenue])/DISTINCTCOUNT([Date]) appears in the Formula box.

▶ 6. Click **Currency** in the Category box to display the values as currency. See Figure 11–47.

Figure 11–47 **Daily Revenue measure**

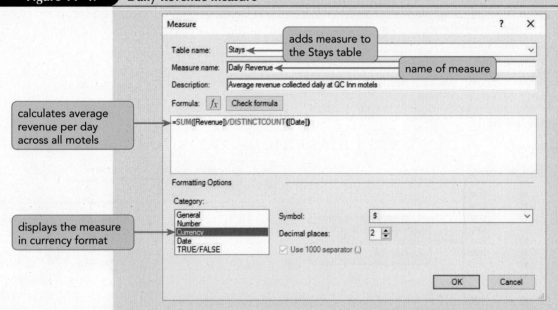

▶ 7. Click **OK**. The measure of average revenue collected daily from across all motels is shown in column E. See Figure 11–48.

Figure 11–48   **Average daily revenue across all motels**

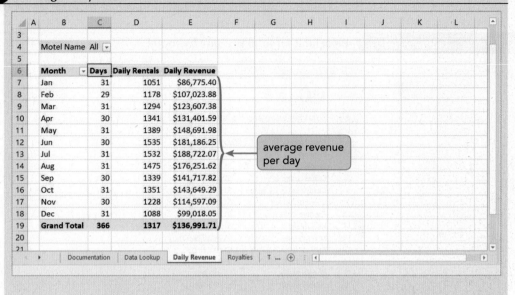

average revenue per day

Tip

To view average daily revenues at specific motels, select the motel name from the PivotTable filter.

In January 2024, the Nebraska/South Dakota sales territory took in more than $86,000 on an average day. In July, at the height of the tourist season, the typical daily revenue collected for the territory was almost $189,000. To view average daily rentals and revenues for other combinations of motels and dates, Anna has only to change the structure of the PivotTable. The Daily Rentals and Daily Revenue measures will automatically recalculate for each cell in the new PivotTable.

The revenues collected by the 24 motels do not all go to QC Inn because the company franchises its motels. Instead, the company receives a percentage, or royalty, of the revenue in exchange for administrative help, infrastructure, advertising, and the right to use the QC Inn name.

Anna wants to track the total royalties collected from the Nebraska/South Dakota motels in the past year. To do that calculation, you will create a measure using data from multiple tables.

Calculating Measures Across Tables and Rows

The great power of DAX and Power Pivot becomes apparent when you need to combine data from multiple tables in a wide variety of ways. In this case, you want to combine data from two tables: the Revenue field from the Stays table that records the amount of revenue collected by each motel and the Royalty field from the Motels table that provides each motel's royalty rate. Motel franchises in the QC Inn chain will pay royalties from 4% of revenue up to 7% based on the contract between the franchise owner and the company.

Anna wants a PivotTable that shows the revenue and royalties for each motel. You will start creating this PivotTable now by inserting a column of total revenue.

To create a PivotTable of total revenue:

▶ **1.** Go to the **Royalties** worksheet.

▶ **2.** In the PivotTable Fields pane, click **All** to see all of the tables in the Data Model.

▶ **3.** Drag the **Motel Name** field from the Motels table into the Rows area box.

> **4.** Drag the **Revenue** field from the Stays table into the Values area, and then change the label from Sum of Revenue to **Total Revenue**. See Figure 11–49.

Figure 11–49 | **PivotTable of total revenue by motel**

To calculate the total royalties owed to the company, you'll multiply the revenue collected by the motel's royalty rate. For example, if a motel collects $10,000 in revenue at a 6% royalty rate, it will owe the chain ($10,000) x (6%) = $600. Anna wants to use this calculation to sum the total royalties QC Inn collects from its franchised motels.

The RELATED Function

For every royalty calculation, you need to use the value of the Royalty field for the motel. You can look up a value from a table in the Data Model using the RELATED function

```
RELATED(Table[field])
```

where `Table[field]` is the table and *field* is the field to retrieve the data from. So, to retrieve the value of the Royalty field in the Motels table, the expression is:

```
RELATED(Motels[Royalty])
```

Tip

You must have defined a table relation to use the RELATED function.

The RELATED function acts like a lookup table, but there's no lookup value. So how does the formula know where to find the correct royalty rate? The answer is that the relation between the Stays table and Motels table has already been defined in the Data Model. If you know the motel that generated the revenue, the table relation tells which record in the Motels table to use for the royalty rate.

The SUMX Function

Royalties are calculated by multiplying revenue by the value of the royalty field. At first, you might try the following formula that multiplies the sum of the Revenue field in the Stays table by the value of the Royalty field in the Motels table:

```
=SUM(Stays[Revenue])*RELATED(Motels[Royalty])
```

But this formula would not work. Nothing in the expression SUM(Stays[Revenue]) indicates which revenue figures are being summed. You could be summing revenues from one motel or from several motels, each with a different royalty rate. Remember that the measure provides the formula, but the PivotTable supplies the data. There's no way to match the sum of the revenues to a single royalty rate.

Instead, you want to calculate the royalty owed each time revenue is collected by a motel and then add those royalties to get the total royalties paid to the company. That kind of sum, which proceeds through a table row-by-row, is calculated using the following SUMX function:

SUMX(*table, expression*)

where *table* is the table to go through row-by-row, and *expression* is an expression to calculate on each row of the table. SUMX then returns the sum of all those individual calculations. So, the expression

[Revenue]*RELATED(Motels[Royalty])

calculates the royalty on a single transaction, which you can then nest within the following SUMX function to sum all the calculations for every record in the Stays table:

SUMX(Stays, [Revenue]*RELATED(Motels[Royalty]))

This measure can then be added to a PivotTable to calculate total royalties for any combination of motels or dates within the year. You'll add this formula as a measure named Royalties to the PivotTable in the Royalties worksheet.

To create the Royalties measure:

▶ **1.** On the ribbon, click the **Power Pivot** tab. In the Calculations group, click the **Measures** button, and then click **New Measure**. The Measure dialog box opens.

▶ **2.** Verify that **Stays** is selected in the Table name box.

▶ **3.** Change the name of the measure to **Royalties** and enter the description **Calculates the total royalties owed to QC Inn** in the Description box.

▶ **4.** In the Formula box after the = symbol, type **SUMX(Stays, [Revenue]*RELATED(Motels[Royalty]))** to enter the formula. Remember, you can avoid typing mistakes by selecting table names, field names, and function names from the box that appears within the Formula box.

▶ **5.** Click **Check formula** to confirm the expression you entered contains no syntax errors.

Trouble? If Excel reports an error, you probably mistyped the formula. Common errors include missing parentheses or square brackets around the field names. Check your formula against the formula in Step 4, correct any mistakes, and then repeat Step 5. If you are still having problems entering the formula correctly, you can copy the expression from the Terms and Definitions worksheet.

▶ **6.** In the Category box, click **Currency** to display the Royalties measure as currency. See Figure 11–50.

Figure 11–50   **Royalties measure**

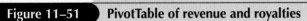

sums royalty values over each record in the Stays table

calculates royalty due for each revenue value

displays total royalties as currency

Measure	?	×

Table name: Stays

Measure name: Royalties

Description: Calculates the total royalties owed to QC Inn

Formula: f_x Check formula

=SUMX(Stays, [Revenue]*RELATED(Motels[Royalty]))

✓ No errors in formula.

Formatting Options

Category:
General
Number
Currency
Date
TRUE/FALSE

Symbol: $

Decimal places: 2

☑ Use 1000 separator (,)

OK   Cancel

7. Click **OK**. The Royalties measure is added to the PivotTable.

8. Click the **Filter button** in cell B4, and then click **More Sort Options**. The Sort (Motel Name) dialog box opens.

9. Click the **Descending (Z to A)** option button, and then select **Royalties** in the box.

10. Click **OK** to return to the PivotTable. The PivotTable is sorted in descending order of royalties. See Figure 11–51.

Figure 11–51   **PivotTable of revenue and royalties**

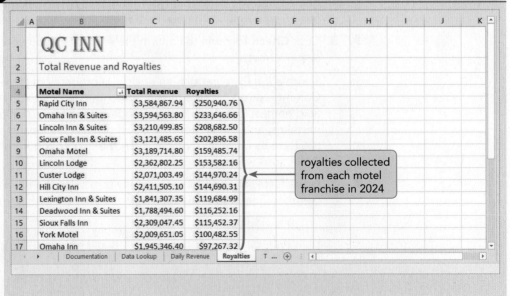

royalties collected from each motel franchise in 2024

Motel Name	Total Revenue	Royalties
Rapid City Inn	$3,584,867.94	$250,940.76
Omaha Inn & Suites	$3,594,563.80	$233,646.66
Lincoln Inn & Suites	$3,210,499.85	$208,682.50
Sioux Falls Inn & Suites	$3,121,485.65	$202,896.58
Omaha Motel	$3,189,714.80	$159,485.74
Lincoln Lodge	$2,362,802.25	$153,582.16
Custer Lodge	$2,071,003.49	$144,970.24
Hill City Inn	$2,411,505.10	$144,690.31
Lexington Inn & Suites	$1,841,307.35	$119,684.99
Deadwood Inn & Suites	$1,788,494.60	$116,252.16
Sioux Falls Inn	$2,309,047.45	$115,452.37
York Motel	$2,009,651.05	$100,482.55
Omaha Inn	$1,945,346.40	$97,267.32

The most royalties were collected from the Rapid City Inn with more than $250,000 in royalties from a total revenue of $3.585 million. The smallest royalty amount came from the Valentine Lodge with more than $35,000 in royalties from more than $880,000 in revenue (row 28). Altogether from the Nebraska/South Dakota sales territory, about $2.825 million in royalties were collected from more than $50 million in total revenue (row 29).

Insight

Exploring the X Functions in DAX

SUMX is one of the summary X functions in DAX. The others are AVERAGEX, COUNTX, MINX, MAXX, and PRODUCTX. As with SUMX, each X function evaluates an expression row-by-row within a table, applying the summary function to the row-by-row values. For example, the following AVERAGEX function goes through every record in the Stays table, calculates the rooms rented divided by the total number of rooms in the motel for each record, and then returns the average of those ratios:

```
=AVERAGEX(Stays, [Rooms Rented]/RELATED(Motels[Total
Rooms]))
```

Similarly, the following COUNTX function counts up the number of days in which every room was rented:

```
=COUNTX(Stays,IF([Rooms Rented]=RELATED(Motels[Total
Rooms]),1))
```

The measure goes through every record in the Stays table using the IF function to test whether the number of rooms rented equals the number of rooms in the motel. If they are equal, the value 1 is returned; otherwise, no numeric value is given. The COUNTX function then counts the number of records containing a numeric value which is the same as counting the number of days the motel was full.

DAX is a powerful language for constructing formulas using data from multiple tables, and the X functions are one of its more useful tools.

Retrieving PivotTable Data with GETPIVOTDATA

The reports you helped Anna create were limited to the 24 motels in Nebraska and South Dakota, but there are over 6,000 QC Inn motels in more than 35 countries and territories. A PivotTable providing summaries on each motel would be large and unwieldy. One solution to that problem is to treat a PivotTable itself as a data source and extract information from it for use in a report using the **GETPIVOTDATA function**. The syntax of the function is:

```
GETPIVOTDATA(data_field, pivot_table, [field1, item1,
field2, item2,...])
```

where *data_field* is the data you want to retrieve from the PivotTable, *pivot_table* is a reference to any cell within the PivotTable, and the *field1*, *item1*, *field2*, *item2*, and so on are optional field/item pairs that indicate the location the cell within the PivotTable. Each field or item value is a text string and must be enclosed within quotation marks.

Note that it doesn't matter how the PivotTable is structured. You can switch rows and columns, add subtotals, add grand totals, and so forth. As long as you specify a data field, a cell (any cell) within the PivotTable, and a list of fields and field items, the GETPIVOTDATA function can locate the value in the PivotTable.

The GETPIVOTDATA function works with both standard PivotTables and PivotTables created under the Data Model. Figure 11–52 shows an example of the GETPIVOTDATA function used with a standard PivotTable.

Figure 11–52   **GETPIVOTDATA function for a standard PivotTable**

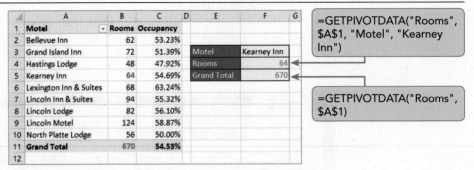

The first GETPIVOTDATA function

`=GETPIVOTDATA("Rooms", $A$1, "Motel", "Kearney Inn")`

returns the value of the Rooms field where Motel equals "Kearney Inn". In Figure 11–52, this is cell B5 in the PivotTable. If the field/item pairs are omitted as in the following function, the GETPIVOTDATA function returns the grand total of the Rooms field:

`=GETPIVOTDATA("Rooms", $A$1)`

With PivotTables based on the Data Model, the GETPIVOTDATA function is more complicated, expressing the fields and items of the PivotTable in terms of measures. For example, the GETPIVOTDATA function for retrieving the number of rooms from the Kearney motel in Figure 11–52 is

`=GETPIVOTDATA("[Measures].[Sum of Rooms]",$A$1,"[Motel_Data].[Motel]", "[Motel_Data].[Motel].&[Kearney Inn]")`

and the GETPIVOTDATA function for retrieving the grand total of rooms across all motels is:

`=GETPIVOTDATA("[Measures].[Sum of Rooms]",$A$1)`

Fortunately, you don't have to write these formulas yourself. If you reference a PivotTable cell, Excel will automatically generate the GETPIVOTDATA function for you.

Reference

Inserting the GETPIVOTDATA function

- Click the cell in which you wish to place the GETPIVOTDATA function.
- Type = and then click the PivotTable cell. Excel enters a reference to the PivotTable cell using the GETPIVOTDATA function.
- Press ENTER to insert the formula.

Anna included a Data Lookup worksheet in which you will use the GETPIVOTDATA function to retrieve data from the Royalties PivotTable. You'll enter the GETPIVOTDATA functions now by referencing cells within the PivotTable.

To insert the GETPIVOTDATA function:

1. Go to the **Data Lookup** worksheet.

2. Click cell **C5** and type **=** to begin the formula.

3. Click the **Royalties** sheet tab, click cell **C5** containing the total revenue for the Rapid City Inn, and then press **ENTER**. The GETPIVOTDATA function in cell C5 references the cell value from the PivotTable.

Next, you'll retrieve the value of the Royalties measure for the Rapid City Inn.

4. Click cell **C6**, type **=** to begin the formula, click cell the **Royalties** sheet tab, click cell **D5**, and then press **ENTER**.

5. Select the range **C5:C6** containing the GETPIVOTDATA functions. See Figure 11–53.

Figure 11–53   **Values referenced from the Royalties PivotTable**

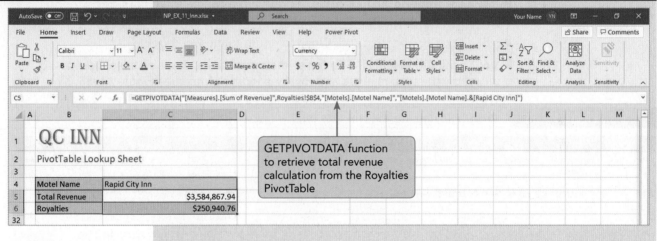

In Excel, the default behavior is to generate a GETPIVOTDATA function whenever you link to a cell within a PivotTable. If that's not what you want, you can change the default behavior: Select the PivotTable. On the PivotTable Analyze tab, in the PivotTable group, click the Options arrow, and then deselect the Generate GetPivotData option. After that, Excel will use familiar worksheet references to cells within a PivotTable in place of the GETPIVOTDATA function.

Anna wants the GETPIVOTDATA function to retrieve revenue and royalty values for any of the 24 motels. You will modify the GETPIVOTDATA functions now, replacing the explicit reference to the Rapid City Inn with a reference to whatever motel is named in cell C4.

To view PivotTable data for any motel:

1. With the range C5:C6 still selected, press **CTRL+H**. The Find and Replace dialog box opens.

2. Type **Rapid City Inn** in the Find what box.

3. Press **TAB**, and then type **"&C4&"** in the Replace with box. See Figure 11–54.

Figure 11–54   **Find and Replace dialog box**

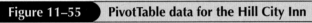

Replace the "Rapid City Inn" text with a reference to the value of cell C4

▶ **4.** Click **Replace All** to replace the text in the two selected cells. Excel reports that two replacements were made.

▶ **5.** Click **OK**, and then click **Close** to return to the workbook.

▶ **6.** In cell **C4**, enter **Hill City Inn** as the motel name. The worksheet updates to show the total revenue and royalties for the motel. See Figure 11–55.

Figure 11–55   **PivotTable data for the Hill City Inn**

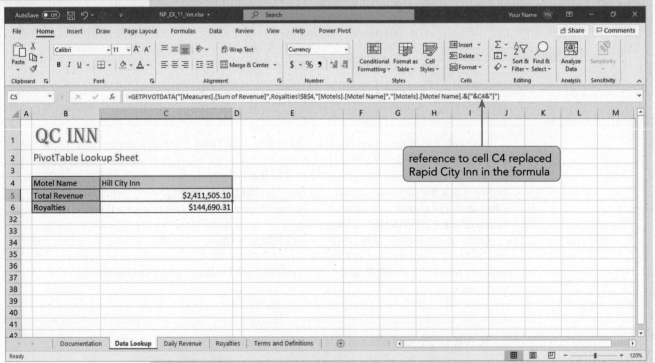

reference to cell C4 replaced Rapid City Inn in the formula

▶ **7. sam** Save the workbook, and then close it.

Anna can build upon this example to create a dashboard with PivotTable lookups. One of the great appeals of the GETPIVOTDATA function is that it gives you the flexibility to display PivotTable results in customized layouts and report styles.

Proskills

Problem Solving: Retrieving Measures from OLAP Cubes

Under the Data Model, you don't need a PivotTable to display PivotTable results. This is because the Data Model stores data in a multidimensional array of fields and measures known as a **Data Cube**. A Data Cube is part of an **Online Analytic Processing (OLAP)** database that is designed for the efficient reporting a large datasets. Rather than calculating and re-calculating a dataset that might have millions of records, an OLAP database has all those measures pre-stored for quick retrieval.

The Data Model is based on a Data Cube model, which is why you can store large datasets in the Data Model and have PivotTables quickly retrieve and display measures without having to wait for Excel to recalculate the PivotTable values.

You calculate measures directly from the Data Model without even needing a PivotTable by using the CUBEVALUE function

```
=CUBEVALUE(connection, [expression1, expression2, …])
```

where *connection* is the connection to an OLAP database like the Data Model and *expression1, expression2,* and so on are OLAP expressions that define how those measures should be filtered and retrieved. For example, the following formula retrieves the Sum of Revenue measure for the York Motel from the Data Model:

```
=CUBEVALUE("ThisWorkbookDataModel",
    "[Measures].[Sum of Revenue]",
    "[Motels].[Motel Name][York Motel]"
```

By adding more expressions to the CUBEVALUE function, you can filter the Sum of Revenue measure to cover any motel or combination of motels within any date interval you choose. The CUBEVALUE function is one of 7 CUBE functions supported by Excel.

Exploring Database Functions

Another way to summarize data from an Excel table or data range without using PivotTables is with a **Database function** (or **Dfunction**). Database functions calculate summary statistics including AVERAGE, COUNT, MAX, MIN, and SUM using criteria specified in a range. The general form of a Database function is

```
Dfunction(database, field, criteria)
```

where *database* specifies the data range containing the data including the column names, *field* is the name of a column from the data range or table, and *criteria* is a range containing filter criteria to apply to the database function. Figure 11–56 lists some of the Database functions used to calculate summary statistics from a database.

| Figure 11–56 | Database functions |

Function	Description
DAVERAGE(*database, field, criteria*)	Calculates the average of the values in the *field* column under criteria specified in the *criteria* range
DCOUNT(*database, field, criteria*)	Counts the numeric values in the *field* column for cells matching the *criteria*
DCOUNTA(*database, field, criteria*)	Counts the nonblank cells in the *field* column for cells matching the *criteria*
DMAX(*database, field, criteria*)	Returns the maximum value of the *field* column for cells matching the *criteria*
DMIN(*database, field, criteria*)	Returns the minimum value of the *field* column for cells matching the *criteria*
DSUM(*database, field, criteria*)	Calculates the sum of the *field* column for cells matching the *criteria*
DSTDEV(*database, field, criteria*)	Calculates the standard deviation of the *field* column for cells matching the *criteria*
DGET(*database, field, criteria*)	Returns the first cell from *field* column matching the *criteria*

Figure 11–57 shows an example of the DAVERAGE, DSUM, and DMAX Database functions used to calculate the average, sum, and maximum value of revenue collected during August of 2024.

| Figure 11–57 | Summary statistics calculated with database functions |

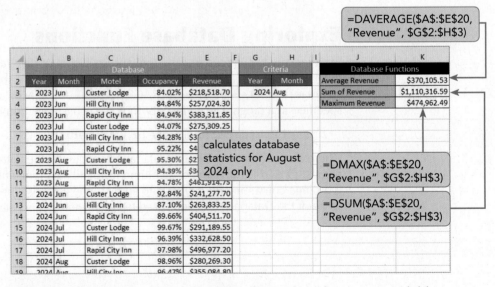

The criteria range operates the same way for the Database functions as it did for Advanced Filter criteria in that:

1. Field names are listed in the first row of the table and must exactly match the field names used from the database. Field names can be repeated in the same row for multiple criteria.

2. Criteria for each field are listed in subsequent rows of criteria range.

3. Criteria within the same row are combined using the AND logical operator.

4. Criteria in different rows are combined using the OR logical operator.

Figure 11–58 shows a criteria range with two rows so that the matching rows from the database contain either Hill City Inn revenue for 2023 or Custer Lodge Revenue for 2024.

Figure 11–58 | **Database calculations with multiple criteria**

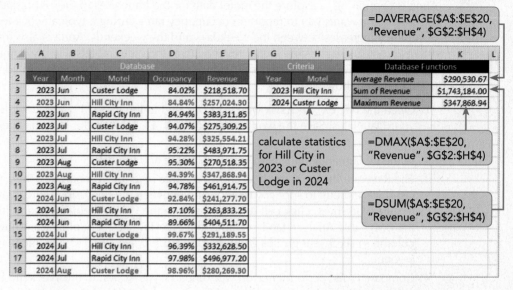

As with advanced filters, you can include operations in the criteria cells. An expression such as "> 300000" could be used to filter results to include only those rows in which revenues were greater than $300,000. If you want a quick way of calculating databases statistics, the Excel Database functions might be a good choice.

You've completed your initial work on the motel data for QC Inn. Anna will want to continue using these PivotTables to explore the data in preparation for the annual report.

Review

Session 11.3 Quick Check

1. What is a standard PivotTable?
2. What function should you use to count the number of unique values within a field?
3. What is the difference between an implicit measure and an explicit measure?
4. Write a DAX formula to calculate the average of the Revenue field values in the Stays table.
5. What DAX function do you use to retrieve a value from a Data Model table based on the table relation?
6. What is the difference between the SUM and SUMX functions?
7. What function do you use to retrieve values from a PivotTable?
8. What function do you use to retrieve calculated values from the Data Model without the use of a PivotTable?
9. What are the three arguments of an Excel Database function?

Practice

Review Assignments

Data Files needed for the Review Assignments: NP_EX_11-3.xlsx, NP_EX_11-4.xlsx

Anna is continuing to explore the motel data for the franchises in the Nebraska/South Dakota sales territory. Anna wants you to report on occupancy rates during a typical week to learn how much occupancy increases between the weekdays and the weekends. Anna is also interested in whether the new motels are showing higher revenue than the older motels. Finally, Anna wants to report the number and percentage of days in which each motel was completely filled during the year. Complete the following:

1. Open the **NP_EX_11-3.xlsx** workbook located in the Excel11 > Review folder included with your Data Files. Save the workbook as **NP_EX_11_Days** in the location specified by your instructor.

2. In the Documentation sheet, enter your name and the date.

3. The Revenue by Age worksheet shows average revenue compared to the age of each motel in years. It's difficult to spot any relationship between the two using individual ages. In the Revenue by Age worksheet, click cell A4, and then use the Group Field command in the Group group on the PivotTable Analyze tab to simplify the PivotTable by grouping the values in the Motel Age column in six 5-year groups going from 0 to 30 to see whether new motels have higher average revenue.

4. Compare motel performance on weekends vs. weekdays. In the Weekend Rates worksheet, manually group the Mon, Tue, Wed, and Thu items in the Weekday field of the PivotTable. Remove the Weekday field from the Columns area and rename Group1 as **Weekdays**. Manually group the Sun, Fri, and Sat items and change the name of that group from Group2 to **Weekends**. Click cell C4, and then use the Active Field box in the Active Field group on the PivotTable Analyze tab to change the name of the grouped field from Weekday2 to **Days**.

5. Enhance the appearance of the PivotTable with color. Click cell D6, click the Conditional Formatting button in the Styles group on the Home tab, and then click the New Rule command. For all cells showing Occupancy Rate values, format the values with a 3-color scale going from red (low occupancy) through yellow and up to green (high occupancy).

6. Explore how occupancy rates change from one day to the next within a typical week. In the Daily Occupancy worksheet, a PivotTable shows the average occupancy by day but organized with the groups you created in Step 4. Remove the Weekday2 group from the Rows area of the PivotTable. Click cell D5, and then click the Field Settings button in the Active Field group on the PivotTable Analyze tab. On the Show Values As tab, select the Difference From calculation with Weekday as the Base field and (previous) as the Base item. Change the Custom Name of the field to **Change in Rate**.

7. Use conditional formatting to indicate whether occupancy rates are going up, down, or remaining steady from one day to the next. Create a new conditional formatting rule that uses the red-yellow-green arrow icon set to highlight all cells showing change in rate values for weekdays. If the cell number is greater than or equal to 0.002 display a green up arrow. If the number is less than –0.002, display a red down arrow; otherwise, display a yellow sideways arrow. Note that Sunday will not have an icon because it's the first day of the week.

8. Examine how Revenue per Available Room or RevPar values change during the week. Go to the Daily RevPar worksheet and press ALT+D and then P to open the PivotTable Wizard. Use the data in the Motels table and select No in Step 2 to create a PivotTable from a new cache. Place the PivotTable report in cell B6 of the RevPar worksheet and rename the PivotTable **RevPar Pivot**. Place the Motel Name field in the Filters area and Weekday in the Rows area.

9. Click cell B6, click the Fields, Items, & Sets button in the Calculations group on the PivotTable Analyze tab, and then select Calculated Field. Create a calculated field named **RevPar** equal to the Revenue field divided by the Motel Rooms field. Change the label of value field from Sum of RevPar to **RevPar** followed by a blank space.

10. Summarize the RevPar values by weekdays and weekends. Click cell B6, click the Fields, Items, & Sets button in the Calculations group on the PivotTable Analyze tab, select Calculated Item, and then add the following calculated items:

    a. The **Weekday Average** calculated item using the formula =AVERAGE(Mon, Tue, Wed, Thu).

    b. The **Weekend Average** calculated item using the formula =AVERAGE(Sun, Fri, Sat).

11. Save the workbook, and then close it.

12. Open the **NP_EX_11-4.xlsx** workbook located in the Excel10 > Review folder included with your Data Files. Save the workbook as **NP_EX_11_Vacancy** in the location specified by your instructor. You'll use this workbook to examine how often the QC Inns motels have no vacancies.

13. In the Documentation sheet, enter your name and the date.

14. Go to the Vacancy Table worksheet. Click the Measures button in the Calculations group on the Power Pivot tab to add a new measure to the Stays table named **Days Filled**. Insert the description **Count of days with no vacancies** to indicate that this measure will calculate the number of days in which a motel was completely filled. Enter the following DAX formula:

    `=SUMX(Stays, IF([Rooms Rented]=RELATED(Motels[Total Rooms]),1,0))`

    (You can also copy this formula from the Terms and Definitions worksheet and paste it into the Measures dialog box. Be sure to type an equal sign (=) before the expression.) In the Formatting Options section, display the measure as a decimal number with no decimal places.

15. Add a second measure to the Stays table named **Percent Filled** with the description **Percent of days with no vacancies** that calculates the percent of days in which the motel was completely filled using the DAX formula and displays the value as a percentage number to two decimal places:

    `=[Days Filled]/[Count of Date]`

16. Make sure that both the Days Filled and the Percent Filled measures are added to the PivotTable. Note that motels will not be filled up except in the busiest of seasons.

17. Change the report layout to a tabular form.

18. Because the table is large and cumbersome, you'll set up a lookup worksheet to retrieve the vacancy data from the PivotTable. Go to the Vacancy Lookup worksheet, click cell C6, type = and then click cell E5 in the Vacancy Table worksheet to insert the GETPIVOTDATA function for that cell. Do the same with cell C7 to insert the GETPIVOTDATA function from cell F5 in the Vacancy Table worksheet.

19. Select the range C6:C7 and use the Find and Replace command to replace all occurrences within the selection of Bellevue Inn with "&C4&" (include the quotation marks). With the range C6:C7 still selected, use the Find and Replace command to replace all occurrences of Jan with "&C5&" (include the quotation marks).

20. Test the vacancy lookup by entering **Custer Lodge** in cell C4 and **Aug** in cell C5 to return the number and percentage of days in August with no vacancies at the Custer Lodge.

21. Save the workbook, and then close it.

Apply

Case Problem 1

Data File needed for this Case Problem: NP_EX_11-5.xlsx

Alcmaeon Selene Marados is an account executive with Alcmaeon, a tech company that specializes in custom software for hospitals and clinics. Selene wants to create a report on software sales to hospitals and clinics in the previous year. Selene has stored sales data in a workbook containing a Data Model with four tables: an Agents table containing information about the sales staff, a Hospitals table containing data on the hospitals and clinics that purchase software licenses from Alcmaeon, a Products table containing data on the software products sold by the company, and a Sales table that contains information on each sales transaction. You will use these tables to generate an analysis of the sales data.

Sales agents working at Alcmaeon are paid a base salary plus a commission based on the percentage of revenue they generate beyond $350,000. Commission rates can vary from 4% to 6%. Selene wants the report to include the total compensation paid to the sales staff from the base salary and their commissions. Complete the following:

1. Open the **NP_EX_11-5.xlsx** workbook located in the Excel11 > Case1 folder included with your Data Files. Save the workbook as **NP_EX_11_Alcmaeon** in the location specified by your instructor.

2. In the Documentation sheet, enter your name and the date.

3. In the Revenue Report worksheet, in cell B4, create a PivotTable named **Revenue by Month**. Place the Date field from the Sales table in the Rows area. After Excel automatically groups the dates, remove the Date field from the Rows area, leaving only the Date (Month) field showing the names of the months. Change the PivotTable report layout to tabular form and do not display any grand totals in either the rows or the columns.

4. Place the Revenue field from the Sales table into the Values area four times and do the following to display sales revenue in different ways in your table:

   a. In the first column, Sum of Revenue, display the rank of the revenue values from largest to smallest and change the field label to **Rank**.

   b. In the second column, Sum of Revenue2, change the field label to **Total Revenue**.

   c. In the third column, Sum of Revenue3, track the increase in revenue over the year by displaying the running total. Change the field label to **Running Total**.

   d. In the last column, Sum of Revenue4, display the revenue values as % Running Total in Date (Month). Change the field label to **Percentage**.

5. Examine how sales vary by region and agent. Go to the Region Report worksheet and create a PivotTable in cell B4 named **Revenue by Region**. Place the Sales Region and the Name fields from the Agents table in the Rows area. Place the Revenue field from the Sales table in the Values area and change the field label from Sum of Revenue to **Total Revenue**. Change the layout to Outline form and add subtotals to the top of each region group.

6. Show the percentage of revenue generated by each agent and each region by placing the Revenue field a second time the Values area, displaying its values as a percent of the parent row total. Change the field label name to **Percent**.

7. To better view the top selling agents and regions, sort the items in the Sales Region column in descending order of the Percent field, and then sort the items in the Name field also in descending order of Percent.

8. Determine how many hospitals bought a software license during the past years and from which agents. In the Hospital Sales worksheet, in cell B4, create a PivotTable named **Clients**. Set the report layout to tabular form, showing grand totals for both rows and columns. Place the Name field from the Agents table in the Rows area and place the Date (Month) field from the Sales table in the Columns area.

9. Place the Hospital field from the Sales table in the Values area. Show how many clients each agent had during the year by displaying the distinct count of the Hospital field. Change the field label to **Clients**.

10. In the PivotTable Options dialog box for the PivotTable, on the Layout & Format tab, enter **0** as the value to show for empty cells.

11. Calculate each agent's total compensation from the past year. In the Sales Commissions worksheet, create a PivotTable in cell B4 named **Commissions**. Set the PivotTable layout to tabular form with no grand totals.

12. Place the Name field from the Agents table in the Rows area. Place the Base Salary field from the Agents table in the Values area. Change the field label to **Base Salary** followed by a blank space. Place the Commission field from the Agents table in the Values area. Change the field label to **Commission Rate**.

13. Place the Revenue field from the Sales table in the Values area. Change the field label to **Revenue Generated**.

14. Create a measure named **Earned Commission** in the Sales table with the description **Commission earned by revenue generated above a minimum amount** that calculates the amount of commission earned by a sales agent for revenue generated above a minimum level. Use the following DAX formula and format values returned by the measure as currency with no decimal places:

    ```
    =(SUM([Revenue]) - SUM(Agents[Sales Minimum]))*SUM(Agents[Commission])
    ```

    (You can copy this formula from the Tables and Measures worksheet if you have trouble entering it; be sure to insert an equal sign to start the formula and match all closing and opening parentheses.)

15. Create a measure named **Total Compensation** with the description **Total compensation from base salary and earned commission** that calculates the total compensation for each sales agent by adding the base salary and the earned commission. Use the following DAX formula and display total compensation in currency with no decimal places:

    ```
    =SUM(Agents[Base Salary])+[Earned Commission]
    ```

16. Make sure that the Earned Commission and Total Compensation measures are added to the PivotTable.

17. Sort the agent names in descending order of the Total Compensation column.

18. Save the workbook, and then close it.

Challenge

Case Problem 2

Data File needed for this Case Problem: NP_EX_11-6.xlsx

Computer Discount Essentials   Jamere Carter manages inventory for Computer Discount Essentials. Part of Jamere's job is to monitor the stocking levels in the company's warehouses to ensure that merchandise is restocked well before the warehouse runs out. Jamere stores inventory data in an Excel workbook with two tables in the Data Model: The Products table describes all the warehouse merchandise, including each item's initial stocking level and the level below which the item must be restocked. The Transactions table contains a daily record of transactions at the warehouse including items shipped out and items restocked. Jamere wants you to create a report on the current state of the warehouse, flagging those items that need immediate restocking and calculating the total value of all items in stock. Complete the following:

1. Open the **NP_EX_11-6.xlsx** workbook located in the Excel11 > Case2 folder included with your Data Files. Save the workbook as **NP_EX_11_CDE** in the location specified by your instructor.

2. In the Documentation sheet, enter your name and the date.

3. In the Inventory Report worksheet, in cell B7, insert a PivotTable named **Inventory Pivot**. Set the PivotTable layout to the tabular form with no grand totals. Set the layout to repeat all item labels.

4. Place the Category, SKU, and Description fields from the Products table in the Rows area.

5. Display the initial quantity of each item stocked in the warehouse by placing the Initial QTY field from the Products table in the Values area and change the field label from Sum of Initial QTY to **Starting QTY**.

6. Display the change in the item quantities over the past year by placing the Change field from the Inventory in the Values area and change the field label from Sum of Change to **Change in QTY**.

7. Determine the current quantity of each item left in the warehouse by adding a measure to the Products table named **Current QTY** with the description **Current quantity in stock**. Enter the DAX formula `=[Sum of Initial QTY]+[Sum of Change]`. Add the measure to the PivotTable, if needed.

8. Determine the value of the items in inventory by creating a measure for the Products table named **Inventory Value** with the description **Total value of the items in the inventory**. Enter the DAX formula `=SUMX(Products, [Unit Value]*[Current QTY])` and display the value as currency to two decimal places. Add the measure to the PivotTable, if needed.

9. Determine which items need to be restocked by creating a measure for the Products table named **Restock Order** with the description **Quantity of item to reorder**. Insert the following DAX formula that uses the SUMX and IF functions to calculate the amount of items that Jamere will have to order to bring the inventory up to the proper level:

`=SUMX(Products, IF([Current QTY]<[Restock Level], [Restock Amount], 0))`

Note that if an item is above the restocking level, this measure will return a value of zero (because no restocking is required). If you are having problems entering the formula, you can copy and paste the measure formula from the Data Summary worksheet.

🜨 **Explore** 10. Click cell I8 and add a conditional format icon set to all cells in the PivotTable showing Restock Order values. If the numeric value of a cell is greater than zero, indicating that the item needs restocking, display a red flag; for all other values do not display any icon. (*Hint*: You can select individual icons by clicking the drop-down list box next to each icon image in the New Formatting Rule dialog box.)

🜨 **Explore** 11. Jamere wants the total value of all items in the inventory displayed above the PivotTable. Because this total is not part of the PivotTable, you need to retrieve the measure directly from the Data Model using the CUBEVALUE function. In cell H5, enter the following formula to calculate the total value of all items in the warehouse by retrieving the Inventory Value measure:

`=CUBEVALUE("ThisWorkbookDataModel","[Measures].[Inventory Value]")`

12. Resize the column widths of the PivotTable so that all values and labels can be read.

13. Jamere wants a table listing the names of the items by warehouse row and bin. In the Warehouse Grid worksheet, create a PivotTable in cell B4 named **Warehouse**, set the layout to the tabular form, and do not display any grand totals for the table.

14. Place the Warehouse Row field from the Products table in the Rows area and place the Storage Bin field from the Products table in the Columns area.

🜨 **Explore** 15. With DAX you can create measures that return text strings in place of numeric values by using the CONCATENATEX function. Display all the items stored in a warehouse row and bin in a comma-separated list by adding the following **Item List** measure to the Products table. Include the description **List of items from the warehouse inventory** and enter the measure formula:

`=CONCATENATEX(Products, [Description], ", ")`

Add the measure to the Values area of the PivotTable, if needed. Confirm that each cell in the PivotTable displays items stored in the matching storage bin and warehouse row.

16. Wrap the text in the cells containing the item lists within each cell. Resize the PivotTable column and row widths to fit the contents.

17. Save the workbook, and then close it.

Objectives

Session 12.1
- Create a WordArt graphic
- Plot data with a funnel chart
- Hide error values with the IFERROR function

Session 12.2
- Validate data entry
- Hide worksheet rows and columns
- Hide worksheets
- Protect worksheets and workbooks from edits
- Unlock worksheet cells to allow edits

Session 12.3
- Display the Developer tab
- Record and run a macro
- Assign a macro to a graphic or macro button
- Edit macro code in an editor

EXCEL

Developing an Excel Application

Creating a Data Entry App

Case | Primrose Community Clinic

Jenya Rattan is a project coordinator for Primrose Community Clinic, a private nonprofit clinic in Toledo, Ohio. Currently, Jenya is directing fundraising efforts for a multimillion-dollar expansion of the clinic. Jenya is using Excel to monitor the fundraising efforts and generate reports for the clinic administrators and trustees. Jenya wants you to help develop an Excel application for entering donor information and reporting on fundraising progress.

Starting Data Files

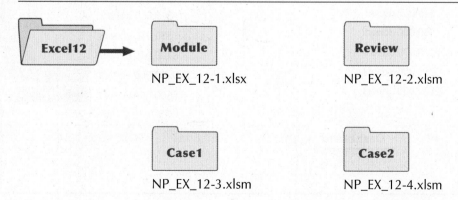

Excel12 → Module
NP_EX_12-1.xlsx

Review
NP_EX_12-2.xlsm

Case1
NP_EX_12-3.xlsm

Case2
NP_EX_12-4.xlsm

Session 12.1 Visual Overview:

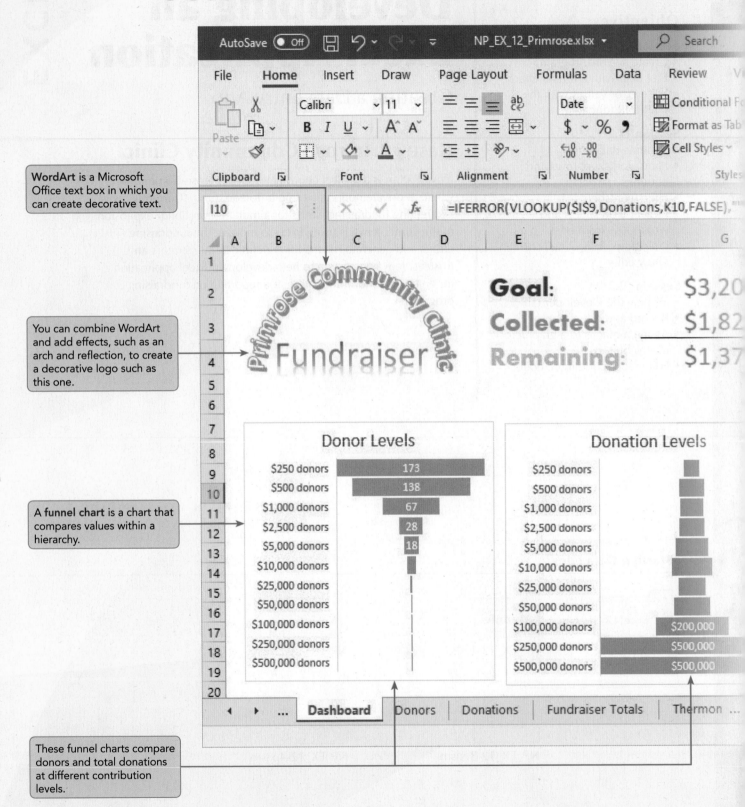

WordArt is a Microsoft Office text box in which you can create decorative text.

You can combine WordArt and add effects, such as an arch and reflection, to create a decorative logo such as this one.

A funnel chart is a chart that compares values within a hierarchy.

These funnel charts compare donors and total donations at different contribution levels.

WordArt and Funnel Charts

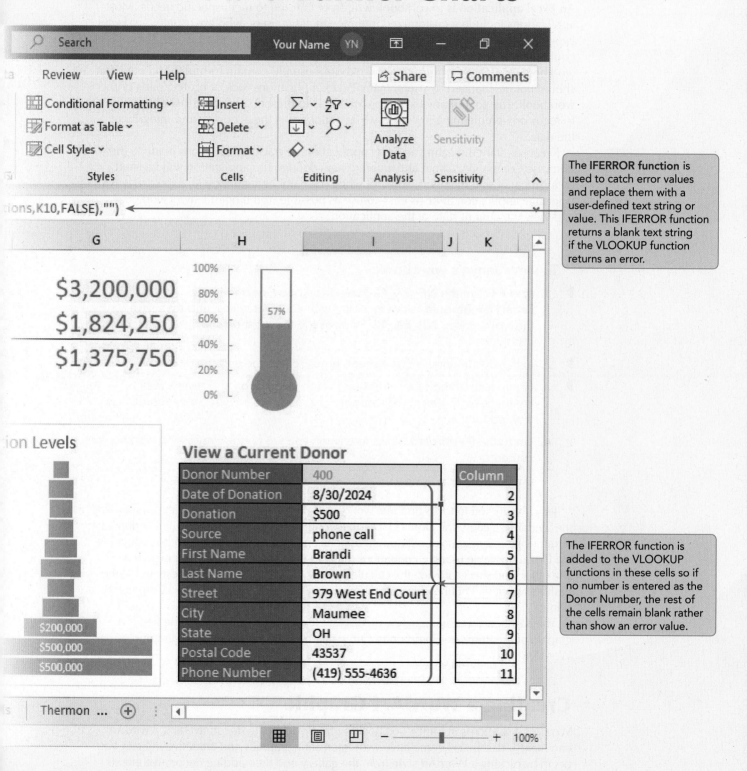

The **IFERROR function** is used to catch error values and replace them with a user-defined text string or value. This IFERROR function returns a blank text string if the VLOOKUP function returns an error.

The IFERROR function is added to the VLOOKUP functions in these cells so if no number is entered as the Donor Number, the rest of the cells remain blank rather than show an error value.

View a Current Donor

			Column
Donor Number	400		
Date of Donation	8/30/2024		2
Donation	$500		3
Source	phone call		4
First Name	Brandi		5
Last Name	Brown		6
Street	979 West End Court		7
City	Maumee		8
State	OH		9
Postal Code	43537		10
Phone Number	(419) 555-4636		11

$3,200,000
$1,824,250
$1,375,750

57%

$200,000
$500,000
$500,000

...ion Levels

...ons,K10,FALSE),"")

Planning an Excel Application

An **Excel application** is a workbook written or tailored to meet specific needs. Most applications include a customized interface to assist users, who are usually not Excel experts, to quickly and easily perform tasks without having to learn Excel. These tasks could include entering data, updating charts, updating PivotTables, and navigating the workbook contents. Because these workbooks usually contain formulas and data that should not be changed by users, many Excel applications lock or protect parts of the workbook. The goal of any Excel application is to present a product that allows users to focus on completing a few tasks while maintaining the accuracy and integrity of the data.

Jenya has started creating an Excel application for tracking donations made to the Primrose Community Clinic and entering new donors. The application will be used by a variety of staff members, some of whom may not be familiar with Excel, so Jenya wants the application to be as easy-to-use as possible. You'll open Jenya's workbook and view the current state of the application.

To view Jenya's workbook:

1. **sam ↓** Open the **NP_EX_12-1.xlsx** workbook located in the **Excel12 > Module** folder included with your Data Files, and then save the workbook as **NP_EX_12_Primrose** in the location specified by your instructor.

2. In the Documentation worksheet, enter your name and the date.

3. Go to each of the other worksheets in the workbook and review their contents. Note that some worksheets already have PivotTable report areas created for you.

4. Go to the **Dashboard** worksheet when you are finished reviewing workbook contents.

Jenya wants you to focus on three worksheets: The Dashboard worksheet summarizing the fundraising effort, the Donors worksheet for entering information about new donors or retrieving information about current donors, and the Donations worksheet containing the Donations table listing all donations made to the clinic since the campaign began. The other worksheets provide the calculations for the charts and tables presented in the dashboard but will not be of interest to other staff members at the Primrose Community Clinic.

The dashboard is missing a few pieces that Jenya wants you to add. The first is a graphic of the Primrose Community Clinic name. You can create such a graphic using WordArt.

Creating a WordArt Graphic

WordArt is a Microsoft Office text box in which you create decorative text. WordArt can make a dashboard come alive with interesting graphics and attractive images. You begin by picking a WordArt style from the gallery and then adding decorative effects using tools on the ribbon.

You'll create a WordArt graphic containing the text "Primrose Community Clinic" to include on the dashboard.

To create a WordArt graphic for the dashboard:

1. On the ribbon, click the **Insert** tab. In the Text group, click the **Text arrow** if necessary to display the menu of text objects, and then click the **WordArt** button. A gallery of WordArt styles appears. Each style is represented by the letter A.

2. Click the WordArt style in the third row and fourth column of the gallery. White text with a dark orange border shadow containing the text "Your text here" appears in the workbook.

3. Type **Primrose Community Clinic** to replace the default text with the name of the clinic.

4. Use your mouse to select all the text in the WordArt box.

5. On the ribbon, click the **Home** tab. In the Font group, click the **Font Size arrow**, and then click **28** as the font size. The WordArt reduces in size.

6. Point to the WordArt border, and then use the Move pointer to drag the WordArt text box so the upper-left corner of the WordArt graphic is in cell A1. See Figure 12–1.

Figure 12–1	WordArt added to the dashboard

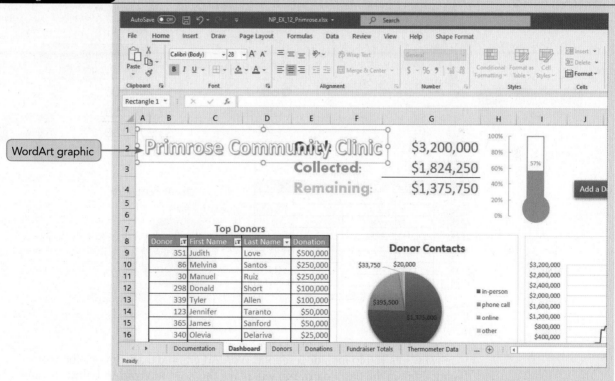

WordArt graphic

The WordArt graphic overlaps other content on the dashboard. You can fix that by formatting it. Among the decorative effects that you can apply to WordArt are drop shadows, glowing edges, reflections, and 3D rotations. You will apply a text effect that places the WordArt text in a semicircular arch.

To transform the WordArt text:

▶ **1.** With the WordArt graphic still selected, click the **Shape Format** tab on the ribbon, and then in the WordArt Styles group, click the **Text Effects** button. A menu of effects appears.

▶ **2.** On the Text Effects menu, point to **Transform**. The Transform gallery with different ways to transform the WordArt opens.

▶ **3.** In the Follow Path section, click the first option to apply the Arch transformation. You can change the height and width of the arch.

▶ **4.** In the Size group, enter **2** in the Shape Height box, press **TAB**, and then enter **2** in the Shape Width box. The text in the WordArt graphic is spread over a bigger arch.

▶ **5.** Drag the WordArt graphic so that the entire graphic is visible at the top of the worksheet. See Figure 12–2.

Figure 12–2	Transformed WordArt graphic

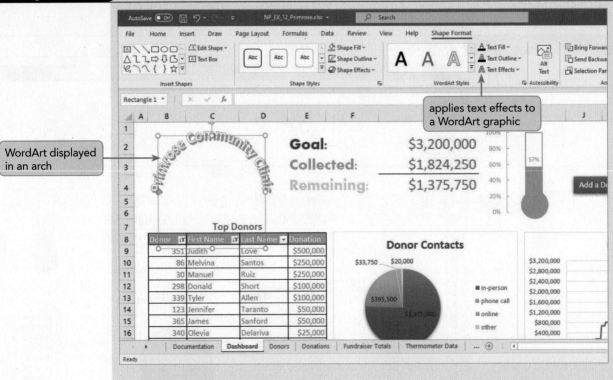

Jenya wants you to include a second WordArt graphic that contains the word "Fundraiser" in the dashboard. You will place this second WordArt below the arch you just created.

To insert the Fundraiser WordArt object:

▶ **1.** On the ribbon, click the **Insert** tab. In the Text group, click the **Text arrow** to view the menu of text objects if necessary, click the **WordArt** button, and then click the WordArt style in the second row and second column of the gallery. A WordArt text box in a blue font with reflected text is inserted in the worksheet.

▶ **2.** Type **Fundraiser** to replace the selected text, and then select **Fundraiser** in the WordArt text box.

▶ **3.** On the ribbon, click the **Home** tab. In the Font group, click the **Font Size arrow**, and then click **24**. The font size of the WordArt is reduced.

▶ **4.** Move the Fundraiser WordArt so it is centered directly under the WordArt arch you created in the previous set of steps. See Figure 12–3.

| Figure 12–3 | **Reflected WordArt graphic** |

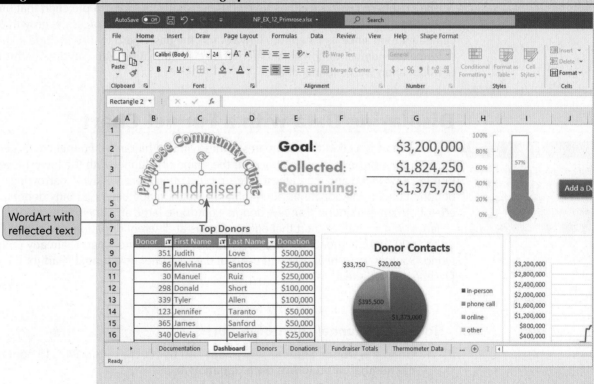

You can modify other parts of the WordArt style using commands and tools on the Shape Format tab. If you want to remove all the decorative features from a WordArt graphic, go to the Shape Format tab, click the WordArt gallery in the WordArt Styles group, and then click Clear WordArt.

Insight

Enhancing your Application with SmartArt

Another way of adding eye-catching graphics to application dashboards is with SmartArt. **SmartArt graphics** are professionally designed business graphics to create illustrations of flow charts, organization charts, cycle charts, and other diagrams. To create a SmartArt graphic, go to the Insert tab, and then in the Illustrations group, click the SmartArt button. The Choose a SmartArt Graphic dialog box opens from which you can choose a SmartArt diagram. The SmartArt graphics are organized into the following diagram categories: List, Process, Cycle, Hierarchy, Relationship, and Pyramid. You can also load SmartArt graphics from an external picture file or from the Microsoft Office website. Once you insert a SmartArt graphic, you can enter text labels to describe the graphic and format it with tools available on the ribbon. As with WordArt, SmartArt graphics support special formatting effects including drop shadows, reflections, glow edges, and 3D rotations.

The Dashboard worksheet has several useful charts including a pie chart that breaks down donations by type of donor contacts and a line chart that tracks the growth of the campaign fund since its inception. Jenya wants the dashboard to also include a chart showing the number of donors at different levels of donation. You can display this kind of information with a funnel chart.

Displaying Data with a Funnel Chart

Tip

Funnel charts are often used to track stages in a production process from initial stages through a completion stage.

A funnel chart is a chart that compares values within a hierarchy. Funnel charts get their name because they often appear in the shape of a funnel with the lowest level forming a wide top and the highest levels representing a progressively narrowing bottom. Fundraising donations often follow a funnel shape because many donors contribute small amounts, but few donors contribute large amounts.

Jenya wants a funnel chart that counts donors at different donation levels from $250 up to $500,000. The donation data you will use for the funnel chart is already in the Donor Sources worksheet. You will use that data to generate a funnel chart for the Dashboard worksheet.

To create a funnel chart of donors:

1. Go to the **Donor Sources** worksheet and select the range **B4:C15** containing the number of donors at each donation level.

2. On the ribbon, click the **Insert** tab, and then in the Charts group, click the **Recommended Charts** button. The Insert Chart dialog box opens.

3. Click the **All Charts** tab, and then in the list of chart types, click **Funnel**. There is one funnel chart available.

4. Click **OK**. The funnel chart is added to the workbook.

5. Move and resize the funnel chart to the **Dashboard** worksheet to cover the range **F20:H32**.

6. Change the chart title to **Donor Levels**.

7. On the Chart Design tab, in the Chart Styles group, click the **Change Colors** button, and then click **Colorful Palette 3**. See Figure 12–4.

| Figure 12–4 | Formatted funnel chart |

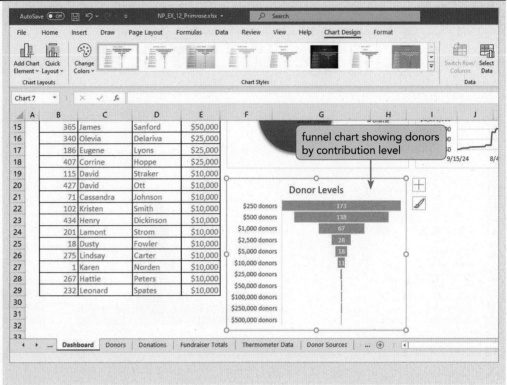

The funnel chart shows the drop-off in donors at higher contribution levels. So far, the campaign has 445 donors with 173 donors contributing at the $250 level, 138 donors at the $500 level, and only a handful donors at the highest levels.

Although few individuals have contributed large amounts to the campaign, the ones who did contributed a lot. Many fundraising efforts follow the 80/20 rule in which 80% of the total donations come from 20% of the donors. Jenya wants a second funnel chart that compares the total amount of contributions given by donors of different levels from $250 up to $500,000. You will create that funnel chart now.

To create a funnel chart of donations:

1. Go to the **Donation Sources** worksheet and select the range **B4:C15** containing the number of donations at each donation level.

2. On the ribbon, click the **Insert** tab, and then in the Charts group, click the **Recommended Charts** button. The Insert Chart dialog box opens.

3. On the Recommended Charts tab, click the **Funnel** chart type, and then click **OK**. The funnel chart of donations at different contribution levels is added to the worksheet.

4. Move and resize the funnel chart to the **Dashboard** worksheet to cover the range **I20:N32**.

5. Change the chart title to **Donation Levels**.

6. On the Chart Design tab, in the Chart Styles group, click the **Change Colors** button, and then click **Colorful Palette 3**. This funnel chart is formatted to match the Donor Levels funnel chart you created. See Figure 12–5.

Figure 12–5   **Funnel chart of total donations by contribution level**

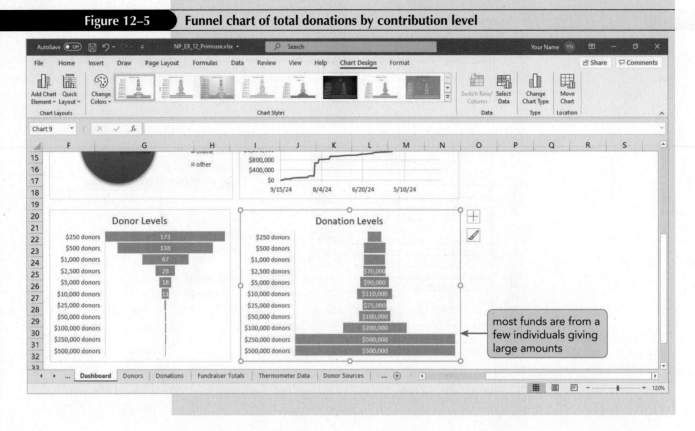

By breaking down donations by donor level, Jenya confirms that although most donors contribute at the lowest level, most of the total money raised comes from a few individuals contributing a lot. These charts illustrate that the success of the fundraising campaign depends in part on finding a few wealthy individuals willing to donate a great amount to the cause.

Insight

Creating a Thermometer Chart

Thermometer charts are fun charts to track progress toward a goal. The Dashboard worksheet includes one to show progress toward reaching the clinic's fundraising goal. Excel does not include a thermometer chart type, but you can create one by using a column chart and then reformatting it. To create a thermometer chart, do the following:

1. Enter the goal and progress toward a goal in a two-by-two table as follows:

Progress	Goal
57%	100%

2. Create a clustered column chart from the data range, and then on the Chart Design tab, in the Data group, click the Switch Row/Column button.
3. Double-click the Progress marker in the column chart to open the Format Data Series pane.
4. In the Series Option section, plot the Progress series on a secondary axis.
5. Set the range for both the primary and secondary axes to go from 0 to 1.

At this point, the two columns of the column chart are superimposed on each other. You can then edit the fill colors and line colors to create the thermometer effect. To make the chart look more like a thermometer, you can place a round shape filled with the progress color at the base of the column.

Because individual donors can have such a large impact on the success of the campaign, Jenya wants the Primrose Community Clinic staffers to be able to easily retrieve information on specific donors. You will add that feature next.

Hiding Error Values with the IFERROR Function

One challenge of creating an Excel application is ensuring that users are not distracted by error values that might appear in a cell. For example, an application might include the following formula to calculate the average value in the range A1:A50:

```
=AVERAGE(A1:A50)
```

However, if the range A1:A50 does not yet contain data, the formula will return the error value #DIV/0!. This error message can be confusing to users who are less familiar with Excel. To prevent this potential confusion, you can enclose formulas within the IFERROR function

```
=IFERROR(value, value_if_error)
```

where *value* is the value returned by a formula with no errors and *value_if_error* specifies a value if the formula does contain an error. Continuing the earlier example, the following formula returns the average of the data in the range A1:A50, but if no data has been entered in the range, it returns an empty text string:

```
=IFERROR(AVERAGE(A1:A50), "")
```

Tip

In place of an empty text string, you can enter a text message that describes the error in more detail.

Jenya stores information about current donors in the Donations worksheet. The Donors worksheet already includes formulas to retrieve donor information based on a donor number. However, if no donor number is provided or an invalid donor number is included, the formulas will return the #N/A value. Jenya wants the VLOOKUP formulas to return an empty text string in place of an error value. You'll revise those formulas now.

To add the IFERROR function to the VLOOKUP formulas:

▶ **1.** Go to **Donors** worksheet and select cell **E5**. In the range F6:F15, the VLOOKUP function retrieves corresponding information for the donor number entered in cell F5. The information is retrieved from the Donations table on the Donations worksheet using column index numbers specified in the range H6:H15. Currently, the table shows the information for the first donor—Karen Norden who donated $10,000.

▶ **2.** Delete the value in cell **F5**. The error value #N/A appears in the range F6:F15 because there is no longer a donor number to look up.

Because Jenya does not want #N/A values appearing in the application, you'll revise the formula in cell F6 by enclosing the VLOOKUP function within an IFERROR function.

▶ **3.** Double-click cell **F6** to select it and enter Edit mode.

▶ **4.** Click directly after = to place the insertion point between the equal sign and VLOOKUP, and then type **IFERROR(** to begin the IFERROR function.

▶ **5.** Press **END** on your keyboard to move the insertion point to the end of the formula.

Be sure to type a comma before typing the *value_if_error* to separate the arguments in the IFERROR function.

6. Type **,"")** to complete the formula, and then press **ENTER**. The formula `=IFERROR(VLOOKUP($F$5,Donations,H6,FALSE),"")` is entered in cell F6. A blank text string appears instead of the #N/A value.

7. Click cell **F6** and drag the fill handle down over the range **F7:F15** to copy the formula into the remaining cells in the range.

8. Click the **Auto Fill Options button**, and then click **Fill Without Formatting** to retain the formats currently used in those cells. No error values appear on the worksheet even when a donor number is not entered. See Figure 12–6.

Figure 12–6   **Error values hidden with the IFERROR function**

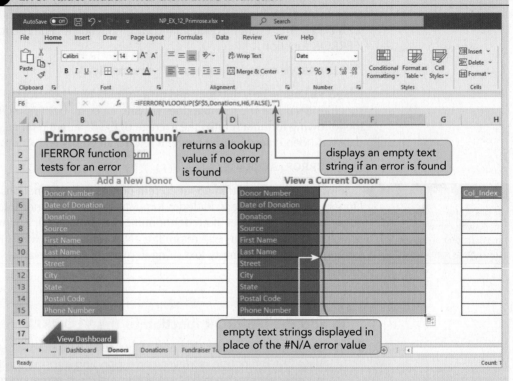

9. In cell **F5**, enter **400** to look up information about the 400th donor. Information on Brandi Brown, who contributed $500 on August 30, 2024, appears.

10. Save the workbook.

The IFERROR function eliminates distracting error values. However, remember to add this function only at the end of application development. When you first start building an application, you want to see all error values, so you can find and fix any mistakes in formulas or data.

Proskills

Written Communication: Handling Error Values

The IFERROR function is one of many functions supplied by Excel to catch errors. Another useful error function is the ISERROR function, which returns a value of TRUE if **value** is an error value and FALSE if it isn't:

```
ISERROR(value)
```

For example, the following expression tests whether cell B10 contains an error value:

```
ISERROR(B10)
```

The advantage of the ISERROR function is that you can enter the formula in one cell, such as B10, and then place an informative message about any errors in cell B10 within an adjacent cell. The following formula nests an ISERROR function within an IF function to display one message if cell B10 is in error and a different message if it is not:

```
=IF(ISERROR(B10), "Input Error", "Input Valid")
```

The ISERROR function returns TRUE for any error value. To test for specific errors or specific data values, use the ISBLANK, ISNA, ISNUMBER, ISREF, ISLOGICAL, ISNONTEXT, or ISTEXT functions. For example, the ISNA function tests whether a cell is displaying the #N/A error value; the ISNUMBER function tests whether a cell contains a numeric value, and so forth. You can learn more about Excel error functions by viewing Excel Help.

Remember that an Excel application is designed for users who are not Excel experts, so you want to take advantage of the Excel error functions to catch errors for them. The end-user should focus on the task at hand, not on interpreting error values generated by the application.

You've completed your initial work on adding new graphics and charts to Jenya's application and you've used the IFERROR function to improve the appearance of the donor lookup. In the next session, you'll add features for entering new donor information that automatically notify the user when incorrect data is entered.

Review

Session 12.1 Quick Check

1. What is WordArt?
2. What is a funnel chart?
3. Convert the formula =B1/B10 into a formula that calculates this value only if there is no error and otherwise displays the message "Error Found".
4. Why would you use the IFERROR function?
5. What Excel function can be used to test whether a cell contains a numeric value?

Session 12.2 Visual Overview:

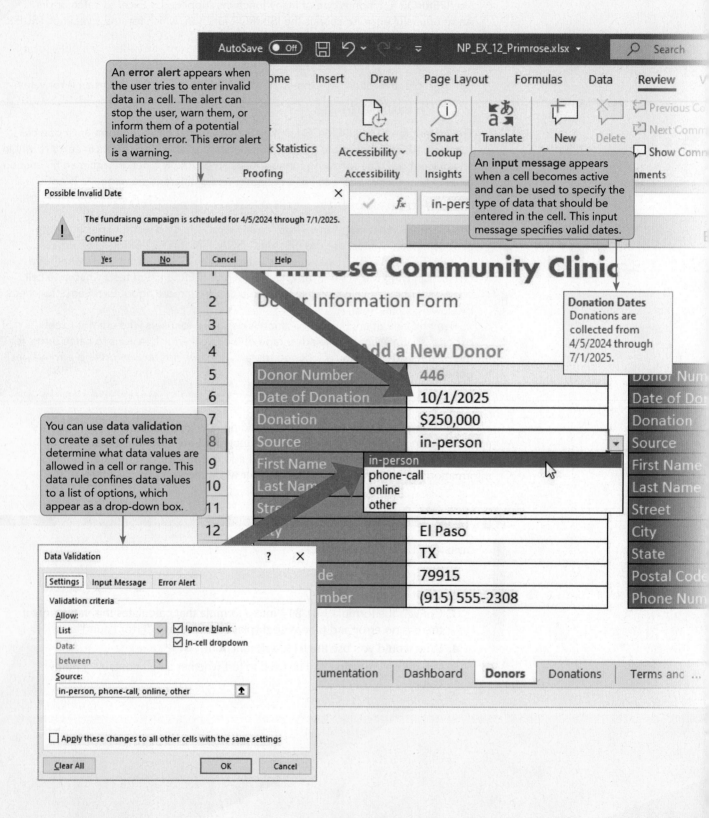

An **error alert** appears when the user tries to enter invalid data in a cell. The alert can stop the user, warn them, or inform them of a potential validation error. This error alert is a warning.

An **input message** appears when a cell becomes active and can be used to specify the type of data that should be entered in the cell. This input message specifies valid dates.

Possible Invalid Date

The fundraisng campaign is scheduled for 4/5/2024 through 7/1/2025.

Continue?

Yes   No   Cancel   Help

Donation Dates Donations are collected from 4/5/2024 through 7/1/2025.

Primrose Community Clinic

Donor Information Form

Add a New Donor

Donor Number	446
Date of Donation	10/1/2025
Donation	$250,000
Source	in-person
First Name	in-person
Last Name	phone-call
Street	online
	other
City	El Paso
State	TX
Postal Code	79915
Phone Number	(915) 555-2308

You can use **data validation** to create a set of rules that determine what data values are allowed in a cell or range. This data rule confines data values to a list of options, which appear as a drop-down box.

Data Validation   ?   X

Settings | Input Message | Error Alert

Validation criteria

Allow:
List
☑ Ignore blank

Data:
between
☑ In-cell dropdown

Source:
in-person, phone-call, online, other

☐ Apply these changes to all other cells with the same settings

Clear All   OK   Cancel

...cumentation | Dashboard | **Donors** | Donations | Terms and ...

Data Validation and Workbook Protection

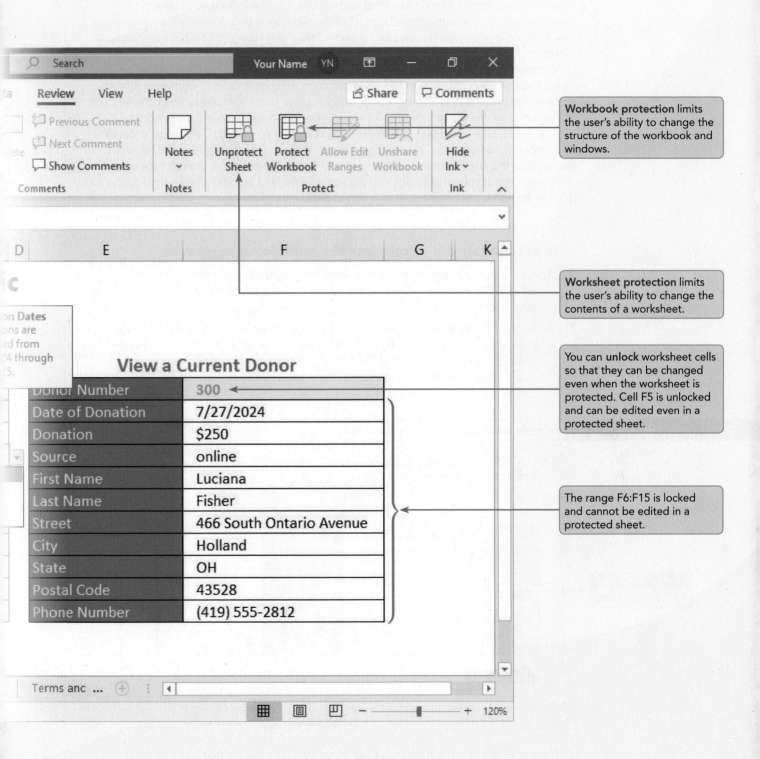

Workbook protection limits the user's ability to change the structure of the workbook and windows.

Worksheet protection limits the user's ability to change the contents of a worksheet.

You can **unlock** worksheet cells so that they can be changed even when the worksheet is protected. Cell F5 is unlocked and can be edited even in a protected sheet.

The range F6:F15 is locked and cannot be edited in a protected sheet.

View a Current Donor

Donor Number	300
Date of Donation	7/27/2024
Donation	$250
Source	online
First Name	Luciana
Last Name	Fisher
Street	466 South Ontario Avenue
City	Holland
State	OH
Postal Code	43528
Phone Number	(419) 555-2812

Validating Data Entry

Excel applications are intended to be used by people with all levels of Excel experience. However, anyone can mistakenly enter wrong data, change formulas, or delete important results. There may also be parts of the workbook you don't want users to even see. To avoid inadvertent changes to the application, you can restrict what users can do within an Excel application.

Whenever possible, you should have Excel calculate values rather than relying on user input. You can apply this rule to Jenya's application, which includes a worksheet form to enter information on new donors and donations. Jenya wants the user to enter the amount of the donation, the donor's contact information, and a donor ID number. The donor IDs are sequential—the first donor in the list is donor ID number 1, the second is donor ID number 2, and so forth. Thus, any new donor will always be assigned an ID that is 1 greater than the largest donor number currently in the donations list. Rather than have users enter that number manually, you'll insert a formula to automatically calculate the ID number based on the numbers already in the donations table.

To enter a formula to calculate the next donor number:

▶ **1.** If you took a break after the previous session, make sure the NP_EX_12_Primrose workbook is open, and the Donors worksheet is the active sheet.

▶ **2.** In cell **C5**, enter `=MAX(Donations[Donor Number])+1` as the formula to calculate the next donor ID with a value that is one greater than the maximum value of the Donor Number field from the Donations table. The cell displays 446 as the ID for the next donor to be added to the donations list. See Figure 12–7.

Figure 12–7	Formula automatically enters the donor number

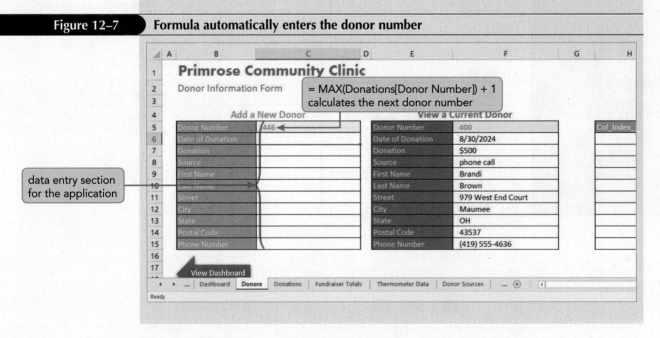

The rest of the fields in the range C6:C15 will contain values that must be entered by the user. You can also restrict the allowable data values for those cells by creating a **validation rule** that defines what data values are allowed and what are not.

Reference

Validating Data

- On the Data tab, in the Data Tools group, click the Data Validation button.
- Click the Settings tab.
- Click the Allow arrow, click the type of data allowed in the cell, and then enter the validation criteria for that data.
- Click the Input Message tab, and then enter a title and text for the input message.
- Click the Error Alert tab, and then, if necessary, click the Show error alert after invalid data is entered check box to insert a checkmark.
- Select an alert style, and then enter the title and text for the error alert message.
- Click OK.

Validating Dates

Tip

Only one validation rule can be assigned to a cell or data range.

Every validation rule is based on **validation criteria** specifying values allowed within a worksheet cell or range. For example, a date value might be limited to a range of dates or a numeric value might be limited to fall between a specified minimum and maximum value. Text values might be confined to a predefined list of possible entries. Figure 12–8 summarizes the types of criteria that Excel supports for validation rules.

Figure 12–8   **Validation criteria**

Type	Description
Any value	Any number, text, or date; removes any existing data validation
Whole Number	Integers only; you can specify the range of acceptable integers
Decimal	Any type of number; you can specify the range of acceptable numbers
List	Any value in a range or entered in the Data Validation dialog box separated by commas
Date	Dates only; you can specify the range of acceptable dates
Time	Times only; you can specify the range of acceptable times
Text Length	Text limited to a specified number of characters
Custom	Values based on the results of a logical formula

In cell C6, users will enter the date in which a new donation is made. The fundraising campaign is scheduled for 4/5/2024 through 7/1/2025, so any date must fall within that interval. You will create a validation rule for cell C6 that limits the cell value to dates between 4/5/2024 and 7/1/2025.

To create a validation rule for dates:

1. If necessary, click cell **C6** to select it.

2. On the ribbon, click the **Data** tab, and then in the Data Tools group, click the **Data Validation** button. The Data Validation dialog box opens.

Tip

To apply the same validation rule to multiple cells, select the range and then create the validation rule using the Data Validation dialog box.

3. If it is not already selected, click the **Settings** tab to display the criteria for the validation rule.

4. Click the **Allow** box, and then click **Date** to specify that dates are allowed in the cell.

5. In the Data box, verify that **between** is selected as the comparison for the date criteria.

6. In the Start date box, enter **4/5/2024** and in the End date box, enter **7/1/2025**. See Figure 12–9.

Figure 12–9	Data Validation dialog box

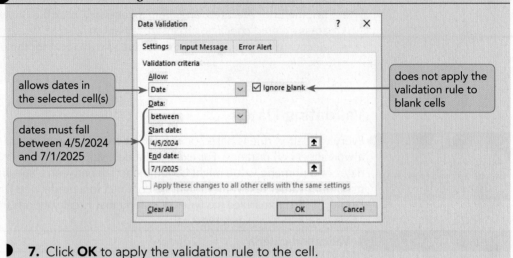

allows dates in the selected cell(s)

dates must fall between 4/5/2024 and 7/1/2025

does not apply the validation rule to blank cells

7. Click **OK** to apply the validation rule to the cell.

To confirm that Excel will not allow invalid dates in the cell, you will try to enter a date that is *not* between 4/5/2024 and 7/1/2025.

To test the date validation rule:

Tip

Validation rules are tested only when the user exits Edit mode.

1. In cell **C6**, type the date **8/1/2025** and press **ENTER**. A message dialog box opens, indicating that the cell value doesn't match the data validation restrictions defined for this cell.

2. Click **Cancel** to close the dialog box and return to the cell with no specified date.

3. In cell **C6**, type **9/18/2024** and press **ENTER**. Because this date satisfies the validation rule, no error message appears, and the date is accepted.

The default error message doesn't explain why the data was invalid. You can provide specific information to the user with a custom error message.

Creating a Validation Error Message

Excel provides three ways of responding to invalid data. In decreasing order of strictness, they are:

1. **Stop**—The user is stopped, and no data entry is allowed in the cell unless it satisfies the validation rule (the default).
2. **Warning**—The user is warned, and data is allowed in the cell only after it is confirmed by the user as being correct.
3. **Information**—The user is informed that possibly invalid data is being entered and is given the opportunity to cancel the data entry.

With each error response, you can create a custom message explaining in more detail why the data was invalid and what the user should do to correct the problem.

Jenya wants the rule for donation dates to display a warning because it is possible that some donations will fall outside of the campaign period. This gives users the ability to still insert a date value that falls outside the stated date range. You will create the warning message now.

To create the warning error message:

▶ **1.** Click cell **C6** to select it, and then on the Data tab, in the Data Tools group, click the **Data Validation** button. The Data Validation dialog box opens.

▶ **2.** Click the **Error Alert** tab. You'll create the warning message on this tab.

▶ **3.** Verify that the **Show error alert after invalid data is entered** check box is selected.

▶ **4.** Click the **Style** box, and then click **Warning** to set the type of error alert.

▶ **5.** Click the **Title** box, and then type **Possible Invalid Date** as the title for the error message.

▶ **6.** Click the **Error message** box, and then type **The fundraising campaign is scheduled for 4/5/2024 through 7/1/2025.** (including the period). See Figure 12–10.

Tip

If you don't want users to be constantly reminded about the validation rule, deselect the Show error alert after invalid data is entered check box.

Figure 12–10   Warning error alert message

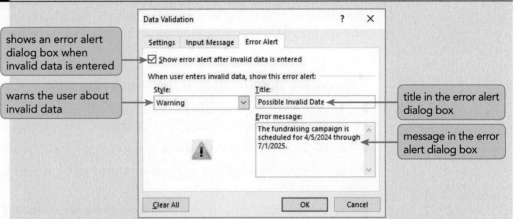

▶ **7.** Click **OK**.

▶ **8.** Click cell **C6**, type **8/1/2025** as the donation date, and then press **ENTER**. The warning message you created appears. See Figure 12–11.

Figure 12–11   Warning alert for an invalid date

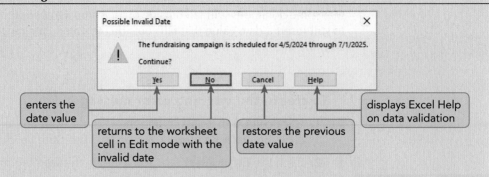

9. Click **Cancel** to stop the attempt at entering a potentially invalid data and return to cell C6, restoring the previous valid date of 9/18/2024.

Rather than constantly notifying users of attempts of entering invalid data, you can make an application more user-friendly by providing the validation rules in advance with an input message.

Creating an Input Message

An input message is a pop-up message appearing next to the cell that gives information about the type of data that is expected in the cell. Jenya wants you to add an input message to cell C6 indicating valid donation dates. You'll add the input message now.

To create the donation dates input message:

1. With cell C6 still selected, on the Data tab, in the Data Tools group, click the **Data Validation** button. The Data Validation dialog box opens.

2. Click the **Input Message** tab. You create the input message on this tab.

3. Click the **Title** box, type **Donation Dates** as the dialog box title, and then press **TAB**.

4. In the Input message box, type **Donations are collected from 4/5/2024 through 7/1/2025.** (including the period). See Figure 12–12.

Figure 12–12   Custom input message

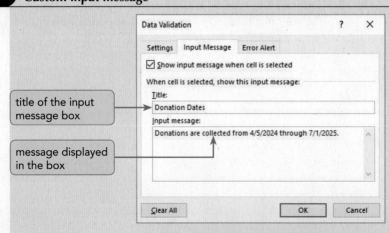

5. Click **OK**. Now when cell C6 is selected, an input message appears next to the cell. See Figure 12–13.

Figure 12–13   Input message box

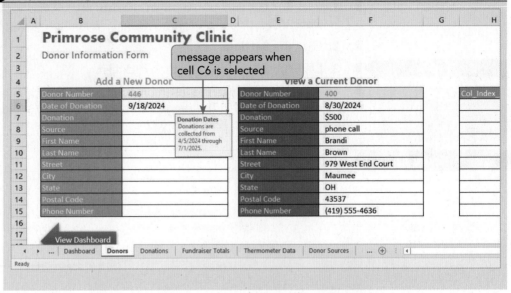

Jenya is confident that with the input message and validation rule, it is unlikely that invalid dates will be entered in cell C6. If at any time you need to remove the validation rule, error message, or input message from a cell or range, you can reopen the Data Validation dialog box and click the Clear Rules button.

Insight

Validating Against Past and Future Dates

Some applications, such as those that track sales or shipping data, limit the data to dates occurring before or after the current date. You can validate those dates using the TODAY function. To allow only dates before or on the current date, do the following:

1. Open the Data Validation dialog box.
2. Click the Allow box, and then click Choose Date.
3. Click the Data box, and then click "less than or equal to".
4. In the End date box, enter =TODAY().
5. Click OK.

Any date value that is less than or equal to the current date will be accepted. To allow only dates on or after the current date, change the value in the Data box to "greater than or equal to" and enter =TODAY() in the Start date box.

Validating Against a List

Another type of validation rule limits data values to a predefined list of accepted choices. Such lists appear within the cells as a drop-down list box from which the user can select a value, removing the need for typing. The list can be based on cells within the worksheet or entered directly into the Data Validation dialog box as a comma-separated list.

In this application, Jenya is tracking donations made in specific amounts from $250 up to $500,000. The donation categories are listed in the range J5:J15 of the Donors worksheet. You'll create a validation rule for cell C7 that limits its possible values to those listed in that range.

To validate the donation amounts against a list of values:

1. Click cell **C7**, and then on the Data tab, in the Data Tools group, click the **Data Validation** button. The Data Validation dialog box opens.

2. Click the **Settings** tab.

3. Click the **Allow** box, and then click **List**.

Tip

To reference cells from another worksheet, use a named range in the expression.

4. Press **TAB** to move the insertion point to the Source box, and then select the range **J5:J15**. The range reference =**$J$5:$J$15** appears in the Source box. See Figure 12–14.

Figure 12–14   List box validation

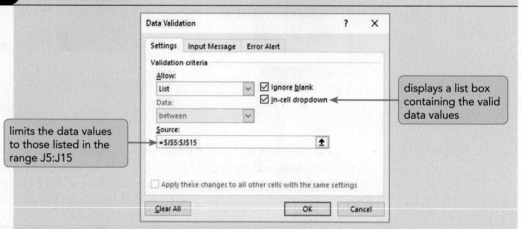

limits the data values to those listed in the range J5:J15

displays a list box containing the valid data values

5. Click **OK** to return to the worksheet.

6. Click the **arrow** button that appears next to cell C7 to display the list box of values, then scroll down and point to **$250,000**. See Figure 12–15.

Figure 12–15   List box values

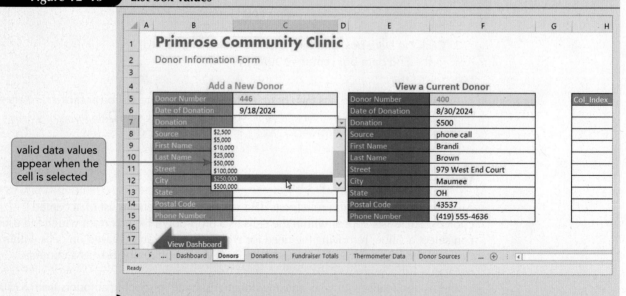

valid data values appear when the cell is selected

7. Click **$250,000**. The selected donation amount is entered in the cell.

In cell C8, users will enter the source of donation. The four possible values are in-person, phone call, online, or other. You'll enter a validation rule for cell C8 to limit values to these four choices by entering them as a comma-separated list in the Data Validation dialog box.

To validate donation source against a comma-separated list of values:

▶ **1.** Click cell **C8**, and then on the Data tab, in the Data Tools group, click the **Data Validation** button. The Data Validation dialog box opens.

▶ **2.** On the Settings tab, click the **Allow** box, and then click **List**.

▶ **3.** Press **TAB** to move the insertion point to the Source box, and then type **in-person, phone call, online, other** (including the commas between each donation source). See Figure 12–16.

Figure 12–16	Comma-separated data values

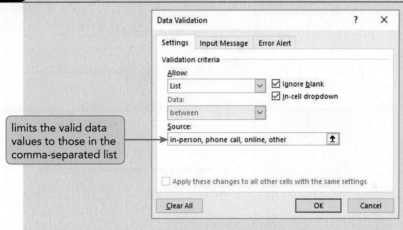

limits the valid data values to those in the comma-separated list

▶ **4.** Click **OK**.

▶ **5.** Click the **arrow** button next to cell C8, and then click **in-person**. The data source is added to the cell.

The only validation rule for the contact information in the range C9:C15 is that they should not be left blank. You can test for empty cells using a custom validation rule.

Creating a Custom Validation Rule

A custom validation rule is based on a logical expression that evaluates something as either TRUE (valid) or FALSE (invalid). For example, the expression `A10 = B10` returns a value of TRUE if cell A10 is equal to cell B10 and FALSE if it is not. The expression can include a reference to the cell for which you are validating, testing whether that cell's value satisfies the conditions of the logical expression.

The logical expression can include any of the Excel functions that evaluate as TRUE or FALSE. That means that the formula `=ISNUMBER(A10)` when applied to cell A10 will validate that cell only if it contains a number. You can combine logical expressions using an AND or an OR function to allow for multiple validation tests within the same cell. For example, the formula `=AND(A10 = B10, ISNUMBER(A10))` passes validation only when cell A10 is equal to cell B10 *and* is a number.

Jenya wants users to be informed that they have entered a blank value for a cell that should have a value. You will use the expression `=NOT(ISBLANK(C9))` to test whether the value in cell C9 is blank or not. If the cell is not blank, the expression returns the value TRUE (valid); otherwise, it returns the value FALSE (invalid). You'll apply this custom validation rule to all of the cells in the range C9:C15 and add an error alert.

To create a custom validation rule for the range C9:C15:

▶ 1. Select the range **C9:C15**, and then on the Data tab, in the Data Tools group, click the **Data Validation** button ⊞. The Data Validation dialog box opens.

▶ 2. On the Settings tab, click the **Allow** box, and then click **Custom**.

▶ 3. Click the **Ignore blank** check box to deselect it. This ensures that Excel does *not* ignore blank cells.

> Be sure to include the equal sign so Excel recognizes the custom validation rule as a formula.

▶ 4. In the Formula box, type **=NOT(ISBLANK(C9))** to test whether the value in cell C9 is blank. See Figure 12–17.

Figure 12–17	Custom validation rule

cell is valid only when not blank

applies the validation rule to all cells, including blank ones

▶ 5. Click the **Error Alert** tab, click the **Style** box, and then click **Information** to select the error alert style.

▶ 6. Press **TAB**, type **Missing Data** in the Title box, press **TAB**, and then type **Do you mean to leave this cell blank?** in the Error message box.

▶ 7. Click **OK** to apply the validation rule to the selected range.

▶ 8. Double-click cell **C9** to enter Edit mode, and then without typing any content, press **ENTER**. The Missing Data dialog box opens, asking whether you intend to leave the cell blank.

▶ 9. Click **OK** to leave cell C9 blank, return to the workbook, and select cell C10.

▶ 10. Repeat Steps 8 and 9 for cell C10 to confirm that the validation rule also applies to this cell.

▶ 11. In the range **C9:C15**, enter the remaining new donor information, as follows: **Kevin** in cell C9, **Nielsen** in cell C10, **100 Main Street** in cell C11, **El Paso** in cell C12, **TX** in cell C13, **79915** in cell C14, and **(915) 555-2308** in cell C15.

Every cell in the range C9:C15 obeys the same validation rule. Because you used a relative reference for the formula, the reference changes as the rule is applied throughout the range. For example, in cell C10, the expression is =NOT(ISBLANK(C10)) and so forth. If you don't want a reference to change, use an absolute cell reference or a defined name in your formula.

Insight

Validating for Uniqueness

Some entries require unique data. For example, if you are entering ID numbers into a workbook, you will need to ensure that those ID numbers are unique and not duplicated. You can use a custom validation rule to test for uniqueness by using the COUNTIF function in the form

```
=COUNTIF(range, cell) = 0
```

where *range* is the *range* containing a list of data values and *cell* is the cell that should not have a value already entered in that list. For example, the following formula tests whether the value in cell B2 has already been entered in the range D1:D100:

```
=COUNTIF($D$1:$D$100, B2) = 0
```

If the cell you are validating is also part of the range containing the data values, the formula has this slightly different form which tests whether the cell value occurs exactly once in the selected range:

```
=COUNTIF(range, cell) = 1
```

The following formula validates the value in cell D1 against the entire range D1:D100.

```
=COUNTIF($D$1:$D$100, D1) = 1
```

If you apply this validation rule to all the cells in the range D1:D100, every cell will be validated for uniqueness within the range. If the range D1:D100 contains ID numbers, each ID must be unique to pass validation.

With custom validation rules and Excel functions, you can create a wide variety of powerful validation criteria in which cell values are validated against values in other cells or calculations of the values in other cells.

Validating Data Already in the Workbook

A validation rule is applied only during data entry when the cell is in Edit mode. Validation rules are not applied to cells already containing data. To check data already in the workbook you can use the Circle Invalid Data command, which does not remove invalid data but does circle it so that you can edit or remove on your own.

To validate data already entered in the workbook, do the following:

1. Enter a validation rule for the range of cells you want to validate.
2. On the Data tab, in the Data Tools group, click the Data Validation arrow, and then click Circle Invalid Data. Red circles surround each cell containing invalid data.
3. To remove the validation circles, edit the cell(s) to make them valid or click the Data Validation arrow and click Clear Validation Circles.

To ensure the integrity of your data, you should use the Circle Invalid Data command on any data table in which you plan to perform an analysis.

Hiding Workbook Content

Excel workbooks often contain content you don't want users to see. You can hide worksheet rows and columns or entire worksheets from the user. Sometimes this is done to prevent users from seeing sensitive material. But more often, it's done to remove distractions such as data that is not important to your users or to keep users from mistakenly editing content that should not be edited. Hiding a row, column, or worksheet does not impact any formula in the workbook. Hidden formulas work the same as visible ones.

Jenya wants you to hide the content of cells H through J in the Donors worksheet because their content is not of interest to the users entering or retrieving donor data.

To hide worksheet columns H through J:

▶ **1.** Select the column headers for column **H** through column **J**.

▶ **2.** Right-click the selected columns, and then click **Hide** on the shortcut menu. The columns are hidden.

▶ **3.** Look at the column headers and notice that they jump from G to K.

Jenya created several worksheets that contain the data used for generating the charts and PivotTables that appear on the Dashboard worksheet. She wants you to hide these sheets from users.

To hide worksheets in the workbook:

▶ **1.** Click the **Fundraiser Totals** sheet tab to select it.

▶ **2.** Use the Sheet Scrolling buttons in the lower-left corner of the workbook window to scroll to the last sheet in the workbook.

▶ **3.** Press **SHIFT**, click the **Donation History** sheet tab, and then release **SHIFT**. The Fundraiser Tools worksheet through the Donation History worksheet are now part of a worksheet group.

▶ **4.** Right-click the worksheet group, and then click **Hide** on the shortcut menu. The worksheet group is hidden, leaving only the Documentation, Dashboard, Donors, Donations, and Terms and Definitions worksheets still visible.

You can make a hidden worksheet visible again. Right-click any sheet tab in the workbook, click Unhide on the shortcut menu, click the name of the hidden worksheet you want, and then click OK to make the selected worksheet reappear. To unhide multiple worksheets, hold the CTRL key as you click each sheet name in the list of hidden worksheets.

Protecting Workbook Contents

A final way of restricting the actions of users in an application is to protect a worksheet or an entire workbook from unauthorized changes. Once a worksheet or workbook is protected, it can be altered only by users who know the password that opens the sheet for editing.

Protecting a Worksheet

When you set up worksheet protection, you specify which actions users are allowed in the protected sheet. The default is to allow users to only select cells, but you can also give users the ability to perform other tasks such as formatting cells, inserting rows and columns, editing scenarios, sorting data, and deleting rows and columns. As long as the worksheet is protected, those limitations are in place. They are removed only after the sheet is no longer protected.

Reference

Protecting a Worksheet

To unlock cells that users can access in a protected worksheet:
- Select the range to unlock so that users can enter data in them.
- On the Home tab, in the Cells group, click the Format button, and then click Format Cells (or press CTRL+1).
- In the Format Cells dialog box, click the Protection tab.
- Click the Locked check box to remove the checkmark.
- Click OK.

To protect a worksheet:
- On the Review tab, in the Protect group, click the Protect Sheet button.
- Enter a password (optional).
- Select all the actions you want to allow users to take when the worksheet is protected.
- Click OK.

Jenya wants you to protect the worksheets in the workbook that appear after the Documentation sheet. You'll protect each of the four sheets now.

To protect a worksheet:

1. Click the **Dashboard** sheet tab.

2. On the ribbon, click the **Review** tab, and then in the Protect group, click the **Protect Sheet** button. The Protect Sheet dialog box opens. See Figure 12–18.

Figure 12–18 Protect Sheet dialog box

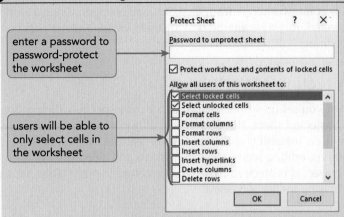

enter a password to password-protect the worksheet

users will be able to only select cells in the worksheet

In the Protect Sheet dialog box, you can specify a password that must be entered before the sheet can be unprotected. You can also go through a checklist of tasks that users are allowed to do within the protected sheet. The default is to allow users to select worksheet cells.

▶ **3.** Click **OK** to protect the sheet without a password and without allowing users to do anything other than selecting cells.

▶ **4.** For each of the three remaining worksheets in the workbook, go to the worksheet, click any cell in the worksheet, and then repeat Steps 2 and 3.

▶ **5.** Go to the **Donors** worksheet and click cell **C6**. You will verify that you cannot enter data into this protected sheet.

▶ **6.** Try to enter a value into the cell. An error message dialog box opens indicating that you cannot make changes on a protected sheet.

▶ **7.** Click **OK**.

Tip

Passwords are case-sensitive. The password "admin" is different from "ADMIN".

If you don't include a password in the Protect Sheet dialog box, any user will be able to unprotect the sheet by clicking the Unprotect Sheet button in the Protect group on the Review tab. If you do include a password, *don't lose it*. Without the password, you won't be able to unprotect the sheet.

Protecting a Workbook

Worksheet protection applies only to the contents of a worksheet, not to the worksheet itself. To keep a worksheet from being modified, you need to protect the workbook. You can protect both the structure and the windows of a workbook. Protecting the structure prevents users from renaming, deleting, hiding, or inserting worksheets. Protecting the windows prevents users from moving, resizing, closing, or hiding parts of the Excel window. The default is to protect only the structure of the workbook, not the windows used to display it.

Reference

Protecting a Workbook

- On the Review tab, in the Protect group, click the Protect Workbook button.
- Click the check boxes to indicate whether you want to protect the workbook's structure, windows, or both.
- Enter a password (optional).
- Click OK.

You can also add a password to the workbook protection. However, the same guidelines apply as for protecting worksheets. Add a password only if you are concerned that others might unprotect the workbook and modify it. If you add a password, keep in mind that it is case-sensitive, and you cannot unprotect the workbook without it.

Jenya asks that you protect the workbook itself so that users cannot inadvertently hide or delete a worksheet.

To protect Jenya's workbook:

1. On the Review tab, in the Protect group, click the **Protect Workbook** button. The Protect Structure and Windows dialog box opens. See Figure 12–19.

Figure 12–19	Protect Structure and Windows dialog box

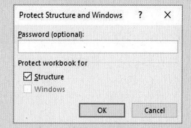

2. Make sure the **Structure** check box is checked and the **Password** box is blank. The Windows check box is unavailable and unchecked.

3. Click **OK** to protect the workbook without specifying a password.

4. Right-click the **Donors** sheet tab, and then on the shortcut menu, notice that the Insert, Delete, Rename, Move or Copy, Tab Color, Hide, and Unhide commands are gray. This indicates that these options for modifying worksheets are no longer available in the protected workbook.

5. Press **ESC** to close the shortcut menu.

Unprotecting a Worksheet and a Workbook

You can always unprotect a protected worksheet to make additional edits to its content. If you assigned a password when you protected the worksheet, you must enter that password to remove worksheet protection. Likewise, you can unprotect a protected workbook to make changes to its structure, such as if you need to insert a new worksheet or rename an existing worksheet. Once you make the changes you need to the worksheet content and workbook structure, you can then reapply worksheet and workbook protection.

Jenya has edits she wants you to make to the Donors worksheet. You will unprotect that worksheet to make the changes. You can leave the other worksheets protected.

To turn off protection for the Donors worksheet:

Tip

To remove workbook protection, click the Protect Workbook button in the Protect group on the Review tab.

1. On the Review tab, in the Protect group, click the **Unprotect Sheet** button. The name of the button changes to Protect Sheet and the Donors worksheet is once again available for editing.

Locking and Unlocking Cells

Most applications don't require that you protect everything. Usually, you want to allow users to edit some cells but not others. In particular, you don't want users to be able to edit cells containing formulas that are important to actions of the application. You can determine which cells users can edit with the locked property.

Every cell in the workbook contains a **locked property** that determines whether changes can be made to that cell. The locked property is unused until the worksheet is protected. Once a worksheet is protected, only those cells that are unlocked can be edited. See Figure 12–20.

Figure 12–20   **Locked and unlocked cells**

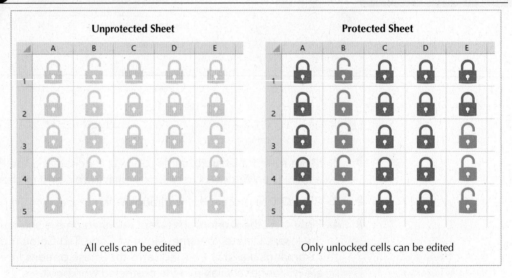

All cells can be edited   Only unlocked cells can be edited

The default is to lock every cell in a worksheet. Once the sheet is protected, *all* cell contents are protected. However, you can unlock some cells to make them editable even with a protected worksheet.

Insight

Highlighting Unlocked Cells

You cannot tell from the worksheet which cells are locked or unlocked until you protect the sheet and attempt to edit cells. However, you can highlight all the unlocked cells with conditional formatting and the CELL function. The **CELL function** is used to retrieve information about a cell and has the syntax:

CELL(*info_type*, *reference*)

where ***info_type*** is the name of information about the cell and ***reference*** is the cell reference. For example, the following formula determines whether cell A1 is locked:

=CELL("protect", A1)

The formula returns a value of 1 for locked cells and 0 for unlocked cells. You can use this formula in a conditional format to highlight unlocked cells in the worksheet. Do the following:

1. Unprotect the worksheet and select all cells in the sheet.
2. On the Home tab, in the Styles group, click the Conditional Formatting button, and then click New Rule.
3. In the New Formatting Rule dialog box, click Use a formula to determine which cells to format.
4. In the Format values where this formula is true box, enter the formula =CELL("protect", A1)=0.
5. Click Format to select a format for cells that are unlocked, and then click OK.
6. Click OK to apply the conditional format.

Every unlocked cell in the selected range will be formatted with the conditional format you chose.

Jenya wants users to be able to edit the cells in the range C6:C15 and cell F5. You'll change the lock property of those cells now.

To unlock the cells in the range C6:C15,F5:

1. Select the nonadjacent range **C6:C15,F5**.

2. On the ribbon, click the **Home** tab. In the Cells group, click the **Format** button, and then click **Format Cells** (or press **CTRL+1**). The Format Cells dialog box opens.

3. Click the **Protection** tab to view protection options for the selected cells.

4. Click the **Locked** check box to remove the checkmark. See Figure 12–21.

Figure 12–21 Protection tab in the Format Cells dialog box

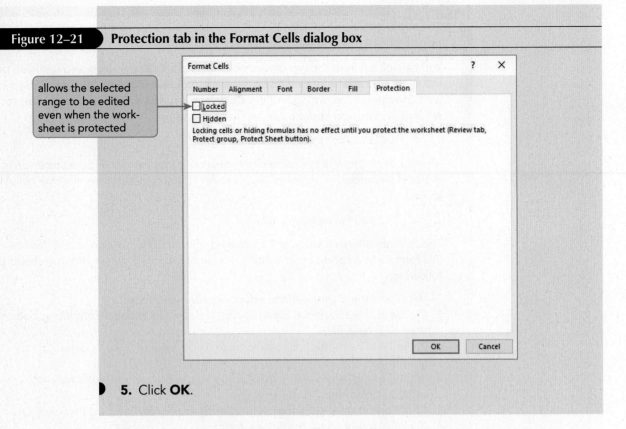

allows the selected range to be edited even when the worksheet is protected

5. Click **OK**.

Next, you will protect the Donors worksheet again and confirm you can edit the unlocked cells even when the sheet is protected.

To protect the Donors worksheet:

1. On the ribbon, click the **Review** tab, and then in the Protect group, click the **Protect Sheet** button. The Protect Sheet dialog box opens.

2. Click **OK** to apply protection to the worksheet.

3. Click cell **F5**, type **300** as the donor number, and then press **ENTER**. The worksheet displays data for Luciana Fisher who donated $250 to the campaign on 7/27/2024. You were able to edit a cell that was unlocked.

4. Double-click cell **F6** to attempt to go into Edit mode. A dialog box opens, alerting you that the cell is protected. You cannot edit a cell that was not unlocked.

5. Click **OK** to close the dialog box.

6. Double-click cell **C11**, change Kevin Nielsen's street address from 100 Main Street to **150 Main Street**, and then press **ENTER**. You can edit this unlocked cell.

7. Save the workbook.

The only cells that users can edit in the Donors worksheet are the cells you want them to edit. Any cell containing a formula or a design element is locked and cannot be edited.

Proskills

Teamwork: Assigning Ranges to Users

A workbook might be shared among several colleagues. But you might want to assign each colleague a different range to edit. The technique of unlocking cells does not distinguish between one user and another. The cells in a workbook are locked or unlocked for every user.

You can fine-tune access to the contents of a workbook using the Allow Edit Ranges button in the Protect group on the Review tab. This tool lets you define who can edit which ranges when the worksheet is protected. You can even create different passwords for each range. Thus, workers in one department can edit one range of data and while workers in another department are limited to a different range.

Editable ranges are a useful tool when you have several groups of employees accessing and editing the workbook. You can then control who has access to existing data and who has the clearance to enter new data.

You've restricted access to Jenya's Excel workbook by controlling what kind of data users can enter, what parts of the workbook are visible to them, and what parts of the workbook can be edited. In the next session, you will finish Jenya's application by creating a macro to insert new donors into the Donations table.

Review

Session 12.2 Quick Check

1. What are three responses to invalid data?
2. Why would you create an input message for a cell?
3. What are two ways of specifying a validation list?
4. Provide a custom validation expression that validates the data only if cell C10 is less than or equal cell D10.
5. When do you use the Circle Invalid Data command?
6. Can you rename a protected worksheet? Explain why or why not.
7. What is a locked cell? When does locking a cell take effect?

Session 12.3 Visual Overview:

The Macros button opens the Macro dialog box, which you use to run or edit macros.

The Record Macro button opens the Record Macro dialog box, which you use to start recording a macro.

The macro security settings control the security level for workbooks containing macros.

In the Record Macro dialog box, you specify a name, shortcut key, location, and description of a macro.

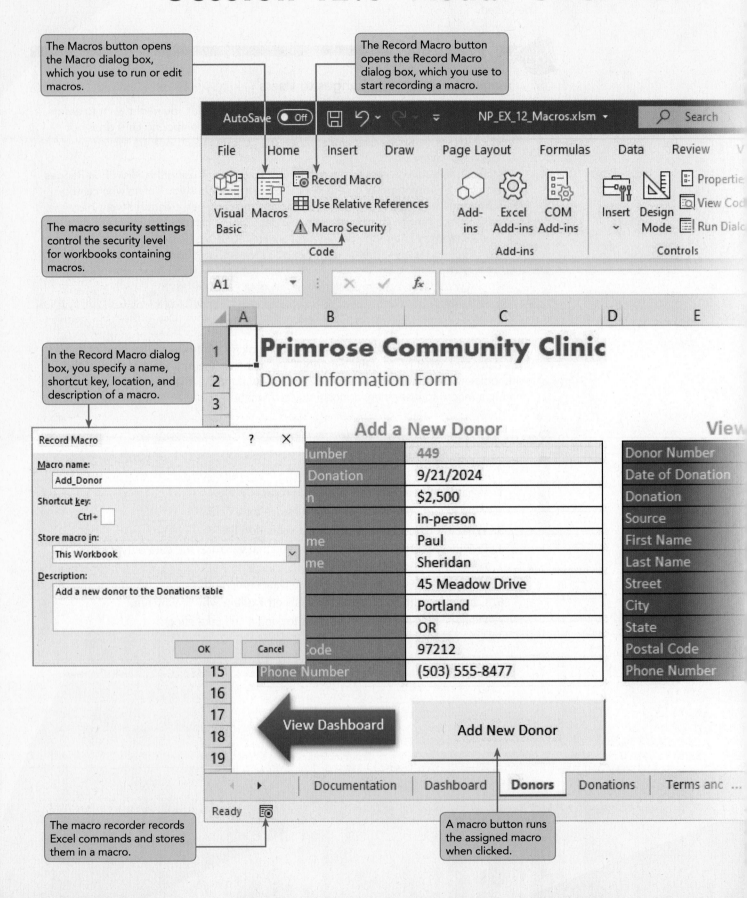

AutoSave ⬤ Off   NP_EX_12_Macros.xlsm ▾   🔎 Search

File   Home   Insert   Draw   Page Layout   Formulas   Data   Review

Visual Basic   Macros   📷 Record Macro   ⊞ Use Relative References   ⚠ Macro Security   Add-ins   Excel Add-ins   COM Add-ins   Insert ▾   Design Mode   📋 Properties   🔍 View Code   ⊞ Run Dialog

Code   Add-ins   Controls

A1

Primrose Community Clinic

Donor Information Form

Add a New Donor   View

Record Macro   ?   ✕

Macro name:
Add_Donor

Shortcut key:
Ctrl+ [ ]

Store macro in:
This Workbook

Description:
Add a new donor to the Donations table

OK   Cancel

Number	449
Donation	9/21/2024
n	$2,500
	in-person
me	Paul
me	Sheridan
	45 Meadow Drive
	Portland
	OR
Code	97212
Phone Number	(503) 555-8477

Donor Number
Date of Donation
Donation
Source
First Name
Last Name
Street
City
State
Postal Code
Phone Number

View Dashboard ⬅   **Add New Donor**

◄ ►   Documentation   Dashboard   **Donors**   Donations   Terms and ...

Ready   📷

The macro recorder records Excel commands and stores them in a macro.

A macro button runs the assigned macro when clicked.

Macros and Visual Basic for Applications

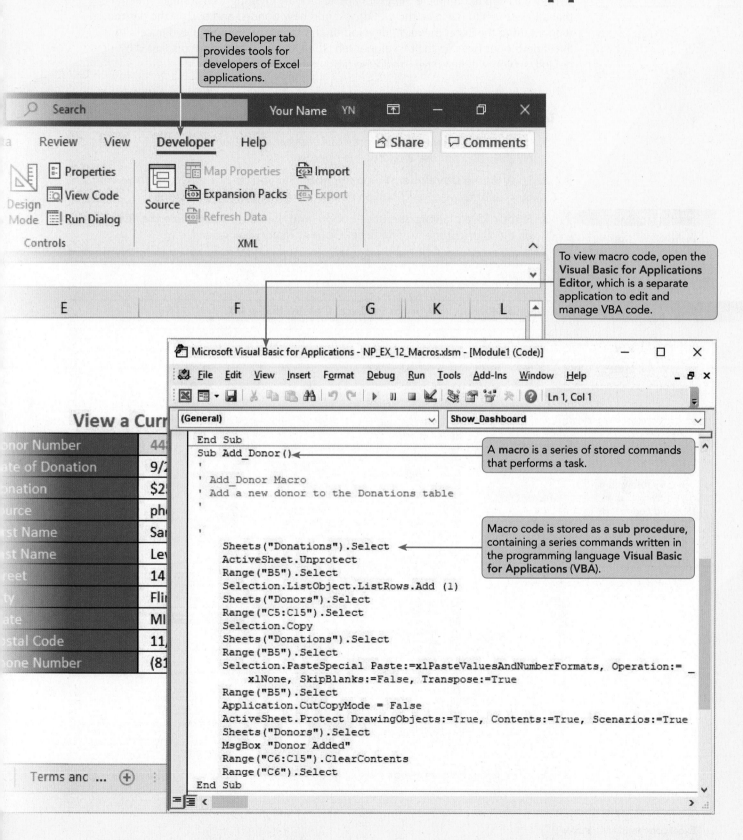

The Developer tab provides tools for developers of Excel applications.

To view macro code, open the **Visual Basic for Applications Editor**, which is a separate application to edit and manage VBA code.

A **macro** is a series of stored commands that performs a task.

Macro code is stored as a sub procedure, containing a series commands written in the programming language Visual Basic for Applications (VBA).

```
    End Sub
    Sub Add_Donor()
    '
    ' Add_Donor Macro
    ' Add a new donor to the Donations table
    '

    '
        Sheets("Donations").Select
        ActiveSheet.Unprotect
        Range("B5").Select
        Selection.ListObject.ListRows.Add (1)
        Sheets("Donors").Select
        Range("C5:C15").Select
        Selection.Copy
        Sheets("Donations").Select
        Range("B5").Select
        Selection.PasteSpecial Paste:=xlPasteValuesAndNumberFormats, Operation:= _
            xlNone, SkipBlanks:=False, Transpose:=True
        Range("B5").Select
        Application.CutCopyMode = False
        ActiveSheet.Protect DrawingObjects:=True, Contents:=True, Scenarios:=True
        Sheets("Donors").Select
        MsgBox "Donor Added"
        Range("C6:C15").ClearContents
        Range("C6").Select
    End Sub
```

Loading the Excel Developer Tab

Jenya wants you to complete the Excel application by creating a customized interface that allows users to navigate the workbook, add new donors, and update the dashboard without using the Excel menu. In developing this interface, you will need access to Excel developer tools on the Developer tab. The Developer tab is not displayed by default, so you will first have to add the tab to the Excel ribbon.

To add the Developer tab to the ribbon:

1. If you took a break after the previous session, make sure the NP_EX_12_Primrose workbook is open.

2. Look for the **Developer** tab on the ribbon. If you do not see it, continue with Step 3; otherwise, read but do not perform the rest of these steps.

Tip
You can also click Options in Backstage view to open the Excel Options dialog box.

3. Right-click a blank spot on the ribbon, and then click **Customize the Ribbon** on the shortcut menu. The Excel Options dialog box opens.

4. In the right pane, click the **Developer** check box to select it. See Figure 12–22.

Figure 12–22   Customize Ribbon category in the Excel Options dialog box

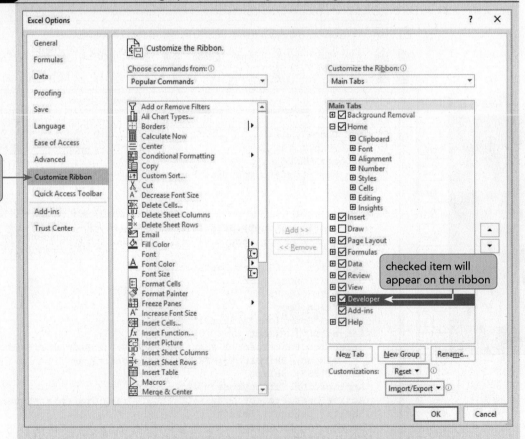

5. Click **OK**. The dialog box closes, and the Developer tab is added to the ribbon.

Now that you've added the Developer tab, you can start working on the next phase in developing an Excel application: creating a macro.

Automating Tasks with Macros

A macro is a collection of commands that accomplish a task. The tasks could be short and straightforward such as switching between one workbook and another, or they can be long and involved such as adding a new record to an Excel table and refreshing the reports that rely on that table. Macros save time by replacing a long sequence of commands with a single command.

Macros are stored as lines of program code, usually attached to the workbook. When you run a macro, Excel accesses the stored code, executing every command in the macro. There are two ways to generate macro code: You can type the code directly into a program editor, or you can record the actions to accomplish the task and have Excel write the macro code for you based on the recording. The best way to start learning about macros is through the recording process.

Recording a Macro

The macro recorder works like any other kind of recorder: You start the recorder, perform whatever tasks you wish, and then stop the recorder. All of your actions are recorded as macro code for later playback.

Reference

Recording a Macro

- Save the workbook before you start the recording.
- On the Developer tab, in the Code group, click the Record Macro button.
- Enter a name for the macro.
- Specify a shortcut key (optional).
- Specify the location to store the macro.
- Enter a description of the macro (optional).
- Click OK to start the macro recorder.
- Perform the tasks you want to automate.
- Click the Stop Recording button.

Jenya wants users of the workbook to be able to quickly access the contents of the dashboard. To accomplish that task, you will record a macro to switch to the Dashboard worksheet from anywhere in the workbook. You'll begin the macro recorder now.

To start the macro recorder:

Always save your workbook before beginning a recording. If you make a mistake in the recording, you can close the file without saving your changes and try again.

1. Save the workbook.

2. Go to the **Documentation** worksheet. This is the starting point of the macro.

3. On the ribbon, click the **Developer** tab.

4. In the Code group, click the **Record Macro** button. The Record Macro dialog box opens.

5. Type **Show_Dashboard** in the Macro name box, and then press **TAB** twice to go to the Store macro in box.

6. If it is not already selected, select **This Workbook** from the Store macro in box to store the macro in the current workbook, and then press **TAB** to go to the Description box.

7. Type **Display the contents of the Dashboard** in the Description box. See Figure 12–23.

Figure 12–23   Record Macro dialog box

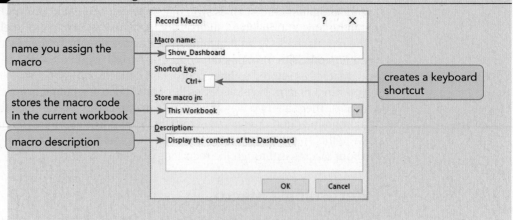

name you assign the macro

creates a keyboard shortcut

stores the macro code in the current workbook

macro description

You are ready to begin recording your actions. From this point on, every command you perform will be recorded as part of the Show_Dashboard macro. In any macro recording, you want to be very careful and precise in following the steps because every command you perform will be recorded in the order you perform them in. You'll start recording the macro now.

To record the macro:

1. Click **OK** to begin the recorder.

2. Click the **Dashboard** sheet tab to make Dashboard the active sheet in the workbook.

3. Click cell **A1** to make it the active cell in the worksheet. Note that even if cell A1 is already the active cell, you still select it to ensure that is always the active cell when a user switches to the dashboard.

4. On the Developer tab, in the Code group, click the **Stop Recording** button. The macro recording is turned off and no additional tasks will be added to the macro code.

Be sure to turn off the macro recorder when you are done. Otherwise, the recorder will add every additional task to the macro code.

The Show_Dashboard macro that you recorded is stored in the current document.

Insight

Creating a Macro Library with the Personal Macro Workbook

Excel has three options for storing macro code: in the current workbook where the macro was recorded, in a new workbook, or in the Personal Macro workbook. The **Personal Macro workbook** is a hidden workbook named Personal.xlsb that opens whenever you start Excel. Every macro in the Personal Macro workbook is accessible to any open workbook, making the Personal Macro workbook an ideal location for a macro library.

The Personal.xlsb file is stored in the Excel XLSTART folder. If you want to share your macro library, you can send colleagues a copy of the workbook or you can make that workbook available on a shared server. An IT department might have such a macro library stored on a shared server with macros tailored to specific needs of its organization or company.

Running a Macro

After recording a macro, you should run it to verify that it works as intended. In running the macro, Excel runs the same commands in the same order that they were recorded, including any mistakes you may have made during the recording!

Reference

Running a Macro

- Press the shortcut key assigned to the macro.
or
- On the Developer tab, in the Code group, click the Macros button.
- Select the macro from the list of macros.
- Click Run.

You will test the Show_Dashboard macro by running it.

To run the Show_Dashboard macro:

1. Go to the **Donors** worksheet as the starting point for running the macro. The macro should work from any worksheet.

2. On the Developer tab, in the Code group, click the **Macros** button (or press **ALT+F8**). The Macro dialog box opens. See Figure 12–24.

| Figure 12–24 | Macro dialog box |

3. Verify the **Show_Dashboard** macro is selected, and then click **Run**. The Dashboard worksheet becomes the active sheet with cell A1 selected.

Trouble? If the macro does not go to the Dashboard worksheet, you probably made a mistake in recording the actions. Close the workbook without saving, and then reopen the workbook and repeat both set of steps in the previous section to record the macro again.

The Show_Dashboard macro will work from any sheet in the workbook, jumping the user to cell A1 in the Dashboard worksheet. Before creating other macros, you should save your workbook and the macro you recorded so you don't lose your work if you make mistakes in recording other macros.

Saving and Opening a Macro-Enabled Workbook

Workbooks that contain macros pose a security risk for Excel because macros could contain viruses or malicious software. The default Excel file format does not support macros. If you want to save a workbook containing macros, you must save it in the macro-enabled workbook format, preserving both your data and the macro code attached to the workbook. You will save the NP_EX_12_Primrose workbook as a macro-enabled workbook.

To save Jenya's workbook as a macro-enabled workbook:

1. On the ribbon, click the **File** tab, and then in the navigation bar, click **Save As**.

2. Type **NP_EX_12_Macros** in the File name box.

3. Click **Save as type** box below the file name box, and then click **Excel Macro-Enabled Workbook (*.xlsm)** so you can save the macro you just recorded with your workbook.

4. Click **Save**. Excel saves the file NP_EX_12_Macros.xlsm to the same folder containing the NP_EX_12_Primrose.xlsx file.

5. Close the workbook.

Next you will reopen the workbook file. When Excel encounters a macro-enabled workbook, it prompts you, for security reasons, to enable the macros in the workbook. If you don't enable the macros, they remain part of the workbook, but you cannot run them. This extra step is done to prevent you from mistakenly opening a third-party workbook containing malicious code. You'll reopen the NP_EX_12_Macros workbook now, enabling the macros it contains.

To open the macro-enabled NP_EX_12_Macros workbook:

1. Open the **NP_EX_12_Macros** workbook. A Message Bar with a security warning that the workbook contains macros that have been disabled appears below the ribbon. See Figure 12–25.

Figure 12–25   Security Warning for a macro-enabled workbook

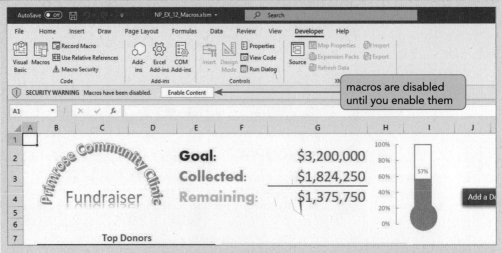

2. Click **Enable Content** to enable the macros in your workbook. The workbook opens.

After you enable content from a macro-enabled workbook, Excel adds the file to a list of trusted documents. As a trusted document, the security warning will not reappear as long as the workbook name or file location remains unchanged.

Assigning Macros to Shapes and Buttons

Macros can be assigned to graphic objects and command buttons so that you and others can quickly run macros by clicking those objects. You do not need the Developer tab to run your macro once it's been recorded.

Assigning a Macro to a Shape

Any object within a workbook that can be clicked can be turned into an object that runs a macro. Assigning a macro to a graphic object simplifies an application for users because they only have to click objects within the workbook, not interact with the Excel ribbon or buttons.

Jenya created an arrow shape containing the text "View Dashboard" on the Donors worksheet. You will assign the Show_Dashboard macro to this object.

To assign a macro to a graphic:

1. Go to the **Donors** worksheet.

2. On the ribbon, click the **Review** tab, and then in the Protect group, click the **Unprotect Sheet** button. You can now make modifications to the worksheet.

3. Right-click the **View Dashboard** arrow graphic in rows 17 through 19, and then click **Assign Macro** on the shortcut menu. The Assign Macro dialog box opens.

4. In the list of macros, click **Show_Dashboard** to select it, and then click **OK**. The macro is assigned to the graphic.

5. Click cell **A1** to deselect the arrow graphic.

6. On the Review tab, in the Protect group, click the **Protect Sheet** button. The Protect Sheet dialog box opens.

7. Click **OK** to again protect the contents of the worksheet. Now you'll test the macro.

8. Click the **View Dashboard** graphic. Cell A1 in the Dashboard worksheet becomes the active cell.

The dashboard also includes a graphic arrow for displaying the contents of the Donors worksheet. You'll create a new macro named Show_Donors_Sheet to show the contents of that sheet.

To record a macro to show the Donors worksheet:

1. Save the workbook so that if you make a mistake you can restart the process of creating the Show_Donors_Sheet macro.

2. On the ribbon, click the **Developer** tab, and then in the Code group, click the **Record Macro** button. The Record Macro dialog box opens.

▶ 3. Type **Show_Donors_Sheet** in the Macro name box, type **Go to the Donors worksheet** in the Description box, and then verify that **This Workbook** appears in the Store macro in box.

▶ 4. Click **OK** to begin the recorder.

▶ 5. Click the **Donors** sheet tab, and then click cell **A1** to select it (even if it is already selected).

▶ 6. Click the **Stop Recording** button to stop the macro recorder and create the Show_Donors_Sheet macro.

Next, you will assign the macro to the Add a Donor graphic arrow on the dashboard.

To assign the Show_Donors_Sheet macro to a graphic object:

▶ 1. Go to the **Dashboard** worksheet.

▶ 2. On the ribbon, click the **Review** tab, and then in the Protect group, click the **Unprotect Sheet** button so you can edit the contents of the worksheet.

▶ 3. Right-click the **Add a Donor** arrow in the upper-right corner of the dashboard, and then click **Assign Macro**. The Assign Macro dialog box opens.

▶ 4. In the macros list, click **Show_Donors_Sheet** to select it, and then click **OK**.

▶ 5. Click cell **A1** to deselect the arrow graphic.

▶ 6. In the Protect group, click the **Protect Sheet** button to open the Protect Sheet dialog box, and then click **OK**. The worksheet is once again protected.

▶ 7. Click the **Add a Donor** arrow and verify that cell A1 in the Donors worksheet becomes the active cell.

Trouble? If the macro fails or reports an error, close the workbook without saving changes, then reopen the workbook, and then repeat the previous two sets of steps to record the macro again.

By using graphic arrows, users can quickly switch between viewing the dashboard and viewing the worksheet containing information on specific donors.

Insight

Assigning Keyboard Shortcuts to Macros

Another way to quickly run a macro is with a keyboard shortcut. You can assign a shortcut key to run the macro within the Record Macro dialog box by selecting CTRL plus a letter or selecting CTRL+SHIFT plus a letter. If you use a shortcut key combination that is already assigned to a default Excel shortcut, the new shortcut you create overrides the default Excel shortcut for the workbook. For example, using CTRL+p to run a macro overrides the default keyboard shortcut for opening the Print screen (CTRL+P).

Some users find macro shortcut keys a quick way to run a macro. Others dislike them because they can sometimes override the original function of the shortcut key, confusing users who use the built-in Excel keyboard shortcuts. The keyboard shortcut exists as long as the macro-enabled workbook is opened. Once you close the workbook, the keyboard shortcut for the macro disappears and any Excel commands assigned to the keyboard combination return.

Another way to assign a macro to a worksheet object is to assign it to a form button.

Assigning a Macro to a Button

The Developer tab includes options for creating **form controls**, which are form elements used for entering data and running commands. You can create form controls for input boxes, check boxes, spinners, and list boxes among other choices. The controls can also be linked to worksheet cells so that a user can set or change a cell value by clicking a form control.

You'll examine one type of form control called a macro button that can be clicked to run a macro. The first macro button will be used with a macro that adds a new donor to the Donations table based on information from the Donors worksheet. You'll start the process of recording the Add_Donor macro.

To begin creating the Add_Donor macro:

1. Save the workbook so that if you make a mistake you can restart the process of creating the Add_Donor macro.

2. On the ribbon, click the **Developer** tab, and then in the Code group, click the **Record Macro** button. The Record Macro dialog box opens.

3. Verify that **This Workbook** appears in the Store macro in box.

4. Type **Add_Donor** in the Macro name box, and then type **Add a new donor to the Donations table** in the Description box.

5. Click **OK** to start the recorder.

After this point every command you enter will be recorded. Note that this macro contains several steps, so take it slow and perform every action precisely as described. Do not omit or add anything. It's often a good idea to practice any set of steps before doing them with the macro recorder. If you do practice the steps, be sure to reset the workbook back to its original conditions before you start the actual recording.

Caution! If at any time you make a mistake as you perform these steps, you can stop the recording, close the workbook without saving changes, and then reopen the workbook and try again starting from the previous set of steps. Another option is to stop the macro, click the Macros button from Code group on the Developer tab, select Add_Donor from the list of macros, click Delete to remove the macro, and repeat the previous set of steps to begin creating the macro again. If you choose this method, make sure that you have reset the workbook to its original condition prior to recording the macro.

To add a new donor to the donations table:

1. Click the **Donations** sheet tab to display the contents of the donations table.

2. On the ribbon, click the **Review** tab, and then in the Protect group, click the **Unprotect Sheet** button to enable you to edit the worksheet.

3. Click cell **B5** to select it.

4. On the ribbon, click the **Home** tab, and then in the Cells group, click the **Insert** button to insert a new record at the top of the Donations table.

5. Click the **Donors** sheet tab to return to the Donors worksheet.

6. Select the range **C5:C15**, and then in the Clipboard group, click the **Copy** button.

7. Click the **Donations** sheet tab.

8. In the Clipboard group, click the **Paste arrow**, and then click **Paste Special** to open the Paste Special dialog box.

9. In the Paste section, click the **Values and number formats** option button, and then at the bottom of the dialog box, click the **Transpose** check box. See Figure 12–26.

Figure 12–26   **Paste Special dialog box**

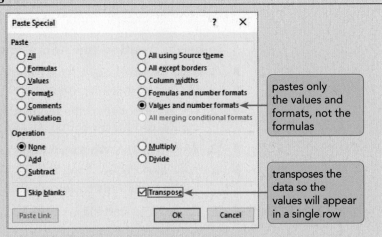

pastes only the values and formats, not the formulas

transposes the data so the values will appear in a single row

10. Click **OK** to paste the copied values into the top row of the Donations table. See Figure 12–27.

Figure 12–27   **New donor added to the Donations table**

new table row contains donation data for Kevin Nielsen

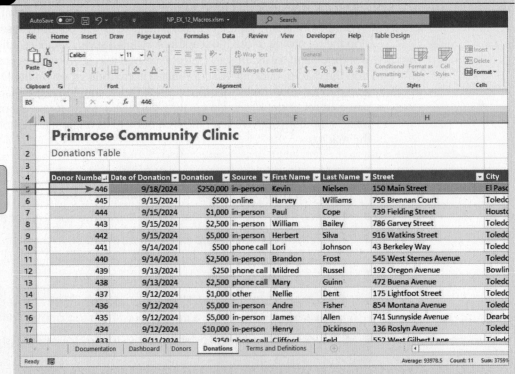

▶ **11.** On the ribbon, click the **Review** tab, and then in the Protect group, click the **Protect Sheet** button to open the Protect Sheet dialog box.

▶ **12.** Click **OK** to again protect the worksheet contents.

▶ **13.** Click the **Donors** sheet tab to return to the Donors worksheet.

▶ **14.** Click cell **C5** to make it the active cell in the worksheet.

▶ **15.** On the ribbon, click the **Developer** tab, and then in the Code group, click the **Stop Recording** button. You have completed recording the macro.

With the Add_Donor macro recorded and saved, you will assign it to a macro button you place on the Donors worksheet.

To create a macro button for the Add_Donor macro:

▶ **1.** On the ribbon, click **Review** tab, and then in the Protect group, click the **Unprotect Sheet** button so that you can add a form control to the worksheet contents.

▶ **2.** On the ribbon, click the **Developer** tab, and then in the Controls group, click the **Insert** button. A gallery of Form Controls appears with a variety of objects that can be placed in the worksheet. See Figure 12–28.

| **Figure 12–28** | Gallery of Form Controls and ActiveX Controls |

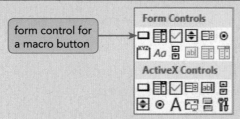

▶ **3.** Click the **Button (Form Control)** icon in the first row and first column of the Form Controls section and then point to cell **C17**.

▶ **4.** Click and drag the pointer over the range **C17:C18** and then release the mouse button. The Assign Macro dialog box opens.

▶ **5.** Click **Add_Donor** in the list of macros to assign to the button, and then click **OK**. A new button appears on the worksheet.

▶ **6.** With the button still selected in the worksheet, type **Add New Donor** as the button label. See Figure 12–29.

Figure 12–29   Button to run the Add_Donor macro

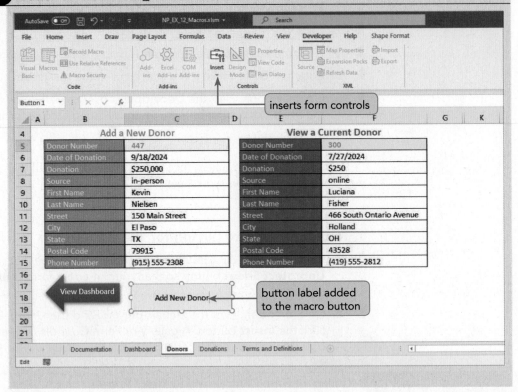

You will test the macro button and the Add_Donor macro now by adding a new donor to the Donations table.

To test the Add_Donor macro:

1. Click cell **C6** to deselect the macro button.

2. On the ribbon, click the **Review** tab, in the Protect group, click the **Protect Sheet** button to open the Protect Sheet dialog box, and then click **OK** to again protect the worksheet contents.

3. In the range **C6:C15**, enter the following data: **9/19/2024** in cell C6, **$10,000** in cell C7, **other** in cell C8, **Laura** in cell C9, **Raymond** in cell C10, **8 Elm Drive** in cell C11, **Columbus** in cell C12, **OH** in cell C13, **43229** in cell C14, and **(614) 555-4856** in cell C15.

4. Click the **Add New Donor** button. Excel runs the Add_Donor macro, adding the data to the Donations table and returning the Donors worksheet.

5. Go to the **Donations** sheet to verify that Laura Raymond's donation was added to the table. See Figure 12–30.

Figure 12–30   **Laura Raymond donation added using a macro**

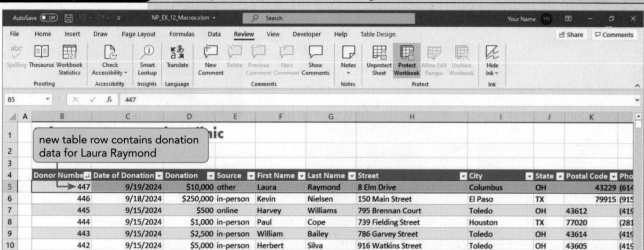

Trouble? If the macro fails or returns an error message, close the workbook without saving changes. Reopen the workbook and repeat each set of steps in this section, beginning with creating the Add_Donor macro. If you still cannot get the macro to work, ask your instructor or technical support person for help.

The donations from the two new donors you added to the Donations table will not be reflected in the statistics shown on the dashboard until you refresh the PivotTable cache. Jenya wants you to create a final macro that updates the PivotTable cache so that the dashboard displays the most current information on the fundraising campaign.

To create the Refresh_Dashboard macro:

1. Go to the **Dashboard** worksheet.

2. Save the workbook so that if you make a mistake you can restart the process of creating the Refresh_Dashboard macro.

3. On the ribbon, click the **Developer** tab, and then in the Code group click the **Record Macro** button. The Record Macro dialog box opens.

4. Enter **Refresh_Dashboard** as the macro name. Verify that **This Workbook** is selected in the Store macro in box. Enter **Refresh the PivotTable cache for the dashboard** in the Description box, and then click **OK** to begin recording.

5. On the ribbon, click the **Review** tab, and then in the Protect group, click the **Unprotect Sheet** button to allow edits in the worksheet.

6. On the ribbon, click the **Data** tab, and then in the Queries & Connections group, click the **Refresh All** button. Excel updates the dashboard to show the impact of the two new donors on the campaign. See Figure 12–31.

Figure 12-31   Refreshed dashboard

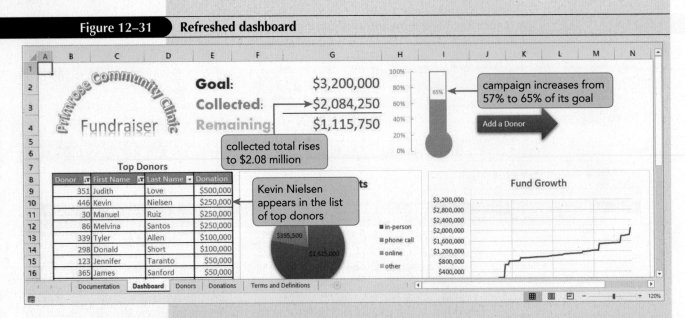

7. On the ribbon, click the **Review** tab, in the Protect group, click the **Protect Sheet** button, and then click the **OK** button in the dialog box to protect the worksheet.

8. On the ribbon, click the **Developer** tab, and then in the Code group, click **Stop Recording**. The Refresh_Dashboard macro is complete.

Jenya wants you to add a macro button to the Dashboard worksheet to run the Refresh_Dashboard macro.

To create a macro button for the Refresh_Dashboard macro:

1. On the ribbon, click the **Review** tab, and then in the Protect group, click the **Unprotect Sheet** button to enable you to add a button to the worksheet.

2. On the ribbon, click the **Developer** tab. In the Controls group, click the **Insert** button, and then click **Button (Form Control)** in the first row and column of the Format Controls section of the gallery.

3. Drag the pointer over the range **J2:L3** of the Dashboard worksheet to create a button. The Assign Macro dialog box opens.

4. Click **Refresh_Dashboard** in the macro list, and then click **OK**. The macro is assigned to the selected button.

5. With the macro button still selected, type **Refresh Dashboard** as the new button label. See Figure 12-32.

Figure 12-32 Refresh Dashboard macro button

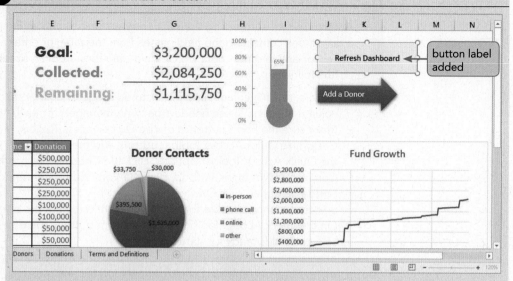

6. Click cell **A1** to deselect the button.

7. On the ribbon, click the **Review** tab, in the Protect group, click the **Protect Sheet** button, and then click **OK** in the dialog box to again protect the worksheet.

8. In the Dashboard worksheet, click the **Refresh Dashboard** button. The contents of the worksheet are refreshed.

   Trouble? If the macro returns an error message, close the workbook without saving changes. Reopen the workbook and repeat the previous set of steps to create the Refresh_Dashboard macro and then repeat this set of steps to create the macro button.

You've now created four macros to make it easier for users of Jenya's workbook to enter new donor information and update the contents of the dashboard. However, to put the finishing touches on the application, you will view and edit the content of the macro code you generated with the macro recorder.

Insight

Data Entry with a Data Form

Another way of automating the data entry process is with an **Excel data form**, which is a dialog box containing the field names from the table or data range along with input boxes for entering new data. To create a data form from an Excel table or data range, do the following:

1. Make sure each column in the structured range of data or the Excel table has column headers. These headers become the labels for each field on the form.
2. Make sure the Form button is on the Quick Access Toolbar. If not, click the Customize Quick Access Toolbar button, and then click More Commands. In the Quick Access Toolbar options, click the Choose commands from box, click Commands Not in the Ribbon, click the Form button in the box, click the Add button, and then click OK.
3. Select the range or table for which you want to create the data form.
4. On the Quick Access Toolbar, click the Form button. The data form opens with the selected fields ready for data entry.
5. Enter data in each box, and then click New to add the complete record to the end of the range or table and create a new record.
6. Click Close to close the data form.

Data forms can be helpful when people who are unfamiliar with Excel need to enter data. They can also be useful when a worksheet is very wide and requires repeated horizontal scrolling.

Working with the VBA Editor

Macro code is written in a programming language called Visual Basic for Applications (VBA), which is the programming language used by all Microsoft Office apps. Once you know the basics of VBA in one Office program, you can apply much of what you learn to create applications for the other programs in the Office suite.

Opening the VBA Editor

The content of a macro code can be accessed in the Visual Basic for Applications editor. The editor is a separate application that works with Excel and other Office programs to fix, edit, and manage VBA code. You'll open the editor now to view the code of the Add_Donor macro.

To view the code of the Add_Donor macro:

1. On the ribbon, click the **Developer** tab, and then in the Code group, click the **Macros** button.

2. With **Add_Donor** highlighted in the list of macros, click the **Edit** button. The Visual Basic for Applications editor opens showing the code of the Add_Donor macro. See Figure 12–33.

Figure 12–33   **VBA Editor window**

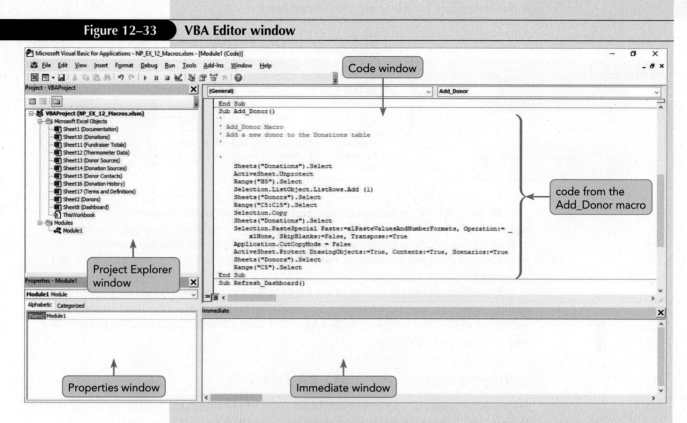

Trouble? Depending on how your computer is configured, the layout and contents of your window might differ from that shown in Figure 12–33. If all the windows of the VBA editor are not shown, you can display them by selecting the name of the window on the View menu.

The VBA Editor opens with the four windows: The Project Explorer window displays a treelike diagram consisting of every open workbook. The Properties window shows the properties associated with the selected object in the Project Explorer window. The Code window contains the VBA code, including the code of every recorded macro. The Immediate window lets you enter and run VBA commands. In this session, you will work with the contents of the Code window.

Understanding Sub Procedures

In VBA, macros are stored in blocks of code called sub procedures, which have the general syntax

```
Sub procedure(arguments)
  'comments
  commands
```

Tip

Every comment line must begin with the ' character.

where ***procedure*** is the name of the sub procedure, ***arguments*** are any arguments used in the sub procedure, ***comments*** are descriptive comments about the sub procedure, and ***commands*** are the command run by the sub procedure. Even without knowing VBA syntax, you can often interpret what each command does by examining the code used in the command. Figure 12–34 describes the content of the Show_Dashboard sub procedure.

Figure 12–34   Sub procedure for the Show_Dashboard macro

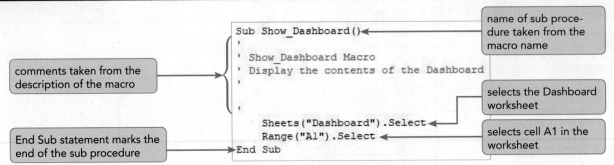

Both the name of the sub procedure and the description are taken from the macro name and macro description entered in the Record Macro dialog box (refer back to Figure 12–23). This sub procedure has only two commands. The first command selects the Dashboard worksheet, and the second command selects cell A1 within that worksheet.

Sub procedures are organized in a folder called a **module**. A VBA project could have multiple modules, and multiple sub procedures within each module. The first module is named Module1, the second is called Module2, and so forth. Modules are primarily a way of grouping related macros.

Editing a Macro with the VBA Editor

Learning the syntax of VBA is beyond the scope of this text, but you can do some simple tasks to add to the code that was generated by the macro recorder. To enter a VBA command, you write the text of the command in the Code window. As you type a command, the editor will provide pop-up windows to assist you in writing error-free code.

Reference

Editing a Macro

- On the Developer tab, in the Code group, click the Macros button, select the macro in the Macro name list, and then click Edit; or on the Developer tab, in the Code group, click the Visual Basic button.
- Use the Visual Basic Editor to edit the macro code.
- On the menu bar, click File, and then click Close and Return to Microsoft Excel.

Jenya wants you to modify the Add_Donor macro so that it displays a message box when a donor has been successfully added to the Donations worksheet. You can display a message box using the VBA command

```
MsgBox message
```

where *message* is the text of the message to display in the box. The following VBA command creates a message box with the text "Donor added":

```
MsgBox "Donor added"
```

Jenya also wants you to clear the data in the range C6:C15 of the Donors worksheet after a donor has been successfully added to the Donations table, in preparation for adding information on the next donor. You can clear the contents of a range using the VBA command

```
Range(range).ClearContents
```

where *range* is the cell range whose contents should be cleared. To clear the contents of the cells in the range C6:C15, you use the VBA command:

```
Range("C6:C15").ClearContents
```

You'll add both commands to the Add_Donor sub procedure now.

To edit the Add_Donor sub procedure:

▶ 1. Scroll down the contents of the Code window until you see the Add_Donor sub procedure. The sub procedure contains a sequence of commands to insert new donor data in the first row of the Donations table.

   Trouble? If you don't see the Add_Donor sub procedure in the Code window, it might have been stored in a different module. Double-click a different module in the Project Explorer window to locate the sub procedure.

▶ 2. Scroll down and click at the end of the `Sheets("Donors").Select` line.

▶ 3. Press **ENTER** to insert a new line.

▶ 4. Type `MsgBox "Donor added"` to create the Donor added message box, and then press **ENTER** to insert a command to display a message box.

▶ 5. Type `Range("C6:C15").ClearContents` to clear the contents of the cells in the range C6:C15. (Do not select the similarly named `ClearComments` in your code, which only clears comments attached to the selected range.) As you type the command, you can select different parts of the command by selecting the command value and pressing TAB. See Figure 12–35.

Figure 12–35	Edited sub procedure

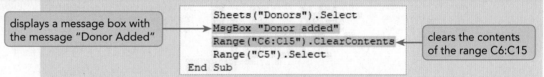

displays a message box with the message "Donor Added"

```
Sheets("Donors").Select
MsgBox "Donor added"
Range("C6:C15").ClearContents
Range("C5").Select
End Sub
```

clears the contents of the range C6:C15

▶ 6. On the menu bar, click **File**, and then click **Close and Return to Microsoft Excel** (or press **CTRL +Q**).

You'll test the revised macro by adding a donor to the Donations list using the Add_Donor macro.

To add a new donor to the Donations list:

▶ 1. Go to the **Donors** worksheet.

▶ 2. In the range **C6:C15**, enter the following data: **9/20/2024** in cell C6, **$250** in cell C7, **phone call** in cell C8, **Sandra** in cell C9, **Lewis** in cell C10, **14 Upton Court** in cell C11, **Flint** in cell C12, **MI** in cell C13, **48532** in cell C14, and **(810) 555-1008** in cell C15.

▶ 3. Click the **Add New Donor** macro button. The donor information is added as a new row in the Donations table. A dialog box with the message "Donor Added" appears.

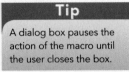

Tip

A dialog box pauses the action of the macro until the user closes the box.

4. Click **OK** to close the dialog box and continue the macro. The data in the range C6:C15 is cleared and the form is ready for information on another donor.

5. Go to the **Donations** worksheet and confirm that the Sandra Lewis has been inserted as a new donor in the table. See Figure 12–36.

Figure 12–36 New donor added to the Donations table

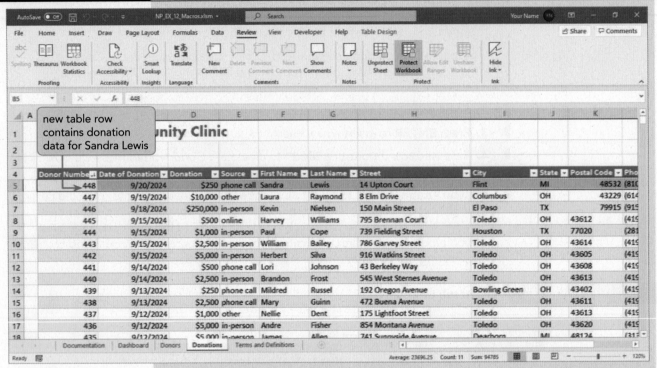

6. Go to the **Dashboard** worksheet, and then click the **Refresh Dashboard** button to update the dashboard with Sandra Lewis' contribution. The amount contributed to the campaign has increased to $2,084,500, which is still 65% of the way to the fundraising goal.

You've finished creating and editing macros. Because you no longer need the Developer tab, you will remove this tab from the ribbon.

To remove the Developer tab from the ribbon:

1. Right-click an empty area of the ribbon, and then click **Customize the Ribbon** on the shortcut menu.

2. In the Main Tabs box on the right, click the **Developer** check box to deselect the Developer tab.

3. Click **OK** to apply the changes to the ribbon. The Developer tab no longer appears on the ribbon.

4. **sam↑** Save the workbook, and then close it.

Jenya is pleased with your work on the Excel application for managing donations to the Primrose Community Clinic. The changes you made to the workbook will enable staffers at the clinic to enter fundraising data without data entry errors and to monitor the progress of the campaign.

Proskills

Decision Making: Planning and Recording a Macro

Planning and practice help to ensure you create an error-free macro. First, decide what you want to accomplish. Then, consider the best way to achieve those results. Next, practice the keystrokes and mouse actions before you begin recording. This may seem like extra work, but it reduces the chance of error when you actually record the macro. As you set up a macro, consider the following:

- Choose a descriptive name that identifies the macro's purpose.
- Weigh the benefits of selecting a shortcut key against its drawbacks. Although a shortcut key is another way to run a macro, you are limited to one-letter shortcuts, which don't identify the shortcut's purpose. Your macro shortcut key might override another shortcut key provided by Microsoft Office.
- Store the macro with the current workbook unless the macro can be used with other workbooks.
- Include a description that provides an overview of the macro and perhaps your name and contact information.

Good decision making includes thinking about what to do and what not to do as you progress to your goals. This is true when developing a macro as well.

Protecting Against Macro Viruses

If you plan on distributing an Excel application to a wider audience, you need to consider how Excel manages security to ward off viruses. A **virus** is a computer program designed to copy itself into other programs with the intention of causing mischief or harm. When unsuspecting users open these infected workbooks, Excel automatically runs the attached virus-infected macro. **Macro viruses** are a type of virus that uses a program's own macro programming language to distribute the virus. Macro viruses can be destructive and can modify or delete files that may not be recoverable. Excel provides several security levels for managing exposure to macro viruses.

Macro Security Settings

The macro security settings control how Excel manages a macro-enabled workbook. For example, one user may choose to run macros only if they are "digitally signed" by a developer who is on a list of trusted sources. Another user might want to see a notification when a workbook contains macros, which the user can then choose to enable or disable. Excel has four levels of macro security settings, as described in Figure 12–37.

Figure 12–37   **Macro security settings**

Setting	Description
Disable all macros without notification	All macros in all workbooks are disabled and no security alerts about macros are displayed. Use this setting if you don't want macros to run.
Disable all macros with notification	All macros in all workbooks are disabled, but security alerts appear when the workbook contains a macro. Use this default setting to choose on a case-by-case basis whether to run a macro.
Disable all macros except digitally signed macros	The same as the "Disable all macros with notification" setting except any macro signed by a trusted publisher runs if you have already trusted the publisher. Otherwise, security alerts appear when a workbook contains a macro.
Enable all macros	All macros in all workbooks run. Use this setting temporarily in such cases as when developing an application that contains macros. This setting is not recommended for regular use.

You set macro security for all Microsoft Office programs in a central location called the **Trust Center**. To access the Trust Center:

1. On the ribbon, click the File tab, and then in the navigation bar, click Options to open the Excel Options dialog box.
2. Click Trust Center in the list of option categories.
3. Click the Trust Center Settings button to view or change specific security settings.

Figure 12–38 shows the Trust Center dialog box opened to the settings for handling macro-enabled workbooks. By default, all potentially dangerous content in a macro-enabled workbook is blocked and the user is notified that some content is disabled. You can place files you consider trustworthy in a location defined as trustworthy. Any workbook opened from a trusted location is considered safe and will not be blocked.

Figure 12–38   **Macro Settings in the Trust Center**

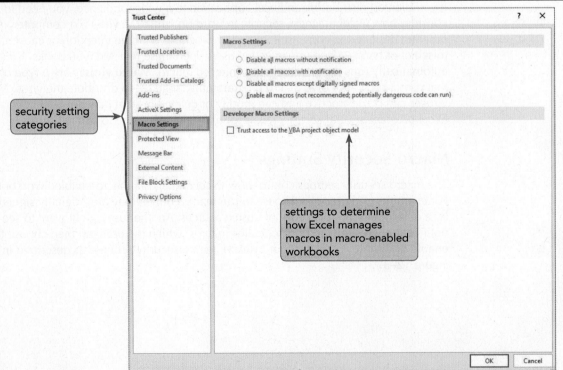

Adding a Digital Signature to a Workbook

Another way to mark a trusted workbook is to assign it a **digital signature**, which marks the workbook as coming from a trusted author. Digital signatures are added as the last step before distributing a workbook to a wide audience of users. Before you can add a digital signature to a workbook, you need to obtain a digital ID (also called a digital certificate) that proves your identity. Digital certificates are typically issued by a certificate authority. After you have a digital certificate, do the following to digitally sign your workbook:

1. On the ribbon, click the File tab, and then, in the navigation bar, click Info.
2. On the Info screen, click the Protect Workbook button, and then click Add a Digital Signature.
3. If the Get a Digital ID dialog box opens, asking if you would like to get a digital ID from a Microsoft Partner, click Yes. Your browser opens to a website with information about digital signature providers and available digital IDs.
4. Select a provider and follow the steps to obtain a digital ID from that provider.

By digitally signing your workbooks, you can assure others that the workbook has not been altered since its creation by the document's author. A digital signature is removed any time the workbook is saved, ensuring that no one (including the original workbook author) can modify the document without removing the digital signature. In this way, a chain of custody is established from document creation to document distribution, ensuring that no third party has altered your Excel application.

Review

Session 12.3 Quick Check

1. What is the Developer tab?
2. What is the Personal Macro workbook?
3. What is the one thing you should do before starting the macro recorder?
4. What is a macro-enabled workbook?
5. How do you assign a macro to a graphic shape or form button?
6. What is VBA?
7. What is a sub procedure?
8. What VBA command would you enter to clear the contents of the data in the range A1:A50?
9. What VBA command would you enter to display a message box with the message "End of Project"?

Practice

Review Assignments

Data File needed for the Review Assignments: NP_EX_12-2.xlsm

Jenya needs to create another Excel application for the Primrose Community Clinic that tracks payments on the pledges made by donors. You will help complete the application by creating a macro that adds donor payments to a table of payments and then updates a dashboard to reflect the current payment status. To maintain data integrity, you will validate the payment information entered by the user and restrict access to parts of the workbook. Complete the following:

1. Open the macro-enabled workbook **NP_EX_12-2.xlsm** located in the Excel12 > Review folder included with your Data Files. Save the workbook as **NP_EX_12_Payments** in the location specified by your instructor.

2. In the Documentation worksheet, enter your name and the date.

3. In the Documentation worksheet, insert a WordArt object from the first row and third column of the WordArt gallery. Change the text to **Primrose Community Clinic**. Select the entire text and change the font size to 28 points. Move the WordArt graphic to the upper-left corner of the worksheet.

4. In the Fully Paid Donations worksheet, insert a funnel chart of the data in the range B4:C15. Move the funnel chart to the Summary worksheet, and resize it to cover the range H8:M20. Change the chart title to **Fully Paid Donors by Donation Level**.

5. In the Payment Form worksheet (which displays the total amount pledged, paid, and owed by donors), use an IFERROR function in cells F4 and F6 to display a blank text string if the formulas in those cells return an error.

6. Hide the Pledge Tables through Fully Paid Donations worksheets.

7. On the Review tab, in the Protect group, use the Protect Workbook button to protect the structure of the workbook. Do not specify a password for the protected workbook.

8. In the Payment Form worksheet, use data validation to add a validation list to cell C4 using the data in the range H4:H451 of the Payment Form worksheet as the source.

9. Create a validation rule for cell C5 to allow date values greater than or equal to 9/20/2024. Add an input message to the cell with the title **Payment Date** and the input message **Enter a date of 9/20/2024 or later**. If an invalid date is entered, display only a warning alert with the title **Invalid Date** and the message **Confirm the date of the payment**.

10. Create a validation rule for cell C6 to allow only decimal numbers between 1 and 500,000.

11. Hide column H in the Payment Form worksheet.

12. Select the range C4:C6, and then use the Protection tab in the Format Cells dialog box to unlock the data in that range.

13. For each of the six visible worksheets, click the Protect Sheet button in the Protect group on the Review tab and protect the sheets, allowing users only to select locked and unlocked cells. Do not specify a password.

14. In the Payment Form worksheet, in the range C4:C6, enter the following data: **18** in cell C4, **9/25/2024** in cell C5, and **$6,750** in cell C6.

15. Display the Developer tab on the ribbon.

16. Save the workbook, and then record a macro in this workbook named **Add_Payment** with the description **Add a new payment to the Payments table**. Record the following steps in the macro:

    a. Go to the Payments worksheet, and then on the Review tab, in Protect group, click the Unprotect Sheet button.

    b. Click B5, and then on the Home tab, in the Cells group, click the Insert button to insert a new row into the table.

    c. Go to the Payment Form worksheet, select range from cell C6 up to cell C4, and then copy the selected data.

    d. Go to the Payments worksheet, and on the Home tab, in the Clipboard group, click the Paste arrow, and then click Paste Special.

e. In the Paste Special dialog box, select the Values and number formats option button and the Transpose check box, and then click OK to paste the payment date into row 5 of the worksheet.

f. Go to the Summary worksheet, and then on the Review tab, in the Protect group, click the Unprotect Sheet button.

g. On the Data tab, in the Queries and Connections group, click the Refresh All button.

h. On the Review tab, in the Protect group, click the Protect Sheet button and allow users to only select lock and unlocked cells.

i. Go to the Payments worksheet, and then on the Review tab, in the Protect group, click the Protect Sheet button and allow users to only select lock and unlocked cells.

j. Go to the Payment Form worksheet, and then click cell C4.

k. Stop the macro recorder.

17. On the Developer tab, in the Code group, click the Macros button, and then click Edit to edit the VBA code for the Add_Payment macro, adding the following new lines of code directly after the command `Range("C4").Select` line near the end of the sub procedure:

```
MsgBox "Payment Entered"
Range("C4:C6").ClearContents
```

18. Close the VBA editor and return to the workbook.

19. Unprotect the Payment Form worksheet, insert a macro button over the range B8:C9, assign the Add_Payment macro to the button, and then enter **Add Payment** as the button label.

20. Protect the Payment Form worksheet again, allowing users only to select locked and unlocked cells.

21. In the range C4:C6, enter the following data: **30** in cell C4, **9/26/2024** in cell C5, and **$10,000** in cell C6.

22. Click the Add Payment macro button to add the data in the Payments table and refresh the contents of the Summary worksheet, and then click OK to close the Payment Entered dialog box.

23. In cell C4, enter **30** and then confirm that $8,750 is still owed on the donor's pledge.

24. In the Summary worksheet, verify that the total amount owed on the pledges is now $828,380.

25. Save the workbook and then close it.

Apply

Case Problem 1

Data File needed for this Case Problem: NP_EX_12-3.xlsm

Invent Software   David Wright is a hiring manager for the Human Resources (HR) department at Invent Software, a growing company that creates software for inventory management. David is using Excel to track the hiring process from initial job postings through interviews to job offers and wants your help in developing an application to automate the process of reporting key hiring metrics. He also wants it to include safeguards to help prevent user error. David already created part of the application and needs you to finish it. Complete the following:

1. Open the **NP_EX_12-3.xlsm** workbook located in the Excel12 > Case1 folder included with your Data Files. Save the workbook as **NP_EX_12_Invent** in the location specified by your instructor.

2. In the Documentation worksheet, enter your name and the date.

3. In the Dashboard worksheet, create the following WordArt object:

a. Insert the WordArt object showing text in a black font with a hard red drop shadow located in the third row and second column of the WordArt gallery.

b. Change the default text to **Invent Software**.

c. Move the WordArt object to the upper-left corner of the worksheet.

d. Apply an 18-point golden glow text effect to the WordArt object, choosing the effect in the fourth row and first column of the gallery of glow effects.

4. Insert a funnel chart of the data in the range F8:G13. Move and resize the chart to cover the range J6:K15. Change the chart title to **Application History**.

5. In cell F19, create a list validation based on the data in the range O8:O18. In cell G19, create a list validation based on the data in the range Q8:Q13. The application will now be able to retrieve data on applicants that match specified search criteria.

6. Use the arrow buttons in cells F19 and G19 to select the values **Accountant** and **Onsite Interview**.

7. In the Dashboard worksheet, hide the contents of columns O through Q.

8. Hide the Applicants, Application PivotTable, and Terms and Definitions worksheets.

9. Protect the workbook. Do not specify a password for the document.

10. In the Dashboard worksheet, unlock cells F19 and G19, and then protect the worksheet to allow only selecting locked and unlocked cells. Do not specify a password for the protected sheet.

11. Save the workbook, and then use the macro recorder to create a macro for this workbook named **Lookup_Applicants** with the description **Retrieve application data using an advanced filter**.

12. Start the recorder, and perform the following tasks to create the macro:

    a. Unprotect the worksheet.

    b. Click the Data tab, and then in the Sort & Filter group, click the Advanced button.

    c. In the Advanced Filter dialog box, click the Copy to another location option button, enter **Applicants[#All]** in the List range box to retrieve data from the Applicants table, verify that **$F$18:$G$19** is displayed in the Criteria range box, and **$F$21:$M$21** is displayed in the Copy to box. Click click OK to apply the advanced filter.

    d. Protect the worksheet.

    e. Stop the recorder.

13. Unprotect the worksheet and create a macro button in the range H17:H19 to run the Lookup_Applicants macro. Change the label of the button to **Retrieve Records**. Protect the worksheet again, allowing users to only select locked and unlocked cells. Do not specify a password.

14. Use VBA to modify the code so the application displays a message indicating the number of records found using the advanced filter. In the Visual Basic for Applications editor, directly before the End Sub statement in the Lookup_Applicants sub procedure, add the following commands:

```
recNum = Application.WorksheetFunction.Count(Range("K:K"))
MsgBox recNum & " record(s) found"
```

15. Close the editor and return to the workbook.

16. Choose Website Designer from the slicer to display a funnel chart of the application history for the Website Designer position.

17. Select Website Designer and Onsite Interview from cells F19 and G19, and then click the Retrieve Records button to retrieve the 24 records of applicants who got only as far as the onsite interview stage.

18. Save the workbook, and then close it.

Challenge

Case Problem 2

Data File needed for this Case Problem: NP_EX_12-4.xlsm

Milwaukee Cheese   Roberta Olson is a dispatch manager for Milwaukee Cheese, a large cheese and dairy supply company operating in the Midwest. One of Roberta's jobs is to provide the shipping assignments to the company drivers among 27 Wisconsin cities. It is company policy that no driver logs more than 350 miles in a single day driving from one distribution center to the next. You will help Roberta develop an Excel application for entering driving assignments that fulfill company policy.

Roberta's worksheet includes a Driving Form worksheet in which you will enter commands to store each leg of a driving itinerary. The legs will then be stored in the Itinerary table of the Driving Itinerary worksheet. The distances between the 27 cities are stored in the Distance Table worksheet. Distances will be automatically calculated for you.

In this application, you will combine validation tests within a single cell using a custom validation formula. For a driving leg to be valid it should start and end in one of the 27 cities, and the total driving distance should not exceed 350 miles. Complete the following:

1. Open the **NP_EX_12-4.xlsm** workbook located in the Excel12 > Case2 folder included with your Data Files. Save the workbook as **NP_EX_12_Cheese** in the location specified by your instructor.

2. In the Documentation worksheet, enter your name and the date.

3. In the Driving Form worksheet, you will enter individual legs of a driving itinerary. The mileage between starting and ending cities is calculated in cell F6. Currently that cell displays an error value because no cities have been specified in cells D6 and E6. Revise the formula in cell F6 so that it displays a blank text string in place of an error value.

4. This form will use the AutoComplete feature to fill in the city names in cells D6 and E6. There is no need to display the city names in rows 7 through 33 for AutoComplete to work. Hide rows 7 through 33 in the worksheet so that content doesn't distract the user.

5. Unlock cells D6 and E6.

   Explore 6. The data in cells D6 and E6 have two validation rules: The city names must be included in the list of cities. The total of the driving mileage in cell F6 and the value stored in the dist range name should be less than or equal to 350. In the range D6:E6, create a custom validation rule using the following formula:
      =AND(COUNTIF(cities,D6)=1,SUM($F$6,dist)<=350)

7. If the validation rule is violated, display a warning box with the title **Invalid Data** and the message **You either mistyped the city name or adding this leg will result in a total driving distance exceeding 350 miles.** (including the period).

8. Hide the Distance Table worksheet.

9. Protect the workbook. Do not specify a password.

10. Protect the contents of the Driving Form and Driving Itinerary worksheets, allowing users to only select locked and unlocked cells. Save the workbook.

11. In the Driving Form worksheet, enter **Milwaukee** as the starting city of the first leg in cell D6, and then enter **West Allis** as the ending city in cell E6. Verify that the distance between the two cities is 7 miles.

12. Save the workbook.

13. Use the macro recorder to create a macro for this workbook named **Add_Leg** with the description **Add a leg to the driving itinerary**.

14. Start the recorder, and then perform the following tasks:

    a. Go to the Driving Itinerary worksheet and unprotect the sheet.

    b. Press F5 and go to the travel_end cell.

    c. Insert a new sheet row above the travel_end cell. (*Hint*: On the Home tab, in the Cells group, click the Insert arrow, and then click Insert Sheet Rows.)

    d. Go to the Driving Form worksheet and copy the values in the range C6:F6.

    e. Return to the Driving Itinerary worksheet and use the Paste Special command to paste the values and number formats into the active cell of the worksheet.

    f. Protect the Driving Itinerary worksheet.

    g. Press F5 and go to the travel_end cell again.

    h. Unprotect the Driving Form worksheet.

    i. Copy the value in cell E6 and paste that value into cell D6.

    j. Click cell E6, and then press DEL to clear the contents of the cell.

    k. Protect the Driving Form worksheet.

    l. Stop the recorder.

15. Unprotect the Driving Form worksheet and insert a macro button in the range D35:E37 to play the Add_Leg macro. Change the label of the macro button to **Add Leg to the Itinerary**. Protect the Driving Form worksheet again.

16. Use the data form to enter the following legs into the driving itinerary: West Allis to Madison, and then Madison to La Crosse.

17. Verify that when you try to enter a fourth driving leg of La Crosse to Marshfield, the application warns you that you are about to exceed the allowed driving distance. Do not enter Marshfield as the last leg of the trip. Instead enter Eau Claire as the last leg.

⊕ **Explore** 18. When a macro switches between worksheets, the quick jump from one sheet to another can be distracting. To correct this problem, edit the Add_Leg sub procedure in the Visual Basic for Applications editor.

     a. Directly after the initial comment section at the top of the sub procedure insert the following command to turn off screen updating while the macro is running:

```
Application.ScreenUpdating = False
```

     b. Directly before the closing End Sub command at the bottom of the sub procedure, insert the following command to turn screen updating back on:

```
Application.ScreenUpdating = True
```

19. Close the editor and then return to the workbook.

20. Save the workbook, and then close it.

INDEX

A

absolute cell references, **EX 3–28,** EX 3–32–3–33, EX 3–34–3–35
    enter, EX 3–34–3–35
    formulas, EX 3–33, EX 3–35
Access database
    query, EX 10–27–10–28
Accounting format, **EX 2–2, EX 2–16**
actions
    redo, EX 1–20
    undo, EX 1–20
activate Solver, EX 8–41–8–42
active cell, **EX 1–3**
active sheet, **EX 1–2**
    change, EX 1–8–1–9
add-in, **EX 8–40**
advanced filter, EX 6–33–6–37. *See also* filter
    criteria range, EX 6–34
    defined, **EX 6–34**
Advanced Filter dialog box, EX 6–36
align cell content, EX 2–20–2–21
amortization schedule, create, EX 9–12–9–19
analysis
    ideas, EX 10–66
analytics, **EX 10–4**
Analyze Data (Ideas) pane, EX 10–66
Analyze Data tool, EX 10–66
AND function, EX 7–17–7–19
    defined, **EX 7–17**
answer report, **EX 8–51**
    create, EX 8–51–8–53
approximate match lookups, **EX 3–41, EX 7–3**
    create, EX 7–6–7–10
arguments, **EX 1–38**
arithmetic operators, **EX 1–34**
Arrange All button, EX 5–2
arrays
    data tables, EX 8–21
    formulas, **EX 8–21**
ascending order sort, **EX 6–13,** EX 6–14. *See also* sort
asset(s)
    calculate depreciation, EX 9–29–9–35
    declining-balance depreciation, EX 9–33
    material, EX 9–29
    noncash, EX 9–29
    straight-line depreciation, EX 9–32
    tangible, EX 9–29
audit workbook, EX 9–51–9–59
AutoComplete, **EX 1–21**
    understand, EX 1–21–1–22
AutoFill, **EX 3–3**
    explore options, EX 3–8–3–10
    fill series, EX 3–10–3–12
    formula, EX 3–8
    formulas and data patterns, EX 3–7–3–12
    options menu, EX 3–9
    extend series, EX 3–10
AutoFit, **EX 1–29**
automate tasks with macros, EX 12–37–12–41
automatic page break, **EX 2–31**
AutoSum, **EX 1–33**
    insert functions, EX 1–39–1–41
average, **EX 3–18**
AVERAGE function, **EX 2–32, EX 3–2,** EX 11–6, EX 11–46
    3-D reference, EX 5–15
AVERAGEIF function, **EX 7–2, EX 7–26**
    applied to media table, EX 7–25
    calculate conditional averages, EX 7–24–7–25
averages, calculate, EX 2–32–2–34
AVERAGEX function, EX 11–61
AVG function, EX 11–53. *See also* AVERAGE function
axis titles
    add, EX 4–28–4–29
    added to chart, EX 4–29
    defined, **EX 4–28**

B

background
    image, add, EX 2–11
    work, EX 2–9–2–11
Backstage view, **EX 1–4**
banded rows, **EX 6–25**
bar charts, **EX 4–18**
base field, **EX 11–26**
base item, **EX 11–26**
BI. *See* business intelligence
bind constraint, **EX 8–53**
bins, **EX 4–46**
blank cell(s)
    calculations, EX 3–23
    role, EX 3–23
border(s), **EX 1–32**
    add to cells, EX 2–21–2–23
borrowing cost, calculate, EX 9–4–9–12
boxplot, EX 6–61
break-even analysis, **EX 8–6**
break-even point, **EX 8–3**
    CVP chart, EX 8–6
    directly calculate, EX 8–14
    explore, EX 8–6–8–7
    find with what-if analysis, EX 8–7–8–9
Bubble map, EX 10–62
business intelligence (BI), **EX 10–4**
    introduce, EX 10–4
buttons
    assign macros, EX 12–41–12–50

C

calculate
  averages, EX 2–32–2–34
  borrowing cost, EX 9–4–9–12
  cost of goods sold, EX 9–26–9–27
  cumulative interest and principal payments, EX 9–16–9–19
  depreciation of assets, EX 9–29–9–35
  distinct counts, EX 11–51–11–53
  formulas, EX 1–34–1–38
  functions, EX 1–38–1–41
  future value with FV function, EX 9–7–9–9
  inflation with FV function, EX 9–9
  interest and principal payments, EX 9–13–9–15
  interest rates with RATE function, EX 9–40–9–41
  internal rate of return, EX 9–46–9–48
  measures across tables and rows, EX 11–57–11–61
  monthly revenues in query, EX 10–13–10–14
  net present value, EX 9–43–9–46
  payment period with NPER function, EX 9–9–9–10
  payments with PMT function, EX 9–5–9–7
  percent differences, EX 11–29–11–31
  present value with PV function, EX 9–10–9–12
  ranks, EX 11–28–11–29
  value of investment, EX 9–47
  values for PivotTable field, EX 11–28
calculated fields, **EX 11–25, EX 11–42**. *See also* field(s)
  behind the math, EX 11–46–11–47
  create, EX 11–39, EX 11–42–11–45
  defined, **EX 6–43**
  Excel table, EX 6–43–6–45
  work, EX 11–39–11–47
calculated items, **EX 11–25, EX 11–39**
  behind the math, EX 11–46–11–47
  create, EX 11–39–11–42
  group, EX 11–42
  set solve order, EX 11–46
  work, EX 11–39–11–47
calculated values, format, EX 3–39–3–40
calculation(s)
  blank cells and zeroes, EX 3–23
  dates and times, EX 3–6–3–7
  design workbook, EX 3–4–3–6
  document, EX 3–5
  measures of central tendency, EX 3–19
  minimums and maximums, EX 3–16–3–18
  PivotTables, EX 11–26–11–31
  run totals with Quick Analysis Tool, EX 3–30–3–31
cascade layout, workbook window, EX 5–7
cash flow, **EX 9–4**
  negative, EX 9–3
  positive, EX 9–2
cash inflow, **EX 9–2**. *See also* positive cash flow
cash outflow, **EX 9–3**. *See also* negative cash flow
category axis, **EX 4–18**
category map, **EX 10–54**
category values, **EX 4–3**
cell(s), **EX 1–3**
  add borders, EX 2–21–2–23
  change, EX 8–22
  copy, EX 1–41–1–43
  dependent, EX 9–39
  find and select, EX 6–26–6–27
  find by type, EX 6–27
  format text selections, EX 2–8
  highlight based on values, EX 2–46–2–48

  highlight unlocked, EX 12–31
  highlight with top/bottom rule, EX 2–48
  input, EX 8–2
  locate, within worksheet, EX 6–26–6–27
  lock, EX 12–30–12–33
  merge, EX 2–23–2–24
  move, EX 1–41–1–43
  objective, EX 8–36, EX 8–42–8–44
  precedent, EX 9–39
  selected, EX 11–31
  show field value, EX 11–31
  show multiple field values, EX 11–31
  unlock, EX 12–30–12–33
  variable, EX 8–42–8–44
  wrap text, EX 1–29–1–30
cell borders, add, EX 1–51–1–52
cell content
  align, EX 2–20–2–21
  edit, EX 1–20–1–21
  format, EX 2–4
  indent, EX 2–21
  rotate, EX 2–24–2–25
CELL function, **EX 12–31**
cell range, **EX 1–2**
  select, EX 1–12–1–13
cell references, **EX 1–10**
  absolute, EX 3–28, EX 3–32–3–33, EX 3–34–3–35
  explore, EX 3–32–3–35
  mixed, EX 3–28, EX 3–33–3–34
  relative, EX 3–28, EX 3–32
cell styles, **EX 2–31**
  apply, EX 2–35–2–38
  create custom, EX 2–37–2–38
  defined, **EX 2–35**
cell text, format, EX 2–4–2–8
central tendency, **EX 3–18**
change
  cells, **EX 8–22**
  PivotTable layout, EX 11–7–11–8
characters, wildcard, EX 6–33
chart(s), **EX 4–4**. *See also* specific types
  add data callout, EX 4–40
  add data tables, EX 4–22
  add gridlines, EX 4–22
  add trendlines, EX 4–39
  axis titles added, EX 4–29
  change color scheme, EX 4–15–4–16
  choose style, EX 4–14–4–15
  color schemes, EX 4–16
  communicate effectively, EX 4–26
  dynamic, EX 6–58–6–61
  extrapolate, EX 9–25
  funnel, EX 12–8–12–11
  hierarchy, EX 4–45–4–46
  histogram, EX 4–46–4–47
  insert graphic shape, EX 4–41–4–42
  interpolate, EX 9–25
  move, EX 4–8–4–9
  net income values, EX 8–19
  Pareto, EX 4–46
  perform what-if analyses, EX 4–16–4–17
  resize, EX 4–8–4–9
  revenue, EX 8–5
  sunburst, EX 4–45–4–46
  templates, create, EX 5–50
  thermometer, EX 12–10

total expenses, EX 8–5
treemap, EX 4–45
variable expenses, EX 8–4
waterfall, EX 4–47–4–48

chart area, **EX 4–3**

chart data source
edit, EX 4–37–4–39
modify, EX 4–38

chart design theory, EX 4–52

chart elements
common, EX 4–10–4–11
defined, **EX 4–10**
format, EX 4–11–4–14
overlay, EX 4–16
work, EX 4–10–4–16

chart formats
copy, EX 4–37
paste, EX 4–37

"chart junk," EX 4–52

chart legend, **EX 4–2**
chart area, EX 4–13
fill color, EX 4–14

chart sheet, **EX 1–8**

chart style
choose, EX 4–14–4–15
preview, EX 4–15

chart title, **EX 4–2**
edit, EX 4–20–4–21

Choose a SmartArt Graphic dialog box, EX 12–8

choose
PivotTable layout, EX 11–7
rate of return, EX 9–44–9–46

clear, **EX 1–46**

Clipboard, **EX 1–37**

clustered column chart, **EX 4–18**
create, EX 4–19–4–20

Clustered Column map, create, EX 10–62

Collapsed PivotTable outline, EX 10–46

color scales, **EX 11–24**
create, EX 11–32
defined, EX 11–34
new format rule, EX 11–34
work, EX 11–34–11–35

column(s)
add multiple fields, EX 7–35–7–36
add new, EX 10–12–10–13
delete, EX 1–46–1–47
freeze, in worksheet, EX 6–9
hide, EX 1–49
insert, EX 1–45–1–46
modify, EX 1–44–1–49
resize, EX 1–27–1–31
set column width, EX 1–27–1–29
unhide, EX 1–49

column chart, **EX 4–18**
clustered, EX 4–19–4–20
compare subtypes, EX 4–18–4–19
create, EX 4–18–4–22
set gap width, EX 4–21
subtypes, EX 4–18–4–19

column headings, **EX 1–3**

column width, set, EX 1–27–1–29

combination chart, **EX 4–3**
add axis title, EX 4–28–4–29
create, EX 4–26–4–30
edit value axis scale, EX 4–29–4–30

comma-separated data values, EX 12–23

Comma Separated Values (CSV) file, **EX 10–4**
data arranged, EX 10–5

Comma style, **EX 2–3**

Compact layout, **EX 11–2**

compare expenses and revenue, EX 8–4–8–5

comparison operator, **EX 3–36**

conditional averages
calculate with AVERAGEIF function, EX 7–24–7–25
defined, **EX 7–24**

conditional count, **EX 7–20**
COUNTIF function, EX 7–20–7–22, EX 7–26

conditional formats, **EX 2–31**
display PivotTables, EX 11–31–11–35
document, EX 2–51–2–52
duplicate values, EX 6–11
dynamic, EX 2–51
highlight data, EX 2–46–2–52
use effectively, EX 2–52

conditional formatting rule
clear, EX 2–51
edit, EX 2–49–2–50

conditional sums
calculate with SUMIF function, EX 7–22–7–24
defined, **EX 7–22**

conference workbook, EX 1–5

confidence bounds, **EX 10–20**

constant(s)
decide where to place, EX 3–6
defined, **EX 3–5**
units, EX 3–5–3–6

constraints, **EX 8–37**
binding, EX 8–53
nonbinding, EX 8–53

cost of goods sold, **EX 9–20**. *See also* cost of sales
calculate, EX 9–26–9–27

cost of sales, **EX 9–20**. *See also* cost of goods sold

Cost-Volume-Profit (CVP)
analysis, **EX 8–4**
chart, **EX 8–6**

cost-volume relationships, EX 8–4–8–9

COUNT function, EX 11–46, EX 11–51–11–52, EX 11–53
3-D reference, EX 5–15
use, EX 1–43–1–44

COUNTIF function, **EX 7–2, EX 7–25,** EX 12–25
applied to Media table, EX 7–22
conditional count, EX 7–20–7–22, EX 7–21, EX 7–26

count caches, EX 11–39

COUNTX function, EX 11–61

Create Forecast Worksheet dialog box, EX 10–19

Create PivotTable dialog box, EX 10–35

criteria filters, EX 6–30–6–32
defined, **EX 6–30**
text, number, and date, EX 6–31

criteria range, **EX 6–34**
three conditions, EX 6–34

CUBEVALUE function, EX 11–65

CUMIPMT function, **EX 9–16**

CUMPRINC function, **EX 9–16**

cumulative interest
    calculate, EX 9–16–9–19

Currency format, **EX 2–16**

Custom AutoFilter dialog box, EX 6–32

custom cell styles
    create, EX 2–37–2–38
    merge, EX 2–38

custom colors, create, EX 2–7

custom input message, EX 12–20

Customize Ribbon category in the Excel Options dialog box, EX 12–36

custom
    validation rule, create, EX 12–23–12–25

custom list

Custom Lists dialog box, EX 6–18, EX 11–11
    defined, **EX 6–17**
    delete, EX 6–18
    sort PivotTables, EX 11–11
    sort, EX 6–17–6–19

D

dashboard
    add histogram, EX 6–58–6–59
    add Order Date timeline, EX 10–38–10–39
    add slicers, EX 10–38–10–39
    create, EX 6–52–6–63
    create dynamic charts, EX 6–58–6–61
    defined, **EX 6–49**
    design, EX 6–55
    filtered by store type and order date, EX 10–41
    slicer, EX 6–49
    SUBTOTAL function, EX 6–55–6–58

data
    date, EX 1–18
    displayed as different chart types, EX 4–18
    display with funnel chart, EX 12–8–12–11
    filter, EX 6–27–6–37
    filter, with slicer(s), EX 6–50–6–52
    handle in Excel, EX 6–4–6–6
    highlight with conditional formats, EX 2–46–2–52
    look up, EX 3–40–3–45
    look up, with tables, EX 6–62–6–63
    numeric, EX 1–18
    retrieve with Index Match lookups, EX 7–14–7–15
    text, EX 1–18
    time, EX 1–18
    transpose, EX 2–41–2–42
    use pane, for view, EX 6–6–6–10
    validate, EX 12–17
    validate, already in workbook, EX 12–25

Data Analysis Expressions (DAX), **EX 11–48**
    introduce, EX 11–53–11–54
    X functions, EX 11–61

data bar rule, modify, EX 4–49–4–50

data bars, **EX 4–33**
    create, EX 4–48–4–50

database, **EX 10–24**
    calculations with multiple criterion, EX 11–67
    design, EX 10–30
    introduce, EX 10–26–10–28
    tables, EX 10–24

Database functions, **EX 11–65**
    explore, EX 11–65–11–67
    summary statistics calculated, EX 11–66

data callouts, **EX 4–32**
    add to chart, EX 4–40
    defined, **EX 4–40**

Data Cube, **EX 11–65**

data definition table, **EX 6–5**
    employee data, EX 6–5

data entry, EX 6–6
    create custom validation rule, EX 12–23–12–25
    create input message, EX 12–20–12–21
    create validation error message, EX 12–18–12–20
    data form, EX 12–50
    validate, EX 12–16–12–25
    validate against list, EX 12–21–12–23
    validate data already in workbook, EX 12–25
    validate dates, EX 12–17–12–18

data form. *See also* Excel data form
    data entry, EX 12–50

data label, **EX 4–2**

data markers, **EX 4–3**
    format, EX 4–24–4–25

Data Model, **EX 10–24**
    advantages of storing data, EX 10–28
    apply slicers and timelines in Power Pivot, EX 10–38–10–41
    calculate distinct counts, EX 11–51–11–53
    create PivotTable, EX 10–34–10–41
    explore, EX 10–28–10–30
    explore in Diagram view, EX 10–32
    import Data dialog box to load data, EX 10–29
    introduce PivotTable design under, EX 11–50–11–51
    load Customers table, EX 10–29
    named sets, EX 11–51
    Power Pivot with data, EX 10–36
    view contents, EX 10–31

data patterns, and AutoFill, EX 3–7–3–12

data query
    edit, EX 10–9–10–10
    month column, add, EX 10–13
    refresh, EX 10–10–10–11
    retrieve data into Excel table, EX 10–8–10–9
    set up, EX 10–12
    use Power Query, EX 10–4–10–8
    write, EX 10–4–10–11

data range
    add subtotal, EX 6–19
    convert, into table, EX 6–37–6–39
    defined, **EX 6–2**
    highlight duplicate values, EX 6–10
    remove duplicate records, EX 6–12–6–13
    sort records, EX 6–13–6–19
    vs. Excel table, EX 6–46

data security, maintain, EX 10–22

data series, **EX 4–6**

data source(s), **EX 4–3**
    Excel table, EX 10–11
    move query, EX 10–15
    select, EX 4–6

data tables
    arrays, EX 8–21
    defined, **EX 8–9**
    modify, EX 8–13–8–14
    one-variable, EX 8–9–8–12, EX 8–12–8–13
    two-variable, EX 8–14–8–21
    work, EX 8–9–8–14

data types, linked, EX 10–59

data validation, **EX 12–14**

Data Validation dialog box, EX 12–18

data values, round, EX 3–13–3–15

Data view, **EX 10–32**

date(s)
    calculate, EX 3–6–3–7
    calculations with working days, EX 3–25
    create validation rule, EX 12–17–12–18
    enter, EX 1–18–1–27
    format, EX 2–19–2–20
    group, EX 11–18–11–21
    validate, EX 12–17–12–18
    validate against past and future, EX 12–21
    warning alert for invalid, EX 12–20

date and time functions, EX 3–23–3–25

date data, **EX 1–18**

Date Filter dialog box, EX 11–21

date filters, EX 11–12

DB function, **EX 9–21**

declining balance depreciation, EX 9–30–9–34
    asset, EX 9–33
    calculate, EX 9–31, EX 9–33
    definition, **EX 9–30**
    straight-line, EX 9–30

default PivotTable options, EX 11–8

defined name, **EX 5–34**
    existing formulas, EX 5–44–5–46
    save time, EX 5–39
    written communication, EX 5–39

delete, **EX 1–46**
    range, EX 1–47–1–49
    records, in Excel table, EX 6–42–6–43
    rows and columns, EX 1–46–1–47
    worksheets, EX 1–17–1–18

delimiter, **EX 10–4**

dependent cells, **EX 9–39**

depreciation of assets
    add to income statement, EX 9–34
    calculate, EX 9–29–9–35
    declining balance depreciation, EX 9–30–9–34
    defined, **EX 9–20**
    schedule, EX 9–35
    straight-line, EX 9–30

descending order sort, **EX 6–13**

design
    footers, EX 2–58–2–60
    headers, EX 2–58–2–60
    workbook for calculations, EX 3–4–3–6

design database, EX 10–30

destination workbook, **EX 5–20**

Developer tab, EX 12–35
    load, EX 12–36

Dfunction, **EX 11–65**. See also Database functions

Diagram view, **EX 10–32**
    explore Data Model, EX 10–32
    Power Pivot, EX 10–32
    switch, EX 10–32
    table relationships, EX 10–33

Diagram View button, Power Pivot, EX 10–24

digital certificates, EX 12–57

digital signature, **EX 12–57**
    add to workbook, EX 12–57

DISCOUNT COUNT function, EX 11–51–11–52

discount counts
    calculate, EX 11–51–11–53

discount rate, **EX 9–38**

display
    all state categories in PivotTable, EX 10–56
    data with funnel chart, EX 12–8–12–11
    multiple subtotal functions, EX 11–6
    PivotChart by Cust ID field, EX 10–52–10–53
    PivotTables with conditional formats, EX 11–31–11–35
    summary calculations, Power Pivot, EX 10–35–10–36
    total revenue by store and product category, EX 10–37

DISTINCTCOUNT function, EX 11–48, EX 11–53

document calculations, EX 3–5

document conditional formats, EX 2–51–2–52

document PivotTables, EX 11–47

drag and drop, **EX 1–41**

drill down, **EX 7–65**
    PivotTable, EX 7–65–7–67
    revenue by Product PivotChart using Quick Explore Tool,
        EX 10–51–10–52

drill up
    hierarchy, **EX 10–46**

duplicate records. See also record(s)
    highlight duplicate values, EX 6–10–6–11
    locate, EX 6–10–6–13
    remove, EX 6–12–6–13

duplicate values
    conditional formatting highlights cells, EX 6–11
    highlight, EX 6–10–6–11

dynamic
    charts, EX 6–58–6–61
    conditional format, EX 2–51
    reference with OFFSET function, EX 7–60

E

Edit Custom Lists button, EX 11–11

Edit Default Layout dialog box, EX 11–8

edit
    category axis, EX 4–24
    cell content, EX 1–20–1–21
    chart data source, EX 4–37–4–39
    chart title, EX 4–20–4–21
    conditional formatting rule, EX 2–49–2–50
    data query, EX 10–9–10–10
    Links dialog box, EX 5–27
    macro with VBA editor, EX 12–52–12–55
    Revenue History query, EX 10–9–10–10
    scenario, EX 8–29–8–30
    trendline, EX 10–16
    value axis scale, EX 4–29–4–30

Edit mode, **EX 1–20**

email address, link, EX 5–31–5–32

enhance application with SmartArt, EX 12–8

error
    trace, EX 9–53–9–55
    values in Balance Sheet worksheet, EX 9–52

error alert, **EX 12–14**

error values, **EX 3–25**
    Balance Sheet worksheet, EX 9–52
    traced, EX 9–53
    common, EX 3–26
    handle, EX 12–13
    hide with IFERROR function, EX 12–11–12–13
    interpret, EX 3–25–3–27
    source, EX 9–54
    trace, EX 9–53

error values (*Continued*)
    use IFERROR function to catch, EX 3–38
    worksheets, EX 3–27

evaluate, formula, EX 9–55–9–57

Evolutionary method, **EX 8–51**

exact match lookup, **EX 3–41**
    find with VLOOKUP function, EX 3–41–3–45

Excel, **EX 1–4**
    apply functions, EX 3–12–3–25
    calculate with formulas, EX 1–34–1–38
    calculate with functions, EX 1–38–1–41
    close workbook, EX 1–13–1–14
    data handle, EX 6–4–6–6
    depreciation functions, EX 9–34
    enter dates, EX 1–23–1–26
    enter numbers, EX 1–26–1–27
    enter text, dates, and numbers, EX 1–18–1–27
    explore workbook, EX 1–8–1–13
    get Help, EX 1–6
    introduce, EX 1–4–1–7
    modify worksheet, EX 1–41–1–43
    navigation keyboard shortcuts, EX 1–10
    plan workbook, EX 1–14–1–15
    programming language, EX 11–39
    resize columns and rows, EX 1–27–1–31
    start new workbook, EX 1–15–1–18
    understand AutoComplete, EX 1–21–1–22
    undo and redo an action, EX 1–20
    use Flash Fill, EX 1–49–1–51
    use in Touch Mode, EX 1–6–1–7
    use keyboard shortcuts to work faster, EX 1–6

Excel add-ins, EX 8–42

Excel application, **EX 12–4**
    plan, EX 12–4

Excel charts. *See also* chart(s)
    get started, EX 4–4–4–5
    types and subtypes, EX 4–4

Excel data form, **EX 12–50**. *See also* data form

Excel Data Model. *See* Data Model

Excel Developer tab, load, EX 12–36

Excel functions
    apply, EX 3–12–3–25
    calculate minimums and maximums, EX 3–16–3–18
    date and time functions, EX 3–23–3–25
    measures of central tendency, EX 3–18–3–21
    nested, EX 3–21–3–23
    role of blanks and zeroes, EX 3–23
    round data values, EX 3–13–3–15

Excel Ideas tool, EX 10–66

Excel Options dialog box, EX 11–11
    Customize Ribbon category, EX 12–36

Excel table, **EX 6–24**
    add and delete records, EX 6–42–6–43
    add Total row, EX 6–41–6–42
    calculated field creation, EX 6–43–6–45
    convert range to table, EX 6–37–6–39
    create, EX 6–37–6–47
    data sources, EX 10–11
    filters, EX 6–25
    load query data, EX 10–8–10–9
    retrieve data, EX 10–8–10–9
    structural elements, EX 6–39
    structural references, EX 6–45–6–47
    styles, use, EX 6–39–6–41
    vs. data range, EX 6–46

Excel templates, EX 5–48

Excel workbook
    return, EX 10–34

Excel XLSTART folder, EX 12–38

expenses
    fixed, EX 9–20
    general, EX 9–20
    interest, EX 9–35–9–36
    projected general, EX 9–29
    project future, EX 9–22–9–29
    revenue, EX 8–4–8–5

explicit measure, **EX 11–49**

exploded pie chart, **EX 4–10**

explore
    Data Model, EX 10–28–10–30
    Data Model in Data view, EX 10–32
    growth trend, EX 9–22–9–23
    linear trend, EX 9–22–9–23
    PivotTable cache, EX 11–35–11–39
    XIRR function, EX 9–49–9–51
    XNPV function, EX 9–49–9–51

exponential trendline, EX 10–17

external reference, **EX 5–20**
    create, EX 5–22–5–25
    enter, EX 5–23
    formula, EX 5–24
    profit and loss values, EX 5–25
    security concerns, EX 5–26–5–27

external workbooks, link, EX 5–22–5–29

extrapolate
    charts, EX 9–25
    series, EX 9–27
    series of values, EX 9–27–9–29

extrapolation, defined, **EX 9–21**

F

field(s)
    defined, **EX 6–3**
    manually sort, EX 11–9
    outline by nested, EX 10–44–10–46
    primary sort, EX 6–15
    Product List hierarchy, EX 10–48
    secondary sort, EX 6–15
    sort by multiple, EX 6–15–6–17
    sort by single, EX 6–13–6–15
    tabulate from multiple tables, Power Pivot, EX 10–37–10–38

Field List pane, 3D Map window, EX 10–60

Field Settings dialog box, EX 11–6

field value
    cells show, EX 11–31

fill colors, **EX 2–3**
    change, EX 2–9–2–10
    set worksheet tab color, EX 2–10
    work, EX 2–9–2–11

fill handle, **EX 3–8**

filter
    based on multiple field, EX 6–29–6–30
    based on one field, EX 6–28–6–29
    buttons, EX 6–52
    data, EX 6–27–6–37
    data with slicers, EX 6–50–6–52
    PivotTable, EX 7–37–7–38, EX 11–12–11–14

filtered pie chart, EX 4–17

filters
    apply advanced, EX 6–33–6–37
    clear, EX 6–33
    criteria, EX 6–30–6–32
    Excel table, EX 6–25
    text, EX 6–33
financial functions
    defined, **EX 9–4**
    introduce, EX 9–4
financial scenarios
    explore with scenario manager, EX 8–24–8–30
financial workbook, EX 9–18
Find and Replace commands, EX 2–31, EX 2–42–2–44
Find and Replace dialog box, EX 6–26–6–27, EX 11–64
fixed expenses, **EX 8–4, EX 9–20.**
    See also general expenses
Flash Fill, **EX 1–49**
    use, EX 1–49–1–51
font(s), **EX 2–2**
    apply, EX 2–4–2–6
    color, apply, EX 2–6–2–8
    Sans serif, EX 2–4
    standard, EX 2–4
    theme, EX 2–4, EX 2–45–2–46
font size, **EX 1–32**
    change, EX 1–52–1–53
font styles, **EX 2–2**
    apply, EX 2–4–2–6
footer(s)
    defined, **EX 2–58**
    design, EX 2–58–2–60
Forecast sheets, **EX 10–18**
    create, EX 10–18–10–23
    generate, EX 10–19
Forecasts with seasonal trend, EX 10–20–10–21
Forecast worksheet, EX 10–21
format, **EX 1–51**
    calculated values, EX 3–39–3–40
    cell content, EX 2–4
    cell text, EX 2–4–2–8
    change labels and number formats, EX 7–40–7–42
    chart elements, EX 4–11–4–14
    conditional and duplicate values, EX 6–11
    data markers, EX 4–24–4–25
    dates and times, EX 2–19–2–20
    input values, EX 3–39–3–40
    map chart, EX 10–58–10–59
    monetary values, EX 2–17
    numbers, EX 2–16–2–20
    output values, EX 3–39–3–40
    PivotTable, EX 7–39–7–45
    result cell, EX 8–17–8–18
    slicer(s), EX 6–54–6–55
    sparkline, EX 4–54
    text selections within cell, EX 2–8
    workbooks for readability and appeal, EX 2–28
    worksheet, EX 1–51–1–53
    worksheet cells, EX 2–20–2–25
    worksheet for print, EX 2–53–2–63
Format Cells dialog box
    alignment, EX 2–25
    border, EX 2–26
    explore, EX 2–25–2–29
    fill, EX 2–26
    font, EX 2–25

number, EX 2–25
    protection, EX 2–26
Format Painter, **EX 2–30**
    copy formats, EX 2–38–2–39
Format pane, **EX 4–3**
Formats
    copy, EX 2–38–2–42
    copy with Format Painter, EX 2–38–2–39
    copy with Paste Options button, EX 2–40
    find and replace, EX 2–42–2–44
    highlight data with conditional, EX 2–46–2–52
    paste, EX 2–38–2–42
form controls, **EX 12–43**
formula(s)
    3-D reference apply, EX 5–14–5–18
    absolute references, EX 3–35
    AutoFill, EX 3–7–3–12
    automatically enter donor number, EX 12–16
    copy, EX 1–37–1–38
    defined, **EX 1–33**
    defined names, EX 5–44–5–46
    enter, EX 1–34–1–37
    evaluate, EX 9–55–9–57
    external references, EX 5–24
    named range, EX 5–39–5–41
    paste, EX 1–37–1–38
    perform what-if analyses, EX 3–45–3–51
    simplify with named ranges, EX 5–36–5–46
    step, EX 9–56
    use absolute references, EX 3–33
    use mixed references, EX 3–34
    use relative references, EX 3–32
    use with sales data, EX 2–12–2–15
    write effective, EX 1–41
formula bar, **EX 1–2**
freeze pane(s), EX 6–8–6–10
    defined, **EX 6–8**
    freeze rows and columns, EX 6–9
function(s)
    3-D reference apply, EX 5–14–5–18
    calculate future value with FV, EX 9–7–9–9
    calculate inflation with FV, EX 9–9
    calculate interest rates with RATE, EX 9–40–9–41
    calculate payment period with NPER, EX 9–9–9–10
    calculate payments with PMT, EX 9–5–9–7
    calculate present value with PV, EX 9–10–9–12
    calculate, EX 1–38–1–41
    defined, **EX 1–33**
    display multiple subtotal, EX 11–6
    excel depreciation, EX 9–34
    explore XIRR, EX 9–49–9–51
    explore XNPV, EX 9–49–9–51
    insert with AutoSum, EX 1–39–1–41
    perform what-if analyses, EX 3–45–3–51
    understand syntax, EX 1–38
    use with sales data, EX 2–12–2–15
    VLOOKUP function, EX 6–62–6–63
function syntax. *See* syntax
funnel chart, **EX 12–2**
    display data, EX 12–8–12–11
    formatted, EX 12–9
    total donations by contribution level, EX 12–10
future value, **EX 9–4**
    calculate with FV function, EX 9–7–9–9
FV function, **EX 9–2**
    calculate future value, EX 9–7–9–9
    calculate inflation, EX 9–9

G

gap width, set, EX 4–21

general expenses, **EX 9–20**. *See also* fixed expenses

General format, **EX 2–16**

generate multiple PivotTables with Show Report Filter Pages, EX 11–15

Get Data dialog box, EX B6

GETPIVOTDATA function, **EX 11–61**
    insert, EX 11–62
    retrieve PivotTable data, EX 11–61–11–65
    standard PivotTable, EX 11–62

Get & Transform Data group, EX 10–3

global optimum, **EX 8–51**

global scope, **EX 5–35**

Goal Seek, **EX 3–48**–3–50
    perform, EX 3–49

grand totals
    calculated formulas applied, EX 11–46
    removed from PivotTable, EX 11–6
    work, EX 11–4–11–6

graphic icons, insert, EX 4–42–4–44

graphic objects
    add to workbook, EX 4–39–4–45
    tools, EX 4–44–4–45

graphic shape, insert, EX 4–41–4–42

GRG Nonlinear method, **EX 8–51**

gridlines, **EX 1–32**, **EX 4–2**
    add to chart, EX 4–22

gross profit, **EX 9–26**

group
    calculated items, EX 11–42
    dates, EX 11–18–11–21
    manual, EX 11–16–11–18
    numeric fields, EX 11–21–11–23
    PivotTable fields, EX 11–15–11–23

Group By dialog box, EX 10–14

grouped worksheets, EX 5–11

Group dialog box, EX 11–16, EX 11–20, EX 11–22

groups, **EX 1–2**

growth trend, **EX 9–21**
    explore, EX 9–22–9–23

H

handle error values, EX 12–13

header(s)
    defined, **EX 2–58**
    design, EX 2–58–2–60

header row, **EX 6–4**

Heat map, EX 10–62

Help, EX 1–6

hide, **EX 1–49**
    columns, EX 1–49
    error values with IFERROR function, EX 12–11–12–13
    rows, EX 1–49
    workbook content, EX 12–25–12–26
    worksheets, EX 1–49

hierarchy, **EX 10–42**
    define, EX 10–47
    drill up, **EX 10–46**

hierarchy charts, **EX 4–45**, EX 4–45–4–46

hierarchy of fields
    create, EX 10–47
    create in Products table, EX 10–47

highlight unlocked cells, EX 12–31

histogram, **EX 4–46**

histogram charts, EX 4–46–4–47

Holoease, EX 9–1

horizontal layout, workbook window, EX 5–7

horizontal lookup tables
    create approximate match lookup, EX 7–12

100% stacked column chart, **EX 4–19**

hyperlink(s), **EX 5–21**
    create, EX 5–29–5–32
    link to email address, EX 5–31–5–32
    link to location within workbook, EX 5–29–5–31
    work, EX 5–29

Hyperlink dialog box, inserting, EX 5–30

I

icon sets, **EX 11–24**
    create, EX 11–32–11–34

IFERROR function, **EX 3–38, EX 12–3**
    error values hidden, EX 12–12
    hide error values, EX 12–11–12–13

IF logical function, **EX 3–28**
    evaluate customer hold time, EX 3–37
    work, EX 3–35–3–38

IFS function
    apply summary, EX 7–19–7–27
    defined, **EX 7–17**
    OR function nested, EX 7–19
    use, EX 7–17

implicit measure, **EX 11–49**

improper scale, EX 4–55

income
    project future, EX 9–22–9–29

income statement, **EX 5–4, EX 9–20**. *See also* profit and loss statement
    add depreciation, EX 9–34–9–35
    add taxes and interest expenses, EX 9–35–9–37
    final, EX 9–51
    revised, EX 9–36

indent cell content, EX 2–21

INDEX function, EX 7–11

Index Match lookups
    retrieve data, EX 7–14–7–15

indirect reference, **EX 5–47**

inflation, calculation with FV function, EX 9–9

input cells, **EX 8–2**

input message, **EX 12–14**
    create, EX 12–20–12–21
    custom, EX 12–20

input message box, EX 12–21

input value(s), **EX 8–2**
    format, EX 3–39–3–40

insert
    GETPIVOTDATA function, EX 11–62
    graphic icons, EX 4–42–4–44
    graphic shape, EX 4–41–4–42
    Hyperlink dialog box, EX 5–30
    PivotTable, EX 7–31–7–32
    Product Revenue PivotTable, EX 10–44

range, EX 1–47–1–49
rows and columns, EX 1–45–1–46
worksheets, EX 1–16–1–17
Insert Calculated Field dialog box, EX 11–43
Insert Slicers dialog box, EX 10–38–10–39
interest, **EX 9–4**
calculate, EX 9–13–9–15
interest expenses
add to income statement, EX 9–35–9–37
interest payments, calculate, EX 9–13–9–15
interest rates
calculate with RATE function, EX 9–40–9–41
investment, EX 9–41
internal rate of return, **EX 9–38**
calculate, EX 9–46–9–48
net present value, EX 9–46
use IRR function, EX 9–47–9–48
international date formats, EX 1–24
interpolate
charts, EX 9–25
series, EX 9–27
start value to end value, EX 9–23–9–25
interpolation, defined, **EX 9–20**
interpret error values, EX 3–25–3–27
INT function, **EX 3–15**
investment(s)
calculate value, EX 9–47
use NPV and IRR to compare, EX 9–48
view payback period, EX 9–41–9–42
work, EX 9–6
IPMT function, **EX 9–2**
IRR function, **EX 9–38**
use, EX 9–47–9–48
use to compare investments, EX 9–48
iterative process
defined, **EX 8–50**
explore, EX 8–50–8–51

K

keyboard shortcuts, **EX 1–6**
use to work faster, EX 1–6
key performance indicator (KPI), **EX 3–37**
KeyTips, **EX 1–6**

L

Label Filter (Motel Name) dialog box, EX 11–12
label filters, EX 11–12
labels, change, EX 7–40–7–42
landscape orientation, **EX 1–55**
language
mashup query, **EX 10–8**
Power Query, EX 10–8
Layer pane, 3D Map window, EX 10–60
layers, **EX 10–43**
lay out PivotTable, EX 11–4–11–8
limits report, **EX 8–51**. See also sensitivity report
linear trend, **EX 9–21**
explore, EX 9–22–9–23
linear trendline
add to scatter chart, EX 10–17
definition, EX 10–17

line chart, **EX 4–2**
create, EX 4–23–4–26
edit category axis, EX 4–24
format data markers, EX 4–24–4–25
link(s), **EX 5–20**
email address, EX 5–31–5–32
external workbooks, EX 5–22–5–29
hyperlinks to location within workbook, EX 5–29–5–31
manage workbooks, EX 5–28
review within workbooks, EX 5–27
linked data types, **EX 10–59**
Links dialog box, editing, EX 5–27
list, validate against, EX 12–21–12–23
list box validation, EX 12–22
list box values, EX 12–22
Live Preview, **EX 2–4**
load
Customers table into Data Model, EX 10–29
Excel Developer tab, EX 12–36
Monthly Revenue query, EX 10–14
query data into Excel table, EX 10–8–10–9
Solver models, EX 8–53–8–57
loan(s)
calculate future value, EX 9–8
calculate number of payments, EX 9–10
future value, EX 9–8
payments required to repay, EX 9–10
present value, EX 9–11
quarterly payment required to repay, EX 9–7
work, EX 9–6
local optimum, **EX 8–51**
local scope, **EX 5–35**
locked property, **EX 12–30**
lock cells, EX 12–30–12–33
logarithmic trendline
definition, EX 10–17
revenue estimated use, EX 10–18
logical comparison operators, EX 3–36
logical functions
apply, EX 7–17
combine conditions with OR and AND functions, EX 7–17–7–19
defined, **EX 3–35**
explore, EX 7–16–7–19
use IFS function, EX 7–17
Long Date format, **EX 2–20**
lookup functions, **EX 3–40**
use, EX 7–4–7–12
lookup table, **EX 3–40**
exact match returned, EX 3–41
lookup values, **EX 3–40**

M

macro(s), **EX 12–35**
assign keyboard shortcuts, EX 12–42
assign to buttons, EX 12–41–12–50
assign to shapes, EX 12–41–12–50
automate tasks, EX 12–37–12–41
edit with VBA editor, EX 12–52–12–55
plan, EX 12–55
record, EX 12–37–12–38, EX 12–55
run, EX 12–39
sub procedure for Show_Dashboard, EX 12–52
Macro dialog box, EX 12–39

macro-enabled workbook
    open, EX 12–40–12–41
    save, EX 12–40–12–41
    security warning, EX 12–40

macro security set, **EX 12–34,** EX 12–55–12–56

Macro Settings in Trust Center, EX 12–56

macro viruses, **EX 12–55**
    add digital signature to workbook, EX 12–57
    macro security set, EX 12–55–12–56
    protect against, EX 12–55–12–57

major tick marks, **EX 4–29**

manual filters, EX 11–12

manual group, **EX 11–16**–11–18

manually sort field, EX 11–9

manual page break, **EX 2–30**

map(s)
    customers mapped by postal code, EX 10–61
    location of Cup and Platter customers, EX 10–61
    specify location, EX 10–58
    total revenue by state, EX 10–56–10–57
    value, **EX 10–54**

map chart, **EX 10–42**
    connect to slicer and timeline filters, EX 10–57
    create, EX 10–54
    format, EX 10–58–10–59
    format options, EX 10–59
    view data, EX 10–53–10–67

map style
    selection, EX 10–62–10–63

margin
    defined, **EX 2–60**
    set left, EX 2–61

mashup query language, **EX 10–8**

MATCH function, EX 7–15
    INDEX, EX 7–15

material assets, EX 9–29

MAX function, **EX 3–2,** EX 11–53
    3-D reference, EX 5–15

MAXIFS function, **EX 7–27**

Maximize button, **EX 1–3**

MAXX function, EX 11–61

mean, **EX 3–18**

measure(s), **EX 11–49**
    add to table, EX 11–54–11–57
    calculate across tables and rows, EX 11–57–11–61
    create, EX 11–53–11–57
    explicit, EX 11–49
    implicit, EX 11–49

measure, create
    add measure to table, EX 11–54–11–57
    introduce DAX, EX 11–53–11–54

measures of central tendency, EX 3–18–3–21
    average, EX 3–18
    calculate, EX 3–19
    mean, EX 3–18
    median, EX 3–18
    mode, EX 3–18

median, **EX 3–18**

MEDIAN function, **EX 3–2**
    3-D reference, EX 5–15

merge, **EX 2–2**
    cells, EX 2–23–2–24

custom cell styles, EX 2–38
    scenarios, EX 8–35

Microsoft Access. *See* Data Model

Microsoft Excel, **EX 1–4**

Microsoft Office text box, EX 12–4

MIN function, **EX 3–2,** EX 11–53
    3-D reference, EX 5–15

MINIFS function, **EX 7–27**

Minimize button, **EX 1–3**

minimums and maximums
    calculate, EX 3–16–3–18

Mini toolbar, **EX 2–8**

minor tick marks, **EX 4–29**

MINX function, EX 11–61

mixed cell references, **EX 3–28,** EX 3–33–3–34
    formulas use, EX 3–34

mixed expense, **EX 8–5**

M language, **EX 10–8**

mode, **EX 3–18**

MODE.MULT function, EX 3–18

MODE.SNGL function, **EX 3–2**

modify
    chart data source, EX 4–38
    data bar rule, EX 4–49–4–50
    data table, EX 8–13–8–14
    PivotTable layout, EX 7–34–7–35
    rows and columns, EX 1–44–1–49
    worksheets, EX 1–41–1–43

module, **EX 12–52**

money
    time value, EX 9–43

Monthly Revenue query
    close and load, EX 10–14
    import values, EX 10–15

monthly revenue values
    calculate, EX 10–13–10–14
    import, EX 10–15

More Sort Options (Motel Name) dialog box, EX 11–10

Mouse Mode, **EX 1–7**

Move or Copy dialog box, EX 5–5, EX 5–6

move
    cell or range, EX 1–41–1–43
    query data source, EX 10–15
    worksheets, EX 5–4

moving average trendline, EX 10–17

MROUND function, **EX 3–15**

multiple fields sort, EX 6–15–6–17

multiple field values, cells show, EX 11–31

multiple PivotTable caches, EX 11–37

multiple sheets, unhide, EX 12–26

Multi-Select button, EX 6–48

N

Name box, **EX 1–2**

named range, **EX 5–34**
    defined in Name box, EX 5–37
    define, EX 5–36–5–38
    determine scope, EX 5–42–5–44
    formulas, EX 5–39–5–41

scope, **EX 5–35**
    simplify formulas, EX 5–36–5–46
named sets, **EX 11–51**
    Data Model, EX 11–51
name constants, EX 5–44
Navigator dialog box, EX 10–28
negative cash flow, **EX 9–3**. *See also* cash outflow
nested fields
    outline by PivotTable, EX 10–44–10–46
nesting functions, EX 3–21–3–23
net present value, **EX 9–38**
    calculate, EX 9–43–9–46
    choose rate of return, EX 9–44–9–46
    time value of money, EX 9–43
    understand, EX 9–45
    use NPV function, EX 9–43–9–44
NETWORKDAYS function, **EX 3–25**
New Formatting Rule dialog box, EX 11–33
New Window button, EX 5–2
nonadjacent range, **EX 1–2**
nonbinding constraint, **EX 8–53**
noncash assets, EX 9–29
Normal view, **EX 1–33**
NPER function, **EX 9–3**
    calculate payment period with function, EX 9–9–9–10
NPV function, **EX 9–38**
    understand, EX 9–45
    use, EX 9–43–9–44
    use to compare investments, EX 9–48
number(s)
    display as text, EX 1–22–1–23
    display percentages, EX 2–19
    enter, EX 1–18–1–27
    format, EX 2–16–2–20
number formats
    apply, EX 2–16–2–19
    change, EX 7–40–7–42
numeric data, **EX 1–18**
numeric fields, group, EX 11–21–11–23

O

objective cell
    defined, **EX 8–36**
    set, EX 8–42–8–44
OFFSET function
    dynamic reference, EX 7–60
OLAP Cube
    retrieve measures, EX 11–65
one-to-many relationship, **EX 10–24, EX 10–27**
one-variable data table, **EX 8–2**
    chart, EX 8–12–8–13
    completed, EX 8–12
    create, EX 8–9–8–12
    example, EX 8–10
    setup, EX 8–11
Online Analytic Processing (OLAP) database, **EX 11–65**
open
    3D maps, EX 10–60
    macro-enabled workbook, EX 12–40–12–41
    VBA editor, EX 12–50–12–51
operators, **EX 1–34**

optimize product mix, EX 8–38–8–40
Options dialog box, EX 11–8
Order Date timeline
    add to dashboard, EX 10–39
    Orders table, EX 10–40
Orders table, Order Date timeline, EX 10–40
OR function, EX 7–17–7–19
    defined, **EX 7–17**
    nested within IF function, EX 7–19
Outline layout, **EX 11–2**
outline(s)
    Collapsed PivotTable, EX 10–46
    PivotTable by nested fields, EX 10–44–10–46
outline view
    create, EX 6–23
    subtotals, EX 6–21–6–23
output values, format, EX 3–39–3–40

P

Page Break Preview, **EX 1–33**
    use, EX 2–53–2–54
page breaks, insert, EX 2–55–2–56
Page Layout, **EX 1–32**
Page Layout view, **EX 1–33**
page margins, setting, EX 2–60–2–63
page orientation, **EX 1–55**
    change, EX 1–55
pane(s)
    defined, **EX 6–2**
    divide workbook window, EX 6–6–6–8
    freeze, EX 6–8–6–10
    unfreeze, in workbook window, EX 6–10
    use, for viewing data, EX 6–6–6–10
Pareto charts, **EX 4–46**
partial lookups
    defined, **EX 7–16**
    perform with wildcards, EX 7–16
Paste Link
    PivotTable data pasted, EX 10–55
Paste Options button
    copy formats, EX 2–40
Paste Special command
    copy formats, EX 2–40
    perform special tasks, EX 2–41
Paste Special dialog box, EX 12–44
paste
    chart formats, EX 4–37
    formats, EX 2–38–2–42
    formulas, EX 1–37–1–38
path, **EX 5–22**
payback period, **EX 9–38**
    view for investment, EX 9–41–9–42
payment period
    calculation with NPER function, EX 9–9–9–10
payments
    calculate interest and principal, EX 9–13–9–15
    calculation with PMT function, EX 9–5–9–7
    initial, in amortization schedule, EX 9–14
    quarterly, required to repay loan, EX 9–7
    required to repay loan, EX 9–10
    total loan, EX 9–18

percentages, display, EX 2–19

Percent style formats, **EX 2–3**

Personal Macro workbook, **EX 12–38**
    create macro library, EX 12–38

Personal.xslb file, EX 12–38

pie chart, **EX 4–2**
    chart with Quick Analysis tool, EX 4–7–4–8
    create, EX 4–6–4–10
    exploded, **EX 4–10**
    filtered, EX 4–17
    move and resize chart, EX 4–8–4–9
    select data source, EX 4–6

pie PivotChart, create, EX 7–56–7–60

PivotCharts
    create, EX 7–52, EX 7–53–7–55
    create, product revenue, EX 10–50–10–51
    defined, **EX 7–51**
    display by Cust ID field, EX 10–52–10–53
    introduce, EX 7–52–7–60
    move to another worksheet, EX 7–55–7–56
    revenue by product, EX 10–50
    structure, EX 7–52

PivotTable(s), EX 12–4
    Add multiple fields to row or column, EX 7–35–7–36
    add Product List hierarchy, EX 10–48
    all cells showing field value, EX 11–31
    all cells showing multiple field values, EX 11–31
    apply slicer to multiple, EX 7–61–7–62
    calculate percent differences, EX 11–29–11–31
    calculate ranks, EX 11–28–11–29
    calculations, EX 11–26–11–31
    change labels and number formats, EX 7–40–7–42
    change PivotTable layout, EX 11–7–11–8
    choose recommended, EX 7–39
    choose report layout, EX 7–45
    choose summary function, EX 7–42–7–43
    collapse and expand categories, EX 10–45
    columns area, EX 7–30
    Count of Date, EX 11–52
    create, EX 7–30–7–45
    create icon set, EX 11–32–11–34
    create layout, EX 7–33–7–34
    create of revenue by state, EX 10–54–10–55
    Daily Rentals measure, EX 11–55
    data pasted using Paste Link, EX 10–55
    defined, **EX 7–28**
    display all state categories, EX 10–56
    display with conditional formats, EX 11–31–11–35
    document, EX 11–47
    drill down, EX 7–65–7–67
    filter, EX 7–37–7–38, EX 11–12–11–14
    filters area, EX 7–30
    format, EX 7–39–7–45
    grand total removed, EX 11–6
    group fields, EX 11–15–11–23, EX 11–16
    insert, EX 7–31–7–32
    insert Product Revenue, EX 10–44
    lay out, EX 11–4–11–8
    make accessible, EX 7–47
    manually sort field, EX 11–9
    modified, EX 7–35
    move, EX 7–44
    outline by nested fields, EX 10–44–10–46
    PivotTable cache shared by multiple, EX 11–36
    reorder categories, EX 7–45
    retrieve data with GETPIVOTDATA function, EX 11–61–11–65
    revenue and royalties, EX 11–60
    revenue by location, EX 11–5
    rows area, EX 7–30

selected cells, EX 11–31
set options, EX 7–46–7–47
set PivotTable design, EX 7–47–7–49
share cache, EX 11–35–11–37
sort by custom list, EX 11–11
sort by value, EX 11–9–11–11
standard, EX 11–50
structure, EX 7–30
style and options, EX 7–48
subtotals removed, EX 11–6
Tabular layout, EX 11–8
Total Revenue by product fields, EX 10–45
use slicers, EX 7–60–7–65
values area, EX 7–30
work with color scales, EX 11–34–11–35
work with grand totals and subtotals, EX 11–4–11–6

PivotTable caches, **EX 7–45, EX 11–35**
    count, EX 11–39
    create new, EX 11–37–11–38
    create PivotTable from new, EX 11–37
    explore, EX 11–35–11–39
    multiple, EX 11–37
    new PivotTable report based on separate, EX 11–38
    shared by multiple PivotTables, EX 11–36
    share cache between PivotTables, EX 11–35–11–37

PivotTable design
    introduce under Data Model, EX 11–50–11–51
    set, EX 7–47–7–49

PivotTable fields
    calculate values, EX 11–28
    group, EX 11–15–11–23, EX 11–16
    group by dates, EX 11–18–11–21
    group by numeric fields, EX 11–21–11–23
    manual group, EX 11–16–11–18

PivotTable Fields pane, EX 7–29

PivotTable layout
    change, EX 11–7–11–8
    choose, EX 11–7
    create, EX 7–33–7–34
    modify, EX 7–34–7–35
    options, EX 11–7

PivotTable Options dialog box, EX 7–47, EX 10–56, EX 11–8, EX 11–11, EX 11–13

PivotTables from the Data Model
    features, EX 11–50

PivotTables options, set, EX 7–46–7–47

PivotTable Tools Analyze tab, EX 11–11, EX 11–16, EX 11–51

PivotTable Wizard, **EX 11–37**

pixel, **EX 1–27**

PMT function, **EX 9–3**
    calculate payments, EX 9–5–9–7

point, **EX 1–30**

polynomial trendline, EX 10–17

portrait orientation, **EX 1–55**

positive cash flow, **EX 9–2**. *See also* cash inflow

Power Pivot
    add Order Date timeline to dashboard, EX 10–39–10–40
    add slicers to dashboard, EX 10–38–10–39
    apply slicers and timelines from Data Model, EX 10–38–10–41
    BI tool, EX 10–30
    connect slicer and timeline, EX 10–40
    create from Data Model, EX 10–34–10–41
    data from Data Model, EX 10–36
    Data Model, EX 10–24, EX 10–25
    Diagram view, EX 10–32
    Diagram View button, EX 10–24

display summary calculations, EX 10–35–10–36
install, EX 10–31
table relationships, EX 10–33
tabulate across fields from multiple tables, EX 10–37–10–38
transform data, EX 10–30–10–34

Power Pivot window, EX 10–31

Power Query, **EX 10–4**
data query, EX 10–4–10–8
language, EX 10–8

Power Query data types, EX B8

Power Query Editor, **EX 10–2**, EX 10–3, EX B7

Power Query Editor window, EX 10–6

power trendline, EX 10–17

PPMT function, **EX 9–3**

precedent cells, **EX 9–39**

present value, **EX 9–4**
calculation with PV function, EX 9–10–9–12

preview
queried data, EX 10–6
Recent History query, EX 10–12

Preview grid, EX 10–2

primary axis, **EX 4–26**

primary sort field, **EX 6–15**

principal, defined, **EX 9–4**

principal payments, calculate, EX 9–13–9–15, EX 9–16–9–19

print
format worksheet, EX 2–53–2–63
workbook, EX 1–53–1–57
worksheet groups, EX 5–13

print area
defined, **EX 2–31**, **EX 2–54**

print options, set, EX 1–56–1–57

print titles, **EX 2–30**
add, EX 2–56–2–58

problem-solving
3-D reference, EX 5–15

Product List hierarchy
add to PivotTable, EX 10–48
drill down, EX 10–49
drill up, EX 10–49
fields, EX 10–48
PivotTable drilled down, EX 10–49

product mix
assume increasing sales for higher-end models, EX 8–39
assume lower sales for higher-end models, EX 8–40
defined, **EX 8–36**
optimize, EX 8–38–8–40

Product PivotChart
drill down revenue by using Quick Explore Tool, EX 10–51–10–52

Product Revenue PivotTable
insert, EX 10–44

Products table
create hierarchy of fields, EX 10–47

PRODUCTX function, EX 11–61

profit and loss (P&L) statement, **EX 5–4, EX 9–20**. *See also* income statement
open workbook, EX 5–4
templates, EX 5–49

project
future income and expenses, EX 9–22

PROPER function
defined, **EX A7**
use, EX A7

protect
against macro viruses, EX 12–55–12–57
workbook, EX 12–28–12–29
workbook contents, EX 12–27–12–33
worksheet, EX 12–27–12–28

Protection tab in Format Cells dialog box, EX 12–32

Protect Sheet dialog box, EX 12–28

PV function, **EX 9–2**
calculate present value, EX 9–10–9–12

Q

Queries & Connections pane, EX 10–3

query, **EX 10–2**
Access database, EX 10–27–10–28
add new column, EX 10–12–10–13
calculate monthly revenues, EX 10–13–10–14
construct, EX 10–5
create Access database table, EX 10–28
create to revenue history data, EX 10–5–10–6
group values, EX 10–13–10–15
import monthly revenue values, EX 10–15
move data source, EX 10–15
preview of data, EX 10–6
set name, EX 10–7
trendline, EX 10–3
view steps, EX 10–7

Query Settings pane, EX 10–2

Query tab, EX 10–9, EX 10–10

Quick Analysis tool, **EX 2–48,** EX 10–53
calculate running totals, EX 3–30–3–31
chart, EX 4–7–4–8

Quick Explore, **EX 10–42**

Quick Explore button, EX 10–51

Quick Explore Tool
drill down revenue by Product PivotChart, EX 10–51–10–52
view data, EX 10–51–10–53

R

*R*2 statistic, **EX 10–18**

random data, generate, EX 3–45

range, **EX 1–2**
assign to users, EX 12–33
copy, EX 1–41–1–43
insert and delete, EX 1–47–1–49
move, EX 1–41–1–43
nonadjacent, **EX 1–2**

range reference, **EX 1–12**

rank(s)
calculate, EX 11–28–11–29
occupancy field calculation, EX 11–29
weekly occupancy rates, EX 11–29

RATE function, **EX 9–39**
calculate interest rates, EX 9–40–9–41

rate of return, **EX 9–38**
choose, EX 9–44–9–46

Recent History query
initial preview, EX 10–12

record(s)
add and delete, in Excel table, EX 6–42–6–43
defined, **EX 6–3**
sort, in data range, EX 6–13–6–19

record macro, EX 12–37–12–38, EX 12–55

Record Macro dialog box, EX 12–34, EX 12–38, EX 12–42

Refresh Dashboard macro button, EX 12–49

refresh
    data query, EX 10–10–10–11
    PivotTable data, **EX 7–66**

Region map, EX 10–62

RELATED function, EX 11–58

relational databases, EX 10–26–10–27, **EX 10–27**

relationship(s)
    one-to-many, **EX 10–24, EX 10–27**
    table, **EX 10–24**

relative cell references, **EX 3–28**, EX 3–32
    formulas use, EX 3–32

Remove Duplicates tool, EX 6–12–6–13

rename worksheets, EX 1–16–1–17

Report Connections button, EX 7–50

resize
    charts, EX 4–8–4–9
    columns and rows, EX 1–27–1–31

Restore Down button, **EX 1–3**

result cells, **EX 8–2**
    format, EX 8–17–8–18

result values, **EX 8–2**

retrieve
    data into Excel table, EX 10–8–10–9

return values, **EX 3–40**

revenue
    chart, EX 8–5
    compare expenses, EX 8–4–8–5

Revenue History dialog box, EX 10–10

Revenue History query, EX 10–9–10–10

revenue trends, annual and monthly, EX 10–22

RGB Color model, **EX 2–7**

ribbon, **EX 1–2**

Ribbon Display Options button, **EX 1–3**

rotate cell contents, EX 2–24–2–25

ROUNDDOWN function, **EX 3–13**

ROUND function, **EX 3–13**

round data values, EX 3–13–3–15

ROUNDUP function, **EX 3–3, EX 3–13**

row(s)
    add multiple fields, EX 7–35–7–36
    banded, EX 6–25
    calculate measures across, EX 11–57–11–61
    change heights, EX 1–30–1–31
    delete, EX 1–46–1–47
    freeze, in worksheet, EX 6–9
    hide, EX 1–49
    insert, EX 1–45–1–46
    modify, EX 1–44–1–49
    resize, EX 1–27–1–31
    subtotal, create, EX 6–19–6–21
    Total, EX 6–25
    unhide, EX 1–49

row headings, **EX 1–2**

row heights, change, EX 1–30–1–31

run macro, EX 12–39

run total(s)
    calculate with Quick Analysis Tool, EX 3–30–3–31
    call durations, EX 3–31

S

sales data
    formulas use, EX 2–12–2–15
    functions use, EX 2–12–2–15

Sans serif fonts, **EX 2–4**. *See also* font(s)

save
    macro-enabled workbook, EX 12–40–12–41
    Solver models, EX 8–53–8–57
    theme, EX 2–46
    workbook, EX 1–18

scale, **EX 1–55, EX 4–29**
    data values differently, EX 4–55
    improper, EX 4–55
    options, set, EX 1–55–1–56
    secondary axis, EX 4–29–4–30

scatter chart, **EX 4–32**
    create, EX 4–34–4–37, EX 10–16
    insert graphic icons, EX 4–42–4–44
    insert graphic shape, EX 4–41–4–42
    linear trendline, add, EX 10–17
    preview, EX 4–35
    removing elements, EX 4–37
    return rate *vs.* volatility, EX 4–34

Scenario Manager, **EX 8–22**
    explore financial scenarios, EX 8–24–8–30

scenario PivotTable report, **EX 8–23**

scenarios
    define, **EX 8–22**, EX 8–25–8–28
    edit, EX 8–29–8–30
    merge, EX 8–35
    view, EX 8–28–8–29

scenario summary reports, **EX 8–23**
    create, EX 8–30–8–35

Scene Options dialog box, EX 10–65

scene(s), **EX 10–43**
    create, EX 10–63–10–64
    play tour, EX 10–66–10–67
    set options, EX 10–64–10–65
    tour with two, EX 10–64

scope, **EX 5–35**
    determine, named range, EX 5–42–5–44

ScreenTip, **EX 1–6**

Search box, **EX 1–3**

seasonal data, **EX 10–18**

seasonal forecast, create, EX 10–20–10–21

secondary axis, **EX 4–26**

secondary sort field, **EX 6–15**

security warning for macro-enabled workbook, EX 12–40

sensitivity report, **EX 8–51**. *See also* limits report

series
    AutoFill used to extend, EX 3–10
    extrapolate, EX 9–27
    fill, EX 3–10–3–12
    interpolate, EX 9–27
    patterns extended with AutoFill, EX 3–10
    values, extrapolate, EX 9–27–9–29

Serif fonts, **EX 2–4**. *See also* font(s)

set
    forecast options, EX 10–19
    query name, EX 10–7
    scene options, EX 10–64–10–65

set up data query, EX 10–12

shapes
    assign macros, EX 12–41–12–50
share cache between PivotTables, EX 11–35–11–37
sheets, **EX 1–3**
sheet tab, **EX 1–3**
shortcut menu, **EX 1–17**
Short Date format, **EX 2–20**
Show Report Filters Pages tool, **EX 11–15**
    generate multiple PivotTables, EX 11–15
significant digits
    defined, **EX 3–18**
    display, EX 3–18
Simplex LP method, **EX 8–51**
single field sort, EX 6–13–6–15
slack, **EX 8–53**
slicer(s), **EX 6–48**, EX 7–60–7–65
    add to dashboard, Power Pivot, EX 10–38–10–39
    apply from Data Model, Power Pivot, EX 10–38–10–41
    apply to multiple PivotTables, EX 7–61–7–62
    choose between filter buttons and, EX 6–52
    connect map chart, EX 10–57
    create, EX 6–50
    dashboard, EX 6–49
    filter data, EX 6–50–6–52
    format, EX 6–54–6–55
SmartArt
    enhance application, EX 12–8
SmartArt diagram, EX 12–8
SmartArt graphics, **EX 12–8**
Solver
    activate, EX 8–41–8–42
    add-in, EX 8–40
    add constraints, EX 8–44–8–50
    constraint types, EX 8–44
    defined, **EX 8–37**
    find optimal solution, EX 8–40–8–50
Solver answer report, create, EX 8–51–8–53
Solver models
    activate Solver, EX 8–41–8–42
    add constraints to Solver, EX 8–44–8–50
    load, EX 8–53–8–57
    save, EX 8–53–8–57
    set objective cell and variable cells, EX 8–42–8–44
Sort (Motel Name) dialog box, EX 11–10
sort
    ascending order, EX 6–13
    custom list, EX 6–17–6–19
    descending order, EX 6–13
    multiple fields, EX 6–15–6–17
    options, choose, EX 6–17
    PivotTable, EX 11–9–11–11
    PivotTables by custom list, EX 11–11
    records in data range, EX 6–13–6–19
    single field, EX 6–13–6–15
    value, EX 11–9–11–11
source workbook, **EX 5–20**
sparkline(s)
    create, EX 4–50–4–57
    defined, **EX 4–33**
    format, EX 4–54
    types, EX 4–51
sparkline axes, EX 4–55–4–57
sparkline groups, EX 4–55–4–57

split bar, **EX 6–2**
Split button, EX 6–7–6–8
spreadsheet(s), **EX 1–4**
    introduce, EX 1–4–1–7
stacked column chart, **EX 4–18**
Stacked Column map, EX 10–62
standard colors, **EX 2–6**
standard fonts, **EX 2–4**. *See also* font(s)
standard PivotTable, **EX 11–50**
    features, EX 11–50
    GETPIVOTDATA function, EX 11–62
status bar, **EX 1–2**
Stores table, Type slicer, EX 10–39
straight-line depreciation, EX 9–30
    asset, EX 9–32
    declining-balance depreciation, EX 9–30
    defined, **EX 9–30**
structural references
    defined, **EX 6–45**
    Excel table, EX 6–45–6–47
sub procedures, **EX 12–35**
    edited, EX 12–53
    Show_Dashboard macro, EX 12–52
    understand, EX 12–51–12–52
Subtotal button, EX 6–3
Subtotal dialog box, EX 6–20
Subtotal & Filters tab, EX 11–6
SUBTOTAL function, **EX 6–48**
    apply, EX 6–56–6–57
    dashboard, EX 6–55–6–58
    display multiple, EX 11–6
    function numbers, EX 6–56
subtotals
    calculate, EX 6–19–6–23
    defined, **EX 6–19**
    outline view, EX 6–21–6–23
    removed from PivotTable, EX 11–6
    row, create, EX 6–19–6–21
    work, EX 11–4–11–6
Subtotal tool, EX 6–2
SUM function, **EX 1–33**, EX 11–6, EX 11–46, EX 11–53
    3-D reference, EX 5–16
SUMIF function, **EX 7–2, EX 7–26**
    calculate conditional sums, EX 7–22–7–24
summary IFS functions
    apply, EX 7–19–7–27
    use, EX 7–25–7–27
SUMX function, EX 11–58–11–61, EX 11–61
sunburst charts, EX 4–45–**4–46**
switch, to Diagram view, EX 10–32
Synchronous Scrolling button, EX 5–3
    between windows, EX 5–9–5–10
syntax, **EX 1–38**
    understand, EX 1–38

T

tab, **EX 1–2**
table(s)
    add measure, EX 11–54–11–57
    calculate measures, EX 11–57–11–61

Table Design tab, EX 10–9

table relationships, **EX 10–24**
    defined in Power Pivot, EX 10–33
    Diagram view, EX 10–33
    manage, EX 10–32–10–34

Tabular layout, **EX 11–3**
    PivotTable, EX 11–8

tangible assets, **EX 9–29**

tasks
    automate, with macros, EX 12–37–12–41

taxes
    add to income statement, EX 9–35–9–37

Tell Me box, **EX 1–3**

template(s), **EX 1–4,** EX 5–34
    chart, EX 5–50
    copy styles, EX 5–53
    create workbook, EX 5–50–5–52
    profit and loss statements, EX 5–49
    workbooks created, EX 5–50

text
    display numbers, EX 1–22–1–23
    enter, EX 1–18–1–19
    find, EX 2–42–2–44
    replace, EX 2–42–2–44
    wrap within cell, EX 1–29–1–30

text data, **EX 1–18**

text filters, EX 6–33

text string, **EX 1–18**

theme(s), **EX 2–4**
    apply, EX 2–44–2–45
    save, EX 2–46
    set theme colors and fonts, EX 2–45–2–46
    work, EX 2–44–2–46

theme colors, **EX 2–6**
    set, EX 2–45–2–46

theme fonts, **EX 2–4**
    set, EX 2–45–2–46

thermometer charts, create, EX 12–10

3-D distortions, EX 4–55

3D maps, **EX 10–43**
    open, EX 10–60
    use Dates and Times, EX 10–63
    visualize data, EX 10–60–10–62

3D Map window, EX 10–60

3-D reference, **EX 5–3**
    apply to formulas and functions, EX 5–14–5–18
    enter, EX 5–15
    problem-solving, EX 5–15
    SUM function, EX 5–16
    wildcards, EX 5–18
    write, EX 5–14–5–18

tiled layout, workbook window, EX 5–7

time(s)
    calculate, EX 3–6–3–7
    format, EX 2–19–2–20

time data, **EX 1–18**

timeline(s), **EX 7–51**
    add Order Date to dashboard, Power Pivot, EX 10–38–10–39
    apply from Data Model, Power Pivot, EX 10–38–10–41
    connect map chart, EX 10–57
    connect slicer and, Power Pivot, EX 10–40

timeline slicer, EX 7–63–7–65
    create, EX 7–63–7–65

time value of money, **EX 9–43**

TODAY function, **EX 3–24**

tools for managing graphic objects, EX 4–44–4–45

top/bottom rule, EX 2–48

total expenses, chart of, EX 8–5

Total row, **EX 6–25**
    add, in Excel table, EX 6–41–6–42

Totals & Filters tab, EX 11–11

Touch Mode, **EX 1–6**
    use Excel, EX 1–6–1–7

Tour Editor pane, 3D Map window, EX 10–60

tours, **EX 10–43**

trace error, EX 9–53–9–55

transformed WordArt graphic, EX 12–6

transpose data, EX 2–41–2–42

transposed pasted range, EX 2–41

treemap chart, **EX 4–45**

trendlines, EX 9–25, **EX 10–3**
    add, EX 10–16
    add to charts, EX 4–39
    defined, **EX 4–39**
    edit, EX 10–16
    exponential, EX 10–17
    judge with $R2$ statistic, EX 10–18
    linear, EX 10–17
    logarithmic, EX 10–17
    moving average, EX 10–17
    polynomial, EX 10–17
    power, EX 10–17
    queries, EX 10–3
    types, EX 10–17

trial and error, **EX 3–45**
    use, EX 3–45–3–48
    what-if analysis, EX 3–45–3–48

Trust Center, **EX 12–56**
    Macro Settings, EX 12–56

Tufte, Edward, EX 4–52

two-variable data table, **EX 8–3**
    chart, EX 8–18–8–21
    completed, EX 8–17
    create, EX 8–14–8–21
    example, EX 8–15
    format result cell, EX 8–17–8–18
    setup, EX 8–16

two-way lookup table, **EX 7–12**
    value retrieved, EX 7–12

U

ungroup, worksheet groups, EX 5–13

unhide
    columns, EX 1–49
    multiple sheets, EX 12–26
    rows, EX 1–49
    worksheets, EX 1–49

uniqueness, validate, EX 12–25

units, and constants, EX 3–5–3–6

unlocked cells
    highlight, EX 12–31

unlock cells, EX 12–30–12–33

unlock worksheet cells, **EX 12–15**

unprotect
    workbook, EX 12–29–12–30
    worksheet, EX 12–29–12–30

V

validate
  data, EX 12–17
  data already in workbook, EX 12–25
  data entry, EX 12–16–12–25
  dates, EX 12–17–12–18
  against list, EX 12–21–12–23
  against past and future dates, EX 12–21
  uniqueness, EX 12–25

validation criteria, EX 12–17

validation error message
  create, EX 12–18–12–20

validation rule, EX 12–16

value(s)
  interpolate from start to end, EX 9–23–9–25
  series of, extrapolate, EX 9–27–9–29
  tracing error, EX 9–53

value axis, **EX 4–18**

value axis scale, edit, EX 4–29–4–30

value field, **EX 7–28**

Value Filter (Motel Name) dialog box, EX 11–14

value filters, EX 11–12

value map, **EX 10–42, EX 10–54**

value map chart
  create, EX 10–54–10–58
  revenue totals, EX 10–57

variable cells
  defined, **EX 8–36**
  set, EX 8–42–8–44

variable expenses, **EX 8–4**
  chart, EX 8–4

VBA editor
  edit macro with VBA editor, EX 12–52–12–55
  open, EX 12–50–12–51
  understand sub procedures, EX 12–51–12–52
  work, EX 12–50–12–55

VBA Editor window, EX 12–51

vertical layout, workbook window, EX 5–7, EX–5–9

vertical lookup table, EX 3–29

view
  contents of Data Model, EX 10–31
  data with map chart, EX 10–53–10–67
  data with Quick Explore Tool, EX 10–51–10–53
  payback period for investment, EX 9–41–9–42
  pretax profits and percentages in other sheets, EX 5–13
  scenarios, EX 8–28–8–29
  steps of query, EX 10–7
  workbook, multiple windows, EX 5–6–5–10

viruses, **EX 12–55**
  protect against macro, EX 12–55–12–57

Visual Basic for Applications (VBA), EX 11–39, **EX 12–35**

Visual Basic for Applications Editor, **EX 12–35**

Visual Basic for Applications (VBA) macro language,
  EX 8–42

visualize
  data with 3D maps, EX 10–60–10–62

VLOOKUP formulas, EX 12–11

VLOOKUP function, **EX 3–28**, EX 6–49, EX 6–62–6–63, EX 11–46,
  EX 12–3
  approximate match, EX 7–8
  find exact match, EX 3–41–3–45

Function Arguments dialog box, EX 3–43
  results, EX 3–43

volatile functions, **EX 3–45**

W

warning alert for invalid date, EX 12–20

warning error alert message, EX 12–19

Watch Window
  definition, **EX 9–55**
  use, EX 9–57–9–59

waterfall charts, **EX 4–47**, EX 4–47–4–48

what-if analysis, **EX 3–45**
  cost-volume relationships, EX 8–4–8–9
  create scenario summary reports, EX 8–30–8–35
  create Solver answer report, EX 8–51–8–53
  create two-variable data table, EX 8–14–8–21
  data tables, work, EX 8–9–8–14
  explore financial scenarios with Scenario Manager, EX 8–24–8–30
  explore iterative process, EX 8–50–8–51
  find break-even point, EX 8–7–8–9
  find optimal solution with Solver, EX 8–40–8–50
  optimize product mix, EX 8–38–8–40
  perform with charts, EX 4–16–4–17
  perform with formulas and functions, EX 3–45–3–51
  save and load Solver models, EX 8–53–8–57
  tool, EX 8–53
  use Goal Seek tool, EX 3–48–3–50
  use trial and error, EX 3–45–3–48

what-if scenarios, EX 8–24

wildcard characters, **EX 6–33**

wildcards, **EX 5–18**
  perform partial lookups, EX 7–16
  3-D reference, EX 5–18

WordArt graphic, **EX 12–2**
  added to dashboard, EX 12–5
  create, EX 12–4–12–8
  reflected, EX 12–7
  transformed, EX 12–6

workbook(s), **EX 1–2**
  add digital signature, EX 12–57
  add graphic objects, EX 4–39–4–45
  arrange multiple windows, EX 5–7, EX 5–9
  arrange Windows dialog box, EX 5–8
  audit, EX 9–51–9–59
  change active sheet, EX 1–8–1–9
  change page orientation, EX 1–55
  change worksheet views, EX 1–53–1–55
  close, EX 1–13–1–14
  created from templates, EX 5–50
  create effective, EX 1–15
  create new viewing window, EX 5–7
  decision-making while link, EX 5–28
  delete worksheets, EX 1–17–1–18
  design for calculations, EX 3–4–3–6
  edit cell content, EX 1–20–1–21
  evaluate formula, EX 9–55–9–57
  explore, EX 1–8–1–13
  financial, EX 9–18
  hide content, EX 12–25–12–26
  link external, EX 5–22–5–29
  link hyperlinks to location within, EX 5–29–5–31
  macro-enabled, EX 12–40–12–41
  manage links, EX 5–28
  modify rows and columns, EX 1–44–1–49
  move worksheets, EX 1–17

navigate within worksheet, EX 1–9–1–11
open, profit and loss statement, EX 5–4
plan, EX 1–14–1–15
print, EX 1–53–1–57
protect, EX 12–28–12–29
protect contents, EX 12–27–12–33
rename and insert worksheets, EX 1–16–1–17
review links, EX 5–27
save, EX 1–18
select cell range, EX 1–12–1–13
set print options, EX 1–56–1–57
set scaling options, EX 1–55–1–56
start new, EX 1–15–1–18
template, EX 5–34
trace error, EX 9–52–9–55
unprotect, EX 12–29–12–30
update links, EX 5–25–5–26
use color to enhance, EX 2–9
use COUNT function, EX 1–43–1–44
validate data already, EX 12–25
view, multiple windows, EX 5–6–5–10
Watch Window, use, EX 9–57–9–58
window layout, EX 5–7
windows in vertical layout, EX 5–7, EX 5–9

workbook contents
    hide, EX 12–25–12–26
    protect, EX 12–27–12–33

workbook contents, protect
    lock and unlock cells, EX 12–30–12–33
    protect workbook, EX 12–28–12–29
    protect worksheet, EX 12–27–12–28
    unprotect, worksheet and workbook, EX 12–29–12–30

workbook protection, **EX 12–15**

workbook templates
    explore, EX 5–47–5–53
    set up, EX 5–48–5–49

workbook window, **EX 1–3**
    divide, into panes, EX 6–6–6–8
    panes, EX 6–3
    split, EX 6–7–6–8
    unfreeze pane(s), EX 6–10

WORKDAY function, **EX 3–25**

work with VBA editor, EX 12–50–12–55

worksheet(s), **EX 1–3**
    add cell borders, EX 1–51–1–52
    change font size, EX 1–52–1–53
    change views, EX 1–53–1–55
    consolidate data from multiple, EX 7–62
    copy, EX 5–4–5–6
    data definition, EX 6–5
    delete, EX 1–17–1–18
    enter text, dates, and numbers, EX 1–18–1–27
    format, EX 1–51–1–53
    format for print, EX 2–53–2–63
    freeze column(s), EX 6–9
    freeze rows, EX 6–9

group and ungroup, EX 5–10, EX 5–11
    hide, EX 1–49
    insert, EX 1–16–1–17
    locate cells within, EX 6–26–6–27
    modify, EX 1–41–1–43
    Move or Copy dialog box, EX 5–5, EX 5–6
    move,, EX 1–17, EX 5–4
    move PivotChart to another, EX 7–55–7–56
    navigate within, EX 1–9–1–11
    protect, EX 12–27–12–28
    reference cells in other, EX 5–14
    remove split bars, EX 6–8
    rename, EX 1–16–1–17
    unhide, EX 1–49
    unprotect, EX 12–29–12–30
    view formulas, EX 1–57–1–59

worksheet cells
    format, EX 2–20–2–25

worksheet formulas, EX 1–57–1–59

worksheet group(s), **EX 5–2**
    edit, EX 5–11–5–13
    print, EX 5–13
    ungroup, EX 5–13

worksheet protection, **EX 12–15**

worksheet tab color, set, EX 2–10

write
    3-D references, EX 5–14–5–18
    data query, EX 10–4–10–11
    financial workbook, EX 9–18
    query to access Two Year Revenue data source, EX 10–11

X

XIRR function
    defined, **EX 9–49**
    explore, EX 9–49–9–51

XLOOKUP function, **EX 7–3**
    approximate match, EX 7–10
    array of values returned, EX 7–13
    engagement grades retrieved, EX 7–11
    function arguments for approximate match, EX 7–11
    perform two-way lookups, EX 7–12–7–14
    syntax, EX 7–9
    transition, EX 7–14
    two-way lookup with nested, EX 7–13

XNPV function
    defined, **EX 9–49**
    explore, EX 9–49–9–51

Z

zeroes
    calculations, EX 3–23
    role, EX 3–23

Zoom controls, **EX 1–3**